Personal Trainer®

Personal Trainer is an Internet-based homework tutor designed specifically for students taking a course in financial accounting. With annotated spreadsheets for students and full gradebook functionality for the instructor, students can complete homework and submit answers electronically.

Xtreme! With Personal Trainer

This hybrid CD-ROM and Internet-based product provides your students with the most media-rich content for any financial accounting text on the market! Using this non-platform-specific product, you can leverage technology to take your students to the outer limits of mastering the introductory financial accounting course!

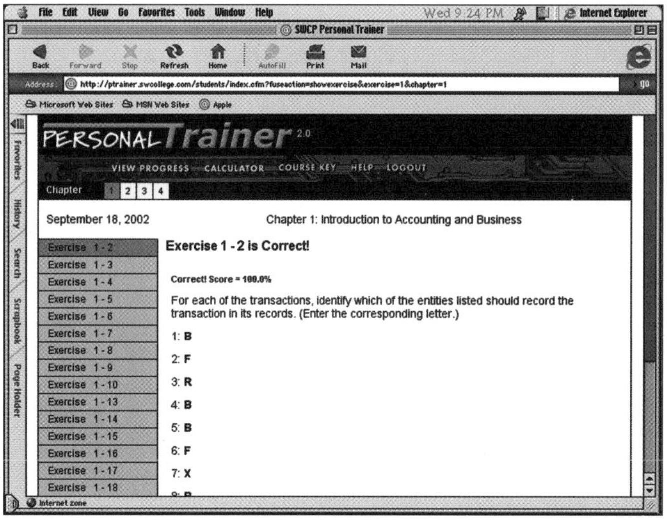

Xtra! for Financial Accounting

This CD-ROM provides *lecture replacement resources* and *access* to games and interactive quizzes so that students can test their understanding of the content. Free when bundled with a new text, students receive an access code so that they can receive Xtra! reinforcement in financial accounting.

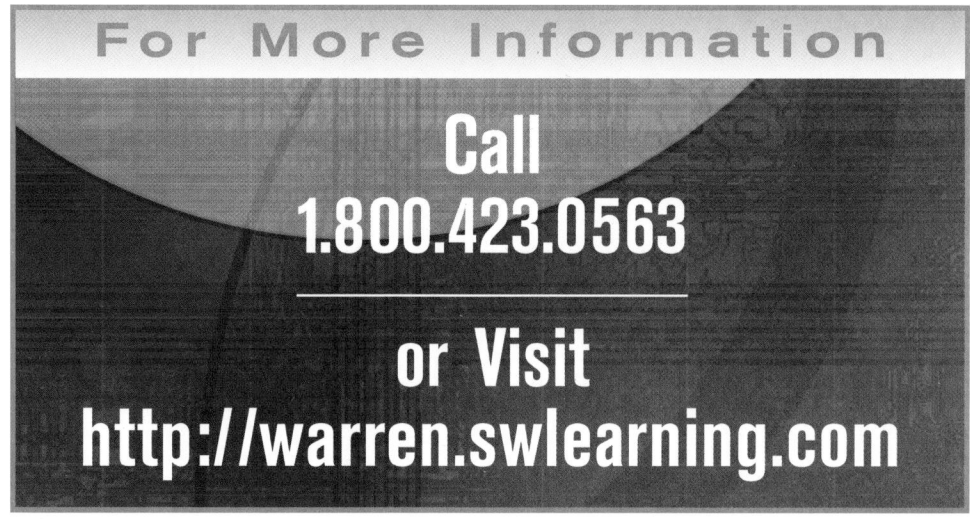

For More Information

Call 1.800.423.0563

or Visit http://warren.swlearning.com

A New Vision for a New Age of Business!

Financial Accounting for Future Business Leaders is designed to be used in a *one-term financial accounting course for undergraduate students at four-year colleges and universities.* As reliable and comprehensive as traditional financial accounting textbooks, this truly innovative text presents accounting concepts, principles, and reporting with an emphasis on cash basis accounting, and within the overarching framework of the statement of cash flows. The text is rich with practical applications to actual business settings, as well as real-world lessons in leadership, ethics, and strategic decision making.

Unlock the Innovative Approach to Teaching Financial Accounting!

A Cash Basis Starting Point

With its focus on training students to think like business leaders and develop an analytical view, Financial Accounting for Future Business Leaders approaches accounting from a new vantage point, beginning with a thorough discussion of cash basis accounting before presenting the accrual basis.

Consistent Attention to Accrual Accounting

Chapter 4 describes and illustrates the nature of business and accounting information systems. As part of the accounting system, the traditional rules of debit and credit are introduced through the use of "T" accounts. Students are guided through an illustration of the accounting cycle to solidify their understanding of accrual accounting before continuing on to more complex topics.

Strong Analytical Focus

- **"Strategy" Boxes:** The concept of business strategy is introduced in Chapter 1 with a description of the types of business strategies. Real-world examples and business strategy cases are included throughout the text, with emphasis on the ways different strategies impact business growth and development.
- **Financial Analysis:** Each chapter describes and illustrates a financial analysis tool useful in analyzing and interpreting financial statements. Real companies are used as examples of the tool in action, and end-of-chapter exercises and problems give students practice in the application of these tools. Additionally, Chapter 14 presents a close examination of the integrated DuPont model for financial analysis and its applications.
- **Extensive End-of-Chapter Materials:** To help develop well-rounded future business leaders, the end-of-chapter materials feature analytical questions, real-data exercises, accounting application problems, and a Building Leadership Skills section consisting of Financial Analysis and Reporting and Responsible Leadership activities.

The Total Spectrum of Technology

Would you like customized content available where you can add your syllabus to a course management system—and you have a Web-assisted or online course? Or would you prefer to add your own materials in addition to the content offered by Warren/Reeve's *Financial Accounting for Future Business Leaders* for your WebCT™ or Blackboard® course? Either way, WebTutor® Advantage with Personal Trainer® is the turnkey solution for you.

WebTutor® Advantage with Personal Trainer®

WebTutor® Advantage with Personal Trainer® on Blackboard® or WebCT™ provides learning reinforcement tools for students. Content includes:

- E-Lectures
- Problem Demonstrations
- Video Clips
- Chapter Summaries and Overviews
- Tutorial Quizzes
- Quiz Bowl
- Discussion Topics
- Flashcards
- Crossword Puzzles
- Links to InfoTrac® and Text Web site
- Testing
- Personal Trainer

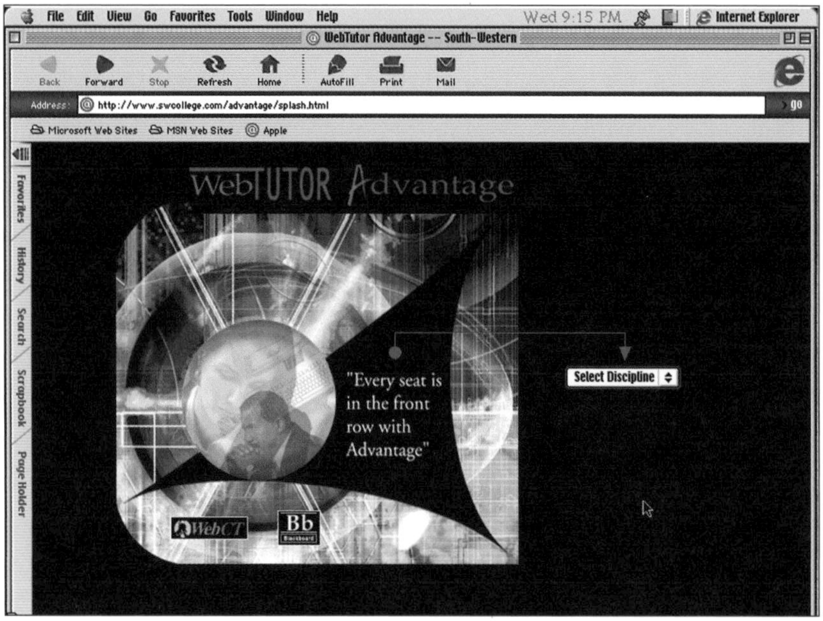

Access certificates for WebTutor® Advantage with Personal Trainer® can be bundled with the textbook or sold separately.

For more information, including a demo, visit **http://webtutor.swlearning.com.** To adopt the course in either WebCT™ or Blackboard, contact your sales representative or sign-up at **http://webtutor.thomsonlearning.com.**

Personal Trainer®

Personal Trainer is an Internet-based homework tutor designed specifically for students taking a course in financial accounting. With annotated spreadsheets for students and full gradebook functionality for the instructor, students can complete homework and submit answers electronically.

Xtreme! With Personal Trainer

This hybrid CD-ROM and Internet-based product provides your students with the most media-rich content for any financial accounting text on the market! Using this non-platform-specific product, you can leverage technology to take your students to the outer limits of mastering the introductory financial accounting course!

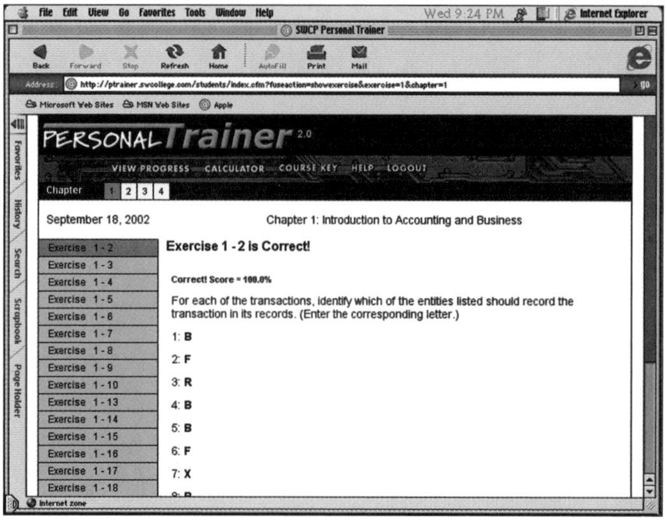

Xtra! for Financial Accounting

This CD-ROM provides *lecture replacement resources* and *access* to games and interactive quizzes so that students can test their understanding of the content. Free when bundled with a new text, students receive an access code so that they can receive Xtra! reinforcement in financial accounting.

A New Vision for a New Age of Business!

Financial Accounting for Future Business Leaders is designed to be used in a *one-term financial accounting course for undergraduate students at four-year colleges and universities.* As reliable and comprehensive as traditional financial accounting textbooks, this truly innovative text presents accounting concepts, principles, and reporting with an emphasis on cash basis accounting, and within the overarching framework of the statement of cash flows. The text is rich with practical applications to actual business settings, as well as real-world lessons in leadership, ethics, and strategic decision making.

Unlock the Innovative Approach to Teaching Financial Accounting!

A Cash Basis Starting Point

With its focus on training students to think like business leaders and develop an analytical view, Financial Accounting for Future Business Leaders approaches accounting from a new vantage point, beginning with a thorough discussion of cash basis accounting before presenting the accrual basis.

Consistent Attention to Accrual Accounting

Chapter 4 describes and illustrates the nature of business and accounting information systems. As part of the accounting system, the traditional rules of debit and credit are introduced through the use of "T" accounts. Students are guided through an illustration of the accounting cycle to solidify their understanding of accrual accounting before continuing on to more complex topics.

Strong Analytical Focus

- **"Strategy" Boxes:** The concept of business strategy is introduced in Chapter 1 with a description of the types of business strategies. Real-world examples and business strategy cases are included throughout the text, with emphasis on the ways different strategies impact business growth and development.
- **Financial Analysis:** Each chapter describes and illustrates a financial analysis tool useful in analyzing and interpreting financial statements. Real companies are used as examples of the tool in action, and end-of-chapter exercises and problems give students practice in the application of these tools. Additionally, Chapter 14 presents a close examination of the integrated DuPont model for financial analysis and its applications.
- **Extensive End-of-Chapter Materials:** To help develop well-rounded future business leaders, the end-of-chapter materials feature analytical questions, real-data exercises, accounting application problems, and a Building Leadership Skills section consisting of Financial Analysis and Reporting and Responsible Leadership activities.

WARREN • REEVE
FINANCIAL ACCOUNTING
FOR FUTURE BUSINESS LEADERS

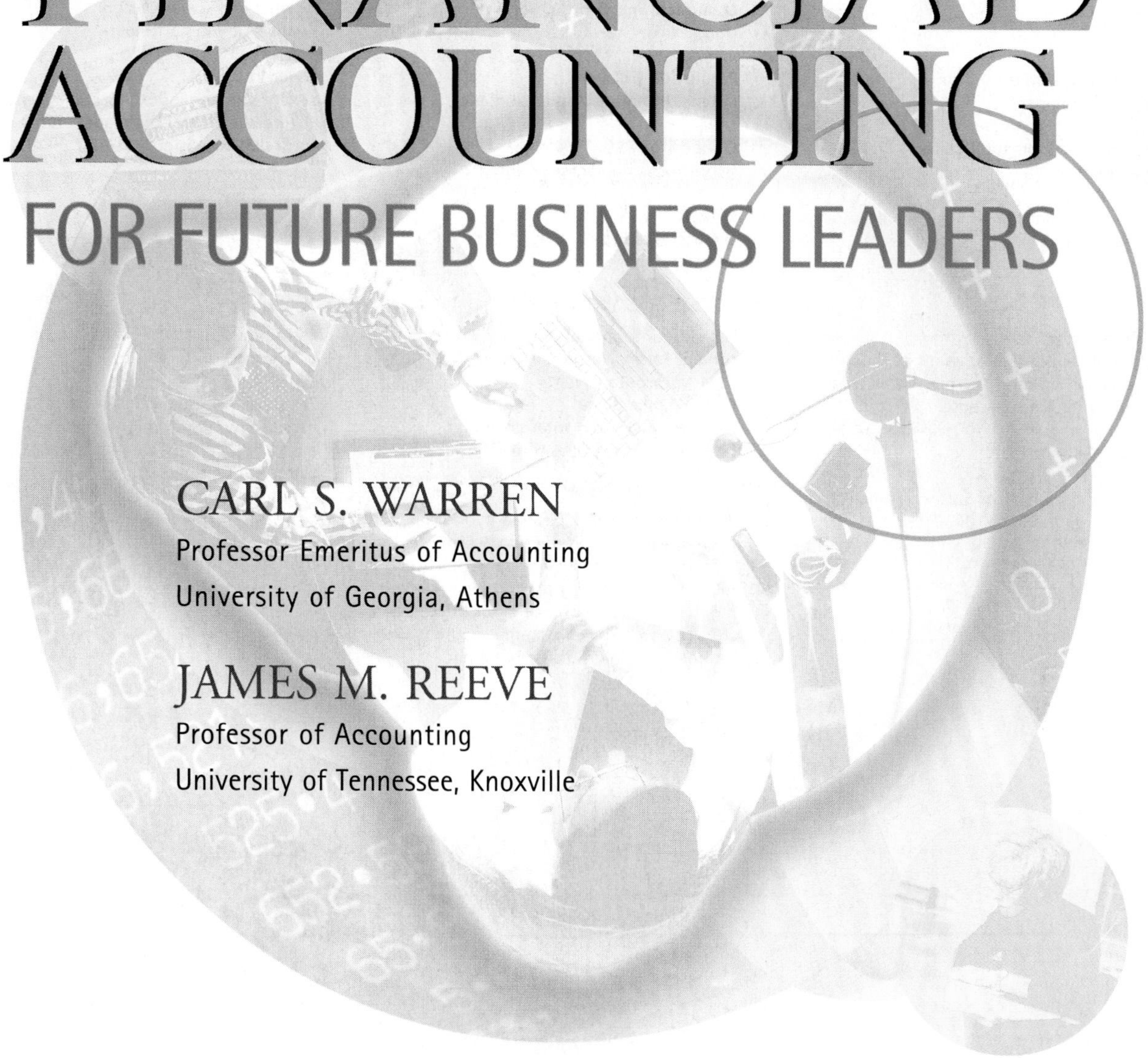

CARL S. WARREN
Professor Emeritus of Accounting
University of Georgia, Athens

JAMES M. REEVE
Professor of Accounting
University of Tennessee, Knoxville

THOMSON™
SOUTH-WESTERN

Australia · Canada · Mexico · Singapore · Spain · United Kingdom · United States

THOMSON
SOUTH-WESTERN

Financial Accounting for Future Business Leaders, 1e

Carl S. Warren, James M. Reeve

Editor-in-Chief:
Jack W. Calhoun

Team Leader:
Melissa S. Acuña

Senior Acquisitions Editor:
Sharon Oblinger

Senior Developmental Editor:
Ken Martin

Marketing Manager:
Keith Chassé

Production Editors:
Salvatore Versetto and Heather Mann

Manufacturing Coordinator:
Doug Wilke

Production House:
Litten Editing and Production, Inc.

Compositor:
GGS Information Services, Inc.

Printer:
Quebecor World
Versailles, KY

Senior Design Project Manager:
Michelle Kunkler

Internal and Cover Design:
Knapke Design, Cincinnati

Cover Images:
© Paul Venning/Index Stock Imagery/ PictureQuest, © Getty Images and © Image Source/ElektraVision

ISBN: 0-324-18145-0

Printed in the United States of America
1 2 3 4 5 06 05 04 03

For more information, contact South-Western, 5191 Natorp Boulevard, Mason, Ohio 45040.
Or you can visit our Internet site at: http://www.swlearning.com

Library of Congress
Control Number: 2002111181

Brief Contents

Contents

Preface

Because sound financial management is the key to success in nearly every business enterprise, students who gain a solid grasp of accounting methods and procedures are particularly well-positioned to become business leaders who will achieve corporate productivity and individual accomplishment. But a good grounding in basic accounting principles is only the first step. We recognize that today's highly competitive workplace demands strong personal leadership skills along with an increased level of professionalism, and we believe that the dynamic nature of the 21st century business world calls for a new perspective on how accounting is taught. To address those needs, we offer *Financial Accounting for Future Business Leaders*, a text written to prepare students for maximum success in the modern marketplace.

A New Vision for a New Age of Business

Financial Accounting for Future Business Leaders is designed to be used in a one-term financial accounting course for undergraduate students at four-year colleges and universities. As reliable and comprehensive as traditional financial accounting textbooks, this truly innovative text presents accounting concepts, principles, and reporting with an emphasis on cash basis accounting, and within the overarching framework of the statement of cash flows. The text is rich with practical applications to actual business settings, as well as real-world lessons in leadership, ethics, and strategic decision making.

An Innovative Approach

With its focus on training students to think like business leaders and develop an analytical view, *Financial Accounting for Future Business Leaders* approaches accounting from a new vantage point, beginning with a thorough discussion of cash basis accounting before presenting the accrual basis. The text emphasizes the *analysis* and *interpretation* of financial statements rather than financial statement *preparation*, and examines the importance of the statement of cash flows in evaluating and interpreting changes in a company's financial condition and results of operations. Students learn to identify the effects that transactions have on the financial statements and thereby understand the multiple levels on which accounting decisions affect a company's growth and performance.

The emphasis on building leadership skills is another distinguishing feature of this text. Key issues for future business leaders are presented in conjunction with related accounting principles. The importance of ethical conduct for business leaders is emphasized through "Ethics In Action" items in each chapter, as well as end-of-chapter ethics cases. Additionally, each chapter's assignment materials include a section entitled "Building Leadership Skills – Financial Reporting and Analysis," which uses cases based upon real companies to teach students to apply decision-making strategies to financial reporting issues and analyses. Another section of assignment materials, "Building Leadership Skills – Responsible Leadership," contains activities that focus on ethics situations and group interactions.

Case 1–5

Financial analysis of Enron Corporation

Enron Corporation, headquartered in Houston, Texas, provides products and services for natural gas, electricity, and communications to wholesale and retail customers. Enron's operations are conducted through a variety of subsidiaries and affiliates that involve transporting gas through pipelines, transmitting electricity, and managing energy commodities. The following data were taken from Enron's December 31, 2000, financial statements.

	In millions
Total revenues	$100,789
Total costs and expenses	98,836
Operating income	1,953
Net income	979
Total assets	65,503
Total liabilities	54,033
Total stockholders' equity	11,470
Net cash flows from operating activities	4,779
Net cash flows from investing activities	(4,264)
Net cash flows from financing activities	571
Net increase in cash	1,086

Unique Pedagogy and Features

Financial Accounting for Future Business Leaders uses unique pedagogical concepts and features to explain major accounting issues and principles from a statement of cash flows perspective, to develop leadership qualities along with accounting skills, and to aid student comprehension. These features go beyond "how" to emphasize "why" generally accepted accounting principles are applied, giving students the knowledge and background essential for the proper interpretation and analysis of financial statements.

Real-World Emphasis

Throughout the text, accounting theory is taught in the context of business reality, both to clarify the concepts and to stimulate student interest in business matters.

- Each chapter begins with a story about a major company, such as Wal-Mart or Hershey Foods, which describes the company's unique aspects and links them to the chapter topics.
- Real-world examples are referenced throughout the narrative of each chapter.
- "Strategy in Business" boxed items utilize real business scenarios to stimulate student interest and to illustrate the effects and importance of business strategies for managers.

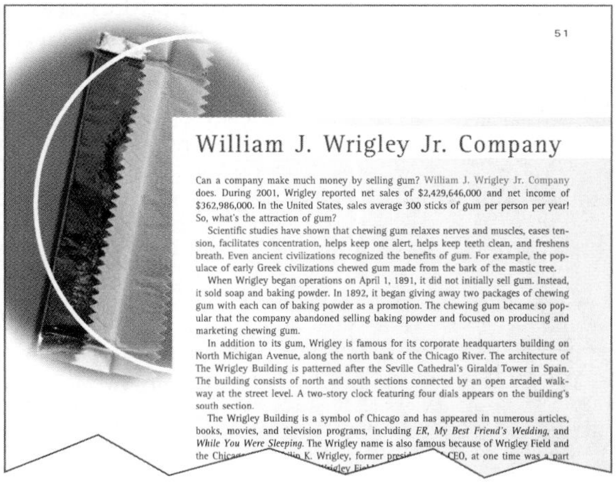
51

William J. Wrigley Jr. Company

Can a company make much money by selling gum? William J. Wrigley Jr. Company does. During 2001, Wrigley reported net sales of $2,429,646,000 and net income of $362,986,000. In the United States, sales average 300 sticks of gum per person per year! So, what's the attraction of gum?

Scientific studies have shown that chewing gum relaxes nerves and muscles, eases tension, facilitates concentration, helps keep one alert, helps keep teeth clean, and freshens breath. Even ancient civilizations recognized the benefits of gum. For example, the populace of early Greek civilizations chewed gum made from the bark of the mastic tree.

When Wrigley began operations on April 1, 1891, it did not initially sell gum. Instead, it sold soap and baking powder. In 1892, it began giving away two packages of chewing gum with each can of baking powder as a promotion. The chewing gum became so popular that the company abandoned selling baking powder and focused on producing and marketing chewing gum.

In addition to its gum, Wrigley is famous for its corporate headquarters building on North Michigan Avenue, along the north bank of the Chicago River. The architecture of The Wrigley Building is patterned after the Seville Cathedral's Giralda Tower in Spain. The building consists of north and south sections connected by an open arcaded walkway at the street level. A two-story clock featuring four dials appears on the building's south section.

The Wrigley Building is a symbol of Chicago and has appeared in numerous articles, books, movies, and television programs, including *ER, My Best Friend's Wedding*, and *While You Were Sleeping*. The Wrigley name is also famous because of Wrigley Field and the Chic[illegible] K. Wrigley, former presi[illegible] CEO, at one time was a part

- Numerous exercises and problems that utilize real companies are included in end-of-chapter materials.
- The Home Depot Annual Report, included at the end of the text, is referenced within various chapters and can be used by instructors to illustrate the financial reporting of a well-known company.

Financial Analysis and Interpretation Tools

Each chapter describes and illustrates a financial analysis tool useful in analyzing and interpreting financial statements, utilizing one or more actual companies as a basis for illustration. In addition, end-of-chapter exercises and problems give students practice in the application of these analysis tools.

Supportive Study Aids

To assist students with no prior accounting background and to improve comprehension for all students, substantial study aids are included throughout the text.

- Following the chapter-opening story, a section entitled "Your Need to Know" describes the importance of the chapter material for future business leaders. These items stimulate student interest in the chapter, focus on key chapter topics, and help students develop a personal connection to the concepts.

> **Your Need To Know**
>
> When you shop at Wal-Mart or Target, go to a movie theatre, buy gas at an Exxon or BP station, buy groceries at Kroger or Supervalu, buy a ticket to fly on United or American Airlines, or order a pizza from Pizza Hut or Domino's, you enter into a transaction that is captured, processed, and recorded by the business. At Wal-Mart, for example, cash register clerks use an electronic scanner to read the bar code off the item purchased. The cash register displays the price, and the cashier completes the transaction when you pay for the merchandise. But the transaction processing doesn't stop at this point. Periodically, each Wal-Mart store sends its sales data to the corporate office for updating the company records. ...includes recording the ... and the cost of merchandise sold as well as up-

> **For 2001, General Motors reported net sales of $177,260 million and net income of $601 million. What were General Motors' total expenses for 2001?**
>
> $176,659 million ($177,260 million − $601 million)

- Question and Answer items are provided throughout each chapter to allow students to check their progress and their understanding of topics as they work through the chapter.
- Each chapter contains an "Illustrative Accounting Application Problem," patterned after an end-of-chapter problem, to assist students in reviewing chapter content and to prepare them for end-of-chapter homework assignments.
- A set of "Self-Study" questions at the end of each chapter directs the student's review of chapter topics and improves comprehension. The answers to the self-study questions are provided at the end of the chapter.
- A "Summary of Learning Goals" and a chapter-specific glossary appear at the end of each chapter to facilitate student review and studying.

Teaching Tools

A good variety of assignment materials helps instructors reinforce concepts presented in class and provides application activities directly related to chapter topics. The end-of-chapter assignment options include Discussion Questions, Exercises, Accounting Application Problems, Cases, and Activities.

- "Building Leadership Skills" cases and activities use real companies to address issues and concepts that require students to employ critical-thinking skills, and are intended to build the leadership skills that will enable students to succeed in their future business careers. The cases and activities serve as an excellent resource for class discussions about real-world business topics and issues.
- Discussion Questions are designed to stimulate critical thinking rather than rote answers.
- Twenty or more exercises per chapter provide the instructor with examples to use during lectures as well as for homework assignments.

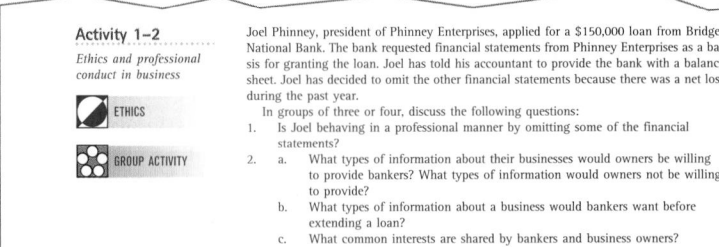

> **Activity 1-2**
> *Ethics and professional conduct in business*
>
> ETHICS
>
> GROUP ACTIVITY
>
> Joel Phinney, president of Phinney Enterprises, applied for a $150,000 loan from Bridger National Bank. The bank requested financial statements from Phinney Enterprises as a basis for granting the loan. Joel has told his accountant to provide the bank with a balance sheet. Joel has decided to omit the other financial statements because there was a net loss during the past year.
>
> In groups of three or four, discuss the following questions:
>
> 1. Is Joel behaving in a professional manner by omitting some of the financial statements?
> 2. a. What types of information about their businesses would owners be willing to provide bankers? What types of information would owners not be willing to provide?
>   b. What types of information about a business would bankers want before extending a loan?
>   c. What common interests are shared by bankers and business owners?

- Accounting Application Problems require the application of one or more accounting topics that have been described and illustrated within the chapter. A and B problems are provided for use by instructors in assigning homework and rotating homework assignments between class sections or academic terms.

An Overview of the Text

The Overarching Framework of the Statement of Cash Flows

Financial Accounting for Future Business Leaders presents comprehensive accounting information organized around the concept of the statement of cash flows.

The text does not assume that students have prior accounting training or experience. It begins by describing basic business concepts and principles and by discussing, within the first three chapters, the interrelationship of the statement of cash flows with the other financial statements Chapter 1 emphasizes the importance of communicating the effects of financing, investing, and operating business activities through the statement of cash flows. Chapter 2 examines the cash basis of accounting in detail, using carefully selected transactions to clearly illustrate the preparation of the statement of cash flows and the interrelationship between the income statement and the statement of cash flows. Although the accrual basis of accounting is introduced in Chapter 3, the statement of cash flows is illustrated and prepared by analyzing cash transactions for the period. An appendix at the end of Chapter 3 allows instructors to cover the reconciliation of net cash flows from operations with net income under the accrual basis.

Exhibit 15

Statement of Cash Flows for Online Solutions

Online Solutions
Statement of Cash Flows
For the Two Months Ended December 31, 2004

Cash flows from operating activities:		
Cash received from customers	$ 14,120 (a)	
Cash received from renting land	360	$ 14,480
Deduct cash payments for expenses:		
Wages	$ 4,275 (b)	
Insurance	2,400	
Supplies	1,900 (c)	
Rent	1,600 (d)	
Utilities	985 (e)	
Miscellaneous	455 (f)	11,615
Net cash flows from operating activities		$ 2,865
Cash flows used for investing activities:		
Purchase of land	$(20,000)	
Purchase of office equipment	(1,800)	
Net cash flows used in investing activities		(21,800)
Cash flows from financing activities:		
Issuance of capital stock	$ 25,000	
Payment of dividends	(4,000)	
Net cash flows from financing activities		21,000
Net increase in cash		$ 2,065
November 1, 2004 cash balance		0
December 31, 2004 cash balance		$ 2,065

Computational Notes:
(a) $14,120 = $7,500 + $3,100 + $650 + $2,870
(b) $4,275 = $2,125 + $950 + $1,200
(c) $1,900 = $950 + $400 + $550
(d) $1,600 = $800 + $800
(e) $985 = $450 + $310 + $225
(f) $455 = $275 + $180

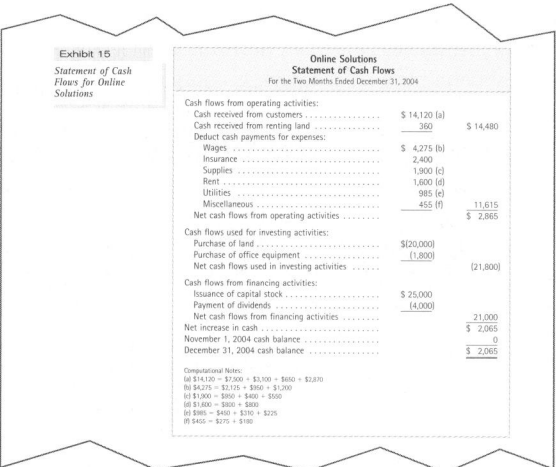

Chapters 4 and 5 continue to provide illustrations and real-world examples of the statement of cash flows, though Chapter 5 takes a particular look at accounting practices in merchandising and manufacturing. Both chapters provide appendixes that demonstrate how the statement of cash flows is prepared. These appendixes allow instructors to present in-depth coverage and discussion of the statement of cash flows, including its importance, preparation, and interrelationship with the other financial statements. Both chapters also contain appendix exercises and problems requiring the preparation of the statement of cash flows.

Chapters 6 through 12 contain boxed statement of cash flow items that further explain how more complex accounting topics impact the statement of cash flows. Chapter 13 is a traditional statement of cash flows chapter that illustrates the indirect and direct methods of cash flows from operating activities. Chapter 14 utilizes the integrated DuPont model for financial analysis and interpretation to teach financial statement analysis.

Other Key Topics Presented in this Text

Financial Accounting for Future Business Leaders examines specialized topics of particular value to students preparing for leadership positions in business.

- **Business Strategy** – The concept of business strategy is introduced in Chapter 1 with a description of the types of business strategies. Real-world examples and business strategy cases are included throughout the text, with emphasis on the ways different strategies impact business growth and development.
- **Employee Fraud** – Chapter 6, "Internal Control and Cash, "includes a discussion of the common elements of employee fraud – one of the most frequent and costly business problems – and successful methods for prevention and detection.
- **Financial Analysis** – Each chapter describes and illustrates a financial analysis tool useful in analyzing and interpreting financial statements. Real companies are used

as examples of the tool in action, and end-of-chapter exercises and problems give students practice in the application of these tools.

- **International Issues** – An examination of accounting principles and rules from other countries establishes student awareness of the global economic community and its impact on business practices.

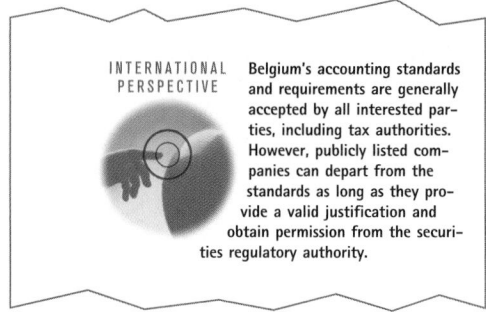

INTERNATIONAL PERSPECTIVE

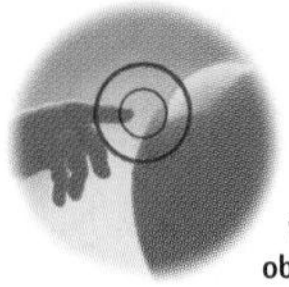

Belgium's accounting standards and requirements are generally accepted by all interested parties, including tax authorities. However, publicly listed companies can depart from the standards as long as they provide a valid justification and obtain permission from the securities regulatory authority.

A Closer Look at Introductory Chapters 1-5

Financial Accounting for Future Business Leaders presents a wealth of information and applications throughout the text, but its innovative approach is most apparent in the introductory chapters that address critical fundamental accounting concepts. We offer a special in-depth discussion of these chapters to help instructors understand the text's unique orientation and organization.

Chapter 1: The Role of Accounting in Business. Because accounting exists within the broader context of business, the text begins by describing basic business concepts and principles. Chapter 1 describes and illustrates business strategies, value chains, and stakeholders. "Strategy in Business" boxed items as well as business strategy cases, found throughout the text, are introduced in this chapter. These strategy items utilize real business scenarios to stimulate student interest as well as to illustrate the effects and importance of business strategies for managers.

Strategy in Business

Got the Flu? Why Not Chew Some Gum?

Facing a slumping market for sugared chewing gum, such as Juicy Fruit and Doublemint, Wm. J. Wrigley Jr. Company is reinventing itself with a strategy to expand its product lines and introduce new chewing gum applications. Wrigley's new products include sugarless breath mints and more powerful flavored mint chewing gum, like Extra Polar Ice. In addition, Wrigley is experimenting with health-care applications of chewing gum. Wrigley's Health Care Division has already developed Surpass, an antacid chewing gum to compete with Rolaids and Mylanta. In addition, Wrigley is experimenting with a cold-relief chewing gum and a gum that would provide dental benefits, such as whitening teeth and reducing plaque. Given that the U.S. population is a
the company figures that pe
might prefer chewing gum t
ing pills for sore throats, col
the flu. The effects of these
strategic initiatives will ulti
be reflected in Wrigley's fin
statements.

Source: Adapted from "A Young Heir Has Ne
Old Company," by David Barboza, *The New Y*
August 28, 2001.

Consistent with the statement of cash flows, Chapter 1 also describes financing, investing, and operating business activities. It does not include examples of transaction recording, but rather emphasizes the basic accounting concepts underlying financial statements. Additionally, the interrelationships among the financial statements are illustrated and emphasized.

Chapter 2: The Cash Basis of Accounting. Unlike other financial accounting textbooks, *Financial Accounting for Future Business Leaders* does not begin with the accrual basis of accounting. Rather, the cash basis of accounting is used to illustrate, record, and summarize the effects of transactions on financial statements. Students can better relate to and comprehend the cash basis, since it mirrors the accounting system they use in their daily lives.

Exhibit 2

Family Health Care Summary of Transactions for September

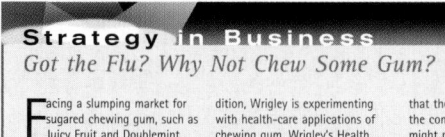

	Assets		= Liabilities	+ Stockholders' Equity		
	Cash	+ Land	= Notes Payable	+ Capital Stock	+ Retained Earnings	
a.	6,000			6,000		Investment
b.	10,000		10,000			Loan from bank
Bal.	16,000		10,000	6,000		
c.	−12,000	12,000				Purchase of land
Bal.	4,000	12,000	10,000	6,000		
d.	5,500				5,500	Fees earned
Bal.	9,500	12,000	10,000	6,000	5,500	
e.	−2,900				−1,125	Wages expense
					−950	Rent expense
					−450	Utilities expense
					−100	Interest expense
					−275	Miscellaneous exp.
Bal.	6,600	12,000	10,000	6,000	2,600	
f.	−1,500				−1,500	Dividends
Bal.	5,100	12,000	10,000	6,000	1,100	

An additional benefit of the cash basis is that it allows students to prepare all the financial statements, including the statement of cash flows, in end-of-chapter exercises and problems. Specifically, by analyzing the effects of transactions on cash, the statement of cash flows can be easily prepared. This approach also simplifies and clarifies the effects transactions have on a company's financial condition and operations, without the complications of adjusting entries. Finally, another benefit of the cash basis is that net income (or net loss) on the income statement equals the net cash from (used by) operating activities on the statement of cash flows. This relationship reinforces the students' understanding of the interrelationships among the financial statements.

Adjustment 1 (Deferred Expense—Prepaid Insurance) This first adjustment recognizes that a portion of the prepaid insurance purchased November 1 expired during November. Family Health Care prepaid two policies—a general business policy for $2,400 (transaction b) and a malpractice policy for $6,000 (transaction c). The general business policy is a two-year policy expiring at a rate of $100 ($2,400 ÷ 24) per month. The malpractice policy is a six-month policy that expires at a rate of $1,000 ($6,000 ÷ 6) per month. The total expired prepaid insurance is thus $1,100 ($100 + $1,000). This adjustment is recorded as shown below.

	Assets						= Liabilities		+ Stockholders' Equity		
	Cash +	Accts. Rec. +	Prepaid Ins. +	Supp. +	Office Equip. +	Land =	Notes Pay. +	Accts. Pay. +	Unearned Revenue +	Capital Stock +	Retained Earnings
Bal.	7,730	1,900	8,400	240	8,500	12,000	16,800	140	1,800	11,000	9,030
a1			−1,100								−1,100 Ins. exp.
Bal.	7,730	1,900	7,300	240	8,500	12,000	16,800	140	1,800	11,000	7,930

Chapter 3: The Accrual Basis of Accounting. Chapter 3 is consistent with our pedagogical philosophy of progressing from simple to more complex concepts and principles. Chapter 3 introduces accrual accounting by continuing the illustration from Chapter 2 (Family Health Care, P.C.). The transactions in Chapter 2 were carefully selected to avoid accrual accounting issues, which allowed the cash basis to serve as a building block for introducing and understanding the accrual basis of accounting. For example, in Chapter 3, Family Health Care enters into accrual and deferral transactions that give rise to receivables, prepaid expenses, depreciation, and payables. This, in turn, leads to a discussion of the need for the adjustment process (and adjusting entries) in preparing financial statements.

By using the Family Health Care illustration throughout Chapters 2 and 3, the text demonstrates that the cash basis provides a net income (and a net cash flow from operations) that implies that Family Health Care's operations are unfavorable. In contrast, using the accrual basis shows that Family Health Care's operations are expanding and rapidly growing. In other words, the chapter illustration shows that the cash basis can give misleading results when a company (Family Health Care) has significant accruals and deferrals.

An appendix at the end of Chapter 3 describes and illustrates the reconciliation of net cash flows from operations and net income. Using simple transactions, students are able to understand why net income and net cash flows from operations differ under the accrual basis.

Chapter 4: Accounting Information Systems. Double-entry accounting and the rules of debit and credit are introduced in Chapter 4 through the use of "T" accounts. An illustration (Online Solutions) using two months of transactions demonstrates the accounting cycle. This illustration also reinforces and reviews the accrual basis concepts presented in Chapter 3. This review provides students with an opportunity to solidify their understanding of accrual accounting before continuing on to more complex topics.

Chapter 5: Merchandising and Manufacturing Accounting. Chapter 5 covers merchandising enterprises. Rather than beginning with transaction analysis, the chapter opens with the comparison of financial statements of a service and merchandising business. Two real companies, H & R Block and Home Depot, are used as a basis for this illustration.

Innovative Technology

Personal Trainer®

This *Homework Tutor* is an Internet-based assistant designed specifically for students taking the introductory course in financial accounting. With the help of warm-ups and hints, students can complete assigned homework or practice by completing unassigned work online. Instructors receive the results, which can be automatically entered into a gradebook for the assigned homework, and can view the efforts of the unassigned work completed by students. Unlike any other tutorial on the market, students receive the pedagogical benefits of the completion of homework assignments and instructors have more time to devote to other classroom activities.

WebTutor® Advantage with Personal Trainer

Available in either WebCT™ or Blackboard® platforms, this rich course management product is a specially designed extension of the classroom experience that enlivens the course by leveraging the power of the Internet with comprehensive educational content. WebTutor Advantage on WebCT™ or Blackboard® includes Personal Trainer to provide a real-time, guided, self-correcting study outside the classroom. Instructors or students can use these resources along with those on the Product Web Site to supplement the classroom experience. Use this effective resource as an integrated solution for your distance learning or web-enhanced course! This powerful, turnkey solution provides the following content customized for this edition:

- **E-Lectures** – PowerPoint® slides of the key topical coverage accompanied by audio explanations provide additional learning support.
- **Interactive Quizzes** – Multiple choice questions that test students' knowledge of the chapter content provide immediate feedback on the accuracy of the response. These quizzes help students pinpoint areas needing more study.
- **Problem Demonstrations** – The chapter review problem is presented, and an audio step-by-step explanation of the solution is provided to guide student understanding.
- **Videos** - Short, high-interest segments focus on chapter-related topics.
- **Reviews of Key Concepts** – Tied to each learning goal, these chapter reviews reinforce important concepts.
- **Flashcards** – A terminology quiz helps students gain a complete understanding of the key terms from the chapter.
- **Spanish Dictionary** – To aid Spanish-speaking students, a Spanish dictionary of key financial accounting terms is provided.
- **Crossword Puzzles** – These interactive puzzles provide an alternative tool for students to test their understanding of terminology.
- **Quiz Bowl Game** – Students can review chapter content using this online game, which is similar to Jeopardy!®.
- **Personal Trainer** – This Internet-based homework tutor, described fully in the preceding section, is a rich tool for students and instructors.

Xtreme! With Personal Trainer

This hybrid CD-ROM and Internet-based product provides your students with the most media-rich content available! Features include:

- Learning Goals that summarize key concepts from each chapter.
- Quizzing that reinforces concepts and helps your students focus their study efforts better.
- Quiz Bowl Game, an innovative and fun way for students to review concepts.
- Crossword puzzles to test students' knowledge of the glossary and make learning "the language of business" more fun.
- E-Lectures that provide a PowerPoint® presentation with audio voiceovers to help students review chapter content or work on difficult topics.
- Problem demonstrations help to guide students to complete homework assignment through the review problems and save you time.
- Video clips that provide real-world examples of applications so that students can make the connection between the accounting concept and its use in the business world.
- Personal Trainer, an online self-grading homework tutorial with a gradebook for monitoring student progress and reporting the details to help you better target your teaching efforts!

Xtra! for Financial Accounting

This CD-ROM provides *lecture replacement resources* and *access* to games and interactive quizzes so that students can test their understanding of the content of the text. Free when bundled with a new text, students receive an access code so that they can receive Xtra! reinforcement in financial accounting.

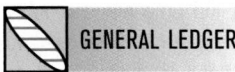

GENERAL LEDGER

General Ledger CD-ROM

Developed for the learning market, students can use this software to learn the benefits of accounting in a computer environment.

Text Web Site

(http://warren.swlearning.com) The Web site for the text offers you and your students a wide array of resources for teaching and learning. Among the many elements available, without charge, to **Students** are:

- *Quizzes with feedback*
- *Hotlinks* to many resources on the Web, including all of the Web sites listed in the text. This provides a quick connection to key information
- *PowerPoint® presentation slides* for review of chapter coverage
- *Excel templates* for selected assignments in the text
- *Crossword puzzles* provide fun testing of vocabulary knowledge
- *Check figures* to selected assignments
- *Learning goals* from the chapter are repeated as a study aid to keep clear focus on the core goals
- *Updates* for the latest information about changes in GAAP and any new, important information related to the text

SPREADSHEET

For Instructors, in addition to full access to the student resources listed above, a password-protected section of the Web site contains a number of resource files, including:

- *Solutions Manual*
- *Instructor's Manual*
- *Solutions to Excel templates*
- *Solution transparencies*
- Additional *updates* pertinent to instructors

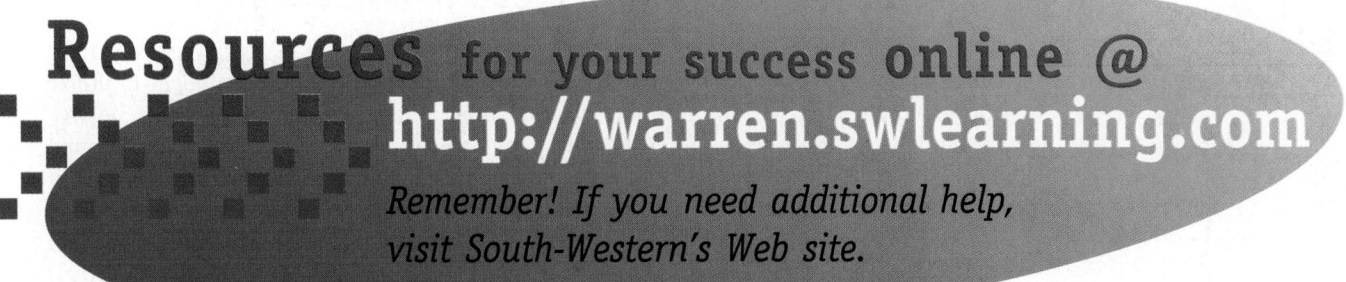

Resources for your success online @
http://warren.swlearning.com
Remember! If you need additional help, visit South-Western's Web site.

Other Helpful Support Materials

For Students:

- *Working Papers* – Why use notebook paper for your homework when you can save time by simply entering the answers in the format preferred by your instructor? This handy book provides all the forms you'll need when your instructor asks you to manually prepare the homework assignments from the text.

STUDENT SOLUTIONS MANUAL

- *Student Solutions Manual* – Solutions for the even-numbered exercises and the alternate accounting application problems are included in this book.

For Instructors:

- *Instructor's Resource Manual* – composed of the Instructor's Manual and the Solutions Manual, this ancillary's content is also available in electronic form on the Instructor's Resource CD-ROM and (restricted) on the product support Web site.
- *Test Bank* – a complete and plentiful set of test items that are also available in electronic form (using ExamView® software, provided) on the Instructor's Resource CD-ROM.
- *Solution Transparencies* – acetate transparencies of the numerical solutions to the exercises and problems.
- *Instructor's Resource CD-ROM with ExamView®*. Key instructor ancillaries (solutions manual, instructor's manual, test bank, and PowerPoint® presentation slides) are provided on CD-ROM–giving instructors the ultimate tool for customizing lectures and presentations. The testbank files on the CD-Rom are provided in ExamView® format. This program is an easy-to-use test creation software compatible with Microsoft® Windows. Instructors can add or edit questions, instructions, and answers, and select questions (randomly or numerically) by previewing them on the screen. Instructors can also create and administer quizzes online, whether over the Internet, a local area network (LAN), or a wide area network (WAN).
- *PowerPoint® Presentation Slides* – Located on the Instructor's Resource CD-Rom and on the text's Web site, these colorful slides reinforce chapter content and provide a rich tool for in-class lectures and out-of-class reviewing.

Additional Financial Accounting Resources

Inside Look: Analysis From All Angles

Accounting is in the news *and* the classroom with access to this new Web site from Thomson/South-Western. The *Access Card* allows the instructor and the student to utilize information related to Enron, Andersen, and other "names in the news" that involve accounting-related concerns. Well-known, popular news sources provide the background for the selected current events. Teaching tools are available to the instructor to implement class discussions, while analysis and questions are available to the student to utilize in many accounting discipline areas. This site is intended to help instructors teach and students to learn about critical current issues and understand them in the context of their accounting studies. **For a Demo, go to http://insidelook.swcollege.com.**

Thomson Analytics—Business School Edition

Bring Wall Street to the classroom with Thomson Analytics–a Web-based portal product that provides integrated access to Thomson Financial content for the purpose of financial analysis. This is an educational version of the same financial resources used by Wall Street analysts on a daily basis!

For **500 companies**, this online resource provides seamless access to:

- **Current and Past Company Data:** Worldscope®, which includes company profiles, financials and accounting results, market per-share data, annual information, and monthly prices going back to 1980.
- **Financial Analyst Data and Forecasts:** I/B/E/S Consensus Estimates, which provides consensus estimates, analyst-by-analyst earnings coverage, and analysts' forecasts.
- **SEC Disclosure Statements:** Disclosure SEC Database, which includes company profiles, annual and quarterly company financials, pricing information, and earnings.

InfoTrac® College Edition

With this resource, your students can receive anytime, anywhere online access to a database of full-text articles from hundreds of popular and scholarly periodicals, such as *Newsweek, Fortune, Entrepreneur, Journal of Accountancy,* and *Nation's Business,* among others. Students can use its fast and easy search tools to find relevant news and analytical information among the tens of thousands of articles in the database–updated daily and going back as far as four years–all at a single Web site. InfoTrac is a great way to expose students to online research techniques, with the security that the content is academically based and reliable. An InfoTrac College Edition subscription card is packaged free with new copies of the text. For more information, visit http://www.swcollege.com/infotrac/infotrac.html.

NewsEdge®

NewsEdge offers the flexibility of delivering news and information that meet the individual needs of your classroom. The content is derived from the world's premier news and information sources. Editorial experts sift through the clutter, delivering only the stories and updates students really need.

An Introduction to Accounting, Business Processes, and ERP

by Phil Reckers, Julie Smith David, and Harriet MacCracken, all of Arizona State University

Utilizing JD Edwards software demos, an industry-leading ERP company, your students will learn an overview of the use of ERP software for accounting and business processes. They will not only learn the advantages of technology in accessing business information but will also learn to apply it in three different business models. After each module, student learning is reinforced by quizzing. Equip your students with this class-tested and easy-to-use experience to help them meet the ever-changing challenges of business and technology!

INTAACT Financial Accounting

This Internet-based tutorial at http://rama.swcollege.com was designed for use in a financial accounting course or in any course where a review of the key financial concepts and terminology is needed. The program offers a visual, user-friendly way to reinforce accounting principles and includes tutorials, demonstration problems, exercises, and an interactive glossary. Users will receive an access certificate that will allow them to do the online tutorial over the full term of a course.

Accounting Career Consultant: Financial Accounting

by Charles Davis and Eric Sandburg

This resource is an online, interactive simulation. It is designed to complement both the classroom instruction and the text presentations. Each module includes links to review questions with customized feedback (approximately 20 questions), links to resources to further augment learning, and company profiles for the businesses discussed.

Accounting Ethics in the Post—Enron Age, 1e

by Iris Stuart, of California State University - Fullerton, and Bruce Stuart

With the Enron/Andersen debacle, ethics is becoming an increasingly important (and interesting) part of accounting education. Ethics coverage is also required by the AACSB for accreditation purposes. Most texts include some limited ethics coverage, but many instructors would like to include more. This timely supplement contains ethics cases based on real situations in the business world. Examples include cases tied to Enron, Global Crossing, and Boston Chicken. Identifying ethical dilemmas and projecting their resolution will allow students to develop essential skills for success in their future careers. In each section of the textbook, the problems will be labeled according to subject matter (i.e. bad debt expense, revenue recognition). This allows the instructor to select problems consistent with the needs of the course.

The Financial Reporting Project and Readings, 3e

by Bruce A. Baldwin, of Arizona State University-West, and Clayton A. Hock, of Miami University

This project book requires students to obtain and analyze "live" financial statements from publicly traded firms. Also included are several high-interest articles from popular publications, such as *The Wall Street Journal* and *Business Week*. The project has a flexible format and accommodates individual or team-based learning. Students are encouraged to compose short written responses to explain their analysis and to express their ideas based on the readings.

The Monopoly Game Practice Set

Robert Knechel, University of Florida

This fun practice set, based on Monopoly, helps students understand accounting transactions as triggered by real business events. Each student's solution is unique but easily graded.

Acknowledgments

We wish to thank the following individuals who reviewed manuscript for the text and provided helpful comments and suggestions.

Craig Bain
Northern Arizona University

Luann Bean
Pittsburg State University

Michael Bitter
Stetson University

Allen Bizzell
Southwest Texas State University

Steven Campbell
University of Idaho

Alan Cherry
Loyola Marymount University

Joann Cross
University of Wisconsin – Oshkosh

Stan Davis
Wake Forest University

Dan Devine
Eastern Michigan University

Martha Doran
San Diego State University

Gloria Grayless
Sam Houston State University

Fred Jacobs
Georgia State University

Carol Johnson
Oklahoma State University

Cathy Larson
Middlesex Community College

Robert McCabe
California State University, Fullerton

Mary Ann Prater
Clemson University

Donald Raux
Siena College

Mary Ann Reynolds
Western Washington University

Anne Rich
Quinnipiac University

Daniel Shim
Sacred Heart University

Aileen Smith
Stephen F. Austin State University

Steven White
Western Kentucky University

About the Authors

Carl S. Warren

Dr. Carl S. Warren is Professor Emeritus of Accounting at the University of Georgia, Athens. For over twenty-five years, Professor Warren taught all levels of classes. In recent years, Professor Warren focused his teaching efforts on principles of accounting and auditing classes. Professor Warren also has taught classes at the University of Iowa, Michigan State University, and University of Chicago. Professor Warren received his doctorate degree (Ph.D.) from Michigan State University and his undergraduate (B.B.A.) and masters (M.A.) degrees from the University of Iowa. Professor Warren enjoys interacting and learning from colleagues on how to improve student learning. Professor Warren's outside interests include writing short stories and novels, painting, handball, golf, skiing, backpacking, and fly-fishing.

James M. Reeve

Dr. James M. Reeve is Professor of Accounting at the University of Tennessee, Knoxville. He received his Ph.D. from Oklahoma State University in 1980. Dr. Reeve is founder of the Cost Management Institute and a member of the Institute for Productivity Through Quality faculty at the University of Tennessee. In addition to his teaching experience, Dr. Reeve brings to this text a wealth of experience consulting on managerial accounting issues with numerous companies, including Procter & Gamble, AMOCO, Rockwell International, Harris Corporation, and Freddie Mac. Dr. Reeve's interests outside the classroom and the business world include golf, skiing, reading, and travel.

Chapter 1
The Role of Accounting in Business

THE LAW OF NAVIGATION

"Anyone can steer the ship, but it takes a leader to chart the course."

–The 21 Irrefutable Laws of Leadership

Dr. John C. Maxwell

Learning Goals

1. Describe the types and forms of businesses, business strategies, value chains, and stakeholders.
2. Describe the three business activities of financing, investing, and operating.
3. Define accounting and its role in business.
4. Describe and illustrate the basic financial statements and how they interrelate.
5. Describe eight basic accounting concepts underlying financial reporting.
6. Describe and illustrate how horizontal analysis can be used to analyze and evaluate a company's performance.

Hershey Foods Corporation

For Milton Hershey, the founder of Hershey Foods Corporation, the ability to overcome failure and to "try, try again" was a key to success. His first encounter with failure came at the age of eighteen when a small candy shop he opened in Philadelphia failed after six years. His next two attempts at the candy-making business also failed—first in Chicago and then in New York. After the New York failure, he returned to Lancaster, Pennsylvania, where once again he tried his luck in the candy business by establishing the Lancaster Caramel Company.

In 1893, Hershey attended the Chicago International Exposition, where he became fascinated with German chocolate-making machinery. He bought the equipment and soon began producing chocolate-coated caramels. The chocolate-coated caramels were so well received that the Hershey Chocolate Company was organized as a subsidiary to the Lancaster Caramel Company. In 1900, Milton Hershey sold the Lancaster Caramel Company for $1 million, but he retained the chocolate machinery and the rights to manufacture chocolate. He believed that a large market existed for chocolate candy that could be mass-produced at an affordable cost.

Today, Hershey Foods Corporation is America's leading chocolate manufacturer, producing more than a billion pounds of chocolate products each year. In addition to candy, the company has expanded to baking chocolate, chocolate drinks, chocolate milk mixes, ice cream toppings, cocoa mixes, and Reese's baking pieces. For the year ending December 31, 2001, the company reported net sales of over $4 billion and net income of over $200 million.

The success of Hershey Foods brought wealth to the Hershey family. So what did Milton and his wife do with their wealth? First, they built a model town that included comfortable homes and an inexpensive public transportation system for their employees. Although Milton and his wife Catherine had no children of their own, they established a school for orphan boys. Following Catharine's premature death in 1918, Milton endowed the school with his stock in the Hershey Chocolate Company. Today, the 10,000-acre school nurtures over 1,100 financially needy boys and girls in grades K-12. Through the Hershey Trust Company, the school controls 76 percent of the voting shares of Hershey Foods Corporation.

The M.S. Hershey Foundation was established in 1935. This foundation supports the Hershey Museum, the Hershey Gardens, the Hershey Theatre, and the Hershey Community Archives. In addition, The Milton S. Hershey Medical Center of Pennsylvania State University was established in 1963 with the aid of a $50 million award from The Milton Hershey School Trust Fund.

In this chapter and throughout this text, we focus on the corporate form of business organization and examples of corporations like Hershey Foods Corporation.

Source: Adapted from the Hershey Foods Corporation and Hershey, Pennsylvania, Web sites.

Your Need to Know

Every day you interact with businesses like Hershey's. You might buy a Hershey's candy bar. You may eat lunch at McDonald's or Burger King, order a cup of coffee from Starbucks or Seattle Coffee, or fill up your car with gas at an Exxon or BP gas station. How do these businesses influence you to buy their products? What are their underlying business strategies?

As we begin our study of accounting in this chapter, we will first discuss the nature, types, activities, and strategies of businesses, such as Hershey, McDonald's, and Starbucks. In doing so, we describe business stakeholders and how businesses add value for their customers (you). We conclude the chapter by discussing the role of accounting in business, including financial statements, basic accounting concepts, and how to use financial statements to evaluate a business's performance.

The Nature of Business

1 Describe the types and forms of businesses, business strategies, value chains, and stakeholders.

You are familiar with many large companies, such as General Motors, Barnes & Noble, and AT&T. You are also familiar with many local businesses, such as gas stations, grocery stores, and restaurants. You may work for one of these businesses. But what do they have in common that identifies them as businesses?

In general, a **business** is an organization in which basic resources (inputs), such as materials and labor, are assembled and processed to provide goods or services (outputs) to customers.[1] Businesses come in all sizes, from a local coffee house to General Motors, which sells several billion dollars worth of cars and trucks each year. The customers of a business are individuals or other businesses who purchase goods or services in exchange for money or other items of value. In contrast, a church is not a business because those who receive its services are not obligated to pay for them.

The objective of most businesses is to maximize profits by providing goods or services that meet customer needs. Profit is the difference between the amount received from customers for goods or services provided and the amount paid for the inputs used to provide the goods or services. Some businesses operate with an objective other than to maximize profits. The objective of such not-for-profit businesses is to provide some benefit to society, such as medical research or conservation of natural resources. In other cases, governmental units such as cities operate water works or sewage treatment plants on a not-for-profit basis. Our focus in this text will be on businesses operated to earn a profit. However, many of the concepts and principles also apply to not-for-profit businesses.

Types of Businesses

There are three different types of businesses that are operated for profit: manufacturing, merchandising, and service businesses. Each type of business has unique characteristics.

Manufacturing businesses change basic inputs into products that are sold to individual customers. Examples of manufacturing businesses and some of their products are shown below.

1 A glossary of terms appears at the end of each chapter in the text.

Manufacturing Business	Product
General Motors	Automobiles, trucks, vans
General Mills	Breakfast cereals
Boeing	Jet aircraft
Nike	Athletic shoes
Coca-Cola	Beverages
Sony	Stereos, televisions, radios

Merchandising businesses also sell products to customers. However, they do not make the products but purchase them from other businesses (such as manufacturers). In this sense, merchandisers bring products and customers together. Examples of merchandising businesses and some of the products they sell are shown below.

Merchandising Business	Product
Wal-Mart	General merchandise
Toys"R"Us	Toys
Barnes & Noble	Books
Best Buy	Consumer electronics
Amazon.com	Books

Service businesses provide services rather than products to customers. Examples of service businesses and the types of services they offer are shown below.

Service Business	Service
Disney	Entertainment
Delta Air Lines	Transportation
Marriott Hotels	Hospitality and lodging
Merrill Lynch	Financial
Sprint	Telecommunications

Forms of Business

A business is normally organized as one of three different forms: proprietorship, partnership, or corporation. A **proprietorship** is owned by one individual. More than 70 percent of the businesses in the United States are organized as proprietorships. The popularity of this form is due to the ease and low cost of organizing. The primary disadvantage of proprietorships is that the financial resources available to the business are limited to the individual owner's resources. Small local businesses such as hardware stores, repair shops, laundries, restaurants, and maid services are often organized as proprietorships.

As a business grows and requires more financial and managerial resources, it may become a partnership. A **partnership** is owned by two or more individuals. Like proprietorships, small local businesses such as automotive repair shops, music stores, beauty shops, and men's and women's clothing stores may be organized as partnerships. Currently, about 10 percent of the businesses in the United States are organized as partnerships.

Like proprietorships, a partnership may outgrow its ability to finance its operations. As a result, it may become a corporation. A **corporation** is organized under state or federal statutes as a separate legal entity. The ownership of a corporation is divided into shares of stock. A corporation issues the stock to individuals or other businesses, who then become owners or stockholders of the corporation.

A primary advantage of the corporate form is the ability to obtain large amounts of resources by issuing shares of stock, which are ownership rights in the corporation. For this reason, most companies that require large investments in equipment and facilities are organized as corporations. For example, Toys"R"Us has raised over $800 million by issuing shares of common stock to finance its operations. Other examples of corporations include General Motors, Ford, International Business Machines (IBM), Coca-Cola, and General Electric.

About 20 percent of the businesses in the United States are organized as corporations. However, since most large companies are organized as corporations, over 90 percent of the total dollars of business receipts are received by corporations. Thus, corporations have a major influence on the economy.

The three types of businesses we discussed earlier—manufacturing, merchandising, and service—may be either proprietorships, partnerships, or corporations. However, because of the large amount of resources required to operate a manufacturing business, most manufacturing businesses are corporations. Likewise, most large retailers such as Wal-Mart, Sears, and JC Penney are corporations. Because most large businesses are corporations, they tend to dominate the economic activity in the United States. For this reason, we focus our attention in this text on the corporate form of organization. However, many of the concepts and principles that we discuss also apply to proprietorships and partnerships.

Business Strategies

How does a business decide which products or services to offer its customers? For example, should Best Buy offer warranty and repair services to its customers? Many factors influence this decision, but ultimately the decision is made on the basis of whether it is consistent with the overall business strategy of the company.

A **business strategy** is an integrated set of plans and actions designed to enable the business to gain an advantage over its competitors, and in doing so, to maximize its profits. The two basic strategies a business may use are a low-cost strategy or a differentiation strategy.

Under a **low-cost strategy**, a business designs and produces products or services of acceptable quality at a cost lower than its competitors. Wal-Mart and Southwest Airlines are examples of businesses with a low-cost strategy. Such businesses often sell no-frills, standardized products to the most typical customer in the industry. Following this strategy, businesses must continually focus on lowering costs.

Businesses may try to achieve lower costs in a variety of ways. For example, a business may employ strict budgetary controls, use sophisticated training programs, implement simple manufacturing technologies, or enter into cost-saving supplier relationships. Such supplier relationships may involve linking the supplier's production process directly

Ethics in Action

Partnership Ethics

In a partnership, the unethical behavior of one partner may broadly impact the whole firm. A partner of Arthur Andersen & Co., a major public accounting firm, pleaded guilty to obstruction of justice in the destruction of documents related to the Enron bankruptcy. As a result of these events, the Justice Department prosecuted and won a case in which the entire firm was accused of obstruction of justice. This worldwide firm then began a decline, as its clients fled in droves. The questionable actions of a few had severe implications for many innocent Andersen partners and employees.

to the client's production processes to minimize inventory costs, variations in raw materials, and record keeping costs.

A primary concern of a business using a low-cost strategy is that a competitor may copy its low costs or develop technological advances that enables it to achieve even lower costs. Another concern is that competitors may differentiate their products in such a way that customers no longer desire a standardized, no-frills product. For example, local pharmacies most often try to compete with Wal-Mart on the basis of personalized service rather than cost.

Under a **differentiation strategy**, a business designs and produces products or services that possess unique attributes or characteristics for which customers are willing to pay a premium price. For the differentiation strategy to be successful, a product or service must be truly unique or perceived as unique in quality, reliability, image, or design. To illustrate, Maytag attempts to differentiate its appliances on the basis of reliability, while Tommy Hilfiger differentiates its clothing on the basis of image.

Businesses using a differentiation strategy often use information systems to capture and analyze customer buying habits and preferences. For example, many grocery stores such as Kroger and Safeway issue magnetic cards to preferred customers that allow the consumer to receive special discounts on purchases. In addition to establishing brand loyalty, the cards allow the stores to track consumer preferences and buying habits for use in purchasing and advertising campaigns.

Companies may enhance differentiation by investing in manufacturing and service technologies, such as flexible manufacturing methods that allow timely product design and delivery. Some companies use marketing and sales efforts to promote product differences. Other companies use unique credit-granting arrangements, emphasize personal relationships with customers, or offer extensive training and after-sales service programs for customers.

A business using a differentiation strategy wants customers to pay a premium price for the differentiated features of its products. However, a business may provide features that exceed the customers' needs. In this case, competitors may be able to offer customers less differentiated products at lower costs. Also, customers' perceptions of the differentiated features may change. As a result, customers may not be willing to continue to pay a premium price for the products. For example, as Tommy Hilfiger clothing becomes more commonplace, customers may be unwilling to pay a premium price for Hilfiger clothing. Over time, customers may also become better educated about the products and the value of the differentiated features. For example, IBM personal computers were once viewed as being differentiated on quality. However, as consumers have become better educated and more experienced with personal computers, Dell and Gateway computers have also become perceived as high quality.

Ethics in Action

Misleading Advertising

One method of creating differentiation is by using advertising to communicate the unique features of a product. However, it is fraudulent to make unsubstantiated claims about products or services. For example, the Federal Trade Commission (FTC) recently warned makers of devices and additives that claim to "improve gas mileage up to 300 percent" to cease from making such "false and grossly exaggerated" claims.

Source: "USA: FTC says gas-saving gadgets inflate online claims," 04/18/2002, Reuters English News Service.

A business may attempt to implement a **combination strategy** that includes elements of both the low-cost and differentiation strategies. That is, a business may attempt to develop a differentiated product at competitive, low-cost prices. For example, Andersen Windows allows customers to design their own windows through the use of its proprietary manufacturing software. By using flexible manufacturing, Andersen Windows can produce a variety of windows in small quantities with a low or moderate cost. Thus, Andersen windows sell at a higher price than standard low-cost windows, but at a lower price than a fully customized window built on site.

As you might expect, a danger of a business using a combination strategy is that its products might not adequately satisfy either end of the market. That is, because its products are differentiated, it cannot establish itself as the low-cost leader, and, at the same time, its products may not be differentiated enough that customers are willing to pay a premium price. In other words, the business may become "stuck in the middle." For example, JC Penney has difficulty competing as a low-cost leader against Wal-Mart, Kmart, Goody's Family Clothing, Fashion USA, T.J. Maxx, and Target. At the same time, JC Penney cannot adequately differentiate its stores and merchandise from such competitors as The Gap, Old Navy, Eddie Bauer, and Talbot's so that it can charge higher prices.

A business may also attempt to implement different strategies for different markets. For example, Toyota segments the market for automobiles by offering the Lexus to image- and quality-conscious buyers. To reinforce this image, Toyota developed a separate dealer network. At the same time, Toyota offers a low-cost automobile, the Echo, to price-sensitive buyers.

Exhibit 1 summarizes the characteristics of the low-cost, differentiation, and combination strategies. In addition, some common examples of businesses that employ each strategy are also listed.

Exhibit 1

Business Strategies and Industries

	Industry					
Business Strategy	**Airline**	**Freight**	**Automotive**	**Retail**	**Financial Services**	**Hotel**
Low cost	Southwest	Union Pacific	Saturn	Sam's Clubs	Schwab	Super 8
Differentiated	Virgin Atlantic	Federal Express	BMW	Talbot's	Morgan Stanley	Ritz Carlton
Combination	Delta	United Postal Service	Ford	Target	Merrill Lynch	Marriott

Value Chain of a Business

Once a business has chosen a strategy, it must implement the strategy in its value chain. A **value chain** is the way a business adds value for its customers by processing inputs into a product or service, as shown in Exhibit 2.

Exhibit 2

The Value Chain

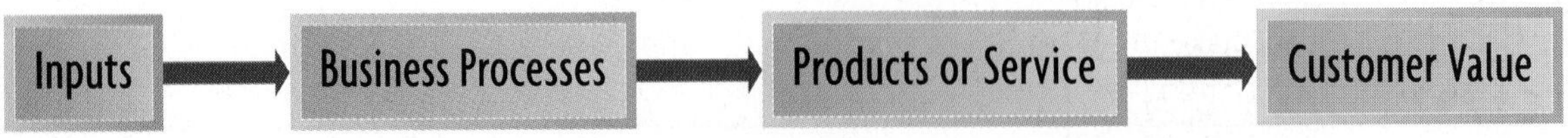

Strategy in Business

It's All in the Name

Intel develops and produces microprocessors for use in electronic equipment, including personal computers and organizers. Beginning with the 8086 processor and continuing with the 286, 386, and 486 processors, Intel's processors were widely used in personal computers during the 1980s and 1990s. Intel's competitors, however, also developed and sold 386 and 486 processors. In doing so, its competitors were able to erode Intel's market share. In responding, Intel named its next microprocessor the "Pentium," rather than the 586, and registered "Pentium" as a trademark. By doing so, Intel prevented its competitors from selling their products as "Pentiums." Thus, Intel developed a "differentiated" brand name that its competitors were unable to duplicate.

To illustrate, Delta Air Lines' value chain consists of taking inputs, such as people, aircraft, and equipment, and processing these inputs into a service of transporting goods and passengers throughout the world. The extent to which customers value Delta's passenger service is reflected by the air fares Delta is able to charge as well as passenger load factors (percentage of seats occupied). For example, the extent to which Delta can, on average, charge higher fares than discount airlines, such as AirTran, implies that passengers value Delta's services more than AirTran's. These services may include newer, more comfortable aircraft, the ability to earn frequent flyer miles, more convenient passenger schedules, passenger lounges for frequent flyers, and international connections.

A business's value chain can be divided into primary and supporting processes. Primary processes are those that are directly involved in creating value for customers. Examples of primary processes include manufacturing, selling, and customer service. Supporting processes are those that facilitate the primary processes. Examples of support processes include purchasing, personnel, and accounting.[2] For Delta Air Lines, primary processes would include aircraft maintenance, baggage handling, ticketing, and flight operations. Secondary processes for Delta Air Lines would include the accounting and finance functions, contracting for fuel deliveries, and investor relations.

Business Stakeholders

A company's business strategy and how well the company implements its strategy directly affect its economic performance and its stakeholders. For example, Kmart was unsuccessful in implementing a business strategy that would allow it to compete effectively against Wal-Mart. The result was that Kmart filed for bankruptcy protection in early 2002, and Kmart stakeholders, including employees, creditors, and stockholders, suffered.

A **business stakeholder** is a person or entity that has an interest in the economic performance and well-being of a business. For example, stockholders, suppliers, customers, and employees are all stakeholders in a corporation. Business stakeholders can be classified into one of the four categories illustrated in Exhibit 3.

---

2 The value chain is described and illustrated in most management textbooks. A more advanced discussion of the value chain can be found in *Competitive Advantage* by Michael E. Porter [The Free Press (New York: 1985)].

Exhibit 3
Business Stakeholders

Business Stakeholder	**Interest in the Business**	**Examples**
Capital market stakeholder	Providers of major financing for the business	Banks, owners, stockholders
Product or service market stakeholders	Buyers of products or services and vendors to the business	Customers and suppliers
Government stakeholders	Collect taxes and fees from the business and its employees	Federal, state, and city governments
Internal stakeholders	Individuals employed by the business	Employees and managers

Capital market stakeholders provide the major financing for the business in order for the business to begin and continue its operations. Banks and other long-term creditors have an economic interest in recovering the amount they loaned the business plus interest. Owners and stockholders want to maximize the economic value of their investments and thus also have an economic interest in the business. Capital market stakeholders expect to receive a return on their investments proportionate to the degree of risk they are taking on their investments. Since banks and long-term creditors have first preference to the assets in case the business fails, their risk is less than that of the owners and stakeholders, and thus their overall return is lower.

Product or service market stakeholders include customers who purchase the business's products or services as well as the vendors who supply inputs to the business. Customers have an economic interest in the continued success of the business. For example, customers of the Internet provider @home.com were initially unable to retrieve their e-mail or connect with the Internet when @home.com declared bankruptcy. Customers who purchase advance tickets on Southwest Airlines have an economic interest in whether Southwest will continue in business. Similarly, suppliers are stakeholders in the continued success of their customers. Suppliers may invest in technology or other capital equipment to meet a customer's buying and manufacturing specifications. If a customer fails or cuts back on purchases during downturns, suppliers may see their business decline also.

Various governments have an interest in the economic performance of businesses. As a result, city and state governments often provide incentives for businesses to locate in their jurisdictions. City, county, state, and federal governments collect taxes from businesses within their jurisdictions. The better a business does, the more taxes the government can collect. In addition, workers are taxed on their wages. In contrast, workers who are laid off and unemployed can file claims for unemployment compensation, which results in a financial burden for the government.

Internal stakeholders include individuals employed by the business. The managers are those individuals who the owners have authorized to operate the business. Managers are primarily evaluated on the economic performance of the business. The managers of businesses that perform poorly are often fired by the owners. Thus, managers have an incentive to maximize the economic value of the business. Owners may offer managers salary contracts that are tied directly to how well the business performs. For example, a manager might receive a percent of the profits or a percent of the increase in profits.

Employees provide services to the company they work for in exchange for pay. Thus, employees have an interest in the economic performance of the business because their jobs depend upon it. During business downturns, it is not unusual for a business to lay off workers for extended periods of time. In the extreme, a business may fail and the employees lose their jobs permanently. Employee labor unions often use the good economic performance of a business to argue for wage increases. In contrast, businesses often use poor economic performance to argue for employee concessions such as wage decreases.

Business Activities

2 Describe the three business activities of financing, investing, and operating.

Regardless of whether the company is Microsoft or General Motors, all businesses are engaged in the activities of financing, investing, and operating. First, a business must obtain the necessary funds to finance the costs to organize, pay legal fees, and pay other startup costs. Next, a business must invest funds in the necessary assets such as building and equipment to begin operations. For example, Milton Hershey invested in the German chocolate-making machinery he saw at the Chicago International Exposition. Finally, a business must utilize its assets and resources to implement its business strategy. Milton Hershey's business strategy was to mass-produce chocolate candies at an affordable cost.

As we will discuss later in this chapter, a major role of accounting is to provide stakeholders with information on the financing, investing, and operating activities of businesses. Financial statements are one source of such information.

Financing Activities

Financing activities involve obtaining funds to begin and operate a business. Businesses seek financing through the use of the capital markets. This financing may take the form of borrowing or issuing shares of ownership. Most major businesses use both means of financing.

When a business borrows money, it incurs a liability. A **liability** is a legal obligation to repay the amount borrowed according to the terms of the borrowing agreement. For example, when you use your credit card, you incur an obligation to pay the issuer (bank). When a business borrows from a vendor or supplier, the liability is called an **account payable**. In such cases, the business is buying on credit and promising to pay according to the terms set forth by the vendor or supplier. Most vendors and suppliers require payment within a relatively short time, such as thirty days. As of December 31, 2001, Hershey Foods Corporation reported approximately $150 million of accounts payable.

A business may borrow money by issuing bonds. *Bonds* are sold to investors and normally require repayment with interest at a specific time in the future. Bonds are a type of long-term financing, with a face amount that is normally due after several years have passed. For example, Lucent Technologies currently has bonds due in 2028. In contrast, the interest on bonds is normally paid semiannually. Bond obligations are reported as **bonds payable**, and any interest that is due is reported as **interest payable**. Examples of well-known companies that have bonds outstanding include American Telephone and Telegraph (ATT), John Deere, and Xerox.

Most large corporations also borrow money by issuing commercial paper and negotiating lines of credit with financial institutions. Commercial paper is debt obligations that are sold to investors, such as banks and insurance companies, based upon the general creditworthiness of the corporation. Similarly, lines of credit are negotiated with financial institutions in such a way that the corporation may borrow on the line of credit as needed. For example, Hershey Foods has a $500 million line of credit with a syndicate of banks. However, as of December 31, 2001, it had borrowed slightly over $250 million on its credit line. When a corporation issues commercial paper or borrows on a line of credit, it incurs a note payable. A **note payable** requires payment of the amount of borrowing plus interest. Notes payable may be issued either on a short-term or a long-term basis.

A business may also finance its operations by issuing shares of ownership. For a corporation, shares of ownership are issued in the form of shares of stock. Although corporations may issue a variety of different types of stock, the basic type of stock issued to owners is called **common stock**. For our purposes, we will use the term **capital stock** to include all the types of stock a corporation may issue.[3] Investors who purchase the stock are referred to as **stockholders**.

The claims of creditors and stockholders on the assets of the corporation are different. In case of a corporation's liquidation or bankruptcy, creditors have first claim on its assets. Only after the creditors' claims are satisfied can the stockholders obtain corporate assets. In addition, while creditors expect to receive timely payments of their claims, which may include interest, stockholders are not entitled to regular payments. However, many corporations distribute earnings to stockholders on a regular basis as long as the claims of creditors are being satisfied. These distributions of earnings to stockholders are called **dividends**. During 2001, Hershey paid stockholders almost $130 million in dividends.

Investing Activities

Once financing has been obtained, a business uses **investing activities** to obtain the necessary resources to start and operate the business. Depending upon the nature of the business, a variety of different resources must be purchased. For example, Milton Hershey purchased the German chocolate-making machinery and later constructed a building to house the Hershey operations. In addition to machinery and buildings, other resources could include computers, office furnishings, trucks, and automobiles. Although most resources have physical characteristics, such as equipment, some resources are intangible in nature. For example, a business may purchase patent rights for use in a manufacturing process or product.

The resources that a business owns are called **assets**. A business may acquire assets through the financing, investing, and operating activities. Assets are acquired through financing activities when the business acquires cash through borrowing or issuing shares of stock. Cash is used to purchase assets through investing activities, such as in the preceding paragraph. Finally, assets may be acquired through operating activities, as we will describe in the next section.

Assets may take a variety of different forms. For example, tangible assets include cash, land, property, plant, and equipment. Assets may also include intangible items, such as rights to patents and rights to payments from customers. Rights to payments from customers are called **accounts receivable**. Other intangible assets, such as goodwill, copyrights, or patents, are often grouped together and reported as **intangible assets**. A business may also prepay for items such as insurance or rent. Such items, which are assets until they are consumed, are normally reported as **prepaid expenses**.

Operating Activities

Once resources have been acquired, a business uses **operating activities** to implement its business strategy. Hershey's strategy was to mass-produce and distribute chocolate candies at affordable prices. When Hershey sold its chocolates, it received revenue from its customers. **Revenue** is the increase in assets from selling products or services. Revenues are often identified according to their source. For example, revenues received from selling products are called *sales*. Revenues received from providing services are called *fees*.

To earn revenue, a business incurs costs, such as wages of employees, salaries of managers, rent, insurance, advertising, freight, and utilities. Costs used to earn revenue are called **expenses**. Depending upon the nature of the cost, expenses may be identified in a variety of ways. For example, the cost of products sold is often referred to as the *cost of merchandise sold, cost of sales*, or *cost of goods sold*. Other expenses are often classified as either *selling expenses* or *administrative expenses*. Selling expenses include those costs directly related to the selling of a product or service. For example, selling expenses include such costs as sales salaries, sales commissions, freight, and advertising costs. Administrative expenses include other costs not directly related to the selling, such as officer salaries and other costs of the corporate office.

---

3 Types of stock are discussed in Chapter 11, "Stockholders' Equity: Capital Stock and Dividends."

As we will discuss later in this chapter, by comparing the revenues for a period with the related expenses, you can determine whether the business earned net income or incurred a net loss. A **net income** results when revenues exceed expenses. A **net loss** results when expenses exceed revenues.

What Is Accounting and Its Role in Business?

3 Define accounting and its role in business.

How do stakeholders get information about the financing, investing, and operating activities of a business? This is the role of accounting. Accounting provides information for managers to use in operating the business. In addition, accounting provides information to other stakeholders to use in assessing the economic performance and condition of the business.

In a general sense, **accounting** can be defined as an information system that provides reports to stakeholders about the economic activities and condition of a business. We will focus our discussions in this text on accounting and its role in business. However, many of the concepts in this text also apply to individuals, governments, and other types of organizations. For example, individuals must account for activities such as hours worked, checks written, and bills due. Stakeholders for individuals include creditors, dependents, and the government. A main interest of the government is making sure that individuals pay the proper taxes.

Accounting is sometimes called the "language of business." This is because accounting is the means by which business information is communicated to the stakeholders. For example, accounting reports summarizing the profitability of a new product help Coca-Cola's management decide whether to continue offering the new product for sale. Likewise, financial analysts use accounting reports in deciding whether to recommend the purchase of Coca-Cola's stock. Banks use accounting reports in deciding the amount of credit to extend to Coca-Cola. Suppliers use accounting reports in deciding whether to offer credit for Coca-Cola's purchases of supplies and raw materials. State and federal governments use accounting reports as a basis for assessing taxes on Coca-Cola.

As we described above, accounting serves many purposes for business. A primary purpose is to summarize the financial performance of the firm for external users, such as banks and governmental agencies. The branch of accounting that is associated with preparing reports for users external to the business is termed *financial accounting.* Accounting also can be used to guide management in making decisions about the business. This branch of accounting is called *managerial accounting.* Financial and managerial accounting overlap in many areas. For example, financial reports for external users are often used by managers in considering the impact of their decisions.

In this text, we focus on financial accounting. The two major objectives of financial accounting are:

1. To report the financial condition of a business at a point in time.
2. To report changes in the financial condition of a business over a period of time.

The relationship between the two financial accounting objectives is shown in Exhibit 4. You may think of the first objective as a still photograph (snapshot) of the business and the second objective as a moving picture (video) of the business. The first objective measures the financial status of a business. This measure is used by stakeholders to evaluate the business's financial health at a point in time. The second objective measures the change in the financial condition of a business for a period of time. This measure is used by stakeholders to predict how a business may perform in the future.

The objectives of accounting are satisfied by (1) recording the economic events affecting a business and then (2) summarizing the impact of these events on the business in financial reports, called **financial statements**. We will describe and illustrate the basic financial statements next.

Exhibit 4

Objectives of Financial Accounting

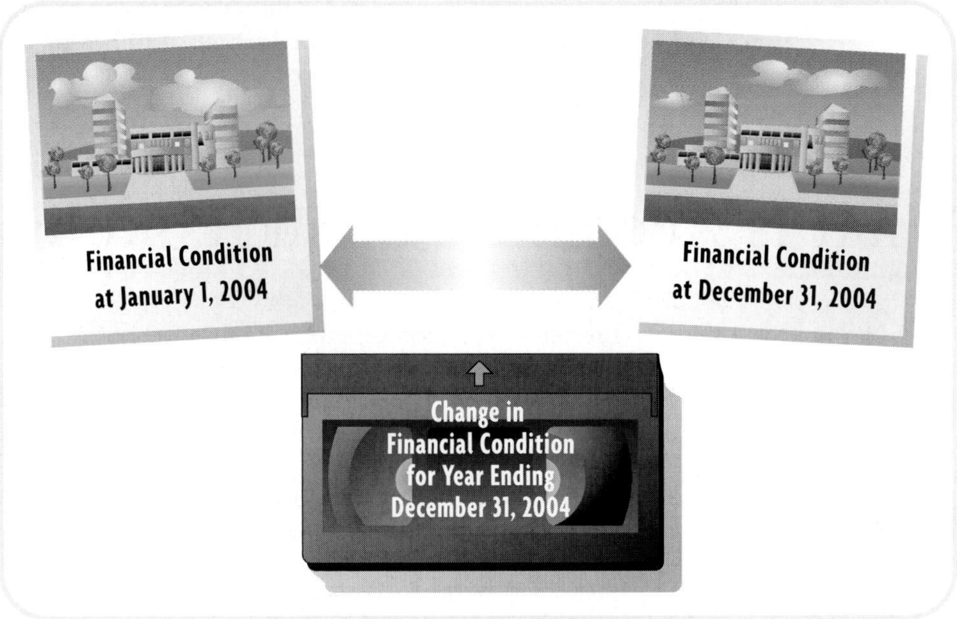

Financial Statements

4 Describe and illustrate the basic financial statements and how they interrelate.

Financial statements report the financial condition of a business at a point in time and changes in the financial condition over a period of time. The four basic financial statements and their relationship to the two objectives of financial accounting are listed below.[4]

Financial Statement	Financial Accounting Objective
Income statement	Reports change in financial condition
Retained earnings statement	Reports change in financial condition
Balance sheet	Reports financial condition
Statement of cash flows	Reports change in financial condition

The income statement is normally prepared first, followed by the retained earnings statement, the balance sheet, and the statement of cash flows. The nature of each statement is described below.

- **Income statement**—A summary of the revenue and the expenses for a specific period of time, such as a month or a year.
- **Retained earnings statement**—A summary of the changes in the earnings retained in the corporation for a specific period of time, such as a month or a year.
- **Balance sheet**—A list of the assets, liabilities, and stockholders' equity as of a specific date, usually at the close of the last day of a month or a year.

4 Instead of the retained earnings statement, companies often prepare a statement of stockholders' equity. This statement reports changes in retained earnings as well as changes in other stockholders' equity items. We describe and illustrate the statement of stockholders' equity in a later chapter, after we have discussed stockholders' equity in more detail.

- **Statement of cash flows**–A summary of the cash receipts and cash payments for a specific period of time, such as a month or a year.

The four financial statements are illustrated in Exhibits 5–8. The data for the statements were adapted from the annual report of Hershey Foods Corporation.[5]

Income Statement

The income statement reports the change in financial condition due to the operations of a business. The time period covered by the income statement may vary depending upon the needs of the stakeholders. Public corporations are required to file quarterly and annual income statements with the Securities and Exchange Commission. The income statement shown in Exhibit 5 for Hershey Foods Corporation is for the year ended December 31, 2001.

Exhibit 5

Income Statement: Hershey Foods Corporation

Hershey Foods Corporation
Income Statement
For the Year Ended December 31, 2001
(in thousands)

Revenues:		
Sales		$4,557,241
Expenses:		
Cost of sales	$2,665,566	
Selling and administrative	1,269,964	
Other expenses	209,077	
Interest	69,093	
Income taxes	136,385	4,350,085
Net income		$ 207,156

Since the focus of business operations is to generate revenues, the income statement begins by listing the revenues for the period. During 2001 Hershey Foods Corporation generated sales of over $4.5 billion. These sales are listed under the revenue caption. You should note that the numbers shown in Exhibit 5 are expressed in thousands of dollars. It is common for large corporations to express their financial statements in thousands and, in some cases, millions of dollars.

Following the revenues, the expenses that were used in generating the revenues are listed. For Hershey Foods, these expenses include cost of sales, selling and administrative, other expenses, interest, and income taxes.[6] By reporting the expenses and the related revenues for a period, the expenses are said to be matched against the revenues. This is known in accounting as the *matching concept.* We will further discuss this concept later in this chapter.

5 The financial statements for Hershey Foods Corporation can be found at www.hersheys.com by clicking on "Investor Relations."

6 Other expenses consist primarily of an asset impairment expense, which we will discuss in a later chapter.

For 2001, General Motors reported net sales of $177,260 million and net income of $601 million. What were General Motors' total expenses for 2001?

$176,659 million ($177,260 million − $601 million)

When revenues exceed expenses for a period, the business has *net income.* If expenses exceed revenues, the business has a *net loss.* Reporting net income means that the business increased its net assets through its operations. That is, the assets created by the revenues coming into the business exceeded the assets used in generating the revenues. The objective of most businesses is to maximize net income or profit. A net loss means that the business decreased its net assets through its operations. While a business might survive in the short-run by reporting net losses, in the long-run a business must report net income to survive.

During 2001, Hershey Foods earned net income of over $200 million dollars. Is this good or bad? Certainly, net income is better than a net loss. However, the stakeholders must assess the economic performance of the corporation according to their own standards. For example, a creditor might be satisfied that the net income is sufficient to assure that it will be repaid. On the other hand, a stockholder might not be satisfied if the corporation's profitability is less than its competitors' profitability. Throughout this text, we describe various methods and analyses of assessing corporate performance.

Retained Earnings Statement

The retained earnings statement reports changes in financial condition due to changes in retained earnings during a period. **Retained earnings** is the portion of a corporation's net income that is retained in the business. A corporation may retain all its net income for use in expanding operations, or it may pay a portion or all its net income to stockholders as dividends. For example, high growth companies like Microsoft and Amazon.com do not pay dividends to stockholders, but rather retain profits for future expansion. In contrast, more mature corporations like Coca-Cola or General Electric routinely pay their stockholders a regular dividend. Thus, investors such as retirees who desire the comfort of a routine dividend payment might invest in Coca-Cola or General Electric. In contrast, younger and more aggressive growth-oriented investors might invest in Microsoft or Amazon.com.

Since retained earnings depend upon net income, the time period covered by the retained earnings statement is the same period as the income statement. Thus, the retained earnings statement for Hershey Foods Corporation shown in Exhibit 6 is for the year ended December 31, 2001.

Exhibit 6

Retained Earnings Statement: Hershey Foods Corporation

Hershey Foods Corporation
Retained Earnings Statement
For the Year Ended December 31, 2001
(in thousands)

Retained earnings, January 1, 2001		$2,702,927
Add net income	$207,156	
Less dividends	154,750	
Increase in retained earnings		52,406
Retained earnings, December 31, 2001		$2,755,333

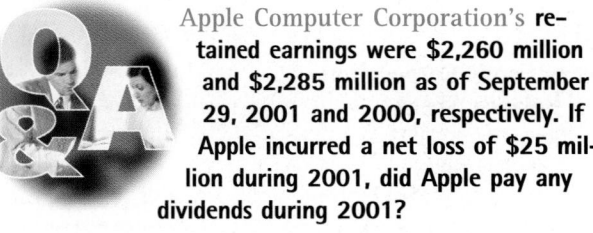

Apple Computer Corporation's **retained earnings were $2,260 million and $2,285 million as of September 29, 2001 and 2000, respectively. If Apple incurred a net loss of $25 million during 2001, did Apple pay any dividends during 2001?**

No. The decrease in retained earnings of $25 million is due entirely to the net loss of $25 million.

You should note that dividends are reported in Hershey's retained earnings statement rather than in the income statement. This is because dividends are not an expense, but are a distribution of net income to stockholders. During 2001, Hershey paid dividends of approximately $155 million and retained approximately $52 million of its net income in the business. Thus, Hershey's retained earnings increased from $2,703 million to $2,755 million during 2001.

Balance Sheet

The balance sheet reports the financial condition as of a point in time. This is in contrast to the income statement, the retained earnings statement, and the statement of cash flows that report changes in financial condition. The financial condition of a business as of a point in time is measured by its total assets and claims or rights to those assets. Thus, the financial condition of a business can be represented as follows:

Assets = Claims (Rights to the Assets)

The claims on a business's assets consist of rights of creditors who have loaned money or extended credit to the business and the rights of stockholders who have invested in the business. As we discussed earlier, the rights of creditors are liabilities. The rights of stockholders are referred to as **stockholders' equity**, which is sometimes referred to as **owners' equity**. Thus, the assets and the claims on those assets can be presented in equation form as follows:

Assets = Liabilities + Stockholders' Equity

This equation is called the **accounting equation.** As we shall discover in later chapters, accounting information systems are developed using this equation as their foundation.

The balance sheet, sometimes called the statement of financial condition, is prepared using the framework of the accounting equation. That is, assets are listed first and added to arrive at total assets. Liabilities are then listed and added to arrive at total liabilities. Stockholders' equity items are listed next and added to arrive at total stockholders' equity. Finally, the total assets must equal the combined total liabilities and stockholders' equity. In other words, the accounting equation must balance; thus, the name balance sheet. The balance sheet for Hershey Foods Corporation as of December 31, 2001, is shown in Exhibit 7.

IBM's **balance sheet as of December 31, 2001, reported assets of $88,313 million and liabilities of $64,699 million. What is IBM's stockholders' equity as of December 31, 2001?**

$23,614 million ($88,313 million − $64,699 million)

As of December 31, 2001, Hershey had total assets of approximately $3.2 billion, of which creditors had claims of $2.1 billion and stockholders had claims of $1.1 billion. One use of the balance sheet by creditors is to determine whether the corporation's assets are sufficient to ensure that they will be paid their claims. In Hershey's case, as of December 31, 2001, the assets of the corporation exceed the creditors' claims by $1.1 billion. Thus, the creditors are reasonably assured that their claims will be repaid.

Statement of Cash Flows

The statement of cash flows reports the change in financial condition due to the changes in cash during a period. During 2001, Hershey's net cash increased by $102 million, as shown in Exhibit 8 on page 19.

Earlier in this chapter, we discussed the three business activities of financing, investing, and operating. Any changes in cash must be related to one of these three activities.

Exhibit 7

Balance Sheet: Hershey Foods Corporation

Hershey Foods Corporation
Balance Sheet
December 31, 2001
(in thousands)

Assets	
Cash	$ 134,147
Accounts receivable	361,726
Inventories	512,134
Prepaid expenses	62,595
Property, plant and equipment	1,534,901
Intangibles	429,128
Other assets	212,799
Total assets	$ 3,247,430
Liabilities	
Accounts payable	$ 133,049
Accrued liabilities	462,901
Notes and other debt	1,245,939
Income taxes	258,337
Total liabilities	$ 2,100,226
Stockholders' Equity	
Capital stock	$ 183,213
Retained earnings	2,755,333
Repurchased stock and other equity items	(1,791,342)
Total stockholders' equity	$ 1,147,204
Total liabilities and stockholders' equity	$ 3,247,430

Thus, the statement of cash flows is organized by reporting the changes in each of these three activities, as shown in Exhibit 8.

In the statement of cash flows, the net cash flows from operating activities is reported first, because cash flows from operating activities are a primary analysis focus for most business stakeholders. For example, creditors are interested in determining whether the company's operating activities are generating enough positive cash flow to repay their debts. Likewise, stockholders are interested in the company's ability to pay dividends. A business cannot survive in the long term unless it generates positive cash flows from operating activities. Thus, employees, managers, and other stakeholders interested in the long-term viability of the business also focus upon the cash flows from operating activities. During 2001, Hershey's operations generated a positive net cash flow of approximately $706 million.

Because of the impact investing activities have on the operations of a business, the cash flows from investing activities are presented following the cash flows from operating activities section. Any cash receipts from selling property, plant, and equipment would be reported in this section. Likewise, any purchases of property, plant, and equipment would be reported as cash payments. Companies that are expanding rapidly, such as startup companies, will normally report negative net cash flows from investing activities. In contrast, companies that are downsizing or selling segments of the business may report positive net cash flows from investing activities.

Exhibit 8

Statement of Cash Flows: Hershey Foods Corporation

Hershey Foods Corporation
Statement of Cash Flows
For the Year Ended December 31, 2001
(in thousands)

Net cash flows from operating activities	$ 706,405
Cash flows from investing activities:	
Investments in property, plant, and equipment	$(187,029)
Proceeds from sale of property, plant, and equipment	63,042
Net cash flows used in investing activities	$(123,987)
Cash flows from financing activities:	
Cash receipts from financing activities, including debt	$ 30,589
Dividends paid to stockholders	(154,750)
Repurchase of stock	(40,322)
Other, including repayment of debt	(315,757)
Net cash flows used in financing activities	$(480,240)
Net increase in cash during 2001	$ 102,178
Cash as of January 1, 2001	31,969
Cash as of December 31, 2001	$ 134,147

As shown in Exhibit 8, Hershey reported negative net cash flows from investing activities of approximately $124 million. Of this negative net cash flow, $187 million was from the purchase of property, plant, and equipment, while approximately $63 million was related to the sale of property, plant, and equipment. Thus, it appears that Hershey is expanding operations.

Cash flows from financing activities are reported next. Any cash receipts from issuing debt or stock would be reported in this section as cash receipts. Likewise, paying debt or dividends would be reported as cash payments. Business stakeholders can analyze cash flows from financing activities to determine whether a business is changing its financing policies.

As shown in Exhibit 8, Hershey paid dividends of approximately $155 million and repaid debt of approximately $316 million. Cash of approximately $31 million was received from financing activities that included additional borrowing from creditors. Finally, Hershey purchased its own stock at a cost of approximately $40 million. A company may purchase its own stock if the corporate management believes its stock is undervalued or for providing stock to employees or managers as part of an incentive (stock option) plan.[7]

The statement of cash flows is completed by determining the increase or decrease in cash flows for the period by adding the net cash flows from operating, investing, and financing activities. Hershey reported a net increase in cash of approximately $102 million. This increase or decrease is added to or subtracted from the cash at the beginning of the period to determine the cash as of the end of the period. Thus, Hershey began the year with approximately $32 million in cash and ended the year with $134 million in cash.

So what does the statement of cash flows reveal about Hershey Foods Corporation during 2001? The statement reveals that Hershey generated over $700 million in cash flows

7 We will discuss the accounting for a company's purchase of its own stock in a later chapter.

from its operations while using cash to expand its operations and pay dividends to stockholders. Overall, Hershey appears to be in a strong operating position to generate cash and pay its creditors.

Interrelationships Among Financial Statements

As we mentioned earlier, financial statements are prepared in the order of the income statement, retained earnings statement, balance sheet, and statement of cash flows. Preparing them in this order is important because the financial statements are interrelated. Using the Hershey Foods Corporation financial statements in Exhibits 5–8, these interrelationships are as follows:[8]

1. The income and retained earnings statements are interrelated. The net income or net loss appearing on the income statement also appears on the retained earnings statement as either an addition (net income) to or deduction (net loss) from the beginning retained earnings. To illustrate, Hershey's net income of $207,156 million is also reported on the retained earnings statement as an addition to the beginning retained earnings.
2. The retained earnings statement and the balance sheet are interrelated. The retained earnings at the end of the period on the retained earnings statement also appears on the balance sheet as a part of stockholders' equity. To illustrate, Hershey's retained earnings of $2,755,333 as of December 31, 2001, is also reported on the balance sheet.
3. The balance sheet and statement of cash flows are interrelated. The cash on the balance sheet also appears as the end-of-the-period cash on the statement of cash flows. To illustrate, the cash of $134,147 reported on Hershey's balance sheet is also reported as the end-of-the-period cash on the statement of cash flows.

Hershey Foods Corporation's **balance sheet in Exhibit 7 reports cash of $134,147 thousand and retained earnings of $2,755,333 thousand. In what other Hershey exhibits do these numbers also appear?**

Cash of $134,147 thousand also appears in Exhibit 8, Statement of Cash Flows; Retained earnings of $2,755,333 thousand also appears in Exhibit 6, Retained Earnings Statement.

The preceding interrelationships are important in analyzing financial statements and the possible impact of economic events or transactions on a business. In addition, these interrelationships serve as a check on whether the financial statements have been prepared correctly. For example, if the ending cash on the statement of cash flows doesn't agree with the balance sheet cash, then an error exists.

Accounting Concepts

5 **Describe eight basic accounting concepts underlying financial reporting.**

In the preceding section, we described and illustrated the four basic corporate financial statements. Just as the rules of football determine the proper manner of scoring touchdowns, accounting "rules," called **generally accepted accounting principles (GAAP)**, determine the proper content of financial statements. GAAP are necessary so that stakeholders can compare the financial condition and operating results across companies and across time. If the management of a company could prepare financial state-

8 Depending upon the method of preparing cash flows from operating activities, net income may also appear on the statement of cash flows. This interrelationship and the method of preparing the statement of cash flows, called "the indirect method," is illustrated in a later chapter. In addition, as we will illustrate in Chapter 2 under the cash basis of accounting, cash flows from operating activities equals net income.

INTERNATIONAL PERSPECTIVE **Belgium's accounting standards and requirements are generally accepted by all interested parties, including tax authorities. However, publicly listed companies can depart from the standards as long as they provide a valid justification and obtain permission from the securities regulatory authority.**

ments as they saw fit, the comparability between companies and across time periods would be difficult, if not impossible. In other words, this would be like allowing a football team to determine the point-count for a touchdown every time it scored.

GAAP are established in the United States by the **Financial Accounting Standards Board (FASB).**[9] In establishing GAAP, the FASB publishes *Statements of Financial Accounting Standards.* Understanding these concepts that support the FASB pronouncements is essential for analyzing and interpreting financial statements. We discuss eight of the most important of these concepts below.

Business Entity Concept

A business entity could be an individual, a not-for-profit organization such as a church, or a for-profit company such as a real estate agency. The **business entity concept** applies accounting to a specific entity for which stakeholders need economic data. Once the entity is identified, the accountant can determine which economic data and activities should be analyzed, recorded, and summarized in the financial statements for stakeholders.

The accounting for Hershey Foods Corporation, a for-profit corporation, is separated from the accounting for other entities. For example, the accounting for transactions and events of individual stockholders, creditors, or other Hershey stakeholders are not included in Hershey Foods Corporation's financial statements. Only the transactions and events of the corporation as a separate entity are included in Hershey's financial statements.

Cost Concept

The **cost concept** determines the amount initially entered into the accounting records for purchases. For example, assume that Hershey purchased land for $2 million as a site for a future plant. The cost of the land to Hershey is the amount that would be entered into the accounting records. The seller may have been asking $2.3 million for the land up to the time of the sale. The land may have been assessed for property tax purposes at $1.5 million. A month after purchasing the land, Hershey may have received an offer of $2.4 million for the land. The only amount that affects the accounting records and the financial statements is the $2 million purchase price.

Going Concern Concept

In most cases, the amount of time that a business will be able to continue in operation is not known, so an assumption must be made. A business normally expects to continue operating for an indefinite period of time. This is called the **going concern concept.**

The going concern concept affects the recording of transactions and thus affects the financial statements. For example, the going concern concept justifies the use of the cost concept for recording purchases, such as the land purchased by Hershey in the preceding example. In this example, Hershey plans to build a plant on the land. Since Hershey does not plan to sell the land, reporting changes in the market value of the land is irrelevant. That is, the amount Hershey could sell the land for if it discontinued operations or went out of business is not important because Hershey plans to continue its operations.

If, however, there is strong evidence that a business is planning to discontinue its operations, then the accounting records should show the values expected to be received. For example, the assets and liabilities of businesses in receivership or bankruptcy are valued from a quitting concern or liquidation point of view, rather than from the going concern point of view.

---

9 The Securities and Exchange Commission also has authority to set accounting principles for publicly held corporations. In almost all cases, the SEC adopts the principles established by the FASB.

Matching Concept

In accounting, revenues for a period are matched with the expenses incurred in generating the revenues. Under this **matching concept**, revenues are normally recorded at the time of the sale of the product or service. This recording of revenues is often referred to as *revenue recognition.* At the point of sale, the sale price has been agreed upon, the buyer acquires ownership of the product or acquires the service, and the seller has a legal claim against the buyer for payment.

The following excerpt from the notes to Hershey's annual report describes when Hershey records sales:

> *. . . The Corporation records sales when . . . a . . . customer order with a fixed price has been received . . . the product has been shipped . . . there is no further obligation to assist in the resale of the product, and collectibility (of the account receivable) is reasonably assured.*

Objectivity Concept

The **objectivity concept** requires that entries in the accounting records and the data reported on financial statements be based on objective evidence. If this concept is ignored, the confidence of users of the financial statements cannot be maintained. For example, evidence such as invoices and vouchers for purchases, bank statements for the amount of cash in the bank, and physical counts of supplies on hand support the accounting records. Such evidence is objective and verifiable. In some cases, judgments, estimates, and other subjective factors may have to be used in preparing financial statements. In such situations, the most objective evidence available should be used.

Unit of Measure Concept

In the United States, the **unit of measure concept** requires that all economic data be recorded in dollars. Other relevant, nonfinancial information may also be recorded, such as terms of contracts. However, it is only through using dollar amounts that the various transactions and activities of a business can be measured, summarized, reported, and compared. Money is common to all business transactions and thus is the unit of measurement for reporting.

Adequate Disclosure Concept

Financial statements, including related footnotes and other disclosures, should contain all relevant data a reader needs to understand the financial condition and performance of a business. This is called the **adequate disclosure concept.** Nonessential data should be excluded in order to avoid clutter. For example, the balance of each cash account is usually not reported separately. Instead, the balances are grouped together and reported as one total.

Accounting Period Concept

The process in which accounting data are recorded and summarized in financial statements is a period process. Data are recorded and the income statement, retained earnings statement, and statement of cash flows are prepared for a period of time such as a month or a year. The balance sheet is then prepared as of the end of the period. After the accounting process is completed for one period, a new period begins and the accounting process is repeated for the new period. This process is based on the **accounting period concept.** Hershey's financial statements shown in Exhibits 5–8 illustrate the accounting period concept for the year ending December 31, 2001.

The financial history of a business may be shown by a series of balance sheets and income statements. If the life of a business is expressed by a line moving from left to right, this series of financial statements may be graphed as follows:

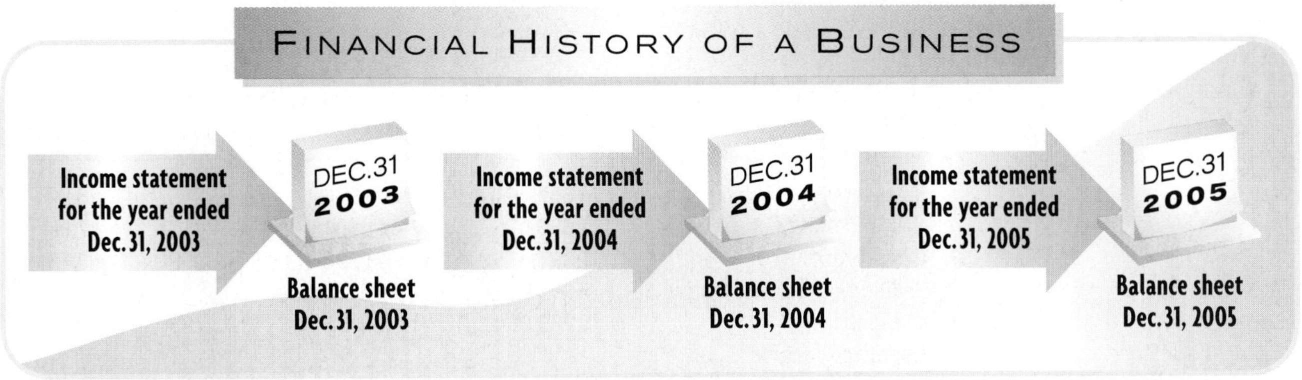

Horizontal Analysis

6 Describe and illustrate how horizontal analysis can be used to analyze and evaluate a company's performance.

The basic financial statements illustrated in this chapter are a primary source of information that financial analysts use in evaluating a company's performance. One method of analyzing financial performance is to compute percentage increases and decreases in related items in comparative financial statements. This type of analysis, called **horizontal analysis**, compares each item on the most recent financial statement with the related item on one or more earlier statements. The amount of the increase or decrease in each item is shown along with the percent increase or decrease.

To illustrate, income statements for Hershey Corporation will be used for the years ending December 31, 2001 and 2000. For analysis purposes, the income statements have been condensed and adapted to emphasize the operating aspects of Hershey's performance. For example, other expenses, interest expense, and income taxes have been omitted from the income statements. This allows us to focus on the basic operating aspects of Hershey's business without being distracted by unusual items, such as other expenses related to asset impairments. The exclusion of income taxes helps simplify the analysis and also recognizes that the amount of income taxes is largely beyond the operating control of the business. Interest expense is omitted, since it deals more with the financing rather than the operating aspects of the business. The resulting comparative income statements are shown in Exhibit 9.

The income statements shown in Exhibit 9 report **gross profit** as sales less the cost of sales. Gross profit represents the amount that Hershey marked up the cost of its products in selling them to its customers. Gross profit is a useful performance measure in analyzing the profitability of the company's products from one period to the next.

Did Hershey improve its operations during the year ending December 31, 2001? Exhibit 9 indicates that Hershey was able to increase its sales by 8 percent, while the cost of sales increased just under 8 percent. This combination of increases and decreases resulted in an increase in gross profit of just over 8 percent. Selling and administrative expenses increased significantly more than sales. This could be due to implementing a new advertising campaign, which may impact sales beyond just the current year.

Exhibit 9

Comparative Income Statements Using Horizontal Analysis: Hershey Foods Corporation

Hershey Foods Corporation
Income Statements
For the Years Ended December 31, 2001 and 2000
(in thousands)

			Increase (Decrease)	
	2001	**2000**	**Amount**	**Percent**
Sales	$4,557,241	$4,220,976	$336,265	8.0%
Cost of sales	2,665,566	2,471,151	194,415	7.9%
Gross profit	$1,891,675	$1,749,825	$141,850	8.1%
Selling and administrative expenses	1,269,964	1,127,175	142,789	12.7%
Operating income before taxes	$ 621,711	$ 622,650	$ (939)	(0.2)%

The overall impact on operations of these changes is that operating income before taxes decreased by 0.2 percent. Before arriving at a final conclusion on Hershey's operating results for 2001, additional analyses as well as comparisons with the operating results of competitors should be performed.[10]

10 Additional financial statement analyses will be discussed and illustrated throughout the remainder of this text.

Summary of Learning Goals

1 Describe the types and forms of businesses, business strategies, value chains, and stakeholders.

The three types of businesses operated for profit include manufacturing, merchandising, and service businesses. Such businesses may be organized as proprietorships, partnerships, or corporations. The two basic business strategies a business may use are low-cost and differentiation strategies. Sometimes a business will implement a combination strategy that includes elements of both the low-cost and differentiation strategies. Once a business has chosen a strategy, it must implement the strategy in its value chain. A business's value chain is the way it adds value for its customers by processing inputs into a product or service. A company's business strategy and value chain are of interest to its stakeholders. Business stakeholders include four categories: capital market stakeholders, product or service market stakeholders, government stakeholders, and internal stakeholders.

2 Describe the three business activities of financing, investing, and operating.

All businesses engage in financing, investing, and operating activities. Financing activities involve obtaining funds to begin and operate a business. Investing activities involve obtaining the necessary resources to start and operate the business. Operating activities involve using the business's resources according to its strategy.

3 Define accounting and its role in business.

Accounting is an information system that provides reports to stakeholders about the economic activities and condition of a business. Accounting is the "language of business."

4 Describe and illustrate the basic financial statements and how they interrelate.

The principal financial statements of a corporation are the income statement, the retained earnings statement, the balance sheet, and the statement of cash flows. The income statement reports a period's net income or net loss, which also appears on the retained earnings statement. The ending retained earnings reported on the retained earnings statement is also reported on the balance sheet. The ending cash balance is reported on the balance sheet and the statement of cash flows.

5 Describe eight basic accounting concepts underlying financial reporting.

The eight basic accounting concepts discussed in this chapter include the business entity, cost, going concern, matching, objectivity, unit of measure, adequate disclosure, and accounting period concepts.

6 Describe and illustrate how horizontal analysis can be used to analyze and evaluate a company's performance.

One method of analyzing financial performance is to compute percentage increases and decreases in related items in comparative financial statements. This type of analysis, called horizontal analysis, compares each item on the most recent financial statement with the related item on one or more earlier statements.

Glossary

Account payable The liability created when a business borrows from a vendor or supplier.

Accounts receivable Rights to payments from customers.

Accounting An information system that provides reports to stakeholders about the economic activities and condition of a business.

Accounting equation Assets = Liabilities + Stockholders' Equity.

Accounting period concept A concept of accounting in which accounting data are recorded and summarized in a period process.

Adequate disclosure concept A concept of accounting that requires that the financial statements include all relevant data a readers needs to understand the financial condition and performance of a business.

Assets The resources owned by a business.

Balance sheet A list of the assets, liabilities, and stockholders' equity *as of a specific date*, usually at the close of the last day of a month or a year.

Bonds payable A type of long-term debt financing with a face amount that is due in the future with interest that is normally paid semiannually.

Business An organization in which basic resources (inputs), such as materials and labor, are assembled and processed to provide goods or services (outputs) to customers.

Business entity concept A concept of accounting that limits the economic data in the accounting system to data related directly to the activities of a specific business or entity.

Business stakeholder A person or entity who has an interest in the economic performance of a business.

Business strategy An integrated set of plans and actions designed to enable the business to gain an advantage over its competitors and, in doing so, maximize its profits.

Capital stock Types of stock a corporation may issue.

Combination strategy A business strategy that includes elements of both the low-cost and differentiation strategies.

Common stock The basic type of stock issued to stockholders of a corporation.

Corporation A business organized under state or federal statutes as a separate legal entity.

Cost concept A concept of accounting that determines the amount initially entered into the accounting records for purchases.

Differentiation strategy A business strategy in which a business designs and produces products or services that possess unique attributes or characteristics for which customers are willing to pay a premium price.

Dividends Distributions of earnings of a corporation to stockholders.

Expenses Costs used to earn revenues.

Financial Accounting Standards Board (FASB) The authoritative body that has the primary responsibility for developing accounting principles.

Financial statements Financial reports that summarize the effects of events on a business.

Financing activities Business activities that involve obtaining funds to begin and operate a business.

Generally accepted accounting principles (GAAP) Rules for how financial statements should be prepared.

Going concern concept A concept of accounting that assumes a business will continue operating for an indefinite period of time.

Gross profit Sales less the cost of sales.

Horizontal analysis A method of analyzing financial performance that computes percentage increases and decreases in related items in comparative financial statements.

Income statement A summary of the revenue and expenses *for a specific period of time,* such as a month or a year.

Intangible assets Assets that are rights to future benefits such as patent or copyright rights.

Interest payable A liability to pay interest on a due date.

Investing activities Business activities that involve obtaining the necessary resources to start and operate the business.

Liabilities The rights of creditors that represent a legal obligation to repay an amount borrowed according to terms of the borrowing agreement.

Low-cost strategy A business strategy in which a business designs and produces products of acceptable quality at a cost lower than competitors.

Manufacturing A type of business that changes basic inputs into products that are sold to individual customers.

Matching concept A concept of accounting in which expenses are matched with the revenue generated during a period by those expenses.

Merchandising A type of business that purchases products from other businesses and sells them to customers.

Net income The excess of revenues over expenses.

Net loss The excess of expenses over revenues.

Note payable A type of short or long-term financing that requires payment of the amount borrowed plus interest.

Objectivity concept A concept of accounting that requires accounting records and the data reported in financial statements be based on objective evidence.

Operating activities Business activities that involve using the business's resources to implement its business strategy.

Owners' equity The rights of the owners of a company.

Partnership A business owned by two or more individuals.

Prepaid expenses An asset resulting from the prepayment of a future expense such as insurance or rent.

Proprietorship A business owned by one individual.

Retained earnings Net income retained in a corporation.

Retained earnings statement A summary of the changes in the retained earnings in a corporation for *a specific period of time,* such as a month or a year.

Revenue The increase in assets from selling products or services to customers.

Service A type of business that provides services rather than products to customers.

Statement of cash flows A summary of the cash receipts and cash payments *for a specific period of time,* such as a month or a year.

Stockholders Investors who purchase stock in a corporation.

Stockholders' equity The rights of the owners of a corporation.

Unit of measure concept A concept of accounting requiring that economic data be recorded in dollars.

Value chain The way a business adds value for its customers by processing inputs into a product or service.

Illustrative Accounting Application Problem

The financial statements at the end of Spratlin Consulting's first month of operations are shown below.

Spratlin Consulting
Income Statement
For the Month Ended June 30, 2004

Fees earned		$36,000
Operating expenses:		
Wages expense	$12,000	
Rent expense	7,640	
Utilities expense	(a)	
Miscellaneous expense	1,320	
Total operating expenses		23,120
Net income		(b)

Spratlin Consulting
Retained Earnings Statement
For the Month Ended June 30, 2004

Net income for June	(c)
Less dividends	(d)
Retained earnings, June 30, 2004	(e)

Spratlin Consulting
Balance Sheet
June 30, 2004

Assets	
Cash	$ 5,600
Land	50,000
Total assets	(f)
Liabilities	
Accounts payable	$ 1,920
Stockholders' Equity	
Capital stock	(g)
Retained earnings	(h)
Total stockholders' equity	(i)
Total liabilities and stockholders' equity	j

Spratlin Consulting
Statement of Cash Flows
For the Month Ended June 30, 2004

Cash flows from operating activities:		
Cash received from customers	$36,000	
Deduct cash payments for operating expenses	(k)	
Net cash flow from operating activities		$14,160
Cash flows from investing activities:		
Cash payments for acquisition of land		(l)
Cash flows from financing activities:		
Cash received from issuing capital stock	$48,000	
Deduct dividends	7,200	
Net cash flow from financing activities		(m)
Net cash flow and June 30, 2004 cash balance		(n)

Instructions

By analyzing the interrelationships among the four financial statements, determine the proper amounts for (a) through (n).

Solution

a. Utilities expense, $2,160 ($23,120 − $10,200 − $5,840 − $3,600 − $1,320)
b. Net income, $12,880 ($36,000 − $23,120)
c. Net income, $12,880 (same as b)
d. Dividends, $7,200 (from statement of cash flows)
e. Retained earnings, $5,680 ($12,880 − $7,200)
f. Total assets, $55,600 ($4,960 + $640 + $50,000)
g. Capital stock, $48,000 (from the statement of cash flows)
h. Retained earnings, $5,680 (same as e)
i. Total stockholders' equity, $53,680 ($48,000 + $5,680)
j. Total liabilities and stockholders' equity, $55,600 ($1,920 + $53,680) (same as f)
k. Cash payments for operating expenses, $21,840 ($36,000 − $14,160)
l. Cash payments for acquisition of land, $50,000 (from balance sheet)
m. Net cash flow from financing activities, $40,800 ($48,000 − $7,200)
n. Net cash flow and June 30, 2004 cash balance, $4,960 ($14,160 − $50,000 + $40,800)

Self-Study Questions

Answers at end of chapter

1. A profit-making business operating as a separate legal entity and in which ownership is divided into shares of stock is known as a:
   A. proprietorship.
   B. service business.
   C. partnership.
   D. corporation.

2. The resources owned by a business are called:
   A. assets.
   B. liabilities.
   C. the accounting equation.
   D. stockholders' equity.

3. A listing of a business entity's assets, liabilities, and stockholders' equity as of a specific date is:
   A. a balance sheet.
   B. an income statement.
   C. the retained earnings statement.
   D. a statement of cash flows.

4. If total assets are $20,000 and total liabilities are $12,000, the amount of stockholders' equity is:
   A. $32,000.
   B. ($32,000).
   C. ($8,000).
   D. $8,000.

5. If revenue was $45,000, expenses were $37,500, and dividends were $10,000, the amount of net income or net loss would be:
   A. $45,000 net income.
   B. $7,500 net income.
   C. $37,500 net loss.
   D. $2,500 net loss.

Discussion Questions

1. What is the objective of most businesses?
2. What is the difference between a manufacturing business and a merchandising business? Give an example of each type of business.
3. What is the difference between a manufacturing business and a service business? Is a restaurant a manufacturing business, a service business, or both?
4. Why are most large companies like Microsoft, Pepsi, Caterpillar, and AutoZone organized as corporations?
5. Both KIA and Porche produce and sell automobiles. Describe and contrast the business strategies of KIA and Porche.

6. Assume that a friend of yours operates a family owned pharmacy. A Super Wal-Mart is scheduled to open in the next several months that will also offer pharmacy services. What business strategy would your friend use to compete with the Super Wal-Mart pharmacy?
7. How does eBay offer value to its customers?
8. A business's stakeholders can be classified into capital market, product or service market, government, and internal stakeholders. Will the interests of all the stakeholders with a classification be the same? Use bankers and stockholders of the capital market as an example in answering this question.
9. The three business activities are financing, investing, and operating. Using United Airlines, give an example of a financing, investing, and operating activity.
10. What is the role of accounting in business?
11. Briefly describe the nature of the information provided by each of the following financial statements: the income statement, the retained earnings statement, the balance sheet, and the statement of cash flows. In your descriptions indicate whether each of the financial statements covers a period of time or is for a specific date.
12. For the year ending February 3, 2001, The Limited Inc. had revenues of $10,104,606,000 and total expenses of $9,676,701,000. Did The Limited (a) incur a net loss or (b) realize net income?
13. What particular item of financial or operating data appears on both the income statement and the retained earnings statement? What item appears on both the balance sheet and the retained earnings statement? What item appears on both the balance sheet and statement of cash flows?
14. Lynda Lyons is the owner of Fast Delivery Service. Recently, Lynda paid interest of $3,500 to First Union on a personal loan of $60,000 that she used to begin the business. Should Fast Delivery Service record the interest payment? Explain.
15. On April 18, Neece Repair Service extended an offer of $95,000 for land that had been priced for sale at $100,000. On April 25, Neece Repair Service accepted the seller's counteroffer of $97,500. Describe how Neece Repair Service should record the land.
16. Land with an assessed value of $200,000 for property tax purposes is acquired by a business for $350,000. Seven years later, the plot of land has an assessed value of $240,000 and the business receives an offer of $400,000 for it. Should the monetary amount assigned to the land in the business records now be increased?

A New Vision for a New Age of Business!

To help you achieve outstanding results in this course, we have developed incredible resources to make learning accounting even easier. You can purchase these supplements by visiting

http://warren.swlearning.com

Xtreme!

0-324-20115-X

This hybrid CD-ROM and Internet-based product provides you with the following media-rich content:

- Learning Objectives that summarize key concepts from each chapter.
- Quizzing that reinforces concepts and helps you better focus your study efforts.
- Quiz Bowl, an innovative and fun way to review concepts.
- Crossword Puzzles to test your knowledge of the glossary.
- E-Lectures that provide a PowerPoint® lecture-style with audio voiceovers to help you review chapter content or work on difficult topics.
- Problem Demonstrations that walk you through an example homework assignment.
- Video clips that provide real-world examples of accounting applications.
- Personal Trainer online tutorial.

Xtra!

0-324-20110-9

This CD-ROM provides lecture replacement resources and access to games and interactive quizzes for testing your understanding of the content of the text.

Personal Trainer

0-324-18192-2

This online tutorial will help you complete the end-of-chapter exercises and problems from the textbook, with warm-ups and hints. You will get immediate feedback to determine if you have done the exercises and problems correctly. This product will not only save you time on your homework but will help you learn the concepts.

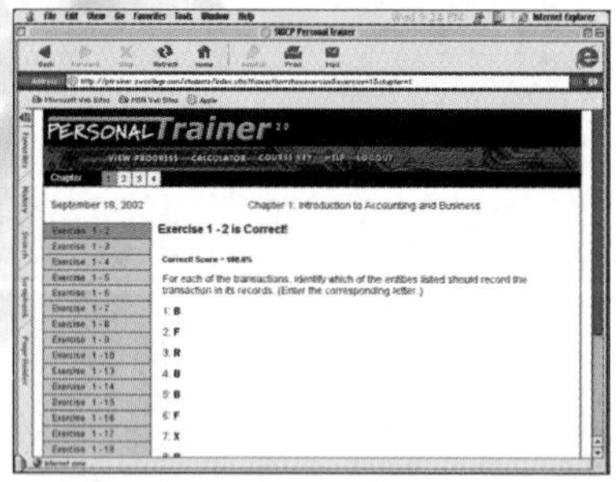

INTACCT
(Internet Accounting Tutor)

0-324-01592-5

rama.swcollege.com

- This product, designed to be used with any financial accounting textbook, will give you reinforcement of key accounting concepts in an interactive format.
- You can see how to apply the concepts with practice problems and demonstration problems.
- You can e-mail your INTACCT homework problems to your instructor to grade.

Working Papers

0-324-18188-4

This supplement contains forms that will help you organize your solutions.

Student Solutions Manual

0-324-18002-0

This manual contains the solutions for the even-numbered exercises and the "B" problems in the text.

Save on these products by purchasing online @

http://warren.swlearning.com

Exercises

Exercise 1–1

Types of businesses

Goal 1

Indicate whether each of the following companies is primarily a service, merchandise, or manufacturing business. If you are unfamiliar with the company, you may use the Internet to locate the company's home page or use the finance Web site of Yahoo.com.

1. Ford Motor
2. Citigroup
3. Sears Roebuck
4. AT&T
5. H&R Block Inc.
6. Boeing
7. First Union Corporation
8. Alcoa
9. CVS
10. Caterpillar
11. FedEx
12. Dow Chemical
13. Gap
14. Hilton Hotels
15. Procter & Gamble

Exercise 1–2

Business strategy

Goal 1

STUDENT SOLUTIONS MANUAL

Identify the primary business strategy of each of the following companies as (a) a low-cost strategy, (b) a differentiation strategy, or (c) a combination strategy. If you are unfamiliar with the company, you may use the Internet to locate the company's home page or use the finance Web site of Yahoo.com.

1. Southwest Airlines
2. Home Depot
3. BMW
4. Coca-Cola
5. Target
6. Goldman Sachs Group
7. Sara Lee
8. Delta Air Lines
9. Circuit City Stores
10. Maytag
11. Office Depot
12. Nike
13. Charles Schwab
14. Dollar General
15. General Motors

Exercise 1–3

Accounting equation

Goal 4

Pearson Co., $9,513

The total assets and total liabilities of Pearson Co. and McDaniel Inc. are shown below.

	Pearson Co.	McDaniel Inc.
Assets	$21,623	$17,551
Liabilities	12,110	10,670

Determine the stockholders' equity of each company.

Exercise 1–4

Accounting equation

Goal 4

Toys"R"Us, $3,418

STUDENT SOLUTIONS MANUAL

The total assets and total liabilities of Toys"R"Us Inc. and Estee Lauder Companies Inc. are shown below.

	Toys"R"Us (in millions)	Estee Lauder Companies (in millions)
Assets	$8,003	$3,219
Liabilities	4,585	1,867

Determine the stockholders' equity of each company.

Exercise 1–5

Accounting equation

Goal 4

a. $51,500

Determine the missing amount for each of the following:

	Assets	=	Liabilities	+	Stockholders' Equity
a.	X	=	$20,000	+	$31,500
b.	$62,750	=	X	+	$10,000
c.	$57,000	=	$38,000	+	X

Exercise 1-6

Accounting equation

Goal 4

a. $1,771

STUDENT SOLUTIONS MANUAL

Determine the missing amounts (in millions) for the 2001 balance sheets (summarized below) for The Limited Inc., Federal Express Corporation, and Eastman Kodak Co.

	The Limited	Federal Express	Eastman Kodak
Assets	$4,088	(b)	$13,362
Liabilities	(a)	$5,323	10,468
Stockholders' equity	2,317	4,248	(c)

Exercise 1-7

Net income and dividends

Goal 4

The income statement of a corporation for the month of January indicates a net income of $52,750. During the same period, $60,000 in cash dividends were paid.

Would it be correct to say that the business incurred a net loss of $7,250 during the month? Discuss.

Exercise 1-8

Net income and stockholders' equity for four businesses

Goal 4

Company Y: Net loss, ($25,000)

STUDENT SOLUTIONS MANUAL

Four different corporations—W, X, Y, and Z—show the same balance sheet data at the beginning and end of a year. These data, exclusive of the amount of stockholders' equity, are summarized as follows:

	Total Assets	Total Liabilities
Beginning of the year	$375,000	$150,000
End of the year	600,000	325,000

On the basis of the above data and the following additional information for the year, determine the net income (or loss) of each company for the year. (*Hint:* First determine the amount of increase or decrease in stockholders' equity during the year.)

Company W: No additional capital stock was issued, and no dividends were paid.
Company X: No additional capital stock was issued, but dividends of $30,000 were paid.
Company Y: Capital stock of $75,000 was issued, but no dividends were paid.
Company Z: Capital stock of $75,000 was issued, and dividends of $30,000 were paid.

Exercise 1-9

Accounting equation and income statement

Goal 4

1. $2,225,583

Staples, Inc., is a leading office products distributor, with a total of 1,307 retail stores in the United States, Canada, the United Kingdom, the Netherlands, and Portugal. The following financial statement data were taken from Staples' financial statements as of February 3, 2001 and 2000:

	2001 (in thousands)	2000 (in thousands)
Total assets	$3,989,413	$3,846,076
Total liabilities	(1)	2,017,263
Total stockholders' equity	1,763,830	(2)
Retained earnings	1,008,021	948,309
Sales	$10,673,671	
Cost of goods sold	8,097,166	
Operating and other expenses	2,332,320	
Income tax expense	184,473	

a. Determine the missing data indicated for (1) and (2).
b. Using the income statement data for 2001, determine the amount of net income or loss.
c. Did Staples pay any dividends to stockholders during 2001? *Hint:* Compare the change in retained earnings to your answer for (b).

Exercise 1-10

Balance sheet items

Goal 4

STUDENT SOLUTIONS MANUAL

From the following list of selected items taken from the records of Kagy Appliance Service as of a specific date, identify those that would appear on the balance sheet.

1. Utilities Expense
2. Fees Earned
3. Prepaid Expenses
4. Wages Expense
5. Accounts Payable
6. Cash
7. Advertising Expense
8. Land
9. Capital Stock
10. Wages Payable

Exercise 1-11

Income statement items

Goal 4

Based on the data presented in Exercise 1-10, identify those items that would appear on the income statement.

Exercise 1-12

Financial statement items

Goal 4

STUDENT SOLUTIONS MANUAL

Identify each of the following items as (a) an asset, (b) a liability, (c) revenue, (d) expense, or (e) dividend:

1. Rent paid for the month
2. Cash sales
3. Equipment
4. Cash paid to stockholders
5. Amounts owed vendors
6. Cash on hand
7. Wages paid to employees
8. Sales commissions paid to salespersons
9. Amounts due from customers
10. Note payable owed to the bank

Exercise 1-13

Retained earnings statement

Goal 4

Retained earnings, June 30, 2003: $393,750

SPREADSHEET

Financial information related to Douma Company for the month ended June 30, 2003, is as follows:

Net income for June	$ 91,250
Dividends during June	15,000
Retained earnings, June 1, 2003	317,500

Prepare a retained earnings statement for the month ended June 30, 2003.

Exercise 1-14

Income statement

Goal 4

Net income: $63,800

STUDENT SOLUTIONS MANUAL

SPREADSHEET

Surgery Services was organized on April 1, 2003. A summary of the revenue and expense transactions for April follows:

Fees earned	$165,800
Wages expense	74,750
Miscellaneous expense	2,250
Rent expense	25,000

Prepare an income statement for the month ended April 30.

Exercise 1-15

Missing amounts from balance sheet and income statement data

Goal 4

(a) $130,250

One item is omitted in each of the following summaries of balance sheet and income statement data for four different corporations, I, II, III, and IV.

	I	II	III	IV
Beginning of the year:				
Assets	$600,000	$125,000	$100,000	(d)
Liabilities	360,000	65,000	76,000	$150,000
End of the year:				
Assets	745,000	175,000	90,000	310,000
Liabilities	325,000	55,000	80,000	170,000
During the year:				
Additional issue of capital stock	(a)	25,000	10,000	50,000
Dividends	40,000	8,000	(c)	75,000
Revenue	197,750	(b)	115,000	140,000
Expenses	108,000	32,000	122,500	160,000

Determine the missing amounts, identifying them by letter. (*Hint:* First determine the amount of increase or decrease in stockholders' equity during the year.)

Exercise 1-16

Balance sheets, net income

Goal 4

b. $11,330

STUDENT SOLUTIONS MANUAL

SPREADSHEET

Financial information related to Revival Interiors for August and September of the current year is as follows:

	August 31, 2004	September 30, 2004
Accounts payable	$ 3,850	$ 4,150
Accounts receivable	8,500	9,780
Capital stock	10,000	10,000
Retained earnings	?	?
Cash	15,000	25,500
Prepaid expenses	750	600

a. Prepare balance sheets for Revival Interiors as of August 31 and as of September 30.
b. Determine the amount of net income for September, assuming that no additional capital stock was issued and no dividends were paid.
c. Determine the amount of net income for September, assuming that no additional capital stock was issued, but dividends of $7,500 were paid.

Exercise 1-17

Financial statements

Goal 4

Each of the following items is shown in the financial statements of ExxonMobil Corporation. Identify the financial statement (balance sheet or income statement) in which each item would appear.

a. Operating expenses
b. Crude oil inventory
c. Income taxes payable
d. Sales
e. Investments
f. Marketable securities
g. Exploration expenses
h. Notes and loans payable
i. Cash equivalents
j. Long-term debt
k. Selling expenses
l. Retained earnings
m. Equipment
n. Accounts payable
o. Prepaid taxes

Exercise 1-18

Statement of cash flows

Goal 4

STUDENT SOLUTIONS MANUAL

Indicate whether each of the following cash activities would be reported on the statement of cash flows as (a) an operating activity, (b) an investing activity, or (c) a financing activity.

1. Paid for advertising
2. Paid for office equipment
3. Issued capital stock
4. Paid officers' salaries
5. Sold services
6. Paid rent
7. Paid dividends
8. Issued a note payable
9. Paid rent
10. Sold excess office equipment

Exercise 1-19

Statement of cash flows

Goal 4

Indicate whether each of the following activities would be reported on the statement of cash flows as (a) an operating activity, (b) an investing activity, or (c) a financing activity.

1. Cash received from investment by stockholders
2. Cash paid for land
3. Cash received from fees earned
4. Cash paid for expenses

Exercise 1-20

Statement of cash flows

Goal 4

Net cash flows from operating activities, $15,150

STUDENT SOLUTIONS MANUAL

SPREADSHEET

Cremation Services was organized on January 1, 2004. A summary of cash flows for January is shown below.

Cash receipts:	
Cash received from customers	$23,500
Cash received for capital stock	90,000
Cash received from note payable	10,000
Cash payments:	
Cash paid out for expenses	$ 8,350
Cash paid out for purchase of furnace	75,000
Cash paid as dividends	5,000

Prepare a statement of cash flows for the month ended January 31, 2004.

Exercise 1-21

Using financial statements

Goal 4

A company's stakeholders often differ in their financial statement focus. For example, some stakeholders focus primarily on the income statement, while others may focus primarily on the statement of cash flows or the balance sheet. For each of the following situations, indicate which financial statement would be the likely focus for the stakeholder. Choose either the income statement, balance sheet, or the statement of cash flows and justify your choice.

Situation One: Assume that you are a banker for Citigroup (capital market stakeholder), considering whether to grant a major credit line (loan) to Wal-Mart. The credit line will allow Wal-Mart to borrow up to $400 million for a five-year period at the market rate of interest.

Situation Two: Assume that you are employed by Sara Lee Corporation (product market stakeholder) and are considering whether to extend credit for a 60-day period to a new grocery store chain that has recently opened throughout the Midwest.

Situation Three: Assume that you are considering investing in Amazon.com (capital market stakeholder).

Situation Four: Assume that you are considering taking a job (internal stakeholder) with either Sears or JC Penney.

Situation Five: Assume that you are considering purchasing a personal computer from Gateway.

Exercise 1–22

Financial statement items

Goal 4

STUDENT SOLUTIONS MANUAL

Starbucks Corporation purchases and roasts high-quality whole bean coffees and sells them, along with fresh, rich-brewed coffees and a variety of other complementary items, primarily through company-operated retail stores.

The following items were adapted from the annual report of Starbucks Corporation for the period ending September 30, 2001:

	In thousands
1. Accounts payable	$ 127,905
2. Accounts receivable	90,455
3. Accrued expenses payable	244,724
4. Additions to property, plant, and equipment	384,215
5. Checks drawn in excess of bank balance	61,987
6. Cost of sales	1,112,785
7. General and administrative expenses	151,416
8. Income tax expense	107,712
9. Net cash provided by operating activities	460,826
10. Net sales	2,648,980
11. Other income (loss)	36,443
12. Other operating expenses	256,827
13. Property, plant, and equipment	1,135,784
14. Retained earnings (September 30, 2001)	589,713
15. Store operating expenses	875,473

Using the following notations, indicate on which financial statement you would find each of the above items. (Note: An item may appear on more than one statement.)

IS	Income statement	BS	Balance sheet
RE	Retained earnings statement	SCF	Statement of cash flows

Exercise 1–23

Income statement

Goal 4

Net income, $181,210

SPREADSHEET

Based on the Starbucks Corporation financial statement data shown in Exercise 1–22, prepare an income statement for the year ending September 30, 2001.

Exercise 1–24

Retained earnings statement

Goal 4

STUDENT SOLUTIONS MANUAL

SPREADSHEET

Based on the Starbucks Corporation financial statement data shown in Exercise 1–22, prepare a retained earnings statement for the year ending September 30, 2001. The retained earnings as of October 1, 2000, was $408,503, and Starbucks paid no dividends during the year.

Exercise 1-25

Financial statement items

Goal 4

Though the McDonald's menu of hamburgers, cheeseburgers, the Big Mac®, Quarter Pounder®, the Filet-O-Fish®, and Chicken McNuggets® is easily recognized, McDonald's financial statements may not be as familiar. The following items were adapted from a recent annual report of McDonald's Corporation:

1. Accounts payable
2. Accrued interest payable
3. Capital stock outstanding
4. Cash
5. Cash provided by operations
6. Food and packaging costs used in operations
7. Income tax expense
8. Interest expense
9. Inventories
10. Long-term debt payable
11. Net income
12. Net increase in cash
13. Notes payable
14. Notes receivable
15. Occupancy and rent expense
16. Payroll expense
17. Prepaid expenses not yet used in operations
18. Property and equipment
19. Retained earnings
20. Sales

Identify the financial statement on which each of the preceding items would appear. An item may appear on more than one statement. Use the following notations:

IS	Income statement
RE	Retained earnings statement
BS	Balance sheet
SCF	Statement of cash flows

Exercise 1-26

Financial statements

Goal 4

Correct Amount of Total Assets is $13,875

STUDENT SOLUTIONS MANUAL

Aspen Realty, organized February 1, 2004, is owned and operated by Lynn Soby. How many errors can you find in the following financial statements for Aspen Realty, prepared after its second month of operations?

Aspen Realty
Income Statement
March 31, 2004

Sales commissions		$37,100
Operating expenses:		
Office salaries expense	$23,150	
Rent expense	7,800	
Miscellaneous expense	550	
Automobile expense	1,975	
Total operating expenses		33,475
Net income		$13,625

Lynn Soby
Retained Earnings Statement
March 31, 2003

Retained earnings, March 1, 2004	$ 2,450
Less dividends during March	1,000
	$ 1,450
Net income for the month	13,625
Retained earnings, March 31, 2004	$15,075

Balance Sheet
For the Month Ended March 31, 2004

Assets		
Cash		$ 2,350
Accounts payable		2,300
Total assets		$ 4,650
Liabilities		
Accounts receivable		$10,200
Prepaid expenses		1,325
Stockholders' Equity		
Capital stock	$ 6,500	
Retained earnings	15,075	21,575
Total liabilities and stockholders' equity		$33,100

Exercise 1–27

Accounting concepts

Goal 5

Match each of the following statements with the appropriate accounting concept. Some concepts may be used more than once, while others may not be used at all. Use the notations below to indicate the appropriate accounting concept.

Accounting Concept	Notation
Accounting period concept	P
Adequate disclosure concept	D
Business entity concept	B
Cost concept	C
Going concern concept	G
Matching concept	M
Objectivity concept	O
Unit of measure concept	U

Statements

1. The changes in financial condition are reported for November.
2. Personal transactions of owners are kept separate from the business.
3. Land worth $500,000 is reported at its original purchase price of $120,000.
4. Assume that a business will continue forever.
5. This concept supports relying on an independent actuary (statistician), rather than the chief operating officer of the corporation, to estimate a pension liability.
6. This concept justifies recording only transactions that are expressed in dollars.
7. Material litigation involving the corporation is described in a footnote.

8. December utilities costs are reported as expenses along with the December revenues.
9. If this concept was ignored, the confidence of users in the financial statements could not be maintained.
10. Changes in the use of accounting methods from one period to the next are described in the notes to the financial statements.

Exercise 1-28

Business entity concept

Goal 5

STUDENT SOLUTIONS MANUAL

Bag-One Sports Inc. sells hunting and fishing equipment and provides guided hunting and fishing trips. Bag-One Sports Inc. is owned and operated by Marc Trailer, a well-known sports enthusiast and hunter. Marc's wife, Robin, owns and operates Red Bird Boutique Inc., a women's clothing store. Marc and Robin have established a trust fund to finance their children's college education. The trust fund is maintained by First Wyoming Bank in the name of the children, Sparrow and Trout.

For each of the following transactions, identify which of the entities listed should record the transaction in its records.

Entities	
B	Bag-One Sports Inc.
F	First Wyoming Bank
R	Red Bird Boutique Inc.
X	None of the above

1. Marc received a cash advance from customers for a guided hunting trip.
2. Robin deposited a $5,000 personal check in the trust fund at First Wyoming Bank.
3. Robin purchased three dozen spring dresses from a Denver designer for a special spring sale.
4. Marc paid a local doctor for his annual physical, which was required by the workmen's compensation insurance policy carried by Bag-One Sports Inc.
5. Marc paid for an advertisement in a hunters' magazine.
6. Robin purchased mutual fund shares as an investment for the children's trust.
7. Marc paid for dinner and a movie to celebrate their tenth wedding anniversary.
8. Robin donated several dresses from inventory for a local charity auction for the benefit of a women's abuse shelter.
9. Marc paid a breeder's fee for an English springer spaniel to be used as a hunting guide dog.
10. Robin paid her dues to the Cheyenne Garden Club.

Accounting Application Problems

Problem 1-1A

Income statement, retained earnings statement, and balance sheet

Goal 4

Net income: $40,865

SPREADSHEET

Following are the amounts of the assets and liabilities of Fly Away Travel Agency at December 31, 2004, the end of the current year, and its revenue and expenses for the year. The retained earnings were $4,500 and the capital stock was $10,000 on January 1, 2004, the beginning of the current year. During the current year, dividends of $30,000 were paid.

Accounts payable	$ 3,200
Accounts receivable	19,500
Cash	7,200
Fees earned	117,480
Miscellaneous expense	1,750
Rent expense	27,000
Prepaid expenses	1,865
Utilities expense	12,365
Wages expense	35,500

Instructions

1. Prepare an income statement for the current year ended December 31, 2004.
2. Prepare a retained earnings statement for the current year ended December 31, 2004.
3. Prepare a balance sheet as of December 31, 2004.

Problem 1-2A

Missing amounts from financial statements

Goal 4

a. $15,000

The financial statements at the end of Magic Realty Inc.'s first month of operations are shown below.

Magic Realty Inc.
Income Statement
For the Month Ended April 30, 2004

Fees earned		$ (a)
Operating expenses:		
Wages expense	$4,250	
Rent expense	1,600	
Utilities expense	(b)	
Miscellaneous expenses	550	
Total operating expenses		8,800
Net income		$6,200

Magic Realty Inc.
Retained Earnings Statement
For the Month Ended April 30, 2004

Net income for April	$ (c)
Less dividends	3,000
Retained earnings, April 30, 2004	$ (d)

Magic Realty Inc.
Balance Sheet
April 30, 2004

Assets		
Cash		$ 2,900
Prepaid expenses		1,100
Land		20,000
Total assets		$ (e)
Liabilities		
Accounts payable		$ 800
Stockholders' Equity		
Capital stock	$20,000	
Retained earnings	(f)	(g)
Total liabilities and stockholders' equity		$ (h)

Magic Realty Inc.
Statement of Cash Flows
For the Month Ended April 30, 2004

Cash flows from operating activities:		
Cash received from customers	$ (i)	
Deduct cash payments for expenses and payments to creditors	9,100	
Net cash flows from operating activities		$ (j)
Cash flows from investing activities:		
Cash payment for purchase of land		(k)
Cash flows from financing activities:		
Cash received from issuing capital stock	(l)	
Deduct dividends	(m)	
Net cash flows from financing activities		(n)
Net cash flow and April 30, 2004 cash balance		$ (o)

Instructions

1. Would you classify a realty business like Magic Realty as a manufacturing, merchandising, or service business?
2. By analyzing the interrelationships between the financial statements, determine the proper amounts for (a) through (o).

Problem 1–3A

Income statement, retained earnings statement, and balance sheet

Goal 4

Net income, $395,839

SPREADSHEET

The following financial data were adapted from the annual report of Best Buy Inc. for the period ending March 31, 2001:

	In thousands
Accounts payable	$ 1,772,722
Accrued liabilities	827,036
Capital stock	493,786
Cash	746,879
Cost of goods sold	12,267,459
Income taxes	245,640
Interest income	37,171
Inventories	1,766,934
Goodwill	385,355
Other assets	183,370
Other liabilities	417,901
Property, plant, and equipment	1,444,172
Receivables	209,031
Sales	15,326,552
Selling, general, and administrative expenses	2,454,785

Instructions

1. Prepare Best Buy's income statement for the year ending March 31, 2001.
2. Prepare Best Buy's retained earnings statement for the year ending March 31, 2001. Note: The Retained Earnings at February 26, 2000, was $828,457. During the year, Best Buy did not pay any dividends.
3. Prepare a balance sheet as of March 31, 2001, for Best Buy.

Problem 1-4A

Statement of cash flows

Goal 4

Net decrease in cash, $3,844

SPREADSHEET

The following cash data were adapted from the annual report of Best Buy Inc. for the period ending March 31, 2001. The cash balance as of April 1, 2000, was $750,723 (in thousands).

	In thousands
Receipts from issuing capital stock	$235,379
Payments for property, plant, and equipment	657,706
Payments for purchase of other long-term assets	372,096
Payments for long-term debt	17,625
Net cash flows from operating activities	808,204

Instructions

Prepare Best Buy's statement of cash flows for the year ending March 31, 2001.

Problem 1-5A

Financial statements, including statement of cash flows

Goal 4

1. Net income, $225,000

SPREADSHEET

Lamar Corporation began operations on January 1, 2004, as an online retailer of computer software and hardware. The following financial statement data were taken from Lamar's records at the end of its first year of operations, December 31, 2004.

Accounts payable	$ 30,000
Accounts receivable	48,000
Capital stock	250,000
Cash	?
Cash payments for operating activities	700,000
Cash receipts from operating activities	837,000
Cost of sales	400,000
Dividends	25,000
Income tax expense	140,000
Income taxes payable	20,000
Interest expense	15,000
Inventories	90,000
Note payable due in 2010	100,000
Property, plant, and equipment	378,000
Retained earnings	?
Sales	885,000
Selling and administrative expense	105,000

Instructions

1. Prepare an income statement for the year ending December 31, 2004.
2. Prepare a retained earnings statement for the year ending December 31, 2004.
3. Prepare a balance sheet as of December 31, 2004.
4. Prepare a statement of cash flows for the year ending December 31, 2004.

Alternate Problem 1-1B

Financial statements

Goal 4

Net income: $27,775

STUDENT SOLUTIONS MANUAL

SPREADSHEET

Below are the amounts of the assets and liabilities of Hiawatha Travel Service at April 30, 2004, the end of the current year, and its revenue and expenses for the year. The retained earnings were $13,000 and the capital stock was $12,000 at May 1, 2003, the beginning of the current year. During the current year, dividends of $15,000 were paid.

Accounts payable	$ 6,100	Rent expense	$ 18,900
Accounts receivable	15,675	Prepaid expenses	1,675
Cash	26,525	Taxes expense	2,800
Fees earned	131,600	Utilities expense	14,800
Miscellaneous expense	1,475	Wages expense	65,850

Instructions

1. Prepare an income statement for the current year ended April 30, 2004.
2. Prepare a retained earnings statement for the current year ended April 30, 2004.
3. Prepare a balance sheet as of April 30, 2004.

Alternate Problem 1–2B

Missing amounts from financial statements

Goal 4

j. $50,550

STUDENT SOLUTIONS MANUAL

The financial statements at the end of Ruby River Realty's first month of operations are shown below.

Ruby River Realty
Income Statement
For the Month Ended June 30, 2004

Fees earned		$23,500
Operating expenses:		
Wages expense	$ (a)	
Rent expense	4,400	
Utilities expense	1,350	
Miscellaneous expense	825	
Total operating expenses		11,950
Net income		$ (b)

Ruby River Realty
Retained Earnings Statement
For the Month Ended June 30, 2004

Net income for June	$ (c)	
Less dividends	(d)	
Retained earnings, June 30, 2004		$ (e)

Ruby River Realty
Balance Sheet
June 30, 2004

Assets		
Cash		$14,750
Prepaid expenses		1,000
Land		(f)
Total assets		$ (g)
Liabilities		
Accounts payable		$ 1,200
Stockholders' Equity		
Capital stock	$ (h)	
Retained earnings	(i)	(j)
Total liabilities and stockholders' equity		$ (k)

Ruby River Realty
Statement of Cash Flows
For the Month Ended June 30, 2004

Cash flows from operating activities:		
Cash received from customers	$ (l)	
Deduct cash payments for expenses and payments to creditors	11,750	
Net cash flow from operating activities		$ (m)
Cash flows from investing activities:		
Cash payments for acquisition of land		$(36,000)
Cash flows from financing activities:		
Cash received from issuing capital stock	$45,000	
Deduct dividends	6,000	
Net cash flow from financing activities		(n)
Net cash flow and June 30, 2004 cash balance		$ (o)

Instructions

1. Would you classify a realty business like Ruby River as a manufacturing, merchandising, or service business?
2. By analyzing the interrelationships among the four financial statements, determine the proper amounts for (a) through (o).

Alternate Problem 1–3B

Income statement, retained earnings statement, and balance sheet

Goal 4

1. Net income, $16,967

STUDENT SOLUTIONS MANUAL

SPREADSHEET

The following financial data were adapted from the annual report of Circuit City Stores Inc. for the period ending May 30, 2001.

	In thousands
Accounts payable	$ 821,591
Accounts receivable	594,228
Accrued liabilities	154,795
Capital stock	768,662
Cash	404,501
Cost of goods sold	2,112,121
Dividends	3,621
Income taxes	10,400
Interest expense	2,992
Inventories	1,731,833
Other assets	103,154
Other liabilities	459,038
Property, plant, and equipment	981,031
Sales	2,678,474
Selling, general, and administrative expenses	535,994

Instructions

1. Prepare Circuit City's income statement for the year ending May 30, 2001.
2. Prepare Circuit City's retained earnings statement for the year ending May 30, 2001. Note: The Retained Earnings at May 31, 2000, was $1,597,315.
3. Prepare a balance sheet as of May 30, 2001 for Circuit City.

Alternate Problem 1-4B

Statement of cash flows

Goal 4

Net decrease in cash, $41,630

STUDENT SOLUTIONS MANUAL

SPREADSHEET

The following cash data were adapted from the annual report of Circuit City Stores Inc. for the period ending May 30, 2001. The cash balance as of May 31, 2000, was $446,131 (in thousands).

	In thousands
Cash receipts from issuing capital stock	$ 7,102
Cash receipts from issuing debt	1,640
Cash receipts from selling property, plant, and equipment	3,248
Cash payments for capital stock repurchases	187
Cash payments for debt	275
Cash payments for dividends	3,621
Cash payments for other investing activities	5,460
Cash payments for property, plant, and equipment	32,852
Net cash flows used in operating activities	(11,225)

Instructions

Prepare Circuit City's statement of cash flows for the year ending May 30, 2001.

Alternate Problem 1-5B

Financial statements, including statement of cash flows

Goal 4

1. Net income, $405,000

STUDENT SOLUTIONS MANUAL

SPREADSHEET

Rigby Corporation began operations on June 1, 2004, as an online retailer of camping and outdoor recreational equipment. The following financial statement data were taken from Rigby's records at the end of its first year of operations, May 31, 2005:

Accounts payable	$ 54,000
Accounts receivable	86,400
Cash	?
Cash receipts from operating activities	1,506,600
Cash payments for operating activities	1,260,000
Capital stock	450,000
Cost of sales	720,000
Dividends	45,000
Income tax expense	252,000
Income taxes payable	36,000
Interest expense	27,000
Inventories	162,000
Note payable due in 2010	180,000
Property, plant, and equipment	680,400
Retained earnings	?
Sales	1,593,000
Selling and administrative expense	189,000

Instructions

1. Prepare an income statement for the year ending May 31, 2005.
2. Prepare a retained earnings statement for the year ending May 31, 2005.
3. Prepare a balance sheet as of May 31, 2005.
4. Prepare a statement of cash flows for the year ending May 31, 2005.

Building Leadership Skills— Financial Analysis and Reporting

Case 1–1

Hershey's annual report

The financial statements of Hershey Foods Corporation are shown in Exhibits 5 through 8 of this chapter. Based upon these statements, answer the following questions.

1. What are Hershey's sales (in thousands)?
2. What is Hershey's cost of sales (in thousands)?
3. What is Hershey's net income (in thousands)?
4. What is Hershey's percent of the cost of sales to sales? Round to one decimal point.
5. The percent that a company adds to its cost of sales to determine the selling price is called a markup. What is Hershey's markup percent? Round to one decimal point.
6. What is the percentage of net income to sales for Hershey? Round to one decimal point.

Case 1–2

Income statement analysis

The following data (in thousands of dollars) were adapted from the December 31, 2001 financial statements of Tootsie Roll Industries Inc.:

Sales	$423,496
Cost of goods sold	216,657
Net income	65,687

1. What is Tootsie Roll's percent of the cost of sales to sales? Round to one decimal point.
2. The percent a company adds to its cost of sales to determine selling price is called a markup. What is Tootsie Roll's markup percent? Round to one decimal point.
3. What is the percentage of net income to sales for Tootsie Roll? Round to one decimal point.
4. Compare your answers to (2) and (3) with those of Hershey Foods Corporation in Case 1. What are your conclusions?

Case 1–3

Horizontal analysis

The following data (in millions of dollars) were adapted from the January 31, 2001 and 2000 financial statements of Kmart Corporation:

For year ending	2001	2000
Sales	$37,028	$35,925
Cost of sales	29,658	28,111
Selling, general, and administrative expenses	7,415	6,514

1. Prepare a horizontal analysis income statement for Kmart Corporation that includes gross profit and operating income before taxes. Round to one decimal place.
2. Comment on the results of your horizontal analysis of Kmart.

Case 1–4

Horizontal analysis

The telecommunications industry suffered a severe business downturn during the early part of this decade. Lucent Technologies is one of the major equipment providers to this industry. At the top of the next page are the comparative income statements for Lucent Technologies for the fiscal years ended September 30, 2001 and 2000.

1. Prepare a horizontal analysis income statement for Lucent Technologies.
2. Interpret your analysis.

Lucent Technologies Inc.
Consolidated Statements of Income
For the Years Ended September 30, 2000 and 2001

	In millions	
	9/30/01	**9/30/00**
Revenues	$ 21,294	$28,904
Costs	19,236	17,190
Gross profit	$ 2,058	$11,714
Operating expenses:		
Selling, general and administrative	$ 7,410	$ 5,610
Research and development	3,520	3,179
Other operating and restructuring expenses	10,157	559
Total operating expenses	$ 21,087	$ 9,348
Operating income (loss)	$(19,029)	$ 2,366
Other income (expense)—net	(357)	333
Interest expense	518	342
Income (loss) from continuing operations before income tax expense (benefit)	$(19,904)	$ 2,357
Income tax expense (benefit)	(5,734)	924
Income (loss) from continuing operations	$(14,170)	$ 1,433

Case 1–5

Financial analysis of Enron Corporation

Enron Corporation, headquartered in Houston, Texas, provides products and services for natural gas, electricity, and communications to wholesale and retail customers. Enron's operations are conducted through a variety of subsidiaries and affiliates that involve transporting gas through pipelines, transmitting electricity, and managing energy commodities. The following data were taken from Enron's December 31, 2000, financial statements.

	In millions
Total revenues	$100,789
Total costs and expenses	98,836
Operating income	1,953
Net income	979
Total assets	65,503
Total liabilities	54,033
Total stockholders' equity	11,470
Net cash flows from operating activities	4,779
Net cash flows from investing activities	(4,264)
Net cash flows from financing activities	571
Net increase in cash	1,086

At the end of 2000, the market price of Enron's stock was approximately $83 per share. As of March 15, 2002, Enron's stock was selling for $0.22 per share.

Review the preceding financial statement data and search the Internet for articles on Enron Corporation. Briefly explain why Enron's stock dropped so dramatically in such a short time.

Building Leadership Skills—Responsible Leadership

Activity 1–1

Business strategy

GROUP ACTIVITY

Assume that you are the chief executive officer for Gold Kist Inc., a national poultry producer. The company's operations include hatching chickens through the use of breeder stock and feeding, raising, and processing the mature chicks into finished products. The finished products include breaded chicken nuggets and patties and deboned, skinless, and marinated chicken. Gold Kist sells its products to schools, military services, fast food chains, and grocery stores.

In groups of four or five, discuss the following business strategy and risk issues:

1. In a commodity business like poultry production, what do you think is the dominant business strategy? What are the implications in this dominant strategy for how you would run Gold Kist?
2. Identify at least two major business risks for operating Gold Kist.
3. How could Gold Kist try to differentiate its products?

Activity 1–2

Ethics and professional conduct in business

ETHICS

GROUP ACTIVITY

Joel Phinney, president of Phinney Enterprises, applied for a $150,000 loan from Bridger National Bank. The bank requested financial statements from Phinney Enterprises as a basis for granting the loan. Joel has told his accountant to provide the bank with a balance sheet. Joel has decided to omit the other financial statements because there was a net loss during the past year.

In groups of three or four, discuss the following questions:

1. Is Joel behaving in a professional manner by omitting some of the financial statements?
2. a. What types of information about their businesses would owners be willing to provide bankers? What types of information would owners not be willing to provide?
   b. What types of information about a business would bankers want before extending a loan?
   c. What common interests are shared by bankers and business owners?

Activity 1–3

Net income vs. cash flow

On January 3, 2004, Dr. Brittany North established Expert Opinion, a medical practice organized as a proprietorship. The following conversation occurred the following August between Dr. North and a former medical school classmate, Dr. Charles Ryder, at an American Medical Association convention in Bermuda.

Dr. Ryder: Brittany, good to see you again. Why didn't you call when you were in Las Vegas? We could have had dinner together.

Dr. North: Actually, I never made it to Las Vegas this year. My husband and kids went up to our Lake Tahoe condo twice, but I got stuck in New York. I opened a new consulting practice this January and haven't had any time for myself since.

Dr. Ryder: I heard about it . . . Expert . . . something . . . right?

Dr. North: Yes, Expert Opinion. My husband chose the name.

Dr. Ryder: I've thought about doing something like that. Are you making any money? I mean, is it worth your time?

Dr. North: You wouldn't believe it. I started by opening a bank account with $30,000, and my July bank statement has a balance of $180,000. Not bad for seven months—all pure profit.

Dr. Ryder: Maybe I'll try it in Las Vegas. Let's have breakfast together tomorrow and you can fill me in on the details.

Comment on Dr. North's statement that the difference between the opening bank balance ($30,000) and the July statement balance ($180,000) is pure profit.

Activity 1-4

The accounting equation

Obtain the annual reports for three well-known companies, such as Ford Motor Co., General Motors, IBM, Microsoft, or Amazon.com. These annual reports can be obtained from a library or the company's 10-K filing with the Securities and Exchange Commission at www.sec.gov/edgar.shtml.

To obtain annual report information, click on "Search for Company Filings." Next, click on "Search EDGAR Historical Archives." Key in the company name. EDGAR will list the reports available for the company. Click on the 10-K (or 10-K405) report for the year you want to download. If you wish, you can save the whole 10-K report to a file and then open it with your word processor.

Examine the balance sheet for each company and determine the total assets, liabilities, and stockholders' equity. Verify that total assets equal the total of the liabilities plus stockholders' equity.

Activity 1-5

Certification requirements for accountants

By satisfying certain specific requirements, accountants may become certified as public accountants (CPAs), management accountants (CMAs), or internal auditors (CIAs). Find the certification requirements for one of these accounting groups by accessing the appropriate Internet site listed below.

Site	Description
www.ais-cpa.com	This site lists the address and/or Internet link for each state's board of accountancy. Find your state's requirements.
www.imanet.org	This site lists the requirements for becoming a CMA.
www.theiia.org	This site lists the requirements for becoming a CIA.

Answers to Self-Study Questions

1. **D** A corporation, organized in accordance with state or federal statutes, is a separate legal entity in which ownership is divided into shares of stock (answer D). A proprietorship (answer A) is an unincorporated business owned by one individual. A service business (answer B) provides services to its customers. It can be organized as a proprietorship, partnership, or corporation. A partnership (answer C) is an unincorporated business owned by two or more individuals.
2. **A** The resources owned by a business are called assets (answer A). The debts of the business are called liabilities (answer B), and the equity of the owners is called stockholders' equity (answer D). The relationship between assets, liabilities, and stockholders' equity is expressed as the accounting equation (answer C).
3. **A** The balance sheet is a listing of the assets, liabilities, and stockholders' equity of a business at a specific date (answer A). The income statement (answer B) is a summary of the revenue and expenses of a business for a specific period of time. The retained earnings statement (answer C) summarizes the changes in retained earnings during a specific period of time. The statement of cash flows (answer D) summarizes the cash receipts and cash payments for a specific period of time.
4. **D** The accounting equation is:

   Assets = Liabilities + Stockholders' Equity

   Therefore, if assets are $20,000 and liabilities are $12,000, stockholders' equity is $8,000 (answer D), as indicated in the following computation:

Assets	= Liabilities + Stockholders' Equity
+$20,000	= +$12,000 + Stockholders' Equity
+$20,000 − $12,000	= Stockholders' Equity
+$8,000	= Stockholders' Equity

5. **B** Net income is the excess of revenue over expenses, or $7,500 (answer B). If expenses exceed revenue, the difference is a net loss. Dividends are the opposite of the stockholders investing in the business and do not affect the amount of net income or net loss.

Chapter 2
The Cash Basis of Accounting

THE LAW OF E.F. HUTTON

"When the real leader speaks, people listen."

–The 21 Irrefutable Laws of Leadership

Dr. John C. Maxwell

Learning Goals

1 Describe the basic elements of a financial accounting system.

2 Describe the cash and accrual bases of accounting.

3 Use the cash basis of accounting to analyze, record, and summarize transactions for a corporation's first period of operations.

4 Use the cash basis of accounting to prepare financial statements for the first period of operations.

5 Use the cash basis of accounting for recording transactions and preparing financial statements for a second period of operations.

6 Describe the advantages and disadvantages of the cash basis of accounting.

7 Describe and illustrate how vertical analysis can be used to analyze and evaluate a company's performance.

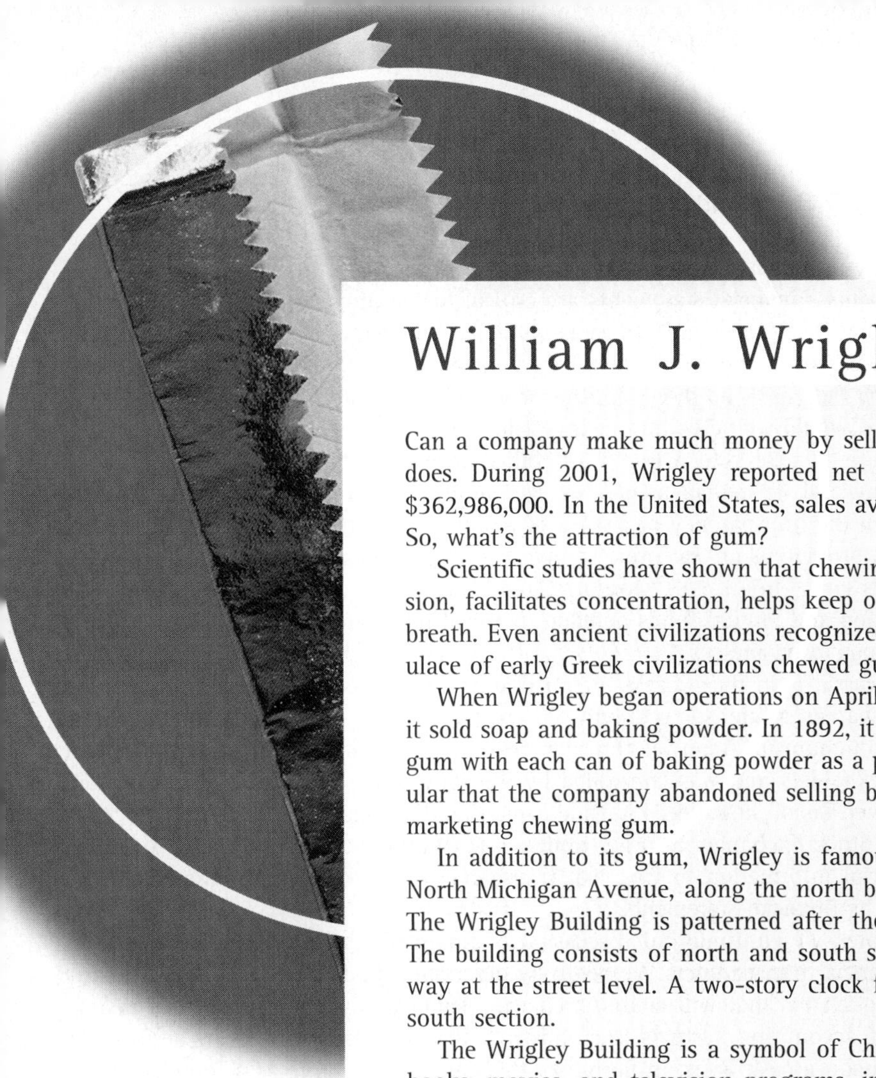

William J. Wrigley Jr. Company

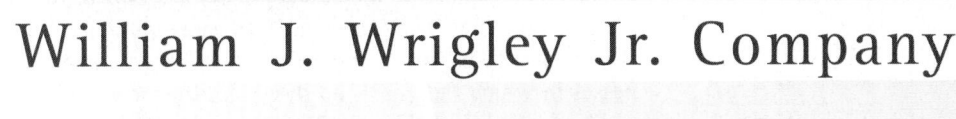

Can a company make much money by selling gum? William J. Wrigley Jr. Company does. During 2001, Wrigley reported net sales of $2,429,646,000 and net income of $362,986,000. In the United States, sales average 300 sticks of gum per person per year! So, what's the attraction of gum?

Scientific studies have shown that chewing gum relaxes nerves and muscles, eases tension, facilitates concentration, helps keep one alert, helps keep teeth clean, and freshens breath. Even ancient civilizations recognized the benefits of gum. For example, the populace of early Greek civilizations chewed gum made from the bark of the mastic tree.

When Wrigley began operations on April 1, 1891, it did not initially sell gum. Instead, it sold soap and baking powder. In 1892, it began giving away two packages of chewing gum with each can of baking powder as a promotion. The chewing gum became so popular that the company abandoned selling baking powder and focused on producing and marketing chewing gum.

In addition to its gum, Wrigley is famous for its corporate headquarters building on North Michigan Avenue, along the north bank of the Chicago River. The architecture of The Wrigley Building is patterned after the Seville Cathedral's Giralda Tower in Spain. The building consists of north and south sections connected by an open arcaded walkway at the street level. A two-story clock featuring four dials appears on the building's south section.

The Wrigley Building is a symbol of Chicago and has appeared in numerous articles, books, movies, and television programs, including *ER*, *My Best Friend's Wedding*, and *While You Were Sleeping*. The Wrigley name is also famous because of Wrigley Field and the Chicago Cubs. Philip K. Wrigley, former president and CEO, at one time was a part owner of both the Cubs and Wrigley Field.

William J. Wrigley Jr. Company's history is part of the lore of Chicago. As the company moves forward, its stakeholders are interested in its future financial condition and success. As we discussed in Chapter 1, the financial condition and changes in financial condition of a business are assessed through analyzing financial statements. In this chapter, we continue our discussion of financial statements by describing and illustrating how financial statements are prepared under a cash basis of accounting.

Source: Adapted from the William J. Wrigley Jr. Company Web site.

Your Need to Know

In Chapter 1 we introduced you to the nature of businesses and the basic concepts of financial statements. Financial statements are critical to the proper functioning of a free-market economy. Disclosures such as those provided by financial statements are termed "financial transparency." Financial transparency encourages individuals to invest in businesses in which they have no direct control or ability to monitor.

For example, would we be willing to invest in the stock of Lucent Technologies, Microsoft, Amazon.com, or Intel without an ability to monitor the economic performance of the company and its management? No, we wouldn't. However, financial statements provide us with the transparency necessary to monitor the performance of these companies and, thus, provide us an incentive to invest in their stocks. Likewise, financial institutions such as First Union, J.P. Morgan Chase, TIAA-CREF, Bank One Corporation, and state pension and mutual funds demand financial transparency before they are willing to loan funds to businesses.

Currently, Russia is in the process of transitioning from a secret economy to a more open and transparent, capitalistic economy. For example, Lucoil is Russia's largest oil company. Under communism, financial transparency was unimportant, since Lucoil had no individual stockholders and was controlled by the state using nonpublic, internal information. However, Lucoil now needs outside capital and is considering listing its stock on the New York Stock Exchange. In order to do so, Lucoil must move from being secretive with its financial information to financial transparency with open publication and dissemination of its financial statements.

In this chapter, we continue our discussion of financial statements and their role in enhancing financial transparency. We begin by describing the basic elements of a financial accounting system that will enable preparing financial statements. We then distinguish types of accounting systems and illustrate the simplest form of an accounting system based upon a cash basis. In doing so, this chapter will serve as a foundation for our later discussions of modern day accounting systems and financial reporting. However, throughout this discussion and the remainder of this text you should not forget that a primary benefit of financial reporting is its role in facilitating the functioning of a free-market economy.

Elements of an Accounting System

1 Describe the basic elements of a financial accounting system.

A financial accounting system is designed to produce financial statements. You should recall from Chapter 1 that the basic financial statements are the income statement, retained earnings statement, balance sheet, and statement of cash flows. So what are the basic elements of an accounting system that will enable the preparation of these statements?

The basic elements of a **financial accounting system** include (1) a set of rules for determining what, when, and the amount that should be recorded for economic events, (2) a framework for preparing financial statements, and (3) one or more controls to determine whether errors may have arisen in the recording process. These basic elements are found in all financial accounting systems—from a local retailer or hardware store to Microsoft, General Motors, Boeing, and William J. Wrigley Jr. Company.

Rules

The set of rules for determining what, when, and the amount that should be recorded for economic events are derived from the eight concepts we discussed in Chapter 1. In addition, the set of rules depends upon whether the business uses the cash basis or the accrual basis of accounting. We will describe and illustrate the set of rules for the cash basis of accounting in this chapter. The set of rules for the accrual basis of accounting are described and illustrated in Chapter 3.

Framework

The accounting equation provides a framework for recording and summarizing economic events and preparing financial statements. You should recall from Chapter 1 that the accounting equation is expressed as follows:

$$Assets = Liabilities + Stockholders' \ Equity$$

Using this equation, accounting systems are designed to record and summarize the effects of economic events on each element of the equation. That is, an economic event is analyzed in terms of its effect on assets, liabilities, or stockholders' equity.

A **transaction** is an economic event that under generally accepted accounting principles affects an element of the accounting equation and, therefore, must be recorded. A transaction may affect only one, two, or all three elements of the accounting equation. For example, equipment purchased for cash affects only assets. That is, one asset (equipment) increases while another asset (cash) decreases. If, on the other hand, the equipment is purchased on credit, both assets (equipment) and liabilities (accounts or notes payable) increase.

The receipt of cash for capital stock affects what elements of the accounting equation?

Total assets (cash) increases, and stockholders' equity (capital stock) increases.

By keeping a running total of the effects of transactions on each element, the equation also provides a framework for summarizing the overall effects of a series of transactions. For example, by keeping a record of increases and decreases in cash, the net change in cash can be determined for a period. Likewise, by keeping a record of sales, the total sales for the period can be determined.

Using the accounting equation as the framework for recording and summarizing transactions also facilitates preparing financial statements. This is because the accounting equation represents all the balance sheet elements and thus the financial condition of a company at a point in time. Changes in financial condition can be measured by analyzing changes in two balance sheets for two periods of time. By doing so, the income statement, retained earnings statement, and statement of cash flows can be prepared. These relationships are illustrated below for an annual accounting period ending on December 31, 2004.

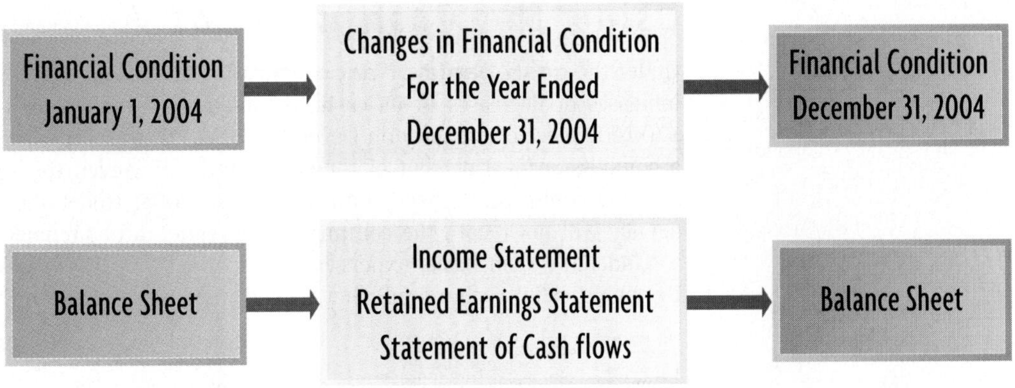

Controls

Using the accounting equation as a framework for designing an accounting system provides the control that, after recording transactions, total assets must equal total liabilities plus total stockholders' equity. If at the end of the period the equality does not hold, then an error has occurred in either recording or summarizing transactions. For example, if a $10,000 purchase of equipment for cash is incorrectly recorded as an increase in both equipment and cash, the total assets will exceed the total liabilities and stockholders' equity by $20,000 at the end of the period. Likewise, if equipment was increased by $10,000, but cash was not decreased by $10,000, the total assets will exceed total liabilities and stockholders' equity by $10,000 at the end of the period. In both cases, the inequality of the equation will indicate that an error has occurred in the recording process.

When $3,000 of cash was received for fees earned, it was erroneously recorded as an increase in cash of $300 and an increase in retained earnings (fees earned) of $3,000. Will the accounting equation balance?

No. Total assets will be less than total liabilities plus stockholders' equity by $2,700.

Before the financial statements are prepared, errors can be discovered and corrected. However, the equality of the equation at the end of the period doesn't necessarily mean that no errors have occurred. For example, assume that a business purchased $10,000 of equipment on credit and recorded the transaction as an increase in equipment of $10,000. However, instead of increasing the liabilities by $10,000, the transaction was recorded as a $10,000 decrease in cash. In this case, the accounting equation still balances, even though cash and liabilities are understated by $10,000. For this reason, accounting systems are designed with additional controls for recording and summarizing transactions. We will discuss these controls in later chapters.

Cash and Accrual Bases of Accounting

2 Describe the cash and accrual bases of accounting.

Accounting systems are based upon either the cash basis or the accrual basis of accounting. The accrual basis is used by large businesses and is required of publicly held corporations, such as Amazon.com and Wm. J. Wrigley Jr. Company. The cash basis of accounting is often used by individuals and small businesses.[1] For example, you probably use a cash basis because your checkbook is your primary accounting record. You keep track of your deposits (cash receipts) and checks (cash payments). Periodically, the bank sends you a statement that you use to verify the accuracy of your record keeping.

Both the cash and accrual bases of accounting use the business entity, cost, going concern, objectivity, unit of measure, adequate disclosure, and accounting period concepts discussed in Chapter 1. As we will discuss in the following paragraphs, the primary difference between the cash and accrual bases of accounting involves the matching concept.

Using the Cash Basis of Accounting

Under the **cash basis of accounting**, a business records only transactions involving increases or decreases of its cash. To illustrate, assume that a real estate agency sells a $300,000 piece of property on December 28, 2003. In selling the property, the agency earns a commission of 8 percent of the selling price. However, the agency does not receive the $24,000 commission check until January 3, 2004. Under the cash basis, the real estate agency will not record the commission (revenue) until January 3, 2004.

Under the cash basis, expenses are recorded only when cash is paid. For example, a December cellular phone bill that is paid in January would be recorded as a January ex-

---

1 Some business may use a modified-cash or tax basis of accounting. These bases of accounting are covered in advanced accounting texts.

Strategy in Business

Got the Flu? Why Not Chew Some Gum?

Facing a slumping market for sugared chewing gum, such as Juicy Fruit and Doublemint, Wm. J. Wrigley Jr. Company is reinventing itself with a strategy to expand its product lines and introduce new chewing gum applications. Wrigley's new products include sugarless breath mints and more powerful flavored mint chewing gum, like Extra Polar Ice. In addition, Wrigley is experimenting with health-care applications of chewing gum. Wrigley's Health Care Division has already developed Surpass, an antacid chewing gum to compete with Rolaids and Mylanta. In addition, Wrigley is experimenting with a cold-relief chewing gum and a gum that would provide dental benefits, such as whitening teeth and reducing plaque. Given that the U.S. population is aging, the company figures that people might prefer chewing gum to taking pills for sore throats, colds, or the flu. The effects of these new strategic initiatives will ultimately be reflected in Wrigley's financial statements.

Source: Adapted from "A Young Heir Has New Plans at Old Company," by David Barboza, *The New York Times*, August 28, 2001.

pense, not a December expense. Thus, under the cash basis, the matching concept does not determine when expenses are recorded. That is, expenses are recorded when paid in cash, not necessarily in the period when the revenue is earned.

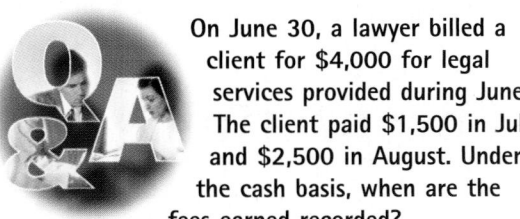

On June 30, a lawyer billed a client for $4,000 for legal services provided during June. The client paid $1,500 in July and $2,500 in August. Under the cash basis, when are the fees earned recorded?

June, $0; July, $1,500; August, $2,500

Using the Accrual Basis of Accounting

Under the **accrual basis of accounting**, revenue is recorded as it is earned, regardless of when cash is received. To illustrate, using the preceding example, the real estate agency would record the commissions (revenue) of $24,000 as earned on December 28, 2003, even though the check (cash) is not received until January 3, 2004. Once revenue has been earned and recorded, any expenses that have been incurred in generating the revenue are recorded and thus matched against that revenue. For example, a December cellular phone bill would be recorded in December as an increase in expenses and liabilities, even though it is not paid until January. In this way, the December phone expense is matched against the revenue it helped generate in December.

Summary of Differences between the Cash and Accrual Bases of Accounting

Exhibit 1 summarizes the basic differences of how revenue and expenses are recorded under the cash and accrual bases of accounting.

Exhibit 1

Cash versus Accrual Accounting

	Cash Basis	Accrual Basis
Revenue is recorded	When cash is received	When revenue is earned
Expense is recorded	When cash is paid	When expense is incurred in generating revenue

Ethics in Action
Channel Stuffing

To boost earnings prior to the end of a reporting period, managers will sometimes engage in the questionable practice of "channel stuffing." Channel stuffing enhances revenue (accrual-basis) by persuading a distributor to take additional products. The practice backfired for Lucent Technologies, which had to take back $452 million of equipment from distributors, causing a reversal of previously recognized revenue.

In the remainder of this chapter, we illustrate recording transactions and preparing financial statements using the cash basis of accounting. We will illustrate the accrual basis of accounting in Chapter 3. Because the cash basis is simpler, it will allow us to better focus on how the accounting equation is used as the framework for accounting systems. In addition, a thorough understanding of the cash basis will enhance your understanding of the accrual basis. In turn, this understanding will facilitate your ability to analyze and interpret the financial statements of publicly held corporations prepared under the accrual basis.

Using the Cash Basis for a Corporation's First Period of Operations

3 Use the cash basis of accounting to analyze, record, and summarize transactions for a corporation's first period of operations.

Using the accounting equation as our basic framework, we will illustrate the recording of transactions under the cash basis of accounting. We will assume that on September 1, 2003, Lee Landry, M.D., organizes a professional corporation to practice general medicine. The business is to be known as Family Health Care, P.C. We describe each transaction or group of similar transactions during September, the first month of operations. We then describe how the accounting equation can be used to analyze the effects of the transactions on the financial condition of the business. We will begin with Dr. Landry's investment to establish the business.

Transaction a Dr. Landry deposits $6,000 in a bank account in the name of Family Health Care, P.C., in return for shares of stock in the corporation. We will refer to stock issued to owners (stockholders) such as Lee Landry as capital stock. The effect of this transaction is to increase the asset (cash), on the left side of the equation, by $6,000. Increases are recorded as positive numbers, while decreases are recorded as negative numbers. Thus, the $6,000 deposit is recorded as a positive addition to Cash. To balance the equation, the stockholders' equity (capital stock) on the right side of the equation is increased by the same amount. This $6,000 is recorded as a positive addition to Capital Stock. The effect of this transaction on Family Health Care's accounting equation is shown below.

	Assets =	Stockholders' Equity	
	Cash =	Capital Stock	
a.	6,000	6,000	Investment by Dr. Landry

Note that the equation relates only to the business, Family Health Care, P.C. Lee Landry's personal assets (such as a home or a personal bank account) and personal liabilities are excluded from the equation. The business is treated as a separate entity, with cash of $6,000 and stockholders' equity of $6,000.

Transaction b Family Health Care's next transaction is to borrow $10,000 from First National Bank to finance its operations. To borrow the $10,000, Lee Landry signed a note payable in the name of Family Health Care. The note payable is a liability or a claim on assets that Family Health Care must satisfy (pay) in the future. In addition, the note payable requires the payment of interest of $100 per month until the note is due in full on September 30, 2009. At the end of September, we will record the payment of $100 of interest.

The items in the equation prior to the borrowing transaction and the effect of the borrowing transaction are shown next. The new amounts or balances of the items are also shown.

	Assets =	Liabilities +	Stockholders' Equity	
	Cash =	Notes Payable +	Capital Stock	
a.	6,000		6,000	
b.	10,000	10,000		Loan from bank
Bal.	16,000	10,000	6,000	

Observe how this transaction changed the mix of assets and liabilities but did not change Family Health Care's stockholders' equity. That is, assets minus liabilities still equals stockholders' equity of $6,000.

Transaction c Next, Family Health Care buys land for $12,000 cash. The land is located near a new suburban hospital that is under construction. Lee Landry plans to rent office space and equipment for several months. When the hospital is completed, Family Health Care will build on the land.

The purchase of the land changes the makeup of the assets, but it does not change the total assets. The effect of this transaction on the accounting equation is shown below.

	Assets		= Liabilities +	Stockholders' Equity	
	Cash +	Land =	Notes Payable +	Capital Stock	
Bal.	16,000		10,000	6,000	
c.	−12,000	12,000			Purchase of land
Bal.	4,000	12,000	10,000	6,000	

Transactions (b) and (c) have not improved the stockholders' equity of Family Health Care. They have simply changed the mix of assets and increased the liability, notes payable. However, the objective of businesses is to improve stockholders' equity through operations.

Ethics in Action
Phony Shares of Stock

Unethical practices can occur in promoting the issuance of stock to stockholders. It would be considered fraudulent to hide known risks from potential stockholders and to use stock proceeds for purposes other than indicated or for selling counterfeit shares. For example, two people pled guilty for fraudulently selling $15 million of phony shares of MindArrow Systems, Inc., stock.

How does a business improve the stockholders' equity? By earning revenues in excess of expenses. Revenues increase stockholders' equity through the business operations, while expenses decrease stockholders' equity. When revenues for a period exceed the expenses used to earn the revenues, the financial condition of the business will have improved. This improvement in financial condition results in an increase in the stockholders' equity of the business. Likewise, if the expenses exceed the revenues for a period of time, the stockholders' equity of the business will decrease. For this reason, transactions involving revenues and expenses are recorded as part of stockholders' equity in the accounting equation. In the following paragraphs, we illustrate the recording of revenue and expense transactions for Family Health Care.

Transaction d During the first month of operations, Family Health Care earns patient fees of $5,500, receiving the amount in cash. These transactions increase cash and the stockholders' equity by $5,500, as shown below.

	Assets			=	Liabilities	+	Stockholders' Equity			
	Cash	+	Land	=	Notes Payable	+	Capital Stock	+	Retained Earnings	
Bal.	4,000		12,000		10,000		6,000			
d.	5,500								5,500	Fees earned
Bal.	9,500		12,000		10,000		6,000		5,500	

Unlike transactions (b) and (c), the stockholders' equity of Family Health Care has increased by $5,500 as a result of this transaction. You should note that the increase in stockholders' equity from revenue is listed in the equation under "Retained Earnings." Retained earnings is the stockholders' equity created by the business operations (revenues less expenses). Transactions affecting earnings are kept separate from transactions related to stockholders' investments (capital stock). This is useful in preparing reports to owners and creditors and in satisfying some states' legal requirements that we will discuss later in the text.

Transaction e For Family Health Care, the expenses paid during the month were as follows: wages, $1,125; rent, $950; utilities, $450; interest, $100; miscellaneous, $275. Miscellaneous expenses include small amounts paid for such items as postage due and newspaper and magazine purchases. This group of expense transactions reduces cash and stockholders' equity, as shown below.

	Assets		=	Liabilities	+	Stockholders' Equity		
	Cash	+ Land	=	Notes Payable	+	Capital Stock	+ Retained Earnings	
Bal.	9,500	12,000		10,000		6,000	5,500	
e.	−2,900						−1,125	Wages expense
							−950	Rent expense
							−450	Utilities expense
							−100	Interest expense
							−275	Misc. exp.
Bal.	6,600	12,000		10,000		6,000	2,600	

Transaction f At the end of the month, Family Health Care pays $1,500 to stockholders (Dr. Lee Landry) as dividends. Dividends are distributions of business earnings to stockholders. Dividend payments reduce cash and stockholders' equity. The effect of this transaction is shown as follows:

	Assets		=	Liabilities	+	Stockholders' Equity		
	Cash	+ Land	=	Notes Payable	+	Capital Stock	+ Retained Earnings	
Bal.	6,600	12,000		10,000		6,000	2,600	
f.	−1,500						−1,500	Dividends
Bal.	5,100	12,000		10,000		6,000	1,100	

You should be careful not to confuse dividends with expenses. Dividends do not represent assets consumed or services used in the process of earning revenues. The decrease in stockholders' equity from dividends is listed in the equation under "Retained Earnings." This is because dividends are considered a distribution of earnings to the owners.

The transactions of Family Health Care are summarized as follows in Exhibit 2. The transactions are identified by letter, and the balance of each item is shown after each transaction.

Exhibit 2

Family Health Care Summary of Transactions for September

	Assets		=	Liabilities	+	Stockholders' Equity		
	Cash	+ Land	=	Notes Payable	+	Capital Stock	+ Retained Earnings	
a.	6,000					6,000		Investment
b.	10,000			10,000				Loan from bank
Bal.	16,000			10,000		6,000		
c.	−12,000	12,000						Purchase of land
Bal.	4,000	12,000		10,000		6,000		
d.	5,500						5,500	Fees earned
Bal.	9,500	12,000		10,000		6,000	5,500	
e.	−2,900						−1,125	Wages expense
							−950	Rent expense
							−450	Utilities expense
							−100	Interest expense
							−275	Miscellaneous exp.
Bal.	6,600	12,000		10,000		6,000	2,600	
f.	−1,500						−1,500	Dividends
Bal.	5,100	12,000		10,000		6,000	1,100	

In reviewing the preceding illustration, you should note the following, which apply to all types of businesses:

1. The effect of every transaction is an increase or a decrease in one or more of the accounting equation elements.
2. The two sides of the accounting equation are always equal.
3. The stockholders' equity is increased by amounts invested by stockholders (capital stock). In addition, stockholders' equity (retained earnings) is increased by revenues and decreased by expenses. Finally, stockholders' equity (retained earnings) is decreased by dividends distributed to stockholders. The effect of these four types of transactions on stockholders' equity is illustrated in Exhibit 3.

A physician refunded $300 to a patient for an incorrect bill. How would you record this transaction?

Decrease assets (cash) $300, and decrease retained earnings (fees earned) by $300.

Exhibit 3

Effects of Transactions on Stockholders' Equity

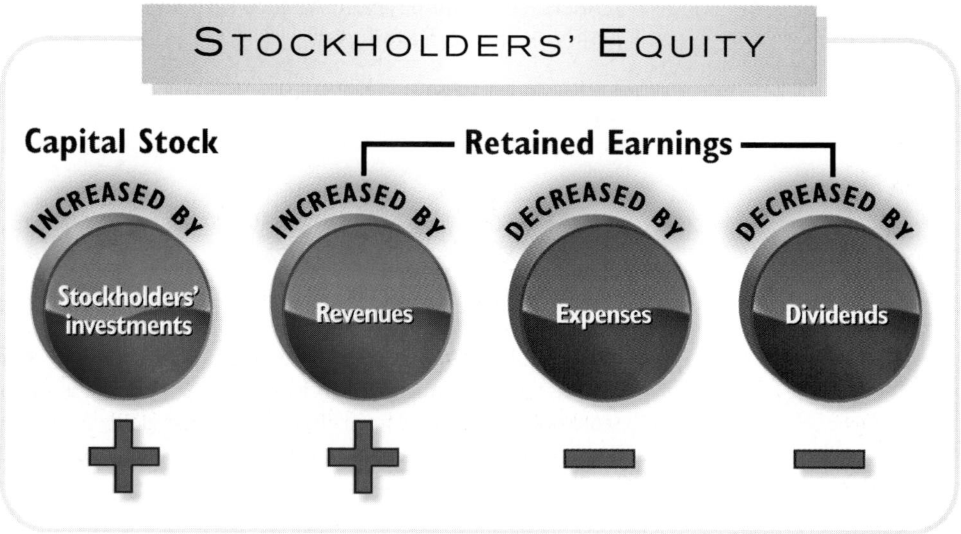

Financial Statements for a Corporation's First Period of Operations

4 Use the cash basis of accounting to prepare financial statements for the first period of operations.

In Exhibit 2, the September transactions for Family Health Care are listed in the order that they occurred. This exhibit, however, is not very user-friendly in that it does not group and summarize like transactions together. As we described and illustrated in Chapter 1, the accounting reports that provide this summarized information are the financial statements.

The September financial statements for Family Health Care are illustrated in Exhibit 4.

Exhibit 4

Family Health Care Financial Statements for September

Family Health Care, P.C.
Retained Earnings Statement
For the Month Ended September 30, 2003

Net income for September	$2,600
Less dividends	1,500
Retained earnings, September 30, 2003	$1,100

Exhibit 4

Concluded

Family Health Care, P.C.
Income Statement
For the Month Ended September 30, 2003

Fees earned		$5,500
Operating expenses:		
Wages expense	$1,125	
Rent expense	950	
Utilities expense	450	
Interest expense	100	
Miscellaneous expenses	275	
Total operating expenses		2,900
Net income		$2,600

Family Health Care, P.C.
Balance Sheet
September 30, 2003

Assets		
Cash		$ 5,100
Land		12,000
Total assets		$17,100
Liabilities		
Notes payable		$10,000
Stockholders' Equity		
Capital stock	$6,000	
Retained earnings	1,100	7,100
Total liabilities and stockholders' equity		$17,100

Family Health Care, P.C.
Statement of Cash Flows
For the Month Ended September 30, 2003

Cash flows from operating activities:			
Cash received from customers			$ 5,500
Deduct cash payments for expenses			2,900
Net cash flow from operating activities			$ 2,600
Cash flows from investing activities:			
Cash payments for acquisition of land			(12,000)
Cash flows from financing activities:			
Cash received from sale of cap. stock	$ 6,000		
Cash received from notes payable	10,000	$16,000	
Deduct cash dividends		1,500	
Net cash flow from financing activities			14,500
Net increase in cash			$ 5,100
September 1, 2003 cash balance			0
September 30, 2003 cash balance			$ 5,100

The data for the statements were taken from the transactions summary shown in Exhibit 2. You should note that each financial statement is identified by the *name* of the business, the *title* of the statement, and the *date* or *period of time.*

Income Statement

As shown in Exhibit 4, the income statement for Family Health Care reports fees earned of $5,500, total operating expenses of $2,900, and net income of $2,600. The $5,500 of fees earned was taken from the Retained Earnings column of Exhibit 2. Likewise, the expenses were summarized from the Retained Earnings column of Exhibit 2 and reported under the heading "Operating expenses." The expenses were listed in order of size, beginning with the largest expense. Miscellaneous expense is usually shown as the last item, regardless of the amount. The total operating expenses were then subtracted from the fees earned to arrive at the net income of $2,600. The effect of this net income will be to increase retained earnings and stockholders' equity.

Retained Earnings Statement

Since Family Health Care has been in operation for only one month, it has no retained earnings at the beginning of September. The ending September balance is the change in retained earnings that results from net income and dividends. This change, $1,100, will be the beginning balance for October.

Balance Sheet

The amounts of Family Health Care's assets, liabilities, and stockholders' equity at the end of September appear on the last line of the summary of transactions. With the addition of a heading, the balance sheet is prepared as shown in Exhibit 4.

In the liabilities section of Family Health Care's balance sheet, notes payable is the only liability. When there are two or more categories of liabilities, each should be listed and the total amount of liabilities reported. Liabilities should be presented in the order that they will be paid in cash. Thus, the notes payable due in 2009 will be listed after the obligations that are due in shorter time periods.

For Family Health Care, the September 30, 2003 stockholders' equity consists of $6,000 of capital stock and retained earnings of $1,100. The retained earnings amount is taken from the retained earnings statement.

INTERNATIONAL PERSPECTIVE

Brazil's accounting standards do not require a statement of cash flows.

Statement of Cash Flows

Family Health Care's statement of cash flows for September shows that cash increased from a zero balance at the beginning of the month to $5,100 at the end of the month. This $5,100 increase in cash was a result of cash flows from operating activities of $2,600. Family Health Care also reported net income of $2,600 for September. Under the cash basis of accounting, the net income and the cash flows from operating activities will be the same. Under the accrual basis of accounting, this will normally not be true.[2]

---

2 In Chapter 3, we will discuss why net income and cash flows from operating activities differ under the accrual basis of accounting.

At January 1, 2004, total assets and total liabilities were $600,000 and $380,000, respectively. At December 31, 2004, total assets and total liabilities were $950,000 and $580,000, respectively. If dividends of $75,000 were paid in 2004, what was the net income or loss?

$225,000 [($950,000 − $580,000) − ($600,000 − $380,000) + $75,000]

In addition to cash inflows of $2,600 from operating activities, Family Health Care spent $12,000 of cash for investing activities involving the purchase of land. This cash outflow related to investing activities was financed by an increased investment of $6,000 by Dr. Landry and $10,000 borrowed through a note payable at First National Bank. Family Health Care also distributed $1,500 in cash dividends during September.

Using the Cash Basis for the Second Period of Operations

5 Use the cash basis of accounting for recording transactions and preparing financial statements for a second period of operations.

To reinforce your understanding of recording transactions and preparing financial statements under the cash basis, we continue with Family Health Care's October transactions. During October, Family Health Care entered into the following transactions:

a. Received fees of $6,400 in cash.
b. Paid expenses in cash, as follows: wages, $1,370; rent, $950; utilities, $540; interest, $100; miscellaneous, $220.
c. Paid dividends of $1,000 in cash.

The preceding October transactions have been analyzed and entered into a summary of transactions for October, as shown in Exhibit 5. You should note that the summary of transactions for October begins with the ending balances as of September 30, 2003.

Exhibit 5

Family Health Care Summary of Transactions for October

	Asset			=	Liabilities	+	Stockholders' Equity			
	Cash	+	Land	=	Notes Payable	+	Capital Stock	+	Retained Earnings	
Bal.	5,100		12,000		10,000		6,000		1,100	
a.	6,400								6,400	Fees earned
Bal.	11,500		12,000		10,000		6,000		7,500	
b.	−3,180								−1,370	Wages expense
									−950	Rent expense
									−540	Utilities expense
									−100	Interest expense
									−220	Miscellaneous exp.
Bal.	8,320		12,000		10,000		6,000		4,320	
c.	−1,000								−1,000	Dividends
Bal.	7,320		12,000		10,000		6,000		3,320	

Family Health Care's financial statements for October are shown in Exhibit 6. These statements were prepared from the summary of transactions in Exhibit 5.

The income statement for October reports net income of $3,220. This is an increase of $620, or 23.8% ($620/$2,600), from September's net income of $2,600. This increase in net income was due to fees increasing from $5,500 to $6,400, a $900, or 16.4% ($900/$5,500),

Exhibit 6

Family Health Care Financial Statements for October

Family Health Care, P.C.
Income Statement
For the Month Ended October 31, 2003

Fees earned		$6,400
Operating expenses:		
Wages expense	$1,370	
Rent expense	950	
Utilities expense	540	
Interest expense	100	
Miscellaneous expenses	220	
Total operating expenses		3,180
Net income		$3,220

Family Health Care, P.C.
Retained Earnings Statement
For the Month Ended October 31, 2003

Retained earnings, October 1, 2003		$1,100
Net income for October	$3,220	
Less dividends	1,000	2,220
Retained earnings, October 31, 2003		$3,320

Family Health Care, P.C.
Balance Sheet
October 31, 2003

Assets		
Cash		$ 7,320
Land		12,000
Total assets		$19,320
Liabilities		
Notes payable		$10,000
Stockholders' Equity		
Capital stock	$6,000	
Retained earnings	3,320	9,320
Total liabilities and stockholders' equity		$19,320

Under the cash basis, what income statement amounts also appear on other financial statements?

The net income or loss appears on the retained earnings statement and the statement of cash flows. Under the cash basis, net income and net cash flows from operating activities are the same.

increase from September. At the same time, total operating expenses increased only $280, or 9.7% ($280/$2,900). This suggests that Family Health Care's operations are profitable and expanding.

The retained earnings statement reports an increase in retained earnings of $2,220. This increase is the result of net income ($3,220) less the dividends ($1,000) paid to Dr. Landry.

Exhibit 6

Concluded

Family Health Care, P.C.
Statement of Cash Flows
For the Month Ended October 31, 2003

Cash flows from operating activities:	
Cash received from customers	$ 6,400
Deduct cash payments for expenses	3,180
Net cash flow from operating activities	$ 3,220
Cash flows from investing activities	0
Cash flows from financing activities:	
Deduct cash dividends	(1,000)
Net increase in cash	$ 2,220
October 1, 2003 cash balance	5,100
October 31, 2003 cash balance	$ 7,320

The balance sheet shows that total assets increased from $17,100 on September 30, 2003 to $19,320 on October 31. This increase of $2,220 was due to an increase in cash from operations ($3,220) less the dividends ($1,000) that were paid to Dr. Landry. Total liabilities remained the same, but retained earnings and stockholders' equity increased by $2,220.

The statement of cash flows shows a net cash receipts from operations ($3,220) and a cash payment for dividends ($1,000). Recall that under the cash basis the net income is the same as the net cash flows from operations. The ending cash balance of $7,320 also appears on the October 31 balance sheet.

Advantages and Disadvantages of the Cash Basis

6 Describe the advantages and disadvantages of the cash basis of accounting.

The primary advantage of the cash basis of accounting is its simplicity. As shown in the illustrations for Family Health Care, it is relatively easy to use the cash basis to record and summarize transactions. In addition, the financial statements are easy to prepare and the net income from operations is the same as the cash flows from operating activities.

The primary disadvantage of the cash basis is that revenues and expenses may not always be properly matched on the income statement. This is because revenues and expenses are recorded only when cash is received or paid. As a result, an expense may be reported in one period and its related revenue in another period, with the result that net income may be distorted. This is the primary reason that generally accepted accounting principles rely upon the accrual basis of accounting. For this same reason, all publicly held corporations are required to use the accrual basis of accounting. If, on the other hand, cash receipts and payments are relatively stable and uniform over time, net income under the cash basis may approximate net income under the accrual basis. In such cases, the ease and simplicity of the cash basis may more than offset the additional costs of using the accrual basis. This is often the case for smaller businesses and individuals.

Vertical Analysis

7 Describe and illustrate how vertical analysis can be used to analyze and evaluate a company's performance.

The basic financial statements illustrated in this and the preceding chapter are primary sources of information that financial analysts and other stakeholders use in evaluating a company's performance. In Chapter 1, we illustrated horizontal analysis as one method of analyzing financial performance. Another method of analyzing comparative financial statements is to compute percentages of each item within a statement to a total within the statement. These percentages can then be compared across years. This type of analysis is called **vertical analysis**.

In vertical analysis of the balance sheet, each asset item is stated as a percent of the total assets. Each liability and stockholders' equity item is stated as a percent of total liabilities and stockholders' equity. To illustrate, Exhibit 7 shows comparative balance sheets for Wm. J. Wrigley Jr. Company, using vertical analysis.[3]

Exhibit 7

Comparative Balance Sheets Using Vertical Analysis: Wm. J. Wrigley Jr. Company

	December 31, 2001		December 31, 2000	
	Amount (thousands)	Percent	Amount (thousands)	Percent
Assets:				
Cash and cash equivalents	$ 307,785	17.4%	$ 300,599	19.1%
Short-term investments	25,450	1.4	29,301	1.9
Accounts receivable	239,885	13.6	191,570	12.2
Inventories	278,981	15.8	253,291	16.1
Property, plant, and equipment	684,379	38.8	607,034	38.5
Other assets	229,168	13.0	192,945	12.3
TOTAL ASSETS	$1,765,648	100.0%	$1,574,740	100.0%
Liabilities:				
Accounts payable	$ 91,225	5.2%	$ 73,129	4.6%
Dividends payable	42,741	2.4	39,467	2.5
Income and other taxes payable	68,467	3.9	60,976	3.9
Long-term liabilities	157,127	8.9	153,633	9.8
Other liabilities	129,891	7.4	114,638	7.3
Total liabilities	$ 489,451	27.7%	$ 441,843	28.1%
Stockholders' equity:				
Total stockholders' equity	$1,276,197	72.3%	$1,132,897	71.9%
TOTAL LIABILITIES AND STOCKHOLDERS' EQUITY	$1,765,648	100.0%	$1,574,740	100.0%

To simplify, the stockholders' equity is shown as a single amount. A review of Exhibit 7 reveals no major changes in the makeup of Wrigley's December 31 balance sheets for 2001 and 2000.

3 These financial statements have been adapted, based upon Securities and Exchange Commission filings.

In vertical analysis of the income statement, each item is stated as a percent of sales. To illustrate, Exhibit 8 shows comparative income statements of Wm. J. Wrigley Jr. Company, using vertical analysis.

Exhibit 8

Comparative Income Statements Using Vertical Analysis Wm. J. Wrigley Jr. Company for Years Ending December 31, 2001 and 2000

	2001		2000	
	Amount (thousands)	Percent	Amount (thousands)	Percent
Net sales	$2,429,646	100.0%	$2,145,706	100.0%
Cost of sales	997,054	41.1	904,266	42.1
Gross profit	$1,432,592	58.9%	$1,241,440	57.9%
Selling and administrative expenses	919,236	37.8	778,197	36.3
Operating income	$ 513,356	21.1%	$ 463,243	21.6%
Other income (expense)	14,010	0.6	16,069	0.7
Income before income taxes	$ 527,366	21.7%	$ 479,312	22.3%
Income taxes	164,380	6.8	150,370	7.0
Net income	$ 362,986	14.9%	$ 328,942	15.3%

Exhibit 8 reveals a slight decline in overall net income from 2000 to 2001 from 15.3% to 14.9% of sales. Gross profit improved from 57.9% to 58.9% of sales due to the decrease in the cost of sales from 42.1% to 41.1%. This increase in gross profit was offset by the increase in selling and administrative expenses from 36.3% to 37.8% of sales. As a result, operating income decreased from 21.6% to 21.1%. Other income and expense remained approximately the same while income taxes decreased as a percent of sales from 7.0% to 6.8%. Further inquiry should be made as to why selling and administrative expenses increased as a percentage of sales. This increase in expenses hurt what was otherwise a positive improvement in operating results.

Summary of Learning Goals

1 Describe the basic elements of a financial accounting system.

The basic elements of a financial accounting system include (1) a set of rules for determining what, when, and the amount that should be recorded for economic events, (2) a framework for facilitating preparation of financial statements, and (3) one or more controls to determine whether errors may have arisen in the recording process.

2 Describe the cash and accrual bases of accounting.

Under the cash basis of accounting, a business records only transactions involving increases or decreases of its cash. Under the accrual basis of accounting, revenue is recorded as it is earned and expenses are recorded when they generate revenue.

3 Use the cash basis of accounting to analyze, record, and summarize transactions for a corporation's first period of operations.

Using the accounting equation as a basic framework, September transactions for Family Health Care are recorded using the cash basis of accounting. In doing so,

(1) every transaction affects one or more elements of the accounting equation; (2) the two sides of the accounting equation are always equal; and (3) stockholders' equity is increased by issuing capital stock and revenues (retained earnings) and is decreased by expenses (retained earnings) and dividends (retained earnings).

4 Use the cash basis of accounting to prepare financial statements for the first period of operations.

The financial statements for Family Health Care for September, its first period of operations, are shown in Exhibit 4. Under the cash basis of accounting, the net income and the cash flows from operating activities are the same as shown in Exhibit 4.

5 Use the cash basis of accounting for recording transactions and preparing financial statements for a second period of operations.

Using the accounting equation as a basic framework, October transactions for Family Health Care are recorded and are summarized in Exhibit 5. The financial statements for Family Health Care for October, its second period of operations, are shown in Exhibit 6.

6 Describe the advantages and disadvantages of the cash basis of accounting.

The primary advantage of the cash basis of accounting is its simplicity. In addition, the financial statements are easy to prepare and the net income from operations is the same as the cash flows from operating activities. The primary disadvantage of the cash basis is that revenues and expenses may not always be properly matched on the income statement.

7 Describe and illustrate how vertical analysis can be used to analyze and evaluate a company's performance.

Vertical analysis is a method of analyzing comparative financial statements in which percentages are computed for each item within a statement to a total within the statement. In vertical analysis of the balance sheet, each asset item is stated at a percent of the total assets. Each liability and stockholders' equity item is stated at a percent of total liabilities and stockholders' equity. In vertical analysis of the income statement, each item is stated as a percent of sales.

Glossary

Accrual basis of accounting A system of accounting in which revenue is recorded as it is earned and expenses are recorded when they generate revenue.

Cash basis of accounting A system of accounting in which only transactions involving increases or decreases of the entity's cash are recorded.

Financial accounting system A system that includes (1) a set of rules for determining what, when, and the amount that should be recorded for economic events, (2) a framework for facilitating preparation of financial statements, and (3) one or more controls to determine whether errors may have arisen in the recording process.

Transaction An economic event that under generally accepted accounting principles affects an element of the accounting equation and, therefore, must be recorded.

Vertical analysis A method of analyzing comparative financial statements in which percentages are computed for each item within a statement to a total within the statement.

Illustrative Accounting Application Problem

Beth Sumner established an insurance agency on April 1, 2004, and completed the following transactions during April:

a. Opened a business bank account in the name of Sumner Insurance Inc. with a deposit of $15,000 in exchange for capital stock.

b. Borrowed $8,000 by issuing a note payable.
c. Received cash from fees earned, $11,500.
d. Paid rent on office and equipment for the month, $3,500.
e. Paid automobile expenses for month, $650, and miscellaneous expenses, $300.
f. Paid office salaries, $1,400.
g. Paid interest on the note payable, $60.
h. Purchased land as a future building site, $20,000.
i. Paid dividends, $1,000.

Instructions

1. Indicate the effect of each transaction and the balances after each transaction, using the following tabular headings:

Assets	=	Liabilities	+	Stockholders' Equity
Cash + Land	=	Notes Payable	+	Capital Stock + Retained Earnings

   Explain the nature of each increase and decrease in stockholders' equity by an appropriate notation at the right of the amount.
2. Prepare an income statement and retained earnings statement for April.
3. Prepare a balance sheet as of April 30, 2004.
4. Prepare a statement of cash flows for April.

Solution

	Assets			=	Liabilities	+	Stockholders' Equity			
	Cash	+	Land	=	Notes Payable	+	Capital Stock	+	Retained Earnings	
a.	+15,000						+15,000			Investment
b.	+8,000				+8,000					
Bal.	23,000				8,000		15,000			
c.	+11,500								+11,500	Fees earned
Bal.	34,500				8,000		15,000		11,500	
d.	−3,500								−3,500	Rent expense
Bal.	31,000				8,000		15,000		8,000	
e.	−950								−650	Auto expense
									−300	Misc. expense
Bal.	30,050				8,000		15,000		7,050	
f.	−1,400								−1,400	Salaries expense
Bal.	28,650				8,000		15,000		5,650	
g.	−60								−60	Interest expense
Bal.	28,590				8,000		15,000		5,590	
h.	−20,000		+20,000							Purchase of land
Bal.	8,590		20,000		8,000		15,000		5,590	
i.	−1,000								−1,000	Dividends
Bal.	7,590		20,000		8,000		15,000		4,590	

(2)

Sumner Insurance Inc.
Income Statement
For the Month Ending April 30, 2004

Revenues:		
Fees earned		$11,500
Expenses:		
Rent expense	$3,500	
Salaries expense	1,400	
Automotive expense	650	
Interest expense	60	
Miscellaneous expense	300	
Total expenses		5,910
Net income		$ 5,590

Sumner Insurance Inc.
Retained Earnings Statement
For the Month Ending April 30, 2004

Net income	$5,590
Less dividends	1,000
Retained earnings, April 30, 2001	$4,590

(3)

Sumner Insurance Inc.
Balance Sheet
April 30, 2004

Assets		
Cash		$ 7,590
Land		20,000
Total assets		$27,590
Liabilities		
Notes payable		$ 8,000
Stockholders' Equity		
Capital stock	$15,000	
Retained earnings	4,590	
Total stockholders' equity		19,590
Total liabilities and stockholders' equity		$27,590

(4)

Sumner Insurance Inc.
Statement of Cash Flows
For the Month Ending April 30, 2004

Cash flows from operating activities:		
Cash receipts from operating activities		$ 11,500
Cash payments for operating activities		5,910
Net cash flows from operating activities		$ 5,590
Cash flows from investing activities:		
Cash payments for land		(20,000)
Cash flows from financing activities:		
Cash receipts from issuing capital stock	$15,000	
Cash receipts from note payable	8,000	
Cash payments for dividends	(1,000)	
Net cash flows used in financing activities		22,000
Net increase in cash during April		$ 7,590
Cash as of April 1, 2004		0
Cash as of April 30, 2004		$ 7,590

Self-Study Questions

Answers at end of chapter

1. The purchase of land for $50,000 cash was incorrectly recorded as an increase in land and an increase in notes payable. Which of the following statements is correct?
   A. The accounting equation will not balance because cash is overstated by $50,000.
   B. The accounting equation will not balance because notes payable are overstated by $50,000.
   C. The accounting equation will not balance because assets will exceed liabilities by $50,000.
   D. Even though a recording error has been made, the accounting equation will balance.

2. The receipt of $8,000 of cash for fees earned was recorded by Langley Consulting as an increase in cash of $8,000 and a decrease in retained earnings (revenues) of $8,000. What is the effect of this error on the accounting equation?
   A. Total assets will exceed total liabilities and stockholders' equity by $8,000.
   B. Total assets will be less than total liabilities and stockholders' equity by $8,000.
   C. Total assets will exceed total liabilities and stockholders' equity by $16,000.
   D. The error will not affect the accounting equation.

3. Assume a lawyer bills his clients $25,000 for fees earned on April 30, 2004. The lawyer collects $18,500 of the billings during May and the remainder in June. Under the cash basis of accounting when would the lawyer record the revenue for fees earned?
   A. April, $25,000; May, $0; and June, $0.
   B. April, $0; May $18,500; and June, $7,500.
   C. April $18,500; May, $6,500; and June, $0.
   D. April $0; May, $18,500; and June, $6,500.

4. Using the information in Question 3, when would the lawyer record the revenue under the accrual basis of accounting?
   A. April, $25,000; May, $0; and June, $0.
   B. April, $0; May $18,500; and June, $7,500.
   C. April $18,500; May, $6,500; and June, $0.
   D. April $0; May, $18,500; and June, $6,500.

5. Which of the following transactions changes only the mix of assets and does not affect liabilities or stockholders' equity?
   A. Borrowed $40,000 from First National Bank.
   B. Purchased land for cash.
   C. Received $3,800 for fees earned.
   D. Paid $4,000 for office salaries.

Discussion Questions

1. What are the basic elements of a financial accounting system? Do these elements apply to all businesses from a local restaurant to General Motors? Explain.
2. Provide an example of a transaction that affects (a) only one element of the accounting equation, (b) two elements of the accounting equation, (c) three elements of the accounting equation.
3. For each of the following errors, indicate whether the error would cause the accounting equation to be out of balance and, if so, indicate how it would be out of balance. (a) The purchase of land for $30,000 cash was recorded as an increase in land of $30,000 and a decrease in cash of $3,000. (b) The receipt of $4,000 for fees earned was recorded as an increase in cash of $4,000 and an increase in liabilities of $4,000. (c) The payment of wages of $2,750 was recorded as a decrease in cash of $2,750 and a decrease in retained earnings (wages expense) of $2,570.
4. Why is the cash basis rather than the accrual basis often used by individuals and small businesses?
5. Under the cash basis of accounting, what are two primary controls for determining the accuracy of a business's or individual's record keeping?
6. Assume that at the end of each month, Leister Consulting Services bills its clients for jobs completed during the month. On October 31, 2004, Leister billed its clients $45,000 for fees earned on jobs completed during October. During November, Leister collected 80 percent of its fees billed on October 31 and collected the remaining 20 percent during December. What would be recorded by Leister as fees earned during October, November, and December under the cash basis and accrual basis of accounting?
7. As of January 31, 2004, Wyle Construction Inc. owed its employees $5,000 for wages. Because the 31st falls on a Saturday, Wyle did not pay its employees until the following Monday, February 2. Under the cash basis, when would the wages expense of $5,000 be recorded? Explain.
8. Fathom Consulting Services acquired land three years ago for $25,000. On September 30, Fathom signed an agreement to sell the land for $80,000. In accordance with the sales agreement, the buyer transferred $80,000 to Fathom's bank account on October 6. Fathom uses the cash basis of accounting. (a) When would Fathom record the sale of the land? (b) How would the elements of the accounting equation be affected by the sale?
9. (a) How does the payment of dividends of $15,000 affect the three elements of the accounting equation? (b) Is net income affected by the payment of dividends? Explain.
10. Assume that Margarita Consulting erroneously recorded the payment of $7,500 of dividends as salary expense. (a) How would this error affect the equality of the accounting equation? (b) How would this error affect the income statement, retained earnings statement, balance sheet, and statement of cash flows?
11. Assume that Blitzkrieg Realty Inc. borrowed $25,000 from First Union Bank and Trust. In recording the transaction, Blitzkrieg erroneously recorded the receipt of $25,000 as an increase in cash, $25,000, and an increase in fees earned, $25,000. (a) How would this error affect the equality of the accounting equation? (b) How would this error affect the income statement, retained earnings statement, balance sheet, and statement of cash flows?
12. Assume that as of January 1, 2004, Palmetto Consulting has total assets of $450,000 and total liabilities of $280,000. As of December 31, 2004, Palmetto has total liabilities of $300,000 and total stockholders' equity of $225,000. (a) What was Palmetto's stockholders' equity as of December 31, 2003? (b) Assume that Palmetto did not pay any dividends during 2004. What was the amount of net income for 2004?

13. Using the January 1 and December 31, 2004 data given in Question 12, answer the following questions. (a) If Palmetto paid $18,000 of dividends during 2004, what was the amount of net income for 2004? (b) Under the cash basis, will Palmetto's cash flows from operating activities be the same as its net income?
14. The primary disadvantage of the cash basis of accounting is that revenues and expenses may not always be properly matched on the income statement. Explain.
15. In Chapter 1, we described and illustrated horizontal analysis. (a) What is the difference between horizontal and vertical analysis? (b) Can horizontal and vertical analysis be used together in analyzing a company?

Resources for your success online @
http://warren.swlearning.com

Remember! If you need additional help, visit South-Western's Web site. See page 30 for a description of the online and printed materials that are available.

Exercises

Exercise 2-1

Accounting equation

Goal 1

a. $80,000

Determine the missing amount for each of the following:

	Assets	=	Liabilities	+	Stockholders' Equity
a.	X	=	$30,500	+	$ 50,000
b.	$360,000	=	X	+	100,000
c.	225,000	=	45,000	+	X

Exercise 2-2

Accounting equation

Goal 1

a. $24,100

STUDENT SOLUTIONS MANUAL

The assets and liabilities (in millions) of Walt Disney Company as of September 30, 2000, were as follows:

Assets	$45,027
Liabilities	20,927

a. Determine the stockholders' equity of Walt Disney as of September 30, 2000.
b. If assets decreased by $1,328 and stockholders' equity decreased by $1,428, what was the increase or decrease in liabilities for the year ending September 30, 2001?
c. What were the total assets, liabilities, and stockholders' equity as of September 30, 2001?
d. Based upon your answer to (c), does the accounting equation balance?

Exercise 2–3

Accounting equation

Goal 1

a. $137

The assets and liabilities (in millions) of Campbell Soup Co. as of July 29, 2000, were as follows:

Assets	$5,196
Liabilities	5,059

a. Determine the stockholders' equity of Campbell Soup as of July 29, 2000.
b. If assets increased by $731 and liabilities increased by $1,115, what was the increase or decrease in stockholders' equity for the year ending July 29, 2001?
c. What were the total assets, liabilities, and stockholders' equity as of July 29, 2001?
d. Based upon your answer to (c), does the accounting equation balance?

Exercise 2–4

Accounting equation

Goal 1

a. $303,516

STUDENT SOLUTIONS MANUAL

One item is omitted in each of the following summaries of balance sheet and income statement data (in millions) for General Motors and Coca-Cola as of December 31, 2001 and 2000.

	General Motors	Coca-Cola
December 31, 2000:		
Assets	$323,969	(e)
Liabilities	(a)	(f)
Stockholders' equity	(b)	$ 9,316
Increase (Decrease) in Assets, Liabilities, and Stockholders' Equity During 2001:		
Assets	$ (20,869)	(g)
Liabilities	(31,437)	$ (467)
Stockholders' equity	10,568	(h)
December 31, 2001:		
Assets	(c)	$22,417
Liabilities	$272,079	(i)
Stockholders' equity	(d)	11,366

Determine the amounts of the missing items (a) through (i).

Exercise 2–5

Accounting equation

Goal 1

b. $230,000

Jason Seagle is the sole stockholder and operator of Go-For-It, a motivational consulting business. At the end of its accounting period, December 31, 2004, Go-For-It has assets of $325,000 and liabilities of $142,000. Using the accounting equation and considering each case independently, determine the following amounts:

a. Stockholders' equity as of December 31, 2004.
b. Stockholders' equity as of December 31, 2005, assuming that assets increased by $84,000 and liabilities increased by $37,000 during 2005.
c. Stockholders' equity as of December 31, 2005, assuming that assets decreased by $8,000 and liabilities increased by $17,000 during 2005.
d. Stockholders' equity as of December 31, 2005, assuming that assets increased by $75,000 and liabilities decreased by $17,500 during 2005.
e. Net income (or net loss) during 2005, assuming that as of December 31, 2005, assets were $425,000, liabilities were $105,000, and there were no additional investments or dividends.

Exercise 2–6

Effect of transactions on stockholders' equity

Goals 3, 4, 5

STUDENT SOLUTIONS MANUAL

For Kroger Co., indicate whether the following transactions would (1) increase, (2) decrease, or (3) have no effect on stockholders' equity.

a. Paid creditors.
b. Made cash sales to customers.
c. Paid interest expense.
d. Purchased store equipment.
e. Paid dividends.
f. Borrowed money from the bank.
g. Sold store equipment at a loss.
h. Paid store rent.
i. Paid taxes.
j. Received interest income.

Exercise 2–7

Effect of transactions on accounting equation

Goals 1, 3, 4, 5

Describe how the following business transactions affect the three elements of the accounting equation.

a. Issued capital stock for cash.
b. Purchased land for cash.
c. Borrowed cash at local bank.
d. Received cash for services performed.
e. Paid for utilities used in the business.

Exercise 2–8

Effect of transactions on accounting equation

Goals 1, 3, 4, 5

(1) Assets increase $50,000

STUDENT SOLUTIONS MANUAL

A vacant lot acquired for $120,000, on which there is a balance owed of $40,000, is sold for $210,000 in cash. The seller pays the $40,000 owed. What is the effect of these transactions on the total amount of the seller's (1) assets, (2) liabilities, and (3) stockholders' equity?

Exercise 2–9

Effect of transactions on stockholders' equity

Goals 3, 4, 5

Indicate whether each of the following types of transactions will (a) increase stockholders' equity or (b) decrease stockholders' equity:

1. Issued capital stock for cash.
2. Received cash for fees earned.
3. Paid cash for rent expense.
4. Paid cash dividends.
5. Paid cash for utilities expense.

Exercise 2–10

Transactions

Goals 1, 3, 4, 5

STUDENT SOLUTIONS MANUAL

The following selected transactions were completed by Speedy Delivery Service during May:

1. Received cash for capital stock, $25,000.
2. Borrowed $15,000 from a local bank.
3. Paid advertising expense, $800.
4. Paid rent for May, $2,500.
5. Received cash from customers, $7,250.
6. Paid creditors, $500.
7. Paid interest on note payable, $400.
8. Purchased land for future building site by paying cash of $20,000.
9. Paid a customer a $200 refund for an overcharge of services.
10. Paid cash dividends, $1,000.

Indicate the effect of each transaction on the accounting equation by listing the numbers identifying the transactions, (1) through (10), in a vertical column, and inserting at the right of each number the appropriate letter from the following list:

a. Increase in an asset, decrease in another asset.
b. Increase in an asset, increase in a liability.
c. Increase in an asset, increase in stockholders' equity.
d. Decrease in an asset, decrease in a liability.
e. Decrease in an asset, decrease in stockholders' equity.

Exercise 2–11

Nature of transactions

Goals 1, 3, 4, 5

b. $1,750

David Saros operates his own catering service. Summary financial data for August are presented in equation form as follows. Each line designated by a number indicates the effect of a transaction on the equation. Each increase and decrease in stockholders' equity, except transaction (4), affects net income.

	Cash	+	Land	=	Liabilities	+	Capital Stock	+	Retained Earnings
Bal.	9,500		10,000		4,350		10,000		5,150
1.	+36,000								+36,000
2.	−15,000		+15,000						
3.	−21,250								−21,250
4.	−1,500								−1,500
Bal.	7,750		25,000		4,350		10,000		18,400

a. Describe each transaction.
b. What is the amount of net decrease in cash during the month?
c. What is the amount of net increase in retained earnings during the month?
d. What is the amount of the net income for the month?
e. How much of the net income for the month was retained in the business?
f. What is the amount of net cash flows from operating activities?
g. What is the amount of net cash flows from investing activities?
h. What is the amount of net cash flows from financing activities?

Exercise 2–12

Net income and dividends

Goals 4, 5

STUDENT SOLUTIONS MANUAL

The income statement of a corporation for the month of April indicates a net income of $42,000. During the same period, $50,000 in cash dividends was paid. Would it be correct to say that the business incurred a net loss of $8,000 during the month? Discuss.

Exercise 2–13

Net income and stockholders' equity for four businesses

Goals 1, 3, 4, 5

Company C: Net income, $165,000

Four different corporations, A, B, C, and D, show the same balance sheet data at the beginning and end of a year. These data, exclusive of the amount of stockholders' equity, are summarized as follows:

	Total Assets	Total Liabilities
Beginning of the year	$525,000	$220,000
End of the year	970,000	425,000

On the basis of the above data and the following additional information for the year, determine the net income (or loss) of each company for the year. (*Suggestion:* First determine the amount of increase or decrease in stockholders' equity during the year.)

Company A: No additional capital stock was issued, and no dividends were paid.
Company B: No additional capital stock was issued, but dividends of $50,000 were paid.
Company C: Capital stock of $75,000 was issued, but no dividends were paid.
Company D: Capital stock of $75,000 was issued, and dividends of $50,000 were paid.

Exercise 2–14

Missing amounts from balance sheet and income statement data

One item is omitted in each of the following summaries of balance sheet and income statement data for four different corporations, I, II, III, and IV.

Goals 1, 3, 4, 5

a. $230,000

STUDENT SOLUTIONS MANUAL

	I	II	III	IV
Beginning of the year:				
Assets	$400,000	$ 95,000	$100,000	(d)
Liabilities	260,000	45,000	80,000	$150,000
End of the year:				
Assets	900,000	125,000	120,000	310,000
Liabilities	500,000	35,000	105,000	170,000
During the year:				
Additional issue of capital stock	(a)	22,000	10,000	50,000
Dividends	40,000	8,000	(c)	75,000
Revenue	250,000	(b)	175,000	140,000
Expenses	180,000	52,000	177,000	160,000

Determine the amounts of the missing items, identifying them by letter. (*Suggestion:* First determine the amount of increase or decrease in stockholders' equity during the year.)

Exercise 2–15

Net income, retained earnings, and dividends

Goals 4, 5

a. $278 increase

Use the following data (in millions) for Campbell Soup Co. for the year ending July 29, 2001, to answer the following questions.

Retained earnings July 29, 2000	$4,373
Retained earnings July 29, 2001	4,651
Net cash from operating activities	1,106
Net decrease in cash	3

a. Determine the net increase or decrease in retained earnings during 2001.
b. If dividends in 2001 are $371, what was the net income or loss for Campbell Soup for the year ending July 29, 2001?
c. Why doesn't your answer in (b) agree with the net cash from operating activities of $1,106 shown above?
d. Why doesn't the net cash from operating activities of $1,106 agree with the net decrease in cash of $3?

Exercise 2–16

Balance sheet, net income, and cash flows

Goals 4, 5

b. $11,000

STUDENT SOLUTIONS MANUAL

SPREADSHEET

Woods Interiors uses the cash basis of accounting. Financial information related to Woods Interiors for September and October of 2004 is as follows:

	September 30, 2004	October 31, 2004
Notes payable	$10,000	$15,000
Land	17,000	25,000
Capital stock	6,000	9,000
Retained earnings	?	?
Cash	18,000	27,000

a. Prepare balance sheets for Woods Interiors as of September 30 and as of October 31, 2004.
b. Determine the amount of net income for October, assuming that dividends of $2,000 were paid.
c. Determine the net cash flows from operating activities.
d. Determine the net cash flows from investing activities.
e. Determine the net cash flows for financing activities.
f. Determine the net increase or decrease in cash.

Exercise 2–17

Income statement

Goals 4, 5

Net income, $11,250

SPREADSHEET

After its first month of operations, the following amounts were taken from the accounting records of Mata Hari Realty Inc. as of April 30, 2004. Mata Hari Realty uses the cash basis of accounting.

Capital stock	$ 5,000	Notes payable	$15,000
Cash	10,750	Rent expense	3,000
Dividends	2,000	Retained earnings	0
Interest expense	1,000	Salaries expense	4,500
Land	18,500	Sales commissions	24,750
Miscellaneous expense	1,250	Utilities expense	3,750

Prepare an income statement for the month ending April 30, 2004.

Exercise 2–18

Retained earnings statement

Goals 4, 5

Retained earnings, April 2, 2004, $9,250

STUDENT SOLUTIONS MANUAL

SPREADSHEET

Using the financial data shown in Exercise 2–17 for Mata Hari Realty Inc., prepare a retained earnings statement for the month ending April 30, 2004.

Exercise 2–19

Balance sheet

Goals 4, 5

Total assets, $29,280

SPREADSHEET

Using the financial data shown in Exercise 2–17 for Mata Hari Realty Inc., prepare a balance sheet as of April 30, 2004.

Exercise 2–20

Statement of cash flows

Goals 4, 5

Net cash flows from financing activities, $18,000

STUDENT SOLUTIONS MANUAL

SPREADSHEET

Using the financial data shown in Exercise 2–17 for Mata Hari Realty Inc., prepare a statement of cash flows for the month ending April 30, 2004.

Exercise 2–21

Effect of transactions on accounting equation

Goals 1, 3, 4, 5

Describe how each of the following transactions of Lucent Technologies Inc. would affect the three elements of its accounting equation.

a. Paid dividends.
b. Made cash sales.
c. Received cash from issuing stock.
d. Paid long-term debt.
e. Received proceeds from selling a portion of manufacturing operations for a gain on the sale.
f. Received cash from the issuance of long-term debt.

g. Paid taxes.
h. Paid research and development expenses for the current year.
i. Paid employee pension expenses for the current year.
j. Purchased machinery and equipment for cash.
k. Paid officer salaries.
l. Paid selling expenses.

Exercise 2-22

Statement of cash flows

Goals 4, 5

STUDENT SOLUTIONS MANUAL

Based upon the financial transactions for Lucent Technologies Inc. shown in Exercise 2-21, indicate whether the transaction would be reported in the cash flows from operating, investing, or financing sections of the statement of cash flows.

Accounting Application Problems

Problem 2-1A

Transactions and financial statements

Goals 1, 3, 4, 5

3. Net income, $4,475

SPREADSHEET GENERAL LEDGER

Jay Marsh established an insurance agency on May 1, 2004, and completed the following transactions during May:

a. Opened a business bank account in the name of Frontier Insurance Inc. with a deposit of $30,000 in exchange for capital stock.
b. Borrowed $10,000 by issuing a note payable.
c. Received cash from fees earned, $8,100.
d. Paid rent on office and equipment for the month, $1,000.
e. Paid automobile expenses for month, $800, and miscellaneous expenses, $250.
f. Paid office salaries, $1,500.
g. Paid interest on the note payable, $75.
h. Purchased land as a future building site, $15,000.
i. Paid dividends, $2,000.

Instructions

1. Indicate the effect of each transaction and the balances after each transaction, using the following tabular headings:

Assets	=	Liabilities	+	Stockholders' Equity
Cash + Land	=	Notes Payable	+	Capital Stock + Retained Earnings

   Explain the nature of each increase and decrease in stockholders' equity by an appropriate notation at the right of the amount.
2. Briefly explain why the stockholders' investments and revenues increased stockholders' equity, while dividends and expenses decreased stockholders' equity.
3. Prepare an income statement and retained earnings statement for May.
4. Prepare a balance sheet as of May 31, 2004.
5. Prepare a statement of cash flows for May.

Problem 2-2A

Cash basis financial statements

Goals 1, 3, 4, 5

1. Net income, $6,600

SPREADSHEET

Scott Douma established Top-Notch Computer Services on July 1, 2004. The effect of each transaction and the balances after each transaction for July are shown in the table at the top of the following page.

Instructions

1. Prepare an income statement for the month ended July 31, 2004.
2. Prepare a retained earnings statement for the month ended July 31, 2004.
3. Prepare a balance sheet as of July 31, 2004.
4. Prepare a statement of cash flows for the month ended July 31, 2004.

	Assets		= Liabilities	+ Stockholders' Equity		
	Cash	+ Land	= Notes Payable	+ Capital Stock	+ Retained Earnings	
a.	+18,000			+18,000		Investment
b.	+12,250				12,250	Fees earned
Bal.	30,250			18,000	12,250	
c.	−2,000				−2,000	Rent expense
Bal.	28,250			18,000	10,250	
d.	+10,000		+10,000			
Bal.	38,250		10,000	18,000	10,250	
e.	−25,000	+25,000				
Bal.	13,250	25,000	10,000	18,000	10,250	
f.	−1,150				−800	Auto expense
					−350	Misc. expense
Bal.	12,100	25,000	10,000	18,000	9,100	
g.	−2,500				−2,500	Salaries expense
Bal.	9,600	25,000	10,000	18,000	6,600	
h.	−1,000				−1,000	Dividends
Bal.	8,600	25,000	10,000	18,000	5,600	

Problem 2–3A

Cash basis financial statements

Goals 4, 5

1. Net income, $82,500

SPREADSHEET

The following amounts were taken from the accounting records of Nutrition Services Inc. as of December 31, 2004. Nutrition Services began its operations on January 1, 2004, and uses the cash basis of accounting.

Capital stock	$ 10,000
Cash	27,500
Dividends	5,000
Fees earned	229,500
Interest expense	1,200
Land	75,000
Miscellaneous expense	6,800
Notes payable	15,000
Rent expense	24,000
Salaries expense	65,000
Taxes expense	18,000
Utilities expense	32,000

Instructions

1. Prepare an income statement for the year ending December 31, 2004.
2. Prepare a retained earnings statement for the year ending December 31, 2004.
3. Prepare a balance sheet as of December 31, 2004.
4. Prepare a statement of cash flows for the year ending December 31, 2004.

Problem 2–4A

Cash basis financial statements

Goals 4, 5

After its second year of operations, the following amounts were taken from the accounting records of Nutrition Services Inc. as of December 31, 2005. Nutrition Services began its operations on January 1, 2004 (see Problem 2–3A) and uses the cash basis of accounting.

1. Net income, $91,500

SPREADSHEET

Capital stock	$ 25,000
Cash	?
Dividends	15,000
Fees earned	254,100
Interest expense	1,600
Land	140,000
Miscellaneous expense	7,000
Notes payable	20,000
Rent expense	28,000
Salaries expense	70,000
Taxes expense	20,000
Utilities expense	36,000

Instructions

1. Prepare an income statement for the year ending December 31, 2005.
2. Prepare a retained earnings statement for the year ending December 31, 2005. Note: The Retained Earnings at January 1, 2005, was $77,500.
3. Prepare a balance sheet as of December 31, 2005.
4. Prepare a statement of cash flows for the year ending December 31, 2005. *Hint:* You should compare the asset and liability amounts of December 31, 2005 with those of December 31, 2004, to determine cash used in investing and financing activities. See Problem 2–3A for the December 31, 2004 balance sheet amounts.

Problem 2–5A

Missing amounts from financial statements

Goals 4, 5

a. $13,000

The financial statements at the end of Harvest Realty Inc.'s first month of operations are shown below. By analyzing the interrelationships between the financial statements, fill in the proper amounts for (a) through (s).

Harvest Realty Inc.
Income Statement
For the Month Ended March 31, 2004

Fees earned		$ (a)
Operating expenses:		
Wages expense	$3,680	
Rent expense	2,000	
Utilities expense	(b)	
Interest expense	200	
Miscellaneous expenses	440	
Total operating expenses		7,500
Net income		$ (c)

Harvest Realty Inc.
Retained Earnings Statement
For the Month Ended March 31, 2004

Retained earnings, March 1, 2004		$ (d)
Net income for March	$5,500	
Less dividends	(e)	(f)
Retained earnings, March 31, 2004		$ (g)

Harvest Realty Inc.
Balance Sheet
March 31, 2004

Assets		
Cash		$ (h)
Land		20,000
Total assets		$26,500
Liabilities		
Notes payable		$12,000
Stockholders' Equity		
Capital stock	$ (i)	
Retained earnings	(j)	(k)
Total liabilities and stockholders' equity		$ (l)

Harvest Realty Inc.
Statement of Cash Flows
For the Month Ended March 31, 2004

Cash flows from operating activities:			
Cash received from customers			$ 13,000
Deduct cash payments for expenses			7,500
Net cash flows from operating activities			$ (m)
Cash flows from investing activities:			
Cash payment for purchase of land			$(20,000)
Cash flows from financing activities:			
Cash received from sale of capital stock	$10,000		
Cash received from notes payable	(n)	$ (o)	
Deduct cash dividends		1,000	
Net cash flows from financing activities			(p)
Net increase in cash			$ (q)
March 1, 2004 cash balance			(r)
March 31, 2004 cash balance			$ (s)

Problem 2–6A

Cash basis financial statements

Goals 4, 5

Spring Creek Realty Inc., organized July 1, 2004, is operated by Bob Gibbs. How many errors can you find in the following financial statements for Spring Creek Realty Inc., prepared after its first month of operations?

Spring Creek Realty Inc.
Income Statement
July 31, 2004

Sales commissions		$46,100
Operating expenses:		
Office salaries expense	$8,150	
Rent expense	3,800	
Automobile expense	1,750	
Dividends	1,000	
Miscellaneous expense	775	
Total operating expenses		15,475
Net income		$20,625

Bob Gibbs
Retained Earnings Statement
July 31, 2003

Net income for the month	$20,625
Retained earnings, July 31, 2004	$20,625

Balance Sheet Inc.
For the Month Ended July 31, 2004

Assets		
Cash		$30,425
Notes payable		10,000
Total assets		$40,425
Liabilities		
Land		$20,200
Stockholders' Equity		
Capital stock	$10,000	
Retained earnings	20,625	30,625
Total liabilities and stockholders' equity		$50,825

Spring Creek Realty Inc.
Statement of Cash Flows
July 31, 2004

Cash flows from operating activities:	
Cash receipts from sales commissions	$ 46,100
Cash flows from investing activities:	
Cash payments for land	(20,200)
Cash flows from financing activities:	
Cash receipts from retained earnings	40,625
Net increase in cash during July	$ 66,525
Cash as of July 1, 2004	0
Cash as of July 31, 2004	$ 66,525

Alternate Problem 2–1B

Transactions and financial statements

Goals 1, 3, 4, 5

3. Net income, $4,410

STUDENT SOLUTIONS MANUAL

SPREADSHEET GENERAL LEDGER

Ruth Kincaid established a real estate agency on October 1, 2004, and completed the following transactions during October:

a. Opened a business bank account in the name of Granite Realty Inc. with a deposit of $20,000 in exchange for capital stock.
b. Borrowed $15,000 by issuing a note payable.
c. Received cash from commissions earned, $9,000.
d. Paid rent on office and equipment for the month, $1,800.
e. Paid automobile expenses for month, $950, and miscellaneous expenses, $550.
f. Paid office salaries, $1,200.
g. Paid interest on the note payable, $90.
h. Purchased land as a future building site, $20,000.
i. Paid dividends, $1,000.

Instructions

1. Indicate the effect of each transaction and the balances after each transaction, using the following tabular headings:

Assets	=	Liabilities	+	Stockholders' Equity
Cash + Land	=	Notes Payable	+	Capital Stock + Retained Earnings

   Explain the nature of each increase and decrease in stockholders' equity by an appropriate notation at the right of the amount.
2. Briefly explain why the stockholders' investments and revenues increased stockholders' equity, while dividends and expenses decreased stockholders' equity.
3. Prepare an income statement and retained earnings statement for October.
4. Prepare a balance sheet as of October 31, 2004.
5. Prepare a statement of cash flows for October.

Alternate Problem 2–2B

Cash basis financial statements

Goals 1, 3, 4, 5

1. Net income, $5,000

STUDENT SOLUTIONS MANUAL

SPREADSHEET

Jay Fleming established A1 Architectural Services on January 1, 2004. The effect of each transaction and the balances after each transaction for January are as follows:

	Assets			=	Liabilities	+	Stockholders' Equity			
	Cash	+	Land	=	Notes Payable	+	Capital Stock	+	Retained Earnings	
a.	+15,000						+15,000			Investment
b.	+9,500								+9,500	Fees earned
Bal.	24,500						15,000		9,500	
c.	−1,500								−1,500	Rent expense
Bal.	23,000						15,000		8,000	
d.	+10,000				+10,000					
Bal.	33,000				10,000		15,000		8,000	
e.	−20,000		+20,000							
Bal.	13,000		20,000		10,000		15,000		8,000	
f.	−1,000								−750	Auto expense
									−250	Misc. expense
Bal.	12,000		20,000		10,000		15,000		7,000	
g.	−2,000								−2,000	Salaries expense
Bal.	10,000		20,000		10,000		15,000		5,000	
h.	−500								−500	Dividends
Bal.	9,500		20,000		10,000		15,000		4,500	

Instructions

1. Prepare an income statement for the month ended January 31, 2004.
2. Prepare a retained earnings statement for the month ended January 31, 2004.
3. Prepare a balance sheet as of January 31, 2004.
4. Prepare a statement of cash flows for the month ended January 31, 2004.

Alternate Problem 2–3B

Cash basis financial statements

Goals 4, 5

1. Net income, $140,000

STUDENT SOLUTIONS MANUAL

SPREADSHEET

The following amounts were taken from the accounting records of Mallard Consulting Services Inc. as of December 31, 2004. Mallard Consulting Services began its operations on January 1, 2004, and uses the cash basis of accounting.

Capital stock	$ 10,000
Cash	39,500
Dividends	25,000
Fees earned	338,300
Interest expense	4,800
Land	125,500
Miscellaneous expense	7,500
Notes payable	40,000
Rent expense	36,000
Salaries expense	80,000
Taxes expense	30,000
Utilities expense	40,000

Instructions

1. Prepare an income statement for the year ending December 31, 2004.
2. Prepare a retained earnings statement for the year ending December 31, 2004.
3. Prepare a balance sheet as of December 31, 2004.
4. Prepare a statement of cash flows for the year ending December 31, 2004.

Alternate Problem 2–4B

Cash basis financial statements

Goals 4, 5

1. Net income, $80,000

STUDENT SOLUTIONS MANUAL

SPREADSHEET

After its second year of operations, the following amounts were taken from the accounting records of Mallard Consulting Services Inc. as of December 31, 2005. Mallard Consulting Services began its operations on January 1, 2004 (see Problem 2–3B), and uses the cash basis of accounting.

Capital stock	$ 20,000
Cash	?
Dividends	20,000
Fees earned	289,000
Interest expense	6,000
Land	171,000
Miscellaneous expense	8,000
Notes payable	50,000
Rent expense	40,000
Salaries expense	90,000
Taxes expense	20,000
Utilities expense	45,000

Instructions

1. Prepare an income statement for the year ending December 31, 2005.
2. Prepare a retained earnings statement for the year ending December 31, 2005. Note: The Retained Earnings at January 1, 2005, was $115,000.
3. Prepare a balance sheet as of December 31, 2005.

4. Prepare a statement of cash flows for the year ending December 31, 2005.
Hint: You should compare the asset and liability amounts of December 31, 2005, with those of December 31, 2004, to determine cash used in investing and financing activities. See Problem 2-3B for the December 31, 2004 balance sheet amounts.

Alternate Problem 2-5B

Missing amounts from financial statements

Goals 4, 5

a. $18,500

STUDENT SOLUTIONS MANUAL

The financial statements at the end of Gallia Consulting Inc.'s first month of operations are shown below. By analyzing the interrelationships between the financial statements, fill in the proper amounts for (a) through (t).

Gallia Consulting Inc.
Income Statement
For the Month Ended June 30, 2004

Fees earned		$ (a)
Operating expenses:		
Wages expense	$4,500	
Rent expense	2,800	
Utilities expense	1,900	
Interest expense	200	
Miscellaneous expenses	600	
Total operating expenses		10,000
Net income		$ (b)

Gallia Consulting Inc.
Retained Earnings Statement
For the Month Ended June 30, 2004

Retained earnings, June 1, 2004		$ (c)
Net income for June	$ (d)	
Less dividends	(e)	(f)
Retained earnings, June 30, 2004		$ (g)

Gallia Consulting Inc.
Balance Sheet
June 30, 2004

Assets		
Cash		$ (h)
Land		18,000
Total assets		$46,500
Liabilities		
Notes payable		$15,000
Stockholders' Equity		
Capital stock	$25,000	
Retained earnings	(i)	(j)
Total liabilities and stockholders' equity		$ (k)

Gallia Consulting Inc.
Statement of Cash Flows
For the Month Ended June 30, 2004

Cash flows from operating activities:			
Cash received from customers			$ (l)
Deduct cash payments for expenses			(m)
Net cash flows from operating activities			$ 8,500
Cash flows from investing activities:			
Cash payment for purchase of land			$(18,000)
Cash flows from financing activities:			
Cash received from sale of capital stock	$ (n)		
Cash received from notes payable	(o)	$ (p)	
Deduct cash dividends		2,000	
Net cash flows from financing activities			(q)
Net increase in cash			$ (r)
June 1, 2004 cash balance			(s)
June 30, 2004 cash balance			$ (t)

Alternate Problem 2–6B

Cash basis financial statements

Goals 4, 5

STUDENT SOLUTIONS MANUAL

OBGYN Consulting Inc., organized February 1, 2004, is operated by Dr. Cline. How many errors can you find in the following financial statements for OBGYN Consulting Inc., prepared after its first month of operations?

OBGYN Consulting Inc.
Income Statement
February 29, 2004

Fees earned		$18,500
Operating expenses:		
Office salaries expense	$8,500	
Rent expense	2,500	
Automobile expense	1,750	
Dividends	1,000	
Miscellaneous expense	550	
Total operating expenses		15,500
Net income		$ 3,000

OBGYN Consulting Inc.
Retained Earnings Statement
February 29, 2005

Net income for the month	$3,000
Retained earnings, February 29, 2004	$3,000

Dr. Cline
Balance Sheet Inc.
For the Month Ended February 29, 2004

Assets		
Cash		$ 6,200
Notes payable		10,000
Total assets		$16,200
Liabilities		
Land		$13,000
Stockholders' Equity		
Capital stock	$5,000	
Retained earnings	3,000	8,000
Total liabilities and stockholders' equity		$21,000

Statement of Cash Flows
February 29, 2004

Cash flows from operating activities:	
Cash receipts from fees earned	$18,500
Net cash from operating activities	$18,500
Cash flows from investing activities:	
Cash payments for land	13,000
Cash flows from financing activities:	
Cash receipts from issuance of capital stock	5,000
Net increase in cash during February	$36,500
Cash as of February 1, 2004	0
Cash as of February 29, 2004	$36,500

Building Leadership Skills—Financial Analysis and Reporting

Case 2–1

Accounting equation

Condensed financial statements for Wm. J. Wrigley Jr. Company for 2001 and 2000 are shown in Exhibits 7 and 8 of this chapter. Based upon these financial statements, answer the following questions:

1. Using the accounting equation, Assets = Liabilities + Stockholders' Equity, fill in the amounts for 2000. Express the amounts in thousands.
2. If during 2001, assets increased by $190,908 and liabilities increased by $47,608, determine the increase or decrease in stockholders' equity during 2001.
3. Based upon your answers to (1) and (2), determine the total stockholders' equity as of December 31, 2001. Does this amount agree with Wrigley's balance sheet shown in Exhibit 7?
4. Based upon Exhibit 7, what percent of Wrigley's total assets was financed by debt during 2001? Assuming you are a long-term creditor of Wrigley, interpret this percent in terms of the chances that you will be repaid by Wrigley.

5. Assuming that in (4) you are a short-term creditor of Wrigley, would your interpretation and analysis of your chances of being repaid change?

Case 2–2

Vertical analysis

The following balance sheets (in millions) were adapted from the December 31, 2001 and 2000 financial statements of Boeing Co.:

	December 31, 2001	December 31, 2000
Assets		
Cash	$ 633	$ 1,010
Receivables	15,554	12,478
Inventories	6,920	6,852
Property, plant, and equipment	8,459	8,814
Intangible assets and goodwill	6,443	5,214
Prepaid pension cost	5,838	4,845
Other assets	4,496	3,464
Total assets	$48,343	$42,677
Liabilities and Stockholders' Equity		
Accounts payable	$13,872	$12,312
Income taxes payable	909	1,866
Notes and other liabilities	22,737	17,479
Total liabilities	$37,518	$31,657
Stockholders' equity	10,825	11,020
Total liabilities and stockholders' equity	$48,343	$42,677

1. Prepare a comparative vertical analysis of the balance sheets for 2001 and 2000. Round to one decimal place.
2. Based upon (1), what is your analysis of Boeing's financial condition in 2001 as compared to 2000?

Case 2–3

Vertical analysis

The following income statement data (in thousands) for Dell Computer Corporation and Gateway Inc. were taken from their recent annual reports:

	Dell	Gateway
Net sales	$31,888,000	$6,079,524
Cost of goods sold	25,445,000	5,241,332
Gross profit	$ 6,443,000	$838,192
Operating expenses	3,780,000	2,022,122
Operating income (loss)	$ 2,663,000	$(1,183,930)

1. Prepare a vertical analysis of the income statement for Dell. Round to one decimal place.
2. Prepare a vertical analysis of the income statement for Gateway. Round to one decimal place.
3. Based upon (1) and (2), how does Dell compare to Gateway?

Case 2–4

Financial information

Yahoo.com finance Internet site provides summary financial information about public companies, such as stock quotes, recent financial filings with the Securities and Exchange Commission, and recent news stories. Go to Yahoo.com's financial Web site (http://finance.yahoo.com/) and enter Wm. J. Wrigley Jr. Company's stock symbol, WWY. Answer the following questions concerning Wm. J. Wrigley Jr. Company by clicking on "Profile" and "Research."

1. At what price did Wrigley's stock last trade?
2. What is the 52-week range of Wrigley's stock?
3. When was the last time Wrigley's stock hit a 52-week high?
4. Over the last six months, has there been any insider selling or buying of Wrigley's stock?
5. Who is the president of Wm. J. Wrigley Jr. Company?
6. What was the salary of the president of Wm. J. Wrigley Jr. Company?
7. What is the annual dividend of Wrigley's stock?
8. How many current broker recommendations are strong buy, buy, hold, sell, or strong sell? What is the average of the broker recommendations?
9. What is the earnings per share of stock for this year?
10. What is the earnings per share estimate for next year?

Case 2–5

Analyzing financial information

In the Business Section of the August 28, 2001 issue of *The New York Times*, there is an article by David Barboza, entitled "A Young Heir Has New Plans At Old Company?" Read the article and answer the following questions:

1. Is the article favorable, neutral, or unfavorable regarding future prospects for Wm. J. Wrigley Jr. Company?
2. Would you invest in Wm. J. Wrigley Jr. Company's stock based only upon this article? If not, what additional information would you want?
3. Would it be a prudent investment strategy to only rely upon published financial statements in deciding to invest in a company's stock?
4. What sources do you think financial analysts use in making investment decisions and recommendations?

Business Leadership Skills—Responsible Leadership

Activity 2–1

Business strategy

GROUP ACTIVITY

Assume that you are considering developing a nationwide chain of women's clothing stores. You have contacted a Houston based firm that specializes in financing new business ventures and enterprises. Such firms, called venture capital firms, finance new businesses in exchange for a percentage of the ownership.

1. In groups of four or five, discuss the different business strategies that you might use in your venture.
2. For each strategy you listed in (1), provide an example of a real world business using the same strategy.
3. What percentage of the ownership would you be willing to give the venture capital firm in exchange for its financing?

Activity 2-2

Cash basis of accounting

Megan Peroni and Shannon Haley both graduated from State University in May 2004. After graduation, Shannon took a job as a staff accountant in the Atlanta office of PricewaterhouseCoopers, an international public accounting firm. Megan began working as a manager in Arrow Electronics, a wholesale computer hardware and software company, but left after only six months to start her own consulting business. The following conversation took place between Megan and Shannon at their first annual alumni function:

Megan: Shannon, good to see you again.
Shannon: Yes. It doesn't seem like it's been almost a year since we graduated.
Megan: That's for sure. It seems like only yesterday we were listening to that boring commencement speaker. I don't even remember her name . . . Monica somebody. Are you still working for PricewaterhouseCoopers?
Shannon: Yes, it's been a great year. I've worked on thirteen companies . . . it's been a fantastic learning experience. Each client has a different culture, management team, strategy, problems, and personality. I've learned something new every day. How about you? Are you still working for Arrow Electronics?
Megan: No, I quit after six months. My customers really didn't know what they needed for computer systems . . . so . . . I quit and started a consulting business. I feel like I'm helping my customers more now than I did before. Besides, I like being my own boss.
Shannon: What's the name of your business?
Megan: I-Chor Consulting. It's been amazing. I started with my savings of $10,000 six months ago. My last bank statement showed I've got more than $120,000–"pure profit" of $110,000 in only six months.
Shannon: That's unbelievable! If you ever need a CPA firm, keep us in mind.
Megan: Sure. What are friends for anyway?

1. Comment on Megan's statement that she's earned $110,000 "pure profit" in only six months.
2. Would the cash basis or the accrual basis of accounting be most appropriate for I-Chor?

Activity 2-3

Cash-basis income statement

ETHICS

Identify the circumstances under which it may be ethical to switch from an accrual-basis to a cash-basis income statement to reflect the results of operations.

Activity 2-4

Cash flows

Amazon.com, an Internet retailer, was incorporated in July 1994 and opened its virtual doors on the Web in July 1995. On the statement of cash flows, would you expect Amazon.com's net cash flows from operating, investing, and financing activities to be positive or negative for 1996, 1997, and 1998? Use the following format for your answers, and briefly explain your logic.

	1998	1997	1996
Net cash flows from operating activities	positive		
Net cash flows from investing activities			
Net cash flows from financing activities			

Activity 2-5

Opportunities for accountants

The increasing complexity of the current business and regulatory environment has created an increased demand for accountants who can analyze business transactions and interpret their effects on the financial statements. In addition, a basic ability to analyze the effects of transactions is necessary to be successful in all fields of business as well as in other disciplines, such as law. To better understand the importance of accounting in today's environment, search the Internet or your local newspaper for job opportunities. One possible Internet site is www.jobweb.com. Then do one of the following:

1. Print a listing of at least two ads for accounting jobs. Alternatively, bring to class at least two newspaper ads for accounting jobs.
2. Print a listing of at least two ads for nonaccounting jobs for which some knowledge of accounting is preferred or necessary. Alternatively, bring to class at least two newspaper ads for such jobs.

Answers to Self-Study Questions

1. **D** Even though a recording error has been made, the accounting equation will balance (answer D). However, assets (cash) will be overstated $50,000 and liabilities (notes payable) will be overstated by $50,000. Answer A is incorrect because although cash is overstated by $50,000, the accounting equation will balance. Answer B is incorrect because although notes payable are overstated by $50,000, the accounting equation will balance. Answer C is incorrect because the accounting equation will balance and assets will not exceed liabilities.
2. **C** Total assets will exceed total liabilities and stockholders' equity by $16,000. This is because stockholders' equity (retained earnings) was decreased instead of increased by $8,000. Thus, stockholders' equity will be understated by a total of $16,000.
3. **D** Under the cash basis of accounting revenues are recorded when the cash is collected, not necessarily when the fees are earned. Thus, no revenue would be recorded in April, $18,500 of revenue would be recorded in May, and $6,500 of revenue would be recorded in June (Answer D).
4. **A** Under the accrual basis of accounting revenues are recorded when the fees are earned. Thus, $25,000 of revenue would be recorded in April and no revenue would be recorded in May or June (Answer A).
5. **B** The purchase of land for cash changes the mix of assets and does not affect liabilities or stockholders' equity (Answer B). Borrowing cash from a bank (Answer A) increases assets and liabilities. Receiving cash for fees earned (Answer C) increases cash and stockholders' equity (retained earnings). Paying office salaries (Answer D) decreases cash and stockholders' equity (retained earnings).

Chapter 3 The Accrual Basis of Accounting

THE LAW OF SOLID GROUND

"Trust is the foundation of leadership."

—The 21 Irrefutable Laws of Leadership

Dr. John C. Maxwell

Learning Goals

1. Describe the accrual basis of accounting.
2. Use the accrual basis of accounting to analyze, record, and summarize transactions.
3. Describe and illustrate the end-of-the-period adjustment process.
4. Prepare accrual-basis financial statements, including a classified balance sheet.
5. Describe how the accrual basis of accounting enhances the interpretation of financial statements.
6. Describe the accounting cycle for the accrual basis of accounting.
7. Describe and illustrate how common-sized financial statements can be used to analyze and evaluate a company's performance.

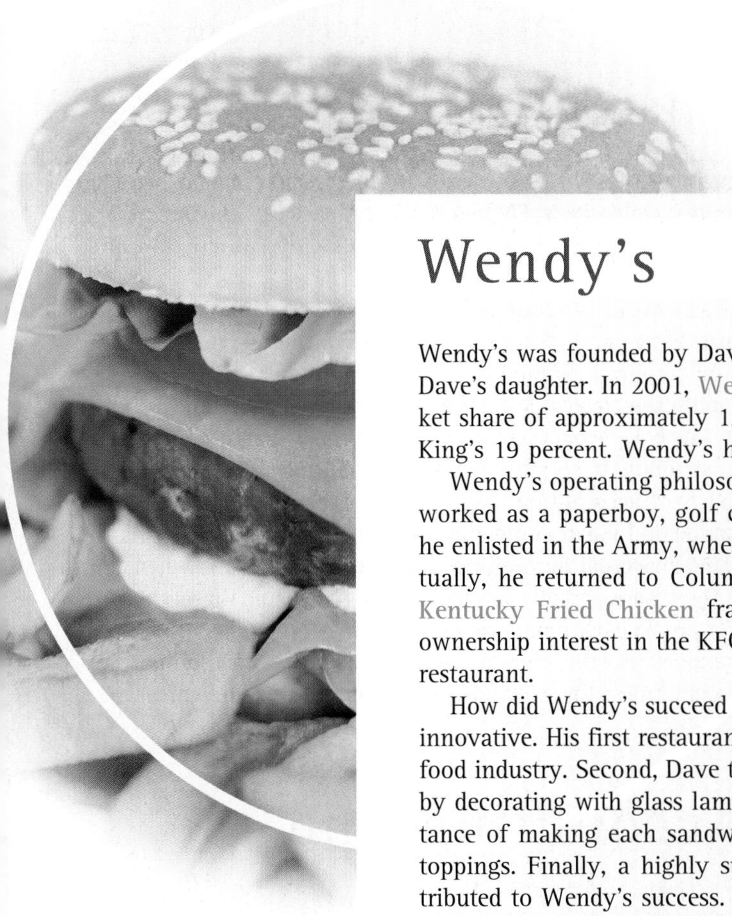

Wendy's

Wendy's was founded by Dave Thomas in 1969 in Columbus, Ohio, and was named after Dave's daughter. In 2001, Wendy's International had sales of $2.3 billion. Wendy's market share of approximately 13 percent is third behind McDonald's 43 percent and Burger King's 19 percent. Wendy's has over 40,000 employees and 6,000 restaurants.

Wendy's operating philosophy is influenced by Dave's background. Growing up, Dave worked as a paperboy, golf caddy, grocery deliverer, and bowling alley pinsetter. Later, he enlisted in the Army, where he served as a manager of the Enlisted Men's Club. Eventually, he returned to Columbus, Ohio, where he helped a former boss turn around a Kentucky Fried Chicken franchise that had been losing money. In 1968, he sold his ownership interest in the KFC franchise to fulfill his life-long dream of opening his own restaurant.

How did Wendy's succeed in the highly competitive fast-food industry? First, Dave was innovative. His first restaurant featured a salad bar. This was a radical change in the fast-food industry. Second, Dave tried to create a family-friendly atmosphere in his restaurants by decorating with glass lamps and bentwood chairs. Third, Dave emphasized the importance of making each sandwich fresh, never frozen, and offering customers a choice of toppings. Finally, a highly successful series of advertising campaigns significantly contributed to Wendy's success.

The premise behind Wendy's advertising was an emphasis on food and quality. One of Wendy's most successful advertising campaigns appeared in the mid-1980s, using the slogan, "Where's the beef?" However, the advertising campaigns that established Dave Thomas as a household name were the campaigns that featured him cooking or serving hamburgers. Sales increased dramatically as the ads continued to run, and Dave became an icon.

Most advertising executives agree that the success of the ads was due to Dave being a "normal" person and not an actor. One executive, Bob Garfield, commented: ". . . such a perfect symbol of the brand, he represented . . . the perennially bewildered guy with the wan smile who could always take refuge in something real, Wendy's hamburgers." But after Dave's death on January 8, 2002, analysts questioned whether Wendy's success could continue without him.

In this chapter, we continue our discussion of financial statements and financial reporting systems. In doing so, we focus on the accrual basis of accounting system that is used by all major businesses, such as Wendy's. Our discussions will include how to record transactions under accrual accounting, how to update accounting records and prepare accrual-basis financial statements, and how to prepare accounting records for the next period.

Source: "Wendy's Loses Its Legend, " by Bruce Horovitz and Theresa Howard, *USA Today*, January 9, 2002; "After Founder Dies, Wendy's Ponders New Ways to Pitch," by Stuart Elliott, *The New York Times*, January 9, 2002; "Dave Thomas, 69, Wendy's Founder, Dies," by Douglas Martin, *The New York Times*, January 9, 2002.

Your Need to Know

Do you subscribe to any magazines? Most of us subscribe to one or more magazines such as *Cosmopolitan, Sports Illustrated, Golf Digest, Fly Rod & Reel, Newsweek, Business Week, Barron's,* or *People.* Magazines usually require us to prepay the yearly subscription price before we receive any issues.

When should the magazine record this revenue from subscriptions? As we discussed in Chapter 2, under the cash basis of accounting a publisher records the revenue when the cash is received. However, large corporations publish most of the popular magazines. For example, AOL Time-Warner publishes over one hundred and thirty magazines including *Fortune, Time, Entertainment Weekly, People,* and *Sports Illustrated.* Large corporations such as AOL-Time Warner must follow generally accepted accounting principles that require the use of the accrual basis of accounting.

In this chapter, we will describe and illustrate how to account for transactions using the accrual basis of accounting. Under accrual accounting, revenues are recorded when they are earned, regardless of when the cash is actually received. Thus, AOL-Time Warner records revenues from magazine subscriptions each month as its magazines are published and delivered. Because all large companies use the accrual basis of accounting, a thorough understanding of accrual basis is important for your business studies and future career.

The Accrual Basis of Accounting and the Matching Concept

1 Describe the accrual basis of accounting.

In Chapter 2, we illustrated the use of the cash basis of accounting for Family Health Care for the months of September and October. In these illustrations, we used many of the accounting concepts we described in Chapter 1. For example, under the business entity concept, we accounted for Family Health Care as a separate entity independent of the owner-manager, Dr. Lee Landry. Under the cost concept, we recorded the purchase of land at the amount that we paid for it. Consistent with the going concern concept, we did not revalue the land for increases or decreases in its market value, but retained the land in the accounting records at its original cost. We also employed the accounting period, full disclosure, objectivity, and the unit of measurement concepts in preparing financial statements for Family Health Care.

The one accounting concept that we did not emphasize in Chapter 2 was the matching concept. This is because we used the cash basis of accounting. Transactions were recorded only when cash was received or paid. For example, when $6,000 of cash was received for Dr. Landry's initial investment in Family Health Care, the transaction was recorded as an increase in assets (cash) and an increase in stockholders' equity (capital stock). Likewise, when $10,000 cash was received from First National Bank as a loan, the transaction was recorded as an increase in assets (cash) and an increase in liabilities (notes payable). The other transactions were recorded in a similar manner as cash was received or paid. This is how individuals normally record transactions. That is, we record only the receipts and payments of cash in our personal records.

Under the cash basis, the matching concept is not emphasized. Rather, the receipt or payment of cash governs the recording process. Revenues and expenses are matched with each other only if cash from revenues is received in the same period as cash is paid for expenses. While the cash basis may work reasonably well for individuals or small businesses, it does not work well for large businesses. This is because the timing of when cash is received or paid can vary widely with the result that net income may become meaningless under the cash basis. For example, a construction company might spend months or years developing land for a business complex or subdivision. During the development of the land, the company would have to pay for materials, wages, insurance, and other construction items. At the same time, cash might not be received until portions of the development are sold. As a result, a series of net losses would be reported during development until some sales occur. Thus, the income statement under the cash basis might not provide a realistic picture of the company's operations. In fact, the development might be highly successful and the early losses misleading.

The accrual basis of accounting is designed to avoid misleading income statement results that could otherwise result from the timing of cash receipts and payments. At the same time, the accrual basis recognizes the importance of reporting cash flows through its emphasis on preparing the statement of cash flows.

Under the accrual basis of accounting, transactions are recorded as they occur and thus affect the accounting equation (assets, liabilities, and stockholders' equity). Since the receipt or payment of cash affects assets (cash), all cash receipts and payments are recorded in the accounts under the accrual basis or the cash basis. However, under the accrual basis, transactions are also recorded even though cash is not received or paid until a later point. For example, Family Health Care may provide services to patients who are covered by health insurance. It then files a claim with the insurance company for the payment. In this case, the services are said to be provided "on account." Likewise, a business may purchase supplies from a vendor, with terms that allow the business to pay for the purchase within a time period, such as ten days. In this case, the supplies are said to be purchased "on account." Each of the preceding illustrations represents a business transaction that affects elements of the accounting equation and is therefore recorded under the accrual basis, *even though cash is not received or paid.*

J. C. Clark, Attorney at Law, drafted a will and estate documents for Max Winder on April 30. Clark billed Winder $1,200 for these services on May 20 and received payment on June 4. In what month should Clark record the revenue under the accrual and cash bases of accounting?

Accrual basis: April; Cash basis: June.

In accounting, we often use the term "recognized" to refer to when a transaction is recorded. Thus, under the cash basis of accounting, transactions are not recognized until cash is received or paid. *Under the accrual basis of accounting, revenue is normally recognized when it is earned.* For Family Health Care, revenue is earned when services have been provided to the customer. At this point, the revenue earning process is complete, and the customer is legally obligated to pay for the services.

Under the accrual basis, the matching concept plays an important role in determining when expenses are recorded. When revenues are earned and recorded, all expenses incurred in generating the revenues must also be recorded, regardless of whether cash has been paid. In this way, revenues and expenses are matched and the net income or net loss for the period can be determined. This is an application of the matching concept that we

Strategy in Business

Not Cutting Corners

Have you ever ordered a hamburger from Wendy's and noticed that the meat patty is square? The square meat patty reflects a business strategy instilled in Wendy's by its founder, Dave Thomas. Mr. Thomas' strategy was to offer high-quality products at a fair price in a friendly atmosphere, without "cutting corners"; hence, the square meat patty. In the highly competitive fast-food industry, Dave Thomas's strategy enabled Wendy's to grow to be the third largest fast-food restaurant in the world, with annual sales of over $7 billion.

Source: "Dave Thomas, 69, Wendy's Founder, Dies," by Douglas Martin, *The New York Times*, January 9, 2002.

discussed in Chapter 1. That is, expenses are recognized and recorded in the same period as the related revenues that they generated.

The accrual basis recognizes liabilities at the time the business incurs the obligation to pay for the services or goods purchased. For example, the purchase of supplies on account would be recorded when the supplies are received and the business has incurred the obligation to pay for the supplies.

Using the Accrual Basis of Accounting for Family Health Care's November Transactions

2 Use the accrual basis of accounting to analyze, record, and summarize transactions.

To illustrate the accrual basis of accounting, we will use the November 2003 Family Health Care transactions. These transactions are as follows:

a. On November 1, received $1,800 from ILS Company as rent for the use of Family Health Care's land as a temporary parking lot from November 2003 through March 2004.
b. On November 1, paid $2,400 for an insurance premium on a two-year, general business policy.
c. On November 1, paid $6,000 for an insurance premium on a six-month medical malpractice policy.
d. Dr. Landry invested an additional $5,000 in the business in exchange for capital stock.
e. Purchased supplies for $240 on account.
f. Purchased $8,500 of office equipment. Paid $1,700 cash as a down payment, with the remainder due in five monthly installments of $1,360, beginning December 1.
g. Provided services of $6,100 to patients on account.
h. Received $5,500 for services provided to patients who paid cash.
i. Received $4,200 from insurance companies, which paid on patients' accounts for services that have been provided.
j. Paid $100 on account for supplies that had been purchased.
k. Expenses paid during November were as follows: wages, $2,790; rent, $800; utilities, $580; interest, $100; miscellaneous, $420.
l. Paid dividends of $1,200 to stockholders (Dr. Landry).

In analyzing and recording the November transactions for Family Health Care, we use the same format as we used in Chapter 2. In so doing, we record increases and decreases for each financial statement element. These separate elements are referred to as **accounts**.

Transaction a *On November 1, received $1,800 from ILS Company as rent for the use of Family Health Care's land as a temporary parking lot from November 2003 through March 2004.* In this transaction, Family Health Care entered into a rental agreement for the use of its land. The agreement required the payment of the rental fee of $1,800 in advance. The rental agreement also gives ILS Company the option of renewing the agreement for another four months.

How does this transaction affect the accounts (elements) of the accounting equation and how should it be recorded? Since cash has been received, cash is increased by $1,800, but what other account should be increased or decreased? Family Health Care has agreed to rent the land to ILS Company for five months and thus has incurred a liability to provide this service–rental of the land. If Family Health Care canceled the agreement on November 1, after accepting the $1,800, it would have to repay that amount to ILS Company.

Thus, Family Health Care should record this transaction as an increase in cash and an increase in a liability for $1,800. Because the liability relates to rental revenue, it is recorded as **unearned revenue**, as shown below.

	Assets			=	Liabilities			+ Stockholders' Equity		
	Cash	+	Land	=	Notes Payable	+	Unearned Revenue	+ Capital Stock	+ Retained Earnings	
Bal.	7,320		12,000		10,000			6,000	3,320	
a.	1,800						1,800			Received rent in advance
Bal.	9,120		12,000		10,000		1,800	6,000	3,320	

As time passes, the liability will decrease and Family Health Care will earn rental revenue. For example, at the end of November, one-fifth of the $1,800 ($360) will have been earned. Later in this chapter, we will discuss how to record the $360 of earned rent revenue at the end of November.

You should note that the beginning balances shown in the preceding equation are the ending balances from October. That is, the cash balance of $7,320 is the ending cash balance as of October 31, 2003. Likewise, the other balances are carried forward from the preceding month. In this sense, the accounting equation represents a cumulative history of the financial results of the business.

Transaction b *On November 1, paid $2,400 for an insurance premium on a two-year, general business policy.* This umbrella policy covers a variety of possible risks to the business, such as fire and theft. By paying the premium, Family Health Care has purchased an asset, insurance coverage, in exchange for cash. Thus, the mix of assets has changed. However, the prepaid insurance coverage is unique in that it expires with the passage of time. At the end of the two-year period, the asset will have completely expired. Such assets are called prepaid expenses or deferred expenses. Thus, the purchase of the insurance coverage is recorded as prepaid insurance, as shown below.

	Assets			= Liabilities		+ Stockholders' Equity		
	Cash	+ Prepaid Insurance	+ Land	= Notes Payable	+ Unearned Revenue	+ Capital Stock	+ Retained Earnings	
Bal.	9,120		12,000	10,000	1,800	6,000	3,320	
b.	−2,400	2,400						Paid insurance for two years
Bal.	6,720	2,400	12,000	10,000	1,800	6,000	3,320	

Later in this illustration, we will discuss how such accounts are updated at the end of an accounting period to reflect the portion of the asset that has expired.

Transaction c *On November 1, paid $6,000 for an insurance premium on a six-month medical malpractice policy.* This transaction is similar to transaction (b), except that Family Health Care has purchased medical malpractice insurance that is renewable every six months. The transaction is recorded as follows:

	Assets			= Liabilities		+ Stockholders' Equity		
	Cash	+ Prepaid Insurance	+ Land	= Notes Payable	+ Unearned Revenue	+ Capital Stock	+ Retained Earnings	
Bal.	6,720	2,400	12,000	10,000	1,800	6,000	3,320	
c.	−6,000	6,000						Paid insurance for 6 months
Bal.	720	8,400	12,000	10,000	1,800	6,000	3,320	

Transaction d *Dr. Landry invested an additional $5,000 in the business in exchange for capital stock.* This transaction is similar to the one in which Dr. Landry initially established Family Health Care. It is recorded as shown below.

	Assets			=	Liabilities		+	Stockholders' Equity	
	Cash	+ Prepaid Insurance	+ Land	=	Notes Payable	+ Unearned Revenue	+	Capital Stock	+ Retained Earnings	
Bal.	720	8,400	12,000		10,000	1,800		6,000	3,320	
d.	5,000							5,000		Investment
Bal.	5,720	8,400	12,000		10,000	1,800		11,000	3,320	

Transaction e *Purchased supplies for $240 on account.* This transaction is similar to transactions (b) and (c), in that purchased supplies are assets until they are used up in generating revenue. Family Health Care has purchased and received the supplies, with a promise to pay in the near future. Such liabilities that are incurred in the normal operations of the business are called **accounts payable.** The transaction is recorded by increasing the asset supplies and increasing the liability accounts payable, as shown below.

	Assets				=	Liabilities		+ Stockholders' Equity			
	Cash	+ Prepaid Ins.	+ Supplies	+ Land	=	Notes Pay.	+ Accts. Pay.	+ Unearned Revenue	+ Capital Stock	+ Retained Earnings	
Bal.	5,720	8,400		12,000		10,000		1,800	11,000	3,320	
e.			240				240				Purchase of supplies
Bal.	5,720	8,400	240	12,000		10,000	240	1,800	11,000	3,320	

Transaction f *Purchased $8,500 of office equipment. Paid $1,700 cash as a down payment, with the remainder due in five monthly installments of $1,360, beginning December 1.* In this transaction, the asset office equipment is increased by $8,500, cash is decreased by $1,700, and notes payable is increased by $6,800. The transaction is recorded as follows:

	Assets					=	Liabilities		+Stockholders' Equity			
	Cash	+ Prepaid Ins.	+ Supplies	+ Office Equip.	+ Land	=	Notes Pay.	+ Accts. Pay.	+ Unearned Revenue	+ Capital Stock	+ Retained Earnings	
Bal.	5,720	8,400	240		12,000		10,000	240	1,800	11,000	3,320	
f.	−1,700			8,500			6,800					Purchase of office equip.
Bal.	4,020	8,400	240	8,500	12,000		16,800	240	1,800	11,000	3,320	

Transaction g *Provided services of $6,100 to patients on account.* This transaction is similar to the revenue transactions that we recorded in September and October, except that the services have been provided on account. Family Health Care will collect cash from the patients' insurance companies in the future. Such amounts that are to be collected in the future and that arise from the normal operations of a business are called **accounts receivable.** Since a valid claim exists against a third party, accounts receivable are assets and the transaction would be recorded as shown.

	Assets						=	Liabilities		+ Stockholders' Equity		
	Cash +	Accts. Rec. +	Prepaid Ins.	+ Supplies	+ Office Equip. +	Land	= Notes Pay.	+ Accts. Pay.	+ Unearned Revenue	+ Capital Stock	+ Retained Earnings	
Bal.	4,020		8,400	240	8,500	12,000	16,800	240	1,800	11,000	3,320	
g.		6,100									6,100	Fees earned
Bal.	4,020	6,100	8,400	240	8,500	12,000	16,800	240	1,800	11,000	9,420	

Transaction h *Received $5,500 for services provided to patients who paid cash.* This transaction is similar to the revenue transactions that we recorded in September and October and is recorded as shown below.

	Assets						=	Liabilities		+ Stockholders' Equity		
	Cash +	Accts. Rec. +	Prepaid Ins.	+ Supplies	+ Office Equip. +	Land	= Notes Pay.	+ Accts. Pay.	+ Unearned Revenue	+ Capital Stock	+ Retained Earnings	
Bal.	4,020	6,100	8,400	240	8,500	12,000	16,800	240	1,800	11,000	9,420	
h.	5,500										5,500	Fees earned
Bal.	9,520	6,100	8,400	240	8,500	12,000	16,800	240	1,800	11,000	14,920	

Transaction i *Received $4,200 from insurance companies, which paid on patients' accounts for services that have been provided.* In this transaction, cash is increased and the accounts receivable is decreased by $4,200. Thus, only the mix of assets changes, and the transaction is recorded as shown below.

	Assets						=	Liabilities		+ Stockholders' Equity		
	Cash +	Accts. Rec. +	Prepaid Ins.	+ Supp.	+ Office Equip. +	Land	= Notes Pay.	+ Accts. Pay.	+ Unearned Revenue	+ Capital Stock	+ Retained Earnings	
Bal.	9,520	6,100	8,400	240	8,500	12,000	16,800	240	1,800	11,000	14,920	
i.	4,200	−4,200										Collected cash
Bal.	13,720	1,900	8,400	240	8,500	12,000	16,800	240	1,800	11,000	14,920	

A customer accidentally pays $2,000 on an account receivable of $1,500. Upon receipt, the business increases cash and decreases accounts receivable. What elements of the accounting equation are affected if the customer later requests a refund and the business pays it?

Cash decreases by $500, and accounts receivable increases by $500.

Transaction j *Paid $100 on account for supplies that had been purchased.* This transaction reduces the cash and the accounts payable by $100, as shown below.

	Assets						=	Liabilities		+ Stockholders' Equity		
	Cash +	Accts. Rec. +	Prepaid Ins.	+ Supp.	+ Office Equip. +	Land	= Notes Pay.	+ Accts. Pay.	+ Unearned Revenue	+ Capital Stock	+ Retained Earnings	
Bal.	13,720	1,900	8,400	240	8,500	12,000	16,800	240	1,800	11,000	14,920	
j.	−100							−100				Paid on acct.
Bal.	13,620	1,900	8,400	240	8,500	12,000	16,800	140	1,800	11,000	14,920	

Assume that you cancel a $300 airline ticket that, though nonrefundable, may be applied to another ticket within one year. When should the airline transfer the $300 from unearned revenue to revenue?

After one year, or when the $300 is applied to another ticket and you use that ticket.

Transaction k *Expenses paid during November were as follows: wages, $2,790; rent, $800; utilities, $580; interest, $100; miscellaneous, $420.* This transaction is similar to the expense transaction that we recorded for Family Health Care in September and October. It is recorded as shown below.

	Assets						=	Liabilities		+ Stockholders' Equity		
	Cash +	Accts. Rec. +	Prepaid Ins. +	Supp. +	Office Equip. +	Land =	Notes Pay. +	Accts. Pay. +	Unearned Revenue +	Capital Stock +	Retained Earnings	
Bal.	13,620	1,900	8,400	240	8,500	12,000	16,800	140	1,800	11,000	14,920	
k.	−4,690										−2,790	Wages exp.
											−800	Rent exp.
											−580	Utilities exp.
											−100	Interest exp.
											−420	Misc. exp.
Bal.	8,930	1,900	8,400	240	8,500	12,000	16,800	140	1,800	11,000	10,230	

Transaction l *Paid dividends of $1,200 to stockholders (Dr. Landry).* This transaction is similar to the dividends transactions of September and October. It is recorded as shown below.

	Assets						=	Liabilities		+ Stockholders' Equity		
	Cash +	Accts. Rec. +	Prepaid Ins. +	Supp. +	Office Equip. +	Land =	Notes Pay. +	Accts. Pay. +	Unearned Revenue +	Capital Stock +	Retained Earnings	
Bal.	8,930	1,900	8,400	240	8,500	12,000	16,800	140	1,800	11,000	10,230	
l.	−1,200										−1,200	Dividends
Bal.	7,730	1,900	8,400	240	8,500	12,000	16,800	140	1,800	11,000	9,030	

The Adjustment Process

3 Describe and illustrate the end-of-the-period adjustment process.

The accrual basis of accounting requires the accounting records to be updated prior to preparing financial statements. This updating process, called the **adjustment process**, is necessary to properly match revenues and expenses. This is an application of the matching concept.

Adjustments are necessary because, at any point in time, some accounts (elements) of the accounting equation will not be up to date. For example, as time passes, prepaid insurance will expire and supplies will be used in operations. However, it is not efficient to record the daily expiration of prepaid insurance or the daily usage of supplies. Rather, the accounting records are normally updated just prior to preparing the financial statements.

You may wonder why we were able to prepare the September and October financial statements for Family Health Care in Chapter 2 without recording any adjustments. The answer is that in September and October, Family Health Care used the cash basis of accounting. Under the cash basis, no adjustments are necessary because transactions are only recorded as cash is received or paid. However, Family Health Care began using the accrual basis in November. Thus, we must now address the adjustment process.

Deferrals and Accruals

The financial statements are affected by two types of adjustments—deferrals and accruals. Whether a deferral or an accrual, each adjustment will affect a balance sheet account and an income statement account.

Deferrals are created by recording a transaction in a way that delays or defers the recognition of an expense or a revenue. Common examples of deferrals are described below.

- **Deferred expenses** or *prepaid expenses* are items that initially have been recorded as assets but are expected to become expenses over time or through the normal operations of the business. For Family Health Care, prepaid insurance is an example of a deferral that will normally require adjustment. Other examples include supplies, prepaid advertising, and prepaid interest. The tuition you pay at the beginning of each term is also an example of a deferred expense to you as a student. McDonald's Corporation reported over $300 million of prepaid expenses and other current assets on a recent balance sheet.
- **Deferred revenues** or *unearned revenues* are items that initially have been recorded as liabilities but are expected to become revenues over time or through the normal operations of the business. For Family Health Care, unearned rent is an example of a deferred revenue. Other examples include tuition received in advance by a school, an annual retainer fee received by an attorney, premiums received in advance by an insurance company, and magazine subscriptions received in advance by a publisher. On a recent balance sheet, Microsoft Corporation reported almost $5 billion of deferred revenue related to its software. Likewise, AOL Time-Warner reported over a billion dollars of deferred revenue on a recent balance sheet.

Accruals are created when a revenue or expense has not been recorded at the end of the accounting period. Accruals are normally the result of revenue being earned or an expense being incurred before any cash is received or paid. For example, employees may earn wages before the end of the year, but may be paid after year-end. That is, employee

Ethics in Action

Free Issue

Office supplies are often available to employees on a "free issue" basis. This means employees do not have to "sign" for the release of office supplies but merely obtain the necessary supplies from a local storage area as needed. Just because supplies are easily available, however, doesn't mean they can be taken for personal use. There are many instances when employees have been terminated for taking supplies home for personal use.

wages may be paid and recorded every Friday, but the accounting period may end on a Tuesday. Thus, at the end of the accounting period, the company owes the employees for their wages on Monday and Tuesday that will be paid on the following Friday. At the end of the accounting period, these wages have been incurred by the company, but have not yet been recorded or paid. Thus, the amount of the wages for Monday and Tuesday is an accrual. Other examples of accruals are described below.

- **Accrued expenses** or accrued liabilities are expenses that have been incurred but have not been recorded in the accounts. An example of an accrued expense is accrued interest on notes payable at the end of a period. Other examples include accrued utility expenses and taxes. On a recent balance sheet, Home Depot reported over $600 million of accrued salaries and related expenses, almost $300 million of sales taxes payable, and over a billion dollars of other accrued expenses.
- **Accrued revenues** or accrued assets are revenues that have been earned but have not been recorded in the accounts. An example of an accrued revenue is fees for services that an attorney has provided but has not billed to the client at the end of the period. Other examples include unbilled commissions by a travel agent, accrued interest on notes receivable, and accrued rent on property rented to others. On a recent balance sheet, General Motors reported over $5.8 billion of accounts receivable.

Assume that you take advantage of an offer by a local funeral home to prepay your funeral, burial, and related expenses. How would the funeral home account for the prepayment?

Increase cash and deferred (unearned) revenue.

Exhibit 1 summarizes the nature of deferrals and accruals and the need for adjustments in order to prepare financial statements.

Exhibit 1

Deferrals and Accruals

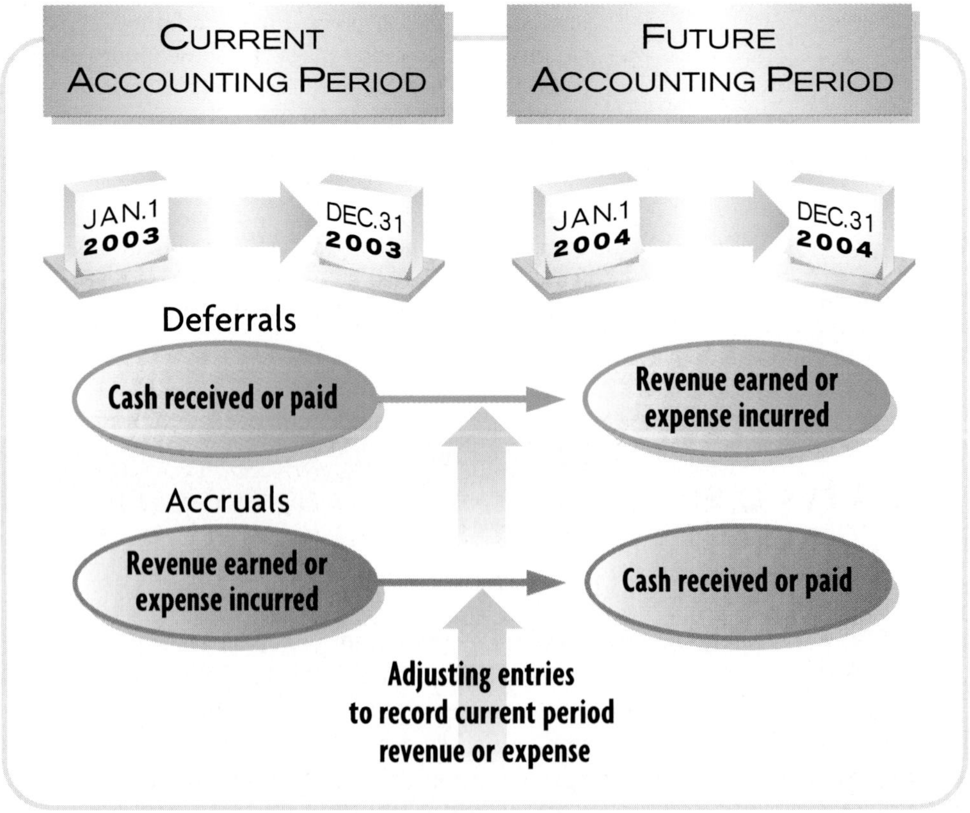

Adjustments for Family Health Care

We now analyze the financial statement accounts for Family Health Care at the end of November to determine whether any adjustments are necessary. Specifically, we will focus on the following adjustment data, which are typical for most businesses.

Deferred expenses:
1. Prepaid insurance expired, $1,100.
2. Supplies used, $150.
3. Depreciation on office equipment, $160.

Deferred revenue:

4. Unearned revenue earned, $360.

Accrued expense:

5. Wages owed but not paid to employees, $220.

Accrued revenue:

6. Services provided but not billed to insurance companies, $750.

Adjustment 1 (Deferred Expense—Prepaid Insurance) This first adjustment recognizes that a portion of the prepaid insurance purchased November 1 expired during November. Family Health Care prepaid two policies–a general business policy for $2,400 (transaction b) and a malpractice policy for $6,000 (transaction c). The general business policy is a two-year policy expiring at a rate of $100 ($2,400 ÷ 24) per month. The malpractice policy is a six-month policy that expires at a rate of $1,000 ($6,000 ÷ 6) per month. The total expired prepaid insurance is thus $1,100 ($100 + $1,000). This adjustment is recorded as shown below.

	Assets						=	Liabilities		+ Stockholders' Equity		
	Cash +	Accts. Rec. +	Prepaid Ins.	+ Supp.	+ Office Equip.	+ Land	= Notes Pay.	+ Accts. Pay.	+ Unearned Revenue	+ Capital Stock	+ Retained Earnings	
Bal.	7,730	1,900	8,400	240	8,500	12,000	16,800	140	1,800	11,000	9,030	
a1			−1,100								−1,100	Ins. exp.
Bal.	7,730	1,900	7,300	240	8,500	12,000	16,800	140	1,800	11,000	7,930	

As of January 1, $450 of supplies are on hand. During January, $1,250 of supplies were purchased on account, and on January 31, $175 of supplies are on hand. What is the supplies expense for January?

$1,525 ($450 + $1,250 − $175)

Adjustment 2 (Deferred Expense—Supplies) This adjustment recognizes the portion of the $240 of supplies purchased during November that have been used. For November, $150 of the supplies were used, leaving $90 of supplies for use during the coming months. Thus, after recording the adjustment, the accounting records should show supplies expense of $150 for November and supplies on hand (an asset) of $90. The second adjustment is recorded as shown below.

	Assets						=	Liabilities		+ Stockholders' Equity		
	Cash +	Accts. Rec. +	Prepaid Ins.	+ Supp.	+ Office Equip.	+ Land	= Notes Pay.	+ Accts. Pay.	+ Unearned Revenue	+ Capital Stock	+ Retained Earnings	
Bal.	7,730	1,900	7,300	240	8,500	12,000	16,800	140	1,800	11,000	7,930	
a2				−150							−150	Supplies exp.
Bal.	7,730	1,900	7,300	90	8,500	12,000	16,800	140	1,800	11,000	7,780	

Adjustment 3 (Deferred Expense—Depreciation) This adjustment recognizes that fixed assets such as office equipment lose their ability to provide service over time. This reduction in the ability of a fixed asset to provide service is called **depreciation**. However, it is difficult to objectively determine the physical decline in the ability of fixed assets to provide service. For this reason, accountants estimate the amount of the cost of long-term assets that becomes expense over the asset's useful life. In a later chapter, we will discuss methods of estimating depreciation. In this chapter, we simply assume that the amount of November depreciation for the office equipment is $160.

To maintain a record of the initial cost of a fixed asset for tax and other purposes, the fixed asset (office equipment) is not reduced directly. Instead, an offsetting or contra asset account, called **accumulated depreciation**, is included in the accounting equation. Thus, the third adjustment is recorded as shown.

	Assets						=	Liabilities			+ Stockholders' Equity		
	Cash +	Accts. Rec. +	Prepaid Ins. +	Supp. +	Office Equip. −	Acc. Dep. +	Land =	Notes Pay. +	Accts. Pay. +	Unearned Revenue +	Capital Stock +	Ret. Earn.	
Bal.	7,730	1,900	7,300	90	8,500		12,000	16,800	140	1,800	11,000	7,780	
a3						160						−160	Dep. exp.
Bal.	7,730	1,900	7,300	90	8,500	160	12,000	16,800	140	1,800	11,000	7,620	

Note that the accumulated depreciation account is subtracted in determining the total assets. To highlight the effect of this account, its balance is shown in color. We should also note three other points related to Adjustment 3. First, land is not depreciated, since it usually does not lose its ability to provide service. Second, the cost of the equipment can be thought of as a deferred expense, since it is recognized as an expense over the equipment's useful life. Third, the cost of the fixed asset less the balance of its accumulated depreciation is called the asset's *carrying value* or *book value*. For example, the carrying value of the office equipment, after the preceding adjustment, is $8,340 ($8,500 − $160).

Adjustment 4 (Deferred Revenue—Unearned Rent) This adjustment recognizes that a portion of the unearned revenue is earned by the end of November. That is, of the $1,800 received for rental of the land for five months (November through March), one-fifth, or $360, would have been earned as of November 30. The fourth adjustment recognizes this decrease in the unearned revenue and the increase in the rental revenue, as shown below.

	Assets						=	Liabilities			+ Stockholders' Equity		
	Cash +	Accts. Rec. +	Prepaid Ins. +	Supp. +	Office Equip. −	Acc. Dep. +	Land =	Notes Pay. +	Accts. Pay. +	Unearned Revenue +	Capital Stock +	Ret. Earn.	
Bal.	7,730	1,900	7,300	90	8,500	160	12,000	16,800	140	1,800	11,000	7,620	
a4										−360		360	Rental rev.
Bal.	7,730	1,900	7,300	90	8,500	160	12,000	16,800	140	1,440	11,000	7,980	

Adjustment 5 (Accrued Expense—Wages) This adjustment recognizes that as of November 30, employees of Family Health Care may have worked one or more days for which they have not been paid. It is rare that the employees are paid the same day that the accounting period ends. Thus, at the end of an accounting period, it is normal for businesses to owe wages to their employees. This is what we defined as an accrued expense earlier in our discussion. The fifth adjustment is recorded by increasing wages payable, a liability, and deducting wages expense from retained earnings, as shown.

	Assets							=	Liabilities				+ Stockholders' Equity	
	Cash +	Accts. Rec. +	Prepaid Ins.	+ Supp.	+ Office Equip.	− Acc. Dep.	+ Land	= Notes Pay.	+ Accts. Pay.	+ Wages Pay	+ Unearned Revenue	+ Capital Stock	+ Retained Earnings	
Bal.	7,730	1,900	7,300	90	8,500	160	12,000	16,800	140		1,440	11,000	7,980	
a5										220			−220	Wages exp.
Bal.	7,730	1,900	7,300	90	8,500	160	12,000	16,800	140	220	1,440	11,000	7,760	

During August, wages expense of $18,950 was reported on the income statement. If wages payable at August 1 was $1,100, and wages of $18,500 were paid during August, how much was accrued wages payable on August 31?

$1,550 ($18,500 − $1,100 = $17,400; $18,950 − $17,400 = $1,550)

Adjustment 6 (Accrued Revenue—Fees Earned) This adjustment recognizes that Family Health Care has provided services to patients that have not yet been billed. Such services are usually provided near the end of the month. This adjustment is recorded by increasing accounts receivable and fees earned, as shown below.

	Assets							=	Liabilities				+ Stockholders' Equity	
	Cash +	Accts. Rec. +	Prepaid Ins.	+ Supp.	+ Office Equip.	− Acc. Dep.	+ Land	= Notes Pay.	+ Accts. Pay.	+ Wages Pay	+ Unearned Revenue	+ Capital Stock	+ Retained Earnings	
Bal.	7,730	1,900	7,300	90	8,500	160	12,000	16,800	140	220	1,440	11,000	7,760	
a6		750											750	Fees earned
Bal.	7,730	2,650	7,300	90	8,500	160	12,000	16,800	140	220	1,440	11,000	8,510	

Family Health Care's transactions for November and the related adjustments are summarized in Exhibit 2. We will prepare Family Health Care's November financial statements using this summary.

Ethics in Action

The Round Trip

A common type of fraud involves artificially inflating revenue. One fraudulent method of inflating revenue is called "round tripping." Under this scheme, a selling company (S) "lends" money to a customer company (C). The money is then used by C to purchase a product from S. Thus, S sells product to C and is paid with the money just loaned to C! This looks like a sale in the accounting records, but in reality, S is shipping product for free. The fraud is exposed when it is determined that there was no intent to repay the original loan.

Exhibit 2

Family Health Care Summary of Transactions and Adjustments for November

	Assets													=
	Cash	+	Accts. Rec.	+	Prepaid Ins.	+	Supp.	+	Office Equip.	−	Acc. Dep.	+	Land	=
Bal.	7,320												12,000	
a.	1,800													
Bal.	9,120												12,000	
b.	−2,400				2,400									
Bal.	6,720				2,400								12,000	
c.	−6,000				6,000									
Bal.	720				8,400								12,000	
d.	5,000													
Bal.	5,720				8,400								12,000	
e.							240							
Bal.	5,720				8,400		240						12,000	
f.	−1,700								8,500					
Bal.	4,020				8,400		240		8,500				12,000	
g.			6,100											
Bal.	4,020		6,100		8,400		240		8,500				12,000	
h.	5,500													
Bal.	9,520		6,100		8,400		240		8,500				12,000	
i.	4,200		−4,200											
Bal.	13,720		1,900		8,400		240		8,500				12,000	
j.	−100													
Bal.	13,620		1,900		8,400		240		8,500				12,000	
k.	−4,690													
Bal.	8,930		1,900		8,400		240		8,500				12,000	
l.	−1,200													
Bal.	7,730		1,900		8,400		240		8,500				12,000	
a1.					−1,100									
Bal.	7,730		1,900		7,300		240		8,500				12,000	
a2.							−150							
Bal.	7,730		1,900		7,300		90		8,500				12,000	
a3.											160			
Bal.	7,730		1,900		7,300		90		8,500		160		12,000	
a4.														
Bal.	7,730		1,900		7,300		90		8,500		160		12,000	
a5.														
Bal.	7,730		1,900		7,300		90		8,500		160		12,000	
a6.			750											
Bal.	7,730		2,650		7,300		90		8,500		160		12,000	

(continued)

Exhibit 2

Concluded

Liabilities				+ Stockholders' Equity		
Notes Pay. +	Accts. Pay. +	Wages Pay. +	Unearned Revenue +	Capital Stock +	Ret. Earn.	
10,000				6,000	3,320	
			1,800			Rental revenue
10,000			1,800	6,000	3,320	
						Paid insurance
10,000			1,800	6,000	3,320	
						Paid insurance
10,000			1,800	6,000	3,320	
				5,000		Investment
10,000			1,800	11,000	3,320	
	240					Purchase of supplies
10,000	240		1,800	11,000	3,320	
6,800						Purchase of office equipment
16,800	240		1,800	11,000	3,320	
					6,100	Fees earned
16,800	240		1,800	11,000	9,420	
					5,500	Fees earned
16,800	240		1,800	11,000	14,920	
						Collected cash
16,800	240		1,800	11,000	14,920	
	−100					Paid on account
16,800	140		1,800	11,000	14,920	
					−2,790	Wages expense
					−800	Rent expense
					−580	Utilities expense
					−100	Interest expense
					−420	Misc. expense
16,800	140		1,800	11,000	10,230	
					−1,200	Dividends
16,800	140		1,800	11,000	9,030	
					−1,100	Ins. expense
16,800	140		1,800	11,000	7,930	
					−150	Supplies expense
16,800	140		1,800	11,000	7,780	
					−160	Depreciation expense
16,800	140		1,800	11,000	7,620	
			−360		360	Rental revenue
16,800	140		1,440	11,000	7,980	
		220			−220	Wages expense
16,800	140	220	1,440	11,000	7,760	
					750	Fees earned
16,800	140	220	1,440	11,000	8,510	

Financial Statements

4 Prepare accrual-basis financial statements, including a classified balance sheet.

In Chapter 2, we prepared financial statements for Family Health Care for September and October. These financial statements were prepared using the cash basis of accounting. In this section, we describe and illustrate financial statements for November, using the accrual basis of accounting. These financial statements are shown in Exhibit 3. They are based on the summary of transactions and adjustments shown in Exhibit 2.

The income statement is prepared by summarizing the revenue and expense transactions listed under the retained earnings column of Exhibit 2. The operating income is determined by deducting the operating expenses from the fees earned from normal operations. The other income–rental revenue–is then added to determine the net income for November.

As reported on the income statement, *revenues* are the increases in the stockholders' equity as a result of providing services or selling products to customers. Examples of revenues include fees earned, fares earned, commissions revenue, interest revenue, and rent revenue.

Revenues from the primary operations of the business are normally reported separately from other revenue. For example, Family Health Care has two types of revenues for November, fees earned and rental revenue. Since the primary operation of the business is providing services to patients, rent revenue is reported under the heading of "Other income."

Expenses on the income statement are assets used up or services consumed in the process of generating revenues. Expenses are matched against their related revenues to determine the net income or net loss for a period. Examples of typical expenses include wages expense, rent expense, utilities expense, supplies expense, and miscellaneous expense. Expenses not related to the primary operations of the business are sometimes reported as "Other expense." Interest expense is an example of an expense often reported separately as an Other expense.

The retained earnings statement is prepared by adding the November net income (from the income statement), less the November dividends, to the beginning amount of retained earnings. This ending amount of retained earnings is included on the balance sheet.

Exhibit 3

Family Health Care Financial Statements for November

Family Health Care, P.C.
Income Statement
For the Month Ended November 30, 2003

Fees earned		$12,350
Operating expenses:		
Wages expense	$3,010	
Insurance expense	1,100	
Rent expense	800	
Utilities expense	580	
Depreciation expense	160	
Supplies expense	150	
Interest expense	100	
Miscellaneous expenses	420	
Total operating expenses		6,320
Operating income		$ 6,030
Other income:		
Rental revenue		360
Net income		$ 6,390

Exhibit 3

Continued

Family Health Care, P.C.
Retained Earnings Statement
For the Month Ended November 30, 2003

Retained earnings, November 1, 2003		$3,320
Net income for November	$6,390	
Less dividends	1,200	5,190
Retained earnings, November 30, 2003		$8,510

Family Health Care, P.C.
Balance Sheet
November 30, 2003

Assets			
Current assets:			
Cash		$ 7,730	
Accounts receivable		2,650	
Prepaid insurance		7,300	
Supplies		90	
Total current assets			$17,770
Fixed assets:			
Office equipment	$8,500		
Less accumulated depreciation	160	$ 8,340	
Land		12,000	
Total fixed assets			20,340
Total assets			$38,110
Liabilities			
Current liabilities:			
Accounts payable		$ 140	
Wages payable		220	
Notes payable		6,800	
Unearned revenue		1,440	
Total current liabilities			$ 8,600
Long-term liabilities:			
Notes payable			10,000
Total liabilities			$18,600
Stockholders' Equity			
Capital stock		$11,000	
Retained earnings		8,510	19,510
Total liabilities and stockholders' equity			$38,110

The capital stock amount on the balance sheet results from adding the additional investment during November to the beginning amount of capital stock. The other balance sheet amounts are the ending balances shown in Exhibit 2.

The balance sheet shown in Exhibit 3 is a classified balance sheet. As the term implies, a **classified balance sheet** is prepared with various sections, subsections, and captions that aid in its interpretation and analysis. In the following paragraphs, we describe some of these sections and subsections.

Exhibit 3

Concluded

Family Health Care, P.C.
Statement of Cash Flows
For the Month Ended November 30, 2003

Cash flows from operating activities:		
Cash received from patients	$ 9,700	
Cash received from rental of land	1,800	$ 11,500
Deduct cash payments for expenses:		
Insurance premiums	$(8,400)	
Supplies	(100)	
Wages	(2,790)	
Rent	(800)	
Utilities	(580)	
Interest	(100)	
Miscellaneous expense	(420)	(13,190)
Net cash flow used in operating activities		$ (1,690)
Cash flows from investing activities:		
Purchase of office equipment		(1,700)
Cash flows from financing activities:		
Additional issuance of capital stock	$ 5,000	
Deduct cash dividends	(1,200)	
Net cash flow from financing activities		3,800
Net increase in cash		$ 410
November 1, 2003 cash balance		7,320
November 30, 2003 cash balance		$ 7,730

Assets are resources such as physical items or rights that are owned by the business. Examples of physical assets include cash, supplies, buildings, equipment, and land. Examples of rights are patent rights or rights to services (prepaid items). Physical assets of a long-term nature are referred to as **fixed assets**. Rights that are long-term in nature are called **intangible assets**.

Assets are normally divided into classes in preparing a classified balance sheet. Three of these classes are (1) current assets, (2) fixed assets, and (3) intangible assets.

Cash and other assets that are expected to be converted to cash or sold or used up within one year or less, through the normal operations of the business, are called **current assets**. In addition to cash, the current assets normally include accounts receivable, notes receivable, supplies, and other prepaid expenses. Accounts receivable and notes receivable are current assets because they will usually be converted to cash within one year or less. **Notes receivable** are written claims against debtors who promise to pay the amount of the note and interest at an agreed-upon rate. A note receivable is the creditor's view of a note payable transaction. As shown in Exhibit 3, Family Health Care has current assets of cash, accounts receivable, prepaid insurance, and supplies as of November 30, 2003.

The fixed assets section may also be labeled as property, plant, and equipment, or plant assets. Fixed assets include equipment, machinery, buildings, and land. Except for land, such fixed assets depreciate over a period of time, as we discussed earlier in this chapter. The cost less accumulated depreciation for each major type of fixed asset is normally reported on the classified balance sheet. As of November 30, 2003, Family Health Care's fixed assets consist of office equipment and land.

Intangible assets represent rights, such as patent rights, copyrights, and goodwill. Goodwill arises from such factors as name recognition, location, product quality, reputation, and managerial skill. Goodwill is reported on the balance sheet when these factors are recognized through a purchase of a company at a premium price. For example, goodwill was recognized when eBay, Inc., purchased PayPal, Inc.

Liabilities are amounts owed to outsiders (creditors). Liabilities are often identified on the balance sheet by titles that include the word *payable*. Examples of liabilities include notes payable and wages payable.

Liabilities are normally divided into two classes on a classified balance sheet. These classes are (1) current liabilities and (2) long-term liabilities.

Liabilities that will be due within a short time (usually one year or less) and that are to be paid out of current assets are called **current liabilities**. The most common current liabilities are notes payable and accounts payable. Other current liabilities reported on the classified balance sheet include wages payable, interest payable, taxes payable, and unearned revenue.

Liabilities that will not be due for a long time (usually more than one year) are called **long-term liabilities**. Long-term liabilities are reported below the current liabilities. As long-term liabilities come due and are to be paid within one year, they are reported as current liabilities. If they are to be renewed rather than paid, they would continue to be classified as long-term. When an asset is pledged as security for a long-term liability, the obligation may be called a *mortgage note payable* or a *mortgage payable*.

Family Health Care's current and long-term liabilities as of November 30, 2003, are shown in Exhibit 3. You should note that $6,800 of the notes payable is due within the next year and therefore is reported as a current liability. The remainder of the notes payable, $10,000, is not due until 2009 and thus is reported as a long-term liability. Family Health Care's other current liabilities consist of accounts payable, wages payable, and unearned revenue.

Stockholders' equity is the stockholders' rights to the assets of the business. For a corporation, the stockholders' equity consists of capital stock and retained earnings. The stockholders' equity section of a classified balance sheet reports each of these two financial statement accounts separately.

The statement of cash flows is prepared by summarizing the cash transactions shown in the cash column of Exhibit 2. The net cash flow from operations is computed by listing the cash receipts from revenue transactions and subtracting the cash payments for operating transactions. The purchase of the office equipment is treated as a separate cash outflow from investment activities. The receipt of the additional investment and the payment of dividends are reported as cash flows from financing activities.

INTERNATIONAL PERSPECTIVE

Bayerische Motoren Werke Aktiengesellschaft **(better known as BMW!) reports fixed assets first on its balance sheet, followed by current assets. It also reports stockholders' equity before the liabilities.**

Interpreting Accrual and Cash Basis Income

5 Describe how the accrual basis of accounting enhances the interpretation of financial statements.

The financial statements of Family Health Care for November illustrate the major differences between the accrual and cash bases of accounting. Note that the $6,390 net income reported in the November income statement is different from the negative $1,690 net cash flow from operating activities reported on the November statement of cash flows.[1] This is in contrast to September and October when these amounts were the same. Under the cash basis of accounting, which Family Health Care used in those months, the net cash flow from operations is the same as the net income. In November, however, Family Health Care began using the accrual basis of accounting.

1 The difference between the net cash flows from operations and the net income can be reconciled by considering the effects of accruals and deferrals. Such a reconciliation is shown in the appendix at the end of this chapter.

The difference between the net income (or loss) and the net cash flow from operating activities can be significant. To illustrate, we have summarized these amounts for Family Health Care below.

	Net Cash Flow from Operations	Net Income
September	$2,600	$2,600
October	3,220	3,220
November	(1,690)	6,390

Under the cash basis, the cash flow from operating activities and the net income for November would be reported as a negative amount (loss) of $1,690. This normally would be interpreted as an unfavorable trend and could imply that Family Health Care is failing. In fact, the accrual basis better reflects what is really happening to Family Health Care. Since September, revenues have more than doubled, increasing from $5,500 to $12,350, and net income has more than doubled. Thus, the accrual basis reflects Family Health Care as a profitable, rapidly expanding business.

Such differences between the cash basis and the accrual basis illustrate why generally accepted accounting principles require the accrual basis for all but the very smallest businesses. You should recognize, however, that the net cash flow from operating activities is an important amount that is useful to readers of the financial statements. For this reason, generally accepted accounting principles require reporting cash flows. In the long run, a business will go bankrupt if it continually experiences negative cash flows from operations, even though it may report net income. A business must generate positive cash flows from operations in order to survive. In the case of Family Health Care, the negative cash flow from operations for November was due in large measure to prepaying insurance premiums of $8,400. Thus, the negative cash flow from operations is temporary for Family Health Care and not a matter of major concern. This illustrates why the financial statements must be analyzed and interpreted together, rather than individually. For example, long-run profitability is best analyzed by focusing on the net income reported under the accrual basis, while the availability of cash to pay debts as they become due is best analyzed by focusing on the net cash flow from operating activities.

The Accounting Cycle

6 Describe the accounting cycle for the accrual basis of accounting.

The process that begins with analyzing transactions and ends with preparing the accounting records for the next accounting period is called the **accounting cycle**. The most important output of the accounting cycle is the financial statements. The basic steps in the accounting cycle are listed below.

1. *Identifying, analyzing, and recording* the effects of transactions on the accounting equation (financial statement accounts).
2. *Identifying, analyzing, and recording* adjustment data.
3. *Preparing* financial statements.
4. *Preparing* the accounting records for the next accounting period.

We have described and illustrated Steps 1–3 in this chapter. In this section, we complete the discussion of the accounting cycle by describing how the accounting records are prepared for the next accounting period.[2]

2 An additional illustration of the complete accounting cycle for Family Health Care is shown in the Illustrative Application Problem at the end of this chapter.

In prior illustrations, we have recorded and accumulated revenue, expense, and dividend transactions under retained earnings, with separate notations describing them. At the end of an accounting period, we then reviewed retained earnings and summarized the revenues and expenses so that they could be reported in the income statement. Likewise, the dividends were summarized in the retained earnings statement.

Because of the volume of transactions during a period, most businesses record revenues, expenses, and dividends as separate elements (accounts) of the accounting equation, as shown in Exhibit 4. This makes the information for preparing the financial statements more readily available. After the financial statements have been prepared, the balances of the revenue, expense, and dividend accounts are transferred to retained earnings. This process, which is shown in Exhibit 4 for Family Health Care, is called the **closing process**. In this way, these accounts begin each period with zero balances, and the transactions of each period are kept separate from one another.

Exhibit 4

Family Health Care Closing Process for November

	Ret. Earn.	− Dividends	+ Fees Earned	+ Rental Rev.	− Wages Exp.	− Ins. Exp.	− Rent Exp.	− Util. Exp.	− Dep. Exp.	− Supp. Exp.	− Int. Exp.	− Misc. Exp.
Bal., Nov. 1, 2003	3,320	1,200	12,350	360	3,010	1,100	800	580	160	150	100	420
Revenue closing	12,710		−12,350	−360								
Expense closing	−6,320				−3,010	−1,100	−800	−580	−160	−150	−100	−420
	9,710	1,200	0	0	0	0	0	0	0	0	0	0
Dividends closing	−1,200	−1,200										
Bal. after closing	8,510	0	0	0	0	0	0	0	0	0	0	0

The net amount of the revenue and expense balances transferred to retained earnings is the net income or net loss for the period. In this example, Family Health Care had a net income of $6,390 ($12,710 − $6,320). Because the balances of the revenue, expense, and dividend accounts are transferred to retained earnings, they are sometimes called temporary accounts.

Common-Sized Financial Statements

7 Describe and illustrate how common-sized financial statements can be used to analyze and evaluate a company's performance.

Common-sized financial statements are often useful in comparing one company to another. In **common-sized financial statements**, all items are expressed in percentages. Such statements are useful in comparing the current period with prior periods, individual businesses, or one business with industry percentages. Industry data are often available from trade associations or financial information services.

To illustrate, common-sized income statement and balance sheet data for Wendy's and McDonald's Corporation are shown in Exhibit 5.[3] The income statement data is expressed as a percent of revenues, thus Exhibit 5 indicates revenues for both companies as 100%. This, in turn, allows for analysis of the income statement components on

3 The financial statements for Wendy's and McDonald's shown in Exhibit 5 were adapted from 10-K Securities and Exchange Commission filings.

Exhibit 5

Common-Sized Financial Statements: Wendy's and McDonald's

Income Statements for the Year Ending December 31, 2001

	Wendy's	McDonald's
Revenues	100.0%	100.0%
Operating expenses	86.2%	81.8%
Operating income	13.8%	18.2%
Other expenses	0.9%	2.5%
Income before taxes	12.9%	15.7%
Income taxes	4.8%	4.7%
Net income	8.1%	11.0%

Balance Sheets as of December 31, 2001

	Wendy's	McDonald's
Currents assets:		
Cash	5.4%	1.9%
Accounts receivable	4.0%	3.9%
Inventories, prepaid, and other assets	3.4%	2.3%
Total current assets	12.8%	8.1%
Property, plant, and equipment	79.0%	76.7%
Other long-term assets	8.2%	15.2%
Total assets	100.0%	100.0%
Current liabilities:		
Accounts payable	5.4%	3.1%
Other liabilities	8.9%	6.9%
Total current liabilities	14.3%	10.0%
Long-term liabilities	36.1%	47.9%
Stockholders' equity	49.6%	42.1%
Total liabilities and stockholders' equity	100.0%	100.0%

a common basis. Without a common basis it is difficult to compare companies. For example, Wendy's total operating expenses are $1,926,545,000 compared to McDonald's $10,913,300,000. So, does this mean that Wendy's has an advantage because of its lower total operating expenses? Exhibit 5 reveals that this is not the case. In fact, Wendy's operating expenses are 86.2% of sales in comparison to 81.8% for McDonald's. As a result, Wendy's operating income is significantly less as a percent of sales, 13.8%, compared to McDonald's 18.2%.

Based upon Exhibit 5, further analyses are called for to determine why Wendy's operating expenses as a percent of sales are significantly higher than McDonald's. For example, the higher operating expenses may be related to the fact that 19.2% of Wendy's revenues come from its franchise restaurants while 26.5% of McDonald's revenues come from franchised restaurants.

Exhibit 5 also reports common-sized balance sheet information for Wendy's and McDonald's. The balance sheet data are expressed as a percent of total assets. Exhibit 5 indicates that Wendy's keeps a higher percent of its assets in the form of cash and equivalents, 5.4%, as compared to 1.9% for McDonald's. Wendy's also has a higher percent of receivables than McDonald's while both companies have 79.0% vs. 76.7% of assets in property, plant, and equipment. Exhibit 5 also reveals that Wendy's finances more of its operations through stockholders' equity, 49.6%, than does McDonald's, 42.1%.

As Exhibit 5 shows, common-sized financial statements facilitate company comparisons and analyses. Such statements are often a starting point for further investigation and analyses of major differences between companies in similar industries. For example, based upon the preceding comparison further inquiries might be made into why Wendy's operating expenses are a higher percent of sales and why Wendy's maintains a higher percent of its total assets in cash and receivables than does McDonald's.

APPENDIX

Reconciliation: Net Cash Flows From Operations and Net Income[4]

In Chapter 2, we illustrated financial statements for Family Health Care for September and October, 2003. During September and October, Family Health Care used the cash basis of accounting. Under the cash basis of accounting, the net cash flows from operating activities shown on the statement of cash flows equals the net income shown in the income statements. For example, Exhibits 4 and 6 in Chapter 2 report net cash flows from operating activities and net income of $2,600 and $3,220 for September and October. Under the cash basis, net cash flows from operating activities will always equal net income. This is not true, however, under the accrual basis of accounting.

During November and December, Family Health Care used the accrual basis of accounting. The November financial statements are illustrated in Exhibit 3 of this chapter. The December financial statements for Family Health Care are illustrated in the Illustrative Problem at the end of this chapter. The net cash flows from operating activities and net income for November and December are shown below.

	Net Cash Flows from Operating Activities	Net Income
November	$(1,690)	$ 6,390
December	8,760	10,825

Under the accrual basis, net cash flows from operating activities will normally not be the same as net income. The difference can be reconciled by considering the effects of accruals and deferrals on the income statement. Exhibit 6 illustrates the November reconciliation of Family Health Care's net income with operating cash flows from operations.

In Exhibit 6, we begin with net income. We then add or deduct the effects of accruals or deferrals that influenced net income under the accrual basis but did not result in the receipt or payment of cash. We thus arrive at net cash flows from operating activities.

The effect of an accrual or deferral on the income statement and net income is reflected in its net increase or decrease during the period. For example, during November depreciation expense of $160 was recorded (a deferred expense) and thus deducted in arriving at net income. Yet, no cash was paid. Thus, to arrive at cash flows from operations, depreciation expense is added back to net income. Likewise, accounts payable increased during November by $140 and a related expense was recorded. But again, no cash was paid.

4 In a later chapter, this reconciliation will be referred to as the indirect method of reporting cash flows from operations.

Exhibit 6

November's Reconciliation of Net Income and Cash Flows from Operations

Net income		$ 6,390
Add:		
Depreciation expense	$ 160	
Increase in accounts payable	140	
Increase in wages payable	220	
Increase in unearned revenue	1,440	1,960
Deduct:		
Increase in accounts receivable	$(2,650)	
Increase in prepaid insurance	(7,300)	
Increase in supplies	(90)	(10,040)
Net cash flows from operating activities		$ (1,690)

Similarly, wages payable increased during November by $220 and the related wages expense was deducted in arriving at net income. However, the $220 was not paid until the next month. Thus, for November, the increases of $140 in accounts payable and $220 in wages payable are added back to net income.

The increase in unearned revenue of $1,440 represents unearned revenue for four months for land rented to ILS Company. ISL Company initially paid Family Heath Care $1,800 in advance. Of the $1,800, one-fifth ($360) was recorded as revenue for November. However, under the cash basis, the entire $1,800 would have been recorded as revenue. Thus, $1,440 (the increase in the unearned revenue) is added back to net income to arrive at cash flows from operations.

During November, accounts receivable increased by $2,650 and thus was recorded as part of revenue in arriving at net income. However, no cash was received. Thus, this increase in accounts receivable is deducted in arriving at cash flows from operations.

The increase in prepaid insurance represents an $8,400 payment of cash for insurance premiums. During November, only $1,100 of the premiums is deducted in arriving at net income. Thus, the remaining $7,300 (the increase in prepaid insurance) is deducted in arriving at cash flows from operations. Similarly, the increase in supplies of $90 is deducted.

You may have noticed a pattern in how we reconciled net income to net cash flows from operations. First, depreciation expense was added. Next, increases in current assets related to operations were deducted, while increases in current liabilities related to operations were added. The increase in the current liability for notes payable of $6,800 was not included in the reconciliation. This is because the notes payable is related to the purchase of office equipment, which, in the statement of cash flows, is an investing activity rather than an operating activity.

During November, all the current asset and liability accruals and deferrals related to operations were increases. This was because Family Health Care used the cash basis during October, and thus there were no deferrals or accruals at the beginning of November.

Exhibit 7

Reconciling Items

Net income		$XXX
Add:		
Depreciation expense	$XXX	
Increases in current liabilities from operations	XXX	
Decreases in current assets from operations	XXX	XXX
Deduct:		
Increases in current assets from operations	$XXX	
Decreases in current liabilities from operations	XXX	XXX
Net cash flows from operations		$XXX

In future periods, there would be both increases and decreases in these items. These increases and decreases would be added or subtracted to arrive at cash flows from operations, as shown in Exhibit 7.

For example, a decrease in accounts receivable implies that cash was collected and thus would be added. In contrast, a decrease in accounts payable implies that cash was paid and thus would be deducted.

Summary of Learning Goals

1 Describe the accrual basis of accounting.

Under the accrual basis of accounting, revenue is recognized when it is earned. When revenues are earned and recorded, all expenses incurred in generating the revenues are recorded so that revenues and expenses are properly matched in determining the net income or loss for the period. Liabilities are recorded at the time a business incurs the obligation to pay for the services or goods purchased.

2 Use the accrual basis of accounting to analyze, record, and summarize transactions.

Every transaction affects one or more elements of the accounting equation, and the two sides of the equation must always be equal. Stockholders' equity is increased by issuing capital stock and revenues (retained earnings) and is decreased by expenses (retained earnings) and dividends (retained earnings).

3 Describe and illustrate the end-of-the-period adjustment process.

The accrual basis of accounting requires the accounting records to be updated prior to preparing financial statements. This updating process, called the adjustment process, is necessary to match revenues and expenses. The adjustment process involves two types of adjustments—deferrals and accruals. Adjustments for deferrals may involve deferred expenses or deferred revenues. Adjustments for accruals may involve accrued expenses or accrued revenues.

4 Prepare accrual-basis financial statements, including a classified balance sheet.

A classified balance sheet includes sections for current assets; property, plant and equipment (fixed assets); and intangible assets. Liabilities are classified as current liabilities or long-term liabilities. The income statement normally reports sections for revenues, operating expenses, other income and expense, and net income.

5 Describe how the accrual basis of accounting enhances the interpretation of financial statements.

The net cash flows from operating activities and net income will differ under the accrual basis of accounting. Under the accrual basis, net income is a better indicator of the long-term profitability of a business. For this reason, the accrual basis of accounting is required by generally accepted accounting principles, except for very small businesses. The accrual basis reports the effects of operations on cash flows through the reporting of net cash flows from operating activities on the statement of cash flows.

6 Describe the accounting cycle for the accrual basis of accounting.

The accounting cycle is the process that begins with the analysis of transactions and ends with preparing the accounting records for the next accounting period. The basic steps in the accounting cycle are (1) identifying, analyzing, and recording the effects of transactions on the accounting equation, (2) identifying, analyzing, and recording adjustment data, (3) preparing financial statements, and (4) preparing the accounting records for the next accounting period.

7 Describe and illustrate how common-sized financial statements can be used to analyze and evaluate a company's performance.

Common-sized financial statements are often useful in comparing one company to another. In common-sized financial statements, all items are expressed in percentages. Such statements are useful in comparing the current period with prior periods, individual businesses, or one business with industry percentages.

Glossary

Account A record for summarizing increases and decreases in a financial statement element.

Accounting cycle The process that begins with the analysis of transactions and ends with preparing the accounting records for the next accounting period.

Accounts payable A liability for an amount incurred from purchases of products or services in the normal operations of a business.

Accounts receivable An asset for amounts due from customers in the normal operations of a business.

Accruals A revenue or expense that has not been recorded.

Accrued expense An expense that has been incurred at the end of an accounting period but has not been recorded in the accounts; sometimes called an accrued liability.

Accrued revenue A revenue that has been earned at the end of an accounting period but has not been recorded in the accounts; sometimes called an accrued asset.

Accumulated depreciation An offsetting or contra asset account used to record depreciation on a fixed asset.

Adjustment process A process required by the accrual basis of accounting in which the accounts are updated prior to preparing financial statements.

Classified balance sheet A balance sheet prepared with various sections, subsections, and captions that aid in its interpretation and analysis.

Closing process The process of transferring the balances of the revenue, expense, and dividends accounts to retained earnings in preparation for the next accounting period.

Common-sized financial statement A financial statement in which all items are expressed in percentages.

Current assets Cash and other assets that are expected to be converted to cash or sold or used up within one year or less, through the normal operations of the business.

Current liabilities Liabilities that will be due within a short time (usually one year or less) and that are to be paid out of current assets.

Deferrals The delayed recording of an expense or revenue.

Deferred expense Items that are initially recorded as assets but are expected to become expenses over time or through the normal operations of the business; sometimes called prepaid expenses.

Deferred revenues Items that are initially recorded as liabilities but are expected to become revenues over time or through the normal operations of the business; sometimes called unearned revenues.

Depreciation The reduction in the ability of a fixed asset to provide service.

Fixed assets Physical assets of a long-term nature; sometimes called plant assets.

Intangible assets Assets that are rights of a long-term nature.

Liabilities Amounts owed to creditors.

Long-term liabilities Liabilities that will not be due for a long time (usually more than one year).

Notes receivable Written claims against debtors who promise to pay the amount of the note plus interest at an agreed-upon rate.

Prepaid expenses Items that are initially recorded as assets but are expected to become expenses over time or through the normal operations of the business; often called deferred expenses.

Stockholders' equity The stockholders' rights to the assets of a business.

Unearned revenues Items that are initially recorded as liabilities but are expected to become revenues over time or through the normal operation of the business; often called deferred revenues.

Illustrative Accounting Application Problem

Assume that the December transactions for Family Health Care are as follows:

a. Received cash of $1,900 from patients for services provided on account during November.
b. Provided services of $10,800 on account.
c. Received $6,500 for services provided for patients who paid cash.
d. Purchased supplies on account, $400.
e. Received $6,900 from insurance companies that paid on patients' accounts for services that had been previously billed.
f. Paid $310 on account for supplies that had been purchased.
g. Expenses paid during December were as follows: wages, $4,200, including $220 accrued at the end of November; rent, $800; utilities, $610; interest, $100; miscellaneous, $520.
h. Paid dividends of $1,200 to stockholders (Dr. Landry).

Instructions:

1. Record the December transactions, using the summary of transactions form shown below. The beginning balances of December 1 have already been entered into the form. After each transaction, you should enter a balance for each item. The transactions are recorded similarly to those for November, except that separate accounts are used for dividends, revenues, and expenses. In addition, you should note that in transaction (g), the $4,200 of wages paid includes wages of $220 that were accrued at the end of November. Thus, only $3,980 ($4,200 − $220) should be recorded as wages expense for December. The remaining $220 reduces the wages payable. You should also note that the balance of retained earnings on December 1, $8,510, is the balance on November 30.

Assets = Liabilities + Stockholders' Equity

	Cash	+ Accts. Rec.	+ Prepaid Ins.	+ Supp.	+ Office Equip.	− Acc. Dep.	+ Land	= Notes Pay.	+ Accts. Pay.	+ Wages Pay.	+ Unearned Revenue	+ Capital Stock
Bal.	7,730	2,650	7,300	90	8,500	160	12,000	16,800	140	220	1,440	11,000

	+ Retained Earnings	− Dividends	+ Fees Earned	+ Rental Rev.	− Wages Exp.	− Ins. Exp.	− Rent Exp.	− Util. Exp.	− Dep. Exp.	− Supp. Exp.	− Int. Exp.	− Misc. Exp.
Bal.	8,510											

2. The adjustment data for December are as follows:

   Deferred expenses:
   1. Prepaid insurance expired, $1,100.
   2. Supplies used, $275.
   3. Depreciation on office equipment, $160.

   Deferred revenues:
   4. Unearned revenue earned, $360.

   Accruals:
   5. Wages owed employees but not paid, $340.
   6. Services provided but not billed to insurance companies, $1,050.

   Enter the adjustments in the Summary of Transactions. Identify each adjustment by "a" and the number of the related adjustment item. For example, the adjustment for prepaid insurance should be identified as (a1).
3. Prepare the December financial statements, including the income statement, retained earnings statement, balance sheet, and statement of cash flows.
4. Close the temporary accounts on the Summary of Transactions.
5. (Appendix) Reconcile the December net income with the net cash flows from operations. (Note: In computing increases and decreases in amounts, use adjusted balances.)

Solution

[Solutions to (1) and (2) are found on pages 122–123. Solution to (3) is on pages 124–125.]

4. Family Health Care Closing Process for December

Retained Earnings	− Dividends	+ Fees Earned	+ Rental Rev.	− Wages Exp.	− Ins. Exp.	− Rent Exp.	− Util. Exp.	− Dep. Exp.	− Supp. Exp.	− Int. Exp.	− Misc. Exp.
8,510	1,200	18,350	360	4,320	1,100	800	610	160	275	100	520
18,710		−18,350	−360								
−7,885				−4,320	−1,100	−800	−610	−160	−275	−100	−520
19,335	1,200	0	0	0	0	0	0	0	0	0	0
−1,200	−1,200										
18,135	0	0	0	0	0	0	0	0	0	0	0

1. Family Health Care Summary of Transactions for December

	Assets							=	Liabilities				+ Stockholders' Equity
	Cash +	Accts. Rec. +	Prepaid Ins.	+ Supp.	+ Office Equip.	− Acc. Dep.	+ Land	= Notes Pay.	+ Accts. Pay.	+ Wages Pay.	+ Unearned Revenue	+ Capital Stock	
Bal.	7,730	2,650	7,300	90	8,500	160	12,000	16,800	140	220	1,440	11,000	
a.	1,900	−1,900											
Bal.	9,630	750	7,300	90	8,500	160	12,000	16,800	140	220	1,440	11,000	
b.		10,800											
Bal.	9,630	11,550	7,300	90	8,500	160	12,000	16,800	140	220	1,440	11,000	
c.	6,500												
Bal.	16,130	11,550	7,300	90	8,500	160	12,000	16,800	140	220	1,440	11,000	
d.				400					400				
Bal.	16,130	11,550	7,300	490	8,500	160	12,000	16,800	540	220	1,440	11,000	
e.	6,900	−6,900											
Bal.	23,030	4,650	7,300	490	8,500	160	12,000	16,800	540	220	1,440	11,000	
f.	−310								−310				
Bal.	22,720	4,650	7,300	490	8,500	160	12,000	16,800	230	220	1,440	11,000	
g.	−6,230									−220			
Bal.	16,490	4,650	7,300	490	8,500	160	12,000	16,800	230	0	1,440	11,000	
h.	−1,200												
Bal.	15,290	4,650	7,300	490	8,500	160	12,000	16,800	230	0	1,440	11,000	

2. Family Health Care Adjustments for December

	Assets							=	Liabilities				+ Stockholders' Equity
	Cash +	Accts. Rec. +	Prepaid Ins.	+ Supp.	+ Office Equip.	− Acc. Dep.	+ Land	= Notes Pay.	+ Accts. Pay.	+ Wages Pay.	+ Unearned Revenue	+ Capital Stock	
Bal.	15,290	4,650	7,300	490	8,500	160	12,000	16,800	230	0	1,440	11,000	
a1			−1,100										
Bal.	15,290	4,650	6,200	490	8,500	160	12,000	16,800	230	0	1,440	11,000	
a2				−275									
Bal.	15,290	4,650	6,200	215	8,500	160	12,000	16,800	230	0	1,440	11,000	
a3						160							
Bal.	15,290	4,650	6,200	215	8,500	320	12,000	16,800	230	0	1,440	11,000	
a4											−360		
Bal.	15,290	4,650	6,200	215	8,500	320	12,000	16,800	230	0	1,080	11,000	
a5										340			
Bal.	15,290	4,650	6,200	215	8,500	320	12,000	16,800	230	340	1,080	11,000	
a6		1,050											
Bal.	15,290	5,700	6,200	215	8,500	320	12,000	16,800	230	340	1,080	11,000	

	+ Retained Earnings	− Dividends	+ Fees Earned	+ Rental Rev.	− Wages Exp.	− Ins. Exp.	− Rent Exp.	− Util. Exp.	− Dep. Exp.	− Supp. Exp.	− Int. Exp.	− Misc. Exp.	
Bal.	8,510												
a.													Collected cash
Bal.	8,510												
b.			10,800										Fees earned
Bal.	8,510		10,800										
c.			6,500										Fees earned
Bal.	8,510		17,300										
d.													Purch. of suppl.
Bal.	8,510		17,300										
e.													Collected cash
Bal.	8,510		17,300										
f.													Paid on account
Bal.	8,510		17,300										
g.					3,980		800	610			100	520	Paid expenses
Bal.	8,510		17,300		3,980		800	610			100	520	
h.		1,200											Paid dividends
Bal.	8,510	1,200	17,300		3,980		800	610			100	520	

	+ Retained Earnings	− Dividends	+ Fees Earned	+ Rental Rev.	− Wages Exp.	− Ins. Exp.	− Rent Exp.	− Util. Exp.	− Dep. Exp.	− Supp. Exp.	− Int. Exp.	− Misc. Exp.	
Bal.	8,510	1,200	17,300		3,980		800	610			100	520	
a1						1,100							Ins. exp.
Bal.	8,510	1,200	17,300		3,980	1,100	800	610	0	0	100	520	
a2										275			Supp. exp.
Bal.	8,510	1,200	17,300		3,980	1,100	800	610	0	275	100	520	
a3									160				Dep. exp.
Bal.	8,510	1,200	17,300		3,980	1,100	800	610	160	275	100	520	
a4				360									Rental rev.
Bal.	8,510	1,200	17,300	360	3,980	1,100	800	610	160	275	100	520	
a5					340								Wages exp.
Bal.	8,510	1,200	17,300	360	4,320	1,100	800	610	160	275	100	520	
a6			1,050										Fees earned
Bal.	8,510	1,200	18,350	360	4,320	1,100	800	610	160	275	100	520	

3.

Family Health Care, P.C.
Income Statement
For the Month Ended December 31, 2003

Fees earned		$18,350
Operating expenses:		
Wages expense	$4,320	
Insurance expense	1,100	
Rent expense	800	
Utilities expense	610	
Supplies expense	275	
Depreciation expense	160	
Interest expense	100	
Miscellaneous expenses	520	
Total operating expenses		7,885
Operating income		$10,465
Other income:		
Rental revenue		360
Net income		$10,825

Family Health Care, P.C.
Balance Sheet
December 31, 2003

Assets			
Current assets:			
Cash		$15,290	
Accounts receivable		5,700	
Prepaid insurance		6,200	
Supplies		215	
Total current assets			$27,405
Fixed assets:			
Office equipment	$8,500		
Less accumulated depreciation	320	$ 8,180	
Land		12,000	
Total fixed assets			20,180
Total assets			$47,585
Liabilities			
Current liabilities:			
Accounts payable		$ 230	
Wages payable		340	
Notes payable		6,800	
Unearned revenue		1,080	
Total current liabilities			$ 8,450
Long-term liabilities:			
Notes payable			10,000
Total liabilities			$18,450
Stockholders' Equity			
Capital stock		$11,000	
Retained earnings		18,135	29,135
Total liabilities and stockholders' equity			$47,585

Family Health Care, P.C.
Retained Earnings Statement
For the Month Ended December 31, 2003

Retained earnings, December 1, 2003		$ 8,510
Net income for December	$10,825	
Less dividends	1,200	9,625
Retained earnings, December 31, 2003		$18,135

Family Health Care, P.C.
Statement of Cash Flows
For the Month Ended December 31, 2003

Cash flows from operating activities:		
Cash received from patients		$15,300
Deduct cash payments for expenses:		
Supplies	$ (310)	
Wages	(4,200)	
Rent	(800)	
Utilities	(610)	
Interest	(100)	
Miscellaneous expense	(520)	(6,540)
Net cash flow from operating activities		$ 8,760
Cash flows from financing activities:		
Deduct cash dividends		(1,200)
Net increase in cash		$ 7,560
December 1, 2003 cash balance		7,730
December 31, 2003 cash balance		$15,290

5. December's Reconciliation of Net Income with Net Cash Flows from Operations

Net income		$10,825
Add:		
Depreciation expense	$ 160	
Increase in accounts payable	90	
Increase in wages payable	120	
Decrease in prepaid insurance	1,100	1,470
Deduct:		
Increase in accounts receivable	$(3,050)	
Increase in supplies	(125)	
Decrease in unearned revenue	(360)	(3,535)
Net cash flows from operating activities		$ 8,760

Self-Study Questions

Answers at end of chapter

1. Assume that a lawyer bills her clients $15,000 on June 30, 2004, for services rendered during June. The lawyer collects $8,500 of the billings during July and the remainder in August. Under the accrual basis of accounting, when would the lawyer record the revenue for the fees?

A. June, $15,000; July, $0; and August, $0
B. June, $0; July, $6,500; and August, $8,500
C. June, $8,500; July, $6,500; and August, $0
D. June, $0; July, $8,500; and August, $6,500

2. On January 24, 2004, Niche Consulting collected $5,700 it had billed its clients for services rendered on December 31, 2003. How would you record the January 24 transaction, using the accrual basis?
   A. Increase Cash, $5,700; decrease Fees Earned, $5,700.
   B. Increase Accounts Receivable, $5,700; increase Fees Earned, $5,700.
   C. Increase Cash, $5,700; decrease Accounts Receivable, $5,700.
   D. Increase Cash, $5,700; increase Fees Earned, $5,700.

3. Which of the following items represents a deferral?
   A. Prepaid insurance
   B. Wages payable
   C. Fees earned
   D. Accumulated depreciation

4. If the supplies account indicated a balance of $2,250 before adjustment on May 31 and supplies on hand at May 31 totaled $950, the adjustment would be:
   A. Increase Supplies, $950; Decrease Supplies Expense, $950.
   B. Increase Supplies, $1,300; Decrease Supplies Expense, $1,300.
   C. Increase Supplies Expense, $950; Decrease Supplies, $950.
   D. Increase Supplies Expense, $1,300; Decrease Supplies, $1,300.

5. The balance in the unearned rent account for Jones Co. as of December 31 is $1,200. If Jones Co. failed to record the adjusting entry for $600 of rent earned during December, the effect on the balance sheet and income statement for December would be:
   A. assets understated by $600; net income overstated by $600.
   B. liabilities understated by $600; net income understated by $600.
   C. liabilities overstated by $600; net income understated by $600.
   D. liabilities overstated by $600; net income overstated by $600.

Discussion Questions

1. Would General Electric and Xerox use the cash basis or the accrual basis of accounting? Explain.
2. How are revenues and expenses reported on the income statement under (a) the cash basis of accounting and (b) the accrual basis of accounting?
3. Fees for services provided are billed to a customer during 2003. The customer remits the amount owed in 2004. During which year would the revenues be reported on the income statement under (a) the cash basis? (b) the accrual basis?
4. Employees performed services in 2003, but the wages were not paid until 2004. During which year would the wages expense be reported on the income statement under (a) the cash basis? (b) the accrual basis?
5. Which of the following accounts would appear only in an accrual basis accounting system and which could appear in either a cash basis or accrual basis accounting system? (a) Capital Stock, (b) Fees Earned, (c) Accounts Payable, (d) Land, (e) Utilities Expense, and (f) Accounts Receivable.
6. Is the land balance before the accounts have been adjusted the amount that should normally be reported on the balance sheet? Explain.
7. Is the supplies balance before the accounts have been adjusted the amount that should normally be reported on the balance sheet? Explain.
8. Why are adjustments needed at the end of an accounting period?
9. What is the difference between the adjusting process and the closing process?
10. Identify the four different categories of adjustments frequently required at the end of an accounting period.

11. If the effect of an adjustment is to increase the balance of a liability account, which of the following statements describes the effect of the adjustment on the other account?
    a. Increases the balance of a revenue account.
    b. Increases the balance of an expense account.
    c. Increases the balance of an asset account.
12. If the effect of an adjustment is to increase the balance of an asset account, which of the following statements describes the effect of the adjustment on the other account?
    a. Increases the balance of a revenue account.
    b. Increases the balance of a liability account.
    c. Increases the balance of an expense account.
13. Does every adjustment have an effect on determining the amount of net income for a period? Explain.
14. (a) Explain the purpose of the two accounts: Depreciation Expense and Accumulated Depreciation. (b) Is it customary for the balances of the two accounts to be equal? (c) In what financial statements, if any, will each account appear?
15. Describe the nature of the assets that compose the following sections of a balance sheet: (a) current assets, (b) property, plant, and equipment.
16. (a) Why is the closing process required at the end of an accounting period? (b) To what account are revenue and expenses closed? (c) To what account is dividends closed?
17. (a) What are common-sized financial statements? (b) Why are common-sized financial statements useful in interpreting and analyzing financial statements?

Resources for your success online @ http://warren.swlearning.com

Remember! If you need additional help, visit South-Western's Web site. See page 30 for a description of the online and printed materials that are available.

Exercises

Exercise 3–1

Accrual basis of accounting

Goal 2

Neal Hastings established Ember Services, P.C., a professional corporation, on January 1 of the current year. Ember Services offers financial planning advice to its clients. The effect of each transaction and the balances after each transaction for January are as follows. Each increase or decrease in stockholders' equity, except transaction (h), affects net income.

	Assets			=	Liabilities	+	Stockholders' Equity	
	Cash +	Accounts Receivable +	Supplies	=	Accounts Payable	+	Capital Stock +	Retained Earnings
a.	+15,000						+15,000	
b.			+1,100		+1,100			
Bal.	15,000		1,100		1,100		15,000	
c.	−775				−775			
Bal.	14,225		1,100		325		15,000	
d.	+9,000							+9,000
Bal.	23,225		1,100		325		15,000	9,000
e.	−4,500							−4,500
Bal.	18,725		1,100		325		15,000	4,500
f.			−850					−850
Bal.	18,725		250		325		15,000	3,650
g.		+2,800						+2,800
Bal.	18,725	2,800	250		325		15,000	6,450
h.	−2,000							−2,000
Bal.	16,725	2,800	250		325		15,000	4,450

a. Describe each transaction.
b. What is the amount of the net income for January?

Exercise 3–2

Classify accruals and deferrals

Goal 3

STUDENT SOLUTIONS MANUAL

Classify the following items as (a) deferred expense (prepaid expense), (b) deferred revenue (unearned revenue), (c) accrued expense (accrued liability), or (d) accrued revenue (accrued asset).

1. Fees earned but not yet received.
2. Taxes owed but payable in the following period.
3. Salary owed but not yet paid.
4. Supplies on hand.
5. Fees received but not yet earned.
6. Utilities owed but not yet paid.
7. A two-year premium paid on a fire insurance policy.
8. Subscriptions received in advance by a magazine publisher.

Exercise 3–3

Classify adjustments

Goal 3

The following accounts were taken from the unadjusted trial balance of O'Neil Co., a congressional lobbying firm. Indicate whether or not each account would normally require an adjusting entry. If the account normally requires an adjusting entry, use the following notation to indicate the type of adjustment:

AE—Accrued Expense
AR—Accrued Revenue
DR—Deferred Revenue
DE—Deferred Expense

To illustrate, the answers for the first two accounts are shown below.

Account	Answer
Dividends	Does not normally require adjustment.
Accounts Receivable	Normally requires adjustment (AR).
Accumulated Depreciation	
Cash	
Interest Payable	
Interest Receivable	

(continued)

Account	Answer
Land	
Office Equipment	
Prepaid Insurance	
Supplies Expense	
Unearned Fees	
Wages Expense	

Exercise 3-4

Adjustment for supplies

Goal 3

a. $1,234

STUDENT SOLUTIONS MANUAL

Answer each of the following independent questions concerning supplies and the adjustment for supplies. (a) The balance in the supplies account, before adjustment at the end of the year, is $1,475. What is the amount of the adjustment if the amount of supplies on hand at the end of the year is $241? (b) The supplies account has a balance of $418, and the supplies expense account has a balance of $1,943 at December 31, 2004. If 2004 was the first year of operations, what was the amount of supplies purchased during the year?

Exercise 3-5

Adjustments for prepaid insurance

Goal 3

The prepaid insurance account had a balance of $3,600 at the beginning of the year. The account was increased for $1,200 for premiums on policies purchased during the year. What is the adjustment required at the end of the year for each of the following independent situations: (a) the amount of unexpired insurance applicable to future periods is $3,450? (b) the amount of insurance expired during the year is $1,875? For (a) and (b), indicate each account affected, whether the account is increased or decreased, and the amount of the increase or decrease.

Exercise 3-6

Adjustment for unearned fees

Goal 3

STUDENT SOLUTIONS MANUAL

The balance in the unearned fees account, before adjustment at the end of the year, is $6,750. What is the adjustment if the amount of unearned fees at the end of the year is $2,800? Indicate each account affected, whether the account is increased or decreased, and the amount of the increase or decrease.

Exercise 3-7

Adjustment for unearned revenue

Goal 3

For the years ending June 30, 2001 and 2000, Microsoft Corporation reported unearned revenue of $4,816 million and $5,614 million, respectively. For the year ending June 30, 2001, Microsoft also reported total revenues of $19,747 million. (a) What adjustment for unearned revenue did Microsoft make at June 30, 2001? Indicate each account affected, whether the account is increased or decreased, and the amount of the increase or decrease. (b) What percentage of total revenues was the adjustment for unearned revenue?

Exercise 3-8

Effect of omitting adjustment

Goal 3

STUDENT SOLUTIONS MANUAL

At the end of March, the first month of the business year, the usual adjustment transferring rent earned to a revenue account from the unearned rent account was omitted. Indicate which items will be incorrectly stated, because of the error, on (a) the income statement for March and (b) the balance sheet as of March 31. Also indicate whether the items in error will be overstated or understated.

Exercise 3-9

Adjustment for accrued salaries

Goal 3

Taylor Fork Realty Co. pays weekly salaries of $13,750 on Friday for a five-day week ending on that day. What is the adjustment at the end of the accounting period, assuming that the period ends (a) on Tuesday, (b) on Wednesday? Indicate each account affected, whether the account is increased or decreased, and the amount of the increase or decrease.

Exercise 3–10

Determine wages paid

Goal 3

STUDENT SOLUTIONS MANUAL

The balances of the two wages accounts at December 31, after adjustments at the end of the first year of operations, are Wages Payable, $1,960, and Wages Expense, $87,430. Determine the amount of wages paid during the year.

Exercise 3–11

Effect of omitting adjustment

Goal 3

Accrued salaries of $3,100 owed to employees for December 30 and 31 are not considered in preparing the financial statements for the year ended December 31, 2003. Indicate which items will be erroneously stated, because of the error, on (a) the income statement for December 2003 and (b) the balance sheet as of December 31, 2003. Also indicate whether the items in error will be overstated or understated.

Exercise 3–12

Effect of omitting adjustment

Goal 3

STUDENT SOLUTIONS MANUAL

Assume that the error in Exercise 3–11 was not corrected and that the $3,100 of accrued salaries was included in the first salary payment in January 2004. Indicate which items will be erroneously stated, because of failure to correct the initial error, on (a) the income statement for January 2004 and (b) the balance sheet as of January 31, 2004.

Exercise 3–13

Effects of errors on financial statements

Goal 3

For a recent period, Circuit City Stores reported accrued expenses of $183,336 thousand. For the same period, Circuit City reported earnings before income taxes of $352,893 thousand. If accrued expenses had not been recorded, what would have been the earnings (loss) before income taxes?

Exercise 3–14

Effects of errors on financial statements

Goal 3

STUDENT SOLUTIONS MANUAL

The balance sheet for Ford Motor Company as of December 31, 2001, includes $23,990 million of accrued expenses as liabilities. Before taxes, Ford Motor Company reported a net loss of $7,584 million. If the accruals had not been recorded at December 31, 2001, how much would net income or net loss before taxes have been for the year ended December 31, 2001?

Exercise 3–15

Effects of errors on financial statements

Goal 3

b. $445,670

The accountant for Maxim Medical Co., a medical services consulting firm, mistakenly omitted adjustments for (a) unearned revenue ($10,390) and (b) accrued wages ($2,440). (a) Indicate the effect of each error, considered individually, on the income statement for the current year ended December 31. Also indicate the effect of each error on the December 31 balance sheet. Set up a table similar to the following, and record your answers by inserting the dollar amount in the appropriate spaces. Insert a zero if the error does not affect the item.

	Error (a)		Error (b)	
	Over-stated	Under-stated	Over-stated	Under-stated
1. Revenue for the year would be	$	$	$	$
2. Expenses for the year would be	$	$	$	$
3. Net income for the year would be	$	$	$	$
4. Assets at December 31 would be	$	$	$	$
5. Liabilities at December 31 would be	$	$	$	$
6. Stockholders' equity at December 31 would be	$	$	$	$

(b) If the net income for the current year had been $437,720, what would be the correct net income if the proper adjustments had been made?

Exercise 3-16

Adjustment for accrued fees

Goal 3

STUDENT SOLUTIONS MANUAL

At the end of the current year, $7,260 of fees have been earned but have not been billed to clients.

a. What is the adjustment to record the accrued fees? Indicate each account affected, whether the account is increased or decreased, and the amount of the increase or decrease.

b. If the cash basis rather than the accrual basis had been used, would an adjustment have been necessary? Explain.

Exercise 3-17

Adjustments for unearned and accrued fees

Goal 3

The balance in the unearned fees account, before adjustment at the end of the year, is $48,000. Of these fees, $16,000 have been earned. In addition, $7,500 of fees have been earned but have not been billed. What are the adjustments to (a) to adjust the unearned fees account and (b) to record the accrued fees? Indicate each account affected, whether the account is increased or decreased, and the amount of the increase or decrease.

Exercise 3-18

Effect of deferred revenue

Goal 3

a. $597 million

STUDENT SOLUTIONS MANUAL

AOL Time Warner Inc. reported unearned revenue of $1,660 million and $1,063 million as of December 31, 2001 and 2000, respectively. For the year ending December 31, 2001, AOL Time Warner reported total revenues of $38,234 million. (a) What was the amount of the adjustment for unearned revenue for 2001? (b) What would have been total revenues under the cash basis?

Exercise 3-19

Effect on financial statements of omitting adjustment

Goal 3

The adjustment for accrued fees was omitted at December 31, the end of the current year. Indicate which items will be in error, because of the omission, on (a) the income statement for the current year and (b) the balance sheet as of December 31. Also indicate whether the items in error will be overstated or understated.

Exercise 3-20

Adjustment for depreciation

Goal 3

STUDENT SOLUTIONS MANUAL

The estimated amount of depreciation on equipment for the current year is $3,000. (a) How is the adjustment recorded? Indicate each account affected, whether the account is increased or decreased, and the amount of the increase or decrease. (b) If the adjustment in (a) was omitted, which items would be erroneously stated on (1) the income statement for the year and (2) the balance sheet as of December 31?

Exercise 3-21

Adjustments

Goal 3

The Purification Company is a consulting firm specializing in pollution control. The following adjustments were made for The Purification Company:

Account	Adjustments Increase (Decrease)
Accounts Receivable	$ 5,100
Supplies	(1,225)
Prepaid Insurance	(1,000)
Accumulated Depreciation—Equipment	1,800
Wages Payable	900
Unearned Rent	(2,500)
Fees Earned	5,100
Wages Expense	900
Supplies Expense	1,225
Rent Revenue	2,500
Insurance Expense	1,000
Depreciation Expense	1,800

Identify each of the six pairs of adjustments. For each adjustment, indicate the account, whether the account is increased or decreased, and the amount of the adjustment. No account is affected by more than one adjustment. Use the following format. The first adjustment is shown as an example.

Adjustment	Account	Increase or Decrease	Amount
1.	Accounts Receivable	Increase	$5,100
	Fees Earned	Increase	5,100

Exercise 3–22

Book value of fixed assets

Goal 4

STUDENT SOLUTIONS MANUAL

Cisco Systems Inc. reported *Property, Plant, and Equipment* of $5,029 million and *Accumulated Depreciation* of $2,438 million at July 28, 2001.

a. What was the book value of the fixed assets at July 28, 2001?
b. Would the book values of Cisco Systems' fixed assets normally approximate their fair market values?

Exercise 3–23

Classify assets

Goal 4

Identify each of the following as (a) a current asset or (b) property, plant, and equipment:

1. Accounts receivable
2. Building
3. Cash
4. Equipment
5. Prepaid insurance
6. Supplies

Exercise 3–24

Balance sheet classification

Goal 4

STUDENT SOLUTIONS MANUAL

At the balance sheet date, a business owes a mortgage note payable of $375,000, the terms of which provide for monthly payments of $12,500. Explain how the liability should be classified on the balance sheet.

Exercise 3–25

Classified balance sheet

Goal 4

Total assets, $96,550

SPREADSHEET

Shoshone Co. offers personal weight reduction consulting services to individuals. After all the accounts have been closed on June 30, 2004, the end of the current fiscal year, the balances of selected accounts from the ledger of Shoshone Co. are as follows:

Accounts Payable	$ 8,750	Prepaid Insurance	$ 3,100
Accounts Receivable	18,725	Prepaid Rent	2,400
Accum. Depr.—Equipment	21,100	Retained Earnings	59,850
Capital Stock	25,000	Salaries Payable	1,750
Cash	2,150	Supplies	675
Equipment	90,600	Unearned Fees	1,200

Prepare a classified balance sheet.

Exercise 3–26

Classified balance sheet

Goal 4

Total assets, $1,222,503

STUDENT SOLUTIONS MANUAL

La-Z-Boy Inc. is one of the world's largest manufacturers of furniture that is best known for its reclining chairs. The following data (in thousands) were adapted from the 2001 annual report of La-Z-Boy Inc.:

Accounts payable	$ 92,830
Accounts receivables	380,867
Accumulated depreciation	252,027
Capital stock	267,530
Cash	23,565

(continued)

SPREADSHEET

Income taxes payable*	$ 11,490
Intangible assets	247,422
Inventories	257,887
Long-term debt*	5,304
Long-term debt**	196,923
Other assets*	46,457
Other assets**	35,964
Other liabilities*	51,361
Other long-term liabilities**	80,519
Notes payable*	10,380
Payroll payable*	78,550
Property, plant, and equipment	482,368
Retained earnings	427,616

For the preceding items, (*) indicates that the item is current in nature, while (**) indicates that the item is long-term in nature.

Prepare a classified balance sheet as of April 28, 2001.

Exercise 3–27

Balance Sheet

Goal 4

List the errors you find in the following balance sheet. Prepare a corrected balance sheet.

ZigZag Services Co.
Balance Sheet
For the Year Ended March 31, 2004

Assets		
Current assets:		
Cash	$ 3,170	
Accounts payable	4,390	
Supplies	750	
Prepaid insurance	1,600	
Land	100,000	
Total current assets		$109,910
Property, plant, and equipment:		
Building	$ 55,500	
Equipment	28,250	
Total property, plant, and equipment		101,750
Total assets		$211,660
Liabilities		
Current liabilities:		
Accounts receivable	$ 8,390	
Accumulated depreciation—building	23,000	
Accumulated depreciation—equipment	16,000	
Net loss	10,000	
Total liabilities		$ 57,390
Stockholders' Equity		
Wages payable		$ 975
Capital stock		40,000
Retained earnings		113,295
Total stockholders' equity		$154,270
Total liabilities and stockholders' equity		$211,660

Exercise 3-28

Identify accounts to be closed

Goal 6

STUDENT SOLUTIONS MANUAL

From the following list, identify the accounts that should be closed at the end of the accounting period:

a.	Accounts Payable	g.	Fees Earned
b.	Accumulated Depreciation–Buildings	h.	Land
c.	Capital Stock	i.	Salaries Expense
d.	Depreciation Expense–Buildings	j.	Salaries Payable
e.	Dividends	k.	Supplies
f.	Equipment	l.	Supplies Expense

Exercise 3-29

Closing process

Goal 6

SPREADSHEET

During the closing process for Matrix Corporation, retained earnings was affected by three separate transactions: an increase of $729,350, a decrease of $512,900, and a decrease of $40,000. For the year ending July 31, 2004, dividends of $40,000 were paid. As of August 1, 2003, the balance of retained earnings was $405,700. (a) What was the net income or loss for the year ending July 31, 2004? (b) Prepare a retained earnings statement for the year.

Exercise 3-30

Closing process

Goal 6

STUDENT SOLUTIONS MANUAL

Image Services Co. offers its services to individuals desiring to improve their personal images. After the accounts have been adjusted at January 31, the end of the fiscal year, the following balances were taken from the ledger of Image Services Co.:

Retained Earnings	$325,750	Rent Expense	$74,000
Dividends	45,000	Supplies Expense	15,500
Fees Earned	380,700	Miscellaneous Expense	4,500
Wages Expense	205,300		

Perform the closing process for (a) revenues, (b) expenses, and (c) dividends. Indicate each account closed, whether the account is increased or decreased, and the amount of the increase or decrease. Close all expenses with one transfer to retained earnings.

Accounting Application Problems

Problem 3-1A

Accrual-basis accounting

Goal 2

SPREADSHEET GENERAL LEDGER

Papaw Health Care Inc. is owned and operated by Dr. Richard Byrne, the sole stockholder. During October 2004, Papaw Health Care entered into the following transactions:

Oct. 1 Received $4,500 from Embark Company as rent for the use of a vacant office in Papaw Health Care's building. Embark paid the rent six months in advance.
1 Paid $2,400 for an insurance premium on a one-year, general business policy.
4 Purchased supplies of $1,200 on account.
5 Collected $5,100 for services provided to customers on account.
11 Paid creditors $900 on account.
18 Invested an additional $25,000 in the business in exchange for capital stock.
20 Billed patients $13,600 for services provided on account.
25 Received $3,800 for services provided to customers who paid cash.
29 Paid expenses as follows: wages, $7,000; utilities, $2,000; rent on medical equipment, $1,500; interest, $125; miscellaneous, $300.
29 Paid dividends of $3,000 to stockholders (Dr. Byrne).

Instructions

Analyze and record the October transactions for Papaw Health Care Inc. Using the following format, record each transaction by date and as a plus or minus in the appropriate accounts. The October 1, 2004 balances are shown in the form.

	Assets							=	Liabilities			+	Stockholders' Equity
	Cash	+ Accts. Rec.	+ Pre. Ins.	+ Supp.	+ Building	− Acc. Dep.	+ Land	=	Accts. Pay.	+ Un. Rent	+ Wages Pay.	+ Notes Pay.	+ Capital Stock
Bal. Oct. 1	5,800	7,500	200	310	50,000	4,000	25,000		2,150	0	0	20,000	25,000

	+ Ret. Earn.	− Dividends	+ Fees Earned	+ Rent Rev.	− Wages Exp.	− Utilities Exp.	− Rent Exp.	− Supplies Exp.	− Dep. Exp.	− Ins. Exp.	− Int. Exp.	− Misc. Exp.
Bal. Oct. 1	37,660	0	0	0	0	0	0	0	0	0	0	0

Problem 3–2A

Adjustment process

Goal 3

SPREADSHEET GENERAL LEDGER

Adjustment data for Papaw Health Care Inc. for October are as follows:

1. Insurance expired, $200.
2. Supplies on hand on October 31, $325.
3. Depreciation on building, $1,000.
4. Unearned rent revenue earned, $750.
5. Wages owed employees but not paid, $800.
6. Services provided but not billed to patients, $2,100.

Instructions

Based upon the transactions recorded in October for Problem 3–1A, record the adjustments for October.

Problem 3–3A

Financial statements and the closing process

Goals 4, 6

1. Net income, $6,140

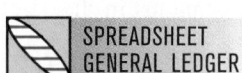

SPREADSHEET GENERAL LEDGER

Data for Papaw Health Care for October are provided in Problem 3–1A and Problem 3–2A

Instructions

1. Prepare an income statement, retained earnings statement, and a classified balance sheet for October. The notes payable is due in 2010.
2. Close the revenue, expense, and dividend accounts.

Problem 3–4A

Statement of cash flows

Goal 4

Net cash flow from operating activities, ($825)

SPREADSHEET GENERAL LEDGER

Data for Papaw Health Care for October are provided in Problems 3–1A, 3–2A, and 3–3A.

Instructions

1. Prepare a statement of cash flows for October. *Hint:* The statement of cash flows is prepared by analyzing and summarizing the cash transactions shown in the summary of transactions for Problem 3–1A.
2. Reconcile the net cash flows from operating activities with the net income for October. *Hint:* See the appendix to this chapter and use adjusted balances in computing increases and decreases in accounts.

Problem 3–5A

Adjustments and errors

Goal 3

Corrected net income, $198,225

SPREADSHEET

At the end of April, the first month of operations, the following selected data were taken from the financial statements of Phil Olson, P.C., a professional services corporation owned and operated by Phil Olson, an attorney at law:

Net income for April	$187,500
Total assets at April 30	498,300
Total liabilities at April 30	67,800
Total stockholders' equity at April 30	430,500

In preparing the statements, adjustments for the following data were overlooked:

a. Unbilled fees earned at April 30, $21,500.

b. Depreciation of equipment for April, $6,000.

c. Accrued wages at April 30, $2,900.
d. Supplies used during April, $1,875.

Instructions

Determine the correct amount of net income for April and the total assets, liabilities, and stockholders' equity at April 30. In addition to indicating the corrected amounts, indicate the effect of each omitted adjustment by setting up and completing a columnar table similar to the following. Adjustment (a) is presented as an example.

	Net Income	Total Assets	Total Liabilities	Total Stockholders' Equity
Reported amounts	$187,500	$498,300	$67,800	$430,500
Corrections:				
Adjustment (a)	+21,500	+21,500	0	+21,500
Adjustment (b)	______	______	______	______
Adjustment (c)	______	______	______	______
Adjustment (d)	______	______	______	______
Corrected amounts	______	______	______	______

Problem 3–6A

Adjustment process and financial statements

Goals 3, 4

2. Net income, $21,040

SPREADSHEET GENERAL LEDGER

Adjustment data for Marasca Laundry Inc. for January 2004 are as follows:

a. Wages accrued but not paid at January 31, $2,100.
b. Depreciation of equipment during the year, $6,600.
c. Laundry supplies on hand at January 31, $900.
d. Insurance premiums expired, $2,800.

Instructions

1. Using the following format, record each adjustment as a plus or minus in the appropriate accounts. The January 31 balances are given.

	Assets					=	Liabilities		+	Stockholders' Equity
	Cash +	Laundry Supplies +	Prepaid Insurance +	Laundry Equipment −	Acc. Dep.	=	Accounts Payable +	Wages Payable	+	Capital Stock
Jan. 31 Balances	11,100	5,560	4,490	95,100	40,200		4,100	0		7,500

	+ Retained Earnings −	Dividends +	Laundry Revenue −	Wages Expense −	Rent Expense −	Utilities Expense −	Dep. Expense −	Laundry Supplies Expense −	Insurance Expense −	Misc. Expense
Jan. 31 Balances	29,250	2,000	150,000	61,400	36,000	13,700	0	0	0	1,700

2. Prepare an income statement and a retained earnings statement for the year ended January 31, 2004, and a classified balance sheet as of January 31, 2004.

Problem 3–7A

Adjustment process and the closing process

Goals 3, 4, 6

Last Chance Corporation offers legal consulting advice to prison inmates. Adjustment data for Last Chance Corporation for June 2004 are as follows:

a. Accrued fees revenue at June 30, $5,000.
b. Insurance expired during the year, $1,900.
c. Supplies on hand at June 30, $450.

2. Net income, $45,900

SPREADSHEET GENERAL LEDGER

d. Depreciation of building for the year, $1,620.
e. Depreciation of equipment for the year, $3,500.
f. Accrued salaries and wages at June 30, $1,750.
g. Unearned rent at June 30, $1,000.

Instructions

1. Using the following format, record each adjustment as a plus or minus in the appropriate accounts. The June 30 balances are shown in the form.

	Cash	+ Accounts Receivable	+ Prepaid Insurance	+ Supplies	+ Land	+ Building	− Acc. Dep. Building	+ Equipment
June 30 Balances	4,200	15,500	3,800	1,950	50,000	137,500	51,700	90,100

	− Acc. Dep. Equip.	= Accounts Payable	+ Salaries and Wages Payable	+ Unearned Rent	+ Capital Stock	+ Retained Earnings	− Dividends	− Fees Revenue
June 30 Balances	35,300	9,500	0	3,000	50,000	111,800	7,500	200,000

	+ Rent Revenue	− Salaries & Wages Expense	− Advertising Expense	− Utilities Expense	− Repairs Expense	− Dep. Exp. Equip.	− Insurance Expense	− Dep. Exp. Building	− Supplies Expense	− Misc. Expense
June 30 Balances	0	80,000	38,200	19,000	11,500	0	0	0	0	2,050

2. Prepare an income statement and a retained earnings statement for the year ended June 30, 2004, and a classified balance sheet as of June 30, 2004.
3. Close the revenue, expense, and dividend accounts.

Alternate Accounting Application Problems

Alternate Problem 3–1B

Accrual-basis accounting

Goal 2

STUDENT SOLUTIONS MANUAL

SPREADSHEET GENERAL LEDGER

Osmosis Health Care Inc. is owned and operated by Dr. Chris Ballard, the sole stockholder. During August, Osmosis Health Care entered into the following transactions:

Aug. 2 Received $9,000 from BFX Company as rent for the use of a vacant office in Osmosis Health Care's building. BFX prepays the rent six months in advance.
2 Paid $3,600 for an insurance premium on a one-year, general business policy.
3 Purchased supplies of $1,450 on account.
6 Collected $5,500 for services provided to customers on account.
9 Paid creditors $2,400 on account.
18 Invested an additional $10,000 in the business in exchange for capital stock.
23 Billed patients $11,500 for services provided on account.
25 Received $4,800 for services provided to customers who paid cash.
30 Paid expenses as follows: wages, $10,250; utilities, $3,800; rent on medical equipment, $2,500; interest, $125; miscellaneous, $340.
31 Paid dividends of $2,000 to stockholders (Dr. Ballard).

Instructions

Analyze and record the August transactions for Osmosis Health Care Inc. Using the following format, record each transaction by date and as a plus or minus in the appropriate accounts. The August 1, 2004 balances are shown in the form.

	Assets							=	Liabilities			+ Stockholders' Equity
	Cash	+ Accts. Rec.	+ Pre. Ins.	+ Supp.	+ Building	− Acc. Dep.	+ Land	= Accts. Pay.	+ Un. Rent	+ Wages Pay.	+ Notes Pay.	+ Capital Stock
Bal. Aug. 1	5,800	8,300	300	180	50,000	4,000	25,000	4,280	0	0	20,000	40,000

	+ Ret. Earn.	− Dividends	+ Fees Earned	+ Rent Rev.	− Wages Exp.	− Utilities Exp.	− Rent Exp.	− Supplies Exp.	− Dep. Exp.	− Ins. Exp.	− Int. Exp.	− Misc. Exp.
Bal. Aug. 1	21,300	0	0	0	0	0	0	0	0	0	0	0

Alternate Problem 3–2B

Adjustment process

Goal 3

STUDENT SOLUTIONS MANUAL

SPREADSHEET GENERAL LEDGER

Adjustment data for Osmosis Health Care Inc. for August are as follows:

1. Insurance expired, $300.
2. Supplies on hand on August 31, $285.
3. Depreciation on building, $1,000.
4. Unearned rent revenue earned, $1,500.
5. Wages owed employees but not paid, $725.
6. Services provided but not billed to patients, $5,500.

Instructions

Based upon the transactions recorded in August for Problem 3–1B, record the adjustments for August.

Alternate Problem 3–3B

Financial statements and the closing process

Goals 4, 6

1. Net income, $2,915

STUDENT SOLUTIONS MANUAL

SPREADSHEET GENERAL LEDGER

Data for Osmosis Health Care Inc. for August are provided in Problem 3–1B and Problem 3–2B.

Instructions

1. Prepare an income statement, retained earnings statement, and a classified balance sheet for August. The notes payable is due in 2015.
2. Close the revenue, expense, and dividend accounts.

Alternate Problem 3–4B

Statement of Cash Flows

Goal 4

1. Net cash flow from operating activities, ($3,715)

STUDENT SOLUTIONS MANUAL

SPREADSHEET GENERAL LEDGER

Data for Osmosis Health Care for August are provided in Problems 3–1B, 3–2B, and 3–3B.

Instructions

1. Prepare a statement of cash flows for August. *Hint:* The statement of cash flows is prepared by analyzing and summarizing the cash transactions shown in the summary of transactions for Problem 3–1B.
2. Reconcile the net cash flows from operating activities with the net income for August. *Hint:* See the appendix to this chapter and use adjusted balances in computing increases and decreases in accounts.

Alternate Problem 3–5B

Adjustments and errors

Goal 3

At the end of March, the first month of operations, the following selected data were taken from the financial statements of Rita Abbott, P.C., a professional services corporation owned and operated by Rita Abbott, an attorney at law:

Net income for March	$372,300	Total liabilities at March 31	158,500
Total assets at March 31	862,000	Total stockholders' equity at March 31	703,500

Corrected net income, $371,425

STUDENT SOLUTIONS MANUAL

SPREADSHEET

In preparing the statements, adjustments for the following data were overlooked:

a. Unbilled fees earned at March 31, $10,100.
b. Depreciation of equipment for March, $7,500.
c. Accrued wages at March 31, $2,100.
d. Supplies used during March, $1,375.

Instructions

Determine the correct amount of net income for March and the total assets, liabilities, and stockholders' equity at March 31. In addition to indicating the corrected amounts, indicate the effect of each omitted adjustment by setting up and completing a columnar table similar to the following. Adjustment (a) is presented as an example.

	Net Income	Total Assets	Total Liabilities	Total Stockholders' Equity
Reported amounts	$372,300	$862,000	$158,500	$703,500
Corrections:				
Adjustment (a)	+10,100	+10,100	0	+10,100
Adjustment (b)	______	______	______	______
Adjustment (c)	______	______	______	______
Adjustment (d)	______	______	______	______
Corrected amounts	______	______	______	______

Alternate Problem 3–6B

Adjustment process and financial statements

Goals 3, 4

2. Net income, $116,810

STUDENT SOLUTIONS MANUAL

Adjustment data for Catnip Laundry Inc. for October 2004 are as follows:

a. Wages accrued but not paid at October 31, $2,500.
b. Depreciation of equipment during the year, $6,600.
c. Laundry supplies on hand at October 31, $900.
d. Insurance premiums expired during the year, $4,500.

Instructions

1. Using the following format, record each adjustment as a plus or minus in the appropriate accounts. The October 31 balances are given.

	Assets					=	Liabilities		+	Stockholders' Equity
	Cash +	Laundry Supplies +	Prepaid Insurance +	Laundry Equipment −	Acc. Dep.	=	Accounts Payable +	Wages Payable	+	Capital Stock
Oct. 31 Balances	18,100	7,640	6,000	395,100	140,200		9,100	0		34,100

	Retained Earnings −	Dividends +	Laundry Revenue −	Wages Expense −	Rent Expense −	Utilities Expense −	Dep. Expense −	Laundry Supplies Expense −	Insurance Expense −	Misc. Expense
Oct. 31 Balances	109,290	3,000	240,900	51,400	36,000	13,650	0	0	0	2,700

SPREADSHEET GENERAL LEDGER

2. Prepare an income statement and a retained earnings statement for the year ended October 31, 2004, and a classified balance sheet as of October 31, 2004.

Alternate Problem 3–7B

Adjustment process and the closing process

Goals 3, 4, 6

2. Net income, $40,130

Pale Corporation offers legal consulting advice to prison inmates. Adjustment data for Pale Corporation for April 2004 are as follows:

a. Accrued fees revenue at April 30, $6,000.
b. Insurance expired during the year, $9,000.
c. Supplies on hand at April 30, $450.
d. Depreciation of building for the year, $1,620.
e. Depreciation of equipment for the year, $3,500.

STUDENT SOLUTIONS MANUAL

SPREADSHEET GENERAL LEDGER

f. Accrued salaries and wages at April 30, $1,200.
g. Unearned rent at April 30, $2,500.

Instructions

1. Using the following format, record each adjustment as a plus or minus in the appropriate accounts. The April 30 balances are shown in the form.

	Cash	+ Accounts Receivable	+ Prepaid Insurance	+ Supplies	+ Land	+ Building	− Acc. Dep. Building	+ Equipment
Apr. 30 Balances	8,200	10,500	13,800	1,950	50,000	132,500	51,700	90,100

	− Acc. Dep. Equip.	= Accounts Payable	+ Salaries & Wages Payable	+ Unearned Rent	+ Capital Stock	+ Retained Earnings	− Dividends	+ Fees Revenue
Apr. 30 Balances	35,300	7,500	0	8,000	50,000	119,100	10,000	198,400

	+ Rent Revenue	− Salaries & Wages Expense	− Advertising Expense	− Utilities Expense	− Repairs Expense	− Dep. Exp. Equip.	− Insurance Expense	− Dep. Exp. Building	− Supplies Expense	− Misc. Expense
Apr. 30 Balances	0	80,200	38,200	19,000	11,500	0	0	0	0	4,050

2. Prepare an income statement and a retained earnings statement for the year ended April 30, 2004, and a classified balance sheet as of April 30, 2004.
3. Close the revenue, expense, and dividend accounts.

Building Leadership Skills— Financial Analysis and Reporting

Case 3–1

Analysis of income statements

Walgreen Company and CVS Corporation operate national chains of drugstores that sell prescription drugs, over-the-counter drugs, and other general merchandise such as greeting cards, beauty and cosmetics, household items, food,and beverages. Walgreen operates approximately 3,600 stores, while CVS Corporation operates approximately 4,200 stores. The following operating data (in thousands) were adapted from the 2001 SEC 10-K filings of Walgreen and CVS.

	CVS	Walgreen
Net sales	$22,241,400	$24,623,000
Cost of sales	16,550,400	18,048,900
Gross profit	$ 5,691,000	$ 6,574,100
Selling, general, and administrative expenses	4,920,400	5,175,800
Operating income	$ 770,600	$ 1,398,300
Other income and expense	(61,000)	24,400
Income before taxes	$ 709,600	$ 1,422,700
Income taxes	296,400	537,100
Net income	$ 413,200	$ 885,600

1. Prepare common-sized income statements for CVS and Walgreen.
2. Compute the average sales per store for CVS and Walgreen. Round to thousands.
3. Analyze and comment on your results in (1) and (2).
4. Broker recommendations are reported on Yahoo.com's financial Web site (http://finance.yahoo.com/). The recommendations are ranked as follows:

Strong Buy	1
Buy	2
Hold	3
Sell	4
Strong Sell	5

Based upon your answer to (3), would you expect that the average broker recommendation for CVS to be higher (less favorable) or lower (more favorable) than for Walgreen? Compare your assessment with the average broker recommendation on Yahoo.com's financial Web site (http://finance.yahoo.com/). To find the broker recommendation, enter the stock symbols for CVS (CVS) and Walgreen (WAG) and click on "research." Appendix C at the end of the text provides more details about using Yahoo Finance for research.

Case 3–2

Cash-basis income statement

The following operating data (in thousands) were adapted from the 2001 SEC 10-K filings of Walgreen and CVS:

	CVS		Walgreen	
	2001	2000	2001	2000
Accounts receivable	$ 966,200	$ 824,500	$ 798,300	$ 614,500
Accounts payable	1,535,800	1,351,500	1,546,800	1,364,000
Accrued expenses payable	1,267,900	1,001,400	937,500	847,700

1. Using the preceding data, adjust the operating income for CVS and Walgreen shown in Case 3–1 to an adjusted cash basis. *Hint:* To convert to a cash basis, you need to compute the change in each accrual accounting item shown above and then either add or subtract the change to the operating income.
2. Compute the net difference between the operating income under the accrual and cash bases.
3. Express the net difference in (2) as a percent of operating income under the accrual basis.
4. Which company's operating income, CVS's or Walgreen's, is closer to the cash basis?
5. Do you think most analysts focus on operating income or net income in assessing the long-term profitability of a company? Explain.

Case 3–3

Cash basis vs. accrual basis financial statements

The local minor league baseball team, *The Hampton Hounds*, began their season in late April, with 5 home dates (and no road games) in April. The team's owner is seeking a short-term loan from the local bank to help fund some improvements. As a result, a statement of cash receipts and disbursements was prepared for the bank for April.

ETHICS

The owner estimates that the average cash receipts from tickets and concessions is $20,000 per home date. The average operating cash disbursements is $4,000 per home date. Players are paid the 15th of every month during the regular season (until Oct. 15th) at an average rate of $18,000 per month per player. All 25 players receive their first paycheck on May 15th. Rent is paid on the stadium on the first of every month during the playing season at a rate of $60,000 per month, with the first payment due on May 1st and the last payment due on September 1st. In addition to individual game sales, the Hounds sold 1,000 season tickets during the month of April at $720 per ticket. There are 160 total games in the season, half of which are home dates.

1. Prepare a statement of cash receipts and disbursements for April.
2. Prepare an accrual basis income statement for April. (*Hint:* Translate expenses into a per game basis and match against the revenue.)
3. Which statement best represents the results of operations for April?
4. Comment on management's intention to use the statement of cash receipts and disbursements to support the request for the bank loan rather than using an accrual-based income statement.

Case 3–4

Effect of events on financial statements

On September 11, 2001, two United Air Lines aircraft were hijacked and destroyed in terrorist attacks on the World Trade Center in New York City and in a crash near Johnstown, Pennsylvania. In addition to the loss of all passengers and crew on board the aircraft, these attacks resulted in numerous deaths and injuries to persons on the ground and massive property damage. In the immediate aftermath of the attacks, the FAA ordered all aircraft operating in the United States grounded immediately. This grounding effectively lasted for three days, and United was able to operate only a portion of its scheduled flights for several days thereafter. Passenger traffic and yields on United's flights declined significantly when flights were permitted to resume, and United refunded significant numbers of tickets for the period from September 11 to September 25.

The following data for United were adapted (in millions) from the Securities and Exchange Commission 10-K filing for the years ending December 31, 2000 and 1999:

	Year Ending December 31,	
	2000	**1999**
Operating income	$ 673	$1,342
Net income	52	1,204
Net cash flows from operating activities	2,358	2,415

1. Based upon the preceding data, develop an expectation of what you believe the operating income, net income, and net cash flows from operating activities would be for United Air Lines for the year ending December 31, 2001. Use the following format for your answers:

	Year Ending December 31, 2001
Operating income	$________
Net income	$________
Net cash flows from operating activities	$________

2. Would you report the loss related to the terrorist attacks separately in the income statement? If so, how?

Case 3–5

Analysis of income and cash flows

The following data (millions) for 2001, 2000, and 1999 were taken from 10-K filings with the Securities and Exchange Commission:

	2001	2000	1999
Company A			
Revenues	$20,092	$19,889	$19,284
Operating income	5,352	3,691	3,982
Net income	3,969	2,177	2,431
Net cash flows from operating activities	4,110	3,585	3,883
Net cash flows from investing activities	(1,188)	(1,165)	(3,421)
Net cash flows from financing activities	(2,830)	(2,072)	(471)
Total assets	22,417	20,834	21,623
Company B			
Revenues	$13,879	$16,741	$14,883
Operating income (loss)	(1,602)	1,637	1,318
Net income (loss)	(1,216)	828	1,208
Net cash flows from operating activities	236	2,898	2,647
Net cash flows from investing activities	(2,696)	(3,396)	(3,962)
Net cash flows from financing activities	3,306	239	2,270
Total assets	23,605	21,931	19,942
Company C			
Revenues	$ 3,122	$ 2,762	$ 1,640
Operating income (loss)	(412)	(864)	(606)
Net income (loss)	(567)	(1,411)	(720)
Net cash flows from operating activities	(120)	(130)	(91)
Net cash flows from investing activities	(253)	164	(952)
Net cash flows from financing activities	107	693	1,104
Total assets	1,638	2,135	2,466
Company D			
Revenues	$49,000	$45,352	$43,082
Operating income (loss)	2,183	1,739	1,534
Net income (loss)	877	613	247
Net cash flows from operating activities	2,281	1,548	1,838
Net cash flows from investing activities	(1,523)	(1,810)	(1,465)
Net cash flows from financing activities	(878)	280	(257)
Total assets	18,190	17,932	16,641

1. Match each of the following companies with the data for Company A, B, C, or D:

   Amazon.com
   Coca-Cola Inc.
   Delta Air Lines
   Kroger

2. Explain the logic underlying your matches.

Case 3-6

Analysis of income statements

Home Depot and Lowe's operate national chains of home improvement stores that sell a wide assortment of building materials and home improvement, lawn, and garden products, such as lumber, paint, wall coverings, lawn mowers, plumbing, and electrical supplies. Home Depot operates approximately 1,300 stores, while Lowe's operates approximately 740 stores. The following operating data (in thousands) were adapted from the 2002 SEC 10-K filings of Home Depot and Lowe's:

	Home Depot	Lowe's
Net sales	$53,553,000	$22,111,108
Cost of sales	37,406,000	15,743,267
Gross profit	$16,147,000	$ 6,367,841
Operating expenses	11,215,000	4,570,053
Operating income	$ 4,932,000	$ 1,797,788
Other income and expense	25,000	(173,537)
Income before taxes	$ 4,957,000	$ 1,624,251
Income taxes	1,913,000	600,989
Net income	$ 3,044,000	$ 1,023,262

1. Prepare common-sized income statements for Home Depot and Lowe's.
2. Compute the average sales per store for Home Depot and Lowe's. Round to thousands.
3. Analyze and comment on your results in (1) and (2).
4. Broker recommendations are reported on Yahoo.com's financial Web site (http://finance.yahoo.com/). The recommendations are ranked as follows:

Strong Buy	1
Buy	2
Hold	3
Sell	4
Strong Sell	5

Based upon your answer to (3), would you expect that the average broker recommendation for Home Depot to be higher (less favorable) or lower (more favorable) than for Lowe's? Compare your assessment with the average broker recommendation on Yahoo.com's financial Web site (http://finance.yahoo.com/). To find the broker recommendation, enter the stock symbols for Home Depot (HD) and Lowe's (LOW) and click on "research." Appendix C at the end of the text provides more details about using Yahoo Finance for research.

Building Leadership Skills—Responsible Leadership

Activity 3–1

Accrued expense

On December 30, 2003, you buy a Ford Expedition. It comes with a three-year, 36,000-mile warranty. On January 21, 2004, you return the Expedition to the dealership for some basic repairs covered under the warranty. The cost of the repairs to the dealership is $315. In what year, 2003 or 2004, should Ford Motor Co. recognize the cost of the warranty repairs as an expense?

Activity 3–2

Account for revenue

State College requires students to pay tuition each term before classes begin. Students who have not paid their tuition are not allowed to enroll or to attend classes.

What accounts do you think would be used by State College to record the receipt of the students' tuition payments? Describe the nature of each account.

Activity 3–3

Accrued revenue

The following is an excerpt from a conversation between Karen Wyer and Jim Harris just before they boarded a flight to Puerto Rico on United Airlines. They are going to Puerto Rico to attend their company's annual sales conference.

Karen: Jim, aren't you taking an accounting course at City College?

Jim: Yes, I decided it's about time I learned something about accounting. You know, our annual bonuses are based upon the sales figures that come from the accounting department.

Karen: I guess I never really thought about it.

Jim: You should think about it! Last year, I placed a $250,000 order on December 23. But when I got my bonus, the $250,000 sale wasn't included. They said it hadn't been shipped until January 4, so it would have to count in next year's bonus.

Karen: A real bummer!

Jim: Right! I was counting on that bonus including the $250,000 sale.

Karen: Did you complain?

Jim: Yes, but it didn't do any good. Jacob, the head accountant, said something about matching revenues and expenses. Also, something about not recording revenues until the sale is final. I figure I'd take the accounting course and find out whether he's just jerking me around.

Karen: I never really thought about it. When do you think United Airlines will record its revenues from this flight?

Jim: Mmm . . . I guess it could record the revenue when it sells the ticket . . . or . . . when the boarding passes are taken at the door . . . or . . . when we get off the plane . . . or when our company pays for the tickets . . . or . . . I don't know. I'll ask my accounting instructor.

Discuss when United Airlines should recognize the revenue from ticket sales to properly match revenues and expenses.

Activity 3–4

Adjustments for financial statements

Several years ago, your father opened Derby Television Repair Inc. He made a small initial investment and added money from his personal bank account as needed. He withdrew money for living expenses at irregular intervals. As the business grew, he hired an assistant. He is now considering adding more employees, purchasing additional service trucks, and purchasing the building he now rents. To secure funds for the expansion, your father submitted a loan application to the bank and included the most recent financial statements (as follows) prepared from accounts maintained by a part-time bookkeeper.

Derby Television Repair Inc. Income Statement For the Year Ended December 31, 2004		
Service revenue		$66,900
Less: Rent paid	$18,000	
Wages paid	16,500	
Supplies paid	7,000	
Utilities paid	3,100	
Insurance paid	3,000	
Miscellaneous payments	2,150	49,750
Net income		$17,150

Derby Television Repair Inc. Balance Sheet December 31, 2004	
Assets	
Cash	$ 3,750
Amounts due from customers	2,100
Truck	25,000
Total assets	$30,850
Equities	
Stockholders' equity	$30,850

After reviewing the financial statements, the loan officer at the bank asked your father if he used the accrual basis of accounting for revenues and expenses. Your father responded that he did, and that is why he included an account for "Amounts Due from Customers." The loan officer then asked whether or not the accounts were adjusted prior to the preparation of the statements. Your father answered that they had not been adjusted.

a. Why do you think the loan officer suspected that the accounts had not been adjusted prior to the preparation of the statements?
b. Indicate possible accounts that might need to be adjusted before an accurate set of financial statements could be prepared.

Activity 3–5

Compare balance sheets

Compare the balance sheets of two different companies, and present to the class a summary of the similarities and differences of the two companies. You may obtain the balance sheets you need from one of the following sources:

1. Your school or local library.
2. The investor relations department of each company.
3. The company's Web site on the Internet.
4. EDGAR (Electronic Data Gathering, Analysis, and Retrieval), the electronic archives of financial statements filed with the Securities and Exchange Commission. The EDGAR address is www.sec.gov/edgarhp.htm. To obtain annual report information, click on "Search for Company Filings," then click on "Search for Companies and Filings." Type in a company name on the "EDGAR Company Search" form. EDGAR will list the reports available for the selected company. A

company's annual report (along with other information) is provided in its annual 10-K report to the SEC. Click on the 10-K (or 10-K405) report for the year you wish to download. If you wish, you can save the whole 10-K report to a file and then open it with your word processor. Appendix C at the end of the text provides more details about using EDGAR for research.

Activity 3-6

Business strategy

GROUP ACTIVITY

Assume that you and two friends are debating whether to open an automotive and service retail chain that will be called Auto-Mart. Initially, Auto-Mart will open three stores locally, but the business plan anticipates going nationwide within five years.

Currently, you and your future business partners are debating whether to focus Auto-Mart on a "do-it-yourself" or "do-it-for-me" business strategy. A "do-it-yourself" business strategy emphasizes the sale of retail auto parts that customers will use themselves to repair and service their cars. A "do-it-for-me" business strategy emphasizes the offering of maintenance and service for customers.

1. In groups of three or four, discuss whether to implement a "do-it-yourself" or "do-it-for-me" business strategy. List the advantages of each strategy and arrive at a conclusion as to which strategy to implement.
2. Provide examples of real world businesses that use "do-it-yourself" or "do-it-for-me" business strategies.

Answers to Self-Study Questions

1. **A** Under the accrual basis of accounting, revenues are recorded when the services are rendered. Since the services were rendered during June, all the fees should be recorded on June 30 (Answer A). This is an example of accrued revenue. Under the cash basis of accounting, revenues are recorded when the cash is collected, not necessarily when the fees are earned. Thus, no revenue would be recorded in June, $8,500 of revenue would be recorded in July, and $6,500 of revenue would be recorded in August (Answer D). Answers B and C are incorrect and are not used under either the accrual or cash bases.
2. **C** The collection of a $5,700 accounts receivable is recorded as an increase in Cash, $5,700, and a decrease in Accounts Receivable, $5,700 (Answer C). The initial recording of the fees earned on account is recorded as an increase in Accounts Receivable and an increase in Fees Earned (Answer B). Services rendered for cash are recorded as an increase in Cash and an increase in Fees Earned (Answer D). Answer A is incorrect and would result in the accounting equation being out of balance because total assets would exceed total liabilities and stockholders' equity by $11,400.
3. **A** A deferral is the delay in recording an expense already paid, such as prepaid insurance (answer A). Wages payable (answer B) is considered an accrued expense or accrued liability. Fees earned (answer C) is a revenue item. Accumulated depreciation (answer D) is a contra account to a fixed asset.
4. **D** The balance in the supplies account, before adjustment, represents the amount of supplies available during the period. From this amount ($2,250) is subtracted the amount of supplies on hand ($950) to determine the supplies used ($1,300). The used supplies is recorded as an increase in Supplies Expense, $1,300, and a decrease in Supplies, $1,300 (Answer D).
5. **C** The failure to record the adjusting entry increasing Rent Revenue, $600, and decreasing Unearned Rent, $600, would have the effect of overstating liabilities by $600 and understating net income by $600 (answer C).

Chapter 4
Accounting Information Systems

THE LAW OF RESPECT

"People naturally follow leaders stronger than themselves."

–The 21 Irrefutable Laws of Leadership

Dr. John C. Maxwell

Learning Goals

1 Describe the nature of business information systems.

2 Describe the nature of accounting information systems.

3 Describe and illustrate the basic elements of transaction processing systems.

4 Describe and illustrate the basic elements of a financial reporting system.

5 Describe and illustrate the computation and use of earnings before interest, taxes, depreciation, and amortization (EBITDA).

Amazon.com

Would you buy stock in a company named "Abracadabra"? Jeff Bezos, the chief executive officer and founder of Amazon.com, initially considered naming the company "Abracadabra" because he liked the way it sounded. However, it was too long for a company name, so he considered shortening it to "Cadabra." When an attorney inadvertently referred to the company as "Cadaver" (a dead body or corpse), Bezos decided to change the name. "Amazon" was chosen because of the South American river that can seem endless.

Bezos first thought about starting an Internet-based business in 1994, after he became aware that the Internet user base was growing at a rate of over 2000 percent per year. He realized that by acting quickly he could gain a first-mover advantage in e-commerce. For example, by being the first online retailer, he could build customer loyalty that later competitors might have difficulty overcoming. In addition, he could develop innovative technology that could be patented or copyrighted to prevent competitors from duplicating. Such innovations included search technologies, secure shopping, fulfillment processes, and one-click shopping.

When did Bezos decide to sell books online? First, online retailing of books would give Amazon several advantages over traditional booksellers, such as Barnes & Noble. A traditional bookstore chain stocks thousands of books in stores throughout the country. In contrast, Amazon could stock only a few books in its warehouse and ship them as ordered. Thus, Amazon could realize significant cost savings from carrying less inventory. In addition, traditional bookstore chains need to cover the costs that result from operating and maintaining hundreds of store locations. By avoiding these traditional costs, Amazon could offer discounted prices that were considerably lower than the traditional stores. For example, Amazon offers discounts of as much as 50 percent on best sellers and 20 percent on other books.

On July 16, 1995, Amazon opened its Web site for business by offering over a million book titles. Within thirty days, it had sold books in all 50 states and in 45 foreign countries. Today, Amazon offers over 18 million products, including music, DVDs, cell phones, computers, cameras, software, tools, toys, and kitchen appliances. Recently, Amazon reported over $1 billion in sales in one quarter alone.

On May 15, 1997, Amazon did an initial public offering (IPO) and sold its stock to the public at a price of $18. The stock has since split numerous times, such that the initial offering price would now be the equivalent of only $1.50. As a result, Jeff and his parents, who initially invested $300,000 of their savings, have become billionaires.

Is Amazon making a profit? In 2001, it reported its first profitable quarter and has yet to report an annual profit. In fact, as of December 31, 2001, Amazon reported negative retained earnings (an accumulated deficit) of $3 billion.

In this chapter, we will describe the basic elements of business and accounting information systems. These elements are used by all businesses, including Amazon.com, to record and summarize transactions for use in decision making and preparing financial statements.

Sources: *Time Magazine*, "1999 Person of the Year, Jeff Bezos," December 27, 1999; and "A Profitable Amazon Looks to Do an Encore," *The New York Times*, by Saul Hansell, January 26, 2002.

Your Need to Know

When you shop at Wal-Mart or Target, go to a movie theatre, buy gas at an Exxon or BP station, buy groceries at Kroger or Supervalu, buy a ticket to fly on United or American Airlines, or order a pizza from Pizza Hut or Domino's, you enter into a transaction that is captured, processed, and recorded by the business. At Wal-Mart, for example, cash register clerks use an electronic scanner to read the bar code off the item purchased. The cash register displays the price, and the cashier completes the transaction when you pay for the merchandise. But the transaction processing doesn't stop at this point. Periodically, each Wal-Mart store sends its sales data to the corporate office for updating the company records. This process includes recording the sales and the cost of merchandise sold as well as updating other records, such as inventory, customer buying habits, and individual store records.

As a customer, understanding how transactions are processed by a business's information system is not usually important to you. If you own a business or work for a business, however, understanding the accounting information system is important to your career. For example, you need to understand how to interpret and analyze business reports. This interpretation and analysis includes understanding how the reports were generated and whether the reports reflect all the relevant data necessary to make business decisions. For example, Wal-Mart analyzes each store's profitability through store income statements. While such income statements may measure store profitability, they do not directly measure customer satisfaction considerations, such as the amount of time customers stand in line waiting to check out, the friendliness of store associates, or the cleanliness of the store.

In this chapter, we begin by discussing the nature of business information systems. We then describe the nature of accounting information systems and their subsystems, including the management reporting, transaction processing, and financial reporting systems. Our primary focus in this chapter is on the elements of transaction processing and financial reporting systems. The elements of these systems are the same for Wal-Mart and Exxon as for the local convenience store or hardware store.

Business Information Systems

1 Describe the nature of business information systems.

In prior chapters, we discussed how businesses report their financial condition and changes in financial condition through financial statements. We described and illustrated how small businesses and individuals use the cash basis of accounting, while large, publicly held companies use the accrual basis of accounting. In those chapters, we used the accounting equation as the framework for recording and summarizing transactions and generating the resulting financial statements. While this framework may be used for a small number of transactions, it is not very efficient for recording millions of transactions daily by large corporations such as Home Depot or Wal-Mart.

In this chapter, we focus on how accounting information systems are designed to efficiently record a large number of transactions. We show how basic controls in the accounting system provide assurance that transactions are accurately recorded. We begin by describing generic business information systems.

A **business information system** collects and processes data and distributes the information to users. All business information systems share common elements that include data sources, data collection, data processing, database management, information generation, and users. These elements of business information systems are shown in Exhibit 1.

In designing a business information system, the end users of the information must first be identified and their information needs determined. Users can be classified as internal users, such as managers and operational employees, and external users, such as creditors, stockholders, regulatory agencies, suppliers and customers. The information needs of internal users vary widely throughout the business in both form and content. In contrast,

Exhibit 1

Business Information Systems

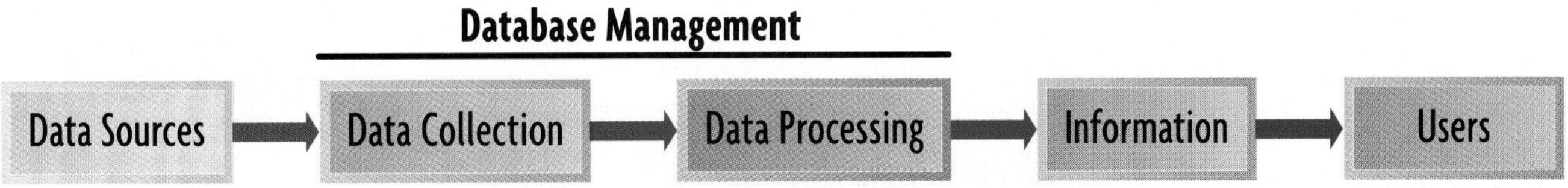

external users require information in standardized formats, such as tax forms, regulatory filings, and financial statements.

Once the information needs of users have been determined, the business information system must be designed to collect the necessary data and process the data into the required information. For example, a business's personnel information system requires data to be collected, such as anticipated and actual work schedules, training needs, accrued vacation time, sick leave, pay scales, and workmen's compensation requirements. Controls should be designed into the collection process to ensure that the data are accurate, timely, and complete. Likewise, controls should be designed into the information system so that errors in processing data are prevented and detected. For example, the personnel system should include a processing control that would prevent an employee from accruing vacation time beyond the total allowable by the business.

In practice, businesses have a variety of information systems. Examples of such systems include sales order, transportation, human resources, purchasing, and accounting systems. Each system should be linked to the other systems for operational efficiency and effectiveness. In the remainder of this chapter, we focus on accounting information systems.

Ethics in Action

Controls to Prevent Fraud

Controls are often placed in accounting information systems to prevent fraud. For example, payroll checks should not be issued to employees without appropriate authorization. Such authorization prevents checks from being issued fraudulently to fictitious employees or for time not worked.

Basic Accounting Systems

2 Describe the nature of accounting information systems.

An **accounting information system** processes financial and operational data into reports useful to internal and external stakeholders. As shown in Exhibit 2, accounting information systems normally consist of the following three subsystems: (1) the management reporting system, (2) the transaction processing system, and (3) the financial reporting system.

Exhibit 2

Accounting Information System

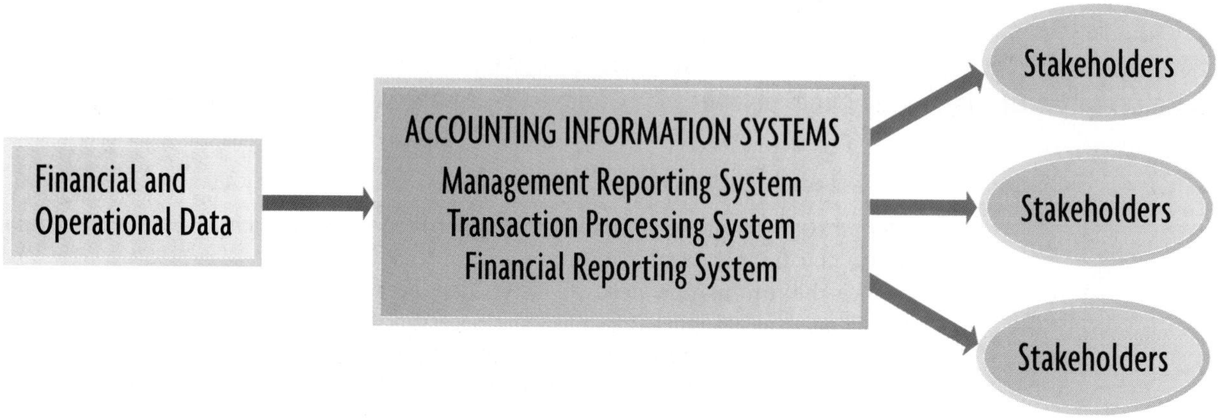

The **management reporting system** provides internal information to assist managers in making decisions. The form and content of the information will vary, depending upon the decisions. The information may include either financial information, such as the effects of a proposed acquisition on the financial statements, or nonfinancial information, such as the number of back orders, on-time deliveries, or customer returns. Examples of such reports could include budgets, variance analyses, cost-volume-profit analyses, sales mix analyses, and employee turnover. The area of accounting that focuses on developing management reporting systems is called *managerial accounting.*

The **transaction processing system** records and summarizes the effects of financial transactions on the business. Large businesses enter into thousands and, in some cases, millions of transactions daily. To efficiently process such a large volume of transactions, most businesses group similar, repetitive transactions into transaction cycles. The most common transaction cycles are the revenue cycle, the purchasing cycle, the payroll cycle, the inventory cycle, and the treasury cycle.

Revenue cycle transactions involve providing services or selling products. They include collecting payments for the services or products. The *purchasing cycle* transactions involve buying assets or services for use in the normal operations of the business. Included in the purchasing cycle is the payment for the goods or services. *Payroll cycle* transactions involve paying employees. *Inventory cycle* transactions involve converting raw materials into a finished product through the use of a production process. Manufacturing businesses have an inventory cycle. Merchandising businesses buy products ready for sale. *Treasury cycle* transactions involve financing the operations of the business. Examples of treasury cycle transactions include issuing capital stock or long-term debt. Paying dividends and redeeming long-term debt would also be types of treasury cycle transactions.

The **financial reporting system** produces financial statements and other reports for external stakeholders. The financial reporting system is closely interrelated to the transaction processing system in that the financial statements summarize the effects of transactions on the financial condition and changes in financial condition of the business. The financial reporting system also summarizes transactions for other stakeholders in reports such as tax returns and other regulatory reports.

Our primary focus in this text is on the transaction processing and financial reporting systems. In this chapter, we describe and illustrate the basic elements of these two systems.

Strategy in Business

What's Next for Amazon?

Amazon.com built its online business strategy on offering books at significant discounts that traditional chains couldn't match. Over the years, Amazon has expanded its online offerings to include DVDs, toys, electronics, and even kitchen appliances. But can its low-cost, discount strategy continue to work across a variety of products? Some have their doubts. The electronics business has lower margins and more competition than books. For example, Dell Computers is already an established low-cost provider of personal computers and software. In addition, some electronic manufacturers such as Sony are protective of their prices and have refused to make Amazon.com an authorized dealer. As Lauren Levitan, a noted financial analyst, recently said, "It's hard to be the low-cost retailer. You have to execute flawlessly on a very consistent basis. Most people who try a low-price strategy fail." This risk of failing at the low-cost strategy was validated by Kmart's filing for bankruptcy protection in 2002 because of its inability to compete with Wal-Mart's low prices.

Source: Saul Hansell, "A Profitable Amazon Looks to Do an Encore," *The New York Times*, January 26, 2002.

Transaction Processing Systems

3 Describe and illustrate the basic elements of transaction processing systems.

The basic elements of transaction processing systems have evolved over centuries, beginning with the earliest known economic activity and ending with today's highly computerized and integrated information systems. These elements include accounts and rules for recording transactions in accounts, journals, and ledgers. In addition, the system should include controls to prevent and detect errors in the recording and summarization process.

The Account

In Chapters 2 and 3, we recorded and summarized transactions by using the accounting equation. Each financial statement item was represented in the equation. Transactions were recorded as pluses or minuses for each item affected by the transaction. Detecting and preventing errors in processing transactions was controlled by monitoring the equality of the accounting equation. That is, total assets must equal total liabilities plus stockholders' equity.

While the simple system illustrated in Chapters 2 and 3 allowed us to record and summarize transactions for a small business with few transactions, it would be inefficient for a large business with thousands or even millions of transactions daily. One element in which transactions are recorded efficiently is the *account.*

An **account**, in its simplest form, has three parts. First, each account has a title, which is the name of the item recorded in the account. Second, each account has a space for recording increases in the amount of the item. Third, each account has a space for recording decreases in the amount of the item. The account form presented below is called a *T account* because it resembles the letter T. The left side of the account is called the *debit* side, and the right side is called the *credit* side.

TITLE	
Left side *Debit*	Right side *Credit*

Amounts entered on the left side of an account, regardless of the account title, are called **debits** to the account. When debits are entered in an account, the account is said to be *debited* (or charged). Amounts entered on the right side of an account are called **credits**, and the account is said to be *credited*. Debits and credits are sometimes abbreviated as *Dr.* and *Cr.*

In the cash account that follows, transactions involving cash receipts are listed on the debit side of the account. The transactions involving cash payments are listed on the credit side. If at any time the total cash receipts ($10,950) is needed, the entries on the debit side of the account are added. The total of the cash payments on the credit side, $6,850 in the example, is determined in a similar manner. Subtracting the payments from the receipts, $10,950 − $6,850, determines the amount of cash on hand, $4,100. This amount is called the **balance of the account**. This balance should be identified as a debit balance in some way, such as showing the balance on the debit side of the account or simply listing it as a debit balance.

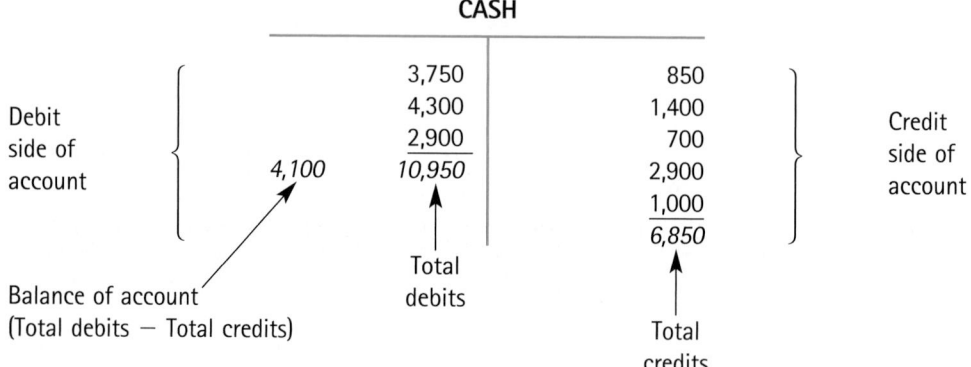

		CASH		
Debit side of account		3,750	850	Credit side of account
		4,300	1,400	
		2,900	700	
	4,100	*10,950*	2,900	
			1,000	
			6,850	
	Balance of account (Total debits − Total credits)	Total debits	Total credits	

Rules of Debit and Credit

Why did we record increases in the cash account as debits and decreases as credits? The simple answer is because of convention. That is, a standardized method of recording increases and decreases in accounts is essential in order that businesses record transactions in a similar manner. If each business recorded transactions differently, the result would be chaotic and comparability between companies would be lost.

The standardized **rules of debit and credit** are shown in Exhibit 3. These standardized rules are used by all businesses—from the corner gas station to the largest public corporation.

Exhibit 3 shows several important characteristics of the rules of debit and credit. First, the normal balance of an account is the side of the account used to record increases. Thus, the normal balance of an asset account is a debit balance, while the normal balance of a liability account is a credit balance. This characteristic is often useful in detecting errors in the recording process. That is, when an account normally having a debit balance actually has a credit balance, or vice versa, an error may have occurred or an unusual situation may exist.

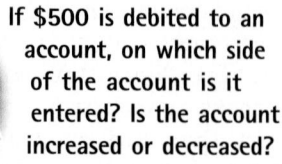

If $500 is debited to an account, on which side of the account is it entered? Is the account increased or decreased?

The $500 is entered on the left side of the account. Whether the $500 increases or decreases the account depends on what kind of account is involved.

To illustrate, assume that at the end of the period the cash account has a credit balance. In this case, either an error has occurred or the company has overdrawn its bank account. Likewise, if accounts payable has a debit balance, then an error has occurred or the company has over-

Exhibit 3

Rules of Debit and Credit

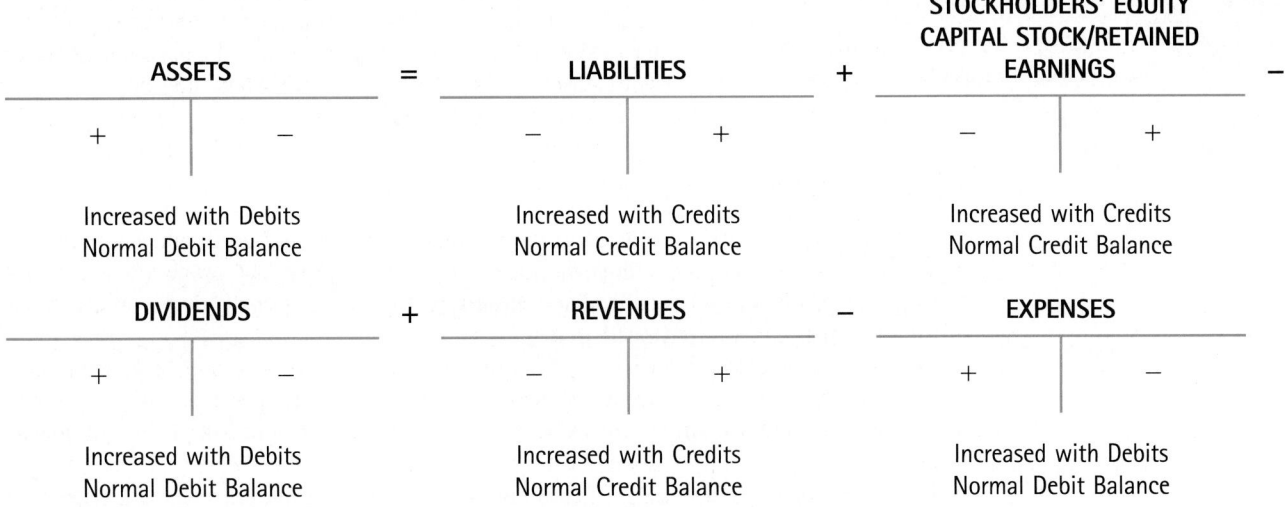

ASSETS		=	LIABILITIES		+	STOCKHOLDERS' EQUITY CAPITAL STOCK/RETAINED EARNINGS		−
+	−		−	+		−	+	
Increased with Debits Normal Debit Balance			Increased with Credits Normal Credit Balance			Increased with Credits Normal Credit Balance		

DIVIDENDS		+	REVENUES		−	EXPENSES	
+	−		−	+		+	−
Increased with Debits Normal Debit Balance			Increased with Credits Normal Credit Balance			Increased with Debits Normal Debit Balance	

paid its accounts payable. On the other hand, a credit balance in the office equipment or land account can only result from an error in the recording process. That is, a company cannot have negative office equipment or land. Thus, the normal balances of accounts provide a degree of control in the recording process.

The second characteristic shown in Exhibit 3 is that accounts on the left side of the accounting equation (the assets side) are increased by debits and have normal debit balances, while accounts on the right side of the accounting equation (liability and stockholders' equity side) are increased by credits and have normal credit balances. On the asset (left hand) side of the equation, the only exception to the preceding relationship is that some asset accounts, called contra asset accounts, are normally increased by credits and have normal credit balances. As the name contra asset implies, these accounts offset the normal debit balances of asset accounts. For example, accumulated depreciation, an offset to plant assets, is increased by credits and has a normal credit balance. Thus, accumulated depreciation is a contra asset account.

On the liability and stockholders' equity (right hand) side of the equation, the only exceptions to the preceding relationship are the dividend and expense accounts. The payment of dividends decreases stockholders' equity (retained earnings); thus, the dividends account is increased by debits and has a normal debit balance. In this sense, the dividends account can be thought of as a type of contra account to retained earnings. However, unlike contra asset accounts, the dividends account is closed to retained earnings at the end of the period. In this way, dividends for each period are recorded and accounted for separately.

Revenue increases stockholders' equity (retained earnings), and thus revenue accounts are increased by credits and have normal credit balances. In contrast, expenses decrease stockholders' equity (retained earnings). Thus, expense accounts are increased by debits and have a normal debit balance. Like dividends, expense accounts can be thought of as a type of contra account. In this case, expenses can be thought of as contra accounts to revenues. Like dividends, revenue and expense accounts are closed at the end of the period.

The third characteristic of the rules of debit and credit is that for each transaction the total debits will equal the total credits. That is, each transaction must be recorded so that the total debits for the transaction will equal the total credits. For example, assume that a company pays cash of $500 for supplies. The asset account supplies will be debited (increased) by $500 and cash will be credited (decreased) by $500. Likewise, if the company provides services and receives $2,000 from customers, cash will be debited (increased) and fees earned will be credited (increased) by $2,000. Debits equaling the credits for each

A credit balance in which of the following accounts—Cash, Dividends, Unearned Revenue—would indicate that an error had occurred?

Dividends. If Cash has a credit balance, the business may have overdrawn its bank account.

transaction provides a degree of control in the recording process.

To summarize, each transaction is recorded under the rules shown in Exhibit 3. Under these rules, the total debits will equal the total credits for each transaction, because the equality of the debits and credits is built into the accounting equation: Assets = Liabilities + Stockholders' Equity.

The Journal

Each transaction is initially entered in chronological order in a record called a **journal**. In this way, the journal documents the history of the company. The process of recording transactions in the journal is called **journalizing**. The specific transaction record entered in the journal is called a **journal entry**.

In practice, most journal entries are automated with the transaction processing system. However, transactions that are unusual, correcting, or infrequent may require manual entries. We stress manual entries in this text to help you understand the automated framework.

A business may use a variety of formats for recording journal entries. It may use one all-purpose journal, sometimes called a *general journal*, or it may use several journals. In the latter case, a *special journal* is designed to record a single kind of transaction that occurs frequently. To simplify, we will use a basic, two-column general journal in the remainder of this chapter to illustrate the manual journalizing of transactions.

Ethics in Action

Will journalizing prevent fraud?

While journalizing transactions reduces the possibility of fraud, it by no means eliminates it. For example, embezzlement can be hidden within the double-entry bookkeeping system by creating fictitious suppliers to whom checks are issued.

Assume that on November 1, 2004, Shannon Hughes organizes a corporation that will be known as Online Solutions. The first phase of Shannon's business plan is to operate Online Solutions as a service business that provides assistance to individuals and small businesses in developing Web pages and in configuring and installing application software. Shannon expects this initial phase of the business to last one to two years. During this period, Shannon will gather information on the software and hardware needs of customers. During the second phase of the business plan, Shannon plans to expand Online Solutions into an Internet-based retailer of software and hardware of individuals and small businesses.

To start the business, Shannon deposits $25,000 in a bank account in the name of Online Solutions in return for shares of stock in the corporation. This first transaction increases cash and capital stock by $25,000. The transaction is entered in the general journal by first listing the date, then the title of the account to be debited and the amount of the debit. Next, the title of the account to be credited is listed below and to the right of the debit, followed by the amount to be credited. The resulting journal entry follows.

2004				
Nov.	1	Cash	25,000	
		Capital Stock		25,000

The increase in the asset is debited to the cash account. The increase in stockholders' equity (capital stock) is credited to the capital stock account. As other assets are acquired, the increases are also recorded as debits to asset accounts. Likewise, other increases in stockholders' equity will be recorded as credits to stockholders' equity accounts.

Online Solutions entered into the following additional transactions during the remainder of November:

Nov. 5 Purchased land for $20,000, paying cash. The land is located in a new business park with convenient access to transportation facilities. Shannon Hughes plans to rent office space and equipment during the first phase of Online Solutions' business plan. During the second phase, Shannon plans to build an office and warehouse on the land.

10 Purchased supplies on account for $1,350.

18 Received $7,500 for services provided to customers for cash.

30 Paid expenses as follows: wages, $2,125; rent, $800; utilities, $450; and miscellaneous, $275.

30 Paid creditors on account, $950.

30 Paid stockholders (Shannon Hughes) dividends of $2,000.

The journal entries to record these transactions are shown below.

Nov.	5	Land	20,000	
		Cash		20,000
	10	Supplies	1,350	
		Accounts Payable		1,350
	18	Cash	7,500	
		Fees Earned		7,500
	30	Wages Expense	2,125	
		Rent Expense	800	
		Utilities Expense	450	
		Miscellaneous Expense	275	
		Cash		3,650
	30	Accounts Payable	950	
		Cash		950
	30	Dividends	2,000	
		Cash		2,000

Posting to the Ledger

As we discussed in the preceding section, a transaction is first recorded in the journal. The journal thus provides a chronological history of transactions. Periodically, the journal entries must be transferred to the accounts. The group of accounts for a business is called its **general ledger**. The list of accounts in the general ledger is called the **chart of accounts**. The accounts are normally listed in the order in which they appear in the financial statements, beginning with the balance sheet and concluding with the income statement. The chart of accounts for Online Solutions is shown in Exhibit 4.

Exhibit 4

Chart of Accounts for Online Solutions

Balance Sheet Accounts

Assets

Cash
Accounts Receivable
Supplies
Prepaid Insurance
Office Equipment
Accumulated Depreciation
Land

Liabilities

Accounts Payable
Wages Payable
Unearned Rent

Stockholders' Equity

Capital Stock
Retained Earnings
Dividends

Income Statement Accounts

Revenue

Fees Earned
Rent Revenue

Expenses

Wages Expense
Rent Expense
Depreciation Expense
Utilities Expense
Supplies Expense
Insurance Expense
Miscellaneous Expense

The process of transferring the debits and credits from the journal entries to the accounts in the ledger is called **posting**. To illustrate the posting process, Online Solutions' November 1st transaction, along with its posting to the cash and capital stock accounts, is shown in Exhibit 5.

Exhibit 5

Posting a Journal Entry

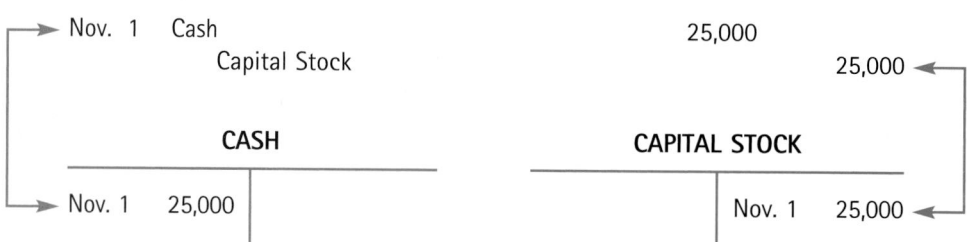

Nov. 1	Cash	25,000	
	Capital Stock		25,000

CASH

Nov. 1 25,000	

CAPITAL STOCK

	Nov. 1 25,000

The debits and credits for each journal entry are posted to the accounts in the order in which they occur in the journal. In posting to the accounts, the date is entered followed by the amount of the entry. After the journal entries are posted, the ledger becomes a chronological history of transactions by account. The posting of Online Solutions' remaining journal entries is shown in Exhibit 6. Posting is performed automatically in computerized systems. In Exhibit 6, however, we illustrate the concept by posting manually.

Trial Balance

How can you be sure that you have not made an error in posting the debits and credits to the ledger? One way is to determine the equality of the debit and credit balances of accounts in the ledger. This equality should be proved at the end of each accounting period, if not more often. Such a proof, called a **trial balance**, may be in the form of a computer printout or in the form shown in Exhibit 7, which lists the balances shown in Exhibit 6.

The trial balance does not provide complete proof of accuracy of the ledger. It indicates only that the debits and the credits are equal. This proof is of value, however, because errors often affect the equality of debits

Cash of $450 was received on account, but was recorded as a $540 debit to Cash and a $540 debit to Accounts Receivable. Would the trial balance totals be equal?

No. The debit total would exceed the credit total by $1,080.

Exhibit 6

Ledger for Online Solutions–November

CASH

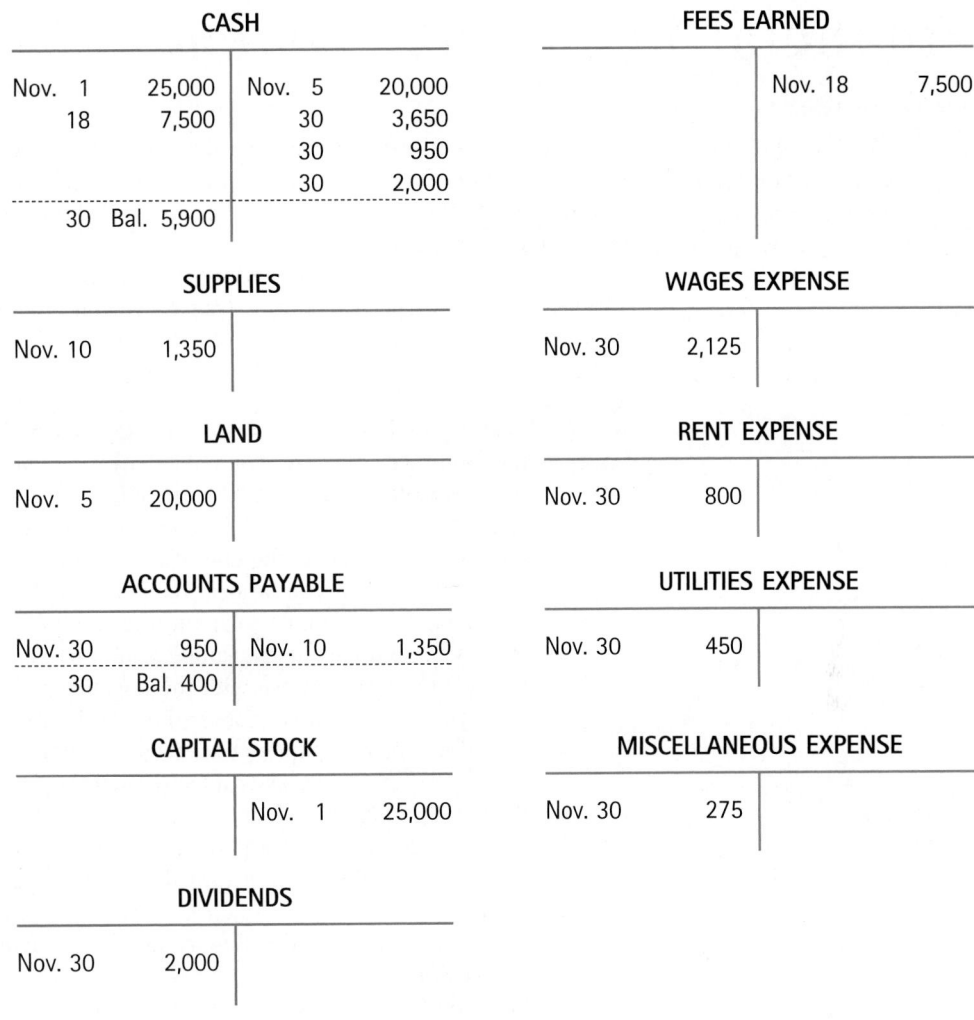

Nov. 1	25,000	Nov. 5	20,000
18	7,500	30	3,650
		30	950
		30	2,000
30 Bal.	5,900		

FEES EARNED

		Nov. 18	7,500

SUPPLIES

Nov. 10	1,350		

WAGES EXPENSE

Nov. 30	2,125		

LAND

Nov. 5	20,000		

RENT EXPENSE

Nov. 30	800		

ACCOUNTS PAYABLE

Nov. 30	950	Nov. 10	1,350
30 Bal.	400		

UTILITIES EXPENSE

Nov. 30	450		

CAPITAL STOCK

		Nov. 1	25,000

MISCELLANEOUS EXPENSE

Nov. 30	275		

DIVIDENDS

Nov. 30	2,000		

Exhibit 7

Trial Balance

Online Solutions
Trial Balance
November 30, 2004

Cash	5,900	
Supplies	1,350	
Land	20,000	
Accounts Payable		400
Capital Stock		25,000
Dividends	2,000	
Fees Earned		7,500
Wages Expense	2,125	
Rent Expense	800	
Utilities Expense	450	
Miscellaneous Expense	275	
	32,900	32,900

and credits. If the two totals of a trial balance are not equal, an error has occurred. In such a case, the error must be located and corrected before financial statements are prepared.

Financial Reporting System

4 Describe and illustrate the basic elements of a financial reporting system.

In the prior section, we described and illustrated the basic elements of a transaction processing system. In this section, we continue this illustration to include the basic elements of a financial reporting system. These elements include adjusting entries, financial statements, and closing entries.

As a review of transaction processing systems and as a basis for illustrating a double-entry accounting financial reporting system, we continue our illustration of Online Solutions. During December, assume that Online Solutions entered into the following transactions:

Dec.	1	Paid a premium of $2,400 for a comprehensive insurance policy covering liability, theft, and fire. The policy covers a two-year period.
	1	Paid rent for December, $800. The company from which Online Solutions is renting its store space now requires the payment of rent on the first of each month, rather than at the end of the month.
	1	Received an offer from a local retailer to rent the land purchased on November 5. The retailer plans to use the land as a parking lot for its employees and customers. Online Solutions agreed to rent the land to the retailer for three months, with the rent payable in advance. Online Solutions received $360 for three months' rent beginning December 1.
	4	Purchased office equipment on account from Executive Supply Co. for $1,800.
	6	Paid $180 for a newspaper advertisement.
	11	Paid creditors $400.
	13	Paid a receptionist and a part-time assistant $950 for two weeks' wages.
	16	Received $3,100 from fees earned for the first half of December.
	16	Earned fees on account totaling $1,750 for the first half of December.
	20	Paid $1,800 to Executive Supply Co. on the debt owed from the December 4 transaction.
	21	Received $650 from customers in payment of their accounts.
	23	Purchased $1,450 of supplies by paying $550 cash and charging the remainder on account.
	27	Paid the receptionist and the part-time assistant $1,200 for two weeks' wages.
	31	Paid $310 telephone bill for the month.
	31	Paid $225 electric bill for the month.
	31	Received $2,870 from fees earned for the second half of December.
	31	Earned fees on account totaling $1,120 for the second half of December.
	31	Paid dividends of $2,000 to stockholders.

The journal entries for the December transactions are shown in Exhibit 8. The posting of the journal entries to the ledger accounts is shown in Exhibit 14.

Exhibit 8

Journal Entries: December Transactions for Online Solutions

Dec.	1	Prepaid Insurance	2,400	
		Cash		2,400
	1	Rent Expense	800	
		Cash		800
	1	Cash	360	
		Unearned Rent		360
	4	Office Equipment	1,800	
		Accounts Payable		1,800

(continued)

Exhibit 8
Concluded

Dec.	6	Miscellaneous Expense	180	
		Cash		180
	11	Accounts Payable	400	
		Cash		400
	13	Wages Expense	950	
		Cash		950
	16	Cash	3,100	
		Fees Earned		3,100
	16	Accounts Receivable	1,750	
		Fees Earned		1,750
	20	Accounts Payable	1,800	
		Cash		1,800
	21	Cash	650	
		Accounts Receivable		650
	23	Supplies	1,450	
		Cash		550
		Accounts Payable		900
	27	Wages Expense	1,200	
		Cash		1,200
	31	Utilities Expense	310	
		Cash		310
	31	Utilities Expense	225	
		Cash		225
	31	Cash	2,870	
		Fees Earned		2,870
	31	Accounts Receivable	1,120	
		Fees Earned		1,120
	31	Dividends	2,000	
		Cash		2,000

Adjusting Entries

In Chapter 3, we described and illustrated various adjustments necessary in preparing financial statements. In this section, we illustrate this process for Online Solutions, using the double-entry accounting system. However, before we begin this process, we prepare the trial balance shown in Exhibit 9 (on page 162) to make sure that no error has occurred in posting December transactions to the general ledger.

The adjustment data for Online Solutions as of December 31, 2004, are as follows:

Supplies on hand at December 31, $760.
Insurance premiums expired during December, $100.
Unearned rent earned during December, $120.
Wages accrued, but not paid at December 31, $250.
Fees revenue earned, but not yet billed, $500.
Depreciation of office equipment during December, $50.

Based upon the preceding adjustment data, the adjusting entries for Online Solutions are shown in Exhibit 10.

Like other journal entries, Online Solutions' **adjusting entries** should be posted to the general ledger, as shown in Exhibit 14. After these entries have been posted, we

Exhibit 9

Trial Balance for Online Solutions

Online Solutions
Trial Balance
December 31, 2004

Cash	2,065	
Accounts Receivable	2,220	
Supplies	2,800	
Prepaid Insurance	2,400	
Office Equipment	1,800	
Land	20,000	
Accounts Payable		900
Unearned Rent		360
Capital Stock		25,000
Dividends	4,000	
Fees Earned		16,340
Wages Expense	4,275	
Rent Expense	1,600	
Utilities Expense	985	
Miscellaneous Expense	455	
	42,600	42,600

Exhibit 10

Adjusting Entries for Online Solutions

Dec. 31	Supplies Expense	2,040	
	Supplies		2,040
31	Insurance Expense	100	
	Prepaid Insurance		100
31	Unearned Rent	120	
	Rent Revenue		120
31	Wages Expense	250	
	Wages Payable		250
31	Accounts Receivable	500	
	Fees Earned		500
31	Depreciation Expense	50	
	Accumulated Depreciation—Office Equipment		50

compute adjusted balances and prepare an **adjusted trial balance** prior to preparing the financial statements. This verifies that no errors have occurred in posting the adjustments. The adjusted trial balance for Online Solutions is shown in Exhibit 11.

Using the adjusted trial balance shown in Exhibit 11, the financial statements for Online Solutions for the two months ending December 31, 2004, can be prepared. The income statement, retained earnings statement, balance sheet, and statement of cash flows for Online Solutions are shown in Exhibit 12.

The income statement, retained earnings statement, and balance sheet for Online Solutions can be prepared directly from the adjusted trial balance shown in Exhibit 11. The statement of cash flows is more complex and requires additional analysis of November and December transactions. In the appendix at the end of this chapter, we describe and illustrate how Online Solutions' statement of cash flows is prepared.

Exhibit 11

Adjusted Trial Balance for Online Solutions

Online Solutions
Adjusted Trial Balance
December 31, 2004

Cash	2,065	
Accounts Receivable	2,720	
Supplies	760	
Prepaid Insurance	2,300	
Office Equipment	1,800	
Accumulated Depreciation		50
Land	20,000	
Accounts Payable		900
Wages Payable		250
Unearned Rent		240
Capital Stock		25,000
Dividends	4,000	
Fees Earned		16,840
Rent Revenue		120
Wages Expense	4,525	
Supplies Expense	2,040	
Rent Expense	1,600	
Utilities Expense	985	
Insurance Expense	100	
Depreciation Expense	50	
Miscellaneous Expense	455	
	43,400	43,400

Exhibit 12

Financial Statements for Online Solutions

Online Solutions
Income Statement
For the Two Months Ended December 31, 2004

Fees earned	$16,840	
Rent revenue	120	
Total revenues		$16,960
Operating expenses:		
Wages expense	$ 4,525	
Supplies expense	2,040	
Rent expense	1,600	
Utilities expense	985	
Insurance expense	100	
Depreciation expense	50	
Miscellaneous expense	455	
Total operating expenses		9,755
Net income		$ 7,205

(continued)

In the Online Solutions illustration, operations began on November 1 and the accounting period was for two months, November and December. Since Shannon Hughes, the sole stockholder, decided to adopt a calendar-year accounting period, Online Solutions' accounts

Exhibit 12
Continued

Online Solutions
Retained Earnings Statement
For the Two Months Ended December 31, 2004

Net income for November and December	$7,205
Less dividends	4,000
Retained earnings, December 31, 2004	$3,205

Online Solutions
Balance Sheet
December 31, 2004

Assets			
Current assets:			
Cash		$ 2,065	
Accounts receivable		2,720	
Supplies		760	
Prepaid insurance		2,300	
Total current assets			$ 7,845
Property, plant, and equipment:			
Land		$20,000	
Office equipment	$1,800		
Less accumulated depreciation	50	1,750	
Total fixed assets			21,750
Total assets			$29,595
Liabilities			
Current liabilities:			
Accounts payable		$ 900	
Wages payable		250	
Unearned rent		240	
Total liabilities			$ 1,390
Stockholders' Equity			
Capital stock		$25,000	
Retained earnings		3,205	28,205
Total liabilities and stockholders' equity			$29,595

(continued)

were closed on December 31, 2004. In future years, the financial statements for Online Solutions will be prepared for twelve months, ending on December 31 each year.

INTERNATIONAL PERSPECTIVE

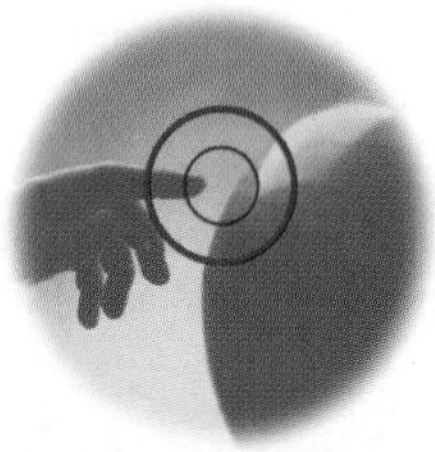

In Mexico, a statement of changes in financial position is required, rather than a statement of cash flows. This statement reports the net changes in current assets and current liabilities, rather than the changes in cash, as in the United States.

The annual accounting period adopted by a business is known as its **fiscal year**. Fiscal years begin with the first day of the month selected and end on the last day of the following twelfth month. The period most commonly used is the calendar year. Other periods are not unusual, especially for businesses organized as corporations. For example, a corporation may adopt a fiscal year that ends when business activities have reached the lowest point in its annual operating cycle. Such a fiscal year is called the

Exhibit 12
Concluded

Online Solutions Statement of Cash Flows For the Two Months Ended December 31, 2004		
Cash flows from operating activities:		
Cash received from customers	$ 14,120	
Cash received from renting land	360	$ 14,480
Deduct cash payments for expenses:		
Wages	$ 4,275	
Insurance	2,400	
Supplies	1,900	
Rent	1,600	
Utilities	985	
Miscellaneous	455	11,615
Net cash flows from operating activities		$ 2,865
Cash flows used for investing activities:		
Purchase of land	$(20,000)	
Purchase of office equipment	(1,800)	
Net cash flows used in investing activities		(21,800)
Cash flows from financing activities:		
Issuance of capital stock	$ 25,000	
Payment of dividends	(4,000)	
Net cash flows from financing activities		21,000
Net increase in cash		$ 2,065
November 1, 2004 cash balance		0
December 31, 2004 cash balance		$ 2,065

natural business year. At the low point in its operating cycle, a business has more time to analyze the results of operations and to prepare financial statements.

Closing Entries

In Chapter 3, we described and illustrated the closing process for Family Health Care. In this section, we illustrate the closing process for Online Solutions. As we illustrated in Chapter 3, revenues, expenses, and dividends are closed to retained earnings at the end of the accounting period. In a double-entry accounting system, a **closing entry** is normally prepared for each of the three categories of accounts that are closed. That is, three separate closing entries are prepared for revenues, expenses, and dividends. For Online Solutions, these three closing entries are shown in Exhibit 13.

After the closing entries have been posted to the ledger, as shown in Exhibit 14, the balance in the retained earnings account will agree with the amount reported on the retained earnings statement and the balance sheet. In addition, the revenue, expense, and dividends accounts will have zero balances.

Post-Closing Trial Balance

A **post-closing trial balance** is normally prepared after the closing entries have been posted to the ledger. This is to make sure that no errors have been made in the posting process and that the ledger is in balance at the beginning of the next period. The accounts and amounts should agree exactly with the accounts and amounts listed on the balance sheet at the end of the period.

Exhibit 13

Closing Entries for Online Solutions

Dec. 31	Fees Earned	16,840	
	Rent Revenue	120	
	Retained Earnings		16,960
31	Retained Earnings	9,755	
	Wages Expense		4,525
	Rent Expense		1,600
	Depreciation Expense		50
	Utilities Expense		985
	Supplies Expense		2,040
	Insurance Expense		100
	Miscellaneous Expense		455
31	Retained Earnings	4,000	
	Dividends		4,000

Exhibit 14

Ledger for Online Solutions—December

CASH

Dec. 1	Balance	5,900	Dec. 1		2,400
1		360	1		800
16		3,100	6		180
21		650	11		400
31		2,870	13		950
			20		1,800
			23		550
			27		1,200
			31		310
			31		225
			31		2,000
		12,880			10,815
31	Balance	2,065			

ACCOUNTS RECEIVABLE

Dec. 16		1,750	Dec. 21		650
31		1,120			
31	Balance	2,220			
31	Adjusting	500			
31	Adj. Bal.	2,720			

SUPPLIES

Dec. 1	Balance	1,350	Dec. 31	Adjusting	2,040
23		1,450			
31	Balance	2,800			
31	Adj. Bal.	760			

PREPAID INSURANCE

Dec. 1		2,400	Dec. 31	Adjusting	100
Dec. 31	Adj. Bal.	2,300			

LAND

Dec. 1	Balance	20,000			

OFFICE EQUIPMENT

Dec. 4		1,800			

ACCUMULATED DEPRECIATION

			Dec. 31	Adjusting	50

ACCOUNTS PAYABLE

Dec. 11		400	Dec. 1	Balance	400
20		1,800	4		1,800
			23		900
		2,200			3,100
			31	Balance	900

WAGES PAYABLE

			Dec. 31	Adjusting	250

Exhibit 14

Concluded

UNEARNED RENT

Dec. 31	Adjusting	120	Dec. 1		360
			31	Balance	240

CAPITAL STOCK

			Dec. 1	Balance	25,000

RETAINED EARNINGS

Dec. 31	Closing	9,755	Dec. 31	Closing	16,960
31	Closing	4,000			
		13,755	31	Balance	3,205

DIVIDENDS

Dec. 1	Balance	2,000	Dec. 31	Closing	4,000
31		2,000			
31	Balance	0			

FEES EARNED

Dec. 31	Closing	16,840	Dec. 1	Balance	7,500
			16		3,100
			16		1,750
			31		2,870
			31		1,120
			31	Balance	16,340
			31	Adjusting	500
			31	Adj. Bal.	16,840
			31	Balance	0

RENT REVENUE

Dec. 31	Closing	120	Dec. 31	Adjusting	120
			31	Balance	0

WAGES EXPENSE

Dec. 1	Balance	2,125	Dec. 31	Closing	4,525
13		950			
27		1,200			
31	Balance	4,275			
31	Adjusting	250			
31	Balance	0			

SUPPLIES EXPENSE

Dec. 1	Balance	800	Dec. 31	Closing	2,040
31	Adjusting	1,240			
31	Adj. Bal.	1,240			
31	Balance	0			

RENT EXPENSE

Dec. 1	Balance	800	Dec. 31	Closing	1,600
1		800			
31	Balance	1,600			
31	Balance	0			

UTILITIES EXPENSE

Dec. 1	Balance	450	Dec. 31	Closing	985
31		310			
31		225			
31	Balance	985			
31	Balance	0			

INSURANCE EXPENSE

Dec. 31		100	Dec. 31	Closing	100
31	Balance	0			

DEPRECIATION EXPENSE

Dec. 31	Adjusting	50	Dec. 31	Closing	50
31	Balance	0			

MISCELLANEOUS EXPENSE

Dec. 1	Balance	275	Dec. 31	Closing	455
6		180			
31	Balance	455			
31	Balance	0			

EBITDA

6 Describe and illustrate the computation and use of earnings before interest, taxes, depreciation, and amortization (EBITDA).

In this chapter, we have illustrated the basic elements of transaction processing and financial reporting accounting systems. The financial statements, which are used by the company's stakeholders, are the major product of these systems. However, stakeholders often adjust financial statement data for use in their analyses. Such adjustments are called *pro forma* or "as if" computations. Because these pro forma computations are adjustments to financial statements, they are not in conformity with generally accepted accounting principles.

One common type of pro forma computation that is widely used and reported in the financial press is **earnings before interest, taxes, depreciation, and amortization (EBITDA)**. EBITDA is used by financial analysts as a rough estimate of operating cash flows that are available to pay interest and other fixed charges. Because the computation of EBITDA is not required by generally accepted accounting principles, its computation may vary from analyst to analyst. For example, the computations of EBITDA (in millions) for Delta Air Lines and Southwest Airlines for the year ended December 31, 2001, are shown below.

Delta Air Lines:	
Operating loss (before interest and taxes)	$(1,602)
Depreciation and amortization	1,283
EBITDA	$ (319)
Southwest Airlines:	
Operating income (before interest and taxes)	$631
Depreciation and amortization	346
EBITDA	$977

The preceding computations reveal that Southwest has a much higher EBITDA than Delta. Thus, Southwest is generating more cash from its operations to pay interest and other fixed charges than is Delta.

You should be careful not to confuse EBITDA with net cash flows from operating activities. For example, Delta and Southwest reported positive net cash flows from operating activities for 2001 of $236 and $1,485 million, respectively. In contrast, the EBITDA

Ethics in Action

Worldcom, Inc.

In their public earnings announcements, companies have recently focused on reporting EBITDA to outside investors. This was done under the belief that EBITDA would be a more realistic measure of earning power in some industries with large depreciation expenses, such as telecommunications. However, alleged accounting fraud at Worldcom, Inc., has changed perceptions. Worldcom is alleged to have caused nearly $4 billion in costs to disappear when reporting EBITDA. As stated recently by Chuck Hill, Director of Research at data provider Thomson Financial/First Call, "I think the days of having EBITDA being the focus of an earnings release are probably numbered."

Source: "Days May Be Numbered for EBITDA Numbers," *The Wall Street Journal*, July 5, 2002.

for Delta and Southwest was ($319) and $977 million, respectively. These differences reflect that net cash flows from operating activities is computed using generally accepted accounting principles. These principles require the consideration of factors other than just interest, taxes, depreciation, and amortization in determining cash flows from operations. For example, increases or decreases in accounts receivable and inventories affect the amount of cash flows from operations. For this reason, EBITDA should be interpreted only as a rough estimate of the cash available to pay interest and other fixed charges, rather than as an estimate of cash flows from operations. In addition, since EBITDA and other "pro forma" estimates are not governed by generally accepted accounting principles, each analyst can decide what to exclude and include in the computations. Thus, what one analyst reports and uses for EBITDA may differ from that of another analyst.

APPENDIX

The Statement of Cash Flows

The income statement, retained earnings statement, balance sheet, and statement of cash flows for Online Solutions are shown in Exhibit 12. The income statement, retained earnings statement, and balance sheet can be prepared directly from the adjusted trial balance shown in Exhibit 11. Preparing the statement of cash flows, however, is more complex.

The statement of cash flows for Online Solutions can be prepared by analyzing the cash account shown in Exhibit 13. Each of the transactions posted to the cash account should be classified as affecting cash flows from operating, investing, or financing activities. This analysis of the cash transactions in chronological order is shown below.

Date		Transaction Description	Cash Flow Activity	Amount Increase (Decrease)
Nov.	1	Issued capital stock	Financing	$ 25,000
	5	Purchased land	Investing	(20,000)
	18	Earned cash fees	Operating	7,500
	30	Paid $3,650 for:		
		Wages	Operating	(2,125)
		Rent	Operating	(800)
		Utilities	Operating	(450)
		Miscellaneous	Operating	(275)
	30	Paid creditors on account for supplies	Operating	(950)
	30	Paid dividends	Financing	(2,000)
Dec.	1	Paid insurance premiums	Operating	(2,400)
	1	Paid rent	Operating	(800)
	1	Received cash for renting land	Operating	360
	6	Paid for adverstisement (misc. expense)	Operating	(180)
	11	Paid creditors on account for supplies	Operating	(400)
	13	Paid employee wages	Operating	(950)
	16	Earned cash fees	Operating	3,100
	20	Paid creditors on account for office equipment	Investing	(1,800)
	21	Received cash from customers on account for fees earned	Operating	650
	23	Paid for supplies	Operating	(550)
	27	Paid employee wages	Operating	(1,200)
	31	Paid telephone bill (utilities expense)	Operating	(310)
	31	Paid electric bill (utilities expense)	Operating	(225)
	31	Earned cash fees	Operating	2,870
	31	Paid dividends	Financing	(2,000)

The statement of cash flows can be prepared from the preceding analysis by grouping the cash receipts and payments for each of the cash flow activities. The resulting statement for Online Solutions is shown in Exhibit 15.

Exhibit 15

Statement of Cash Flows for Online Solutions

Online Solutions
Statement of Cash Flows
For the Two Months Ended December 31, 2004

Cash flows from operating activities:		
Cash received from customers	$ 14,120 (a)	
Cash received from renting land	360	$ 14,480
Deduct cash payments for expenses:		
Wages	$ 4,275 (b)	
Insurance	2,400	
Supplies	1,900 (c)	
Rent	1,600 (d)	
Utilities	985 (e)	
Miscellaneous	455 (f)	11,615
Net cash flows from operating activities		$ 2,865
Cash flows used for investing activities:		
Purchase of land	$(20,000)	
Purchase of office equipment	(1,800)	
Net cash flows used in investing activities		(21,800)
Cash flows from financing activities:		
Issuance of capital stock	$ 25,000	
Payment of dividends	(4,000)	
Net cash flows from financing activities		21,000
Net increase in cash		$ 2,065
November 1, 2004 cash balance		0
December 31, 2004 cash balance		$ 2,065

Computational Notes:
(a) $14,120 = $7,500 + $3,100 + $650 + $2,870
(b) $4,275 = $2,125 + $950 + $1,200
(c) $1,900 = $950 + $400 + $550
(d) $1,600 = $800 + $800
(e) $985 = $450 + $310 + $225
(f) $455 = $275 + $180

You should note that the net cash flows from operating activities of $2,865 is not the same as the net income of $7,205. As discussed in Chapter 3, this difference is due to the effect of accruals and deferrals on determining net income under the accrual basis of accounting. In the Appendix to Chapter 3, we showed how the net cash flows from operations can be reconciled with net income. This reconciliation is illustrated in Exhibit 16 for Online Solutions.

Exhibit 16

Reconciliation of Net Income with Net Cash Flows from Operating Activities

Online Solutions
Reconciliation of Net Income
with Net Cash Flows from Operating Activities

Net income		$ 7,205
Add:		
Depreciation expense	$ 50	
Increase in accounts payable	900	
Increase in wages payable	250	
Increase in unearned rent	240	1,440
Deduct:		
Increase in accounts receivable	$(2,720)	
Increase in supplies	(760)	
Increase in prepaid insurance	(2,300)	(5,780)
Net cash flows from operating activities		$ 2,865

Summary of Learning Goals

1 Describe the nature of business information systems.

A business information system collects and processes data into information that is distributed to users. Business information systems share common elements that include data sources, data collection, data processing, database management, information generation, and users.

2 Describe the nature of accounting information systems.

An accounting information system is a type of business information system that processes financial and operational data into reports useful to internal and external stakeholders. Accounting information systems consist of the (1) management reporting system, (2) the transaction processing system, and (3) the financial reporting system.

3 Describe and illustrate the basic elements of transaction processing systems.

The basic elements of transaction processing systems include accounts and rules for recording transactions in accounts, journals, and ledgers. In addition, the processing system should include controls to prevent and detect errors in the recording and summarization process. An account is used to record increases and decreases in financial statement elements. The rules of debit and credit are used to determine how increases and decreases are recorded in the various accounts. A journal is a chronological record of each transaction. The ledger is the summary of all the accounts for a business. The trial balance provides the control that the total of accounts with debit balances must equal the total of accounts with credit balances.

4 Describe and illustrate the basic elements of a financial reporting system.

The basic elements of a financial reporting system include adjusting entries, financial statements, and closing entries. Adjusting entries are necessary under the accrual basis of accounting to bring the accounts up to date for preparing financial statements. Closing entries transfer the balances of the revenue, expense, and dividend accounts to retained earnings.

5 Describe and illustrate the computation and use of earnings before interest, taxes, depreciation, and amortization (EBITDA).

Earnings before interest, taxes, depreciation, and amortization (EBITDA) is a type of pro forma computation used by financial analysts as a rough estimate of operating cash flows that are available to pay interest and other fixed charges.

Glossary

Account The element of an accounting system that summarizes the increases and decreases in each financial statement item.

Accounting information system An information system that consists of management reporting, transaction processing, and financial reporting subsystems that processes financial and operational data into reports useful to internal and external stakeholders.

Adjusted trial balance The trial balance prepared after the adjusting entries have been posted to the ledger.

Adjusting entries The entries necessary to bring the accounts up to date before preparing financial statements.

Balance of an account The amount of the difference between the debits and the credits that have been entered into an account.

Business information system A system that collects and processes company data into information that is distributed to users.

Chart of accounts The list of accounts in the general ledger.

Closing entries The entries necessary at the end of an accounting period to transfer the balances of revenue, expense, and dividend accounts to retained earnings.

Credits Amounts entered on the right side of an account.

Debits Amounts entered on the left side of an account.

Earnings before interest, taxes, depreciation, and amortization (EBITDA) A type of pro forma computation used by financial analysts as a rough estimate of operating cash flows that are available to pay interest and other fixed charges.

Financial reporting system A subsystem of accounting that produces financial statements and other reports for external stakeholders.

Fiscal year The annual accounting period adopted by a business.

General ledger The group of accounts of a business.

Journal The record in which the effects of transactions are recorded in chronological order.

Journal entry The transaction record entered in the journal.

Journalizing The process of recording transactions in the journal.

Management reporting system A subsystem of accounting that provides internal information to assist managers in making decisions.

Natural business year The fiscal year that ends when a business's activities reach their lowest point in the operating cycle.

Post-closing trial balance The trial balance prepared after the closing entries have been posted to the ledger.

Posting The process of transferring the debits and credits from the journal entries to the accounts in the ledger.

Rules of debit and credit Standardized rules for recording increases and decreases in accounts.

Transaction processing system A subsystem of accounting that records and summarizes the effects of financial transactions on the business.

Trial balance A summary listing of the accounts and their balances in the ledger.

Illustrative Accounting Application Problem

J. F. Outz, M.D., has been practicing as a cardiologist for three years in a professional corporation known as Hearts, P.C. During April 2004, Hearts completed the following transactions.

Apr. 1 Paid office rent for April, $800.
3 Purchased equipment on account, $2,100.
5 Received cash on account from patients, $3,150.
8 Purchased X-ray film and other supplies on account, $245.
9 One of the items of equipment purchased on April 3 was defective. It was returned with the permission of the supplier, who agreed to reduce the account for the amount charged for the item, $325.
12 Paid cash to equipment supplier on account, $1,250.
17 Paid cash for renewal of a six-month property insurance policy, $370.
20 Paid cash to laboratory on account, $200.
24 Paid cash for laboratory analysis, $545.
25 Recorded fees charged to patients on account for services performed in April, $5,145.
27 Paid cash dividends, $1,250.

Apr. 28 Recorded the cash received in payment of services (on a cash basis) to patients during April, $1,720.
28 Paid salaries of receptionist and nurses, $1,725.
30 Paid various utility expenses, $360.
30 Paid miscellaneous expenses, $132.

Hearts' accounts and balances (all normal balances) as of April 1 are listed as follows: Cash, $4,123; Accounts Receivable, $4,725; Supplies, $290; Prepaid Insurance, $465; Equipment, $21,745; Accumulated Depreciation, $3,100; Accounts Payable, $765; Salary Payable; Capital Stock, $10,000; Retained Earnings, $17,483; Dividends; Professional Fees; Salary Expense; Rent Expense; Laboratory Expense; Insurance Expense; Utilities Expense; Supplies Expense; Depreciation Expense; Miscellaneous Expense.

Instructions

1. Enter the April 1 balances in standard T accounts. Identify each amount as "Balance." (*Hint:* Verify the equality of the debit and credit balances in the ledger before proceeding with the next instruction.)
2. Journalize each transaction in a two-column journal.
3. Post the journal entries to the T accounts, placing the date to the left of each amount to identify the transaction. Determine the account balances after all posting is complete.
4. Prepare an unadjusted trial balance as of April 30, 2004.
5. Data necessary to determine the end-of-month adjustments are as follows:
   a. Supplies on hand at April 30, $185.
   b. Professional fees accrued on April 30, $1,375.
   c. Insurance premiums expired during April, $435.
   d. Depreciation on equipment during April, $80.
   e. Salaries accrued at April 30, $300.

   Journalize and post the necessary adjusting entries for April. Identify each adjusting entry in the account as "Adjusting." For the adjusted accounts, determine an adjusted balance.
6. Prepare an adjusted trial balance as of April 30, 2004.
7. Prepare an income statement, a retained earnings statement, and a classified balance sheet.
8. Journalize and post the closing entries for April. Identify each entry in the accounts as "Closing."
9. Prepare a post-closing trial balance as of April 30, 2004.
10. (Appendix) Prepare a statement of cash flows for April. Note that the April 12 payment of $1,250 on account was for the equipment purchase. The April 20 payment of $200 on account was for laboratory expense.
11. (Appendix) Reconcile net income with net cash flows from operations for April. Note that only $45 of the increase in Accounts Payable represents operating activities. The remaining $525 increase in Accounts Payable relates to the purchase of equipment, an investing activity.

Solution to Illustrative Problem

2.

Apr.	1	Rent Expense	800	
		Cash		800
	3	Equipment	2,100	
		Accounts Payable		2,100

(continued)

Apr.	5	Cash	3,150	
		Accounts Receivable		3,150
	8	Supplies	245	
		Accounts Payable		245
	9	Accounts Payable	325	
		Equipment		325
	12	Accounts Payable	1,250	
		Cash		1,250
	17	Prepaid Insurance	370	
		Cash		370
	20	Accounts Payable	200	
		Cash		200
	24	Laboratory Expense	545	
		Cash		545
	25	Accounts Receivable	5,145	
		Professional Fees		5,145
	27	Dividends	1,250	
		Cash		1,250
	28	Cash	1,720	
		Professional Fees		1,720
	28	Salary Expense	1,725	
		Cash		1,725
	30	Utilities Expense	360	
		Cash		360
	30	Miscellaneous Expense	132	
		Cash		132

1. and 3.

CASH

April 1	Balance	4,123	April 1		800
5		3,150	12		1,250
28		1,720	17		370
			20		200
			24		545
			27		1,250
			28		1,725
			30		360
			30		132
		8,993			6,632
30	Balance	2,361			

ACCOUNTS RECEIVABLE

April 1	Balance	4,725	April 5		3,150
25		5,145			
30	Balance	6,720			
30	Adjusting	1,375			
30	Adj. Bal.	8,095			

SUPPLIES

April 1	Balance	290			
8		245			
30	Balance	535	April 30	Adjusting	350
30	Adj. Bal.	185			

PREPAID INSURANCE

April	1	Balance	465				
	17		370				
	30	Balance	835	April	30	Adjusting	435
	30	Adj. Bal.	400				

EQUIPMENT

April	1	Balance	21,745	April	9		325
	3		2,100				
	30	Balance	23,520				

ACCUMULATED DEPRECIATION

				April	30	Balance	3,100
					30	Adjusting	80
					30	Adj. Bal.	3,180

ACCOUNTS PAYABLE

April	9		325	April	1	Balance	765
	12		1,250		3		2,100
	20		200		8		245
					30	Balance	1,335

SALARY PAYABLE

				April	30	Adjusting	300

CAPITAL STOCK

				April	1	Balance	10,000

RETAINED EARNINGS

April	30	Closing	4,727	April	1	Balance	17,483
	30	Closing	1,250		30	Closing	8,240
					30	Balance	19,746

DIVIDENDS

April	27		1,250	April	30	Closing	1,250
	30	Balance	0				

PROFESSIONAL FEES

				April	25		5,145
					28		1,720
					30	Balance	6,865
					30	Adjusting	1,375
April	30	Closing	8,240		30	Adj. Bal.	8,240
					30	Balance	0

SALARY EXPENSE

April	28		1,725				
	30	Adjusting	300				
	30	Adj. Bal.	2,025	April	30	Closing	2,025
	30	Balance	0				

RENT EXPENSE

April	1		800	April	30	Closing	800
	30	Balance	0				

LABORATORY EXPENSE

April	24		545	April	30	Closing	545
	30	Balance	0				

INSURANCE EXPENSE

April	30	Adjusting	435	April	30	Closing	435
	30	Balance	0				

UTILITIES EXPENSE

April	30		360	April	30	Closing	360
	30	Balance	0				

SUPPLIES EXPENSE

April	30	Adjusting	350	April	30	Closing	350
	30	Balance	0				

DEPRECIATION EXPENSE

April	30	Adjusting	80	April	30	Closing	80
	30	Balance	0				

MISCELLANEOUS EXPENSE

April	30		132	April	30	Closing	132
	30	Balance	0				

4.

Hearts, P. C.
Unadjusted Trial Balance
April 30, 2004

Cash	2,361	
Accounts Receivable	6,720	
Supplies	535	
Prepaid Insurance	835	
Equipment	23,520	
Accumulated Depreciation		3,100
Accounts Payable		1,335
Capital Stock		10,000
Retained Earnings		17,483
Dividends	1,250	
Professional Fees		6,865
Salary Expense	1,725	
Rent Expense	800	
Laboratory Expense	545	
Utilities Expense	360	
Miscellaneous Expense	132	
	38,783	38,783

5.

a.	Supplies Expense	350	
	Supplies		350
b.	Accounts Receivable	1,375	
	Professional Fees		1,375
c.	Insurance Expense	435	
	Prepaid Insurance		435
d.	Depreciation Expense	80	
	Accumulated Depreciation		80
e.	Salary Expense	300	
	Salary Payable		300

6.

Hearts, P. C.
Adjusted Trial Balance
April 30, 2004

Cash	2,361	
Accounts Receivable	8,095	
Supplies	185	
Prepaid Insurance	400	
Equipment	23,520	
Accumulated Depreciation		3,180
Accounts Payable		1,335
Salary Payable		300
Capital Stock		10,000
Retained Earnings		17,483
Dividends	1,250	
Professional Fees		8,240
Salary Expense	2,025	
Rent Expense	800	
Laboratory Expense	545	
Insurance Expense	435	
Utilities Expense	360	
Supplies Expense	350	
Depreciation Expense	80	
Miscellaneous Expense	132	
	40,538	40,538

7.

Hearts, P.C.
Income Statement
For the Month Ended April 30, 2004

Professional fees		$8,240
Operating expenses:		
Salary expense	$2,025	
Rent expense	800	
Laboratory expense	545	
Insurance expense	435	
Utilities expense	360	
Supplies expense	350	
Depreciation expense	80	
Miscellaneous expense	132	
Total operating expenses		4,727
Net income		$3,513

(continued)

Hearts, P.C.
Retained Earnings Statement
For the Month Ended April 30, 2004

Retained earnings, April 1, 2004		$17,483
Net income for April	$3,513	
Less dividends	1,250	
Increase in retained earnings		2,263
Retained earnings, April 30, 2004		$19,746

Hearts, P.C.
Balance Sheet
April 30, 2004

Assets		
Current assets:		
Cash	$ 2,361	
Accounts receivable	8,095	
Supplies	185	
Prepaid insurance	400	
Total current assets		$11,041
Property, plant, and equipment:		
Equipment	$23,520	
Accumulated depreciation	3,180	
Total property, plant, and equipment		20,340
Total assets		$31,381
Liabilities		
Current liabilities:		
Accounts payable	$ 1,335	
Salary payable	300	
Total liabilities		$ 1,635
Stockholders' Equity		
Capital stock	$10,000	
Retained earnings	19,746	29,746
Total liabilities and stockholders' equity		$31,381

8.

Professional Fees	8,240	
Retained Earnings		8,240
Retained Earnings	4,727	
Salary Expense		2,025
Rent Expense		800
Laboratory Expense		545
Insurance Expense		435
Utilities Expense		360
Supplies Expense		350
Depreciation Expense		80
Miscellaneous Expense		132
Retained Earnings	1,250	
Dividends		1,250

9.

Hearts, P. C.
Post-Closing Trial Balance
April 30, 2004

Cash	2,361	
Accounts Receivable	8,095	
Supplies	185	
Prepaid Insurance	400	
Equipment	23,520	
Accumulated Depreciation		3,180
Accounts Payable		1,335
Salary Payable		300
Capital Stock		10,000
Retained Earnings		19,746
	34,561	34,561

10.

Hearts, P.C.
Statement of Cash Flows
For the Month Ended April 30, 2004

Cash flows from operating activities:		
Cash received from customers		$ 4,870 (a)
Deduct cash payments for operating expenses:		
Salary	$1,725	
Rent	800	
Laboratory	745 (b)	
Utilities	360	
Insurance	370	
Miscellaneous	132	4,132
Net cash flows from operating activities		$ 738
Net cash flows used for investing activities:		
Purchase equipment		$(1,250)
Net cash flows used for financing activities:		
Payment of dividends		$(1,250)
Net decrease in cash		$(1,762)
April 1, 2004 cash balance		4,123
April 30, 2004 cash balance		$ 2,361

(a) $3,150 + $1,720
(b) $545 + $200

11.

Net income		$3,513
Add:		
Depreciation	$ 80	
Decrease in supplies	105	
Decrease in prepaid insurance	65	
Increase in accounts payable (from operations)	45	
Increase in salary payable	300	595
Deduct:		
Increase in accounts receivable		3,370
Net cash flows from operating activities		$ 738

Self-Study Questions

Answers at end of chapter

1. A debit may signify:
   A. an increase in an asset account.
   B. a decrease in an asset account.
   C. an increase in a liability account.
   D. an increase in the capital stock account.

2. The type of account with a normal credit balance is:
   A. an asset.
   B. dividends.
   C. a revenue.
   D. an expense.

3. A debit balance in which of the following accounts would indicate a likely error?
   A. Accounts Receivable
   B. Cash
   C. Fees Earned
   D. Miscellaneous Expense

4. Which of the following entries closes the dividends account at the end of the period?
   A. Debit the dividends account, credit the capital stock account.
   B. Debit the retained earnings account, credit the dividends account.
   C. Debit the capital stock account, credit the dividends account.
   D. Debit the dividends account, credit the retained earnings account.

5. Which of the following accounts would not be closed to the retained earnings account at the end of a period?
   A. Fees Earned
   B. Wages Expense
   C. Rent Expense
   D. Accumulated Depreciation

Discussion Questions

1. When you registered for this class and paid your tuition, you interacted with the college's information systems. (a) Are the registration and tuition payment systems business information systems? (b) Which system is part of the college's accounting system?
2. What is the difference between an account and a ledger?
3. Do the terms *debit* and *credit* signify increase or decrease, or can they signify either? Explain.
4. What is the effect (increase or decrease) of a debit to an expense account (a) in terms of stockholders' equity and (b) in terms of expense?
5. What is the effect (increase or decrease) of a credit to a revenue account (a) in terms of stockholders' equity and (b) in terms of revenue?

6. Meadows Company adheres to a policy of depositing all cash receipts in a bank account and making all payments by check. The cash account as of July 31 has a credit balance of $900, and there is no undeposited cash on hand. (a) Assuming that no errors occurred during journalizing or posting, what caused this unusual balance? (b) Is the $900 credit balance in the cash account an asset, a liability, stockholders' equity, a revenue, or an expense?
7. Shaw Company performed services in October for a specific customer for a fee of $4,230. Payment was received the following November. (a) Was the revenue earned in October or November? (b) What accounts should be debited and credited in (1) October and (2) November?
8. What proof is provided by a trial balance?
9. If the two totals of a trial balance are equal, does it mean that there are no errors in the accounting records? Explain.
10. Assume that when a purchase of supplies of $1,050 for cash was recorded, both the debit and the credit were journalized and posted as $1,500. (a) Would this error cause the trial balance to be out of balance? (b) Would the trial balance be out of balance if the $1,050 entry had been journalized correctly, but the credit to Cash had been posted as $1,500?
11. Banks rely heavily upon customers' deposits as a source of funds. Demand deposits normally pay interest to the customer, who is entitled to withdraw at any time without prior notice to the bank. Checking and NOW (negotiable order of withdrawal) accounts are the most common form of demand deposits for banks. Assume that ABC Storage has a checking account at American Savings Bank. What type of account (asset, liability, stockholders' equity, revenue, expense, dividends) does the account balance of $13,850 represent from the viewpoint of (a) ABC Storage and (b) American Savings Bank?
12. Why are closing entries required at the end of an accounting period?
13. What is the difference between adjusting entries and closing entries?
14. What types of accounts are closed by transferring their balances (a) as a debit to Retained Earnings, (b) as a credit to Retained Earnings?
15. What is the purpose of the post-closing trial balance?
16. The fiscal years for several well-known companies were as follows:

Company	Fiscal Year Ending
Kmart	January 30
JC Penney	January 26
Zayre Corp.	January 26
Toys"R"Us, Inc.	February 3
Federated Department Stores	February 3
The Limited, Inc.	February 2

What general characteristic shared by these companies explains why they do not have fiscal years ending December 31?

Resources for your success **online @ http://warren.swlearning.com**

Remember! If you need additional help, visit South-Western's Web site. See page 30 for a description of the online and printed materials that are available.

Exercises

Exercise 4–1

Chart of accounts

Goal 3

The following accounts appeared in recent financial statements of Continental Airlines:

Accounts Payable	Flight Equipment
Aircraft Fuel Expense	Landing Fees
Air Traffic Liability	Passenger Revenue
Cargo and Mail Revenue	Purchase Deposits for Flight Equipment
Commissions	Spare Parts and Supplies

Identify each account as either a balance sheet account or an income statement account. For each balance sheet account, identify it as an asset, a liability, or stockholders' equity. For each income statement account, identify it as a revenue or an expense.

Exercise 4–2

Normal account balances

Goal 3

STUDENT SOLUTIONS MANUAL

For each account listed in Exercise 4–1, indicate whether its normal balance is a debit or a credit.

Exercise 4–3

Chart of accounts

Goal 3

The following accounts have been adapted from recent financial statements of AOL Time Warner:

Accounts Receivable
Accumulated Depreciation
Advertising Revenues
Cable Television Equipment
Compact Discs and DVD Merchandise
Interest Expense
Music Catalogs and Copyrights
Notes Payable (due December 6, 2019)
Property, Plant and Equipment
Retained Earnings
Royalties and Programming Costs Payable
Selling, General and Administrative Expense
Short-Term Investments
Unearned Subscriptions

Identify each account as either a balance sheet account or an income statement account. For each balance sheet account, identify it as an asset, a liability, or stockholders' equity. For each income statement account, identify it as a revenue or an expense.

Exercise 4–4

Normal account balances

Goal 3

STUDENT SOLUTIONS MANUAL

For each account listed in Exercise 4–3, indicate whether its normal balance is a debit or a credit.

Exercise 4–5

Normal entries for accounts

Goal 3

During the month, Quark Labs Co. has a substantial number of transactions affecting each of the following accounts. State for each account whether it is likely to have (a) debit entries only, (b) credit entries only, or (c) both debit and credit entries.

1. Accounts Payable
2. Accounts Receivable
3. Cash
4. Fees Earned
5. Dividends
6. Miscellaneous Expense
7. Supplies Expense

Exercise 4–6

Normal balances of accounts

Goal 3

STUDENT SOLUTIONS MANUAL

Identify each of the following accounts of Century Services Co. as asset, liability, stockholders' equity, revenue, or expense, and state in each case whether the normal balance is a debit or a credit.

a. Accounts Payable
b. Accounts Receivable
c. Cash
d. Capital Stock
e. Dividends
f. Equipment
g. Fees Earned
h. Rent Expense
i. Salary Expense
j. Supplies

Exercise 4–7

Rules of debit and credit

Goal 3

The following table summarizes the rules of debit and credit. For each of the items (a) through (n), indicate whether the proper answer is a debit or a credit.

	Increase	Decrease	Normal Balance
Balance sheet accounts:			
Asset	Debit	Credit	(a)
Liability	(b)	(c)	(d)
Stockholders' Equity:			
Capital Stock	(e)	(f)	Credit
Retained Earnings	Credit	(g)	(h)
Dividends	(i)	Credit	(j)
Income statement accounts:			
Revenue	(k)	Debit	(l)
Expense	(m)	Credit	(n)

Exercise 4–8

Identifying transactions

Goals 3, 4

STUDENT SOLUTIONS MANUAL

World Co. is a travel agency. The nine transactions recorded by World during April, its first month of operations, are indicated in the following T accounts:

CASH

(1)	30,000	(2)	1,500
(7)	9,500	(3)	10,000
		(4)	4,050
		(6)	7,500
		(8)	3,000

EQUIPMENT

(3)	30,000		

DIVIDENDS

(8)	3,000		

ACCOUNTS RECEIVABLE

(5)	13,000	(7)	9,500

ACCOUNTS PAYABLE

(6)	7,500	(3)	20,000

SERVICE REVENUE

		(5)	13,000

SUPPLIES

(2)	1,500	(9)	1,050

CAPITAL STOCK

		(1)	30,000

OPERATING EXPENSES

(4)	4,050		
(9)	1,050		

Indicate for each debit and each credit: (a) whether an asset, liability, stockholders' equity, dividends, revenue, or expense account was affected and (b) whether the account was increased (+) or decreased (−). Present your answers in the following form, with transaction (1) given as an example:

	Account Debited		Account Credited	
Transaction	Type	Effect	Type	Effect
(1)	asset	+	stockholders' equity	+

Exercise 4–9

Journal entries

Goals 3, 4

Based upon the T accounts in Exercise 4–8, prepare the nine journal entries from which the postings were made.

Exercise 4–10

Trial balance

Goals 3, 4

STUDENT SOLUTIONS MANUAL

SPREADSHEET

Based upon the data presented in Exercise 4–8, prepare a trial balance, listing the accounts in their proper order.

Exercise 4–11

Classification of accounts, normal balances

Goals 3, 4

The following accounts (in millions) were adapted from the financial statements of Apple Computer, Inc. for the year ending September 29, 2001:

Accounts Payable	$ 801	Other Assets	$ 516
Accounts Receivable	466	Other Income (net)	319
Accrued Expenses Payable	717	Other Liabilities	266
Capital Stock	1,660	Other Operating Expenses	11
Cash	2,310	Property, Plant, and Equipment	564
Cost of Sales	4,128	Research and Development Expenses	430
Inventories	11	Retained Earnings, September 30, 2000	2,285
Investments	2,154	Sales	5,363
Long-Term Debt	317	Selling, General, and Administrative Expenses	1,138

(a) Identify each account as either a balance sheet account or an income statement account. (b) For each balance sheet account, identify it as an asset, a liability, or stockholders' equity. For each income statement account, identify it as a revenue or an expense. (c) Indicate the normal balance of the account.

Exercise 4–12

Trial balance

Goals 3, 4

Total debit column, $11,728

STUDENT SOLUTIONS MANUAL

SPREADSHEET

Using the data from Exercise 4–11, prepare a trial balance for Apple Computer as of September 29, 2001. List the accounts in the order they would appear in the ledger of Apple Computer.

Exercise 4–13

Income statement, retained earnings statement

Goals 3, 4

Net loss, $25

SPREADSHEET

Using the data from Exercise 4–11 and 4–12, prepare (a) an income statement and (b) a retained earnings statement for the year ending September 29, 2001, for Apple Computer.

Exercise 4–14

Closing entries, post-closing trial balance

Goals 3, 4

Total debit column, $6,021

STUDENT SOLUTIONS MANUAL

SPREADSHEET

Using the data from Exercises 4–11 and 4–12, (a) journalize the closing entries and (b) prepare a post-closing trial balance for Apple Computer.

Exercise 4–15

Cash account balance

Goals 3, 4

b. $8,500

During the month, Kapok Co. received $312,800 in cash and paid out $295,000 in cash.

a. Do the data indicate that Kapok Co. earned $17,800 during the month? Explain.
b. If the balance of the cash account is $26,300 at the end of the month, what was the cash balance at the beginning of the month?

Exercise 4–16

Account balances

Goals 3, 4

a. $11,550

STUDENT SOLUTIONS MANUAL

a. On June 1, the cash account balance was $3,850. During June, cash receipts totaled $11,850, and the June 30 balance was $4,150. Determine the cash payments made during June.
b. On May 1, the accounts receivable account balance was $18,500. During May, $21,000 was collected from customers on account. Assuming that the May 31 balance was $27,500, determine the fees billed to customers on account during May.
c. During January, $60,500 was paid to creditors on account, and purchases on account were $77,700. Assuming that the January 31 balance of Accounts Payable was $31,000, determine the account balance on January 1.

Exercise 4–17

Transactions

Goals 3, 4

The Wildcat Co. has the following accounts in its ledger: Cash; Accounts Receivable; Supplies; Office Equipment; Accounts Payable; Capital Stock; Dividends; Fees Earned; Rent Expense; Advertising Expense; Utilities Expense; Miscellaneous Expense.

Journalize the following selected transactions in a journal:

Mar.	1	Paid rent for the month, $2,500.
	2	Paid advertising expense, $600.
	4	Paid cash for supplies, $1,050.
	6	Purchased office equipment on account, $4,500.
	8	Received cash from customers on account, $3,600.
	12	Paid creditor on account, $2,150.
	20	Paid dividends, $1,000.
	25	Paid cash for repairs to office equipment, $120.
	30	Paid telephone bill for the month, $195.
	31	Earned fees for the month and billed to customers, $11,150.
	31	Paid electricity bill for the month, $280.

Exercise 4–18

Journalizing and posting

Goals 3, 4

STUDENT SOLUTIONS MANUAL

On November 12, 2004, Trux Co. purchased $1,720 of supplies on account.

a. Journalize the November 12, 2004 transaction.

b. Prepare a T account for Supplies. Enter a debit balance of $390 as of November 1, 2004.

c. Prepare a T account for Accounts Payable. Enter a credit balance of $9,681 as of November 1, 2004.

d. Post the November 12, 2004 transaction to the accounts and determine account balances.

Exercise 4–19

Transactions and T accounts

Goals 3, 4

The following selected transactions were completed during September of the current year:

1. Billed customers for fees earned, $8,210.
2. Purchased supplies on account, $1,070.
3. Received cash from customers on account, $6,150.
4. Paid creditors on account, $750.

a. Journalize the above transactions in a journal, using the appropriate number to identify the transactions.

b. Post the entries prepared in (a) to the following T accounts: Cash, Supplies, Accounts Receivable, Accounts Payable, Fees Earned. To the left of each amount posted in the accounts, place the appropriate number to identify the transactions.

Exercise 4–20

Trial balance

Goals 3, 4

STUDENT SOLUTIONS MANUAL

SPREADSHEET

The accounts in the ledger of Bogart Park Co. as of August 31 of the current year are listed in alphabetical order, as shown below. All accounts have normal balances. The balance of the cash account has been intentionally omitted.

Accounts Payable	$ 13,710
Accounts Receivable	27,500
Capital Stock	75,000
Cash	?
Dividends	25,000
Fees Earned	333,500
Insurance Expense	5,000
Land	125,000
Miscellaneous Expense	9,900
Notes Payable	40,000
Prepaid Insurance	3,150
Rent Expense	58,000

Retained Earnings	$ 35,290
Supplies	4,100
Supplies Expense	5,900
Unearned Rent	6,000
Utilities Expense	41,500
Wages Expense	175,000

Prepare a trial balance, listing the accounts in their proper order and inserting the missing figure for cash.

Exercise 4–21

Effect of errors on trial balance

Goals 3, 4

Indicate which of the following errors, each considered individually, would cause the trial balance totals to be unequal:

a. Payment of dividends of $3,500 was journalized and posted as a debit of $5,300 to Salary Expense and a credit of $3,500 to Cash.
b. A payment of $6,100 for equipment purchased was posted as a debit of $1,600 to Equipment and a credit of $1,600 to Cash.
c. A fee of $1,850 earned and due from a client was not debited to Accounts Receivable or credited to a revenue account, because the cash had not been received.
d. A receipt of $325 from an account receivable was journalized and posted as a debit of $325 to Cash and a credit of $325 to Fees Earned.
e. A payment of $1,075 to a creditor was posted as a debit of $1,075 to Accounts Payable and a debit of $1,075 to Cash.

Exercise 4–22

Errors in trial balance

Goals 3, 4

Total debit column, $167,255

STUDENT SOLUTIONS MANUAL

The following preliminary trial balance of Entrée Co., a sports ticket agency, does not balance:

Entrée Co.
Trial Balance
December 31, 2004

Cash	75,350	
Accounts Receivable	23,600	
Prepaid Insurance		3,300
Equipment	86,000	
Accounts Payable		9,450
Unearned Rent		2,570
Capital Stock	30,000	
Retained Earnings	61,615	
Dividends	10,000	
Service Revenue		64,940
Wages Expense		33,400
Advertising Expense	5,200	
Miscellaneous Expense		1,380
	291,765	115,040

When the ledger and other records are reviewed, you discover the following: (1) the debits and credits in the cash account total $75,350 and $53,975, respectively; (2) a billing of $1,000 to a customer on account was not posted to the accounts receivable account; (3) a payment of $1,500 made to a creditor on account was not posted to the accounts

payable account; (4) the balance of the unearned rent account is $2,750; (5) the correct balance of the equipment account is $68,000; and (6) each account has a normal balance.
Prepare a corrected trial balance.

Exercise 4–23

Effect of errors on trial balance

Goals 3, 4

The following errors occurred in posting from a journal:

1. A debit of $750 to Accounts Payable was posted as a credit.
2. A credit of $350 to Cash was posted as $530.
3. A debit of $800 to Cash was posted to Miscellaneous Expense.
4. A debit of $1,050 to Supplies was posted twice.
5. A debit of $1,575 to Wages Expense was posted as $5,175.
6. A credit of $3,175 to Accounts Payable was not posted.
7. An entry debiting Accounts Receivable and crediting Fees Earned for $4,500 was not posted.

Considering each case individually (i.e., assuming that no other errors had occurred), indicate: (a) by "yes" or "no" whether the trial balance would be out of balance; (b) if answer to (a) is "yes," the amount by which the trial balance totals would differ; and (c) whether the debit or credit column of the trial balance would have the larger total. Answers should be presented in the following form, with error (1) given as an example:

Error	(a) Out of Balance	(b) Difference	(c) Larger Total
1.	yes	$1,500	credit

Exercise 4–24

Errors in trial balance

Goals 3, 4

STUDENT SOLUTIONS MANUAL

How many errors can you find in the following trial balance? All accounts have normal balances.

Goulet Co.
Trial Balance
For the Month Ending January 31, 2004

Cash	8,010	
Accounts Receivable		16,400
Prepaid Insurance	2,400	
Equipment	52,000	
Accounts Payable	1,850	
Salaries Payable		750
Capital Stock		18,000
Retained Earnings		21,600
Dividends		5,000
Service Revenue		78,700
Salary Expense	28,400	
Advertising Expense		7,200
Miscellaneous Expense	1,490	
	94,150	94,150

Exercise 4–25

Adjusting entries

Goals 3, 4

On December 31, the end of the current year, the following data were accumulated to assist the accountant in preparing the adjusting entries for Epoch Realty:

a. The supplies account balance on December 31 is $1,750. The supplies on hand on December 31 are $245.

b. The unearned rent account balance on December 31 is $6,750, representing the receipt of an advance payment on December 1 of three months' rent from tenants.
c. Wages accrued but not paid at December 31 are $1,800.
d. Fees accrued but unbilled at December 31 are $10,600.
e. Depreciation of office equipment for the year is $3,100.

Journalize the adjusting entries required at December 31.

Exercise 4–26

Adjusting entries

Goals 3, 4

STUDENT SOLUTIONS MANUAL

Francesca Services Co. offers cleaning services to business clients. The trial balance for Francesca Services Co. before adjustments is shown below.

Francesca Services Co.
Unadjusted Trial Balance
December 31, 2004

Cash	4	
Accounts Receivable	25	
Supplies	4	
Prepaid Insurance	6	
Land	25	
Equipment	16	
Accumulated Depr.—Equip.		1
Accounts Payable		13
Wages Payable		0
Capital Stock		7
Retained Earnings		49
Dividends	4	
Fees Earned		30
Wages Expense	8	
Rent Expense	4	
Insurance Expense	0	
Utilities Expense	2	
Depreciation Expense	0	
Supplies Expense	0	
Miscellaneous Expense	2	
Totals	100	100

The data for year-end adjustments are as follows:

a. Fees earned but not yet billed, $3.
b. Supplies on hand, $1.
c. Insurance premiums expired, $5.
d. Depreciation expense, $2.
e. Wages accrued but not paid, $1.

Prepare the adjusting entries for Francesca Services Co.

Exercise 4–27

Adjusted trial balance

Goals 3, 4

Total debit column, $106

SPREADSHEET

Based upon the data in Exercise 4–26, adjust the account balances shown and prepare an adjusted trial balance for Francesca Services Co.

Exercise 4–28

Financial statements

Goal 4

Net income, $6

STUDENT SOLUTIONS MANUAL

SPREADSHEET

Based upon the data in Exercise 4–27, prepare an income statement, retained earnings statement, and balance sheet for Francesca Services Co.

Exercise 4–29

Closing entries

Goal 4

Based upon the data in Exercises 4–26 and 4–27, prepare the closing entries for Francesca Services Co.

Exercise 4–30

Statement of retained earnings

Goals 3, 4

STUDENT SOLUTIONS MANUAL

SPREADSHEET

Greenhorn Services Co. offers its services to new arrivals in the Belgrade area. Selected accounts from the ledger of Greenhorn Services Co. for the current fiscal year ended July 31, 2004, are as follows:

RETAINED EARNINGS

July 31	11,000	Bal. Aug. 1, 2003	183,750
31	577,150	July 31	621,400
		Bal. July 31, 2004	217,000

DIVIDENDS

Oct. 30	2,000	July 31	11,000
Jan. 31	2,000		
Apr. 30	2,000		
July 31	5,000		

Prepare a retained earnings statement for the year ending July 31, 2004.

Exercise 4–31

Statement of retained earnings; net loss

Goals 3, 4

SPREADSHEET

Selected accounts from the ledger of Yankee Sports for the current fiscal year ended October 31, 2004, are as follows:

RETAINED EARNINGS

Oct. 31	6,000	Bal. Nov. 1, 2003	310,300
31	523,400	July 31	475,250
		Bal. Oct. 31, 2004	256,150

DIVIDENDS

Jan. 31	2,000	Oct. 31	6,000
Apr. 30	2,000		
July 31	1,000		
Oct. 31	1,000		

Prepare a retained earnings statement for the year.

Accounting Application Problems

Problem 4–1A

Journal entries and trial balance

Goal 3

3. Total debit column, $23,550

SPREADSHEET GENERAL LEDGER

On May 1, 2004, Jim Lindley established Homestead Realty, which completed the following transactions during the month:

a. Jim Lindley transferred cash from a personal bank account to an account to be used for the business in exchange for capital stock, $7,500.
b. Paid rent on office and equipment for the month, $2,500.
c. Purchased supplies on account, $1,200.
d. Paid creditor on account, $900.
e. Earned sales commissions, receiving cash, $15,750.
f. Paid automobile expenses (including rental charge) for month, $2,400, and miscellaneous expenses, $1,250.
g. Paid office salaries, $4,500.
h. Determined that the cost of supplies used was $875.
i. Paid dividends, $2,500.

Instructions

1. Journalize entries for transactions (a) through (i), using the following accounts: Cash; Supplies; Accounts Payable; Capital Stock; Dividends; Sales Commissions Earned; Office Salaries Expense; Rent Expense; Automobile Expense; Supplies Expense; Miscellaneous Expense.
2. Post the journal entries to T accounts, placing the appropriate letter to the left of each amount to identify the transactions. Determine the account balances, after all posting is complete.
3. Prepare a trial balance as of May 31, 2004.
4. Determine the following:
   a. Amount of total revenue recorded in the ledger.
   b. Amount of total expenses recorded in the ledger.
   c. Assuming that no adjustments are necessary, what is the amount of net income for May?

Problem 4–2A

Journal entries and trial balance

Goal 3

3. Total debit column, $47,400

SPREADSHEET GENERAL LEDGER

On April 5 of the current year, John Bike established an interior decorating business, Tucson Designs. During the remainder of the month, John completed the following transactions related to the business:

April 5 John transferred cash from a personal bank account to an account to be used for the business in exchange for capital stock, $18,000.
6 Paid rent for the period of April 6 to the end of the month, $2,000.
7 Purchased office equipment on account, $10,500.
8 Purchased a used truck for $18,000, paying $10,000 cash and giving a note payable for the remainder.
10 Purchased supplies for cash, $1,315.
12 Received cash for job completed, $7,300.
20 Paid annual premiums on property and casualty insurance, $1,200.
23 Recorded jobs completed on account and sent invoices to customers, $4,950.
24 Received an invoice for truck expenses, to be paid in May, $450.
29 Paid utilities expense, $750.
29 Paid miscellaneous expenses, $210.
30 Received cash from customers on account, $2,200.
30 Paid wages of employees, $3,000.
30 Paid creditor a portion of the amount owed for equipment purchased on April 7, $1,800.
30 Paid dividends, $3,500.

Instructions

1. Journalize each transaction in a two-column journal, referring to the following chart of accounts in selecting the accounts to be debited and credited.

Cash	Capital Stock
Accounts Receivable	Dividends
Supplies	Fees Earned
Prepaid Insurance	Wages Expense
Equipment	Rent Expense
Truck	Utilities Expense
Notes Payable	Truck Expense
Accounts Payable	Miscellaneous Expense

2. Post the journal to a ledger of T accounts. For accounts with more than one posting, determine the account balance.
3. Prepare a trial balance for Tucson Designs as of April 30.

Problem 4–3A

Journal entries and trial balance

Goal 3

3. Total debit column, $158,650

SPREADSHEET GENERAL LEDGER

Eastside Realty acts as an agent in buying, selling, renting, and managing real estate. The account balances at the end of March 2004 of the current year are as follows:

Cash	8,150	
Accounts Receivable	28,750	
Prepaid Insurance	1,100	
Office Supplies	1,050	
Land	0	
Office Equipment	8,500	
Accumulated Depreciation		2,400
Accounts Payable		900
Salary and Commissions Payable		0
Unearned Fees		1,500
Notes Payable		0
Capital Stock		10,000
Retained Earnings		32,750
Dividends	0	
Fees Earned		0
Salary and Commission Expense	0	
Rent Expense	0	
Office Supplies Expense	0	
Advertising Expense	0	
Automobile Expense	0	
Insurance Expense	0	
Depreciation Expense	0	
Miscellaneous Expense	0	
	47,550	47,550

The following business transactions were completed by Eastside Realty during April 2004:

Apr. 1 Paid rent on office for April, $4,000.
2 Purchased office supplies on account, $1,375.
5 Paid annual insurance premiums, $1,650.
8 Received cash from clients on account, $27,500.
15 Purchased land for a future building site for $75,000, paying $7,500 in cash and giving a non-interest-bearing note payable due in 2006 for the remainder.

Apr. 17 Paid creditors on account, $900.
20 Returned a portion of the office supplies purchased on April 2, receiving full credit for their cost, $275.
24 Paid advertising expense, $1,100.
25 Billed clients for fees earned, $38,400.
27 Paid salaries and commissions, $11,500.
28 Paid automobile expense (including rental charges for an automobile), $715.
29 Paid miscellaneous expenses, $215.
30 Received cash from client for fees earned, $5,000.
30 Paid dividends, $2,000.

Instructions

1. Record the April 1 balance of each account in the appropriate column of a T account. Write *Balance* to identify the opening amounts.
2. Journalize the transactions for April in a two-column journal.
3. Post the journal entries to the T accounts, placing the date to the left of each amount to identify the transaction. Determine the balances for all accounts with more than one posting.
4. Prepare an unadjusted trial balance of the ledger as of April 30.

Problem 4–4A

Adjusting entries, financial statements, closing entries

Goals 3, 4

4. Total debit column, $160,925

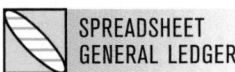

SPREADSHEET GENERAL LEDGER

The data necessary to adjust Eastside Realty accounts from Problem 4–3A as of April 30, 2004, are as follows:

a. Prepaid insurance expired during April, $250.
b. Office supplies on hand at April 30, $875.
c. Depreciation on office equipment, $125.
d. Unearned fees earned during April, $500.
e. Accrued fees as of April 30, $1,400.
f. Accrued salary and commissions as of April 30, $750.

Instructions:

1. Journalize the necessary adjusting entries for April.
2. Post the adjusting entries to T accounts. Identify each adjusting entry as "Adjusting." For those accounts that were adjusted, determine an adjusted balance.
3. Prepare an adjusted trial balance as of April 30.
4. Prepare an income statement, a retained earnings statement, and a classified balance sheet.
5. Journalize and post the closing entries for April. Identify each entry as "Closing." Determine post-closing balances.
6. Prepare a post-closing trial balance as of April 30, 2004.
7. (Appendix) Prepare a statement of cash flows for April. Note that the April 17 payment on account of $900 was for a March purchase of supplies on account.
8. (Appendix) Reconcile net income with net cash flows from operations for April.

Problem 4–5A

Adjustments and financial statements

Goals 3, 4

SPREADSHEET GENERAL LEDGER

Figure-Eight Company maintains and repairs warning lights, such as those found on radio towers and lighthouses. Figure-Eight Company prepared the following unadjusted trial balance at October 31, 2004, the end of the current fiscal year:

2. Total debit column, $389,280

Figure-Eight Company
Unadjusted Trial Balance
October 31, 2004

Cash	5,500	
Accounts Receivable	16,500	
Prepaid Insurance	3,000	
Supplies	1,950	
Land	70,000	
Building	100,500	
Accumulated Depreciation—Building		81,700
Equipment	72,400	
Accumulated Depreciation—Equipment		63,800
Accounts Payable		4,100
Unearned Rent		1,500
Capital Stock		18,000
Retained Earnings		39,700
Dividends	4,000	
Fees Revenue		171,200
Salaries and Wages Expense	60,200	
Advertising Expense	18,500	
Utilities Expense	15,100	
Repairs Expense	9,300	
Miscellaneous Expense	3,050	
	380,000	380,000

The data needed to determine year-end adjustments are as follows:

a. Fees revenue accrued at October 31 is $2,500.
b. Insurance expired during the year is $2,000.
c. Supplies on hand at October 31 are $450.
d. Depreciation of building for the year is $1,620.
e. Depreciation of equipment for the year is $3,160.
f. Accrued salaries and wages at October 31 are $2,000.
g. Unearned rent at October 31 is $500.

Instructions

1. Prepare the adjusting entries.
2. Based upon (1), prepare an adjusted trial balance.
3. Prepare an income statement for the year ended October 31.
4. Prepare a retained earnings statement for the year ended October 31.
5. Prepare a classified balance sheet as of October 31.
6. Prepare the closing entries.
7. Prepare a post-closing trial balance.

Alternate Accounting Application Problems

Alternate Problem 4–1B

Journal entries and trial balance

Goal 3

3. Total debit column, $33,500

STUDENT SOLUTIONS MANUAL

SPREADSHEET GENERAL LEDGER

On December 1, 2004, Mary Jo Croy established Preferred Realty, which completed the following transactions during the month:

a. Mary Jo Croy transferred cash from a personal bank account to an account to be used for the business in exchange for capital stock, $10,000.
b. Purchased supplies on account, $1,900.
c. Earned sales commissions, receiving cash, $22,600.
d. Paid rent on office and equipment for the month, $4,500.
e. Paid creditor on account, $1,000.
f. Paid dividends, $3,000.
g. Paid automobile expenses (including rental charge) for month, $1,900, and miscellaneous expenses, $1,050.
h. Paid office salaries, $4,000.
i. Determined that the cost of supplies used was $905.

Instructions

1. Journalize entries for transactions (a) through (i), using the following accounts: Cash; Supplies; Accounts Payable; Capital Stock; Dividends; Sales Commissions Earned; Rent Expense; Office Salaries Expense; Automobile Expense; Supplies Expense; Miscellaneous Expense.
2. Post the journal entries to T accounts, placing the appropriate letter to the left of each amount to identify the transactions. Determine the account balances, after all posting is complete.
3. Prepare a trial balance as of December 31, 2004.
4. Determine the following:
   a. Amount of total revenue recorded in the ledger.
   b. Amount of total expenses recorded in the ledger.
   c. Assuming that no adjustments are necessary, what is the amount of net income for December?

Alternate Problem 4–2B

Journal entries and trial balance

Goal 3

3. Total debit column, $33,480

STUDENT SOLUTIONS MANUAL

SPREADSHEET GENERAL LEDGER

On October 10 of the current year, Kirk Hurwitz established an interior decorating business, Marquis Designs. During the remainder of the month, Kirk Hurwitz completed the following transactions related to the business:

Oct. 10 Kirk transferred cash from a personal bank account to an account to be used for the business in exchange for capital stock, $15,000.
10 Paid rent for the period of October 10 to the end of the month, $1,600.
11 Purchased a truck for $15,000, paying $5,000 cash and giving a note payable for the remainder.
13 Purchased equipment on account, $3,500.
14 Purchased supplies for cash, $1,050.
14 Paid annual premiums on property and casualty insurance, $750.
15 Received cash for job completed, $3,100.
21 Paid creditor for equipment purchased on October 13, $3,500.
24 Recorded jobs completed on account and sent invoices to customers, $5,100.
26 Received an invoice for truck expenses, to be paid in November, $280.
27 Paid utilities expense, $1,205.
27 Paid miscellaneous expenses, $180.
29 Received cash from customers on account, $2,420.
30 Paid wages of employees, $2,500.
31 Paid dividends, $1,000.

Instructions

1. Journalize each transaction in a two-column journal, referring to the following chart of accounts in selecting the accounts to be debited and credited.

Cash	Capital Stock
Accounts Receivable	Dividends
Supplies	Fees Earned
Prepaid Insurance	Wages Expense
Equipment	Rent Expense
Truck	Utilities Expense
Notes Payable	Truck Expense
Accounts Payable	Miscellaneous Expense

2. Post the journal to a ledger of T accounts. For accounts with more than one posting, determine the account balance.
3. Prepare a trial balance for Marquis Designs as of October 31.

Alternate Problem 4–3B

Journal entries and trial balance

Goal 4

4. Total debit column, $121,900

STUDENT SOLUTIONS MANUAL

SPREADSHEET GENERAL LEDGER

Yellowstone Realty acts as an agent in buying, selling, renting, and managing real estate. The account balances at the end of May 2004 of the current year are as follows:

Cash	6,150	
Accounts Receivable	18,750	
Prepaid Insurance	1,800	
Office Supplies	1,200	
Land	0	
Office Equipment	13,100	
Accumulated Depreciation		3,600
Accounts Payable		800
Salary and Commissions Payable		0
Unearned Fees		1,800
Notes Payable		0
Capital Stock		25,000
Retained Earnings		9,800
Dividends	0	
Fees Earned		0
Salary and Commission Expense	0	
Rent Expense	0	
Office Supplies Expense	0	
Advertising Expense	0	
Automobile Expense	0	
Insurance Expense	0	
Depreciation Expense	0	
Miscellaneous Expense	0	
	41,000	41,000

The following business transactions were completed by Yellowstone Realty during June 2004:

June 1 Paid rent on office for June, $2,500.
2 Purchased office supplies on account, $1,375.
5 Paid annual insurance premiums, $2,400.
8 Received cash from clients on account, $16,300.
10 Purchased land for a future building site for $60,000, paying $6,000 in cash and giving a non-interest-bearing note payable due in 2006 for the remainder.
16 Paid creditors on account, $800.

June 18 Returned a portion of the office supplies purchased on June 2, receiving full credit for their cost, $175.
24 Paid advertising expense, $850.
25 Billed clients for fees earned, $23,500.
27 Paid salaries and commissions, $7,500
28 Paid automobile expense (including rental charges for an automobile), $750.
29 Paid miscellaneous expenses, $250.
30 Received cash from client for fees earned, $3,000.
30 Paid dividends, $1,000.

Instructions

1. Record the June 1 balance of each account in the appropriate column of a T account. Write *Balance* to identify the opening amounts.
2. Journalize the transactions for June in a two-column journal.
3. Post the journal entries to the T accounts, placing the date to the left of each amount to identify the transaction. Determine the balances for all accounts with more than one posting.
4. Prepare an unadjusted trial balance of the ledger as of June 30.

Alternate Problem 4-4B

Adjusting entries, financial statements, closing entries

Goals 3, 4

3. Total debit column, $124,000

STUDENT SOLUTIONS MANUAL

SPREADSHEET GENERAL LEDGER

The data necessary to adjust Yellowstone Realty accounts from Problem 4-3B as of June 30, 2004, are as follows:

a. Prepaid insurance expired during June, $350.
b. Office supplies on hand at June 30, $725.
c. Depreciation on office equipment, $200.
d. Unearned fees earned during June, $600.
e. Accrued fees as of June 30, $1,200.
f. Accrued salary and commissions as of June 30, $700.

Instructions:

1. Journalize the necessary adjusting entries for June.
2. Post the adjusting entries to T accounts. Identify each adjusting entry as "Adjusting." For those accounts that were adjusted, determine an adjusted balance.
3. Prepare an adjusted trial balance as of June 30.
4. Prepare an income statement, a retained earnings statement, and a classified balance sheet.
5. Journalize and post the closing entries for June. Identify each entry as "Closing." Determine post-closing balances.
6. Prepare a post-closing trial balance as of June 30, 2004.
7. (Appendix) Prepare a statement of cash flows for June. Note that the June 16 payment on account of $800 was for a May purchase of supplies on account.
8. (Appendix) Reconcile net income with net cash flows from operations for June.

Alternate Problem 4-5B

Adjustments and financial statements

Goals 3, 4

STUDENT SOLUTIONS MANUAL

SPREADSHEET GENERAL LEDGER

Sanguine Company offers legal consulting advice to immigrants. Sanguine Company prepared the following trial balance at June 30, 2004, the end of the current fiscal year:

2. Total debit column, $502,320

Sanguine Company
Unadjusted Trial Balance
June 30, 2004

Cash	2,200	
Accounts Receivable	7,500	
Prepaid Insurance	1,800	
Supplies	1,350	
Land	50,000	
Building	137,500	
Accumulated Depreciation—Building		51,700
Equipment	90,100	
Accumulated Depreciation—Equipment		35,300
Accounts Payable		3,500
Unearned Rent		3,000
Capital Stock		70,000
Retained Earnings		142,500
Dividends	10,000	
Fees Revenue		188,400
Salaries and Wages Expense	101,200	
Advertising Expense	58,200	
Utilities Expense	19,000	
Repairs Expense	11,500	
Miscellaneous Expense	4,050	
	494,400	494,400

The data needed to determine year-end adjustments are as follows:

a. Accrued fees revenue at June 30 is $1,750.
b. Insurance expired during the year is $800.
c. Supplies on hand at June 30 are $650.
d. Depreciation of building for the year is $1,620.
e. Depreciation of equipment for the year is $3,500.
f. Accrued salaries and wages at June 30 are $1,050.
g. Unearned rent at June 30 is $1,000.

Instructions

1. Prepare the adjusting entries.
2. Based upon (1), prepare an adjusted trial balance.
3. Prepare an income statement for the year ended June 30.
4. Prepare a retained earnings statement for the year ended June 30.
5. Prepare a classified balance sheet as of June 30.
6. Prepare the closing entries.
7. Prepare a post-closing trial balance.

Building Leadership Skills—Financial Analysis and Reporting

Case 4–1

The Gap is a global specialty retailer operating stores selling casual apparel, personal care, and other accessories for men, women, and children under The Gap, Banana Republic, and Old Navy brands. The Gap designs virtually all of its products, which are manufactured by independent sources and sold under The Gap's name brands.

The following operating data (in thousands) were adapted from the 2002 SEC 10-K filings of The Gap for the years ending February 2, 2002, and February 3, 2001:

	2002	2001
Net sales	$13,847,873	$13,673,460
Costs and expenses		
Cost of goods sold	$ 9,704,389	$ 8,599,442
Operating expenses	3,805,968	3,629,257
Interest expense	109,190	74,891
Other income	(13,315)	(12,015)
	$13,606,232	$12,291,575
Income before taxes	$ 241,641	$ 1,381,885
Income taxes	249,405	504,388
Net income (loss)	$ (7,764)	$ 877,497
Depreciation and amortization	$ 810,486	$ 590,365

1. Compute EBITDA for 2002 and 2001.
2. Compute the ratio of EBITDA to interest expense for 2002 and 2001. Round to one decimal place.
3. Based upon (1) and (2), discuss the trends in EBITDA and the ratio of EBITDA to interest expense.
4. Is EBITDA normally the same as the amount reported for net cash flows from operating activities? Explain.

Case 4–2

The following excerpt is taken from the notes to the financial statements for The Gap:

> *Our credit agreements are subject to our not exceeding a debt to EBITDA ratio of 3:1.*

Financial requirements such as that shown above are called loan or credit covenants. The violation of a loan or credit covenant can result in the debt becoming due immediately, as well as requirements to pay additional interest and penalties. For purposes of determining compliance with the preceding covenant, only long-term debt is considered. The long-term debt of The Gap at the end of 2002 and 2001 was $1,961,397 and $780,246, respectively.

1. Based upon your answer to Case 4–1, determine whether The Gap is in compliance with the loan covenant for 2002 and 2001. Round to one decimal place.

(continued)

2. Assume that long-term debt does not change during 2003. Also, assume the following operating data for 2003:

Interest expense	$125,000
Depreciation and amortization	800,000
Net loss before income taxes	(200,000)

Given this information, will The Gap violate its loan covenant in 2003? Show your computations. Round to one decimal place.

3. Assuming that during 2003 the long-term debt does not change, how much would EBITDA have to decline before The Gap would violate the covenant?

Case 4–3

The following excerpt describing EBITDA is from the Securities and Exchange Commission 10-K filing by AOL Time Warner for the year ending December 31, 2001:

> *AOL Time Warner evaluates operating performance based on several factors, including its primary financial measure of operating income (loss) before non-cash depreciation of tangible assets and amortization of goodwill and intangible assets (EBITDA). AOL Time Warner considers EBITDA an important indicator of the operational strength and performance of its businesses, including the ability to provide cash flows to service debt and fund capital expenditures. In addition, EBITDA eliminates the uneven effect across all business segments of considerable amounts of noncash depreciation of tangible assets and amortization of goodwill and intangible assets recognized in business combinations accounted for by the purchase method. As such, the following comparative discussion of the results of operations of AOL Time Warner includes, among other factors, an analysis of changes in EBITDA. However, EBITDA should be considered in addition to, not as a substitute for, operating income (loss), net income (loss) and other measures of financial performance reported in accordance with generally accepted accounting principles.*

The following income statement (in millions) is adapted from the 2001 10-K filing of AOL Time Warner:

Revenues	$ 38,234
Cost of revenues	(20,704)
Gross profit	$ 17,530
Selling, administrative, and other expenses	(9,846)
Amortization of goodwill and other intangible assets	(7,231)
Operating income	$ 453
Interest expense	(1,379)
Other expenses	(3,849)
Loss before taxes	$ (4,775)
Taxes	(146)
Net loss	$ (4,921)

Included in the preceding income statement is depreciation of property, plant, and equipment of $1,972.

1. Compute the EBITDA for 2001.
2. Compute the percentage of EBITDA to total revenues for 2001. Round to one decimal place after converting to a percentage.
3. Compute the ratio of EBITDA to interest expense for 2001. Round to one decimal place.
4. Compute the ratio of long-term debt to EBITDA for 2001. The long-term debt as of December 31, 2001, was $22,792. Round to one decimal place.
5. Comment on the ability of AOL Time Warner to meet its interest obligations.

Case 4–4

AOL Time Warner's operations consist of various business segments. The following revenue and EBITDA data (in millions) are from the Securities and Exchange Commission 10-K filing by AOL Time Warner for the year ending December 31, 2001:

	Revenues	EBITDA
America Online	$ 8,718	$2,945
Cable	6,992	3,199
Filmed entertainment	8,759	1,017
Networks	7,050	1,797
Music	3,929	419
Publishing	4,810	909
Offsetting corporate adjustments	(2,024)	(630)
Total	$38,234	$9,656

1. Compute the percentage of EBITDA to revenues for each of the business segments. Ignore the offsetting corporate adjustments in your computations. Round to one decimal place.
2. Based upon (1), comment on the ability of each of the business segments to generate EBITDA per revenue dollar.

Case 4–5

The following income statement (in thousands) is from the Securities and Exchange Commission 10-K filing by Amazon.com for the year ending December 31, 2001:

Net sales		$3,122,433
Cost of sales		2,323,875
Gross profit		$ 798,558
Operating expenses:		
Fulfillment expenses	$374,250	
Marketing expenses	138,283	
Technology and content expenses	241,165	
General and administrative expenses	89,862	
Stock-based compensation expense	4,637	
Amortization of goodwill and other intangible assets	181,033	
Restructuring and other expenses	181,585	
Total operating expenses		1,210,815
Loss from operations before interest and taxes		$ (412,257)

Included in the preceding income statement is total depreciation expense of $83,444.

1. Compute the EBITDA for 2001.
2. Based upon (1), comment on Amazon.com's EBITDA.

Case 4–6

ETHICS

Worldcom, Inc., allegedly reported nearly $4 billion as fixed assets on its balance sheet, rather than as operating expense on its income statement. Of this amount, $3.06 billion should have been expensed in 2001, rather than capitalized as a fixed asset. As a result of this discovery, Worldcom lost credibility with investors, and its common stock lost nearly all of its value. Worldcom made public disclosures of its net income, as required, but also focused its earning announcements on EBITDA. The income statement for the year ended December 31, 2001, reported the following:

Worldcom, Inc.
Income Statement
For the Year Ended December 31, 2001

	(in millions)
Revenues	$35,179
Operating expenses:	
Line costs	$14,739
Selling, general and administrative	11,046
Depreciation and amortization	5,880
Total	$31,665
Operating income	$ 3,514
Other income (expense):	
Interest expense	(1,533)
Miscellaneous income	447
Income before income taxes	$ 2,428
Provision for income taxes	927
Net income	$ 1,501

1. Determine EBITDA, using the reported figures.
2. Determine EBITDA as it should have been reported in 2001 if costs were properly expensed, rather than capitalized.
3. Assume that fixed assets are depreciated on the straight-line basis for five years. Under this assumption, what would be the correct net income (loss) before income taxes for 2001?

Case 4–7

On the Internet, go to the google.com Web site and perform an advanced search for "EBITDA." Review the articles for a discussion of the advantages and disadvantages of using EBITDA as a financial analysis tool. Pick one or more articles, read them, and summarize your findings.

Building Leadership Skills—Responsible Leadership

Activity 4–1

Business strategy

Mohawk Industries is a leading distributor of carpets and rugs in the United States. The company sells its carpets and rugs to locally-owned, independent carpet retailers, home centers such as Home Depot and Lowe's, and department stores such as Sears. Mohawk's carpets are marked under the brand names that include "Aladdin, Mohawk Home, Bigelow, Custom Weave, Durkan, Karastan, and Townhouse."

1. List some factors that increase the demand for carpet.
2. From a strategic viewpoint, do you think Mohawk should view itself as a carpet or floorcovering manufacturer? Discuss the advantages and disadvantages of Mohawk viewing itself as a floorcovering manufacturer rather than just a carpet manufacturer.
3. Read Mohawk's latest 10-K filing with the Securities and Exchange Commission by using EdgarScan (http://edgarscan.pwcglobal.com). Does Mohawk view itself as a carpet manufacturer or as a floorcovering manufacturer? Explain.

Activity 4–2

Ethics and professional conduct in business

ETHICS

At the end of the current month, Dana Fossum prepared a trial balance for City Motors Co. The credit side of the trial balance exceeds the debit side by a significant amount. Dana has decided to add the difference to the balance of the miscellaneous expense account in order to complete the preparation of the current month's financial statements by a 5 o'clock deadline. Dana will look for the difference next week when she has more time.

Discuss whether Dana is behaving in a professional manner.

Activity 4–3

Recording transactions

The following discussion took place between Marc Bolli, the office manager of Landmark Data Company, and a new accountant, Kelly Holt.

Kelly: I've been thinking about our method of recording entries. It seems that it's inefficient.
Marc: In what way?
Kelly: Well—correct me if I'm wrong—it seems like we have unnecessary steps in the process. We could easily develop a trial balance by posting our transactions directly into the ledger and bypassing the journal altogether. In this way we could combine the recording and posting processes into one step and save ourselves a lot of time. What do you think?
Marc: We need to have a talk.

What should Marc say to Kelly?

Activity 4–4

Debits and credits

GROUP ACTIVITY

The following excerpt is from a conversation between Jill Rhyne, the president and chief operating officer of Lodge Construction Co., and her neighbor, Sean Resnik:

Sean: Jill, I'm taking a course in night school, "Intro to Accounting." I was wondering—could you answer a couple of questions for me?
Jill: Well, I will if I can.
Sean: Okay, our instructor says that it's critical we understand the basic concepts of accounting, or we'll never get beyond the first test. My problem is with those rules of debit and credit . . . you know, assets increase with debits, decrease with credits, etc.

Jill: Yes, pretty basic stuff. You just have to memorize the rules. It shouldn't be too difficult.

Sean: Sure, I can memorize the rules, but my problem is I want to be sure I understand the basic concepts behind the rules.

For example, why can't assets be increased with credits and decreased with debits like revenue? As long as everyone did it that way, why not? It would seem easier if we had the same rules for all increases and decreases in accounts.

Also, why is the left side of an account called the debit side? Why couldn't it be called something simple . . . like the "LE" for Left Entry? The right side could be called just "RE" for Right Entry.

Finally, why are there just two sides to an entry? Why can't there be three or four sides to an entry?

In a group of four or five, select one person to play the role of Jill and one person to play the role of Sean.

1. After listening to the conversation between Jill and Sean, help Jill answer Sean's questions.
2. What information (other than just debit and credit journal entries) could the accounting system gather that might be useful to Jill in managing Lodge Construction Co.?

Activity 4–5

Financial statements

The following is an excerpt from a telephone conversation between Gail Richie, president of Flanders Supplies Co., and Gary Weir, owner of On-Time Employment Co.:

Gail: Gary, you're going to have to do a better job of finding me a new computer programmer. That last guy was great at programming, but he didn't have any common sense.

Gary: What do you mean? The guy had a master's degree with straight A's.

Gail: Yes, well, last month he developed a new financial reporting system. He said we could do away with manually posting journal entries and preparing financial statements. The computer would automatically generate our financial statements with "a push of a button."

Gary: So what's the big deal? Sounds to me like it would save you time and effort.

Gail: Right! The balance sheet showed a minus for supplies!

Gary: Minus supplies? How can that be?

Gail: That's what I asked.

Gary: So, what did he say?

Gail: Well, after he checked the program, he said that it must be right. The minuses were greater than the pluses . . .

Gary: Didn't he know that supplies can't have a credit balance–it must have a debit balance?

Gail: He asked me what a debit and credit were.

Gary: I see your point.

1. Comment on (a) the desirability of computerizing Flanders Supplies Co.'s financial reporting system, (b) the elimination of manually posting journal entries and preparing financial statements in a computerized accounting system, and (c) the computer programmer's lack of accounting knowledge.
2. Explain to the programmer why supplies could not have a credit balance.

Activity 4–6

Financial statements

Assume that you recently accepted a position with the Big Timber National Bank as an assistant loan officer. As one of your first duties, you have been assigned the responsibility of evaluating a loan request for $50,000 from Megabit.com, a small corporation. In support of the loan application, Erica Salley, owner, submitted a "Statement of Accounts" (trial balance) for the first year of operations ended December 31, 2004.

1. Explain to Erica Salley why a set of financial statements (income statement, retained earnings statement, and balance sheet) would be useful to you in evaluating the loan request.
2. In discussing the "Statement of Accounts" with Erica Salley, you discovered that the accounts had not been adjusted at December 31. Analyze the "Statement of Accounts" (shown below) and indicate possible adjusting entries that might be necessary before an accurate set of financial statements could be prepared.

Megabit.com
Statement of Accounts
December 31, 2004

Cash	3,120	
Billings Due from Others	10,150	
Supplies (chemicals, etc.)	14,950	
Trucks	32,750	
Equipment	26,150	
Amounts Owed to Others		6,700
Investment in Business		57,260
Service Revenue		117,300
Wages Expense	70,100	
Utilities Expense	16,900	
Rent Expense	4,800	
Insurance Expense	1,400	
Other Expenses	940	
	181,260	181,260

3. Assuming that an accurate set of financial statements will be submitted by Erica Salley in a few days, what other considerations or information would you require before making a decision on the loan request?

Answers to Self-Study Questions

1. **A** A debit may signify an increase in an asset account (answer A) or a decrease in a liability or capital stock account. A credit may signify a decrease in an asset account (answer B) or an increase in a liability or capital stock account (answers C and D).
2. **C** Liability, capital stock, and revenue (answer C) accounts have normal credit balances. Asset (answer A), dividends (answer B), and expense (answer D) accounts have normal debit balances.
3. **C** Accounts Receivable (answer A), Cash (answer B), and Miscellaneous Expense (answer D) would all normally have debit balances. Fees Earned should normally have a credit balance. Hence, a debit balance in Fees Earned (answer C) would indicate a likely error in the recording process.
4. **B** The entry to close the dividends account is to debit the retained earnings account and credit the dividends account (answer B).
5. **D** Since all revenue and expense accounts are closed at the end of the period, Fees Earned (answer A), Wages Expense (answer B), and Rent Expense (answer C) would all be closed to Retained Earnings. Accumulated Depreciation (answer D) is a contra asset account that is not closed.

Chapter 5
Accounting for Merchandise Operations

THE LAW OF MAGNETISM

"Who you are is who you attract."

–The 21 Irrefutable Laws of Leadership

Dr. John C. Maxwell

Learning Goals

1. Distinguish the operating activities of a service business from those of a merchandise business.
2. Describe and illustrate the financial statements of a merchandising business.
3. Describe the accounting for the sale of merchandise.
4. Describe the accounting for the purchase of merchandise.
5. Describe the accounting for transportation costs and sales taxes.
6. Illustrate the dual nature of merchandising transactions.
7. Describe the accounting for merchandise shrinkage.
8. Describe and illustrate the effects of inventory misstatements on the financial statements.
9. Describe and illustrate the use of gross profit and operating income in analyzing a company's operations.

JC Penney

You are probably familiar with the "Golden Rule," which is "Do unto others as you would have them do unto you." In Kemmer, Wyoming, a young entrepreneur opened his first retail store and called it the Golden Rule. Why? Because he believed that his customers deserved to be treated fairly by providing money-back returns, standardized pricing, and quality merchandise with a smile. This was a radical departure from existing retail practice, which could best be described as "let the customer beware." He stated, "In setting up a business under the name and meaning of the Golden Rule, I was publicly binding myself, in my business relations, to a principle which had been a real and intimate part of my family upbringing. To me the sign on the store was much more than a trade name. . . . We took our slogan 'Golden Rule Store' with strict literalness. Our idea was to make money and build business through serving the community with fair dealing and honest value."

From these humble beginnings, this company has grown under the founder's name to become the largest department store chain and catalog general merchandiser in the U.S. Who was this humble entrepreneur? James Cash Penney. His company, of course, is JC Penney. Mr. Penney's life could be summed up well by a statement he made in the latter part of his life: "Life's greatest pleasure and satisfaction is found in giving; and the greatest gift of all gifts is that of one's self."

Your Need to Know

Merchandising has existed since the days of the traveling merchant, trade festivals, and village bartering. The way we buy goods (and services) has undergone significant changes and will continue to change with consumer tastes and technology. For example, in the past twenty years we have seen the emergence of (1) discount merchandising, (2) category killers, and (3) Internet retailing.

Wal-Mart, which led the development of discount merchandising, has become the world's largest retailer. Wal-Mart's growth is centered on providing the consumer with everyday discount pricing over a broad array of household products. Category killers include Toys"R"Us (toys), Best Buy (electronics), Home Depot (home improvement), and Office Depot (office supplies), which provide a wide selection of attractively priced goods within a particular product segment. Internet retailers, such as Amazon.com and Lands' End, allow time-conscious consumers to shop quickly and effortlessly.

Merchandising will undoubtedly continue to evolve as consumer lifestyles and technologies change in the future. In this chapter, we introduce you to the accounting issues unique to merchandisers. We emphasize merchandisers at this point in the text because merchandising is significant in its own right, and because even nonmerchandisers have similar accounting issues to those discussed in this chapter.

Merchandise Operations

1 Distinguish the operating activities of a service business from those of a merchandise business.

In prior chapters, we described and illustrated how businesses report their financial condition and changes in financial condition using the cash and accrual bases of accounting. In these prior chapters, we focused on service businesses. In this chapter, we describe and illustrate the accounting for merchandise operations.

How do the operating activities of a service business, such as a consulting firm, law practice, or architectural firm, differ from a merchandising business, such as Home Depot or Wal-Mart? The differences are best illustrated by focusing on the income statements of the two types of businesses.

The condensed income statement of H&R Block Inc. is shown in Exhibit 1.[1] H&R Block is a service business that primarily offers tax planning and preparation to its customers.

The condensed income statement of Home Depot Inc. is shown in Exhibit 2.[2] Home Depot is the world's largest home improvement retailer and the second largest retailer in the United States, based on net sales volume.

Assume that operating income is $45,000, gross profit is $100,000, and the cost of goods sold is $525,000. What are the net sales and the total operating expenses?

Net sales: $625,000 ($100,000 + $525,000)
Operating expenses: $55,000 ($100,000 − $45,000)

The revenue activities of a service business involve providing services to customers. On the income statement for a service business, the revenues from services are reported as revenues or fees earned. The operating expenses incurred in providing services are subtracted from the revenues to arrive at operating income. Any other income or expense is then added or subtracted to arrive at income before taxes. Net income is determined by subtracting income taxes. Exhibit 1 shows that H&R Block earned operating profits of $465 million based upon revenues of over $3 billion. Adding other income and subtracting income taxes results in net income of $277 million.

In contrast, the revenue activities of a merchandising business involve the buying and selling of merchandise. A merchandise business must first purchase merchandise to sell to its customers. The revenue received for

1 Adapted from H&R Block's 10-K filing with the Securities and Exchange Commission.

2 Adapted from Home Depot's 10-K filing with the Securities and Exchange Commission.

Exhibit 1

H&R Block Income Statement

H&R Block Inc.
Condensed Income Statement
For the Year Ending April 30, 2001
(in millions)

Revenue	$3,002
Operating expenses	2,537
Operating income	$ 465
Other income	8
Income before taxes	$ 473
Income taxes	196
Net income	$ 277

Exhibit 2

Home Depot Income Statement

Home Depot Inc.
Condensed Income Statement
For the Year Ending December 28, 2001
(in millions)

Net sales	$45,738
Cost of merchandise sold	32,057
Gross profit	$13,681
Operating expenses	9,490
Operating income	$ 4,191
Other income	26
Income before taxes	$ 4,217
Income taxes	1,636
Net income	$ 2,581

merchandise sold to customers less any merchandise returned or any discounts is reported as **net sales**. The related **cost of merchandise sold** is then determined and matched against the net sales. **Gross profit** is determined by subtracting the cost of merchandise sold from net sales. Gross profit gets its name from the fact that it is the profit before deducting operating expenses. Operating expenses are then subtracted in arriving at operating income. Like a service business, other income or expense is then added or subtracted to arrive at income before taxes. Subtracting income taxes yields net income.

Exhibit 2 shows that Home Depot earned a gross profit of almost $13.7 billion, based upon net sales of $45.7 billion. Operating expenses reduce gross profit to an operating income of $4.2 billion. Adding other income and subtracting income taxes results in net income of $2.6 billion.

In addition to operating and income statement differences, merchandise inventory on hand (not sold) at the end of the accounting period is reported on the balance sheet as **merchandise inventory**. Since merchandise is normally sold within a year, it is reported as a current asset on the balance sheet.

Strategy in Business

Under One Roof at JC Penney

Most businesses cannot be all things to all people. Businesses must seek a position in the marketplace to serve a unique customer need. Companies that are unable to do this can be squeezed out of the marketplace. The mall-based department store has been under pressure from both ends of the retail spectrum. At the discount store end of the market, Wal-Mart has been a formidable competitor. At the high end, specialty retailers have established strong presence in identifiable niches, such as electronics and apparel. Over a decade ago, JC Penney abandoned its "hard goods," such as electronics and sporting goods, in favor of providing "soft goods" because of the emerging strength of specialty retailers in the hard goods segments. JC Penney is positioning itself against these forces by *"exceeding the fashion, quality, selection, and service components of the discounter, equaling the merchandise intensity of the specialty store, and providing the selection and 'under one roof' shopping convenience of the department store."* JC Penney merchandise strategy is focused toward customers it terms the "modern spender" and "starting outs." It views these segments as most likely to value its higher-end merchandise offered under the convenience of "one roof."

Financial Statements for a Merchandising Business

2 Describe and illustrate the financial statements of a merchandising business.

In this section, we continue the illustration from Chapter 4, illustrating the financial statements for Online Solutions after it becomes a retailer of computer hardware and software. These financial statements are similar to those for a service business.[3]

During 2005, we assume that Shannon Hughes implemented the second phase of Online Solutions' business plan. Accordingly, Shannon notified clients that beginning January 1, 2006, Online Solutions would be terminating its consulting services. Instead, it would become an Internet-based retailer.

Online's business strategy is to focus on offering personalized service to individuals and small businesses who are upgrading or purchasing new computer systems. Online's personal service before the sale will include a no-obligation, on-site assessment of the customer's computer needs. By providing tailor-made solutions, personalized service, and follow-up, Shannon feels that Online can compete effectively against larger retailers, such as Dell or Gateway. Initially, Shannon plans to grow Online Solutions regionally. If successful, Shannon plans to take the company public.

3 The closing process, which is not illustrated, is also similar to a service business.

Multiple-Step Income Statement

The 2007 income statement for Online Solutions' second year as an Internet retailer is shown in Exhibit 3.[4] This form of income statement, called a **multiple-step income statement**, contains several sections, subsections, and subtotals.

Exhibit 3

Multiple-Step Income Statement

Online Solutions
Income Statement
For the Year Ended December 31, 2007

Net sales	$708,255
Cost of merchandise sold	525,305
Gross profit	$182,950
Operating expenses	105,710
Operating income	$ 77,240
Other income and expense (net)	(1,840)
Operating income before taxes	$ 75,400
Income taxes	15,000
Net income	$ 60,400

Net sales for Online Solutions is determined as follows:

Sales		$720,185
Less sales returns and allowances	$6,140	
Less sales discounts	5,790	11,930
Net sales		$708,255

Sales is the total amount charged customers for merchandise sold, including cash sales and sales on account. Both sales returns and allowances and sales discounts are subtracted in arriving at net sales.

Sales returns and allowances are granted by the seller to customers for damaged or defective merchandise. For example, rather than have a buyer return merchandise, a seller may offer a $500 allowance to the customer as compensation for damaged merchandise. Sales returns and allowances are recorded when the merchandise is returned or when the allowance is granted by the seller.

Sales discounts are granted by the seller to customers for early payment of amounts owed. For example, a seller may offer a customer a 2% discount on a sale of $10,000 if the customer pays within ten days. If the customer pays within the ten-day period, the seller receives cash of $9,800 and the buyer receives a discount of $200 ($10,000 × 2%). Sales discounts are recorded when the customer pays the bill.

Cost of merchandise sold is the cost of the merchandise sold to customers. To illustrate the determination of the cost of merchandise sold, assume that Online Solutions purchased $340,000 of merchandise during 2006. If the inventory at December 31, 2006, the end of the year, is $59,700, the cost of the merchandise sold during 2006 is determined as shown on the next page.

Assume that sales are $790,000, sales discounts are $35,000, and net sales are $680,000. What are the sales returns and allowances?

$75,000 ($790,000 − $35,000 − $680,000)

4 We use the Online Solutions income statement for 2007 as a basis for illustration because, as will be shown, it allows us to better illustrate the computation of the cost of merchandise sold.

Purchases	$340,000
Less merchandise inventory, December 31, 2006	59,700
Cost of merchandise sold	$280,300

As we discussed in the preceding section, sellers may offer customers sales discounts for early payment of their bills. Such discounts are referred to as **purchases discounts** by the buyer. Purchase discounts reduce the cost of merchandise. A buyer may return merchandise to the seller (a **purchase return**), or the buyer may receive a reduction in the initial price at which the merchandise was purchased (a **purchase allowance**). Like purchase discounts, purchases returns and allowances reduce the cost of merchandise purchased during a period. In addition, transportation costs paid by the buyer for merchandise also increase the cost of merchandise purchased.

To continue the illustration, assume that during 2007 Online Solutions purchased additional merchandise of $521,980. It received credit for purchases returns and allowances of $9,100, took purchases discounts of $2,525, and paid transportation costs of $17,400. The purchases returns and allowances and the purchases discounts are deducted from the total purchases to yield the *net purchases.* The transportation costs are added to the net purchases to yield the *cost of merchandise purchased,* as shown below.

Purchases		$521,980
Less: Purchases returns and allowances	$9,100	
Purchases discounts	2,525	11,625
Net purchases		$510,355
Add transportation in		17,400
Cost of merchandise purchased		$527,755

Assume that purchases are $480,000, purchases returns and allowances are $25,000, and purchases discounts are $60,000. What are the net purchases?

$395,000 ($480,000 − $25,000 − $60,000)

The ending inventory of Online Solutions on December 31, 2006, $59,700, becomes the beginning inventory for 2007. This beginning inventory is added to the cost of merchandise purchased to yield **merchandise available for sale**. The ending inventory, which is assumed to be $62,150, is then subtracted from the merchandise available for sale to yield the cost of merchandise sold, as shown in Exhibit 4.

Exhibit 4

Cost of Merchandise Sold

Merchandise inventory, January 1, 2007			$ 59,700
Purchases		$521,980	
Less: Purchases returns and allowances	$9,100		
Purchases discounts	2,525	11,625	
Net purchases		$510,355	
Add transportation in		17,400	
Cost of merchandise purchased			527,755
Merchandise available for sale			$587,455
Less merchandise inventory, December 31, 2007			62,150
Cost of merchandise sold			$525,305

If merchandise available for sale is $1,375,000 and the cost of merchandise sold is $950,000, what is the ending merchandise inventory?

$425,000 ($1,375,000 − $950,000)

The cost of merchandise sold was determined by deducting the merchandise on hand at the end of the period from the merchandise available for sale during the period. The merchandise on hand at the end of the period is determined by taking a physical count of inventory on hand. This method of determining the cost of merchandise sold and the amount of merchandise on hand is called the **periodic method** of accounting for merchandise inventory. Under the periodic method, the inventory records do not show the amount available for sale or the amount sold during the period. In contrast, under the **perpetual method** of accounting for merchandise inventory, each purchase and sale of merchandise is recorded in the inventory and the cost of merchandise sold accounts. As a result, the amount of merchandise available for sale and the amount sold are continuously (perpetually) disclosed in the inventory records.

Most large retailers and many small merchandising businesses use computerized perpetual inventory systems. Such systems normally use bar codes, such as the one on the back of this textbook. An optical scanner reads the bar code to record merchandise purchased and sold. Merchandise businesses using a perpetual inventory system report the cost of merchandise sold as a single line on the income statement, as shown in Exhibit 3 for Online Solutions. Merchandise businesses using the periodic inventory method report the cost of merchandise sold by using the format shown in Exhibit 4. Because of its wide use, we will use the perpetual inventory method throughout the remainder of this chapter.

Exhibit 3 shows that Online Solutions reported gross profit of $182,950 in 2007. *Operating income*, sometimes called **income from operations**, is determined by subtracting operating expenses from gross profit. Most merchandising businesses classify operating expenses as either selling expenses or administrative expenses. Expenses that are incurred directly in the selling of merchandise are **selling expenses**. They include such expenses as salespersons' salaries, store supplies used, depreciation of store equipment, and advertising. Expenses incurred in the administration or general operations of the business are **administrative expenses** or *general expenses*. Examples of these expenses are office salaries, depreciation of office equipment, and office supplies used. Credit card expense is also normally classified as an administrative expense. Although selling and administrative expenses may be reported separately, many companies report operating expenses as a single item, as shown in Exhibit 3.

As we will illustrate later in this chapter, operating income is often used in financial analysis to judge the efficiency and profitability of operations. For example, operating income divided by total assets or net sales is often used in comparing merchandise businesses.

Online Solutions' income statement in Exhibit 3 also reports other income and expense. Revenue from sources other than the primary operating activity of a business is classified as **other income**. In a merchandising business, these items include income from interest, rent, and gains resulting from the sale of fixed assets.

Expenses that cannot be traced directly to operations are identified as **other expense**. Interest expense that results from financing activities and losses incurred in the disposal of fixed assets are examples of these items.

Other income and other expense are offset against each other on the income statement and are reported as a net amount, as shown in Exhibit 3. If the total of other income exceeds the total of other expense, the difference is added to income from operations. If the reverse is true, the difference is subtracted from income from operations.

Deducting income taxes from income before taxes yields the net income. As we illustrated in Chapter 4, net income or loss is closed to Retained Earnings at the end of the period.

Single-Step Income Statement

An alternate form of income statement is the **single-step income statement**. As shown in Exhibit 5, the income statement for Online Solutions deducts the total of all expenses *in one step* from the total of all revenues.

The single-step form emphasizes total revenues and total expenses as the factors that determine net income. A criticism of the single-step form is that such amounts as gross profit and income from operations are not readily available for analysis.

Exhibit 5

Single-Step Income Statement

Online Solutions Income Statement For the Year Ended December 31, 2007		
Revenue:		
Net sales		$708,255
Expenses:		
Cost of merchandise sold	$525,305	
Operating expenses	105,710	
Income taxes	15,000	
Other income and expense (net)	1,840	647,855
Net income		$ 60,400

Retained Earnings Statement

The retained earnings statement for Online Solutions is shown in Exhibit 6. This statement is prepared in the same manner that we described previously for a service business.

Exhibit 6

Retained Earnings Statement

Online Solutions Retained Earnings Statement For the Year Ended December 31, 2007		
Retained earnings, January 1, 2007		$128,800
Net income for the year	$60,400	
Less dividends	18,000	
Increase in retained earnings		42,400
Retained earnings, December 31, 2007		$171,200

Balance Sheet

As we discussed and illustrated in previous chapters, the balance sheet may be presented in a downward sequence in three sections, beginning with the assets. This form of balance sheet is called the **report form**.[5] The 2007 balance sheet for Online Solutions is shown in Exhibit 7. In this balance sheet, note that merchandise inventory at the end of the period is reported as a current asset and that the current portion of the note payable is $5,000.

Statement of Cash Flows

The statement of cash flows for Online Solutions is shown in Exhibit 8 (on page 218). It indicates that cash increased during 2007 by $11,450. This increase is generated from

5 The balance sheet may also be presented in an account form, with assets on the left-hand side and the liabilities and stockholders' equity on the right-hand side.

Exhibit 7

Balance Sheet

Online Solutions Balance Sheet December 31, 2007			
Assets			
Current assets:			
Cash		$ 52,950	
Accounts receivable		76,080	
Merchandise inventory		62,150	
Office supplies		480	
Prepaid insurance		2,650	
Total current assets			$194,310
Property, plant, and equipment:			
Land		$ 20,000	
Store equipment	$27,100		
Less accumulated depreciation	5,700	21,400	
Office equipment	$15,570		
Less accumulated depreciation	4,720	10,850	
Total property, plant, and equipment			52,250
Total assets			$246,560
Liabilities			
Current liabilities:			
Accounts payable		$ 22,420	
Note payable (current portion)		5,000	
Salaries payable		1,140	
Unearned rent		1,800	
Total current liabilities			$ 30,360
Long-term liabilities:			
Note payable (final payment due 2017)			20,000
Total liabilities			$ 50,360
Stockholders' Equity			
Capital stock		$ 25,000	
Retained earnings		171,200	196,200
Total liabilities and stockholders' equity			$246,560

a positive cash flow from operating activities of $47,120, which is partially offset by negative cash flows from investing and financing activities of $12,670 and $23,000, respectively.

The net cash flows from operating activities is shown in Exhibit 8 using a method known as the **indirect method**. This method, which reconciles net income with net cash flows from operating activities, is widely used among publicly held corporations.[6] Finally, you should note that the December 31, 2007 cash balance reported on the statement of cash flows agrees with the amount reported for cash on the December 31, 2007 balance sheet shown in Exhibit 7.

6 The preparation of the statement of cash flows using the indirect method is further discussed and illustrated in the Appendix to this chapter.

Exhibit 8

Statement of Cash Flows for Merchandising Business

Online Solutions
Statement of Cash Flows
For the Year Ended December 31, 2007

Cash flows from operating activities:		
Net income		$ 60,400
Add: Depreciation expense—store equipment	$ 3,100	
Depreciation expense—office equipment	2,490	
Decrease in office supplies	120	
Decrease in prepaid insurance	350	
Increase in accounts payable	8,150	14,210
Deduct:		
Increase in accounts receivable	$(24,080)	
Increase in merchandise inventory	(2,450)	
Decrease in salaries payable	(360)	
Decrease in unearned rent	(600)	(27,490)
Net cash flows from operating activities		$ 47,120
Cash flows from investing activities:		
Purchase of store equipment	$ (7,100)	
Purchase of office equipment	(5,570)	
Net cash flows used in investing activities		(12,670)
Cash flows from financing activities:		
Payment of note payable	$ (5,000)	
Payment of dividends	(18,000)	
Net cash flows used in financing activities		(23,000)
Net increase in cash		$ 11,450
January 1, 2007 cash balance		41,500
December 31, 2007 cash balance		$ 52,950

Sales Transactions

3 Describe the accounting for the sale of merchandise.

In the remainder of this chapter, we illustrate transactions that affect the financial statements of a merchandising business. These transactions affect the reporting of net sales, cost of merchandise sold, gross profit, and merchandise inventory.

Sales of merchandise are recorded in a journal and posted to the accounts in a ledger, using the rules of debit and credit that we illustrated in Chapter 4. The only difference between the illustrations in Chapter 4 and those in this chapter is that we are now focusing on sales of merchandise rather than services. Because the operating activities of a merchandise business differ from those of a service business, the chart of accounts will also differ to reflect the difference in operations. Thus, instead of fees earned, sales of merchandise are recorded in a sales account.

To illustrate, assume that on January 3 Online Solutions sells merchandise costing $1,200 for $1,800. The customer charges the purchase on a MasterCard. Because MasterCard sales receipts are deposited directly in the bank, credit card sales involving MasterCard or VISA are recorded as cash sales. Thus, the entry to record the sale of $1,800 is as follows:

Jan. 3	Cash	1,800	
	Sales		1,800

Under the perpetual inventory system, the cost of merchandise sold and the reduction of merchandise inventory on hand are recorded at the time of sale. In this way, the merchandise inventory account indicates the amount of merchandise on hand at all times. Thus, on January 3, Online Solutions also updates the merchandise inventory account with the following entry:

Jan. 3	Cost of Merchandise Sold	1,200	
	Merchandise Inventory		1,200

Ethics in Action

Skimming

Credit card fraud and identity theft are significant concerns among credit card issuers and users. One of the fastest growing credit card frauds is called *skimming.* Skimming occurs when your credit card is out of your possession during a legitimate restaurant transaction. In this scam, a server illegally swipes your credit card by using a small, hand-held scanner concealed in an apron. The hand-held scanner illegally transmits the information from the magnetic strip on your card, such as your name, card number, and routing information, to a computer. The information can then be used for making counterfeit cards.

Sales of merchandise on account would be recorded in the same manner as cash sales, except that Accounts Receivable rather than Cash is debited at the time of sale. An individual account for each customer is maintained in a **subsidiary ledger**. The total of the subsidiary ledger is represented in the general ledger by a **controlling account**. In the case of the accounts receivable subsidiary ledger, the accounts receivable account is the controlling account. Likewise, a subsidiary ledger is also maintained for other accounts, such as the merchandise inventory and accounts payable accounts. The relationship between the general ledger, controlling accounts, and subsidiary ledgers is shown in Exhibit 9.

Instead of MasterCard or VISA a customer may use a nonbank credit card, such as American Express. In this case, the sale is recorded as a sale on account and the seller must collect the receivable from the credit card company. For example, a seller submits a monthly bill to American Express for sales to its customers, and American Express remits the amount of the sales less a service fee. The service fee is recorded as an expense.

To illustrate, assume that during January Online Solutions sold merchandise costing \$68,000 to American Express customers for \$100,000. At the end of January, Online

Exhibit 9

General Ledger, Controlling Accounts, and Subsidiary Ledgers

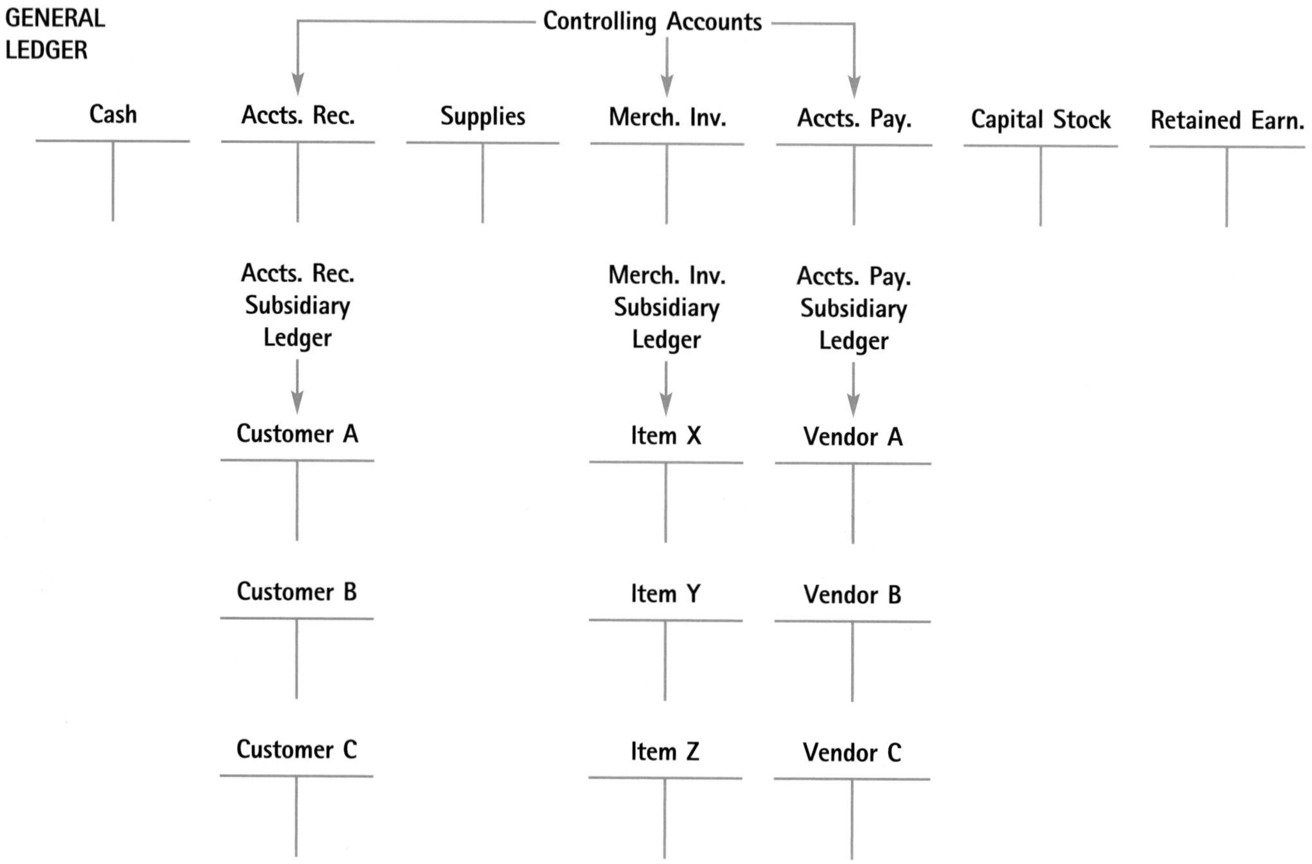

submitted a bill to American Express and received cash less a 4% service fee on February 15. The entries to record the sales and the receipt of cash are shown below.

Jan.	31	Accounts Receivable—American Express	100,000	
		Sales		100,000
	31	Cost of Merchandise Sold	68,000	
		Merchandise Inventory		68,000
Feb.	15	Cash	96,000	
		Credit Card Expense	4,000	
		Accounts Receivable—American Express		100,000

Sales Discounts

The **credit terms** of a sale on account are normally indicated on the **invoice** or bill that the seller sends to the customer. If payment is required on delivery, the terms are *cash* or *net cash*. Otherwise, the buyer is allowed an amount of time, known as the **credit period**, in which to pay. The credit period usually begins with the date of the sale as shown on the invoice. If payment is due within a stated number of days after the date of the invoice, such as 30 days, the terms are *net 30 days*. These terms may be written as *n/30*. If payment is due by the end of the month in which the sale was made, the terms are written as *n/eom*.

As a means of encouraging the buyer to pay before the end of the credit period, the seller may offer a discount, called a *sales discount*. For example, a seller may offer a 2% discount if the buyer pays within 10 days of the invoice date. If the buyer does not take the discount, the total amount is due within 30 days. These terms are expressed as *2/10, n/30* and are read as *2% discount if paid within 10 days, net amount due within 30 days.*

Sales discounts reduce sales and, therefore, the sales account could be debited. However, managers may want to know the amount of the sales discounts for a period in deciding whether to change credit terms. For this reason, the seller records the sales discounts in a separate account. The sales discounts account is a *contra* (or *offsetting*) account to Sales.

To illustrate, assume that Online Solutions receives cash within the discount period from a $1,500 credit sale to Omega Technologies. The sale of merchandise costing $850 was made on January 12, with the terms 2/10, n/30. The initial sale and the receipt of the cash are recorded as follows:

Jan. 12	Accounts Receivable—Omega Tech.	1,500	
	Sales		1,500
12	Cost of Merchandise Sold	850	
	Merchandise Inventory		850
22	Cash	1,470	
	Sales Discounts	30	
	Accounts Receivable—Omega Tech.		1,500

Sales Returns and Allowances

Merchandise that has been sold may be returned to the seller (*sales return*). In addition, because of defects or for other reasons, the seller may reduce the initial price at which the goods were sold (*sales allowance*). If the return or allowance is for a sale on account, the seller normally issues a **credit memorandum**. This memorandum is sent to the customer and indicates the amount the seller is crediting the customer's account receivable for the return or allowance.

Sales returns and allowances reduce sales revenue. They also result in additional shipping and other expenses. Since managers often want to know the amount of returns and allowances for a period, the seller records sales returns and allowances in a separate sales returns and allowances account. Sales Returns and Allowances may be viewed as a *contra* (or *offsetting*) account to Sales.

To illustrate, assume that on January 13 Online Solutions issued a $2,000 credit memorandum to Krier Company for merchandise that was returned. The merchandise was sold on account and the cost of the merchandise sold was $1,200. The entries to record the issuance of the credit memorandum and the receipt of the returned merchandise are as follows:

Jan. 13	Sales Returns and Allowances	2,000	
	Accounts Receivable—Krier Company		2,000
13	Merchandise Inventory	1,200	
	Cost of Merchandise Sold		1,200

$10,000 of merchandise is purchased 2/10, n/30; $4,500 is returned; and the invoice is paid within the discount. What was the amount paid?

$5,390 [$5,500 − ($5,500 × 2%)]

Using a perpetual inventory system, the second entry is necessary so that the merchandise inventory account is up to date and reflects the actual merchandise on hand.

What if the customer pays for the merchandise and later returns the merchandise? In this case, the seller issues a credit memorandum, and the credit may be applied against other accounts receivable owed by the customer, or cash may be refunded. If cash is refunded, the seller credits Cash, rather than Accounts Receivable, for the amount of the refund.

Ethics in Action

The Case of the Fraudulent Price Tags

One of the challenges for a retailer is policing its sales return policy. There are many ways in which customers can unethically or illegally abuse such policies. In one case, a couple was accused of attaching Marshall's store price tags to cheaper merchandise bought or obtained elsewhere. The couple then returned the cheaper goods and received the substantially higher refund amount. Company security officials discovered the fraud and had the couple arrested after they had allegedly bilked the company for over $1 million.

Purchase Transactions

4 Describe the accounting for the purchase of merchandise.

As we indicated earlier in this chapter, most large retailers and many small merchandising businesses use computerized perpetual inventory systems. Under the perpetual inventory system, cash purchases of merchandise are recorded as follows:

Jan. 3	Merchandise Inventory	2,500	
	Cash		2,500

Purchases of merchandise on account are recorded as follows:

Jan. 6	Merchandise Inventory	1,800	
	Accounts Payable—Smith Corporation		1,800

Purchase Discounts

As we mentioned in our discussion of sales transactions, a seller may offer the buyer credit terms that include a discount for early payment. The buyer refers to such discounts as *purchases discounts*, which reduce the cost of merchandise purchased. Under the perpetual inventory system, the buyer initially debits the merchandise inventory account for the amount of the invoice. When paying the invoice, the buyer credits the merchandise inventory account for the amount of the discount. In this way, the merchandise inventory shows the *net* cost to the buyer.

To illustrate, assume that Online Solutions purchased the $1,800 merchandise from Smith Corporation in the preceding entry on January 6 under the terms 1/15, n/30. The entry to record the payment within the discount period is as follows:

Jan. 21	Accounts Payable—Smith Corporation	1,800	
	Merchandise Inventory		18
	Cash		1,782

If Online Solutions does not pay within the discount period, the entry to record the payment is as follows:

Feb. 5	Accounts Payable—Smith Corporation	1,800	
	Cash		1,800

Purchases Returns and Allowances

When merchandise is returned (*purchase return*) or a price adjustment is requested (*purchase allowance*), the buyer (debtor) usually sends the seller a letter or a debit memorandum. A **debit memorandum** informs the seller of the amount the buyer proposes to *debit* to the account payable due the seller. It also states the reasons for the return or the request for a price reduction.

The buyer may use a copy of the debit memorandum as the basis for recording the return or allowance or wait for approval from the seller (creditor). To illustrate, assume that on January 22 Online Solutions returns $5,000 of merchandise purchased from Quantum Inc. and issues an accompanying debit memorandum. The return is recorded as follows:

Jan. 22	Accounts Payable—Quantum Inc.	5,000	
	Merchandise Inventory		5,000

When a buyer returns merchandise or has been granted an allowance prior to paying the invoice, the amount of the debit memorandum is deducted from the invoice amount. The amount is deducted before any purchase discount is computed. For example, assume that the merchandise returned to Quantum on January 22 was only part of an overall purchase of $9,000 with terms 2/10, n/30. If Online pays within the discount period, it would deduct a discount of $80, or ($9,000 − $5,000) × 2%.

Transportation Costs and Sales Taxes

5 Describe the accounting for transportation costs and sales taxes.

Merchandise businesses incur transportation costs in selling and purchasing merchandise. In addition, a retailer must also collect sales taxes in most states. In this section, we briefly discuss the unique aspects of accounting for transportation costs and sales taxes.

Transportation Costs

Does the buyer or the seller pay transportation costs? It depends upon when the ownership (title) of the merchandise passes from the seller to the buyer.[7] The terms of a sale should indicate when the ownership (title) of the merchandise passes to the buyer. The ownership of the merchandise may pass to the buyer when the seller delivers the merchandise to the transportation company or freight carrier. For example, DaimlerChrysler records the sale and the transfer of ownership of its vehicles to dealers when the vehicles are shipped. In this case, the terms are said to be **FOB (free on board) shipping point**. This term means that DaimlerChrysler is responsible for the transportation charges to the shipping point, which is where the shipment originates. The dealer then pays the transportation costs to the final destination. Such costs are part of the dealer's total cost of purchasing inventory and should be added to the cost of the inventory by debiting Merchandise Inventory.

To illustrate, assume that on January 19, Online Solutions buys merchandise from Data Max on account, $2,900, terms FOB shipping point, and prepays the transportation cost of $150. Online records these two transactions as follows:

Jan.	19	Merchandise Inventory	2,900	
		Accounts Payable—Data Max		2,900
	19	Merchandise Inventory	150	
		Cash		150

The ownership of the merchandise may pass to the buyer when the buyer receives the merchandise. In this case, the terms are said to be **FOB (free on board) destination**. This term means that the seller delivers the merchandise to the buyer's final destination, free of transportation charges to the buyer. The seller thus pays the transportation costs to the final destination. The seller debits Transportation Out or Delivery Expense, which is reported on the seller's income statement as an expense.

To illustrate, assume that on January 24, Online Solutions sells merchandise to Miller Company on account, $4,700, terms FOB destination. The cost of the merchandise sold is $2,750, and Online pays the transportation cost of $350. Online records the sale, the cost of the sale, and the transportation cost as shown on the next page.

Sometimes FOB shipping point and FOB destination are expressed in terms of the location at which the title to the merchandise passes to the buyer. For example, if Toyota Motor Co.'s assembly plant in Osaka, Japan, sells automobiles to a dealer in Chicago, FOB shipping point could be expressed as FOB Osaka. Likewise, FOB destination could be expressed as FOB Chicago.

Shipping terms, the passage of title, and whether the buyer or seller pays the transportation costs are summarized in Exhibit 10.

---

7 The transfer of ownership (title) also determines whether the buyer or seller must pay other costs, such as the cost of insurance while the merchandise is in transit.

Jan.	24	Accounts Receivable—Miller Company	4,700	
		Sales		4,700
	24	Cost of Merchandise Sold	2,750	
		Merchandise Inventory		2,750
	24	Transportation Out	350	
		Cash		350

Exhibit 10

Transportation Terms

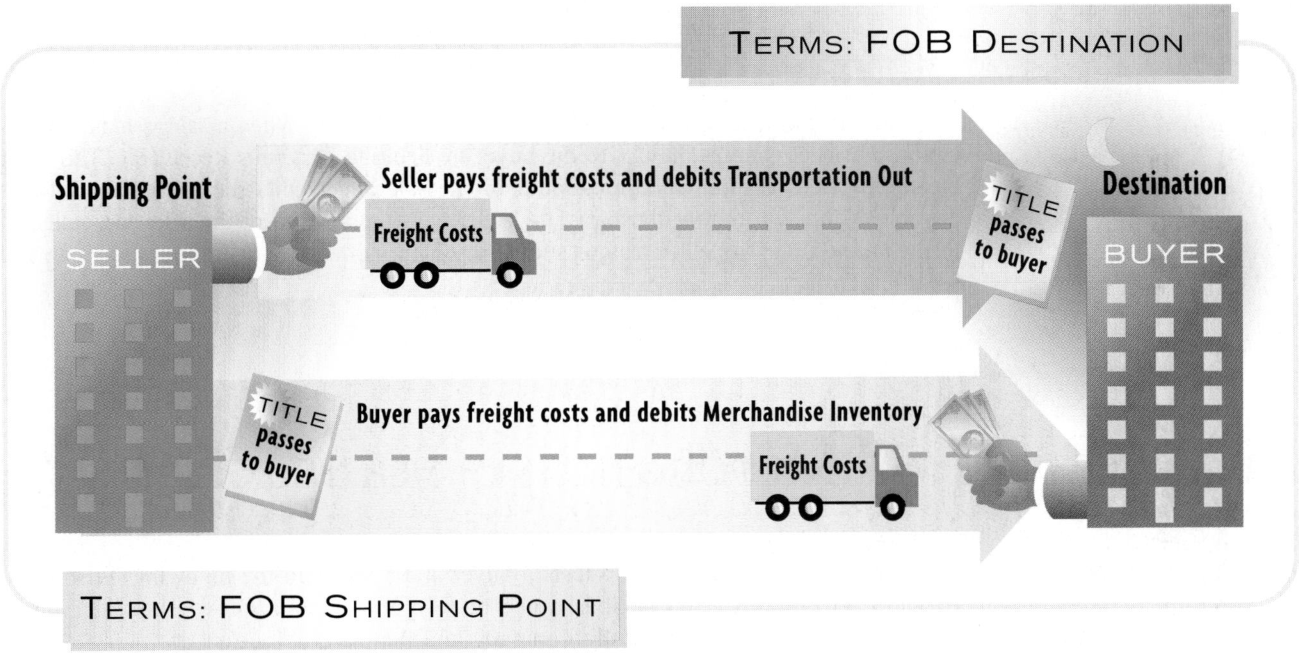

As a convenience to the buyer, the seller may prepay the transportation costs, even though the terms are FOB shipping point. The seller will then add the transportation costs to the invoice. The buyer will debit Merchandise Inventory for the total amount of the invoice, including the transportation costs.

To illustrate, assume that on January 14, Online Solutions sells merchandise to Golden Company on account, $8,000, terms 2/10, n/30, FOB shipping point. Online pays the transportation cost of $500 and adds it to the invoice. The cost of the merchandise sold is $4,800. Online records these transactions as follows:

Jan.	14	Accounts Receivable—Golden Company	8,000	
		Sales		8,000

(continued)

Jan. 14	Cost of Merchandise Sold	4,800	
	Merchandise Inventory		4,800
14	Accounts Receivable—Golden Company	500	
	Cash		500

$8,000 of merchandise is purchased 1/15, n/30, FOB shipping point. The seller pays $500 shipping charges as an accommodation. If paid within the discount period, how much will the buyer remit?

$8,420 [$8,000 − ($8,000 × 1%) + $500]

When the seller prepays transportation costs for the buyer, any sales discount applies only to the amount of the merchandise sale. For example, if Golden Company pays within the discount period, it would remit cash of $8,340 [$8,000 − ($8,000 × 2%) + $500].

Sales Taxes

Almost all states and many other taxing units levy a tax on sales of merchandise.[8] The liability for the sales tax is incurred when the sale is made.

At the time of a cash sale, the seller collects the sales tax. When a sale is made on account, the seller charges the tax to the buyer by debiting Accounts Receivable. The seller credits the sales account for the amount of the sale and credits the tax to Sales Taxes Payable. Normally on a regular basis, the seller pays the amount of the sales tax collected to the taxing unit. The seller records such a payment by debiting Sales Taxes Payable and crediting Cash.

Dual Nature of Merchandise Transactions

6 Illustrate the dual nature of merchandising transactions.

Each merchandising transaction affects a buyer and a seller. In the following illustration, we show how the same transactions would be recorded by both the seller and the buyer. In this example, the seller is Scully Company and the buyer is Burton Co.

Transaction	Scully Company (Seller)			Burton Co. (Buyer)		
July 1. Scully Company sold merchandise on account to Burton Co., $7,500, terms FOB shipping point, n/45. The cost of the merchandise sold was $4,500.	Accounts Receivable—Burton Co.	7,500		Merchandise Inventory	7,500	
	Sales		7,500	Accounts Payable—Scully Co.		7,500
	Cost of Merchandise Sold	4,500				
	Merchandise Inventory		4,500			

(continued)

8 Businesses that purchase merchandise for resale to others are normally exempt from paying sales taxes on their purchases. Only final buyers of merchandise normally pay sales taxes.

Transaction	Scully Company (Seller)			Burton Co. (Buyer)		
July 2. Burton Co. paid transportation charges of $150 on July 1 purchase from Scully Company.	No entry.			Merchandise Inventory	150	
				Cash		150
July 5. Scully Company sold merchandise on account to Burton Co., $5,000, terms FOB destination, n/30. The cost of the merchandise sold was $3,500.	Accounts Receivable—Burton Co.	5,000		Merchandise Inventory	5,000	
	Sales		5,000	Accounts Payable—Scully Co.		5,000
	Cost of Merchandise Sold	3,500				
	Merchandise Inventory		3,500			
July 7. Scully Company paid transportation costs of $250 for delivery of merchandise sold to Burton Co. on July 5.	Transportation Out	250		No entry.		
	Cash		250			
July 13. Scully Company issued Burton Co. a credit memorandum for merchandise returned, $1,000. The merchandise had been purchased by Burton Co. on account on July 5. The cost of the merchandise returned was $700.	Sales Returns & Allowances	1,000		Accounts Payable—Scully Co.	1,000	
	Accounts Receivable—Burton Co.		1,000	Merchandise Inventory		1,000
	Merchandise Inventory	700				
	Cost of Merchandise Sold		700			
July 15. Scully Company received payment from Burton Co. for purchase of July 5.	Cash	4,000		Accts. Pay.—Scully Co.	4,000	
	Accts. Rec.—Burton Co.		4,000	Cash		4,000
July 18. Scully Company sold merchandise on account to Burton Co., $12,000, terms FOB shipping point, 2/10, n/eom. Scully Company prepaid transportation costs of $500, which were added to the invoice. The cost of the merchandise sold was $7,200.	Acct. Rec.—Burton Co.	12,000		Merchandise Inventory	12,500	
	Sales		12,000	Accts. Pay.—Scully Co.		12,500
	Acct. Rec.—Burton Co.	500				
	Cash		500			
	Cost of Merch. Sold	7,200				
	Merchandise Inventory		7,200			
July 28. Scully Company received payment from Burton Co. for purchase of July 18, less discount (2% × $12,000).	Cash	12,260		Acct. Pay.—Scully Co.	12,500	
	Sales Discounts	240		Merch. Inventory		240
	Acct. Rec.—Burton Co.		12,500	Cash		12,260

Merchandise Shrinkage

7 Describe the accounting for merchandise shrinkage.

Under the perpetual inventory system, a separate merchandise inventory account is maintained in the ledger. During the accounting period, this account shows the amount of merchandise for sale at any time. However, merchandising businesses may experience some loss of inventory due to shoplifting, employee theft, or errors in recording or counting inventory. As a result, the **physical inventory** taken at the end of the accounting period may differ from the amount of inventory shown in the inventory records. Normally, the amount of merchandise for sale, as indicated by the balance of the merchandise inventory account, is larger than the total amount of merchandise counted during the physical inventory. For this reason, the difference is often called **inventory shrinkage** or *inventory shortage*. One recent study estimated that inventory shrinkage exceeds $30 billion annually in the United States.[9]

To illustrate, Online Solutions' inventory records, called the **book inventory**, indicate that $63,950 of merchandise should be available for sale on December 31, 2007. The physical inventory taken on December 31, 2007, however, indicates that only $62,150 of merchandise is actually available for sale. The inventory shrinkage for the year ending December 31, 2007, is $1,800 as shown below.

December 31, 2007 unadjusted book inventory	$63,950
December 31, 2007 physical inventory	62,150
Inventory shrinkage	$ 1,800

The adjusting entry to record the shrinkage is as follows:

Dec. 31	Cost of Merchandise Sold	1,800	
	Merchandise Inventory		1,800

After this entry has been recorded, the adjusted Merchandise Inventory (book inventory) in the accounting records agrees with the actual physical inventory at the end of the period. Since no system of procedures and safeguards can totally eliminate it, inventory

Ethics in Action
The Cost of Employee Theft

A recent survey reported that the 30 largest retail store chains have lost over $5 billion to shoplifting and employee theft. Of this amount only 3.45% of the losses resulted in any recovery. The stores apprehended over 600,000 shoplifters and 78,000 dishonest employees during 2001. Approximately one out of every 27 employees was apprehended for theft from his or her employer. Each dishonest employee stole approximately 8 times the amount stolen by shoplifters ($900 vs. $114).

Source: Jack L. Hayes International, *Fourteenth Annual Retail Theft Survey*, 2001.

9 "New Study Finds U.S. Retailers Losing $32 Billion to Theft," PR Newswire, November 23, 2001.

shrinkage is often considered a normal cost of operations. If the amount of the shrinkage is abnormally large, it may be disclosed separately on the income statement. In such cases, the shrinkage may be recorded in a separate account, such as Loss from Merchandise Inventory Shrinkage.

Effects of Inventory Misstatements on the Financial Statements

8 Describe and illustrate the effects of inventory misstatements on the financial statements.

Any error in the physical inventory count at the end of the accounting period affects the income statement and balance sheet. This is because the physical inventory count is the basis for determining the amount of inventory shrinkage. As we illustrated in the preceding section, the adjusting entry for inventory shrinkage affects the cost of merchandise sold and merchandise inventory. Thus, if the physical inventory is misstated, then the amount of inventory shrinkage is misstated and the cost of merchandise sold will be misstated after the inventory shrinkage adjustment is recorded. Because net income is closed to Retained Earnings at the end of the accounting period, retained earnings and total assets are misstated. This misstatement of total assets, current assets, and merchandise inventory equals the misstatement of stockholders' equity. These effects are shown in Exhibit 11.

Exhibit 11

Effects of Inventory Misstatements

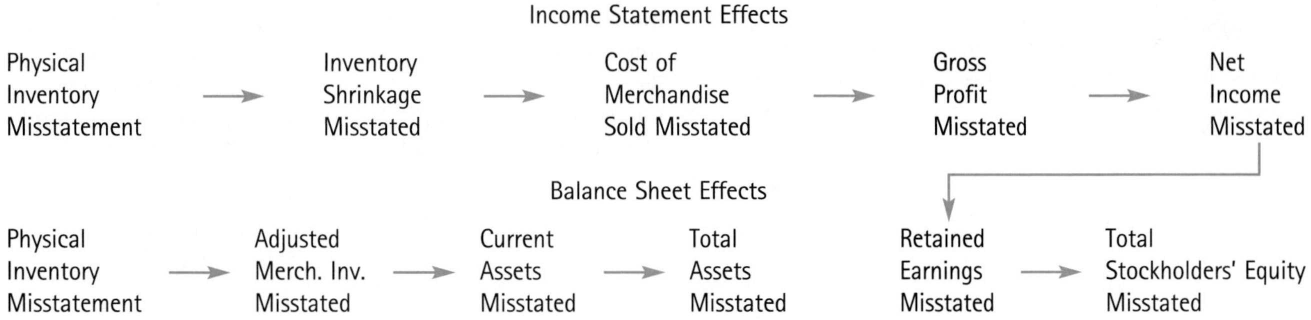

To illustrate, assume that in taking the physical inventory on December 31, 2007, Sapra Company incorrectly counted its physical inventory as $115,000 instead of $125,000. Because the ending physical inventory is understated, the inventory shrinkage and the cost of merchandise sold will be overstated by $10,000, as shown below.

	Amount of Misstatement Overstated (Understated)
December 31, 2007 unadjusted book inventory	Correct
Less December 31, 2007 physical inventory	$(10,000)
Inventory shrinkage (cost of merchandise sold)	$ 10,000

Recall from the preceding section that the amount of inventory shrinkage is recorded by adjusting the cost of merchandise sold. Thus, an overstatement of the inventory shrinkage overstates the cost of merchandise sold. Because the cost of merchandise sold is overstated, gross profit and net income for 2007 will be understated by $10,000. Since net income is closed to Retained Earnings at the end of 2007, the total stockholders' equity on the December 31, 2007 balance sheet will also be understated by $10,000.

As we discussed, the ending physical inventory determines the ending (adjusted) merchandise inventory reported on the balance sheet. Thus, on the December 31, 2007 balance sheet, merchandise inventory, current assets, and total assets are understated by $10,000 ($125,000 − $115,000).

The effects of the misstatement on Sapra Company's 2007 financial statements are summarized below.

2007 Financial Statements	Amount of Misstatement Overstated (Understated)
Balance Sheet as of December 31, 2007:	
Merchandise inventory	$(10,000)
Current assets	(10,000)
Total assets	(10,000)
Total stockholders' equity (retained earnings)	(10,000)
Income Statement for Year Ended Dec. 31, 2007:	
Cost of merchandise sold	$ 10,000
Gross profit	(10,000)
Net income	(10,000)

If the ending physical inventory is understated by $6,000, what is the effect on total assets, retained earnings, the cost of merchandise sold, and gross profit?

Total assets: understated $6,000; Retained earnings: understated $6,000; Cost of merchandise sold: overstated $6,000; Gross profit: understated $6,000.

If the $10,000 understatement of merchandise inventory at the end of 2007 is not detected, the misstatement will also affect the 2008 financial statements. This is because the merchandise inventory at the end of 2007 becomes the beginning merchandise inventory for 2008. Thus, the book inventory during 2008 will be understated throughout the year, and as a result, the unadjusted book inventory on December 31, 2008, will be understated by $10,000. Assuming that the physical inventory count at the end of 2008 is correct, the merchandise shrinkage will be understated by $10,000, as shown below.

	Amount of Misstatement Overstated (Understated)
December 31, 2008 unadjusted book inventory	$(10,000)
Less December 31, 2008 physical inventory	Correct
Inventory shrinkage (cost of merchandise sold)	$(10,000)

Since inventory shrinkage is understated by $10,000, the cost of merchandise sold will be understated and gross profit will be overstated by $10,000 for 2008. Because the December 31, 2008 physical inventory is correct and the accounting records are adjusted to the physical count, the adjusted balance of merchandise inventory will be correct on the December 31, 2008 balance sheet. Likewise, the 2008 overstatement of net income offsets the 2007 understatement of net income, with the result that the December 31, 2008 stockholders' equity (retained earnings) is correct. Thus, the effects of inventory misstatements if not detected reverse themselves in the following period, and the balance sheet at the end of the second period will be correct, as shown on the following page.

2008 Financial Statements	Amount of Misstatement Overstated (Understated)
Balance Sheet as of December 31, 2008:	
Merchandise inventory	Correct
Current assets	Correct
Total assets	Correct
Total stockholders' equity (retained earnings)	Correct
Income Statement for Year Ended December 31, 2008:	
Cost of merchandise sold	$(10,000)
Gross profit	10,000
Net income	10,000

In the examples of inventory misstatements, we assumed that an error occurred in the physical inventory count. This could occur because the quantities of inventory were miscounted or summarized (added) incorrectly. Other types of errors that could misstate the inventory could include using incorrect costs or including items not owned by the business. For example, merchandise businesses often carry items on consignment from other retailers. Items on **consignment** are owned by another retailer, called a **consignor**. The retailer carrying the item is a **consignee**. The consignee normally earns a commission or fee when the consigned goods are sold. Since consigned merchandise is normally displayed along with the consignee's own merchandise, consigned merchandise on hand at the end of the year may be incorrectly included in the consignee's physical inventory. This would overstate the ending physical inventory and misstate the financial statements. Likewise, merchandise out on consignment might be overlooked in counting the consignor's inventory, and thus understate the consignor's physical inventory.

INTERNATIONAL PERSPECTIVE

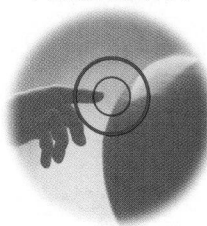

Home Depot operates five stores in Chile, which does not have specific standards for start-up and organizational costs. Another South American country—Venezuela—has no standards for inventories.

Inventory misstatements may also arise for merchandise in transit at year-end. For example, merchandise may be ordered FOB shipping point near the end of the year. In such cases, it is likely that the merchandise is in transit at year-end. In determining the ending physical inventory it would be easy to overlook this merchandise in transit, since it is not on hand. The result would be that the physical inventory is understated. Similarly, merchandise sold FOB destination could be in transit at year-end. Even though the merchandise is not on hand, it is still owned by the seller and should be included in the seller's ending physical inventory.

Gross Profit and Operating Profit Analysis

9 Describe and illustrate the use of gross profit and operating income in analyzing a company's operations.

Gross profit and operating income are two important profitability measures analysts use in assessing the efficiency and effectiveness of a merchandiser's operations. In this section, we use these measures to assess JC Penney operating performance for the past several years.

Like many financial statement measures, sometimes referred to as *performance metrics*, gross profit and operating income are best analyzed over time as a percent rather than as amounts. Since gross profit and operating income are income statement amounts, they are normally expressed as a percent of net sales. Doing so allows us to better analyze the operating performance over time.

Gross profit and operating profit as a percent of net sales for JC Penney are shown in Exhibit 12. The data, shown for the past three years, are taken from the Securities and Exchange Commission annual filings (Form 10-K) for JC Penney.

Exhibit 12

JC Penney Operating Ratios

	For the Years Ending . . . (in millions)		
	Jan. 26, 2002	Jan. 27, 2001	Jan. 29, 2000
Net sales	$32,004	$31,846	$31,743
Cost of merchandise sold	22,789	23,031	22,286
Gross profit	$ 9,215	$ 8,815	$ 9,457
Operating expenses	8,459	8,637	8,604
Operating income	$ 756	$ 178	$ 853
Gross profit percent	28.8%	27.7%	29.8%
Operating income percent	2.4%	0.6%	2.7%

As you can see in Exhibit 12, the gross profit as a percent of net sales was at its highest in fiscal 1999, dipped in fiscal 2000, and recovered partially in fiscal 2001 at nearly 29% of sales.[10] The gross profit improvement in fiscal 2001 was credited by Penney's management to better merchandise assortments, improved inventory productivity, and centralized buying that allowed buyers advantages in negotiating price reductions from their suppliers. Operating income as a percent of sales followed a similar dipping, then recovery trend. Operating income as a percent of sales in fiscal 2001 was 1.8 percentage points better than the previous year (2.4% − 0.6%). The gross profit percent improvement accounts for 1.1 percentage points (28.8% − 27.7%). The remaining 0.7 percentage point improvement was credited by Penney's management to lower catalog book and marketing costs, lower telemarketing costs, and a shift from development to maintenance of JCPenney.com.

APPENDIX

Statement of Cash Flows: The Indirect Method

Online Solutions' statement of cash flows for year ended December 31, 2007, is shown in Exhibit 8. The operating activities section of this statement was prepared using a method known as the *indirect method.* This method is used by over 90 percent of publicly held companies.

The use of the indirect method only affects net cash flows from operating activities. The other method of preparing the net cash flows from operating activities section is called the *direct method.* The direct method analyzes each transaction and its effect on cash flows.[11] In contrast, the indirect method analyzes only the changes in accounts.

A major reason that the indirect method is so popular is that it is normally less costly to use. However, regardless of whether the indirect or direct method is used, the reporting of net cash flows from investing and financing activities is not affected. In this appendix, we illustrate the use of the indirect method of preparing the statement of cash flows.

The indirect method reconciles net income with net cash flows from operating activities. Net income is adjusted for the effects of accruals and deferrals that affected the net

10 The income statement is dated at the end of the first month of the year, but represents most (11 months) of the previous year's activity. Thus, a statement dated January 26, 2002, is said to be for fiscal year 2001.

11 We used the direct method to prepare the statement of cash flows in the appendix to Chapter 4.

income but did not result in the receipt or payment of cash. The resulting amount is the net cash flows from operating activities.

The indirect method converts net income determined under the accrual basis of accounting to what it would have been under the cash basis of accounting. In other words, net cash flows from operating activities is equivalent to net income using the cash basis of accounting.

To illustrate, assume that accounts receivable increases during the period by $10,000. This increase is included in the period's revenue and thus increases net income. However, cash was not collected. Thus, an increase in accounts receivable must be deducted from net income under the indirect method. Likewise, depreciation expense is deducted in arriving at net income, but does not involve any cash payments. Thus, depreciation expense is added to net income under the indirect method.

The typical adjustments to convert net income to net cash flows from operating activities, using the indirect method, are shown in Exhibit 13.

Exhibit 13

Indirect Method Adjustments

Net income			$XXX
Add:	Depreciation	$XXX	
	Decreases in current assets (accounts receivables, inventories, prepaid expenses)	XXX	
	Increases in current liabilities (accounts payable, notes payable, accrued expenses)	XXX	XXX
Deduct:	Increases in current assets (accounts receivables, inventories, prepaid expenses)	$XXX	
	Decreases in current liabilities (accounts payable, notes payable, accrued expenses)	XXX	XXX
Net cash flows from operating activities			$XXX

You should note that, except for depreciation, the adjustments in Exhibit 13 are for changes in the current assets and current liabilities. This is because changes in the current assets and current liabilities are related to operations and thus net income. For example, changes in inventories are related to sales, while changes in accounts payable are related to expenses.

Cash Flows from Operating Activities

The statement of cash flows shown in Exhibit 8 for Online Solutions was prepared using the indirect method. To prepare the operating activities section, we need to determine depreciation and the changes in the current assets and the liabilities during the year. This information is included in Exhibit 14, which shows the comparative balance sheets for Online Solutions as of December 31, 2007 and 2006, and related changes.

Based on Exhibit 14, the net cash flows from operating activities is shown below.

Net income			$ 60,400
Add:	Depreciation expense—store equipment	$ 3,100	
	Depreciation expense—office equipment	2,490	
	Decrease in office supplies	120	
	Decrease in prepaid insurance	350	
	Increase in accounts payable	8,150	14,210
Deduct:			
	Increase in accounts receivable	$(24,080)	
	Increase in merchandise inventory	(2,450)	
	Decrease in salaries payable	(360)	
	Decrease in unearned rent	(600)	(27,490)
Net cash flows from operating activities			$ 47,120

Exhibit 14

Online Solutions' Comparative Balance Sheets

Online Solutions
Balance Sheets

	December 31,		Changes
	2007	2006	Increase (Decrease)
Assets			
Current assets:			
Cash	$ 52,950	$ 41,500	$11,450
Accounts receivable	76,080	52,000	24,080
Merchandise inventory	62,150	59,700	2,450
Office supplies	480	600	(120)
Prepaid insurance	2,650	3,000	(350)
Total current assets	$194,310	$156,800	$37,510
Property, plant, and equipment:			
Land	$ 20,000	$ 20,000	$ 0
Store equipment	27,100	20,000	7,100
Accumulated depreciation—store equipment	(5,700)	(2,600)	(3,100)
Office equipment	15,570	10,000	5,570
Accumulated depreciation—office equipment	(4,720)	(2,230)	(2,490)
Total property, plant, and equipment	$ 52,250	$ 45,170	$ 7,080
Total assets	$246,560	$201,970	$44,590
Liabilities			
Current liabilities:			
Accounts payable	$ 22,420	$ 14,270	$ 8,150
Notes payable (current portion)	5,000	5,000	0
Salaries payable	1,140	1,500	(360)
Unearned rent	1,800	2,400	(600)
Total current liabilities	$ 30,360	$ 23,170	$ 7,190
Long-term liabilities:			
Notes payable (final payment due 2017)	20,000	25,000	(5,000)
Total liabilities	$ 50,360	$ 48,170	$ 2,190
Stockholders' Equity			
Capital stock	$ 25,000	$ 25,000	$ 0
Retained earnings	171,200	128,800	42,400
Total stockholders' equity	$196,200	$153,800	$42,400
Total liabilities and stockholders' equity	$246,560	$201,970	$44,590

The depreciation expense of $3,100 for store equipment is determined from the increase in the accumulated depreciation for store equipment. Likewise, the depreciation expense of $2,490 for office equipment is determined from the increase in the accumulated depreciation for office equipment. The changes in the current assets and current liabilities are also taken from Exhibit 14.

Cash Flows Used for Investing Activities

The cash flows for investing activities section can also be prepared by analyzing the changes in the accounts shown in Exhibit 14. For Online Solutions, the cash flows used for investing activities is composed of two items. First, additional store equipment of $7,100 was purchased, as shown by the increase in the store equipment. Likewise, additional office equipment of $5,570 was purchased. Thus, cash of $12,670 was used for investing activities, as shown in Exhibit 8.

Cash Flows Used for Financing Activities

The cash flows for financing activities can also be determined from Exhibit 14. For Online Solutions, the cash flows used for financing activities is composed of two items. First, dividends of $18,000 are reported on the retained earnings statement shown in Exhibit 6. Since no dividends payable appears on the balance sheets, cash dividends of $18,000 must have been paid during the year. In addition, notes payable decreased by $5,000 during the year. Thus, cash must have been used in paying off $5,000 of the notes. Thus, cash of $23,000 was used for financing activities, as shown in Exhibit 8.

Summary of Learning Goals

1 Distinguish the operating activities of a service business from those of a merchandise business.

The revenue activities of a service enterprise involve providing services to customers. In contrast, the revenue activities of a merchandising business involve the buying and selling of merchandise.

2 Describe and illustrate the financial statements of a merchandising business.

The multiple-step income statement of a merchandiser reports sales, sales returns and allowances, sales discounts, and net sales. The cost of the merchandise sold is subtracted from net sales to determine the gross profit. The cost of merchandise sold is determined by using either the periodic or perpetual method. Operating income is determined by subtracting operating expenses from gross profit. Operating expenses are normally classified as selling or administrative expenses. Net income is determined by subtracting income taxes and other expense and adding other income. The income statement may also be reported in a single-step form. The retained earnings statement and the statement of cash flows are similar to those for a service business. The balance sheet reports merchandise inventory at the end of the period as a current asset.

3 Describe the accounting for the sale of merchandise.

Sales of merchandise for cash or on account are recorded by crediting Sales. The cost of merchandise sold and the reduction in merchandise inventory are also recorded for the sale. For sales of merchandise on account, the credit terms may allow sales discounts for early payment. Such discounts are recorded by the seller as a debit to Sales Discounts. Sales discounts are reported as a deduction from the amount initially recorded in Sales. Likewise, when merchandise is returned or a price adjustment is granted, the seller debits Sales Returns and Allowances. For sales on account, a subsidiary ledger is maintained for individual customer accounts receivable.

Under the perpetual inventory system, the cost of merchandise sold and the reduction of merchandise inventory on hand are recorded at the time of sale. In this way, the merchandise inventory account indicates the amount of merchandise on hand at all times. Likewise, any returned merchandise is recorded in the merchandise inventory account, with a related reduction in the cost of merchandise sold.

4 Describe the accounting for the purchase of merchandise.

Purchases of merchandise for cash or on account are recorded by debiting Merchandise Inventory. For purchases of merchandise on account, the credit terms may allow cash discounts for early payment. Such purchases discounts are viewed as a reduction in the cost of the merchandise purchased. When merchandise is returned or a price adjustment is granted, the buyer credits Merchandise Inventory.

5 Describe the accounting for transportation costs and sales taxes.

When merchandise is shipped FOB shipping point, the buyer pays the transportation costs and debits Merchandise Inventory. When merchandise is shipped FOB destination, the seller pays the transportation costs and debits Transportation Out or Delivery Expense. If the seller prepays transportation costs as a convenience to the buyer, the seller debits Accounts Receivable for the costs.

The liability for sales tax is incurred when the sale is made and is recorded by the seller as a credit to the sales taxes payable account. When the amount of the sales tax is paid to the taxing unit, Sales Taxes Payable is debited and Cash is credited.

6 Illustrate the dual nature of merchandising transactions.

Each merchandising transaction affects a buyer and a seller. The illustration in this chapter shows how the same transactions would be recorded by both.

7 Describe the accounting for merchandise shrinkage.

The physical inventory taken at the end of the accounting period may differ from the amount of inventory shown in the inventory records. The difference, called inventory shrinkage, requires an adjusting entry debiting Cost of Merchandise Sold and crediting Merchandise Inventory. After this entry has been recorded, the adjusted Merchandise Inventory (book inventory) in the accounting records agrees with the actual physical inventory at the end of the period.

8 Describe and illustrate the effects of inventory misstatements on the financial statements.

Any errors in the physical inventory count at the end of the accounting period affect the income statement and balance sheet. If the physical inventory is misstated, the amount of inventory shrinkage is misstated and the cost of merchandise sold will be misstated after the inventory shrinkage adjustment is recorded. Because net income is closed to Retained Earnings at the end of the accounting period, the retained earnings and total stockholders' equity are also misstated. Likewise, merchandise inventory, current assets, and total assets are misstated. This misstatement of total assets, current assets, and merchandise inventory equals the misstatement of stockholders' equity. The effects of inventory misstatements on the financial statements are shown in Exhibit 11.

9 Describe and illustrate the use of gross profit and operating income in analyzing a company's operations.

Gross profit and operating income are two important profitability measures analysts use in assessing the efficiency and effectiveness of a merchandiser's operations. Gross profit and operating income are normally analyzed over time as a percent of net sales.

Glossary

Administrative expenses Expenses incurred in the administration or general operations of the business.

Book inventory The amount of inventory recorded in the accounting records.

Consignee The retailer carrying an item for sale (consignment) that is owned by another retailer (consignor).

Consignment Merchandise that is owned by a retailer (consignor) that is being carried for sale by another retailer (consignee).

Consignor A retailer who allows another retailer (consignee) to carry and sale its merchandise (consignment).

Controlling account The account in the general ledger that summarizes the balances of the accounts in a subsidiary ledger.

Cost of merchandise sold The cost that is reported as an expense when merchandise is sold.

Credit memorandum A form used by a seller to inform the buyer of the amount the seller proposes to credit to the account receivable due from the buyer.

Credit period The amount of time the buyer is allowed in which to pay the seller.

Credit terms Terms for payment on account by the buyer to the seller.

Debit memorandum A form used by a buyer to inform the seller of the amount the buyer proposes to debit to the account payable due the seller.

FOB (free on board) destination Freight terms in which the seller pays the transportation costs from the shipping point to the final destination.

FOB (free on board) shipping point Freight terms in which the buyer pays the transportation costs from the shipping point to the final destination.

Gross profit Sales minus the cost of merchandise sold.

Income from operations (operating income) The excess of gross profit over total operating expenses.

Indirect method A method of preparing the statement of cash flows that reconciles net income with net cash flows from operating activities.

Inventory shrinkage The amount by which the merchandise for sale, as indicated by the balance of the merchandise inventory account, is larger than the total amount of merchandise counted during the physical inventory.

Invoice The bill that the seller sends to the buyer.

Merchandise available for sale The cost of merchandise available for sale to customers.

Merchandise inventory Merchandise on hand (not sold) at the end of an accounting period.

Multiple-step income statement A form of income statement that contains several sections, subsections, and subtotals.

Net sales Revenue received for merchandise sold to customers less any sales returns and allowances and sales discounts.

Other expense Expenses that cannot be traced directly to operations.

Other income Revenue from sources other than the primary operating activity of a business.

Periodic inventory method The inventory method in which the inventory records do not show the amount available for sale or sold during the period.

Perpetual inventory system The inventory system in which each purchase and sale of merchandise is recorded in an inventory account.

Physical inventory A detailed listing of the merchandise for sale at the end of an accounting period.

Purchase return or allowance From the buyer's perspective, returned merchandise or an adjustment for defective merchandise.

Purchases discounts Discounts taken by the buyer for early payment of an invoice.

Report form The form of balance sheet in which assets, liabilities, and stockholders' equity are reported in a downward sequence.

Sales The total amount charged to customers for merchandise sold, including cash sales and sales on account.

Sales discounts From the seller's perspective, discounts that a seller may offer the buyer for early payment.

Sales return or allowance From the seller's perspective, returned merchandise or an adjustment for defective merchandise.

Selling expenses Expenses that are incurred directly in the selling of merchandise.

Single-step income statement A form of income statement in which the total of all expenses is deducted from the total of all revenues.

Subsidiary ledger A ledger containing individual accounts with a common characteristic.

Illustrative Accounting Application Problem

The following transactions were completed by Montrose Company during May of the current year. Montrose Company uses a perpetual inventory system.

May 3 Purchased merchandise on account from Floyd Co., $4,000, terms FOB shipping point, 2/10, n/30, with prepaid transportation costs of $120 added to the invoice.

5 Purchased merchandise on account from Kramer Co., $8,500, terms FOB destination, 1/10, n/30.

6 Sold merchandise on account to C. F. Howell Co., $2,800, terms 2/10, n/30. The cost of the merchandise sold was $1,125.

8 Purchased office supplies for cash, $150.

10 Returned merchandise purchased on May 5 from Kramer Co., $1,300.

13 Paid Floyd Co. on account for purchase of May 3, less discount.

14 Purchased merchandise for cash, $10,500.

15 Paid Kramer Co. on account for purchase of May 5, less return of May 10 and discount.

16 Received cash on account from sale of May 6 to C. F. Howell Co., less discount.

19 Sold merchandise on nonbank credit cards and reported accounts to the card company, American Express, $2,450. The cost of the merchandise sold was $980.

May 22 Sold merchandise on account to Comer Co., $3,480, terms 2/10, n/30. The cost of the merchandise sold was $1,400.

24 Sold merchandise for cash, $4,350. The cost of the merchandise sold was $1,750.

25 Received merchandise returned by Comer Co. from sale on May 22, $1,480. The cost of the returned merchandise was $600.

31 Received cash from card company for nonbank credit card sales of May 19, less $140 service fee.

Instructions

1. Journalize the preceding transactions.
2. Journalize the adjusting entry for merchandise inventory shrinkage, $3,750.

Solution

1.

May	3	Merchandise Inventory	4,120	
		Accounts Payable—Floyd Co.		4,120
	5	Merchandise Inventory	8,500	
		Accounts Payable—Kramer Co.		8,500
	6	Accounts Receivable—C. F. Howell Co.	2,800	
		Sales		2,800
	6	Cost of Merchandise Sold	1,125	
		Merchandise Inventory		1,125
	8	Office Supplies	150	
		Cash		150
	10	Accounts Payable—Kramer Co.	1,300	
		Merchandise Inventory		1,300
	13	Accounts Payable—Floyd Co.	4,120	
		Merchandise Inventory		80
		Cash		4,040
		[$4,000 − (2% × $4,000) + $120]		
	14	Merchandise Inventory	10,500	
		Cash		10,500
	15	Accounts Payable—Kramer Co.	7,200	
		Merchandise Inventory		72
		Cash		7,128
		[($8,500 − $1,300) × 1% = $72; $8,500 − $1,300 − $72 = $7,128]		
	16	Cash	2,744	
		Sales Discounts	56	
		Accounts Receivable—C. F. Howell Co.		2,800
	19	Accounts Receivable—American Express	2,450	
		Sales		2,450
	19	Cost of Merchandise Sold	980	
		Merchandise Inventory		980
	22	Accounts Receivable—Comer Co.	3,480	
		Sales		3,480

May	22	Cost of Merchandise Sold	1,400	
		Merchandise Inventory		1,400
	24	Cash	4,350	
		Sales		4,350
	24	Cost of Merchandise Sold	1,750	
		Merchandise Inventory		1,750
	25	Sales Returns and Allowances	1,480	
		Accounts Receivable—Comer Co.		1,480
	25	Merchandise Inventory	600	
		Cost of Merchandise Sold		600
	31	Cash	2,310	
		Credit Card Expense	140	
		Accounts Receivable—American Express		2,450

2.

May	31	Cost of Merchandise Sold	3,750	
		Merchandise Inventory		3,750

Self-Study Questions

Answers at end of chapter

1. If merchandise purchased on account is returned, the buyer may inform the seller of the details by issuing:
   A. a debit memorandum
   B. a credit memorandum
   C. an invoice
   D. a bill

2. If merchandise is sold on account to a customer for $1,000, terms FOB shipping point, 1/10, n/30, and the seller prepays $50 in transportation costs, the amount of the discount for early payment would be:
   A. $0
   B. $5.00
   C. $10.00
   D. $10.50

3. The income statement in which the total of all expenses is deducted from the total of all revenues is termed:
   A. multiple-step form
   B. single-step form
   C. direct form
   D. report form

4. On a multiple-step income statement, the excess of net sales over the cost of merchandise sold is called:
   A. operating income
   B. income from operations
   C. gross profit
   D. net income

5. As of December 31, 2004, Ames Corporation incorrectly counted its physical inventory as $275,000 instead of $300,000. The effect on the income statement is:
   A. Cost of merchandise sold is understated by $25,000
   B. Gross profit is overstated by $25,000
   C. Operating income is understated by $25,000
   D. Inventory shrinkage is understated by $25,000

Discussion Questions

1. What distinguishes a merchandising business from a service business?
2. Can a business earn a gross profit but incur a net loss? Explain.
3. What is the difference between the cost of merchandise purchased and the cost of merchandise available for sale? Can they be the same amount? Explain.
4. What is the difference between the cost of merchandise available for sale and the cost of merchandise sold? Can they be the same amount? Explain.
5. Name at least three accounts that would normally appear in the financial statements of a merchandising business, but would not appear in the chart of accounts of a service business.
6. How does the accounting for sales to customers using bank credit cards, such as MasterCard and VISA, differ from accounting for sales to customers using nonbank credit cards, such as American Express? Explain.
7. Sometimes a retailer will not accept American Express, but will accept MasterCard or VISA. Why would a retailer accept one and not the other?
8. At some Texaco, Chevron, or Conoco gasoline stations, the cash price per gallon is 3 or 4 cents less than the credit price per gallon. As a result, many customers pay cash rather than use their credit cards. Why would a gasoline station owner establish such a policy?
9. Assume that you purchased merchandise with credit terms 2/10, n/30. On the date the invoice is due, you don't have the cash to pay the invoice. However, you can borrow the necessary money at an 8% annual interest rate. Should you borrow the money to pay the invoice? Explain.
10. What is the nature of (a) a credit memorandum issued by the seller of merchandise, (b) a debit memorandum issued by the buyer of merchandise?
11. Who bears the transportation costs when the terms of sale are (a) FOB shipping point, (b) FOB destination?
12. When you purchase a new car, the "sticker price" includes a "destination" charge. Are you purchasing the car FOB shipping point or FOB destination? Explain.
13. Hansen Office Equipment, which uses a perpetual inventory system, experienced a normal inventory shrinkage of $12,860. (a) What accounts would be debited and credited to record the adjustment for the inventory shrinkage at the end of the accounting period? (b) What are some causes of inventory shrinkage?
14. Assume that Hansen Office Equipment in Question 13 experienced an abnormal inventory shrinkage of $210,500. It has decided to record the abnormal inventory shrinkage so that it would be separately disclosed on the income statement. What account would be debited for the abnormal inventory shrinkage?
15. Assume that Dugal Inc. (the consignee) included $32,000 of inventory held on consignment for Martin Company (the consignor) as part of its physical inventory. (a) What is the effect of this error on Dugal's financial statements? (b) Would Dugal's error also cause a misstatement in Martin's financial statements? Explain.

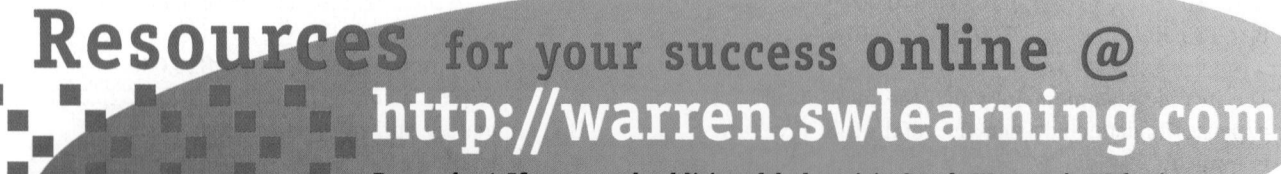

Resources for your success online @ http://warren.swlearning.com

Remember! If you need additional help, visit South-Western's Web site. See page 30 for a description of the online and printed materials that are available.

Exercises

Exercise 5-1

Determining gross profit

Goals 1, 9

a. $6,574

Walgreen Company operates drugstores throughout the United States, selling prescription drugs, general merchandise, cosmetics, food, and beverages. For 2001, Walgreen reported (in millions) net sales of $24,623, cost of sales of $18,049, and operating income of $1,398.

a. Determine Walgreen's gross profit.
b. Determine the gross profit as a percent of net sales. Round to one decimal place.
c. Determine the operating income as a percent of net sales. Round to one decimal place.

Exercise 5-2

Determining gross profit

Goals 1, 9

a. $5,691

STUDENT SOLUTIONS MANUAL

CVS Corporation operates drugstores throughout the United States, selling prescription drugs, general merchandise, cosmetics, greeting cards, food, and beverages. For 2001, CVS reported (in millions) net sales of $22,241, cost of sales of $16,550, and operating income of $771.

a. Determine CVS's gross profit.
b. Determine the gross profit as a percent of net sales. Round to one decimal place.
c. Determine the operating income as a percent of net sales. Round to one decimal place.

Exercise 5-3

Analyzing gross profit and operating income

Goal 9

Based upon the data shown in Exercises 5-1 and 5-2, comment on the operating performance of Walgreen in comparison to CVS.

Exercise 5-4

Determining gross profit

Goals 1, 9

a. $316,000

STUDENT SOLUTIONS MANUAL

During the current year, merchandise is sold for $170,000 cash and for $620,000 on account. The cost of the merchandise sold is $474,000.

a. What is the amount of the gross profit?
b. Compute the gross profit as a percent of sales.
c. Will the income statement necessarily report a net income? Explain.

Exercise 5-5

Determining gross profit

Goals 1, 9

a. $7,984

Office Depot operates a chain of office supply stores throughout the United States. For 2001, Office Depot reported (in millions) net sales of $11,154, gross profit of $3,170, and operating income of $354.

a. Determine the cost of goods sold.
b. Determine the cost of goods sold as a percent of net sales. Round to one decimal place.
c. Determine the gross profit as a percent of net sales. Round to one decimal place.
d. Determine the operating income as a percent of net sales. Round to one decimal place.
e. What is the difference between the gross profit as a percent of net sales and the operating income as a percent of net sales? Explain.

Exercise 5-6

Income statement for merchandiser

Goal 2

STUDENT SOLUTIONS MANUAL

For the fiscal year, sales were $7,230,000, sales discounts were $320,000, sales returns and allowances were $580,000, and the cost of merchandise sold was $4,338,000. What was the amount of net sales and gross profit?

Exercise 5–7

Identify items missing in determining cost of merchandise sold

Goal 2

For (a) through (d), identify the items designated by X.

a. Purchases − (X + X) = Net purchases.
b. Net purchases + X = Cost of merchandise purchased.
c. Merchandise inventory (beginning) + Cost of merchandise purchased = X.
d. Merchandise available for sale − X = Cost of merchandise sold.

Exercise 5–8

Cost of merchandise sold and related items

Goal 2

a. Cost of merchandise sold, $592,050

STUDENT SOLUTIONS MANUAL

SPREADSHEET

The following data were extracted from the accounting records of My Computers Company for the year ended November 30, 2004:

Merchandise Inventory, December 1, 2003	$ 75,750
Merchandise Inventory, November 30, 2004	88,200
Purchases	625,000
Purchases Returns and Allowances	14,500
Purchases Discounts	12,950
Sales	870,625
Transportation In	6,950

a. Prepare the cost of merchandise sold section of the income statement for the year ended November 30, 2004, using the periodic inventory method.
b. Determine the gross profit to be reported on the income statement for the year ended November 30, 2004.

Exercise 5–9

Cost of merchandise sold

Goal 2

How many errors can you find in the following schedule of cost of merchandise sold for the current year ended December 31, 2004?

Cost of merchandise sold:			
Merchandise inventory, December 31, 2004			$ 75,000
Purchases		$500,000	
Plus: Purchases returns and allowances	$12,500		
Purchases discounts	6,500	19,000	
Gross purchases		$519,000	
Less transportation in		12,400	
Cost of merchandise purchased			506,600
Merchandise available for sale			$581,600
Less merchandise inventory, January 1, 2004			81,300
Cost of merchandise sold			$500,300

Exercise 5–10

Income statement for merchandiser

Goal 2

STUDENT SOLUTIONS MANUAL

The following expenses were incurred by a merchandising business during the year. In which expense section of the income statement should each be reported: (a) selling, (b) administrative, or (c) other?

1. Advertising expense
2. Depreciation expense on office equipment
3. Insurance expense on store equipment
4. Interest expense on notes payable
5. Office supplies used
6. Rent expense on office building
7. Salaries of office personnel
8. Salary of sales manager

Exercise 5–11

Single-step income statement

Summary operating data for The Lifeboat Company during the current year ended April 30, 2004, are as follows: cost of merchandise sold, $1,460,000; administrative expenses,

Goal 2

SPREADSHEET

$225,000; interest expense, $37,500; rent revenue, $30,000; net sales, $3,600,000; and selling expenses, $375,000. Prepare a single-step income statement.

Exercise 5–12

Determining amounts for items omitted from income statement

Goal 2

a. $10,000

STUDENT SOLUTIONS MANUAL

Two items are omitted in each of the following four lists of income statement data. Determine the amounts of the missing items, identifying them by letter.

Sales	$298,000	$500,000	$700,000	$ (g)
Sales returns and allowances	(a)	15,000	(e)	30,500
Sales discounts	8,000	8,000	10,000	37,000
Net sales	280,000	(c)	665,000	(h)
Cost of merchandise sold	(b)	285,000	(f)	540,000
Gross profit	130,000	(d)	200,000	150,000

Exercise 5–13

Multiple-step income statement

Goal 2

How many errors can you find in the following income statement?

The Functor Company
Income Statement
For the Year Ended July 31, 2004

Revenue from sales:			
Sales		$3,000,000	
Add: Sales returns and allowances	$58,000		
Sales discounts	14,500	72,500	
Gross sales			$3,072,500
Cost of merchandise sold			1,495,000
Income from operations			$1,577,500
Operating expenses:			
Selling expenses		$ 145,000	
Transportation out		5,300	
Administrative expenses		87,200	
Total operating expenses			237,500
			$1,340,000
Other expense:			
Interest revenue			47,500
Gross profit			$1,292,500

Exercise 5–14

Multiple-step income statement

Goal 2

a. Net income, $97,500

STUDENT SOLUTIONS MANUAL

SPREADSHEET

On August 31, 2004, the balances of the accounts appearing in the ledger of Noble Company, a furniture wholesaler, are as follows:

Administrative Expenses	$ 60,000	Office Supplies	$ 10,600
Building	512,500	Retained Earnings	558,580
Capital Stock	50,000	Salaries Payable	3,220
Cash	48,500	Sales	775,000
Cost of Merchandise Sold	450,000	Sales Discounts	20,000
Dividends	25,000	Sales Returns and Allowances	45,000
Interest Expense	7,500	Selling Expenses	95,000
Merchandise Inventory	130,000	Store Supplies	7,700
Notes Payable	25,000		

a. Prepare a multiple-step income statement for the year ended August 31, 2004.
b. Compare the major advantages and disadvantages of the multiple-step and single-step forms of income statements.

Exercise 5–15

Sales-related transactions, including the use of credit cards

Goal 3

Journalize the entries for the following transactions:

a. Sold merchandise for cash, $15,000. The cost of the merchandise sold was $8,500.
b. Sold merchandise on account, $7,500. The cost of the merchandise sold was $4,000.
c. Sold merchandise to customers who used MasterCard and VISA, $7,750. The cost of the merchandise sold was $3,850.
d. Sold merchandise to customers who used American Express, $8,100. The cost of the merchandise sold was $5,860.
e. Paid an invoice from First National Bank for $350, representing a service fee for processing MasterCard and VISA sales.
f. Received $7,776 from American Express Company after a $324 collection fee had been deducted.

Exercise 5–16

Sales returns and allowances

Goal 3

STUDENT SOLUTIONS MANUAL

During the year, sales returns and allowances totaled $112,150. The cost of the merchandise returned was $67,300. The accountant recorded all the returns and allowances by debiting the sales account and crediting Cost of Merchandise Sold for $112,150.

Was the accountant's method of recording returns acceptable? Explain. In your explanation, include the advantages of using a sales returns and allowances account.

Exercise 5–17

Sales-related transactions

Goal 3

After the amount due on a sale of $5,500, terms 2/10, n/eom, is received from a customer within the discount period, the seller consents to the return of the entire shipment. The cost of the merchandise returned was $3,380. (a) What is the amount of the refund owed to the customer? (b) Journalize the entries made by the seller to record the return and the refund.

Exercise 5–18

Sales-related transactions

Goal 3

STUDENT SOLUTIONS MANUAL

The debits and credits for three related transactions are presented in the following T accounts. Describe each transaction.

CASH

(5)	7,425		

SALES

		(1)	10,000

ACCOUNTS RECEIVABLE

(1)	10,000	(3)	2,500
		(5)	7,500

SALES DISCOUNTS

(5)	75		

MERCHANDISE INVENTORY

(4)	1,500	(2)	6,000

SALES RETURNS AND ALLOWANCES

(3)	2,500		

COST OF MERCHANDISE SOLD

(2)	6,000	(4)	1,500

Exercise 5-19

Sales-related transactions

Goal 3

Merchandise is sold on account to a customer for $15,000, terms FOB shipping point, 3/10, n/30. The seller paid the transportation costs of $625. Determine the following: (a) amount of the sale, (b) amount debited to Accounts Receivable, (c) amount of the discount for early payment, and (d) amount due within the discount period.

Exercise 5-20

Purchase-related transaction

Goal 4

STUDENT SOLUTIONS MANUAL

Degas Company purchased merchandise on account from a supplier for $3,500, terms 2/10, n/30. Degas Company returned $750 of the merchandise and received full credit.

a. If Degas Company pays the invoice within the discount period, what is the amount of cash required for the payment?

b. Under a perpetual inventory system, what account is credited by Degas Company to record the return?

Exercise 5-21

Determining amounts to be paid on invoices

Goal 4

Determine the amount to be paid in full settlement of each of the following invoices, assuming that credit for returns and allowances was received prior to payment and that all invoices were paid within the discount period.

	Merchandise	Transportation Paid by Seller		Returns and Allowances
a.	$4,000	—	FOB shipping point, 1/10, n/30	$1,200
b.	1,500	$50	FOB shipping point, 2/10, n/30	700
c.	9,500	—	FOB destination, n/30	400
d.	2,500	75	FOB shipping point, 1/10, n/30	600
e.	5,000	—	FOB destination, 2/10, n/30	—

Exercise 5-22

Purchase-related transactions

Goal 4

STUDENT SOLUTIONS MANUAL

A retailer is considering the purchase of ten units of a specific item from either of two suppliers. Their offers are as follows:

A: $500 a unit, total of $5,000, 2/10, n/30, plus transportation costs of $175.
B: $510 a unit, total of $5,100, 1/10, n/30, no charge for transportation.

Which of the two offers, A or B, yields the lower price?

Exercise 5-23

Purchase-related transactions

Goal 4

The debits and credits from four related transactions are presented in the following T accounts. Describe each transaction.

CASH

		(2)	75
		(4)	3,920

ACCOUNTS PAYABLE

(3)	1,000	(1)	5,000
(4)	4,000		

MERCHANDISE INVENTORY

(1)	5,000	(3)	1,000
(2)	75	(4)	80

Exercise 5-24

Purchase-related transactions

Goal 4

STUDENT SOLUTIONS MANUAL

Citron Co., a women's clothing store, purchased $12,000 of merchandise from a supplier on account, terms FOB destination, 2/10, n/30. Citron Co. returned $3,500 of the merchandise, receiving a credit memorandum, and then paid the amount due within the discount period. Journalize Citron Co.'s entries to record (a) the purchase, (b) the merchandise return, and (c) the payment.

Exercise 5–25

Purchase-related transactions

Goal 4

Journalize entries for the following related transactions of Aloha Company:

a. Purchased $9,000 of merchandise from Green Co. on account, terms 2/10, n/30.
b. Paid the amount owed on the invoice within the discount period.
c. Discovered that $2,000 of the merchandise was defective and returned items, receiving credit.
d. Purchased $1,000 of merchandise from Green Co. on account, terms n/30.
e. Received a check for the balance owed from the return in (c), after deducting for the purchase in (d).

Exercise 5–26

Sales tax

Goal 5

STUDENT SOLUTIONS MANUAL

A sale of merchandise on account for $3,000 is subject to a 6% sales tax. (a) Should the sales tax be recorded at the time of sale or when payment is received? (b) What is the amount of the sale? (c) What is the amount debited to Accounts Receivable? (d) What is the title of the account to which the $180 is credited?

Exercise 5–27

Sales tax transactions

Goal 5

Journalize the entries to record the following selected transactions:

a. Sold $6,000 of merchandise on account, subject to a sales tax of 5%. The cost of the merchandise sold was $3,600.
b. Paid $4,380 to the state sales tax department for taxes collected.

Exercise 5–28

Sales-related transactions

Goal 3

STUDENT SOLUTIONS MANUAL

Sterile Co., a furniture wholesaler, sells merchandise to Bawd Co. on account, $8,000, terms 2/15, n/30. The cost of the merchandise sold is $4,800. Sterile Co. issues a credit memorandum for $500 for merchandise returned and subsequently receives the amount due within the discount period. The cost of the merchandise returned is $300. Journalize Sterile Co.'s entries for (a) the sale, including the cost of the merchandise sold, (b) the credit memorandum, including the cost of the returned merchandise, and (c) the receipt of the check for the amount due from Bawd Co.

Exercise 5–29

Purchase-related transactions

Goal 4

Based on the data presented in Exercise 5-30, journalize Bawd Co.'s entries for (a) the purchase, (b) the return of the merchandise for credit, and (c) the payment of the invoice within the discount period.

Exercise 5–30

Normal balances of merchandise accounts

Goals 3, 4, 5

STUDENT SOLUTIONS MANUAL

What is the normal balance of the following accounts: (a) Cost of Merchandise Sold, (b) Merchandise Inventory, (c) Sales, (d) Sales Discounts, (e) Sales Returns and Allowances, (f) Transportation Out?

Exercise 5–31

Adjusting entry for merchandise inventory shrinkage

Goal 7

Nocturnal Inc.'s perpetual inventory records indicate that $417,200 of merchandise should be on hand on October 31, 2004. The physical inventory indicates that $400,680 of merchandise is actually on hand. Journalize the adjusting entry for the inventory shrinkage for Nocturnal Inc. for the year ended October 31, 2004.

Exercise 5–32

Effects of inventory misstatements

Goal 8

1. 2003 net income overstated, $15,000

STUDENT SOLUTIONS MANUAL

Following are descriptions of two independent situations that involve inventory misstatements.

1. Ending merchandise inventory is overstated by $15,000 on December 31, 2003. Ending merchandise inventory is correct on December 31, 2004.
2. Ending merchandise inventory is understated by $8,000 on December 31, 2003. Ending merchandise inventory is overstated by $12,000 on December 31, 2004.

For each situation, indicate the effects of the misstatements on the financial statements for 2003 and 2004. Use the following format for your answers:

	Amount of Misstatement Overstatement (Understatement)	
	2003	**2004**
Balance Sheet (December 31):		
Merchandise inventory	_____	_____
Current assets	_____	_____
Total assets	_____	_____
Retained earnings	_____	_____
Total stockholders' equity	_____	_____
Income Statement:		
Cost of merchandise sold	_____	_____
Gross profit	_____	_____
Net income	_____	_____

Exercise 5–33

Effects of inventory misstatements

Goal 8

1. 2004 net income overstated, $5,000

Following are descriptions of two independent situations that involve inventory misstatements.

1. Ending merchandise inventory is overstated by $13,000 on December 31, 2003. Ending merchandise inventory is overstated by $18,000 on December 31, 2004.
2. Ending merchandise inventory is understated by $9,000 on December 31, 2003. Ending merchandise inventory is understated by $6,000 on December 31, 2004.

For each situation, indicate the effects of the misstatements on the financial statements for 2003 and 2004. Use the following format for your answers:

	Amount of Misstatement Overstatement (Understatement)	
	2003	**2004**
Balance Sheet (December 31):		
Merchandise inventory	_____	_____
Current assets	_____	_____
Total assets	_____	_____
Retained earnings	_____	_____
Total stockholders' equity	_____	_____
Income Statement:		
Cost of merchandise sold	_____	_____
Gross profit	_____	_____
Net income	_____	_____

Exercise 5-34

Effects of inventory misstatements

Goal 8

STUDENT SOLUTIONS MANUAL

Merchandise of $31,000 was ordered on December 26, 2003, FOB destination, and was received on December 30, 2003. The invoice from the vendor was not received until January 7, 2004, and the related accounts payable journal entry was not recorded until January 7, 2004. However, since the merchandise was on hand at December 31, 2003, it was included in the physical inventory and properly assigned a cost.

Assume that the accounts payable was recorded on January 7, 2004, as a debit to Merchandise Inventory and a credit to Accounts Payable for $31,000. Also, assume that the December 31, 2004 physical inventory is correct. Indicate the effects of the inventory misstatements on the financial statements for 2003 and 2004, using the following format for your answers:

	Amount of Misstatement Overstatement (Understatement)	
	2003	**2004**
Balance Sheet (December 31):		
Merchandise inventory	_____	_____
Total assets	_____	_____
Accounts payable	_____	_____
Total liabilities	_____	_____
Retained earnings	_____	_____
Total stockholders' equity	_____	_____
Income Statement:		
Cost of merchandise sold	_____	_____
Gross profit	_____	_____
Net income	_____	_____

Exercise 5-35

Effects of inventory misstatements

Goal 8

Merchandise of $25,000 was ordered on December 29, 2003, FOB shipping point. The vendor paid the shipping charges of $500 as an accommodation to the buyer. The invoice from the vendor was not received until January 3, 2004, and the related accounts payable journal entry was not recorded until January 3, 2004. The merchandise was shipped on December 30, 2003, and was received on January 5, 2004. Since the merchandise was in transit, it was not included in the physical count of inventory on December 31, 2003.

Assume that the accounts payable was recorded on January 3, 2004, as a debit to Merchandise Inventory and a credit to Accounts Payable for $25,500. Also, assume that the December 31, 2004 physical inventory is correct. Indicate the effects of the inventory misstatements on the financial statements for 2003 and 2004, using the following format for your answers:

	Amount of Misstatement Overstatement (Understatement)	
	2003	**2004**
Balance Sheet (December 31):		
Merchandise inventory	_____	_____
Total assets	_____	_____
Accounts payable	_____	_____
Total liabilities	_____	_____
Retained earnings	_____	_____
Total stockholders' equity	_____	_____
Income Statement:		
Cost of merchandise sold	_____	_____
Gross profit	_____	_____
Net income	_____	_____

Exercise 5-36

Gross profit and operating income

Goal 9

STUDENT SOLUTIONS MANUAL

Staples, Inc., operates a chain of office supply stores throughout the United States. For 2001 and 2000, Staples reported (in millions) the following operating data:

	2001	2000
Net sales	$10,674	$8,937
Cost of goods sold	8,097	6,722
Gross profit	$ 2,577	$2,215
Operating income	$ 289	$ 534

a. Compute the percent of gross profit and operating income to net sales. Round to one decimal place.
b. Based upon (a), comment on Staples' operating performance in 2001 as compared to 2000.

Accounting Application Problems

Problem 5-1A

Multiple-step income statement, retained earnings statement, and report form of balance sheet

Goal 2

1. Net income, $100,000

SPREADSHEET

The following selected accounts and their current balances appear in the ledger of Mandolin Co. for the fiscal year ended March 31, 2004:

Cash	$ 33,750	Sales	$1,275,000
Notes Receivable	120,000	Sales Returns and Allowances	23,100
Accounts Receivable	121,000	Sales Discounts	21,900
Merchandise Inventory	175,000	Cost of Merchandise Sold	775,000
Office Supplies	5,600	Sales Salaries Expense	173,200
Prepaid Insurance	3,400	Advertising Expense	43,800
Office Equipment	85,000	Depreciation Expense—Store Equipment	6,400
Accumulated Depreciation—Office Equipment	12,800	Miscellaneous Selling Expense	1,600
Store Equipment	153,000	Office Salaries Expense	84,150
Accumulated Depreciation—Store Equipment	34,200	Rent Expense	31,350
Accounts Payable	55,600	Depreciation Expense—Office Equipment	12,700
Salaries Payable	2,400	Insurance Expense	3,900
Note Payable (final payment due 2013)	56,000	Office Supplies Expense	1,300
Capital Stock	75,000	Miscellaneous Administrative Expense	1,600
Retained Earnings	395,750	Interest Revenue	11,000
Dividends	35,000	Interest Expense	6,000

Instructions

1. Prepare a multiple-step income statement.
2. Prepare a retained earnings statement.
3. Prepare a report form of balance sheet, assuming that the current portion of the note payable is $7,500.
4. Briefly explain how multiple-step and single-step income statements differ.

Problem 5-2A

Single-step income statement and retained earnings statement

Goal 2

SPREADSHEET

Selected accounts and related amounts for Mandolin Co. for the fiscal year ended March 31, 2004, are presented in Problem 5-1A.

Instructions

1. Prepare a single-step income statement.
2. Prepare a retained earnings statement.

Problem 5-3A

Sales-related transactions

Goals 3, 5

GENERAL LEDGER

The following selected transactions were completed by Fastball Supply Co., which sells office supplies primarily to wholesalers and occasionally to retail customers:

July	2	Sold merchandise on account to Magnolia Co., $10,500, terms FOB destination, 2/10, n/30. The cost of the merchandise sold was $6,000.
	3	Sold merchandise for $2,000 plus 5% sales tax to cash customers. The cost of merchandise sold was $1,100.
	4	Sold merchandise on account to McNutt Co., $2,800, terms FOB shipping point, n/eom. The cost of merchandise sold was $1,800.
	5	Sold merchandise for $1,400 plus 5% sales tax to customers who used MasterCard. Deposited credit card receipts into the bank. The cost of merchandise sold was $750.
	12	Received check for amount due from Magnolia Co. for sale on July 2.
	14	Sold merchandise to customers who used American Express cards, $8,600. The cost of merchandise sold was $6,200.
	16	Sold merchandise on account to Westpark Co., $12,000, terms FOB shipping point, 1/10, n/30. The cost of merchandise sold was $7,200.
	18	Issued credit memorandum for $3,000 to Westpark Co. for merchandise returned from sale on July 16. The cost of the merchandise returned was $1,800.
	19	Sold merchandise on account to Hempel Co., $7,500, terms FOB shipping point, 1/10, n/30. Added $85 to the invoice for transportation costs prepaid. The cost of merchandise sold was $4,500.
	26	Received check for amount due from Westpark Co. for sale on July 16 less credit memorandum of July 18 and discount.
	27	Received $9,410 from American Express for $10,000 of sales reported July 1-12.
	28	Received check for amount due from Hempel Co. for sale of July 19.
	31	Received check for amount due from McNutt Co. for sale of July 4.
	31	Paid Fast Delivery Service $1,050 for merchandise delivered during July to customers, under shipping terms of FOB destination.
Aug.	3	Paid First National Bank $690 for service fees for handling MasterCard sales during July.
	15	Paid $3,100 to state sales tax division for taxes owed on July sales.

Instructions

Journalize the entries to record the transactions of Fastball Supply Co.

Problem 5-4A

Purchase-related transactions

Goals 4, 5

GENERAL LEDGER

The following selected transactions were completed by Bushwhack Company during October of the current year:

Oct.	1	Purchased merchandise from Riverhill Co., $10,500, terms FOB destination, n/30.
	3	Purchased merchandise from Windsor Co., $8,000, terms FOB shipping point, 2/10, n/eom. Prepaid transportation costs of $150 were added to the invoice.
	4	Purchased merchandise from Picadilly Co., $7,500, terms FOB destination, 2/10, n/30.
	6	Issued debit memorandum to Picadilly Co. for $1,000 of merchandise returned from purchase on October 4.

Oct. 13 Paid Windsor Co. for invoice of October 3, less discount.
14 Paid Picadilly Co. for invoice of October 4, less debit memorandum of October 6 and discount.
19 Purchased merchandise from Ivy Co., $5,000, terms FOB shipping point, n/eom.
19 Paid transportation charges of $120 on October 19 purchase from Ivy Co.
20 Purchased merchandise from Hatcher Co., $8,000, terms FOB destination, 1/10, n/30.
30 Paid Hatcher Co. for invoice of October 20, less discount.
31 Paid Riverhill Co. for invoice of October 1.
31 Paid Ivy Co. for invoice of October 19.

Instructions
Journalize the entries to record the transactions of Bushwhack Company for October.

Problem 5–5A

Sales-related and purchase-related transactions

Goals 3, 4, 5, 6

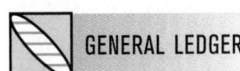

GENERAL LEDGER

The following were selected from among the transactions completed by The Knapsack Company during April of the current year:

Apr. 3 Purchased merchandise on account from Velcro Co., $24,000, terms FOB destination, 2/10, n/30.
4 Sold merchandise for cash, $5,100. The cost of the merchandise sold was $3,000.
5 Purchased merchandise on account from Summit Co., $7,500, terms FOB shipping point, 2/10, n/30, with prepaid transportation costs of $200 added to the invoice.
6 Returned $4,000 of merchandise purchased on April 3 from Velcro Co.
11 Sold merchandise on account to Bowles Co., $1,800, terms 1/10, n/30. The cost of the merchandise sold was $1,050.
13 Paid Velcro Co. on account for purchase of April 3, less return of April 6 and discount.
14 Sold merchandise on nonbank credit cards and reported accounts to the card company, American Express, $7,850. The cost of the merchandise sold was $3,900.
15 Paid Summit Co. on account for purchase of April 5, less discount.
21 Received cash on account from sale of April 11 to Bowles Co., less discount.
24 Sold merchandise on account to Hardigree Co., $4,200, terms 1/10, n/30. The cost of the merchandise sold was $1,850.
28 Received cash from American Express for nonbank credit card sales of April 14, less $314 service fee.
30 Received merchandise returned by Hardigree Co. from sale on April 24, $1,100. The cost of the returned merchandise was $600.

Instructions
Journalize the transactions.

Problem 5–6A

Sales-related and purchase-related transactions for seller and buyer

Goals 3, 4, 5, 6

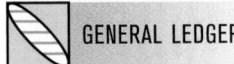

GENERAL LEDGER

The following selected transactions were completed during July between Snap Company and Buckle Co.:

July 1 Snap Company sold merchandise on account to Buckle Co., $11,750, terms FOB destination, 2/15, n/eom. The cost of the merchandise sold was $7,000.
2 Snap Company paid transportation costs of $350 for delivery of merchandise sold to Buckle Co. on July 1.
5 Snap Company sold merchandise on account to Buckle Co., $17,500, terms FOB shipping point, n/eom. The cost of the merchandise sold was $10,000.
6 Buckle Co. returned $2,000 of merchandise purchased on account on July 1 from Snap Company. The cost of the merchandise returned was $1,200.
9 Buckle Co. paid transportation charges of $200 on July 5 purchase from Snap Company.

July 15 Snap Company sold merchandise on account to Buckle Co., $20,000, terms FOB shipping point, 1/10, n/30. Snap Company paid transportation costs of $1,750, which were added to the invoice. The cost of the merchandise sold was $12,000.

16 Buckle Co. paid Snap Company for purchase of July 1, less discount and less return of July 6.

25 Buckle Co. paid Snap Company on account for purchase of July 15, less discount.

31 Buckle Co. paid Snap Company on account for purchase of July 5.

Instructions

Journalize the July transactions for (1) Snap Company and (2) Buckle Co.

Appendix Problem 5–7A

Statement of Cash Flows Using Indirect Method

For the year ending December 31, 2004, Seamless Systems Inc. reported net income of $30,200 and paid dividends of $9,000. Comparative balance sheets as of December 31, 2004 and 2003, are as follows:

Seamless Systems Inc.
Balance Sheets

	December 31,		Changes
	2004	**2003**	**Increase (Decrease)**
Assets			
Current assets:			
Cash	$ 26,475	$ 20,750	$ 5,725
Accounts receivable	38,040	26,000	12,040
Merchandise inventory	31,075	29,850	1,225
Office supplies	240	300	(60)
Prepaid insurance	1,325	1,500	(175)
Total current assets	$ 97,155	$ 78,400	$18,755
Property, plant, and equipment:			
Land	$ 10,000	$ 10,000	$ 0
Store equipment	13,550	10,000	3,550
Accumulated depreciation—store equipment	(2,850)	(1,300)	(1,550)
Office equipment	7,785	5,000	2,785
Accumulated depreciation—office equipment	(2,360)	(1,115)	(1,245)
Total property, plant, and equipment	$ 26,125	$ 22,585	$ 3,540
Total assets	$123,280	$100,985	$22,295
Liabilities			
Current liabilities:			
Accounts payable	$ 11,210	$ 7,135	$ 4,075
Notes payable (current portion)	2,500	2,500	0
Salaries payable	570	750	(180)
Unearned rent	900	1,200	(300)
Total current liabilities	$ 15,180	$ 11,585	$ 3,595
Long-term liabilities:			
Notes payable (final payment due 2009)	10,000	12,500	(2,500)
Total liabilities	$ 25,180	$ 24,085	$ 1,095

(continued)

	December 31,		Changes
	2004	2003	Increase (Decrease)
Stockholders' Equity			
Capital stock	$ 12,500	$ 12,500	$ 0
Retained earnings	85,600	64,400	21,200
Total stockholders' equity	$ 98,100	$ 76,900	$21,200
Total liabilities and stockholders' equity	$123,280	$100,985	$22,295

1. Net cash flow from operating activities, $23,560

SPREADSHEET

Instructions

1. Prepare a statement of cash flows, using the indirect method.
2. Why is depreciation added to net income in determining net cash flows from operating activities? Explain.

Alternative Accounting Application Problems

Alternate Problem 5–1B

Multiple-step income statement, retained earnings statement, and report form of balance sheet

Goal 2

1. Net income, $68,000

STUDENT SOLUTIONS MANUAL

SPREADSHEET

The following selected accounts and their current balances appear in the ledger of Cypress Co. for the fiscal year ended June 30, 2004:

Cash	$ 26,500	Sales	$1,500,000
Notes Receivable	50,000	Sales Returns and Allowances	21,000
Accounts Receivable	62,000	Sales Discounts	11,000
Merchandise Inventory	100,000	Cost of Merchandise Sold	1,070,000
Office Supplies	2,600	Sales Salaries Expense	210,000
Prepaid Insurance	6,800	Advertising Expense	28,300
Office Equipment	64,000	Depreciation Expense—Store Equipment	4,600
Accumulated Depreciation—Office Equipment	10,800	Miscellaneous Selling Expense	1,100
Store Equipment	117,500	Office Salaries Expense	41,000
Accumulated Depreciation—Store Equipment	48,600	Rent Expense	22,150
Accounts Payable	27,000	Insurance Expense	12,750
Salaries Payable	2,000	Depreciation Expense—Office Equipment	9,000
Note Payable (final payment due 2013)	30,000	Office Supplies Expense	900
Capital Stock	60,000	Miscellaneous Administrative Expense	1,200
Retained Earnings	208,000	Interest Revenue	5,000
Dividends	25,000	Interest Expense	4,000

Instructions

1. Prepare a multiple-step income statement.
2. Prepare a retained earnings statement.
3. Prepare a report form of balance sheet, assuming that the current portion of the note payable is $2,500.
4. Briefly explain how multiple-step and single-step income statements differ.

Alternate Problem 5–2B

Single-step income statement and retained earnings statement

Goal 2

STUDENT SOLUTIONS MANUAL

SPREADSHEET

Selected accounts and related amounts for Cypress Co. for the fiscal year ended June 30, 2004, are presented in Alternate Problem 5–1B.

Instructions

1. Prepare a single-step income statement.
2. Prepare a retained earnings statement.

Alternate Problem 5–3B

Sales-related transactions

Goals 3, 5

STUDENT SOLUTIONS MANUAL

GENERAL LEDGER

The following selected transactions were completed by Sprinkle Supplies Co., which sells irrigation supplies primarily to wholesalers and occasionally to retail customers.

May 1 Sold merchandise on account to Lynlex Co., $4,500, terms FOB shipping point, n/eom. The cost of merchandise sold was $2,300.

2 Sold merchandise for $5,000 plus 6% sales tax to cash customers. The cost of merchandise sold was $3,750.

5 Sold merchandise on account to Maple Company, $11,500, terms FOB destination, 1/10, n/30. The cost of merchandise sold was $7,000.

8 Sold merchandise for $4,150 plus 6% sales tax to customers who used VISA cards. Deposited credit card receipts into the bank. The cost of merchandise sold was $2,800.

13 Sold merchandise to customers who used American Express cards, $4,500. The cost of merchandise sold was $2,600.

14 Sold merchandise on account to Blech Co., $7,500, terms FOB shipping point, 1/10, n/30. The cost of merchandise sold was $4,000.

15 Received check for amount due from Maple Company for sale on May 5.

16 Issued credit memorandum for $800 to Blech Co. for merchandise returned from sale on May 14. The cost of the merchandise returned was $360.

18 Sold merchandise on account to Fortson Company, $6,850, terms FOB shipping point, 2/10, n/30. Paid $210 for transportation costs and added them to the invoice. The cost of merchandise sold was $4,100.

24 Received check for amount due from Blech Co. for sale on May 14 less credit memorandum of May 16 and discount.

27 Received $7,680 from American Express for $8,000 of sales reported during the week of May 1–12.

28 Received check for amount due from Fortson Company for sale of May 18.

31 Paid Anywhere Delivery Service $1,500 for merchandise delivered during May to customers under shipping terms of FOB destination.

31 Received check for amount due from Lynlex Co. for sale of May 1.

June 3 Paid First National Bank $525 for service fees for handling MasterCard sales during May.

10 Paid $1,100 to state sales tax division for taxes owed on May sales.

Instructions

Journalize the entries to record the transactions of Sprinkle Supplies Co.

Alternate Problem 5–4B

Purchase-related transactions

Goals 4, 5

The following selected transactions were completed by Beagley Co. during March of the current year:

Mar. 1 Purchased merchandise from Lumpkin Co., $9,000, terms FOB shipping point, 2/10, n/eom. Prepaid transportation costs of $350 were added to the invoice.

5 Purchased merchandise from Guthrie Co., $9,200, terms FOB destination, n/30.

10 Paid Lumpkin Co. for invoice of March 1, less discount.

STUDENT SOLUTIONS MANUAL

GENERAL LEDGER

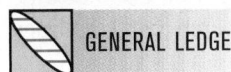

Mar. 13 Purchased merchandise from Mickle Co., $7,500, terms FOB destination, 1/10, n/30.
14 Issued debit memorandum to Mickle Co. for $2,500 of merchandise returned from purchase on March 13.
18 Purchased merchandise from Aschor Company, $11,500, terms FOB shipping point, n/eom.
18 Paid transportation charges of $200 on March 18 purchase from Aschor Company.
19 Purchased merchandise from Hatcher Co., $7,500, terms FOB destination, 2/10, n/30.
23 Paid Mickle Co. for invoice of March 13, less debit memorandum of March 14 and discount.
29 Paid Hatcher Co. for invoice of March 19, less discount.
31 Paid Aschor Company for invoice of March 18.
31 Paid Guthrie Co. for invoice of March 5.

Instructions

Journalize the entries to record the transactions of Beagley Co. for March.

Alternate Problem 5-5B

Sales-related and purchase-related transactions

Goals 3, 4, 5, 6

STUDENT SOLUTIONS MANUAL

GENERAL LEDGER

The following were selected from among the transactions completed by Pelops Company during March of the current year:

Mar. 3 Purchased merchandise on account from Spruce Co., $11,700, terms FOB shipping point, 2/10, n/30, with prepaid transportation costs of $620 added to the invoice.
5 Purchased merchandise on account from Blake Co., $10,000, terms FOB destination, 1/10, n/30.
6 Sold merchandise on account to Howell Co., $4,500, terms 2/10, n/30. The cost of the merchandise sold was $1,850.
7 Returned $1,800 of merchandise purchased on March 5 from Blake Co.
13 Paid Spruce Co. on account for purchase of March 3, less discount.
15 Paid Blake Co. on account for purchase of March 5, less return of March 7 and discount.
16 Received cash on account from sale of March 6 to Howell Co., less discount.
19 Sold merchandise on nonbank credit cards and reported accounts to the card company, American Express, $4,450. The cost of the merchandise sold was $2,950.
22 Sold merchandise on account to Morton Co., $3,480, terms 2/10, n/30. The cost of the merchandise sold was $1,400.
23 Sold merchandise for cash, $7,350. The cost of the merchandise sold was $3,750.
25 Received merchandise returned by Morton Co. from sale on March 22, $1,480. The cost of the returned merchandise was $600.
31 Received cash from American Express for nonbank credit card sales of March 19, less $290 service fee.

Instructions

Journalize the transactions.

Alternate Problem 5-6B

Sales-related and purchase-related transactions for seller and buyer

Goals 3, 4, 5, 6

The following selected transactions were completed during November between Subliminal Company and Bungee Company:

Nov. 2 Subliminal Company sold merchandise on account to Bungee Company, $12,000, terms FOB shipping point, 2/10, n/30. Subliminal Company paid transportation costs of $500, which were added to the invoice. The cost of the merchandise sold was $7,500.
8 Subliminal Company sold merchandise on account to Bungee Company, $13,500, terms FOB destination, 1/15, n/eom. The cost of the merchandise sold was $9,500.

STUDENT SOLUTIONS MANUAL

GENERAL LEDGER

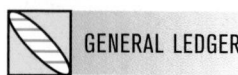

Nov. 8 Subliminal Company paid transportation costs of $750 for delivery of merchandise sold to Bungee Company on November 8.

12 Bungee Company returned $3,000 of merchandise purchased on account on November 8 from Subliminal Company. The cost of the merchandise returned was $1,600.

12 Bungee Company paid Subliminal Company for purchase of November 2, less discount.

23 Bungee Company paid Subliminal Company for purchase of November 8, less discount and less return of November 12.

24 Subliminal Company sold merchandise on account to Bungee Company, $9,000, terms FOB shipping point, n/eom. The cost of the merchandise sold was $5,400.

26 Bungee Company paid transportation charges of $250 on November 24 purchase from Subliminal Company.

30 Bungee Company paid Subliminal Company on account for purchase of November 24.

Instructions

Journalize the November transactions for (1) Subliminal Company and (2) Bungee Company.

Appendix Alternate Problem 5–7B

Statement of Cash Flows Using Indirect Method

STUDENT SOLUTIONS MANUAL

For the year ending December 31, 2004, Bauer Systems Inc. reported net income of $120,800 and paid dividends of $36,000. Comparative balance sheets as of December 31, 2004 and 2003 are as follows:

Bauer Systems Inc.
Balance Sheets

	December 31,		Changes
	2004	**2003**	**Increase (Decrease)**
Assets			
Current assets:			
Cash	$105,900	$ 83,000	$ 22,900
Accounts receivable	152,160	104,000	48,160
Merchandise inventory	124,300	119,400	4,900
Office supplies	960	1,200	(240)
Prepaid insurance	5,300	6,000	(700)
Total current assets	$388,620	$313,600	$ 75,020
Property, plant, and equipment:			
Land	$ 40,000	$ 40,000	$ 0
Store equipment	54,200	40,000	14,200
Accumulated depreciation—store equipment	(11,400)	(5,200)	(6,200)
Office equipment	31,140	20,000	11,140
Accumulated depreciation—office equipment	(9,440)	(4,460)	(4,980)
Total property, plant, and equipment	$104,500	$ 90,340	$ 14,160
Total assets	$493,120	$403,940	$ 89,180

(continued)

	December 31,		Changes
	2004	2003	Increase (Decrease)
Liabilities			
Current liabilities:			
Accounts payable	$ 44,840	$ 28,540	$ 16,300
Notes payable (current portion)	10,000	10,000	0
Salaries payable	2,280	3,000	(720)
Unearned rent	3,600	4,800	(1,200)
Total current liabilities	$ 60,720	$ 46,340	$ 14,380
Long-term liabilities:			
Notes payable (final payment due 2009)	40,000	50,000	(10,000)
Total liabilities	$100,720	$ 96,340	$ 4,380
Stockholders' Equity			
Capital stock	$ 50,000	$ 50,000	$ 0
Retained earnings	342,400	257,600	84,800
Total stockholders' equity	$392,400	$307,600	$ 84,800
Total liabilities and stockholders' equity	$493,120	$403,940	$ 89,180

1. Net cash flow from operating activities, $94,240

SPREADSHEET

Instructions

1. Prepare a statement of cash flows, using the indirect method.
2. Under the indirect method, why is net income adjusted for changes in accruals and deferrals? Explain.

Building Leadership Skills— Financial Analysis and Reporting

Case 5–1

Analysis of gross profit and operating income

Federated Department Stores, Inc., is one of the leading operators of full-line department stores in the United States, operating under the names Bloomingdale's, The Bon Marche, Burdines, Goldsmith's, Lazarus, Macy's and Rich's. The following operating data (in millions) for the past three years is taken from Federated's income statement:

	For the Years Ended		
	Feb. 2, 2002	Feb. 3, 2001	Jan. 29, 2000
Net sales	$15,651	$16,638	$16,029
Cost of merchandise sold	9,584	9,955	9,576
Operating expenses	4,801	4,912	4,760

1. Compute the gross profit for each year.
2. Compute the operating income for each year.
3. Compute the gross profit as a percentage of net sales for each year. Round to one decimal place.
4. Compute the operating income as a percentage of net sales for each year. Round to one decimal place.
5. Based upon this analysis, comment on the trends in operating performance for the past three years.
6. Based upon this analysis, compare Federated's operating performance with JC Penney's performance shown in this chapter (see Exhibit 12).

Case 5–2

Analysis of gross profit and operating income

Nordstrom, Inc. is a fashion specialty retailer offering a wide selection of high-quality apparel, shoes, and accessories for women, men, and children in the United States through 80 full-line Nordstrom stores, 46 Nordstrom rack and clearance stores, 4 Faconnable boutiques, and 2 free-standing shoe stores. The following operating data (in millions) were taken from 10K filings with the Securities and Exchange Commission:

	For Year Ending January 31		
	2002	2001	2000
Net sales	$5,634	$5,529	$5,149
Cost of goods sold	3,766	3,650	3,359
Gross profit	$1,868	$1,879	$1,790
Selling, general, admin. exp.	1,722	1,747	1,524
Operating income	$ 146	$ 132	$ 266

1. Compute gross profit as a percent of net sales for each year. Round to one decimal place.
2. Compute operating income as a percent of net sales for each year. Round to one decimal place.
3. Based upon (1) and (2), comment on Nordstrom's operating performance.

Case 5–3

Analysis of gross profit and operating income

Target Corporation (formerly Dayton Hudson Corporation) is a general merchandise retailer, comprised of three operating segments: Target, Mervyn's, and Marshall Field's. Target, an upscale discount chain located in 47 states, contributed 82 percent of the 2001 total revenues. Mervyn's, a middle-market promotional department store located in 14 states in the West, South, and Midwest, contributed 10 percent of total revenues. Marshall Field's (including stores formerly named Dayton's and Hudson's), a traditional department store located in 8 states in the upper Midwest, contributed 8 percent of total revenues. The following operating data (in millions) were taken from 10K filings with the Securities and Exchange Commission:

	For Year Ending		
	Feb. 2 2002	Feb. 3 2001	Jan. 31 2000
Net sales	$39,888	$36,362	$33,212
Cost of goods sold	27,246	25,295	23,029
Gross profit	$12,642	$11,067	$10,183
Operating income	$ 2,680	$ 2,478	$ 2,329

1. Compute gross profit as a percent of net sales for each year. Round to one decimal place.
2. Compute operating income as a percent of net sales for each year. Round to one decimal place.
3. Based upon (1) and (2), comment on Target's operating performance.

Case 5–4

Comparative analysis of operating performance

Using the data provided in Cases 5–2 and 5–3, compare the operating performances of Nordstrom and Target.

Case 5–5

Effects of inventory misstatements

Following are descriptions of two independent situations that involve inventory misstatements.

Castellon Corporation

On December 30, 2003, Castellon Corporation sold merchandise that cost $42,000 for $75,000, FOB shipping point. During the morning of December 31, 2003, the merchandise was counted as part of the physical inventory since it was still on hand. Late in the afternoon of December 31, the merchandise was picked up by the freight company hired by the customer to deliver the merchandise. Castellon Corporation's accounting department did not record the sale and related cost of merchandise sold until January 3, 2004. Castellon Corporation did not discover the preceding errors in 2004, and the customer paid the receivable later in January 2004.

Crumbley Jewelry

On December 31, 2003, Crumbley Jewelry failed to include in its inventory count $85,000 of its inventory that was out on consignment with other jewelers. Of this amount, $30,000 was sold the last week of December 2003 for $72,000. Crumbley Jewelry was notified of these consignment sales on January 3, and, as a result, recorded the $72,000 of sales on January 3, 2004. On January 20, the consignee remitted the $72,000 to Crumbley Jewelry. On December 31, 2004, Crumbley again failed to include in its inventory count $75,000 of its inventory that was out on consignment with other jewelers. None of the jewelry out on consignment on December 31, 2004, had been sold as of that date. Crumbley had not discovered any of the errors by that date.

For each of the companies, indicate the effects of the inventory misstatements on the financial statements for 2003 and 2004.

Building Leadership Skills—Responsible Leadership

Activity 5-1

Ethics and professional conduct in business

ETHICS

On October 1, 2004, Couperin Company, a garden retailer, purchased $15,000 of corn seed, terms 2/10, n/30, from Kernel Co. Even though the discount period had expired, Bryant Harness subtracted the discount of $300 when he processed the documents for payment on October 15, 2004.

Discuss whether Bryant Harness behaved in a professional manner by subtracting the discount, even though the discount period had expired.

Activity 5-2

Purchases discounts and accounts payable

The Movie Store Co. is owned and operated by Amy Lell. The following is an excerpt from a conversation between Amy Lell and Tammi Beach, the chief accountant for The Movie Store.

Amy: Tammi, I've got a question about this recent balance sheet.
Tammi: Sure, what's your question?
Amy: Well, as you know, I'm applying for a bank loan to finance our new store in Three Forks, and I noticed that the accounts payable are listed as $130,000.
Tammi: That's right. Approximately $100,000 of that represents amounts due our suppliers, and the remainder is miscellaneous payables to creditors for utilities, office equipment, supplies, etc.
Amy: That's what I thought. But as you know, we normally receive a 2% discount from our suppliers for earlier payment, and we always try to take the discount.
Tammi: That's right. I can't remember the last time we missed a discount.
Amy: Well, in that case, it seems to me the accounts payable should be listed minus the 2% discount. Let's list the accounts payable due suppliers as $98,000, rather than $100,000. Every little bit helps. You never know. It might make the difference between getting the loan and not.

How would you respond to Amy Lell's request?

Activity 5-3

Determining cost of purchase

The following is an excerpt from a conversation between Gina Bellamy and Kim Craft. Gina is debating whether to buy a stereo system from Mega Sound, a locally owned electronics store, or Decibel Electronics, a mail-order electronics company.

Gina: Kim, I don't know what to do about buying my new stereo.
Kim: What's the problem?
Gina: Well, I can buy it locally at Mega Sound for $495.00. However, Decibel Electronics has the same system listed for $499.99.
Kim: So what's the big deal? Buy it from Mega Sound.
Gina: It's not quite that simple. Decibel said something about not having to pay sales tax, since I was out-of-state.
Kim: Yes, that's a good point. If you buy it at Mega Sound, they'll charge you 5% sales tax.

Gina: But Decibel Electronics charges $12.50 for shipping and handling. If I have them send it next-day air, it'll cost $25 for shipping and handling.

Kim: I guess it is a little confusing.

Gina: That's not all. Mega Sound will give an additional 1% discount if I pay cash. Otherwise, they will let me use my MasterCard, or I can pay it off in three monthly installments.

Kim: Anything else???

Gina: Well . . . Decibel says I have to charge it on my MasterCard. They don't accept checks.

Kim: I am not surprised. Many mail-order houses don't accept checks.

Gina: I give up. What would you do?

1. Assuming that Decibel Electronics doesn't charge sales tax on the sale to Gina, which company is offering the best buy?
2. What might be some considerations other than price that might influence Gina's decision on where to buy the stereo system?

Activity 5-4

Sales discounts

Your sister operates Hercules Parts Company, a mail-order boat parts distributorship that is in its third year of operation. The following income statement was recently prepared for the year ended July 31, 2003:

Hercules Parts Company
Income Statement
For the Year Ended July 31, 2003

Revenues:		
Net sales		$600,000
Interest revenue		5,000
Total revenues		$605,000
Expenses:		
Cost of merchandise sold	$420,000	
Selling expenses	66,000	
Administrative expenses	34,000	
Interest expense	10,000	
Total expenses		530,000
Net income		$ 75,000

Your sister is considering a proposal to increase net income by offering sales discounts of 2/15, n/30, and by shipping all merchandise FOB shipping point. Currently, no sales discounts are allowed and merchandise is shipped FOB destination. These credit terms are estimated to increase net sales by 10%. The ratio of the cost of merchandise sold to net sales is expected to be 70%. All selling and administrative expenses are expected to remain unchanged, except for store supplies, miscellaneous selling, office supplies, and miscellaneous administrative expenses, which are expected to increase proportionately with increased net sales. The amounts of these preceding items for the year ended July 31, 2003, were as follows:

Store supplies expense	$5,000
Miscellaneous selling expense	2,000
Office supplies expense	1,000
Miscellaneous administrative expense	1,800

The other income and other expense items will remain unchanged. The shipment of all merchandise FOB shipping point will eliminate all transportation-out expenses, which for the year ended July 31, 2003, were $20,150.

1. Prepare a projected single-step income statement for the year ending July 31, 2004, based on the proposal.
2. a. Based on the projected income statement in (1), would you recommend the implementation of the proposed changes?
   b. Describe any possible concerns you may have related to the proposed changes described in (1).

Activity 5-5

Shopping for a television

GROUP ACTIVITY

Assume that you are planning to purchase a 50-inch Sony television. In groups of three or four, determine the lowest cost for the television, considering the available alternatives and the advantages and disadvantages of each alternative. For example, you could purchase locally, through mail order, or through an Internet shopping service. Consider such factors as delivery charges, interest-free financing, discounts, coupons, and availability of warranty services. Prepare a report for presentation to the class.

Answers to Self-Study Questions

1. **A** A debit memorandum (answer A), issued by the buyer, indicates the amount the buyer proposes to debit to the accounts payable account. A credit memorandum (answer B), issued by the seller, indicates the amount the seller proposes to credit to the accounts receivable account. An invoice (answer C) or a bill (answer D), issued by the seller, indicates the amount and terms of the sale.
2. **C** The amount of discount for early payment is $10 (answer C), or 1% of $1,000. Although the $50 of transportation costs paid by the seller is debited to the customer's account, the customer is not entitled to a discount on that amount.
3. **B** The single-step form of income statement (answer B) is so named because the total of all expenses is deducted in one step from the total of all revenues. The multiple-step form (answer A) includes numerous sections and subsections with several subtotals. The report form (answer D) is a common form of the balance sheet.
4. **C** Gross profit (answer C) is the excess of net sales over the cost of merchandise sold. Operating income (answer A) or income from operations (answer B) is the excess of gross profit over operating expenses. Net income (answer D) is the final figure on the income statement after all revenues and expenses have been reported.
5. **C** Operating income is understated by $25,000 (answer C). The cost of merchandise sold is overstated, not understated (answer A). Gross profit is understated, not overstated (answer B). Inventory shrinkage is overstated, not understated (answer D).

Chapter 6
Internal Control and Cash

THE LAW OF CONNECTION
"Leaders touch a heart before they ask for a hand."
–The 21 Irrefutable Laws of Leadership
Dr. John C. Maxwell

Learning Goals

1. Describe and illustrate the objectives and elements of internal control.
2. Describe and illustrate methods of preventing and detecting employee fraud.
3. Describe and illustrate the application of internal controls to cash.
4. Describe the nature of a bank account and its use in controlling cash.
5. Describe and illustrate the use of a bank reconciliation in controlling cash.
6. Describe the accounting for special-purpose cash funds.
7. Describe and illustrate the reporting of cash and cash equivalents in the financial statements.
8. Describe, illustrate, and interpret the cash flow to net income ratio and the cash to monthly cash expenses ratio.

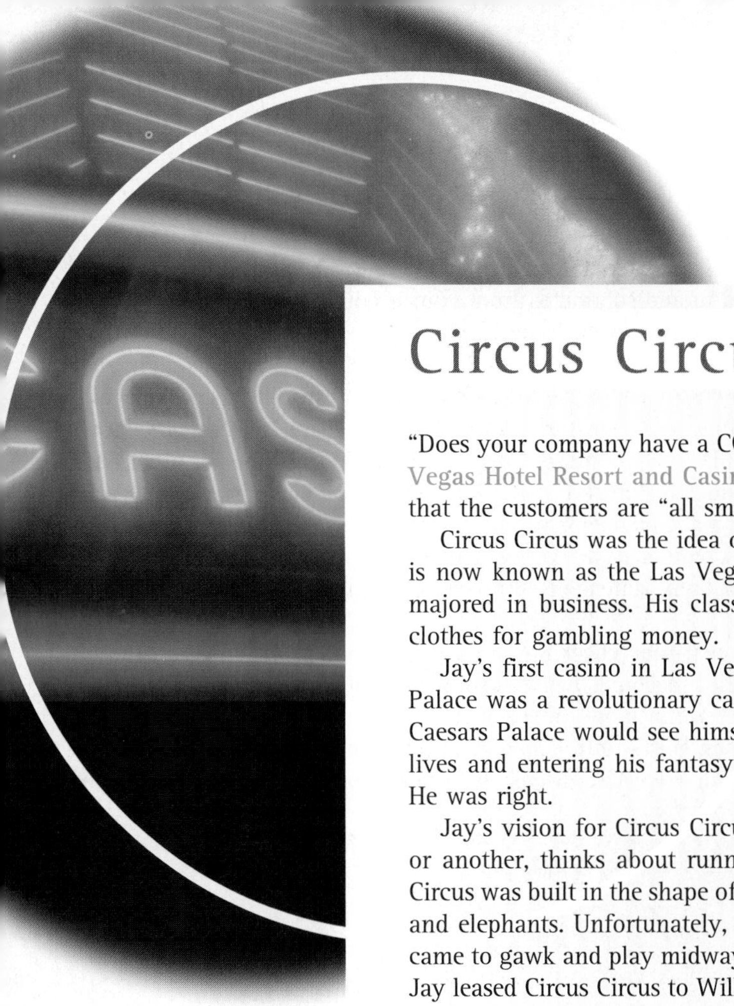

Circus Circus

"Does your company have a CCO?" CCO stands for Chief Clown Officer. Circus Circus Las Vegas Hotel Resort and Casino has a CCO, whose primary responsibility is to make sure that the customers are "all smiles" after their experience at Circus Circus.

Circus Circus was the idea of Jay Sarno, one of the creative geniuses that shaped what is now known as the Las Vegas strip. He attended the University of Missouri, where he majored in business. His classmates remember him as a gambler who would pawn his clothes for gambling money.

Jay's first casino in Las Vegas was Caesars Palace. When it opened in 1964, Caesars Palace was a revolutionary casino concept. Jay's vision was that each customer entering Caesars Palace would see himself or herself as Caesar or Cleopatra. Escaping their former lives and entering his fantasy world, Jay felt customers would gamble and spend more. He was right.

Jay's vision for Circus Circus was based upon the theme that every child, at one time or another, thinks about running away from home and joining the circus. Thus, Circus Circus was built in the shape of a tent and featured a midway, complete with flying trapezes and elephants. Unfortunately, Circus Circus wasn't profitable. Without a hotel, customers came to gawk and play midway games, but didn't gamble enough. Thus, in the early 1970s, Jay leased Circus Circus to William G. Bennett and his partners, who eventually bought the casino.

William Bennett brought a business perspective to the hotel-casino industry. Prior to that time, most of the people running the hotels and casinos were promoted from the gambling ranks, such as former blackjack dealers. Bennett began recruiting managers with business backgrounds and then teaching them the casino business. He built a 395-room Circus Circus hotel tower. He also focused on how to make slot machines more profitable and popular. In doing so, he established separate slot machine departments and managers. Prior to this time, slots were managed by individuals from the live gaming end of the casinos, such as blackjack dealers. As a result, the managers didn't fully appreciate the importance or profitability of slots and often neglected them as a source of revenue.

William Bennett continued Jay Sarno's escapist theme by building the theme of the $300 million Excalibur–the legend of King Arthur–in the form of a 4,000-room storybook castle. Excalibur was followed by the $375-million, Egyptian-themed Luxor. Bennett also developed Laughlin, Nevada as a major gaming destination. On the banks of the Colorado River, he bought and developed the Edgewater Hotel and Casino, with a family, camping, and water sport emphasis.

During the 1980s, Bennett and his partners took their company public with a stock offering. Eventually, Bennett sold his interest in the company and became a multimillionaire. After his departure, the company built the Mandalay Bay Resort and Casino and renamed the company, the Mandalay Resort Group.

As you might expect, the hotel-casino industry handles and generates a tremendous amount of cash in its operations. For example, Mandalay Resort generates over $400 million of net cash flows from its operating activities. Thus, it is important that companies have effective controls over their operations and, in particular, over cash. In this chapter, we first focus on the objectives and elements of internal controls. We then apply these control concepts to employee fraud and cash.

Source: Adapted from the Web site of Circus Circus and The Mandalay Resort Group, Inc., and the *Las Vegas Review-Journal*, "The First 100 Persons Who Shaped Southern Nevada."

Your Need to Know

Once a month, you may receive a bank statement that lists the deposits, withdrawals, and checks that have been added to and subtracted from your account balance. The statement may also be accompanied by your canceled checks.

New forms of payments are now arising that don't involve checks at all. Retailers, such as grocery stores, now allow customers to pay for merchandise by swiping their bank cards at check-out, causing an immediate transfer of funds out of a bank account. Banks are allowing regular monthly bills, such as utility bills, to be paid directly out of a checking account, using electronic fund transfers. Internet payments can be made by using services such as Paypal®, which will make payments to third parties directly out of a checking account. In all of these cases, you need to verify actual fund transfers with the correct amounts by comparing your bank statement with electronic invoices, receipts, and other evidence of payment.

Many banks are making real-time checking account information available on the Internet to account owners. Thus, account owners using this feature are now able to manage and control their accounts in a more timely way.

Like individuals, businesses must control their cash and other assets to guard against errors and fraud. In this chapter we will discuss how companies control their cash and other assets.

Internal Control

1 Describe and illustrate the objectives and elements of internal control.

Internal controls help businesses guide their operations and prevent abuses. For example, assume that you own and manage a lawn care service. Your business uses several employee teams, and you provide each team with vehicle and lawn equipment. What are some of the issues you would face as a manager in controlling the operations of this business? Below are some examples.

- Lawn care must be provided on time.
- The quality of lawn care services must meet customer expectations.
- Employees must provide work for the hours they are paid.
- Lawn care equipment should be used for business purposes only.
- Vehicles should be used for business purposes only.
- Customers must be billed and bills collected for services rendered.

How would you address these issues? You could, for example, develop a schedule at the beginning of each day and then inspect the work at the end of the day to verify that it was completed according to quality standards. You could have "surprise" inspections by arriving on site at random times to verify that the teams are working according to schedule. You could require employees to "clock in" at the beginning of the day and "clock out" at the end of the day to make sure that they are paid for hours worked. You could require the work teams to return the vehicles and equipment to a central location to prevent unauthorized use. You could keep a log of odometer readings at the end of each day to verify that the vehicles have not been used for "joy riding." You could bill customers after you have inspected the work and then monitor the collection of all receivables. All of these are examples of internal control.

Objectives of Internal Control

The objectives of **internal control** are to provide reasonable assurance that:

1. assets are safeguarded and used for business purposes.
2. business information is accurate.
3. employees comply with laws and regulations.

Internal control can safeguard assets by preventing theft, fraud, misuse, or misplacement. One of the most serious breaches of internal control is employee fraud. **Employee fraud** is the intentional act of deceiving an employer for personal gain. Such deception may range from purposely overstating expenses on a travel expense report to embezzling millions of dollars through complex schemes. In a separate section of this chapter, we address how to prevent and detect employee fraud.

Accurate information is necessary for operating a business successfully. The safeguarding of assets and accurate information often go hand-in-hand. The reason is that employees attempting to defraud a business will also need to adjust the accounting records in order to hide the fraud.

Businesses must comply with applicable laws, regulations, and financial reporting standards. Examples of such standards and laws include environmental regulations, contract terms, safety regulations, and generally accepted accounting principles (GAAP).

Elements of Internal Control

How does management achieve its internal control objectives? Management is responsible for designing and applying five **elements of internal control** to meet the three internal control objectives. These elements are (1) the control environment, (2) risk assessment, (3) control procedures, (4) monitoring, (5) information and communication.[1]

The elements of internal control are illustrated in Exhibit 1. In this exhibit, these elements form an umbrella over the business to protect it from control threats. The business's

Exhibit 1

Elements of Internal Control

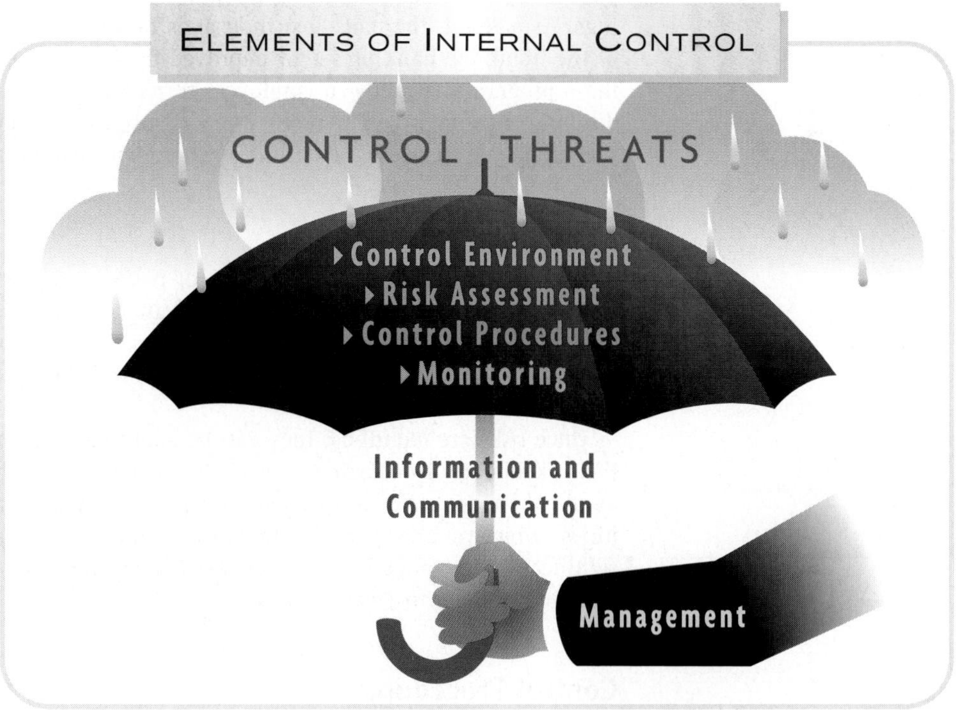

1 *Internal Control—Integrated Framework by the Committee of Sponsoring Organizations of the Treadway Commission (COSO)*, pp. 12–14. This document provides a professionally sponsored framework for internal control.

control environment is represented by the size of the umbrella. Risk assessment, control procedures, and monitoring are the fabric that keeps the umbrella from leaking. Information and communication links the umbrella to management. In the following paragraphs, we discuss each of these elements.

Control Environment

A business's control environment is the overall attitude of management and employees about the importance of controls. One of the factors that influences the control environment is *management's philosophy and operating style.* A management that overemphasizes operating goals and deviates from control policies may indirectly encourage employees to ignore controls. For example, the pressure to achieve revenue targets may encourage employees to fraudulently record sham sales. On the other hand, a management that emphasizes the importance of controls and encourages adherence to control policies will create an effective control environment.

The business's *organizational structure,* which is the framework for planning and controlling operations, also influences the control environment. For example, a department store chain might organize each of its stores as separate business units. Each store manager has full authority over pricing and other operating activities. In such a structure, each store manager has the responsibility for establishing an effective control environment.

Personnel policies also affect the control environment. Personnel policies involve the hiring, training, evaluation, compensation, and promotion of employees. In addition, job descriptions, employee codes of ethics, and conflict-of-interest policies are part of the personnel policies. Such policies can enhance the internal control environment if they provide reasonable assurance that only competent, honest employees are hired and retained.

To illustrate the importance of the control environment, the head of a bank's loan department perpetrated a fraud by accepting kickbacks from customers with poor credit ratings. As a result, the bank lost thousands of dollars from bad loans. After the discovery of the fraud, the bank president improved the bank's control environment by implementing a program that allowed employees to report suspicious conduct anonymously. In addition to encouraging employees to report suspicious conduct, the employees were warned that employee fraud might occur anywhere and involve anyone.

Risk Assessment

All organizations face risks. Examples of risk include changes in customer requirements, competitive threats, regulatory changes, changes in economic factors such as interest rates, and employee violations of company policies and procedures. Management should assess these risks and take necessary actions to control them, so that the objectives of internal control can be achieved.

Once risks are identified, they can be analyzed to estimate their significance, to assess their likelihood of occurring, and to determine actions that will minimize them. For example, the manager of a warehouse operation may analyze the risk of employee back injuries, which might give rise to lawsuits. If the manager determines that the risk is significant, the company may purchase back support braces for its warehouse employees and require them to wear the braces.

Control Procedures

Control procedures are established to provide reasonable assurance that business goals will be achieved, including the prevention of fraud. In the following paragraphs, we will briefly discuss control procedures that can be integrated throughout the accounting system. These procedures are listed in Exhibit 2.

Exhibit 2

Internal Control Procedures

Competent Personnel, Rotating Duties, and Mandatory Vacations The successful operation of an accounting system requires procedures to ensure that people are able to perform the duties to which they are assigned. Hence, it is necessary that all accounting employees be adequately trained and supervised in performing their jobs. It may also be advisable to rotate duties of clerical personnel and mandate vacations for nonclerical personnel. These policies encourage employees to adhere to prescribed procedures. In addition, existing errors or fraud may be detected. For example, numerous cases of employee fraud have been discovered after a long-term employee, who never took vacations, missed work because of an illness or other unavoidable reasons.

Separating Responsibilities for Related Operations To decrease the possibility of inefficiency, errors, and fraud, the responsibility for related operations should be divided among two or more persons. For example, the responsibilities for purchasing, receiving, and paying for computer supplies should be divided among three persons or departments. If the same person orders supplies, verifies the receipt of the supplies, and pays the supplier, the following abuses are possible:

1. Orders may be placed on the basis of friendship with a supplier, rather than on price, quality, and other objective factors.
2. The quantity and quality of supplies received may not be verified, thus causing payment for supplies not received or poor-quality supplies.
3. Supplies may be stolen by the employee.
4. The validity and accuracy of invoices may be verified carelessly, thus causing the payment of false or inaccurate invoices.

The "checks and balances" provided by dividing responsibilities among various departments requires no duplication of effort. The business documents prepared by one department are designed to coordinate with and support those prepared by other departments.

Separating Operations, Custody of Assets, and Accounting Control policies should establish the responsibilities for various business activities. To reduce the possibility of errors and fraud, the responsibilities for operations, custody of assets, and accounting should be separated. The accounting records then serve as an independent check on the individuals who have custody of the assets and who engage in the business operations. For example, the employees entrusted with handling cash receipts from credit customers should not record cash receipts in the accounting records. To do so would allow employees to borrow or steal cash and hide the theft in the records. Likewise, if those engaged in operating activities also record the results of operations, they could distort the accounting reports to show favorable results. For example, a store manager whose year-end bonus is based upon operating profits might be tempted to record fictitious sales in order to receive a larger bonus.

Proofs and Security Measures Proofs and security measures should be used to safeguard assets and ensure reliable accounting data. This control procedure applies to many different techniques, such as authorization, approval, and reconciliation procedures. For example, employees who travel on company business may be required to obtain a department manager's approval on a travel request form.

Other examples of control procedures include the use of bank accounts and other measures to ensure the safety of cash and valuable documents. A cash register that displays the amount recorded for each sale and provides the customer a printed receipt can be an effective part of the internal control structure. An all-night convenience store could use the following security measures to deter robberies:

1. Locate the cash register near the door, so that it is fully visible from outside the store; have two employees work late hours; employ a security guard.
2. Deposit cash in the bank daily, before 5 p.m.
3. Keep only small amounts of cash on hand after 5 p.m. by depositing excess cash in a store safe that can't be opened by employees on duty.
4. Install cameras and alarm systems.

Monitoring

Monitoring the internal control system locates weaknesses and improves control effectiveness. The internal control system can be monitored through either ongoing efforts by management or by separate evaluations. Ongoing monitoring efforts may include observing both employee behavior and warning signs from the accounting system. The indicators shown in Exhibit 3 may be clues to internal control problems.[2]

Separate monitoring evaluations are generally performed when there are major changes in strategy, senior management, business structure, or operations. In large businesses, internal auditors who are independent of operations normally are responsible for monitoring the internal control system. Internal auditors can report issues and concerns to an audit committee of the board of directors, who are independent of management. In addition, external auditors also evaluate internal control as a normal part of their annual financial statement audit.

Information and Communication

Information and communication are essential elements of internal control. Information about the control environment, risk assessment, control procedures, and monitoring are needed by management to guide operations and ensure compliance with reporting, legal, and regulatory requirements. Management can also use external information to assess events and conditions that impact decision making and external reporting. For example, management uses information from the Financial Accounting Standards Board (FASB) to assess the impact of possible changes in reporting standards.

---

2 Edwin C. Bliss, "Employee Theft," *Boardroom Reports*, July 15, 1994, pp. 5–6.

Exhibit 3

Indicators of Internal Control Problems

CLUES TO POTENTIAL PROBLEMS

Warning signs with regard to people

1. Abrupt change in lifestyle (without winning the lottery).
2. Close social relationships with suppliers.
3. Refusing to take a vacation.
4. Frequent borrowing from other employees.
5. Excessive use of alcohol or drugs.

Warning signs from the accounting system

1. Missing documents or gaps in transaction numbers (could mean documents are being used for fraudulent transactions).
2. An unusual increase in customer refunds (refunds may be phony).
3. Differences between daily cash receipts and bank deposits could mean receipts are being pocketed before being deposited).
4. Sudden increase in slow payments (employee may be pocketing the payment).
5. Backlog in recording transactions (possibly an attempt to delay detection of fraud).

Prevention and Detection of Employee Fraud

2 Describe and illustrate methods of preventing and detecting employee fraud.

The theft of assets by employees from their employer is employee fraud. Employee fraud may involve small amounts, such as the taking of office supplies for personal use or making long-distance telephone calls from work. Employee fraud also can involve the theft of millions of dollars through complex schemes. For example, an employee may process payments for goods or services not received. The payments for the goods or services may be made to phantom (fictitious) companies controlled by the employee.

The following three elements are common to most employee fraud:[3]

1. an employee's perceived financial need
2. an opportunity to use a fraudulent scheme to satisfy the need
3. a rationalization that the fraud is justified

For example, an employee may need cash to pay for a spouse's or a child's medical expenses. In order for employee fraud to occur, the employee must also have the opportunity

3 Donald R. Cressey, "Management Fraud, Accounting Controls, and Criminological Theory," *Management Fraud*, Robert K. Elliott and John J. Willingham, Petrocelli Books (New York: 1980).

to satisfy the need. This opportunity may involve physical access to assets such as cash, or it may involve the ability to obtain cash or assets by authorization of fictitious transactions. For example, a store manager of a local retail chain may have the ability to authorize the purchase of office equipment for the store as long as the amount is under $3,000. Subsequently, the store manager purchases a personal computer, has it delivered to his home address, and then later sells it. The store manager rationalizes the theft as justified because he feels that the owner is underpaying him.

In the following paragraphs, we describe and illustrate controls for preventing and detecting employee fraud. Many of these controls are similar to the control procedures that we discussed earlier in this chapter. However, the magnitude, seriousness, and frequency of employee fraud warrant a separate emphasis on controls to prevent and detect it.

Preventive Controls

In trying to prevent employee fraud, a business should focus primarily upon designing controls to prevent the opportunity of employees to steal assets. Businesses have little control over employees' personal financial needs and their ability to rationalize the theft of assets. Controls to prevent the opportunity of employees to steal assets can be grouped into those involving (1) physical safeguarding of assets and (2) proper authorization and approval procedures.

Physical Safeguarding Physical safeguarding of assets involves controlling the company's assets in such a way that an employee's ability to steal the assets is limited. For example, in a department store, valuable inventory such as jewelry should be locked in a vault at the end of each day. Similarly, inventory in a manufacturing plant should be stored in a guarded, fenced-in area away from the employees' parking lot. A manufacturer might routinely inspect employees' lunch boxes and bags when they leave the plant in order to prevent the theft of tools. Retailers should deposit cash at least once each day, if not more frequently, to prevent the build-up of large amounts of cash on hand that may be susceptible to theft.

Authorization and Approval Proper authorization and approval procedures can be effectively used to prevent employee fraud. For example, the owner of a small company may prepare an approved vendor list for the purchase of supplies, merchandise, or services. Any changes to the list or purchases from vendors not on the list must be approved by the owner. This control would effectively reduce the chances that an employee might set up a "phantom vendor" who would be paid for purchases or services that were not provided. An approved vendor list would also reduce the possibility that an employee might be receiving kickbacks from vendors for purchases that are not the proper quality or the best price.

Proper authorization and approval procedures could also be used in a variety of other situations. For example, a procedure that requires a properly authorized, approved, and completed materials requisition before the release of inventory helps prevent employee theft of inventory. Likewise, proper authorization and approval procedures for hiring, firing, and increasing pay reduce the chances of theft related to overpayment of employees or the payment of fictitious employees. Finally, requiring proper supporting documentation for the payment of vendor invoices, such as an authorized purchase order and a receiving report, provides assurance that the company is paying only for goods actually received and ordered.

Detective Controls

Businesses should also design controls to detect employee fraud. These controls include periodic reviews, independent checks, and reconciliations. The effectiveness of these detective controls, however, depends upon separating the custody of assets from the accounting for the assets. The separation of duties is often essential for the detection of employee fraud. Otherwise, an employee might steal assets and cover up the theft by changing the accounting records.

The accounting system should also be designed so that each asset is recorded as soon as practical. By doing so, an initial accountability for the asset is established. Shortages and possible employee fraud can be detected by comparing the assets on hand with the accounting records. To illustrate, when a retailer receives inventory, a receiving report should be prepared. The receiving report includes a detailed description of the item and the quantity received. A copy of the receiving report is sent to accounting, a copy is maintained in the receiving area, and a copy accompanies the inventory to the inventory storage area or to the retail floor. In this way, if the inventory is later missing, the documentation can be traced back to determine where it was last accounted for, and the party responsible for the missing inventory can be isolated. For example, if the copy of the receiving report kept in the receiving department includes the signature of the storage supervisor, indicating that the missing inventory was delivered to storage, then the receiving department is relieved of responsibility and the focus shifts to the storage area. If the storage area records indicate that the missing inventory was delivered to the sales floor, the focus would then shift to the floor area supervisor.

Periodic Reviews Periodic reviews of the accounting records are useful in identifying unusual transactions or accounts for further investigation. For example, a review of the accounts receivable subsidiary ledger may reveal several overdue accounts from normally good customers. Further investigation may reveal that the customers in fact paid their bills, but that the mail clerk or some other employee has stolen their payments. Likewise, a review of the payroll records may identify fictitious employees or employees who were fired or laid off months ago. The review of the payroll may also reveal unauthorized pay increases. A review of the inventory records or purchase records may reveal purchases that are not in line with normal business operations. For example, the review of the supporting documentation for a purchase of inventory, such as a freight bill, may indicate that the inventory was delivered to a residential address. Further investigation may reveal that the address is that of a purchasing agent who ordered the inventory for personal use.

Independent Checks Independent checks are useful in detecting employee fraud. Independent checks normally involve physically examining an asset or other item of interest and then comparing the results of this investigation against the accounting records. For example, inventory should be physically counted at least once a year and the results compared against the inventory that should be on hand according to the accounting records. Shoplifting results in a discrepancy between a retailer's physical inventory and the book inventory. However, wide discrepancies may also indicate employee theft. Likewise, physically counting fixed assets and comparing the count against the subsidiary ledger for fixed assets may detect missing assets. For example, the failure to locate a microcomputer or printer may indicate employee theft. Independent checks can also be used to detect fictitious employees on the payroll. For example, if fictitious employees are suspected, the owner or other manager might be present when the payroll is distributed to employees. In order to receive their payroll checks employees are asked to show identification, such as a driver's license. Any payroll checks that are not picked up represent those that are possibly related to fictitious employees.

Reconciliations Reconciliations are useful in detecting employee theft. Reconciliations involve comparisons within the accounting records and comparisons of the accounting records to external sources of information. A reconciliation differs from an independent check in that the objective of the independent check is to determine the amount of the difference between the physical examination of an item and the accounting records. In contrast, reconciliations are based upon the premise that agreement should exist, and management can focus on finding and correcting differences. For example, the accounts receivable controlling account should agree with the sum of the individual balances in the customers (accounts receivable) subsidiary ledger. If the two do not agree, then an error such as an incorrect recording of a transaction in a customer's account may have occurred. If an error has occurred, it must be tracked down and corrected. Similarly, businesses should reconcile the amount of recorded cash sales for the day with the amount of the daily cash deposit. Unexplained differences in reconciliations are often due to employee fraud. For example, an inability to reconcile the cash sales with the cash deposit may be the result of an employee's theft of a portion of a day's cash sales.

Risk Factors Relating to Employee Fraud

The American Institute of Certified Public Accountants has developed a set of risk factors related to employee fraud.[4] These factors are grouped into two categories: (1) susceptibility of assets to theft and (2) lack of controls.

Susceptibility of Assets The more assets that are susceptible to theft, the greater the opportunity, and thus the greater the risk of employee theft. Cash is, of course, the asset most susceptible to theft. Inventories that are small in size, high in value, and high in demand are also highly susceptible to theft. Examples of such inventories include drugs, diamonds, and computer chips. Easily convertible assets, such as microcomputers that are small in size, highly marketable, or lack ownership identification, are also highly susceptible to theft.

Lack of Controls Lack of preventive or detective controls such as we described in the preceding paragraphs increase the risk of employee fraud. The specific risk factors related to lack of controls are as follows:

1. Lack of proper record keeping for assets susceptible to theft.
2. Lack of proper segregation of duties.
3. Lack of independent checks.
4. Lack of a proper system for authorization and approval of transactions.
5. Lack of proper physical safeguarding of assets susceptible to theft.
6. Lack of timely and proper documentation for transactions.
7. Lack of proper management oversight.
8. Lack of proper screening procedures for employees in sensitive positions.
9. Lack of mandatory vacations for employees in sensitive positions.

We discussed the first six risk factors in the section on controls to prevent and detect employee fraud. The last three factors warrant additional discussion. The lack of proper management oversight provides the employee with the opportunity to commit theft. The lack of mandatory vacations for employees in sensitive positions increases the risk that an employee who has stolen assets will not be caught. That is, an employee involved in stealing assets has a greater chance of getting caught when the substitute employee performs these duties. Obviously, a company that allows vacationing employees to catch up on their work when they return, rather than use substitute employees, defeats the purpose of requiring vacations.

Proper screening of employees who are hired for sensitive positions also helps to reduce the risk of employee theft. For example, hiring a cash register clerk who has been

4 *Statement on Auditing Standards No. 82*, "Consideration of Fraud in a Financial Statement Audit," American Institute of Certified Public Accountants (New York: 1997).

previously convicted of shoplifting is simply asking for trouble. However, proper hiring practices have their limits. Time and time again, employees caught stealing assets have been properly screened, with no prior indication of any tendencies suggesting a risk of fraud. In other words, hiring practices are not a substitute for effective preventive and detective controls for employee fraud.

Examples of Employee Fraud

The importance of controls for preventing and detecting employee fraud can be illustrated through actual cases. In this section, we describe frauds that could have been prevented or detected before they became significant.[5]

Case 1: Fictitious Invoices

Facts: An accounts payable clerk altered the name and address of an inactive vendor and opened a commercial account at a local bank under the assumed name. The clerk then entered fictitious invoices into the accounts payable system for payment. The clerk was able to steal thousands of dollars over several months.

Control Failure: Payments were not properly approved by an employee independent of the accounts payable (accounting) function.

Corrective Action: A policy was implemented that required proper approval of all payments by an employee independent of the accounts payable function. In addition, an approved vendor listing for all purchases was developed. Now, any purchases from a vendor not on the list must be approved by a senior manager.

Case 2: Fictitious Certificates of Deposit

Facts: A new accounts officer at a bank embezzled customer funds for over 16 years. The officer printed his own certificates of deposit, which looked exactly like the bank's certificates. When a customer came to purchase a certificate, the officer would issue a fake certificate and pocket the customer's money. When the fake certificates matured, he would attempt to convince the customer to roll the CD over to a new higher yielding (fake) certificate. If a customer insisted upon cashing in the fake certificate, he would terminate another customer's legitimate CD and use the proceeds to pay the holder of the fake CD. Over the 16 years, the officer stole approximately $5 million.

Control Failure: The officer's transactions were not reviewed on a periodic basis. The officer was not required to take vacations. The officer also handled customer cash receipts and had authority to change the accounting records of the customers.

Corrective Action: Sensitive transactions are now reviewed on a surprise basis. All employees are required to take vacations. Individuals who handle cash do not have authority to change or otherwise alter the accounting records.

Case 3: Missing School Funds

Facts: A secretary at a middle school stole approximately $20,000 by converting student checks and activity fees to cash and by taking undeposited faculty vending machine receipts.

5 The cases are adapted from the "Roundtable" and "Fraud Findings" sections of the *Internal Auditor* magazine, published by the Institute of Internal Auditors.

Control Failure: An initial accountability was never established for faculty vending machine receipts, and deposited receipts were never reconciled with vending machine usage records. A reconciliation of student checks and activity fees with student records and enrollment figures was not performed. Finally, background checks were not performed on clerical employees. The secretary had a prior criminal record.

Corrective Action: Background checks are now required on all employees of the school. An employee independent of the handling of cash, student activity fees, and student book fees performs a periodic reconciliation with attendance and enrollment figures. Each day, vending machine receipts are collected and recorded. The receipts are periodically reconciled with machine usage.

Case 4: Parking Ticket Shortage

Facts: Citizens of a small town could pay parking fines by inserting the ticket with the amount of the fine into a locked box outside of the town hall. An analysis later discovered that approximately $8,000 was missing for a period of 18 months.

Control Failure: The key to the locked box was readily available to a variety of employees. Thus, no one could be held responsible for the missing cash.

Corrective Action: The key to the locked box was assigned to the person collecting the cash and was kept in a safe until needed for collections. A person independent of the collections was assigned the responsibility of reconciling the parking tickets from the locked box with the cash deposits.

Case 5: National Flood Insurance Claims

Facts: The claims agent would develop fictitious claims, arrange for the claims manager to issue a check for the claim, and then recall the checks. The claims agent would then pass the checks to an accomplice, who would cash the checks and split the money with the claims agent. The fraud totaled approximately $85,000 before it was detected.

Control Failure: The recalled checks were forwarded to the claims agent requesting the check for follow-up and disposition.

Corrective Action: A procedure was implemented that prohibited recalled checks from being returned to the claims agent requesting the checks. In addition, the numbers of recalled checks processed by each claims agent were reviewed for unusual trends or numbers of recalled checks.

Case 6: Payroll Fraud

Facts: A payroll assistant was responsible for entering payroll hours, with no review or reconciliation, and for receiving, sorting, and distributing the payroll checks. These duties were assigned to the payroll assistant because he was "most familiar with the company's employees." By issuing duplicate payroll checks, the assistant stole $4,000 in two months. In addition, the assistant submitted fictitious hours for part-time summer interns during periods when the interns were not working. The assistant then intercepted and cashed the interns' checks and thus stole another $36,000.

Control Failure: Duties were not separated, and the payroll assistant had too much control and responsibility.

Corrective Action: The job of entering the payroll data was separated from the job of handling the payroll checks. In addition, a reconciliation of the hours worked, the employees, and the amounts paid is now performed each payroll period.

Ethics in Action
Tips on Preventing Employee Fraud in Small Companies

- Do not have the same employee write company checks and keep the books. Look for payments to vendors you don't know or payments to vendors whose names appear to be misspelled.
- If your business has a computer system, restrict access to accounting files as much as possible. Also, keep a backup copy of your accounting files and store it at an off-site location.
- Be wary of anybody working in finance that declines to take vacations. They may be afraid that a replacement will uncover fraud.
- Require and monitor supporting documentation (such as vendor invoices) before signing checks.
- Track the number of credit card bills you sign monthly.
- Limit and monitor access to important documents and supplies, such as blank checks and signature stamps.
- Check W-2 forms against your payroll annually to make sure you're not carrying any fictitious employees.
- Rely on yourself, not an audit, to spot fraud.

Source: Steve Kaufman, "Embezzlement Common at Small Companies," Knight-Ridder Newspapers, reported in *Athens Daily News/Athens Banner-Herald*, March 10, 1996, page 4D.

Cash Controls Over Receipts and Payments

3 Describe and illustrate the application of internal controls to cash.

Cash includes coins, currency (paper money), checks, money orders, and money on deposit that is available for unrestricted withdrawal from banks and other financial institutions. Normally, you can think of cash as anything that a bank would accept for deposit in your account. For example, a check made payable to you could normally be deposited in a bank and thus is considered cash.

We will assume in this chapter that a business maintains only *one* bank account, represented in the ledger as *Cash*. In practice, however, a business may have several bank accounts, such as one for general cash payments and another for payroll. For each of its bank accounts, the business will maintain a ledger account, one of which may be called *Cash in Bank—First Bank*, for example. It will also maintain separate ledger accounts for special-purpose cash funds, such as travel reimbursements. We will introduce some of these other cash accounts later in this chapter.

Because of the ease with which money can be transferred, cash is the asset most likely to be diverted and used improperly by employees. In addition, many transactions either directly or indirectly affect the receipt or the payment of cash. Businesses must therefore design and use controls that safeguard cash and control the authorization of cash transactions. In the following paragraphs, we will discuss these controls.

Control of Cash Receipts

To protect cash from theft and misuse, a business must control cash from the time it is received until it is deposited in a bank. Businesses normally receive cash from two main sources: (1) customers purchasing products or services and (2) customers making payments on account. For example, fast-food restaurants, such as McDonald's, Wendy's, and Burger

King, receive cash primarily from over-the-counter sales to customers. Mail-order and Internet retailers, such as Lands' End, Orvis, L.L. Bean, and Amazon.com, receive cash (checks) primarily through the mail and from credit card companies.

Controlling Cash Received from Cash Sales

Regardless of the source of cash receipts, every business must properly safeguard and record its cash receipts. One of the most important controls to protect cash received in over-the-counter sales is a cash register. When a clerk (cashier) enters the amount of a sale, the cash register normally displays the amount. This is a control to ensure that the clerk has charged you the correct amount. You also receive a receipt to verify the accuracy of the amount.

At the beginning of a work shift, each cash register clerk is given a cash drawer that contains a predetermined amount of cash for making change for customers. The amount in each drawer is sometimes called a *change fund*. At the end of the shift, the clerk and the supervisor count the cash in that clerk's cash drawer. The amount of cash in each drawer should equal the beginning amount of cash plus the cash sales for the day. However, errors in recording cash sales or errors in making change cause the amount of cash on hand to differ from this amount. Such differences are recorded in a **cash short and over account.**

At the end of the accounting period, a debit balance in the cash short and over account is included in Miscellaneous Expense in the income statement. A credit balance is included in the Other Income section. If a clerk consistently has significant cash short and over amounts, the supervisor may require the clerk to take additional training.

A cash register begins with $300, recorded cash sales are $13,644, and cash of $13,959 is on hand. What is the cash short or over?

Cash over is $15.

After a cash register clerk's cash has been counted and recorded on a memorandum form, the cash is then placed in a store safe in the Cashier's Department until it can be deposited in the bank. The supervisor forwards the clerk's cash register tapes to the Accounting Department, where they serve as the basis for recording the transactions for the day.

Some retail companies use debit card systems to transfer and record the receipt of cash. In a debit card system, a customer pays for goods at the time of purchase by presenting a plastic card. The card authorizes the electronic transfer of cash from the customer's checking account to the retailer's bank account.

Controlling Cash Received in the Mail

Cash is received in the mail when customers pay their bills. This cash is usually in the form of checks and money orders. Most companies' invoices are designed so that customers return a portion of the invoice, called a *remittance advice*, with their payment. The employee who opens the incoming mail should initially compare the amount of cash received with the amount shown on the remittance advice. If a customer does not return a remittance advice, an employee prepares one. Like the cash register, the remittance advice serves as a record of cash initially received. It also helps ensure that the posting to the customer's account is accurate. Finally, as a preventive control, the employee opening the mail normally also stamps checks and money orders "For Deposit Only" in the bank account of the business.

All cash received in the mail is sent to the Cashier's Department. An employee there combines it with the receipts from cash sales and prepares a bank deposit ticket. The remittance advices and their summary totals are delivered to the Accounting Department. An accounting clerk then prepares the records of the transactions and posts them to the customer accounts.

When cash is deposited in the bank, the bank normally stamps a duplicate copy of the deposit ticket with the amount received. This bank receipt is returned to the Accounting Department, where a clerk compares the receipt with the total amount that should have been deposited. This control helps ensure that all the cash is deposited and that no cash is lost or stolen on the way to the bank. Any shortages are thus promptly detected.

Strategy in Business
Turn Off the Light?

Kmart recently filed for bankruptcy. What happened? What went wrong?

Most analysts blame Kmart's problems on a strategy that relied heavily upon advertising circulars to get customers into its stores. Such circulars, which are expensive to produce, accounted for 10.6% of Kmart's operating expenses, as compared to 2.2% for Target and 0.4% for Wal-Mart. In addition, Kmart continued to use its "blue-light specials," in which merchandise prices would be reduced at periodic intervals for customers who were shopping within its stores. These specials created inventory shortages as merchandise sold out and suppliers could not accurately predict customer needs. As a result, suppliers increased Kmart's prices, which in turn were passed on to customers. In contrast, Wal-Mart employs an "always low price" strategy for getting customers into its stores. Kmart reacted by promoting a "Blue-Light Always" program, developing a Bluelight.com Web site, and reducing its use of ad circulars. Unfortunately, Kmart's traditional customers who were used to the circulars stopped shopping at Kmart. In addition, Kmart couldn't compete with Wal-Mart's efficiency and low costs. Thus, Kmart filed for bankruptcy with the hope of reorganizing and once again becoming competitive and profitable.

Sources: Amy Merrick, "Expensive Ad Circulars Precipitate Kmart President's Departure," *The Wall Street Journal*, January 18, 2002; Michael Levy and Dhruv Grewal, "So Long, Kmart Shoppers," *The Wall Street Journal*, January 28, 2002; and "Blue Light Blues," *The Economist*, January 18, 2002.

Separating the duties of the Cashier's Department, which handles cash, and the Accounting Department, which records cash, is a preventive control. If Accounting Department employees both handle and record cash, an employee could steal cash and change the accounting records to hide the theft.

Control of Cash Payments

The control of cash payments should provide reasonable assurance that payments are made for only authorized transactions. In addition, controls should ensure that cash is used efficiently. For example, controls should ensure that all available discounts, such as purchase and trade discounts, are taken.

In a small business, an owner/manager may sign all checks, based upon personal knowledge of goods and services purchased. In a large business, however, employees who do not have such a complete knowledge of the transactions often prepare checks. In a large business, for example, the duties of purchasing goods, inspecting the goods received, and verifying the invoices are usually performed by different employees. These duties must be coordinated to ensure that checks for proper amounts are issued to creditors. One system used for this purpose is the voucher system.

Voucher System

A **voucher system** is a set of procedures for authorizing and recording liabilities and cash payments. A **voucher** is any document that serves as proof of authority to pay cash. For example, an invoice properly approved for payment could be considered a voucher. In many businesses, however, a voucher is a special form for recording relevant data about a liability and the details of its payment.

A voucher is normally prepared after all necessary supporting documents have been received. For example, when a voucher is prepared for the purchase of goods, the voucher should be supported by the supplier's invoice, a purchase order, and a receiving report.

After a voucher is prepared, it is submitted to the proper manager for approval. Once approved, the voucher is recorded in the accounts and filed by due date. Upon payment, the voucher is recorded in the same manner as the payment of an account payable.

A voucher system may be either manual or computerized. In a computerized system, properly approved supporting documents (such as purchase orders and receiving reports) would be entered directly into computer files. At the due date, the checks would be automatically generated and mailed to creditors. At that time, the voucher would be automatically transferred to a paid voucher file. In some cases, payments may be made electronically rather than by check.

Electronic Funds Transfer

With rapidly changing technology, new systems are being devised to more efficiently record and transfer cash among companies. Such systems often use **electronic funds transfer (EFT)**. In an EFT system, computers, rather than paper (money, checks, etc.), are used to effect cash transactions. For example, a business may pay its employees by means of EFT. Under such a system, employees may authorize the deposit of their payroll checks directly into checking accounts. Each pay period, the business electronically transfers the employees' net pay to their checking accounts through the use of computer systems and networks. Likewise, many companies are using EFT systems to pay their suppliers and other vendors.

Electronic funds transfer is also becoming more widely accepted by individuals. For example, TeleCheck Services, Inc., offers an online real-time check payment option for purchases made over the Internet. "It is apparent from the rapid growth of online sales that many consumers are as comfortable writing checks for Internet purchases as they are at their local brick-and-mortar store," explains Steve Shaper, chief executive officer of TeleCheck.

Bank Accounts

4 Describe the nature of a bank account and its use in controlling cash.

Most of you are familiar with bank accounts. You probably have a checking account at a local bank, credit union, savings and loan association, or other financial institution. In this section, we discuss the use of bank accounts by businesses. We then discuss the use of bank accounts as an additional control over cash.

Use of Bank Accounts

A business often maintains several bank accounts. For example, a business with several branches or retail outlets such as Sears or The Gap will often maintain a bank account for each location. In addition, businesses usually maintain a separate bank account for payroll and other special purposes.

A major reason that businesses use bank accounts is for control purposes. Use of bank accounts reduces the amount of cash on hand at any one time. For example, many merchandise businesses deposit cash receipts twice daily to reduce the amount cash on hand that is susceptible to theft. Likewise, using a payroll account allows for paying employees by check rather than by distributing a large amount of cash each payroll period.

In addition to reducing the amount of cash on hand, bank accounts provide an independent recording of cash transactions that can be used as a verification of the business's recording of transactions. That is, the use of bank accounts provides a double recording of cash transactions. The company's cash account corresponds to the bank's liability (deposit) account for the company. As we will discuss and illustrate in the next section, this double recording of cash transactions allows for a reconciliation of the cash account on the company's records with the cash balance recorded by the bank.

Finally, the use of bank accounts facilitates the transfer of funds. For example, electronic funds transfer systems require bank accounts for the transfer of funds between companies. Within a company, cash can be transferred between bank accounts through the use of wire transfers. In addition, online banking through the use of the Internet allows companies to transfer funds and pay bills electronically as well as monitor their cash balances on a real-time basis.

Bank Statement

Banks usually maintain a record of all checking account transactions. A summary of all transactions, called a **bank statement**, is mailed to the depositor, usually each month. Like any account with a customer or a creditor, the bank statement shows the beginning balance, additions, deductions, and the balance at the end of the period. A typical bank statement is shown in Exhibit 4.

The depositor's checks received by the bank during the period may accompany the bank statement, arranged in the order of payment. The paid checks are stamped "Paid," together with the date of payment. Other entries that the bank has made in the depositor's account may be described in debit or credit memorandums enclosed with the statement.

Exhibit 4

Bank Statement

MEMBER FDIC

VALLEY NATIONAL BANK
OF LOS ANGELES

LOS ANGELES, CA 90020-4253 (310)851-5151

POWER NETWORKING
1000 Belkin Street
Los Angeles, CA 90014 -1000

PAGE 1

ACCOUNT NUMBER 1627042

FROM 6/30/06 TO 7/31/06

	BALANCE	4,218.60
22	DEPOSITS	13,749.75
52	WITHDRAWALS	14,698.57
3	OTHER DEBITS AND CREDITS	90.00CR
	NEW BALANCE	3,359.78

CHECKS AND OTHER DEBITS			DEPOSITS	DATE	BALANCE
819.40	122.54		585.75	07/01	3,862.41
369.50	732.26	20.15	421.53	07/02	3,162.03
600.00	190.70	52.50	781.30	07/03	3,100.13
25.93	160.00		662.50	07/05	3,576.70
921.20	NSF 300.00		503.18	07/07	2,858.68
32.26	535.09		932.00	07/29	3,404.40
21.10	126.20		705.21	07/30	3,962.31
	SC 18.00		MS 408.00	07/30	4,352.31
26.12	1,615.13		648.72	07/31	3,359.78

EC — ERROR CORRECTION
MS — MISCELLANEOUS
NSF — NOT SUFFICIENT FUNDS
OD — OVERDRAFT
PS — PAYMENT STOPPED
SC — SERVICE CHARGE

* * * * * * * * *

THE RECONCILEMENT OF THIS STATEMENT WITH YOUR RECORDS IS ESSENTIAL.
ANY ERROR OR EXCEPTION SHOULD BE REPORTED IMMEDIATELY.

You should note that a depositor's checking account balance *in the bank's records* is a liability with a credit balance. Debit memorandums issued by the bank on a depositor's account therefore decrease the depositor's balance. Likewise, credit memorandums increase the depositor's balance. A bank issues a debit memorandum to charge (decrease) a depositor's account for service charges or for deposited checks returned because of insufficient funds. Likewise, a bank issues a credit memorandum when it increases the depositor's account for collecting a note receivable for the depositor, making a loan to the depositor, receiving a wire deposit, or adding interest to the depositor's account.

On the bank's records, are customer service charges recorded as a debit or a credit to the depositor's account?

Debit.

Bank Accounts as a Control Over Cash

As we mentioned earlier, a bank account is one of the primary tools a business uses to control cash. For example, businesses often require that all cash receipts be initially deposited in a bank account. Likewise, businesses usually use checks or bank account transfers to make all cash payments, except for very small amounts. When such a system is used, there is a double record of cash transactions–one by the business and the other by the bank.

A business can use a bank statement to compare the cash transactions recorded in its accounting records to those recorded by the bank. The cash balance shown by a bank statement is usually different from the cash balance shown in the accounting records of the business, as shown in Exhibit 5.

Exhibit 5

Power Networking's Records and Bank Statement

Bank Statement			Power Networking Records	
Beginning Balance . . .		$ 4,218.60	Beginning Balance . . .	$ 4,227.60
Additions:				
Deposits		13,749.75	Deposits	14,565.95
Miscellaneous		408.00		
Deductions:				
Checks		14,698.57	Checks	16,243.56
NSF Check	$300			
Service Charge	18	318.00		
Ending Balance		$ 3,359.78	Ending Balance	$ 2,549.99

Power Networking should determine the reason for the difference in these two amounts.

This difference may be the result of a delay by either party in recording transactions. For example, there is a time lag of one day or more between the date a check is written and the date that it is presented to the bank for payment. If the depositor mails deposits to the bank or uses the night depository, a time lag between the date of the deposit and the date that it is recorded by the bank is also probable. The bank may also debit or credit the depositor's account for transactions about which the depositor will not be informed until later.

The difference may be the result of errors made by either the business or the bank in recording transactions. For example, the business may incorrectly post to Cash a check written for $4,500 as $450. Likewise, a bank may incorrectly record the amount of a check.

Ethics in Action

Check fraud

Check fraud involves counterfeiting, altering, or otherwise manipulating the information on checks in order to fraudulently cash a check. According to the National Check Fraud Center, check fraud and counterfeiting are among the fastest growing problems affecting the financial system, generating over $10 billion in losses annually. Criminals perpetrate the fraud by taking blank checks from your checkbook, finding a canceled check in the garbage, or removing a check you have mailed to pay bills. Consumers can prevent check fraud by carefully storing blank checks, placing outgoing mail in postal mailboxes, and shredding canceled checks.

Bank Reconciliation

5 Describe and illustrate the use of a bank reconciliation in controlling cash.

For effective control, the reasons for the difference between the cash balance on the bank statement and the cash balance in the accounting records should be determined by preparing a bank reconciliation. A **bank reconciliation** is a listing of the items and amounts that cause the cash balance reported in the bank statement to differ from the balance of the cash account in the ledger.

A bank reconciliation is usually divided into two sections. The first section begins with the cash balance according to the bank statement and ends with the adjusted balance. The second section begins with the cash balance according to the depositor's records and ends with the adjusted balance. The two amounts designated as the adjusted balance must be equal. The content of the bank reconciliation is shown below.

Cash balance according to bank statement		$XXX
Add: Additions by depositor not on bank statement	$XX	
Bank errors	XX	XX
		$XXX
Deduct: Deductions by depositor not on bank statement	$XX	
Bank errors	XX	XX
Adjusted balance		$XXX

Cash balance according to depositor's records		$XXX
Add: Additions by bank not recorded by depositor	$XX	
Depositor errors	XX	XX
		$XXX
Deduct: Deductions by bank not recorded by depositor	$XX	
Depositor errors	XX	XX
Adjusted balance		$XXX

(The two adjusted balances must be equal.)

The following steps are useful in finding the reconciling items and determining the adjusted balance of Cash:

1. Compare each deposit listed on the bank statement with unrecorded deposits appearing in the preceding period's reconciliation and with deposit receipts or other records of deposits. *Add deposits not recorded by the bank to the balance according to the bank statement.*

2. Compare paid checks with outstanding checks appearing on the preceding period's reconciliation and with recorded checks. *Deduct checks outstanding that have not been paid by the bank from the balance according to the bank statement.*
3. Compare bank credit memorandums to entries in the journal. For example, a bank would issue a credit memorandum for a note receivable and interest that it collected for a depositor. *Add credit memorandums that have not been recorded to the balance according to the depositor's records.*
4. Compare bank debit memorandums to entries recording cash payments. For example, a bank normally issues debit memorandums for service charges and check printing charges. A bank also issues debit memorandums for not-sufficient-funds checks. A *not-sufficient-funds (NSF) check* is a customer's check that was recorded and deposited but was not paid when it was presented to the customer's bank for payment. NSF checks are normally charged back to the customer as an account receivable. *Deduct debit memorandums that have not been recorded from the balance according to the depositor's records.*
5. List any errors discovered during the preceding steps. For example, if an amount has been recorded incorrectly by the depositor, the amount of the error should be added to or deducted from the cash balance according to the depositor's records. Similarly, errors by the bank should be added to or deducted from the cash balance according to the bank statement.

Is an NSF check added to or deducted from the bank balance according to the depositor's records?

Deducted.

To illustrate a bank reconciliation, we will use the bank statement for Power Networking in Exhibit 4. This bank statement shows a balance of $3,359.78 as of July 31. The cash balance in Power Networking's ledger as of the same date is $2,549.99. The following reconciling items are revealed by using the steps outlined above:

Deposit of July 31, not recorded on bank statement	$ 816.20
Checks outstanding: No. 812, $1,061.00; No. 878, $435.39; No. 883, $48.60	1,544.99
Note plus interest of $8 collected by bank (credit memorandum), not recorded in the journal	408.00
Check from customer (Thomas Ivey) returned by bank because of insufficient funds (NSF)	300.00
Bank service charges (debit memorandum), not recorded in the journal	18.00
Check No. 879 for $732.26 to Taylor Co. on account, recorded in the journal as $723.26	9.00

The bank reconciliation based on the bank statement and the reconciling items is shown in Exhibit 6.

Any items in the second section of the bank reconciliation must be recorded in the depositor's accounts. This section begins with the cash balance according to the depositor's records. For example, journal entries should be made for any unrecorded bank memorandums and any depositor's errors. The journal entries for Power Networking, based on the preceding bank reconciliation, are as follows:

July	31	Cash	408	
		Notes Receivable		400
		Interest Income		8
	31	Accounts Receivable—Thomas Ivey	300	
		Miscellaneous Expense	18	
		Accounts Payable—Taylor Co.	9	
		Cash		327

Exhibit 6

Bank Reconciliation for Power Networking

Power Networking
Bank Reconciliation
July 31, 2006

Cash balance according to bank statement		$3,359.78	Cash balance according to depositor's records		$2,549.99
Add deposit of July 31, not recorded by bank		816.20	Add note and interest collected by bank		408.00
		$4,175.98			$2,957.99
			Deduct: Check returned because of insufficient funds	$300.00	
Deduct outstanding checks:					
No. 812	$1,061.00		Bank service charge	18.00	
No. 878	435.39		Error in recording		
No. 883	48.60	1,544.99	Check No. 879	9.00	327.00
Adjusted balance		$2,630.99	Adjusted balance		$2,630.99

No entries are necessary on the depositor's records as a result of the information included in the first section of the bank reconciliation. This section begins with the cash balance according to the bank statement. However, the bank should be notified of any errors that need to be corrected on its records.

After the entries on page 282 have been posted, the cash account will have a debit balance of $2,630.99. This balance agrees with the adjusted cash balance shown on the bank reconciliation. This is the amount of cash available as of July 31 and the amount that would be reported on Power Networking's July 31 balance sheet.

Although businesses may reconcile their bank accounts in a slightly different format from what we described above, the objective is the same: to control cash by reconciling the company's records to the records of an independent outside source, the bank. In doing so, any errors or misuse of cash may be detected.

For effective control, the bank reconciliation should be prepared by an employee who does not take part in or record cash transactions. When these duties are not properly separated, mistakes are likely to occur, and it is more likely that cash will be stolen or

Ethics in Action
Bank Error in Your Favor

You may sometime have a bank error in your favor, such as a misposted deposit. Such errors are not a case of "found money," as in the Monopoly® game. Bank control systems quickly discover most errors and make automatic adjustments. Even so, you have a legal responsibility to report the error and return the money to the bank.

otherwise misapplied. For example, an employee who takes part in all of these duties could prepare and cash an unauthorized check, omit it from the accounts, and omit it from the reconciliation.

Special-Purpose Cash Funds

6 Describe the accounting for special-purpose cash funds.

It is usually not practical for a business to write checks to pay small amounts, such as postage. Yet, these small payments may occur often enough to add up to a significant total amount. Thus, it is desirable to control such payments. For this purpose, a special cash fund, called a **petty cash fund**, is used.

In addition, businesses often use other cash funds to meet special needs, such as travel expenses for salespersons. For example, each salesperson might be given $200 for travel-related expenses. Periodically, the salesperson submits a detailed expense report and the travel funds are replenished. Also, as we discussed earlier in this chapter, retail businesses use change funds for making change for customers. Finally, most businesses use a payroll bank account to pay employees. Such cash funds are called **special-purpose funds**.

A special-purpose cash fund is initially established by first estimating the amount of cash needed for payments from the fund during a period, such as a week or a month. After necessary approvals, a check is written and cashed for this amount. The money obtained from cashing the check is then given to an employee, called the custodian, who is authorized to disburse monies from the fund. For control purposes, the company may place restrictions on the maximum amount and the types of payments that can be made from the fund.

To illustrate, a petty cash fund of $500 is established. Each time monies are paid from petty cash, the custodian records the payment on a petty cash receipt form. At periodic intervals, or when it is depleted or reaches a minimum amount, the petty cash fund is replenished. When the fund is replenished, the accounts debited are determined by summarizing the petty cash receipts. A check is then written for this amount.

Financial Statement Reporting of Cash

7 Describe and illustrate the reporting of cash and cash equivalents in the financial statements.

Cash is the most liquid asset, and therefore it is listed as the first asset in the Current Assets section of the balance sheet. Most companies present only a single cash amount on the balance sheet by combining all their bank and cash fund accounts.

A company may have cash in excess of its operating needs. In such cases, the company normally invests in highly liquid investments in order to earn interest. These investments are called **cash equivalents**.[6] Examples of cash equivalents include U.S. Treasury Bills, notes issued by major corporations (referred to as commercial paper), and money market funds. Companies that have invested excess cash in cash equivalents usually report *Cash and cash equivalents* as one amount on the balance sheet.

To illustrate, Microsoft Corp. disclosed the details of its cash and cash equivalents in the notes to its financial statements as follows:

6 To be classified as a cash equivalent, according to FASB Statement 95, the investment is expected to be converted to cash within 90 days.

June 30,	2000	2001
	(in millions)	
Cash and equivalents:		
Cash	$ 849	$1,145
Commercial paper	1,986	894
Certificates of deposit	1,017	286
U.S. government and agency securities	729	400
Corporate notes and bonds	265	1,130
Municipal securities	—	67
Cash and equivalents	$4,846	$3,922

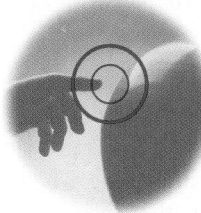

INTERNATIONAL PERSPECTIVE

In the United Kingdom, the statement of cash flows is prepared using a narrower definition of "cash" than in the United States. Specifically, the U.K. does not include cash equivalents, such as certificates of deposit, in its definition of cash as does the United States.

Banks may require depositors to maintain minimum cash balances in their bank accounts. Such a balance is called a *compensating balance.* This requirement is often imposed by the bank as a part of a loan agreement or line of credit. A *line of credit* is a preapproved amount the bank is willing to lend to a customer upon request. If significant, compensating balance requirements should be disclosed in notes to the financial statements.

Cash Ratios

8 Describe, illustrate, and interpret the cash flow to net income ratio and the cash to monthly cash expenses ratio.

Analyzing cash and cash flows is essential to interpreting financial statements. The statement of cash flows reports cash flows from operating, investing, and financing activities. In addition, two cash ratios useful for analyzing and interpreting operating performance are (1) cash flow to net income and (2) cash to monthly cash expenses.

Ratio of Cash Flow to Net Income

The accrual basis of accounting is used by all public companies in determining and reporting net income. As we illustrate throughout this text, accrual accounting records revenues when earned and expenses when incurred and not necessarily when cash is received or paid. This process gives rise to accruals and deferrals that are updated and adjusted at the end of each reporting period. As a result, net cash flows from operations is rarely the same as net income.

When the amount of accruals and deferrals is large, the difference between net cash flows from operations and net income will also be large. The effect of accruals and deferrals on net income can be measured by the ratio of net cash flows from operations to net income. Accordingly, significant changes in this ratio from year to year should be investigated for the underlying causes. For example, implementing a new accounting standard may significantly affect net income and comparability between years. On the other hand, management could change methods of estimating and recording accruals, deferrals, and depreciation. Such changes also affect the current period's net income comparability with prior years.

To illustrate, the ratio of cash flow to net income for Hershey Foods for 2001 and 2000 is shown below.

	2001	2000
Net cash flows from operations (in millions)	$706	$412
Net income	207	335
Cash flow ratio	3.4	1.2

The cash flow ratio increased from 1.2 in 2000 to 3.4 in 2001. While net cash flows from operations increased during 2001, net income decreased, and thus the cash flow ratio increased. Why did this happen? A review of the statement of cash flows for Hershey reveals that during 2001 depreciation and amortization expense increased by $15 million. In addition, Hershey wrote off $172 million for business realignment initiatives and $53 million for asset impairments. If we adjust for these three accrual accounting effects, the revised cash flow ratio is 1.6 [$706 ÷ ($207 + $15 − $172 + $53)]. Thus, these three accrual accounting effects on net income explain most of the change in the cash flow ratio.

If net income is $580,000 and net cash flows from operations are $725,000, what is the cash ratio?

1.25 ($725,000 ÷ $580,000).

Ratio of Cash to Monthly Cash Expenses

As we illustrated for Federal Express, the cash flow ratio is useful for identifying when significant changes may have occurred in accrual accounting methods. Another cash ratio that is especially useful for startup companies is the ratio of cash to monthly cash expenses.

In their first few years of operations, startup companies often report losses and negative net cash flows. In these cases, the ratio of cash to monthly cash expenses (net cash flow used for operating activities) is useful for assessing how long a company can continue to operate without additional financing or without generating positive cash flows from operations. In computing cash to monthly cash expenses, the amount of cash on hand can be taken from the balance sheet, while the monthly cash expenses can be estimated from the operating activities section of the statement of cash flows.

To illustrate this ratio, we use Pets.com, a former online retailer of pet products. Pets.com was organized in 1999 by raising over $90 million from private investors. Selling stock to the public in February 2000 raised an additional $77 million. For the three months ending March 31, 2000, Pets.com reported the following data (in thousands):

Revenues	$ 7,651
Net loss	(39,088)
Net cash flows from operating activities	(27,475)
Cash as of March 31, 2000	70,342

Based upon the preceding data, the monthly cash expenses, sometimes referred to as *cash burn*, was $9,158 per month ($27,475 ÷ 3). Thus, as of March 31, 2000, the cash to monthly cash expenses ratio was 7.7 ($70,342 ÷ $9,158). In other words, as of March 31, 2000, Pets.com would run out of cash in less than eight months unless it changed its operations or was able to raise additional financing. Failing to do either of these, the Board of Directors of Pets.com approved a plan of liquidation and dissolution in November 2000.

If net cash flows from operating activities are ($540,000) and cash at the end of the year is $292,500, how many months will pass before the company runs out of cash?

6.5 months [$292,500 ÷ ($540,000 ÷ 12)].

Focus on Cash Flow

Reconciling Net Income and Cash Flows From Operating Activities

In preparing the statement of cash flows, generally accepted accounting principles require a company to reconcile net income with cash flows from operating activities. This reconciliation for Mandalay Resort Group is shown below for the year ended January 31, 2001.

		Year ended January 31, 2001 (in thousands)
Net income		$119,700
Adjustments to reconcile net income to net cash provided by operating activities:		
Depreciation and amortization	$217,984	
Increase (decrease) in deferred income tax	25,023	
Increase in allowance for doubtful accounts	(19,514)	
Increase (decrease) in interest payable	33,727	
Increase in accrued pension cost	4,363	
(Increase) decrease in other current assets	7,462	
Increase in other current liabilities	18,584	
(Increase) decrease in other noncurrent assets	(551)	
Other items	28,788	
Total adjustments		315,866
Net cash provided by operating activities		$435,566

The preceding reconciliation begins by adding back depreciation and amortization of $217,984. This is because depreciation and amortization are deducted as expenses in arriving at net income, but they do not impact cash. That is, no cash related to yearly depreciation or amortization is paid.

The other reconciling items involve increases or decreases in other financial statement accounts. The logic behind including these reconciling items involves the accounting equation. Specifically, the accounting equation must always balance.

$$\text{Assets} = \text{Liabilities} + \text{Stockholders' Equity}$$

Therefore, changes in the cash account can be determined by analyzing changes in the other accounts:

$$\text{Changes in Cash} = \text{Changes in Liabilities} + \text{Changes in Stockholders' Equity} - \text{Changes in Noncash Assets}$$

As shown in the illustration for Mandalay Resorts, some changes in the noncash accounts affect the reporting of cash flows from operating activities. Changes in noncash accounts also affect the reporting of cash flows from financing and investing activities.

Summary of Learning Goals

1 Describe and illustrate the objectives and elements of internal control.

The objectives of internal control are to provide reasonable assurance that (1) assets are safeguarded and used for business purposes, (2) business information is accurate, and (3) laws and regulations are complied with. The elements of internal control are the control environment, risk assessment, control procedures, monitoring, and information and communication.

2 Describe and illustrate methods of preventing and detecting employee fraud.

Controls to prevent the opportunity of employees to steal assets can be grouped into those involving (1) physical safeguarding of assets and (2) proper authorization and approval procedures. Controls to detect employee fraud include (1) periodic reviews, (2) independent checks, and (3) reconciliations.

3 Describe and illustrate the application of internal controls to cash.

One of the most important controls to protect cash received in over-the-counter sales is a cash register. A remittance advice is a preventive control for cash received through the mail. Separating the duties of handling cash and recording cash is also a preventive control. A voucher system is a control system for cash payments that uses a set of procedures for authorizing and recording liabilities and cash payments.

4 Describe the nature of a bank account and its use in controlling cash.

Businesses use bank accounts as a means of controlling cash. Bank accounts reduce the amount of cash on hand and facilitate the transfer of cash between businesses and locations. In addition, banks send monthly statements to their customers (depositors), summarizing all of the transactions for the month. The bank statement allows a business to reconcile the cash transactions recorded in the accounting records to those recorded by the bank.

5 Describe and illustrate the use of a bank reconciliation in controlling cash.

The first section of the bank reconciliation begins with the cash balance according to the bank statement. This balance is adjusted for the depositor's changes in cash that do not appear on the bank statement and for any bank errors. The second section begins with the cash balance according to the depositor's records. This balance is adjusted for the bank's changes in cash that do not appear on the depositor's records and for any depositor errors. The adjusted balances for the two sections must be equal. No entries are necessary on the depositor's records as a result of the information included in the first section of the bank reconciliation. However, the items in the second section must be journalized on the depositor's records.

6 Describe the accounting for special-purpose cash funds.

Businesses often use special-purpose cash funds, such as a petty cash fund or travel funds, to meet specific needs. Each fund is initially established by cashing a check for the amount of cash needed. The cash is then given to a custodian who is authorized to disburse monies from the fund. At periodic intervals or when it is depleted or reaches a minimum amount, the fund is replenished and the disbursements recorded.

7 Describe and illustrate the reporting of cash and cash equivalents in the financial statements.

Cash is listed as the first asset in the Current Assets section of the balance sheet. Companies that have invested excess cash in highly liquid investments usually report *Cash and cash equivalents* on the balance sheet.

8 Describe, illustrate, and interpret the cash flow to net income ratio and the cash to monthly cash expenses ratio.

Two cash ratios useful for analyzing and interpreting operating performance are (1) cash flow to net income and (2) cash to monthly cash expenses. The effect of accruals and deferrals on net income can be measured by the ratio of net cash flows from operations to net income. The ratio of cash to monthly cash expenses is useful for assessing how long a company can continue to operate without additional financing or without generating positive cash flows from operations.

Glossary

Bank reconciliation The analysis that details the items responsible for the difference between the cash balance reported in the bank statement and the balance of the cash account in the ledger.

Bank statement A summary of all transactions is mailed to the depositor by the bank each month.

Cash Coins, currency (paper money), checks, money orders, and money on deposit that is available for unrestricted withdrawal from banks and other financial institutions.

Cash equivalents Highly liquid investments that are usually reported with cash on the balance sheet.

Cash short and over account An account used to record the difference between the amount of cash in a cash register and the amount of cash that should be on hand according to the records.

Electronic funds transfer (EFT) A system in which computers rather than paper (money, checks, etc.) are used to effect cash transactions.

Elements of internal control The control environment, risk assessment, control activities, information and communication, and monitoring.

Employee fraud The intentional act of deceiving an employer for personal gain.

Internal controls The policies and procedures used to safeguard assets, ensure accurate business information, and ensure compliance with laws and regulations.

Petty cash fund A special-purpose cash fund to pay relatively small amounts.

Special-purpose fund A cash fund used for a special business need.

Voucher Any document that serves as proof of authority to pay cash.

Voucher system A set of procedures for authorizing and recording liabilities and cash payments.

Illustrative Accounting Application Problem

The bank statement for Urethane Company for June 30, 2004, indicates a balance of $9,143.11. All cash receipts are deposited each evening in a night depository, after banking hours. The accounting records indicate the following summary data for cash receipts and payments for June:

Cash balance as of June 1	$ 3,943.50
Total cash receipts for June	28,971.60
Total amount of checks issued in June	28,388.85

Comparing the bank statement and the accompanying canceled checks and memorandums with the records reveals the following reconciling items:

a. The bank had collected for Urethane Company $1,030 on a note left for collection. The face of the note was $1,000.
b. A deposit of $1,852.21, representing receipts of June 30, had been made too late to appear on the bank statement.
c. Checks outstanding totaled $5,265.27.
d. A check drawn for $139 had been incorrectly charged by the bank as $157.
e. A check for $30 returned with the statement had been recorded in the depositor's records as $240. The check was for the payment of an obligation to Avery Equipment Company for the purchase of office supplies on account.
f. Bank service charges for June amounted to $18.20.

Instructions

1. Prepare a bank reconciliation for June.
2. Journalize the entries that should be made by Urethane Company.

Solution

1.

Urethane Company
Bank Reconciliation
June 30, 2004

Cash balance according to bank statement		$ 9,143.11
Add: Deposit of June 30 not recorded by bank	$1,852.21	
Bank error in charging check as $157 instead of $139	18.00	1,870.21
		$11,013.32
Deduct: Outstanding checks		5,265.27
Adjusted balance		$ 5,748.05
Cash balance according to depositor's records		$ 4,526.25*
Add: Proceeds of note collected by bank, including $30 interest	$1,030.00	
Error in recording check	210.00	1,240.00
		$ 5,766.25
Deduct: Bank service charges		18.20
Adjusted balance		$ 5,748.05

*$3,943.50 + $28,971.60 − $28,388.85

2.

Cash	1,240.00	
Notes Receivable		1,000.00
Interest Revenue		30.00
Accounts Payable—Avery Equipment		210.00
Miscellaneous Administrative Expense	18.20	
Cash		18.20

Self-Study Questions

Answers at end of chapter

1. Which of the following is *not* an element of internal control?
   A. control environment
   B. monitoring
   C. compliance with laws and regulations
   D. control procedures

2. The policies and procedures used by management to protect assets from misuse, ensure accurate business information, and ensure compliance with laws and regulations are called:
   A. internal controls.
   B. systems analysis.
   C. systems design.
   D. systems implementation.

3. In preparing a bank reconciliation, the amount of checks outstanding would be:
   A. added to the cash balance according to the bank statement.
   B. deducted from the cash balance according to the bank statement.
   C. added to the cash balance according to the depositor's records.
   D. deducted from the cash balance according to the depositor's records.

4. Journal entries based on the bank reconciliation are required for:
   A. additions to the cash balance according to the depositor's records.
   B. deductions from the cash balance according to the depositor's records.
   C. both A and B.
   D. neither A nor B.

5. A petty cash fund is:
   A. used to pay relatively small amounts.
   B. established by estimating the amount of cash needed for disbursements of relatively small amounts during a specified period.
   C. reimbursed when the amount of money in the fund is reduced to a predetermined minimum amount.
   D. all of the above.

Discussion Questions

1. (a) Name and describe the five elements of internal control. (b) Is any one element of internal control more important than another?
2. How does a policy of rotating clerical employees from job to job aid in strengthening the control procedures within the control environment? Explain.
3. Why should the responsibility for a sequence of related operations be divided among different persons? Explain.
4. Why should the employee who handles cash receipts not have the responsibility for maintaining the accounts receivable records? Explain.
5. In an attempt to improve operating efficiency, one employee was made responsible for all purchasing, receiving, and storing of supplies. Is this organizational change wise from an internal control standpoint? Explain.
6. The ticket seller at a movie theater doubles as a ticket taker for a few minutes each day while the ticket taker is on a break. Which control procedure of a business's system of internal control is violated in this situation?
7. Why should the responsibility for maintaining the accounting records be separated from the responsibility for operations? Explain.
8. Assume that the accounts payable clerk for Script Inc. stole $50,000 by paying fictitious invoices for goods that were never received. The clerk set up accounts in the names of the fictitious companies and cashed the checks at a local bank. (a) Describe how the clerk could have rationalized (justified) her behavior. (b) Describe a control procedure that would have prevented or detected the fraud.
9. Before a voucher for the purchase of merchandise is approved for payment, supporting documents should be compared to verify the accuracy of the liability. Give an example of a supporting document for the purchase of merchandise.
10. The accounting clerk pays all obligations by prenumbered checks. What are the strengths and weaknesses in the internal control over cash payments in this situation?
11. The balance of Cash is likely to differ from the bank statement balance. What two factors are likely to be responsible for the difference?
12. What is the purpose of preparing a bank reconciliation?
13. Do items reported as credits on the bank statement represent (a) additions made by the bank to the depositor's balance or (b) deductions made by the bank from the depositor's balance? Explain.
14. Heifer Inc. has a petty cash fund of $500. (a) Since the petty cash fund is only $500, should Heifer Inc. implement controls over petty cash? (b) What controls, if any, could be used for the petty cash fund?
15. (a) How are cash equivalents reported in the financial statements? (b) What are some examples of cash equivalents?

Resources for your success online @ http://warren.swlearning.com

Remember! If you need additional help, visit South-Western's Web site. See page 30 for a description of the online and printed materials that are available.

Exercises

Exercise 6–1

Internal controls

Goals 1, 2, 3

Connie Stevens has recently been hired as the manager of Big Apple Deli. Big Apple Deli is a national chain of franchised delicatessens. During her first month as store manager, Connie encountered the following internal control situations:

a. Big Apple Deli has one cash register. Prior to Connie's joining the deli, each employee working on a shift would take a customer order, accept payment, and then prepare the order. Connie made one employee on each shift responsible for taking orders and accepting the customer's payment. Other employees prepare the orders.

b. Since only one employee uses the cash register, that employee is responsible for counting the cash at the end of the shift and verifying that the cash in the drawer matches the amount of cash sales recorded by the cash register. Connie expects each cashier to balance the drawer to the penny *every* time—no exceptions.

c. Connie caught an employee putting a box of 100 single-serving bags of potato chips in his car. Not wanting to create a scene, Connie smiled and said, "I don't think you're putting those chips on the right shelf. Don't they belong inside the deli?" The employee returned the chips to the stockroom.

State whether you agree or disagree with Connie's method of handling each situation and explain your answer.

Exercise 6–2

Internal controls

Goals 1, 2, 3

STUDENT SOLUTIONS MANUAL

Summer Breeze is a retail store specializing in women's clothing. The store has established a liberal return policy for the holiday season in order to encourage gift purchases. Any item purchased during November and December may be returned through January 31, with a receipt, for cash or exchange. If the customer does not have a receipt, cash will still be refunded for any item under $25. If the item is more than $25, a check is mailed to the customer.

Whenever an item is returned, a store clerk completes a return slip, which the customer signs. The return slip is placed in a special box. The store manager visits the return counter approximately once every two hours to authorize the return slips. Clerks are instructed to place the returned merchandise on the proper rack on the selling floor as soon as possible.

This year, returns at Summer Breeze have reached an all-time high. There are a large number of returns under $25 without receipts.

a. How can sales clerks employed at Summer Breeze use the store's return policy to steal money from the cash register?

b.
   1. What internal control weaknesses do you see in the return policy that make cash thefts easier?
   2. Would issuing a store credit in place of a cash refund for all merchandise returned without a receipt reduce the possibility of theft? List some advantages and disadvantages of issuing a store credit in place of a cash refund.

3. Assume that Summer Breeze is committed to the current policy of issuing cash refunds without a receipt. What changes could be made in the store's procedures regarding customer refunds in order to improve internal control?

Exercise 6-3

Internal controls for bank lending

Goals 1, 2, 3

United Savings Bank provides loans to businesses in the community through its Commercial Lending Department. Small loans (less than $100,000) may be approved by an individual loan officer, while larger loans (greater than $100,000) must be approved by a board of loan officers. Once a loan is approved, the funds are made available to the loan applicant under agreed-upon terms. The president of United Savings Bank has instituted a policy whereby she has the individual authority to approve loans up to $5,000,000. The president believes that this policy will allow flexibility to approve loans to valued clients much quicker than under the previous policy.

As an internal auditor of United Savings Bank, how would you respond to this change in policy?

Exercise 6-4

Internal controls

Goals 1, 2, 3

STUDENT SOLUTIONS MANUAL

One of the largest fraud losses in history involved a securities trader for the Singapore office of Barings Bank, a British merchant bank. The trader established an unauthorized account number that was used to hide $1.4 billion in losses. Even after Barings's internal auditors noted that the trader both executed trades and recorded them, management did not take action. As a result, a lone individual in a remote office bankrupted an internationally recognized firm overnight.

What general weaknesses in Barings's internal controls contributed to the occurrence and size of the fraud?

Exercise 6-5

Internal controls

Goals 1, 2, 3

In the Equity Funding fraud, approximately $2 billion of insurance policies that were claimed to have been sold by the company were bogus. The bogus policies, which were supported by falsified policy applications, were listed along with real policies on Equity Funding's computer files (records). Equity Funding personnel, including the computer programmers, kept these files in a separate room where they were easily accessible. In addition, computer programmers and other company personnel had access to the computer.

What general weaknesses in Equity Funding's internal controls contributed to the occurrence and size of the fraud?

Exercise 6-6

Financial statement fraud

Goals 1, 2, 3

STUDENT SOLUTIONS MANUAL

The former chairman, the CFO, and the controller of Donnkenny, an apparel company that makes sportswear for Pierre Cardin and Victoria Jones, pleaded guilty to financial statement fraud. These managers used false journal entries to record fictitious sales, hid inventory in public warehouses so that it could be recorded as "sold," and required sales orders to be backdated so that the sale could be moved back to an earlier period. The combined effect of these actions caused $25 million out of $40 million in quarterly sales to be phony.

a. Why might control procedures listed in this chapter be insufficient in stopping this type of fraud?
b. How could this type of fraud be stopped?

Exercise 6-7

Internal control of cash receipts

Goals 1, 2, 3

The procedures used for over-the-counter receipts are as follows. At the close of each day's business, the sales clerks count the cash in their respective cash drawers, after which they determine the amount recorded by the cash register and prepare the memorandum cash form, noting any discrepancies. An employee from the cashier's office counts the cash, compares the total with the memorandum, and takes the cash to the cashier's office.

a. Indicate the weak link in internal control.
b. How can the weakness be corrected?

Exercise 6-8

Internal control of cash receipts

Goals 1, 2, 3

STUDENT SOLUTIONS MANUAL

Kathy Beal works at the drive-through window of Fletch's Burgers. Occasionally, when a drive-through customer orders, Kathy fills the order and pockets the customer's money. She does not ring up the order on the cash register.

Identify the internal control weaknesses that exist at Fletch's Burgers, and discuss what can be done to prevent this theft.

Exercise 6-9

Internal control of cash receipts

Goals 1, 2, 3

The mailroom employees send all remittances and remittance advices to the cashier. The cashier deposits the cash in the bank and forwards the remittance advices and duplicate deposit slips to the Accounting Department.

a. Indicate the weak link in internal control in the handling of cash receipts.
b. How can the weakness be corrected?

Exercise 6-10

Entry for cash sales; cash short

Goals 1, 2, 3

STUDENT SOLUTIONS MANUAL

The actual cash received from cash sales was $18,153.79, and the amount indicated by the cash register total was $18,178.31.

a. Determine the amount of cash short or over.
b. Journalize the entry to record the cash receipts and cash sales.

Exercise 6-11

Entry for cash sales; cash over

Goals 1, 2, 3

The actual cash received from cash sales was $9,357.69, and the amount indicated by the cash register total was $9,346.22.

a. Determine the amount of cash short or over.
b. Journalize the entry to record the cash receipts and cash sales.

Exercise 6-12

Internal control of cash payments

Goals 1, 2, 3

STUDENT SOLUTIONS MANUAL

Fiedler Co. is a medium-size merchandising company. An investigation revealed that in spite of a sufficient bank balance, a significant amount of available cash discounts had been lost because of failure to make timely payments. In addition, it was discovered that several purchases invoices had been paid twice.

Outline procedures for the payment of vendors' invoices, so that the possibilities of losing available cash discounts and of paying an invoice a second time will be minimized.

Exercise 6-13

Internal control of cash payments

Goals 1, 2, 3

Herringbone Company, a communications equipment manufacturer, recently fell victim to an embezzlement scheme masterminded by one of its employees. To understand the scheme, it is necessary to review Herringbone's procedures for the purchase of services.

The purchasing agent is responsible for ordering services (such as repairs to a photocopy machine or office cleaning) after receiving a service requisition from an authorized manager. However, since no tangible goods are delivered, a receiving report is not prepared. When the Accounting Department receives an invoice billing Herringbone for a service call, the accounts payable clerk calls the manager who requested the service in order to verify that it was performed.

The embezzlement scheme involves Kellie Barth, the manager of plant and facilities. Kellie arranged for her uncle's company, Barth Industrial Supply and Service, to be placed on Herringbone's approved vendor list. Kellie did not disclose the family relationship.

On several occasions, Kellie would submit a requisition for services to be provided by Barth Industrial Supply and Service. However, the service requested was really not needed, and it was never performed. Barth would bill Herringbone for the service and then split the cash payment with Kellie.

Explain what changes should be made to Herringbone's procedures for ordering and paying for services in order to prevent such occurrences in the future.

Exercise 6–14

Bank reconciliation

Goals 4, 5

STUDENT SOLUTIONS MANUAL

Identify each of the following reconciling items as: (a) an addition to the cash balance according to the bank statement, (b) a deduction from the cash balance according to the bank statement, (c) an addition to the cash balance according to the depositor's records, or (d) a deduction from the cash balance according to the depositor's records. (None of the transactions reported by bank debit and credit memorandums have been recorded by the depositor.)

1. Outstanding checks, $3,512.30.
2. Deposit in transit, $10,000.
3. Note collected by bank, $8,000.
4. Check for $89 incorrectly charged by bank as $98.
5. Check drawn by depositor for $200 but incorrectly recorded as $2,000.
6. Check of a customer returned by bank to depositor because of insufficient funds, $775.
7. Bank service charges, $25.

Exercise 6–15

Entries based on bank reconciliation

Goals 4, 5

Which of the reconciling items listed in Exercise 6–14 require an entry in the depositor's accounts?

Exercise 6–16

Bank reconciliation

Goals 4, 5

Adjusted balance, $8,961.45

STUDENT SOLUTIONS MANUAL

SPREADSHEET

The following data were accumulated for use in reconciling the bank account of Juno Co. for July:

a. Cash balance according to the depositor's records at July 31, $8,530.20.
b. Cash balance according to the bank statement at July 31, $3,457.25.
c. Checks outstanding, $1,276.20.
d. Deposit in transit, not recorded by bank, $6,780.40.
e. A check for $270 in payment of an account was erroneously recorded in the check register as $720.
f. Bank debit memorandum for service charges, $18.75.

Prepare a bank reconciliation, using the format shown in Exhibit 6.

Exercise 6–17

Entries for bank reconciliation

Goals 4, 5

Using the data presented in Exercise 6–16, journalize the entry or entries that should be made by the depositor.

Exercise 6–18

Entries for note collected by bank

Goals 4, 5

STUDENT SOLUTIONS MANUAL

Accompanying a bank statement for Lyric Company is a credit memorandum for $12,500, representing the principal ($12,000) and interest ($500) on a note that had been collected by the bank. The depositor had been notified by the bank at the time of the collection, but had made no entries. Journalize the entry that should be made by the depositor to bring the accounting records up to date.

Exercise 6–19

Bank reconciliation

Goals 4, 5

Adjusted balance, $13,445.00

SPREADSHEET

An accounting clerk for Noxious Co. prepared the following bank reconciliation:

Noxious Co.
Bank Reconciliation
March 31, 2004

Cash balance according to depositor's records		$10,100.75
Add: Outstanding checks	$7,557.12	
Error by Noxious Co. in recording Check No. 1621 as $2,510 instead of $2,150	360.00	
Note for $2,500 collected by bank, including interest	3,000.00	10,917.12
		$21,017.87
Deduct: Deposit in transit on March 31	$6,150.00	
Bank service charges	15.75	6,165.75
Cash balance according to bank statement		$14,852.12

a. From the data in the above bank reconciliation, prepare a new bank reconciliation for Noxious Co., using the format shown in the illustrative problem.

b. If a balance sheet were prepared for Noxious Co. on March 31, 2004, what amount should be reported for cash?

Exercise 6–20

Bank reconciliation

Goals 4, 5

Corrected adjusted balance, $9,998.02

STUDENT SOLUTIONS MANUAL

SPREADSHEET

How many errors can you find in the following bank reconciliation?

Protractor Co.
Bank Reconciliation
For the Month Ended November 30, 2004

Cash balance according to bank statement . .			$ 9,767.76
Add outstanding checks:			
No. 721		$ 545.95	
739		172.75	
743		459.60	
744		601.50	1,779.80
			$11,547.56
Deduct deposit of November 30, not recorded by bank			2,010.06
Adjusted balance			$10,537.50
Cash balance according to depositor's records			$ 4,363.62
Add: Proceeds of note collected by bank:			
Principal	$5,000.00		
Interest	750.00	$5,750.00	
Service charges		20.00	5,770.00
			$10,133.62
Deduct: Check returned because of insufficient funds		$ 635.60	
Error in recording November 10 deposit of $3,718 as $3,178		540.00	1,175.60
Adjusted balance			$ 8,958.02

Exercise 6–21

Using bank reconciliation to determine cash receipts stolen

Goals 4, 5

SPREADSHEET

Ovation Co. records all cash receipts on the basis of its cash register tapes. Ovation Co. discovered during November 2004 that one of its sales clerks had stolen an undetermined amount of cash receipts when he took the daily deposits to the bank. The following data have been gathered for November:

Cash in bank according to the general ledger	$11,573.22
Cash according to the November 30, 2004 bank statement	14,271.14
Outstanding checks as of November 30, 2004	2,901.38
Bank service charge for November	25.10
Note receivable, including interest, collected by bank in November	3,060.00

No deposits were in transit on November 30, which fell on a Sunday.

a. Determine the amount of cash receipts stolen by the sales clerk.
b. What accounting controls would have prevented or detected this theft?

Exercise 6–22

Variation in cash flows

Goal 7

STUDENT SOLUTIONS MANUAL

Toys"R"Us is one of the world's leading retailers of toys, children's apparel, and baby products, operating nearly 1,600 retail stores. For a recent year, Toys"R"Us reported the following net cash flows from operating activities:

First quarter ending May 5, 2001	$(437,000,000)
Second quarter ending August 4, 2001	(43,000,000)
Third quarter ending November 3, 2001	(80,000,000)
Year ending February 2, 2002	504,000,000

Explain how Toys"R"Us can report negative net cash flows from operating activities during the first three quarters yet report net positive cash flows for the year.

Exercise 6–23

Cash flow to net income ratio

Goal 8

a. 2001: 1.8

Avon Products Inc. is a global manufacturer and marketer of beauty products. Avon distributes its products to customers in the United States through over 450,000 independent sales representatives. The following operating results (in thousands) are for years ending December 31:

	2001	2000
Net cash flows from operating activities	$754,900	$323,900
Net income	430,000	478,400

a. Compute the ratio of cash flow to net income for each year. Round to one decimal place.
b. Is there a significant difference between the ratios for 2001 and 2000? If so, what are some possible causes for the difference?

Exercise 6–24

Cash flow to net income ratio

Goal 8

a. 2001: 1.4

STUDENT SOLUTIONS MANUAL

Colgate-Palmolive is a consumer products company with the leading toothpaste brand in the United States. In addition, Colgate sells bar and liquid hand soaps, shower gels, shampoos, conditioners, deodorants, antiperspirants, and shaving products. The following operating results (in millions) are for years ending December 31:

	2001	2000
Net cash flows from operating activities	$1,600	$1,536
Net income	1,147	1,064

a. Compute the ratio of cash flow to net income for each year. Round to one decimal place.

b. Is there a significant difference between the ratios for 2001 and 2000? If so, what are some possible causes for the difference?

Exercise 6–25

Cash to monthly cash expenses ratio

Goal 8

During 2004, Tempura Inc. has monthly cash expenses of $40,000. On December 31, 2004, the cash balance is $720,000.

a. Compute the ratio of cash to monthly cash expenses.

b. Based upon (a), what are the implications for Tempura Inc.?

Exercise 6–26

Cash to monthly cash expenses ratio

Goal 8

STUDENT SOLUTIONS MANUAL

EMusic.com was organized as an online music network that would allow its customers to sample and purchase music on the Internet, using the Mp3 format. Through relationships with leading artists and licensing agreements with recording labels, EMusic.com offered over 125,000 tracks of digital music for purchase. EMusic.com raised over $80 million by issuing stock, and it reported the following financial data (in thousands) for the year ending June 30, 2000:

Net cash flows from operating activities	$(42,976)
Cash, June 30, 2000	14,591

a. Determine the monthly cash expenses. Round to the nearest dollar.

b. Determine the ratio of cash to monthly cash expenses. Round to one decimal place.

c. Based upon your analysis, do you believe EMusic.com is still in business?

Exercise 6–27

Cash to monthly cash expenses ratio

Goal 8

Stamps.com provides Internet-based services for mailing or shipping letters, packages, or parcels in the United States. Stamps.com permits individuals, home offices, or small businesses to print U.S. postage or shipping labels, using any ordinary PC, any ordinary inkjet or laser printer, and an Internet connection. Stamps.com reported the following financial data (in thousands) for the year ending December 31, 2001:

Net cash flows from operating activities	$ (38,797)
Cash, December 31, 2001	101,703

a. Determine the monthly cash expenses. Round to the nearest dollar.
b. Determine the ratio of cash to monthly cash expenses. Round to one decimal place.
c. Based upon your analysis, do you believe Stamps.com is still in business?

Accounting Application Problems

Problem 6–1A

Evaluating internal control of cash

Goals 1, 2, 3

The following procedures were recently installed by Gambrel Company:

a. Along with petty cash expense receipts for postage, office supplies, etc., several post-dated employee checks are in the petty cash fund.
b. The accounts payable clerk prepares a voucher for each disbursement. The voucher along with the supporting documentation is forwarded to the treasurer's office for approval.
c. At the end of each day, an accounting clerk compares the duplicate copy of the daily cash deposit slip with the deposit receipt obtained from the bank.
d. The bank reconciliation is prepared by the cashier, who works under the supervision of the treasurer.
e. At the end of the day, cash register clerks are required to use their own funds to make up any cash shortages in their registers.
f. All mail is opened by the mail clerk, who forwards all cash remittances to the cashier. The cashier prepares a listing of the cash receipts and forwards a copy of the list to the accounts receivable clerk for recording in the accounts.
g. After necessary approvals have been obtained for the payment of a voucher, the treasurer signs and mails the check. The treasurer then stamps the voucher and supporting documentation as paid and returns the voucher and supporting documentation to the accounts payable clerk for filing.
h. At the end of each day, any deposited cash receipts are placed in the bank's night depository.

Instructions:

Indicate whether each of the procedures of internal control over cash represents (1) a strength or (2) a weakness. For each weakness, indicate why it exists.

Problem 6–2A

Bank reconciliation and entries

Goals 4, 5

Adjusted balance, $20,395.95

SPREADSHEET

The cash account for Wok Co. at November 30, 2004, indicated a balance of $16,190.95. The bank statement indicated a balance of $21,016.30 on November 30, 2004. Comparing the bank statement and the accompanying canceled checks and memorandums with the records revealed the following reconciling items:

a. Checks outstanding totaled $5,169.75.
b. A deposit of $4,189.40, representing receipts of November 30, had been made too late to appear on the bank statement.
c. The bank had collected $4,500 on a note left for collection. The face of the note was $4,000.
d. A check for $2,850 returned with the statement had been incorrectly recorded by Wok Co. as $2,580. The check was for the payment of an obligation to Kiser Co. for the purchase of office equipment on account.
e. A check drawn for $1,375 had been erroneously charged by the bank as $1,735.
f. Bank service charges for November amounted to $25.00.

Instructions:

1. Prepare a bank reconciliation.
2. Journalize the necessary entries. The accounts have not been closed.

Problem 6–3A

Bank reconciliation and entries

Goals 4, 5

Adjusted balance, $3,599.87

SPREADSHEET

The cash account for Magneto Co. at August 1, 2004, of the current year indicated a balance of $2,705.37. During August, the total cash deposited was $21,077.75, and checks written totaled $21,770.25. The bank statement indicated a balance of $3,465.50 on August 31, 2004. Comparing the bank statement, the canceled checks, and the accompanying memorandums with the records revealed the following reconciling items:

a. Checks outstanding totaled $2,003.84.
b. A deposit of $1,148.21, representing receipts of August 31, had been made too late to appear on the bank statement.
c. The bank had collected for Magneto Co. $1,620 on a note left for collection. The face of the note was $1,500.
d. A check for $110 returned with the statement had been incorrectly charged by the bank as $1,100.
e. A check for $86 returned with the statement had been recorded by Magneto Co. as $68. The check was for the payment of an obligation to Adgate Co. on account.
f. Bank service charges for August amounted to $15.

Instructions:

1. Prepare a bank reconciliation as of August 31.
2. Journalize the necessary entries. The accounts have not been closed.

Problem 6–4A

Bank reconciliation and entries

Goals 4, 5

Adjusted balance, $10,622.02

SPREADSHEET

Kudzu Company deposits all cash receipts in a night depository, after banking hours. The data required to reconcile the bank statement as of June 30 have been taken from various documents and records and are reproduced as follows. The sources of the data are printed in capital letters. All checks were written for payments on account.

CASH ACCOUNT:
Balance as of June 1 $7,317.40

CASH RECEIPTS FOR MONTH OF JUNE $8,451.58

DUPLICATE DEPOSIT TICKETS:
Date and amount of each deposit in June:

Date	Amount	Date	Amount	Date	Amount
June 1	$1,080.50	June 10	$ 896.61	June 22	$897.34
3	854.17	15	882.95	24	942.71
8	840.50	17	1,246.74	29	810.06

CHECKS WRITTEN:
Number and amount of each check issued in June:

Check No.	Amount	Check No.	Amount	Check No.	Amount
740	$237.50	747	Void	754	$249.75
741	495.15	748	$450.90	755	272.75
742	501.90	749	640.13	756	113.95
743	671.30	750	276.77	757	407.95
744	506.88	751	299.37	758	159.60
745	117.25	752	537.01	759	501.50
746	298.66	753	380.95	760	486.39

Total amount of checks issued in June $7,605.66

JUNE BANK STATEMENT:

MEMBER FDIC

AMERICAN NATIONAL BANK OF DETROIT

DETROIT, MI 48201-2500 (313)933-8547

KUDZU COMPANY

	ACCOUNT NUMBER	
	FROM 6/01/20–	TO 6/30/20–
	BALANCE	7,447.20
9	DEPOSITS	8,691.77
20	WITHDRAWALS	7,345.91
4	OTHER DEBITS AND CREDITS	2,298.70CR
	NEW BALANCE	11,091.76

CHECKS AND OTHER DEBITS				DEPOSITS	DATE	BALANCE
No.731	162.15	No.738	251.40	690.25	06/01	7,723.90
No.739	60.55	No.740	237.50	1,080.50	06/02	8,506.35
No.741	495.15	No.742	501.90	854.17	06/04	8,363.47
No.743	671.30	No.744	506.88	840.50	06/09	8,025.79
No.745	117.25	No.746	298.66	MS 2,500.00	06/09	10,109.88
No.748	450.90	No.749	640.13	MS 125.00	06/09	9,143.85
No.750	276.77	No.751	299.37	896.61	06/11	9,464.32
No.752	537.01	No.753	380.95	882.95	06/16	9,429.31
No.754	449.75	No.756	113.95	1,606.74	06/18	10,472.35
No.757	407.95	No.760	486.39	897.34	06/23	10,475.35
				942.71	06/25	11,418.06
		NSF	291.90		06/28	11,126.16
		SC	34.40		06/30	11,091.76

EC — ERROR CORRECTION
MS — MISCELLANEOUS
NSF — NOT SUFFICIENT FUNDS
OD — OVERDRAFT
PS — PAYMENT STOPPED
SC — SERVICE CHARGE

* * * * * * * * *

THE RECONCILEMENT OF THIS STATEMENT WITH YOUR RECORDS IS ESSENTIAL.
ANY ERROR OR EXCEPTION SHOULD BE REPORTED IMMEDIATELY.

BANK RECONCILIATION FOR PRECEDING MONTH:

Kudzu Company
Bank Reconciliation
May 31, 20–

Cash balance according to bank statement		$7,447.20
Add deposit for May 31, not recorded by bank		690.25
		$8,137.45
Deduct outstanding checks:		
No. 731	$162.15	
736	345.95	
738	251.40	
739	60.55	820.05
Adjusted balance		$7,317.40
Cash balance according to depositor's records		$7,352.50
Deduct service charges		35.10
Adjusted balance		$7,317.40

Instructions:

1. Prepare a bank reconciliation as of June 30. If errors in recording deposits or checks are discovered, assume that the errors were made by the company. Assume that all deposits are from cash sales. All checks are written to satisfy accounts payable.
2. Journalize the necessary entries. The accounts have not been closed.
3. What is the amount of cash that should appear on the balance sheet as of June 30?
4. If in preparing the bank reconciliation you note that a canceled check for $270 has been incorrectly recorded by the bank as $720, briefly explain how the error would be included in the bank reconciliation and how it should be corrected.

Alternate Accounting Application Problems

Alternate Problem 6-1B

Evaluating internal control of cash

Goals 1, 2, 3

STUDENT SOLUTIONS MANUAL

The following procedures were recently installed by The Recipe Company:

a. The bank reconciliation is prepared by the accountant.
b. Disbursements are made from the petty cash fund only after a petty cash receipt has been completed and signed by the payee.
c. Checks received through the mail are given daily to the accounts receivable clerk for recording collections on account and for depositing in the bank.
d. At the end of a shift, each cashier counts the cash in his or her cash register, unlocks the tape, and compares the amount of cash with the amount on the tape to determine cash shortages and overages.
e. Each cashier is assigned a separate cash register drawer to which no other cashier has access.
f. All sales are rung up on the cash register, and a receipt is given to the customer. All sales are recorded on a tape locked inside the cash register.
g. Vouchers and all supporting documents are perforated with a PAID designation after being paid by the treasurer.

Instructions:

Indicate whether each of the procedures of internal control over cash represents (1) a strength or (2) a weakness. For each weakness, indicate why it exists.

Alternate Problem 6-2B

Bank reconciliation and entries

Goals 4, 5

Adjusted balance, $21,506.10

STUDENT SOLUTIONS MANUAL

SPREADSHEET

The cash account for Viaduct Systems at March 31, 2004, indicated a balance of $17,474.35. The bank statement indicated a balance of $23,391.40 on March 31, 2004. Comparing the bank statement and the accompanying canceled checks and memorandums with the records reveals the following reconciling items:

a. Checks outstanding totaled $5,010.80.
b. A deposit of $3,215.50, representing receipts of March 31, had been made too late to appear on the bank statement.
c. The bank had collected $3,600 on a note left for collection. The face of the note was $3,000.
d. A check for $1,050 returned with the statement had been incorrectly recorded by Viaduct Systems as $1,500. The check was for the payment of an obligation to Bates Co. for the purchase of office supplies on account.
e. A check drawn for $878 had been incorrectly charged by the bank as $788.
f. Bank service charges for March amounted to $18.25.

Instructions:

1. Prepare a bank reconciliation.
2. Journalize the necessary entries. The accounts have not been closed.

Alternate Problem 6–3B

Bank reconciliation and entries

Goals 4, 5

Adjusted balance, $12,001.88

STUDENT SOLUTIONS MANUAL

SPREADSHEET

The cash account for Actuator Co. on June 1, 2004, indicated a balance of $6,911.95. During June, the total cash deposited was $70,500.40, and checks written totaled $67,568.47. The bank statement indicated a balance of $13,880.45 on June 30, 2004. Comparing the bank statement, the canceled checks, and the accompanying memorandums with the records revealed the following reconciling items:

a. Checks outstanding totaled $6,180.27.
b. A deposit of $4,481.70, representing receipts of June 30, had been made too late to appear on the bank statement.
c. A check for $310 had been incorrectly charged by the bank as $130.
d. A check for $257.25 returned with the statement had been recorded by Actuator Co. as $527.25. The check was for the payment of an obligation to Sylvester & Son on account.
e. The bank had collected for Actuator Co. $1,908 on a note left for collection. The face of the note was $1,800.
f. Bank service charges for June amounted to $20.

Instructions:

1. Prepare a bank reconciliation as of June 30.
2. Journalize the necessary entries. The accounts have not been closed.

Alternate Problem 6–4B

Bank reconciliation and entries

Goals 4, 5

Adjusted balance, $14,219.09

STUDENT SOLUTIONS MANUAL

SPREADSHEET

Mademoiselle Interiors deposits all cash receipts in a night depository, after banking hours. The data required to reconcile the bank statement as of August 31 have been taken from various documents and records and are reproduced as follows. The sources of the data are printed in capital letters. All checks were written for payments on account.

CASH ACCOUNT:
Balance as of August 1 $10,578.00

CASH RECEIPTS FOR MONTH OF AUGUST 6,305.60

DUPLICATE DEPOSIT TICKETS:
Date and amount of each deposit in August:

Date	Amount	Date	Amount	Date	Amount
Aug. 2	$569.50	Aug. 12	$580.70	Aug. 23	$ 731.45
5	701.80	16	600.10	27	601.50
10	819.24	20	701.26	31	1,000.05

CHECKS WRITTEN:
Number and amount of each check issued in August:

Check No.	Amount	Check No.	Amount	Check No.	Amount
614	$243.50	621	$309.50	628	$ 737.70
615	350.10	622	Void	629	329.90
616	279.90	623	Void	630	882.80
617	395.50	624	770.01	631	1,081.56
618	435.40	625	158.63	632	62.40
619	320.10	626	550.03	633	310.08
620	238.87	627	318.73	634	103.30

Total amount of checks issued in August $7,878.01

AUGUST BANK STATEMENT:

MEMBER FDIC
AMERICAN NATIONAL BANK OF DETROIT
DETROIT, MI 48201-2500 (313)933-8547

MADEMOISELLE INTERIORS

	ACCOUNT NUMBER	
	FROM 8/01/20–	TO 8/31/20–
	BALANCE	10,422.80
9	DEPOSITS	6,086.35
20	WITHDRAWALS	7,514.11
4	OTHER DEBITS AND CREDITS	5,150.50CR
	NEW BALANCE	14,145.54

CHECKS AND OTHER DEBITS					DEPOSITS	DATE	BALANCE
No.580	310.10	No.612	92.50		780.80	08/01	10,801.00
No.613	137.50	No.614	243.50		569.50	08/03	10,989.50
No.615	350.10	No.616	279.90		701.80	08/06	11,061.30
No.617	395.50	No.618	435.40		819.24	08/11	11,049.64
No.619	320.10	No.620	238.87		580.70	08/13	11,071.37
No.621	309.50	No.624	707.01		MS 5,000.00	08/14	15,054.86
No.625	158.63	No.626	550.03		MS 400.00	08/14	14,746.20
No.627	318.73	No.629	329.90		600.10	08/17	14,697.67
No.630	882.80	No.631	1,081.56	NSF 225.40		08/20	12,507.91
No.632	62.40	No.633	310.08		701.26	08/21	12,836.69
					731.45	08/24	13,568.14
					601.50	08/28	14,169.64
		SC	24.10			08/31	14,145.54

EC — ERROR CORRECTION
MS — MISCELLANEOUS
NSF — NOT SUFFICIENT FUNDS
OD — OVERDRAFT
PS — PAYMENT STOPPED
SC — SERVICE CHARGE

* * * * * * * * *

THE RECONCILEMENT OF THIS STATEMENT WITH YOUR RECORDS IS ESSENTIAL.
ANY ERROR OR EXCEPTION SHOULD BE REPORTED IMMEDIATELY.

BANK RECONCILIATION FOR PRECEDING MONTH:

Mademoiselle Interiors
Bank Reconciliation
July 31, 20–

Cash balance according to bank statement		$10,422.80
Add deposit of July 31, not recorded by bank		780.80
		$11,203.60
Deduct outstanding checks:		
No. 580	$310.10	
No. 602	85.50	
No. 612	92.50	
No. 613	137.50	625.60
Adjusted balance		$10,578.00
Cash balance according to depositor's records		$10,605.70
Deduct service charges		27.70
Adjusted balance		$10,578.00

Instructions:

1. Prepare a bank reconciliation as of August 31. If errors in recording deposits or checks are discovered, assume that the errors were made by the company. Assume that all deposits are from cash sales. All checks are written to satisfy accounts payable.
2. Journalize the necessary entries. The accounts have not been closed.
3. What is the amount of cash that should appear on the balance sheet as of August 31?
4. If in preparing the bank reconciliation you note that a canceled check for $275 has been incorrectly recorded by the bank as $725, briefly explain how the error would be included in the bank reconciliation and how it should be corrected.

Building Leadership Skills– Financial Analysis and Reporting Cases

Case 6–1

Control environment of a public corporation

Adolph Coors Company is a multinational brewer, marketer, and seller of beer and other malt-based beverages. For the year ending December 31, 2001, Coors reported sales of almost $2.9 billion and net income of $123 million. For large corporations such as Coors, maintaining a strong control environment is an everyday challenge. One method of maintaining a strong control environment is to have a strong Board of Directors that is actively engaged in overseeing the business.

Using the Internet, access the Coors December 30, 2001 10-K filing with the Securities and Exchange Commission. You can use the PriceWaterhouseCoopers Web site, http://edgarscan.pwcglobal.com, to search for company filings by name. Based upon the 10-K filing, answer the following questions:

1. List the members of the Board of Directors of Coors and identify whether any Board member is a manager with Coors.
2. Based upon your answer to (1), what percentage of the Board is not part of Coors' management team? Round to one decimal place.
3. Based upon your answer to (1), what percentage of the Board is a member of the Coors' family? Round to one decimal place.
4. What are the primary duties and responsibilities of the Audit Committee of the Board of Directors?
5. Who makes up the Audit Committee of the Board of Directors?
6. Was the Audit Committee active throughout the year?
7. Based upon your answers to (1)–(6), do you believe that the Board of Directors and the Audit Committee of the Board facilitate an effective control environment at Coors?

Case 6–2

Responsibility for internal controls of a public corporation

CVS Corporation is a leader in the retail drugstore industry in the United States, with net sales of $22.2 billion in fiscal 2001. As of December 2001, CVS operated over 4,000 retail and specialty pharmacy stores in 33 states and the District of Columbia.

Using the Internet, access the CVS December 29, 2001 10-K filing with the Securities and Exchange Commission. You can use the PriceWaterhouseCoopers Web site, http://edgarscan.pwcglobal.com, to search for company filings by name. Based upon the 10-K filing, answer the following questions:

1. Who is responsible for the integrity and objectivity of the financial statements of CVS?
2. What is the system of internal controls of CVS designed to accomplish?
3. In addition to management, who reviews the system of internal controls for improvements and modifications necessary because of changing business conditions?

(continued)

4. Who are the independent auditors of CVS?
5. Do you think having the Chief Executive Officer and Chief Financial Officer of CVS serve on its Audit Committee is a good way to foster an effective control environment?
6. Do members of the management team of CVS serve on the Audit Committee of the Board of Directors?

Case 6–3

Real-time financial statements

In the past, Cisco Systems needed over two weeks to adjust and close its accounting records each quarter in order to prepare financial statements. Using Internet technology to link its accounting information to its underlying business events, Cisco now uses what it calls a "virtual close." This means that the books are available for management decision making on a real-time basis. No longer does Cisco Systems' management need to wait until the end of an accounting period and closing cycle to receive financial information for decision making. Day-by-day financial information is accumulated and summarized for management so that it is able to plan and react to business conditions as required.

Which elements of Cisco's internal control would be most enhanced by a virtual close?

Case 6–4

Ratio of cash flow to net income

Home Depot, Inc. is the world's largest home improvement retailer, operating over 1,300 stores. The following data (in millions) for the years 2002 and 2001 were taken from Home Depot's 10-K filing with the Securities and Exchange Commission:

	For Year Ending:	
	February 2, 2002	**January 28, 2001**
CASH FLOWS FROM OPERATIONS:		
Net income	$3,044	$ 2,581
Reconciliation of Net income to Net Cash Provided by Operations:		
Depreciation and Amortization	764	601
Increase in Receivables, net	(119)	(246)
Increase in Merchandise Inventories	(166)	(1,075)
Increase in Accounts Payable and Accrued Liabilities	2,078	754
Increase in Income Taxes Payable	272	151
Other	90	30
Net Cash Provided by Operations	5,963	2,796

1. Compute the ratio of cash flow to net income for 2002 and 2001. Round to one decimal place.
2. Using the Internet, access the February 3, 2002 Home Depot 10-K filing with the Securities and Exchange Commission. Based upon the 10-K filing, determine whether the differences between 2002 and 2001 in inventories and accounts payable are due to changes in accounting methods or operational decisions by management.

Case 6–5

Ratio of cash flow to net income

Sears, Roebuck and Co. operates retail stores that sell a variety of merchandise, including Sears brands, such as Kenmore, Craftsman, and WeatherBeater. The following data (in millions) for the years 2001 and 2000 were taken from the Sears 10-K filing with the Securities and Exchange Commission:

	For the Years Ending:	
	December 29, 2001	December 30, 2000
Net cash flows from operating activities	$2,262	$2,702
Net income	735	1,343

1. Compute the ratio of cash flow to net income for 2001 and 2000. Round to one decimal place.
2. Compute the ratio of cash flow to net income after adjusting the 2001 net income for the selected changes shown below. Round to one decimal place.

Depreciation and amortization	decreased $150
Uncollectible receivable expense	increased 460
Asset impairment expense	increased 277

3. Does management's choice of accounting methods and estimates affect net income? Explain.

Case 6–6

Cash to monthly cash expenses ratio

Webvan was organized as an Internet retailer offering delivery of a variety of products, including food, nonprescription drugs, housewares, pet supplies, CDs, and books. The products were offered for sale and delivery through the Webvan's Webstore, which allowed customers to create a personal shopping list and schedule their deliveries. In 1999, Webvan raised over $400 million through issuing stock to the public. The following financial data (in thousands) were reported for the years ending December 31, 2000 and 1999:

	2000	1999
Net cash flows from operating activities	$(263,080)	$(58,798)
Cash, December 31	40,293	60,220

1. Determine the monthly cash expenses for each year. Round to the nearest dollar.
2. Determine the ratio of cash to monthly cash expenses for each year. Round to one decimal place.
3. Based on your analysis of (1) and (2), do you believe Webvan is still in business?

Case 6–7

Cash to monthly cash expenses ratio

Garden.com, Inc. was organized as an online gardening store. Through its Web site, http://www.garden.com, it provided customers with gardening information and resources and offered a broad selection of products and gardening advice. During 2000 and 1999, Garden.com raised over $70 million through issuing stock. The following financial data (in thousands) were reported for the years ending June 30, 2000 and 1999:

	2000	1999
Net cash flows from operating activities	$(32,764)	$(18,474)
Cash, June 30	9,047	15,340

1. Determine the monthly cash expenses for each year. Round to the nearest dollar.
2. Determine the ratio of cash to monthly cash expenses for each year. Round to one decimal place.
3. Based on your analysis of (1) and (2), do you believe Garden.com is still in business?

Case 6–8

Cash to monthly cash expenses ratio

Fashionmall.com, Inc. operates multiple Internet fashion Web sites, including http://www.fashionmall.com, http://www.outletmall.com, and http://www.boo.com. Fashionmall.com generates revenues by charging fees for the placement of store links and advertising on its Web sites. Its customers include traditional and online retailers and catalogs as well as manufacturers, magazines, and advertisers. During 1999, Fashionmall.com raised approximately $35 million from issuing stock to the public. The following financial data (in thousands) were reported for the years ending December 31, 2001 and 2000:

	2001	2000
Net cash flows from operating activities	$ (316)	$ (4,992)
Cash, December 31	15,947	26,592

1. Determine the monthly cash expenses for each year. Round to the nearest dollar.
2. Determine the ratio of cash to monthly cash expenses for each year. Round to one decimal place.
3. Based on your analysis of (1) and (2), do you believe Fashionmall.com is still in business?

Building Leadership Skills—Responsible Leadership

Activity 6–1

Ethics and professional conduct in business

ETHICS

In preparing the bank reconciliation for The Breadbasket Co., Lee Roberts, the assistant controller, discovered that City National Bank incorrectly recorded a $718 check written by The Breadbasket Co. as $178. Lee has decided not to notify the bank but wait for the bank to detect the error. Lee plans to record the $540 error as Other Income if the bank fails to detect the error within the next three months.

Discuss whether Lee is behaving in a professional manner.

Activity 6–2

Internal controls

The following is an excerpt from a conversation between two sales clerks, Karol Bolton and Bill Hall. Both Karol and Bill are employed by Zoom Electronics, a locally owned and operated computer retail store.

Karol: Did you hear the news?
Bill: What news?
Karol: Melanie and Richard were both arrested this morning.
Bill: What? Arrested? You're putting me on!
Karol: No, really! The police arrested them first thing this morning. Put them in handcuffs, read them their rights—the whole works. It was unreal!
Bill: What did they do?
Karol: Well, apparently they were filling out merchandise refund forms for fictitious customers and then taking the cash.
Bill: I guess I never thought of that. How did they catch them?
Karol: The store manager noticed that returns were twice that of last year and seemed to be increasing. When he confronted Melanie, she became flustered and admitted to taking the cash, apparently over $1,800 in just three months. They're going over the last six months' transactions to try to determine how much Richard stole. He apparently started stealing first.

Suggest appropriate control procedures that would have prevented or detected the theft of cash.

Activity 6–3

Internal controls

The following is an excerpt from a conversation between Jill Allen, store manager of Ethnic Grocery Stores, and Gary Malone, president of Ethnic Grocery Stores.

Gary: Jill, I'm concerned about this new scanning system.
Jill: What's the problem?
Gary: Well, how do we know the clerks are ringing up all the merchandise?
Jill: That's one of the strong points about the system. The scanner automatically rings up each item, based on its bar code. We update the prices daily, so we're sure that the sale is rung up for the right price.
Gary: That's not my concern. What keeps a clerk from pretending to scan items and then simply not charging his friends? If his friends were buying 10-15 items, it would be easy for the clerk to pass through several items with his finger over the bar code or just pass the merchandise through the scanner with the wrong side showing. It would look normal for anyone observing. In the old days, we at least could hear the cash register ringing up each sale.
Jill: I see your point.

Suggest ways that Ethnic Grocery Stores could prevent or detect the theft of merchandise as described.

Activity 6–4

Ethics and professional conduct in business

ETHICS

Devon Payne and Meredith Sibley are both cash register clerks for Mammoth Markets. Kelley Russell is the store manager for Mammoth Markets. The following is an excerpt of a conversation between Devon and Meredith:

Devon: Meredith, how long have you been working for Mammoth Markets?
Meredith: Almost five years this October. You just started two weeks ago . . . right?
Devon: Yes. Do you mind if I ask you a question?
Meredith: No, go ahead.

Devon: What I want to know is, have they always had this rule that if your cash register is short at the end of the day, you have to make up the shortage out of your own pocket?
Meredith: Yes, as long as I've been working here.
Devon: Well, it's the pits. Last week I had to pay in almost $30.
Meredith: It's not that big a deal. I just make sure that I'm not short at the end of the day.
Devon: How do you do that?
Meredith: I just short-change a few customers early in the day. There are a few jerks that deserve it anyway. Most of the time, their attention is elsewhere and they don't think to check their change.
Devon: What happens if you're over at the end of the day?
Meredith: Kelley lets me keep it as long as it doesn't get to be too large. I've not been short in over a year. I usually clear about $10 to $20 extra per day.

Discuss this case from the viewpoint of proper controls and professional behavior.

Activity 6–5

Bank reconciliation and internal control

The records of Pegasus Company indicate a March 31 cash balance of $9,806.05, which includes undeposited receipts for March 30 and 31. The cash balance on the bank statement as of March 31 is $8,004.95. This balance includes a note of $2,500 plus $200 interest collected by the bank but not recorded in the journal. Checks outstanding on March 31 were as follows: No. 670, $481.20; No. 679, $510; No. 690, $616.50; No. 1996, $127.40; No. 1997, $520; and No. 1999, $851.50.

On March 3, the cashier resigned, effective at the end of the month. Before leaving on March 31, the cashier prepared the following bank reconciliation:

Cash balance per books, March 31		$ 9,806.05
Add outstanding checks:		
No. 1996	$127.40	
1997	520.00	
1999	851.50	1,198.90
		$11,004.95
Less undeposited receipts		3,000.00
Cash balance per bank, March 31		$ 8,004.95
Deduct unrecorded note with interest		2,700.00
True cash, March 31		$ 5,304.95

Calculator Tape of Outstanding Checks:

0.00 *
127.40 +
520.00 +
851.50 +
1,198.90 *

Subsequently, the owner of Pegasus Company discovered that the cashier had stolen all undeposited receipts in excess of the $3,000 on hand on March 31. The owner, a close family friend, has asked your help in determining the amount that the former cashier has stolen.

1. Determine the amount the cashier stole from Pegasus Company. Show your computations in good form.
2. How did the cashier attempt to conceal the theft?
3. a. Identify two major weaknesses in internal controls, which allowed the cashier to steal the undeposited cash receipts.
   b. Recommend improvements in internal controls, so that similar types of thefts of undeposited cash receipts can be prevented.

Activity 6-6

Observe internal controls over cash

GROUP ACTIVITY

Select a business in your community and observe its internal controls over cash receipts and cash payments. The business could be a bank or a bookstore, restaurant, department store, or other retailer. In groups of three or four, identify and discuss the similarities and differences in each business's cash internal controls.

Activity 6-7

Invest excess cash

You have $50,000 cash. Go to the Web site of (or visit) a local bank and collect information about the savings and checking options that are available. Identify the option that is best for you and why it is best.

Answers to Self-Study Questions

1. **C** Compliance with laws and regulations (answer C) is an objective, not an element, of internal control. The control environment (answer A), monitoring (answer B), control procedures (answer D), risk assessment, and information and communication are the five elements of internal control.
2. **A** The policies and procedures that are established to safeguard assets, ensure accurate business information, and ensure compliance with laws and regulations are called internal controls (answer A). The three steps in setting up an accounting system are (1) analysis (answer B), (2) design (answer C), and (3) implementation (answer D).
3. **B** On any specific date, the cash account in a depositor's ledger may not agree with the account in the bank's ledger because of delays and/or errors by either party in recording transactions. The purpose of a bank reconciliation, therefore, is to determine the reasons for any differences between the two account balances. All errors should then be corrected by the depositor or the bank, as appropriate. In arriving at the adjusted (correct) cash balance according to the bank statement, outstanding checks must be deducted (answer B) to adjust for checks that have been written by the depositor but that have not yet been presented to the bank for payment.
4. **C** All reconciling items that are added to (answer A) and deducted from (answer B) the cash balance according to the depositor's records on the bank reconciliation (answer C) require that journal entries be made by the depositor to correct errors made in recording transactions or to bring the cash account up to date for delays in recording transactions.
5. **D** To avoid the delay, annoyance, and expense that are associated with paying all obligations by check, relatively small amounts (answer A) are paid from a petty cash fund. The fund is established by estimating the amount of cash needed to pay these small amounts during a specified period (answer B), and it is then reimbursed when the amount of money in the fund is reduced to a predetermined minimum amount (answer C).

Chapter 7
Receivables

THE LAW OF THE INNER CIRCLE
"A leader's potential is determined by those closest to him or her."
–The 21 Irrefutable Laws of Leadership
Dr. John C. Maxwell

Learning Goals

1. Describe the common classifications of receivables.
2. Summarize and provide examples of internal control procedures that apply to receivables.
3. Describe the nature of and the accounting for uncollectible receivables.
4. Describe the allowance method of accounting for uncollectible receivables.
5. Describe the direct write-off method of accounting for uncollectible receivables.
6. Describe the nature, characteristics, and accounting for notes receivable.
7. Describe the reporting of receivables on the balance sheet.
8. Describe the principles of managing accounts receivable.
9. Compute and interpret the accounts receivable turnover and the number of days' sales in receivables.

Starbucks Corporation

Starbucks was founded by Jerry Baldwin (an English teacher), Zev Siegel (a history teacher), and Gordon Bowker (a writer). All three shared a passion for fine coffee and tea. It was Gordon's idea to open a coffee shop in Seattle, and, with each investing $1,350 and with a $5,000 loan from a bank, they started Starbucks.

But they needed a name for their company. Gordon suggested *Pequod*, the name of the ship in Melville's *Moby Dick*. "Who would want to drink a cup of "Pee-quod?" the others protested. After researching turn-of-the-century mining camps on Mt. Rainer, they came up with Starbo, which after lengthy discussion became Starbucks, the first mate on the *Pequod*. The Starbucks logo is based upon a sixteenth-century wood carving of a two-tailed mermaid, or siren, around which was circled the company's name. The siren is intended to portray the seductive nature of Starbucks' coffees.

From its early beginnings in the 1970s until the mid-1980s, Starbucks Coffee, Tea, and Spice remained small, with only four Seattle stores. But Howard Schultz would soon change that. Starbucks first came to the attention of Schultz in 1981 when he was working for a Swedish kitchen equipment maker in New York. Noticing that Starbucks had ordered a large number of specialty coffee makers, he became curious and decided to visit the company on his next trip to the northwest.

Recognizing the potential of Starbucks, Schultz called one of the co-founders, Jerry Baldwin, and inquired about a job. But the co-founders were uncomfortable with Schultz's high-energy style and turned him down. However, Schultz wouldn't take "no" for an answer. A year later, the co-founders finally relented and hired Schultz as director of marketing and operations of the four Seattle stores.

Schultz left Starbucks after several years to start his own chain of specialty coffee stores. Schultz modeled his stores after espresso bars that he had visited while in Milan, Italy. These coffee bars not only served coffee, but they also served an important social role within the local communities. A year after opening his first coffee bar in Seattle, Schultz purchased the original Starbucks for almost $4 million and began to build a modern-day business success story.

With the backing of local investors, Schultz expanded Starbucks by opening stores in Chicago, Vancouver, Portland, and Los Angeles. After building a new roasting plant and expanding its headquarters in Seattle, Schultz decided to take Starbucks public in 1992. Starbucks is currently traded on NASDAQ under the symbol SBUX.

So what's Howard Schultz up to now? He gave up his chief executive officer (CEO) and president's role to Orin Smith, so that he can focus on Starbucks' global strategy. His formal title is Chief Global Strategist. In addition, he bought the Seattle Supersonics NBA basketball team for $250 million.

With its diverse business operations, Starbucks has a variety of assets, including over $95 million of accounts receivable at the end of its 2001 accounting period. In this chapter, we describe and illustrate accounting for such receivables and estimating the amount of receivables that will be uncollectible. For example, Starbucks estimates that over $4.5 million of its $95 million of receivables will be uncollectible.

Sources: Howard Schultz and Dori Jones Yang, *Pour Your Heart Into It* (Hyperion, New York: 1997); Starbucks Web site; "Biography, Howard Schultz, Starbucks," Myprimetime.com; "Stories of Entrepreneurs—Howard Schultz, Starbucks Coffee," National Commission on Entrepreneurship Web site.

Your Need to Know

Businesses and individuals engage in transactions that involve the exchange of goods and services for money. There are a number of ways that this is accomplished so that both parties are certain that value is being given and received as promised. In the simplest arrangement, an individual both makes payment and receives goods at the time of the transaction. If you purchase a CD player, you pay for the player and receive the player at the same time. There is no need for trusting the other party for future fulfillment of part of the transaction, since the transaction elements are simultaneous.

At other times, however, the transaction elements are not simultaneous; that is, one party is delayed in either providing the cash or the product/service. For example, the purchase of land often requires the buyer to provide "earnest money" to the seller. An independent third party, called an escrow agent, holds the money until final closing. This payment becomes part of the cash used to purchase the land upon closing. If the land is not purchased, however, the earnest money may be forfeited. Thus, the advance payment is used to show serious intent by the purchaser, but is held by an escrow agent to facilitate trust.

Goods and services may also be delivered before payment is received. This is most common when companies do business with each other. Unlike the individual consumer purchasing the CD player, a person purchasing for a business does not have control of the business checkbook. Rather, the supplier will invoice the customer for payment at a later time. This delay in payment facilitates internal control by separating the purchase decision from payment. For example, Hershey Foods Company will invoice Kroger supermarkets for delivery of chocolate candy to the store. Kroger will pay for the candy after delivery according to the terms of the invoice. This gives Kroger time to process the invoice. Hershey trusts Kroger to pay the invoice because of their successful history as business partners, coupled with Kroger's financial strength. Indeed, as an individual you might be able to move from cash-based transactions to transactions on a personal account. For example, a copy shop may agree to an account relationship after establishing trust from a history of cash-basis transactions.

Trust is a large part of business. Trust allows companies to avoid simultaneous cash transactions and use trade credit. Trade credit gives rise to accounts receivable for the seller, which is often a significant current asset for many businesses. In this chapter, we will discuss how to account for, disclose, manage, and analyze accounts and notes receivable.

Classification of Receivables

1 Describe the common classifications of receivables.

Many companies sell on credit in order to sell more services or products. The receivables that result from such sales are normally classified as accounts receivable or notes receivable. The term **receivables** includes all money claims against other entities, including people, business firms, and other organizations. These receivables are usually a significant portion of the total current assets. For example, an annual report of La-Z-Boy Chair Company reported that receivables made up over 60 percent of La-Z-Boy's current assets.

Accounts Receivable

The most common transaction creating a receivable is selling merchandise or services on credit. The receivable is recorded as a debit to the accounts receivable account. Such **accounts receivable** are normally expected to be collected within a relatively short period, such as 30 or 60 days. They are classified on the balance sheet as a current asset.

Notes Receivable

Notes receivable are amounts that customers owe for which a formal, written instrument of credit has been issued. As long as notes receivable are expected to be collected within a year, they are normally classified on the balance sheet as a current asset.

Notes are often used for credit periods of more than sixty days. For example, a dealer in automobiles or furniture may require a down payment at the time of sale and accept a note or a series of notes for the remainder. Such arrangements usually provide for monthly payments. For example, if you have purchased an automobile on credit, you probably signed a note. From your viewpoint, the note is a note payable. From the creditor's viewpoint, the note is a note receivable.

Notes may be used to settle a customer's account receivable. Notes and accounts receivable that result from sales transactions are sometimes called *trade receivables.* Unless stated otherwise, we will assume that all notes and accounts receivable in this chapter are from sales transactions.

Other Receivables

Other receivables are normally listed separately on the balance sheet. If they are expected to be collected within one year, they are classified as current assets. If collection is expected beyond one year, they are classified as noncurrent assets and reported under the caption *Investments. Other receivables* include interest receivable, taxes receivable, and receivables from officers or employees.

Ethics in Action
Sales and Collection Fraud

A sales transaction may involve "sales fraud" or "collection fraud." Sales fraud occurs when money is received in advance of the sale and the goods are either not delivered or are not what was promised. This type of fraud has occurred in eBay auctions where buyers must pay for the goods prior to receiving them. eBay's seller ratings help reduce the incidence of fraudulent sellers. In collection fraud, the goods are delivered to a customer that does not intend to pay for them. This type of fraud is common among customers of small businesses that fail to screen such customers by using credit reports and analyses.

Internal Controls for Receivables

2 Summarize and provide examples of internal control procedures that apply to receivables.

The principles of internal control that we discussed in Chapter 6 can be used to safeguard receivables. For example, the four functions of credit approval, sales, accounting, and collections should be separated, as shown in Exhibit 1.

Exhibit 1

Separating the Receivables Functions

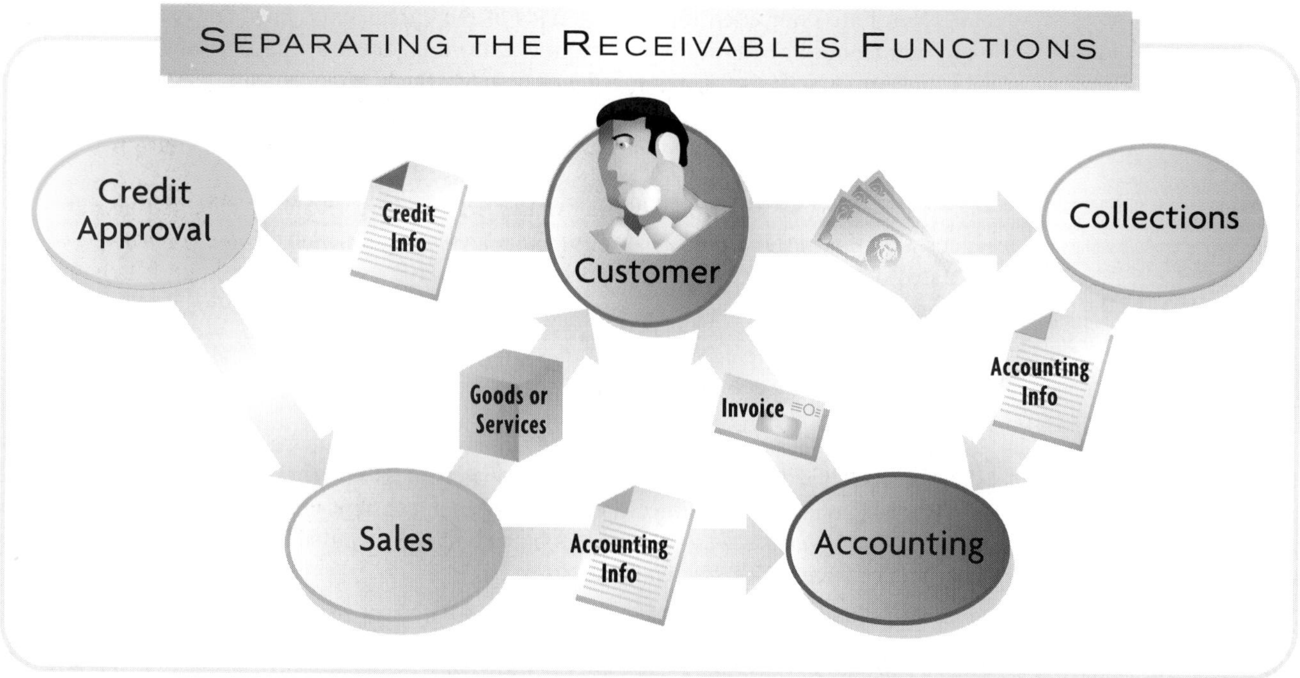

The individuals responsible for sales should be separate from the individuals accounting for the receivables and approving credit. By doing so, the accounting and credit approval functions serve as independent checks on sales. The employee who handles the accounting for receivables should not be involved with collecting receivables. Separating these functions reduces the possibility of errors and the misuse of funds.

Strategy in Business

Coffee Anyone?

Starbucks' objective is to become the leading retailer of specialty coffee. When planning new stores, Starbucks focuses on high-traffic, high-visibility locations that offer convenient access for pedestrians and drivers. Starbucks varies the size and format of its stores to fit the location. As a result, you may find Starbucks in a variety of locations, including downtown and suburban retail centers, office buildings, and university campuses. In addition to its retail operations, Starbucks is also attempting to develop its brand through a number of other distribution channels. These channels include Internet and mail-order access, grocery stores and supermarkets, warehouse clubs, hotels, airlines, and restaurants. Finally, Starbucks has entered into a variety of business alliances and joint ventures. One of these joint ventures is with Pepsi for the marketing of a bottled coffee drink, Frappuccino. Another is with Dreyer's Grand Ice Cream for marketing premium coffee ice creams.

Source: Starbucks Corporation Form 10-K filing with the Securities and Exchange Commission for the year ending September 30, 2001.

To illustrate the need to separate functions, assume that the accounts receivable billing clerk has access to cash receipts from customer collections. The clerk can steal a customer's cash payment and then alter the customer's monthly statement to indicate that the payment was received. The customer would not complain and the theft could go undetected.

To further illustrate the need for internal control of receivables, assume that salespersons have authority to approve credit. If the salespersons are paid commissions, say 10 percent of sales, they can increase their commissions by approving poor credit risks. Thus, the credit approval function is normally assigned to individuals outside the sales area.

Uncollectible Receivables

3 Describe the nature of and the accounting for uncollectible receivables.

In prior chapters, we described and illustrated the accounting for transactions involving sales of merchandise or services on credit. A major issue that we have not yet discussed in recording these transactions is that some of the customers will not pay their accounts. That is, some accounts receivable will be uncollectible.

Retail businesses may shift the risk of uncollectible receivables to other companies. For example, some retailers do not accept sales on account, but will only accept cash or credit cards. Such policies shift the risk to the credit card companies. Other retailers, however, such as Macy's, Sears, and JC Penney, have issued their own credit cards.

Companies may sell their receivables to other companies. This is often the case when a company issues its own credit card. Selling receivables is called *factoring* the receivables, and the buyer of the receivables is called a *factor*. An advantage of factoring is that the company selling its receivables receives immediate cash for operating and other needs. In addition, depending upon the factoring agreement, some of the risk of uncollectible accounts may be shifted to the factor.

Regardless of the care used in granting credit and the collection procedures used, a part of the credit sales will not be collectible. The operating expense incurred because of the failure to collect receivables is called **uncollectible accounts expense**, *bad debts expense*, or *doubtful accounts expense.*

Once a receivable is past due, companies should use procedures to maximize the collection of an account. After repeated attempts at collection, such procedures may include turning an account over to a collection agency.

When does an account or a note become uncollectible? There is no general rule for determining when an account is uncollectible. A debtor that fails to pay an account according to a sales contract or fails to pay a note on the due date does not necessarily mean that the account is uncollectible. The debtor's bankruptcy is one of the most significant indications of partial or complete uncollectibility. Other indications include the closing of the customer's business and the failure of repeated attempts to collect.

There are two methods of accounting for receivables that appear to be uncollectible. The **allowance method** provides an expense for uncollectible receivables in advance of their write-off.[1] The other procedure, called the **direct write-off method**, recognizes the expense only when accounts are judged to be worthless. We discuss each of these methods next.

---

1 The allowance method is not acceptable for federal income tax purposes for most taxpayers.

Allowance Method for Uncollectibles

4 Describe the allowance method of accounting for uncollectible receivables.

Most large businesses use the allowance method to estimate the uncollectible portion of their receivables. To illustrate this method, we will use assumed data for Richards Company. This new business began in August and chose to use the calendar year as its fiscal year. The accounts receivable account has a balance of $1,000,000 at the end of December.

The customer accounts making up the $1,000,000 balance in Accounts Receivable include some that are past due. However, Richards doesn't know which specific accounts will be uncollectible. Some accounts will be collected only in part, and others will become worthless. Based on a careful study, Richards estimates that a total of $40,000 will eventually be uncollectible. The following adjusting entry at the end of the fiscal period records this estimate:

Dec. 31	Uncollectible Accounts Expense	40,000	
	Allowance for Doubtful Accounts		40,000

Since the $40,000 reduction in accounts receivable is an estimate, specific customer accounts cannot be reduced or credited. Instead, a *contra asset* account entitled **Allowance for Doubtful Accounts** is credited.

As with all adjustments, the preceding entry serves two purposes. First, it reduces the value of the receivables to the amount of cash expected to be realized in the future. This amount, which is $960,000 ($1,000,000 − $40,000), is called the **net realizable value** of the receivables. Second, the adjusting entry matches the $40,000 expense of uncollectible accounts with the related revenues of the period.

If the balance of accounts receivable is $380,000 and the balance of the allowance for doubtful accounts is $56,000, what is the net realizable value of the receivables?

$324,000 ($380,000 − $56,000)

After the adjusting entry has been recorded, Accounts Receivable still has a balance of $1,000,000. This balance represents the total claims against customers on account. The balance of $40,000 in Allowance for Doubtful Accounts reduces the total Accounts Receivable to its net realizable value of $960,000. Uncollectible Accounts Expense of $40,000 is reported in the current-period income statement.

Write-Offs to the Allowance Account

When a customer's account is identified as uncollectible, it is written off against the allowance account. For example, John Parker's account of $6,000 with Richards Company is written off as follows:

Jan. 21	Allowance for Doubtful Accounts	6,000	
	Accounts Receivable—John Parker		6,000

The total write-offs against the allowance account during a period will rarely be equal to the amount in the account at the beginning of the period. The allowance account will have a credit balance at the end of the period if the write-offs during the period are less than the beginning balance. It will have a debit balance if the write-offs exceed the beginning balance. However, after the year-end adjusting entry is recorded, the allowance account should have a credit balance. The flow into and out of the allowance account can be illustrated as follows:

What happens if an account receivable that has been written off against the allowance account is later collected? In such cases, the account is reinstated by an entry that reverses the write-off entry. The cash received in payment is then recorded as a receipt on account. For example, assume that John Parker's account of $6,000 written off in the preceding entry is later collected on June 10. Richards Company records the reinstatement and the collection as follows:

June	10	Accounts Receivable—John Parker	6,000	
		Allowance for Doubtful Accounts		6,000
	10	Cash	6,000	
		Accounts Receivable—John Parker		6,000

Estimating Uncollectibles

How is the amount of uncollectible accounts estimated? The estimate of uncollectibles at the end of a fiscal period is based on past experience and forecasts of the future. When the general economy is doing well, the amount of uncollectible expense is normally less than it would be when the economy is doing poorly. The estimate of uncollectibles is usually based on either (1) the amount of sales, as shown on the income statement for the period, or (2) the amount of the receivables, as shown on the balance sheet at the end of the period, and the age of the receivable accounts.

Estimate Based on Sales Accounts receivable are created by credit sales. The amount of credit sales during the period may be used to estimate the amount of uncollectible accounts expense. This estimate is added to whatever balance exists in Allowance for Doubtful Accounts. For example, assume that the allowance account has a credit balance of $7,000 before any adjustment. It is estimated from past experience that 1% of the credit sales will be uncollectible. If credit sales for the period are $3,000,000, the adjustment for uncollectible accounts at the end of the period is as follows:

Dec. 31	Uncollectible Accounts Expense	30,000	
	Allowance for Doubtful Accounts		30,000

Before the year-end adjustment, Allowance for Doubtful Accounts has a credit balance of $45,000. Uncollectible accounts are estimated as 2% of credit sales of $1,200,000. The accounts receivable balance before adjustment is $290,000. What is (1) the uncollectible expense for the period, (2) the balance of Allowance for Doubtful Accounts after adjustment, and (3) the net realizable value of the receivables after adjustment?

(1) $24,000 (2% × $1,200,000); (2) $69,000 ($24,000 + $45,000); and (3) $221,000 ($290,000 − $69,000)

After the adjustment is recorded, the balance of the allowance account is $37,000. If there had been a debit balance of $2,000 in the allowance account before the year-end adjustment, the amount of the adjustment would still have been $30,000. The balance in the allowance account would have been $28,000 ($30,000 − $2,000).

The percentage of uncollectible accounts will vary across companies and industries. For example, in their annual reports, JC Penney reported 1.7% of its receivables as uncollectible, Deere & Company (manufacturer of John Deere tractors, etc.) reported only 1.0% of its dealer receivables as uncollectible, and Columbia HCA Healthcare Corporation reported 45.6% of its receivables as uncollectible.

The estimate-based-on-sales method *emphasizes the matching of uncollectible accounts expense with the related sales of the period.* Thus, this method places more emphasis on the income statement than on the balance sheet.

Estimate Based on Analysis of Receivables The longer an account receivable remains outstanding, the less likely that it will be collected. Thus, we can base the estimate of uncollectible accounts on how long the accounts have been outstanding. For this purpose, we can use a process called **aging the receivables.**

Receivables are aged by preparing a schedule that classifies each receivable by its due date. The number of days an account is past due is the number of days between the due date of the account and the date the aging schedule is prepared. To illustrate, assume that Rodriguez Company is preparing an aging schedule as of August 31. Its $160 account receivable for Saxon Woods Company was due on May 29. As of August 31, Saxon's account is 94 days past due, as shown below.

Number of days past due in May	2 days	(31 − 29)
Number of days past due in June	30 days	
Number of days past due in July	31 days	
Number of days past due in August	31 days	
Total number of days past due	94 days	

A portion of the aging schedule for Rodriguez is shown in Exhibit 2. The schedule shows the total amount of receivables in each aging class.

Exhibit 2

Aging of Accounts Receivable

			Days Past Due					
Customer	Balance	Not Past Due	1–30	31–60	61–90	91–180	181–365	over 365
Ashby & Co.	$ 150			$ 150				
B. T. Barr	610					$ 350	$260	
Brock Co.	470	$ 470						
Saxon Woods Co.	160					160		
Total	$86,300	$75,000	$4,000	$3,100	$1,900	$1,200	$800	$300

Rodriguez Company uses a sliding scale of percentages, based on industry or company experience, to estimate the amount of uncollectibles in each aging class, as shown in Exhibit 3. The total of these amounts is the desired balance for the Allowance for Doubtful Accounts, $3,390.

Exhibit 3

Estimate of Uncollectible Accounts

		Estimated Uncollectible Accounts	
Age Interval	Balance	Percent	Amount
Not past due	$75,000	2%	$1,500
1–30 days past due	4,000	5	200
31–60 days past due	3,100	10	310
61–90 days past due	1,900	20	380
91–180 days past due	1,200	30	360
181–365 days past due	800	50	400
Over 365 days past due	300	80	240
Total	$86,300		$3,390

Comparing the estimate of $3,390 with the unadjusted balance of the allowance account determines the amount of the adjustment for Uncollectible Accounts Expense. For example, assume that the unadjusted balance of the allowance account is a credit balance of $510. The amount to be added to this balance is therefore $2,880 ($3,390 − $510). The adjustment is recorded as follows:

Dec.	31	Uncollectible Accounts Expense	2,880	
		Allowance for Doubtful Accounts		2,880

Before the year-end adjustment, Allowance for Doubtful Accounts has a debit balance of $3,000. Using the aging-of-receivables method, the desired balance of the allowance for doubtful accounts is estimated as $55,000. The accounts receivable balance before adjustment is $290,000. What is (1) the uncollectible expense for the period, (2) the balance of Allowance for Doubtful Accounts after adjustment, and (3) the net realizable value of the receivables after adjustment?

(1) $58,000 ($3,000 + $55,000); (2) $55,000; and (3) $235,000 ($290,000 − $55,000)

After the adjustment is recorded, the credit balance in the allowance account is $3,390, the desired amount. The net realizable value of the receivables is $82,910 ($86,300 − $3,390). If the unadjusted balance of the allowance account had been a debit balance of $300, the amount of the adjustment would have been $3,690 ($3,390 + $300).

Estimates of the uncollectible accounts expense based on the analysis of receivables *emphasizes the current net realizable value of the receivables.* Thus, this method places more emphasis on the balance sheet than on the income statement.

Direct Write-Off Method for Uncollectibles

5 Describe the direct write-off method of accounting for uncollectible receivables.

The allowance method emphasizes reporting uncollectible accounts expense in the period in which the related sales occur. This method matches expenses with related revenues, and thus the allowance method is the preferred method of accounting for uncollectible receivables.

There are situations, however, where it is impossible to accurately estimate the uncollectibles. Also, if a business sells most of its goods or services on a cash basis, the amount of uncollectible expense is probably small. In such cases, receivables are also a small part of the current assets. Examples of such businesses are a restaurant, an attorney's office, and a small retail store, such as a hardware store. In such cases, the direct write-off method of recording uncollectible expense may be used.

Under the direct write-off method, uncollectible accounts expense is not recorded until an account is determined to be worthless. Thus, an allowance account and an adjusting entry are not needed at the end of the period. When an account is determined to be uncollectible, it is written off as follows:

May	10	Uncollectible Accounts Expense	4,200	
		Accounts Receivable—D. L. Ross		4,200

What if a customer later pays on an account that has been written off? If this happens, the account is reinstated by reversing the earlier write-off entry. For example, assume that the account written off in the May 10 entry is collected on November 21 of the same fiscal year. The reinstatement and receipt of cash is recorded as follows:

Nov.	21	Accounts Receivable—D. L. Ross	4,200	
		Uncollectible Accounts Expense		4,200
	21	Cash	4,200	
		Accounts Receivable—D. L. Ross		4,200

Notes Receivable

6 Describe the nature, characteristics, and accounting for notes receivable.

A claim supported by a note has some advantages over a claim in the form of an account receivable. By signing a note, the debtor recognizes the debt and agrees to pay it according to the terms listed. A note is thus a stronger legal claim.

Characteristics of Notes Receivable

A note receivable, or promissory note, is a written promise to pay a sum of money on demand or at a definite time. It is payable to the order of a person or firm or to the bearer or holder of the note. It is signed by the person or firm that makes the promise. The one to whose order the note is payable is called the *payee*, and the one making the promise is called the *maker.*

The date a note is to be paid is called the *due date* or *maturity date.* The period of time between the issuance date and the due date of a short-term note may be stated in either days or months. When the term of a note is stated in days, the due date is the specified number of days after its issuance. To illustrate, the due date of the 90-day note dated March 16 is June 14th, as shown below.

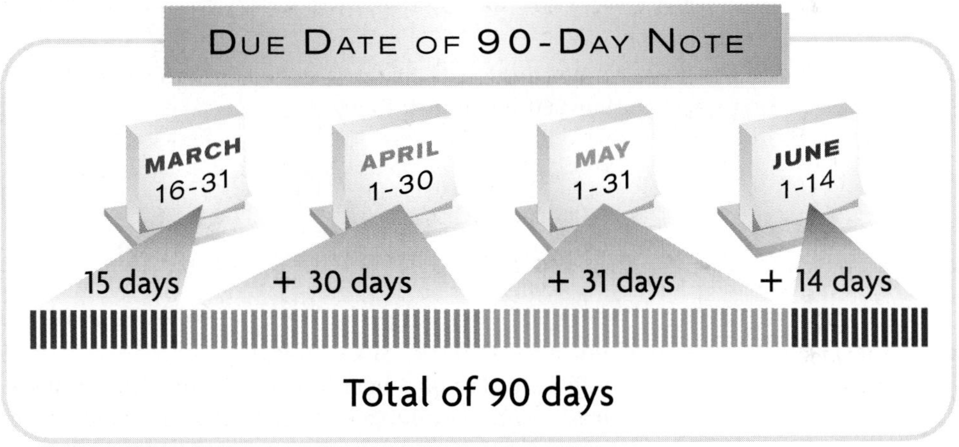

The term of a note may be stated as a certain number of months after the issuance date. In such cases, the due date is determined by counting the number of months from the issuance date. For example, a three-month note dated June 5 would be due on September 5. A two-month note dated July 31 would be due on September 30.

What is the due date of a 120-day note receivable dated September 9?

January 7 [21 days in September (30 days − 9 days) + 31 days in October + 30 days in November + 31 days in December + 7 days in January = 120 days]

A note normally specifies that interest be paid for the period between the issuance date and the due date.[2] Notes covering a period of time longer than one year normally provide for interest to be paid annually, semiannually, quarterly, or monthly. When the term of the note is less than one year, the interest is usually payable at the time the note is paid.

The interest rate on notes is normally stated in terms of a year, regardless of the actual period of time involved. Thus, the interest on $2,000 for one year at 12% is $240

2 You may occasionally see references to non-interest-bearing notes receivable. Such notes are not widely used and carry an assumed or implicit interest rate.

(12% × $2,000). The interest on $2,000 for 90 days at 12% is $60 ($2,000 × 12% × 90/360). To simplify computations, we will use 360 days per year. In practice, companies such as banks and mortgage companies use the exact number of days in a year, 365.

What is the maturity value of a $15,000, 90-day, 12% note?

$15,450 [$15,000 + ($15,000 × 0.12 × 90/360)]

The amount that is due at the maturity or due date of a note receivable is its **maturity value**. The maturity value of a note is the sum of the face amount and the interest. For example, the maturity value of a $25,000, 9%, 120-day note receivable is $25,750 [$25,000 + ($25,000 × 9% × 120/360)].

Accounting for Notes Receivable

A customer may use a note to replace an account receivable. To illustrate, assume that a company accepts a 30-day, 12% note dated November 21, 2005, in settlement of the account of W. A. Bunn Co., which is past due and has a balance of $6,000. The company records the receipt of the note as follows:

Nov. 21	Notes Receivable—W. A. Bunn	6,000	
	Accounts Receivable—W. A. Bunn		6,000

When the note matures, the company records the receipt of $6,060 ($6,000 principal plus $60 interest) as follows:

Dec. 21	Cash	6,060	
	Notes Receivable—W. A. Bunn		6,000
	Interest Revenue		60

If the maker of a note fails to pay the debt on the due date, the note is a **dishonored note receivable**. A company that holds a dishonored note transfers the face value of the note plus any interest due back to an accounts receivable account. For example, assume that the $6,000, 30-day, 12% note received from W. A. Bunn Co. and recorded on November 21 is dishonored at maturity. The company holding the note transfers the note and interest back to the customer's account, as follows:

Dec. 21	Accounts Receivable—W. A. Bunn	6,060	
	Notes Receivable—W. A. Bunn		6,000
	Interest Revenue		60

The company has earned the interest of $60, even though the note is dishonored. If the account receivable is uncollectible, the company will write off $6,060 against the Allowance for Doubtful Accounts.

If a note matures in a later fiscal period, the company holding the note records an adjustment for the interest accrued in the period in which the note is received. For example, assume that Crawford Company uses a 90-day, 12% note dated December 1, 2005, to settle its account, which has a balance of $4,000. Assuming that the accounting period ends on December 31, the holder of the note records the transactions as follows:

2005				
Dec.	1	Notes Receivable—Crawford Co.	4,000	
		Accounts Receivable—Crawford Co.		4,000
	31	Interest Receivable	40	
		Interest Revenue		40
2006				
Mar.	1	Cash	4,120	
		Notes Receivable—Crawford Co.		4,000
		Interest Receivable		40
		Interest Revenue		80

The interest revenue account is closed at the end of each accounting period. The amount of interest revenue is normally reported in the Other Income section of the income statement.

Reporting Receivables on the Balance Sheet

7 Describe the reporting of receivables on the balance sheet.

All receivables expected to be realized in cash within a year are presented in the Current Assets section of the balance sheet. These assets are normally listed in the order of their liquidity, that is, the order in which they are expected to be converted to cash during normal operations. The receivables are presented on Starbucks' balance sheet as shown below.[3]

ASSETS	Sept. 30, 2001	Oct. 1, 2000
	(in thousands)	
Current assets:		
Cash and cash equivalents	$113,237	$ 70,817
Marketable securities	107,312	61,336
Accounts receivable, net of allowances of $4,590 and $2,941, respectively	90,425	76,385
Inventories	221,253	201,656
Prepaid expenses and other current assets	61,698	48,040
Total current assets	$593,925	$458,234

INTERNATIONAL PERSPECTIVE

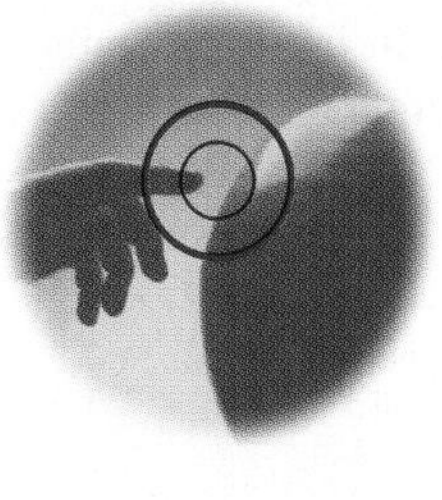

In Hungary, allowances for bad debts are reported as liabilities on the balance sheet, and receivables are shown at their gross amounts.

Starbucks reports net accounts receivable of $90,425 and $76,385. The allowances for doubtful accounts of $4,590 and $2,941 are subtracted from the total accounts receivable to arrive at the net receivables. Alternatively, the allowances for each year could be shown in a note to the financial statements.

3 Adapted from Starbucks Corporation 10-K dated September 30, 2001.

Other disclosures related to receivables are presented either on the face of the financial statements or in the accompanying notes.[4] Such disclosures include the market (fair) value of the receivables if significantly different from the reported value. In addition, if unusual credit risks exist within the receivables, the nature of the risks should be disclosed. For example, if the majority of the receivables are due from one customer or are due from customers located in one area of the country or one industry, these facts should be disclosed.

Starbucks did not report any unusual credit risks related to its receivables. However, the following credit risk disclosure appeared in the financial statements of Deere & Company:

> *Credit receivables have significant concentrations of credit risk in the agricultural, industrial, lawn and grounds care, and recreational (non-Deere equipment) business sectors. . . . The portion of credit receivables related to the agricultural equipment business was 60%; that related to the industrial equipment business was 12%; that related to the lawn and grounds care equipment business was 7%; and that related to the recreational equipment business was 21%. On a geographic basis, there is not a disproportionate concentration of credit risk in any area. . . .*

Managing Accounts Receivable

8 Describe the principles of managing accounts receivable.

Businesses grant credit in order to earn additional profits from customers who would otherwise not purchase the company's goods or services. Thus, the overall objective of managing accounts receivable is to help the company earn profits. The basic steps in managing accounts receivables include the following:

1. Screening customers
2. Determining credit terms
3. Monitoring collections

Screening Customers

Screening customers involves assessing which customers should be granted credit. Too strict a credit-screening process causes the company to lose revenues and profits from customers who would otherwise pay their accounts on time. Too loose a credit-screening process causes the company to extend credit to customers who do not pay. Not only does the company lose any profits on nonpaying customers, but the company also incurs the expense of providing the goods or services to the customers as well as the additional expense of trying to collect the amounts due. For this reason, too loose a credit-screening process can be more costly than too tight a policy.

Most businesses have formal credit-screening procedures that include customer-submitted documentation of creditworthiness. For example, if you apply for a credit card, you have to fill out an application form. Likewise, if you apply for a student loan or home mortgage, you have to fill out a loan application form. In addition, loan applications normally require the customer to also submit other documents, such as recent tax returns or bank statements.

Business customers that apply for credit often are asked to submit recent financial statements with their credit applications. Sometimes the seller will also require a letter of credit

---

4 *Statements of Financial Accounting Standards, No. 105*, "Disclosures of Information about Financial Instruments with Off-Balance Sheet Risk and Financial Instruments with Concentrations of Credit Risk," and *No. 107*, "Disclosures about Fair Value of Financial Instruments," Financial Accounting Standards Board, Norwalk.

from the business's bank. The letter of credit documents that the business has funds available to pay the seller. Letters of credit are often required when a buyer is purchasing goods from overseas sellers. In rare cases, a seller may also require the customer's bank to guarantee the credit of the buyer.

Once the seller receives the buyer's credit application and documents, the seller analyzes the buyer's creditworthiness. In addition to analyzing the application and documents submitted by the buyer, the seller usually requests an independent credit report and often will contact the buyer's banking and other credit references. The *Dun & Bradstreet Reference Book of American Business* provides credit ratings for many business customers. The amount of analysis for a customer will, of course, vary with the size of the buyer's purchases. For example, credit card applications with credit limits of $1,500 do not receive as much analysis and independent verification as a business's credit application for a $500,000 purchase.

Determining Credit Terms

Once a seller has decided to grant credit to a buyer, the seller must determine credit terms for the sale. Credit terms include determining the amount of credit, called the *credit limit*, and the payment terms. The credit limit is set consistent with the creditworthiness of the customer. New customers often receive a small limit that is increased over time as the customer pays accounts and thus establishes a good credit history with the seller.

The payment terms are often set so that they are consistent with the seller's industry and competitors. For example, MasterCard and Visa's payment terms require full or partial payment within 30 days. Any amounts due after 30 days are subject to interest charges. Likewise, businesses often set payment terms of 2/10, n/30. As we discussed in Chapter 5, these terms offer the buyer a 2% discount if the invoice is paid within 10 days, with the entire amount due within 30 days. Regardless of the payment terms, the seller should communicate them to the buyer at the time of sale. In most cases, the payment terms are stated on the sales invoice.

Monitoring Collections

Effective internal controls over receivables and credit granting require the seller to monitor collections of receivables on a routine basis. One means of monitoring receivables and collections is to prepare an aging schedule. We illustrated the aging of receivables earlier in this chapter.

Ethics in Action

Seller Beware

A company in financial distress will still try to purchase goods and services on account. In these cases, rather than "buyer beware," it is more like "seller beware." Sellers must be careful in advancing credit to such companies, because trade creditors have low priority for cash payments in the event of bankruptcy. To help suppliers, third-party services specialize in evaluating financially distressed customers. These services analyze credit risk for these firms by evaluating recent management payment decisions (who is getting paid and when), court actions (if in bankruptcy), and other supplier credit tightening or suspension actions. Such information helps a supplier monitor and tune trade credit amounts and terms with the financially distressed customer.

In addition to preparing aging schedules, sellers should monitor concentrations of credit risk in any one customer or class of customers. For example, a concentration of credit risk with any one customer could subject a seller to a large accounts receivable write-off if the customer experiences financial difficulty or goes bankrupt. As we discussed in the preceding section, generally accepted accounting principles require the disclosure of credit risks in notes to the financial statements. An example of such a disclosure for Deere & Company was shown in the preceding section. An example of a credit risk note for Delta Air Lines is shown below.

Our accounts receivable are generated largely from the sale of passenger airline tickets and cargo transportation services to customers. The majority of these sales are processed through major credit card companies, resulting in accounts receivable which are generally short-term in duration. We also have receivables from the sale of mileage credits to partners, such as credit card companies, hotels and car rental agencies, that participate in our SkyMiles program. We believe that the credit risk associated with these receivables is minimal and that the allowance for bad debts that we have provided is sufficient.

Accounts Receivable Turnover and Days' Sales in Receivables

9 Compute and interpret the accounts receivable turnover and the number of days' sales in receivables.

In addition to preparing an aging of receivables schedule and monitoring concentrations of credit risk, several financial statement ratios are also useful in monitoring receivables and their collection. Two of these ratios are described and illustrated in the following paragraphs.

Businesses granting long credit terms normally have relatively greater amounts tied up in accounts receivable than those granting short credit terms. In either case, businesses normally desire to collect receivables as promptly as possible. The cash collected from receivables improves solvency and lessens the risk of loss from uncollectible accounts. Two financial measures that are especially useful in evaluating the efficiency in collecting receivables are (1) the accounts receivable turnover and (2) the number of days' sales in receivables.

The **accounts receivable turnover** measures how frequently during the year the accounts receivable are being converted to cash. For example, with credit terms of 2/10, n/30 days, the accounts receivable should turn over more than twelve times per year. The accounts receivable turnover is computed as follows:[5]

$$\text{Accounts receivable turnover} = \frac{\text{Net sales}}{\text{Average accounts receivable}}$$

The average accounts receivable can be determined by using monthly data or by simply adding the beginning and ending accounts receivable balances and dividing by two. For example, using the following financial data for Starbucks, the 2001 accounts receivable turnover is computed as 31.8, as shown below.

	Sept. 30, 2001	Oct. 1, 2000	Oct. 3, 1999
Net revenues	$2,648,980	$2,177,614	$1,680,145
Net accounts receivable	90,425	76,385	47,646

5 If known, credit sales should be used in the numerator. Because credit sales are not normally known by external users, we use net sales in the numerator.

$$\text{Accounts receivable turnover} = \frac{\text{Net sales}}{\text{Average accounts receivable}} = \frac{\$2{,}648{,}980}{(\$90{,}425 + \$76{,}385)/2} = 31.8$$

By computing the accounts receivable turnover for the prior year, shown below, we can determine whether Starbucks' management of accounts receivable has improved.

$$\text{Accounts receivable turnover} = \frac{\text{Net sales}}{\text{Average accounts receivable}} = \frac{\$2{,}177{,}614}{(76{,}385 + \$47{,}646)/2} = 35.1$$

What is the accounts receivable turnover if the net sales is $1,280,000 and the average accounts receivable is $200,000?

6.4 [$1,280,000/$200,000]

The 2000 accounts receivable turnover for Starbucks is 35.1. Thus, Starbucks did not improve its management of accounts receivable during 2001.

The **number of days' sales in receivables** is an estimate of the length of time the accounts receivable have been outstanding. With credit terms of 2/10, n/30 days, the number of days' sales in receivables should be less than 20 days. It is computed as follows:

$$\text{Number of days' sales in receivables} = \frac{\text{Accounts receivable, end of year}}{\text{Average daily sales}}$$

Average daily sales in receivables are determined by dividing net sales by 365 days. For example, using the preceding data for Starbucks, the number of days' sales in receivables is 12.5 and 12.8 for 2001 and 2000, respectively.

		2001	2000
Number of days' sales in receivables =	$\frac{\text{Accounts receivable, end of year}}{\text{Average daily sales}}$ =	$\frac{\$90{,}425}{(\$2{,}648{,}980/365)}$	$\frac{\$76{,}385}{(\$2{,}177{,}614/365)}$
		12.5 days	12.8 days

The number of days' sales in receivables has declined during 2001. Generally, this would be viewed as a favorable trend. That is, the efficiency in collecting accounts receivable has improved when the number of days' sales in receivables decreases. However, these measures should also be compared with similar companies within the industry. For example, Diedrich Coffee Inc. is a specialty coffee roaster, wholesaler, and retailer. Diedrich reports an accounts receivable turnover of 35.4 and 8.7 days' sales in receivables. While Diedrich is significantly smaller than Starbucks, the differences in the days' sales in receivables could be worth investigating.

Focus on Cash Flow

Accounts Receivable and Cash Flows

Most retail companies sell merchandise for cash and on account. When merchandise is sold on account, an account receivable is recorded. If accounts receivable increase from one period to the next, then the amount of revenue shown on the

(continued)

income statement does not represent the amount of cash received from revenue during the period. Instead, part of the revenue includes sales on account (accounts receivable) not collected during the period. Thus, to determine the cash flows from revenue activities, any increase or decrease in accounts receivable must be considered.

For example, assume that Bower Company reports total revenues of $760,000 during 2005 and that accounts receivable increased during the year from $45,000 to $63,000. Thus, the amount of cash received from Bower's revenues during 2005 is not $760,000, but rather $742,000. That is, of the $760,000 of total revenue during the year, $18,000 ($63,000 − $45,000) represents revenue that was created by increasing sales on account. Likewise, assume that instead of increasing by $18,000, Bower's accounts receivable had decreased by $15,000 (from $45,000 to $30,000) during 2005. In this case, the cash received from revenue activities would have been $775,000 ($760,000 + $15,000).

In reporting cash flows from operating activities on the statement of cash flows, companies are required to reconcile net income with cash flows from operating activities. In doing so, companies must consider the effect of increases and decreases of their accounts receivable on their cash flows from revenue activities. As illustrated above, if accounts receivable increase, the increase must be deducted in arriving at cash flows. During 2001, Starbucks' accounts receivable increased by $14,040 ($90,425 − $76,385). Thus, on its statement of cash flows, Starbucks must deduct this increase to arrive at cash flows from operating activities, as shown below.[6]

Net earnings	$181,210
Increase in accounts receivable	(14,040)
~~	
Net cash flows from operating activities	$460,826

6 Adapted from Starbucks Corporation Form 10-K filing with the Securities and Exchange Commission. Small differences in reported amounts may appear due to reclassifications within the financial statements.

Summary of Learning Goals

1 Describe the common classifications of receivables.

The term receivables includes all money claims against other entities, including people, business firms, and other organizations. Receivables are normally classified as accounts receivable, notes receivable, or other receivables.

2 Summarize and provide examples of internal control procedures that apply to receivables.

The internal controls that apply to receivables include the separation of responsibilities for related functions. In this way, the work of one employee can serve as a check on the work of another employee.

3 Describe the nature of and the accounting for uncollectible receivables.

The two methods of accounting for uncollectible receivables are the allowance method and the direct write-off method. The allowance method provides in advance for uncollectible receivables. The direct write-off method recognizes the expense only when the account is judged to be uncollectible.

4 Describe the allowance method of accounting for uncollectible receivables.

A year-end adjusting entry provides for (1) the reduction of the value of the receivables to the amount of cash expected to be realized from them in the future and (2) the allocation to the current period of the expected expense resulting from such reduction. The adjusting entry debits Uncollectible Accounts Expense and credits Allowance for Doubtful Accounts. When an account is believed to be uncollectible, it is written off against the allowance account.

When the estimate of uncollectibles is based on the amount of sales for the period, the adjusting entry is made without regard to the balance of the allowance account. When the estimate of uncollectibles is based on the amount and the age of the receivable accounts at the end of the period, the adjusting entry is recorded so that the balance of the allowance account will equal the estimated uncollectibles at the end of the period.

The allowance account, which will have a credit balance after the adjusting entry has been posted, is a contra asset account. The uncollectible accounts expense is generally reported on the income statement as an administrative expense.

5 Describe the direct write-off method of accounting for uncollectible receivables.

Under the direct write-off method, the entry to write off an account debits Uncollectible Accounts Expense and credits Accounts Receivable. Neither an allowance account nor an adjusting entry is needed at the end of the period.

6 Describe the nature, characteristics, and accounting for notes receivable.

A note is a written promise to pay a sum of money on demand or at a definite time. Characteristics of notes that affect how they are recorded and reported include the due date, interest rate, and maturity value. The basic formula for computing interest on a note is: Principal $\times$ Rate $\times$ Time $=$ Interest. The due date is the date a note is to be paid, and the period of time between the issuance date and the due date is normally stated in either days or months. The maturity value of a note is the sum of the face amount and the interest.

A note received in settlement of an account receivable is recorded as a debit to Notes Receivable and a credit to Accounts Receivable. When a note matures, Cash is debited, Notes Receivable is credited, and Interest Revenue is credited. If the maker of a note fails to pay the debt on the due date, the note is said to be dishonored. The holder of a dishonored note debits an accounts receivable account for the amount of the claim against the maker of the note.

7 Describe the reporting of receivables on the balance sheet.

All receivables that are expected to be realized in cash within a year are presented in the Current Assets section of the balance sheet. It is normal to list the assets in the order of their liquidity, which is the order in which they can be converted to cash in normal operations. In addition to the allowance for doubtful accounts, additional receivable disclosures include the market (fair) value and unusual credit risks.

8 Describe the principles of managing accounts receivable.

Businesses grant credit in order to earn additional profits from customers who would otherwise not purchase the company's goods or services. Thus, the overall objective of managing accounts receivable is to help the company earn profits. The basic steps in managing accounts receivable include (1) screening customers, (2) determining credit terms, and (3) monitoring collections.

9 Compute and interpret the accounts receivable turnover and the number of days' sales in receivables.

The accounts receivable turnover is net sales divided by average accounts receivable. It measures how frequently accounts receivable are being converted into cash. The number of days' sales in receivables is the end-of-year accounts receivable divided by the average daily sales. It measures the length of time the accounts receivable have been outstanding.

Glossary

Accounts receivable A receivable created by selling merchandise or services on credit.

Accounts receivable turnover Measures how frequently during the year the accounts receivable are being converted to cash.

Aging the receivables The process of analyzing the accounts receivable and classifying them according to various age groupings, with the due date being the base point for determining age.

Allowance for doubtful accounts The contra asset account for accounts receivable.

Allowance method The method of accounting for uncollectible accounts that provides an expense for uncollectible receivables in advance of their write-off.

Direct write-off method The method of accounting for uncollectible accounts that recognizes the expense only when accounts are judged to be worthless.

Dishonored note receivable A note that the maker fails to pay on the due date.

Maturity value The amount that is due at the maturity or due date of a note.

Net realizable value The amount of cash expected to be realized in the future from a receivable.

Notes receivable Amounts customers owe, for which a formal, written instrument of credit has been issued.

Number of days' sales in receivables An estimate of the length of time the accounts receivable have been outstanding.

Receivables All money claims against other entities, including people, business firms, and other organizations.

Uncollectible accounts expense The operating expense incurred because of the failure to collect receivables.

Illustrative Accounting Application Problem

Ditzler Company, a construction supply company, uses the allowance method of accounting for uncollectible accounts receivable. Selected transactions completed by Ditzler Company are as follows:

Feb.	1	Sold merchandise on account to Ames Co., $8,000. The cost of the merchandise sold was $4,500.
Mar.	15	Accepted a 60-day, 12% note for $8,000 from Ames Co. on account.
Apr.	9	Wrote off a $2,500 account from Dorset Co. as uncollectible.
	21	Loaned $7,500 cash to Jill Klein, receiving a 90-day, 14% note.
May	14	Received the interest due from Ames Co. and a new 90-day, 14% note as a renewal of the loan. (Record both the debit and the credit to the notes receivable account.)
June	13	Reinstated the account of Dorset Co., written off on April 9, and received $2,500 in full payment.
July	20	Jill Klein dishonored her note.
Aug.	12	Received from Ames Co. the amount due on its note of May 14.
	19	Received from Jill Klein the amount owed on the dishonored note, plus interest for 30 days at 15%, computed on the maturity value of the note.
Dec.	16	Accepted a 60-day, 12% note for $12,000 from Global Company on account.
	31	It is estimated that 3% of the credit sales of $1,375,000 for the year ended December 31 will be uncollectible.

Instructions

1. Journalize the transactions.
2. Journalize the adjusting entry to record the accrued interest on December 31 on the Global Company note.

Solution

1.

Feb.	1	Accounts Receivable—Ames Co.	8,000	
		Sales		8,000
	1	Cost of Merchandise Sold	4,500	
		Merchandise Inventory		4,500

Mar.	15	Notes Receivable—Ames Co.	8,000	
		Accounts Receivable—Ames Co.		8,000
Apr.	9	Allowance for Doubtful Accounts	2,500	
		Accounts Receivable—Dorset Co.		2,500
	21	Notes Receivable—Jill Klein	7,500	
		Cash		7,500
May	14	Notes Receivable—Ames Co.	8,000	
		Cash	160	
		Notes Receivable—Ames Co.		8,000
		Interest Revenue		160
June	13	Accounts Receivable—Dorset Co.	2,500	
		Allowance for Doubtful Accounts		2,500
	13	Cash	2,500	
		Accounts Receivable—Dorset Co.		2,500
July	20	Accounts Receivable—Jill Klein	7,762.50	
		Notes Receivable—Jill Klein		7,500.00
		Interest Revenue		262.50
Aug.	12	Cash	8,280	
		Notes Receivable—Ames Co.		8,000
		Interest Revenue		280
	19	Cash	7,859.53	
		Accounts Receivable—Jill Klein		7,762.50
		Interest Revenue		97.03
		($7,762.50 × 15% × 30/360)		
Dec.	16	Notes Receivable—Global Company	12,000	
		Accounts Receivable—Global Company		12,000
	31	Uncollectible Accounts Expense	41,250	
		Allowance for Doubtful Accounts		41,250

2.

Dec.	31	Interest Receivable	60	
		Interest Revenue		60
		($12,000 × 12% × 15/360)		

Self-Study Questions

Answers at end of chapter

1. At the end of the fiscal year, before the accounts are adjusted, Accounts Receivable has a balance of $200,000 and Allowance for Doubtful Accounts has a credit balance of $2,500. If the estimate of uncollectible accounts determined by aging the receivables is $8,500, the amount of uncollectible accounts expense is:
   - A. $2,500
   - B. $6,000
   - C. $8,500
   - D. $11,000

2. At the end of the fiscal year, Accounts Receivable has a balance of $100,000 and Allowance for Doubtful Accounts has a balance of $7,000. The expected net realizable value of the accounts receivable is:
   A. $7,000
   B. $93,000
   C. $100,000
   D. $107,000

3. What is the maturity value of a 90-day, 12% note for $10,000?
   A. $8,800
   B. $10,000
   C. $10,300
   D. $11,200

4. What is the due date of a $12,000, 90-day, 8% note receivable dated August 5?
   A. October 31
   B. November 2
   C. November 3
   D. November 4

5. When a note receivable is dishonored, Accounts Receivable is debited for what amount?
   A. The face value of the note
   B. The maturity value of the note
   C. The maturity value of the note less accrued interest
   D. The maturity value of the note plus accrued interest

Discussion Questions

1. What are the three classifications of receivables?
2. What types of transactions give rise to accounts receivable?
3. In what section of the balance sheet should a note receivable be listed if its term is (a) 120 days, (b) 6 years?
4. Give two examples of other receivables.
5. The accounts receivable clerk is also responsible for handling cash receipts. Which principle of internal control is violated in this situation?
6. Which of the two methods of accounting for uncollectible accounts provides for the recognition of the expense at the earlier date?
7. What kind of an account (asset, liability, etc.) is Allowance for Doubtful Accounts, and is its normal balance a debit or a credit?
8. After the accounts are adjusted and closed at the end of the fiscal year, Accounts Receivable has a balance of $783,150 and Allowance for Doubtful Accounts has a balance of $41,694. Describe how the accounts receivable and the allowance for doubtful accounts are reported on the balance sheet.
9. A firm has consistently adjusted its allowance account at the end of the fiscal year by adding a fixed percent of the period's net sales on account. After five years, the balance in Allowance for Doubtful Accounts has become very large in relationship to the balance in Accounts Receivable. Give two possible explanations.
10. Which of the two methods of estimating uncollectibles provides for the most accurate estimate of the current net realizable value of the receivables?
11. For a business, what are the advantages of a note receivable in comparison to an account receivable?
12. Fryer Company issued a note receivable to Corbett Company. (a) Who is the payee? (b) What is the title of the account used by Corbett Company in recording the note?
13. If a note provides for payment of principal of $75,000 and interest at the rate of 8%, will the interest amount to $6,000? Explain.
14. The maker of a $6,000, 10%, 120-day note receivable failed to pay the note on the due date of April 30. What accounts should be debited and credited by the payee to record the dishonored note receivable?
15. The note receivable dishonored in Question 14 is paid on May 30 by the maker, plus interest for 30 days, 9%. What entry should be made to record the receipt of the payment?
16. Under what caption should accounts receivable be reported on the balance sheet?

17. To reduce its uncollectible accounts expense, Adang Inc. decided to quit granting credit to customers. Is this a wise decision by Adang Inc.? Explain.
18. The accounts receivable turnover increased, while the number of days' sales in receivables decreased for the current year for Nackerud Co. Are changes for the current year good or bad? Explain.

Exercises

Exercise 7–1

Classifications of receivables

Goal 1

The Boeing Company is one of the world's major aerospace firms, with operations involving commercial aircraft, military aircraft, missiles, satellite systems, and information and battle management systems. As of December 31, 2001, Boeing had $2,597 million of receivables involving U.S. government contracts and $679 million of receivables involving commercial aircraft customers, such as Delta Air Lines and United Airlines. Should Boeing report these receivables separately in the financial statements, or combine them into one overall accounts receivable amount? Explain.

Exercise 7–2

Internal control procedures

Goal 2

STUDENT SOLUTIONS MANUAL

Lunar Company sells carpeting. Over 60% of its carpet sales are on credit. The following procedures are used by Lunar to process this large number of credit sales and the subsequent collections:

a. All credit sales to a first-time customer must be approved by the Credit Department. Salespersons will assist the customer in filling out a credit application, but an employee in the Credit Department is responsible for verifying employment and checking the customer's credit history before granting credit.
b. Lunar's standard credit period is 30 days. The Credit Department may approve an extension of this repayment period of up to one year. Whenever an extension is granted, the customer signs a promissory note. Up to 10% of the credit sales in any one year are for repayment periods exceeding 30 days.
c. A formal ledger is not maintained for customers who sign promissory notes. Lunar simply keeps a copy of each signed note in a file cabinet. These unpaid notes are filed by due date.
d. Lunar employs an accounts receivable clerk. The clerk is responsible for recording customer credit sales (based on sales tickets), receiving cash from customers, giving customers credit for their payments, and handling all customer billing complaints.

(continued)

e. The general ledger controlling account for Accounts Receivable is maintained by the General Accounting Department at Lunar. This department records total credit sales, based on credit sales information from the store's electronic cash register, and total customer receipts, based on the bank deposit slip.

State whether each of these procedures is appropriate or inappropriate, considering the principles of internal control. If inappropriate, state which internal control procedure is violated.

Exercise 7-3

Nature of uncollectible accounts

Goal 3

a. 4.3%

Hilton Hotels Corporation owns and operates casinos at several of its hotels, located primarily in Nevada. At the end of one fiscal year, the following accounts and notes receivable were reported (in thousands):

Hotel accounts and notes receivable	$75,796	
Less: Allowance for doubtful accounts	3,256	
		$72,540
Casino accounts receivable	$26,334	
Less: Allowance for doubtful accounts	6,654	
		19,680

a. Compute the percentage of the allowance for doubtful accounts to the gross hotel accounts and notes receivable for the end of the fiscal year.
b. Compute the percentage of the allowance for doubtful accounts to the gross casino accounts receivable for the end of the fiscal year.
c. Discuss possible reasons for the difference in the two ratios computed in (a) and (b).

Exercise 7-4

Number of days past due

Goal 4

The Body Shop, 58 days

STUDENT SOLUTIONS MANUAL

Diamond Auto Supply distributes new and used automobile parts to local dealers throughout the Southeast. Diamond's credit terms are n/30. As of the end of business on July 31, the following accounts receivable were past due.

Account	Due Date	Amount
The Body Shop	June 3	$3,000
Custom Auto	July 1	2,500
Hometown Repair	March 22	500
Jake's Auto Repair	May 19	1,000
Like New	June 18	750
Sally's	April 12	1,800
Uptown Auto	May 8	500
Westside Repair & Tow	May 31	1,100

Determine the number of days each account is past due.

Exercise 7–5

Aging-of-receivables schedule

Goal 4

SPREADSHEET

The accounts receivable clerk for Romance Mattress Company prepared the following partially completed aging-of-receivables schedule as of the end of business on November 30:

Customer	Balance	Not Past Due	Days Past Due			
			1–30	31–60	61–90	Over 90
Aaron Brothers Inc.	2,000	2,000				
Abell Company	1,500		1,500			
Zollo Company	5,000			5,000		
Subtotals	872,500	540,000	180,000	78,500	42,300	31,700

The following accounts were unintentionally omitted from the aging schedule:

Customer	Balance	Due Date
Tamika Industries	$25,000	August 24
Ruppert Company	8,500	September 3
Welborne Inc.	35,000	October 17
Kristi Company	6,500	November 5
Simrill Company	12,000	December 3

a. Determine the number of days past due for each of the preceding accounts.
b. Complete the aging-of-receivables schedule.

Exercise 7–6

Estimating allowance for doubtful accounts

Goal 4

$62,690

STUDENT SOLUTIONS MANUAL

SPREADSHEET

Romance Mattress Company has a past history of uncollectible accounts, as shown below. Estimate the allowance for doubtful accounts, based on the aging-of-receivables schedule you completed in Exercise 7–5.

Age Class	Percentage Uncollectible
Not past due	2%
1–30 days past due	4
31–60 days past due	10
61–90 days past due	20
Over 90 days past due	40

Exercise 7–7

Adjustment for uncollectible accounts

Goal 4

Using the data in Exercise 7–5, assume that the allowance for doubtful accounts for Romance Mattress Company has a credit balance of $6,890 before adjustment on November 30. Journalize the adjusting entry for uncollectible accounts as of November 30.

Exercise 7–8

Estimating doubtful accounts

Goal 4

STUDENT SOLUTIONS MANUAL

SPREADSHEET

Phoenician Co. is a wholesaler of office supplies. An aging of the company's accounts receivable on December 31, 2003, and a historical analysis of the percentage of uncollectible accounts in each age category are as follows:

Age Interval	Balance	Percent Uncollectible
Not past due	$350,000	1%
1–30 days past due	90,000	3
31–60 days past due	17,000	6
61–90 days past due	13,000	10
91–180 days past due	9,400	60
Over 180 days past due	3,600	80
	$483,000	

Estimate what the proper balance of the allowance for doubtful accounts should be as of December 31, 2003.

Exercise 7–9

Entry for uncollectible accounts

Goal 4

Using the data in Exercise 7–8, assume that the allowance for doubtful accounts for Phoenician Co. had a debit balance of $1,891 as of December 31, 2003.

Journalize the adjusting entry for uncollectible accounts as of December 31, 2003.

Exercise 7–10

Providing for doubtful accounts

Goal 4

a. $15,000
b. $14,600

STUDENT SOLUTIONS MANUAL

At the end of the current year, the accounts receivable account has a debit balance of $775,000, and net sales for the year total $6,000,000. Determine the amount of the adjusting entry to provide for doubtful accounts under each of the following assumptions:

a. The allowance account before adjustment has a credit balance of $4,750. Uncollectible accounts expense is estimated at 1/4 of 1% of net sales.
b. The allowance account before adjustment has a credit balance of $3,750. An aging of the accounts in the customer ledger indicates estimated doubtful accounts of $18,350.
c. The allowance account before adjustment has a debit balance of $5,050. Uncollectible accounts expense is estimated at 1/2 of 1% of net sales.
d. The allowance account before adjustment has a debit balance of $5,050. An aging of the accounts in the customer ledger indicates estimated doubtful accounts of $31,400.

Exercise 7–11

Entries to write off accounts receivable

Goals 4, 5

Query.com, a computer consulting firm, has decided to write off the $4,800 balance of an account owed by a customer. Journalize the entry to record the write-off, (a) assuming that the allowance method is used, and (b) assuming that the direct write-off method is used.

Exercise 7–12

Entries for uncollectible receivables, using allowance method

Goal 4

STUDENT SOLUTIONS MANUAL

Journalize the following transactions in the accounts of Rhino Company, a restaurant supply company that uses the allowance method of accounting for uncollectible receivables:

Jan. 13 Sold merchandise on account to Renee Hart, $8,100. The cost of the merchandise sold was $4,750.

Feb. 12 Received $2,000 from Renee Hart and wrote off the remainder owed on the sale of January 13 as uncollectible.

July 3 Reinstated the account of Renee Hart that had been written off on February 12 and received $6,100 cash in full payment.

Exercise 7–13

Entries for uncollectible accounts, using direct write-off method

Goal 5

Journalize the following transactions in the accounts of Menthol Co., a hospital supply company that uses the direct write-off method of accounting for uncollectible receivables:

Aug.	8	Sold merchandise on account to Dr. Beth Mears, $10,500. The cost of the merchandise sold was $6,175.
Sept.	7	Received $8,000 from Dr. Beth Mears and wrote off the remainder owed on the sale of August 8 as uncollectible.
Dec.	20	Reinstated the account of Dr. Beth Mears that had been written off on September 7 and received $2,500 cash in full payment.

Exercise 7–14

Effect of doubtful accounts on net income

Goals 4, 5

STUDENT SOLUTIONS MANUAL

During its first year of operations, Yarmouth Automotive Supply Co. had net sales of $3,050,000, wrote off $52,800 of accounts as uncollectible using the direct write-off method, and reported net income of $112,800. If the allowance method of accounting for uncollectibles had been used, 2% of net sales would have been estimated as uncollectible. Determine what the net income would have been if the allowance method had been used.

Exercise 7–15

Effect of doubtful accounts on net income

Goals 4, 5

Using the data in Exercise 7–14, assume that during the second year of operations Yarmouth Automotive Supply Co. had net sales of $3,800,000, wrote off $64,500 of accounts as uncollectible using the direct write-off method, and reported net income of $162,300.

a. Determine what net income would have been in the second year if the allowance method (using 2% of net sales) had been used in both the first and second years.

b. Determine what the balance of the allowance for doubtful accounts would have been at the end of the second year if the allowance method had been used in both the first and second years.

Exercise 7–16

Determine due date and interest on notes

Goal 6

a. May 5, $150

STUDENT SOLUTIONS MANUAL

Determine the due date and the amount of interest due at maturity on the following notes:

	Date of Note	Face Amount	Term of Note	Interest Rate
a.	March 6	$10,000	60 days	9%
b.	May 20	6,000	60 days	10
c.	June 2	7,500	90 days	12
d.	August 30	15,000	120 days	10
e.	October 1	12,500	60 days	12

Exercise 7–17

Entries for notes receivable

Goal 6

b. $15,300

Funchal Interior Decorators issued a 90-day, 8% note for $15,000, dated April 6, to Maderia Furniture Company on account.

a. Determine the due date of the note.

b. Determine the maturity value of the note.

c. Journalize the entries to record the following: (1) receipt of the note by the payee, and (2) receipt by the payee of payment of the note at maturity.

Exercise 7–18

Entries for notes receivable

Goal 6

The series of seven transactions recorded in the following T accounts were related to a sale to a customer on account and the receipt of the amount owed. Briefly describe each transaction.

STUDENT SOLUTIONS MANUAL

CASH

(7)	23,028		

NOTES RECEIVABLE

(5)	22,000	(6)	22,000

ACCOUNTS RECEIVABLE

(1)	25,000	(3)	3,000
(6)	22,725	(5)	22,000
		(7)	22,725

SALES RETURNS AND ALLOWANCES

(3)	3,000		

MERCHANDISE INVENTORY

(4)	1,800	(2)	15,000

COST OF MERCHANDISE SOLD

(2)	15,000	(4)	1,800

SALES

		(1)	25,000

INTEREST REVENUE

		(6)	725
		(7)	303

Exercise 7–19

Entries for notes receivable, including year-end entries

Goal 6

The following selected transactions were completed by Lupine Co., a supplier of elastic bands for clothing:

2003

Dec. 13 Received from Stout Co., on account, a $30,000, 120-day, 9% note dated December 13.

31 Recorded an adjusting entry for accrued interest on the note of December 13.

2004

Apr. 12 Received payment of note and interest from Stout Co.

Journalize the transactions.

Exercise 7–20

Entries for receipt and dishonor of note receivable

Goal 6

STUDENT SOLUTIONS MANUAL

Journalize the following transactions of Galaxy Theater Productions:

July 3 Received a $50,000, 90-day, 7% note dated July 3 from Hermes Company on account.

Oct. 1 The note is dishonored by Hermes Company.

31 Received the amount due on the dishonored note plus interest for 30 days at 9% on the total amount charged to Hermes Company on October 1.

Exercise 7–21

Entries for receipt and dishonor of notes receivable

Goals 4, 6

Journalize the following transactions in the accounts of Dimitrious Co., which operates a riverboat casino:

Apr. 1 Received a $10,000, 30-day, 6% note dated April 1 from Wilcox Co. on account.

Apr. 18	Received a $12,000, 30-day, 9% note dated April 18 from Aaron Co. on account.
May 1	The note dated April 1 from Wilcox Co. is dishonored, and the customer's account is charged for the note, including interest.
June 17	The note dated April 18 from Aaron Co. is dishonored, and the customer's account is charged for the note, including interest.
July 30	Cash is received for the amount due on the dishonored note dated April 1 plus interest for 90 days at 8% on the total amount debited to Wilcox Co. on May 1.
Sept. 3	Wrote off against the allowance account the amount charged to Aaron Co. on June 17 for the dishonored note dated April 18.

Exercise 7–22

Receivables in the balance sheet

Goal 7

STUDENT SOLUTIONS MANUAL

SPREADSHEET

List any errors you can find in the following partial balance sheet.

Dragonfly Company
Balance Sheet
December 31, 2003

Assets		
Current assets:		
Cash		$ 63,750
Notes receivable	$200,000	
Less interest receivable	12,000	188,000
Accounts receivable	$376,180	
Plus allowance for doubtful accounts	30,500	406,680

Exercise 7–23

Accounts receivable turnover

Goal 9

a. 2002: 19.5

Circuit City is a national retailer of brand-name consumer electronics including televisions, DVD players, compact disc players, personal computers, printers, video games, DVD movies, and music. For the fiscal years 2002 and 2001, Circuit City reported the following (in thousands):

	Year Ending February 28,	
	2002	**2001**
Net sales	$12,791,468	$12,959,028
Accounts Receivable	726,541	585,761

Assume that the accounts receivable (in thousands) were $593,276 at March 1, 2000.

a. Compute the accounts receivable turnover for 2002 and 2001. Round to one decimal place.
b. What conclusions can be drawn from these analyses regarding Circuit City's efficiency in collecting receivables?

Exercise 7–24

Days' sales in receivables

Goal 9

a. 2002: 20.7 days

STUDENT SOLUTIONS MANUAL

Use the Circuit City data in Exercise 7–23 to analyze days' sales in receivables.

a. Compute the days' sales in receivables at the end of 2002 and 2001. Round to one decimal place.
b. What conclusions can be drawn from these analyses regarding Circuit City's efficiency in collecting receivables?

Exercise 7–25

Accounts receivable turnover and days' sales in receivables

Goal 9

a. 2002: 108.2

The Limited Inc. sells women's and men's clothing through specialty retail stores, including Structure, Limited, Express, Lane Bryant, and Lerner New York. The Limited sells women's intimate apparel and personal care products through Victoria Secret and Bath & Body Works stores. For the fiscal years 2002 and 2001, The Limited reported the following (in thousands):

	Year Ending February 2,	
	2002	2001
Net sales	$9,363,000	$10,105,000
Accounts Receivable	79,000	94,000

Assume that the accounts receivable (in thousands) were $109,000 at the beginning of the 2001 fiscal year.

a. Compute the accounts receivable turnover for 2002 and 2001. Round to one decimal place.
b. Compute the days' sales in receivables at the end of 2002 and 2001. Round to one decimal place.
c. What conclusions can be drawn from these analyses regarding The Limited's efficiency in collecting receivables?

Exercise 7–26

Accounts receivable turnover and days' sales in receivables

Goal 9

a. 2001: 7.2

STUDENT SOLUTIONS MANUAL

H.J. Heinz Company was founded in 1869 at Sharpsburg, Pennsylvania, by Henry J. Heinz. The company manufactures and markets food products throughout the world, including ketchup, condiments and sauces, frozen food, pet food, soups, and tuna. For the fiscal years 2001 and 2000, H.J. Heinz reported the following (in thousands):

	Year Ending May 2,	
	2001	2000
Net sales	$9,430,422	$9,407,949
Accounts Receivable	1,383,550	1,237,804

Assume that the accounts receivable (in thousands) were $1,163,915 at the beginning of the 2000 fiscal year.

a. Compute the accounts receivable turnover for 2001 and 2000. Round to one decimal place.
b. Compute the days' sales in receivables at the end of 2001 and 2000. Round to one decimal place.
c. What conclusions can be drawn from these analyses regarding Heinz's efficiency in collecting receivables?

Exercise 7–27

Accounts receivable turnover

Goal 9

Use the data in Exercises 7–25 and 7–26 to analyze the accounts receivable turnover ratios of The Limited and H.J. Heinz Company.

a. Compute the average accounts receivable turnover ratio for The Limited and H.J. Heinz Company for the years shown in Exercises 7–25 and 7–26.
b. Does The Limited or H.J. Heinz Company have the higher average accounts receivable turnover ratio?
c. Explain the logic underlying your answer in (b).

Accounting Application Problems

Problem 7–1A

Entries related to uncollectible accounts

Goal 4

3. $755,050

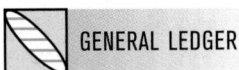

GENERAL LEDGER

The following transactions were completed by The AllStar Gallery during the current fiscal year ended December 31:

Feb. 21	Reinstated the account of Merryl Alber, which had been written off in the preceding year as uncollectible. Journalized the receipt of $2,025 cash in full payment of Alber's account.
Mar. 31	Wrote off the $5,500 balance owed by Amos Co., which is bankrupt.
July 7	Received 35% of the $8,000 balance owed by Morton Co., a bankrupt business, and wrote off the remainder as uncollectible.
Aug. 29	Reinstated the account of Louis Sabo, which had been written off two years earlier as uncollectible. Recorded the receipt of $1,200 cash in full payment.
Dec. 31	Wrote off the following accounts as uncollectible (compound entry): Dailey Co., $10,050; Sun Co., $7,260; Zheng Furniture, $3,775; Carey Wenzel, $2,820.
31	Based on an analysis of the $787,550 of accounts receivable, it was estimated that $32,500 will be uncollectible. Journalized the adjusting entry.

Instructions

1. Record the January 1 credit balance of $30,000 in a T account for Allowance for Doubtful Accounts.
2. Journalize the transactions. Post each entry that affects the following T accounts and determine the new balances:

   Allowance for Doubtful Accounts
   Uncollectible Accounts Expense

3. Determine the expected net realizable value of the accounts receivable as of December 31.
4. Assuming that instead of basing the provision for uncollectible accounts on an analysis of receivables, the adjusting entry on December 31 had been based on

(continued)

an estimated expense of 1/2 of 1% of the net sales of $7,400,000 for the year; determine the following:

a. Uncollectible accounts expense for the year.
b. Balance in the allowance account after the adjustment of December 31.
c. Expected net realizable value of the accounts receivable as of December 31.

Problem 7-2A

Aging of receivables; estimating allowance for doubtful accounts

Goal 4

3. $57,283

SPREADSHEET

Lipshy Wigs Company supplies wigs and hair care products to beauty salons throughout California and the Pacific Northwest. The accounts receivable clerk for Lipshy Wigs prepared the following partially completed aging-of-receivables schedule as of the end of business on December 31, 2003:

		Not	Days Past Due				
Customer	**Balance**	**Past Due**	**1–30**	**31–60**	**61–90**	**91–120**	**Over 120**
Austin Beauty	10,000	10,000					
Blount Wigs	5,500			5,500			
Zabka's	2,900		2,900				
Subtotals	780,000	398,600	197,250	98,750	33,300	29,950	22,150

The following accounts were unintentionally omitted from the aging schedule:

Customer	Due Date	Balance
Houseal Uniquely Yours	July 1, 2003	$ 900
Country Designs	Aug. 2, 2003	4,000
Treat's	Sept. 9, 2003	1,200
Molina's Beauty Store	Sept. 29, 2003	1,100
Ginburg Supreme	Oct. 10, 2003	1,500
Steve's Hair Products	Oct. 17, 2003	600
Hairy's Hair Care	Oct. 31, 2003	2,000
VanDiver's Images	Nov. 18, 2003	700
Lopez's Blond Bombs	Nov. 28, 2003	1,800
Josset Ritz	Nov. 30, 2003	3,500
Cool Designs	Dec. 1, 2003	1,000
Buttram Images	Jan. 3, 2004	6,200

Lipshy Wigs has a past history of uncollectible accounts by age category, as follows:

Age Class	Percentage Uncollectible
Not past due	1%
1–30 days past due	4
31–60 days past due	8
61–90 days past due	15
91–120 days past due	30
Over 120 days past due	80

Instructions

1. Determine the number of days past due for each of the preceding accounts.
2. Complete the aging-of-receivables schedule.
3. Estimate the allowance for doubtful accounts, based on the aging-of-receivables schedule.
4. Assume that the allowance for doubtful accounts for Lipshy Wigs has a credit balance of $11,350 before adjustment on December 31, 2003. Illustrate the effect on the accounts and financial statements of the adjustment for uncollectible accounts.

Problem 7–3A

Compare two methods of accounting for uncollectible receivables

Goals 4, 5

1. Year 4: Balance of allowance account, end of year, $6,750

SPREADSHEET

Minaret Company, which operates a chain of 30 electronics supply stores, has just completed its fourth year of operations. The direct write-off method of recording uncollectible accounts expense has been used during the entire period. Because of substantial increases in sales volume and the amount of uncollectible accounts, the firm is considering changing to the allowance method. Information is requested as to the effect that an annual provision of 1/2% of sales would have had on the amount of uncollectible accounts expense reported for each of the past four years. It is also considered desirable to know what the balance of Allowance for Doubtful Accounts would have been at the end of each year. The following data have been obtained from the accounts:

			Year of Origin of Accounts Receivable Written Off as Uncollectible			
Year	Sales	Uncollectible Accounts Written Off	1st	2nd	3rd	4th
1st	$ 750,000	$ 600	$ 600			
2nd	820,000	1,650	750	$ 900		
3rd	1,050,000	6,200	1,800	1,400	$3,000	
4th	2,250,000	9,150		1,900	2,950	$4,300

Instructions

1. Assemble the desired data, using the following column headings:

	Uncollectible Accounts Expense			
Year	Expense Actually Reported	Expense Based on Estimate	Increase (Decrease) in Amount of Expense	Balance of Allowance Account, End of Year

2. Experience during the first four years of operations indicated that the receivables were either collected within two years or had to be written off as uncollectible. Does the estimate of 1/2% of sales appear to be reasonably close to the actual experience with uncollectible accounts originating during the first two years? Explain.

Problem 7–4A

Details of notes receivable and related entries

Goal 6

1. Note 2: Due date, Sept. 4; Interest due at maturity, $150

Diaz Co. produces advertising videos. During the last six months of the current fiscal year, Diaz Co. received the following notes:

	Date	Face Amount	Term	Interest Rate
1.	May 17	$12,000	45 days	8%
2.	July 6	10,000	60 days	9
3.	Aug. 1	16,500	90 days	8
4.	Sept. 1	20,000	90 days	7
5.	Nov. 29	18,000	60 days	9
6.	Dec. 18	36,000	60 days	12

Instructions

1. Determine for each note (a) the due date and (b) the amount of interest due at maturity, identifying each note by number.
2. Journalize the entry to record the dishonor of Note (3) on its due date.
3. Journalize the adjusting entry to record the accrued interest on Notes (5) and (6) on December 31.
4. Journalize the entries to record the receipt of the amounts due on Notes (5) and (6) in January and February.

Problem 7–5A

Notes receivable entries

Goal 6

GENERAL LEDGER

The following data relate to notes receivable and interest for Robbins Co., a financial services company. (All notes are dated as of the day they are received.)

Mar.	1	Received a $13,000, 9%, 60-day note on account.
	21	Received a $7,500, 8%, 90-day note on account.
Apr.	30	Received $13,195 on note of March 1.
May	16	Received a $40,000, 7%, 90-day note on account.
	31	Received a $6,000, 8%, 30-day note on account.
June	19	Received $7,650 on note of March 21.
	30	Received $6,040 on note of May 31.
July	1	Received a $5,000, 12%, 30-day note on account.
	31	Received $5,050 on note of July 1.
Aug.	14	Received $40,700 on note of May 16.

Instructions

Journalize the entries to record the transactions.

Problem 7–6A

Sales and notes receivable transactions

Goal 6

GENERAL LEDGER

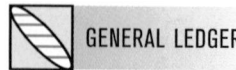

The following were selected from among the transactions completed during the current year by Sonora Co., an appliance wholesale company:

Jan.	7	Sold merchandise on account to Thi Co., $7,500. The cost of merchandise sold was $3,800.
Mar.	8	Accepted a 60-day, 8% note for $7,500 from Thi Co. on account.
May	7	Received from Thi Co. the amount due on the note of March 8.
June	1	Sold merchandise on account to Kihl's for $5,000. The cost of merchandise sold was $3,500.
	5	Loaned $11,000 cash to Michele Duncan, receiving a 30-day, 6% note.
	11	Received from Kihl's the amount due on the invoice of June 1, less 2% discount.
July	5	Received the interest due from Michele Duncan and a new 60-day, 9% note as a renewal of the loan of June 5. (Record both the debit and the credit to the notes receivable account.)

Sept. 3 Received from Michele Duncan the amount due on her note of July 5.
4 Sold merchandise on account to Stover Co., $8,000. The cost of merchandise sold was $5,500.
Oct. 4 Accepted a 60-day, 6% note for $8,000 from Stover Co. on account.
Dec. 3 Stover Co. dishonored the note dated October 4.
29 Received from Stover Co. the amount owed on the dishonored note, plus interest for 26 days at 6% computed on the maturity value of the note.

Instructions

Journalize the transactions. Round to the nearest dollar.

Alternate Accounting Application Problems

Alternate Problem 7-1B

Entries related to uncollectible accounts

Goal 4

3. $623,050

STUDENT SOLUTIONS MANUAL

GENERAL LEDGER

The following transactions were completed by Cascade Contractors Co. during the current fiscal year ended December 31:

Mar. 17 Received 80% of the $17,500 balance owed by Baxter Co., a bankrupt business, and wrote off the remainder as uncollectible.
Apr. 20 Reinstated the account of Susan Evans, which had been written off in the preceding year as uncollectible. Journalized the receipt of $3,782 cash in full payment of Evans' account.
July 29 Wrote off the $4,500 balance owed by Cofer Co., which has no assets.
Oct. 31 Reinstated the account of Mostafa Co., which had been written off in the preceding year as uncollectible. Journalized the receipt of $7,500 cash in full payment of the account.
Dec. 31 Wrote off the following accounts as uncollectible (compound entry): Grovner Co., $1,950; Nance Co., $2,600; Powell Distributors, $3,500; J.J. Levi, $5,200.
31 Based on an analysis of the $635,750 of accounts receivable, it was estimated that $12,700 will be uncollectible. Journalized the adjusting entry.

Instructions

1. Record the January 1 credit balance of $10,050 in a T account for Allowance for Doubtful Accounts.
2. Journalize the transactions. Post each entry that affects the following selected T accounts and determine the new balances:

   Allowance for Doubtful Accounts
   Uncollectible Accounts Expense

3. Determine the expected net realizable value of the accounts receivable as of December 31.
4. Assuming that instead of basing the provision for uncollectible accounts on an analysis of receivables, the adjusting entry on December 31 had been based on an estimated expense of 1/4 of 1% of the net sales of $5,100,000 for the year; determine the following:
   a. Uncollectible accounts expense for the year.
   b. Balance in the allowance account after the adjustment of December 31.
   c. Expected net realizable value of the accounts receivable as of December 31.

Alternate Problem 7–2B

Aging of receivables; estimating allowance for doubtful accounts

Goal 4

3. $69,810

STUDENT SOLUTIONS MANUAL

SPREADSHEET

Wickman Company supplies flies and fishing gear to sporting goods stores and outfitters throughout the western United States. The accounts receivable clerk for Wickman prepared the following partially completed aging-of-receivables schedule as of the end of business on December 31, 2003:

			Days Past Due					
Customer	**Balance**	**Not Past Due**	**1–30**	**31–60**	**61–90**	**91–120**	**Over 120**
Alexandra Fishery	15,000	15,000					
Cutthroat Sports	5,500			5,500			
Yellowstone Sports	2,900		2,900				
Subtotals	880,000	448,600	247,250	98,750	33,300	29,950	22,150

The following accounts were unintentionally omitted from the aging schedule.

Customer	Due Date	Balance
Adel Sports & Flies	June 21, 2003	$1,500
Buzzer Sports	July 30, 2003	3,000
Marabou Flies	Sept. 9, 2003	2,500
Midge Co.	Sept. 30, 2003	1,100
Adventure Outfitters	Oct. 10, 2003	2,500
Pheasant Tail Sports	Oct. 17, 2003	600
Red Tag Sporting Goods	Oct. 30, 2003	2,000
Ross Sports	Nov. 18, 2003	500
Sawyer's Pheasant Tail	Nov. 28, 2003	1,800
Tent Caddis Outfitters	Nov. 30, 2003	3,500
Wulff Company	Dec. 1, 2003	1,000
Zug Bug Sports	Jan. 6, 2004	6,200

Wickman Company has a past history of uncollectible accounts by age category, as follows:

Age Class	Percentage Uncollectible
Not past due	2%
1–30 days past due	4
31–60 days past due	8
61–90 days past due	20
91–120 days past due	40
Over 120 days past due	80

Instructions

1. Determine the number of days past due for each of the preceding accounts.
2. Complete the aging-of-receivables schedule.
3. Estimate the allowance for doubtful accounts, based on the aging-of-receivables schedule.

4. Assume that the allowance for doubtful accounts for Wickman Company has a debit balance of $1,800 before adjustment on December 31, 2003. Journalize the adjusting entry for uncollectible accounts.

Alternate Problem 7–3B

Compare two methods of accounting for uncollectible receivables

Goals 4, 5

1. Year 4: Balance of allowance account, end of year, $12,250

STUDENT SOLUTIONS MANUAL

SPREADSHEET

Interlink Company, a telephone service and supply company, has just completed its fourth year of operations. The direct write-off method of recording uncollectible accounts expense has been used during the entire period. Because of substantial increases in sales volume and the amount of uncollectible accounts, the firm is considering changing to the allowance method. Information is requested as to the effect that an annual provision of 3/4% of sales would have had on the amount of uncollectible accounts expense reported for each of the past four years. It is also considered desirable to know what the balance of Allowance for Doubtful Accounts would have been at the end of each year. The following data have been obtained from the accounts:

			Year of Origin of Accounts Receivable Written Off as Uncollectible			
Year	Sales	Uncollectible Accounts Written Off	1st	2nd	3rd	4th
1st	$ 650,000	$2,500	$2,500			
2nd	760,000	2,950	1,900	$1,050		
3rd	950,000	5,700	700	4,000	$1,000	
4th	1,800,000	7,800		1,200	2,550	$4,050

Instructions

1. Assemble the desired data, using the following column headings:

	Uncollectible Accounts Expense			
Year	Expense Actually Reported	Expense Based on Estimate	Increase (Decrease) in Amount of Expense	Balance of Allowance Account, End of Year

2. Experience during the first four years of operations indicated that the receivables were either collected within two years or had to be written off as uncollectible. Does the estimate of 3/4% of sales appear to be reasonably close to the actual experience with uncollectible accounts originating during the first two years? Explain.

Alternate Problem 7–4B

Details of notes receivable and related entries

Goal 6

1. Note 2: Due date, July 15; Interest due at maturity, $175

STUDENT SOLUTIONS MANUAL

Matrix Co. wholesales bathroom fixtures. During the current fiscal year, Matrix Co. received the following notes:

	Date	Face Amount	Term	Interest Rate
1.	March 3	$36,000	60 days	8%
2.	June 15	17,500	30 days	12
3.	Aug. 20	9,200	120 days	6
4.	Oct. 31	12,000	60 days	9
5.	Nov. 23	15,000	60 days	6
6.	Dec. 27	9,000	30 days	12

Instructions

1. Determine for each note (a) the due date and (b) the amount of interest due at maturity, identifying each note by number.
2. Journalize the entry to record the dishonor of Note (3) on its due date.
3. Journalize the adjusting entry to record the accrued interest on Notes (5) and (6) on December 31.
4. Journalize the entries to record the receipt of the amounts due on Notes (5) and (6) in January.

Alternate Problem 7–5B

Notes receivable entries

Goal 6

STUDENT SOLUTIONS MANUAL

GENERAL LEDGER

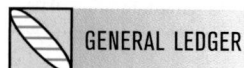

The following data relate to notes receivable and interest for Teleport Optic Co., a cable manufacturer and supplier. (All notes are dated as of the day they are received.)

June	1	Received a $15,800, 9%, 60-day note on account.
July	16	Received a $30,000, 10%, 120-day note on account.
	31	Received $16,037 on note of June 1.
Sept.	1	Received a $24,000, 9%, 60-day note on account.
Oct.	31	Received $24,360 on note of September 1.
Nov.	8	Received a $24,000, 7%, 30-day note on account.
	13	Received $31,000 on note of July 16.
	30	Received a $15,000, 10%, 30-day note on account.
Dec.	8	Received $24,140 on note of November 8.
	30	Received $15,125 on note of November 30.

Instructions

Journalize entries to record the transactions.

Alternate Problem 7–6B

Sales and notes receivable transactions

Goal 6

STUDENT SOLUTIONS MANUAL

GENERAL LEDGER

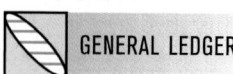

The following were selected from among the transactions completed by Greco Co. during the current year. Greco Co. sells and installs home and business security systems.

Jan.	8	Loaned $6,000 cash to Mark Tift, receiving a 90-day, 8% note.
Feb.	3	Sold merchandise on account to Messina and Son, $18,000. The cost of the merchandise sold was $10,000.
Feb.	12	Sold merchandise on account to Gwyn Co., $25,000. The cost of merchandise sold was $15,000.
Mar.	5	Accepted a 60-day, 6% note for $18,000 from Messina and Son on account.
	14	Accepted a 60-day, 12% note for $25,000 from Gwyn Co. on account.
Apr.	8	Received the interest due from Mark Tift and a new 90-day, 9% note as a renewal of the loan of January 8. (Record both the debit and the credit to the notes receivable account.)
May	4	Received from Messina and Son the amount due on the note of March 5.
	13	Gwyn Co. dishonored its note dated March 14.
June	12	Received from Gwyn Co. the amount owed on the dishonored note, plus interest for 30 days at 12% computed on the maturity value of the note.
July	7	Received from Mark Tift the amount due on his note of April 8.
Aug.	23	Sold merchandise on account to MacKenzie Co., $8,000. The cost of the merchandise sold was $5,000.
Sept.	2	Received from MacKenzie Co. the amount of the invoice of August 23, less 1% discount.

Instructions

Journalize the transactions.

Building Leadership Skills— Financial Analysis and Reporting

Case 7-1

Accounts receivable turnover and days' sales in receivables

Best Buy Company is a specialty retailer of consumer electronics, including personal computers, entertainment software, and appliances. Best Buy operates retail stores in addition to the Best Buy, Media Play, On Cue, and Magnolia Hi-Fi Web sites. For the fiscal years ending March 3, 2002 and 2001, Best Buy reported the following (in millions):

	Year Ending March 3,	
	2002	2001
Net sales	$19,597	$15,327
Accounts receivable at end of year	247	209

Assume that the accounts receivable (in millions) were $189 at the beginning of the 2001 fiscal year.

1. Compute the accounts receivable turnover for 2002 and 2001. Round to one decimal place.
2. Compute the days' sales in receivables at the end of 2002 and 2001.
3. What conclusions can be drawn from (1) and (2) regarding Best Buy's efficiency in collecting receivables?
4. Based upon (1), how many days does it take Best Buy to convert its receivables to cash in 2002?
5. For 2002, why aren't the answers to (2) and (4) the same?
6. For its fiscal years ending in 2002 and 2001, Circuit City has an accounts receivable turnover of 19.5 and 22.0, respectively. Compare Best Buy's efficiency in collecting receivables with that of Circuit City. (Note: The data for Circuit City's 2002 and 2001 fiscal years are shown in Exercise 7-23.)
7. What assumption did we make about sales for the Circuit City and Best Buy ratio computations that might distort the two company ratios and therefore cause the ratios not to be comparable?

Case 7-2

Accounts receivable turnover and days' sales in receivables

Apple Computer Inc. designs, manufactures, and markets personal computers and related personal computing and communicating solutions for sale primarily to education, creative, consumer, and business customers. Substantially all of the company's net sales over the last five years are from sales of its Apple Macintosh line of personal computers and related software and peripherals. For the fiscal years ending September 29, 2001 and 2000, Apple reported the following (in millions):

	Year Ending September 29,	
	2001	2000
Net sales	$5,363	$7,983
Accounts receivable at end of year	466	953

Assume that the accounts receivable (in millions) were $681 at the beginning of the 2000 fiscal year.

1. Compute the accounts receivable turnover for 2001 and 2000. Round to one decimal place.
2. Compute the days' sales in receivables at the end of 2001 and 2000.
3. What conclusions can be drawn from (1) and (2) regarding Apple's efficiency in collecting receivables?
4. Using the Internet, access the Apple September 29, 2001, 10-K filing with the Securities and Exchange Commission. You can use the PriceWaterhouseCoopers Web site http://edgarscan.pwcglobal.com to search for company filings by name. Search the 10-K filing for the term "receivable." Identify two companies that had accounts receivable with Apple at the end of fiscal years 2001 and 2000.

Case 7–3

Accounts receivable turnover and days' sales in receivables

Earthlink, Inc., is a nationwide Internet Service Provider (ISP). Earthlink provides a variety of services to its customers, including narrowband access, broadband or high-speed access, and Web hosting services. For the years ending December 31, 2001 and 2000, Earthlink reported the following (in thousands):

	Year Ending December 31,	
	2001	2000
Net sales	$1,244,928	$986,630
Accounts receivable at end of year	40,624	49,568

Assume that the accounts receivable (in thousands) were $16,367 at January 1, 2000.

1. Compute the accounts receivable turnover for 2001 and 2000. Round to one decimal place.
2. Compute the days' sales in receivables at the end of 2001 and 2000.
3. What conclusions can be drawn from (1) and (2) regarding Earthlink's efficiency in collecting receivables?
4. Given the nature of Earthlink's operations, do you believe Earthlink's accounts receivable turnover ratio would be higher or lower than a typical manufacturing company, such as Boeing or Kellogg? Explain.

Case 7–4

Accounts receivable turnover

General Electric (GE) is one of the largest and most diversified industrial corporations in the world. GE's products include major appliances, lighting products, medical diagnostic imaging equipment, motors, locomotives, and commercial and military aircraft jet engines. Through the National Broadcasting Company (NBC), GE offers network television services, operates television stations, and provides cable, Internet, and programming services. Through General Electric Capital Services (GECS), GE offers consumer financing, commercial and industrial financing, real estate financing, asset management and leasing, mortgage services, and insurance services.

For the years ending December 31, 2001 and 2000, GE reported the following data (in millions):

	December 31,	
	2001	2000
GE (without GECS):		
Total accounts receivable from sales of goods and services	$ 10,167	$ 10,077
Allowance for doubtful accounts	362	350
Net accounts receivable	$ 9,805	$ 9,727
GECS:		
Total accounts receivable from financing	$178,833	$147,333
Allowance for doubtful accounts	4,801	4,034
Net accounts receivable	$174,032	$143,299
Sales for GE (without GECS) for year ending December 31, 2001		$68,018
Revenue for GECS from services for year ending December 31, 2001		$54,726

1. Compute the accounts receivable turnover for GE, excluding GECS, for 2001. Use net accounts receivable and round to one decimal place in your computations.
2. Compute the accounts receivable turnover for GECS for 2001. Use net accounts receivable and round to one decimal place in your computations.
3. Comment on the interpretation of the accounts receivable turnover for GECS.
4. As of December 31, 2001 and 2000, compute the percent of the allowance for doubtful accounts to total accounts receivable for GE, without GECS. Round to one decimal place.
5. As of December 31, 2001 and 2000, compute the percent of the allowance for doubtful accounts to total accounts receivable for GECS. Round to one decimal place.
6. Compare (4) and (5) and explain why one percentage is higher than the other.

Case 7–5

Accounts receivable turnover

The accounts receivable turnover ratio will vary across companies, depending upon the nature of the company's operations. For example, an accounts receivable turnover of six for an Internet Services Provider is unacceptable, but might be excellent for a manufacturer of specialty milling equipment. A list of well-known companies is listed below.

Alcoa	Delta Air Lines	Kroger
AutoZone	Gillette	Maytag Corporation
Barnes & Noble	Home Depot	Wal-Mart
Coca-Cola	IBM	Whirlpool

1. Using the PriceWaterhouseCoopers Web site, http://edgarscan.pwcglobal.com, look up each of company by entering its name. Click on each company's name and then scroll down to the bottom of the page to "Set Preferences." Select "Receivables Turnover" in the Ratios list. Then click "Save Preferences."
2. Categorize each of the preceding companies as to whether its turnover ratio is above or below 15.
3. Based upon (2), identify a characteristic of companies with accounts receivable turnover ratios above 15.

Building Leadership Skills—Responsible Leadership

Activity 7–1

Ethics and professional conduct in business

ETHICS

Tricia Fenton, vice-president of operations for Billings National Bank, has instructed the bank's computer programmer to use a 365-day year to compute interest on depository accounts (payables). Tricia also instructed the programmer to use a 360-day year to compute interest on loans (receivables).

Discuss whether Tricia is behaving in a professional manner.

Activity 7–2

Collecting accounts receivable

The following is an excerpt from a conversation between the office manager, Jamie Luthi, and the president of Jefferson Construction Supplies Co., David King. Jefferson sells building supplies to local contractors.

Jamie: David, we're going to have to do something about these overdue accounts receivable. One-third of our accounts are over 60 days past due, and I've had accounts that have stayed open for almost a year!

David: I didn't realize it was that bad. Any ideas?

Jamie: Well, we could stop giving credit. Make everyone pay with cash or a credit card. We accept MasterCard and Visa already, but only the walk-in customers use them. Almost all of the contractors put purchases on their bills.

David: Yes, but we've been allowing credit for years. As far as I know, all of our competitors allow contractors credit. If we stopped giving credit, we'd lose many of our contractors. They'd just go elsewhere. You know, some of these guys run up bills as high as $40,000 or $60,000. There's no way they could put that kind of money on a credit card.

Jamie: That's a good point. But we've got to do something.

David: How many of the contractor accounts do you actually end up writing off as uncollectible?

Jamie: Not many. Almost all eventually pay. It's just that they take so long!

Suggest one or more solutions to Jefferson's problem concerning the collection of accounts receivable.

Activity 7–3

Value of receivables

The following is an excerpt from a conversation between Kay Kinder, the president and owner of Retriever Wholesale Co., and Michele Stephens, Retriever's controller. The conversation took place on January 4, 2003, shortly after Michele began preparing the financial statements for the year ending December 31, 2002.

Michele: Kay, I've completed my analysis of the collectibility of our accounts receivable. My staff and I estimate that the allowance for doubtful accounts should be somewhere between $60,000 and $90,000. Right now, the balance of the allowance account is $18,000.

Kay: Oh, no! We are already below the estimated earnings projection I gave the bank last year. We used that as a basis for convincing the bank to loan us $100,000. They're going to be upset! Is there any way we can increase the allowance without the adjustment increasing expenses?

Michele: I'm afraid not. The allowance can only be increased by debiting the uncollectible accounts expense account.

Kay: Well, I guess we're stuck. The bank will just have to live with it. But let's increase the allowance by only $42,000. That gets us into our range of estimates with the minimum expense increase.

Michele: Kay, there is one more thing we need to discuss.

Kay: What now?

Michele: Jill, my staff accountant, noticed that you haven't made any payments on your receivable for over a year. Also, it has increased from $20,000 last year to $80,000. Jill thinks we ought to reclassify it as a noncurrent asset and report it as an "other receivable."

Kay: What's the problem? Didn't we just include it in accounts receivable last year?

Michele: Yes, but last year it was immaterial.

Kay: Look, I'll make a $60,000 payment next week. So let's report it as we did last year.

If you were Michele, how would you address Kay's suggestions?

Activity 7-4

Estimate uncollectible accounts

For several years, sales have been on a "cash only" basis. On January 1, 2000, however, Sheepshank Co. began offering credit on terms of n/30. The amount of the adjusting entry to record the estimated uncollectible receivables at the end of each year has been 1/4 of 1% of credit sales, which is the rate reported as the average for the industry. Credit sales and the year-end credit balances in Allowance for Doubtful Accounts for the past four years are as follows:

Year	Credit Sales	Allowance for Doubtful Accounts
2000	$7,800,000	$ 5,100
2001	8,000,000	11,100
2002	8,100,000	16,850
2003	9,250,000	25,375

Carisa Parker, president of Sheepshank Co., is concerned that the method used to account for and write off uncollectible receivables is unsatisfactory. She has asked for your advice in the analysis of past operations in this area and for recommendations for change.

1. Determine the amount of (a) the addition to Allowance for Doubtful Accounts and (b) the accounts written off for each of the four years.
2. a. Advise Carisa Parker as to whether the estimate of 1/4 of 1% of credit sales appears reasonable.
   b. Assume that after discussing (a) with Carisa Parker, she asked you what action might be taken to determine what the balance of Allowance for Doubtful Accounts should be at December 31, 2003, and what possible changes, if any, you might recommend in accounting for uncollectible receivables. How would you respond?

Activity 7-5

Granting credit

GROUP ACTIVITY

In groups of three or four, determine how credit is typically granted to customers. Interview an individual responsible for granting credit for a bank, a department store, an automobile dealer, or other business in your community. You should ask such questions as the following:

1. What procedures are used to decide whether to grant credit to a customer?
2. What procedures are used to try to collect from customers who are delinquent in their payments?
3. Approximately what percentage of customers' accounts are written off as uncollectible in a year?

Summarize your findings in a report to the class.

Activity 7-6

Collection of receivables

Go to the Web page of two department store chains, Federated Department Stores Inc. and Dillard's Inc. The Internet sites for these companies are:

www.federated-fds.com
www.dillards.com

Using the financial information provided at each site, calculate the most recent accounts receivable turnover for each company, and identify which company is collecting its receivables faster.

Answers to Self-Study Questions

1. **B** The estimate of uncollectible accounts, \$8,500 (answer C), is the amount of the desired balance of Allowance for Doubtful Accounts after adjustment. The amount of the current provision to be made for uncollectible accounts expense is thus \$6,000 (answer B), which is the amount that must be added to the Allowance for Doubtful Accounts credit balance of \$2,500 (answer A), so that the account will have the desired balance of \$8,500.
2. **B** The amount expected to be realized from accounts receivable is the balance of Accounts Receivable, \$100,000, less the balance of Allowance for Doubtful Accounts, \$7,000, or \$93,000 (answer B).
3. **C** Maturity value is the amount that is due at the maturity or due date. The maturity value of \$10,300 (answer C) is determined as follows:

Face amount of note	\$10,000
Plus interest (\$10,000 × 0.12 × 90/360)	300
Maturity value of note	\$10,300

4. **C** November 3 is the due date of a \$12,000, 90-day, 8% note receivable dated August 5 [26 days in August (31 days − 5 days) + 30 days in September + 31 days in October + 3 days in November].
5. **B** If a note is dishonored, Accounts Receivable is debited for the maturity value of the note (answer B). The maturity value of the note is its face value (answer A) plus the accrued interest. The maturity value of the note less accrued interest (answer C) is equal to the face value of the note. The maturity value of the note plus accrued interest (answer D) is incorrect, since the interest would be added twice.

Chapter 8
Inventories

The Law of Empowerment

"Only secure leaders give power to others."

—The 21 Irrefutable Laws of Leadership

Dr. John C. Maxwell

Learning Goals

1. Identify the types of inventory used by merchandisers and manufacturers.
2. Summarize and provide examples of internal control procedures that apply to inventories.
3. Describe three inventory cost flow assumptions and how they impact the income statement and balance sheet.
4. Determine the cost of inventory under the perpetual inventory system, using the first-in, first-out; last-in, first-out; and average cost methods.
5. Determine the cost of inventory under the periodic inventory system, using the first-in, first-out; last-in, first-out; and average cost methods.
6. Compare and contrast the use of the three inventory costing methods.
7. Determine the proper valuation of inventory at other than cost, using the lower-of-cost-or-market and net realizable value concepts.
8. Describe how inventories are being reduced through quick response.
9. Determine and interpret the inventory turnover ratio, the number of days' sales in inventory, and lifo reserve adjustments.

Adolph Coors Company

The Adolph Coors Company has a unique culture and history that is unlike most other companies. The company was founded in 1873 by Adolph Coors, who was orphaned at 15 and learned the brewing business in Germany as an apprentice. After arriving in the United States in 1863, Adolph worked in a brewery in Illinois before moving to Colorado and starting a bottling business in Denver. During weekends and time off, Adolph searched the foothills west of Denver for a location to build a brewery. On the banks of Clear Creek, he found an abandoned tannery. The site was particularly appealing to Adolph because of its cool, crystal-clear spring water, which he considered the most important ingredient in beer. The Coors Brewery is still located on Clear Creek, just east of Golden, Colorado.

How many of today's companies do you think would survive if their primary products were legislated out of existence? Not many . . . but Coors did. The temperance movement in the early 1900s resulted in the 18th Amendment to the U.S. Constitution, which provided for the prohibition of alcohol at the state level. In November 1914, Colorado voted to make the manufacture and sale of alcoholic beverages illegal as of January 1, 1916. On December 31, 1915, Coors dumped 561 barrels of beer—17,391 gallons—into Clear Creek.

How did the company survive prohibition? As early as 1908, Adolph Coors began diversifying the operations of the company into real estate, cement, cooking china, and porcelain. In a move that helped save the company, he convinced the Mars Company to use Coors as its main supplier of malted milk. He then converted the brewery for manufacturing malted milk and a near-beer called Mannah.

Once prohibition was repealed in 1933, the company again prospered by brewing and distributing beer as well as engaging in other businesses. The Coors porcelain business eventually was spun off as Coors Ceramics in 1985 and is now part of Coorstek, with revenues in excess of $400 million.

In addition to its reputation as a brewery, Coors is also known for its innovations and environmental concerns. For example, Coors developed the first recyclable, all-aluminum beverage can in 1959. Before aluminum cans, beverage cans were made of tin, which not only leaked and created environmental problems, but affected the taste of the beer. With the introduction of the new aluminum cans, Coors offered a penny for every can returned to the brewery for recycling. The first aluminum can with a press-tab lid was introduced in 1973, and the first twist-off-cap bottle was introduced in 1976.

In 2001, Adolph Coors Company had net sales of almost $2.5 billion, an operating income of $900 million, and net income of $123 million. Included in Coors' total assets of $1.7 billion were $115 million of raw materials, work in process, finished products, and packaging materials inventories. How does Coors account for and report these inventories? Does the manufacture of products with expiration dates, such as Coors beer, affect the accounting for and reporting of inventories? What techniques and performance measures are available for determining how a company manages its inventories? In this chapter, we focus on inventories and answer each of these questions.

Source: Adapted from *Coors: A Rocky Mountain Legend* by Russ Banham, Greenwich Publishing Group, Inc. (1998).

Your Need to Know

What is the role of inventory in a business? From a consumer's perspective, inventory allows us to compare items, touch items, purchase on impulse, and take immediate delivery of a product upon purchase. For example, Circuit City Stores has an inventory of TVs available for customer purchase. In other cases, consumers are willing to wait for the product to be produced to their unique specifications. Boeing, for example, builds aircraft only after an order is received.

Inventory provides protection against disruptions in production, transportation, or other processes in the value chain.[1] For example, an unexpected strike by a supplier's employees can halt production for a manufacturer or cause lost sales for a merchandiser. Inventory also allows a business to meet unexpected increases in the demand for its product.

In addition to the benefits of inventory, there are costs to holding inventory. These include the costs to acquire, hold, store, handle, and finance inventory. In addition, inventories are subject to obsolescence. For example, many food products at the grocery store are freshness dated, so that if the product is not sold by the freshness date it must be discarded. Thus, management must balance the benefits of holding inventory against these costs.

In this chapter, we will define inventory for manufacturers and merchandisers, illustrate inventory valuation approaches, and introduce ratios used to analyze management's effective use of inventory.

Inventory Classification for Merchandisers and Manufacturers

1 Identify the types of inventory used by merchandisers and manufacturers.

In Chapter 5, we defined a merchandiser as a company that purchases products for resale, such as apparel, consumer electronics, hardware, or food items. We stated that the merchandise on hand (not sold) at the end of the period was a current asset called **merchandise inventory**. Inventory sold becomes the *cost of merchandise sold.* Merchandise inventory is a significant current asset for most merchandising companies, as illustrated for four well-known merchandising companies in Exhibit 1.

Exhibit 1

Size of Merchandise Inventory for Merchandising Businesses

	Merchandise Inventory as a % of Current Assets	Merchandise Inventory as a % of Total Assets
Wal-Mart	82%	28%
Best Buy	60	36
Home Depot	84	31
Kroger	75	22

In contrast, manufacturing companies convert raw materials into final products, which are often sold to merchandising businesses. A manufacturing company has three types of inventory, as illustrated in Exhibit 2.

1 The value chain was defined and illustrated in Chapter 1.

Exhibit 2

Manufacturing Inventories

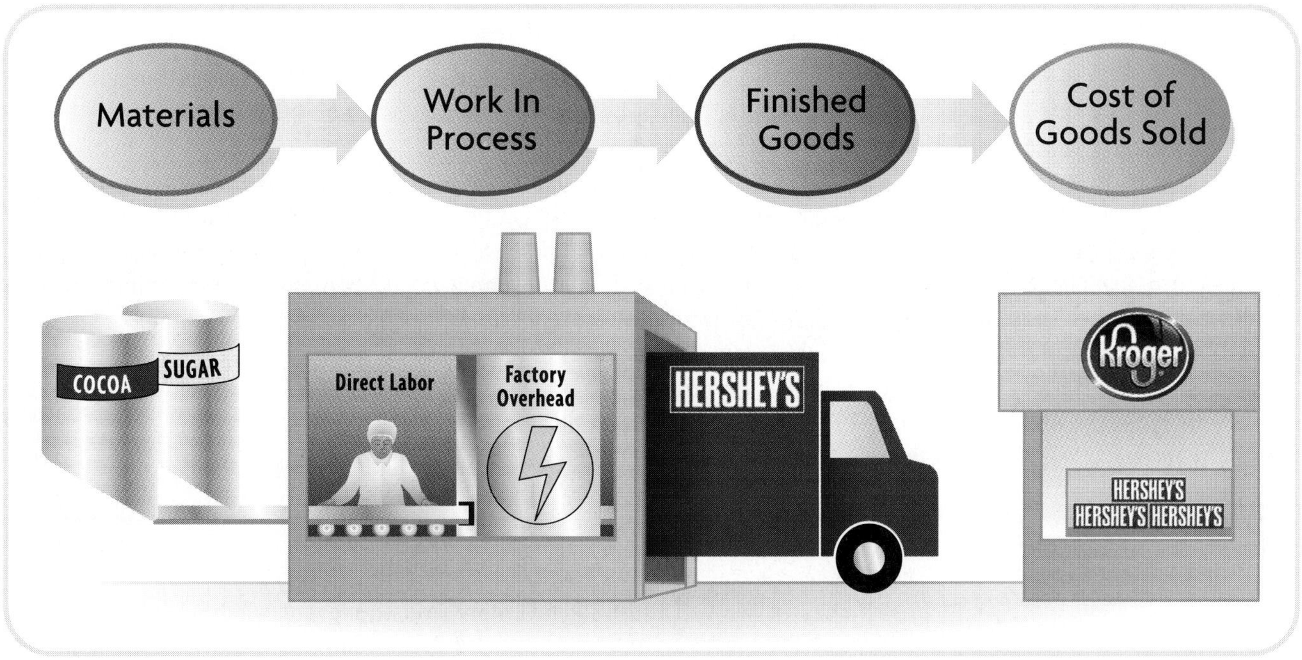

Materials inventory consists of the cost of raw materials used in manufacturing a product. For example, Hershey Foods Corporation uses cocoa and sugar in making chocolate. The cost of cocoa and sugar held in the storage silos at the end of the period would be reported on the balance sheet as materials inventory.

Work in process inventory consists of the costs for partially completed product. These costs include the *direct materials*, which are a product's component materials that are introduced into the manufacturing process. For example, Hershey introduces cocoa and sugar in the process of making chocolate. Other costs are also added in the manufacturing process, such as direct labor and factory overhead costs. *Direct labor costs* are the wages of factory workers directly involved with making a product. *Factory overhead costs* are all factory costs other than direct labor and materials, such as equipment depreciation, supervisory salaries, and power costs. The balance sheet reports the work in process inventory at the end of the period as a current asset.

Finished goods inventory consists of the costs of direct materials, direct labor, and factory overhead for completed production. The finished goods inventory for Hershey Foods is the cost of packaged chocolate held in a finished goods warehouse at the end of the period. When the finished goods are sold, the costs are transferred to the **cost of goods sold** or the *cost of merchandise sold* on the income statement.

Manufacturing inventories are often disclosed in the footnotes to the financial statements of a manufacturer. For example, Hershey Foods Corporation reported inventories of $650,273,000 in the current asset section of the balance sheet, with the following additional footnote reference:

Materials	$263,658,000
Work in Process	47,866,000
Finished Goods	338,749,000
Total Inventories	$650,273,000

Strategy in Business

A Beer Run?

Adolph Coors Company has an estimated 11 percent market share in the United States, in contrast with Anheuser-Busch's 50 percent and Miller Brewing's 20 percent shares. Because of its smaller size, Coors has difficulty competing domestically with Anheuser-Busch and Miller, who often offer rebates and other incentives to their distributors to sell their beer. Coors recently decided to expand operations outside the United States by purchasing Carling beer from Interbrew SA for $1.7 billion. Carling is Britain's best-selling beer. So what is Coors' underlying strategy? In addition to allowing Coors to obtain an immediate international presence in Europe, Carling provides Coors with a beer for possible import into the United States. Carling also provides Coors with another brand to offer its distributors, and thus take advantage of offering as many beers as possible through its distribution channel. However, adding Carling to its product will increase Coors' inventory, thus increasing its related costs of shipping, handling, storing, and financing inventory.

Source: Adapted from "Coors Gets Europe Access in Carling Deal," by Gary McWilliams and Philip Shishkin, *The Wall Street Journal*, December 26, 2001, and "Coors Acquires A Big Brand in Britain," by Suzanne Kapner, *The New York Times*, December 25, 2001.

In this chapter, we will illustrate inventory accounting and analysis issues from the perspective of the merchandising business. However, many of the points apply equally well to a manufacturer. The accounting for manufacturing inventories is covered in a managerial accounting course.

Internal Control of Inventory

2 Summarize and provide examples of internal control procedures that apply to inventories.

What costs should be included in inventory? As we illustrated in earlier chapters, the cost of merchandise is its purchase price, less any purchases discounts. These costs are usually the largest portion of the inventory cost. Merchandise inventory also includes other costs, such as transportation, import duties, property taxes, and insurance costs. The underlying accounting concept is that the inventory cost must include all the costs of ownership. For example, the CarMax division of Circuit City Stores, Inc. states:

> *Parts and labor used to recondition vehicles, as well as transportation and other incremental expenses associated with acquiring vehicles, are included in the CarMax Group's inventory.*

For companies such as Circuit City, good internal control over inventory must be maintained. Two primary objectives of internal control over inventory are safeguarding the inventory and properly reporting it in the financial statements. These internal controls can be either preventive or detective in nature. A preventive control is designed to prevent errors or misstatements from occurring. A detective control is designed to detect an error or misstatement after it has occurred.

Control over inventory should begin as soon as the inventory is received. Receiving reports should be completed by the company's receiving department in order to establish the initial accountability for the inventory. To make sure the inventory received is what was ordered, each receiving report should agree with the company's original purchase order for the merchandise. Likewise, the price at which the inventory was ordered, as shown on the purchase order, should be compared to the price at which the vendor billed the company, as shown on the vendor's invoice. After the receiving report, purchase order, and vendor's invoice have been reconciled, the company should record the inventory and related account payable in the accounting records.

Controls for safeguarding inventory include developing and using security measures to prevent inventory damage or customer or employee theft. For example, inventory should be stored in a warehouse or other area to which access is restricted to authorized employees. When shopping, you may have noticed how retail stores protect inventory from customer theft. Retail stores often use such devices as two-way mirrors, cameras, and security guards. High-priced items are often displayed in locked cabinets. Retail clothing stores often place plastic alarm tags on valuable items such as leather coats. Sensors at the exit doors set off alarms if the tags have not been removed by the clerk. These controls are designed to prevent customers from shoplifting.

Using a perpetual inventory system for merchandise also provides an effective means of control over inventory. The amount of each type of merchandise is always readily available in a subsidiary **inventory ledger**. In addition, the subsidiary ledger can be an aid in maintaining inventory quantities at proper levels. Frequently comparing balances with predetermined maximum and minimum levels allows for the timely reordering of merchandise and prevents the ordering of excess inventory.

To ensure the accuracy of the amount of inventory reported in the financial statements, a merchandising business should take a **physical inventory** (i.e., count the merchandise). In a perpetual inventory system, the physical inventory is compared to the recorded inventory in order to determine the amount of shrinkage or shortage. If the inventory shrinkage is unusually large, management can investigate further and take any necessary corrective action. Knowing that a physical inventory will be taken also helps prevent employee thefts or misuses of inventory.

Most companies take their physical inventories when their inventory levels are the lowest. For example, most retailers take their physical inventories in late January or early February, which is after the holiday selling season but before restocking for spring.

Inventory Cost Flow Assumptions

3 Describe three inventory cost flow assumptions and how they impact the income statement and balance sheet.

When you arrive in line to purchase a movie ticket, the tickets are sold on a first-in, first-out (fifo) order. That is, those who arrive first in line purchase their tickets before those who arrive later. In this section, we will see how this ordering concept is used to value inventory. This issue arises when identical units of merchandise are acquired at different unit costs during a period. When the company sells one of these identical items, it must determine a unit cost so that it can record the proper accounting entry. To illustrate, assume that three identical units of Item X are purchased during May, as shown below.

		Item X	Units	Cost
May	10	Purchase	1	$ 9
	18	Purchase	1	13
	24	Purchase	1	14
	Total		3	$36
	Average cost per unit			$12

Assume that the company sells one unit on May 30 for $20. If this unit can be identified with a specific purchase, the *specific identification method* can be used to determine the cost of the unit sold. For example, if the unit sold was purchased on May 18, the cost assigned to the unit would be $13, and the gross profit would be $7 ($20 − $13). If, however, the unit sold was purchased on May 10, the cost assigned to the unit would be $9, and the gross profit would be $11 ($20 − $9). The specific identification method is normally used by companies that sell relatively expensive items, such as jewelry or automobiles. For example, Oakwood Homes Corp., a manufacturer and seller of mobile homes, stated in the footnotes to its annual report:

> *Inventories are valued at the lower of cost or market, with cost determined using the specific identification method for new and used manufactured homes. . . .*

The specific identification method is not practical unless each unit can be identified accurately. An automobile dealer, for example, may be able to use this method, since each automobile has a unique serial number. For many businesses, however, identical units cannot be separately identified, and a cost flow must be assumed. That is, which units have been sold and which units are still in inventory must be assumed.

Three common cost flow assumptions are used in business. Each of these assumptions is identified with an inventory costing method, as shown below.

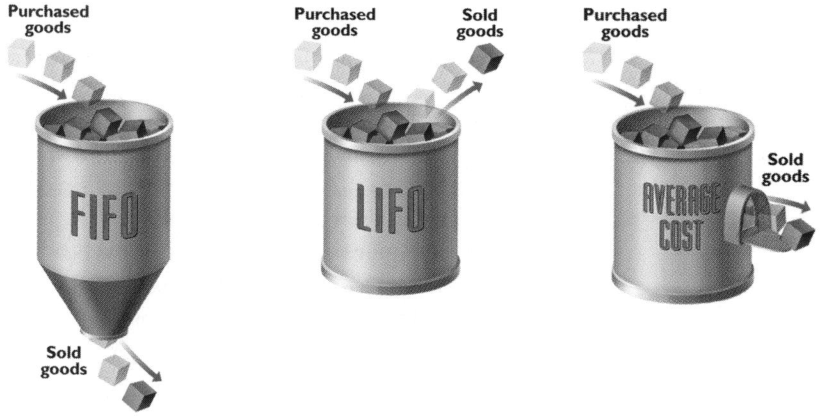

When the **first-in, first-out (fifo) method** is used, the ending inventory is made up of the most recent costs. When the **last-in, first-out (lifo) method** is used, the ending inventory is made up of the earliest costs. When the **average cost method** is used, the cost of the units in inventory is an average of the purchase costs.

To illustrate, we use the preceding example to prepare the income statement for May and the balance sheet as of May 31 for each of the cost flow methods. These financial statements are shown in Exhibit 3.

As you can see, selecting an inventory costing method can have a significant impact on the financial statements. For this reason, the selection has important implications for

Exhibit 3

Effect of Inventory Costing Methods on Financial Statements

Fifo Method

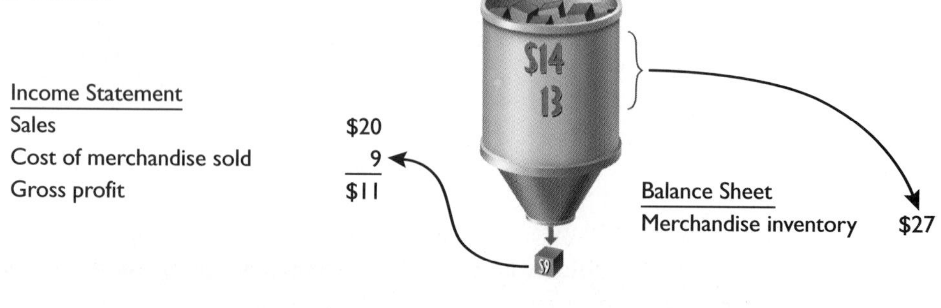

Exhibit 3

Concluded

Lifo Method

Income Statement	
Sales	$20
Cost of merchandise sold	14
Gross profit	$ 6

Balance Sheet	
Merchandise inventory	$22

Average Cost Method

Income Statement	
Sales	$20
Cost of merchandise sold	12
Gross profit	$ 8

Balance Sheet	
Merchandise inventory	$24

managers and others in analyzing and interpreting the financial statements. The chart in Exhibit 4 shows the frequency with which fifo, lifo, and the average methods are used in practice for firms exceeding $1 billion in sales.

Exhibit 4

*Inventory Costing Methods**

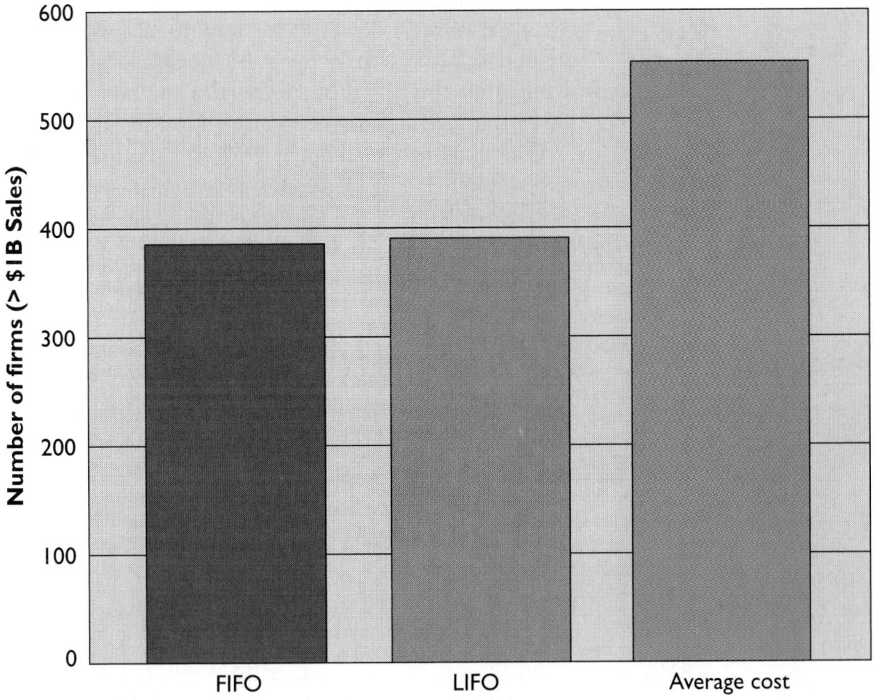

Source: Derived from Disclosure financial database

*Firms may be counted more than once for using multiple methods.

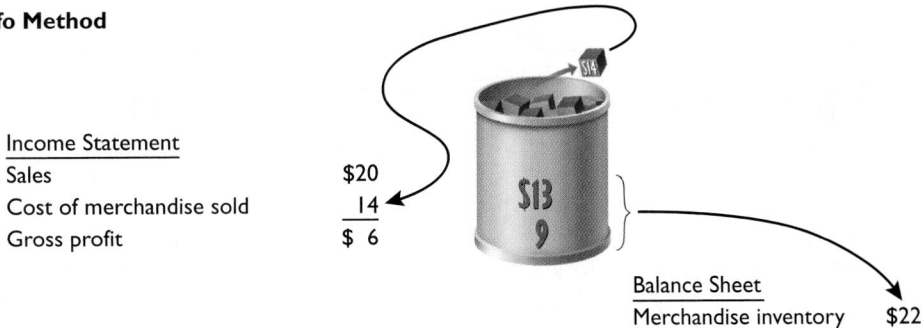

Inventory Costing Methods under a Perpetual Inventory System

4 Determine the cost of inventory under the perpetual inventory system, using the first-in, first-out; last-in, first-out; and average cost methods.

In a perpetual inventory system, all merchandise increases and decreases are recorded in a manner similar to recording increases and decreases in cash. The merchandise inventory account at the beginning of an accounting period indicates the merchandise in stock on that date. Purchases are recorded by debiting *Merchandise Inventory* and crediting *Cash* or *Accounts Payable*. On the date of each sale, the cost of the merchandise sold is recorded by debiting *Cost of Merchandise Sold* and crediting *Merchandise Inventory*.

As we illustrated in the preceding section, a cost flow must be assumed when identical units of an item are purchased at different unit costs during a period. In such cases, the fifo, lifo, or average cost method is used. We illustrate each of these methods, using the data for Item 127B, shown below.

		Item 127B	Units	Cost
Jan.	1	Inventory	10	$20
	4	Sale	7	
	10	Purchase	8	21
	22	Sale	4	
	28	Sale	2	
	30	Purchase	10	22

First-In, First-Out Method

Most businesses dispose of goods in the order in which the goods are purchased. This would be especially true of perishables and goods whose styles or models often change. For example, grocery stores shelve their milk products by expiration dates. Likewise, men's and women's clothing stores display clothes by season. At the end of a season, they often have sales to clear their stores of off-season or out-of-style clothing. Thus, the fifo method is often consistent with the *physical flow* or movement of merchandise. To the extent that this is the case, the fifo method provides results that are about the same as those obtained by identifying the specific costs of each item sold and in inventory.

When the fifo method of costing inventory is used, costs are included in the cost of merchandise sold in the order in which they were incurred. To illustrate, Exhibit 5 shows the journal entries for purchases and sales and the inventory subsidiary ledger account for Item 127B. The number of units in inventory after each transaction, together with total costs and unit costs, are shown in the account. We assume that the units are sold for $30 each on account.

You should note that after the 7 units were sold on January 4, there was an inventory of 3 units at $20 each. The 8 units purchased on January 10 were acquired at a unit cost of $21. Therefore, the inventory after the January 10 purchase is reported on two lines: 3 units at $20 each and 8 units at $21 each. Next, note that the $81 cost of the 4 units sold on January 22 is made up of the remaining 3 units at $20 each and 1 unit at $21. At this point, 7 units are in inventory at a cost of $21 per unit. The remainder of the illustration is explained in a similar manner.

Last-In, First-Out Method

When the lifo method is used in a perpetual inventory system, the cost of the units sold is the cost of the most recent purchases. To illustrate, Exhibit 6 shows the journal entries for purchases and sales and the subsidiary ledger account for Item 127B, prepared on a lifo basis.

Exhibit 5

Entries and Perpetual Inventory Account (Fifo)

Jan. 4	Accounts Receivable	210	
	Sales		210
4	Cost of Merchandise Sold	140	
	Merchandise Inventory		140
10	Merchandise Inventory	168	
	Accounts Payable		168
22	Accounts Receivable	120	
	Sales		120
22	Cost of Merchandise Sold	81	
	Merchandise Inventory		81
28	Accounts Receivable	60	
	Sales		60
28	Cost of Merchandise Sold	42	
	Merchandise Inventory		42
30	Merchandise Inventory	220	
	Accounts Payable		220

Item 127B

	Purchases			Cost of Merchandise Sold			Inventory		
Date	Quantity	Unit Cost	Total Cost	Quantity	Unit Cost	Total Cost	Quantity	Unit Cost	Total Cost
Jan. 1							10	20	200
4				7	20	140	3	20	60
10	8	21	168				3	20	60
							8	21	168
22				3	20	60			
				1	21	21	7	21	147
28				2	21	42	5	21	105
30	10	22	220				5	21	105
							10	22	220

Exhibit 6

Entries and Perpetual Inventory Account (Lifo)

Jan. 4	Accounts Receivable	210	
	Sales		210
4	Cost of Merchandise Sold	140	
	Merchandise Inventory		140
10	Merchandise Inventory	168	
	Accounts Payable		168
22	Accounts Receivable	120	
	Sales		120
22	Cost of Merchandise Sold	84	
	Merchandise Inventory		84
28	Accounts Receivable	60	
	Sales		60
28	Cost of Merchandise Sold	42	
	Merchandise Inventory		42
30	Merchandise Inventory	220	
	Accounts Payable		220

Item 127B

	Purchases			Cost of Merchandise Sold			Inventory		
Date	Quantity	Unit Cost	Total Cost	Quantity	Unit Cost	Total Cost	Quantity	Unit Cost	Total Cost
Jan. 1							10	20	200
4				7	20	140	3	20	60
10	8	21	168				3	20	60
							8	21	168
22				4	21	84	3	20	60
							4	21	84
28				2	21	42	3	20	60
							2	21	42
30	10	22	220				3	20	60
							2	21	42
							10	22	220

If you compare the ledger accounts for the fifo perpetual system and the lifo perpetual system, you should discover that the accounts are the same through the January 10 purchase. Using lifo, however, the cost of the 4 units sold on January 22 is the cost of the units from the January 10 purchase ($21 per unit). The cost of the 7 units in inventory after the sale on January 22 is the cost of the 3 units remaining from the beginning inventory and the cost of the 4 units remaining from the January 10 purchase. The remainder of the lifo illustration is explained in a similar manner.

When the lifo method is used, the inventory ledger is sometimes maintained in units only. The units are converted to dollars when the financial statements are prepared at the end of the period.

The use of the lifo method was originally limited to rare situations in which the units sold were taken from the most recently acquired goods. For tax reasons, which we will discuss later, its use has greatly increased during the past few decades. Lifo is now often used, even when it does not represent the physical flow of goods.

Average Cost Method

When the average cost method is used in a perpetual inventory system, an average unit cost for each type of item is computed each time a purchase is made. This unit cost is then used to determine the cost of each sale until another purchase is made and a new average is computed. This averaging technique is called a *moving average*. Since the average cost method is rarely used in a perpetual inventory system, we do not illustrate it in this chapter.

Computerized Perpetual Inventory Systems

The records for a perpetual inventory system may be maintained manually. However, such a system is costly and time consuming for businesses with a large number of inventory items with many purchase and sales transactions. In most cases, the record keeping for perpetual inventory systems is computerized.

An example of using computers in maintaining perpetual inventory records for retail stores is described below.

1. The relevant details for each inventory item, such as a description, quantity, and unit size, are stored in an inventory record. The individual inventory records make up the computerized inventory file, the total of which agrees with the balance of the inventory ledger account.
2. Each time an item is purchased or returned by a customer, the inventory data are entered into the computer's inventory records and files.
3. Each time an item is sold, a salesclerk scans the item's bar code with an optical scanner. The scanner reads the magnetic code and rings up the sale on the cash register. The inventory records and files are then updated for the cost of goods sold. For example, Wal-Mart, Target, Sears, and other retailers use bar code scanners to update inventory records and sales.
4. After a physical inventory is taken, the inventory count data are entered into the computer. These data are compared with the current balances, and a listing of the overages and shortages is printed. The inventory balances are then adjusted to the quantities determined by the physical count.

Such systems can be extended to aid managers in controlling and managing inventory quantities. For example, items that are selling fast can be reordered before the stock is depleted. Past sales patterns can be analyzed to determine when to mark down merchandise for sales and when to restock seasonal merchandise. In addition, such systems can provide managers with data for developing and fine-tuning their marketing strategies. For example, such data can be used to evaluate the effectiveness of advertising campaigns and sales promotions.

Inventory Costing Methods under a Periodic Inventory System

5 Determine the cost of inventory under the periodic inventory system, using the first-in, first-out; last-in, first-out; and average cost methods.

When the periodic inventory system is used, only revenue is recorded each time a sale is made. No entry is made at the time of the sale to record the cost of the merchandise sold. At the end of the accounting period, a physical inventory is taken to determine the cost of the inventory and the cost of the merchandise sold. Like the perpetual inventory system, a cost flow assumption must be made when identical units are acquired at different unit costs during a period. In such cases, the fifo, lifo, or average cost method is used.

What is the cost of merchandise sold if the beginning inventory is $50,000, the ending inventory is $65,000, the net purchases are $400,000, and the transportation in is $12,000?

$397,000 ($50,000 + $400,000 + $12,000 − $65,000)

First-In, First-Out Method

To illustrate the use of the fifo method in a periodic inventory system, we assume the following data:

Jan. 1	Inventory:	200 units at	$ 9	$ 1,800
Mar. 10	Purchase:	300 units at	10	3,000
Sept. 21	Purchase:	400 units at	11	4,400
Nov. 18	Purchase:	100 units at	12	1,200
Available for sale during year		1,000		$10,400

The physical count on December 31 shows that 300 units have not been sold. Using the fifo method, the cost of the 700 units sold is determined as follows:

Earliest costs, Jan. 1:	200 units at	$ 9	$1,800
Next earliest costs, Mar. 10:	300 units at	10	3,000
Next earliest costs, Sept. 21:	200 units at	11	2,200
Cost of merchandise sold:	700		$7,000

Deducting the cost of merchandise sold of $7,000 from the $10,400 of merchandise available for sale yields $3,400 as the cost of the inventory at December 31. The $3,400 inventory is made up of the most recent costs incurred for this item. Exhibit 7 shows the relationship of the cost of merchandise sold during the year and the inventory at December 31.

Last-In, First-Out Method

When the lifo method is used, the cost of merchandise sold is made up of the most recent costs. Based on the data in the fifo example, the cost of the 700 units of inventory is determined as follows:

Most recent costs, Nov. 18:	100 units at	$12	$1,200
Next most recent costs, Sept. 21:	400 units at	11	4,400
Next most recent costs, Mar. 10:	200 units at	10	2,000
Cost of merchandise sold:	700		$7,600

Exhibit 7

First-In, First-Out Flow of Costs

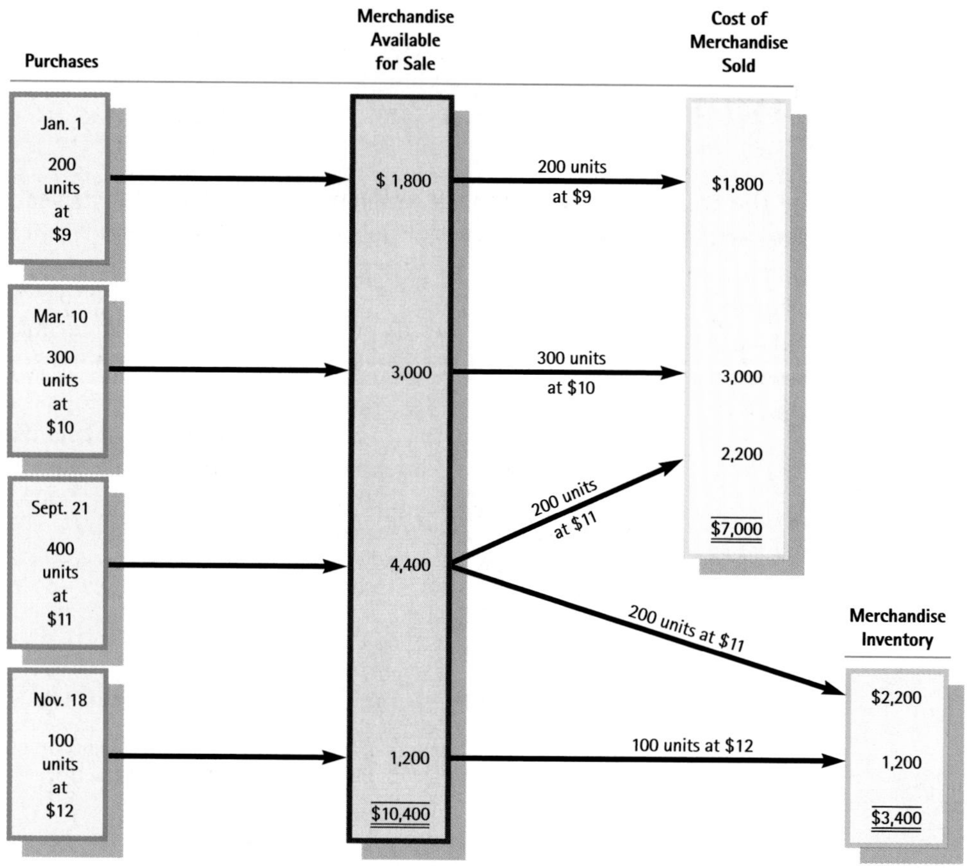

Deducting the cost of merchandise sold of $7,600 from the $10,400 of merchandise available for sale yields $2,800 as the cost of the inventory at December 31. The $2,800 inventory is made up of the earliest costs incurred for this item. Exhibit 8 shows the relationship of the cost of merchandise sold during the year and the inventory at December 31.

Average Cost Method

The average cost method is sometimes called the ***weighted average method.*** When this method is used, costs are matched against revenue according to an average of the unit cost of the goods sold. The same weighted average unit costs are used in determining the cost of the merchandise inventory at the end of the period. For businesses in which merchandise sales may be made up of various purchases of identical units, the average method approximates the physical flow of goods.

The weighted average unit cost is determined by dividing the total cost of the units of each item available for sale during the period by the related number of units of that item. Using the same cost data as in the fifo and lifo examples, the average cost of the 1,000 units, $10.40, and the cost of the 700 units, $7,280, are determined as follows:

Average unit cost: $10,400/1,000 units = $10.40

Cost of merchandise sold: 700 units at $10.40 = $7,280

Deducting the cost of merchandise sold of $7,280 from the $10,400 of merchandise available for sale yields $3,120 as the cost of the inventory at December 31.

Exhibit 8

Last-In, First-Out Flow of Costs

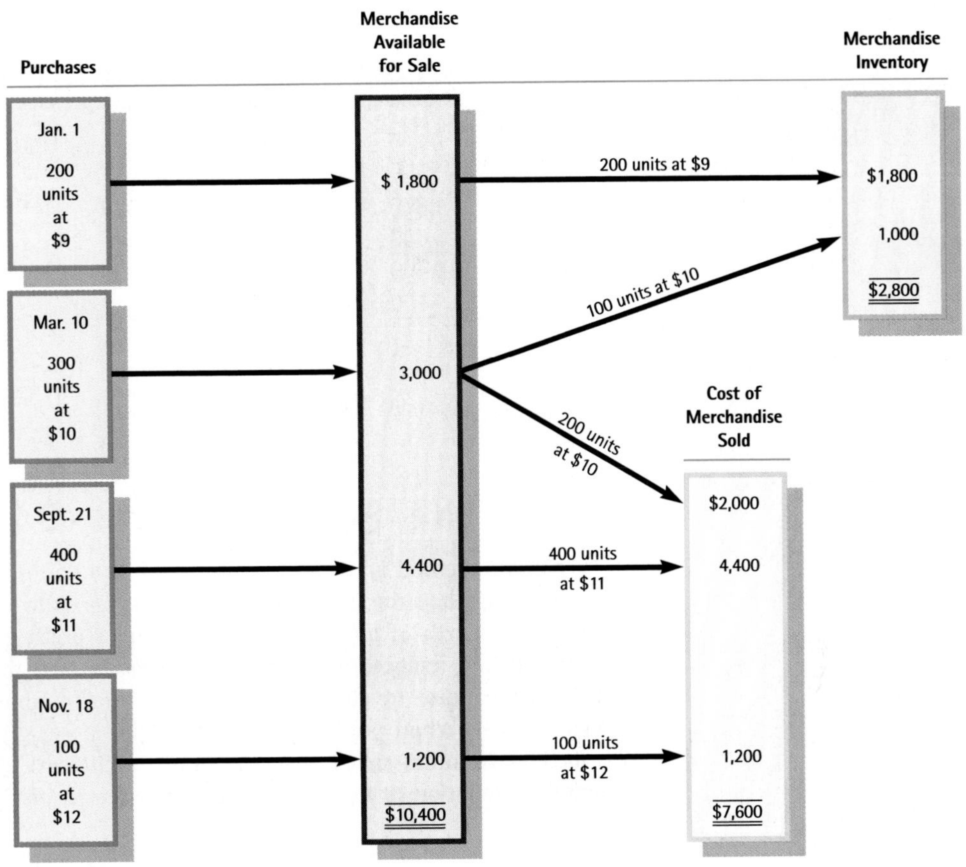

Comparing Inventory Costing Methods

6 Compare and contrast the use of the three inventory costing methods.

As we have illustrated, a different cost flow is assumed for each of the three alternative methods of costing inventories. You should note that if the cost of units had remained stable, all three methods would have yielded the same results. Since prices do change, however, the three methods will normally yield different amounts for (1) the cost of the merchandise sold for the period, (2) the gross profit (and net income) for the period, and (3) the ending inventory. Using the preceding examples for the periodic inventory system and assuming that net sales were $15,000, the partial income statements shown at the top of the next page indicate the effects of each method when prices are rising.[2]

As these partial income statements show, the fifo method yielded the lowest amount for the cost of merchandise sold and the highest amount for gross profit (and net income). It also yielded the highest amount for the ending inventory. On the other hand, the lifo method yielded the highest amount for the cost of merchandise sold, the lowest amount for gross profit (and net income), and the lowest amount for ending inventory. The average cost method yielded results that were between those of fifo and lifo.

2 Similar results would also occur when comparing inventory costing methods under a perpetual inventory system.

Partial Income Statements

	First-In, First-Out		Average Cost		Last-In, First-Out	
Net sales		$15,000		$15,000		$15,000
Cost of merchandise sold:						
Beginning inventory	$ 1,800		$ 1,800		$ 1,800	
Purchases	8,600		8,600		8,600	
Merchandise available for sale	$10,400		$10,400		$10,400	
Less ending inventory	3,400		3,120		2,800	
Cost of merchandise sold		7,000		7,280		7,600
Gross profit		$ 8,000		$ 7,720		$ 7,400

Use of the First-In, First-Out Method

When the fifo method is used during a period of inflation or rising prices, the earlier unit costs are lower than the more recent unit costs, as shown in the preceding fifo example. Much of the benefit of the larger amount of gross profit is lost, however, because the inventory must be replaced at ever higher prices. In fact, the balance sheet will report the ending merchandise inventory at an amount that is about the same as its current replacement cost. When prices are increasing, the larger gross profits that result from the fifo method are often called *inventory profits* or *illusory profits*. You should note that in a period of deflation or declining prices, the effect is just the opposite.

Use of the Last-In, First-Out Method

When the lifo method is used during a period of inflation or rising prices, the results are opposite those of the other two methods. As shown in the preceding example, the lifo method will yield a higher amount of cost of merchandise sold, a lower amount of gross profit, and a lower amount of inventory at the end of the period than the other two methods. The reason for these effects is that the cost of the most recently acquired units is about the same as the cost of their replacement. In a period of inflation, the more recent unit costs are higher than the earlier unit costs. Thus, it can be argued that the lifo method more nearly matches current costs with current revenues. For example, DaimlerChrysler's reason for changing from the fifo method to the lifo method was stated in the following footnote that accompanied its financial statements:

> *DaimlerChrysler changed its method of accounting from first-in, first-out (fifo) to last-in, first-out (lifo) for substantially all of its domestic productive inventories. The change to lifo was made to more accurately match current costs with current revenues.*

The rules used for external financial reporting need not be the same as those used for income tax reporting. One exception to this general rule is the use of lifo. If a firm elects to use lifo inventory valuation for tax purposes, then the business must also use lifo for external financial reporting. This is called the **lifo conformity rule**. Thus, in periods of rising prices, lifo offers an income tax savings because it reports the lowest amount of net income of the three methods. Many managers elect to use lifo because of the tax savings, even though the reported earnings will be lower.

The ending inventory on the balance sheet may be quite different from its current replacement cost (or fifo estimate). In such cases, the financial statements will include a note that states the estimated difference between the lifo inventory and the inventory if fifo had been used. An example of such a note is shown below for the Kmart Corporation.

> *The last-in, first-out ("LIFO") method . . . was used to determine the cost for $5,537, . . . of inventory as of fiscal year-end 2001. . . . Inventories valued on LIFO were $269 . . . lower than amounts that would have been reported using the first-in, first-out ("FIFO") method at fiscal year-end 2001. . . .*

In periods of rising prices, the inventory under lifo would be less than under fifo, as was the case for Kmart. Again, you should note that in a period of deflation or falling price levels, the effects are just the opposite.

Use of the Average Cost Method

As you might have already reasoned, the average cost method is, in a sense, a compromise between fifo and lifo. The effect of price trends is averaged in determining the cost of merchandise sold and the ending inventory. For a series of purchases, the average cost will be the same, regardless of the direction of price trends. For example, reversing the sequence of unit costs presented in the preceding illustration would not affect the reported cost of merchandise sold, gross profit, or ending inventory.

Valuation of Inventory at Other Than Cost

7 Determine the proper valuation of inventory at other than cost, using the lower-of-cost-or-market and net realizable value concepts.

Merchandise inventory is usually presented in the Current Assets section of the balance sheet, following receivables. The method of determining the cost of the inventory (fifo, lifo, or average) should be shown. It is not unusual for large businesses with varied activities to use different costing methods for different segments of their inventories. The details may be disclosed in parentheses on the balance sheet or in a footnote to the financial statements.

Inventory is valued at other than cost when (1) the cost of replacing items in inventory is below the recorded cost, and (2) the inventory is not salable at normal sales prices. This latter case may be due to imperfections, shop wear, style changes, or other causes. In either situation, the method of valuing the inventories (cost or lower of cost or market) should also be disclosed on the balance sheet.

Valuation at Lower of Cost or Market

If the cost of replacing an item in inventory is lower than the original purchase cost, the **lower-of-cost-or-market (LCM) method** is used to value the inventory. *Market,* as used in *lower of cost or market,* is the cost to replace the merchandise on the inventory date. This market value is based on quantities normally purchased from the usual source of supply. In businesses where inflation is the norm, market prices rarely decline. In businesses where technology changes rapidly (e.g., microcomputers and televisions), market declines are common. The primary advantage of the lower-of-cost-or-market method is that the gross profit (and net income) is reduced in the period in which the market decline occurred, rather than waiting until the inventory is sold.

In applying the lower-of-cost-or-market method, the cost and replacement cost can be determined in one of three ways. Cost and replacement cost can be determined for (1) each item in the inventory, (2) major classes or categories of inventory, or (3) the inventory as a whole. In practice, the cost and replacement cost of each item are usually determined.

If the cost of an item is $410, its current replacement cost is $400, and its selling price is $525, at what amount should the item be included in the inventory according to the LCM method?

$400

To illustrate, assume that 400 identical units of Item A are in inventory, acquired at a unit cost of $10.25 each. If at the inventory date the item would cost $10.50 to replace, the cost price of $10.25 would be multiplied by 400 to determine the inventory value. On the other hand, if the item could be replaced at $9.50 a unit, the replacement cost of $9.50 would be used for valuation purposes.

Exhibit 9 illustrates a method of organizing inventory data and applying lower-of-cost-or-market to each inventory item. The amount of the market decline, $450 ($15,520 − $15,070), may be reported as a separate item on the income statement or included in the cost of merchandise sold. Regardless, net income will be reduced by the amount of the market decline.

Exhibit 9

Determining Inventory at Lower of Cost or Market

				Total		
Commodity	Inventory Quantity	Unit Cost Price	Unit Market Price	Cost	Market	Lower of C or M
A	400	$10.25	$ 9.50	$ 4,100	$ 3,800	$ 3,800
B	120	22.50	24.10	2,700	2,892	2,700
C	600	8.00	7.75	4,800	4,650	4,650
D	280	14.00	14.75	3,920	4,130	3,920
Total				$15,520	$15,472	$15,070

INTERNATIONAL PERSPECTIVE

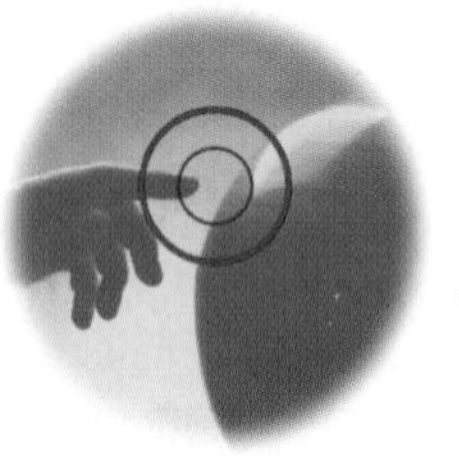

In Japan, inventories are generally valued at cost rather than lower of cost or net realizable value.

Valuation at Net Realizable Value

As you would expect, merchandise that is out of date, spoiled, or damaged or that can be sold only at prices below cost should be written down. Such merchandise should be valued at net realizable value. **Net realizable value** is the estimated selling price less any direct cost of disposal, such as sales commissions. For example, assume that damaged merchandise costing $1,000 can be sold for only $800, and direct selling expenses are estimated to be $150. This inventory should be valued at $650 ($800 − $150), which is its net realizable value. For example, Sotheby's Holdings Inc., a major art provider of art auction services, described inventory acquired under distressed circumstances in footnotes to its financial statements. This inventory was valued below cost, as shown below.

	As of December 31	
	2001	2000
	(Thousands of Dollars)	
Inventory, at cost	$17,590	$22,080
Net realizable value allowances	(6,044)	(8,058)
Total	$11,546	$14,022

Quick Response

8 Describe how inventories are being reduced through quick response.

To satisfy consumer demand, with the least amount of inventory and inefficiency, merchandisers and manufacturers are embracing **quick response** or *efficient consumer response* strategies. Quick response is used to optimize inventory levels in the value chain by electronically sharing common forecast, inventory, sales, and payment information between manufacturers and merchandisers, using the Internet or other electronic means. Using quick response, a merchandiser electronically transmits daily sales information to the manufacturer. The manufacturer uses this sales information to ship replacement stock to the merchandiser, usually within days of receiving the sales information. Shared forecasts are used to help the manufacturer plan for sales promotions or other seasonal factors that may require more or less goods than the replaced amounts. For example, VF Corporation, the manufacturer of Wrangler® jeans, reduced its inventory and increased sales by entering into a quick response program with Federated Department Stores (Bloomingdale's, Macy's). Under this program, VF receives sales information from Federated cash register scanners in the morning and ships goods directly to the retail store within 24 hours.

Prior to the quick response program, VF took about 30 days to deliver product to the selling floor after an order was received. Both VF and Federated saw significant improvements from the quick response strategy. VF estimated that jean sales improved by 40% as a result of having the right colors and sizes on Federated's shelves, while Federated eliminated over $100 million in inefficient paperwork by using electronic ordering. Both firms saw significant reduction in inventories.

Throughout the last two decades, inventory management techniques, such as quick response, have reduced the relative size of inventory by 35 percent for U.S. firms.[3] This has caused the economy to respond more quickly to changes in consumer demand and to be less wasteful in inventory costs. Managing inventory efficiently requires that the amount of inventory be known at all times. Accountants provide this information to managers to help guide inventory policy, so that the costs identified above are minimized.

Inventory Analysis and Interpretation

9 Determine and interpret the inventory turnover ratio, the number of days' sales in inventory, and lifo reserve adjustments.

As with many types of financial analyses, the efficiency and effectiveness of managing inventory can be analyzed by using more than one measure. Two such measures are the inventory turnover and the number of days' sales in inventory.

Inventory Efficiency Ratios

Inventory turnover measures the relationship between the volume of goods (merchandise) sold and the amount of inventory carried during the period. It is computed as follows:

$$\text{Inventory turnover} = \frac{\text{Cost of merchandise sold*}}{\text{Average inventory}}$$

*For a manufacturing company, the numerator would be cost of goods sold.

The average inventory is computed using weekly, monthly, or annual figures. To simplify, we determine the average inventory by dividing the sum of the inventories at the

3 Bernard DeGrove and Kevin Mellyn, "The Argument for Financial-Chain Management," *eCFO* (December 2000).

beginning and end of the year by 2. As long as the amount of inventory held throughout the year is stable, this average will be accurate enough for our analysis.

To illustrate, the following data have been taken from recent annual reports for Safeway Inc. and Zale Corporation:

	Safeway Inc	Zale Corp.
Cost of merchandise sold	$22,482,400,000	$920,003,000
Inventories:		
Beginning of year	$2,444,900,000	$571,669,000
End of year	$2,508,000,000	$630,450,000
Average	$2,476,450,000	$601,059,500
Inventory turnover	9.1	1.5

The inventory turnover is 9.1 for Safeway and 1.5 for Zale. Generally, the larger the inventory turnover, the more efficient and effective the management of the inventory. However, differences in companies and industries are too great to allow specific statements as to what is a good inventory turnover. For example, Safeway is the second largest food retailer in the United States. Because most of Safeway's inventory is perishable, we would expect it to have a high inventory turnover. In contrast, Zale Corporation is the largest specialty retailer of fine jewelry in the United States. Thus, we would expect Zale to have a lower inventory turnover than Safeway, since jewelry is not perishable.

The **number of days' sales in inventory** approximates the length of time it takes to acquire, sell, and replace the inventory. It is computed as follows:

$$\text{Number of days' sales in inventory} = \frac{\text{Inventory, end of year}}{\text{Average daily cost of merchandise sold}}$$

The average daily cost of merchandise sold is determined by dividing the cost of merchandise sold by 365. The number of days' sales in inventory for Safeway and Zale is computed as shown below.

	Safeway	Zale
Average daily cost of merchandise sold:		
$22,482,400,000/365	$61,595,616	
$920,003,000/365		$2,520,556
Ending inventory	$2,508,000,000	$630,450,000
Number of days' sales in inventory	41 days	250 days

Generally, the lower the number of days' sales in inventory, the better. As with inventory turnover, we should expect differences among industries, such as those for Safeway and Zale.

Inventory ratios can also be used to evaluate inventory performance trends over time. For example, Exhibit 10 shows the inventory turnover ratio for Best Buy Co. for five recent years. Over the five-year period, Best Buy has improved its inventory turnover from 4.6 to 7.6 turns per year. Best Buy credited this strong improvement to quick response policies, lower markdowns, and faster-moving product assortments.

Lifo Reserve and the Balance Sheet

We discussed in a previous section that, in periods of rising prices, the inventory valuation under fifo will approximate current cost, while a comparative lifo valuation would be smaller, because it is made up of older cost layers. In some cases, the inventory valuation could be much smaller if the lifo layers were very old. For example, General Motors

Exhibit 10

Best Buy Inventory Turnover over Five Years

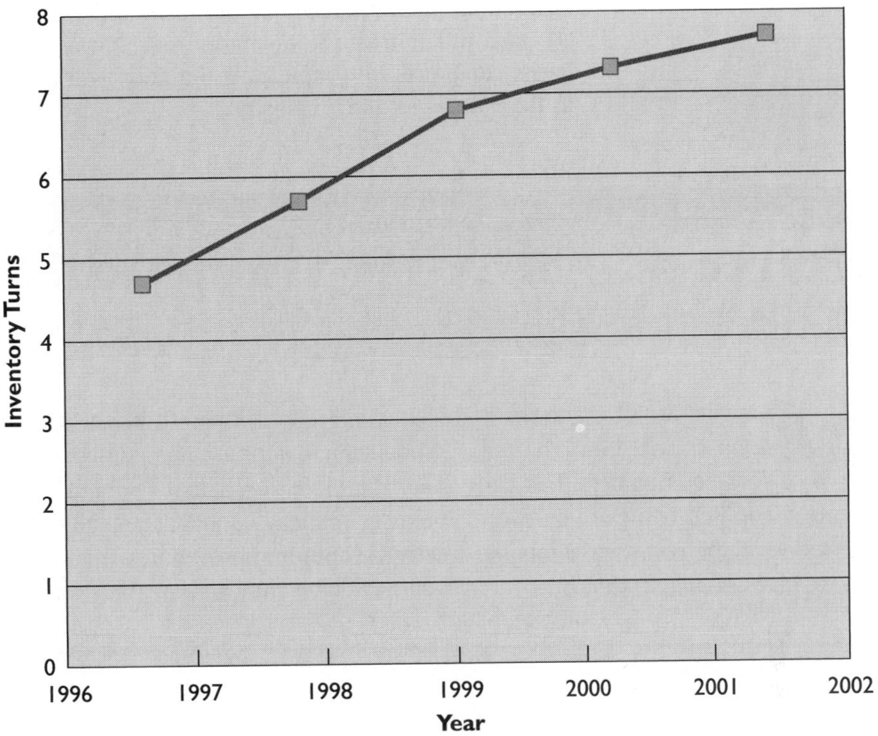

Corporation reported inventory under lifo at $10,945 million, while the comparative fifo valuation was $12,874 million. This difference can make it very difficult to compare companies that are using two different inventory valuation methods. To help analysts with this problem, businesses using lifo must report a lifo reserve. The **lifo reserve** is the difference between comparative inventories valued at fifo[4] and lifo, and is computed as follows:

Lifo reserve = Inventory (fifo) − Inventory (lifo)

Thus, the lifo reserve for General Motors can be shown to be:

$1,929 million = $12,874 million − $10,945 million

The reported lifo inventory, lifo reserve, and relative size of the lifo reserve for some selected businesses are shown in Exhibit 11. As can be seen, the lifo reserve can represent a sizable portion of the current value (fifo) of the inventory. The reason for the wide

Exhibit 11

Lifo Reserve Relative Sizes

Company	(in millions) Lifo Reported Inventory	Lifo Reserve	Fifo Equivalent	% Lifo Reserve to Fifo
ChevronTexaco Corporation	$ 610	$ 861	$ 1,471	58.5%
Exxon Mobil Corporation	8,304	6,706	15,010	44.7%
Caterpillar Inc.	2,692	2,065	4,757	43.4%
General Motors Corporation	10,945	1,929	12,874	15.0%
The Kroger Company	4,066	496	4,562	10.9%
General Electric Company	7,812	845	8,657	9.8%
Wal-Mart Stores, Inc.	21,442	202	21,644	0.9%

4 The actual rule states "replacement cost," which is often similar to fifo.

differences in the percent of the lifo reserve to fifo is a result of two major factors: (1) price inflation of the inventory and (2) the age of the inventory. Generally, old lifo layers combined with rapid price inflation will result in large lifo reserves, such as seen in the natural resource industry.

Ethics in Action
Where's the Bonus?

Managers are often given bonuses based on reported earnings numbers. This can create a conflict. Lifo can improve the value of the company through lower taxes, as illustrated by General Motors. However, lifo also produces a lower earnings number and, therefore, lower management bonuses. Ethically, managers should select accounting procedures that will maximize the value of the firm, rather than their own compensation. Compensation specialists can help avoid this ethical dilemma by adjusting the bonus plan for the accounting procedure differences.

Analysts should use the lifo reserve to adjust inventory efficiency ratios when a company is using lifo valuation. Performing this adjustment restates the lifo inventory to current cost valuation. Thus, for a company using lifo, the inventory turnover and number of days' sales in inventory would be computed as;

$$\text{Inventory turnover} = \frac{\text{Cost of merchandise sold}}{\text{Average inventory} + \text{Average lifo reserve}}$$

$$\text{Number of days' sales in inventory} = \frac{\text{Inventory, end of year} + \text{Lifo reserve, end of year}}{\text{Average daily cost of merchandise sold}}$$

The average lifo reserve in the inventory turnover ratio would be computed in the same way as the average inventory. That is, the beginning and ending balance are summed and then divided by 2. In this way, the inventory figure in the denominator is expressed in more current dollar terms and avoids the distortion of old lifo cost layers. To illustrate the computations, the following information was reported by General Motors Corporation.

	Inventory (Lifo valuation in millions)	Lifo Reserve (in millions)
Beginning balance	$10,638	$1,890
Ending balance	10,945	1,929
Average balance (sum divided by 2)	10,791	1,909

General Motors had a cost of goods sold of $145,664 (in millions); therefore, the adjusted inventory turnover ratio would be:

$$\frac{\$145{,}664}{\$10{,}791 + \$1{,}909} = 11.47$$

Without the lifo reserve adjustment, the inventory turnover would be 13.50 ($145,664/ $10,791).

Likewise, the adjusted number of days' sales in inventory would be calculated as:

$$\frac{\$10{,}945 + \$1{,}929}{\$145{,}664/365} = 32.26 \text{ days}$$

Without the lifo reserve adjustment, the number of days' sales in inventory would be 27.43 days ($10,945/($145,664 ÷ 365)).

Lifo Reserve and the Income Statement

As we discussed earlier, management may desire lifo valuation for tax purposes in periods of rising prices because the most recent costs are included in the cost of merchandise (goods) sold. These recent costs are the highest costs, resulting in a comparatively smaller

Focus on Cash Flow

Inventories and Cash Flows

If a company increases its inventory balances from period to period, then the amount of cash invested in inventory is increasing. In contrast, if the inventory balances are decreasing, cash is being returned to the business. This is why companies use inventory reduction strategies, such as quick response, in order to capture one-time cash benefits from reducing inventory. On the other hand, if management grows inventory in anticipation of sales that do not materialize, then cash will be used.

The impact of changes in inventory balances is shown in the operating activities section of the statement of cash flows. For example, Krispy Kreme Doughnuts Inc. reported the following (in thousands):

Net income	$14,725
Inventory, January 30, 2000	9,979
Inventory, January 31, 2001	12,031

The operating section of the statement of cash flows is reproduced for Krispy Kreme below, with the shaded area showing the impact of inventory changes.

$ in thousands **For the Fiscal Year Ended**	**Jan. 28, 2001**
Operating activities:	
Net earnings	$14,725
Depreciation, amortization and other noncash charges	9,907
Changes in operating assets and liabilities:	
Receivables	(3,434)
Merchandise inventories	(2,052)
Other assets	1,239
Accounts payable	1,591
Other current liabilities	8,600
Total cash provided by operating activities	$30,576

As you can see, the increase in inventory from $9,979 to $12,031 is reflected as a use of $2,052 cash on the statement of cash flows. Krispy Kreme is a growing business; thus, using cash to increase inventories would be expected.

net income than would be the case under fifo. Naturally, a smaller net income results in comparatively lower income taxes. The size of the lifo reserve multiplied by the tax rate is an estimate of the tax deferral a business enjoyed since using lifo. For example, if we assume a 35 percent tax rate, General Motors has deferred over $675 million dollars ($1,929,000,000 × 35%) since adopting lifo. Thus, management can make a strong case for using lifo in periods of rising prices.

If a lifo business dips into old lifo cost layers, either as a result of more efficient inventory management policies, unexpected demand relative to production, or eliminating unpopular products, the lifo reserve is *liquidated.* For example, Kmart Corporation recently reduced its lifo reserve from $202 million to $194 million, or a lifo liquidation of $8 million. A lifo liquidation causes the recapture of old cost layers back into the cost of merchandise (goods) sold. Thus, lifo liquidations cause the cost of merchandise sold to be lower, and operating income and income taxes to be larger, than would be the case if recent-cost goods were sold. These negative tax consequences are a disincentive to embracing inventory reduction strategies, such as quick response. Often, managers of lifo businesses must "bite the tax bullet" in order to gain the long-term benefits of faster inventory turnover.

Summary of Learning Goals

1 Identify the types of inventory used by merchandisers and manufacturers.

The inventory of a merchandiser is called merchandise inventory. The cost of merchandise inventory that is sold is reported on the income statement. Manufacturers typically have three types of inventory: materials, work-in-process, and finished goods. When finished goods are sold, the cost is reported on the income statement as cost of goods sold.

2 Summarize and provide examples of internal control procedures that apply to inventories.

Internal control procedures for inventories include those developed to protect the inventories from damage, employee theft, and customer theft. In addition, a physical inventory count should be taken periodically to detect shortages as well as to deter employee thefts.

3 Describe three inventory cost flow assumptions and how they impact the income statement and balance sheet.

The three common cost flow assumptions used in business are the (1) first-in, first-out method, (2) last-in, first-out method, and (3) average cost method. Each method normally yields different amounts for the cost of merchandise sold and the ending merchandise inventory. Thus, the choice of a cost flow assumption directly affects the income statement and balance sheet.

4 Determine the cost of inventory under the perpetual inventory system, using the first-in, first-out; last-in, first-out; and average cost methods.

In a perpetual inventory system, the number of units and the cost of each type of merchandise are recorded in a subsidiary inventory ledger, with a separate account for each type of merchandise. Inventory costs and the amounts charged against revenue are illustrated using the fifo and lifo methods.

5 Determine the cost of inventory under the periodic inventory system, using the first-in, first-out; last-in, first-out; and average cost methods.

In a periodic inventory system, a physical inventory is taken to determine the cost of the inventory and the cost of merchandise sold. Inventory costs and the amounts charged against revenue are illustrated using fifo, lifo, and average cost methods.

6 Compare and contrast the use of the three inventory costing methods.

The three inventory costing methods will normally yield different amounts for (1) the ending inventory, (2) the cost of the merchandise sold for the period, and (3) the gross profit (and net income) for the period. During periods of inflation, the fifo method yields the lowest amount for the cost of merchandise sold, the highest amount for gross profit (and net income), and the highest amount for the ending inventory. The lifo method yields the opposite results. During periods of deflation, the preceding effects are reversed. The average cost method yields results that are between those of fifo and lifo.

7 Determine the proper valuation of inventory at other than cost, using the lower-of-cost-or-market and net realizable value concepts.

If the market price of an item of inventory is lower than its cost, the lower market price is used to compute the value of the item. Market price is the cost to replace the merchandise on the inventory date. It is possible to apply the lower of cost or market to each item in the inventory, to major classes or categories, or to the inventory as a whole.

Merchandise that can be sold only at prices below cost should be valued at net realizable value, which is the estimated selling price less any direct costs of disposal.

8 Describe how inventories are being reduced through quick response.

Quick response is used to optimize inventory levels in the value chain by electronically sharing common forecast, inventory, sales, and payment information between manufacturers and merchandisers, using the Internet or other electronic means. Using shared information in this way allows manufacturers to more quickly ship goods to replace sold items on the retailer's shelves.

9 Determine and interpret the inventory turnover ratio, the number of days' sales in inventory, and lifo reserve adjustments.

The inventory turnover ratio, computed as the cost of merchandise sold divided by the average inventory, measures the relationship between the volume of goods (merchandise) sold and the amount of inventory carried during the period. The number of days' sales in inventory, computed as the ending inventory divided by the average daily cost of merchandise sold, measures the length of time it takes to acquire, sell, and replace the inventory. The lifo reserve is the difference between the inventory valued under fifo and the inventory valued under lifo. Lifo firms should adjust their inventory turnover and number of days' sales in inventory ratios for the lifo reserve in order to reflect more current costs in the ending inventory.

Glossary

Average cost method The method of inventory costing that is based upon the assumption that costs should be charged against revenue by using the weighted average unit cost of the items sold.

Cost of goods sold The cost of product sold.

Finished goods inventory The cost of finished products on hand that have not been sold.

First-in, first-out (fifo) method A method of inventory costing based on the assumption that the costs of merchandise sold should be charged against revenue in the order in which the costs were incurred.

Inventory ledger The subsidiary ledger that shows the amount of each type of inventory.

Inventory turnover A ratio that measures the relationship between the volume of goods (merchandise) sold and the amount of inventory carried during the period.

Last-in, first-out (lifo) method A method of inventory costing based on the assumption that the most recent merchandise inventory costs should be charged against revenue.

Lifo conformity rule A financial reporting rule requiring a firm that elects to use lifo inventory valuation for tax purposes to also use lifo for external financial reporting.

Lifo reserve A required disclosure for lifo firms, showing the difference between inventory valued under fifo and inventory valued under lifo.

Lower-of-cost-or-market (LCM) method A method of valuing inventory that reports the inventory at the lower of its cost or current market value (replacement cost).

Materials inventory The cost of materials that have not yet entered into the manufacturing process.

Merchandise inventory Merchandise on hand and available for sale to customers.

Net realizable value The estimated selling price of an item of inventory less any direct costs of disposal, such as sales commissions.

Number of days' sales in inventory A measure of the length of time it takes to acquire, sell, and replace the inventory.

Physical inventory The detailed listing of merchandise on hand.

Quick response A method for optimizing inventory levels in the value chain by electronically sharing common forecast, inventory, sales, and payment information between manufacturers and merchandisers, using the Internet or other electronic means.

Work in process inventory The direct materials costs, the direct labor costs, and the factory overhead costs that have entered into the manufacturing process, but are associated with product that has not been finished.

Illustrative Accounting Application Problem

Stewart Co.'s beginning inventory and purchases during the year ended December 31, 2005, were as follows:

		Units	Unit Cost	Total Cost
January 1	Inventory	1,000	$50.00	$ 50,000
March 10	Purchase	1,200	52.50	63,000
June 25	Sold 800 units			
August 30	Purchase	800	55.00	44,000
October 5	Sold 1,500 units			
November 26	Purchase	2,000	56.00	112,000
December 31	Sold 1,000 units			
Total		5,000		$269,000

Instructions

1. Determine the cost of inventory on December 31, 2005, using the perpetual inventory system and each of the following inventory costing methods:
   a. first-in, first-out
   b. last-in, first-out
2. Determine the cost of inventory on December 31, 2005, using the periodic inventory system and each of the following inventory costing methods:
   a. first-in, first-out
   b. last-in, first-out
   c. average cost
3. Assume that the cost of merchandise sold was $173,800 for 2005 and the inventory valuation is as determined in (1a). Determine the:
   a. inventory turnover ratio
   b. number of days' sales in inventory ratio

Solution

1. a. First-in, first-out method: $95,200

Date	Purchases			Cost of Merchandise Sold			Inventory		
	Quantity	Unit Cost	Total Cost	Quantity	Unit Cost	Total Cost	Quantity	Unit Cost	Total Cost
2005 Jan. 1							1,000	50.00	50,000
Mar. 10	1,200	52.50	63,000				1,000	50.00	50,000
							1,200	52.50	63,000
June 25				800	50.00	40,000	200	50.00	10,000
							1,200	52.50	63,000
Aug. 30	800	55.00	44,000				200	50.00	10,000
							1,200	52.50	63,000
							800	55.00	44,000
Oct. 5				200	50.00	10,000	700	55.00	38,500
				1,200	52.50	63,000			
				100	55.00	5,500			
Nov. 26	2,000	56.00	112,000				700	55.00	38,500
							2,000	56.00	112,000
Dec. 31				700	55.00	38,500	1,700	56.00	95,200
				300	56.00	16,800			

b. Last-in, first-out method: $91,000 ($35,000 + $56,000)

Date	Purchases			Cost of Merchandise Sold			Inventory		
	Quantity	Unit Cost	Total Cost	Quantity	Unit Cost	Total Cost	Quantity	Unit Cost	Total Cost
2005 Jan. 1							1,000	50.00	50,000
Mar. 10	1,200	52.50	63,000				1,000	50.00	50,000
							1,200	52.50	63,000
June 25				800	52.50	42,000	1,000	50.00	50,000
							400	52.50	21,000
Aug. 30	800	55.00	44,000				1,000	50.00	50,000
							400	52.50	21,000
							800	55.00	44,000
Oct. 5				800	55.00	44,000	700	50.00	35,000
				400	52.50	21,000			
				300	50.00	15,000			
Nov. 26	2,000	56.00	112,000				700	50.00	35,000
							2,000	56.00	112,000
Dec. 31				1,000	56.00	56,000	700	50.00	35,000
							1,000	56.00	56,000

2. a. First-in, first-out method: 1,700 units at $56 = $95,200

b. Last-in, first-out method:

1,000 units at $50.00	$50,000
700 units at $52.50	36,750
1,700 units	$86,750

c. Average cost method:

Average cost per unit: $269,000 ÷ 5,000 units = $53.80

Inventory, December 31, 2005: 1,700 units at $53.80 = $91,460

3. a. $$\textit{Inventory turnover} = \frac{\textit{Cost of merchandise sold}}{\textit{Average inventory}}$$

$$\textit{Inventory turnover} = \frac{\$173{,}800}{(\$50{,}000 + \$95{,}200)/2}$$

$$\textit{Inventory turnover} = 2.39$$

b. $$\textit{Number of days' sales in inventory} = \frac{\textit{Inventory, end of year}}{\textit{Average daily cost of merchandise sold}}$$

$$\textit{Number of days' sales in inventory} = \frac{\$95{,}200}{\$173{,}800/365}$$

$$\textit{Number of days' sales in inventory} = 199.9 \textit{ days}$$

Self-Study Questions

Answers at end of chapter

1. The direct labor cost should be recognized first in which inventory account?
   A. materials inventory
   B. merchandise inventory
   C. finished goods inventory
   D. work in process inventory

2. The following units of a particular item were purchased and sold during the period:

Beginning inventory	40 units at $20
First purchase	50 units at $21
Second purchase	50 units at $22
First sale	110 units
Third purchase	50 units at $23
Second sale	45 units

   What is the cost of the 35 units on hand at the end of the period as determined under the perpetual inventory system by the lifo costing method?
   A. $715 C. $700
   B. $705 D. $805

3. The following units of a particular item were available for sale during the period:

Beginning inventory	40 units at $20
First purchase	50 units at $21
Second purchase	50 units at $22
Third purchase	50 units at $23

   What is the unit cost of the 35 units on hand at the end of the period as determined under the periodic inventory system by the fifo costing method?
   A. $20 C. $22
   B. $21 D. $23

4. If merchandise inventory is being valued at cost and the price level is steadily rising, the method of costing that will yield the highest net income is:
   A. lifo C. average
   B. fifo D. periodic

5. The average lifo reserve for a company is $10,000. The average inventory is $50,000, and the cost of merchandise sold is $175,000. Determine the appropriate inventory turnover ratio.
   A. 2.92 C. 3.7
   B. 3.5 D. 4.375

Discussion Questions

1. How are manufacturing inventories different than those of a merchandiser?
2. What security measures may be used by retailers to protect merchandise inventory from customer theft?

3. Which inventory system (perpetual or periodic) provides the more effective means of controlling inventories? Why?
4. Before inventory purchases are recorded, the receiving report should be reconciled to what documents?
5. Why is it important to periodically take a physical inventory if the perpetual system is used?
6. Do the terms *fifo* and *lifo* refer to techniques used in determining quantities of the various classes of merchandise on hand? Explain.
7. Does the term *last-in* in the lifo method mean that the items in the inventory are assumed to be the most recent (last) acquisitions? Explain.
8. If merchandise inventory is being valued at cost and the price level is steadily rising, which of the three methods of costing—fifo, lifo, or average cost—will yield (a) the highest inventory cost, (b) the lowest inventory cost, (c) the highest gross profit, (d) the lowest gross profit?
9. Which of the three methods of inventory costing—fifo, lifo, or average cost—will in general yield an inventory cost most nearly approximating current replacement cost?
10. If inventory is being valued at cost and the price level is steadily rising, which of the three methods of costing—fifo, lifo, or average cost—will yield the lowest annual income tax expense? Explain.
11. Can a company change its method of costing inventory? Explain.
12. Because of imperfections, an item of merchandise cannot be sold at its normal selling price. How should this item be valued for financial statement purposes?
13. How is the method of determining the cost of the inventory and the method of valuing it disclosed in the financial statements?
14. Why would a company such as the Target Corporation prefer a quick response inventory policy?
15. What is the lifo reserve and why would an analyst use lifo reserve information to adjust inventory efficiency ratios?

Resources for your success online @
http://warren.swlearning.com

Remember! If you need additional help, visit South-Western's Web site. See page 30 for a description of the online and printed materials that are available.

Exercises

Exercise 8–1

Manufacturing Inventories

Goal 1

Qualcomm Incorporated is a leading developer and manufacturer of digital wireless telecommunications products and services. Qualcomm reported the following inventories on September 30, 2001, in the footnotes to its financial statements:

	September 30, 2001
	(In thousands)
Raw materials	$18,251
Work in process	3,346
Finished goods	74,266
	$95,863

a. Why does Qualcomm report three different inventories?
b. What costs are included in each of the three classes of inventory?

Exercise 8–2

Television costs of Walt Disney Company

Goal 1

STUDENT SOLUTIONS MANUAL

The Walt Disney Company shows "television costs" as an asset on its balance sheet. In the footnotes to its financial statements, the following television cost disclosure was made:

	Sept. 30, 2001	Sept. 30, 2000
Television costs:		
Released, less amortization	$ 649	$ 682
Completed, not released	62	42
In-process	407	328
In development or pre-production	41	33
	$1,159	$1,085

a. Interpret the four television cost asset categories.
b. How are these classifications similar or dissimilar to the inventory classifications used in a manufacturing firm?

Exercise 8–3

Internal control of inventories

Goal 2

Langley Hardware Store currently uses a periodic inventory system. Kevin White, the owner, is considering the purchase of a computer system that would make it feasible to switch to a perpetual inventory system.

Kevin is unhappy with the periodic inventory system because it does not provide timely information on inventory levels. Kevin has noticed on several occasions that the store runs out of good-selling items, while too many poor-selling items are on hand.

Kevin is also concerned about lost sales while a physical inventory is being taken. Langley Hardware currently takes a physical inventory twice a year. To minimize distractions, the store is closed on the day inventory is taken. Kevin believes that closing the store is the only way to get an accurate inventory count.

Will switching to a perpetual inventory system strengthen Langley Hardware's control over inventory items? Will switching to a perpetual inventory system eliminate the need for a physical inventory count? Explain.

Exercise 8–4

Internal control of inventories

Goal 2

STUDENT SOLUTIONS MANUAL

Flyer's Luggage Shop is a small retail establishment located in a large shopping mall. This shop has implemented the following procedures regarding inventory items:

a. Since the display area of the store is limited, only a sample of each piece of luggage is kept on the selling floor. Whenever a customer selects a piece of luggage, the salesclerk gets the appropriate piece from the store's stockroom. Since all salesclerks need access to the stockroom, it is not locked. The stockroom is adjacent to the break room used by all mall employees.
b. Since the shop carries mostly high-quality, designer luggage, all inventory items are tagged with a control device that activates an alarm if a tagged item is removed from the store.
c. Whenever Flyer's receives a shipment of new inventory, the items are taken directly to the stockroom. Flyer's accountant uses the vendor's invoice to record the amount of inventory received.

State whether each of these procedures is appropriate or inappropriate, considering the principles of internal control. If it is inappropriate, state which internal control procedure is violated.

Exercise 8–5

Perpetual inventory using fifo

Goals 3, 4

Inventory balance, June 30, $806

SPREADSHEET

Beginning inventory, purchases, and sales data for portable CD players are as follows:

June	1	Inventory	25 units at $41
	6	Sale	16 units
	13	Purchase	18 units at $42
	18	Sale	12 units
	22	Sale	4 units
	30	Purchase	8 units at $43

The business maintains a perpetual inventory system, costing by the first-in, first-out method. Determine the cost of the merchandise sold for each sale and the inventory balance after each sale, presenting the data in the form illustrated in Exhibit 5.

Exercise 8–6

Perpetual inventory using lifo

Goals 3, 4

Inventory balance, June 30, $797

STUDENT SOLUTIONS MANUAL

SPREADSHEET

Assume that the business in Exercise 8–5 maintains a perpetual inventory system, costing by the last-in, first-out method. Determine the cost of merchandise sold for each sale and the inventory balance after each sale, presenting the data in the form illustrated in Exhibit 6.

Exercise 8–7

Perpetual inventory using lifo

Goals 3, 4

Inventory balance, October 31, $1,680

SPREADSHEET

Beginning inventory, purchases, and sales data for cell phones for October are as follows:

Inventory		Purchases		Sales	
Oct. 1	30 units at $110	Oct. 6	10 units at $120	Oct. 11	9 units
		21	15 units at $130	16	24 units
				31	8 units

Assuming that the perpetual inventory system is used, costing by the lifo method, determine the cost of the inventory balance at October 31, presenting data in the form illustrated in Exhibit 6.

Exercise 8–8

Perpetual inventory using fifo

Goals 3, 4

Inventory balance, October 31, $1,820

STUDENT SOLUTIONS MANUAL

SPREADSHEET

Assume that the business in Exercise 8–7 maintains a perpetual inventory system, costing by the first-in, first-out method. Determine the cost of the inventory balance at October 31, presenting the data in the form illustrated in Exhibit 5.

Exercise 8–9

Fifo, lifo costs under perpetual inventory system

Goals 3, 4

a. $800

The following units of a particular item were available for sale during the year:

Beginning inventory	19 units at $46
Sale	15 units at $90
First purchase	32 units at $48
Sale	25 units at $90
Second purchase	40 units at $50
Sale	35 units at $90

The firm uses the perpetual inventory system, and there are 16 units of the item on hand at the end of the year. What is the total cost of the ending inventory according to (a) fifo, (b) lifo?

Exercise 8–10

Periodic inventory by three methods

Goals 3, 5, 6

b. $990

STUDENT SOLUTIONS MANUAL

The units of an item available for sale during the year were as follows:

Jan. 1	Inventory	25 units at $24
Feb. 4	Purchase	10 units at $25
July 20	Purchase	30 units at $28
Dec. 30	Purchase	35 units at $30

There are 40 units of the item in the physical inventory at December 31. The periodic inventory system is used. Determine the inventory cost by (a) the first-in, first-out method, (b) the last-in, first-out method, and (c) the average cost method.

Exercise 8–11

Periodic inventory by three methods; cost of merchandise sold

Goals 3, 5, 6

a. Inventory, $1,254

The units of an item available for sale during the year were as follows:

Jan. 1	Inventory	21 units at $60
Mar. 4	Purchase	29 units at $65
Aug. 7	Purchase	10 units at $68
Nov. 15	Purchase	15 units at $70

There are 18 units of the item in the physical inventory at December 31. The periodic inventory system is used. Determine the inventory cost and the cost of merchandise sold by three methods, presenting your answers in the following form:

	Cost	
Inventory Method	**Merchandise Inventory**	**Merchandise Sold**
a. First-in, first-out	$	$
b. Last-in, first-out		
c. Average cost		

Exercise 8–12

Comparing inventory methods

Goal 6

STUDENT SOLUTIONS MANUAL

Assume that a firm separately determined inventory under fifo and lifo and then compared the results.

1. In each space below, place the correct sign [less than (<), greater than (>), or equal (=)] for each comparison, assuming periods of rising prices.

a. Lifo inventory	________	Fifo Inventory
b. Lifo cost of goods sold	________	Fifo cost of goods sold
c. Lifo net income	________	Fifo net income
d. Lifo income tax	________	Fifo income tax

2. Why would management prefer to use lifo over fifo in periods of rising prices?

Exercise 8–13

Lower-of-cost-or-market inventory

Goal 7

SPREADSHEET

On the basis of the following data, determine the value of the inventory at the lower of cost or market. Assemble the data in the form illustrated in Exhibit 9.

Commodity	Inventory Quantity	Unit Cost Price	Unit Market Price
X3	9	$300	$320
Y10	16	110	115
A19	12	275	260
J2	15	51	45
J8	25	96	100

Exercise 8–14

Merchandise inventory on the balance sheet

Goal 7

STUDENT SOLUTIONS MANUAL

Based on the data in Exercise 8-13 and assuming that cost was determined by the fifo method, show how the merchandise inventory would appear on the balance sheet.

Exercise 8–15

Quick response

Goal 8

Assume that a company initiated a quick response program.

a. What impact would the program have on the inventory balance and cash flow?
b. What impact would the program have on cost of goods sold, assuming that the firm used lifo?

Exercise 8–16

Inventory turnover

Goal 9

STUDENT SOLUTIONS MANUAL

The following data were taken from recent annual reports of Gateway, Inc., a vendor of personal computers and related products, and American Greetings Corporation, a manufacturer and distributor of greeting cards and related products:

	Gateway	American Greetings
Cost of goods sold	$5,921,651,000	$757,080,000
Inventory, end of year	167,924,000	251,289,000
Inventory, beginning of the year	152,531,000	271,205,000

a. Determine the inventory turnover for Gateway and American Greetings. Round to two decimal places.
b. Would you expect American Greetings' inventory turnover to be higher or lower than Gateway's? Why?

Exercise 8–17

Manufacturing inventories and analysis

Goals 1, 9

Number of days' sales in inventory of raw materials, 16.7

The inventories of Anheuser-Busch Companies, Inc., were recently reported on the balance sheet as follows:

	(in millions)
Raw materials	$347.3
Work in process	82.9
Finished goods	178.1
Total	$608.3

The cost of goods sold reported on the income statement was $7,592 million.

a. What do the three inventory classes on Anheuser-Busch's balance sheet represent?

(continued)

b. Calculate the number of days' sales in inventory for raw materials and finished goods and for the total. Round to two decimal places.
c. Interpret your calculations in (b).

Exercise 8–18

Inventory turnover and number of days' sales in inventory

Goal 9

a. Albertson's, 42.96 days

STUDENT SOLUTIONS MANUAL

Kroger Co., Albertson's Inc., and Safeway Inc. are the three largest grocery chains in the United States. Inventory management is an important aspect of the grocery retail business. The balance sheets for these three companies indicated the following merchandise inventory information:

	Merchandise Inventory	
	Fiscal 2001 end-of-year balance (in millions)	Fiscal 2000 end-of-year balance (in millions)
Albertson's	$3,196	$3,364
Kroger	4,178	4,063
Safeway	2,578	2,508

The cost of goods sold for each company during fiscal year 2001 was:

	Cost of goods sold for fiscal year 2001 (in millions)
Albertson's	$27,155
Kroger	36,398
Safeway	23,697

a. Determine the number of days' sales in inventory and inventory turnover for the three companies for fiscal year 2001.
b. Interpret your results in (a).
c. If Albertson's had Safeway's number of days' sales in inventory, how much additional cash flow would have been generated from the hypothetically smaller inventory relative to its actual ending inventory position for fiscal year 2001?

Exercise 8–19

Lifo reserve and inventory ratios

Goals 1,9

b. Inventory turnover considering the lifo reserve, 4.63

The inventory footnote for Eastman Kodak Company was as follows:

NOTE 3: INVENTORIES (in millions)	2001	2000
At fifo or average cost (approximates current cost)		
Finished goods	$ 851	$1,155
Work in process	318	423
Raw materials and supplies	412	589
	1,581	2,167
Lifo reserve	(444)	(449)
Total	$1,137	$1,718

a. Estimate the lifetime tax deferral of using lifo, assuming a corporate tax rate of 35%.
b. Prepare a table showing the inventory turnover and number of days' sales in inventory for 2001, both with and without the lifo reserve, and the percentage difference between the two. Show supporting calculations. The cost of goods sold for 2001 was $8,670 million.

Exercise 8-20

Lifo liquidation

Goal 9

STUDENT SOLUTIONS MANUAL

The financial statements of Ford Motor Company disclosed the following footnote information about its inventories:

> *Reduction of inventory in 2001 resulted in a decrement of a base-year lifo layer, reducing cost of sales by $63 million.*

What is meant by a "decrement of a base-year lifo layer," and what impact would you expect this to have on the income statement?

Accounting Application Problems

Problem 8-1A

Fifo perpetual inventory

Goals 3, 4

3. $7,480

SPREADSHEET

The beginning inventory of floor mats at Eagle Office Supplies and data on purchases and sales for a three-month period are as follows:

Date		Transaction	Number of Units	Per Unit	Total
Sept.	1	Inventory	250	$ 6.10	$1,525
	8	Purchase	750	6.20	4,650
	20	Sale	450	9.00	4,050
	30	Sale	350	9.00	3,150
Oct.	8	Sale	50	9.10	455
	10	Purchase	500	6.10	3,050
	27	Sale	350	9.20	3,220
	31	Sale	200	9.15	1,830
Nov.	5	Purchase	750	6.00	4,500
	13	Sale	350	10.00	3,500
	23	Purchase	400	5.95	2,380
	30	Sale	500	10.00	5,000

Instructions

1. Record the inventory, purchases, and cost of merchandise sold data in a perpetual inventory record similar to the one illustrated in Exhibit 5, using the first-in, first-out method.
2. Determine the total sales and the total cost of floor mats sold for the period. Record the entries in the sales and cost of merchandise sold accounts. Assume that all sales were on account.
3. Determine the gross profit from sales for the period.
4. Determine the ending inventory cost.

Problem 8-2A

Lifo perpetual inventory

Goals 3, 4

2. Gross profit, $7,510

SPREADSHEET

The beginning inventory of floor mats at Eagle Office Supplies and data on purchases and sales for a three-month period are shown in Problem 8-1A.

Instructions

1. Record the inventory, purchases, and cost of merchandise sold data in a perpetual inventory record similar to the one illustrated in Exhibit 6, using the last-in, first-out method.
2. Determine the total sales, the total cost of floor mats sold, and the gross profit from sales for the period.
3. Determine the ending inventory cost.

Problem 8–3A

Periodic inventory by three methods

Goals 3, 5

1. $7,875

SPREADSHEET

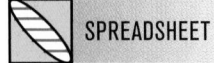

Sixpack Appliances uses the periodic inventory system. Details regarding the inventory of appliances at July 1, 2003, purchases invoices during the year, and the inventory count at June 30, 2004, are summarized as follows:

		Purchases Invoices			
Model	Inventory, July 1	1st	2nd	3rd	Inventory Count, June 30
A103	7 at $242	6 at $250	5 at $260	10 at $259	9
C743	6 at 80	5 at 82	8 at 89	8 at 90	7
F1010	2 at 108	2 at 110	3 at 128	3 at 130	3
H142	8 at 88	4 at 79	3 at 85	6 at 92	8
P813	2 at 250	2 at 260	4 at 271	4 at 272	5
Q661	5 at 160	4 at 170	4 at 175	7 at 180	8
W490	–	4 at 150	4 at 200	4 at 202	5

Instructions

1. Determine the cost of the inventory on June 30, 2004, by the first-in, first-out method. Present data in columnar form, using the following headings:

Model	Quantity	Unit Cost	Total Cost

If the inventory of a particular model comprises one entire purchase plus a portion of another purchase acquired at a different unit cost, use a separate line for each purchase.

2. Determine the cost of the inventory on June 30, 2004, by the last-in, first-out method, following the procedures indicated in (1).
3. Determine the cost of the inventory on June 30, 2004, by the average cost method, using the columnar headings indicated in (1).
4. Discuss which method (fifo or lifo) would be preferred for income tax purposes in periods of (a) rising prices and (b) declining prices.

Problem 8–4A

Lower-of-cost-or-market inventory

Goal 7

Total LCM, $38,835

SPREADSHEET

Data on the physical inventory of Minish Company as of December 31, 2005, are presented below.

Description	Inventory Quantity	Unit Market Price
A10	40	$ 57
B23	15	200
D82	20	140
E34	125	26
F17	18	550
H99	70	15
K41	5	390
M21	400	6
R72	100	17
T15	7	235
BD1	150	18
MS3	9	700

Quantity and cost data from the last purchase invoice of the year and the next-to-the-last purchase invoice are summarized as follows:

	Last Purchase Invoice		Next-to-the-Last Purchase Invoice	
Description	Quantity Purchased	Unit Cost	Quantity Purchased	Unit Cost
A10	25	$ 60	30	$ 58
B23	30	208	20	205
D82	10	145	25	142
E34	150	25	100	24
F17	10	565	10	560
H99	100	15	100	14
K41	10	387	5	384
M21	500	6	500	6
R72	80	19	50	18
T15	5	255	4	260
BD1	100	20	75	19
MS3	7	701	6	699

Instructions

Determine the inventory at cost and also at the lower of cost or market, using the first-in, first-out method. Record the appropriate unit costs on an inventory sheet and complete the pricing of the inventory. When there are two different unit costs applicable to an item, proceed as follows:

1. Draw a line through the quantity, and insert the quantity and unit cost of the last purchase.
2. On the following line, insert the quantity and unit cost of the next-to-the-last purchase.
3. Total the cost and market columns and insert the lower of the two totals in the Lower of C or M column. The first item on the inventory sheet has been completed below as an example.

Inventory Sheet
December 31, 2005

				Total		
Description	Inventory Quantity	Unit Cost Price	Unit Market Price	Cost	Market	Lower of C or M
A10	~~40~~ 25	$60	$57	$1,500	$1,425	
	15	58		870	855	
				$2,370	$2,280	$2,280

Alternate Accounting Application Problems

Alternate Problem 8–1B

Fifo perpetual inventory

The beginning inventory of drift boats at River's Edge Co. and data on purchases and sales for a three-month period are as follows:

Goals 3, 4

3. $239,800

STUDENT SOLUTIONS MANUAL

SPREADSHEET

Date		Transaction	Number of Units	Per Unit	Total
Mar.	1	Inventory	15	$2,200	$ 33,000
	8	Purchase	25	2,250	56,250
	11	Sale	10	5,000	50,000
	22	Sale	13	5,000	65,000
Apr.	3	Purchase	15	2,300	34,500
	10	Sale	10	5,100	51,000
	21	Sale	5	5,100	25,500
	30	Purchase	25	2,350	58,750
May	5	Sale	20	5,150	103,000
	13	Sale	12	5,150	61,800
	21	Purchase	20	2,400	48,000
	28	Sale	15	5,200	78,000

Instructions

1. Record the inventory, purchases, and cost of merchandise sold data in a perpetual inventory record similar to the one illustrated in Exhibit 5, using the first-in, first-out method.
2. Determine the total sales and the total cost of drift boats sold for the period. Record the entries in the sales and cost of merchandise sold accounts. Assume that all sales were on account.
3. Determine the gross profit from sales of drift boats for the period.
4. Determine the ending inventory cost.

Alternate Problem 8–2B

Lifo perpetual inventory

Goals 3, 4

2. Gross profit, $237,800

STUDENT SOLUTIONS MANUAL

SPREADSHEET

The beginning inventory of drift boats and data on purchases and sales for a three-month period are shown in Alternate Problem 8–1B.

Instructions

1. Record the inventory, purchases, and cost of merchandise sold data in a perpetual inventory record similar to the one illustrated in Exhibit 6, using the last-in, first-out method.
2. Determine the total sales, the total cost of drift boats sold, and the gross profit from sales for the period.
3. Determine the ending inventory cost.

Alternate Problem 8–3B

Periodic inventory by three methods

Goals 3, 5

1. $11,580

STUDENT SOLUTIONS MANUAL

SPREADSHEET

Yellowstone Appliances uses the periodic inventory system. Details regarding the inventory of appliances at January 1, 2004, purchases invoices during the year, and the inventory count at December 31, 2004, are summarized on the following page.

Model	Inventory, January 1	Purchases Invoices 1st	2nd	3rd	Inventory Count, December 31
109A	4 at $140	6 at $144	8 at $148	7 at $156	5
110B	3 at 208	3 at 212	5 at 213	4 at 225	5
127X	2 at 520	2 at 527	2 at 530	2 at 535	3
143T	6 at 520	8 at 531	4 at 549	6 at 542	7
144Z	9 at 213	7 at 215	6 at 222	6 at 225	10
160M	6 at 305	3 at 310	3 at 316	4 at 317	5
180X	–	4 at 222	4 at 232	–	2

Instructions

1. Determine the cost of the inventory on December 31, 2004, by the first-in, first-out method. Present data in columnar form, using the following headings:

Model	Quantity	Unit Cost	Total Cost

   If the inventory of a particular model comprises one entire purchase plus a portion of another purchase acquired at a different unit cost, use a separate line for each purchase.
2. Determine the cost of the inventory on December 31, 2004, by the last-in, first-out method, following the procedures indicated in (1).
3. Determine the cost of the inventory on December 31, 2004, by the average cost method, using the columnar headings indicated in (1).
4. Discuss which method (fifo or lifo) would be preferred for income tax purposes in periods of (a) rising prices and (b) declining prices.

Alternate Problem 8–4B

Lower-of-cost-or-market inventory

Goal 7

Total LCM, $38,480

STUDENT SOLUTIONS MANUAL

SPREADSHEET

Data on the physical inventory of Trailblazer Co. as of December 31, 2005, are presented below.

Description	Inventory Quantity	Unit Market Price
A10	40	$ 57
B23	15	200
D82	20	140
E34	125	26
F17	18	550
H99	70	15
K41	5	390
M21	400	6
R72	100	17
T15	7	235
BD1	150	18
MS3	9	700

Quantity and cost data from the last purchases invoice of the year and the next-to-the-last purchases invoice are summarized as follows:

	Last Purchases Invoice		Next-to-the-Last Purchases Invoice	
Description	Quantity Purchased	Unit Cost	Quantity Purchased	Unit Cost
A10	25	$ 60	40	$ 58
B23	25	190	15	191
D82	16	143	15	142
E34	150	25	100	27
F17	6	550	15	540
H99	75	14	100	13
K41	8	400	4	398
M21	500	6	500	7
R72	70	17	50	16
T15	5	250	4	260
BD1	120	19	115	17
MS3	8	701	7	699

Instructions

Determine the inventory at cost and also at the lower of cost or market, using the first-in, first-out method. Record the appropriate unit costs on an inventory sheet and complete the pricing of the inventory. When there are two different unit costs applicable to an item, proceed as follows:

1. Draw a line through the quantity, and insert the quantity and unit cost of the last purchase.
2. On the following line, insert the quantity and unit cost of the next-to-the-last purchase.
3. Total the cost and market columns and insert the lower of the two totals in the Lower of C or M column. The first item on the inventory sheet has been completed below as an example.

Inventory Sheet
December 31, 2005

				Total		
Description	Inventory Quantity	Unit Cost Price	Unit Market Price	Cost	Market	Lower of C or M
A10	~~40~~ 25	$60	$57	$1,500	$1,425	
	15	58		870	855	
				$2,370	$2,280	$2,280

Building Leadership Skills—Financial Analysis and Reporting

Case 8–1

Fifo vs. lifo

The following footnote was taken from the 2001 financial statements of Walgreen Co.:

Inventories are valued on a . . . last-in, first-out (lifo) cost . . . basis. At August 31, 2001 and 2000, inventories would have been greater by $637,600,000 and

$574,800,000 respectively, if they had been valued on a lower of first-in, first-out (fifo) cost or market basis.

Additional data are as follows:

Earnings before income taxes, 2001	$1,422,700,000
Total lifo inventories, August 31, 2001	3,482,400,000

Based on the preceding data, determine (a) what the total inventories at August 31, 2001, would have been, using the fifo method, and (b) what the earnings before income taxes for the year ended August 31, 2001, would have been if fifo had been used instead of lifo.

Case 8–2

Comparing inventory ratios for two companies using different inventory valuations

Neiman Marcus Group uses the fifo method for valuing its merchandise inventories, while Sears Roebuck Co. uses the lifo method. The balance sheet inventory disclosures for Neiman Marcus and Sears Roebuck Co. are as follows for financial statements dated in 2001:

	End-of-Period Inventory	Beginning-of-Period Inventory
Neiman Marcus Group	$ 648,867,000	$ 575,344,000
Sears Roebuck Co.	4,912,000,000	5,618,000,000

The cost of merchandise sold reported by each company for the fiscal 2001 period was:

	Neiman Marcus Group	Sears Roebuck Co.
Cost of merchandise sold	$2,020,954,000	$26,322,000,000

In addition, Sears disclosed a lifo reserve of $591,000,000 for the end of 2001 and a lifo reserve of $566,000,000 for the beginning of 2001.

a. Determine the inventory turnover and number of days' sales in inventory for Neiman Marcus and Sears under a comparable basis.
b. Interpret your results.

Case 8–3

SAKS Incorporated inventory note

SAKS Incorporated disclosed the following footnote regarding its merchandise inventories for its February 2, 2002 financial statements:

MERCHANDISE INVENTORIES AND COST OF SALES Merchandise inventories are . . . stated at the lower of cost (last-in, first-out ["lifo"]), or market and include freight and certain buying and distribution costs. The company also takes markdowns related to slow moving inventory, ensuring an appropriate inventory valuation. At February 2, 2002 and February 3, 2001, the lifo value of inventories exceeded market value and, as a result, inventory was stated at the lower market amount.

Consignment merchandise on hand of $110,567 and $99,737 at February 2, 2002, and February 3, 2001, respectively, is not reflected in the consolidated balance sheets.

a. Why were inventories recorded at market value?
b. What are consignment inventories and why were they excluded from the balance sheet valuation?

Case 8–4

Number of days' sales in inventory—Wal-Mart and retail industry

Wal-Mart Stores, Inc., disclosed the following inventory and cost of goods sold for five recent fiscal years:

	In millions				
	2001	2000	1999	1998	1997
Cost of goods sold	$171,562	$150,255	$129,664	$108,725	$93,438
Ending inventory	22,614	21,442	19,793	17,076	16,497

The industry average number of days' sales in inventory from Disclosure Worldwide® database was reported as:

	2001	2000	1999	1998	1997
Number of days' sales in inventory	68.62	69.32	70.53	73.41	74.76

a. Calculate the number of days' sales in inventory for Wal-Mart Stores for each of the five years.
b. Prepare a line graph of the five-year number of days' sales in inventory ratio of Wal-Mart Stores and the industry average for each of the five years.
c. Interpret your graph.

Case 8–5

Inventory ratios for Dell and HP

Dell Computer Corporation and Hewlett-Packard Company (HP) are both manufacturers of computer equipment and peripherals. However, the two companies follow two different strategies. Dell follows a build-to-order strategy, where the consumer orders the computer from a Web page. The order is then manufactured and shipped to the customer within days of the order. In contrast, HP follows a build-to-stock strategy, where the computer is first built for inventory, then sold from inventory to retailers, such as Best Buy. The following financial statement information is provided for Dell and HP for fiscal year 2001 (in millions):

	Dell	HP
Inventory, beginning of period	$ 400	$ 5,699
Inventory, end of period	278	5,204
Cost of goods sold	25,661	28,370

The two strategies can be seen in the difference between the inventory turnover and number of days' sales in inventory ratio for the two companies.

a. Determine the inventory turnover ratio and number of days' sales in inventory ratio for each company.
b. Interpret the difference between the ratios for the two companies.

Case 8–6

Costing inventory

Lectern Company began operations in 2004 by selling a single product. Data on purchases and sales for the year were as follows:

Date	Units Purchased	Unit Cost	Total Cost
Purchases:			
April 8	3,875	$12.20	$ 47,275
May 10	4,125	13.00	53,625
June 4	5,000	13.20	66,000
July 10	5,000	14.00	70,000
August 3	3,400	14.25	48,450
October 5	1,600	14.50	23,200
November 1	1,000	14.95	14,950
December 10	1,000	16.00	16,000
	25,000		$339,500
Sales:			
April	2,000		
May	2,000		
June	2,500		
July	3,000		
August	3,500		
September	3,500		
October	2,250		
November	1,250		
December	1,000		
Total units	21,000		
Total sales	$552,000		

On January 3, 2005, the president of the company, Kevin Ivey, asked for your advice on costing the 4,000-unit physical inventory that was taken on December 31, 2004. Moreover, since the firm plans to expand its product line, he asked for your advice on the use of a perpetual inventory system in the future.

1. Determine the cost of the December 31, 2004 inventory under the periodic system, using the (a) first-in, first-out method, (b) last-in, first-out method, and (c) average cost method.
2. Determine the gross profit for the year under each of the three methods in (1).
3. a. Explain varying viewpoints on why each of the three inventory costing methods may best reflect the results of operations for 2004.
   b. Which of the three inventory costing methods may best reflect the replacement cost of the inventory on the balance sheet as of December 31, 2004?
   c. Which inventory costing method would you choose to use for income tax purposes? Why?
   d. Discuss the advantages and disadvantages of using a perpetual inventory system. From the data presented in this case, is there any indication of the adequacy of inventory levels during the year?

Building Leadership Skills—Responsible Leadership

Activity 8–1

Ethics and professional conduct in business

ETHICS

Xanadu Co. is experiencing a decrease in sales and operating income for the fiscal year ending December 31, 2004. Neil Whyte, controller of Xanadu Co., has suggested that all orders received before the end of the fiscal year be shipped by midnight, December 31, 2004, even if the shipping department must work overtime. Since Xanadu Co. ships all merchandise FOB shipping point, it would record all such shipments as sales for the year ending December 31, 2004, thereby offsetting some of the decreases in sales and operating income.

Discuss whether Neil Whyte is behaving in a professional manner.

Activity 8–2

Lifo and inventory flow

The following is an excerpt from a conversation between John Lacy, the warehouse manager for Leconte Wholesale Co., and its accountant, Leanne Huskey. Leconte Wholesale operates a large regional warehouse that supplies produce and other grocery products to grocery stores in smaller communities.

John: Leanne, can you explain what's going on here with these monthly statements?
Leanne: Sure, John. How can I help you?
John: I don't understand this last-in, first-out inventory procedure. It just doesn't make sense.
Leanne: Well, what it means is that we assume that the last goods we receive are the first ones sold. So the inventory is made up of the items we purchased first.
John: Yes, but that's my problem. It doesn't work that way! We always distribute the oldest produce first. Some of that produce is perishable! We can't keep any of it very long or it'll spoil.
Leanne: John, you don't understand. We only assume that the products we distribute are the last ones received. We don't actually have to distribute the goods in this way.
John: I always thought that accounting was supposed to show what really happened. It all sounds like "make believe" to me! Why not report what really happens?

Respond to John's concerns.

Activity 8–3

Observe internal controls over inventory

GROUP ACTIVITY

Select a business in your community and observe its internal controls over inventory. In groups of three or four, identify and discuss the similarities and differences in each business's inventory controls. Prepare a written summary of your findings.

Activity 8–4

Compare inventory cost flow assumptions

GROUP ACTIVITY

In groups of three or four, examine the financial statements of a well-known retailing business. You may obtain the financial statements you need from one of the following sources:

1. Your school or local library.
2. The investor relations department of the company.
3. The company's Web site on the Internet.
4. EDGAR (Electronic Data Gathering, Analysis, and Retrieval), the electronic archives of financial statements filed with the Securities and Exchange Commission. SEC documents can be retrieved using the EdgarScan service from PricewaterhouseCoopers at http://edgarscan.pwcglobal.com. To obtain annual

report information, click on "Edgarscan," then type in a company name in the appropriate space. EdgarScan will list the reports available to you for the company you've selected. Select the most recent annual report filing, identified as a 10-K or 10-K405. EdgarScan provides an outline of the report, including the separate financial statements. You can double-click the income statement and balance sheet for the selected company into an Excel spreadsheet for further analysis.

Determine the cost flow assumption(s) that the company is using for its inventory, and determine whether the company is using the lower-of-cost-or-market rule. Prepare a written summary of your findings.

Answers to Self-Study Questions

1. **D** The direct labor costs are introduced into production initially as work in process. Once the units are completed, these costs are transferred to finished goods inventory (answer C). Materials inventory (answer A) includes only material costs, not direct labor cost. Merchandise inventory (answer B) is not used in a manufacturing setting, hence does not include direct labor cost.
2. **A** The lifo method of costing is based on the assumption that costs should be charged against revenue in the reverse order in which costs were incurred. Thus, the oldest costs are assigned to inventory. Thirty of the 35 units would be assigned a unit cost of $20 (since 110 of the beginning inventory units were sold on the first sale), and the remaining 5 units would be assigned a cost of $23, for a total of $715 (answer A).
3. **D** The fifo method of costing is based on the assumption that costs should be charged against revenue in the order in which they were incurred (first-in, first-out). Thus, the most recent costs are assigned to inventory. The 35 units would be assigned a unit cost of $23 (answer D).
4. **B** When the price level is steadily rising, the earlier unit costs are lower than recent unit costs. Under the fifo method (answer B), these earlier costs are matched against revenue to yield the highest possible net income. The periodic inventory system (answer D) is a system and not a method of costing.
5. **A** The inventory turnover ratio should be adjusted by the lifo reserve as follows:

$$\text{Inventory turnover} = \frac{\text{Cost of merchandise sold}}{\text{Average inventory} + \text{Average lifo reserve}}$$

$$\text{Inventory turnover} = \frac{\$175{,}000}{\$50{,}000 + \$10{,}000}$$

$$\text{Inventory turnover} = 2.92 \text{ (rounded)}$$

Chapter 9
Fixed Assets and Intangible Assets

THE LAW OF REPRODUCTION
"It takes a leader to raise up a leader."
—The 21 Irrefutable Laws of Leadership
Dr. John C. Maxwell

Learning Goals

1. Define, classify, and account for the cost of fixed assets.
2. Compute depreciation, using the following methods: straight-line, units-of-production, and declining-balance.
3. Compute and record depletion of natural resources.
4. Account for the disposal of fixed assets.
5. Classify fixed asset costs as either capital expenditures or revenue expenditures according to their project stage.
6. Analyze the utilization of fixed assets.
7. Describe and account for intangible assets, such as patents, copyrights, and goodwill.
8. Describe how depreciation expense is reported in an income statement, and prepare a balance sheet that includes fixed assets and intangible assets.

Southwest Airlines

On June 18, 1971, Southwest Airlines began serving Dallas, Houston, and San Antonio with three Boeing 737 aircraft. As of December 31, 2001, Southwest operated 355 Boeing 737 aircraft and provided service to 58 cities in 30 states. During 2001, Southwest generated over $5.5 billion of revenue and earned over $600 million of operating income and over $500 million of net income. Southwest flew more than 64 million passengers, with over 900,000 departures, making it the fourth largest carrier in the United States, based on passengers flown, and the second largest, based on scheduled domestic departures. But it wasn't easy.

In 1967, when the entrepreneurs who started Southwest (Rollin King and Herb Kelleher) applied for a certificate to fly between the three Texas cities, Braniff, Continental, and Texas International launched an attack against the new airline. These airlines argued that the markets Southwest wanted to serve were already saturated. After Southwest's application was finally approved, the other airlines began legal proceedings that lasted more than three years. Southwest's legal expenses were so great that it almost went out of business before it ever put a plane in the air. Ultimately, the Texas Supreme Court intervened, and Southwest made its first flight.

As with most new companies, Southwest's primary difficulty was raising enough capital to finance its operations. Initially, it was able to raise over $500,000, but that money was quickly eaten up by legal expenses in fighting Braniff and the other airlines. When Lamar Muse was hired by Southwest as its chief executive officer in January of 1971, Southwest had only $142 in the bank and $80,000 in overdue bills. Muse estimated that he'd need over $7 million to buy equipment and get through Southwest's first year. He raised $300,000 through personal friends and contacts and arranged for Southwest's initial public stock offering. But, Southwest needed airplanes.

Fortunately for Southwest, there was an airline slump in the early 1970s. As a result, Boeing had overproduced its 737-200 aircraft and was searching for buyers. Muse was able to negotiate the purchase of three 737-200s for a bargain price of $4 million. In addition, Boeing agreed to finance 90 percent of the deal.

Southwest's ability to start operations still hinged on a successful public offering of its stock. Determined to keep it grounded, Braniff and Texas International applied pressure on some of Southwest's underwriters to pull out of the initial public offering. Fortunately, Muse was able to find another brokerage firm to take the stock, and it was sold to the public on June 8, 1971.

So what is the key to Southwest's success over the years? Fixed assets are a major part of the story. Southwest only operates one aircraft, the Boeing 737. This simplifies its scheduling, maintenance, flight operations, and training activities and allows it to compete effectively. For example, Southwest's average passenger fare during 2001 was just over $83—and it earned a profit!

In this chapter, we will focus on the accounting for and reporting of fixed assets, such as Southwest's 737 aircraft. We describe and illustrate determining the cost of a fixed asset, depreciation methods, fixed asset disposals, and how to analyze the efficiency of fixed asset usage.

Source: Adapted from *Nuts! Southwest Airlines' Crazy Recipe for Business and Personal Success* by Kevin and Jackie Freiberg, Broadway Books, New York (1996).

Your Need to Know

Fixed assets are a key element of implementing a business's strategy. Many businesses need fixed assets in order to operate. For example, a manufacturer needs equipment in order to make its product. Since equipment and other fixed assets use significant business resources, managers must clearly understand their business goals and strategies before making significant fixed asset purchases.

A business strives to have the right quantity and the right type of fixed assets. Overinvesting in fixed assets can lead a company into financial difficulty. For example, Renaissance Cruise Lines, the world's fifth largest leisure cruise line, expanded aggressively during the late 1990s. The company declared bankruptcy in late 2001 because it was unable to book enough passengers on its ten ships to be profitable. Many argue that some Internet companies (e.g., Pets.com, eToys, and Webvan) failed because they invested significant resources in fixed assets without a clear strategy for earning profits. In contrast, underinvesting in fixed assets can limit a business. For example, Pacific Gas and Electric Co. underinvested in power-generating equipment, resulting in electricity shortages in portions of California.

In this chapter, we will illustrate accounting for fixed asset acquisitions, use, and dispositions. We will also illustrate tools for analyzing a business's effectiveness in managing fixed assets. Finally, we will describe accounting for intangible assets.

Nature of Fixed Assets

1 Define, classify, and account for the cost of fixed assets.

Why is a "major purchase" different than other expenditures that you make? More than likely, the purchase is expensive and long-lived. As a result, you are careful when making these types of purchases. The same is true for a business. A business makes "major purchases" of equipment, furniture, tools, machinery, buildings, and land. These assets, which are called **fixed assets**, are long-term or relatively permanent assets. They are *tangible assets* because they exist physically. They are owned and used by the business and are not offered for sale as part of normal operations. Other descriptive titles for these assets are *plant assets* or *property, plant, and equipment.*

The fixed assets of a business can be a significant part of the total assets. Exhibit 1 shows the percent of fixed assets to total assets for some select companies, divided between service, manufacturing, and merchandising firms. As you can see, the fixed assets for most firms

Exhibit 1

Fixed Assets as a Percent of Total Assets—Selected Companies

	Fixed Assets as a Percentage of Total Assets
Service Firms	
Pacific Gas and Electric Co.	47%
Sprint Corporation	59%
Computer Associates	6%
Manufacturing Firms	
Sun Microsystems Inc.	15%
Boeing Co.	21%
Dupont E I De Nemours & Co.	36%
Merchandising Firms	
Barnes & Noble Inc.	49%
Kroger Company	48%
Wal-Mart Stores Inc.	52%

Strategy in Business
Hub-and-Spoke or Point-to-Point?

Southwest Airlines uses a simple fare structure, featuring low, unrestricted, unlimited, everyday coach fares. These fares are possible by Southwest's use of a point-to-point, rather than hub-and-spoke, business strategy. United, Delta, and American employ a hub-and-spoke strategy in which an airline establishes major hubs that serve as connecting links to other cities. For example, Delta has established major connecting hubs in Atlanta, Cincinnati, and Salt Lake City. In contrast, Southwest focuses on point-to-point service between selected cities with over 300 one-way, nonstop city pairs with an average length of 500 miles and average flying time of 1.5 hours. As a result, Southwest minimizes connections, delays, and total trip time. Southwest also focuses on serving conveniently located satellite or downtown airports, such as Dallas Love Field, Houston Hobby, and Chicago Midway. Because these airports are normally less congested than hub airports, Southwest is better able to maintain high employee productivity and reliable ontime performance. This operating strategy permits the company to achieve high asset utilization of its fixed assets, such as its 737 aircraft. For example, aircraft are scheduled to spend only 25 minutes at the gate, thereby reducing the number of aircraft and gate facilities that would otherwise be required.

comprise a significant proportion of their total assets. In contrast, Computer Associates is a consulting firm that relies less on fixed assets to deliver value to customers.

Classifying Costs

Exhibit 2 displays questions that help classify costs. If the purchased item is long-lived, then it should be *capitalized,* which means it should appear on the balance sheet as an asset. Otherwise, the cost should be reported as an expense on the income statement. Capitalized costs are normally expected to last more than a year. If the asset is also used for a productive purpose, which involves a repeated use or benefit, then it should be classified as a fixed asset, such as land, buildings, or equipment. An asset need not actually be used on an ongoing basis or even often. For example, standby equipment for use in the event of a breakdown of regular equipment or for use only during peak periods is included in fixed assets. Fixed assets that have been abandoned or are no longer used should not be classified as a fixed asset.

St. Mary's Hospital maintains an auxiliary generator for use in electrical outages. Such outages are rare, and the generator has not been used for the past two years. Should the generator be reported as a fixed asset on St. Mary's balance sheet?

Yes. Even though the generator has not been used recently, it should be reported as a fixed asset.

Fixed assets are owned and used by the business and are not offered for resale. Long-lived assets held for resale are not classified as fixed assets, but should be listed on the balance sheet in a section entitled *investments.* For example, undeveloped land acquired as an investment for resale would be classified as an investment, not land.

The Cost of Fixed Assets

The costs of acquiring fixed assets include all amounts spent to get the asset in place and ready for use. For example, freight costs and the costs of installing equipment are included as part of the asset's total cost. The direct costs associated with new construction, such as labor and materials, should be debited to a "construction in progress" asset account. When

Exhibit 2
Classifying Costs

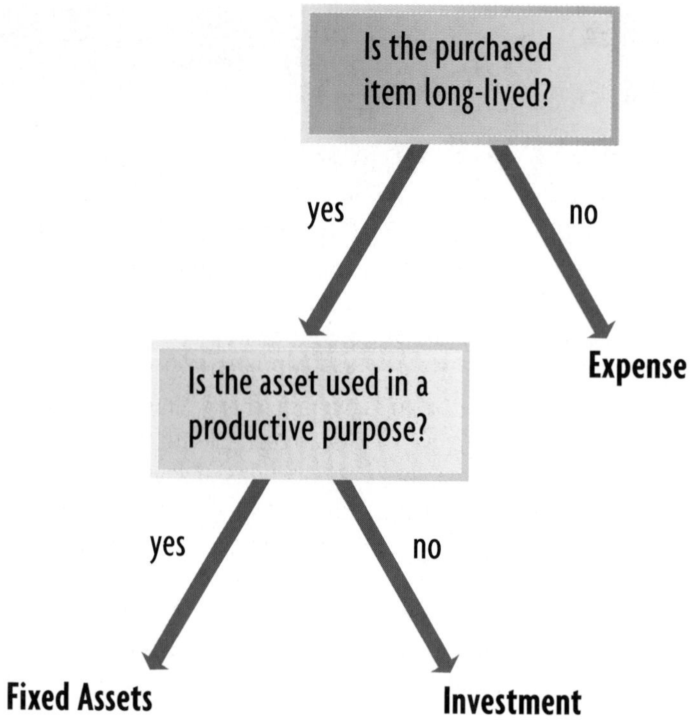

the construction is complete, the costs should be reclassified by crediting the construction in progress account and debiting the appropriate fixed asset account. For growing companies, construction in progress can be significant. For example, Intel Corporation disclosed $4.8 billion of construction in progress, which was 32 percent of its total fixed assets.

The details of fixed assets are disclosed on the face of the balance sheet or the footnotes to the financial statements. For example, Marriott International Inc. had the following fixed asset disclosures on a recent balance sheet:

	($ in millions)
Land	$ 597
Buildings	1,240
Furniture and equipment	647
Timeshare properties	914
Construction in progress	349
Total	$3,747

INTERNATIONAL PERSPECTIVE

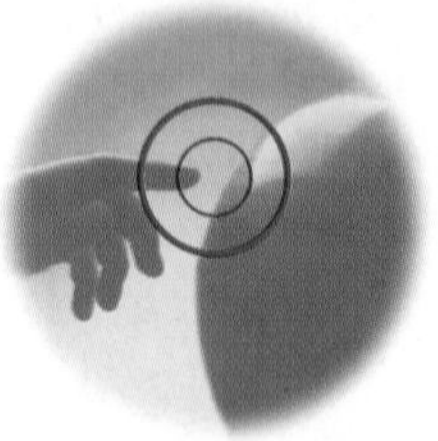

Venezula's accounting standards do not include standards for accounting for property, plant, and equipment and intangible assets.

These categories are typical for a lodging company. Other types of companies would have categories to fit their particular business.

Exhibit 3 summarizes some of the common costs of acquiring fixed assets. These costs should be recorded by debiting the related fixed asset account, such as Land,[1] Building, Land Improvements, or Machinery and Equipment.

1 As discussed here, land is assumed to be used only as a location or site and not for its mineral deposits or other natural resources.

Exhibit 3

Costs of Acquiring Fixed Assets

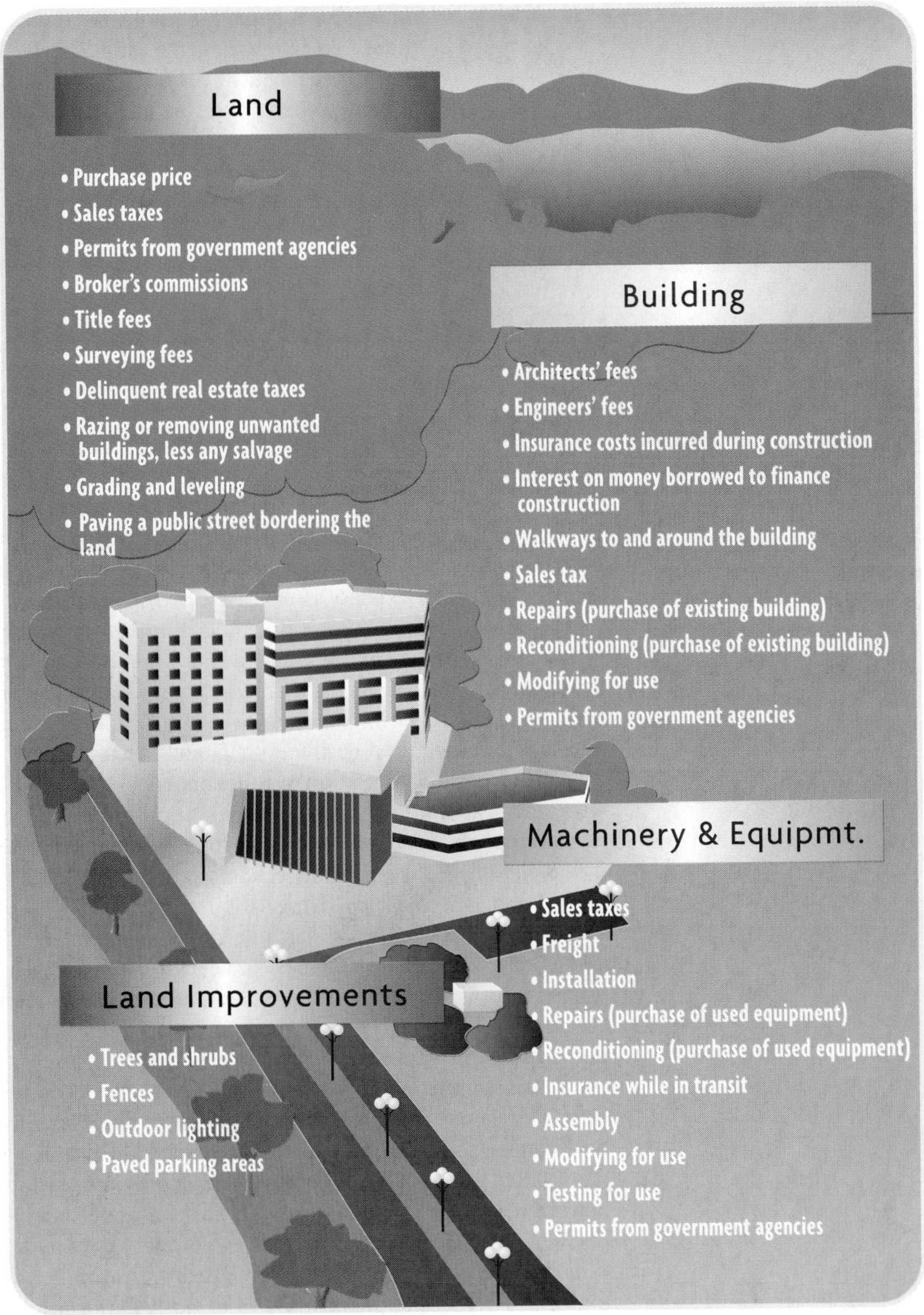

Land
• Purchase price
• Sales taxes
• Permits from government agencies
• Broker's commissions
• Title fees
• Surveying fees
• Delinquent real estate taxes
• Razing or removing unwanted buildings, less any salvage
• Grading and leveling
• Paving a public street bordering the land
Building
• Architects' fees
• Engineers' fees
• Insurance costs incurred during construction
• Interest on money borrowed to finance construction
• Walkways to and around the building
• Sales tax
• Repairs (purchase of existing building)
• Reconditioning (purchase of existing building)
• Modifying for use
• Permits from government agencies
Machinery & Equipmt.
• Sales taxes
• Freight
• Installation
• Repairs (purchase of used equipment)
• Reconditioning (purchase of used equipment)
• Insurance while in transit
• Assembly
• Modifying for use
• Testing for use
• Permits from government agencies
Land Improvements
• Trees and shrubs
• Fences
• Outdoor lighting
• Paved parking areas

Only costs necessary for preparing a long-lived asset for use should be included as a cost of the asset. Unnecessary costs that do not increase the asset's usefulness are recorded as an expense. For example, the following costs are included as an expense:

- Vandalism
- Mistakes in installation
- Uninsured theft
- Damage during unpacking and installing
- Fines for not obtaining proper permits from governmental agencies

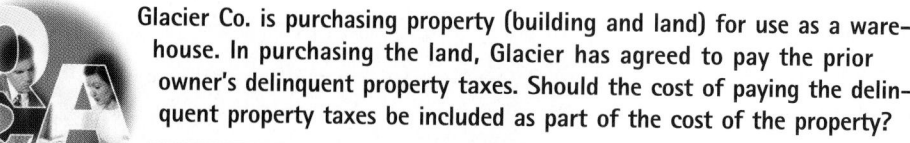

Glacier Co. is purchasing property (building and land) for use as a warehouse. In purchasing the land, Glacier has agreed to pay the prior owner's delinquent property taxes. Should the cost of paying the delinquent property taxes be included as part of the cost of the property?

Yes. All costs of acquiring the property, including the delinquent property taxes, should be included as part of the total cost of the property.

Accounting for Depreciation

2 Compute depreciation, using the following methods: straight-line, units-of-production, and declining-balance.

As we have discussed in earlier chapters, land has an unlimited life and therefore can provide unlimited services. On the other hand, other fixed assets such as equipment, buildings, and land improvements lose their ability, over time, to provide services. As a result, the costs of equipment, buildings, and land improvements should be transferred to expense accounts in a systematic manner during their expected useful lives. This periodic transfer of cost to expense is called **depreciation**.

The adjusting entry to record depreciation is usually made at the end of each month or at the end of the year. This entry debits *Depreciation Expense* and credits a *contra asset* account entitled *Accumulated Depreciation* or *Allowance for Depreciation*. The use of a contra asset account allows the original cost to remain unchanged in the fixed asset account.[2]

Factors that cause a decline in a fixed asset's ability to provide services may be identified as physical depreciation or functional depreciation. *Physical depreciation* occurs from wear and tear from use and from the effects of weather conditions. *Functional depreciation* occurs when a fixed asset is no longer able to provide services at the level for which it was intended. Advances in technology have made functional depreciation an increasingly important cause of depreciation. For example, a personal computer made in the 1980s is not able to provide an Internet connection.

The term *depreciation* as used in accounting is often misunderstood because the same term is also used in business to mean a decline in the market value of an asset. However, the amount of a fixed asset's unexpired cost reported in the balance sheet usually does not agree with the amount that could be realized from its sale. Fixed assets are held for use in a business rather than for sale. Since the business is assumed to be a going concern, a decision to dispose of a fixed asset is based mainly on the usefulness of the asset to the business and not on its market value.

Another common misunderstanding is that depreciation provides cash needed to replace fixed assets as they wear out. This misunderstanding probably occurs because depreciation, unlike most expenses, does not require an outlay of cash in the period in which it is recorded. The cash account is neither increased nor decreased by the periodic entries that transfer the cost of fixed assets to depreciation expense accounts.

Factors in Computing Depreciation Expense

Three factors are considered in determining the amount of depreciation expense to be recognized each period. These three factors are (a) the fixed asset's initial cost, (b) its expected useful life, and (c) its estimated value at the end of its useful life. This third factor is called the **residual value**, *scrap value*, *salvage value*, or *trade-in value*. Exhibit 4 shows the relationship among the three factors and the periodic depreciation expense.

---

2 Depreciation on fixed assets used to manufacture product is debited to Factory Overhead, which eventually becomes part of the cost of goods sold on the income statement. This is discussed more fully in cost accounting texts.

Exhibit 4

Factors that Determine Depreciation Expense

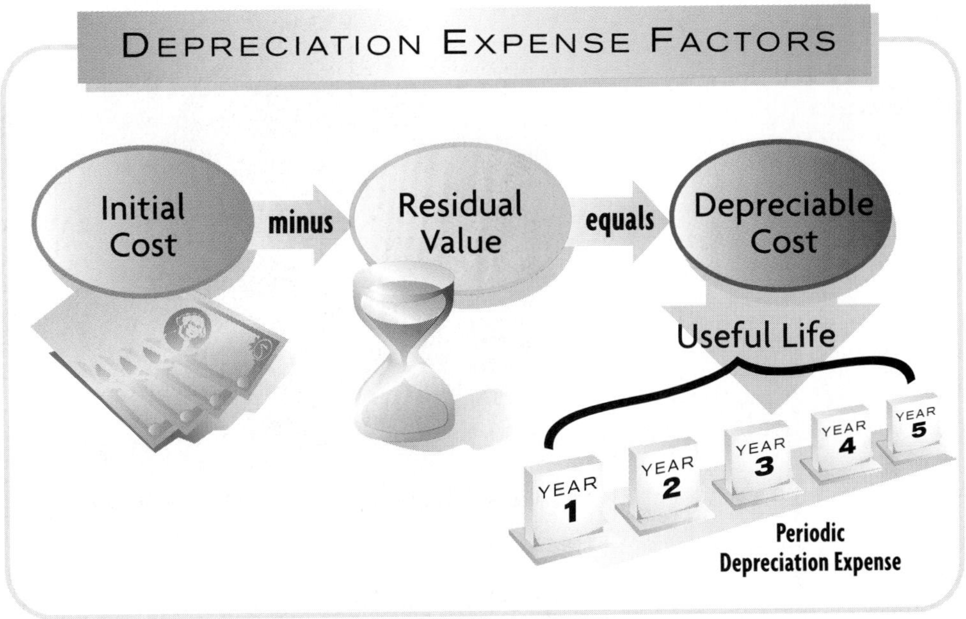

A fixed asset's residual value at the end of its expected useful life must be estimated at the time the asset is placed in service. If a fixed asset is expected to have little or no residual value when it is taken out of service, then its initial cost should be spread over its expected useful life as depreciation expense. If, however, a fixed asset is expected to have a significant residual value, the difference between its initial cost and its residual value, called the asset's *depreciable cost*, is the amount that is spread over the asset's useful life as depreciation expense.

A fixed asset's *expected useful life* must also be estimated at the time the asset is placed in service. Estimates of expected useful lives are available from various trade associations and other publications. It is not uncommon for different companies to have different useful lives for similar assets. For example, the primary useful life for buildings is 50 years for JC Penney Co., while the useful life for buildings for Tandy Corporation, which operates Radio Shack, varies from 10 to 40 years. For federal income tax purposes, the Internal Revenue Service (IRS) has established guidelines for useful lives. For example, the IRS useful life guideline for most vehicles is 5 years, while the designated life for most machinery and equipment is 7 years. These guidelines may also be helpful in determining depreciation for financial reporting purposes. Companies often use different useful lives for similar assets.

Guidelines are also necessary for determining when an asset is placed into and out of service. In practice, many businesses assume that assets placed in or taken out of service during the first half of a month are treated as if the event occurred on the first day of *that* month. That is, these businesses compute depreciation on these assets for the entire month. Likewise, all fixed asset additions and deductions during the second half of a month are treated as if the event occurred on the first day of the *next* month. We will follow this practice in this chapter.

A business is not required to use a single method of computing depreciation for all its depreciable assets. The methods used in the accounts and financial statements may also differ from the methods used in determining income taxes and property taxes. The three methods used most often are (1) straight-line, (2) units-of-production, and (3) declining-balance. Exhibit 5 shows the extent of the use of these methods in financial statements.

Exhibit 5

Use of Depreciation Methods

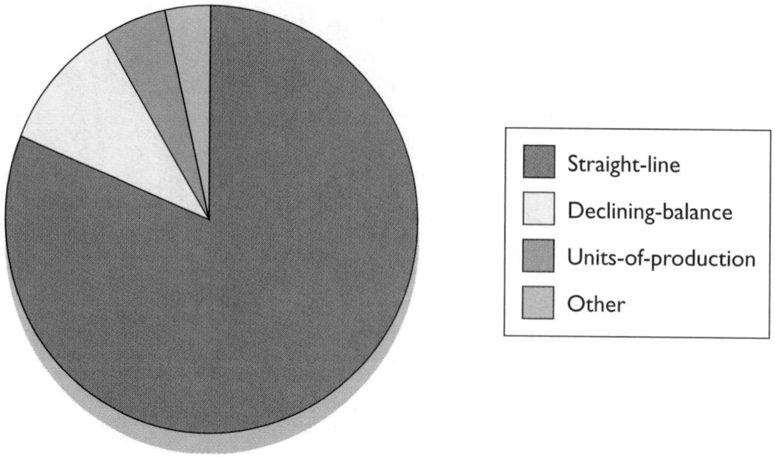

Source: *Accounting Trends & Techniques*, 55th ed., American Institute of Certified Public Accountants, New York, 2001.

Straight-Line Method

The **straight-line method** provides for the same amount of depreciation expense for each year of the asset's useful life. For example, assume that the cost of a depreciable asset is \$24,000, its estimated residual value is \$2,000, and its estimated life is 5 years. The annual depreciation is computed as follows:

$$\frac{\text{\$24,000 cost} - \text{\$2,000 estimated residual value}}{\text{5 years estimated life}} = \text{\$4,400 annual depreciation}$$

The adjusting entry for depreciation would be recorded as:

Dec. 31	Depreciation Expense	4,400	
	Accumulated Depreciation		4,400

A truck that cost \$35,000 has a residual value of \$5,000 and a useful life of 12 years. What are (a) the depreciable cost, (b) the straight-line rate, and (c) the annual straight-line depreciation?

(a) \$30,000 (\$35,000 − \$5,000), (b) 8 1/3% (1/12), (c) \$2,500 (\$30,000 × 8 1/3%).

When an asset is used for only part of a year, the annual depreciation is prorated. For example, assume that the fiscal year ends on December 31 and that the asset in the above example is placed in service on October 1. The depreciation for the first fiscal year of use would be \$1,100 (\$4,400 × 3/12).

For ease in applying the straight-line method, the annual depreciation may be converted to a percentage of the depreciable cost. This percentage is determined by dividing 100% by the number of years of useful life. For example, a useful life of 20 years converts to a 5% rate (100%/20), 8 years converts to a 12.5% rate (100%/8), and so on.[3] In the above example, the annual depreciation of \$4,400 can be computed by multiplying the depreciable cost of \$22,000 by 20% (100%/5).

The straight-line method is simple and is widely used. It provides a reasonable transfer of costs to periodic expense when the asset's use and the related revenues from its use are about the same from period to period.

3 The depreciation rate may also be expressed as a fraction. For example, the annual straight-line rate for an asset with a 3-year useful life is 1/3.

Units-of-Production Method

Sometimes the use of the fixed asset varies significantly from period to period, such as might be the case for vehicles, aircraft, or construction equipment. When the amount of use of a fixed asset varies from year to year, the units-of-production method may be more appropriate than the straight-line method. In such cases, the units-of-production method better matches the depreciation expense with the related revenue.

The **units-of-production method** provides for the same amount of depreciation expense for each unit produced or each unit of capacity used by the asset. For example, Norfolk Southern Corporation depreciates rail track on the basis of gross-ton miles, which is its unit of capacity.

To apply this method, the useful life of the asset is expressed in terms of units of productive capacity, such as hours or miles. The total depreciation expense for each accounting period is then determined by multiplying the unit depreciation by the number of units produced or used during the period. For example, assume that a machine with a cost of $24,000 and an estimated residual value of $2,000 is expected to have an estimated life of 10,000 operating hours. The depreciation for a unit of one hour is computed as follows:

$$\frac{\$24{,}000 \text{ cost} - \$2{,}000 \text{ estimated residual value}}{10{,}000 \text{ estimated hours}} = \$2.20 \text{ hourly depreciation}$$

A truck that cost $35,000 has a residual value of $5,000 and a useful life of 125,000 miles. What are (a) the depreciation rate per mile and (b) the first year's depreciation if 18,000 miles were driven?

(a) $0.24 per mile [($35,000 − $5,000)/125,000 miles], (b) $4,320 (18,000 miles × $0.24 per mile)

Assuming that the machine was in operation for 2,100 hours during a year, the depreciation for that year would be $4,620 ($2.20 × 2,100 hours).

Declining-Balance Method

The **declining-balance method** provides for a declining periodic expense over the estimated useful life of the asset. To apply this method, the annual straight-line depreciation rate is doubled. For example, the declining-balance rate for an asset with an estimated life of 5 years is 40%, which is double the straight-line rate of 20% (100%/5).

For the first year of use, the cost of the asset is multiplied by the declining-balance rate. After the first year, the declining **book value** or *net book value* (initial asset cost minus accumulated depreciation) of the asset is multiplied by this rate. To illustrate, the annual declining-balance depreciation for an asset with an estimated 5-year life and a cost of $24,000 is shown below.

Year	Cost	Accum. Depr. at Beginning of Year	Book Value at Beginning of Year	Rate	Depreciation for Year	Book Value at End of Year
1	$24,000		$24,000.00	40%	$9,600.00	$14,400.00
2	24,000	$ 9,600.00	14,400.00	40%	5,760.00	8,640.00
3	24,000	15,360.00	8,640.00	40%	3,456.00	5,184.00
4	24,000	18,816.00	5,184.00	40%	2,073.60	3,110.40
5	24,000	20,889.60	3,110.40	—	1,110.40	2,000.00

A truck that cost $35,000 has a residual value of $5,000 and a useful life of 12 years. What is the double-declining balance depreciation for the second full year of use?

$4,861 {[$35,000 − ($35,000 × 16 2/3%)] × 16 2/3%}

You should note that when the declining-balance method is used, the estimated residual value is *not* considered in determining the depreciation rate. It is also ignored in computing the periodic depreciation. However, the asset should not be depreciated below its estimated residual value. In the above example, the estimated residual value was $2,000. Therefore, the depreciation for the fifth year is $1,110.40 ($3,110.40 − $2,000.00) instead of $1,244.16 (40% × $3,110.40).

In the example, we assumed that the first use of the asset occurred at the beginning of the fiscal year. This is normally not the case in practice, however, and depreciation for the first partial year of use must be computed. For example, assume that the asset above was in service at the end of the *third* month of the fiscal year. In this case, only a portion (9/12) of the first full year's depreciation of $9,600 is allocated to the first fiscal year. Thus, depreciation of $7,200 (9/12 × $9,600) is allocated to the first partial year of use. The depreciation for the second fiscal year would then be $6,720 [40% × ($24,000 − $7,200)].

Comparing Depreciation Methods

The straight-line method provides for the same periodic amounts of depreciation expense over the life of the asset. The units-of-production method provides for periodic amounts of depreciation expense that vary, depending upon the amount the asset is used.

The declining-balance method provides for a higher depreciation amount in the first year of the asset's use, followed by a gradually declining amount. For this reason, the declining-balance method is called an **accelerated depreciation method**. It is most appropriate when the decline in an asset's productivity or earning power is greater in the early years of its use than in later years. Further, using this method is often justified because repairs tend to increase with the age of an asset. The reduced amounts of depreciation in later years are thus offset to some extent by increased repair expenses.

The periodic depreciation amounts for the straight-line method and the declining-balance method are compared in Exhibit 6. This comparison is based on an asset cost of $24,000, an estimated life of 5 years, and an estimated residual value of $2,000.

Exhibit 6

Comparing Depreciation Methods

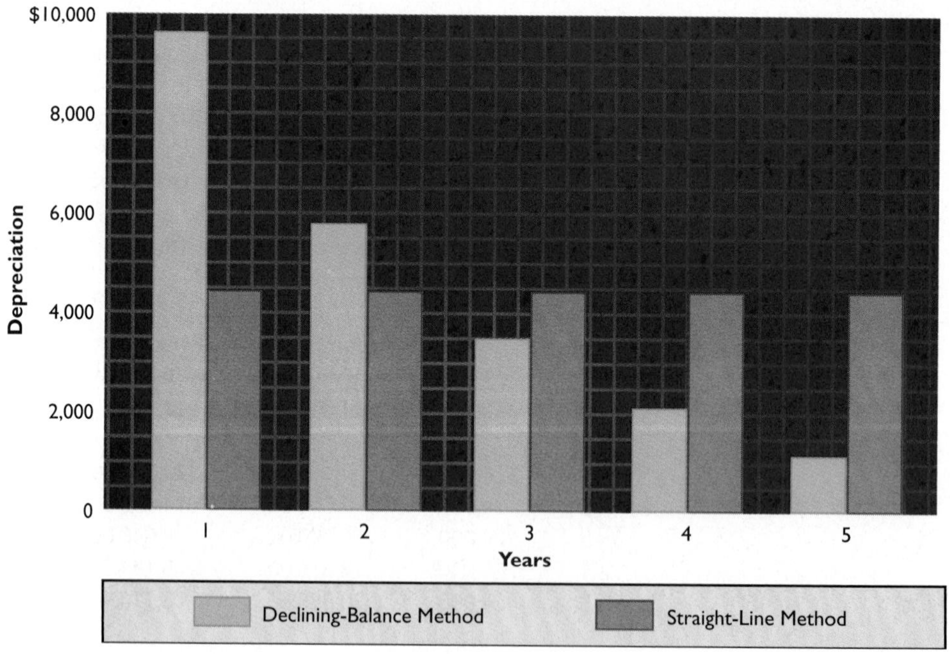

Depreciation for Federal Income Tax

The Internal Revenue Code specifies the *Modified Accelerated Cost Recovery System (MACRS)* for use by businesses in computing depreciation for tax purposes. MACRS specifies eight classes of useful life and depreciation rates for each class. The two most common classes, other than real estate, are the 5-year class and the 7-year class.[4] The 5-year class includes automobiles and light-duty trucks, and the 7-year class includes most machinery and equipment. The depreciation deduction for these two classes is similar to that computed using the declining-balance method.

In using the MACRS rates, residual value is ignored, and all fixed assets are assumed to be put in and taken out of service in the middle of the year. For the 5-year-class assets, depreciation is spread over six years, as shown in the following MACRS schedule of depreciation rates:

Year	5-Year-Class Depreciation Rates
1	20.0%
2	32.0
3	19.2
4	11.5
5	11.5
6	5.8
	100.0%

What is the third-year MACRS depreciation for an automobile that cost $26,000 and has a residual value of $6,500?

$4,992 ($26,000 × 19.2%)

To simplify its record keeping, a business will sometimes use the MACRS method for both financial statement and tax purposes. This is acceptable if MACRS does not result in significantly different amounts than would have been reported using one of the three depreciation methods discussed earlier in this chapter.

Using MACRS for both financial statement and tax purposes may, however, hurt a business. In one case, a business that had used MACRS depreciation for its financial statements lost a $1 million order because its fixed assets had low book values. The bank viewed these low book values as inadequate, so it would not loan the business the amount needed to produce the order.[5]

Revising Depreciation Estimates

Revising the estimates of the residual value and the useful life is normal. When these estimates are revised, they are used to determine the depreciation expense in future periods. They do not affect the amounts of depreciation expense recorded in earlier years.

To illustrate, assume that a fixed asset purchased for $130,000 was originally estimated to have a useful life of 10 years and a residual value of $10,000. The asset has been depreciated for 5 years by the straight-line method at a rate of $12,000 per year (($130,000 − $10,000)/10). At the end of five years, the asset's book value (undepreciated cost) is $70,000, determined as follows:

Asset cost	$130,000
Less accumulated depreciation ($12,000 per year × 5 years)	60,000
Book value (undepreciated cost), end of fifth year	$ 70,000

4 Real estate is in 27 1/2-year classes and 31 1/2-year classes and is depreciated by the straight-line method.

5 Lee Berton, "Do's and Don'ts," *The Wall Street Journal*, June 10, 1988, p. 34R.

An asset with an original cost of $80,000 and a residual value of $12,000 was estimated to have an 8-year life. After 3 years, the asset is estimated to have a remaining life of 10 years, with no change in residual value. What is the revised depreciation expense for the fourth year?

$4,250. The depreciation expense per year for the first 3 years is $8,500 per year [($80,000 − $12,000)/8]. The book value at the end of the third year is $54,500 [$80,000 − (3 × $8,500)]. The remaining book value less the residual value divided by the remaining life is ($54,500 − $12,000)/10.

During the sixth year, the company estimates that the *remaining* useful life is 9 years (instead of 5) and that the residual value is $7,000 (instead of $10,000). The depreciation expense for each of the remaining 9 years is $7,000, computed as follows:

Book value (undepreciated cost), end of fifth year	$70,000
Less revised estimated residual value	7,000
Revised remaining depreciable cost	$63,000
Revised annual depreciation expense ($63,000/9)	$ 7,000

Exhibit 7 shows the book value of the asset over its original and revised lives. Notice that the book value declines at a slower rate beginning at the end of year five and continuing until it reaches the salvage value of $7,000 at the revised end of the asset's useful life.

Exhibit 7

Book Value of Asset with Change in Estimate

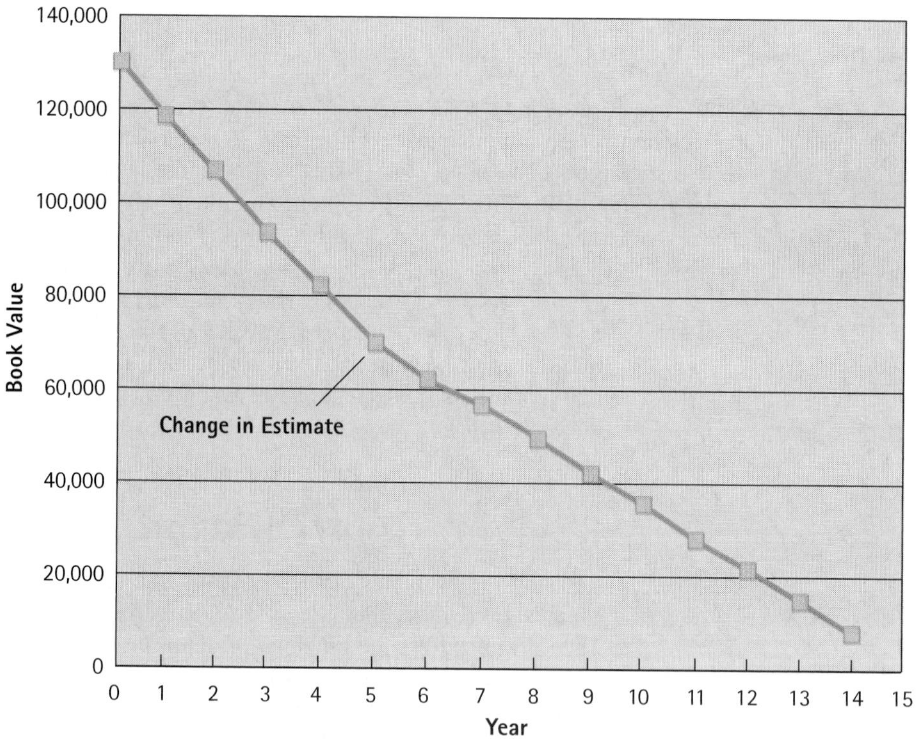

A change in estimate should be disclosed in the footnotes to the financial statements. An example of such a disclosure is shown for St. Paul Companies as follows:

Acceleration of Software Depreciation. . . . The resulting strategy to standardize technology throughout . . . and maintain one data center in St. Paul, Minnesota, resulted in the identification of duplicate software applications. As a result, the estimated useful life for that software was shortened, resulting in an additional charge to earnings.

Natural Resources

3 Compute and record depletion of natural resources.

The fixed assets of some businesses include timber, metal ores, minerals, or other natural resources. As these businesses harvest or mine and then sell these resources, a portion of the cost of acquiring them must be debited to an expense account. This process of transferring the cost of natural resources to an expense account is called **depletion**. The amount of depletion is determined by multiplying the quantity extracted during the period by the depletion rate. This rate is computed by dividing the cost of the mineral deposit by its estimated size.

Computing depletion is similar to computing units-of-production depreciation. To illustrate, assume that a business paid $400,000 for the mining rights to a mineral deposit estimated at 1,000,000 tons of ore. The depletion rate is $0.40 per ton ($400,000/1,000,000 tons). If 90,000 tons are mined during the year, the periodic depletion is $36,000 (90,000 tons × $0.40). The adjusting entry to record the depletion is shown below.

Dec. 31	Depletion Expense	36,000	
	Accumulated Depletion		36,000

Like the accumulated depreciation account, Accumulated Depletion is a *contra asset* account. It is reported on the balance sheet as a deduction from the cost of the mineral deposit.

A business purchased mineral rights to 250,000 tons of ore for $1,500,000. If 35,000 tons of ore were mined in the first year, what are (a) the depletion rate per ton and (b) the depletion expense for the first year?

(a) $6 per ton ($1,500,000/250,000 tons); (b) $210,000 (35,000 tons × $6)

Fixed Asset Disposals

4 Account for the disposal of fixed assets.

Fixed assets that are no longer useful may be discarded, sold, or traded[6] for other fixed assets. The details of the entry to record a disposal will vary. In all cases, however, the book value of the asset is removed from the accounts. The entry to record the disposal of a fixed asset debits the asset's accumulated depreciation account for its balance on the date of disposal and credits the asset account for the cost of the asset.

Discarding Fixed Assets

A fixed asset is not removed from the accounts only because it has been fully depreciated. If the asset is still used by the business, the cost and accumulated depreciation remain in the ledger. This maintains accountability for the asset in the ledger. If the book

6 Accounting for fixed asset exchanges (trades) is a topic covered in advanced accounting courses.

value of the asset is removed from the ledger, the accounts contain no evidence of the continued existence of the asset. In addition, the cost and the accumulated depreciation data on such assets are often needed for property tax and income tax reports.

When fixed assets are no longer useful to the business and have no residual or market value, they are discarded. To illustrate, assume that an item of equipment acquired at a cost of $25,000 is fully depreciated, with no salvage value at December 31, the end of the preceding fiscal year. On February 14, the equipment is discarded. The entry to record this is as follows:

Feb. 14	Accumulated Depreciation	25,000	
	Equipment		25,000

If an asset has not been fully depreciated, depreciation should be recorded prior to removing it from service and from the accounting records. To illustrate, assume that equipment costing $6,000 is depreciated at an annual straight-line rate of 10%. In addition, assume that on December 31 of the preceding fiscal year, the accumulated depreciation balance, after adjusting entries, is $4,750. Finally, assume that the asset is removed from service on the following March 24. The entry to record the depreciation for the three months of the current period prior to the asset's removal from service is as follows:

Mar. 24	Depreciation Expense—Equipment	150	
	Accumulated Depreciation—Equipment		150
	To record current depreciation on equipment discarded ($600 × 3/12).		

The discarding of the equipment is then recorded by the following entry:

Mar. 24	Accumulated Depreciation—Equipment	4,900	
	Loss on Disposal of Fixed Assets	1,100	
	Equipment		6,000

The loss of $1,100 is recorded because the balance of the accumulated depreciation account ($4,900) is less than the balance in the equipment account ($6,000). Losses on the discarding of fixed assets are nonoperating items and are normally reported in the Other Expense section of the income statement.

Selling Fixed Assets

The entry to record the sale of a fixed asset is similar to the entry illustrated above, except that the cash or other asset received must also be recorded. If the selling price is more than the book value of the asset, the transaction results in a gain. If the selling price is less than the book value, there is a loss. For example, H.J. Heinz Company recognized a gain of $18.2 million on the sale of an office building in the United Kingdom because the selling price exceeded the book value.

To illustrate a sale transaction, assume that equipment is acquired at a cost of $10,000 and is depreciated at an annual straight-line rate of 10%. The building is sold for cash on October 12 of the eighth year of its use. The balance of the accumulated depreciation account as of the preceding December 31 is $7,000. The entry to update the depreciation for the nine months of the current year is as follows:

Oct.	12	Depreciation Expense	750	
		Accumulated Depreciation		750

After the current depreciation is recorded, the book value of the asset is $2,250 ($10,000 − $7,750). The entry to record the sale, assuming the asset was sold for $1,000 is:

Oct.	12	Cash	1,000	
		Accumulated Depreciation	7,750	
		Loss on Disposal of Fixed Asset	1,250	
		Equipment		10,000

The loss can be verified as the difference between the cash proceeds upon sale and the book value of the asset, as follows:

Cash proceeds		$1,000
Book value of equipment:		
Equipment initial cost	$10,000	
Accumulated depreciation	7,750	
Equipment book value		2,250
Loss on disposal of fixed asset		$1,250

Provide the journal entry if the asset described in the text illustration was sold for $2,800.

Oct.	12	Cash	2,800	
		Accumulated Depreciation	7,750	
		Gain on Disposal of Fixed Asset		550
		Equipment		10,000

Project Stage Capital and Revenue Expenditures

5 Classify fixed asset costs as either capital expenditures or revenue expenditures according to their project stage.

The costs incurred for fixed assets can be classified into four stages: preliminary, preacquisition, acquisition or construction, and in-service. These stages are illustrated in Exhibit 8.

The *preliminary stage* occurs *before* management believes acquiring a fixed asset is probable. During this stage, a company may conduct feasibility studies, marketing studies, and financial analyses to determine the viability of a fixed asset acquisition. These costs are not associated with a particular fixed asset, so must be treated as revenue

Exhibit 8

Fixed asset project stages

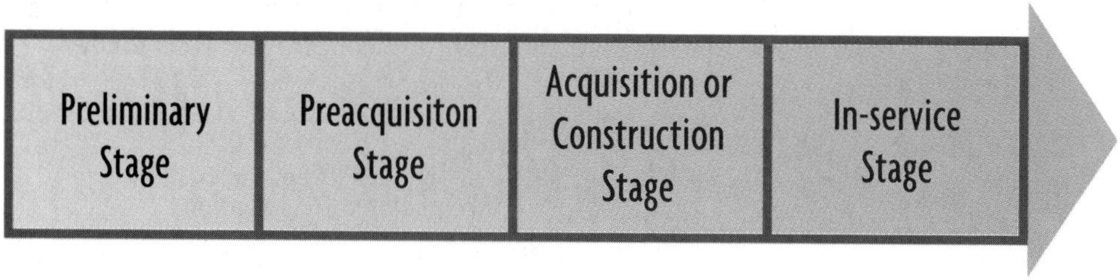

expenditures.[7] A **revenue expenditure** is a cost that benefits only the current period and is debited to an expense account.

At the *preacquisition stage*, acquiring the fixed asset has become probable, but has not yet occurred. Costs that are incurred during this stage, such as surveys, zoning, and engineering studies, can be associated with a specific fixed asset and should be treated as a capital expenditure. As we stated previously, **capital expenditures** are the costs of acquiring, constructing, adding, or replacing fixed assets.

During the *acquisition* or *construction stage*, the acquisition has occurred or construction has begun, but the fixed asset is not yet ready for use. Costs directly identified with the fixed asset during this stage should be capitalized in a construction in progress account. General and administrative costs should *not* be allocated to fixed asset acquisition or construction for capitalization. These costs are debited to the appropriate general and administrative expense account. When the fixed asset is ready for use, the capitalized costs should be transferred from construction in progress to the related fixed asset account.

During the *in-service stage*, the fixed asset is complete and ready for use. During this stage, the fixed asset should be depreciated as described in the previous section. In addition, normal, recurring, or periodic repairs and maintenance activities related to fixed assets during this stage should be charged to maintenance expense for the period. Costs incurred to either acquire additional components of fixed assets or replace existing components of fixed assets should be capitalized, as described in the next section.

Ethics in Action

Capital Crime

One of the largest alleged accounting frauds in history involved the improper accounting for capital expenditures. Worldcom, Inc., the second largest telecommunications company in the United States, improperly treated maintenance expenditures on its telecommunications network as capital expenditures. As a result, the company had to restate its prior years' earnings downward by nearly $4 billion to correct this error. The company declared bankruptcy within months of disclosing the error.

An in-service stage fixed asset may include one or more components. A *component* is a tangible portion of a fixed asset that can be separately identified as an asset and depreciated over its own separate expected useful life. For example, the roof or elevator bank

7 Payments made to acquire options to purchase fixed assets should be capitalized.

of a building could be identified as components that are depreciated separately from the building itself. When a company *acquires* or *constructs a new component*, the costs should be capitalized as described for the previous project stages. Once installed, the component would be depreciated over its useful service life. For example, on April 1, Boxter Company purchased and installed a new crane within a warehouse for $150,000. This cost would be capitalized as a separate component as follows:

April 1	Crane	150,000	
	Cash		150,000

A company can also *replace a component*. Replacements are accounted for in two steps. First, the book value of the replaced component is debited to Depreciation Expense and credited to Accumulated Depreciation. This treatment is consistent with a change of estimate. That is, the fixed asset component is now recognized as being fully depreciated upon replacement. In addition, any costs to remove the old component should be charged to expense. Second, the identifiable direct costs associated with the new component are then capitalized. To illustrate, assume that Boxter removes a warehouse roof on August 1 at a cost of $1,000. As of August 1, the old roof has a remaining book value (initial cost less accumulated depreciation) of $9,000.[8] On August 5, the new roof is completed at a cost of $60,000 and is estimated to have a 20-year life, which is the remaining life of the building. First, the cost of removing the old roof must be expensed, and the book value of the replaced roof must be completely depreciated, as follows:

Identify each of the items related to a truck as capitalized or expensed: (a) a snowplow attachment that allows the truck to be used for snow removal, (b) a new transmission, (c) a hydraulic hitch to replace a manual hitch, (d) the cost of scheduled maintenance.

(a) capitalize (new component), (b) capitalize (replaced component), (c) capitalize (replaced component), (d) expense (normal repair)

Aug. 1	Removal Expenses	1,000	
	Cash		1,000
Aug. 1	Depreciation Expense	9,000	
	Accumulated Depreciation—Warehouse		9,000

As a result of this entry, the book value of the old roof is now zero. Next, the cost of the new roof must be capitalized as a separate component as follows:

Aug. 5	Warehouse	60,000	
	Cash		60,000

Using the straight-line method, the new roof will be depreciated over 20 years at $3,000 per year ($60,000 ÷ 20 years).

8 The depreciation expense would be adjusted to reflect depreciation to August 1, as illustrated previously for asset disposals.

Analyzing Fixed Assets

6 Analyze the utilization of fixed assets.

Business success for many firms is influenced by the utilization of fixed assets. Fixed assets that sit idle do not generate revenue and, hence, do not provide a return on investment. Thus, analysts examine the utilization of the fixed assets. The two major types of analyses are operational utilization analysis and financial utilization analysis.

Operational Utilization Analysis

The operating statistics of fixed assets for some fixed asset-intensive industries are provided by the reports filed with the SEC (Securities and Exchange Commission) and, hence, are publicly available for analysis. These operational measures are typically determined by the following general ratio:

$$\text{Operational utilization (general ratio)} = \frac{\text{Annual usage of the fixed asset}}{\text{Total annual fixed asset capacity}}$$

The closer the operational utilization approaches 100 percent, the more efficient the fixed assets. Naturally, a 100 percent utilization would be rare; however, much smaller percentages could indicate a problem. Exhibit 9 provides the ratio name and calculation for several operational utilization ratios for a number of industries.

Exhibit 9

Operational Utilization Ratio Examples

Industry	Ratio Name	Ratio Calculation
Airline	Load factor	Seat miles sold/Available seat miles
Cable	Penetration	Subscribers/Potential connections on network
Hotel	Occupancy	Nights sold/Available nights
Power generation	Utilization	Net generating output/Total generating capacity

To illustrate, the occupancy rate reported to the SEC for Starwood Hotels & Resorts (Sheraton® and Westin® hotel brands) was 71.6 percent. This percentage is determined by dividing the total room nights sold by the total available nights. The available nights are the number of rooms multiplied by 365 operating days in the year. The comparable ratio for Marriott International, Inc. was 78.2 percent. We could conclude that Marriott has utilized its hotel assets more efficiently than Starwood because more room nights were sold as a percent of available nights.

Financial Utilization Analysis

Fixed assets can also be evaluated by their ability to generate revenue, using two basic methods. The first approach determines the revenue per unit of fixed assets, while the second determines the number of revenue dollars per dollar of fixed assets.

Revenue per Unit of Fixed Assets The general formula for the revenue per unit of fixed assets is determined as follows:

$$\text{Revenue per unit of fixed assets} = \frac{\text{Total revenues}}{\text{Number of fixed asset units}}$$

This type of ratio is used only when the fixed asset units in the denominator are reasonably related to revenues. Otherwise, such a ratio is not generally meaningful. Examples of this ratio for a number of industries are shown in Exhibit 10.

Exhibit 10

Revenue per Unit of Fixed Asset Ratio Examples

Industry	Ratio Name	Ratio Calculation
Airline	Revenue per available seat mile	Total revenues/Available seat miles
Brokerage	Revenue per share traded	Total commission revenue/Total number of shares traded
Hotel	Revenue per available room night	Total revenues/Available room nights
Restaurant	Revenue per restaurant	Total revenues/Total restaurants
Retail	Revenue per square foot	Total revenues/Total square feet of retail floor space

Using the hotel industry as an example, the total number of available room nights is a physical measure of the hotel's revenue capacity. This is a better measure of capacity than is the "number of hotels," for example, since each hotel is a different size. Each "room night" is reasonably similar; thus, the ratio can be interpreted. The revenues per available room night for Starwood and Marriott were reported to be \$115 and \$117, respectively. Both hotels are generating nearly the same revenue for each available room night. In contrast, Choice Hotels International, Inc. (Comfort Inn®, Quality Inn® and EconoLodge® brand names) has a revenue per available room night of only \$54, which is consistent with its mid-market strategy.

Fixed Asset Turnover Ratio The second asset utilization measure is called the fixed asset turnover ratio. The **fixed asset turnover ratio** measures the number of dollars of revenue earned per dollar of fixed assets, and is calculated as:

$$\text{Fixed asset turnover} = \frac{\text{Revenue}}{\text{Average Book Value of Fixed Assets}}$$

Unlike the revenue per unit of fixed asset ratio, this ratio can be calculated for any company because it uses publicly available financial statement information. To illustrate the calculation, the following fixed asset balance sheet information is available for Marriott:

	December 28, 2001 (in millions)	December 29, 2000 (in millions)
Property and equipment (net)	\$2,930	\$3,011

In addition, Marriott reported revenue of \$10,152 million for 2001. Thus, the fixed asset turnover is:

$$\text{Fixed asset turnover} = \frac{\$10{,}152}{(\$3{,}011 + 2{,}930)/2} = 3.42 \text{ turns}$$

For every dollar of fixed assets, Marriott earns \$3.42 of revenue. The larger this ratio, the more efficiently a business is using its fixed assets. This ratio can be compared to other companies in the industry to evaluate overall fixed asset turnover performance. For example, the fixed asset turnover ratios for Starwood and Choice Hotels are 0.55 and 2.29,

Strategy in Business

Rent or Own?

You might hire a copy shop to copy a school paper, rather than acquiring a copy machine to make your own copies. In the same way, companies must decide which activities they should perform and which activities they should hire other companies to perform for them. The activities that are performed internally usually require fixed assets. Fixed assets, in turn, place a firm at risk, since these assets must be used in order to have a financial return. Thus, some firms limit internal activities to their core competencies, or those activities that provide the company a strategic comparative advantage. Under this philosophy, non-core activities are purchased from others. Sara Lee Corporation embraces this strategic philosophy by becoming "an asset-less company." That is, Sara Lee has retained only its core activities and has asked suppliers to perform its non-core activities, such as manufacturing. In contrast, General Mills, a Sara Lee competitor, owns its manufacturing facilities. This difference in strategic philosophy can be seen in the companies' respective fixed asset turnover ratios, 8.3 for Sara Lee and 4.7 for General Mills.

respectively. Marriott is operating its hotel assets very efficiently. This is partially explained by Marriott's franchising strategy, which allows it to earn franchising fees without owning hotel fixed assets.

Exhibit 11 shows the fixed asset turnover ratio for a number of different businesses. The smaller ratios are associated with companies that require large fixed asset investments. The larger fixed asset turnover ratios are associated with firms that are more labor-intensive and require little fixed asset investment.

Exhibit 11

Fixed Asset Turnover Ratios

Company	Fixed Asset Turnover Ratio
Computer Associates International Inc. (consulting)	7.36
eBay, Inc.	3.45
International Paper Co.	1.76
Manpower, Inc. (temporary employment)	56.00
Ruby Tuesday, Inc. (restaurant)	2.83
Southwest Airlines Co.	0.97
Sprint Corporation (telecommunications)	0.93

Intangible Assets

7 Describe and account for intangible assets, such as patents, copyrights, and goodwill.

Patents, copyrights, trademarks, and goodwill are long-lived assets that are useful in the operations of a business and are not held for sale. These assets are called **intangible assets** because they do not exist physically.

The basic principles of accounting for intangible assets are like those described earlier for fixed assets. The major concerns are determining (1) the initial cost and (2) the **amortization**—the amount of cost to transfer to expense. Amortization results from the passage of time or a decline in the usefulness of the intangible asset.

Patents

Manufacturers may acquire exclusive rights to produce and sell goods with one or more unique features. Such rights are granted by **patents**, which the federal government issues to inventors. These rights continue in effect for 20 years. A business may purchase patent rights from others, or it may obtain patents developed by its own research and development efforts.

The initial cost of a purchased patent, including any related legal fees, is debited to an asset account. This cost is written off, or amortized, over the years of the patent's expected usefulness. This period of time may be less than the remaining legal life of the patent. The estimated useful life of the patent may also change as technology or consumer tastes change.

The straight-line method is normally used to determine the periodic amortization. When the amortization is recorded, it is debited to an expense account and credited directly to the patents account. A separate contra asset account is usually *not* used for intangible assets.

To illustrate, assume that at the beginning of its fiscal year, a business acquires patent rights for $100,000. The patent had been granted 6 years earlier by the Federal Patent Office. Although the patent will not expire for 14 years, its remaining useful life is estimated as 5 years. The adjusting entry to amortize the patent at the end of the fiscal year is as follows:

Dec. 31	Amortization Expense—Patents	20,000	
	Patents		20,000

Rather than purchase patent rights, a business may incur significant costs in developing patents through its own research and development efforts. Such *research and development costs* are usually accounted for as current operating expenses in the period in which they are incurred. Expensing research and development costs is justified because the future benefits from research and development efforts are highly uncertain.

Copyrights and Trademarks

The exclusive right to publish and sell a literary, artistic, or musical composition is granted by a **copyright**. Copyrights are issued by the federal government and extend for 70 years beyond the author's death. The costs of a copyright include all costs of creating the work plus any administrative or legal costs of obtaining the copyright. A copyright that is purchased from another should be recorded at the price paid for it. Copyrights are amortized over their estimated useful lives. For example, Sony Corporation states the following amortization policy with respect to its artistic and music intangible assets:

> *Intangibles, which mainly consist of artist contracts and music catalogs, are being amortized on a straight-line basis principally over 16 years and 21 years, respectively.*

INTERNATIONAL PERSPECTIVE

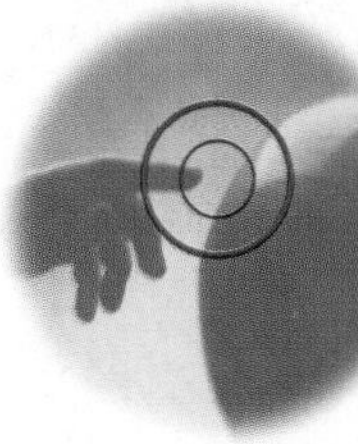

Pirated software is a major concern of software companies. For example, during a recent global sweep, Microsoft seized nearly five million units of counterfeit Microsoft software with an estimated retail value of $1.7 billion. U.S. copyright laws and practices are sometimes ignored or disputed in other parts of the world.

A **trademark** is a name, term, or symbol used to identify a business and its products. For example, the distinctive red-and-white Coca-Cola logo is an example of a trademark. Most businesses identify their trademarks with ® in their advertisements and on their products. Under federal law, businesses can protect against others using their trademarks by registering them for 10 years and renewing the registration for 10-year periods thereafter. Like a copyright, the legal costs of registering a

Ethics in Action

21st Century Pirates

Businesses must honor the copyrights held by software companies by eliminating pirated software from corporate computers. The Business Software Alliance (BSA) represents the largest software companies in campaigns to investigate illegal use of unlicensed software by businesses. The BSA estimates software industry losses of nearly $12 billion annually from software piracy. Employees using pirated software on business assets risk bringing legal penalties to themselves and their employers.

trademark with the federal government are recorded as an asset. Thus, even though the Coca-Cola trademarks are extremely valuable, they are not shown on the balance sheet, because the legal costs for establishing these trademarks are immaterial. If, however, a trademark is purchased from another business, the cost of its purchase is recorded as an asset. The cost of a trademark is in most cases considered to have an indefinite useful life. Thus, trademarks are not amortized over a useful life, as are the previously discussed intangible assets. Rather, trademarks should be tested periodically for impaired value. When a trademark is impaired from competitive threats or other circumstances, the trademark should be written down and a loss recognized.

Goodwill

In business, **goodwill** refers to an intangible asset of a business that is created from such favorable factors as location, product quality, reputation, and managerial skill. Goodwill allows a business to earn a rate of return on its investment that is often in excess of the normal rate for other firms in the same business.

Generally accepted accounting principles permit goodwill to be recorded in the accounts only if it is objectively determined by a transaction. An example of such a transaction is the purchase of a business at a price in excess of the net assets (assets − liabilities) of the acquired business. The excess is recorded as goodwill and reported as an intangible asset. Unlike other intangible assets, goodwill is not amortized. However, a loss should be recorded if the business prospects of the acquired firm become significantly impaired. This loss would normally be disclosed in the Other Expense section of the income statement. To illustrate, AOL Time Warner recorded one of the largest losses in corporate history (nearly $54 billion) for the write-down of goodwill associated with the AOL and Time Warner merger. The entry is recorded as:

Loss from Impaired Goodwill	54,000,000,000	
Goodwill		54,000,000,000

Exhibit 12 shows the frequency of intangible asset disclosures for a sample of 600 large firms. As you can see, goodwill is the most frequently reported intangible asset. This is because goodwill arises from merger transactions, which are very common.

Exhibit 12

Frequency of Intangible Asset Disclosures for 600 Firms

Intangible Asset Category	Number of Firms
Goodwill	495
Trademarks and brand names	94
Patents	78
Customer lists	36
Technology	35
Franchises and licenses	35
Other	93

Source: *Accounting Trends & Techniques*, 55th ed., American Institute of Certified Public Accountants, New York, 2001. Note: Some firms have multiple disclosures.

Ethics in Action

When Does Goodwill Become Worthless?

The timing and amount of goodwill write-offs can be very subjective. Managers and their accountants should fairly estimate the value of goodwill and record goodwill impairment when it occurs. It would be unethical to delay a write-down of goodwill when it is determined that the asset is impaired.

Reporting Fixed Assets and Intangible Assets

8 Describe how depreciation expense is reported in an income statement, and prepare a balance sheet that includes fixed assets and intangible assets.

The amount of depreciation and amortization expense for a period should be reported separately in the income statement or disclosed in a footnote. A general description of the method or methods used in computing depreciation should also be reported, as illustrated below for Sony Corporation.

> *Depreciation of property, plant and equipment is principally computed on a declining-balance method for Sony Corporation and Japanese subsidiaries and on a straight-line method for foreign subsidiary companies at rates based on estimated useful lives of assets, principally ranging from 15 years up to 50 years for buildings and from 2 years up to 10 years for machinery and equipment.*

The amount of each major class of fixed assets should be disclosed in the balance sheet or in footnotes. The related accumulated depreciation should also be disclosed, either by major class or in total. The fixed assets may be shown at their *book value* (cost less accumulated depreciation), which can also be described as their *net* amount. If there are too many classes of fixed assets, a single amount may be presented in the balance sheet, supported by a separate detailed listing. Fixed assets are normally presented under the more descriptive caption of *property, plant, and equipment.*

Intangible assets are usually reported in the balance sheet in a separate section immediately following the fixed assets. The balance of each major class of intangible assets should be disclosed at an amount net of the amortization taken to date. Exhibit 13 is a partial balance sheet that shows the reporting of fixed assets and intangible assets for Sony Corporation.

Exhibit 13

Fixed Assets and Intangible Assets in the Balance Sheet

Sony Corporation
Partial Balance Sheet
March 31, 2002

	In Millions (Yen)
Property, Plant, and Equipment:	
Land	¥ 195,292
Buildings	891,436
Machinery and Equipment	2,216,347
Construction in Progress	66,825
	¥3,369,900
Less: Accumulated Depreciation	1,958,234
Net Property, Plant and Equipment	¥1,411,666
Intangible Assets:	
Copyrights, trademarks, and other intangibles	¥1,108,816
Goodwill	317,240

Focus on Cash Flow

Fixed Assets, Depreciation, and Cash Flow

Depreciation and amortization are deducted from revenues in determining the net income. However, depreciation and amortization expense do not reduce cash. Thus, in the operating activities section of the statement of cash flows, the depreciation and amortization expense for the period should be added back to net income in order to adjust the accrual net income amount to reflect operating cash flow.

In addition, any gains or losses on the sale of fixed assets are included in the proceeds disclosed in the investing section of the statement of cash flows. For example, if an asset with a book value of $1,000,000 were sold for $1,200,000, then $1,200,000 would be disclosed on the statement of cash flows as proceeds from the sale of fixed assets. However, any gain or loss is also included in net income. To avoid double counting the gain or loss, the operating section of the statement of cash flows should remove the impact of gains or losses from the net income number. That is, gains should be subtracted from net income, while losses should be added back. In the example above, the $200,000 gain should be subtracted from net income in the operating activities section of the statement of cash flows.

To illustrate these disclosures, the partial operating activities section of the statement of cash flows for Apple Computer, Inc. shows depreciation and amortization, gain, and loss adjustments in order to reconcile net income to cash generated by operating activities:

Apple Computer, Inc.
Partial Statement of Cash Flows—Operating Activities

Operating Activities	
Net income	$786,000,000
Adjustments to reconcile net income to cash generated by operating activities:	
Depreciation and amortization	84,000,000
Provision for deferred income taxes	163,000,000
Loss on sale of property, plant, and equipment	3,000,000
Gains from sales of equity investment	(367,000,000)

The proceeds from the sale of fixed assets and the cash used to purchase fixed assets are disclosed in the investing section of the statement of cash flows. These are both illustrated for Apple Computer, Inc. as follows:

Apple Computer, Inc.
Partial Statement of Cash Flows—Investing Activities

Investing	
Purchase of short-term investments	$(4,267,000,000)
Proceeds from maturities of short-term investments	3,331,000,000
Purchases of long-term investments	(232,000,000)
Proceeds from sale of property, plant, and equipment	11,000,000
Purchase of property, plant, and equipment	(107,000,000)
Proceeds from sales of equity investment	372,000,000
Other	(38,000,000)
Cash used for investing activities	$ (930,000,000)

Summary of Learning Goals

1 Define, classify, and account for the cost of fixed assets.

Fixed assets are long-term tangible assets that are owned by a business and are used in the normal operations of the business. Examples of fixed assets are equipment, buildings, and land. The initial cost of a fixed asset includes all amounts spent to get the asset in place and ready for use. For example, sales tax, freight, insurance in transit, and installation costs are all included in the cost of a fixed asset. As time passes, all fixed assets except land lose their ability to provide services. As a result, the cost of a fixed asset should be transferred to an expense account, in a systematic manner, during the asset's expected useful life. This periodic transfer of cost to expense is called depreciation.

2 Compute depreciation, using the following methods: straight-line, units-of-production, and declining-balance.

In computing depreciation, three factors need to be considered: (1) the fixed asset's initial cost, (2) the useful life of the asset, and (3) the residual value of the asset.

The straight-line method spreads the initial cost less the residual value equally over the useful life. The units-of-production method spreads the initial cost less the residual value equally over the units expected to be produced by the asset during its useful life. The declining-balance method is applied by multiplying the declining book value of the asset by twice the straight-line rate.

3 Compute and record depletion of natural resources.

The amount of periodic depletion is computed by multiplying the quantity of minerals extracted during the period by a depletion rate. The depletion rate is computed by dividing the cost of the mineral deposit by its estimated size. The entry to record depletion debits a depletion expense account and credits an accumulated depletion account.

4 Account for the disposal of fixed assets.

The journal entries to record disposals of fixed assets will vary. In all cases, however, any depreciation for the current period should be recorded, and the book value of the asset is then removed from the accounts. The entry to remove the book value from the accounts is a debit to the asset's accumulated depreciation account and a credit to the asset account for the cost of the asset. For assets retired from service, a loss may be recorded for any remaining book value of the asset.

When a fixed asset is sold, the book value is removed and the cash or other asset received is also recorded. If the selling price is more than the book value of the asset, the transaction results in a gain. If the selling price is less than the book value, there is a loss.

5 Classify fixed asset costs as either capital expenditures or revenue expenditures according to their project stage.

Fixed assets are acquired and used through the following four stages: preliminary, preacquistion, acquisition or construction, and in-service. The costs incurred during the preliminary stage are generally expensed, while the direct costs incurred during the preacquisition and acquisition stages are capitalized. During the in-service stage ordinary and normal repairs are expensed, while new and replaced components are capitalized.

6 Analyze the utilization of fixed assets.

Business success for many firms is influenced by the utilization of their fixed assets. Fixed asset utilization can be measured using operational and financial data. Operational utilization statistics evaluate the used portion of fixed assets to the total fixed asset capacity. Financial measures of asset utilization include (1) the revenue per unit of fixed assets and (2) the fixed asset turnover ratio (sales divided by average book value of fixed assets).

7 Describe and account for intangible assets, such as patents, copyrights, and goodwill.

Long-term assets that are without physical attributes but are used in the business are classified as intangible assets. Examples of intangible assets are patents, copyrights, trademarks, and goodwill. The initial cost of an intangible asset should be debited to an asset account. For patents and copyrights, this cost should be written off, or amortized, over the years of the asset's expected usefulness by debiting an expense account and crediting the intangible asset account. Trademarks and goodwill are not amortized, but are written down only upon impairment.

8 Describe how depreciation expense is reported in an income statement, and prepare a balance sheet that includes fixed assets and intangible assets.

The amount of depreciation expense and the method or methods used in computing depreciation should be disclosed in the financial statements. In addition, each major class of fixed assets should be disclosed, along with the related accumulated depreciation. Intangible assets are usually presented in the balance sheet in a separate section immediately following the fixed assets. Each major class of intangible assets should be disclosed at an amount net of the amortization recorded to date.

Glossary

Accelerated depreciation method A depreciation method that provides for a higher depreciation amount in the first year of the asset's use, followed by a gradually declining amount of depreciation.

Amortization The periodic transfer of the cost of an intangible asset to expense.

Book value The cost of a fixed asset minus accumulated depreciation on the asset.

Capital expenditures The cost of acquiring fixed assets, adding a component, or replacing a component of fixed assets.

Copyright An exclusive right to publish and sell a literary, artistic, or musical composition.

Declining-balance method A method of depreciation that provides periodic depreciation expense based on the declining book value of a fixed asset over its estimated life.

Depletion The process of transferring the cost of natural resources to an expense account.

Depreciation The systematic periodic transfer of the cost of a fixed asset to an expense account during its expected useful life.

Fixed asset turnover ratio A ratio that measures the number of dollars of revenue earned per dollar of fixed assets, and is calculated as total revenue divided by the average book value of fixed assets.

Fixed assets Long-lived or relatively permanent tangible assets that are used in the normal business operations.

Goodwill An intangible asset of a business that is created from such favorable factors as location, product quality, reputation, and managerial skill, as verified from a merger transaction.

Intangible assets Long-lived assets that are useful in the operations of a business, are not held for sale, and are without physical qualities.

Patents Exclusive rights to produce and sell goods with one or more unique features.

Residual value The estimated value of a fixed asset at the end of its useful life.

Revenue expenditures Costs that benefit only the current period or costs incurred for normal maintenance and repairs of fixed assets.

Straight-line method A method of depreciation that provides for equal periodic depreciation expense over the estimated life of a fixed asset.

Trademark A name, term, or symbol used to identify a business and its products.

Units-of-production method A method of depreciation that provides for depreciation expense based on the expected productive capacity of a fixed asset.

Illustrative Accounting Application Problem

McCollum Company, a furniture wholesaler, acquired new equipment at a cost of $150,000 at the beginning of the fiscal year. The equipment has an estimated life of 5 years and an estimated residual value of $12,000. Ellen McCollum, the president, has requested information regarding alternative depreciation methods.

Instructions

1. Determine the annual depreciation for each of the five years of estimated useful life of the equipment, the accumulated depreciation at the end of each year, and the book value of the equipment at the end of each year by (a) the straight-line method and (b) the declining-balance method (at twice the straight-line rate).

2. Assume that the equipment was depreciated under the declining-balance method. In the first week of the fifth year, the equipment was sold for $25,000. Record the entry for the sale.

Solution

1.

	Year	Depreciation Expense	Accumulated Depreciation, End of Year	Book Value, End of Year
a.	1	$27,600*	$ 27,600	$122,400
	2	27,600	55,200	94,800
	3	27,600	82,800	67,200
	4	27,600	110,400	39,600
	5	27,600	138,000	12,000

*$27,600 = ($150,000 − $12,000) ÷ 5

	Year	Depreciation Expense	Accumulated Depreciation, End of Year	Book Value, End of Year
b.	1	$60,000**	$ 60,000	$ 90,000
	2	36,000	96,000	54,000
	3	21,600	117,600	32,400
	4	12,960	130,560	19,440
	5	7,440***	138,000	12,000

**$60,000 = $150,000 × 40%

***The asset is not depreciated below the estimated residual value of $12,000.

2.

Cash	25,000	
Accumulated Depreciation—Equipment	130,560	
Equipment		150,000
Gain on Disposal of Fixed Assets		5,560

Self-Study Questions

Answers at end of chapter

1. Which of the following expenditures incurred in connection with acquiring machinery is a proper charge to the asset account?
   A. Freight
   B. Installation costs
   C. Both A and B
   D. Neither A nor B

2. What is the amount of depreciation using the declining-balance method (twice the straight-line rate) for the second year of use for equipment costing $9,000, with an estimated residual value of $600 and an estimated life of 3 years?
   A. $6,000
   B. $3,000
   C. $2,000
   D. $400

3. An example of an accelerated depreciation method is:
   A. Straight-line
   B. Declining-balance
   C. Units-of-production
   D. Depletion

4. A component of a fixed asset with a book value of $5,000 is replaced at the beginning of the year with a new component capitalized at a cost of $40,000. The replacement component has a five-year estimated life. How much depreciation expense is recognized for the year?
   A. $3,000
   B. $5,000
   C. $8,000
   D. $13,000

5. A company shows the book value of fixed assets at the beginning of the year of $80,000 and a balance at the end of the year of $120,000. Total revenues were $500,000 for the year. What is the fixed asset turnover ratio?
   A. 0.20
   B. 4.0
   C. 5.0
   D. 6.0

Discussion Questions

1. Which of the following qualities are characteristics of fixed assets? (a) tangible, (b) capable of repeated use in the operations of the business, (c) held for sale in the normal course of business, (d) used continuously in the operations of the business, (e) long-lived
2. Penguin Office Equipment Co. has a fleet of automobiles and trucks for use by salespersons and for delivery of office supplies and equipment. Sioux City Auto Sales Co. has automobiles and trucks for sale. Under what caption would the automobiles and trucks be reported on the balance sheet of (a) Penguin Office Equipment Co., (b) Sioux City Auto Sales Co.?
3. Spiral Co. acquired an adjacent vacant lot with the hope of selling it in the future at a gain. The lot is not intended to be used in Spiral's business operations. Where should such real estate be listed in the balance sheet?
4. Tensile Company solicited bids from several contractors to construct an addition to its office building. The lowest bid received was for $340,000. Tensile Company decided to construct the addition itself at a cost of $325,000. What amount should be recorded in the building account?
5. Are the amounts at which fixed assets are reported in the balance sheet their approximate market values as of the balance sheet date? Discuss.
6. a. Does recognizing depreciation in the accounts provide a special cash fund for the replacement of fixed assets? Explain.
   b. Describe the nature of depreciation as the term is used in accounting.
7. Name the three factors that need to be considered in determining the amount of periodic depreciation.
8. Trigger Company purchased a machine that has a manufacturer's suggested life of 15 years. The company plans to use the machine on a special project that will last 11 years. At the completion of the project, the machine will be sold. Over how many years should the machine be depreciated?
9. Is it necessary for a business to use the same method of computing depreciation (a) for all classes of its depreciable assets, (b) in the financial statements and in determining income taxes?
10. Of the three common depreciation methods, which is most widely used?
11. a. Why is an accelerated depreciation method often used for income tax purposes?
    b. What is the Modified Accelerated Cost Recovery System (MACRS), and under what conditions is it used?
12. A company revised the estimated useful lives of its fixed assets, which resulted in an increase in the remaining lives of several assets. Do GAAP permit the company to include, as income of the current period, the cumulative effect of the changes, which reduces the depreciation expense of past periods? Discuss.
13. For some of the fixed assets of a business, the balance in Accumulated Depreciation is exactly equal to the cost of the asset. (a) Is it permissible to record additional depreciation on the assets if they are still useful to the business? Explain. (b) When should an entry be made to remove the cost and the accumulated depreciation from the accounts?
14. In what sections of the income statement are gains and losses from the disposal of fixed assets presented?
15. Differentiate between the accounting for capital expenditures and revenue expenditures.
16. Immediately after a used truck is acquired, a new motor is installed at a total cost of $4,750. Is this a capital expenditure or a revenue expenditure?
17. How would you evaluate the effective use of fixed assets?

18. a. Over what period of time should the cost of a patent acquired by purchase be amortized?
    b. In general, what is the required treatment for research and development costs?
    c. How should goodwill be amortized?

Resources for your success online @ http://warren.swlearning.com

Remember! If you need additional help, visit South-Western's Web site. See page 30 for a description of the online and printed materials that are available.

Exercises

Exercise 9–1

Costs of acquiring fixed assets

Goal 1

Tracie Klein owns and operates Walcott Print Co. During July, Walcott Print Co. incurred the following costs in acquiring two printing presses. One printing press was new, and the other was used by a business that recently filed for bankruptcy.

Costs related to new printing press:

1. Sales tax on purchase price
2. Insurance while in transit
3. Freight
4. Special foundation
5. New parts to replace those damaged in unloading
6. Fee paid to factory representative for installation

Costs related to secondhand printing press:

7. Freight
8. Installation
9. Repair of vandalism during installation
10. Replacement of worn-out parts
11. Repair of damage incurred in reconditioning the press
12. Fees paid to attorney to review purchase agreement

a. Indicate which costs incurred in acquiring the new printing press should be debited to the asset account.

b. Indicate which costs incurred in acquiring the secondhand printing press should be debited to the asset account.

Exercise 9–2

Cost of land

Goal 1

STUDENT SOLUTIONS MANUAL

A company has developed a tract of land into a ski resort. The company has cut the trees, cleared and graded the land and hills, and constructed ski lifts. (a) Should the tree cutting, land clearing, and grading costs of constructing the ski slopes be debited to the land account? (b) If such costs are debited to Land, should they be depreciated?

Exercise 9–3

Cost of land

Goal 1

$138,250

Birch Delivery Company acquired an adjacent lot to construct a new warehouse, paying $25,000 and giving a short-term note for $100,000. Legal fees paid were $1,750, delinquent taxes assumed were $7,500, and fees paid to remove an old building from the land were $5,500. Materials salvaged from the demolition of the building were sold for $1,500. A contractor was paid $412,500 to construct a new warehouse. Determine the cost of the land to be reported on the balance sheet.

Exercise 9–4

Nature of depreciation

Goal 1

STUDENT SOLUTIONS MANUAL

Yarborough Metal Casting Co. reported $575,000 for equipment and $217,500 for accumulated depreciation—equipment on its balance sheet.

Does this mean (a) that the replacement cost of the equipment is $575,000 and (b) that $217,500 is set aside in a special fund for the replacement of the equipment? Explain.

Exercise 9–5

Straight-line depreciation rates

Goal 2

a. 25%

Convert each of the following estimates of useful life to a straight-line depreciation rate, stated as a percentage, assuming that the residual value of the fixed asset is to be ignored: (a) 4 years, (b) 5 years, (c) 10 years, (d) 20 years, (e) 25 years, (f) 40 years, (g) 50 years.

Exercise 9–6

Straight-line depreciation

Goal 2

$11,750

STUDENT SOLUTIONS MANUAL

A refrigerator used by a meat processor has a cost of $112,000, an estimated residual value of $18,000, and an estimated useful life of 8 years. What is the amount of the annual depreciation computed by the straight-line method?

Exercise 9–7

Depreciation by units-of-production method

Goal 2

$3,220

A diesel-powered generator with a cost of $375,000 and estimated residual value of $30,000 is expected to have a useful operating life of 75,000 hours. During November, the generator was operated 700 hours. Determine the depreciation for the month.

Exercise 9–8

Depreciation by units-of-production method

Goal 2

a. Truck #1, credit Accumulated Depreciation, $8,400

STUDENT SOLUTIONS MANUAL

Prior to adjustment at the end of the year, the balance in Trucks is $176,600 and the balance in Accumulated Depreciation—Trucks is $60,500. Details of the subsidiary ledger are as follows:

Truck No.	Cost	Estimated Residual Value	Estimated Useful Life	Accumulated Depreciation at Beginning of Year	Miles Operated During Year
1	$75,000	$5,000	250,000 miles	$21,000	30,000 miles
2	38,600	3,600	200,000	31,500	25,000
3	35,000	3,000	100,000	8,000	36,000
4	28,000	4,000	120,000	—	21,000

a. Determine the depreciation rate per mile and the amount to be credited to the accumulated depreciation section of each of the subsidiary accounts for the miles operated during the current year.

b. Record the depreciation entry for the year.

Exercise 9–9

Depreciation by two methods

Goal 2

a. $15,400

A backhoe acquired on January 2 at a cost of $154,000 has an estimated useful life of 10 years. Assuming that it will have no residual value, determine the depreciation for each of the first two years (a) by the straight-line method and (b) by the declining-balance method, using twice the straight-line rate.

Exercise 9–10

Depreciation by two methods

Goal 2

a. $8,100

STUDENT SOLUTIONS MANUAL

A dairy storage tank acquired at the beginning of the fiscal year at a cost of $70,000 has an estimated residual value of $5,200 and an estimated useful life of 8 years. Determine the following: (a) the amount of annual depreciation by the straight-line method and (b) the amount of depreciation for the first and second year computed by the declining-balance method (at twice the straight-line rate).

Exercise 9–11

Partial-year depreciation

Goal 2

a. First year, $7,350

Sandblasting equipment acquired at a cost of $64,000 has an estimated residual value of $5,200 and an estimated useful life of 6 years. It was placed in service on April 1 of the current fiscal year, which ends on December 31. Determine the depreciation for the current fiscal year and for the following fiscal year by (a) the straight-line method and (b) the declining-balance method, at twice the straight-line rate.

Exercise 9–12

Change in estimate

Goal 2

a. $12,000

STUDENT SOLUTIONS MANUAL

A warehouse with a cost of $500,000 has an estimated residual value of $20,000, an estimated useful life of 40 years, and is depreciated by the straight-line method. (a) What is the amount of the annual depreciation? (b) What is the book value at the end of the twentieth year of use? (c) If at the start of the twenty-first year the remaining life is estimated to be 15 years and the residual value is estimated to be $5,000, what is the depreciation expense for each of the remaining 15 years?

Exercise 9–13

Book value of fixed assets

Goal 2

The following data were taken from recent annual reports of Interstate Bakeries Corporation (IBC). Interstate Bakeries produces, distributes, and sells fresh bakery products nationwide through supermarkets, convenience stores, and its 67 bakeries and 1,500 thrift stores.

	June 2, 2001 (in thousands)	June 2, 2002 (in thousands)
Land and buildings	$ 418,928	$ 426,322
Machinery and equipment	1,038,323	1,051,861
Accumulated depreciation	582,941	633,178

a. Compute the book value of the fixed assets for the two comparative years and explain the differences, if any.
b. Would you normally expect the book value of fixed assets to increase or decrease during the year?

Exercise 9–14

Depletion entries

Goal 3

STUDENT SOLUTIONS MANUAL

Anaconda Co. acquired mineral rights for $30,000,000. The mineral deposit is estimated at 50,000,000 tons. During the current year, 7,500,000 tons were mined and sold for $6,500,000.

a. Determine the amount of depletion expense for the current year.
b. Provide the adjusting entry to recognize the expense.

Exercise 9–15

Depletion entries

Goal 3

Coeur d'Alene Mines Corporation is a North American-based silver mining company. During 2001 Coeur d'Alene Mines produced 10.9 million ounces of silver. Coeur d'Alene Mines' properties had proven reserves of 88.1 million ounces on December 31, 2000. Coeur's December 31, 2000 balance sheet indicated the following:

Operational mining properties	$113,409,000
Less: Accumulated depletion	(71,225,000)
Book value of mining properties	$ 42,184,000

a. Determine the amount of depletion expense for 2001, using the mining property balances at the end of 2000. Round to two decimal places.

b. Provide the adjusting entry to recognize the 2001 depletion expense.

Exercise 9–16

Entries for sale of fixed asset

Goal 4

STUDENT SOLUTIONS MANUAL

Metal recycling equipment acquired on January 3, 2001, at a cost of $117,500, has an estimated useful life of 8 years, an estimated residual value of $7,500, and is depreciated by the straight-line method.

a. What was the book value of the equipment at December 31, 2004, the end of the fiscal year?

b. Assuming that the equipment was sold on July 1, 2005, for $53,500, record the entries for (1) depreciation for the six months of the current year ending December 31, 2005, and (2) the sale of the equipment.

Exercise 9–17

Disposal of fixed asset

Goal 4

b. $21,250

Equipment acquired on January 3, 2002, at a cost of $71,500, has an estimated useful life of 4 years and an estimated residual value of $4,500.

a. What was the annual amount of depreciation for the years 2002, 2003, and 2004, using the straight-line method of depreciation?

b. What was the book value of the equipment on January 1, 2005?

c. Assuming that the equipment was sold on January 2, 2005, for $18,000, record the entry for the sale.

d. Assuming that the equipment had been sold on January 2, 2005, for $23,000 instead of $18,000, record the entry for the sale.

Exercise 9–18

Capital and revenue expenditures

Goal 5

STUDENT SOLUTIONS MANUAL

Yeats Co. incurred the following costs related to trucks and vans used in operating its delivery service:

1. Installed a hydraulic lift to a van.
2. Removed a two-way radio from one of the trucks and installed a new radio with a greater range of communication.
3. Overhauled the engine on one of the trucks that had been purchased four years ago.
4. Changed the oil and greased the joints of all the trucks and vans.
5. Performed annual maintenance on trucks.
6. Installed security systems on three of the newer trucks.
7. Replaced two of the trucks' shock absorbers with new shock absorbers that allow for the delivery of heavier loads.
8. Repaired a flat tire on one of the vans.
9. Rebuilt the transmission on one of the vans that had been driven only 25,000 miles. The van was no longer under warranty.
10. Tinted the back and side windows of one of the vans to discourage the theft of its contents.

Classify each of the costs as a capital expenditure or a revenue expenditure. For those costs identified as capital expenditures, classify each as an additional or replacement component.

Exercise 9-19

Capital and revenue expenditures

Goal 5

Faith Inman owns and operates Yellow Ribbon Transport Co. During the past year, Faith incurred the following costs related to her 18-wheel truck:

1. Replaced the hydraulic brake system that had begun to fail during her latest trip through the Smoky Mountains.
2. Overhauled the engine.
3. Replaced a headlight that had burned out.
4. Removed the old CB radio and replaced it with a newer model with a greater range.
5. Replaced a shock absorber that had worn out.
6. Installed fog lights.
7. Installed a wind deflector on top of the cab to increase fuel mileage.
8. Modified the factory-installed turbo charger with a special-order kit designed to add 30 more horsepower to the engine performance.
9. Installed a television in the sleeping compartment of the truck.
10. Replaced the old radar detector with a newer model that detects the KA frequencies now used by many of the state patrol radar guns. The detector is wired directly into the cab, so that it is partially hidden. In addition, Faith fastened the detector to the truck with a locking device that prevents its removal.

Classify each of the costs as a capital expenditure or a revenue expenditure. For those costs identified as capital expenditures, classify each as an additional or replacement component.

Exercise 9-20

Fixed asset component replacement

Goals 2, 5

c. Depreciation Expense, $2,250

STUDENT SOLUTIONS MANUAL

Jacobs Company replaced carpeting throughout its general offices. The old carpet was removed at a cost of $1,500 on March 15. The book value of the old carpet was determined to be $6,000 on March 15. New carpet was purchased and installed during the last two weeks of March for a total cost of $45,000. The carpet is estimated to have a 15-year useful life.

a. Record the cost of removing the old carpet.
b. Prepare the two journal entries necessary for recording the replacement of the old carpet with the new carpet.
c. Record the December 31 adjusting entry for the partial-year depreciation expense for the carpet, assuming that Jacobs uses the straight-line method.

Exercise 9-21

Fixed asset component replacement

Goal 5

b. $29,000

Dale's Edge, Inc. purchased and installed an alarm system for its retail store on January 1, 1997, at a cost of $50,000. The alarm system was estimated to have a ten-year life with no salvage value. On January 1, 2004, the alarm system was replaced with a system having more advanced technology. The removal of the old alarm system cost $2,000. The new system cost $120,000 and is estimated to have a ten-year life, with no residual value.

a. Determine the total depreciation expense for 2004 related to the alarm system component.
b. Determine the total expense reported in the income statement in 2004 from these transactions.

Exercise 9-22

Fixed asset turnover ratio

Goal 6

STUDENT SOLUTIONS MANUAL

Verizon Communications Inc. is a major telecommunications company in the United States. Verizon's balance sheet disclosed the following information regarding fixed assets:

	Dec. 31, 2001 (in millions)	Dec. 31, 2000 (in millions)
Plant, property, and equipment	$169,586	$158,957
Less accumulated depreciation	95,167	89,453
	$ 74,419	$ 69,504

Verizon's revenue for 2001 was $67,190 million. The fixed asset turnover for the telecommunications industry averages 1.10.

a. Determine Verizon's fixed asset turnover ratio.
b. Interpret Verizon's fixed asset turnover ratio.

Exercise 9-23

Amortization entries

Goal 7

Langohr Company acquired patent rights on January 3, 2001, for $675,000. The patent has a useful life equal to its legal life of 18 years. On January 5, 2004, Langohr successfully defended the patent in a lawsuit at a cost of $45,000.

a. Determine the patent amortization expense for the current year ended December 31, 2004.
b. Record the adjusting entry to recognize the amortization.

Exercise 9-24

Goodwill impairment

Goal 7

STUDENT SOLUTIONS MANUAL

On January 1, 2002, Delta Financial, Inc. purchased the assets of Guardsman Insurance Co. for $23,000,000, a price reflecting an $8,000,000 goodwill premium. On December 31, 2004, Delta determined that the goodwill from the Guardsman acquisition was impaired and had a value of $2,500,000.

a. Determine the book value of the goodwill on December 31, 2004, prior to making the impairment adjusting entry.
b. Record the goodwill impairment adjusting entry for December 31, 2004.

Exercise 9-25

Balance sheet presentation

Goal 8

How many errors can you find in the following partial balance sheet?

Rosedale Company
Balance Sheet
December 31, 2004

Assets

	Replacement Cost	Accumulated Depreciation	Book Value
Total current assets			$397,500
Property, plant, and equipment:			
Land	$ 75,000	$ 20,000	$ 55,000
Buildings	160,000	76,000	84,000
Factory equipment	350,000	192,000	158,000
Office equipment	120,000	77,000	43,000
Patents	80,000	—	80,000
Goodwill	45,000	5,000	40,000
Total property, plant, and equipment	$830,000	$370,000	$460,000

Accounting Application Problems

Problem 9-1A

Allocate payments and receipts to fixed asset accounts

Goal 1

SPREADSHEET

The following payments and receipts are related to land, land improvements, and buildings acquired for use in a wholesale ceramic business. The receipts are identified by an asterisk.

a.	Fee paid to attorney for title search	$ 3,500
b.	Cost of real estate acquired as a plant site: Land	200,000
	Building	55,000
c.	Delinquent real estate taxes on property, assumed by purchaser	18,750
d.	Cost of razing and removing building	4,800
e.	Proceeds from sale of salvage materials from old building	3,100*
f.	Special assessment paid to city for extension of water main to the property	5,000
g.	Premium on 1-year insurance policy during construction	6,600
h.	Cost of filling and grading land	29,700
i.	Cost of repairing windstorm damage during construction	1,500
j.	Cost of paving parking lot to be used by customers	12,500
k.	Cost of trees and shrubbery planted	15,000
l.	Architect's and engineer's fees for plans and supervision	40,000
m.	Cost of repairing vandalism damage during construction	1,500
n.	Interest incurred on building loan during construction	48,000
o.	Cost of floodlights installed on parking lot	13,500
p.	Money borrowed to pay building contractor	500,000*
q.	Payment to building contractor for new building	750,000
r.	Proceeds from insurance company for windstorm and vandalism damage	3,000*
s.	Refund of premium on insurance policy (g) canceled after 11 months	750*

Instructions

1. Assign each payment and receipt to Land (unlimited life), Land Improvements (limited life), Building, or Other Accounts. Indicate receipts by an asterisk. Identify each item by letter and list the amounts in columnar form, as follows:

Item	Land	Land Improvements	Building	Other Accounts

2. Determine the amount debited to Land, Land Improvements, and Building.
3. The costs assigned to the land, which is used as a plant site, will not be depreciated, while the costs assigned to land improvements will be depreciated. Explain this seemingly contradictory application of the concept of depreciation.

Problem 9-2A

Compare three depreciation methods

Goal 2

2003: straight-line depreciation, $105,000

SPREADSHEET

Diamondback Company purchased packaging equipment on January 3, 2003, for $340,000. The equipment was expected to have a useful life of 3 years, or 18,000 operating hours, and a residual value of $25,000. The equipment was used for 7,500 hours during 2003, 6,000 hours in 2004, and 4,500 hours in 2005.

Instructions

Determine the amount of depreciation expense for the years ended December 31, 2003, 2004, and 2005, by (a) the straight-line method, (b) the units-of-production method, and (c) the declining-balance method, using twice the straight-line rate. Also determine the total depreciation expense for the three years by each method. The following columnar headings are suggested for recording the depreciation expense amounts:

	Depreciation Expense		
Year	Straight-Line Method	Units-of-Production Method	Declining-Balance Method

Problem 9-3A

Depreciation by three methods; partial years

Goal 2

a. 2003: $17,000

SPREADSHEET

Newbauer Company purchased plastic laminating equipment on July 1, 2003, for $108,000. The equipment was expected to have a useful life of 3 years, or 13,600 operating hours, and a residual value of $6,000. The equipment was used for 2,400 hours during 2003, 4,500 hours in 2004, 5,000 hours in 2005, and 1,700 hours in 2006.

Instructions

Determine the amount of depreciation expense for the years ended December 31, 2003, 2004, 2005, and 2006, by (a) the straight-line method, (b) the units-of-production method, and (c) the declining-balance method, using twice the straight-line rate.

Problem 9-4A

Depreciation by two methods; sale of fixed asset

Goals 2, 4

1. b. Year 1: $50,000 depreciation expense

SPREADSHEET

New lithographic equipment, acquired at a cost of $125,000 at the beginning of a fiscal year, has an estimated useful life of 5 years and an estimated residual value of $10,000. The manager requested information regarding the effect of alternative methods on the amount of depreciation expense each year. On the basis of the data presented to the manager, the declining-balance method was selected. In the first week of the fifth year, the equipment was sold for $23,000.

Instructions

1. Determine the annual depreciation expense for each of the estimated 5 years of use, the accumulated depreciation at the end of each year, and the book value of the equipment at the end of each year by (a) the straight-line method and (b) the declining-balance method (at twice the straight-line rate). The following columnar headings are suggested for each schedule:

Year	Depreciation Expense	Accumulated Depreciation, End of Year	Book Value, End of Year

2. Record the entry for the sale.
3. Record the entry for the sale, assuming a sales price of $11,000.

Problem 9-5A

Transactions for fixed assets

Goals 1, 2, 4, 5

June 30, 2004, Gain on Disposal, $750

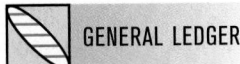

GENERAL LEDGER

The following are transactions and adjusting entries completed by Trailways Furniture Co. during a 3-year period. All are related to the use of delivery equipment. The declining-balance method (at twice the straight-line rate) of depreciation is used.

2003

Jan.	3	Purchased a used delivery truck for $26,500, paying cash.
	5	Paid $4,000 for a new transmission for the truck. The old transmission was estimated to have a component book value of $500. The new transmission is expected to have a useful life equal to the remaining life of the truck.
Aug.	16	Paid garage $285 for miscellaneous repairs to the truck.
Dec.	31	Recorded depreciation on the truck and transmission component for the fiscal year. The estimated useful life of the truck and transmission is 4 years, with a residual value of $6,000 for the truck.

2004	
Jan. 1	Purchased a new truck for $65,000, paying cash.
June 30	Sold the used truck for $12,000. (Record depreciation to date in 2004 for the truck and transmission component.)
Aug. 10	Paid garage $175 for miscellaneous repairs to the truck.
Dec. 31	Recorded depreciation on the truck. It has an estimated residual value of $7,500 and an estimated life of 5 years.
2005	
July 1	Purchased a new truck for $84,000, paying cash.
Oct. 1	Sold the truck purchased January 1, 2004, for $26,750. (Record depreciation for the year.)
Dec. 31	Recorded depreciation on the remaining truck. It has an estimated residual value of $5,000 and an estimated useful life of 8 years.

Instructions

Record the transactions and the adjusting entries.

Problem 9–6A

Amortization and depletion entries

Goals 3, 7

1. (a) $121,600

Data related to the acquisition of timber rights and intangible assets during the current year ended December 31 are as follows:

a. Timber rights on a tract of land were purchased for $480,000 on July 12. The stand of timber is estimated at 1,500,000 board feet. During the current year, 380,000 board feet of timber were cut.
b. Goodwill in the amount of $5,000,000 was purchased on January 3.
c. Governmental and legal costs of $80,000 were incurred on October 2 in obtaining a patent with an estimated economic life of 10 years. Amortization is to be for one-quarter of a year.

Instructions

1. Determine the amount of the amortization or depletion expense for the current year for each of the previous items.
2. Record the adjusting entries required for the amortization or depletion for each item.

Alternate Problem 9–1B

Allocate payments and receipts to fixed asset accounts

Goal 1

STUDENT SOLUTIONS MANUAL

SPREADSHEET

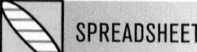

The following payments and receipts are related to land, land improvements, and buildings acquired for use in a wholesale apparel business. The receipts are identified by an asterisk.

a.	Finder's fee paid to real estate agency	$ 10,000
b.	Cost of real estate acquired as a plant site: Land	250,000
	Building	50,000
c.	Fee paid to attorney for title search	2,500
d.	Delinquent real estate taxes on property, assumed by purchaser	18,500
e.	Cost of razing and removing building	11,250
f.	Proceeds from sale of salvage materials from old building	3,500*
g.	Cost of filling and grading land	15,500
h.	Special assessment paid to city for extension of water main to the property	9,000
i.	Architect's and engineer's fees for plans and supervision	50,000
j.	Premium on 1-year insurance policy during construction	5,700
k.	Cost of repairing windstorm damage during construction	3,500
l.	Cost of repairing vandalism damage during construction	800
m.	Cost of paving parking lot to be used by customers	17,500
n.	Cost of trees and shrubbery planted	20,000
o.	Proceeds from insurance company for windstorm and vandalism damage	4,300*

p.	Interest incurred on building loan during construction	$ 65,000
q.	Money borrowed to pay building contractor	1,000,000*
r.	Payment to building contractor for new building	1,250,000
s.	Refund of premium on insurance policy (j) canceled after 10 months	1,050*

Instructions

1. Assign each payment and receipt to Land (unlimited life), Land Improvements (limited life), Building, or Other Accounts. Indicate receipts by an asterisk. Identify each item by letter and list the amounts in columnar form, as follows:

Item	Land	Land Improvements	Building	Other Accounts

2. Determine the amount debited to Land, Land Improvements, and Building.
3. The costs assigned to the land, which is used as a plant site, will not be depreciated, while the costs assigned to land improvements will be depreciated. Explain this seemingly contradictory application of the concept of depreciation.

Alternate Problem 9–2B

Compare three depreciation methods

Goal 2

2003: straight-line depreciation, $57,500

STUDENT SOLUTIONS MANUAL

SPREADSHEET

Sunlight Company purchased waterproofing equipment on January 2, 2003, for $255,000. The equipment was expected to have a useful life of 4 years, or 28,750 operating hours, and a residual value of $25,000. The equipment was used for 8,500 hours during 2003, 8,100 hours in 2004, 7,800 hours in 2005, and 4,350 hours in 2006.

Instructions

Determine the amount of depreciation expense for the years ended December 31, 2003, 2004, 2005, and 2006, by (a) the straight-line method, (b) the units-of-production method, and (c) the declining-balance method, using twice the straight-line rate. Also determine the total depreciation expense for the four years by each method. The following columnar headings are suggested for recording the depreciation expense amounts:

	Depreciation Expense		
Year	Straight-Line Method	Units-of-Production Method	Declining-Balance Method

Alternate Problem 9–3B

Depreciation by three methods; partial years

Goal 2

a. 2003, $10,200

STUDENT SOLUTIONS MANUAL

SPREADSHEET

Autostock Company purchased tool sharpening equipment on July 1, 2003, for $64,800. The equipment was expected to have a useful life of 3 years, or 15,300 operating hours, and a residual value of $3,600. The equipment was used for 3,100 hours during 2003, 5,000 hours in 2004, 4,900 hours in 2005, and 2,300 hours in 2006.

Instructions

Determine the amount of depreciation expense for the years ended December 31, 2003, 2004, 2005, and 2006, by (a) the straight-line method, (b) the units-of-production method, and (c) the declining-balance method, using twice the straight-line rate.

Alternate Problem 9–4B

Depreciation by two methods; sale of fixed asset

Goals 2, 4

1. b. Year 1, $50,000 depreciation expense

STUDENT SOLUTIONS MANUAL

SPREADSHEET

New tire retreading equipment, acquired at a cost of $100,000 at the beginning of a fiscal year, has an estimated useful life of 4 years and an estimated residual value of $10,000. The manager requested information regarding the effect of alternative methods on the amount of depreciation expense each year. On the basis of the data presented to the manager, the declining-balance method was selected. In the first week of the fourth year, the equipment was sold for $18,000.

Instructions

1. Determine the annual depreciation expense for each of the estimated 4 years of use, the accumulated depreciation at the end of each year, and the book value of the equipment at the end of each year by (a) the straight-line method and (b) the declining-balance method (at twice the straight-line rate). The following columnar headings are suggested for each schedule:

Year	Depreciation Expense	Accumulated Depreciation, End of Year	Book Value, End of Year

2. Record the entry for the sale.
3. Record the entry for the sale, assuming a sales price of $5,000.

Alternate Problem 9–5B

Transactions for fixed assets

Goals 1, 2, 4, 5

Apr. 30, 2004 Loss on Disposal, $3,687.50

STUDENT SOLUTIONS MANUAL

GENERAL LEDGER

The following transactions and adjusting entries were completed by Heritage Furniture Co. during a 3-year period. All are related to the use of delivery equipment. The declining-balance method (at twice the straight-line rate) of depreciation is used.

2003

Jan. 2 Purchased a used delivery truck for $37,000, paying cash.

5 Paid $5,000 to replace the engine. The old engine was estimated to have a component book value of $1,000. The new engine is expected to have a useful life equal to the remaining life of the truck.

Apr. 7 Paid garage $125 for changing the oil, replacing the oil filter, and tuning the engine on the delivery truck.

Dec. 31 Recorded depreciation on the truck and engine component for the fiscal year. The estimated useful life of the truck and engine is 8 years, with a residual value of $3,000 for the truck.

2004

Jan. 1 Purchased a new truck for $80,000, paying cash.

Mar. 13 Paid garage $180 to tune the engine and make other minor repairs on the truck.

Apr. 30 Sold the used truck for $24,500. (Record depreciation to date in 2004 for the truck and engine component.)

Dec. 31 Recorded depreciation on the truck. It has an estimated trade-in value of $4,000 and an estimated life of 10 years.

2005

July 1 Purchased a new truck for $45,000, paying cash.

Oct. 2 Sold the truck purchased Jan. 1, 2004, for $63,075. (Record depreciation for the year.)

Dec. 31 Recorded depreciation on the remaining truck. It has an estimated residual value of $4,500 and an estimated useful life of 10 years.

Instructions

Record the transactions and the adjusting entries.

Alternate Problem 9–6B

Amortization and depletion entries

Goals 3, 7

1. (b) $4,700

STUDENT SOLUTIONS MANUAL

Data related to the acquisition of timber rights and intangible assets during the current year ended December 31 are as follows:

a. Goodwill in the amount of $1,875,000 was purchased on January 4.
b. Governmental and legal costs of $75,200 were incurred on July 2 in obtaining a patent with an estimated economic life of 8 years. Amortization is to be for one-half year.
c. Timber rights on a tract of land were purchased for $520,000 on April 2. The stand of timber is estimated at 2,000,000 board feet. During the current year, 250,000 board feet of timber were cut.

Instructions

1. Determine the amount of the amortization or depletion expense for the current year for each of the foregoing items.
2. Record the adjusting entries required for the amortization or depletion expense for each item.

Building Leadership Skills–Financial Analysis and Reporting

Case 9–1

Comparing book value and depreciation expense for two companies

Micron Technology, Inc. is in the semiconductor industry. This industry requires extensive capital investments in fabrication facilities in order to maintain technological competitiveness. E. I. De Nemours DuPont & Co. is one of the leading chemical companies in the world. DuPont requires significant investment in chemical processing facilities. Chemical products have longer lives than do semiconductor products. The following selected fixed asset information is provided from financial statements dated 2001 (all numbers in millions):

	Property, Plant, and Equipment Initial Cost	Accumulated Depreciation	Depreciation Expense
Micron Technology, Inc.	$ 8,199	$ 3,495	$1,050
DuPont	33,778	20,491	1,320

a. Determine the book value of the fixed assets for each company.
b. Estimate the total useful life of the fixed assets, assuming straight-line depreciation and no salvage value.
c. Estimate the percent of accumulated depreciation to the total initial cost of property, plant, and equipment for each company.
d. Interpret the differences between Micron and DuPont from your calculations in (b) and (c).

Case 9–2

Financial and operational utilization analyses in the airline industry

The financial performance of the airline industry is sensitive to aircraft utilization and cost control. The industry uses a number of common measures to evaluate financial performance. Three of these are:

Passenger Load Factor = RPM/ASM
Operating Revenue per Available Seat Mile = Operating Revenue/ASM
Operating Cost per Available Seat Mile = Operating Cost/ASM

Where,

Available seat mile (ASM): the total number of seats *available* for transporting passengers multiplied by the total number of miles flown during a reporting period.

Revenue passenger mile (RPM): the total number of seats *purchased* by passengers multiplied by the total number of miles flown during a reporting period.

The following table provides some operating statistics for 2001 for four passenger airlines:

	Available Seat Miles (in millions)	Revenue Passenger Miles (in millions)	Operating Revenue (in millions)	Operating Cost (in millions)
Northwest Airlines Inc.	98,356	73,126	$ 9,019	$ 9,619
Delta Air Lines Inc.	147,837	101,717	13,879	14,991
U.S. Airways Group Inc.	66,744	45,979	7,288	8,316
Southwest Airlines Inc.	65,295	44,494	5,555	4,924

a. Prepare a table showing for each airline the load factor, operating revenue per ASM, operating cost per ASM, and operating margin (profit) per ASM. Round to four decimal places.

b. Interpret the results in (a) for the four airlines.

Case 9–3

Fixed asset turnover: three industries

The following table shows the revenues and average net fixed assets for fiscal year 2001 for three different companies from three different industries: retailing, manufacturing, and communications.

	Revenues (millions)	Average Net Fixed Assets (millions)
Wal-Mart Stores, Inc.	$217,799	$40,086
Alcoa, Inc.	22,859	12,416
Comcast Corp.	9,674	6,265

a. For each company, determine the fixed asset turnover ratio.

b. Explain Wal-Mart's ratio relative to the other two companies.

Case 9–4

Interpreting railroad operating and financial utilization statistics

The freight statistics for the Burlington Northern Santa Fe Corp's. rail operations for three years are provided from public disclosures as follows:

	Year Ended December 31,		
	2001	2000	1999
Revenue ton miles (millions)	501,829	491,959	493,207
Freight revenue per thousand revenue ton miles	$18.11	$18.52	$18.40
Average haul per ton (miles)	992	996	994

a. What is a "revenue ton mile"? (*Hint:* Note that the revenue ton miles are not expressed on dollar terms.)

b. How would you interpret the trend in "freight revenue per thousand revenue ton miles" over the three years indicated?

c. Estimate the number of tons moved in 2001.

d. Estimate Burlington Northern's total revenue for 2001.

Case 9–5

Operating utilization statistics

Duke Energy Corp. is an integrated energy and energy services provider that generates and distributes electricity in North Carolina and South Carolina. Operating statistics for electricity generation and sales are provided from its public reports for a recent fiscal year, as follows:

Sources of Electric Energy, GWh*	
Generated—net output:	
Coal	43,526
Nuclear	41,073
Hydro	394
Oil and gas	459
Total generation	85,452

Electric Energy Sales, GWh*	
Residential	22,884
General service	22,845
Industrial:	
Textile	10,819
Other	18,952
Other energy and wholesale	8,671
Total GWh sales billed	84,171

*Gigawatt-hour

In addition, at this time, Duke operated three nuclear generating stations with a combined net capacity of 5,409 MW (megawatts), eight coal-fired stations with a combined capacity of 7,572 MW, 31 hydroelectric stations with a combined capacity of 2,693 MW, and six combustion turbine stations with a combined capacity of 2,081 MW.

The megawatt (MW) rating is the peak capacity of the unit at a point in time. Translating this peak capacity into annual MWh (megawatt-hours) requires multiplying this amount times 24 hours per day times 340 days in the year (assuming 25 days for repair). A gigawatt is 1,000 megawatts.

a. Determine the utilization of the coal, nuclear, hydro, and oil and gas turbine generation assets. (*Hint:* You must translate the megawatt rating into gigawatt capacity for 340 days.)
b. Why are the utilization statistics different across the different generating sources?
c. What percent of total electric sales (in GWh) is nonresidential?
d. Why are operating statistics like this useful to analysts?

Case 9–6

Effect of depreciation on net income

Heimlich Construction Co. specializes in building replicas of historic houses. Ami Lamb, president of Heimlich, is considering the purchase of various items of equipment on July 1, 2002, for $150,000. The equipment would have a useful life of 5 years and no residual value. In the past, all equipment has been leased. For tax purposes, Ami is considering depreciating the equipment by the straight-line method. She discussed the matter with her CPA and learned that, although the straight-line method could be elected, it was to her advantage to use the modified accelerated cost recovery system (MACRS) for tax purposes. She asked for your advice as to which method to use for tax purposes.

1. Compute depreciation for each of the years (2002, 2003, 2004, 2005, 2006, and 2007) of useful life by (a) the straight-line method and (b) MACRS. In using the straight-line method, one-half year's depreciation should be computed for 2002 and 2007. Use the MACRS rates presented in the chapter.
2. Assuming that income before depreciation and income tax is estimated to be $150,000 uniformly per year and that the income tax rate is 30%, compute the net income for each of the years 2002, 2003, 2004, 2005, 2006, and 2007, if (a) the straight-line method is used and (b) MACRS is used.
3. What factors would you present to Ami in considering a depreciation method?

Business Leadership Skills—Responsible Leadership

Activity 9-1

Ethics and professional conduct in business

ETHICS

Stuart Madden, CPA, is an assistant to the controller of Tri-State Co. In his spare time, Stuart also prepares tax returns and performs general accounting services for clients. Frequently, Stuart performs these services after his normal working hours, using Tri-State Co.'s computers and laser printers. Occasionally, Stuart's clients will call him at the office during regular working hours.

Discuss whether Stuart is performing in a professional manner.

Activity 9-2

Ethics and professional conduct in business

ETHICS

The following is an excerpt from a conversation between the chief executive officer, Lee Baker, and the chief financial officer, Maurice Townley, of Nile Group, Inc.:

Baker (CEO): Maurice, as you know, the auditors are coming in to audit our year-end financial statements pretty soon. Do you see any problems on the horizon?

Townley (CFO): Well, you know about our "famous" Hill Companies acquisition a couple of years ago. We booked $1,000,000 of goodwill from that acquisition, and the accounting rules require us to recognize any impairment of goodwill.

Baker (CEO): Uh oh.

Townley (CFO): Yeah, right. We had to shut the old Hill Company operations down this year because those products were no longer selling. Thus, our auditor is going to insist that we write off the $1,000,000 of goodwill to reflect the impaired value.

Baker (CEO): We can't have that—at least not this year. Do everything you can to push back on this one. We just can't take that kind of a hit this year. The most we could stand is $200,000. Maurice, keep the write-off to $200,000 and promise anything in the future. Then we'll deal with that when we get there.

How should Townley respond to the CEO?

Activity 9-3

Financial vs. tax depreciation

The following is an excerpt from a conversation between two employees of Stanza Co., Geoff Haines and Allison Foster. Geoff is the accounts payable clerk, and Allison is the cashier.

Geoff: Allison, could I get your opinion on something?

Allison: Sure, Geoff.

Geoff: Do you know Kris, the fixed assets clerk?

Allison: I know who she is, but I don't know her real well. Why?

Geoff: Well, I was talking to her at lunch last Monday about how she liked her job, etc. You know, the usual . . . and she mentioned something about having to keep two sets of books . . . one for taxes and one for the financial statements. That can't be good accounting, can it? What do you think?

Allison: Two sets of books? It doesn't sound right.

Geoff: It doesn't seem right to me either. I was always taught that you had to use generally accepted accounting principles. How can there be two sets of books? What can be the difference between the two?

How would you respond to Allison and Geoff if you were Kris?

Activity 9-4

Shopping for a delivery truck

GROUP ACTIVITY

Assume you are planning to acquire a vehicle. In groups of three or four, go to a local dealer and identify the costs that would be incurred for acquiring the vehicle. Classify the costs as capital or revenue expenditures.

Activity 9-5

Applying for patents, copyrights, and trademarks

GROUP ACTIVITY

Go to the Internet and review the procedures for applying for a patent, a copyright, or a trademark. One Internet site that is useful for this purpose is:

www.idresearch.com

Prepare a written summary of these procedures.

Answers to Self-Study Questions

1. **C** All amounts spent to get a fixed asset (such as machinery) in place and ready for use are proper charges to the asset account. In the case of machinery acquired, the freight (answer A) and the installation costs (answer B) are both (answer C) proper charges to the machinery account.
2. **C** The periodic charge for depreciation under the declining-balance method (twice the straight-line rate) for the second year is determined by first computing the depreciation charge for the first year. The depreciation for the first year of $6,000 (answer A) is computed by multiplying the cost of the equipment, $9,000, by 2/3 (the straight-line rate of 1/3 multiplied by 2). The depreciation for the second year of $2,000 (answer C) is then determined by multiplying the book value at the end of the first year, $3,000 (the cost of $9,000 minus the first-year depreciation of $6,000), by 2/3. The third year's depreciation is $400 (answer D). It is determined by multiplying the book value at the end of the second year, $1,000, by 2/3, thus yielding $667. However, the equipment cannot be depreciated below its residual value of $600; thus, the third-year depreciation is $400 ($1,000 − $600).
3. **B** A depreciation method that provides for a higher depreciation amount in the first year of the use of an asset and a gradually declining periodic amount thereafter is called an accelerated depreciation method. The declining-balance method (answer B) is an example of such a method.
4. **D** The book value of the replaced component ($5,000) should be charged (debited) to depreciation expense. In addition, the new component has a full year of depreciation equal to $8,000 ($40,000 ÷ 5 years). Thus, added together, the correct depreciation expense is $13,000 for the year (answer D).
5. **C** Fixed asset turnover ratio = revenues ÷ average book value of fixed assets, or $500,000/[($80,000 + $120,000)/2], or 5.0 (answer C).

Chapter 10
Liabilities

The Law of Buy-In
"People buy into the leader, then the vision."
—The 21 Irrefutable Laws of Leadership
Dr. John C. Maxwell

Learning Goals

1. Define and give examples of liabilities.
2. Manage accounts payable, using the days' purchases in accounts payable ratio.
3. Describe the accounting for short-term notes payable and maturities currently due.
4. Describe the accounting treatment for contingent liabilities, including product warranties.
5. Describe the accounting for employer liabilities for payroll and fringe benefits.
6. Analyze and interpret current position with the current and quick ratios.
7. Describe the characteristics of long-term liabilities.
8. Describe the accounting for bonds payable issuances and redemptions, and interpret bonds payable footnote disclosures.
9. Describe the accounting for the purchase, interest, discount and premium amortization, and sale of bond investments.
10. Analyze and interpret long-term liability position with the number of times interest charges are earned and the ratio of total liabilities to total assets.

Holiday Inn

Have you ever been unhappy, dissatisfied, or even mad at the quality of service or product you've purchased? If so, maybe you should start your own business! Kemmons Wilson did.

It began in the summer of 1951, when Kemmons and Dorothy Wilson and their five children were traveling by car from Memphis to Washington, D.C. Along the way, Wilson was unhappy with the inconsistency in the cleanliness and size of motel accommodations. He was particularly upset with having to pay an extra $2 for each of his children to stay in their room, turning a $6 room into a $16 room.

Wilson began making plans to build a "family friendly" motel chain—that people could trust without having to inspect the rooms; that would allow children to stay free with their parents; that would become known for its consistent "brand" of cleanliness and service. Each motel would include comfortable beds, an attached restaurant, and a swimming pool for the kids.

Upon returning to Memphis, Wilson hired a draftsman to begin drawing up plans. The night before the plans were to be delivered, the draftsman watched a Bing Crosby movie, titled *Holiday Inn*, and the name for the motels was born.

The first Holiday Inn was opened on August 1, 1952, on the outskirts of Memphis. Aided by the development of the interstate highway systems throughout the United States during the 50s and 60s, Holiday Inn expanded rapidly. In just five years, the 100th Holiday Inn was opened in Tallahassee, Florida, and in just under ten years, the 1,000th Holiday Inn opened in San Antonio. Today, Holiday Inn has over 1,500 properties in 75 countries.

Known as "the home away from home," Wilson pioneered many of the amenities that today's travelers take for granted—ice machines, soft drink machines, TVs, and air conditioning. The biggest and most influential innovation was Holiday Inn's computerized reservation system. Launched in 1965, the system was an immediate hit and gave the chain an immense advantage over its competitors.

Wilson retired as chairman of the board of Holiday Inn in 1979, but he is still active in more than sixty business ventures. As a mentor of future entrepreneurs, he offers the following advice:

> *Work only half a day; it makes no difference which half—it can be either the first 12 hours or the last 12 hours.*
>
> *Do not be afraid of taking a chance. Remember that a broken watch is exactly right at least twice every 24 hours.*
>
> *No job is hard as long as you are smart enough to find someone else to do it for you.*

In August 1989, the Holiday Inn Corporation was sold to a British company, and its headquarters was moved from Memphis to London. The company has since expanded to include Holiday Inn Select, Holiday Inn SunSpree Resorts, Holiday Inn Express, and Staybridge Suites.

Thousands of employees work for the Holiday Inn and the related companies that Kemmons Wilson began in 1952. In this chapter, we discuss accounting for employee payroll and related fringe benefits, such as health and retirement benefits.

Source: Adapted from "Come Inn Off The Highway," by Laura Bly, *USA Today*, May 24, 2002; Kemmons Wilson's Home Page.

Your Need to Know

Using credit to finance trade and purchase fixed assets is probably as old as commerce itself. The Babylonians were lending money as early as 1300 B.C., and the Bible indicates the use of debt in the time of Moses. The proper use of debt can help a business reach its business objectives. On the other hand, too much debt can be a financial burden that can even lead to bankruptcy. Thus, just like for individuals, businesses must manage debt carefully.

One of the basic guidelines in managing *liabilities*, or debt, is to closely match the maturity of the liability with the underlying asset. The *maturity* is the time period that the liability is outstanding prior to its due date. Thus, debt can be short-term in nature (due within a year) or long-term (due beyond one year). For example, if a business used debt to finance the purchase of a building, then the debt maturity should approximate the life of the building. Thus, the cash flows from operating the building could be used to pay back the loan over the life of the building. It would be unwise for the business to finance a building with a current liability that was due within the year. This is because the business would need to constantly refinance the current liability over the life of the building, which would be expensive. In addition, business conditions might change, making it difficult to refinance the short-term debt, and thus creating a cash crunch. It would be similar to you trying to finance the purchase of a house with your credit card, rather than obtaining a mortgage.

In this chapter we will discuss the nature, accounting, and analysis of current and long-term debt. Using debt wisely is critical to successful business management.

The Nature of Liabilities

1 **Define and give examples of liabilities.**

When a business or a bank advances *credit*, it is making a loan. In these circumstances, it is called a **creditor** (or *lender*). Individuals or businesses that receive the credit are called **debtors** (or *borrowers*). Debt is an obligation that is recorded as a liability. *Long-term liabilities* are obligations due for a period of time greater than one year. Thus, a 30-year mortgage taken out to purchase property would be an example of a long-term liability. In contrast, *current liabilities* are obligations that will be paid out of current assets and are due within a short time, usually within one year.

Most current liabilities arise from two basic transactions:

1. Receiving goods or services prior to making payment.
2. Receiving payment prior to delivering goods or services.

An example of the first type of transaction is *accounts payable* arising from purchases of merchandise for resale. An example of the second type of transaction is *unearned rent* arising from the receipt of rent in advance. Some additional examples of current liabilities that we discussed in previous chapters are:

- Taxes payable–the amount of taxes owed to governmental units
- Interest payable–the amount of interest owed on borrowed funds
- Wages payable–the amount owed to employees

In the first half of this chapter, we will discuss common current liabilities. We will discuss long-term liabilities in the last half of the chapter.

Accounts Payable

2 Manage accounts payable, using the days' purchases in accounts payable ratio.

We have defined accounts payable earlier in this text as the amount owed to suppliers for purchased items. The accounts payable for many businesses is often the largest current liability. Exhibit 1 illustrates the size of the current liability balance as a percent of total current liabilities for a number of different companies. The average percent of accounts payable to total current liabilities for large companies is 36.2%.[1]

Exhibit 1

Accounts Payable as a Percent of Total Current Liabilities

Company	Accounts Payable as a Percent of Total Current Liabilities
Alcoa Inc.	24%
American Express Co.	12
BellSouth	17
Gap Inc	38
IBM	23
Nissan Motor Co.	31
Rite-Aid Corp.	54
Texaco	55

Analysts and managers often monitor accounts payable by measuring the speed with which suppliers are paid. Many suppliers have payment terms that provide a discount for timely payment. As we discussed in Chapter 5, it is often advantageous to pay within the discount period. One method of evaluating how quickly suppliers are being paid is with the **days' purchases in accounts payable ratio**. The formula for the ratio is:

$$\text{Days' purchases in accounts payable ratio} = \frac{\text{Average accounts payable}}{\text{Cost of merchandise sold} + \text{change in inventory}} \times 365 \text{ days}$$

The change in inventory (ending inventory minus beginning inventory) is added to the denominator in order to adjust the cost of merchandise sold to approximate the total purchases. To illustrate this ratio, consider the information for Circuit City Stores, Inc., and Best Buy Co., Inc., for fiscal year 2001:

	(in millions)				
	Beginning Accounts Payable	Ending Accounts Payable	Beginning Inventory	Ending Inventory	Cost of Merchandise Sold
Circuit City	$ 903	$1,107	$1,758	$1,633	$10,050
Best Buy	1,773	2,449	1,767	2,258	15,167

The days' purchases in accounts payable ratio for both companies would be calculated as follows on the next page.

1 Determined from *Disclosure* database of public companies exceeding $10 billion in sales.

$$\text{Circuit City: } \frac{(\$903 + \$1{,}107)/2}{\$10{,}050 + (\$1{,}633 - \$1{,}758)} \times 365 \text{ days} = 37 \text{ days}$$

$$\text{Best Buy: } \frac{(\$1{,}773 + \$2{,}449)/2}{\$15{,}167 + (\$2{,}258 - \$1{,}767)} \times 365 \text{ days} = 49 \text{ days}$$

Circuit City is paying its accounts payable faster than Best Buy. Managers would interpret this ratio based on the credit terms and standard industry practices. For example, if the credit terms for Best Buy were net 30, then the ratio would indicate that the accounts payable are being paid slower than promised. This could have a negative impact on supplier relationships. In addition, analysts often interpret this ratio in light of industry practices. Unexpectedly large values of this ratio often indicate liquidity problems.

Notes Payable and Maturities Currently Due

3 Describe the accounting for short-term notes payable and maturities currently due.

A note payable may be issued when merchandise or other assets are purchased, or a note may be issued in exchange for cash from a bank. A note may also be issued to creditors to temporarily satisfy an account payable created earlier. For example, assume that a business issues a 90-day, 12% note for $1,000, dated August 1, 2004, to Murray Co. for a $1,000 overdue account. The issuance of the note is recorded as follows:

Aug.	1	Accounts Payable—Murray Co.	1,000	
		Notes Payable		1,000

When the note matures, the entry to record the payment of the $1,000 principal plus $30 interest ($1,000 × 12% × 90/360) is as follows:

Oct.	30	Notes Payable	1,000	
		Interest Expense	30	
		Cash		1,030

The interest expense is reported in the Other Expense section of the income statement for the year ended December 31, 2004. The interest expense account is closed at December 31.

The preceding entries for notes payable are similar to those we discussed in Chapter 7 for notes receivable. Notes payable entries are presented from the viewpoint of the borrower, while notes receivable entries are presented from the viewpoint of the creditor or lender. To illustrate, the following entries are journalized for a borrower (Bowden Co.), who issues a note payable to a creditor (Coker Co.):

	Bowden Co. (Borrower)	Coker Co. (Creditor)
May 1. Bowden Co. purchased merchandise on account from Coker Co., $10,000, 2/10, n/30. The merchandise cost Coker Co. $7,500.	Merchandise Inventory 10,000 Accounts Payable 10,000	Accounts Receivable 10,000 Sales 10,000 Cost of Merchandise Sold 7,500 Merchandise Inventory 7,500
May 31. Bowden Co. issued a 60-day, 12% note for $10,000 to Coker Co. on account.	Accounts Payable 10,000 Notes Payable 10,000	Notes Receivable 10,000 Accounts Receivable 10,000
July 30. Bowden Co. paid Coker Co. the amount due on the note of May 31. Interest: $10,000 × 12% × 60/360.	Notes Payable 10,000 Interest Expense 200 Cash 10,200	Cash 10,200 Interest Revenue 200 Notes Receivable 10,000

Discounted Notes Payable

Sometimes a borrower will issue a creditor a discounted note rather than an interest-bearing note. Although such a note does not specify an interest rate, the creditor sets a rate of interest and deducts the interest from the face amount of the note. This interest is called the **discount**. The rate used in computing the discount is called the **discount rate**. The borrower is given the remainder, called the **proceeds**.

In buying a used delivery truck, a business issues an $8,000, 60-day note dated July 15, which the truck's seller discounts at 12%. What is the cost of the truck (the proceeds)?

$7,840 [$8,000 − ($8,000 × 12% × 60/360)]

To illustrate, assume that on August 10, Cary Company issues a $20,000, 90-day note to Seinfeld Company in exchange for inventory. Seinfeld discounts the note at a rate of 15%. The amount of the discount, $750, is debited to *Interest Expense.* The proceeds, $19,250, are debited to *Merchandise Inventory. Notes Payable* is credited for the face amount of the note, which is also its maturity value. This entry is shown below.

Aug.	10	Merchandise Inventory	19,250	
		Interest Expense	750	
		Notes Payable		20,000

When the note is paid, the entry is recorded as follows:[2]

Nov.	8	Notes Payable	20,000	
		Cash		20,000

Current Maturities of Long-Term Debt

Long-term liability maturities that are due within the coming year must be classified as a current liability. The total amount of the loan due after the coming year is classified as a

2 If the accounting period ends before a discounted note is paid, an adjusting entry should record the prepaid (deferred) interest that is not yet an expense. This deferred interest would be deducted from Notes Payable.

long-term liability. To illustrate, Starbucks Corp. reported the following scheduled debt payments in the footnotes to its annual report for the fiscal year ending September 30, 2001:

Fiscal year ending	(in thousands)
2002	$ 697
2003	710
2004	722
2005	735
2006	748
Thereafter	2,871
Total principal payments	$6,483

The debt of $697,000 due in 2002 would be reported as a current liability on the September 30, 2001 balance sheet. The remaining debt of $5,786,000 ($6,483,000 − $697,000) would be reported as a long-term liability on the balance sheet.

Contingent Liabilities

4 Describe the accounting treatment for contingent liabilities, including product warranties.

Some past transactions will result in liabilities if certain events occur in the future. These potential obligations are called **contingent liabilities**. For example, Ford Motor Company would have a contingent liability for the estimated costs associated with warranty work on new car sales. The obligation is contingent upon a *future event*, namely, a customer requiring warranty work on a vehicle. The obligation is the result of a *past transaction*, which is the original sale of the vehicle.

If a contingent liability is *probable* and the amount of the liability can be *reasonably estimated*, it should be recorded in the accounts. Ford Motor Company's vehicle warranty costs are an example of a *recordable* contingent liability. The warranty costs are *probable* because warranty repairs will be required on some vehicles. In addition, the costs can be *estimated* from past warranty experience.

INTERNATIONAL PERSPECTIVE

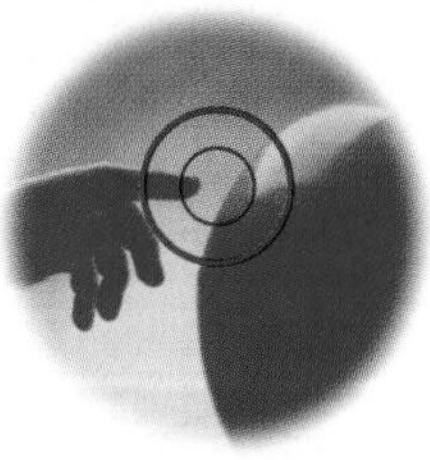

Morocco's accounting standards have no specific rules requiring disclosures of contingent liabilities.

To illustrate, assume that during June a company sells a product for $60,000 on which there is a 36-month warranty for repairing defects. Past experience indicates that the average cost to repair defects is 5% of the sales price over the warranty period. The entry to record the estimated product warranty expense for June is as follows:

June 30	Product Warranty Expense	3,000	
	Product Warranty Payable		3,000

A business sells to a customer $120,000 of commercial audio equipment with a one-year repair and replacement warranty. Historically, the average cost to repair or replace is 2% of sales. How is this contingent liability recorded?

Product Warranty Expense	2,400	
Product Warranty Payable		2,400

This transaction matches revenues and expenses properly by recording warranty costs in the same period in which the sale is recorded. When the defective product is repaired, the repair costs are recorded by debiting *Product Warranty Payable* and crediting *Cash*, *Supplies*, or other appropriate accounts. Thus, if a customer required a $200 part replacement on August 16, the entry is:

Aug. 16	Product Warranty Payable	200	
	Supplies		200

If a contingent liability is probable but cannot be *reasonably estimated* or is only *possible*, then the nature of the contingent liability should be disclosed in the footnotes to the financial statements. Professional judgment is required in distinguishing between contingent liabilities that are probable versus those that are only possible. Common examples of contingent liabilities disclosed in notes to the financial statements are litigation, environmental matters, guarantees, and sale of receivables. The following example of a contingency disclosure, related to litigation, was taken from a recent annual report of eBay Inc:

> *...eBay was served with a lawsuit.... The lawsuit was filed on behalf of a purported class of eBay users who purchased allegedly forged autographed sports memorabilia on eBay. The lawsuit claims eBay was negligent in permitting certain named (and other unnamed) defendants to sell allegedly forged autographed sports memorabilia on eBay.... Management believes that the ultimate resolution of these disputes will not have a material adverse impact on eBay's consolidated financial positions, results of operations, or cash flows.*

eBay's disclosure did not result in recognized losses, because potential litigation losses were not viewed as probable. The accounting treatment of contingent liabilities is summarized in Exhibit 2.

Exhibit 2

Accounting Treatment of Contingent Liabilities

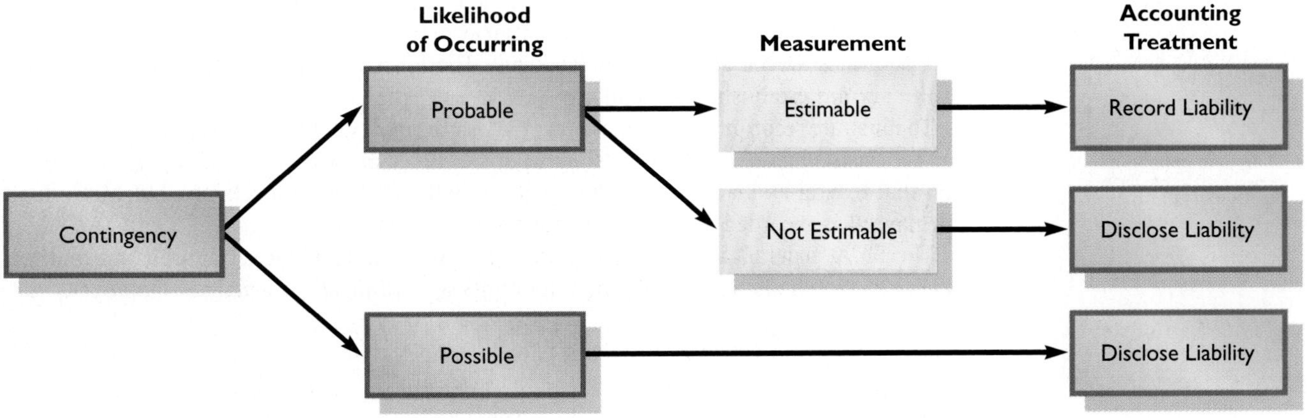

Ethics in Action

The Price of a Clean Environment

Environmental and public health claims are quickly growing into some of the largest contingent liabilities facing companies. For example, tobacco, asbestos, and environmental clean-up claims have reached billions of dollars and have led to a number of corporate bankruptcies. Managers must be careful that today's decisions don't become tomorrow's nightmare.

Employer Liabilities

5 Describe the accounting for employer liabilities for payroll and fringe benefits.

In accounting, the term **payroll** refers to the amount paid to employees for the services they provide during a period. A business's payroll is usually significant for several reasons. First, the payroll and related payroll taxes have a significant effect on net income. Second, the payroll is subject to various federal and state regulations. Finally, the payroll usually has a significant effect on employee morale.

Recording Payroll

Employee salaries and wages are expenses to an employer. The total earnings of an employee for a payroll period, including bonuses and overtime pay, are called **gross pay**. From this amount one or more *deductions* are subtracted to arrive at the net pay. **Net pay** is the amount the employer must pay the employee. The deductions for federal taxes are usually the largest deduction. Deductions may also be required for state or local income taxes. Other deductions may be made for FICA, medical insurance, contributions to pensions, and for items authorized by individual employees.

Most of us have Federal Insurance Contributions Act (FICA) tax withheld from our payroll checks. Employers are required to withhold a portion of the earnings of each of the employees. The amount of **FICA tax** withheld is the employees' contribution to two federal programs: social security and Medicare. The FICA tax rate and the amounts subject to the tax are established annually by law.[3]

To illustrate recording payroll, assume that McDermott Co. had a gross payroll of $13,800 for the week ending April 11. Assume that the FICA tax was 7.5% of the gross payroll, and that federal and state withholding was $1,655 and $280, respectively. The McDermott Co. payroll is recorded at the top of the following page.

The FICA, federal, and state taxes withheld from the employees' earnings are not expenses to the employer. Rather, these amounts are withheld on behalf of employees.

3 The social security portion of the FICA tax is limited to a specified amount of annual compensation for each individual. The 2002 limitation is $84,000. The Medicare portion is not subject to a limitation. Throughout this text, we will simplify by assuming that all compensation is within the social security limitation. Thus, under this assumption, the social security and Medicare tax rates can be combined into a single tax rate, termed FICA tax.

Apr. 11	Wage and Salary Expense	13,800	
	FICA Tax Payable		1,035
	Employees Federal Income Tax Payable		1,655
	Employees State Income Tax Payable		280
	Cash		10,830

Ethics in Action
Phantom Employees

Companies must guard against the fraudulent creation and cashing of payroll checks. Numerous payroll frauds involve supervisors adding fictitious employees to or failing to remove departing employees from the payroll, and then cashing the check. Requiring proper authorization and approval of employee additions, removals, or changes in pay rates can minimize this type of fraud.

Liability for Employer Payroll Taxes

In addition to amounts withheld on behalf of employees, most employers are also subject to federal and state payroll taxes based on the amount paid to their employees. Such taxes are an operating expense of the business. Exhibit 3 summarizes the responsibility for employee and employer payroll taxes.

Exhibit 3

Responsibility for Tax Payments

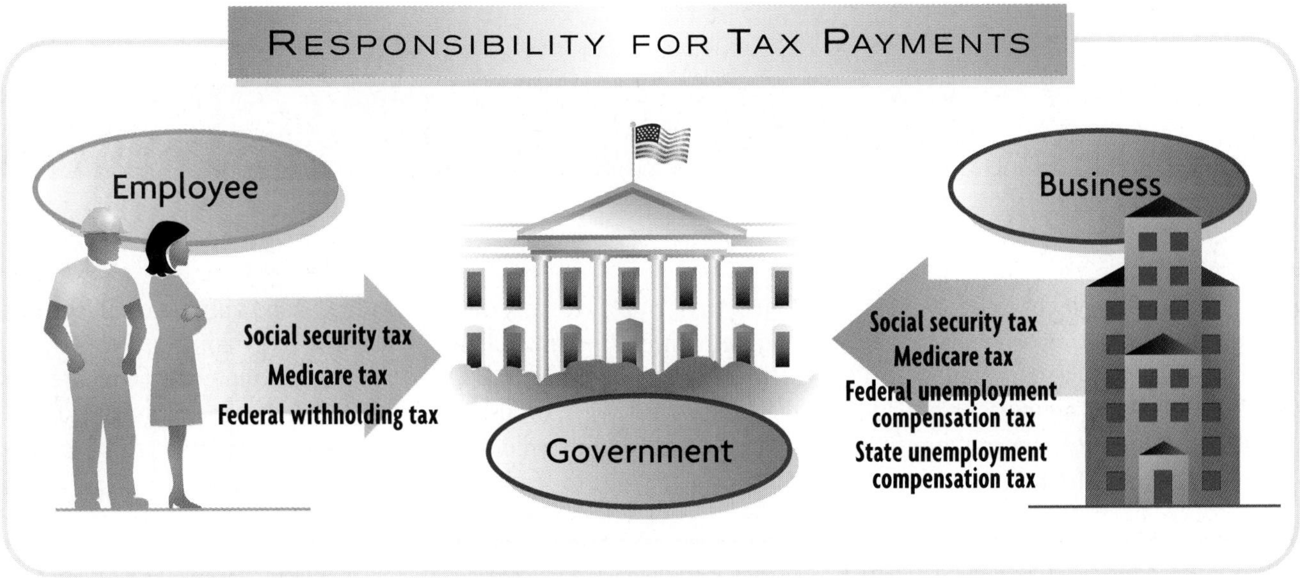

FICA Tax Employers are required to contribute to the social security and Medicare programs for each employee. The employer must match the employee's contribution to each program.

Federal Unemployment Compensation Tax The Federal Unemployment Tax Act (FUTA) provides for temporary payments to those who become unemployed as a result of layoffs due to economic causes beyond their control. Types of employment subject to this program are similar to those covered by FICA taxes. The FUTA tax rate and maximum earnings of each employee subject to the tax are established annually by law.

State Unemployment Compensation Tax State Unemployment Tax Acts (SUTA) also provide for payments to unemployed workers. The amounts paid as benefits are obtained, for the most part, from a tax levied upon employers only. The employment experience and the status of each employer's tax account are reviewed annually, and the tax rates are adjusted accordingly.

Recording and Paying Payroll Taxes

The employer's payroll taxes become liabilities when the related payroll is *paid* to employees. The payroll information of McDermott Co. indicates that the amount of FICA tax withheld is $1,035 on April 11. Since the employer must match the employees' FICA contributions, the employer's social security payroll tax will also be $1,035. Further, assume that the SUTA and FUTA taxes are $145 and $25, respectively. The entry to record the payroll tax expense for the week and the liability for the taxes accrued is shown below.

Apr. 11	Payroll Tax Expense	1,205	
	FICA Tax Payable		1,035
	SUTA Tax Payable		145
	FUTA Tax Payable		25

Payroll tax liabilities are paid to appropriate taxing authorities on a quarterly basis. The quarterly entry would debit the various taxes payable and credit Cash.

Ethics in Action
Pyramiding

Failure to pay payroll taxes on the proper reporting dates can result in severe penalties. These penalties are put in place to dissuade business owners from financing losses from tax payments withheld from employees and due to taxing authorities. One fraudulent practice is termed "pyramiding." Pyramiding occurs when a business withholds taxes from its employees but intentionally fails to remit them to the taxing authorities. Businesses involved in pyramiding frequently file for bankruptcy to eliminate the liability and then start a new business under a different name to begin a new scheme.

Employees' Fringe Benefits

Many companies provide their employees a variety of benefits in addition to salary and wages earned. Such **fringe benefits** may take many forms, including vacations, medical benefits, and post-retirement benefits such as pension plans. When the employer pays part or all of the cost of the fringe benefits, these costs must be recognized as expenses. To properly match revenues and expenses, the estimated cost of these benefits should be recorded as an expense during the period in which the employee earns the benefit.

Exhibit 4 shows benefit dollars as a percent of total benefits for 864 companies surveyed by the U.S. Chamber of Commerce.

Exhibit 4

Benefit Dollars as a Percent of Total

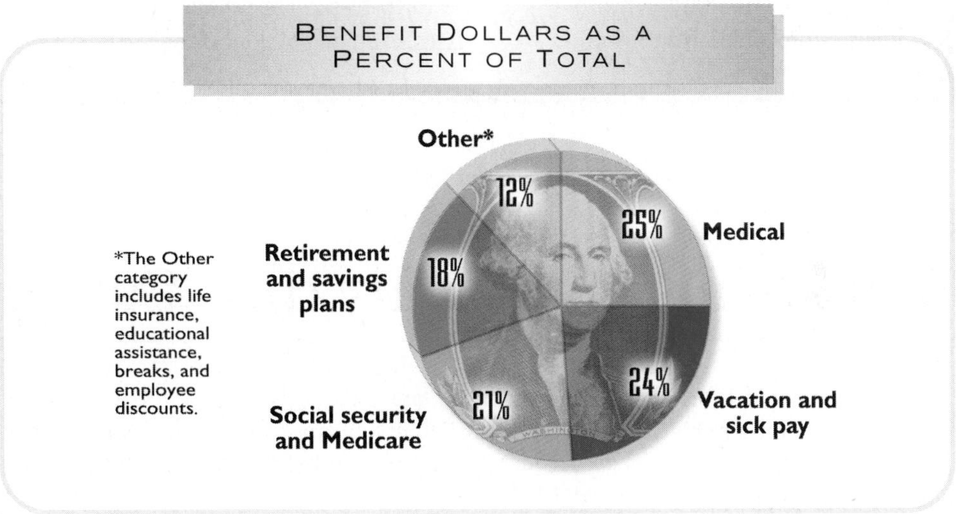

Source: U.S. Chamber of Commerce.

We will use vacation pay to illustrate fringe benefit accounting. Most employers grant vacation rights, sometimes called *compensated absences*, to their employees. Such rights give rise to a recordable contingent liability. The liability for employees' vacation pay should be accrued as a liability as the vacation rights are earned. The entry to accrue vacation pay may be recorded in total at the end of each fiscal year, or it may be recorded at the end of each pay period. To illustrate this latter case, assume that employees earn one day of vacation for each month worked during the year. Assume also that the estimated vacation pay for the payroll period ending May 5 is $2,000. The entry to record the accrued vacation pay for this pay period is shown as follows:

May 5	Vacation Pay Expense	2,000	
	Vacation Pay Payable		2,000

If employees are required to take all their vacation time within one year, the vacation pay payable is reported on the balance sheet as a current liability. If employees are allowed to accumulate their vacation time, the estimated vacation pay liability that is applicable to time that will *not* be taken within one year is a long-term liability.

When payroll is prepared for the period in which employees have taken vacations, the vacation pay payable is reduced. The entry debits *Vacation Pay Payable* and credits *Salaries Payable* and the other related accounts for taxes and withholdings.

Strategy in Business
People Count

Businesses that provide services to customers depend upon the hiring and retaining of good employees. *Fortune* annually publishes a list of "Best Companies to Work For." In 2002, Edward Jones, a brokerage firm headquartered in St. Louis, headed the list of "Best Companies." Edward Jones rose from a ranking of nine in 2001 to one in 2002. Charles Schwab, another brokerage firm, fell from five to forty-six. For service businesses like Edward Jones and Charles Schwab, attracting and retaining employees through perks and other incentives makes good business strategy.

Source: *Fortune*, "Best Companies to Work For," 2002.

Disclosing and Analyzing Current Liabilities

6 Analyze and interpret current position with the current and quick ratios.

Current liabilities are usually listed on the balance sheet on the basis of size and maturity date of the liability. Current maturities of long-term debt followed by accounts payable are frequently the first two listed items. The current asset and current liability sections of recent balance sheets for Barnes & Noble, Inc., and Borders Group, Inc., are shown in Exhibit 5.

Exhibit 5

Partial Balance Sheets for Barnes & Noble and Borders Group

	Barnes & Noble (in thousands) February 2, 2002	Borders Group (in thousands) January 27, 2002
Current assets:		
Cash and cash equivalents	$ 108,218	$ 190,200
Receivables, net	98,570	73,100
Merchandise inventories	1,285,005	1,178,800
Prepaid expenses and other current assets	99,201	–
Total current assets	$1,590,994	$1,442,100
Current liabilities:		
Short-term borrowings and current portion of long-term debt		$ 83,800
Accounts payable	$ 695,284	638,200
Accrued liabilities	444,944	385,200
Total current liabilities	$1,140,228	$1,107,200

Current liabilities are evaluated in relation to current assets, because current assets are normally used to pay current liabilities. When current assets are not deemed sufficient to pay current liabilities, the current liabilities may be refinanced through long-term debt. Using long-term debt in this way is generally considered undesirable.

Financial ratios that measure the degree to which current assets are available to satisfy current liabilities are called **liquidity** ratios. One of the most popular liquidity ratios is the **current ratio**, which is calculated as:

$$\text{Current Ratio} = \frac{\text{Current Assets}}{\text{Current Liabilities}}$$

The current ratio measures the degree to which current assets are available to pay the current liabilities. For example, a current ratio of 2.0 would indicate that current assets are twice as large as current liabilities. A current ratio exceeding 2.0 would generally indicate favorable liquidity, although this guideline may differ across industries.

A second liquidity ratio used by analysts is the **quick ratio** or *acid-test ratio*, which is calculated as:

$$\text{Quick Ratio} = \frac{\text{Quick Assets}}{\text{Current Liabilities}}$$

Quick assets are cash, cash equivalents, and receivables that can be quickly converted into cash. Notice that inventories and prepaid items are excluded from the numerator. Thus, the quick ratio measures the "instant" current debt-paying ability of a company. A quick ratio exceeding 1.0 is often considered desirable, which again may differ for some industries. A ratio less than one would indicate that current liabilities cannot be covered by cash and "near cash" assets.

To illustrate the current and quick ratios, refer to the partial balance sheet information for Barnes & Noble, Inc., and Borders Group, Inc., in Exhibit 5. The current ratios for Barnes & Noble and Borders would be calculated as,

$$\text{Barnes \& Noble: } \frac{\$1,590,994}{\$1,140,228} = 1.40 \qquad \text{Borders: } \frac{\$1,442,100}{\$1,107,200} = 1.30$$

The quick ratio for both companies would be:

$$\text{Barnes \& Noble: } \frac{\$108,218 + \$98,570}{\$1,140,228} = 0.18 \qquad \text{Borders: } \frac{\$190,200 + \$73,100}{\$1,107,200} = 0.24$$

Both companies' ratios are less than the "rule of thumb" guidelines. This is not surprising, since retail bookselling companies, such as Barnes & Noble and Borders, are not expected to have large accounts receivable balances. Most of their sales would be cash and credit card; thus, they can satisfy current liabilities as sales are made, without having to wait for collections.

In comparing the two companies, Barnes & Noble has a stronger current ratio. The reason for this strength is primarily the result of the additional short-term borrowings that are part of Borders' current liabilities. These additional current liabilities will increase the denominator and, thereby, depress Borders' current ratio, relative to Barnes & Noble. Borders' quick ratio is slightly higher than Barnes & Noble's quick ratio, indicating a slightly stronger quick asset position.

Exhibit 6 shows the current ratios for pairs of companies in five different industries. The current and quick ratios across each of these industries are different, indicating the importance of comparing ratios within an industry. For example, software companies and cruise lines won't have much inventory in their current assets, in contrast to companies in retail, consumer appliance manufacturing, and brewing. In addition, some of the company pairs are different within each industry. Further analysis of the balance sheet would be required to uncover the reason for the differences between companies within an industry, as we did with the book retailers.

Exhibit 6

Current Ratios for Pairs of Companies in Five Different Industries

Company	Current Ratio	Quick Ratio
Barnes & Noble, Inc.	1.40	0.18
Borders	1.30	0.24
Microsoft Corp.	3.11	2.77
Oracle Corp.	2.29	2.12
Adolph Coors Company	1.31	0.78
Anheuser-Busch Companies, Inc.	0.92	0.45
Maytag Corporation	1.11	0.58
Whirlpool Corporation	0.98	0.56
Carnival Cruise Lines	0.32	0.17
Royal Caribbean Cruise Lines	0.34	0.25

Nature of Long-Term Liabilities

7 Describe the characteristics of long-term liabilities.

Most of us have financed (purchased on credit) an automobile, a computer, or a home. Similarly, corporations often finance their operations by purchasing on credit and issuing long-term notes or bonds. We have discussed accounts payable and notes payable earlier in this chapter. A **bond** is simply a form of a long-term interest-bearing note. Like a note, a bond requires periodic interest payments, and the face amount must be repaid at the maturity date. Bondholders are creditors of the issuing corporation, and their claims on the assets of the corporation rank ahead of stockholders.

A corporation that issues bonds enters into a contract, called a **bond indenture** or *trust indenture*, with the bondholders. A bond issue is normally divided into a number of individual bonds. Usually the face value of each bond, called the *principal*, is $1,000 or a multiple of $1,000. The interest on bonds may be payable annually, semiannually, or quarterly. Most bonds pay interest semiannually.

The prices of bonds are quoted as a percentage of the bonds' face value. Thus, investors could purchase or sell AOL Time Warner bonds quoted at 109 7/8 for $1,098.75. Likewise, bonds quoted at 109 could be purchased or sold for $1,090.

When all bonds of an issue mature at the same time, they are called *term bonds*. If the maturities are spread over several dates, they are called *serial bonds*. For example, one-tenth of an issue of $1,000,000 bonds, or $100,000, may mature 16 years from the issue date, another $100,000 in the 17th year, and so on until the final $100,000 matures in the 25th year.

Bonds that may be exchanged for other securities, such as common stock, are called *convertible bonds*. Bonds that a corporation reserves the right to redeem before their maturity are called *callable bonds*. Bonds issued on the basis of the general credit of the corporation are called *debenture bonds*.

Once bonds are issued, periodic interest payments and repayment of the face value of the bonds are required. That is, if these payments are not made, the bondholders could seek court action and could force the company into bankruptcy. For example, Regal Cinemas, the largest movie exhibitor in the United States, expanded aggressively through the late 1990s and early 2000s by using long-term debt. Unfortunately, a downturn in revenues resulted in insufficient cash to support interest and debt payments. As a result, creditors forced Regal into bankruptcy proceedings and thus became the new owners.

Issuing, Redeeming, and Disclosing Bonds Payable

8 **Describe the accounting for bonds payable issuances and redemptions, and interpret bonds payable footnote disclosures.**

When a corporation issues bonds, the price that buyers are willing to pay for the bonds depends upon the following three factors:

1. The face amount of the bonds, which is the amount due at the maturity date.
2. The periodic interest to be paid on the bonds.
3. The market rate of interest.

The face amount and the periodic interest to be paid on the bonds are identified in the bond indenture. The periodic interest is expressed as a percentage of the face amount of the bond. This percentage or rate of interest is called the **contract rate** or *coupon rate.*

The *market* or **effective rate of interest** is determined by transactions between buyers and sellers of similar bonds. The market rate of interest is affected by a variety of factors, including investors' assessment of current economic conditions as well as future expectations.

If the contract rate of interest equals the market rate of interest, the bonds will sell at their face amount. If the market rate is higher than the contract rate, the bonds will sell at a **discount**, or less than their face amount. Why is this the case? Buyers are not willing to pay the face amount for bonds whose contract rate is lower than the market rate. The discount, in effect, represents the amount necessary to make up for the difference in the market and the contract interest rates. In contrast, if the market rate is lower than the contract rate, the bonds will sell at a **premium**, or more than their face amount. In this case, buyers are willing to pay more than the face amount for bonds whose contract rate is higher than the market rate.

If IBM $7^1/_4$% bonds maturing in 2005 are listed as selling for $104^3/_8$, is the market rate of interest higher or lower than that for similar bonds?

Lower

Bonds Issued at Face Amount

Assume that on January 1, 2004, a corporation issues for cash $100,000 of 12%, five-year bonds, with interest of $6,000 payable *semiannually.* The market rate of interest at the time the bonds are issued is 12%. Since the contract rate and the market rate of interest are the same, the bonds will sell at their face amount, as discussed in the previous section.

The following entry records the $100,000 bonds issued at their face amount:

Jan. 1	Cash	100,000	
	Bonds Payable		100,000

Every six months after the bonds have been issued, interest payments of $6,000 are made. The first interest payment is recorded as shown below.

June 30	Interest Expense	6,000	
	Cash		6,000

At the maturity date, the payment of the principal of $100,000 is recorded as follows:

Dec. 31	Bonds Payable	100,000	
	Cash		100,000

Bonds Issued at a Discount

What if the market rate of interest is higher than the contract rate of interest? If the market rate of interest is 13% and the contract rate is 12% on the five-year, $100,000 bonds, the bonds will sell at a discount. If the $100,000 face value bonds are issued for $96,406, the issuance is recorded as follows:[4]

Jan. 1	Cash	96,406	
	Discount on Bonds Payable	3,594	
	Bonds Payable		100,000

The $3,594 discount may be viewed as the amount that is needed to entice investors to accept a contract rate of interest that is below the market rate. You may think of the discount as the market's way of adjusting a bond's contract rate of interest to the higher market rate of interest. Using this logic, generally accepted accounting principles require that bond discounts be amortized as interest expense over the life of the bond.

Amortizing a Bond Discount

There are two methods of amortizing a bond discount or premium: (1) the **straight-line method** and (2) the **effective interest rate method**, often called the *interest method.* Both methods amortize the same total amount of discount over the life of the bonds. The interest method is required by generally accepted accounting principles. However, the straight-line method is acceptable if the results obtained do not materially differ from the results that would be obtained by using the interest method. Because the straight-line method illustrates the basic concept of amortizing discounts and is simpler, we will use it in this chapter.

The straight-line method of amortizing a bond discount provides for amortization in equal periodic amounts. Applying this method to the preceding example yields amortization of 1/10 of $3,594, or $359.40, each half-year. The amount of the interest

If the amount of a bond discount on a newly issued 6%, 5-year, $100,000 bond is $28,092, what are (a) the semiannual straight-line amortization of the discount and (b) the annual interest expense?

(a) $2,809.20, (b) $11,618.40 ($2,809.20 + $2,809.20 + $6,000)

4 The prices of bonds issued at a discount or premium can be determined using present value techniques. This topic is covered in advanced courses.

expense on the bonds is the same, $6,359.40 ($6,000 + $359.40) for each half-year. The entry to record the first interest payment and the amortization of the related discount is shown below.

June 30	Interest Expense	6,359.40	
	Discount on Bonds Payable		359.40
	Cash		6,000.00

Bonds Issued at a Premium

If the market rate of interest is 11% and the contract rate is 12% on the five-year, $100,000 bonds, the bonds will sell at a premium. Recall that bonds will sell at a premium when the market rate of interest is less than the contract rate.

If the $100,000 face value bonds are sold for $103,769, the issuance is recorded as:

Jan. 1	Cash	103,769	
	Bonds Payable		100,000
	Premium on Bonds Payable		3,769

If the amount of a bond premium on a newly issued 13%, 5-year, $100,000 bond is $11,581, what are (a) the semiannual straight-line amortization of the premium and (b) the annual interest expense?

(a) $1,158.10, (b) $10,683.80 ($13,000 − $1,158.10 − $1,158.10)

Amortizing a Bond Premium

The amortization of bond premiums is basically the same as that for bond discounts, except that interest expense is decreased. In the above example, the straight-line method yields amortization of 1/10 of $3,769, or $376.90, each half year. The entry to record the first interest payment and the amortization of the related premium is as follows:

June 30	Interest Expense	5,623.10	
	Premium on Bonds Payable	376.90	
	Cash		6,000

Zero-Coupon Bonds

Some corporations issue bonds that provide for only the payment of the face amount at the maturity date. Such bonds are called *zero-coupon bonds*. Because they do not provide for interest payments, these bonds sell at a large discount. For example, $1,000 of General Motor Acceptance Corp. (GMAC) face value zero-coupon bonds maturing in 2015 were selling for $362 on April 5, 2002.

The accounting for zero-coupon bonds is similar to that for interest-bearing bonds that have been sold at a discount. The discount is amortized as interest expense over the life of the bonds. To illustrate, assume that a $100,000 zero-coupon bond due in 5 years is issued at $53,273 on January 1, 2004. The entry to record the issuing of the bonds follows on the next page.

2004				
Jan.	1	Cash	53,273	
		Discount on Bonds Payable	46,727	
		Bonds Payable		100,000

The adjusting entry on December 31, 2004, would be:

2004				
Dec.	31	Interest Expense ($46,727/5)	9,345	
		Discount on Bonds Payable		9,345

Bond Redemption

A corporation may call or redeem bonds before they mature. This is often done if the market rate of interest declines significantly after the bonds have been issued. In this situation, the corporation may sell new bonds at a lower interest rate and use the funds to redeem the original bond issue. The corporation can thus save on future interest expenses.

A corporation often issues callable bonds to protect itself against significant declines in future interest rates. However, callable bonds are more risky for investors, who may not be able to replace the called bonds with investments paying an equal amount of interest.

Callable bonds can be redeemed by the issuing corporation within the period of time and at the price stated in the bond indenture. Normally, the call price is above the face value. A corporation may also redeem its bonds by purchasing them on the open market.

A corporation usually redeems its bonds at a price different from that of the carrying amount (or book value) of the bonds. The **carrying amount** of bonds payable is the balance of the bonds payable account (face amount of the bonds) less any unamortized discount or plus any unamortized premium. If the price paid for redemption is below the bond carrying amount, the difference in these two amounts is recorded as a gain. If the price paid for the redemption is above the carrying amount, a loss is recorded. Gains and losses on the redemption of bonds are reported as an extraordinary item on the income statement.

To illustrate, assume that on June 30 a corporation has a bond issue of $100,000 outstanding, on which there is an unamortized premium of $4,000. Assuming that the corporation purchases one-fourth ($25,000) of the bonds for $24,000 on June 30, the redemption is recorded as follows:

June	30	Bonds Payable	25,000	
		Premium on Bonds Payable	1,000	
		Cash		24,000
		Gain on Redemption of Bonds		2,000

In the preceding entry, only a portion of the premium relating to the redeemed bonds is written off. The difference between the carrying amount of the bonds purchased, $26,000 ($25,000 + $1,000), and the price paid for the redemption, $24,000, is recorded as a gain.

If the corporation calls the entire bond issue for $105,000 on June 30, the redemption is recorded as follows:

June 30	Bonds Payable	100,000	
	Premium on Bonds Payable	4,000	
	Loss on Bonds Payable	1,000	
	Cash		105,000

A $250,000 bond issue on which there is an unamortized discount of $20,000 is redeemed for $235,000. What is the gain or loss on the redemption of the bonds?

$5,000 loss ($250,000 − $20,000 − $235,000)

Long-Term Liability Disclosure

The carrying value, interest rate, and maturity of long-term liabilities must be disclosed on the financial statements or in the footnotes to the financial statements.[5] To illustrate, the Coca-Cola Company disclosed the following long-term debt in the footnotes to its financial statements:

	(in millions)	
December 31,	**2001**	**2000**
$6\frac{5}{8}$% U.S. dollar notes due 2002	$ 150	$150
6% U.S. dollar notes due 2003	150	150
$5\frac{3}{4}$% U.S. dollar notes due 2009	399	399
$5\frac{3}{4}$% U.S. dollar notes due 2011	498	—
$7\frac{3}{8}$% U.S. dollar notes due 2093	116	116
Other, due 2002 to 2013	62	41
	$1,375	$856
Less current portion	156	21
	$1,219	$835

Coca-Cola uses the term "notes," which is similar to a bond. Notice also that the current maturities are subtracted from the long-term debt total. As discussed previously, this is done because the current maturities are included in the current liabilities.

Investments in Bonds

9 Describe the accounting for the purchase, interest, discount and premium amortization, and sale of bond investments.

In the previous sections, we discussed bonds and the related transactions of the issuing corporation (the debtor). However, these transactions also affect investors. In this section, we discuss the accounting for bonds from the investors' point of view.

Accounting for Bond Investments—Purchase, Interest, and Amortization

Bonds may be purchased either directly from the issuing corporation or through an organized bond exchange. Bond exchanges publish daily bond quotations. These quotations normally include the bond interest rate, maturity date, volume of sales, and the high, low,

5 *Statement of Financial Accounting Standards No. 129*, "Disclosure Information About Capital Structure," Financial Accounting Standards Board (Norwalk, Connecticut: 1997).

and closing prices for each corporation's bonds traded during the day. Prices for bonds are quoted as a percentage of the face amount. Thus, the price of a $1,000 bond quoted at $99\frac{1}{2}$ would be $995, while the price of a bond quoted at $104\frac{1}{4}$ would be $1,042.50.

As with other assets, the cost of a bond investment includes all costs related to the purchase. For example, for bonds purchased through an exchange, the amount paid as a broker's commission should be included as part of the cost of the investment.

When bonds are purchased between interest dates, the buyer normally pays the seller the interest accrued from the last interest payment date to the date of purchase. The amount of the interest paid is normally debited to *Interest Revenue*, since it is an offset against the amount that will be received at the next interest date.

To illustrate, assume that an investor purchases a $1,000 bond at 102 plus a brokerage fee of $5.30 and accrued interest of $10.20. The investor records the transaction as follows:

Apr. 2	Investment in Lewis Co. Bonds	1,025.30	
	Interest Revenue	10.20	
	Cash		1,035.50

The cost of the bond is recorded in a single investment account. The face amount of the bond and the premium (or discount) are normally not recorded in separate accounts. This is different from the accounting for bonds payable. Separate premium and discount accounts are usually not used by investors, because they usually do not hold bond investments until the bonds mature.

When bonds held as long-term investments are purchased at a price other than the face amount, the premium or discount should be amortized over the remaining life of the bonds. The amortization of premiums and discounts affects the investment and interest accounts as shown below.

Premium Amortization:			*Discount Amortization:*		
Interest Revenue	XXX		Investment in Bonds	XXX	
Investment in Bonds		XXX	Interest Revenue		XXX

The amount of the amortization can be determined by using either the straight-line method or the interest method. Unlike bonds payable, the amortization of premiums and discounts on bond investments is usually recorded at the end of the period, rather than when interest is received.

To illustrate the accounting for bond investments, assume that on July 1, 2003, Crenshaw Inc. purchases $50,000 of 8% bonds of Deitz Corporation, due in $8\frac{3}{4}$ years. Crenshaw Inc. purchases the bonds directly from Deitz Corporation at a price of $41,706 plus interest of $1,000 ($50,000 × 8% × 3/12) accrued from April 1, 2003, the date of the last semiannual interest payment. Entries in the accounts of Crenshaw Inc. at the time of purchase and for the remainder of the fiscal period ending December 31, 2003, are as follows:

Date		Description		Debit	Credit
2003					
July	1	Investment in Deitz Corp. Bonds		41,706	
		Interest Revenue		1,000	
		Cash			42,706
		Purchased investment in bonds, plus accrued interest:			
		Cost of $50,000 of Deitz Corp. bonds	$41,706		
		Interest accrued ($50,000 × 8% × 3/12)	1,000		
		Total	$42,706		
Oct.	1	Cash		2,000	
		Interest Revenue			2,000
		Received semiannual interest for April 1 to October 1 ($50,000 × 8% × 6/12).			
Dec.	31	Interest Receivable		1,000	
		Interest Revenue			1,000
		Adjusting entry for interest accrued from October 1 to December 31 ($50,000 × 8% × 3/12).			
	31	Investment in Deitz Corp. Bonds		474	
		Interest Revenue			474
		Adjusting entry for amortization of discount for July 1 to December 31:			
		Face value of bonds	$50,000		
		Cost of bond investment	41,706		
		Discount on bond investment	$ 8,294		
		Number of months to maturity (8¾ years × 12)	105 months		
		Monthly amortization ($8,294/105 months, rounded to nearest dollar)	$79 per mo.		
		Amortization for 6 months ($79 × 6)	$474		

The effect of these entries on the interest revenue account is shown below.

Interest Revenue

July 1	1,000	Oct. 1	2,000
		Dec. 31	1,000
		31	474
			3,474
		Bal.	*2,474*

Accounting for Bond Investments—Sale

Many long-term investments in bonds are sold before their maturity date. When this occurs, the seller receives the sales price (less commissions and other selling costs) plus any accrued interest since the last interest payment date. Before recording the cash proceeds, the seller should amortize any discount or premium for the current period up to the date of sale. Any gain or loss on the sale is then recorded when the cash proceeds are recorded. Such gains and losses are normally reported in the Other Income section of the income statement.

To illustrate, assume that the Deitz Corporation bonds in the preceding example are sold for $47,350 plus accrued interest on June 30, 2010. The *carrying amount* of the bonds (cost plus amortized discount) as of January 1, 2010 (78 months after their purchase) is $47,868 [$41,706 + ($79 per month × 78 months)]. The entries to amortize the discount for the current year and to record the sale of the bonds are as follows:

2010				
June 30	Investment in Deitz Corp. Bonds		474	
	Interest Revenue			474
	Amortized discount for current year ($79 × 6 months).			
30	Cash		48,350	
	Loss on Sale of Investments		992	
	Interest Revenue			1,000
	Investment in Deitz Corp. Bonds			48,342
	Received interest and proceeds from sale of bonds.			
	Interest for April 1 to June 30 = $50,000 × 8% × $^3/_{12}$ = $1,000			
	Carrying amount of bonds on Jan. 1, 2010	$47,868		
	Discount amortized, Jan. 1 to June 30, 2010	474		
	Carrying amount of bonds on June 30, 2010	$48,342		
	Proceeds of sale	47,350		
	Loss on sale	$ 992		

If the Deitz Corporation bonds had been sold on September 30 instead of June 30, what would have been the amount of the loss?

$1,229 {$47,350 − [$48,342 + ($79 × 3 months)]}

Balance Sheet Presentation of Bond Investments

Investments in bonds or other debt securities that management intends to hold to their maturity are called **held-to-maturity securities**. Such securities are classified as long-term investments under the caption Investments. These investments are reported at their cost less any amortized premium or plus any amortized discount. In addition, the market (fair) value of the bond investments should be disclosed, either on the face of the balance sheet or in an accompanying note.

Analyze and Interpret Leverage

10 Analyze and interpret long-term liability position with the number of times interest charges are earned and the ratio of total liabilities to total assets.

As an individual, if you have an annual salary of $50,000 per year, you should not borrow $500,000 for a new house. The reason is because your monthly income cannot support the monthly debt payments. Similarly, managers set long-term debt levels that can be supported by the company's income. The ability of a business to meet its fixed financial obligations (debts) is called **leverage**. We will describe two leverage ratios.

The first leverage ratio measures the relationship between a company's income and its interest expense on debt. The ratio is called the **number of times interest charges are earned** during the year (or *interest coverage ratio*), and is calculated as:

$$\text{Number of times interest charges are earned} = \frac{\text{Income before income tax} + \text{Interest expense}}{\text{Interest Expense}}$$

The calculation uses "income *before* income tax" in the numerator, because the amount available to make interest payments is not affected by taxes on income. This is because interest is deductible in determining taxable income. In interpreting the ratio, the higher the ratio, the greater the chance that interest payments will continue to be made if earnings decrease. In contrast, the lower the ratio, the higher the chance the company will be unable to support its required interest payments from current period earnings.[6]

To illustrate this ratio, the following financial statement information was taken from a recent annual report for SBC Communications, Inc., a telecommunications company:

Interest expense	$1,592 million
Income before taxes	$12,888 million

The number of times interest charges are earned, 9.1, is calculated using the formula above as follows:

$$\text{Number of times interest charges are earned} = \frac{\$12{,}888 \text{ million} + \$1{,}592 \text{ million}}{\$1{,}592 \text{ million}} = 9.1$$

The number of times interest charges are earned indicates that the creditors of SBC have their interest receipts protected by over nine times earnings. This would be considered very adequate in most circumstances. The number of times interest charges are earned for some other companies in SBC's industry are as follows:

Telecommunication Company	Number of Times Interest Charges Are Earned
AT&T Corp.	1.82
Bellsouth Corp.	5.97
Qwest Communications	1.12
Sprint Corp.	0.29
Verizon Communications Inc.	6.11

6 A similar analysis can also be applied to dividends on preferred stock. In such cases, net income would be divided by the amount of preferred dividends to yield the number of times preferred dividends were earned. This measure gives an indication of the relative assurance of continued dividend payments to preferred stockholders.

As can be seen, SBC's interest coverage appears to be one of the best in this industry. In contrast, Sprint Corp. and Qwest Communications have poor interest coverage. The reason for the poor interest coverage is either due to poor earnings (small numerator) or large interest expense (large denominator), or a combination of both. The second leverage measure helps isolate the cause.

The second leverage measure compares the total liabilities to the amount of total assets. To illustrate, assume that you borrowed $80,000 and used $20,000 of your own funds to purchase a $100,000 house. Your debt as a percentage of the total value of the house would be 80% ($80,000/$100,000). In a similar way, analysts can measure a company's relative use of debt by measuring the ratio of the total liabilities to the total assets of the company. The **ratio of total liabilities to total assets** is calculated as:[7]

$$\textit{Ratio of total liabilities to total assets} = \frac{\textit{Total Liabilities}}{\textit{Total Assets}}$$

To illustrate, annual report information for SBC disclosed the following:

Total liabilities	$68,188 million
Total assets	$98,651 million

Thus, the ratio of total liabilities to total assets would be:

$$\frac{\$68,188 \text{ million}}{\$98,651 \text{ million}} = 69\%$$

This ratio should be interpreted by comparing it to some other companies in the industry. This is because some industries use more debt than others. The ratio of total liabilities to total assets for the selected companies in the telecommunication industry is as follows:

Telecommunication Company	Ratio of Total Liabilities to Total Assets
AT&T Corp.	53%
Bellsouth Corp.	67%
Qwest Communications	44%
Sprint Corp.	67%
Verizon Communications Inc.	66%

From this information we can conclude that SBC's debt at 69% of total assets is slightly higher than other companies in the industry. In addition, we can determine that neither Qwest nor Sprint are using debt excessively. Indeed, Qwest appears to be using less debt than other companies in the industry. Thus, the low number of times interest charges are earned for Qwest and Sprint appears to be caused more by low earnings, rather than excessive debt.

7 The ratio of total liabilities to total stockholders' equity is another common leverage measure. This ratio is algebraically related to the ratio of total liabilities to total assets, and thus conveys the same relative information.

Focus on Cash Flow

Liabilities

In the statement of cash flows, the net income is adjusted by the change in current liabilities in determining the cash flows from operating activities. That is, increases in current liabilities are added to net income, while decreases in current liabilities are deducted from net income. The operating activities section of the statement of cash flows is reproduced below for **Amazon.com, Inc.** for a recent year.

Amazon.com, Inc.
Partial Statement of Cash Flows—Operating Activities Section

OPERATING ACTIVITIES:	(in thousands)
Net loss	$(1,411,273)
Adjustments to reconcile net loss to net cash provided by (used in) operating activities	994,850
Changes in operating assets and liabilities:	
Inventories	46,083
Prepaid expenses and other current assets	(8,585)
Accounts payable	22,357
Accrued expenses and other current liabilities	93,967
Unearned revenue	97,818
Interest payable	34,341
Net cash provided by (used in) operating activities	$ (130,442)

The shaded area shows the changes in current liability adjustments to net income. In this case, all the changes were increases, which were added to net income in order to obtain the net cash used in operating activities.

The financing activities section of the statement of cash flows will disclose the increases and decreases in cash from long-term liability financing. Increases in long-term liabilities will result in an increase in cash, while a decrease will result in a use of cash. This disclosure is shown below for Amazon.com, Inc.

The shaded area shows both proceeds from issuing new debt and the use of cash from retiring debt.

Amazon.com, Inc.
Partial Statement of Cash Flows—Financing Section

FINANCING ACTIVITIES:	(in thousands)
Proceeds from exercise of stock options	$ 44,697
Proceeds from long-term debt	681,499
Repayment of long-term debt	(16,927)
Financing costs	(16,122)
Net cash provided by financing activities	$693,147

Summary of Learning Goals

1 Define and give examples of liabilities.

Current liabilities are obligations that are to be paid out of current assets and are due within a short time, usually within one year. Current liabilities arise from either (1) receiving goods or services prior to making payment or (2) receiving payment prior to delivering goods or services.

2 Manage accounts payable, using the days' purchases in accounts payable ratio.

The days' purchases in accounts payable ratio measures the timeliness of vendor payments. Management and analysts can use this ratio to evaluate payment speed (in days) in relation to credit terms. Late payments can indicate liquidity problems or poor treatment of vendors.

3 Describe the accounting for short-term notes payable and maturities currently due.

A note issued to a creditor to temporarily satisfy an account payable is recorded as a debit to *Accounts Payable* and a credit to *Notes Payable.* At the time the note is paid, *Notes Payable* and *Interest Expense* are debited and *Cash* is credited. Notes may also be issued to purchase merchandise or other assets or to borrow money from a bank. When a discounted note is issued, *Interest Expense* is debited for the interest deduction at the time of issuance, an asset account is debited for the proceeds, and *Notes Payable* is credited for the face value of the note. The face value and the maturity value of a discounted note are equal. Maturities of notes payable currently due are disclosed as a current liability.

4 Describe the accounting treatment for contingent liabilities, including product warranties.

A contingent liability is a potential obligation that results from a past transaction but depends on a future event. If the contingent liability is both probable and estimable, the liability should be recorded. If the contingent liability is reasonably possible or is not estimable, it should be disclosed in the footnotes to the financial statements. An example of a recordable contingent liability is product warranties. If a company grants a warranty on a product, an estimated warranty expense and liability should be recorded in the period of the sale. The expense and the liability are recorded by debiting *Product Warranty Expense* and crediting *Product Warranty Payable.*

5 Describe the accounting for employer liabilities for payroll and fringe benefits.

The employer's liability for payroll includes the wages payable plus deductions from employees' gross pay. In addition, the employer's liability includes employer taxes, such as the employer's share of FICA plus federal and state unemployment insurance. Employers may also incur employment-related expenses and associated liabilities for fringe benefits, such as vacation pay, pensions, and medical benefits.

6 Analyze and interpret current position with the current and quick ratios.

The current ratio and quick ratio (or acid-test ratio) are measures of a business's ability to pay current liabilities within a short period of time. The current ratio is current assets divided by current liabilities. The quick ratio is quick assets divided by current liabilities.

7 Describe the characteristics of long-term liabilities.

The characteristics of bonds depend upon the type of bonds issued by a corporation. Bonds that may be issued include term bonds, serial bonds, convertible bonds, callable bonds, and debenture bonds.

8 Describe the accounting for bonds payable issuances and redemptions, and interpret bonds payable footnote disclosures.

A bond issuance is recorded by debiting Cash for the proceeds received and crediting Bonds Payable for the face amount of the bonds. Any difference between the face amount of the bonds and the proceeds is debited to Discount on Bonds Payable or credited to Premium on Bonds Payable.

A discount or premium on bonds payable is amortized to interest expense over the life of the bonds. The entry to amortize a discount debits Interest Expense and credits Discount on Bonds Payable. The entry to amortize a premium debits Premium on Bonds Payable and credits Interest Expense.

When a corporation redeems bonds, Bonds Payable is debited for the face amount of the bonds, the premium (discount) on bonds account is debited (credited) for its balance, Cash is credited, and any gain or loss on the redemption is recorded.

The interest rate, carrying amount, and maturity of long-term bonds or notes payable are disclosed either on the face of the financial statements or in the notes.

9 Describe the accounting for the purchase, interest, discount and premium amortization, and sale of bond investments.

A long-term investment in bonds is recorded by debiting Investment in Bonds. When bonds are purchased between interest dates, the amount of the interest paid should be debited to Interest Revenue. Any discount or premium on bond investments should be amortized, using the straight-line or effective interest rate methods. The amortization of a discount is recorded by debiting Investment in Bonds and crediting Interest Revenue. The amortization of a premium is recorded by debiting Interest Revenue and crediting Investment in Bonds.

When bonds held as long-term investments are sold, any discount or premium for the current period should first be amortized. Cash is then debited for the proceeds of the sale, Investment in Bonds is credited for its balance, and any gain or loss is recorded.

Investments in bonds that are held-to-maturity securities are reported as Investments at cost less any amortized premium or plus any amortized discount.

10 Analyze and interpret long-term liability position with the number of times interest charges are earned and the ratio of total liabilities to total assets.

The number of times interest charges are earned during the year is a measure of the risk that interest payments to debtholders will continue to be made if earnings decrease. It is computed by dividing income before income tax plus interest expense by interest expense. The ratio of total liabilities to total assets measures the percent of total assets funded by debt. The larger this ratio, the greater the leverage risk.

Glossary

Bond A form of interest-bearing note used by corporations to borrow on a long-term basis.

Bond indenture The contract between a corporation issuing bonds and the bondholders.

Carrying amount The balance of the bonds payable account (face amount of the bonds) less any unamortized discount or plus any unamortized premium.

Contingent liability An obligation from a past transaction that is contingent upon a future event. An example would be product warranty payable.

Contract rate The periodic interest to be paid on the bonds that is identified in the bond indenture; expressed as a percentage of the face amount of the bond.

Creditor A lender of money, such as a bank or bondholder.

Current ratio A financial ratio that is computed by dividing current assets by current liabilities.

Days' purchases in accounts payable ratio A measure of the vendor payment velocity (measured in days of accounts payable to gross purchases).

Debtor A borrower of money.

Discount The interest deducted from the maturity value of a note or the excess of the face amount of bonds over their issue price.

Discount rate The rate used in computing the interest to be deducted from the maturity value of a note.

Effective interest rate method A method of amortizing a bond discount or premium, using present value techniques.

Effective rate of interest The market rate of interest at the time bonds are issued.

FICA tax Federal Insurance Contributions Act tax used to finance federal programs for old-age and disability benefits (social security) and health insurance for the aged (Medicare).

Fringe benefits Benefits provided to employees in addition to wages and salaries.

Gross pay The total earnings of an employee for a payroll period.

Held-to-maturity securities Investments in bonds or other debt securities that management intends to hold to their maturity.

Leverage The ability of a business to meet its fixed financial obligations (debts).

Liquidity Measures the ability of a business to pay or otherwise satisfy its current liabilities.

Net pay Gross pay less payroll deductions; the amount the employer is obligated to pay the employee.

Number of times interest charges are earned A ratio that measures the risk that interest payments to debtholders will continue to be made if earnings decrease.

Payroll The total amount paid to employees for a certain period.

Premium The excess of the issue price of bonds over their face amount.

Proceeds The net amount available from discounting a note payable.

Quick assets Cash, cash equivalents, and receivables that can be quickly converted into cash.

Quick ratio A financial ratio that measures the ability to pay current liabilities with quick assets (cash, marketable securities, accounts receivable).

Ratio of total liabilities to total assets The percent of total assets that are funded by total liabilities; a measure of solvency.

Straight-line method A method of amortizing a bond discount or premium in equal periodic amounts.

Illustrative Accounting Application Problem

The fiscal year of Russell Inc., a manufacturer of acoustical supplies, ends December 31. Selected transactions for the period 2003 through 2010, involving bonds payable issued by Russell Inc., are as follows:

2003

June 30 Issued $2,000,000 of 25-year, 7% callable bonds dated June 30, 2003, for cash of $1,920,000. Interest is payable semiannually on June 30 and December 31.

Dec. 31 Paid the semiannual interest on the bonds.

31 Recorded straight-line amortization of $1,600 of discount on the bonds.

31 Closed the interest expense account.

2004

June 30 Paid the semiannual interest on the bonds.

Dec. 31 Paid the semiannual interest on the bonds.

31 Recorded straight-line amortization of $3,200 of discount on the bonds.

31 Closed the interest expense account.

2010

June 30 Recorded the redemption of the bonds, which were called at 101½. The balance in the bond discount account is $57,600 after the payment of interest and amortization of discount have been recorded. (Record the redemption only.)

Instructions

1. Record the entries for the preceding transactions.
2. Determine the amount of interest expense for 2003 and 2004.
3. Estimate the effective annual interest rate by dividing the interest expense for 2003 by the bond carrying amount at the time of issuance and multiplying by 2.
4. Determine the carrying amount of the bonds as of December 31, 2004.

Solution

1.

2003				
June 30	Cash		1,920,000	
	Discount on Bonds Payable		80,000	
		Bonds Payable		2,000,000
Dec. 31	Interest Expense		70,000	
		Cash		70,000
31	Interest Expense		1,600	
		Discount on Bonds Payable		1,600
31	Income Summary		71,600	
		Interest Expense		71,600
2004				
June 30	Interest Expense		70,000	
		Cash		70,000
Dec. 31	Interest Expense		70,000	
		Cash		70,000
31	Interest Expense		3,200	
		Discount on Bonds Payable		3,200
31	Income Summary		143,200	
		Interest Expense		143,200
2010				
June 30	Bonds Payable		2,000,000	
	Loss on Redemption of Bonds Payable		87,600	
		Discount on Bonds Payable		57,600
		Cash		2,030,000

2. a. 2003—$71,600
   b. 2004—$143,200

3. $71,600 ÷ $1,920,000 = 3.73% rate for six months of a year
   3.73% × 2 = 7.46% annual rate

4.

Initial carrying amount of bonds	$1,920,000
Discount amortized on December 31, 2003	1,600
Discount amortized on December 31, 2004	3,200
Carrying amount of bonds, December 31, 2004	$1,924,800

Self-Study Questions

Answers at end of chapter

1. A business issued a $5,000, 60-day note to a supplier, which discounted the note at 12%. The proceeds are:
   A. $4,400
   B. $4,900
   C. $5,000
   D. $5,100

2. Which of the following taxes are employers usually not required to withhold from employees?
   A. Federal income tax
   B. Federal unemployment compensation tax
   C. Medicare tax
   D. State and local income taxes

3. A firm's current assets include $100,000 cash, $300,000 accounts receivable, and $400,000 inventory. The current liabilities are $200,000. What are the current and quick ratios?

A.	0.5, 2.0	C.	2.0, 4.0
B.	4.0, 0.5	D.	4.0, 2.0

4. If a firm purchases $100,000 of bonds of X Company at 101 plus accrued interest of $2,000 and pays broker's commissions of $50, the amount debited to Investment in X Company Bonds would be:

A.	$100,000	C.	$103,000
B.	$101,050	D.	$103,050

5. A firm reported net income before tax of $500,000 and paid dividends of $200,000. The firm has $1,000,000 face value 10% bonds outstanding. What is the number of times interest charges are earned?

A.	3.0	C.	5.0
B.	4.0	D.	6.0

Discussion Questions

1. What two types of transactions cause most current liabilities?
2. When are short-term notes payable issued?
3. When should the liability associated with a product warranty be recorded? Discuss.
4. Compaq Computer Corporation reported $752 million of product warranties in the current liabilities section of a recent balance sheet. How would costs of repairing a defective product be recorded?
5. The "Questions and Answers Technical Hotline" in the *Journal of Accountancy* included the following question:

   Several years ago, Company B instituted legal action against Company A. Under a memorandum of settlement and agreement, Company A agreed to pay Company B a total of $17,500 in three installments–$5,000 on March 1, $7,500 on July 1, and the remaining $5,000 on December 31. Company A paid the first two installments during its fiscal year ended September 30. Should the unpaid amount of $5,000 be presented as a current liability at September 30?

   How would you answer this question?
6. What programs are funded by the FICA (Federal Insurance Contributions Act) tax?
7. For each of the following payroll-related taxes, indicate whether it generally applies to (a) employees only, (b) employers only, (c) both employees and employers:
   1. Social security tax
   2. Medicare tax
   3. Federal income tax
   4. Federal unemployment compensation tax
   5. State unemployment compensation tax
8. To match revenues and expenses properly, should the expense for employee vacation pay be recorded in the period during which the vacation privilege is earned or during the period in which the vacation is taken? Discuss.
9. How would you interpret a four-year trend in the current ratio, which has declined from 2.0 to 0.50?
10. Describe the two distinct obligations incurred by a corporation when issuing bonds.
11. If you asked your broker to purchase for you a 6% bond when the market interest rate for such bonds was 7%, would you expect to pay more or less than the face amount for the bond? Explain.
12. A corporation issues $10,000,000 of 6% bonds to yield interest at the rate of 5%. (a) Was the amount of cash received from the sale of the bonds greater or less than $10,000,000? (b) Identify the following terms related to the bond issue:

(1) face amount, (2) market or effective rate of interest, (3) contract rate of interest, and (4) maturity amount.

13. If bonds issued by a corporation are sold at a premium, is the market rate of interest greater or less than the contract rate?
14. The following data relate to a $1,000,000, 6% bond issue for a selected semiannual interest period:

Bond carrying amount at beginning of period	$1,150,000
Interest paid at end of period	30,000
Interest expense allocable to the period	28,750

(a) Were the bonds issued at a discount or at a premium? (b) What is the unamortized amount of the discount or premium account at the beginning of the period? (c) What account was debited to amortize the discount or premium?

15. Would a zero-coupon bond ever sell for its face amount?
16. Bonds Payable has a balance of $750,000, and Discount on Bonds Payable has a balance of $12,500. If the issuing corporation redeems the bonds at 99, is there a gain or loss on the bond redemption?
17. Where are investments in bonds that are classified as held-to-maturity securities reported on the balance sheet?
18. At what amount are held-to-maturity investments in bonds reported on the balance sheet?
19. What is the number of times interest charges are earned if the business has net income before taxes of $600,000 and a $1,500,000 face value bond payable with a coupon rate of 10%?

Resources for your success online @ http://warren.swlearning.com

Remember! If you need additional help, visit South-Western's Web site. See page 30 for a description of the online and printed materials that are available.

Exercises

Exercise 10-1

Current liabilities

Goal 1

Total current liabilities, $218,000

SPREADSHEET

Net World Magazine Inc. sold 4,800 annual subscriptions of *Net World* for $45 each during December 2003. These new subscribers will receive monthly issues, beginning in January 2004. In addition, the business had taxable income of $160,000 during the first calendar quarter of 2004. The federal tax rate is 35%. A quarterly tax payment will be made on April 7, 2004.

Prepare the current liabilities section of the balance sheet for Net World Magazine Inc. on March 31, 2004.

Exercise 10-2

Number of days' purchases in accounts payable ratio

Goal 2

a. 45.625 days

STUDENT SOLUTIONS MANUAL

Harkin Chocolate Stores Inc. purchases candy from suppliers on terms net 30. The comparative balance sheet for Harkin disclosed the following selected balances:

	Dec. 31, 2004	Dec. 31, 2003
Inventory	$150,000	$170,000
Accounts Payable	95,000	125,000

The cost of merchandise sold for 2004 was $900,000.

a. Calculate the number of days' purchases in accounts payable ratio.
b. Interpret the ratio.

Exercise 10-3

Number of days' purchases in accounts payable ratio

Goal 2

DeWitt Company's number of days' purchases in accounts payable was 31 days for 2003. The December 31, 2003 balance sheet showed balances for Inventory and Accounts Payable of $300,000 and $250,000, respectively. The cost of merchandise sold for 2004 was $1,700,000. The December 31, 2004 inventory balance was $50,000 higher, and the accounts payable balance was $200,000 higher than at the beginning of the year.

a. Calculate the number of days' purchases in accounts payable ratio for 2004.
b. Interpret the ratio.

Exercise 10-4

Entries for discounting notes payable

Goal 3

STUDENT SOLUTIONS MANUAL

National Electric Lighting Co. issues a 90-day note for $500,000 to Home Products Supply Co. for merchandise inventory. Home Products discounts the note at 10%.

a. Journalize National Electric's entries to record:
   1. the issuance of the note.
   2. the payment of the note at maturity.
b. Journalize Home Products' entries to record:
   1. the receipt of the note.
   2. the receipt of the payment of the note at maturity.

Exercise 10-5

Evaluate alternative notes

Goal 3

A borrower has two alternatives for a loan: (1) issue a $60,000, 90-day, 8% note or (2) issue a $60,000, 90-day note that the creditor discounts at 8%.

a. Calculate the amount of the interest expense for each option.
b. Determine the proceeds received by the borrower in each situation.
c. Which alternative is more favorable to the borrower? Explain.

Exercise 10-6

Entries for notes payable

Goal 3

STUDENT SOLUTIONS MANUAL

A business issued a 60-day, 9% note for $20,000 to a creditor on account. Record the entries for (a) the issuance of the note and (b) the payment of the note at maturity, including interest.

Exercise 10-7

Fixed asset purchases with note

Goal 3

On June 30, Zelda Game Company purchased land for $250,000 and a building for $730,000, paying $380,000 cash and issuing an 8% note for the balance, secured by a mortgage on the property. The terms of the note provide for 20 semiannual payments of $30,000 on the principal plus the interest accrued from the date of the preceding payment. Record the entries for (a) the transaction on June 30, (b) the payment of the first installment on December 31, and (c) the payment of the second installment the following June 30.

Exercise 10-8

Notes payable and maturities currently due

Goal 3

STUDENT SOLUTIONS MANUAL

The Baltimore Construction Company borrowed $1,000,000 on July 1, 2003, at an annual interest rate of 12%. The note payable is to be repaid in annual installments of $250,000, plus accrued interest, on each June 30th beginning June 30, 2004, until the note is paid in full (on June 30, 2007). Determine the current liabilities disclosed on the December 31, 2003 balance related to this transaction.

Exercise 10-9

Accrued product warranty

Goal 4

Precision Audio Company warrants its products for one year. The estimated product warranty is 3% of sales. Assume that sales were $600,000 for January. In February, a customer received warranty repairs requiring $310 of parts and $460 of labor.

a. Record the adjusting entry required at January 31, the end of the first month of the current year, to record the accrued product warranty.
b. Record the entry for the warranty work provided in February.

Exercise 10-10

Accrued product warranty

Goal 4

a. 0.77%

STUDENT SOLUTIONS MANUAL

During a recent year, Motorola, Inc., had sales of $29,398,000,000. An analysis of Motorola's product warranty payable account for the year was as follows:

Product warranty payable, January 1	$ 337,000,000
Product warranty expense	226,000,000
Warranty claims paid	(230,000,000)
Product warranty payable, December 31	$ 333,000,000

a. Determine the product warranty expense as a percent of sales.
b. Record the adjusting entry for the product warranty expense for the year.

Exercise 10-11

Contingent liabilities

Goal 4

Several months ago, Endurance Battery Company experienced a hazardous materials spill at one of its plants. As a result, the Environmental Protection Agency (EPA) fined the company $170,000. The company is contesting the fine. In addition, an employee is seeking $500,000 damages related to the spill. Lastly, a homeowner has sued the company for $120,000. The homeowner lives 20 miles from the plant, but believes that the incident has reduced her home's resale value by $120,000.

Endurance Battery's legal counsel believes that it is probable that the EPA fine will stand. In addition, counsel indicates that an out-of-court settlement of $250,000 has recently been reached with the employee. The final papers will be signed next week. Counsel believes that the homeowner's case is much weaker and will be decided in favor of Endurance. Other litigation related to the spill is possible, but the damage amounts are uncertain.

a. Record the contingent liabilities associated with the hazardous materials spill.
b. Prepare a footnote disclosure relating to this incident.

Exercise 10-12

Contingent liabilities

Goal 4

STUDENT SOLUTIONS MANUAL

The following note accompanied recent financial statements for eBay, Inc.:

> *. . . The Company was sued by Network Engineering Software, Inc. . . . for the Company's alleged willful and deliberate violation of a patent. The suit seeks unspecified monetary damages as well as an injunction against the Company's operations. It also seeks treble damages and attorneys' fees and costs. The Company believes that it has meritorious defenses against this suit and intends to vigorously defend itself. The Company could be forced to incur material expenses during this defense, and if it were to lose this suit, its business would be harmed.*

Was a liability recorded by eBay, Inc., for this contingent liability? Why or why not?

Exercise 10–13

Calculate payroll

Goal 5

b. Net pay, $989.75

An employee earns $26 per hour and $1\frac{1}{2}$ times that rate for all hours in excess of 40 hours per week. Assume that the employee worked 50 hours during the week. Assume further that the FICA tax rate was 7.5% and federal income tax to be withheld was $333.

a. Determine the gross pay for the week.
b. Determine the net pay for the week.

Exercise 10–14

Summary payroll data

Goal 5

a. (3) Total earnings, $211,000

STUDENT SOLUTIONS MANUAL

In the following summary of data for a payroll period, some amounts have been intentionally omitted:

Earnings:	
1. At regular rate	?
2. At overtime rate	$ 32,500
3. Total earnings	?
Deductions:	
4. FICA tax	15,165
5. Income tax withheld	29,500
6. Medical insurance	3,150
7. Union dues	?
8. Total deductions	50,000
9. Net amount paid	161,000
Accounts debited:	
10. Factory Wages	121,600
11. Sales Salaries	?
12. Office Salaries	34,300

a. Calculate the amounts omitted in lines (1), (3), (7), and (11).
b. Record the entry for the payroll accrual.
c. Record the entry for paying the payroll.

Exercise 10–15

Payroll tax entries

Goal 5

According to a summary of the payroll of All Sport Publishing Co., $700,000 of payroll was subject to the 7.5% FICA tax. Also, $15,000 was subject to state and federal unemployment taxes.

a. Calculate the employer's payroll taxes using the following rates: state unemployment, 4.3%; federal unemployment, 0.8%.
b. Record the entry for the accrual of payroll taxes.

Exercise 10–16

Recording payroll and payroll taxes

Goal 5

STUDENT SOLUTIONS MANUAL

Tower Controls Co. had a gross salary payroll of $550,000 for the month ending March 31. The complete payroll is subject to a FICA tax rate of 7.5%. Only $20,000 of this payroll is subject to state and federal unemployment taxes of 4% and 0.5%, respectively. The employees' income tax withholding is $104,500.

a. Record the March 31 payroll.
b. Record the March 31 payroll taxes.

Exercise 10–17

Accrued vacation pay

Goal 5

A business provides its employees with varying amounts of vacation per year, depending on the length of employment. The estimated amount of the current year's vacation pay is $224,400. Record the adjusting entry required on January 31, the end of the first month of the current year, to accrue the vacation pay.

Exercise 10-18

Current and quick ratios

Goal 6

a. Apple Computer Inc. current ratio, 3.39

STUDENT SOLUTIONS MANUAL

The current assets and current liabilities for Apple Computer Inc. and Gateway Inc. are shown as follows at the end of a recent fiscal period:

	Apple Computer Inc. (in thousands) Sept. 29, 2001	Gateway Inc. (in thousands) Dec. 31, 2001
Current assets:		
Cash and cash equivalents	$2,310,000	$ 730,999
Short-term investments	2,026,000	435,055
Accounts receivable	466,000	219,974
Inventories	11,000	120,270
Other current assets*	330,000	616,626
Total current assets	$5,143,000	$2,122,924
Current liabilities:		
Accounts payable	$ 801,000	$ 341,122
Accrued and other current liabilities	717,000	804,906
Total current liabilities	$1,518,000	$1,146,028

*These represent deferred tax assets, prepaid expenses, and other nonquick current assets.

a. Determine the current and quick ratios for both companies.
b. Interpret the ratio differences between the two companies.

Exercise 10-19

Bond price

Goal 8

IBM Corporation 7% bonds due in 2025 were reported in *The Wall Street Journal* as selling for 101⅛ on April 5, 2002.

Were the bonds selling at a premium or at a discount on April 5, 2002? Explain.

Exercise 10-20

Entries for issuing bonds

Goal 8

STUDENT SOLUTIONS MANUAL

Elba Co. produces and distributes fiber-optic cable for use by telecommunications companies. Elba Co. issued $12,000,000 of 15-year, 9% bonds on April 1 of the current year, with interest payable on April 1 and October 1. The fiscal year of the company is the calendar year. Record the entries for the following selected transactions for the current year:

Apr. 1	Issued the bonds for cash at their face amount.
Oct. 1	Paid the interest on the bonds.
Dec. 31	Recorded accrued interest for three months.

Exercise 10-21

Entries for issuing bonds and amortizing discount by straight-line method

Goal 8

b. $513,065

On the first day of its fiscal year, Electrokinetics Company issued $5,000,000 of five-year, 8% bonds to finance its operations of producing and selling home electronics equipment. Interest is payable semiannually. The bonds were issued at an effective interest rate of 11%, resulting in Electrokinetics Company receiving cash of $4,434,676.

a. Record the entries for the following:
   1. Sale of the bonds.
   2. First semiannual interest payment. (Amortization of discount is to be recorded annually.)
   3. Second semiannual interest payment.
   4. Amortization of discount at the end of the first year, using the straight-line method. (Round to the nearest dollar.)
b. Determine the amount of the bond interest expense for the first year.

Exercise 10–22

Computing bond proceeds, entries for bond issuing, and amortizing premium by straight-line method

Goal 8

STUDENT SOLUTIONS MANUAL

Fajitas Corporation wholesales oil and grease products to equipment manufacturers. On March 1, 2003, Fajitas Corporation issued $10,000,000 of five-year, 11% bonds. The bonds were issued for $10,386,057 to yield an effective interest rate of 10%. Interest is payable semiannually on March 1 and September 1. Record the entries for the following:

a. Sale of bonds on March 1, 2003.

b. First interest payment on September 1, 2003, and amortization of bond premium for six months, using the straight-line method. (Round to the nearest dollar.)

Exercise 10–23

Entries for issuing and calling bonds; loss

Goal 8

Farouk Corp., a wholesaler of office furniture, issued $15,000,000 of 30-year, 8% callable bonds on March 1, 2003, with interest payable on March 1 and September 1. The fiscal year of the company is the calendar year. Record the entries for the following selected transactions:

2003

Mar. 1 Issued the bonds for cash at their face amount.

Sept. 1 Paid the interest on the bonds.

2007

Sept. 1 Called the bond issue at 101, the rate provided in the bond indenture. (Omit entry for payment of interest.)

Exercise 10–24

Entries for issuing and calling bonds; gain

Goal 8

STUDENT SOLUTIONS MANUAL

Gehrig Corp. produces and sells automotive and aircraft safety belts. To finance its operations, Gehrig Corp. issued $20,000,000 of 25-year, 9% callable bonds on June 1, 2003, with interest payable on June 1 and December 1. The fiscal year of the company is the calendar year. Record the entries for the following selected transactions:

2003

June 1 Issued the bonds for cash at their face amount.

Dec. 1 Paid the interest on the bonds.

2008

Dec. 1 Called the bond issue at 99, the rate provided in the bond indenture. (Omit entry for payment of interest.)

Exercise 10–25

Entries for purchase and sale of investment in bonds; loss

Goal 9

Gloucester Co. sells optical supplies to opticians and ophthalmologists. Record the entries for the following selected transactions of Gloucester Co.:

a. Purchased for cash $300,000 of Glitz Co. 8% bonds at $102\frac{1}{2}$ plus accrued interest of $6,000.

b. Received first semiannual interest.

c. At the end of the first year, amortized $250 of the bond premium.

d. Sold the bonds at $98\frac{1}{2}$ plus accrued interest of $2,000. The bonds were carried at $302,500 at the time of the sale.

Exercise 10–26

Entries for purchase and sale of investment in bonds; gain

Goal 9

STUDENT SOLUTIONS MANUAL

Nelson Company develops and sells graphics software for use by architects. Record the entries for the following selected transactions of Nelson Company:

a. Purchased for cash $180,000 of Sequoyah Co. 5% bonds at 96 plus accrued interest of $1,500.

b. Received first semiannual interest.

c. Amortized $1,440 on the bond investment at the end of the first year.

d. Sold the bonds at 99 plus accrued interest of $3,000. The bonds were carried at $176,300 at the time of the sale.

Exercise 10-27

Number of times interest charges earned

Goal 10

a. 2001: 0.81

The following data were taken from recent annual reports of Trump Hotels and Casino Resorts, Inc., which owns and operates casino-based entertainment resorts in Atlantic City, New Jersey.

	2001	2000
Interest expense	$220,633,000	$220,217,000
Income before income tax	(41,139,000)	(77,267,000)

a. Determine the number of times interest charges were earned for the current and preceding years. Round to two decimal places.
b. What conclusions can you draw?

Exercise 10-28

Long-term solvency ratios for comparative years

Goal 10

a. 2002: 26.51%

STUDENT SOLUTIONS MANUAL

Krispy Kreme Doughnuts, Inc. manufactures and sells doughnuts. The liabilities and stockholders' equity at the end of two recent periods is summarized as follows:

	Feb. 3, 2002 (in millions)	Jan. 28, 2001 (in millions)
Total liabilities	$ 67,709	$45,814
Capital stock	118,742	83,132
Retained earnings	68,925	42,547

In addition, the income statement for these two periods showed the following income before tax and interest expense information:

	For the Year Ended	
	Feb. 3, 2002 (in millions)	Jan. 28, 2001 (in millions)
Interest expense	$ 337	$ 607
Income before income tax	42,546	23,783

a. Determine the ratio of total liabilities to total assets at the end of the two accounting periods. Round to two decimal places.
b. Determine the number of times interest charges were earned for the two fiscal years.
c. Interpret the change in the two ratios across the two periods.

Accounting Application Problems

Problem 10-1A

Current liability transactions

Goals 3, 4

GENERAL LEDGER

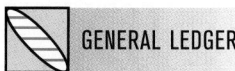

The following items were selected from among the transactions completed by Pride Polymers during the current year:

Apr. 7 Borrowed $15,000 from First Financial Corporation, issuing a 60-day, 12% note for that amount.
May 10 Purchased equipment by issuing a $120,000, 120-day note to Milford Equipment Co., which discounted the note at the rate of 10%.

June	6	Paid First Financial Corporation the interest due on the note of April 7 and renewed the loan by issuing a new 30-day, 16% note for $15,000. (Record both the debit and credit to the notes payable account.)
July	6	Paid First Financial Corporation the amount due on the note of June 6.
Aug.	3	Purchased merchandise on account from Hamilton Co., $36,000, terms, n/30.
Sept.	2	Issued a 60-day, 15% note for $36,000 to Hamilton Co., on account.
	7	Paid Milford Equipment Co. the amount due on the note of May 10.
Nov.	1	Paid Hamilton Co. the amount owed on the note of September 2.
	15	Purchased store equipment from Shingo Equipment Co. for $100,000, paying $23,000 and issuing a series of seven 12% notes for $11,000 each, coming due at 30-day intervals.
Dec.	15	Paid the amount due Shingo Equipment Co. on the first note in the series issued on November 15.
	21	Settled a product liability lawsuit with a customer for $65,000, to be paid in January. Pride Polymers accrued the loss in a litigation claims payable account.

Instructions

1. Record the transactions.
2. Record the adjusting entry for each of the following accrued expenses at the end of the current year:
   a. Product warranty cost, $11,200.
   b. Interest on the six remaining notes owed to Shingo Equipment Co.

Problem 10–2A

Payroll accounts and year-end entries

Goal 5

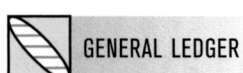

GENERAL LEDGER

The following accounts, with the balances indicated, appear in the ledger of Yellowstone Outdoor Equipment Company on December 1 of the current year:

Salaries Payable	—
FICA Tax Payable	$ 6,667
Employees Federal Income Tax Payable	8,566
Employees State Income Tax Payable	8,334
State Unemployment Tax Payable	840
Federal Unemployment Tax Payable	210
Bond Deductions Payable	1,400
Medical Insurance Payable	3,600
Sales Salaries Expense	640,200
Officers Salaries Expense	283,800
Office Salaries Expense	94,600
Payroll Taxes Expense	79,114

The following transactions relating to payroll, payroll deductions, and payroll taxes occurred during December:

Dec.	1	Issued Check No. 728 to Pico Insurance Company for $3,600, in payment of the semiannual premium on the group medical insurance policy.
	2	Issued Check No. 729 to First National Bank for $15,233, in payment for $6,667 of FICA tax and $8,566 of employees' federal income tax due.
	3	Issued Check No. 730 for $1,400 to First National Bank to purchase U.S. savings bonds for employees.
	14	Recorded the entry for the biweekly payroll. A summary of the payroll record follows:

Salary distribution:		
Sales	$29,000	
Officers	13,200	
Office	4,500	$46,700

Deductions:		
FICA tax	$ 3,270	
Federal income tax withheld	8,313	
State income tax withheld	2,102	
Savings bond deductions	700	
Medical insurance deductions	600	14,985
Net amount		$31,715

14 Issued Check No. 738 in payment of the net amount of the biweekly payroll.

14 Recorded the entry for payroll taxes on employees' earnings of December 14: FICA tax, $3,270; state unemployment tax, $180; federal unemployment tax, $45.

17 Issued Check No. 744 to First National Bank for $14,853, in payment for $6,540 of FICA tax and $8,313 of employees' federal income tax due.

28 Recorded the entry for the biweekly payroll. A summary of the payroll record follows:

Salary distribution:		
Sales	$29,500	
Officers	13,100	
Office	4,400	$47,000
Deductions:		
FICA tax	$ 3,243	
Federal income tax withheld	8,366	
State income tax withheld	2,115	
Savings bond deductions	700	14,424
Net amount		$32,576

28 Issued Check No. 782 for the net amount of the biweekly payroll.

28 Recorded the entry for payroll taxes on employees' earnings of December 28: FICA tax, $3,243; state unemployment tax, $110; federal unemployment tax, $28.

30 Issued Check No. 791 for $12,551 to First National Bank in payment of employees' state income tax due on December 31.

30 Issued Check No. 792 to First National Bank for $1,400 to purchase U.S. savings bonds for employees.

Instructions

1. Record the transactions.
2. Record the following adjusting entries on December 31:
   a. Salaries accrued: sales salaries, $2,950; officers' salaries, $1,310; office salaries, $440. The payroll taxes are immaterial and are not accrued.
   b. Vacation pay, $12,900.

Problem 10–3A

Bond premium; entries for bonds payable transactions

Goal 8

3. $415,075

Moresby Inc. produces and sells voltage regulators. On July 1, 2003, Moresby Inc. issued $8,000,000 of ten-year, 11% bonds priced at $8,498,492 to yield an effective interest rate of 10%. Interest on the bonds is payable semiannually on December 31 and June 30. The fiscal year of the company is the calendar year.

Instructions

1. Record the entry for the amount of the cash proceeds from the sale of the bonds.

(continued)

2. Record the entries for the following:
   a. The first semiannual interest payment on December 31, 2003, including the amortization of the bond premium, using the straight-line method.
   b. The interest payment on June 30, 2004, and the amortization of the bond premium, using the straight-line method.
3. Determine the total interest expense for 2003.
4. Will the bond proceeds always be greater than the face amount of the bonds when the contract rate is greater than the market rate of interest? Explain.

Problem 10-4A

Bond discount; entries for bonds payable transactions

Goal 8

3. $481,155

On July 1, 2003, Cucumber Communications Equipment Inc. issued $10,000,000 of ten-year, 9% bonds priced at $9,376,895 to yield an effective interest rate of 10%. Interest on the bonds is payable semiannually on December 31 and June 30. The fiscal year of the company is the calendar year.

Instructions

1. Record the entry for the amount of the cash proceeds from the sale of the bonds.
2. Record the entries for the following:
   a. The first semiannual interest payment on December 31, 2003, and the amortization of the bond discount, using the straight-line method. (Round to the nearest dollar.)
   b. The interest payment on June 30, 2004, and the amortization of the bond discount, using the straight-line method.
3. Determine the total interest expense for 2003.
4. Will the bond proceeds always be less than the face amount of the bonds when the contract rate is less than the market rate of interest? Explain.

Problem 10-5A

Entries for bonds payable transactions

Goal 8

2. a. $1,252,787

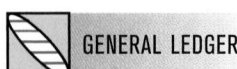

GENERAL LEDGER

Downing Co. produces and sells synthetic string for tennis rackets. The following transactions were completed by Downing Co., whose fiscal year is the calendar year:

2003

July 1 Issued $20,000,000 of 5-year, 14% callable bonds dated July 1, 2003, at an effective rate of 12%, receiving cash of $21,472,126. Interest is payable semiannually on December 31 and June 30.

Dec. 31 Paid the semiannual interest on the bonds.

31 Recorded bond premium amortization of $147,213, which was determined by using the straight-line method.

2004

June 30 Paid the semiannual interest on the bonds.

Dec. 31 Paid the semiannual interest on the bonds.

31 Recorded bond premium amortization of $294,425, which was determined by using the straight-line method.

2005

July 1 Recorded the redemption of the bonds, which were called at 102. The balance in the bond premium account is $883,275 after the payment of interest and amortization of premium have been recorded. (Record the redemption only.)

Instructions

1. Record the entries for the foregoing transactions.
2. Indicate the amount of the interest expense in (a) 2003 and (b) 2004.
3. Determine the carrying amount of the bonds as of December 31, 2004.

Problem 10-6A

Entries for bond investments

Goal 9

GENERAL LEDGER

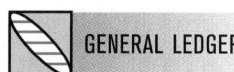

The following selected transactions relate to certain securities acquired by Custom Blueprints Inc., whose fiscal year ends on December 31:

2003

Sept.	1	Purchased $500,000 of Donner Company 20-year, 9% bonds dated July 1, 2003, directly from the issuing company, for $482,150 plus accrued interest of $7,500.
Dec.	31	Received the semiannual interest on the Donner Company bonds.
	31	Recorded bond discount amortization of $300 on the Donner Company bonds. The amortization amount was determined by using the straight-line method.

(Assume that all intervening transactions and adjustments have been properly recorded and that the number of bonds owned has not changed from December 31, 2003, to December 31, 2007.)

2008

June	30	Received the semiannual interest on the Donner Company bonds.
Oct.	31	Sold one-half of the Donner Company bonds at 96½ plus accrued interest. The broker deducted $400 for commission, etc., remitting the balance. Prior to the sale, $375 of discount on one-half of the bonds was amortized, reducing the carrying amount of those bonds to $243,400.
Dec.	31	Received the semiannual interest on the Donner Company bonds.
	31	Recorded bond discount amortization of $450 on the Donner Company bonds.

Instructions

Record the entries for the foregoing transactions.

Alternate Accounting Application Problems

Alternate Problem 10-1B

Liability transactions

Goals 3, 4

STUDENT SOLUTIONS MANUAL

GENERAL LEDGER

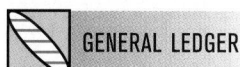

The following items were selected from among the transactions completed by Renaissance Products Co. during the current year:

Feb.	15	Purchased merchandise on account from Ranier Co., $24,000, terms n/30.
Mar.	17	Issued a 30-day, 8% note for $24,000 to Ranier Co., on account.
Apr.	16	Paid Ranier Co. the amount owed on the note of March 17.
July	15	Borrowed $20,000 from Security Bank, issuing a 90-day, 8% note.
	25	Purchased tools by issuing a $90,000, 120-day note to Sun Supply Co., which discounted the note at the rate of 7%.
Oct.	13	Paid Security Bank the interest due on the note of July 15 and renewed the loan by issuing a new 30-day, 9% note for $20,000. (Record both the debit and credit to the notes payable account.)
Nov.	12	Paid Security Bank the amount due on the note of October 13.
	22	Paid Sun Supply Co. the amount due on the note of July 25.
Dec.	1	Purchased office equipment from Valley Equipment Co. for $95,000, paying $15,000 and issuing a series of ten 12% notes for $8,000 each, coming due at 30-day intervals.
	17	Settled a product liability lawsuit with a customer for $46,000, payable in January. Renaissance accrued the loss in a litigation claims payable account.
	31	Paid the amount due Valley Equipment Co. on the first note in the series issued on December 1.

Instructions

1. Record the transactions.
2. Record the adjusting entry for each of the following accrued expenses at the end of the current year: (a) product warranty cost, $18,250; (b) interest on the nine remaining notes owed to Valley Equipment Co.

Alternate Problem 10-2B

Payroll accounts and year-end entries

Goal 5

STUDENT SOLUTIONS MANUAL

GENERAL LEDGER

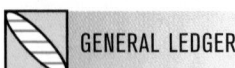

The following accounts, with the balances indicated, appear in the ledger of Mid States CableView Co. on December 1 of the current year:

Salaries Payable	–
FICA Tax Payable	$ 9,657
Employees Federal Income Tax Payable	12,321
Employees State Income Tax Payable	11,988
State Unemployment Tax Payable	1,180
Federal Unemployment Tax Payable	310
Bond Deductions Payable	1,200
Medical Insurance Payable	6,000
Operations Salaries Expense	847,000
Officers Salaries Expense	376,200
Office Salaries Expense	242,000
Payroll Taxes Expense	113,689

The following transactions relating to payroll, payroll deductions, and payroll taxes occurred during December:

Dec. 2 Issued Check No. 728 for $1,200 to First National Bank to purchase U.S. savings bonds for employees.

3 Issued Check No. 729 to First National Bank for $21,978, in payment of $9,657 of FICA tax and $12,321 of employees' federal income tax due.

14 Record the entry for the biweekly payroll. A summary of the payroll record follows:

Salary distribution:		
Operations	$38,000	
Officers	17,400	
Office	10,800	$66,200
Deductions:		
FICA tax	$ 4,634	
Federal income tax withheld	11,784	
State income tax withheld	2,979	
Savings bond deductions	600	
Medical insurance deductions	1,000	20,997
Net amount		$45,203

14 Issued Check No. 738 in payment of the net amount of the biweekly payroll.

14 Record the entry for payroll taxes on employees' earnings of December 14: FICA tax, $4,634; state unemployment tax, $285; federal unemployment tax, $75.

17 Issued Check No. 744 to First National Bank for $21,052, in payment of $9,268 of social security tax and $11,784 of employees' federal income tax due.

18 Issued Check No. 750 to Pico Insurance Company for $6,000, in payment of the semiannual premium on the group medical insurance policy.

28 Record the entry for the biweekly payroll. A summary of the payroll record follows:

Salary distribution:		
Operations	$39,000	
Officers	17,500	
Office	11,000	$67,500
Deductions:		
FICA tax	$ 4,658	
Federal income tax withheld	12,015	
State income tax withheld	3,038	
Savings bond deductions	600	20,311
Net amount		$47,189

28 Issued Check No. 782 in payment of the net amount of the biweekly payroll.
28 Record the entry for payroll taxes on employees' earnings of December 28: FICA tax, $4,658; state unemployment tax, $171; federal unemployment tax, $43.
30 Issued Check No. 791 to First National Bank for $1,200 to purchase U.S. savings bonds for employees.
30 Issued Check No. 792 for $18,005 to First National Bank in payment of employees' state income tax due on December 31.

Instructions

1. Record the transactions.
2. Record the following adjusting entries on December 31:
   a. Salaries accrued: operations salaries, $3,900; officers' salaries, $1,750; office salaries, $1,100. The payroll taxes are immaterial and are not accrued.
   b. Vacation pay, $11,000.

Alternate Problem 10–3B

Bond premium; entries for bonds payable transactions

Goal 8

3. $645,226

STUDENT SOLUTIONS MANUAL

Parnell Corporation produces and sells burial vaults. On July 1, 2003, Parnell Corporation issued $12,000,000 of ten-year, 12% bonds priced at $13,495,471 to yield an effective interest rate of 10%. Interest on the bonds is payable semiannually on December 31 and June 30. The fiscal year of the company is the calendar year.

Instructions

1. Record the entry for the amount of the cash proceeds from the sale of the bonds.
2. Record the entries for the following:
   a. The first semiannual interest payment on December 31, 2003, and the amortization of the bond premium, using the straight-line method. (Round to the nearest dollar.)
   b. The interest payment on June 30, 2004, and the amortization of the bond premium, using the straight-line method.
3. Determine the total interest expense for 2003.
4. Will the bond proceeds always be greater than the face amount of the bonds when the contract rate is greater than the market rate of interest? Explain.

Alternate Problem 10–4B

Bond discount; entries for bonds payable transactions

Goal 8

3. $418,010

On July 1, 2003, Raptor Corporation, a wholesaler of used robotic equipment, issued $7,500,000 of ten-year, 10% bonds priced at $6,639,795 to yield an effective interest rate of 12%. Interest on the bonds is payable semiannually on December 31 and June 30. The fiscal year of the company is the calendar year.

Instructions

1. Record the entry for the amount of the cash proceeds from the sale of the bonds.

(continued)

STUDENT SOLUTIONS MANUAL

2. Record the entries for the following:
   a. The first semiannual interest payment on December 31, 2003, and the amortization of the bond discount, using the straight-line method. (Round to the nearest dollar.)
   b. The interest payment on June 30, 2004, and the amortization of the bond discount, using the straight-line method.
3. Determine the total interest expense for 2003.
4. Will the bond proceeds always be less than the face amount of the bonds when the contract rate is less than the market rate of interest? Explain.

Alternate Problem 10-5B

Entries for bonds payable transactions

Goal 8

2. a. $477,220

STUDENT SOLUTIONS MANUAL

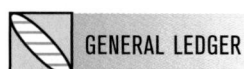

GENERAL LEDGER

The following transactions were completed by Shadwell Inc., whose fiscal year is the calendar year:

2003

July 1 Issued $10,000,000 of 5-year, 8% callable bonds dated July 1, 2003, at an effective rate of 10%, receiving cash of $9,227,796. Interest is payable semiannually on December 31 and June 30.

Dec. 31 Paid the semiannual interest on the bonds.

31 Recorded bond discount amortization of $77,220, which was determined by using the straight-line method.

2004

June 30 Paid the semiannual interest on the bonds.

Dec. 31 Paid the semiannual interest on the bonds.

31 Recorded bond discount amortization of $154,440, which was determined by using the straight-line method.

2005

June 30 Recorded the redemption of the bonds, which were called at $98\frac{1}{2}$. The balance in the bond discount account is $463,324 after payment of interest and amortization of discount have been recorded. (Record the redemption only.)

Instructions

1. Record the entries for the foregoing transactions.
2. Indicate the amount of the interest expense in (a) 2003 and (b) 2004.
3. Determine the carrying amount of the bonds as of December 31, 2004.

Alternative Problem 10-6B

Entries for bond investments

Goal 9

STUDENT SOLUTIONS MANUAL

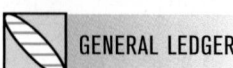

GENERAL LEDGER

Genesis Inc. develops and leases databases of publicly available information. The following selected transactions relate to certain securities acquired as a long-term investment by Genesis Inc., whose fiscal year ends on December 31:

2003

Sept. 1 Purchased $240,000 of Joshua Company 10-year, 8% bonds dated July 1, 2003, directly from the issuing company, for $247,375 plus accrued interest of $3,200.

Dec. 31 Received the semiannual interest on the Joshua Company bonds.

31 Recorded bond premium amortization of $250 on the Joshua Company bonds. The amortization amount was determined by using the straight-line method.

(Assume that all intervening transactions and adjustments have been properly recorded and that the number of bonds owned has not changed from December 31, 2003, to December 31, 2008.)

2009

June 30 Received the semiannual interest on the Joshua Company bonds.

Aug. 31 Sold one-half of the Joshua Company bonds at 102 plus accrued interest. The broker deducted $500 for commission, etc., remitting the balance. Prior to the sale, $250 of premium on one-half of the bonds is to be amortized, reducing the carrying amount of those bonds to $121,438.

Dec. 31 Received the semiannual interest on the Joshua Company bonds.

31 Recorded bond premium amortization of $375 on the Joshua Company bonds.

Instructions

Record the entries for the foregoing transactions.

Building Leadership Skills—Financial Analysis and Reporting

Case 10–1

Days' purchases in accounts payable ratio

Quality Stores Inc., a home and garden retailer, released the following selected financial information.

	(in thousands)
Accounts Payable (Feb. 3, 2001)	$132,319
Accounts Payable (Jan. 29, 2000)	124,012
Inventory (Feb. 3, 2001)	325,116
Inventory (Jan. 29, 2000)	365,383
Cost of Merchandise Sold (year ended Feb. 3, 2001)	826,539

Management's discussion on February 3, 2001, in the company's annual report, included the following:

> *Further, former management had instituted an ill-advised "trade-dating-for-discounts" strategy, which positioned the Company's trade payables as past due based on unusually short dating. At the same time, the spring overbuy problem prevented the Company from taking advantage of the discounts, leaving the Company with past due amounts as a result of the short dating and without the ability to earn the larger discounts that were based on that shorter dating.*
>
> *At February 3, 2001, approximately $81.2 million of trade payables were past current terms.*

Quality Stores declared bankruptcy in November of 2001.

a. Determine the days' purchases in accounts payable ratio for Quality Stores, Inc.
b. Interpret this ratio in light of management's comments and Wal-Mart's days' purchases in accounts payable ratio of 34 days.

Case 10–2

Short- and long-term debt disclosures

K2 Inc. is a sporting goods and recreational equipment company. The footnotes to its financial statements provide details of its long-term debt on December 31, 2001, as follows on the next page.

	2001 (in thousands)	2000
Notes payable due in seven equal annual principal installments through 2009, with annual interest payable at 9.01%	$ 50,000	$50,000
Notes payable due in six equal annual principal installments through 2004, with semiannual interest payable at 8.89%	13,336	17,780
Bank revolving credit line due September 30, 2004	26,500	6,500
Foreign lines of credit and other	13,878	150
	$103,714	$74,430
Less amounts due within one year	5,886	4,594
	$ 97,828	$69,836

The principal amount of long-term debt maturing in each of the five years following 2001 is:

	(in thousands)
2002	$ 5,886
2003	50,527
2004	11,587
2005	7,143
2006	7,143
Thereafter	21,428
	$103,714

a. Estimate the amount of interest expense on the December 31, 2001 debt balances, assuming that the bank and foreign credit lines had an interest rate of 8.75%.
b. Why might the actual annual interest expense reported for 2001 be different than the number calculated in (a)?
c. What percent of the total debt is due within one year of December 31, 2001? Round to two decimal places.
d. Where are the current maturities of long-term debt disclosed on the financial statements?
e. Why does the debt repayment schedule increase in 2003 and 2004, then drop in 2005 and 2006?

Case 10–3

Contingent liability disclosure

A contingent liability note disclosure from the Goodyear Tire and Rubber Co.'s December 31, 2000 financial statements is reproduced as follows:

At December 31, 2000, the Company had recorded liabilities aggregating $78.3 million for anticipated costs related to various environmental matters, primarily the remediation of numerous waste disposal sites and certain properties sold by the Company. These costs include legal and consulting fees, site studies, the design and implementation of remediation plans, post-remediation monitoring and related activities and will be paid over several years. The amount of the Company's ultimate liability in respect of these matters may be affected by several uncertainties, primarily the ultimate cost of required remediation and the extent to which other responsible parties contribute.

On January 20, 2001, the *Buffalo News* reported the following:

The federal government has settled its lawsuit with Goodyear Tire & Rubber Co. over contamination of the former Forest Glen mobile home park, paving the way for the recycling of the property as an industrial site.

Under the settlement, filed Friday in federal court, Goodyear will pay an estimated $13 million to clean up the site to federal specifications. Goodyear also will pay more than $9 million to reimburse the federal government for its cleanup and for damage to the environment caused by the waste.[8]

a. How would the $78.3 million in environmental liabilities be reported on Goodyear's financial statements, assuming that $50 million of this amount was estimated to be paid in 2001? Provide the journal entry.

b. How would Goodyear account for the Forest Glen cleanup payments during 2001, assuming that the cost was accrued on December 31, 2000?

Case 10–4

Current and quick ratios—industry comparison

The standard industrial classification (SIC) code is a four-digit number for classifying companies into different industries. SIC code 4813 is the four-digit code for telephone communications, including such companies as Sprint Corp. and BellSouth Corp. SIC code 5311 is the general department stores classification code, including such companies as Sears Roebuck & Co. and Saks, Inc. The average current and quick ratios for these two industries are provided in the table below.

	SIC Code 4813	SIC Code 5311	Difference
Average current ratio	0.5800	1.9080	1.3280
Average quick ratio	0.4275	0.7170	0.2895
Difference	0.1525	1.1910	

Representative current asset and current liability information from a recent balance sheet for two companies in these industries is shown as follows:

	BellSouth Corp., Dec. 31, 2001 (in millions)	JC Penney, Jan. 26, 2002 (in millions)
Cash	$ 592	$2,840
Accounts receivable	5,206	698
Merchandise inventory		4,930
Materials and supplies	382	
Other	675	209
Total current assets	$ 6,855	$8,677
Accounts payable	$ 1,656	$3,465
Short-term debt	5,111	935
Other*	3,301	99
Total current liabilities	$10,068	$4,499

*For BellSouth, this amount includes customer deposits and accrued expenses.

a. Why is the average current ratio of department stores 1.328 greater than the average current ratio of telephone communication companies?

(continued)

8 Andrew Z. Galarneau, *Buffalo News*, p. B3, January 20, 2001.

b. Why is the average quick ratio of department stores 0.2895 greater than the average quick ratio of telephone communication companies?
c. Why are the differences between the current and quick ratios much larger for department stores than they are for telephone communication equipment companies (1.191 vs. 0.1525)?

Case 10–5

Current and quick ratios across time

The current assets and current liabilities for Texas Instruments Inc. for five recent years are shown as follows (in millions):

	12/31/01	12/31/00	12/31/99	12/31/98	12/31/97
Cash	$ 431	$ 745	$ 781	$ 632	$1,015
Marketable Securities	2,513	3,258	2,045	1,709	2,005
Accounts Receivable	1,198	2,204	1,909	1,373	1,705
Inventories	751	1,233	894	618	742
Other Current Assets*	882	675	724	667	636
Total Current Assets	$5,775	$8,115	$6,353	$4,999	$6,103
Notes Payable	$ 38	$ 148	$ 331	$ 267	$ 71
Accounts Payable	1,205	1,921	1,722	1,606	2,082
Accrued Expenses	10	421	374	153	189
Income Taxes Payable	327	323	270	197	154
Total Current Liabilities	$1,580	$2,813	$2,697	$2,223	$2,496

*These are prepaid expenses and other nonquick assets.

a. Calculate and graph the current and quick ratios for the five comparative years.
b. Interpret your graph.

Case 10–6

Long-term solvency measures for two aerospace companies

The Lockheed Martin Corp. and Northrop Grumman Corp. are two major defense contractors. A partial balance sheet for the end of a recent fiscal year is shown as follows (in millions):

	Lockheed Martin Dec. 31, 2001	Northrop Grumman Dec. 31, 2001
Liabilities and stockholders' equity:		
Total current liabilities	$ 9,689	$ 5,132
Long-term debt	7,422	5,033
Post-retirement benefit liabilities	1,565	1,931
Deferred income taxes	992	669
Other noncurrent liabilities	1,543	730
Total stockholders' equity	6,443	7,391
Total liabilities and stockholders' equity	$27,654	$20,886

The interest expense, income tax expense, and net income (before unusual items) were as follows for both companies:

	Lockheed Martin 2001	Northrop Grumman 2001
Interest expense	$700	$373
Income tax expense	109	272
Net income from continuing operations	(79)	427

a. Determine the total liabilities to total assets ratio for each company.
b. Determine the number of times interest charges are earned for each company.
c. Interpret your results.

Case 10–7

Ratio of total liabilities to total assets–banking industry

The ratio of total liabilities to total assets for the 12 largest bank holding companies reported to the SEC for a recent year are shown in the table below. The average ratio of total liabilities to total assets for the group is 92.6%. This means that the average debt held by these banks is over 92% of their total assets, which is much more than in any other industry.

Bank Holding Company (>$10B sales)	Ratio of Total Liabilities to Total Assets
Bank of America Corp.	0.918
Bank One Corp.	0.930
Citicorp	0.913
Fleetboston Financial Corp.	0.909
Household International Inc.	0.885
HSBC Holdings PLC	0.934
J P Morgan & Co. Inc.	0.951
J P Morgan Chase & Co.	0.932
Mitsubishi Tokyo Financial Group	0.955
Wachovia Corp.	0.939
Washington Mutual Inc.	0.947
Wells Fargo & Co.	0.899
Average	0.926

Why are these ratios so large?

Business Leadership Skills– Responsible Leadership

Activity 10–1

Business strategy

One reason that PepsiCo purchased Quaker Oats in 2001 was to acquire rights to its sports drink, Gatorade. However, Gatorade is under increasing pressure from its competitors, including Coca-Cola's Powerade. As a result, PepsiCo is initiating an aggressive advertising campaign to promote and grow sales of Gatorade.

GROUP ACTIVITY

In groups of three or four, answer the following questions:

1. Go to the Gatorade Web site at http://gatorade.com. (a) How and why was Gatorade developed? (b) What is Gatorade's share of the sports-drink market?
2. Drinks can be labeled as sports, lifestyle, or active thirst drinks. (a) How would you describe each of these drink labels? (b) Give an example of what you would label a sports, lifestyle, and active thirst drink.
3. Do you think PepsiCo's advertising campaign will focus on Gatorade as a sports, lifestyle, or active thirst drink? Explain.

Activity 10–2

Employment ethics

ETHICS

Marge McMaster is a certified public accountant (CPA) and a staff assistant for Tester and Morris, a local CPA firm. The firm's policy had been to provide a holiday bonus equal to two weeks' salary to all employees. The firm's new management team announced on November 25 that a bonus equal to only one week's salary would be made available to employees this year. Marge thought that this policy was unfair because she and her co-workers planned on the full two-week bonus. The two-week bonus had been given for ten straight years, so it seemed as though the firm had breached an implied commitment. Thus, Marge decided that she would make up the lost bonus week by working an extra six hours of overtime per week over the next five weeks until the end of the year. Tester and Morris' policy is to pay overtime at 150% of straight time.

Marge's supervisor was surprised to see overtime being reported, since there is generally very little additional or unusual client service demands at the end of the calendar year. However, the overtime was not questioned, since firm employees are on the "honor system" in reporting their overtime.

Discuss whether the firm is acting in an ethical manner by changing the bonus. Is Marge behaving in an ethical manner?

Activity 10–3

Salary survey

Several Internet services provide career guidance, classified employment ads, placement services, résumé posting, career questionnaires, and salary surveys. Select one of the following Internet sites to determine current average salary levels for one of your career options:

www.cfstaffing.com/salary/index.html	Accounting salary information
www.joboptions.com	Links to computer, engineering, finance, marketing, and accounting salary information
www.occ.com	Online Career Center, with links to salary information
www.imanet.org	Institute of Management Accountants salary survey information (see Career Center)

Activity 10–4

General Electric bond issuance

ETHICS

General Electric Capital, a division of General Electric, uses long-term debt extensively. In early 2002, GE Capital issued $11 billion in long-term debt to investors, then within days filed legal documents to prepare for another $50 billion long-term debt issue. As a result of the $50 billion filing, the price of the initial $11 billion offering declined (due to higher risk of more debt).

> *Bill Gross, a manager of a bond investment fund, "denounced a 'lack in candor' related to GE's recent debt deal. 'It was the most recent and most egregious example of how bondholders are mistreated.' Gross argued that GE was not forthright when GE Capital recently issued $11 billion in bonds, one of the largest issues ever from a U.S. corporation. What bothered Gross is that three days after the issue the company announced its intention to sell as much as $50 billion in additional debt, warrants, preferred stock, guarantees, letters of credit and promissory notes at some future date."*

In your opinion, did GE Capital act unethically by selling $11 billion of long-term debt without telling those investors that a few days later it would be filing documents to prepare for another $50 billion debt offering?

Source: Jennifer Ablan, "Gross Shakes the Bond Market; GE Calms It, a Bit," *Barron's*, March 25, 2002.

Activity 10-5

Investing in bonds

GROUP ACTIVITY

Select a bond from listings that appear daily in *The Wall Street Journal*, and summarize the information related to the bond you select. Include the following information in your summary:

1. Contract rate of interest
2. Year when the bond matures
3. Current yield (effective rate of interest)
4. Closing price of bond (indicate date)
5. Other information noted about the bond, such as whether it is a zero-coupon bond (see the Explanatory Notes to the listings)

In groups of three or four, share the information you developed about the bond you selected. As a group, select one bond in which to invest $100,000, and prepare a justification for your choice for presentation to the class. For example, your justification should include a consideration of risk and return.

Activity 10-6

Bond ratings

Moody's Investors Service maintains a Web site at www.Moodys.com. One of the services offered at this site is a listing of announcements of recent bond rating changes. Visit this site and read over some of these announcements. Write down several of the reasons provided for rating downgrades and upgrades. If you were a bond investor or bond issuer, would you care if Moody's changed the rating on your bonds? Why or why not?

Answers to Self-Study Questions

1. **B** The net amount available to a borrower from discounting a note payable is called the proceeds. The proceeds of $4,900 (answer B) is determined as follows:

Face amount of note	$5,000
Less discount ($5,000 × 12% × 60/360)	100
Proceeds	$4,900

2. **B** Employers are usually required to withhold a portion of their employees' earnings for payment of federal income taxes (answer A), Medicare tax (answer C), and state and local income taxes (answer D). Generally, federal unemployment compensation taxes (answer B) are levied against the employer only and thus are not deducted from employee earnings.

3. **D** Current ratio: $800,000/$200,000 = 4.0
Quick ratio: ($100,000 + $300,000)/$200,000 = 2.0

4. **B** The amount debited to the investment account is the cost of the bonds, which includes the amount paid to the seller for the bonds (101% × $100,000) plus broker's commissions ($50), or $101,050 (answer B). The $2,000 of accrued interest that is paid to the seller should be debited to Interest Revenue, since it is an offset against the amount that will be received as interest at the next interest date.

5. **D** The number of times interest charges are earned is determined as: ($500,000 + $100,000)/$100,000, or 6.0.

Chapter 11
Stockholders' Equity: Capital Stock and Dividends

THE LAW OF VICTORY

"Leaders find a way for the team to win"

–The 21 Irrefutable Laws of Leadership

Dr. John C. Maxwell

Learning Goals

1 Describe the nature of the corporate form of organization.

2 List the major sources of paid-in capital, including the various classes of stock.

3 Describe the financial statement effects of issuing stock.

4 Describe the financial statement effects of treasury stock transactions.

5 Describe the effect of stock splits on the financial statements.

6 Analyze the impact of issuing common stock or bonds.

7 Describe the financial statement effects of cash dividends and stock dividends.

8 Compute and interpret the dividend yield and dividend payout ratio on common stock.

9 Describe financial statement presentations of stockholders' equity.

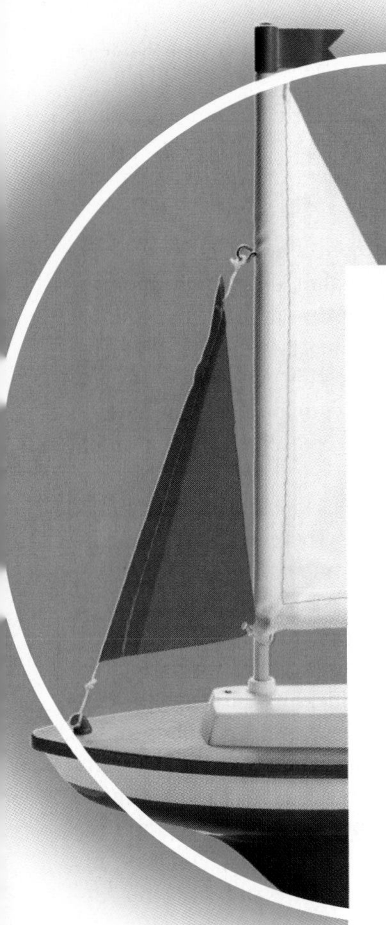

Mattel, Inc.

Mattel, Inc. designs, manufactures, and markets a broad variety of toy products, including the famous Barbie dolls and Hot Wheels. Its worldwide sales total almost $5 billion. The co-founders of Mattel were Harold "Matt" Matson and Ruth and Elliott Handler, who combined "Matt" and "Elliott" to form the name "Mattel."

Mattel didn't begin business as a toy manufacturer. Instead, its initial products when it began operations in the 1940s were picture frames! However, Mattel quickly moved into the toy business, producing dollhouse furniture, ukuleles, plastic pianos, music boxes, and toy guns. In the mid-1950s, ABC approached Mattel with an offer to sponsor a 15-minute segment of a new network television show. Mattel had to commit for a full year at a cost of $500,000. This was over three times Mattel's budgeted advertising and almost equal to its net worth at that time. The show was "The Mickey Mouse Club," produced by Walt Disney.

As a result of its nationwide television exposure, Mattel's sales increased from $5 million to $14 million in just three years. But Mattel's biggest success was yet to come.

In 1956 while touring Switzerland on vacation, the Handlers spotted a store window featuring eleven-inch, adult-styled toy dolls. Both Ruth and her daughter fell in love with the dolls, and the idea was born to produce an adult-looking doll for girls. The final product, named after Ruth's daughter, finally appeared in 1959 as Barbie. Soon afterwards, a companion male doll appeared–Ken, named after Ruth's son. Mattel's sales and profits exploded.

Today, more than one billion Barbie dolls have been sold in over 150 countries. Some of the more interesting Barbie doll facts include the following:

> *Today's Barbie is more beautiful than the first Barbie. The first Barbie was designed to not be so pretty as to intimidate young girls.*
>
> *Barbie initially came as a blonde, brunette, or redhead. Ruth's daughter was a redhead, but the blonde Barbie was by far the most popular.*
>
> *The first Barbie sold for $3. The accompanying clothes were packaged separately and priced between $1 and $3. The business strategy was to make the profits on the accessories.*
>
> *Over time, Barbie has evolved with society and modern culture. For example, during the Kennedy presidency, Barbie had a Jacqueline Kennedy hairdo.*
>
> *In response to criticism that Barbie's figure created unrealistic expectations for young girls, Mattel began offering Barbie in a variety of career choices, such as doctors and astronauts.*

Like most large businesses, Mattel is a corporation, with total stockholders' equity of over $1.7 billion. Included in Mattel's stockholders' equity are common stock of $436 million, additional paid-in capital of $1.6 billion, and treasury stock of $162 million. In this chapter, we illustrate and discuss the common components of stockholders' equity, including common stock, additional paid-in capital, and treasury stock.

Source: Adapted from *Dream Doll: The Ruth Handler Story*, by Ruth Handler, with Jacqueline Shannon (Longmeadow Press, Stamford, Connecticut: 1994); "Ruth Handler, Whose Barbie Gave Dolls Curves, Dies at 85," by Sarah Kershaw, *The New York Times*, April 29, 2002; and "Flatter, Smarter, and Socially Sensitive," by Tamar Lewin, *The New York Times*, November 29, 1997.

Your Need to Know

If you purchased 100 shares of Microsoft Corp., you would own a small interest in the company. These shares might increase in value or decrease in value, depending upon the market's perception of the future earnings prospects of the firm. In addition, the number of shares outstanding might impact the value of your shares. Thus, you would want the financial statements to inform you of any changes in your underlying proportion of ownership. For example, new issues of common stock would dilute your proportional interest in the firm, while reductions in the outstanding stock would increase your proportional interest in the firm.

The shares might also pay a dividend, which is a return of cash to the stockholders. Would you invest in a company that didn't pay any dividends? There are many companies that do not pay dividends, yet they remain attractive investments. Why is this?

To answer this question a firm's dividend policy should be viewed from a longer-term perspective. A firm should use excess cash from operations to maximize the shareholders' wealth. If a firm's internal investment opportunities provide returns that exceed what individual shareholders could earn on their own, then the shareholders would want the firm to retain the cash for internal investment. On the other hand, if the internal opportunities are limited, then the shareholders would want the cash distributed as dividends. In this way, the shareholders could directly put the dividends to good use. So the amount of the dividends should be related, in part, to the investment opportunities facing the firm. This is why growth companies, such as Microsoft and Cisco Systems, do not pay any dividends, while other companies, such as Procter & Gamble, Coca-Cola, and Bank of America, pay dividends.

In this chapter, we will present accounting for common stock and dividends. We will also present some analysis tools for evaluating common stock and dividend policy.

Nature of a Corporation

1 Describe the nature of the corporate form of organization.

More than 70 percent of all businesses are proprietorships and 10 percent are partnerships. Most of these businesses are small businesses. The remaining 20 percent of businesses are corporations. Many corporations are large, and, as a result, they generate more than 90 percent of the total business dollars in the United States.

Characteristics of a Corporation

Corporations have several advantages and disadvantages over proprietorships or partnerships. These are described in Exhibit 1.

A *corporation* is a legal entity, distinct and separate from the individuals who create and operate it. As a legal entity, a corporation may acquire, own, and dispose of property in

Exhibit 1

Advantage and Disadvantages of the Corporate Form

Advantages	**Disadvantages**
Separate legal existence	Owner is separate from management
Continuous life	Double taxation of dividends
An ability to raise large amounts of capital	
Owners can transfer ownership rights without affecting the corporation	
Limited liability	

its own name. It may also incur liabilities and enter into contracts. As a result of being a separate legal entity, the corporation's life continues independent of the owners (as long as it is financially successful). For example, General Electric was founded in 1892 by Thomas Edison, and it exists today, long after the founder's death.

Because a corporation is a legal entity, it can sell shares of ownership, called **stock**, without affecting its operations or continued existence. The **stockholders** or *shareholders* who own the stock own the corporation. Corporations whose shares of stock are traded in public markets are called *public corporations*. The Coca-Cola Corporation is a well-known public corporation. Corporations whose shares are not traded publicly are usually owned by a small group of investors and are called *nonpublic* or *private corporations*. The Mars Candy Company, which is owned by the Mars family, is a well-known private corporation.

Corporations can become large because they have the ability to raise large amounts of capital by selling stock broadly to the general public. Moreover, stockholders can buy and sell stock between themselves without affecting the corporation.

The stockholders of a corporation have *limited liability*. This means that a corporation's creditors usually may not go beyond the assets of the corporation to satisfy their claims. Thus, the financial loss that a stockholder may suffer is limited to the amount invested. This feature has contributed to the rapid growth of the corporate form of business.

Among the disadvantages, the stockholders do not directly control a corporation. Thus, stockholders must protect their interests by electing a *board of directors* that is responsible for representing stockholder interests. The board meets periodically to establish corporate policies. It also selects the chief executive officer (CEO) and other major officers to manage the corporation's day-to-day affairs. When owner and manager interests diverge, the board of directors should represent the shareholders' interests. If the board is not sufficiently independent of management, it is possible for shareholder interests to be poorly represented.

As a separate entity, a corporation is subject to taxes. For example, corporations must pay federal income taxes on their income.[1] Thus, corporate income that is distributed to stockholders in the form of *dividends* has already been taxed. In turn, stockholders must

Ethics in Action
The Responsible Board

Recent corporate failures, such as Enron and Global Crossing, have highlighted the roles of boards of directors in executing their responsibilities. New standards for corporate governance are being suggested, such as (1) independent directors to oversee management, (2) board member expertise and education, (3) separation of the Board Chairmanship from the CEO position, (4) transparent disclosure of all board activities and transactions with the corporation (insider trades), and (5) an independent audit committee. Indeed, one study found that "audit committees of companies where financial statement fraud has occurred generally were less independent, less expert, met less often and were less likely to have internal audit support."

Sources: R. Luke, "Inquisitive Directors: Tough Audit Questions Loom Large Since Enron, *Atlanta Journal–Constitution*, March 29, 2002; and *21st Century Governance Principles for U.S. Corporations* (Corporate Governance Center), 2002.

---

1 Many states also require corporations to pay income taxes.

pay income taxes on the dividends they receive. This *double taxation* of corporate earnings is a major disadvantage of the corporate form.[2]

Forming a Corporation

The first step in forming a corporation is to file an *application of incorporation* with the state. State incorporation laws differ, and corporations often organize in those states with the more favorable laws. For this reason, more than half of the largest companies are incorporated in Delaware. Exhibit 2 lists some corporations that you may be familiar with, their states of incorporation, and the location of their headquarters.

Exhibit 2

Examples of Corporations and Their States of Incorporation

Corporation	State of Incorporation	Headquarters
Caterpillar, Inc.	Delaware	Peoria, Ill.
Delta Air Lines, Inc.	Delaware	Atlanta, Ga.
Dow Chemical Company	Delaware	Midland, Mich.
General Electric Company	New York	Fairfield, Conn.
The Home Depot	Delaware	Atlanta, Ga.
Kellogg Company	Delaware	Battle Creek, Mich.
3M	Delaware	St. Paul, Minn.
May Department Stores	New York	St. Louis, Mo.
RJ Reynolds Tobacco	Delaware	Winston-Salem, N.C.
Sun Microsystems, Inc	Delaware	Palo Alto, CA.
The Washington Post Company	Delaware	Washington, D.C.
Whirlpool Corporation	Delaware	Benton Harbor, Mich.

After the application of incorporation has been approved, the state grants a *charter* or *articles of incorporation*. The articles of incorporation formally create the corporation.[3] The corporate management and board of directors then prepare a set of *bylaws*, which are the rules and procedures for conducting the corporation's affairs.

Ethics in Action

Avoiding Corporate Income Taxes

Corporations can be formed for not-for-profit purposes by making a request to the Internal Revenue Service under Internal Revenue Code section 501(c)3. Such corporations are exempt from federal taxes. Forming businesses inside a 501(c)3 exempt organization that competes with profit-making (and hence, tax-paying) businesses is very controversial. For example, should the local YMCA receive a tax exemption for providing similar services as the local health club business? The IRS is now challenging such businesses and is withholding 501(c)3 status to many organizations due to this issue.

---

2 Under the *Internal Revenue Code*, a corporation with a few stockholders may elect to be treated like a partnership for income tax purposes. Such corporations are known as Subchapter S corporations.

3 The articles of incorporation may also restrict a corporation's activities in certain areas, such as owning certain types of real estate, conducting certain types of business activities, or purchasing its own stock.

Significant costs may be incurred in organizing a corporation. These costs include legal fees, taxes, state incorporation fees, license fees, and promotional costs. Such costs are recorded as an expense for the period incurred.

Sources of Paid-In Capital

2 List the major sources of paid-in capital, including the various classes of stock.

The managers of a corporation are responsible for establishing the capital structure of a company. The *capital structure* of a company is the percentage of total assets that is financed by creditors and the percentage that is financed by owners. The financing from owners comes from two main sources of stockholders' equity: (1) paid-in capital (or contributed capital) and (2) retained earnings. The main source of paid-in capital is from issuing stock, which we will discuss in the next sections.

Common Stock

When only one class of stock is issued, it is called **common stock**. In this case, each share of common stock has equal rights. The major rights that accompany ownership of a share of stock are as follows:

1. The right to vote in matters concerning the corporation.
2. The right to share in distributions of earnings.
3. The right to share in assets on liquidation.

Number of shares authorized, issued, and outstanding

The distribution of earnings is called a *dividend*. The board of directors of a corporation has the sole authority to distribute dividends to the stockholders. When such action is taken, the directors are said to declare a dividend. Since dividends are normally based on earnings, a corporation cannot guarantee dividends. For example, AT&T recently slashed its dividend by 80 percent due to financial constraints in the company.

The number of shares of stock that a corporation is *authorized* to issue is stated in its charter. The term *issued* refers to the shares issued to the stockholders. A corporation may, under circumstances we discuss later in this chapter, reacquire some of the stock that it has issued. The stock remaining in the hands of stockholders is then called **outstanding stock**. The relationship between authorized, issued, and outstanding stock is shown in the graphic at the left.

Shares of stock are often assigned a monetary amount, called **par**. Corporations may issue *stock certificates* to stockholders to document their ownership. Printed on a stock certificate is the par value of the stock, the name of the stockholder, and the number of shares owned. Stock may also be issued without par, in which case it is called *no-par stock*. Some states require the board of directors to assign a **stated value** to no-par stock.

Because corporations have limited liability, creditors have no claim against the personal assets of stockholders. However, some state laws require that corporations maintain a minimum *stockholder* contribution to protect creditors. This minimum amount is called *legal capital*. The amount of required legal capital varies among the states, but it usually includes the amount of par or stated value of the shares of stock issued.

Q&A: On its balance sheet, a corporation reports the following three numbers related to its common stock: 200,000 shares; 150,000 shares; and 138,000 shares. What is the number of shares authorized, issued, outstanding, and reacquired?

200,000 shares authorized; 150,000 shares issued; 138,000 shares outstanding; 12,000 (150,000 − 138,000) shares reacquired.

Market for Common Stock

A public company may sell common stock to the general public, which can then be traded on a stock exchange. There are three major types of stock market transactions:

1. *An initial public offering (IPO).* An IPO is a company's first issue of common stock to the public, and thus the first step to becoming a publicly owned company. Closely held companies become publicly owned through an IPO. For example, United Parcel Service was one of the largest privately held companies in the U.S., until it conducted an IPO to raise capital for expansion. IPOs are also common for corporate spin-offs into separate publicly held companies. For example, Philip Morris Co. sold Kraft Foods Inc. to the public through an IPO. Kraft is now a separate publicly owned company. The issuing company will often use *investment bankers* to help sell an IPO to the general public. This is called the *primary market.*
2. *Additional shares sold by an established public company.* Established publicly owned companies can raise additional equity capital by selling common stock to the public. Since the company already has publicly traded shares, such an issuance is not an IPO. The company can issue additional shares through the primary market. Alternatively, shares can be sold directly to large sophisticated investors in what is termed a *private placement.*
3. *Market exchanges between owners of a publicly held company.* By far the most widespread stock market transactions occur between buyers and sellers of outstanding common stock. These transactions occur on the *secondary market.* The largest secondary markets in the United States are the NYSE (New York Stock Exchange) and NASDAQ (National Association of Security Dealers Automated Quotation). The market price can be determined for any company listed on an organized exchange from numerous Internet sites and from daily financial publications. A sample quotation from the *Wall Street Journal* for Wal-Mart Stores, Inc., is explained as follows:

YTD % CHG	52 Weeks Hi	Lo	Stock	Sym	Div	Yld %	PE	Vol 100s	LAST	Net Chg
−0.2	58^{75}	41^{50}	WalMart	WMT	.28	.5	37	60421	53^{04}	+0.03

The preceding quotation is interpreted as follows:

YTD % CHG	The year-to-date cumulative percentage change in the price
Hi	Highest price during the past 52 weeks
Lo	Lowest price during the past 52 weeks
Stock	Name of the company
Sym	Stock exchange symbol (WMT for Wal-Mart)
Div	Dividends paid per share during the past year
Yld %	Annual dividend yield per share, based on the closing price (Wal-Mart's 0.5% yield on common stock is computed as $0.28/$53.04)
PE	Price-earnings ratio on common stock (price ÷ earnings per share)
Vol	The volume of stock traded in 100s for that day
LAST	Closing price for the day
Net Chg	The net change in price from the previous day

Preferred Stock

To appeal to a broader investment market, a corporation may issue one or more classes of stock with various preference rights. A common example of such a right is the preference to dividends. Such a stock is generally called a **preferred stock**. Similar to common stock, preferred stock trades in the secondary markets, such as the New York Stock Exchange.

Ethics in Action

What's the Real Value?

Stock fraud often involves illegal methods to sell stock or other investments at a price that is higher than its actual value. This can be done through illegally manipulating the stock price, selling stock in nonexistent companies, or using the proceeds of later investors to pay off earlier investors (pyramid scheme). You can avoid these kinds of fraud by following three rules:

1. Don't invest in small new companies that have market prices below $1, based on hot tips from callers in high-pressure "boiler rooms."
2. Don't invest on advice from acquaintances in social or religious groups, without checking the merits yourself.
3. Don't invest in unsolicited "risk-free" and "guaranteed" investments that promise quick profits if you act immediately.

The dividend rights of preferred stock are usually stated in monetary terms or as a percent of par. For example, *$4 preferred stock* has a right to an annual $4 per share dividend. If the par value of the preferred stock was $50, the same right to dividends could be stated as *8% ($4/$50) preferred stock.*

A corporation cannot guarantee dividends, even to preferred stockholders. However, because they have first rights to any dividends, the preferred stockholders have a greater chance of receiving regular dividends than do the common stockholders.

Cumulative preferred stock has a right to receive regular dividends that have been passed (not declared) before any common stock dividends are paid. Noncumulative preferred stock does not have this right. Dividends that have been passed are said to be *in arrears.* Such dividends should be disclosed, normally in a footnote to the financial statements.

To illustrate how dividends on cumulative preferred stock are calculated, assume that a corporation has 1,000 shares of $4 cumulative preferred stock and 4,000 shares of common stock outstanding, and that no dividends were paid in 2003 and 2004. In 2005, the board of directors declares dividends of $22,000. Exhibit 3 shows how the dividends paid in 2005 are distributed between the preferred and common stockholders.

Exhibit 3

Dividends to Cumulative Preferred Stock

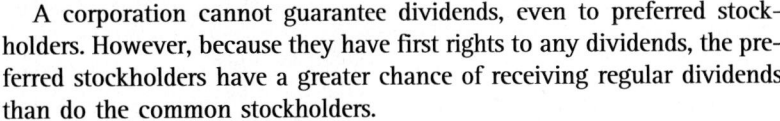

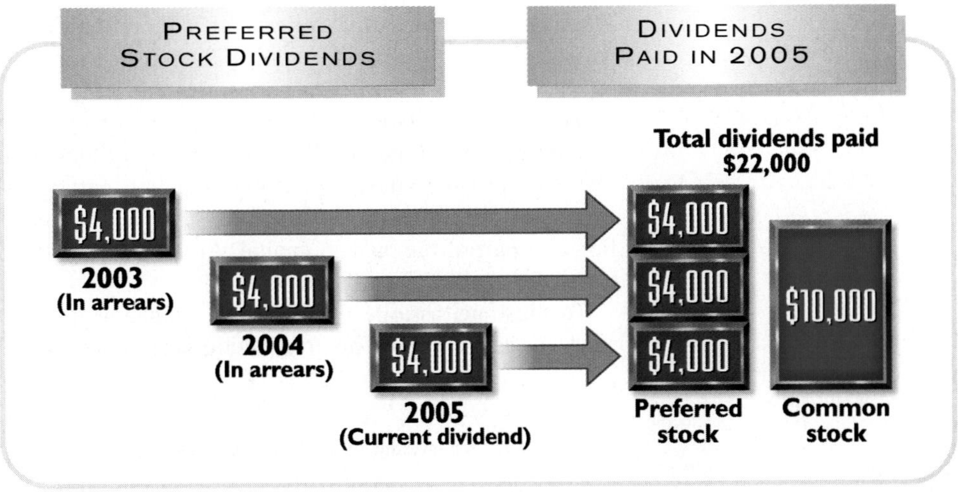

Exhibit 3
Concluded

Amount distributed		$22,000
Preferred dividend (1,000 shares):		
2003 dividend in arrears	$4,000	
2004 dividend in arrears	4,000	
2005 dividend	4,000	12,000
Common dividend (4,000 shares)		$10,000
Dividends per share:		
Preferred		$ 12.00
Common		2.50

Issuing Stock

3 Describe the financial statement effects of issuing stock.

A separate account is used for recording the amount of each class of stock issued to investors in a corporation. For example, assume that a corporation is authorized to issue 10,000 shares of preferred stock, $100 par, and 100,000 shares of common stock, $20 par. One-half of each class of authorized shares is issued at par for cash. The corporation's stock issue is recorded as follows:[4]

Cash	1,500,000	
Preferred Stock		500,000
Common Stock		1,000,000

Stock is often issued by a corporation at a price other than its par. This is because the par value of a stock is simply its legal capital. The price at which stock can be sold by a corporation depends on a variety of factors, such as:

1. The financial condition, earnings record, and dividend record of the corporation.
2. Investor expectations of the corporation's potential earning power.
3. General business and economic conditions and prospects.

Premium on Stock

When stock is issued for a price that is more than its par, the stock has sold at a **premium**. Thus, if stock with a par of $1 is issued for a price of $55, the stock has sold at a premium of $54.

When stock is issued at a premium, Cash or other asset accounts are debited for the amount received. Common Stock or Preferred Stock is then credited for the par amount. The excess of the amount paid over par is a part of the total investment of the stockholders in the corporation. Therefore, such an amount in excess of par should be classified as a part of the paid-in capital. An account entitled *Paid-In Capital in Excess of Par* is usually credited for this amount.

To illustrate, assume that Caldwell Company issues 2,000 shares of $1 par common stock for cash at $55. This transaction is recorded on the next page.

---

4 The accounting for investments in stocks from the point of view of the investor is discussed in the next chapter.

Cash	110,000	
Common Stock		2,000
Paid-In Capital in Excess of Par—Common Stock		108,000
Issued $1 par common stock at $55.		

When stock is issued in exchange for assets other than cash, such as land, buildings, and equipment, the assets acquired should be recorded at their fair market value. If this value cannot be objectively determined, the fair market price of the stock issued may be used.

To illustrate, assume that a corporation acquired land for which the fair market value cannot be determined. In exchange, the corporation issued 10,000 shares of its $10 par preferred stock. Assuming that the stock has a current market price of $12 per share, this transaction is recorded as follows:

Land	120,000	
Common Stock		100,000
Paid-In Capital in Excess of Par—Preferred Stock		20,000
Issued $10 par preferred stock at $12 per share, for land.		

No-Par Stock

In most states, both preferred and common stock may be issued without a par value. When no-par stock is issued, the entire proceeds are credited to the stock account. This is true, even though the issue price varies from time to time. For example, assume that a corporation issues 10,000 shares of no-par common stock at $40 a share, and at a later date issues 1,000 additional shares at $36. The no-par stock is recorded as follows:

Cash	400,000	
Common Stock		400,000
Cash	36,000	
Common Stock		36,000

Some states require that the entire proceeds from the issue of no-par stock be recorded as legal capital. In this case, the preceding entries would be proper. In other states, no-par stock may be assigned a *stated value per share*. The stated value is recorded like a par value, and the excess of the proceeds over the stated value is recorded as follows:

Cash	400,000	
Common Stock		250,000
Paid-In Capital in Excess of Stated Value		150,000
Issued 10,000 shares of no-par common at $40; stated value, $25.		

(continued)

Cash	36,000	
Common Stock		25,000
Paid-In Capital in Excess of Stated Value		11,000
Issued 1,000 shares of no-par common at $36; stated value, $25.		

Stock Options

One method of motivating employees to behave in the best interests of the owners is to provide the employees with common stock at a discount from the market price. A common method for doing this is by way of an employee **stock option**. Over 95 percent of large companies use stock option plans to reward employees. Stock options can be very lucrative for senior executives. For example, stock option gains represented 58 percent of the total senior executive compensation in 2001. Sanford Weill, CEO of Citigroup, cashed in over $200 million in stock options in 2001, thus making him one of the highest paid CEOs in the U.S.

Stock options grant an employee the right to purchase common stock at a fixed price for a limited period of time. The stock option price is called the *exercise price*, and the limited time period is called the *exercise period*. Stock options are often granted to employees at an exercise price equal to the market price on the grant date. If the market price of the stock exceeds the exercise price at any time during the exercise period, it is beneficial for the employee to exercise the option. Exercising the stock option allows the employee to purchase the common stock at a price below the prevailing market price, which may then be sold to realize gains.

Stock options can have many unique features. For example, the employee receiving the stock option may be required to hold the option for a period of time until it can be exercised. Such a waiting period is called a *vesting period*. Due to the complexity of stock options, the accounting treatment is covered in advanced accounting courses.

Treasury Stock

4 Describe the financial statement effects of treasury stock transactions.

A corporation may buy its own stock to provide shares for resale to employees, for reissuing shares as a bonus to employees, or for supporting the market price of the stock. For example, General Motors bought back its common stock and stated that two primary uses of this stock would be for stock option plans and employee savings plans. Such stock that a corporation has once issued and then reacquired is called **treasury stock**. The 2001 edition of *Accounting Trends & Techniques* indicated that over 68 percent of the companies surveyed reported treasury stock.

A commonly used method of accounting for the purchase and resale of treasury stock is the *cost method*.[5] When the stock is purchased by the corporation, the account *Treasury Stock* is debited for its cost (the price paid for it). The par value and the price at which the stock was originally issued are ignored. When the stock is resold, Treasury Stock is credited for its cost, and any difference between the cost and the selling price is normally debited or credited to *Paid-In Capital from Sale of Treasury Stock*.

To illustrate, assume that the paid-in capital of a corporation is as shown on the next page.

5 Another method that is infrequently used, called the *par value method*, is discussed in advanced accounting texts.

Common stock, $25 par (20,000 shares authorized and issued)	$500,000	
Excess of issue price over par	150,000	$650,000

The purchase of 1,000 shares of treasury stock at a price of $45 per share is recorded as follows:

Treasury Stock	45,000	
Cash		45,000

If 200 shares of treasury stock were resold at $60 per share, it is recorded as:

Cash	12,000	
Treasury Stock		9,000
Paid-In Capital from Sale of Treasury Stock		3,000

If at a later date another 200 shares of treasury stock are sold for $40 per share, it would be recorded as:

Cash	8,000	
Paid-In Capital from Sale of Treasury Stock	1,000	
Treasury Stock		9,000

INTERNATIONAL PERSPECTIVE

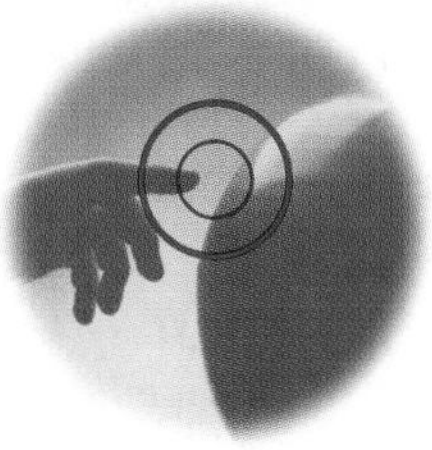

In Finland, treasury shares can be shown as assets, rather than as a reduction of stockholders' equity.

As shown above, a sale of treasury stock may result in a decrease in paid-in capital. To the extent that Paid-In Capital from Sale of Treasury Stock has a credit balance, it should be debited for any decrease. Any remaining decrease should then be debited to the retained earnings account.

At the end of the period, the balance in the treasury stock account is reported as a deduction from the total of the paid-in capital and retained earnings. The balance of Paid-In Capital from Sale of Treasury Stock is reported as part of the paid-in capital, as shown in Exhibit 4.

Exhibit 4

Stockholders' Equity Section with Treasury Stock

Stockholders' Equity			
Paid-in capital:			
Common stock, $25 par (20,000 shares authorized and issued)	$500,000		
Excess of issue price over par	150,000		
From sale of treasury stock	2,000		
Total paid-in capital		$652,000	
Retained earnings		130,000	
Total		$782,000	
Deduct treasury stock (600 shares at cost)		27,000	
Total stockholders' equity			$755,000

Stock Splits

5 Describe the effect of stock splits on the financial statements.

Corporations sometimes reduce the par or stated value of their common stock and issue a proportionate number of additional shares. When this is done, a corporation is said to have *split* its stock, and the process is called a **stock split**.

When stock is split, the reduction in par or stated value applies to all shares, including the unissued, issued, and treasury shares. A major objective of a stock split is to reduce the market price per share of the stock. This, in turn, should attract more investors to enter the market for the stock and broaden the types and numbers of stockholders.

To illustrate a stock split, assume that Rojek Corporation has 10,000 shares of $100 par common stock outstanding with a current market price of $150 per share. The board of directors declares a 5-for-1 stock split, reduces the par to $20, and increases the number of shares to 50,000. The amount of common stock outstanding is $1,000,000 both before and after the stock split. Only the number of shares and the par value per share are changed. Each Rojek Corporation shareholder owns the same total par amount of stock before and after the stock split. For example, a stockholder who owned 4 shares of $100 par stock before the split (total par of $400) would own 20 shares of $20 par stock after the split (total par of $400).

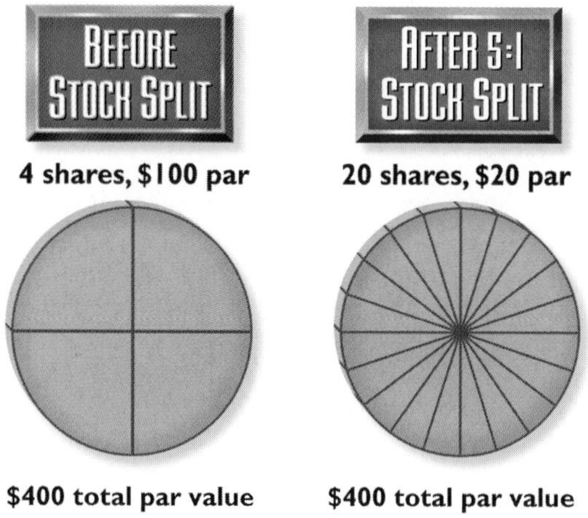

Since there are more shares outstanding after the stock split, we would expect the market price of the stock to fall. In the preceding example, there would be 5 times as many shares outstanding after the split. Thus, we would expect the market price of the stock to fall from $150 to approximately $30 ($150/5).

Sometimes a firm will authorize a *reverse stock split*, where the number of shares outstanding is reduced in order to increase the market price of the stock. A common rationale for a reverse stock split is to increase the market value of the stock above minimum listing requirements for a stock exchange. For example, NASDAQ requires a minimum market price of $1 per share. Firms that drop below the $1 market price will sometimes authorize a reverse stock split in order to increase the market price above the minimum requirement. Iomega Corp. justified its reverse 1:5 stock split when shares were trading near $1, stating:

> *. . . a reverse split will boost shares to above $5 each. Getting it to $5 would make it more attractive to institutional investors.*

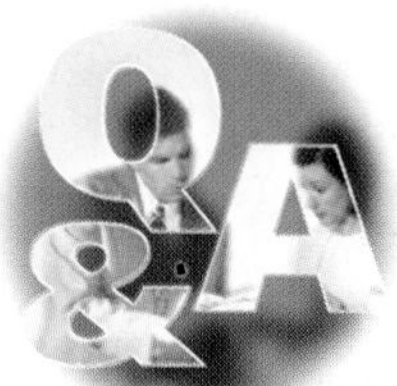

LTM Corporation announced a 4-for-1 stock split of its $50 par value common stock, which is currently trading for $120 per share. What is the new par value and the estimated market price of the stock after the split?

$12.50 ($50/4) par value; $30 ($120/4) estimated market price.

Since a stock split changes only the par or stated value and the number of shares outstanding, it is not recorded by a journal entry. Although the accounts are not affected, the details of stock splits are normally disclosed in the notes to the financial statements.

Analyzing Financing Alternatives

6 Analyze the impact of issuing common stock or bonds.

Significant changes in the capital stock accounts can impact a shareholder's ownership interest in the firm. Such changes in the capital accounts can occur when there are significant corporate financing transactions. Shareholders should analyze the impact of proposed financing alternatives in order to evaluate the status of their ownership interests. To illustrate, assume that Manning International, Inc. has 500,000 shares of common stock outstanding and is seeking additional financing to support a $1,500,000 investment at the beginning of the year. The additional financing can be obtained by either issuing common stock at a price of $15 per share or by issuing 10% bonds with a $1,500,000 face value. Assume that the earnings before interest and taxes (EBIT) for the year is $1,220,000 without the impact of the financing. During the year, we assume that the financing will be invested to earn a 12% pre-tax return on investment. Which financing alternative is most beneficial to the stockholders? The answer to this question depends on the market price for the common stock, as we will explain next.

Exhibit 5 shows the impact on earnings per share for the two financing options compared to no financing. Both financing options create funds that can be invested to produce a pre-tax return of $180,000 ($1,500,000 × 12%). In the first column, the additional common stock has no additional impact on net income; therefore, taxes are deducted from the EBIT to obtain a net income of $840,000. An additional 100,000 shares are issued at a price of $15 per share to obtain the $1,500,000 financing objective. The earnings per share is, thus, $1.40 ($840,000 ÷ 600,000 shares). Compared to the third column, this earnings per share is smaller than the $1.464 earnings per share from assuming that the financing was never obtained. The reduction in earnings per share from issuing more common stock is termed *earnings per share dilution.* Shareholders will wish to avoid dilution. Shareholders can avoid dilution in this case when common stock is issued at a higher price (reducing the number of shares offered), or the investment earns a higher return on investment.

Exhibit 5

Common Stock and Bond Financing Alternatives on Earnings per Share

	Common Stock Financing	Bond Financing	No Financing
Earnings before interest and taxes—base case (EBIT)	$1,220,000	$1,220,000	$1,220,000
Return on investment (12% × $1,500,000)	180,000	180,000	–
Interest on bonds (10% × $1,500,000)	–	(150,000)	–
Earnings before taxes	$1,400,000	$1,250,000	$1,220,000
Income tax (@40%)	560,000	500,000	488,000
Net income	$ 840,000	$ 750,000	$ 732,000
Base number of shares outstanding	500,000	500,000	500,000
Plus additional shares issued	100,000		
Total shares outstanding	600,000	500,000	500,000
Earning per share (EPS)	$1.40	$1.50	$1.464

The second column shows the earnings per share from issuing bonds. In addition to the $180,000 return on investment, the bond interest expense of $150,000 (10% × $1,500,000) must be deducted from the EBIT before deducting taxes. The net income after deducting taxes would be $750,000. With bond financing, the number of common shares outstanding would remain unchanged. Thus, the earnings would be $1.50 per share ($750,000 ÷ 500,000 shares). As can be seen, the bond alternative avoids dilution.[6] This will not always be the case.

For common stock financing, a low market price would require more shares to be issued in order to raise $1,500,000, while a high market price would require fewer shares to be issued. Dilution would be less for higher market prices and greater for lower market prices. Exhibit 6 shows the earnings per share for common stock and bond financing

6 A bond or other security that avoids dilution is also called "anti-dilutive."

Exhibit 6

Earnings Per Share Under Different Common Stock Market Prices

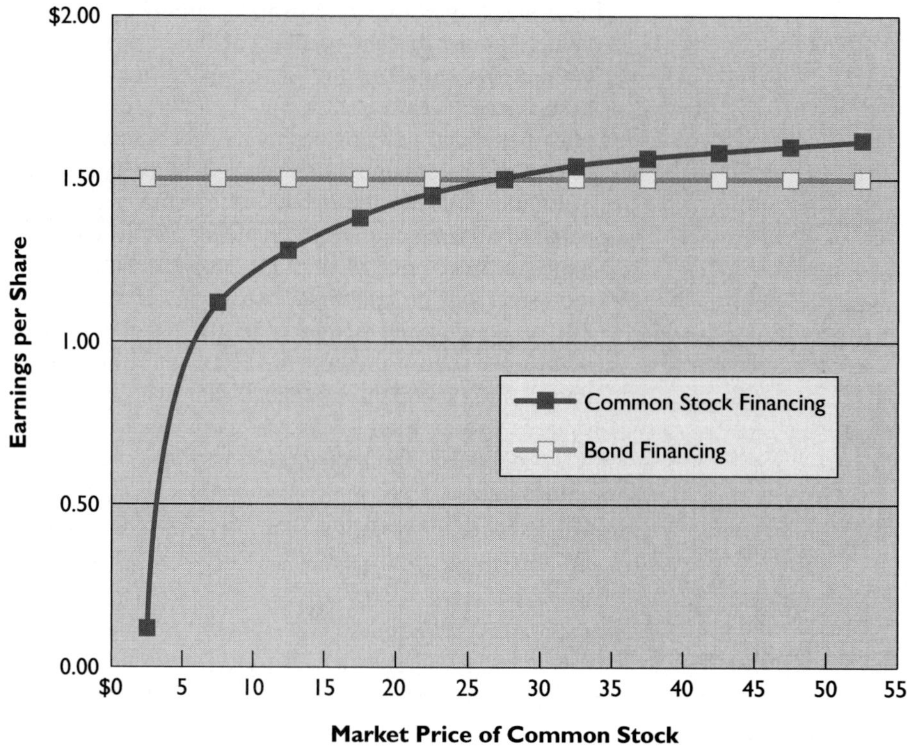

for different common stock market price assumptions. The curved line shows the earnings per share for issuing common stock under different market price assumptions, for a given 12% return on investment. For example, we previously determined (in Exhibit 5) that the earnings per share is $1.40 for a market price of $15 per share. The bond financing is unaffected by the common stock market price, and thus is a straight line at $1.50 per share. If common stock were issued at a market price of $25 per share, the earnings per share under the bond and common stock financing options will be equal, as shown in Exhibit 6. At market prices above $25 per share, the earnings per share under common stock financing will be greater, whereas at a market price below $25 per share, the earnings per share under bond financing would be greater.[7]

Accounting for Dividends

7 Describe the financial statement effects of cash dividends and stock dividends.

When a board of directors declares a cash dividend, it authorizes the distribution of a portion of the corporation's cash to stockholders. When a board of directors declares a stock

7 The $25 market price equality point can be calculated by the following equation:

$$\frac{\text{Target Financing} \times \text{Bond Financing EPS}}{\text{Net income under common stock financing} - (\text{Base common shares} \times \text{Bond Financing EPS})}$$

or

$$\frac{\$1{,}500{,}000 \times \$1.50}{\$840{,}000 - (500{,}000 \times \$1.5)} = \frac{\$2{,}250{,}000}{\$840{,}000 - \$750{,}000} = \$25 \text{ per share}$$

dividend, it authorizes the distribution of a portion of its stock. In both cases, the declaration of a dividend reduces the retained earnings of the corporation.[8]

Cash Dividends

A cash distribution of earnings by a corporation to its shareholders is called a **cash dividend**. Although dividends may be paid in the form of other assets, cash dividends are the most common form.

A corporation must usually meet three conditions in order to pay a cash dividend:

1. Sufficient retained earnings
2. Sufficient cash
3. Formal action by the board of directors

A large amount of retained earnings does not always mean that a corporation is able to pay dividends. As we indicated earlier in the chapter, the balances of the cash and retained earnings account are often unrelated. Thus, a large retained earnings account does not mean that there is cash available to pay dividends.

A corporation's board of directors is not required by law to declare dividends. This is true, even if both retained earnings and cash are large enough to justify a dividend. However, many corporations try to maintain a stable dividend record in order to make their stock attractive to investors. Although dividends may be paid once a year or semiannually, most corporations pay dividends quarterly. In years of high profits, a corporation may declare a *special* or *extra* dividend.

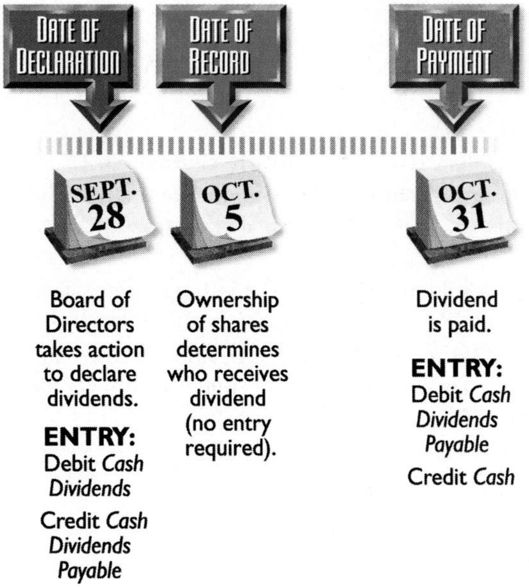
DATE OF DECLARATION
DATE OF RECORD
DATE OF PAYMENT
SEPT. 28
OCT. 5
OCT. 31
Board of Directors takes action to declare dividends.
ENTRY: Debit Cash Dividends Credit Cash Dividends Payable
Ownership of shares determines who receives dividend (no entry required).
Dividend is paid.
ENTRY: Debit Cash Dividends Payable Credit Cash

You may have seen announcements of dividend declarations in financial newspapers or investor services. An example of such an announcement is shown below.

> *On September 28, the board of directors of* Campbell Soup Co. *declared a quarterly cash dividend of $0.1575 per common share to stockholders of record as of the close of business on October 5, payable on October 31.*

This announcement includes three important dates: the *date of declaration* (September 28), the *date of record* (October 5), and the *date of payment* (October 31). During the period of time between the record date and the payment date, the stock price is usually quoted as selling *ex-dividends*. This means that, since the date of record has passed, a new investor will not receive the dividend.

To illustrate, assume that on *December 1* the board of directors of Hiber Corporation declares the following quarterly cash dividends. The date of record is *December 10*, and the date of payment is *January 2*.

	Dividend per Share	Total Dividends
Preferred stock, $100 par, 5,000 shares outstanding	$2.50	$12,500
Common stock, $10 par, 100,000 shares outstanding	$0.30	30,000
Total		$42,500

8 In rare cases, when a corporation is reducing its operations or going out of business, a dividend may be a distribution of paid-in capital. Such a dividend is called a *liquidating dividend*.

Hiber Corporation records the $42,500 liability for the dividends on December 1, the declaration date, as follows:[9]

Dec. 1	Retained Earnings	42,500	
	Cash Dividends Payable		42,500

No entry is required on the date of record, December 10, since this date merely determines which stockholders will receive the dividend. On the date of payment, January 2, the corporation records the $42,500 payment of the dividends as follows:

Jan. 2	Cash Dividends Payable	42,500	
	Cash		42,500

If Hiber Corporation's fiscal year ends December 31, Cash Dividends Payable will be listed on the December 31 balance sheet as a current liability.

If a corporation that holds treasury stock declares a cash dividend, the dividends are not paid on the treasury shares. To do so would place the corporation in the position of earning income through dealing with itself. For example, if Hiber Corporation in the preceding illustration had held 5,000 shares of its own common stock, the cash dividends on the common stock would have been $28,500 [(100,000 − 5,000) × $0.30] instead of $30,000.

Stock Dividends

A distribution of shares of stock to stockholders is called a **stock dividend**. Usually, such distributions are in common stock and are issued to holders of common stock. Stock dividends are different from cash dividends, in that there is no distribution of cash or other assets to stockholders.

The effect of a stock dividend on the stockholders' equity of the issuing corporation is to transfer retained earnings to paid-in capital. For public corporations, the amount transferred from retained earnings to paid-in capital is normally the *fair value* (market price) of the shares issued in the stock dividend.[10] To illustrate, assume that the stockholders' equity accounts of Hendrix Corporation as of December 15 are as follows:

Common stock, $20 par (2,000,000 shares issued)	$40,000,000
Paid-in capital in excess of par—common stock	9,000,000
Retained earnings	26,600,000

On December 15, the board of directors declares a stock dividend of 5% or 100,000 shares (2,000,000 shares × 5%) to be issued on January 10 to stockholders of record on December 31. The market price of the stock on the declaration date is $31 a share. The declaration is recorded as shown on the next page.[11]

9 Alternatively, the debit could be to "Cash Dividends," which is then closed to Retained Earnings.

10 The use of fair market value is justified as long as the number of shares issued for the stock dividend is small (less than 25% of the shares outstanding).

11 Alternatively, the debit could be to "Stock Dividend," which is then closed to Retained Earnings.

Retained Earnings (100,000 shares × $31 market price)	3,100,000	
Stock Dividends Distributable (100,000 × $20 par)		2,000,000
Paid-In Capital in Excess of Par—Common Stock		1,100,000

The stock dividends distributable account is listed in the Paid-In Capital section of the balance sheet. Thus, the effect of the stock dividend is to transfer $3,100,000 of retained earnings to paid-in capital.

On January 10, the number of shares outstanding is increased by 100,000 by the following entry to record the issue of the stock:

Jan. 10	Stock Dividends Distributable	2,000,000	
	Common Stock		2,000,000

A stock dividend does not change the assets, liabilities, or total stockholders' equity of the corporation. Likewise, it does not change a stockholder's proportionate interest (equity) in the corporation. For example, if a stockholder owned 1,000 of a corporation's 10,000 shares outstanding, the stockholder owns 10% (1,000/10,000) of the corporation. After declaring a 6% stock dividend, the corporation will issue 600 additional shares (10,000 shares × 6%), and the total shares outstanding will be 10,600. The stockholder of 1,000 shares will receive 60 additional shares and will now own 1,060 shares, which is still a 10% equity.

Analyze Dividends

8 Compute and interpret the dividend yield and dividend payout ratio on common stock.

Shareholders and analysts evaluate both the *amount* of dividends paid and the likelihood that the dividends will be *maintained* in the future. The dividend yield measures the amount, while the dividend payout ratio can be used to evaluate dividend maintenance.

Dividend Yield

The amount of the cash dividend can be evaluated as a rate of return on the value of an investment. This rate of return is called a **dividend yield**. Although the dividend yield can be computed for both preferred and common stock, it is most often computed for common stock. This is because most preferred stock has a stated dividend rate or amount. In contrast, the dividend and market price of common stock normally varies with the profitability of the corporation.

The dividend yield is computed by dividing the annual dividend paid per share of common stock by the market price per share of common stock at a specific date, as shown below.

$$\text{Dividend Yield} = \frac{\text{Cash Dividend per Share of Common Stock}}{\text{Market Price per Share of Common Stock}}$$

To illustrate, the market price of Procter & Gamble Co.'s (P&G) common stock was $91.20 as of the close of business, April 16, 2002. During the past year, P&G had paid dividends of $1.52 per share. Thus, the dividend yield of P&G's common stock is 1.67% ($1.52/$91.20). Because the market price of a corporation's stock will vary from day to day, its dividend yield will also vary from day to day. Fortunately, the dividend yield is provided with newspaper listings of market prices and most Internet quotation services, such as from Yahoo's Finance Web site.

The recent dividend yields for some selected companies are as follows:

Company	Dividend Yield
Ford Motor Company	7.30%
Hewlett-Packard Company	2.08
Coca-Cola Company	1.45
Home Depot Inc.	0.45
Oracle Corporation	None
ExxonMobil Corporation	2.40
Duke Energy Corporation	2.90

As can be seen, the dividend yield varies widely across firms. Which dividend yield is right for an investor? The answer depends on the investor's objectives. The dividend yield on common stock is of special interest to investors whose main objective is to receive a current dividend return on their investment. In addition, a stock with a healthy dividend yield should be less likely to decline significantly in market price, because the increasing yield would attract buyers. However, a high dividend yield also restricts a company's growth because cash is used for dividends rather than for business objectives. Investors must also be careful in purchasing common stock with very high dividend yields, such as with Ford above. Such high dividends may be "too good to be true." The high dividend yield may not be *safe*, meaning that financial difficulties may force management to reduce the dividend in the future.

In contrast, investors whose main objective is a rapid increase in the market price of their investments may not desire a high dividend yield. For example, technology companies often do not pay dividends, but instead, reinvest their earnings in research and development, such as with Oracle Corporation above. Investors expect such stocks to increase in market price as a result of this reinvestment. Since many factors affect stock prices, an investment strategy relying solely on increases in market prices is more risky than a strategy based on dividend yields.

Dividend Payout Ratio

Investors purchasing common stock for their dividends need to assess the likelihood that the existing dividend can be maintained, which is termed *dividend safety*. While evaluating the safety of the dividend involves many considerations, one important measure is the amount of the dividend as a percent of net income. The **dividend payout ratio** is the ratio of the cash dividend to the net income of the company, determined as follows:

$$\text{Dividend payout ratio} = \frac{\text{Annual cash dividends}}{\text{Annual net income}} = \frac{\text{Annual cash dividend per share}}{\text{Annual earnings per share}}$$

To illustrate, Citigroup Inc., a major financial services company, recently reported earnings of $13,519 million and paid cash dividends of $2,654 million. The dividend payout ratio would be:

$$\frac{\$2,654}{\$13,519} = 19.6\%$$

This ratio means that Citigroup paid out less than 20 percent of its annual earnings in dividends. This is a reasonable payout ratio that would be considered maintainable. In contrast, Ford Motor had a dividend payout ratio of nearly 80 percent, which might not be considered sustainable in the long term.[12]

Exhibit 7 shows the dividend payout ratios for a number of different industries. As can be seen, the dividend policies are not consistent across industries. Indeed, some industries, such as airlines and telecommunications, are paying out more in dividends than they are earning. They cannot sustain this payout ratio in the long term. As of this writing, both industries are experiencing low profitability, while dividends have yet to be cut to reflect this reality. In contrast, software and consumer electronics industries have very small payout ratios, which reflect their high internal growth prospects. That is, management from these industries chooses to retain earnings for financing growth, rather than pay them out as dividends.

Exhibit 7

Dividend Payout Ratios for Selected Industries

Industry (large companies only)	Dividend Payout Ratio
Airlines	190%
Automotive	31
Consumer electronics	2
Consumer products	34
Electric and gas utilities	23
Electronic manufacturing	9
Financial services	9
Food and beverage	23
Petrochemical	11
Retail	13
Software	1
Telecommunications	111

Reporting Stockholders' Equity

9 Describe financial statement presentations of stockholders' equity.

Significant changes in stockholders' equity are reported for the period in which they occur. These changes are reported in a **statement of stockholders' equity**. This statement is often prepared in a columnar format, where each column represents a major stockholders' equity classification. Changes in each classification are then described in the left-hand column, starting with the beginning balance in the first row and ending with the ending balance in the last row. Exhibit 8 illustrates the statement of stockholders' equity for Outback Steakhouse, Inc.

Reporting Retained Earnings

Most corporations report changes in retained earnings by preparing a separate "retained earnings" column in the statement of stockholders' equity, as shown for Outback Steakhouse in Exhibit 8. The beginning balance of the retained earnings is adjusted for net income (add) or loss (deduct) and dividends (deduct). Other adjustments may come from treasury stock reissuances, as discussed earlier, and prior period adjustments.

Prior period adjustments or *earnings restatements* result from material errors in a prior period's net income arising from mathematical mistakes or from mistakes in

12 After this writing, Ford eventually cut its dividend in half.

Exhibit 8

Statement of Stockholders' Equity

Outback Steakhouse, Inc.
Statement of Stockholders' Equity
For the Year Ended December 31, 2001 (in thousands)

	Common Stock Shares	Common Stock Amount	Additional Paid-In Capital	Retained Earnings	Treasury Stock	Total
Balance, December 31, 2000	76,632	$785	$214,541	$638,383	$(46,119)	$807,590
Issuance of common stock	40	1	6,107			6,108
Purchase of treasury stock	(1,210)				(31,250)	(31,250)
Reissuance of treasury stock	1,451			(9,346)	35,365	26,019
Net income				133,377		133,377
Balance, December 31, 2001	76,913	$786	$220,648	$762,414	$(42,004)	$941,844

applying accounting principles. If the effects of material errors are not discovered within the same fiscal period in which they occurred, they should not be included in determining net income for the current period. Instead, corrections of such errors are reported as an adjustment to the retained earnings balance at the beginning of the period in which the error is discovered and corrected. For example, Xerox Corp. reduced retained earnings in 2002 by $2 billion from erroneously applying accounting principles for lease revenues in its 1997–2001 financial statements.

The retained earnings available for use as dividends may also be restricted by action of a corporation's board of directors. The amount restricted is called an **appropriation.** Appropriated retained earnings must be disclosed, usually in the notes to the financial statements. The board may restrict retained earnings because of legal or contractual requirements. In addition, the board may also restrict retained earnings voluntarily, so that more money is available for expanding the business.

Reporting Stockholders' Equity on the Balance Sheet

The stockholders' equity section of the balance sheet is illustrated for Outback Steakhouse in Exhibit 9. Notice that the balances shown in the last row of the Statement of Stockholders' Equity in Exhibit 8 are the balances that are disclosed on the balance sheet in Exhibit 9. The balance sheet also commonly discloses the authorized, issued, and outstanding shares, as well as the par value of various classes of stock. In addition, relevant rights and privileges of the various classes of stock outstanding must be disclosed.[13] Examples of types of information that must be disclosed include dividend and liquidation preferences, rights to participate in earnings, conversion rights, and redemption rights. Such information may be disclosed on the face of the balance sheet or in the accompanying notes.

13 *Statement of Financial Accounting Standards No. 129*, "Disclosure Information about Capital Structure," Financial Accounting Standards Board (Norwalk, Connecticut: 1997).

Exhibit 9

Stockholders' Equity Section of the Balance Sheet

Stockholders' Equity
Outback Steakhouse, Inc.
December 31, 2001 (in thousands)

Stockholders' Equity	
Common stock, $0.01 par value, 200,000 shares authorized; 78,554 shares issued; and 76,913 outstanding as of December 31, 2001	$ 786
Additional paid-in capital	220,648
Retained earnings	762,414
	$983,848
Less treasury stock, 1,641 shares at December 31, 2001, at cost	(42,004)
Total stockholders' equity	$941,844

Focus on Cash Flow
Capital Stock and Dividends

Changes in the stockholders' equity accounts can have a significant impact on cash flows. Issuing common stock will increase cash flows, while purchasing treasury stock will reduce cash flows. In addition, cash dividends reduce cash flows. Changes in stockholders' equity and dividends are disclosed in the financing section of the statement of cash flows, as illustrated for Eli Lilly & Co. below.

Ely Lilly & Co.
Partial Statement of Cash Flows—Financing Activities

Cash Flows From Financing Activities:	
Dividends paid	$(1,126,000,000)
Purchase of common stock and other capital transactions	(1,052,800,000)
Issuances under stock plans	178,400,000
Net change in short-term borrowings	(203,000,000)
Proceeds from issuance of long-term debt	1,100,000
Repayments of long-term debt	(27,200,000)
Net Cash Used for Financing Activities	$(2,229,500,000)

As can be seen from the figures in color, Eli Lilly has paid over a billion dollars in dividends and another billion dollars for treasury stock. The $178 million issued under stock plans are proceeds from common stock issuances to employees under an employee stock option plan.

Summary of Learning Goals

1 Describe the nature of the corporate form of organization.

Corporations have a separate legal existence, transferable units of stock, and limited stockholders' liability. Corporations may be either public or private corporations, and they are subject to federal income taxes.

The documents included in forming a corporation include an application of incorporation, articles of incorporation, and bylaws. Costs often incurred in organizing a corporation include legal fees, taxes, state incorporation fees, and promotional costs. Such costs are debited to an expense account entitled Organization Costs.

2 List the major sources of paid-in capital, including the various classes of stock.

The main source of paid-in capital is from issuing stock. The two primary classes of stock are common stock and preferred stock. Preferred stock may be cumulative or noncumulative. In addition to the issuance of stock, paid-in capital may arise from donations of assets and from treasury stock transactions.

3 Describe the financial statement effects of issuing stock.

When a corporation issues stock at par for cash, the cash account is debited and the class of stock issued is credited for its par amount. When a corporation issues stock at more than par, Paid-In Capital in Excess of Par is credited for the difference between the cash received and the par value of the stock. When stock is issued in exchange for assets other than cash, the assets acquired should be recorded at their fair market value.

When no-par stock is issued, the entire proceeds are credited to the stock account. No-par stock may be assigned a stated value per share, and the excess of the proceeds over the stated value may be credited to Paid-In Capital in Excess of Stated Value.

4 Describe the financial statement effects of treasury stock transactions.

When a corporation buys its own stock, the cost method of accounting is normally used. Treasury Stock is debited for its cost, and Cash is credited. If the stock is resold, Treasury Stock is credited for its cost and any difference between the cost and the selling price is normally debited or credited to Paid-In Capital from Sale of Treasury Stock.

5 Describe the effect of stock splits on the financial statements.

When a corporation reduces the par or stated value of its common stock and issues a proportionate number of additional shares, a stock split has occurred. There are no changes in the balances of any corporation accounts, and no entry is required for a stock split.

6 Analyze the impact of issuing common stock or bonds.

Common stock dilution occurs when a common stock issuance results in an earnings per share decline. Dilution can be avoided by issuing common stock when the stock price is high. When capital is raised through debt, a return in excess of the interest rate will cause earnings per share to increase. In comparing the earnings per share between a debt or common stock offering, the common stock offering will be favored when the stock price is high. The opposite is the case when the common stock price is low.

7 Describe the financial statement effects of cash dividends and stock dividends.

The entry to record a declaration of cash dividends debits Retained Earnings and credits Dividends Payable for each class of stock. The payment of dividends is recorded in the normal manner. When a stock dividend is declared, Retained Earnings is debited for the fair value of the stock to be issued. Stock Dividends Distributable is credited for the par or stated value of the common stock to be issued. The difference between the fair value of the stock and its par or stated value is credited to Paid-In Capital in Excess of Par—Common Stock. When the stock is issued on the date of payment, Stock Dividends Distributable is debited and Common Stock is credited for the par or stated value of the stock issued.

8 Compute and interpret the dividend yield and dividend payout ratio on common stock.

The dividend yield indicates the rate of return to stockholders in terms of cash dividend distributions. It is computed by dividing the annual dividends paid per share of common stock by the market price per share at a specific date. This ratio is of special interest to investors whose main objective is to receive a current dividend return on their investment.

The dividend payout ratio measures dividend safety by computing the percentage of net income paid out in dividends. When this ratio is high, or exceeds 1.0, it suggests a dividend rate that will be difficult to maintain.

9 Describe financial statement presentations of stockholders' equity.

The Statement of Stockholders' Equity discloses changes in the stockholders' equity accounts, in columnar format. The balance of each account at the bottom of the column reconciles with the balance sheet disclosure of each account. Retained earnings can be influenced by prior period adjustments and appropriations. Prior period adjustments are restatements of prior period earnings due to errors or mistakes in the application of accounting principles. Appropriations are an act of the board of directors to restrict an amount of retained earnings available for use as dividends.

Glossary

Appropriation An act by the board of directors to restrict the amount of retained earnings available for use as dividends.

Cash dividend A cash distribution of earnings by a corporation to its shareholders.

Common stock The stock outstanding when a corporation has issued only one class of stock.

Cumulative preferred stock A class of preferred stock that has a right to receive regular dividends that have been passed (not declared) before any common stock dividends are paid.

Dividend payout ratio A ratio computed by dividing the annual cash dividends (per share) by the annual net income (per share); indicates dividend safety.

Dividend yield A ratio computed by dividing the annual dividends paid per share of common stock by the market price per share at a specific date; indicates the rate of return to stockholders in terms of cash dividend distributions.

Outstanding stock The stock in the hands of stockholders.

Par The monetary amount printed on a stock certificate.

Preferred stock A class of stock with preferential rights over common stock.

Premium The excess of the issue price of a stock over its par value.

Prior period adjustment An adjustment to retained earnings arising from material errors in a prior period's net income as a result of mathematical mistakes or mistakes in applying accounting principles.

Stated value A value, similar to par value, approved by the board of directors of a corporation for no-par stock.

Statement of stockholders' equity This statement is often prepared in a columnar format, where each column shows the change in each major stockholders' equity classification.

Stock Shares of ownership of a corporation.

Stock dividend A distribution of shares of stock to stockholders.

Stock option The right to purchase common stock at a fixed price over a limited period of time, often used to provide employee incentives to enhance stock price.

Stock split A reduction in the par or stated value of a common stock and the issuance of a proportionate number of additional shares.

Stockholders The owners of a corporation.

Treasury stock Stock that a corporation has once issued and then reacquires.

Illustrative Accounting Application Problem

Altenburg Inc. is a lighting fixture wholesaler located in Arizona. During its current fiscal year, ended December 31, 2004, Altenburg Inc. completed the following selected transactions:

Feb. 3 Purchased 2,500 shares of its own common stock at $26, recording the stock at cost. (Prior to the purchase, there were 40,000 shares of $20 par common stock outstanding.)

May 1	Declared a semiannual dividend of $1 on the 10,000 shares of preferred stock and a 30¢ dividend on the common stock to stockholders of record on May 31, payable on June 15.
June 15	Paid the cash dividends.
Sept. 23	Sold 1,000 shares of treasury stock at $28, receiving cash.
Nov. 1	Declared semiannual dividends of $1 on the preferred stock and 30¢ on the common stock. In addition, a 5% common stock dividend was declared on the common stock outstanding, to be capitalized at the fair market value of the common stock, which is estimated at $30.
Dec. 1	Paid the cash dividends and issued the certificates for the common stock dividend.

Instructions

Journalize the entries to record the transactions for Altenburg Inc.

Solution

2004			
Feb. 3	Treasury Stock	65,000	
	Cash		65,000
May 1	Retained Earnings	21,250	
	Cash Dividends Payable		21,250
	(10,000 × $1) + [(40,000 − 2,500) × $0.30]		
June 15	Cash Dividends Payable	21,250	
	Cash		21,250
Sept. 23	Cash	28,000	
	Treasury Stock		26,000
	Paid-In Capital from Sale of Treasury Stock		2,000
Nov. 1	Retained Earnings	21,550	
	Cash Dividends Payable		21,550
	(10,000 × $1) + [(40,000 − 1,500) × $0.30]		
1	Retained Earnings	57,750	
	Stock Dividends Distributable		38,500
	Paid-In Capital in Excess of Par		19,250
	(40,000 − 1,500) × 5% × $30		
Dec. 1	Cash Dividends Payable	21,550	
	Stock Dividends Distributable	38,500	
	Cash		21,550
	Common Stock		38,500

Self-Study Questions

Answers at end of chapter

1. If a corporation has outstanding 1,000 shares of $9 cumulative preferred stock of $100 par and dividends have been passed for the preceding three years, what is the amount of preferred dividends that must be declared in the current year before a dividend can be declared on common stock?

   A. $9,000 C. $36,000
   B. $27,000 D. $45,000

2. Paid-in capital for a corporation may arise from which of the following sources?
   A. Issuing cumulative preferred stock
   B. Receiving donations of real estate
   C. Selling the corporation's treasury stock
   D. All of the above

3. If a corporation reacquires its own stock, the stock is listed on the balance sheet in the:
   A. Current Assets section.
   B. Long-Term Liabilities section.
   C. Stockholders' Equity section.
   D. Investments section.

4. A corporation has issued 25,000 shares of $100 par common stock and holds 3,000 of these shares as treasury stock. If the corporation declares a $2 per share cash dividend, what amount will be recorded as cash dividends?
   A. $22,000 C. $44,000
   B. $25,000 D. $50,000

5. A corporation declares a cash dividend of $2.40 per common share for the current year. The market price of common stock is $48 per share at the end of the year, while the book value (stockholders' equity divided by shares outstanding) per share is $32 per share. The earnings per share is $4.00 for the current year. Determine the dividend yield and dividend payout ratio (in that order).
   A. 60%, 5% C. 5%, 60%
   B. 7.5%, 67% D. 7.5%, 60%

Discussion Questions

1. Contrast the owners' liability to creditors of (a) a partnership (partners) and (b) a corporation (stockholders).
2. Why is it said that the earnings of a corporation are subject to *double taxation*? Discuss.
3. Why are most large businesses organized as corporations?
4. Of two corporations organized at approximately the same time and engaged in competing businesses, one issued $50 par common stock, and the other issued $1 par common stock. Do the par designations provide any indication as to which stock is preferable as an investment? Explain.
5. a. Differentiate between common stock and preferred stock.
   b. Describe briefly cumulative preferred stock.
6. A stockbroker advises a client to "buy cumulative preferred stock. . . . With that type of stock, . . . [you] will never have to worry about losing the dividends." Is the broker right?
7. What is the difference between the primary and secondary markets?
8. If common stock of $100 par is sold for $130, what is the $30 difference between the issue price and par called?
9. What are some of the factors that influence the market price of a corporation's stock?
10. When a corporation issues stock at a premium, is the premium income? Explain.
11. Land is acquired by a corporation for 15,000 shares of its $25 par common stock, which is currently selling for $70 per share on a national stock exchange. What accounts should be credited to record the transaction?
12. Indicate which of the following accounts would be reported as part of paid-in capital on the balance sheet:
    a. Retained Earnings
    b. Common Stock
    c. Preferred Stock
13. a. In what respect does treasury stock differ from unissued stock?
    b. How should treasury stock be presented on the balance sheet?
14. A corporation reacquires 5,000 shares of its own $40 par common stock for $370,000, recording it at cost. (a) What effect does this transaction have on

revenue or expense of the period? (b) What effect does it have on stockholders' equity?

15. The treasury stock in Question 14 is resold for $400,000. (a) What is the effect on the corporation's revenue of the period? (b) What is the effect on stockholders' equity?
16. What is the primary purpose of a stock split?
17. Explain how shareholders can avoid earnings per share dilution?
18. What are the conditions for declaring and paying a cash dividend?
19. The dates associated with a cash dividend are October 1, November 15, and December 30. Identify each date.
20. A corporation with both cumulative preferred stock and common stock outstanding has a substantial credit balance in its retained earnings account at the beginning of the current fiscal year. Although net income for the current year is sufficient to pay the preferred dividend of $100,000 each quarter and a common dividend of $300,000 each quarter, the board of directors declares dividends only on the preferred stock. Suggest possible reasons for passing the dividends on the common stock.
21. An owner of 200 shares of Dunston Company common stock receives a stock dividend of 4 shares. (a) What is the effect of the stock dividend on the stockholder's proportionate interest (equity) in the corporation? (b) How does the total equity of 204 shares compare with the total equity of 200 shares before the stock dividend?
22. a. Where should a declared but unpaid cash dividend be reported on the balance sheet?
    b. Where should a declared but unissued stock dividend be reported on the balance sheet?
23. What is the purpose of the Statement of Stockholders' Equity?

Resources for your success online @
http://warren.swlearning.com

Remember! If you need additional help, visit South-Western's Web site. See page 30 for a description of the online and printed materials that are available.

Exercises

Exercise 11-1

Market for common stock

Goals 2, 8

Use either the Internet or the newspaper to determine the following for the Coca-Cola Company:

a. What stock exchange trades the common stock?
b. What is the exchange abbreviation for the common stock?
c. What is the annual dividend per share?
d. What is the current market price?
e. What is the current dividend yield?

Exercise 11–2

Dividends per share

Goal 2

Preferred stock, 3rd year: $2.00

STUDENT SOLUTIONS MANUAL

Masini Inc., a developer of radiology equipment, has stock outstanding as follows: 20,000 shares of $2 noncumulative preferred stock of $100 par, and 250,000 shares of $50 par common. During its first five years of operations, the following amounts were distributed as dividends: first year, none; second year, $30,000; third year, $90,000; fourth year, $200,000; fifth year, $240,000. Calculate the dividends per share on each class of stock for each of the five years.

Exercise 11–3

Dividends per share

Goal 2

Preferred stock, 3rd year: $4.00

Mystic.com, a computer software development firm, has stock outstanding as follows: 10,000 shares of $1.50 cumulative preferred stock of $50 par, and 50,000 shares of $100 par common. During its first five years of operations, the following amounts were distributed as dividends: first year, none; second year, $5,000; third year, $80,000; fourth year, $180,000; fifth year, $75,000. Calculate the dividends per share on each class of stock for each of the five years.

Exercise 11–4

Entries for issuing par stock

Goal 3

STUDENT SOLUTIONS MANUAL

On March 10, Candler Inc., a marble contractor, issued for cash 30,000 shares of $20 par common stock at $30, and on August 9, it issued for cash 5,000 shares of $100 par preferred stock at $105.

a. Record the entries for March 10 and August 9.
b. What is the total amount invested (total paid-in capital) by all stockholders as of August 9?

Exercise 11–5

Entries for issuing no-par stock

Goal 3

On November 2, Catalpa Corp., a carpet wholesaler, issued for cash 5,000 shares of no-par common stock (with a stated value of $25) at $75, and on December 3, it issued for cash 1,000 shares of $50 par preferred stock at $65.

a. Record the entries for November 2 and December 3, assuming that the common stock is to be credited with the stated value.
b. What is the total amount invested (total paid-in capital) by all stockholders as of December 3?

Exercise 11–6

Issuing stock for assets other than cash

Goal 3

STUDENT SOLUTIONS MANUAL

On February 27, Sims Corporation, a wholesaler of hydraulic lifts, acquired land in exchange for 4,000 shares of $10 par common stock with a current market price of $73. Journalize the entry to record the transaction.

Exercise 11–7

Issuing stock

Goal 3

Gyro.com, with an authorization of 25,000 shares of preferred stock and 100,000 shares of common stock, completed several transactions involving its stock on October 1, the first day of operations. The trial balance at the close of the day follows:

Cash	565,000	
Land	40,000	
Buildings	95,000	
Preferred $5 Stock, $100 par		100,000
Paid-In Capital in Excess of Par—Preferred Stock		35,000
Common Stock, $75 par		450,000
Paid-In Capital in Excess of Par—Common Stock		115,000
	700,000	700,000

All shares within each class of stock were sold at the same price. The preferred stock was issued in exchange for the land and buildings.

Record the two entries to record the transactions summarized in the trial balance.

Exercise 11–8

Issuing stock

Goal 3

STUDENT SOLUTIONS MANUAL

Fourier Products Inc., a wholesaler of office products, was organized on January 6 of the current year, with an authorization of 50,000 shares of $2 noncumulative preferred stock, $100 par and 250,000 shares of $10 par common stock. The following selected transactions were completed during the first year of operations:

Jan. 6	Issued 25,000 shares of common stock at par for cash.
Feb. 28	Issued 11,500 shares of common stock in exchange for land, buildings, and equipment with fair market prices of $20,000, $100,000, and $18,000, respectively.
Mar. 15	Issued 5,000 shares of preferred stock at $102 for cash.

Record the transactions.

Exercise 11–9

Issuing stock

Goals 2, 3

MGM Grand, Inc., an entertainment, hotel, and gaming company, made the following news announcement:

> *LAS VEGAS, April 17 (2000) /PRNewswire/–MGM Grand, Inc. (NYSE: MGG) today announced that it has placed 46.5 million shares of its common stock at $26.50 per share with a limited number of financial institutions and Tracinda Corporation, its principal stockholder. The private placement raises $1.23 billion of new equity. MGM Grand expects to utilize the proceeds in connection with its pending acquisition of Mirage Resorts, Incorporated (NYSE: MIR).*

The article further stated that Tracinda Corporation's interest would decline from 64.4% to 60% of the outstanding shares as a result of this placement.

a. MGM common stock has a $0.01 par value. Provide the journal entry that would be made by MGM to record the proceeds from this common stock issuance.
b. What is a private placement?
c. Why would Tracinda Corporation approve the reduction of its ownership?

Exercise 11–10

Treasury stock transactions

Goal 4

b. $8,500 credit

STUDENT SOLUTIONS MANUAL

Chico Springs Inc. bottles and distributes spring water. On March 1 of the current year, Chico reacquired 5,500 shares of its common stock at $40 per share. On July 8, Chico sold 3,500 of the reacquired shares at $43 per share. The remaining 2,000 shares were sold at $39 per share on December 19.

a. Record the transactions of March 1, July 8, and December 19.
b. What is the balance in Paid-In Capital from Sale of Treasury Stock on December 31 of the current year?
c. Where will the balance in Paid-In Capital from Sale of Treasury Stock be reported on the balance sheet?
d. For what reasons might Chico Springs have purchased the treasury stock?

Exercise 11–11

Treasury stock transactions

Goal 4

b. $9,000 credit

Aorta Inc. develops and produces spraying equipment for lawn maintenance and industrial uses. On September 6 of the current year, Aorta Inc. reacquired 6,000 shares of its common stock at $90 per share. On November 15, 2,000 of the reacquired shares were sold at $93 per share, and on December 21, 3,000 of the reacquired shares were sold at $91.

a. Record the transactions of September 6, November 15, and December 21.
b. What is the balance in Paid-In Capital from Sale of Treasury Stock on December 31 of the current year?

c. What is the balance in Treasury Stock on December 31 of the current year?
d. How will the balance in Treasury Stock be reported on the balance sheet?

Exercise 11–12

Treasury stock transactions

Goal 4

b. $3,000 credit

STUDENT SOLUTIONS MANUAL

Heavenly Inc. bottles and distributes spring water. On July 1 of the current year, Heavenly Inc. reacquired 3,000 shares of its common stock at $40 per share. On August 10, Heavenly Inc. sold 1,500 of the reacquired shares at $43 per share. The remaining 1,500 shares were sold at $39 per share on December 19.

a. Journalize the transactions of July 1, August 10, and December 19.
b. What is the balance in Paid-In Capital from Sale of Treasury Stock on December 31 of the current year?
c. Where will the balance in Paid-In Capital from Sale of Treasury Stock be reported on the balance sheet?
d. For what reasons might Heavenly Inc. have purchased the treasury stock?

Exercise 11–13

Effect of stock split

Goal 5

Headwaters Corporation wholesales ovens and ranges to restaurants throughout the Northwest. Headwaters Corporation, which had 30,000 shares of common stock outstanding, declared a 3-for-1 stock split (2 additional shares for each share issued).

a. What will be the number of shares outstanding after the split?
b. If the common stock had a market price of $120 per share before the stock split, what would be an approximate market price per share after the split?

Exercise 11–14

Common stock dilution

Goal 6

STUDENT SOLUTIONS MANUAL

Crawford Corp. issued 5,000 shares of $1 par common stock at a price of $25.25 per share on January 1, 2004. The proceeds will be used to invest in a project that is expected to generate a 20% annual after-tax return. The base earnings per share without the impact of the new investment is $4.00 for each of the 100,000 common shares.

a. Determine the earnings per share for 2004.
b. Is the stock issuance expected to dilute earnings per share?

Exercise 11–15

Effect of cash dividend, stock dividend, and stock split

Goals 5, 7

Indicate whether the following actions would (+) increase, (-) decrease, or (0) not affect Collier Inc.'s total assets, liabilities, and stockholders' equity:

	Assets	Liabilities	Stockholders' Equity
(1) Declaring a stock dividend	______	______	______
(2) Issuing stock certificates for the stock dividend declared in (1)	______	______	______
(3) Declaring a cash dividend	______	______	______
(4) Paying the cash dividend declared in (3)	______	______	______
(5) Authorizing and issuing stock certificates in a stock split	______	______	______

Exercise 11–16

Selected stock and dividend transactions

Goals 5, 7

STUDENT SOLUTIONS MANUAL

Selected transactions completed by Aft Boating Supply Corporation during the current fiscal year are as follows:

Jan. 7 Split the common stock 4 for 1 and reduced the par from $100 to $25 per share. After the split, there were 200,000 common shares outstanding.

(continued)

Mar. 1 Declared semiannual dividends of $2 on 8,000 shares of preferred stock and $0.10 on the common stock to stockholders of record on March 31, payable on April 15.

Apr. 15 Paid the cash dividends.

Nov. 1 Declared semiannual dividends of $2 on the preferred stock and $0.25 on the common stock (before the stock dividend). In addition, a 1% common stock dividend was declared on the common stock outstanding. The fair market value of the common stock is estimated at $30.

Dec. 15 Paid the cash dividends and issued the certificates for the common stock dividend.

Record the transactions.

Exercise 11–17

Entries for cash dividends

Goal 7

The important dates in connection with a cash dividend of $75,000 on a corporation's common stock are January 4, February 3, and March 5. Record the entries required on each date.

Exercise 11–18

Entries for stock dividends

Goal 7

b. (1) $362,500
(3) $833,500

STUDENT SOLUTIONS MANUAL

Heartwood Inc. is an HMO for twelve businesses in the Cleveland area. The following account balances appear on the balance sheet of Heartwood: Common stock (100,000 shares authorized), $50 par, $300,000; Paid-in capital in excess of par—common stock, $62,500; and Retained earnings, $471,000. The board of directors declared a 1% stock dividend when the market price of the stock was $76 a share. Heartwood reported no income or loss for the current year.

a. Record the entries to record (1) the declaration of the dividend, capitalizing an amount equal to market value, and (2) the issuance of the stock certificates.
b. Determine the following amounts before the stock dividend was declared: (1) total paid-in capital, (2) total retained earnings, and (3) total stockholders' equity.
c. Determine the following amounts after the stock dividend was declared: (1) total paid-in capital, (2) total retained earnings, and (3) total stockholders' equity.

Exercise 11–19

Interpret stock exchange listing

Goals 2, 8

a. $90

The Wall Street Journal reported the following stock exchange information for General Electric Co. on February 21, 2002:

YTD % CHG	52 Weeks Hi	52 Weeks Lo	Stock	Sym	Div	Yld %	PE	Vol 100s	LAST	Net Chg
−6.3	53^{55}	28^{50}	GenElec	GE	.72	1.9	27	219362	37^{57}	+1.17

a. If you owned 500 shares of GE, what amount would you receive as a quarterly dividend?
b. Calculate and prove the dividend yield. Round percentage to two decimal places.
c. What is GE's percentage change in market price from the February 20, 2002, close? Round percentage to two decimal places.
d. What was the price of GE common stock at the beginning of the first trading day of the year? (Hint: Use the YTD % CHG column and the current price.)
e. If you bought 500 shares of GE at the close price on February 21, 2002, how much would it cost and who gets the money?

Exercise 11-20

Dividend yield and payout ratio

Goal 8

STUDENT SOLUTIONS MANUAL

At the market close of February 25, 2002, Bank of America Corp. had a closing stock price of $63.25. In addition, Bank of America had earnings per share of $4.18 and dividend per share was $2.40. Determine Bank of America's (a) dividend yield and (b) dividend payout ratio. Round percentages to two decimal places.

Exercise 11-21

Dividend yield and payout ratio

Goal 8

General Motors Corporation had earnings per share of $1.77 for 2001 and $6.68 for 2000. In addition, the dividend was $2.00 per share during these two years. The market price for GM closed at $48 per share on December 31, 2001.

a. Determine the dividend yield for General Motors on December 31, 2001. Round percentages to two decimal places.
b. Determine the 2000 and 2001 dividend payout ratio for General Motors. Round percentages to two decimal places.
c. Interpret these measures.

Exercise 11-22

Statement of stockholders' equity and cash flows

Goals 8, 9

STUDENT SOLUTIONS MANUAL

Procter & Gamble Co. is the largest manufacturer of consumer household products in the United States. The following selected entries were disclosed on the statement of stockholders' equity for a recent year:

(in 000,000s)	Common Stock	Preferred Stock	Additional Paid-In Capital	Retained Earnings	Total
Net earnings				$ 2,922	$ 2,922
Dividends to:					
Common shareholders				(1,822)	(1,822)
Preferred shareholders				(121)	(121)
Treasury purchases	$(18)		$ 6	(1,238)	(1,250)
Common stock issuances (option plan)	6		223		229

a. For all items except net earnings, identify the disclosure location, amount, and direction (inflow or outflow) on the statement of cash flows.
b. Determine the dividend payout ratio. Round percentage to two decimal places.

Accounting Application Problems

Problem 11-1A

Dividends on preferred and common stock

Goal 2

1. Common dividends in 2002: $31,000

SPREADSHEET

Magnifico Inc. owns and operates movie theaters throughout Georgia and Mississippi. Magnifico has declared the following annual dividends over a six-year period: 2000, $32,000; 2001, $65,000; 2002, $84,000; 2003, $60,000; 2004, $72,000; and 2005, $95,000. During the entire period, the outstanding stock of the company was composed of 25,000 shares of cumulative, $2 preferred stock, $100 par, and 50,000 shares of common stock, $7 par.

Instructions

1. Calculate the total dividends and the per-share dividends declared on each class of stock for each of the six years. There were no dividends in arrears on January 1, 2000. Summarize the data in tabular form, using the following column headings:

		Preferred Dividends		Common Dividends	
Year	Total Dividends	Total	Per Share	Total	Per Share
2000	$32,000				
2001	65,000				
2002	84,000				
2003	60,000				
2004	72,000				
2005	95,000				

2. Calculate the average annual dividend per share for each class of stock for the six-year period.
3. Assuming that the preferred stock was sold at par and common stock was sold at $8 at the beginning of the six-year period, calculate the percentage return on initial shareholders' investment, based on the average annual dividend per share (a) for preferred stock and (b) for common stock.

Problem 11–2A

Stock transactions for corporate expansion

Goal 3

On January 1 of the current year, the following accounts and their balances appear in the ledger of Osaka Corp., a meat processor:

Preferred $4 Stock, $100 par (20,000 shares authorized, 7,500 shares issued)	$ 750,000
Paid-In Capital in Excess of Par—Preferred Stock	150,000
Common Stock, $50 par (100,000 shares authorized, 40,000 shares issued)	2,000,000
Paid-In Capital in Excess of Par—Common Stock	300,000
Retained Earnings	805,000

At the annual stockholders' meeting on February 20, the board of directors presented a plan for modernizing and expanding plant operations at a cost of approximately $1,200,000. The plan provided (a) that a building, valued at $375,000, and the land on which it is located, valued at $75,000, be acquired in accordance with preliminary negotiations by the issuance of 8,000 shares of common stock, (b) that 5,000 shares of the unissued preferred stock be issued through an underwriter, and (c) that the corporation borrow $200,000. The plan was approved by the stockholders and accomplished by the following transactions:

Mar. 7 Issued 8,000 shares of common stock in exchange for land and a building, according to the plan.

21 Issued 5,000 shares of preferred stock, receiving $125 per share in cash from the underwriter.

29 Borrowed $200,000 from U.S. East National Bank, giving a 7% mortgage note.

No other transactions occurred during March.

Instructions

Record the transactions.

Problem 11–3A

Selected stock transactions

Goals 3, 4, 7

The following selected accounts appear in the ledger of Cyma Environmental Corporation on July 1, 2004, the beginning of the current fiscal year:

GENERAL LEDGER

Preferred 3% Stock, $75 par (10,000 shares authorized, 7,000 shares issued)	$525,000
Paid-In Capital in Excess of Par—Preferred Stock	60,000
Common Stock, $10 par (50,000 shares authorized, 30,000 shares issued)	300,000
Paid-In Capital in Excess of Par—Common Stock	100,000
Retained Earnings	937,000

During the year, the corporation completed a number of transactions affecting the stockholders' equity. They are summarized as follows:

a. Issued 10,000 shares of common stock at $20, receiving cash.
b. Sold 1,000 shares of preferred 3% stock at $90.
c. Purchased 5,000 shares of treasury common for $105,000.
d. Sold 3,000 shares of treasury common for $75,000.
e. Sold 1,000 shares of treasury common for $20,000.
f. Declared cash dividends of $2.25 per share on preferred stock and $0.50 per share on common stock.
g. Paid the cash dividends.

Instructions

Record the transactions. Identify each entry by letter.

Problem 11–4A

Entries for selected corporate transactions

Goals 3, 4, 7

3. $2,901,100

SPREADSHEET GENERAL LEDGER

Sasquatch Enterprises Inc. manufactures bathroom fixtures. The stockholders' equity accounts of Sasquatch Enterprises Inc., with balances on January 1 of the current fiscal year, are as follows:

Common Stock, $20 stated value (100,000 shares authorized, 80,000 shares issued)	$1,600,000
Paid-In Capital in Excess of Stated Value	300,000
Retained Earnings	625,000
Treasury Stock (4,000 shares, at cost)	120,000

The following selected transactions occurred during the year:

Jan. 30	Paid cash dividends of $1 per share on the common stock. The dividend had been properly recorded when declared on December 30 of the preceding fiscal year for $76,000.
Feb. 19	Issued 10,000 shares of common stock for $350,000.
Apr. 1	Sold all of the treasury stock for $140,000.
July 1	Declared a 5% stock dividend on common stock, to be capitalized at the market price of the stock, which is $42 a share.
Aug. 11	Issued the certificates for the dividend declared on July 1.
Oct. 20	Purchased 7,500 shares of treasury stock for $285,000.
Dec. 27	Declared a $0.90-per-share dividend on common stock.

In addition, Sasquatch had net income of $369,400 during the current year.

Instructions

1. Enter the January 1 balances in T accounts for the stockholders' equity accounts listed. Also prepare T accounts for the following: Paid-In Capital from Sale of Treasury Stock and Stock Dividends Distributable.
2. Record the transactions and post to the six selected accounts. In addition, post the net income closed to retained earnings.
3. Determine the total stockholders' equity on December 31.

Problem 11-5A

Entries for selected corporate transactions

Goals 3, 4, 5, 7

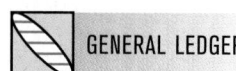

GENERAL LEDGER

Selected transactions completed by Silver Gate Boating Supply Corporation during the current fiscal year are as follows:

Jan.	6	Split the common stock 4 for 1 and reduced the par from $100 to $25 per share. After the split, there were 150,000 common shares outstanding.
Mar.	13	Purchased 7,500 shares of the corporation's own common stock at $35, recording the stock at cost.
May	1	Declared semiannual dividends of $2 on 18,000 shares of preferred stock and $0.60 on the common stock to stockholders of record on May 20, payable on June 1.
June	1	Paid the cash dividends.
Sept.	17	Sold 2,500 shares of treasury stock at $40, receiving cash.
Nov.	2	Declared semiannual dividends of $2 on the preferred stock and $0.60 on the common stock (before the stock dividend). In addition, a 2% common stock dividend was declared on the common stock outstanding. The fair market value of the common stock is estimated at $38.
Dec.	3	Paid the cash dividends and issued the certificates for the common stock dividend.

Instructions

Record the transactions.

Alternate Accounting Application Problems

Alternate Problem 11-1B

Dividends on preferred and common stock

Goal 2

1. Common dividends in 2000: $10,000

STUDENT SOLUTIONS MANUAL

SPREADSHEET

LaMancha Corp. manufactures mountain bikes and distributes them through retail outlets in Idaho and Montana. LaMancha Corp. has declared the following annual dividends over a six-year period: 2000, $25,000; 2001, $8,000; 2002, $10,000; 2003, $4,000; 2004, $50,000; and 2005, $75,500. During the entire period, the outstanding stock of the company was composed of 5,000 shares of cumulative $3 preferred stock, $50 par, and 50,000 shares of common stock, $5 par.

Instructions

1. Calculate the total dividends and the per-share dividends declared on each class of stock for each of the six years. There were no dividends in arrears on January 1, 2000. Summarize the data in tabular form, using the following column headings:

		Preferred Dividends		Common Dividends	
Year	Total Dividends	Total	Per Share	Total	Per Share
2000	$25,000				
2001	8,000				
2002	10,000				
2003	4,000				
2004	50,000				
2005	75,500				

2. Calculate the average annual dividend per share for each class of stock for the six-year period.
3. Assuming that the preferred stock was sold at par and common stock was sold at $11 at the beginning of the six-year period, calculate the percentage return on initial shareholders' investment, based on the average annual dividend per share (a) for preferred stock and (b) for common stock.

Alternate Problem 11–2B

Stock transaction for corporate expansion

Goal 3

STUDENT SOLUTIONS MANUAL

Neural Corp. produces medical lasers for use in hospitals. The following accounts and their balances appear in the ledger of Neural Corp. on June 30 of the current year:

Preferred $5 Stock, $100 par (20,000 shares authorized, 10,000 shares issued)	$1,000,000
Paid-In Capital in Excess of Par—Preferred Stock	150,000
Common Stock, $25 par (100,000 shares authorized, 60,000 shares issued)	1,500,000
Paid-In Capital in Excess of Par—Common Stock	200,000
Retained Earnings	915,000

At the annual stockholders' meeting on July 21, the board of directors presented a plan for modernizing and expanding plant operations at a cost of approximately $2,000,000. The plan provided (a) that the corporation borrow $650,000, (b) that 5,000 shares of the unissued preferred stock be issued through an underwriter, and (c) that a building, valued at $750,000, and the land on which it is located, valued at $100,000, be acquired in accordance with preliminary negotiations by the issuance of 20,000 shares of common stock. The plan was approved by the stockholders and accomplished by the following transactions:

Aug. 3 Borrowed $650,000 from First National Bank, giving an 8% mortgage note.
12 Issued 5,000 shares of preferred stock, receiving $120 per share in cash from the underwriter.
30 Issued 20,000 shares of common stock in exchange for land and a building, according to the plan.

No other transactions occurred during August.

Instructions

Record the foregoing transactions.

Alternate Problem 11–3B

Selected stock transactions

Goals 3, 4, 7

STUDENT SOLUTIONS MANUAL

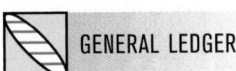

GENERAL LEDGER

Cutthroat Corporation sells and services pipe-welding equipment in Montana. The following selected accounts appear in the ledger of Cutthroat Corporation on January 1, 2004, the beginning of the current fiscal year:

Preferred 2% Stock, $100 par (40,000 shares authorized, 15,000 shares issued)	$1,500,000
Paid-In Capital in Excess of Par—Preferred Stock	112,500
Common Stock, $10 par (800,000 shares authorized, 400,000 shares issued)	4,000,000
Paid-In Capital in Excess of Par—Common Stock	600,000
Retained Earnings	3,450,000

During the year, the corporation completed a number of transactions affecting the stockholders' equity. They are summarized as follows:

a. Purchased 25,000 shares of treasury common for $550,000.
b. Sold 8,000 shares of treasury common for $192,000.
c. Sold 6,000 shares of preferred 2% stock at $110.
d. Issued 50,000 shares of common stock at $20, receiving cash.
e. Sold 7,000 shares of treasury common for $140,000.
f. Declared cash dividends of $2 per share on preferred stock and $0.25 per share on common stock.
g. Paid the cash dividends.

Instructions

Record the transactions. Identify each entry by letter.

Alternate Problem 11-4B

Entries for selected corporate transactions

Goals 3, 4, 7

3. $2,032,410

STUDENT SOLUTIONS MANUAL

SPREADSHEET GENERAL LEDGER

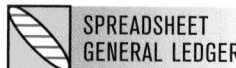

Loran Enterprises Inc. produces aeronautical navigation equipment. The stockholders' equity accounts of Loran Enterprises Inc., with balances on January 1 of the current fiscal year, are as follows:

Common Stock, $10 stated value (100,000 shares authorized, 75,000 shares issued)	$750,000
Paid-In Capital in Excess of Stated Value	150,000
Retained Earnings	597,750
Treasury Stock (5,000 shares, at cost)	90,000

The following selected transactions occurred during the year:

Jan. 15 Paid cash dividends of $0.80 per share on the common stock. The dividend had been properly recorded when declared on December 28 of the preceding fiscal year for $56,000.
Feb. 28 Sold all of the treasury stock for $125,000.
Apr. 5 Issued 10,000 shares of common stock for $300,000.
July 30 Declared a 3% stock dividend on common stock, to be capitalized at the market price of the stock, which is $28 a share.
Aug. 30 Issued the certificates for the dividend declared on July 30.
Sept. 3 Purchased 4,000 shares of treasury stock for $116,000.
Dec. 30 Declared an $0.80-per-share dividend on common stock.

In addition, Loran had net income of $382,500 during the current year.

Instructions

1. Enter the January 1 balances in T accounts for the stockholders' equity accounts listed. Also prepare T accounts for the following: Paid-In Capital from Sale of Treasury Stock and Stock Dividends Distributable.
2. Record the transactions and post to the six selected accounts. In addition, post the net income closed to retained earnings.
3. Determine the total stockholders' equity on December 31.

Alternate Problem 11-5B

Entries for selected corporate transactions

Goals 3, 4, 5, 7

STUDENT SOLUTIONS MANUAL

GENERAL LEDGER

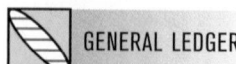

Ocean Atlantic Corporation manufactures and distributes leisure clothing. Selected transactions completed by Ocean Atlantic during the current fiscal year are as follows:

Jan. 3 Split the common stock 5 for 1 and reduced the par from $50 to $10 per share. After the split, there were 125,000 common shares outstanding.
Mar. 15 Declared semiannual dividends of $3 on 10,000 shares of preferred stock and $0.40 on the 125,000 shares of $10 par common stock to stockholders of record on March 31, payable on April 15.
Apr. 15 Paid the cash dividends.
May 8 Purchased 15,000 shares of the corporation's own common stock at $20, recording the stock at cost.
June 10 Sold 5,000 shares of treasury stock at $23, receiving cash.
Sept. 15 Declared semiannual dividends of $3 on the preferred stock and $0.40 on the common stock (before the stock dividend). In addition, a 2% common stock dividend was declared on the common stock outstanding, to be capitalized at the fair market value of the common stock, which is estimated at $25.
Oct. 15 Paid the cash dividends and issued the certificates for the common stock dividend.

Instructions

Record the transactions.

Building Leadership Skills—Financial Analysis and Reporting

Case 11–1

Dividend information on the Internet

Yahoo's Web portal provides stock market information for publicly traded companies. Go to finance.yahoo.com on the Internet. Enter the symbol for Philip Morris Companies, Inc., using the "Symbol Lookup" feature. (Note the single "l" in Philip.) Double-click on the symbol for the detailed market information for Philip Morris. Once at the detailed Philip Morris page view, answer the follow questions:

a. What is Philip Morris's historical, trailing twelve months (ttm) earnings per share?
b. What is Philip Morris's annual dividend per share?
c. What is Philip Morris's closing stock price from the previous day?
d. Calculate Philip Morris's dividend yield, using the closing stock price from (c).
e. What calendar date is the dividend "ex-dividend," and what does this mean?
f. What calendar date is the dividend date, and what does this mean?

Case 11–2

Capital stock dilution

Solectron Corp. is a major contract manufacturer in the electronics industry. During the fiscal year ending on August 31, 2001, the company issued 42,100,000 shares to the public at a price of $33.50 (rounded) to yield proceeds of $1,410,600,000. The company had 605 million shares outstanding prior to this offering. The company had an after-tax loss of $123,500,000 during the fiscal year ended August 31, 2001. Assume the proceeds of this offering can produce a pre-tax 12% return. Additionally, assume a 40% corporate tax rate.

a. Assume that the reported loss does not include the impact of investing the common stock proceeds. Determine the base earnings per share without the impact of the issuance.
b. Determine the pro forma (estimated) earnings per share, assuming that the proceeds from the common stock issuance can be invested to produce a 12% before-tax return and all else remained unchanged.
c. Is the issuance dilutive?
d. If Solectron issued 10% bonds, rather than common stock, what would be the pro forma (estimated) earnings per share if the proceeds earned a 12% before-tax return and all else remained unchanged?

Case 11–3

Capital stock dilution

Corning Inc. is a leading manufacturer of optical fiber, advanced materials, and information displays. *The Wall Street Journal* reported on November 6, 2000:

> *CORNING, N.Y.—Corning Inc. said it priced the offering of 30 million shares of newly issued common stock at $71.25 a share. Goldman, Sachs & Co. is the underwriter and lead manager of the offering. . . . Proceeds from the offering will be used to partially fund Corning's acquisition of Pirelli SpA's 90% interest in Optical Technologies USA Corp. and for general corporate purposes.*

The purchase of Optical Technologies USA Corp. was completed in December 2000. Corning had 781 million shares outstanding prior to the stock issuance. Income before taxes for 2000 was $691 million. Common stock has a par value $0.50 per share. Assume a corporate tax rate of 35%.

a. Provide the journal entry for the common stock issue in November 2000.
b. If the proceeds used to purchase Optical Technologies USA Corp. generated a 20% before-tax return in 2001, what would be the expected (pro forma) earnings per share in 2001, assuming no other change in operations?
c. Is the answer in (b) dilutive to earnings per share?
d. If Corning used 9% debt, rather than common stock, to finance the purchase of Optical Technologies, what would be the expected (pro forma) earnings per share in 2001, assuming no other change in operations?

Case 11–4

Dividend yield

The recent market price per share and dividend per share are provided for five large financial services and insurance companies traded on the New York Stock Exchange in the following table:

	Market Price per Share	Dividend per Share
AIG	$71.50	$0.17
John Hancock Financial Services	38.15	0.31
Lincoln National	51.05	1.28
Hartford Financial Services Group	67.00	1.04
ING Groep, NV	22.77	0.86

a. Determine the dividend yield for the five companies. Round percentages to two decimal places.
b. Why are the dividend yields different, even though these companies are from the same industry?
c. Should you avoid investing in a company with a low dividend yield?

Case 11–5

Statement of stockholders' equity

Thomas Nelson, Inc., is a publisher of Bibles and other religious materials. The statement of stockholders' equity for Thomas Nelson is as follows:

Thomas Nelson, Inc.
Statement of Stockholders' Equity
For the Fiscal Year Ended March 31, 2001
(in thousands, except share and per share data)

	Common Stock	Class B Common Stock	Additional Paid-In Capital	Retained Earnings	Total
Balance at March 31, 2000	$13,145.0	$1,086	$43,126.0	$74,375	$131,732
Net loss				(2,834)	(2,834)
Class B stock converted to common	25.0	(25)			–
Common stock issued:					
Acquisition of interest in subsidiary	108.0		652.0		760
Option plans—2,424 common shares	2.4		57.6		60
Dividends declared—$0.16 per share				(2,292)	(2,292)
Incentive plan stock awards—1,635 common shares	1.6		9.4		11
Balance at March 31, 2001	$13,282.0	$1,061	$43,845.0	$69,249	$127,437

a. What is the par value of the common stock? Round to nearest dollar.
b. How much did employees pay for common stock under the option plan? Round to nearest cent.
c. Record the entry for the common stock issuance under the option plan. (Hint: The issuance is recorded like any issuance.)

d. Provide a summary journal entry for the dividends paid for the year.
e. Does the dividend amount seem reasonable?

Case 11-6

Amazon.com: capitalizing a startup

The following chart shows the retained earnings balance for Amazon.com, Inc., from its initial public offering date until December 31, 2001:

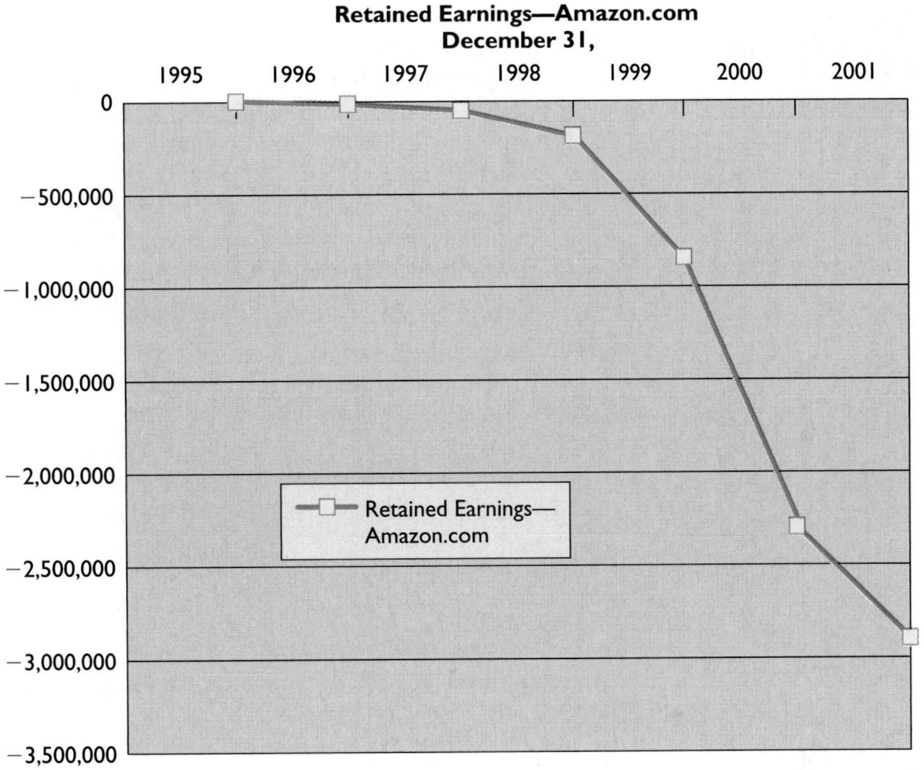

As can be seen, Amazon.com has accumulated deficits during the first seven years of its life as a public company. Below are the comparative liabilities and stockholders' equity for Amazon.com for this time period:

Liabilities and Stockholders' Equity

	12/31/01	12/31/00	12/31/99	12/31/98	12/31/97	12/31/96
Total current liabilities	$ 921,414	$ 974,956	$ 733,234	$ 161,575	$ 44,551	$ 4,870
Long-term debt	2,156,133	2,127,464	1,466,338	348,140	76,702	–
Total liabilities	$ 3,077,547	$ 3,102,420	$2,199,572	$ 509,715	$121,253	$ 4,870
Common stock	$ 3,732	$ 3,571	$ 3,452	$ 3,186	$ 1,449	$ 159
Paid-in capital in excess of par value	1,462,769	1,338,303	1,194,369	298,537	66,586	9,873
Retained earnings	(2,860,578)	(2,293,301)	(882,028)	(162,060)	(37,514)	(6,025)
Other equities	(45,923)	(15,824)	(49,515)	(918)	(1,930)	(606)
Total stockholders' equity	$(1,440,000)	$ (967,251)	$ 266,278	$ 138,745	$ 28,591	$ 3,401
Total liabilities & stockholders' equity	$ 1,637,547	$ 2,135,169	$2,465,850	$ 648,460	$149,844	$ 8,271

Given these accumulated deficits, where does Amazon.com obtain the funds to stay in business?

Building Leadership Skills—Responsible Leadership

Activity 11-1

Business strategy

GROUP ACTIVITY

7-Eleven operates more than 22,000 convenience food stores worldwide. 7-Eleven stores are normally less than 3,000 square feet and carry a variety of items, including soft drinks, candy and snacks, cigarettes, milk, and t-shirts. Many stores also sell CITGO-brand gasoline. 7-Eleven faces increasing competition from other convenience store chains as well as from grocery and supermarket chains, grocery wholesalers and buying clubs, gasoline/miniconvenience stores, food stores, and fast food chains as well as variety, drug, and candy stores. In groups of three to four, answer the following questions:

1. Go to the 7-Eleven Web site (http://www.7-eleven.com). How did the name 7-Eleven orginate?
2. How many items do you think an average 7-Eleven carries?
3. Excluding gasoline, rank the following "seven" categories of merchandise in the order in which you believe they generate the most sales for 7-Eleven. Rank the merchandise category with the most sales 1, the second most sales 2, and so on.

   Merchandise Category
   - baked and fresh foods, such as bread and rolls
   - beer and wine
   - beverages, such as soft drinks and coffee
   - candy and snacks
   - dairy products
   - nonfood products and services, such as automobile oil, toothpaste, coolers, money orders, and lottery tickets
   - tobacco products

4. Describe some ways (strategies) that you think 7-Eleven can increase its same-store sales in the face of increasing competition.

Activity 11-2

Common stock issuance

ETHICS

Holly Abernathy and Garreth Scott are organizing Derby Unlimited Inc. to undertake a high-risk gold-mining venture in Canada. Holly and Garreth tentatively plan to request authorization for 100,000,000 shares of common stock to be sold to the general public. Holly and Garreth have decided to establish par of $1 per share in order to appeal to a wide variety of potential investors. Holly and Garreth feel that investors would be more willing to invest in the company if they received a large quantity of shares for what might appear to be a "bargain" price.

Discuss whether Holly and Garreth are behaving in a professional manner.

Activity 11-3

Board of directors' actions

ETHICS

In early 2002, Bernie Ebbers, the CEO of Worldcom Group, a major telecommunications company, was having some personal financial troubles. Ebbers pledged a large stake of his Worldcom stock as security for some personal loans. As the price of Worldcom stock sank, Ebbers' bankers threatened to sell his stock in order to protect their loans. To avoid having his stock sold, Ebbers asked the board of directors of Worldcom to loan him nearly $400 million of corporate assets at 2.5% interest to pay off his bankers. The board agreed to lend him the money.

Comment on the decision of the board of directors in this situation.

Activity 11-4

Issuing stock

Omen Inc. began operations on January 8, 2004, with the issuance of 500,000 shares of $100 par common stock. The sole stockholders of Omen Inc. are Fay Barnes and Dr. Joseph Cawley, who organized Omen Inc. with the objective of developing a new flu vaccine.

Dr. Cawley claims that the flu vaccine, which is nearing the final development stage, will protect individuals against 99% of the flu types that have been medically identified. To complete the project, Omen Inc. needs $10,000,000 of additional funds. The local banks have been unwilling to loan the funds because of the lack of sufficient collateral and the riskiness of the business.

The following is a conversation between Fay Barnes, the chief executive officer of Omen Inc., and Dr. Joseph Cawley, the leading researcher.

Barnes: What are we going to do? The banks won't loan us any more money, and we've got to have $10 million to complete the project. We are so close! It would be a disaster to quit now. The only thing I can think of is to issue additional stock. Do you have any suggestions?

Cawley: I guess you're right. But if the banks won't loan us any more money, how do you think we can find any investors to buy stock?

Barnes: I've been thinking about that. What if we promise the investors that we will pay them 2% of net sales until they have received an amount equal to what they paid for the stock?

Cawley: What happens when we pay back the $10 million? Do the investors get to keep the stock? If they do, it'll dilute our ownership.

Barnes: How about, if after we pay back the $10 million, we make them turn in their stock for $200 per share? That's twice what they paid for it, plus they would have already gotten all their money back. That's a $200 profit per share for the investors.

Cawley: It could work. We get our money, but don't have to pay any interest, dividends, or the $200 until we start generating net sales. At the same time, the investors could get their money back plus $200 per share.

Barnes: We'll need current financial statements for the new investors. I'll get our accountant working on them and contact our attorney to draw up a legally binding contract for the new investors. Yes, this could work.

In late 2004, the attorney and the various regulatory authorities approved the new stock offering, and 100,000 shares of common stock were privately sold to new investors at the stock's par of $100.

In preparing financial statements for 2004, Fay Barnes and Tanya Kuchar, the controller for Omen Inc., have the following conversation.

Kuchar: Fay, I've got a problem.

Barnes: What's that, Tanya?

Kuchar: Issuing common stock to raise that additional $10 million was a great idea. But . . .

Barnes: But what?

Kuchar: I've got to prepare the 2004 annual financial statements, and I am not sure how to classify the common stock.

Barnes: What do you mean? It's common stock.

Kuchar: I'm not so sure. I called the auditor and explained how we are contractually obligated to pay the new stockholders 2% of net sales until $100 per share is paid. Then, we may be obligated to pay them $200 per share.

Barnes: So . . .

Kuchar: So the auditor thinks that we should classify the additional issuance of $10 million as debt, not stock! And, if we put the $10 million on the balance sheet as debt, we will violate our other loan agreements with the banks. And, if these agreements are violated, the banks may call in all our debt immediately. If they do that, we are in deep trouble. We'll probably have to file for bankruptcy. We just don't have the cash to pay off the banks.

1. Discuss the arguments for and against classifying the issuance of the $10 million of stock as debt.
2. What do you think might be a practical solution to this classification problem?

Activity 11-5

Earnings restatement

The following press report was issued in May 2001 by Robotic Vision Systems, Inc., a manufacturer of vision enabled systems for the electronics industry:

> *At this time, the Company estimates that as a result of the restatement (to correct certain accounting errors involving the recognition of revenue at its Acuity CiMatrix division), the revenue for the fiscal year ended September 30, 2000 to be approximately $223.5 million, or 1.9% less than that reported earlier and the net income for such period to be approximately $10.9 million, or 10.6% less than that reported earlier. The Company also estimates the revenue for the quarter ended December 31, 2000 to be approximately $32.6 million, or 0.8% more than that reported earlier and the net loss for such period to be approximately $13.8 million, or 0.7% less than that reported earlier. (Source: Robotic Vision Systems, Inc. Delays Release of Second Quarter Earnings,* 05/15/2001, PR Newswire.*)*

1. How would Robotic Vision account for these errors in the 2001 financial statements?
2. How do you believe investors will respond to prior period restatement errors?

Activity 11-6

Board of directors' dividend decisions

Ball-Peen Inc. has paid quarterly cash dividends since 1990. These dividends have steadily increased from $0.05 per share to the latest dividend declaration of $0.40 per share. The board of directors would like to continue this trend and is hesitant to suspend or decrease the amount of quarterly dividends. Unfortunately, sales dropped sharply in the fourth quarter of 2003 because of worsening economic conditions and increased competition. As a result, the board is uncertain as to whether it should declare a dividend for the last quarter of 2003.

On November 1, 2003, Ball-Peen Inc. borrowed $500,000 from City National Bank to use in modernizing its retail stores and to expand its product line in reaction to its competition. The terms of the 10-year, 12% loan require Ball-Peen Inc. to:

a. Pay monthly interest on the last day of the month.
b. Pay $50,000 of the principal each November 1, beginning in 2004.
c. Maintain a current ratio (current assets ÷ current liabilities) of 2.
d. Maintain a minimum balance (a compensating balance) of $25,000 in its City National Bank account.

On December 31, 2003, $125,000 of the $500,000 loan had been disbursed in modernization of the retail stores and in expansion of the product line. Ball-Peen Inc.'s balance sheet as of December 31, 2003, appears on the next page.

The board of directors is scheduled to meet January 6, 2004, to discuss the results of operations for 2003 and to consider the declaration of dividends for the fourth quarter of 2003. The chairman of the board has asked for your advice on the declaration of dividends.

1. What factors should the board consider in deciding whether to declare a cash dividend?
2. The board is considering the declaration of a stock dividend instead of a cash dividend. Discuss the issuance of a stock dividend from the point of view of (a) a stockholder and (b) the board of directors.

Ball-Peen Inc. Balance Sheet December 31, 2003			
Assets			
Current assets:			
Cash		$ 40,000	
Marketable securities		375,000	
Accounts receivable	$ 91,500		
Less allowance for doubtful accounts	6,500	85,000	
Merchandise inventory		125,000	
Prepaid expenses		4,500	
Total current assets			$ 629,500
Property, plant, and equipment:			
Land		$150,000	
Buildings	$950,000		
Less accumulated depreciation	215,000	735,000	
Equipment	$360,000		
Less accumulated depreciation	10,000	350,000	
Total property, plant, and equipment			1,235,000
Total assets			$1,864,500
Liabilities			
Current liabilities:			
Accounts payable	$ 71,800		
Notes payable (City National Bank)	50,000		
Salaries payable	3,200		
Total current liabilities		$125,000	
Long-term liabilities:			
Notes payable (City National Bank)		450,000	
Total liabilities			$ 575,000
Stockholders' Equity			
Paid-in capital:			
Common stock, $20 par (50,000 shares authorized, 25,000 shares issued)	$500,000		
Excess of issue price over par	40,000		
Total paid-in capital		$540,000	
Retained earnings		749,500	
Total stockholders' equity			1,289,500
Total liabilities and stockholders' equity			$1,864,500

Activity 11-7

Profiling a corporation

GROUP ACTIVITY

Select a public corporation you are familiar with or which interests you. Using the Internet, your school library, and other sources, develop a short (2 to 5 pages) profile of the corporation. Include in your profile the following information:

1. Name of the corporation.
2. State of incorporation.
3. Nature of its operations.
4. Total assets for the most recent balance sheet.
5. Total revenues for the most recent income statement.
6. Net income for the most recent income statement.

(continued)

7. Classes of stock outstanding.
8. Market price of the stock outstanding.
9. High and low prices of the stock for the past year.
10. Dividends paid for each share of stock during the past year.

In groups of three or four, discuss each corporate profile. Select one of the corporations, assuming that your group has $100,000 to invest in its stock. Summarize why your group selected the corporation it did and how financial accounting information may have affected your decision. Keep track of the performance of your corporation's stock for the remainder of the term.

Note: Most major corporations maintain "home pages" on the Internet. This home page provides a variety of information on the corporation and often includes the corporation's financial statements. In addition, the New York Stock Exchange Web site (www.nyse.com) includes links to the home pages of many listed companies. Financial statements can also be accessed using EDGAR, the electronic archives of financial statements filed with the Securities and Exchange Commission (SEC).

SEC documents can also be retrieved using the EdgarScan™ service from PricewaterhouseCoopers at edgarscan.pwcglobal.com. To obtain annual report information, key in a company name in the appropriate space. EdgarScan will list the reports available to you for the company you've selected. Select the most recent annual report filing, identified as a 10-K or 10-K405. EdgarScan provides an outline of the report, including the separate financial statements, which can also be selected in an Excel® spreadsheet.

Answers to Self-Study Questions

1. **C** If a corporation has cumulative preferred stock outstanding, dividends that have been passed for prior years plus the dividend for the current year must be paid before dividends may be declared on common stock. In this case, dividends of $27,000 ($9,000 × 3) have been passed for the preceding three years, and the current year's dividends are $9,000, making a total of $36,000 (answer C) that must be paid to preferred stockholders before dividends can be declared on common stock.
2. **D** Paid-in capital is one of the two major subdivisions of the stockholders' equity of a corporation. It may result from many sources, including the issuance of cumulative preferred stock (answer A), the receipt of donated real estate (answer B), or the sale of a corporation's treasury stock (answer C).
3. **C** Reacquired stock, known as treasury stock, should be listed in the Stockholders' Equity section (answer C) of the balance sheet. The price paid for the treasury stock is deducted from the total of all the stockholders' equity accounts.
4. **C** If a corporation that holds treasury stock declares a cash dividend, the dividends are not paid on the treasury shares. To do so would place the corporation in the position of earning income through dealing with itself. Thus, the corporation will record $44,000 (answer C) as cash dividends [(25,000 shares issued less 3,000 shares held as treasury stock) × $2 per share dividend].
5. **C** The dividend yield is 5% ($2.40 ÷ $48.00). The dividend payout ratio is 60% ($2.40 ÷ $4.00). The book value per share is not used in any of the calculations.

Chapter 12
Special Income and Investment Reporting Issues

THE LAW OF PRIORITIES

"Leaders understand that activity is not necessarily accomplishment."

—*The 21 Irrefutable Laws of Leadership*

Dr. John C. Maxwell

Learning Goals

1. Describe the accounting for and interpretation of deferred income taxes.
2. Prepare an income statement reporting the following unusual items: discontinued operations, extraordinary items, and changes in accounting principles.
3. Describe the accounting for and interpretation of fixed asset impairments and restructuring charges.
4. Prepare an income statement reporting earnings per share data.
5. Describe the concept and the reporting of comprehensive income.
6. Describe the accounting for investments in stocks.
7. Describe alternative methods of combining businesses and how consolidated financial statements are prepared.
8. Compute and interpret the price-earnings and price-book ratios.

Bose Corporation

Have you ever purchased a product and later became frustrated that it didn't perform as you expected? If so, maybe you should start your own company and make a better product. That is what Professor Amar Bose of MIT did in 1964 when he and five of his former students founded the Bose Corporation.

So why did he decide to organize his own company? While working on his graduate degrees at MIT, Bose decided to purchase a new stereo system. After analyzing the technical specifications of various systems, he purchased a system that appeared to offer the best sound. However, he was shocked by the system's poor sound quality and inability to provide sound comparable to a live performance. He then began extensive research on sound, which eventually led to his career in psychoacoustics—the study of sound as perceived by humans.

Through his research, Bose discovered that 80 percent of the sound heard by the audience in a concert hall is indirect sound. In other words, 80 percent of the sound you hear is sound that has bounced off the ceiling and walls rather than sound you hear directly from the stage musicians. This discovery led to the 1968 development of the Bose 901® Direct/Reflecting® speaker, which reflects 89 percent of the sound off the walls, thus better simulating the listening experience of a live concert hall. Prior to the development of the 901, speakers were developed in a vacuum, without consideration of how the surroundings would affect sound.

The 901 was acknowledged internationally for its life-like sound, and it became an industry standard for over 25 years. In the meantime, Bose developed the Auditioner® audio demonstrator, which takes the specifications of a room or concert hall and simulates exactly how a Bose speaker system will sound in the room or hall—even before it is built.

Early on, Bose also discovered the importance of listening to your customers. His first speaker, the 2201, was an excellent speaker but was never commercially successful. While customers liked the sound, the speakers were too large and clumsy. Bose then began to focus on developing compact speakers that delivered great sound. Today, in Bose retail stores, customers are offered demonstrations of Bose systems. The stunning sound show is conducted with customers sitting on a sofa opposite a large television and two giant speakers. After the show, the salesperson lifts the giant (fake) speakers to reveal tiny Bose speakers the size of a baseball.

Bose Corporation employs over 7,000 people and generates over $1.2 billion in revenues, which have doubled in the past five years. Bose speakers and sound systems can be found in Olympic stadiums, Broadway theatres, the Sistine Chapel, and the Space Shuttle. Meanwhile, Amar Bose, who has earned over two dozen patents, is still on the faculty of MIT, where he teaches acoustics and supervises graduate and undergraduate students.

While Amar Bose's engineering training was invaluable in developing his products, he had to learn a lot about building and running a business. With little business background, he had to learn how to read an income statement, hire and fire employees, and raise the money necessary to finance his company. Since the inception of his company, Bose has undoubtedly also had to learn about special income reporting issues, such as deferred taxes, fixed asset impairments, restructuring charges, earnings per share, and comprehensive income. In this chapter, we discuss these as well as other special income and investment reporting issues.

Sources: Adapted from the Bose Corporation Web Page; "Vox populi," *The Economist*, January 15, 2000; and "Amar Bose," Infoplease.com.

Your Need to Know

How much did Nortel Networks earn during the quarter ending September 30, 2001? The answer depends on whom you ask. According to Nortel's GAAP-based financial statements, it lost $1.08 per share. However, the company's management provided two additional "pro forma" earnings per share disclosures outside the published financial statements: a $0.68 loss that excluded acquisition and restructuring costs, and a $0.27 loss that further excluded inventory write-downs and bad debt provisions on accounts receivable. Which number is correct? The audited number reported to the SEC is a $1.08 loss, which is thus the "official" number. However, investors and analysts want to know the amount of earnings that are recurring and represent ongoing operations. As a result, the management of Nortel reported the two additional pro forma numbers to provide that insight. Paul Volcker, former chairman of the Federal Reserve, states: "It's an effort (by management) to provide some continuity and some reflection of the underlying progress of the company."

Management has broad discretion in defining pro forma disclosures. Critics argue that providing management such broad discretion can be misleading to investors. What may be "unusual" for one management team might not be for another. Dell Computer Company is an example of how this broad discretion can be used. Dell reported gains from venture investments on a separate line in the income statement, as required by GAAP. However, when these gains turned to losses during the early 2000s, Dell excluded the losses from "pro forma" numbers reported to the investing community. Dell responded to this approach by pointing out that investors have both the GAAP numbers, which included the losses, and the pro forma numbers, which did not, and could use them as they wish.

Defining and reporting earnings is an important part of the financial disclosure process. As a user of financial statements, you will need to evaluate the reported earnings numbers to understand the underlying earning power of the company. In this chapter, we will discuss a number of special topics that impact earnings disclosures.

Corporate Income Taxes

1 Describe the accounting for and interpretation of deferred income taxes.

Under the United States tax code, corporations are taxable entities that must pay federal income taxes. Depending upon where it is located, a corporation may also be required to pay state and local income taxes. Although we limit our discussion to federal income taxes, the basic concepts also apply to other income taxes.

Payment of Income Taxes

Most corporations are required to pay estimated federal income taxes in four installments throughout the year. For example, assume that a corporation with a calendar-year accounting period estimates its income tax expense for the year as $84,000. The entry to record the first of the four estimated tax payments of $21,000 (1/4 of $84,000) is as follows:

April 15	Income Tax Expense	21,000	
	Cash		21,000

At year-end, the actual taxable income and the related tax are determined. If additional taxes are owed, the additional liability is recorded. If the total estimated tax payments are greater than the tax liability based on actual taxable income, the overpayment should be debited to a receivable account and credited to *Income Tax Expense.*

Income taxes are normally disclosed as a deduction at the bottom of the income statement in determining net income, as shown in the following excerpt from an income statement for The Procter & Gamble Company:

Year Ended June 30, 2001	**(Amounts in millions)**
Net Sales	$39,244
Cost of products sold	22,102
Marketing, research, and administrative expenses	12,406
Operating Income	$ 4,736
Interest expense	794
Other income, net	674
Earnings Before Income Taxes	$ 4,616
Income taxes	1,694
Net Earnings	$ 2,922

Other common terms used for income taxes on the income statement and in footnote disclosures include *provision for income taxes* and *income tax expense.*

The ratios of reported income tax expense to earnings before taxes are shown below for some selected industries. As can be seen, taxes are a significant expense for most companies.

Industry	**Percent of Reported Income Tax Expense to Earnings before Taxes**
Automobiles	33%
Banking	35
Computers	35
Food	35
Integrated oil	39
Pharmaceuticals	30
Retail	39
Telecommunication	37
Transportation	38

The reported income tax expense is normally between 30%–40% of earnings before taxes. Differences in these rates between industries can be due to tax regulations unique to various industries.

Temporary Differences between Taxable Income and Reported Income

The **taxable income** of a corporation is determined according to the tax laws and is reported to taxing authorities on the corporation's tax return. It is often different from the income before income taxes reported in the income statement according to generally accepted accounting principles. As a result, the *income tax based on taxable income (tax return)* usually differs from the *income tax based on income before taxes (income statement),* as illustrated in Exhibit 1.

Exhibit 1

Tax Differences between Tax Return and Income Statement

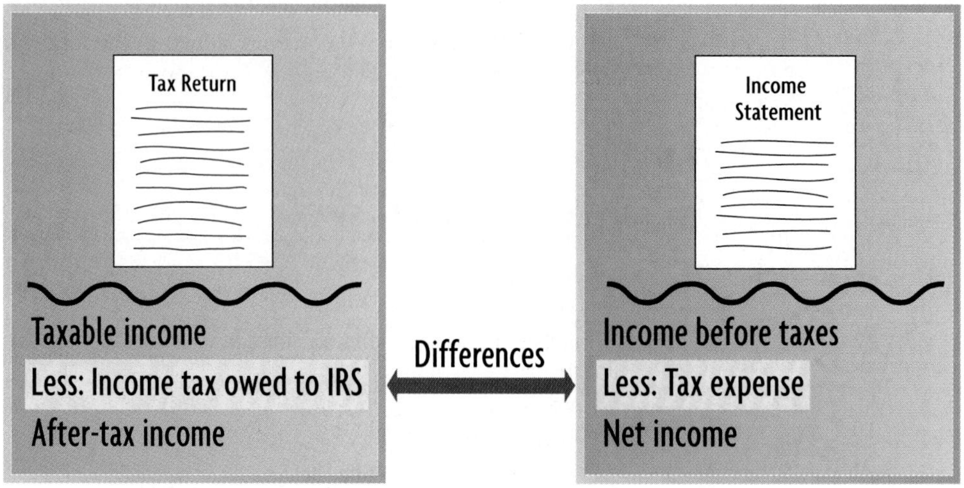

Some differences between taxable income and income before income taxes are created because items are recognized in one period for tax purposes and in another period for income statement purposes. Such differences, called **temporary differences**, reverse or turn around in later years. Some examples of items that create temporary differences are listed below.

1. *Revenues or gains are taxed* **after** *they are reported in the income statement.* Example: In some cases, companies who make sales under an installment plan recognize revenue for financial reporting purposes when a sale is made but defer recognizing revenue for tax purposes until cash is collected.
2. *Expenses or losses are deducted in determining taxable income* **after** *they are reported in the income statement.* Example: Product warranty expense estimated and reported in the year of the sale for financial statement reporting is deducted for tax reporting when paid.
3. *Revenues or gains are taxed* **before** *they are reported in the income statement.* Example: Cash received in advance for magazine subscriptions is included in taxable income when received, but included in the income statement only when earned in a future period.
4. *Expenses or losses are deducted in determining taxable income* **before** *they are reported in the income statement.* Example: MACRS depreciation is used for tax purposes, and the straight-line method is used for financial reporting purposes.

Since temporary differences reverse in later years, they do not change or reduce the total amount of taxable income over the life of a business. Exhibit 2 illustrates the reversing nature of temporary differences in which a business uses MACRS depreciation for tax purposes and straight-line depreciation for financial statement purposes. MACRS recognizes more depreciation in the early years, but less depreciation in the later years. The total depreciation expense is the same for both methods over the life of the asset.

As Exhibit 2 illustrates, temporary differences affect only the timing of when revenues and expenses are recognized for tax purposes. As a result, the total amount of taxes paid does not change. Only the timing of the payment of taxes is affected. In most cases, managers use tax-planning techniques so that temporary differences delay or defer the payment of taxes to later years. As a result, at the end of each year the amount of the current tax liability and the postponed (deferred) liability must be recorded.

To illustrate, assume that at the end of the first year of operations a corporation reports $300,000 income before income taxes on its income statement. If we assume an income tax rate of 40%, the income tax expense reported on the income statement is $120,000 ($300,000 × 40%).[1] However, to reduce the amount owed for current income taxes, the

1 For purposes of illustration, the 40% rate is assumed to include all federal, state, and local income taxes.

Exhibit 2

Temporary Differences

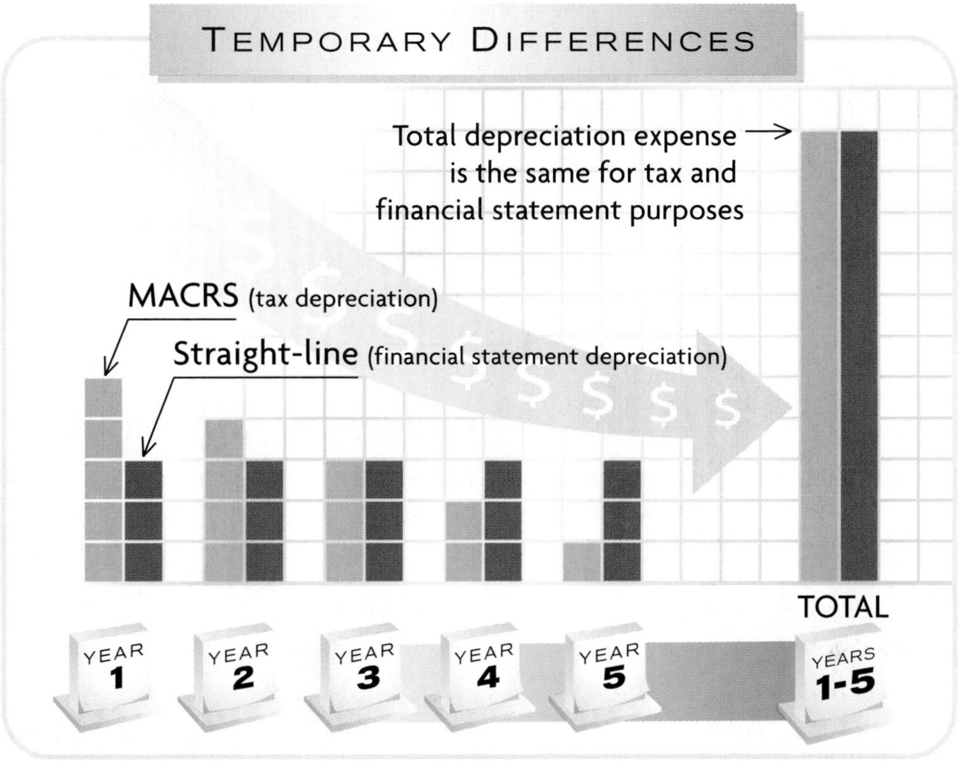

A corporation has $300,000 income before income taxes, a 40% tax rate, and $130,000 taxable income. What is the amount of deferred income tax?

$68,000 [($300,000 × 40%) − ($130,000 × 40%)]

corporation uses tax planning to reduce the taxable income to $100,000. Thus, the income tax actually due for the year is only $40,000 ($100,000 × 40%). The $80,000 ($120,000 − $40,000) difference between the two tax amounts is created by timing differences in recognizing revenue. This amount is deferred to future years. The example is summarized below.

Income tax based on $300,000 reported income at 40%	$120,000
Income tax based on $100,000 taxable income at 40%	40,000
Income tax deferred to future years	$ 80,000

Allocation of Income Taxes[2]

Income tax is allocated between financial statement periods in order to match the current year's tax expense against the current year's revenue on the income statement, using the following journal entry:

Income Tax Expense	120,000	
Income Tax Payable		40,000
Deferred Income Tax Payable		80,000

2 The accounting for deferred income taxes is a complex advanced topic that we only briefly describe here. Although *Statement of Financial Accounting Standards No. 101* requires that the income tax be determined residually from the temporary differences, we present a simplified approach that determines the deferred income tax as the difference between the tax expense and the tax payable.

The income tax expense reported on the income statement is the total tax, $120,000, expected to be paid on the income for the year. In future years, the $80,000 in *Deferred Income Tax Payable* will be transferred to *Income Tax Payable* as the timing differences reverse and the taxes become due. For example, if $48,000 of the deferred tax reverses and becomes due in the second year, the following journal entry would be made in the second year:

Deferred Income Tax Payable	48,000	
Income Tax Payable		48,000

Reporting and Analyzing Deferred Taxes

INTERNATIONAL PERSPECTIVE

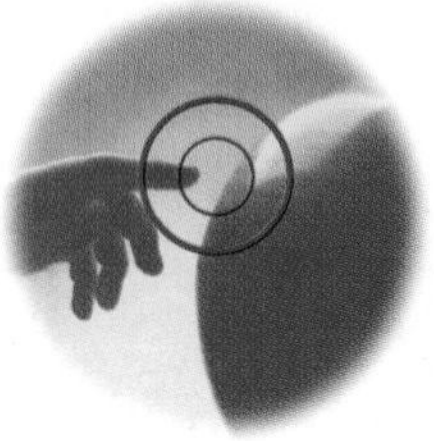

Egypt's accounting standards do not require the recording of deferred taxes.

The balance of *Deferred Income Tax Payable* at the end of a year is reported as a liability. The amount due within one year is classified as a current liability. The remainder is classified as a long-term liability or reported in a Deferred Credits section following the Long-Term Liabilities section.[3] A partial balance sheet of Costco Wholesale Corp. illustrates the long-term deferred tax liability presentation:

Total current liabilities (including $105,492,000 deferred income taxes)	$4,112,189,000
Long-term debt	859,393,000
Deferred income taxes and other long-term liabilities	119,434,000
Total liabilities	$5,091,016,000

Additional disclosures required in the notes identify the timing difference components of deferred tax assets and liabilities, and the current and deferred portion of the tax expense. For example, the deferred tax liability components for Costco were disclosed in the income tax note as follows:

Property and equipment	$127,243,000
Merchandise inventories	40,601,000
Other	40,976,000
Total deferred tax liabilities	$208,820,000

The total deferred tax liabilities are primarily caused by timing differences in accounting for depreciation of property and equipment and inventory. Of the $208,820,000 deferred tax liabilities, only $103,328,000 were classified as *noncurrent*, while the remainder was classified as a current liability.

Deferred income tax liabilities will normally result in future cash outflows when the temporary differences reverse and create higher taxes at future dates. However, what happens to this liability if the firm incurs losses or enters bankruptcy? The deferred tax liabilities are paid only if there is taxable income on the tax return. A firm does not owe taxes when there are losses. In addition, unlike a bank loan, the IRS has no claim on the assets of a company to satisfy deferred tax liabilities in the event of bankruptcy. Deferred tax liabilities are not contractual claims, but are viewed by analysts as contingent claims based on the financial health and existence of the firm. This is why companies may properly elect to disclose deferred tax liabilities with other contingencies on the balance sheet.

3 In some cases, a deferred tax asset may arise for tax benefits to be received in the future. Such deferred tax assets are reported as either a current or a long-term asset, depending on when the benefits are expected to be realized.

Permanent Differences

A corporation's taxable income and its income before taxes may also differ because certain revenues are exempt from tax and certain expenses are not deductible in determining taxable income. Such differences, which will not reverse with the passage of time, are sometimes called *permanent differences.* For example, interest income on municipal bonds may be exempt from taxation. Such differences create no special financial reporting problems, since the amount of income tax determined according to the tax laws is the *same* amount reported on the income statement.

Unusual Items Affecting Net Income

2 Prepare an income statement reporting the following unusual items: discontinued operations, extraordinary items, and changes in accounting principles.

Generally accepted accounting principles identify three types of unusual items that require specialized reporting on the income statement below the income from continuing operations line:

1. The results of discontinued operations.
2. Extraordinary items that result in a gain or loss.
3. A change from one generally accepted accounting principle to another.

These items are reported separately, as shown in the income statement for Jones Corporation in Exhibit 3. Many different terms and formats may be used. For example, the related tax effects of unusual items may be reported with the item with which they are associated or in the notes to the statement. Approximately 29% of U.S. companies reported one of these unusual items on their income statements for a recent fiscal year.[4]

In the following paragraphs, we briefly discuss each of the three types of unusual items. We assume that these items are material to the financial statements. Immaterial items would not affect the normal financial statement presentation.

Discontinued Operations

A gain or loss from disposing of a business segment or component of an entity is reported on the income statement as a gain or loss from **discontinued operations**. The term *business segment* refers to a major line of business for a company, such as a division or a department or a certain class of customer. A *component* of an entity is the lowest level at which the operations and cash flows can be clearly distinguished, operationally and for financial reporting purposes, from the rest of the entity.[5] Examples would be an individual store for a retailer, a territory for a sales organization, or a product category for a consumer products company. To illustrate the disclosure, assume that Jones Corporation has separate divisions that produce electrical products, hardware supplies, and lawn equipment. Jones sells its electrical products division at a loss. As shown in Exhibit 3, this loss is deducted from Jones' income from continuing operations (income from its hardware and lawn equipment divisions). In addition, Note A discloses the identity of the segment sold, the disposal date, a description of the segment's assets and liabilities, and the manner of disposal.

---

4 Determined from U.S. firms in excess of $5 billion sales on Disclosure® database.

5 *Statement of Financial Accounting Standards No. 144,* "Accounting for the Impairment or Disposal of Long-Lived Assets," Financial Accounting Standards Board (Norwalk, Connecticut: 2002), para. 41.

Exhibit 3

Unusual Items in Income Statement

Jones Corporation
Income Statement
For the Year Ended December 31, 2005

Net sales	$ 9,600,000
Cost of merchandise sold	5,600,000
Gross profit	$ 4,000,000
Operating expenses	(2,490,000)
Fixed asset impairment write-down	(200,000)
Income from continuing operations before income tax	$ 1,310,000
Income tax expense	620,000
Income from continuing operations	$ 690,000
Loss on discontinued operations (Note A)	100,000
Income before extraordinary items and cumulative effect of a change in accounting principle	$ 590,000
Extraordinary item:	
Gain on condemnation of land, net of applicable income tax of $65,000	150,000
Cumulative effect on prior years of changing to a different depreciation method (Note B)	92,000
Net income	$ 832,000

Note A.
On July 1 of the current year, the electrical products division of the corporation was sold at a loss of $100,000, net of applicable income tax of $50,000. The net sales of the division for the current year were $2,900,000. The assets sold were composed of inventories, equipment, and plant totaling $2,100,000. The purchaser assumed liabilities of $600,000.

Note B.
Depreciation of all property, plant, and equipment has been computed by the straight-line method in 2005. Prior to 2005, depreciation of equipment for one of the divisions had been computed on the double-declining-balance method. In 2005, the straight-line method was adopted for this division in order to achieve uniformity and to better match depreciation charges with the estimated economic utility of such assets. Consistent with APB Opinion No. 20, this change in depreciation has been applied to prior years. The effect of the change was to increase income by $30,000 before extraordinary items for 2005. The adjustment of $92,000 (after reduction for income tax of $88,000) to apply the new method to prior years is also included in income for 2005.

Extraordinary Items

Extraordinary items result from events and transactions that (1) are significantly different (unusual) from the typical or the normal operating activities of the business and (2) occur infrequently. The gains and losses that result from natural disasters that occur infrequently, such as floods, earthquakes, and fires, are extraordinary items. Gains or losses from condemning land or buildings for public use are also extraordinary. Such gains and losses, other than those from disposing of a business segment, should be reported in the income statement as extraordinary items, as shown in Exhibit 3.

Sometimes extraordinary items result in unusual financial results. For example, Delta Air Lines once reported an extraordinary gain of over $5.5 million as a result of the crash of one of its 727s. The plane that crashed was insured for $6.5 million, but its book value in Delta's accounting records was $962,000.

Gains and losses on the disposal of fixed assets are *not* extraordinary items. This is because (1) they are not unusual and (2) they recur from time to time in the normal operations of a business. Likewise, gains and losses from the sale of investments are usual and recurring for most businesses.

Changes in Accounting Principles

Businesses are often required to change their accounting principles when the Financial Accounting Standards Board (FASB) issues a new accounting standard. In addition, a business may voluntarily change from one generally accepted accounting principle to another. For example, a corporation may change from the fifo to the lifo method of costing inventory to better match revenues and expenses. Changes in generally accepted accounting principles should be disclosed in the financial statements (or in notes to the statements) of the period in which they occur. This disclosure should include the following:

1. The nature of the change.
2. The justification for the change.
3. The effect on the current year's net income.
4. The cumulative effect of the change on the net income of prior periods.

To illustrate, assume that one of Jones Corporation's divisions changes from the double-declining-balance method to the straight-line method of depreciation. As shown in Exhibit 3, the cumulative effect of this change is reported after the extraordinary items. The effect on the prior period is explained in Note B. If financial statements for prior periods are also presented, they should be restated as if the change had been made in the prior periods, and the effect of the restatement should be reported either on the face of the statements or in a note.

Unusual Items Affecting Income from Continuing Operations

3 **Describe the accounting for and interpretation of fixed asset impairments and restructuring charges.**

Reporting unusual items below the income from continuing operations on the income statement allows investors to isolate the effects of these items on income and cash flows from the ongoing and recurring operations of the business. However, other material unusual items should be reported as separate line items *above* the income from continuing operations as a part of continuing operations. Two such common disclosures are fixed asset impairments and restructuring charges.

Both asset impairments and restructuring charges are controversial features of financial reporting, since they often represent significant and unusual losses to an organization. Some critics argue that management is not timely in recognizing these events. Regardless, separate disclosure of these items helps users estimate and interpret operating performance.

Fixed Asset Impairments

Fixed asset impairments occur when the fair value of a fixed asset that is held or used falls below its book value and is not expected to recover. Such impairments should be recognized on the income statement as a loss at the time of the impairment, as shown for Jones Corporation in Exhibit 3. Examples of events that might cause an unrecoverable asset impairment are material decreases in the market price of the fixed asset, significant changes in the business or regulatory climate related to the fixed asset, adverse conditions affecting the use of the fixed asset, or expected cash flow losses from using the fixed asset. For example, Office Depot Inc. suffered impaired fixed assets and made the following disclosure in a recent annual report:

Our review also involved an extensive evaluation of all company assets. This evaluation resulted in a total charge . . . ., which consists of $56.6 million primarily related to impaired long-lived assets in our closing stores, $17.6 million in other fixed asset write-offs (mainly outdated technology-related assets and old signage), ...

When an asset is impaired, the cost of the asset is reduced or *written down*. The journal entry to record Office Depot's 74.2 million impairment of fixed assets was:

Loss on Fixed Asset Impairment	74,200,000	
Fixed Assets (stores and fixtures)		74,200,000

This loss reduces the book value of the fixed asset immediately, and thus reduces the depreciation expense for future periods. When these assets are sold, the gain or loss on the sale would be based on the lowered book value. Thus, asset impairment accounting recognizes the loss when it is first identified, rather than during the use or the sale of the asset.

Ethics in Action

When Is an Asset Impaired?

The asset impairment rule is designed to reduce the subjectivity of timing asset write-downs. Write-downs should occur when the impairment is deemed permanent. In practice, however, there is still judgment in determining when such impairment has occurred. Thus, the timing of asset write-downs remains somewhat controversial. Ethical managers will attempt to recognize asset write-downs when they occur, not when it's most convenient.

Restructuring Charges

Restructuring charges are the accrued employee termination benefits associated with a management-approved employee termination plan.[6] The employee termination benefits should not be associated with future services, but, rather, should represent severance compensation. The charge for the termination benefits is reported as an expense on the income statement at the time the plan is approved by senior management. For example, Quaker Oats Company adopted a plan to close several facilities and reduce employee administrative headcount. The accrued severance and termination benefits from this restructuring plan totaled $74,200,000. The restructuring charge would be recorded as:

Restructuring Charge	74,200,000	
Employee Termination Benefit Obligation		74,200,000

6 *Emerging Issues Task Force 94-3: Liability Recognition for Certain Employee Termination Benefits and Other Costs to Exit an Activity (including Certain Costs Incurred in a Restructuring)*, Financial Accounting Standards Board (Norwalk, Connecticut: 1994).

The restructuring charge is normally reported as a separate expense in determining continuing operations. The employee termination benefit obligation would be shown as a current or a long-term liability, depending on benefit payment terms. The actual benefits paid to terminated employees should be charged (debited) against the liability. For example, the payment by Quaker Oats of $9,000,000 of termination benefits during the current period from a prior-period obligation is recorded as:

Employee Termination Benefit Obligation	9,000,000	
Cash		9,000,000

The following note discloses the termination benefit obligation accrual and adjustment for Quaker Oats:

Supply chain reconfiguration project	$64,400,000
Other U.S. organizational adjustments	9,400,000
Other Beverages Europe restructuring	400,000
Current period restructuring charge	$74,200,000
Adjustment to prior-period obligation	(9,000,000)
Total employee termination benefit obligation	$65,200,000

Ethics in Action

When Is a Loss Not a Loss?

The SEC stated that it would seek enforcement action against companies issuing earnings releases that exclude costs related to mergers, stock options, unusual events, in-process research and development, or other items without proper reconciliation to GAAP-based earnings. Such pro forma disclosures are made by managers in addition to required GAAP disclosures to show "core" earnings apart from unusual items. SEC chairman Pitt stated that "pro forma numbers making a loss look like a profit, without explaining clearly how, were likely to be viewed as fraudulent."

Earnings per Common Share

4 Prepare an income statement reporting earnings per share data.

The amount of net income is often used by investors and creditors in evaluating a company's profitability. However, net income by itself is difficult to use in comparing companies of different sizes. Also, trends in net income may be difficult to evaluate, using only net income, if there have been significant changes in a company's stockholders' equity. Thus, the profitability of companies is often expressed as earnings per share.

Earnings per common share (EPS), sometimes called *basic earnings per share*, is the net income per share of common stock outstanding during a period.

Because of its importance, earnings per share is reported in the financial press, Internet financial services, and by various investor services, such as Moody's and Standard & Poor's. Changes in earnings per share can lead to significant changes in the price of a corporation's stock in the marketplace. For example, the stock of Scientific-Atlanta Inc. surged by over 13 percent to \$39 per share after the company announced earnings per share of 53 cents as compared to 25 cents per share a year earlier. Wall Street analysts had been expecting earnings per share of 41 cents.

Corporations whose stock is traded in a public market must report earnings per common share on their income statements.[7] If no preferred stock is outstanding, the earnings per common share is calculated as follows:

$$\text{Earnings per common share} = \frac{\text{Net income}}{\text{Number of common shares outstanding}}$$

When the number of common shares outstanding has changed during the period, a weighted average number of shares outstanding is used. If a company has preferred stock outstanding, the net income must be reduced by the amount of any preferred dividends, as shown below.

$$\text{Earnings per common share} = \frac{\text{Net income} - \text{Preferred stock dividends}}{\text{Number of common shares outstanding}}$$

Comparing the earnings per share of two or more years, based on only the net incomes of those years, could be misleading. For example, assume that Jones Corporation, whose partial income statement for 2005 was presented in Exhibit 3, reported \$700,000 net income for 2004. Also assume that no extraordinary or other unusual items were reported in 2004. Jones has no preferred stock outstanding and has 200,000 common shares outstanding in 2004 and 2005. The earnings per common share is \$3.50 (\$700,000/200,000 shares) for 2004 and \$4.16 (\$832,000/200,000 shares) for 2005. Comparing the two earnings per share amounts suggests that operations have improved. However, the 2005 earnings per share comparable to the \$3.50 is \$3.45, which is the income from continuing operations of \$690,000 divided by 200,000 shares. The latter amount indicates a slight downturn in normal earnings.

When unusual items below continuing operations exist, earnings per common share should be reported for those items. To illustrate, a partial income statement for Jones Corporation, showing earnings per common share, is shown in Exhibit 4. In this income statement, Jones reports all the earnings per common share amounts on the face of the income statement. However, only earnings per share amounts for income from continuing operations and net income are required to be presented on the face of the statement. The other per share amounts may be presented in the notes to the financial statements.[8]

In the preceding paragraphs, we have assumed a simple capital structure with only common stock or common stock and preferred stock outstanding. Often, however, corporations have complex capital structures with various types of securities outstanding, such as convertible preferred stock, options, warrants, and contingently issuable shares. In such cases, the possible effects of converting such securities to common stock must be calculated and reported as *earnings per common share assuming dilution or diluted earnings per share*.[9] This topic is discussed further in advanced accounting texts.

---

7 *Statement of Financial Accounting Standards No. 128*, "Earnings per Share," Financial Accounting Standards Board (Norwalk, Connecticut: 1997).

8 Ibid., pars. 36 & 37.

9 Ibid., pars. 11–39.

Exhibit 4

Income Statement with Earnings per Share

Jones Corporation
Income Statement
For the Year Ended December 31, 2005

Earnings per common share:	
Income from continuing operations	$3.45
Loss on discontinued operations (Note A)	0.50
Income before extraordinary items and cumulative effect of a change in accounting principle	$2.95
Extraordinary item:	
Gain on condemnation of land, net of applicable income tax of $65,000	0.75
Cumulative effect on prior years of changing to a different depreciation method (Note B)	0.46
Net income	$4.16

Strategy in Business

Tinkering with Success?

Lego is a privately held Danish company that built its reputation on interlocking play bricks. From the early 1970s, generations of children have built houses, cars, and trucks with the famous bricks. However, younger and younger children are demanding more sophisticated toys. Within the toy industry, this phenomenon is known as "age compression." As a result, Lego has expanded beyond plastic bricks into ready-to-play figures and licensed its brand name to manufacturers of wristwatches and children's apparel. In addition, Lego decided to open Legoland theme parks throughout the world, including parks outside London and San Diego. Has Lego's strategy worked? It's too soon to tell, although Lego recently reported its largest loss ever of over $100 million.

Source: Adapted from John Tagliabue, "Lego Tinkered with Success, and Is Now Paying a Price," *The Wall Street Journal*, December 25, 2001.

Comprehensive Income

5 Describe the concept and the reporting of comprehensive income.

Companies must report traditional net income plus or minus *other* comprehensive income items to arrive at comprehensive income.[10] **Comprehensive income** is defined as all changes in stockholders' equity during a period except those resulting from dividends and stockholders' investments.

10 *Statement of Financial Accounting Standards No. 130*, "Reporting Comprehensive Income," Financial Accounting Standards Board (Norwalk, Connecticut: 1997).

Other comprehensive income items include foreign currency items, pension liability adjustments, and unrealized gains and losses on investments. These "other" comprehensive income transactions are reported in a middle ground that requires disclosure of these items, but does not include them as part of reported earnings on the income statement. The FASB wanted these items disclosed separately from earnings in order to avoid potential confusion in interpreting the income statement. Such a disclosure is somewhat controversial, because it begs the question: are these items part of earnings or are they not?

To the extent that other comprehensive income items give rise to tax effects, the taxes should be allocated to these items, as we illustrated earlier in this chapter. The cumulative effects of other comprehensive income items must be reported separately from retained earnings and paid-in capital on the balance sheet. When other comprehensive income items are not present, the income statement and balance sheet formats are similar to those we have illustrated in this and preceding chapters.

Companies may report comprehensive income on the income statement, in a separate statement of comprehensive income, or in the statement of stockholders' equity. Over 70 percent of surveyed firms disclosed comprehensive income in the statement of stockholders' equity.[11] In addition, companies may use terms other than comprehensive income, such as *total nonowner changes in equity*.

To illustrate comprehensive income disclosure, JDS Uniphase Corp., a designer and manufacturer of fiberoptic communications equipment, reported other comprehensive items in a separate statement in the notes to its financial statements, as follows:

	Years Ended June 30,	
	2002	2001
	(in millions)	
Net loss	$(8,738.3)	$(56,121.9)
Other comprehensive items:		
Changes in net unrealized gains (losses) on available-for-sale investments	(2.5)	7.7
Changes in foreign currency translation	0.9	
Other changes	2.2	(14.9)
Total comprehensive loss	$(8,737.7)	$(56,129.1)

The *accumulated other comprehensive loss* is the last line of the stockholders' equity section of the balance sheet for JDS Uniphase, as shown at the top of the following page. This balance accumulates the other comprehensive income or loss separately from retained earnings. Thus, the additional other comprehensive income of $0.6 million for 2002 is added to the accumulated other comprehensive loss of $24.4 million to yield the ending loss balance of $23.8 million.

You should note that the other comprehensive income items do not affect net income or retained earnings as we have discussed and illustrated. In the next section, we will illustrate the reporting of unrealized gains and losses on investments as part of other comprehensive income.

11 *Accounting Trends and Techniques* (2001 Edition), AICPA, p. 401.

JDS Uniphase Corporation
Stockholders' Equity

	In Millions	
Stockholders' equity:	June 30, 2002	June 30, 2001
Common stock, $0.001 par value	$ 1.4	$ 1.3
Common stock to be issued	111.7	90.8
Additional paid-in capital	68,399.0	68,046.8
Deferred compensation	(54.2)	(183.6)
Accumulated deficit	(65,962.7)	(57,224.4)
Accumulated other comprehensive loss	(23.8)	(24.4)
Total stockholders' equity	$ 2,471.4	$ 10,706.5

Accounting for Investments in Stocks

6 Describe the accounting for investments in stocks.

Corporations not only issue stock, but they also purchase stocks of other companies for investment purposes. Like individuals, businesses have a variety of reasons for investing in stocks, called **equity securities**. A business may purchase stocks as a means of earning a return (income) on excess cash that it does not need for its normal operations. Such investments are usually for a short period of time. In other cases, a business may purchase the stock of another company as a means of developing or maintaining business relationships with the other company. A business may also purchase common stock as a means of gaining control of another company's operations. In these two latter cases, the business usually intends to hold the investment for a long period of time.

The equity securities in which a business invests may be classified as trading securities or available-for-sale securities. **Trading securities** are securities that management intends to actively trade for profit. Businesses holding trading securities are those whose normal operations involve buying and selling securities. Examples of such businesses include banks and insurance companies. **Available-for-sale securities** are securities that management expects to sell in the future, but are not actively traded for profit. For example, Warren Buffett, one of the wealthiest men in the world, invests through a public company called Berkshire Hathaway Inc. Berkshire Hathaway has over $35 billion of equity investment holdings listed on its balance sheet as "available-for-sale" securities. Some of these investments include Coca-Cola Company, Gillette Company, and American Express. Available-for-sale securities may be classified as either current or noncurrent, depending on management's investment intent. Securities that are held to effectively control an entity are accounted for under the equity method. In this section, we describe and illustrate the accounting for available-for-sale and equity method investments. The accounting for trading securities is described and illustrated in advanced accounting texts.

Available-for-Sale Equity Investments

Rather than allow excess cash to be idle until it is needed, a business may invest all or part of it in income-yielding securities. Since these investments can be quickly sold and converted to cash as needed, they are called **temporary investments** or *marketable securities*. Although such investments may be retained for several years, they continue to be classified as temporary, provided they meet two conditions. First, the securities must be readily marketable and can be sold for cash at any time. Second, management must intend to sell the securities when the business needs cash for operations.

Temporary investments are recorded in a current asset account, *Marketable Securities*, at their cost. This cost includes all amounts spent to acquire the securities, such as broker's commissions. Any dividends received on the investment are recorded as a debit to *Cash* and a credit to *Dividend Revenue*.[12]

To illustrate, assume that on June 1 Crabtree Co. purchased 2,000 shares of Inis Corporation common stock at $89.75 per share plus a brokerage fee of $500. On October 1, Inis declared a $0.90 per share cash dividend payable on November 30. Crabtree's entries to record the stock purchase and the receipt of the dividend are as follows:

June	1	Marketable Securities	180,000	
		Cash		180,000
		($89.75 × 2,000 shares) + $500		
Nov.	30	Cash	1,800	
		Dividend Revenue		1,800

On the balance sheet, temporary investments are reported at their fair market value. Market values are normally available from stock quotations in financial newspapers, such as *The Wall Street Journal*. Any difference between the fair market values of the securities and their cost is an **unrealized holding gain or loss**. This gain or loss is termed "unrealized" because a transaction (the sale of the securities) is necessary before a gain or loss becomes real (realized).

To illustrate, assume that Crabtree Co.'s portfolio of temporary investments has the following fair market values and unrealized gains and losses on December 31, 2005:

Common Stock	Cost	Market	Unrealized Gain (Loss)
Edwards Inc.	$150,000	$190,000	$ 40,000
SWS Corp.	200,000	200,000	—
Inis Corporation	180,000	210,000	30,000
Bass Co.	160,000	150,000	(10,000)
Total	$690,000	$750,000	$ 60,000

If income taxes of $18,000 are allocated to the unrealized gain, Crabtree's temporary investments should be reported at their total cost of $690,000 plus the unrealized gain (net of applicable income tax) of $42,000 ($60,000 − $18,000), as shown in Exhibit 5.

The unrealized gain (net of applicable taxes) of $42,000 should also be reported as an *other comprehensive income item*, as we mentioned in the preceding section. For example, assume that Crabtree Co. has net income of $720,000 for the year ended December 31, 2005. Crabtree elects to report net income and comprehensive income on one financial statement, *Statement of Income and Comprehensive Income*, as shown in Exhibit 6.

12 Stock dividends received on an investment are not journalized, since they have no effect on the investor's assets and revenues.

Exhibit 5

Temporary Investments on the Balance Sheet

Crabtree Co. Balance Sheet December 31, 2005		
Assets		
Current assets:		
Cash		$119,500
Temporary investments in marketable securities at cost	$690,000	
Plus unrealized gain (net of applicable income tax of $18,000)	42,000	732,000

Exhibit 6

Statement of Income and Comprehensive Income

Crabtree Co. Statement of Income and Comprehensive Income For the Year Ended December 31, 2005	
Net income	$720,000
Other comprehensive income:	
Unrealized gain on temporary investments in marketable securities (net of applicable income tax of $18,000)	42,000
Comprehensive income	$762,000

Unrealized losses are reported in a similar manner. Unrealized gains and losses are reported as other comprehensive income items until the related securities are sold. When temporary securities are sold, the unrealized gains or losses become realized and are included in determining net income.[13]

The accounting for long-term available-for-sale securities is similar to that for short-term investments in stocks. Such long-term investments in stocks are not intended as a source of cash in the normal operations of the business and sometimes include securities that are not readily marketable. They are reported in the balance sheet under the caption **Investments**, which usually follows the Current Assets section. For example, Delta Air Lines disclosed investments in Priceline.com preferred stock as a noncurrent investment at appraised fair market value, which is consistent with available-for-sale treatment.

Equity Method

The **equity method** is used for long-term investments in stocks where the investor (the buyer of the stock) has a significant influence over the operating or financing activities of the investee (the company whose stock is owned). Evidence of such influence includes the percentage of ownership, the existence of intercompany transactions, and the interchange of managerial personnel. Generally, if the investor owns 20% or more of the voting stock of the investee, the investor is assumed to have significant influence over the investee.[14]

---

13 To avoid double-counting, realized gains and losses must be removed from comprehensive income. These adjustments are discussed in advanced accounting texts.

14 For investments of less than 20% of the voting stock of the investee, the cost method is used. Using the cost method is similar to the accounting for short-term investments in stock.

Under the equity method, the net income and cash dividends of the investee are recorded as follows:

1. The investor's share of the periodic net income of the investee is recorded as an *increase in the investment account* and as *revenue for the period.* Likewise, the investor's share of an investee's net loss is recorded as a *decrease in the investment account* and as a *loss for the period.*
2. The investor's share of cash dividends from the investee is recorded as an *increase in the cash account* and a *decrease in the investment account.*

To illustrate the equity method, assume that on January 2, Hally Inc. pays cash of \$350,000 for 40% of the common stock and net assets of Brock Corporation. Assume also that, for the year ending December 31, Brock Corporation reports net income of \$105,000 and declares and pays \$45,000 in dividends. Hally Inc. (the investor) records these transactions as follows:

Jan. 2	Investment in Brock Corp. Stock	350,000	
	Cash		350,000
	Purchased 40% of Brock Corp. Stock.		
Dec. 31	Investment in Brock Corp. Stock	42,000	
	Income of Brock Corp.		42,000
	\$105,000 × 40%		
Dec. 31	Cash	18,000	
	Investment in Brock Corp. Stock		18,000
	45,000 × 40%		

The combined effect of recording 40% of Brock Corporation's net income and dividends is to increase Hally's interest in the net assets of Brock by \$24,000 (\$42,000 − \$18,000), as shown below.

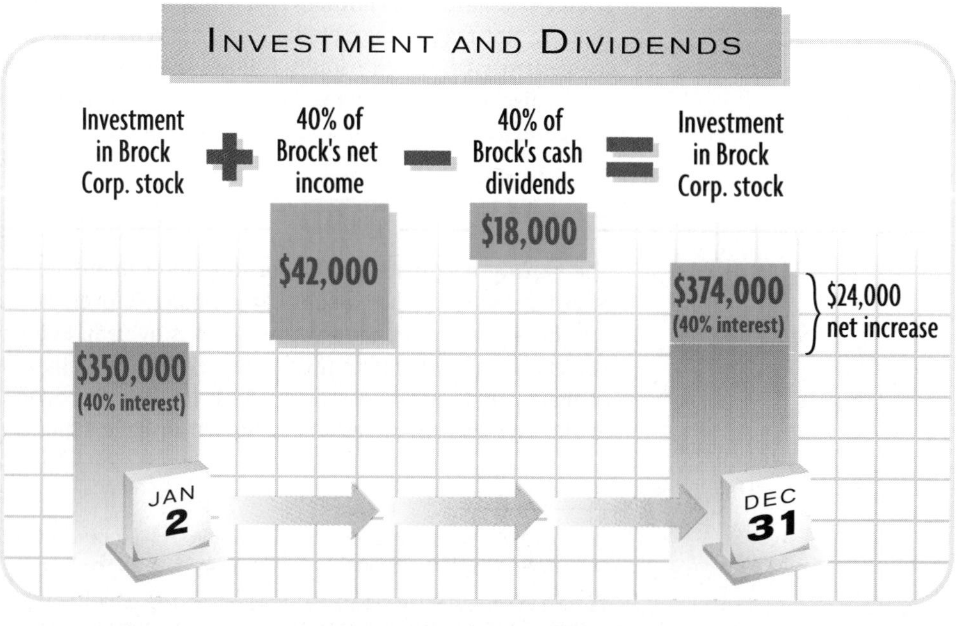

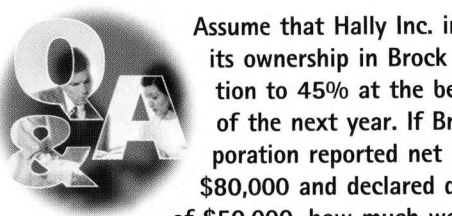

Assume that Hally Inc. increased its ownership in Brock Corporation to 45% at the beginning of the next year. If Brock Corporation reported net income of $80,000 and declared dividends of $50,000, how much would Hally Inc. debit Investment in Brock Corp. Stock?

$13,500 [($80,000 × 45%) − ($50,000 × 45%)]

The equity method causes the investment account to mirror the proportional changes in the book value of the investee. Thus, Brock Corp's. book value increased by $60,000 ($105,000 − $45,000), while the investment in Brock account increased by Hally's proportional share of that increase, or $24,000 ($60,000 × 40%). Both the book value of Brock Corp. and Hally's investment in Brock increased at the same rate from the base cost.

To illustrate equity-method disclosure, Delta Air Lines Inc. showed the following investment on its balance sheet:

	(in millions)	
	December 31,	
	2001	**2000**
OTHER ASSETS:		
Investments in associated companies	180	222

The investments in associated companies was described in its footnotes as follows:

> *We use the equity method to account for our 40% ownership interest in* WORLDSPAN, L.P. (Worldspan)*, a computer reservations system partnership. Our equity earnings from this investment totaled $19 million in 2001, $59 million in 2000, and $30 million in 1999.*

Sale of Investments in Stocks

Accounting for the sale of stock is the same for both short-term and long-term investments. When shares of stock are sold, the investment account is credited for the carrying amount (book value) of the shares sold. The cash or receivables account is debited for the proceeds (sales price less commission and other selling costs). Any difference between the proceeds and the carrying amount is recorded as a gain or loss on the sale and is included in determining net income.

To illustrate, assume that an investment in Drey Inc. stock has a carrying amount of $15,700 when it is sold on March 1. If the proceeds from the sale of the stock are $17,500, the entry to record the transaction is as follows:

Mar. 1	Cash	17,500	
	Investment in Drey Inc. Stock		15,700
	Gain on Sale of Investments		1,800

Equity-method investments recognize unrealized income and losses during the holding period of the investment, as illustrated in the previous section. As a result, the gain or loss on the sale will be influenced by the amount of these previously recognized amounts.

That is, since the book value of equity-method investments changes with unrealized income and losses, the realized gain or loss on the sale must be affected. In contrast, non-equity-method investments recognize the complete gain or loss in the period of sale, without any holding-period recognition.[15]

Ethics in Action

Enron

Enron Corporation, once the seventh largest company in the United States, crashed into bankruptcy in a matter of months. Much of Enron's travails were related to undisclosed losses from complex financial transactions with certain partnerships that were run by its own officers, including the CFO. Enron management came under severe criticism for (1) providing minimum disclosure about these partnership investments to the investing public, and (2) allowing senior officers to hold significant individual investments in these partnerships. Regarding the potential conflict of interest, Wayne Shaw, a professor of accounting, stated, "If it was the CFO, why was he put in a position where no one knew what he was doing? If the blame's being placed on one party, you have to wonder about the internal controls of the company. There's got to be checks and balances, and they weren't there." The lesson from Enron is that unconsolidated investments may require significant additional disclosures in the footnotes and that senior officers should avoid a conflict of interest caused by holding individual interests in the investee while being an officer of the investor.

Business Combinations

7 Describe alternative methods of combining businesses and how consolidated financial statements are prepared.

Each year, many businesses combine in order to produce more efficiently or to diversify product lines. Business combinations often involve complex accounting principles and terminology. Our objective in this section is to introduce you to some of the unique terminology and concepts related to business combinations. We also briefly describe the use and preparation of consolidated financial statements.

Mergers and Consolidations

One corporation may acquire all the assets and liabilities of another corporation, which is then dissolved. This joining of two corporations is called a **merger**. The acquiring company may use cash, debt, or its own stock as the payment. Whatever the form of payment, the amount received by the dissolving corporation is distributed to its stockholders in final liquidation. For example, Mattel Inc. acquired Mindscape Inc. for $152 million in cash and stock. As a result of the merger, Mindscape no longer exists as a separate company.

15 There is holding-period recognition of unrealized gains or losses in other comprehensive income, but these amounts are not disclosed on the income statement until sale.

A new corporation may be created, and the assets and liabilities of two or more existing corporations transferred to it. This type of combination is called a **consolidation**. The new corporation usually issues its own stock in exchange for the net assets acquired. The original corporations are then dissolved. For example, AOL Time Warner Inc. became the new consolidated company that resulted from combining two individual corporations—America Online and Time Warner.

Parent and Subsidiary Corporations

Business combinations may also occur when one corporation buys a controlling share of the outstanding voting stock of one or more other corporations. In this case, none of the corporations dissolve. The corporations continue as separate legal entities in a parent-subsidiary relationship. The corporation owning all or a majority of the voting stock of the other corporation is called the **parent company**. The corporation that is controlled is called the **subsidiary company**. Two or more corporations closely related through stock ownership are sometimes called *affiliated* companies. An example of an affiliated company is Waldenbooks, a subsidiary of Kmart.

A corporation (the acquiring company) may acquire the controlling share of the voting common stock of another corporation (the target company) by paying cash, exchanging other assets, issuing debt, or using some combination of these methods. In addition, a parent-subsidiary relationship may be created by exchanging the voting common stock of the acquiring corporation (the parent) for the common stock of the acquired corporation (the subsidiary). Regardless if there is an outright purchase of assets, common stock, or common stock exchange, the transaction is recorded like a normal purchase of assets, and the combination is accounted for by the **purchase method**.

Under the purchase method, the subsidiary's net assets are reported in the consolidated balance sheet at their fair market value at the time of the purchase. In some cases, a parent may pay more than the fair market value of a subsidiary's net assets because the subsidiary has prospects for high future earnings. The difference between the amount paid by the parent and the fair market value of the subsidiary's net assets is reported on the consolidated balance sheet as an intangible asset. This asset is identified as *Goodwill* or *Excess of cost of business acquired over related net assets.*

Footnotes should disclose the purchase price of a business combination, as illustrated for Starbucks Corp. below.

> *During fiscal 2000, Starbucks acquired the outstanding stock of* Tympanum, Inc. *(d/b/a "Hear Music"), a music retailer, and of* Coffee Partners Co. Ltd., *the company licensed to operate Starbucks stores in Thailand ("Thailand operations").*
>
> *Goodwill resulting from business acquisitions represents the excess purchase price paid over net assets of businesses acquired. . . .*

Consolidated Financial Statements

Although parent and subsidiary corporations may operate as a single economic unit, they continue to maintain separate accounting records and prepare their own periodic financial statements. At the end of the year, the financial statements of the parent and subsidiary are combined and reported as a single company. These combined financial statements are called **consolidated financial statements**. Such statements are usually identified by adding "and subsidiary(ies)" to the name of the parent corporation or by adding "consolidated" to the statement title.

To the stockholders of the parent company, consolidated financial statements are more meaningful than separate statements for each corporation. This is because the parent company, in substance, controls the subsidiaries, even though the parent and its subsidiaries are separate entities.

When a consolidated balance sheet is prepared, the ownership interest of the parent in the subsidiary's stock, which is the balance in the parent's investment in subsidiary account, must be eliminated. This is done by eliminating the parent's investment in subsidiary account against the balances of the subsidiary's stockholders' equity accounts.

If the parent owns less than 100% of the subsidiary stock, the subsidiary stock owned by outsiders is *not* eliminated but is normally reported immediately following the consolidated total liabilities. This amount is described as the **minority interest**. An example from a partial balance sheet of Fox Entertainment Group, Inc., is shown below.

	June 30, 2002
TOTAL LIABILITIES	$9,903,000,000
Minority interest in subsidiaries	$ 878,000,000
STOCKHOLDERS' EQUITY:	
Class A common stock	$ 3,000,000

When the data on the financial statements of the parent and its subsidiaries are combined to form the consolidated statements, intercompany transactions are given special attention. Examples of such transactions are the parent purchasing goods from the subsidiary and the subsidiary loaning money to the parent. These transactions affect the individual accounts of the parent and subsidiary and thus the financial statements of both companies.[16] Since a consolidated entity cannot transact with itself, these intercompany transactions must not be shown in the consolidated statements.

Many U.S. corporations own subsidiaries in foreign countries. Such corporations are often called *multinational corporations*. The financial statements of the foreign subsidiary are usually prepared in the foreign currency. Before the financial statements of foreign subsidiaries are consolidated with their domestic parent's financial statements, the amounts shown on the statements for the foreign companies must be converted to U.S. dollars. For example, General Motors Corporation is a multinational company that consolidates its foreign subsidiaries, such as the European Opel division, into U.S. dollars.

Market-Based Financial Measures

8 Compute and interpret the price-earnings and price-book ratios.

Two ratios used by investors to compare the market price of common stock to an accounting measure are the price-earnings ratio and the market-to-book-value ratios.

Price-Earnings Ratio

A firm's growth potential and future earnings prospects are indicated by how much the market is willing to pay per dollar of a company's earnings. This ratio, called the **price-earnings ratio**, or *P/E ratio*, is commonly included in stock market quotations reported

16 Examples of accounts often affected by intercompany transactions include *Accounts Receivable* and *Accounts Payable*, *Interest Receivable* and *Interest Payable*, and *Interest Expense* and *Interest Revenue*.

by the financial press. A high P/E ratio indicates that the market expects high growth and earnings in the future. Likewise, a low P/E ratio indicates lower growth and earnings expectations.

The price-earnings ratio on common stock is computed by dividing the stock's market price per share at a specific date by the company's annual basic earnings per share, as shown below.

$$\text{Price-earnings ratio} = \frac{\text{Market price per share of common stock}}{\text{Earnings per share of common stock (basic)}}$$

Investors that invest in high price-earnings-ratio companies are often referred to as *growth* investors. Growth investors pay a high price for shares because they expect the company to grow and provide a superior return. That is, high price-earnings ratios can be related to investor optimism. Examples of growth companies are Intel Corp. (P/E 62), Microsoft Corp. (P/E 58), and Genentech Inc. (P/E 222). Growth companies are considered risky because high growth expectations are already reflected in the market price. Thus, if the company's high growth expectations are not realized, the stock price will likely fall.

In contrast, investors in low price-earnings-ratio companies are often referred to as *value* investors. Value investors seek companies with stable and predictable earnings. The value investor believes that the low price-earnings ratio investment is safer than high price-earnings investments, since the stock is priced at a "bargain" level. Value investing is generally considered the "tortoise" strategy to the growth investor's "hare" strategy. Examples of value stocks are Citigroup (P/E 9), Florida Power and Light (P/E 12.67), and DaimlerChrysler (P/E 5.4).

To illustrate the calculation and analysis of the price-earnings ratio, consider the following market price per share, earnings per share, and price-earnings ratio information for Dell Computer Company:

	Market Price per Share	Earnings per Share (Basic)	Price-Earnings Ratio
1999	$52.5	$0.58	91 ($52.5/$0.58)
2000	38.5	0.66	58 ($38.5/$0.66)
2001	26.1	0.87	30 ($26.1/$0.87)

As can be seen, the price-earnings ratio dropped significantly for Dell over the three-year period. Apparently, investors reduced their growth expectations for this company, and the price-earnings ratio declined accordingly. Thus, even though Dell's earnings per share improved over this period, the stock price actually dropped. The price-earnings ratio for Dell Computer can be compared to the price-earnings ratio for a market index, such as Standard & Poor's 500®.[17] Exhibit 7 shows a graph of Dell's price-earnings ratio plotted with the price-earnings ratio of the Standard & Poor's 500 index. As can be seen, Dell's historical 1999 price-earnings ratio was much greater than the general market, reflecting Dell's expected high growth rate at this time. However, Dell's price-earnings ratio dropped to a level much nearer the overall market. Thus, investors changed their expectations of Dell Computer to more nearly reflect the "average" company's return potential.

Price-Book Ratio

The **price-book ratio** is the ratio of the market value of a share of common stock to the book value of a share of common stock. A price-book value of 1.0 suggests that a

17 The Standard & Poor's 500 index is an index of the largest 500 companies in the United States. Dell Computer is one of the companies in the index. The price-earnings ratio for an index is determined by dividing the market price of the index by the total earnings per share of all the stocks within the index.

Exhibit 7

Price-Earnings Ratios for Dell Computer Company and a Market Index

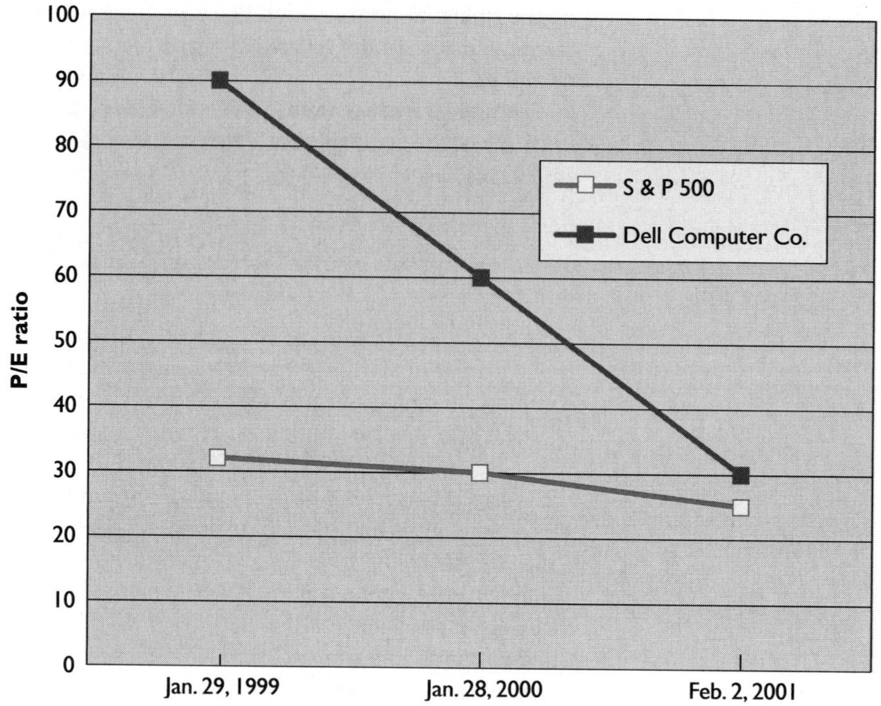

company's market value is equal to the balance sheet estimate of the value (book value). Most companies would be expected to have a price-book ratio greater than 1.0. This is because the going concern value of the company should exceed the sum of the historical costs of the net assets. To illustrate the calculation, the market price per share of Alcoa, Inc., on May 7, 2002, was $34 per share. The book value per share is determined by dividing the total shareholders' equity (book value) by the common shares outstanding. We must first determine the ***book value per share*** of Alcoa, Inc. from the most recent balance sheet information, as shown below.

Total stockholders' equity	$10,519,000,000
Common shares outstanding—basic (balance sheet date)	854,000,000

$$\text{Book value per share} = \frac{\text{Total stockholders' equity}}{\text{Common shares outstanding}}$$

$$\text{Book value per share} = \frac{\$10,519,000,000}{854,000,000}, \text{ or } \$12.32 \text{ (rounded)}$$

Thus, the price-book ratio would be:

$$\text{Price-book ratio} = \frac{\text{Market price per share}}{\text{Book value per share}}$$

$$\text{Price-book ratio} = \frac{\$34}{\$12.32}$$

$$\text{Price-book ratio} = 2.76$$

Alcoa's market price is 2.76 times greater than the book value of the firm. This ratio can be compared to Alcoa's historical price-book ratio or with that of other firms in the aluminum industry to aid in interpreting the ratio. For example, the average price-book ratio for other firms in Alcoa's industry is 0.97. Thus, Alcoa has a significant price premium to book value, compared to other firms in its industry. This suggests that investors view Alcoa very favorably.

Firms with significant unrecorded intangible assets, such as from brand name recognition, patents, or technologies, may have price-book ratios greatly in excess of 1.0. Thus, many analysts believe that this ratio is less meaningful for such "new economy" companies, since the historical cost balance sheet fails to capture the intangible asset value of these firms. Examples include (price-book ratio in parentheses): Oracle Corporation (14.3), Accenture Ltd. (84.31), Amgen Inc. (12.18), and eBay Inc. (14.54).

Focus on Cash Flow

Investments and Cash Flows

Long-term investments in subsidiaries are shown in the investing activities section of the statement of cash flows. Increases in investments are a use of cash, while sales of investments provide cash. For example, the investing activities sections of the statements of cash flows for two recent comparative years of Anheuser-Busch Companies Inc. are as follows:

Years Ended December 31 (in millions)	**2001**	**2000**
CASH FLOW FROM INVESTING ACTIVITIES:		
Capital expenditures	$(1,022.0)	$(1,074.5)
New business acquisitions	(370.4)	(42.9)
Proceeds from sale of business	110.0	—
Cash used for investing activities	$(1,282.4)	$(1,117.4)

As can be seen, Anheuser-Busch received cash proceeds of $110 million from the sale of Sea World Cleveland to Six Flags, Inc. Anheuser-Busch used cash to make investments of $370.4 million, including an equity interest in Compania Cervecerias Unidas S.A. (CCU), the largest brewer in Chile.

Under the equity method of accounting for income from an investment, the amount of income recognized on the income statement may exceed the amount received in cash as a dividend. This difference is termed the undistributed net earnings from equity investments. Since this amount does not impact cash flow, the operating activities section of the statement of cash flows must reduce the accrual net income number for undistributed net earnings from equity investments. This is illustrated for Anheuser-Busch as follows:

(continued)

Years Ended December 31 (in millions)	2001	2000
CASH FLOW FROM OPERATING ACTIVITIES:		
Net income	$1,704.5	$1,551.6
Adjustments to reconcile net income to cash provided by operating activities:		
Depreciation and amortization	834.5	803.5
Deferred income taxes	(18.9)	28.7
Undistributed earnings of affiliated companies	(223.5)	(185.2)
Other, net	7.2	31.4
Operating cash flow before change in working capital	$2,303.8	$2,230.0
Decrease/(increase) in working capital	56.8	27.5
Cash provided by operating activities	$2,360.6	$2,257.5

Anheuser-Busch showed $240.1 million of equity income on its income statement for the year 2001. However, only $16.6 million was actually received as a dividend. Thus, the net income must be reduced by $223.5 million ($240.1 million − $16.6 million) in 2001 to reflect the cash flow from operations.

Summary of Learning Goals

1 Describe the accounting for and interpretation of deferred income taxes.

Corporations are subject to federal income tax and are required to make estimated payments throughout the year. To record the payment of estimated tax, Income Tax is debited and Cash is credited. If additional taxes are owed at the end of the year, Income Tax is debited and Income Tax Payable is credited for the amount owed. If the estimated tax payments are greater than the actual tax liability, a receivable account is debited and Income Tax is credited.

The tax effects of temporary differences between taxable income and income before income taxes must be allocated between periods. The journal entry for such allocations normally debits Income Tax and credits Income Tax Payable and Deferred Income Tax Payable.

2 Prepare an income statement reporting the following unusual items: discontinued operations, extraordinary items, and changes in accounting principles.

A gain or loss resulting from the disposal of a business segment should be identified on the income statement, net of related income tax. The results of continuing operations should also be identified.

Gains and losses may result from events and transactions that are unusual and occur infrequently. Such extraordinary items, net of related income tax, should be identified on the income statement.

A change in an accounting principle results from the adoption of a generally accepted accounting principle different from the one used previously for reporting purposes. The effect of the change in principle on net income in the current period, as well as the cumulative effect on income of prior periods, should be disclosed in the financial statements. The effects of a change in an accounting principle should be reported net of related income tax.

3 Describe the accounting for and interpretation of fixed asset impairments and restructuring charges.

Fixed asset impairments occur when the fair value of a fixed asset falls below its book value and is not expected to recover. The asset is written down and a loss is recognized. The loss is disclosed above the income from continuing operations. Restructuring charges are the accrued employee termination benefits associated with a management-approved employee termination plan. The accrued expenses associated with such a plan are recognized in the period that senior executives approve the plan. The expense is disclosed on the income statement above the income from continuing operations. A liability is accrued for future cash outflows associated with the restructuring.

4 Prepare an income statement reporting earnings per share data.

Earnings per share is reported on the income statements of public corporations. If there are unusual items on the income statement, the per share amount should be presented for each of these items as well as net income.

5 Describe the concept and the reporting of comprehensive income.

Comprehensive income is all changes in stockholders' equity during a period except those resulting from dividends and stockholders' investments. Companies must report traditional net income plus or minus other comprehensive income items to arrive at comprehensive income. Other comprehensive income items include transactions and events that are excluded from net income, such as unrealized gains and losses on certain investments in debt and equity securities.

6 Describe the accounting for investments in stocks.

A business may purchase stock as a means of earning a return (income) on excess cash that it does not need for its normal operations. Such investments are recorded in a marketable securities account. Their cost includes all amounts spent to acquire the securities. Any dividends received on an investment are recorded as a debit to Cash and a credit to Dividend Revenue. On the balance sheet, temporary investments are reported at their fair market values. Any difference between the fair market values of the securities and their cost is an unrealized holding gain or loss (net of applicable taxes) that is reported as an other comprehensive income item.

Long-term investments in stocks are not intended as a source of cash in the normal operations of the business. They are reported at fair market value in the balance sheet under the caption Investments (similar to short-term investments). The equity method is used for long-term investments in stock in which there is influence over the investee.

The accounting for the sale of stock is the same for both short-term and long-term investments. The investment account is credited for the carrying amount (book value) of the shares sold, the cash or receivables account is debited for the proceeds, and any difference between the proceeds and the carrying amount is recorded as a gain or loss on the sale.

7 Describe alternative methods of combining businesses and how consolidated financial statements are prepared.

Businesses may combine in a merger or a consolidation. Business combinations may also occur when one corporation acquires a controlling share of the outstanding voting stock of another corporation. In this case, a parent-subsidiary relationship exists, and the companies are called affiliated or associated companies.

Although the corporations that make up a parent-subsidiary affiliation may operate as a single economic unit, they usually continue to maintain separate accounting records and prepare their own periodic financial statements. The financial statements prepared by combining the parent and subsidiary statements are called consolidated financial statements.

When a parent corporation purchases less than 100% of the subsidiary's stock, the remaining stockholders' equity is identified as the minority interest. The minority interest is reported on the consolidated balance sheet, usually preceding stockholders' equity.

8 Compute and interpret the price-earnings and price-book ratios.

The assessment of a firm's growth potential and future earnings prospects is indicated by the price-earnings ratio, or P/E ratio. It is computed by dividing the stock's market price per share at a specific date by the company's annual earnings per share. The price-book ratio compares the market value of a share of common stock to the book value of a share of common stock. This ratio measures the degree to which the market value exceeds the net assets valued under historical cost principles.

Glossary

Available-for-sale securities Securities that management expects to sell in the future but which are not actively traded for profit.

Comprehensive income All changes in stockholders' equity during a period except those resulting from dividends and stockholders' investments.

Consolidated financial statements Financial statements resulting from combining parent and subsidiary statements.

Consolidation The creation of a new corporation by the transfer of assets and liabilities of two or more existing corporations, which are then dissolved.

Discontinued operations Operations of a major line of business or component for a company, such as a division, a department, or a certain class of customer, that have been disposed of.

Earnings per common share (EPS) Net income per share of common stock outstanding during a period.

Equity method A method of accounting for an investment in common stock by which the investment account is adjusted for the investor's share of periodic net income and cash dividends of the investee.

Equity securities The common and preferred stock of a firm.

Extraordinary items Events and transactions that (1) are significantly different (unusual) from the typical or the normal operating activities of a business and (2) occur infrequently.

Fixed asset impairments A condition when the fair value of a fixed asset falls below its book value and is not expected to recover.

Investments The balance sheet caption used to report long-term investments in stocks not intended as a source of cash in the normal operations of the business.

Merger The joining of two corporations in which one company acquires all the assets and liabilities of another corporation, which is then dissolved.

Minority interest The portion of a subsidiary corporation's stock owned by outsiders.

Parent company The corporation owning all or a majority of the voting stock of the other corporation.

Price-book ratio The ratio of the market value of a share of common stock to the book value of a share of common stock.

Price-earnings ratio The ratio computed by dividing a corporation's stock market price per share at a specific date by the company's annual earnings per share.

Purchase method The accounting method used when a corporation acquires the controlling share of the voting common stock of another corporation by paying cash, exchanging other assets, issuing debt, or some combination of these methods.

Restructuring charge The cost of accrued employee termination benefits associated with a management-approved employee termination plan.

Subsidiary company The corporation that is controlled by a parent company.

Taxable income The income according to the tax laws that is used as a base for determining the amount of taxes owed.

Temporary differences Differences between taxable income and income before income taxes, created because items are recognized in one period for tax purposes and in another period for income statement purposes. Such differences reverse or turn around in later years.

Temporary investments The balance sheet caption used to report investments in income-yielding securities that can be quickly sold and converted to cash as needed.

Trading securities Securities that management intends to actively trade for profit.

Unrealized holding gain or loss The difference between the fair market values of the securities and their cost.

Illustrative Accounting Application Problem

The following data were selected from the records of Botanica Greenhouses Inc. for the current fiscal year ended August 31, 2003:

Administrative expenses	$ 82,200
Cost of merchandise sold	700,000
Gain on condemnation of land	25,000
Income tax:	
Applicable to continuing operations	27,200
Applicable to gain on condemnation of land	10,000
Applicable to loss from disposal of a segment of the business (reduction)	24,000

(continued)

Interest expense	$ 15,200
Loss from disposal of a segment of the business	60,200
Restructuring charge	50,000
Sales	1,097,500
Selling expenses	182,100

Instructions

Prepare a multiple-step income statement, concluding with a section for earnings per share in the form illustrated in this chapter. There were 10,000 shares of common stock (no preferred) outstanding throughout the year. Assume that the gain on condemnation of land is an extraordinary item.

Solution

Botanica Greenhouses Inc.
Income Statement
For the Year Ended August 31, 2003

Sales		$1,097,500
Cost of merchandise sold		700,000
Gross profit		$ 397,500
Operating expenses:		
Selling expenses	$182,100	
Administrative expenses	82,200	
Total operating expenses		264,300
Income from operations		$ 133,200
Other expense:		
Interest expense		(15,200)
Restructuring charge		(50,000)
Income from continuing operations before income tax		$ 68,000
Income tax expense		27,200
Income from continuing operations		$ 40,800
Loss from disposal of a segment of the business	$ 60,200	
Less applicable income tax	24,000	36,200
Income before extraordinary item		$ 4,600
Extraordinary item:		
Gain on condemnation of land	$ 25,000	
Less applicable income tax	10,000	15,000
Net income		$ 19,600
Earnings per share:		
Income from continuing operations		$ 4.08
Loss on discontinued operations		3.62
Income before extraordinary item		$ 0.46
Extraordinary item		1.50
Net income		$ 1.96

Self-Study Questions

Answers at end of chapter

1. During its first year of operations, a corporation elected to use the straight-line method of depreciation for financial reporting purposes and MACRS in determining taxable income. If the income tax is 40% and the amount of depreciation expense is $60,000 under the straight-line method and $100,000 under MACRS, what is the amount of income tax deferred to future years?
   A. $16,000 C. $40,000
   B. $24,000 D. $60,000

2. A material gain resulting from condemning land for public use would be reported on the income statement as:
   A. an extraordinary item.
   B. an other income item.
   C. revenue from sales.
   D. a change in estimate.

3. Gwinnett Corporation's temporary investments cost $100,000 and have a market value of $120,000 at the end of the accounting period. Assuming a tax rate of 40%, the difference between the cost and market value would be reported as a:
   A. $12,000 realized gain.
   B. $12,000 unrealized gain.
   C. $20,000 realized gain.
   D. $20,000 unrealized gain.

4. Cisneros Corporation owns 75% of Harrell Inc. During the current year, Harrell Inc. reported net income of $150,000 and declared dividends of $40,000. How much would Cisneros Corporation increase Investment in Harrell Inc. Stock for the current year?
   A. $0 C. $82,500
   B. $30,000 D. $112,500

5. Harkin Company has a market price of $60 per share on December 31. The total stockholders' equity is $2,400,000 and the net income is $600,000. There are 200,000 shares outstanding. Determine the price-earnings and price-book ratios:
   A. 5, 20 C. 20, 5
   B. 3, 5 D. 20, 12

Discussion Questions

1. A corporation has paid estimated federal income tax during the year on the basis of its estimated income. Indicate the accounts that would be debited and credited at the end of the year if the corporation (a) owes an additional tax; (b) overpaid its tax.
2. How would the amount of deferred income tax payable be reported in the balance sheet if (a) it is payable within one year; (b) it is payable beyond one year?
3. What two criteria must be met to classify an item as an extraordinary item on the income statement?
4. During the current year, 40 acres of land that cost $200,000 were condemned for construction of an interstate highway. Assuming that an award of $350,000 in cash was received and that the applicable income tax on this transaction is 40%, how would this information be presented in the income statement?
5. A corporation realized a material gain when its facilities at a designated floodway were acquired by an urban renewal agency. How should the gain be reported in the income statement?
6. An annual report of Ford Motor Company disclosed the sale of Ford's ownership interest in Visteon Corporation, a major automotive components manufacturer. The estimated after-tax loss on the disposal of these operations was $2.3 billion. Indicate how the loss from discontinued operations should be reported by Ford Motor Co. on its income statement.
7. If significant changes are made in the accounting principles applied from one period to the next, why should the effect of these changes be disclosed in the financial statements?

8. A corporation reports earnings per share of $1.38 for the most recent year and $1.10 for the preceding year. The $1.38 includes a $0.45-per-share gain from insurance proceeds related to a fully depreciated asset that was destroyed by fire. (a) Should the composition of the $1.38 be disclosed in the financial reports? (b) On the basis of the limited information presented, would you conclude that operations had improved or declined?
9. The Maxwell Company owns an equipped plant that has a book value of $150 million. Due to a permanent decline in consumer demand for the products produced by this plant, the market value of the plant and equipment is appraised at $20 million. Describe the accounting treatment for this impairment.
10. How should the severance costs of terminated employees be accounted for?
11. How should earnings per share be reported when there are unusual items disclosed below the income from continuing operations?
12. How is comprehensive income determined?
13. a. List some examples of other comprehensive income items.
    b. Does the reporting of comprehensive income affect the determination of net income and retained earnings?
14. Why might a business invest in another company's stock?
15. How are temporary investments in marketable securities reported on the balance sheet?
16. How are unrealized gains and losses on temporary investments in marketable securities reported on the statement of income and comprehensive income?
17. a. What method of accounting is used for long-term investments in stock in which there is significant influence over the investee?
    b. Under what caption are long-term investments in stock reported on the balance sheet?
18. Plaster Inc. received a $0.15-per-share cash dividend on 50,000 shares of Gestalt Corporation common stock, which Plaster Inc. carries as a long-term investment. Assuming that Plaster Inc. uses the equity method of accounting for its investment in Gestalt Corporation, what account would be credited for the receipt of the $7,500 dividend?
19. Parent Corporation owns 90% of the outstanding common stock of Subsidiary Corporation, which has no preferred stock. (a) What is the term applied to the remaining 10% interest? (b) On the consolidated balance sheet, where is the amount of Subsidiary's book equity allocable to outsiders reported?
20. An annual report of The Campbell Soup Company reported on its income statement $2.4 million as "equity in earnings of affiliates." Journalize the entry that Campbell would have made to record this equity in earnings of affiliates.

Resources for your success online @
http://warren.swlearning.com

Remember! If you need additional help, visit South-Western's Web site. See page 30 for a description of the online and printed materials that are available.

Exercises

Exercise 12–1

Income tax entries

Goal 1

Journalize the entries to record the following selected transactions of Supernal Grave Markers Inc.:

Apr. 15 Paid the first installment of the estimated income tax for the current fiscal year ending December 31, $80,000. No entry had been made to record the liability.

June 15 Paid the second installment of $80,000.

Sept. 15 Paid the third installment of $80,000.

Dec. 31 Recorded the estimated income tax liability for the year just ended and the deferred income tax liability, based on the transactions above and the following data:

Income tax rate	40%
Income before income tax	$1,200,000
Taxable income according to tax return	850,000

Jan. 15 Paid the fourth installment of $100,000.

Exercise 12–2

Deferred income taxes

Goal 1

STUDENT SOLUTIONS MANUAL

Integrated Systems, Inc., recognized service revenue of $300,000 on the financial statements in 2004. Assume, however, that the Tax Code requires this amount to be recognized for tax purposes in 2005. The taxable income for 2004 and 2005 is $2,000,000 and $2,500,000, respectively. Assume a tax rate of 40%.

Prepare the journal entries to record the tax expense, deferred taxes, and taxes payable for 2004 and 2005, respectively.

Exercise 12–3

Extraordinary item

Goal 2

A company received life insurance proceeds on the death of its president before the end of its fiscal year. It intends to report the amount in its income statement as an extraordinary item. Would this be in conformity with generally accepted accounting principles? Discuss.

Exercise 12–4

Extraordinary item

Goal 2

STUDENT SOLUTIONS MANUAL

On May 11, 1996, ValuJet tragically lost its Flight 592 en route from Miami to Atlanta. One hundred and ten people lost their lives. The crash cost ValuJet millions of dollars, including $2 million the company paid to the Federal Aviation Administration (FAA) to compensate it for the costs of the special inspections that were conducted. Do you believe that the costs related to this crash should be reported as an extraordinary item on the 1996 income statement of ValuJet?

Exercise 12–5

Identifying extraordinary items

Goal 2

Assume that the amount of each of the following items is material to the financial statements. Classify each item as either normally recurring (NR) or extraordinary (E).

a. Interest revenue on notes receivable.
b. Uninsured flood loss. (Flood insurance is unavailable because of periodic flooding in the area.)
c. Loss on sale of fixed assets.
d. Salaries of corporate officers.
e. Gain on sale of land condemned for public use.
f. Uncollectible accounts expense.
g. Uninsured loss on building due to hurricane damage. The firm was organized in 1920 and had not previously incurred hurricane damage.
h. Loss on disposal of equipment considered to be obsolete because of development of new technology.

Exercise 12-6

Income statement

Goals 2, 3, 4

Net income, $77,000

STUDENT SOLUTIONS MANUAL

SPREADSHEET

Trafalgar Inc. produces and distributes equipment for sailboats. On the basis of the following data for the current fiscal year ended June 30, 2004, prepare a multiple-step income statement for Trafalgar Inc., including an analysis of earnings per share in the form illustrated in this chapter. There were 10,000 shares of $150 par common stock outstanding throughout the year.

Administrative expenses	$ 26,750
Cost of merchandise sold	604,500
Cumulative effect on prior years of changing to a different depreciation method (decrease in income)	60,000
Gain on condemnation of land (extraordinary item)	37,750
Income tax reduction applicable to change in depreciation method	18,200
Income tax applicable to gain on condemnation of land	7,750
Income tax reduction applicable to loss from discontinued operations	56,000
Income tax applicable to ordinary income	105,200
Loss on discontinued operations	125,000
Restructuring charge	80,000
Sales	1,050,000
Selling expenses	75,750

Exercise 12-7

Asset impairment disclosures

Goals 2, 3

The Cochran Group is a merchandiser with over 300 stores. As a result of deteriorating property conditions, the property and fixtures for these stores were appraised at $320,000 below their carrying value in 2004. In July 2005, management sold 100 of these stores for a loss of $500,000.

a. Record the fixed asset impairment.
b. How should the impairment be disclosed on the 2004 financial statements?
c. How should the sale of 100 stores be disclosed on the 2005 financial statements?

Exercise 12-8

Restructuring charge

Goal 3

STUDENT SOLUTIONS MANUAL

Worldcom, Inc., the second largest telecommunications company in the United States, experienced reduced demand for telecommunication services and filed for bankruptcy. As a result, it announced a 6% reduction in its workforce, or 3,700 positions, on April 3, 2002. Assume that each employee received a severance package equal to 25% of his or her annual salary, half to be paid on July 31, 2002, and half on January 31, 2003. Assume that the average annual salary of the eliminated positions was $50,000.

a. Record the restructuring charge on April 3, 2002.
b. Record the severance payments on July 31, 2002, and January 31, 2003.
c. How would the restructuring charge and liability be disclosed on the calendar year-end financial statements for 2002?

Exercise 12-9

Income statement

Goals 2, 4

Correct net income, $362,000

Boss Sound Inc. sells automotive and home stereo equipment. It has 50,000 shares of $100 par common stock and 10,000 shares of $2, $100 par cumulative preferred stock outstanding as of December 31, 2004. It also holds 10,000 shares of common stock as treasury stock as of December 31, 2004. How many errors can you find in the following income statement for the year ended December 31, 2004?

Boss Sound Inc.
Income Statement
For the Year Ended December 31, 2004

Net sales		$9,450,000
Cost of merchandise sold		7,100,000
Gross profit		$2,350,000
Operating expenses:		
Selling expenses	$920,000	
Administrative expenses	380,000	1,300,000
Income from continuing operations before income tax		$1,050,000
Income tax expense		420,000
Income from continuing operations		$ 730,000
Cumulative effect on prior years' income (decrease) of changing to a different depreciation method (net of applicable income tax of $86,000)		(204,000)
Correction of error (understatement) in December 31, 2003 physical inventory (net of applicable income tax of $20,000)		30,000
Income before condemnation of land and discontinued operations		$ 556,000
Extraordinary item:		
Gain on condemnation of land, net of applicable income tax of $80,000		120,000
Loss on discontinued operations (net of applicable income tax of $76,000)		(184,000)
Net income		$ 492,000
Earnings per common share:		
Income from continuing operations		$ 14.60
Cumulative effect on prior years' income (decrease) of changing to a different depreciation method		(4.08)
Correction of error (understatement) in December 31, 2003 physical inventory		0.60
Income before extraordinary item and discontinued operations		$ 11.12
Extraordinary item		2.40
Loss on discontinued operations		(3.68)
Net income		$ 9.84

Exercise 12–10

Asset impairment

Goal 3

STUDENT SOLUTIONS MANUAL

Sears Roebuck & Co., one of the largest retailers in the world, reported asset impairments in its notes to recent financial statements as follows:

> *Asset impairments–The Company recorded a special charge . . . for the write-down of property and equipment to fair value, less costs to sell. The impaired assets consist of land, abandoned leasehold improvements and equipment used at the stores.*

	Initial Expense	Cash Payments	Asset Write-Downs	Ending Liability Balance
Asset impairments (000,000)	$94	$–	$(69)	$25

a. Record the initial asset impairment.
b. Record the asset write-down.
c. Why is the asset written down at a time after the impairment is identified?

Exercise 12-11

Earnings per share with preferred stock

Goal 4

Alpha-Omega Lighting Company had earnings for 2004 of $820,000. The company had 120,000 shares of common stock outstanding during the year. In addition, the company issued 50,000 shares of $100 par value preferred stock on July 1, 2003. The preferred stock dividend of $8 per share has been declared in 2004. There were no transactions in either common or preferred stock during 2004.

Determine the basic earnings per share for Alpha-Omega.

Exercise 12-12

Accumulated other comprehensive income

Goals 5, 6

b. Accumulated other comprehensive income, Dec. 31, 2003, $42,000

STUDENT SOLUTIONS MANUAL

The temporary investments of Security Network, Inc., include only 10,000 shares of EKO Arts, Inc., common stock purchased on January 10, 2003, for $25 per share. As of the December 31, 2003 balance sheet date, assume that the share price declined to $18 per share. As of the December 31, 2004, balance sheet date, the share price rose to $30 per share. The investment was held through December 31, 2004. Assume a tax rate of 40%.

a. Determine the net after-tax unrealized gain or loss from holding the EKO Arts common stock for 2003 and 2004.
b. What is the balance of the Accumulated Other Comprehensive Income or Deficit for December 31, 2003 and December 31, 2004.
c. Where is the Accumulated Other Comprehensive Income or Deficit disclosed on the financial statements?

Exercise 12-13

Temporary investments in marketable securities

Goal 6

During 2004, its first year of operations, Genotype Corporation purchased the following securities as a temporary investment:

Security	Shares Purchased	Cost	Cash Dividends Received
Research Inc.	1,000	$25,000	$ 800
Crisp Corp.	2,500	36,000	1,200

a. Record the purchase of the temporary investments for cash.
b. Record the receipt of the dividends.

Exercise 12-14

Financial statement reporting of temporary investments

Goals 5, 6

b. Comprehensive income, $81,200

STUDENT SOLUTIONS MANUAL

SPREADSHEET

Using the data for Genotype Corporation in Exercise 12-13, assume that as of December 31, 2004, the Research Inc. stock had a market value of $28 per share and the Crisp Corp. stock had a market value of $14 per share. For the year ending December 31, 2004, Genotype Corporation had net income of $80,000. Its tax rate is 40%.

a. Prepare the balance sheet presentation for the temporary investments.
b. Prepare a statement of income and comprehensive income presentation for the temporary investments.

Exercise 12-15

Entries for investment in stock, receipt of dividends, and sale of shares

Goal 6

On February 27, Gourmet Corporation acquired 3,000 shares of the 50,000 outstanding shares of Goulash Co. common stock at 58 plus commission charges of $420. On July 8, a cash dividend of $1 per share and a 2% stock dividend were received. On December 7, 1,000 shares were sold at 62, less commission charges of $375. Record the entries for (a) the purchase of the stock, (b) the receipt of dividends, and (c) the sale of the 1,000 shares.

Exercise 12–16

Equity method

Goal 6

STUDENT SOLUTIONS MANUAL

The following note to the consolidated financial statements for The Goodyear Tire and Rubber Co. relates to the principles of consolidation used in preparing the financial statements:

> *The Company's investments in 20% to 50% owned companies in which it has the ability to exercise significant influence over operating and financial policies are accounted for by the equity method. Accordingly, the Company's share of the earnings of these companies is included in consolidated net income.*

Is it a requirement that Goodyear use the equity method in this situation? Explain.

Exercise 12–17

Entries using equity method for stock investment

Goal 6

At a total cost of $13,500,000, Southern Corporation acquired 150,000 shares of Northern Corp. common stock as a long-term investment. Southern Corporation uses the equity method of accounting for this investment. Northern Corp. has 500,000 shares of common stock outstanding, including the shares acquired by Southern Corporation. Journalize the entries by Southern Corporation to record the following information:

a. Northern Corp. reports net income of $8,500,000 for the current period.

b. A cash dividend of $1.25 per common share is paid by Northern Corp. during the current period.

Exercise 12–18

Equity method for stock investment–Toys"R"Us Inc.

Goal 6

STUDENT SOLUTIONS MANUAL

Toys"R"Us Inc. is a major retailer of toys in the United States. A recent balance sheet disclosed a long-term investment in Toys-Japan, a public company trading on the Tokyo over-the-counter market. The balance sheet disclosure for two recent comparative years was as follows:

	Feb. 2, 2002	Feb. 3, 2001
Investment in Toys-Japan (in millions)	123	108

In addition, the Toys"R"Us income statement disclosed equity earnings in its Toys-Japan investment as follows:

	For Years Ended	
	Feb. 2, 2002	Feb. 3, 2001
Equity in net earnings of Toys-Japan (in millions)	29	31

The statement of cash flows indicates that the entire equity in the net earnings of Toys–Japan was deducted from net earnings in determining cash flow from operating activities.

The notes to the financial statements provided the following additional information about this investment:

The company accounts for its investment in the common stock of Toys-Japan under the "equity method" of accounting since the initial public offering on April 24, 2000. The quoted market value of the company's investment in Toys-Japan was $283 at February 2, 2002.

a. Explain the change in the Investment in Toys-Japan account for the fiscal year ended February 2, 2002.
b. Why is the Investment in Toys-Japan not recognized at market value?

Exercise 12–19

Price-earnings ratio calculation

Goals 4, 8

a. Price-earnings ratio, Jan. 28, 2001, 61.67

The following comparative income statements are provided for Krispy Kreme Doughnuts, Inc.:

Krispy Kreme Doughnuts, Inc.
Comparative Income Statements

	In Thousands, Except per Share Accounts	
Year Ended	**Jan. 28, 2001**	**Feb. 3, 2002**
Total revenues	$300,715	$394,354
Operating expenses	(250,690)	(316,946)
General and administrative expenses	(20,061)	(27,562)
Depreciation and amortization expenses	(6,457)	(7,959)
Income from operations	$ 23,507	$ 41,887
Interest income	2,325	2,980
Interest expense	(607)	(337)
Equity loss in joint ventures	(706)	(602)
Minority interest	(716)	(1,147)
Loss on sale of property and equipment	(20)	(235)
Income before income taxes	$ 23,783	$ 42,546
Provision for income taxes	9,058	16,168
Net income	$ 14,725	$ 26,378
Basic earnings per share	$ 0.30	$ 0.49
Diluted earnings per share	$ 0.27	$ 0.45

The average stock prices for each of the two fiscal years were as follows:

Fiscal year ended February 3, 2002	$31.50
Fiscal year ended January 28, 2001	18.50

a. Determine the price-earnings ratio for Krispy Kreme Doughnuts, Inc., for each of the two fiscal years, using basic earnings per share and the average market price.
b. What conclusions can you reach by considering the price-earnings ratio?
c. Why is the diluted earnings per share less than the basic earnings per share?

Exercise 12-20

Price-book ratio calculations

Goal 8

a. eBay, 9.6

STUDENT SOLUTIONS MANUAL

Below are some financial statistics for eBay, Inc., the largest online auction provider, and Burlington Northern Santa Fe, a large North American railroad.

	eBay	Burlington Northern Santa Fe
Total stockholders' equity, Dec. 31, 2001	$1,429,138,000	$7,849,000,000
Common shares outstanding, Dec. 31, 2001	268,971,000	387,890,000
Market price, Dec. 31, 2001	$51 per share	$28 per share

a. Determine the price-book ratio for each company.
b. Explain the difference in the price-book ratio between the two companies.

Exercise 12-21

Price-earnings and price-book ratio calculations

Goal 8

a. 2001: 17.49

ExxonMobil Corp. is one of the largest companies in the world. The company explores, develops, refines, and markets petroleum products. The basic earnings per share for three comparative years were as follows:

	Years Ended December 31,		
	2001	2000	1999
Basic earnings per share	$2.23	$2.55	$1.14

The company disclosed the following information from the statement of stockholders' equity (in millions):

	Dec. 31, 2001	Dec. 31, 2000	Dec. 31, 1999
Total stockholders' equity	$73,162	$70,757	$63,466
Common shares outstanding	6,809	6,903	6,955

The market price at the end of each year was $38, $42, and $39 for December 31, 1999, 2000, and 2001, respectively.
a. Determine the price-earnings ratio for 1999, 2000, and 2001.
b. Determine the price-book ratio for 1999, 2000, 2001.
c. Interpret your results over the three years.

Accounting Application Problems

Problem 12-1A

Income tax allocation

Goal 1

1. Year-end balance, 3rd year, $72,000

SPREADSHEET

Differences between the accounting methods applied to accounts and financial reports and those used in determining taxable income yielded the following amounts for the first four years of a corporation's operations:

	First Year	Second Year	Third Year	Fourth Year
Income before income taxes	$300,000	$450,000	$400,000	$500,000
Taxable income	250,000	300,000	420,000	510,000

The income tax rate for each of the four years was 40% of taxable income, and each year's taxes were promptly paid.

Instructions

1. Determine for each year the amounts described by the following captions, presenting the information in the form indicated:

			Deferred Income Tax Payable	
Year	Income Tax Deducted on Income Statement	Income Tax Payments for the Year	Year's Addition (Deduction)	Year-End Balance

2. Total the first three amount columns.

Problem 12-2A

Income tax; income statement

Goals 2, 3, 4, 5

Net income, $57,000

SPREADSHEET

The following data were selected from the records of Mantra Greenhouses Inc. for the current fiscal year ended June 30, 2004:

Advertising expense	$ 40,000
Cost of merchandise sold	266,000
Depreciation expense—office equipment	5,000
Depreciation expense—store equipment	29,000
Gain from disposal of a segment of the business	37,500
Income tax:	
Applicable to continuing operations	32,000
Applicable to gain from disposal of a segment of the business	15,000
Applicable to loss on condemnation of land (reduction)	9,000
Insurance expense	8,000
Interest expense	15,000
Loss on condemnation of land	22,500
Miscellaneous administrative expense	6,000
Miscellaneous selling expense	5,000
Office salaries expense	50,000
Rent expense	21,000
Restructuring charge	150,000
Sales	815,000
Sales commissions expense	140,000
Unrealized gain on temporary investments	25,000

Instructions

Prepare a multiple-step income statement, concluding with a section for earnings per share in the form illustrated in this chapter. There were 75,000 shares of common stock (no preferred) outstanding throughout the year. Assume that the loss on condemnation of land is an extraordinary item. Other comprehensive income items are disclosed in the statement of stockholders' equity.

Problem 12-3A

Income statement, retained earnings statement, balance sheet

Goals 1, 2, 3, 4, 5

Net income, $313,500

SPREADSHEET

The data on the following page were taken from the records of Pushkin Corporation for the year ended October 31, 2004.

Income statement data:	
Administrative expenses	$ 100,000
Cost of merchandise sold	732,000
Gain on condemnation of land	30,000
Income tax:	
Applicable to continuing operations	234,000
Applicable to loss from disposal of a segment of the business	37,000
Applicable to gain on condemnation of land	12,000
Interest expense	8,000
Interest revenue	5,000
Loss from disposal of a segment of the business	92,500
Loss from fixed asset impairment	200,000
Sales	2,020,000
Selling expenses	400,000
Retained earnings and balance sheet data:	
Accounts payable	$ 149,500
Accounts receivable	309,050
Accumulated depreciation	3,050,000
Accumulated other comprehensive income	30,000
Allowance for doubtful accounts	21,500
Cash	145,500
Common stock, $15 par (400,000 shares authorized; 152,000 shares issued)	2,280,000
Deferred income taxes payable (current portion, $4,700)	25,700
Dividends:	
Cash dividends for common stock	120,000
Cash dividends for preferred stock	75,000
Stock dividends for common stock	60,000
Dividends payable	30,000
Equipment	9,541,050
Income tax payable	55,900
Interest receivable	2,500
Merchandise inventory (October 31, 2004), at lower of cost (fifo) or market	425,000
Notes receivable	77,500
Paid-in capital from sale of treasury stock	16,000
Paid-in capital in excess of par—common stock	666,250
Paid-in capital in excess of par—preferred stock	240,000
Patents	55,000
Preferred 5% stock, $100 par (30,000 shares authorized; 15,000 shares issued)	1,500,000
Prepaid expenses	15,900
Retained earnings, November 1, 2003	2,518,150
Treasury stock (2,000 shares of common stock at cost of $35 per share)	70,000

Instructions

1. Prepare a multiple-step income statement for the year ended October 31, 2004, concluding with earnings per share. In computing earnings per share, assume that the average number of common shares outstanding was 150,000 and preferred dividends were $75,000. Assume that the gain on condemnation of land is an extraordinary item.
2. Prepare a retained earnings statement for the year ended October 31, 2004.
3. Prepare a balance sheet in report form as of October 31, 2004.

Problem 12-4A

Entries for investments in stock

Goal 6

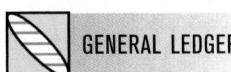

GENERAL LEDGER

Thematic Company is a wholesaler of men's hair products. The following transactions relate to certain securities acquired by Thematic Company, whose fiscal year ends on December 31:

2002

Jan. 3 Purchased 3,000 shares of the 40,000 outstanding common shares of Perch Corporation at 89 plus commissions and other costs of $594.

July 2 Received the regular cash dividend of $1 a share on Perch Corporation stock.

Dec. 5 Received the regular cash dividend of $1 a share plus an extra dividend of $0.10 a share on Perch Corporation stock.

(Assume that all intervening transactions have been recorded properly, the market value of the shares has not changed, and the number of shares of stock owned have not changed from December 31, 2002, to December 31, 2004.)

2005

Jan. 2 Purchased a controlling interest in Villard Inc. for $890,000 by purchasing 20,000 shares directly from the estate of the founder of Villard. There are 80,000 shares of Villard Inc. stock outstanding.

July 6 Received the regular cash dividend of $1 a share and a 3% stock dividend on the Perch Corporation stock.

Oct. 23 Sold 750 shares of Perch Corporation stock at 90. The broker deducted commissions and other costs of $140, remitting the balance.

Dec. 10 Received a cash dividend at the new rate of $1.10 a share on the Perch Corporation stock.

31 Received $24,000 of cash dividends on Villard Inc. stock. Villard Inc. reported net income of $315,000 in 2005. Thematic uses the equity method of accounting for its investment in Villard Inc.

Instructions

Record the entries for the preceding transactions.

Alternate Problems

Alternate Problem 12-1B

Income tax allocation

Goal 1

1. Year-end balance, 3rd year, $56,000

STUDENT SOLUTIONS MANUAL

SPREADSHEET

Differences between the accounting methods applied to accounts and financial reports and those used in determining taxable income yielded the following amounts for the first four years of a corporation's operations:

	First Year	Second Year	Third Year	Fourth Year
Income before income taxes	$350,000	$440,000	$520,000	$695,000
Taxable income	270,000	350,000	550,000	710,000

The income tax rate for each of the four years was 40% of taxable income, and each year's taxes were promptly paid.

Instructions

1. Determine for each year the amounts described by the captions on the following page, presenting the information in the form indicated.

Year	Income Tax Deducted on Income Statement	Income Tax Payments for the Year	Deferred Income Tax Payable: Year's Addition (Deduction)	Deferred Income Tax Payable: Year-End Balance

2. Total the first three amount columns.

Alternate Problem 12–2B

Income tax; income statement

Goals 2, 3, 4, 5

Net income, $51,500

STUDENT SOLUTIONS MANUAL

SPREADSHEET

SUV Inc. produces and sells off-road motorcycles and jeeps. The following data were selected from the records of SUV Inc. for the current fiscal year ended October 31, 2004:

Advertising expense	$ 60,000
Cost of merchandise sold	553,500
Depreciation expense—office equipment	6,000
Depreciation expense—store equipment	21,500
Gain on condemnation of land	31,250
Income tax:	
Applicable to continuing operations	36,250
Applicable to loss from disposal of a segment of the business (reduction)	5,000
Applicable to gain on condemnation of land	12,500
Interest revenue	7,500
Loss from disposal of a segment of the business	26,000
Loss from fixed asset impairment	150,000
Miscellaneous administrative expense	10,000
Miscellaneous selling expense	4,500
Office salaries expense	68,000
Rent expense	20,000
Sales	1,100,000
Sales salaries expense	120,000
Store supplies expense	4,000
Unrealized loss on temporary investments	15,000

Instructions

Prepare a multiple-step income statement, concluding with a section for earnings per share (rounded to the nearest cent) in the form illustrated in this chapter. There were 25,000 shares of common stock (no preferred) outstanding throughout the year. Assume that the gain on condemnation of land is an extraordinary item. Other comprehensive income items are disclosed in the statement of stockholders' equity.

Alternate Problem 12–3B

Income statement, retained earnings statement, balance sheet

Goals 1, 2, 3, 4, 5

Net income, $255,000

STUDENT SOLUTIONS MANUAL

SPREADSHEET

The following data were taken from the records of Onyx Corporation for the year ended July 31, 2004:

Income statement data:	
Administrative expenses	$ 130,000
Cost of merchandise sold	884,000
Gain on condemnation of land	25,000
Income tax:	
Applicable to continuing operations	220,000
Applicable to loss from disposal of a segment of the business	54,000
Applicable to gain on condemnation of land	10,000
Interest expense	7,500
Interest revenue	1,500

(continued)

Loss from disposal of a segment of the business	$ 134,000
Restructuring charge	300,000
Sales	2,400,000
Selling expenses	540,000
Retained earnings and balance sheet data:	
Accounts payable	$ 149,500
Accounts receivable	276,050
Accumulated depreciation	3,050,000
Accumulated other comprehensive loss	40,000
Allowance for doubtful accounts	11,500
Cash	125,500
Common stock, $10 par (500,000 shares authorized; 251,000 shares issued)	2,510,000
Deferred income taxes payable (current portion, $4,700)	25,700
Dividends:	
Cash dividends for common stock	80,000
Cash dividends for preferred stock	120,000
Stock dividends for common stock	40,000
Dividends payable	25,000
Equipment	11,064,050
Income tax payable	55,900
Interest receivable	2,500
Merchandise inventory (July 31, 2004), at lower of cost (fifo) or market	522,500
Paid-in capital from sale of treasury stock	5,000
Paid-in capital in excess of par—common stock	437,500
Paid-in capital in excess of par—preferred stock	240,000
Patents	55,000
Preferred 8% stock, $100 par (30,000 shares authorized; 15,000 shares issued)	1,500,000
Prepaid expenses	15,900
Retained earnings, August 1, 2003	4,116,400
Treasury stock (1,000 shares of common stock at cost of $40 per share)	40,000

Instructions

1. Prepare a multiple-step income statement for the year ended July 31, 2004, concluding with earnings per share. In computing earnings per share, assume that the average number of common shares outstanding was 250,000 and preferred dividends were $120,000. Assume that the gain on condemnation of land is an extraordinary item.
2. Prepare a retained earnings statement for the year ended July 31, 2004.
3. Prepare a balance sheet in report form as of July 31, 2004.

Alternate Problem 12-4B

Entries for investments in stock

Goal 6

STUDENT SOLUTIONS MANUAL

GENERAL LEDGER

Wilhelm Company produces and sells theater costumes. The following transactions relate to certain securities acquired by Wilhelm Company, whose fiscal year ends on December 31:

2002

Feb. 10 Purchased 4,000 shares of the 150,000 outstanding common shares of Moore Corporation at 42 plus commissions and other costs of $300.

June 15 Received the regular cash dividend of $0.80 a share on Moore Corporation stock.

Dec. 15 Received the regular cash dividend of $0.80 a share plus an extra dividend of $0.05 a share on Moore Corporation stock.

(Assume that all intervening transactions have been recorded properly, the market value of the shares has not changed, and the number of shares of stock owned have not changed from December 31, 2002, to December 31, 2004.)

(continued)

2005

Jan. 3 Purchased a controlling interest in Sirloin Inc. for $750,000 by purchasing 40,000 shares directly from the estate of the founder of Sirloin. There are 100,000 shares of Sirloin Inc. stock outstanding.

Apr. 1 Received the regular cash dividend of $0.80 a share and a 2% stock dividend on the Moore Corporation stock.

July 20 Sold 1,000 shares of Moore Corporation stock at 43. The broker deducted commissions and other costs of $150, remitting the balance.

Dec. 15 Received a cash dividend at the new rate of $0.90 a share on the Moore Corporation stock.

31 Received $30,000 of cash dividends on Sirloin Inc. stock. Sirloin Inc. reported net income of $245,000 in 2005. Wilhelm uses the equity method of accounting for its investment in Sirloin Inc.

Instructions

Journalize the entries for the preceding transactions.

Building Leadership Skills— Financial Reporting and Analysis

Case 12–1

Restructuring and unusual charges

Dow Jones & Co. is the publisher of *The Wall Street Journal.* On January 24, 2002, a news release reported the following:

> *Charges for special items in the fourth quarter of 2001 totaled $27.2 million, or $0.32 per diluted share, primarily for costs to permanently relocate certain personnel out of the Company's World Financial Center headquarters, consolidate certain international operations, reduce headcount in other areas, restructure a SmartMoney office lease (recorded in Equity Investments). . . .*

a. Should these charges be treated as an extraordinary item? Why or why not?

b. Provide the original journal entry for recording the charge assuming that the relocation costs were estimated to be $20,000,000, the consolidation and headcount reduction costs were $5,000,000, and the lease restructure was $2,200,000.

c. Assume that $1,000,000 was paid on January 12, 2002, for severance pay related to the headcount reduction announced in 2001. Provide the journal entry.

Case 12–2

Extraordinary item—9/11 incident

The following news item was published on October 7, 2001, less than one month after the September 11 terrorist incident at the World Trade Center:

> *Many companies already are blaming the September 11 terrorist attacks for a slowdown in profits. But accounting rule-makers aren't letting them off the hook so easily. A task force of the Financial Accounting Standards Board recently decided against allowing companies to treat costs related to the disaster as an "extraordinary item" in their financial statements. That means the costs must be considered part of normal business operations and deducted from the company's operating profit.*
>
> *The FASB was worried that companies would blame the attack for a variety of unrelated costs—essentially hiding bad business decisions or other problems and making profits seems better than they were.*

There also was concern that it was too difficult to tell what costs were related to terrorism and what weren't. The impact of Sept. 11 has been so pervasive, affecting virtually every company, that "it almost made it ordinary," says task-force member Dick Stock.

"The task force understood this was an extraordinary event in the English-language sense of the word," says FASB Chairman Tim Lucas. "But in the final analysis, we decided it wasn't going to improve the financial-reporting system to show it as an extraordinary item."

Source: Steve Liesman, "In Translation: What's Extraordinary—and What's Not," *The Wall Street Journal*, October 7, 2001.

Why would the FASB say that the September 11 terrorist incident was not "extraordinary"?

Case 12–3

Restructuring charge

Levi Strauss & Co. is a leading manufacturer of casual apparel. The notes to its financial statements for fiscal year ended November 25, 2001, disclosed the following:

U.S. Reorganization Initiatives

	(Dollars in Thousands)			
	Balance at 11/26/00	Charges	Reductions	Balance at 11/25/01
Severance and Employee Benefits	$–	$20,331	$(342)	$19,989
Total	$–	$20,331	$(342)	$19,989

a. Provide the journal entry for the fiscal-year 2001 restructuring charges.
b. How is the $19,989,000 balance on November 24, 2001, disclosed on the financial statements?
c. Provide the journal entry for the reductions.
d. What impact did these restructuring charges have on the year ending November 25, 2001, income statement?
e. What impact did these restructuring events have on the year ending November 25, 2001, cash flows from operating activities?

Case 12–4

Asset impairments and restructuring charges

Lucent Technologies Inc. is a major manufacturer of telecommunications equipment. In the notes to its annual report, the following table displayed the activity and balances of the restructuring account for the year ended September 30, 2001:

	Deductions (in millions)			
	Total Charges	Net Cash Payments	Noncash Charges	September 30, 2001 Liability
Restructuring costs				
Employee separations	$ 3,440	$179	$2,673	$ 588
Contract settlements	944	334	—	610
Facility closings	304	8	—	296
Other	79	(46)	—	125
Total restructuring costs	$ 4,767	$475	$2,673	$1,619
Asset write-downs				
Goodwill and other acquired intangibles	4,081	—	$4,081	—
Inventory	1,259	—	1,259	—
Capitalized software	362	—	362	—
Property, plant and equipment, net	425	—	425	—
Other	522	—	522	—
Total asset write-downs	$ 6,649	—	$6,649	—
Total	$11,416	$475	$9,322	$1,619

a. What is the total expense from restructuring and asset impairments (write-downs) shown on the September 30, 2001, income statement?
b. What would be the impact of these events in the operating activities section of the statement of cash flows for the year ended September 30, 2001?
c. Why is there no ending liability balance for the asset impairments (write-downs)?
d. Why are all the charges for asset impairments (write-downs) considered "noncash"?
e. How is the $1,619,000,000 September 30, 2001 reserve balance disclosed on the financial statements?

Case 12–5

Comprehensive income

The Stockholders' Equity section of Electronics Boutique Holdings Corp., an electronic game retailer, for two recent comparative dates was as shown at the top of the following page. The accumulated other comprehensive loss increased from $1,551,809 to $2,609,427 as the result of a foreign currency loss of $1,057,618 from international operations.

a. Explain the concept of other comprehensive loss items.
b. What might cause the foreign currency loss (in very general terms)?

Electronics Boutique Holdings Corp.
Stockholders' Equity Section of the Balance Sheet

	Feb. 3, 2001	Feb. 2, 2002
Stockholders' equity		
Preferred stock—authorized 25,000,000 shares; $0.01 par value; no shares issued and outstanding at February 3, 2001, and February 2, 2002	—	—
Common stock—authorized 100,000,000 shares; $0.01 par value; 22,304,722 and 25,782,857 shares issued and outstanding at February 3, 2001, and February 2, 2002, respectively	$ 223,047	$ 257,829
Additional paid-in capital	77,060,816	166,312,221
Accumulated other comprehensive loss	(1,551,809)	(2,609,427)
Retained earnings	55,487,842	73,199,503
Total stockholders' equity	$131,219,896	$237,160,126

Building Leadership Skills—Responsible Leadership

Activity 12–1

Ethics and professional conduct in business

ETHICS

At a recent dinner party, you met Steph Melick, the controller for Mojave Inc. Steph has worked for Mojave for the past seven years. During your conversation, you complained about having to pay your third-quarter estimated taxes on Monday, September 15. In response, Steph indicated that she always *underpays* her estimated taxes. That way, she can use her money as long as possible. Is it appropriate to deliberately underpay your estimated taxes?

Activity 12–2

Ethics and professional conduct in business

ETHICS

Reed Osborn is the president and chief operating officer of Ratchet Corporation, a developer of personal financial planning software. During the past year, Ratchet Corporation was forced to sell ten acres of land to the city of Houston for expansion of a freeway exit. The corporation fought the sale, but after condemnation hearings, a judge ordered it to sell the land. Because of the location of the land and the fact that Ratchet Corporation had purchased the land over 15 years ago, the corporation recorded a $0.20-per-share gain on the sale. Always looking to turn a negative into a positive, Reed Osborn has decided to announce the corporation's earnings per share of $1.05, without identifying the $0.20 impact of selling the land. Although he will retain majority ownership, Reed plans on selling 20,000 of his shares in the corporation sometime within the next month. Are Reed's plans to announce earnings per share of $1.05 without mentioning the $0.20 impact of selling the land ethical and professional?

Activity 12-3

Reporting extraordinary item

Ulster Inc. is in the process of preparing its annual financial statements. Ulster Inc. is a large citrus grower located in central Florida. The following is a discussion between Jason Kirk, the controller, and April Gwinn, the chief executive officer and president of Ulster Inc.

April: Jason, I've got a question about your rough draft of this year's income statement.
Jason: Sure, April. What's your question?
April: Well, your draft shows a net loss of $750,000.
Jason: That's right. We'd have had a profit, except for this year's frost damage. I figured that the frost destroyed over 30 percent of our crop. We had a good year otherwise.
April: That's my concern. I estimated that if we eliminate the frost damage, we'd show a profit of . . . let's see . . . about $250,000.
Jason: That sounds about right.
April: This income statement seems misleading. Why can't we show the loss on the frost damage separately? That way the bank and our outside investors will be able to see that this year's loss is just temporary. I'd hate to get them upset over nothing.
Jason: Maybe we can do something. I recall from my accounting courses something about showing unusual items separately. Let's see . . . yes, I remember. They're called extraordinary items.
April: Well, we haven't had any frost damage in over five years. This year's damage is certainly extraordinary. Let's do it!

Discuss the appropriateness of revising Ulster Inc.'s income statement to report the frost damage separately as an extraordinary item.

Activity 12-4

Consolidated financial statements

Charlene Seymour, your grandmother, recently retired, sold her condominium in New York City and moved to a retirement community in Florida. With some of the proceeds from the sale of her condominium, she is considering investing $800,000 in the stock market.

In the process of selecting among alternative stock investments, your grandmother collected annual reports from fifteen different companies. In reviewing these reports, however, she has become confused and has questions concerning several items that appear in the financial reports. She has asked for your help and has written down the following questions for you to answer:

a. *In reviewing the annual reports, I noticed many references to "consolidated financial statements." What are consolidated financial statements?*
b. *"Excess of cost of business acquired over related net assets" appears on the consolidated balance sheets in several annual reports. What does this mean? Is it an asset (it appears with other assets)?*
c. *What is minority interest?*
d. *A footnote to one of the consolidated statements indicated interest and the amount of a loan from one company to another had been eliminated. Is this good accounting? A loan is a loan. How can a company just eliminate a loan that hasn't been paid off?*
e. *How can financial statements for an American company (in dollars) be combined with a German subsidiary (in marks)?*

1. Briefly respond to each of your grandmother's questions.
2. While discussing the items in (1) with your grandmother, she asked for your advice on whether she should limit her investment to one stock. What would you advise?

Activity 12–5

Extraordinary items and discontinued operations

GROUP ACTIVITY

In groups of three or four students, search company annual reports, news releases, or the Internet for extraordinary items and announcements of discontinued operations. Identify the most unusual extraordinary item in your group. Also, select a discontinued operation of a well-known company that might be familiar to other students or might interest them.

Prepare a brief analysis of the earnings per share impact of both the extraordinary item and the discontinued operation. Estimate the *potential* impact on the company's market price by multiplying the current price-earnings ratio by the earnings per share amount of each item.

One Internet site that has annual reports is EDGAR (Electronic Data Gathering, Analysis, and Retrieval), the electronic archives of financial statements filed with the Securities and Exchange Commission. SEC documents can be retrieved using the EdgarScan service from PricewaterhouseCoopers at http://edgarscan.pwcglobal.com.

To obtain annual report information, type in a company name in the appropriate space. EdgarScan will list the reports available to you for the company you've selected. Select the most recent annual report filing, identified as a 10-K or 10-K405. EdgarScan provides an outline of the report, including the separate financial statements. You can double click the income statement and balance sheet for the selected company into an Excel™ spreadsheet for further analysis.

Answers to Self-Study Questions

1. **A** The amount of income tax deferred to future years is $16,000 (answer A), determined as follows:

Depreciation expense, MACRS	$100,000
Depreciation expense, straight-line method	60,000
Excess expense in determining taxable income	$ 40,000
Income tax rate	× 40%
Income tax deferred to future years	$ 16,000

2. **A** Events and transactions that are distinguished by their unusual nature and by the infrequency of their occurrence, such as a gain on condemning land for public use, are reported in the income statement as extraordinary items (answer A).

3. **B** The difference between the cost of temporary investments held as available-for-sale securities and their market value is reported as an unrealized gain, net of applicable income taxes, as shown below.

Market value of investments	$120,000
Cost of investments	100,000
	$ 20,000
Applicable taxes (40%)	8,000
Unrealized gain, net of taxes	$ 12,000

The unrealized gain of $12,000 (answer B) is reported on the balance sheet as an addition to the cost of the investments and as part of other comprehensive income.

4. **C** Under the equity method of accounting for investments in stocks, Cisneros Corporation records its share of both net income and dividends of Harrell Inc. in Investment in Harrell Inc. Stock. Thus, Investment in Harrell Inc. Stock would increase by $82,500 [($150,000 × 75%) − ($40,000 × 75%)] for the current year. $30,000 (answer B) is only Cisneros Corporation's share of Harrell's dividends for the current year. $112,500 (answer D) is only Cisneros Corporation's share of Harrell's net income for the year.

5. **C**

$$\text{Price-earnings ratio: } \frac{\text{Market price per common share}}{\text{Earnings per share}},$$

$$\text{or } \frac{\$60}{\$600{,}000/200{,}000} = 20$$

$$\text{Price-book ratio: } \frac{\text{Market price per share}}{\text{Book value per share}},$$

$$\text{or } \frac{\$60}{\$2{,}400{,}000/200{,}000} = 5.0$$

Chapter 13
Statement of Cash Flows

THE LAW OF SACRIFICE

"A leader must give to go up."

–The 21 Irrefutable Laws of Leadership

Dr. John C. Maxwell

Learning Goals

1. Summarize the types of cash flow activities reported in the statement of cash flows.
2. Prepare a statement of cash flows, using the indirect method.
3. Prepare a statement of cash flows, using the direct method.
4. Calculate and interpret the cash conversion cycle, flow ratio, and free cash flow.

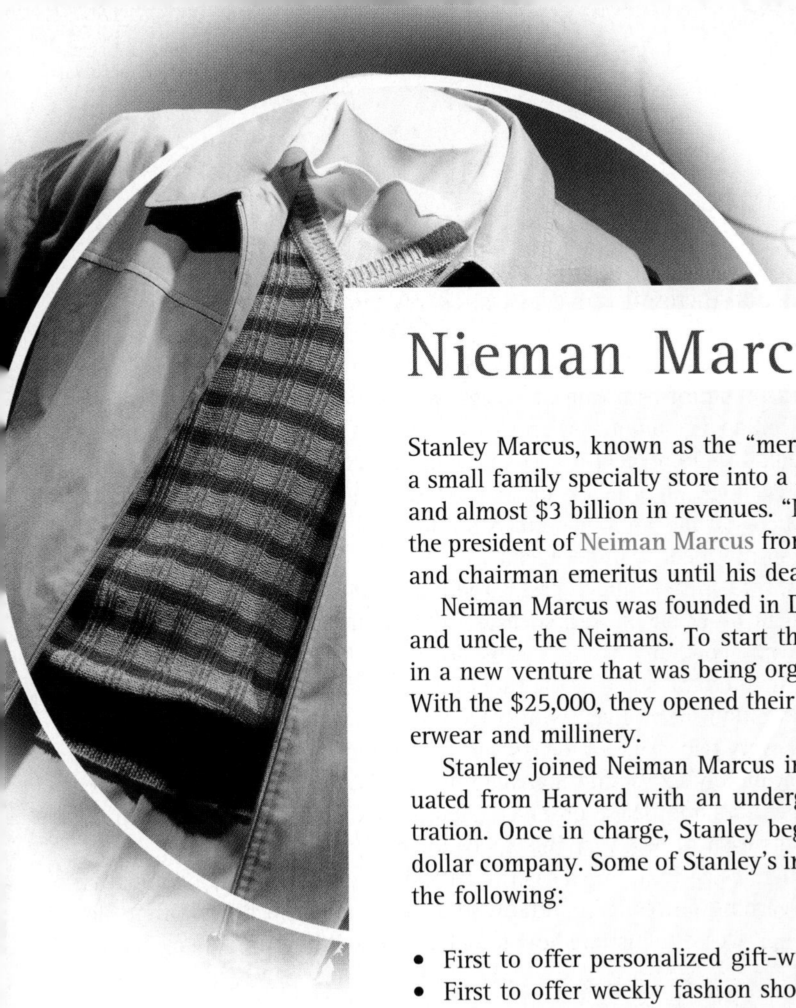

Nieman Marcus

Stanley Marcus, known as the "merchant prince of Texas," is credited with transforming a small family specialty store into a high-end, specialty-retail chain with over thirty stores and almost $3 billion in revenues. "Mr. Stanley," as he was known by the employees, was the president of Neiman Marcus from 1950–1972, chairman of the board from 1972–1976, and chairman emeritus until his death at the age of 96.

Neiman Marcus was founded in Dallas, Texas, in 1907 by Stanley's father and his aunt and uncle, the Neimans. To start their business, the founders sold their $25,000 interest in a new venture that was being organized in Atlanta, Georgia—the Coca-Cola Company. With the $25,000, they opened their first store in downtown Dallas, offering women's outerwear and millinery.

Stanley joined Neiman Marcus in 1926 at the urging of his father. Stanley had graduated from Harvard with an undergraduate degree and a Masters of Business Administration. Once in charge, Stanley began transforming Neiman Marcus into today's billion dollar company. Some of Stanley's innovations that facilitated this transformation included the following:

- First to offer personalized gift-wrapping for customers
- First to offer weekly fashion shows
- First retail apparel store outside New York to advertise in national fashion magazines

The most legendary Stanley innovation was the Neiman Marcus Christmas catalog featuring "His and Hers" gifts for the super wealthy. Some of the featured gifts included his and hers jet aircraft, his and hers miniature submarines, his and hers hot-air balloons, and his and hers camels. One year, Stanley even offered for sale his and her Egyptian mummies, one male and one female.

Some of the retailing principles that Stanley emphasize throughout his career included the following:

- There is never a good sale for Neiman Marcus, unless it's a good buy for the customer.
- Quality is remembered long after the price is forgotten.
- If you force a bad buy on a customer, he will never forgive you.
- At Neiman's we never sell to the people who need something; we have to sell to people who want something.
- We don't train salespeople—we educate them.
- There is no substitute for a good salesperson.
- Focus on quality and service, and sales will take care of themselves.

Neiman Marcus merged in 1969 with Broadway-Hale Stores, which later merged with another retailing group to form Carter, Hawley, Hale Inc. Today, Neiman Marcus is publicly traded as the Neiman Marcus Group.

The major reason that Neiman Marcus merged its operations was its inability to raise cash for expansion on its own. In this chapter, we focus on the importance of the statement of cash flows in assessing and analyzing cash flows and the cash needs of a company.

Sources: Adapted from the Neiman Marcus Internet Web Page; "Obituary—Stanley Marcus," *The Economist*, February 2, 2002; "Neiman Marcus," *The Handbook of Texas Online*; John F. Yarbrough, "Life of a Salesman," *abcnews.go.com*.

Your Need to Know

Microsoft Corporation has nearly $36 billion of cash and temporary marketable securities, which is 60 percent of Microsoft's total assets. This is the largest cash position held by any U.S. company. To give some perspective, General Electric comes in second at $8 billion in cash and marketable securities. How did Microsoft generate so much cash? This cash comes from Microsoft's profit-making activities, which are able to generate cash at the rate of nearly $1 billion per month. Microsoft's Windows®-based software products produce gross profits equal to 90 percent of revenue and produce income from operations of over 40 percent of revenues. Margins of this size generate huge cash inflows from operations. As a result, Microsoft has no long-term liabilities. It generates more than enough cash from operations, so that debt is unnecessary.

What should Microsoft do with so much cash? There are many choices available to the company. It can invest in other businesses, such as its $1 billion acquisition of the successful accounting software company, Great Plains Software. In addition, Microsoft uses cash to buy back its own common stock at the rate of $5 billion per year in order to support its employee stock option plans. Even with these uses of cash, Microsoft's cash position has nearly doubled every two years for the last ten years. Some are now even suggesting that Microsoft cannot profitably invest and manage this much cash. That is, it has allowed its cash position to grow *too* large. These observers suggest that the company is maturing and should start using its cash to begin paying dividends back to shareholders.

How a company generates cash and uses cash is critical to understanding a company's prospects. Thus, while earning power is important, so also are the cash flows. Often they are related. In this chapter, we will illustrate how to determine and interpret the cash flows of a company.

Reporting Cash Flows

1 Summarize the types of cash flow activities reported in the statement of cash flows.

The **statement of cash flows** reports a firm's major cash inflows and outflows for a period.[1] The statement of cash flows is a required disclosure that explains how a company generates and uses cash during an accounting period. It provides useful information about a firm's ability to generate cash from operations, maintain and expand its operating capacity, meet its financial obligations, and pay dividends. It is useful to managers in evaluating past operations and in planning future investing and financing activities. It is useful to investors, creditors, and others in assessing a firm's profit potential. In addition, cash flows are particularly important in evaluating firms in financial distress, because the ultimate cause of bankruptcy is lack of cash. Thus, the statement is also used to assess the firm's ability to pay its maturing debt.

The statement of cash flows reports cash flows by three types of activities:

1. **Cash flows from operating activities** are cash flows from transactions that affect net income. Examples of such transactions include the purchase and sale of merchandise by a retailer.
2. **Cash flows from investing activities** are cash flows from transactions that affect the investments in noncurrent assets. Examples of such transactions include the sale and purchase of fixed assets, such as equipment and buildings.
3. **Cash flows from financing activities** are cash flows from transactions that affect the equity and debt of the business. Examples of such transactions include issuing or retiring debt securities as well as paying dividends.

---

1 As used in this chapter, cash refers to cash and cash equivalents. Examples of cash equivalents include marketable securities, certificates of deposit, U.S. Treasury bills, and money market funds.

In the statement of cash flows, the cash flows from operating activities are normally presented first, followed by the cash flows from investing activities and financing activities. The total of the net cash flow from these activities is the net increase or decrease in cash for the period. The cash balance at the beginning of the period is added to the net increase or decrease in cash, resulting in the cash balance at the end of the period. The ending cash balance on the statement of cash flows equals the cash reported on the balance sheet.

Exhibit 1 shows common cash flow transactions reported in each of the three sections of the statement of cash flows. By reporting cash flows by operating, investing, and financing activities, significant relationships within and among the activities can be evaluated. For example, the cash receipts from issuing bonds can be related to repayments of borrowings when both are reported as financing activities. Also, the impact of each of the three activities (operating, investing, and financing) on cash flows can be identified. This allows investors and creditors to evaluate the effects of cash flows on a firm's profits and ability to pay debt.

INTERNATIONAL PERSPECTIVE

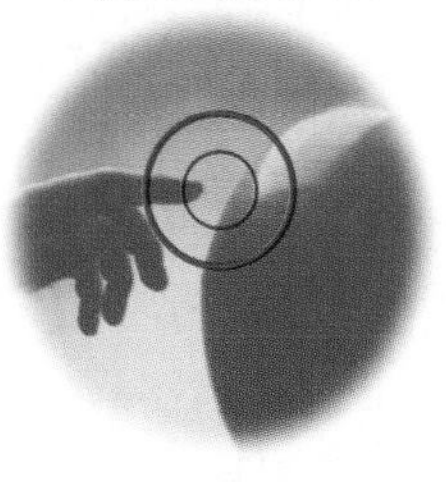

Under Austrian accounting rules, there are no specific disclosures regarding a statement of cash flows.

Exhibit 1

Cash Flows

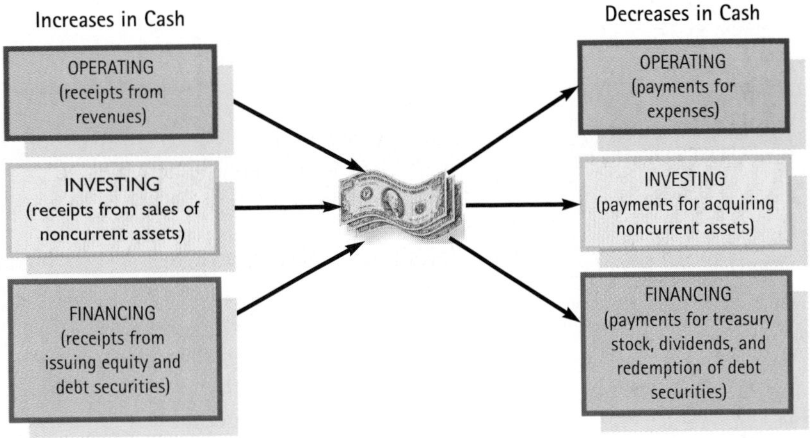

Cash Flows from Operating Activities

The most important cash flows of a business often relate to operating activities. There are two alternative methods for reporting cash flows from operating activities in the statement of cash flows. These methods are (1) the direct method and (2) the indirect method.

The **direct method** reports the sources of operating cash and the uses of operating cash. The major source of operating cash is cash received from customers. The major uses of operating cash include cash paid to suppliers for merchandise and services and cash paid to employees for wages. The difference between these operating cash receipts and cash payments is the net cash flow from operating activities.

The primary advantage of the direct method is that it reports the sources and uses of cash in the statement of cash flows. Its primary disadvantage is that the necessary data may not be readily available and may be costly to gather.

The **indirect method** reports the operating cash flows by beginning with net income and adjusting it for revenues and expenses that do not involve the receipt or payment of cash. In other words, accrual net income is adjusted to determine the net amount of cash flows from operating activities.

A major advantage of the indirect method is that it focuses on the differences between net income and cash flows from operations. In this sense, it shows the relationship between the income statement, the balance sheet, and the statement of cash flows. Because the data are readily available, the indirect method is normally less costly to use than the direct method. Because of these advantages, most firms use the indirect method to report cash flows from operations.

Exhibit 2 illustrates the cash flow from operating activities section of the statement of cash flows under the direct and indirect methods. Both statements are for Family Health Care for the month ended November 2003, and the first statement was shown in Chapter 3, Exhibit 3. Both statements show the same amount of net cash flow from operating activities, regardless of the method. We will illustrate both methods in detail later in this chapter.

Exhibit 2

Cash Flow from Operations: Direct and Indirect Methods

Direct Method		
Cash flows from operating activities:		
Cash received from patients	$9,700	
Cash received from rental of land	1,800	$ 11,500
Deduct cash payments for expenses:		
Insurance premiums	$8,400	
Supplies	100	
Wages	2,790	
Rent	800	
Utilities	580	
Interest	100	
Miscellaneous expense	420	(13,190)
Net cash flow from operating activities		$ (1,690)
Indirect Method		
Cash flows from operating activities:		
Net income, per income statement		$ 6,390
Add: Depreciation expense	$ 160	
Increase in accounts payable	140	
Increase in wages payable	220	
Increase in unearned revenue	1,440	1,960
		$ 8,350
Deduct: Increase in accounts receivable	$2,650	
Increase in prepaid insurance	7,300	
Increase in supplies	90	(10,040)
Net cash flow from operating activities		$ (1,690)

Cash Flows from Investing Activities

Cash inflows from investing activities normally arise from selling fixed assets, investments, and intangible assets. Cash outflows normally include payments to acquire fixed assets, investments, and intangible assets. For example, Walt Disney Company recently invested $2.9 billion cash to acquire Fox Family Worldwide, Inc., which was the Fox Family Channel that is being changed to the ABC Family Channel®.

Cash flows from investing activities are reported on the statement of cash flows by first listing the cash inflows. The cash outflows are then presented. If the inflows are greater than the outflows, *net cash flow provided by investing activities* is reported. If the inflows are less than the outflows, *net cash flow used for investing activities* is reported.

The cash flows from investing activities section in the statement of cash flows for Family Health Care is shown below.

Cash flows from investing activities:	
Purchase of office equipment	$(1,700)

Cash Flows from Financing Activities

Cash inflows from financing activities normally arise from issuing debt or equity securities. Examples of such inflows include issuing bonds, notes payable, and preferred and common stocks. For example, Sprint Corporation recently received cash proceeds of $2.2 billion by issuing debt. Often companies that are expanding operations will seek cash from debt and equity offerings; such is the case with Sprint as it builds out its cellular phone network. Cash outflows from financing activities include paying cash dividends, repaying debt, and acquiring treasury stock. For example, Intel Corporation used $3.2 billion cash to acquire treasury stock to use for its stock option plans.

Cash flows from financing activities are reported on the statement of cash flows by first listing the cash inflows. The cash outflows are then presented. If the inflows are greater than the outflows, *net cash flow provided by financing activities* is reported. If the inflows are less than the outflows, *net cash flow used for financing activities* is reported.

The cash flows from financing activities section in the statement of cash flows for Family Health Care is shown below.

Cash flows from financing activities:	
Additional issuance of capital stock	$ 5,000
Deduct cash dividends	(1,200)
Net cash flow from financing activities	$ 3,800

Ethics in Action
What Is the Real Cash Flow?

The Securities and Exchange Commission disagreed with a cash flow disclosure from a complex natural gas trading arrangement of Dynegy Inc., a major energy provider and trader. As a result, the company was required to remove $300 million from cash flow from operations (a drop of 37%) and put it into the financing section. Although this change did not impact net cash flow from all sources, it did change the interpretation of cash flows. As quoted by one source, "The restatement is a big blow to the many investors who held onto the cash flow statement as a beacon of truth even as their faith in the earnings figure was shattered in recent months. . . ." Dynegy's share price dropped 67% within two months of this announcement.

Source: Henny Sender, "'Reliable' Cash Flow Has Shortcomings—Sums Aren't Always What They Seem," *The Wall Street Journal*, May 9, 2002.

Noncash Investing and Financing Activities

A business may enter into investing and financing activities that do not directly involve cash. For example, it may issue common stock to retire long-term debt. Such a transaction does not have a direct effect on cash. However, the transaction does eliminate the need for future cash payments to pay interest and retire the bonds. Thus, because of their future effect on cash flows, such transactions should be reported to readers of the financial statements.

When noncash investing and financing transactions occur during a period, their effect is reported in a separate schedule. This schedule usually appears at the bottom of the statement of cash flows. For example, in such a schedule, Amazon.com, Inc., disclosed the issuance of $217 million in common stock for Internet acquisitions. Other examples of noncash investing and financing transactions include acquiring fixed assets by issuing bonds or capital stock and issuing common stock in exchange for convertible preferred stock.

No Cash Flow per Share

The term *cash flow per share* is sometimes reported in the financial press. Often, the term is used to mean "cash flow from operations per share." Such reporting may be misleading to users of the financial statements. For example, users might interpret cash flow per share as the amount available for dividends. This would not be the case if most of the cash generated by operations is required for repaying loans or for reinvesting in the business. Users might also think that cash flow per share is equivalent or perhaps superior to earnings per share. For these reasons, the financial statements, including the statement of cash flows, should not report cash flow per share.

Strategy in Business

Fashion Blues

During the 1990s, The Gap became the nation's largest specialty apparel retailer, with sales rising from $1.93 billion in 1990 to $11.64 billion in 1999. The Gap achieved this rapid growth by employing a strategy that emphasized simple, high-quality, casual clothing. Its strategy was aided by the shift in the 1990s to casual attire in the workplace. However, The Gap's same-store sales and profits have plummeted over the past year and a half. Perhaps never before have so many shoppers stopped patronizing a retail chain so quickly. So what happened?

Many former customers blame The Gap's changing fashion mix towards more far-fetched fashions, such as a denim trenchcoat with faux-fur collar, a bleached graphic T shirt, and fuschia-glittered disco jeans. In other words, The Gap became too trendy for its targeted customers, who are between the ages of 20 and 30. In addition, as The Gap expanded its trendy fashions, it curtailed customer choices within its basic apparel. For example, one former customer visited a Gap store in search of Capri pants but wasn't pleased with what she found. "You can't take pink and baby-blue to work, " she said.

Source: Adapted from "Gap's Image Is Wearing Out," by Amy Merrick, *The Wall Street Journal*, December 6, 2001.

Statement of Cash Flows—The Indirect Method

2 Prepare a statement of cash flows, using the indirect method.

The indirect method of reporting cash flows from operating activities is normally less costly and more efficient than the direct method. In addition, when the direct method is used, the indirect method must also be used in preparing a supplemental reconciliation of net income with cash flows from operations. The 2001 edition of *Accounting Trends & Techniques* reported that 593 out of 600 surveyed companies used the indirect method. For these reasons, we will discuss first the indirect method of preparing the statement of cash flows.

To collect the data for the statement of cash flows, all the cash receipts and cash payments for a period could be analyzed. However, this procedure is expensive and time-consuming. A more efficient approach is to analyze the changes in the noncash balance sheet accounts. The logic of this approach is that a change in any balance sheet account (including cash) can be analyzed in terms of changes in the other balance sheet accounts. To illustrate, the accounting equation is rewritten below to focus on the cash account:

$$\text{Assets} = \text{Liabilities} + \text{Stockholders' Equity}$$
$$\text{Cash} + \text{Noncash Assets} = \text{Liabilities} + \text{Stockholders' Equity}$$
$$\text{Cash} = \text{Liabilities} + \text{Stockholders' Equity} - \text{Noncash Assets}$$

Any change in the cash account results in a change in one or more noncash balance sheet accounts. That is, if the cash account changes, then a liability, stockholders' equity, or noncash asset account must also change.

Additional data are also obtained by analyzing the income statement accounts and supporting records. For example, since the net income or net loss for the period is closed to *Retained Earnings*, a change in the retained earnings account can be partially explained by the net income or net loss reported on the income statement.

There is no order in which the noncash balance sheet accounts must be analyzed. However, it is usually more efficient to analyze the accounts in the reverse order in which they appear on the balance sheet. Thus, the analysis of retained earnings provides the starting point for determining the cash flows from operating activities, which is the first section of the statement of cash flows.

The comparative balance sheet for Rundell Inc. on December 31, 2005 and 2004, is used to illustrate the indirect method. This balance sheet is shown in Exhibit 3. Selected ledger accounts and other data are presented as needed.[2]

Retained Earnings

The comparative balance sheet for Rundell Inc. shows that retained earnings increased $80,000 during the year. Analyzing the entries posted to the retained earnings account indicates how this change occurred. The retained earnings account for Rundell Inc. is shown below.

RETAINED EARNINGS

Dec. 31	Cash dividends	28,000	Jan. 1	Balance	202,300
			Dec. 31	Net income	108,000
					310,300
			Dec. 31	Balance	282,300

The retained earnings account must be carefully analyzed because some of the entries to retained earnings may not affect cash. For example, a decrease in retained earnings resulting from issuing a stock dividend does not affect cash. Such transactions are not reported on the statement of cash flows.

For Rundell Inc., the retained earnings account indicates that the $80,000 change resulted from net income of $108,000 and cash dividends declared of $28,000. The effect of each of these items on cash flows is discussed in the following sections.

2 An appendix that discusses using a work sheet as an aid in assembling data for the statement of cash flows is presented at the end of this chapter. This appendix illustrates a work sheet that can be used with the indirect method and a work sheet that can be used with the direct method of reporting cash flows from operating activities.

Exhibit 3

Comparative Balance Sheet

Rundell Inc.
Comparative Balance Sheet
December 31, 2005 and 2004

	2005	2004	Increase Decrease*
Assets			
Cash	$ 97,500	$ 26,000	$ 71,500
Accounts receivable (net)	74,000	65,000	9,000
Inventories	172,000	180,000	8,000*
Land	80,000	125,000	45,000*
Building	260,000	200,000	60,000
Accumulated depreciation—building	(65,300)	(58,300)	(7,000)
Total assets	$618,200	$537,700	$ 80,500
Liabilities			
Accounts payable (merchandise creditors)	$ 43,500	$ 46,700	$ 3,200*
Accrued expenses payable (operating expenses)	26,500	24,300	2,200
Income taxes payable	7,900	8,400	500*
Dividends payable	14,000	10,000	4,000
Bonds payable	100,000	150,000	50,000*
Total liabilities	$191,900	$239,400	$ 47,500*
Stockholders' Equity			
Common stock ($2 par)	$ 24,000	$ 16,000	$ 8,000
Paid-in capital in excess of par	120,000	80,000	40,000
Retained earnings	282,300	202,300	80,000
Total stockholders' equity	$426,300	$298,300	$128,000
Total liabilities and stockholders' equity	$618,200	$537,700	$ 80,500

Cash Flows from Operating Activities

The net income of $108,000 reported by Rundell Inc. normally is not equal to the amount of cash generated from operations during the period. This is because net income is determined using the accrual method of accounting.

Under the accrual method of accounting, revenues and expenses are recorded at different times from when cash is received or paid. For example, merchandise may be sold on account and the cash received at a later date.

Likewise, insurance expense represents the amount of insurance expired during the period. The premiums for the insurance may have been paid in a prior period. Thus, the net income reported on the income statement must be adjusted in determining cash flows from operating activities. The typical adjustments to net income are summarized in Exhibit 4.[3]

Some of the adjustment items in Exhibit 4 are for expenses that affect noncurrent accounts but not cash. For example, depreciation of fixed assets and amortization of intangible assets are deducted from revenue but do not affect cash.

Some of the adjustment items in Exhibit 4 are for revenues and expenses that affect current assets and current liabilities but not cash flows. For example, a sale of $10,000

3 Other items that also require adjustments to net income to obtain cash flow from operating activities include amortization of bonds payable discounts (add), losses on debt retirement (add), amortization of bonds payable premium (deduct), and gains on retirement of debt (deduct).

Exhibit 4

Adjustments to Net Income—Indirect Method

Net income, per income statement		$XX
Add: Depreciation of fixed assets and amortization of intangible assets	$XX	
Decreases in current assets (receivables, inventories, prepaid expenses)	XX	
Increases in current liabilities (accounts and notes payable, accrued liabilities)	XX	
Losses on disposal of assets	XX	XX
Deduct: Increases in current assets (receivables, inventories, prepaid expenses)	$XX	
Decreases in current liabilities (accounts and notes payable, accrued liabilities)	XX	
Gains on disposal of assets	XX	XX
Net cash flow from operating activities		$XX

on account increases accounts receivable by $10,000. However, cash is not affected. Thus, the increase in accounts receivable of $10,000 between two balance sheet dates is deducted from net income in arriving at cash flows from operating activities.

Cash flows from operating activities should not include investing or financing transactions. For example, assume that land costing $50,000 was sold for $90,000 (a gain of $40,000). The sale should be reported as an investing activity: "Cash receipts from the sale of land, $90,000." However, the $40,000 gain on the sale of the land is included in net income on the income statement. Thus, the $40,000 gain is deducted from net income in determining cash flows from operations in order to avoid "double counting" the cash flow from the gain. Losses from the sale of fixed assets are added to net income in determining cash flows from operations.

The effect of dividends payable on cash flows from operating activities is omitted from Exhibit 4. Dividends payable is omitted because dividends do not affect net income. Later in the chapter, we will discuss how dividends are reported in the statement of cash flows. In the following paragraphs, we will discuss each of the adjustments that change Rundell Inc.'s net income to "Cash flows from operating activities."

Depreciation

The comparative balance sheet in Exhibit 3 indicates that Accumulated Depreciation—Building increased by $7,000. As shown below, this account indicates that depreciation for the year was $7,000 for the building.

ACCUMULATED DEPRECIATION—BUILDING

	Jan. 1	Balance	58,300
	Dec. 31	Depreciation for year	7,000
	Dec. 31	Balance	*65,300*

The $7,000 of depreciation expense reduced net income but did not require an outflow of cash. Thus, the $7,000 is added to net income in determining cash flows from operating activities, as follows:

Cash flows from operating activities:		
Net income	$108,000	
Add depreciation	7,000	$115,000

In a recent year, Cablevision Systems had a net loss of $449 million, but a positive cash flow from operating activities of $456 million. This difference was mostly due to $734 million in depreciation and amortization expenses. Younger companies in industries requiring huge infrastructure investments, such as cable or cellular systems, will often have net losses coupled with positive cash flows from operations during their early years of operations.

Net income was $45,000 for the year. The accumulated depreciation balance increased by $15,000 over the year. There were no sales of fixed assets or changes in noncash current assets or liabilities. What is the cash flow from operations?

$60,000 ($45,000 + $15,000)

Current Assets and Current Liabilities

As shown in Exhibit 4, decreases in noncash current assets and increases in current liabilities are added to net income. In contrast, increases in noncash current assets and decreases in current liabilities are deducted from net income. The current asset and current liability accounts of Rundell Inc. are as follows:

	December 31		
Accounts	2005	2004	Increase Decrease*
Accounts receivable (net)	$ 74,000	$ 65,000	$9,000
Inventories	172,000	180,000	8,000*
Accounts payable (merchandise creditors)	43,500	46,700	3,200*
Accrued expenses payable (operating expenses)	26,500	24,300	2,200
Income taxes payable	7,900	8,400	500*

The $9,000 increase in *accounts receivable* indicates that the sales on account during the year are $9,000 more than collections from customers on account. The amount reported as sales on the income statement therefore includes $9,000 that did not result in a cash inflow during the year. Thus, $9,000 is deducted from net income.

The $8,000 decrease in *inventories* indicates that the merchandise sold exceeds the cost of the merchandise purchased by $8,000. The amount deducted as cost of merchandise sold on the income statement therefore includes $8,000 that did not require a cash outflow during the year. Thus, $8,000 is added to net income.

The $3,200 decrease in *accounts payable* indicates that the amount of cash payments for merchandise exceeds the merchandise purchased on account by $3,200. The amount reported on the income statement for cost of merchandise sold therefore excludes $3,200 that required a cash outflow during the year. Thus, $3,200 is deducted from net income.

The $2,200 increase in *accrued expenses payable* indicates that the amount incurred during the year for operating expenses exceeds the cash payments by $2,200. The amount reported on the income statement for operating expenses therefore includes $2,200 that did not require a cash outflow during the year. Thus, $2,200 is added to net income.

The $500 decrease in *income taxes payable* indicates that the amount paid for taxes exceeds the amount incurred during the year by $500. The amount reported on the income statement for income tax therefore is less than the amount paid by $500. Thus, $500 is deducted from net income.

Net income was $36,000 for the year. Accounts receivable increased $3,000, and accounts payable increased $5,000. What is the cash flow from operations?

$38,000 ($36,000 − $3,000 + $5,000)

Ethics in Action
The Effect of Credit on Cash Flow

Management will sometimes feel pressured to boost earnings by relaxing credit policies. Thus, it is able to create more sales on account, but at a higher collection risk. The result is a temporary positive impact on the income statement. However, cash flow may be negatively impacted if high-credit-risk customers delay payment or are unable to pay. For example, Lucent Technologies, Inc., extended billions of dollars in credit to upstart telecom companies to support its equipment sales. Loans to companies like Winstar and One.Tel Ltd. were eventually written off to the tune of $1 billion. This has prompted shareholder lawsuits accusing Lucent's directors of "mismanaging the top U.S. maker of phone equipment by lending the company's money to financially shaky customers to promote sales."

Source: *Omaha World-Herald*, "Lucent to Cut Almost Half Its Work Force. Troubled Phone Equipment Maker to Eliminate 20,000 Jobs, Take a Charge of as Much as $9 Billion," July 24, 2001.

Gain on Sale of Land

The ledger or income statement of Rundell Inc. indicates that the sale of land resulted in a gain of $12,000. As we discussed previously, the sale proceeds, which include the gain and the carrying value of the land, are included in cash flows from investing activities.[4] The gain is also included in net income. Thus, to avoid double reporting, the gain of $12,000 is deducted from net income in determining cash flows from operating activities:

Cash flows from operating activities:	
Net income	$108,000
Deduct gain on sale of land	12,000

Reporting Cash Flows from Operating Activities

We have now presented all the necessary adjustments to convert the net income to cash flows from operating activities for Rundell Inc. These adjustments are summarized in Exhibit 5 in a format suitable for the statement of cash flows.

Exhibit 5

Cash Flows from Operating Activities—Indirect Method

Cash flows from operating activities:			
Net income		$108,000	
Add: Depreciation	$ 7,000		
Decrease in inventories	8,000		
Increase in accrued expenses	2,200	17,200	
		$125,200	
Deduct: Increase in accounts receivable	$ 9,000		
Decrease in accounts payable	3,200		
Decrease in income taxes payable	500		
Gain on sale of land	12,000	24,700	
Net cash flow from operating activities			$100,500

4 Reporting the proceeds (cash flows) from the sale of land as part of investing activities is discussed later in this chapter.

Cash Flows Used for Payment of Dividends

According to the retained earnings account of Rundell Inc., shown earlier in the chapter, cash dividends of $28,000 were declared during the year. However, the dividends payable account, shown below, indicates that dividends of only $24,000 were paid during the year.

DIVIDENDS PAYABLE

Jan. 10	Cash paid	10,000	Jan. 1	Balance	10,000
July 10	Cash paid	14,000	June 20	Dividends declared	14,000
			Dec. 20	Dividends declared	14,000
		24,000			38,000
			Dec. 31	Balance	14,000

The $24,000 of dividend payments represents a cash outflow that is reported in the financing activities section as follows:

Cash flows from financing activities:	
Cash paid for dividends	$24,000

For some mature companies, cash outflows for dividends can be significant. For example, in a recent year Bank of America Corp. paid over $3.3 billion in dividends, which was equal to 65% of cash flows from operations.

Common Stock

The common stock account increased by $8,000, and the paid-in capital in excess of par—common stock account increased by $40,000, as shown below. These increases resulted from issuing 4,000 shares of common stock for $12 per share.

COMMON STOCK

	Jan. 1	Balance	16,000
	Nov. 1	4,000 shares issued for cash	8,000
	Dec. 31	Balance	*24,000*

PAID-IN CAPITAL IN EXCESS OF PAR

	Jan. 1	Balance	80,000
	Nov. 1	4,000 shares issued for cash	40,000
	Dec. 31	Balance	*120,000*

This cash inflow is reported in the financing activities section as follows:

Cash flows from financing activities:	
Cash received from sale of common stock	$48,000

Bonds Payable

The bonds payable account decreased by $50,000, as shown on the next page. This decrease resulted from retiring the bonds by a cash payment for their face amount.

BONDS PAYABLE

June 30	Retired by payment of cash at face amount	50,000	Jan. 1	Balance	150,000
			Dec. 31	Balance	*100,000*

This cash outflow is reported in the financing activities section as follows:

Cash flows from financing activities:	
Cash paid to retire bonds payable	$50,000

Building

The building account increased by $60,000, and the accumulated depreciation–building account increased by $7,000, as shown below.

BUILDING

Jan. 1	Balance	200,000	
Dec. 27	Purchased for cash	60,000	
Dec. 31	Balance	*260,000*	

ACCUMULATED DEPRECIATION—BUILDING

	Jan. 1	Balance	58,300
	Dec. 31	Depreciation for year	7,000
	Dec. 31	Balance	*65,300*

The purchase of a building for cash of $60,000 is reported as an outflow of cash in the investing activities section, as follows:

Cash flows from investing activities:	
Cash paid for purchase of building	$60,000

A building with a cost of $145,000 and accumulated depreciation of $35,000 was sold for a $10,000 gain. How much cash was generated from this investing activity?

$120,000 ($145,000 − $35,000 + $10,000)

The credit in the accumulated depreciation–building account, shown earlier, represents depreciation expense for the year. This depreciation expense of $7,000 on the building has already been considered as an addition to net income in determining cash flows from operating activities, as reported in Exhibit 5.

Land

The $45,000 decline in the land account resulted from two separate transactions, as shown below.

LAND

Jan. 1	Balance	125,000	June 8	Sold for $72,000 cash	60,000
Oct. 12	Purchased for cash	15,000			
		140,000			
Dec. 31	Balance	80,000			

The first transaction is the sale of land with a cost of $60,000 for $72,000 in cash. The $72,000 proceeds from the sale are reported in the investing activities section, as follows:

Cash flows from investing activities:	
Cash received from sale of land	
(includes $12,000 gain reported in net income)	$72,000

The proceeds of $72,000 include the $12,000 gain on the sale of land and the $60,000 cost (book value) of the land. As shown in Exhibit 5, the $12,000 gain is also deducted from net income in the cash flows from operating activities section. This is necessary so that the $12,000 cash inflow related to the gain is not included twice as a cash inflow.

The second transaction is the purchase of land for cash of $15,000. This transaction is reported as an outflow of cash in the investing activities section, as follows:

Cash flows from investing activities:	
Cash paid for purchase of land	$15,000

Preparing the Statement of Cash Flows

The statement of cash flows for Rundell Inc. is prepared from the data assembled and analyzed above, using the indirect method. Exhibit 6 shows the statement of cash flows prepared by Rundell Inc. The statement indicates that the cash position increased by $71,500 during the year. The most significant increase in net cash flows, $100,500, was from operating activities. The most significant use of cash, $26,000, was for financing activities.

Exhibit 6

Statement of Cash Flows–Indirect Method

Rundell Inc.
Statement of Cash Flows
For the Year Ended December 31, 2005

Cash flows from operating activities:			
Net income		$108,000	
Add: Depreciation	$ 7,000		
Decrease in inventories	8,000		
Increase in accrued expenses	2,200	17,200	
		$125,200	
Deduct: Increase in accounts receivable	$ 9,000		
Decrease in accounts payable	3,200		
Decrease in income taxes payable	500		
Gain on sale of land	12,000	24,700	
Net cash flow from operating activities			$100,500
Cash flows from investing activities:			
Cash from sale of land		$ 72,000	
Less: Cash paid to purchase land	$15,000		
Cash paid for purchase of building	60,000	75,000	
Net cash flow used for investing activities			(3,000)
Cash flows from financing activities:			
Cash received from sale of common stock		$ 48,000	
Less: Cash paid to retire bonds payable	$50,000		
Cash paid for dividends	24,000	74,000	
Net cash flow used for financing activities			(26,000)
Increase in cash			$ 71,500
Cash at the beginning of the year			26,000
Cash at the end of the year			$ 97,500

Statement of Cash Flows—The Direct Method

3 Prepare a statement of cash flows, using the direct method.

As we discussed previously, the manner of reporting cash flows from investing and financing activities is the same under the direct and indirect methods. In addition, the direct method and the indirect method will report the same amount of cash flows from operating activities. However, the methods differ in how the cash flows from operating activities data are obtained, analyzed, and reported.

To illustrate the direct method, we will use the comparative balance sheet and the income statement for Rundell Inc. In this way, we can compare the statement of cash flows under the direct method and the indirect method.

Exhibit 7 shows the changes in the current asset and liability account balances for Rundell Inc. The income statement in Exhibit 7 shows additional data for Rundell Inc.

Exhibit 7

Balance Sheet and Income Statement Data for Direct Method

Rundell Inc.
Schedule of Changes in Current Accounts

Accounts	December 31 2005	December 31 2004	Increase Decrease*
Cash	$ 97,500	$ 26,000	$71,500
Accounts receivable (net)	74,000	65,000	9,000
Inventories	172,000	180,000	8,000*
Accounts payable (merchandise creditors)	43,500	46,700	3,200*
Accrued expenses payable (operating expenses)	26,500	24,300	2,200
Income taxes payable	7,900	8,400	500*
Dividends payable	14,000	10,000	4,000

Rundell Inc.
Income Statement
For the Year Ended December 31, 2005

Sales		$1,180,000
Cost of merchandise sold		790,000
Gross profit		$ 390,000
Operating expenses:		
Depreciation expense	$ 7,000	
Other operating expenses	196,000	
Total operating expenses		203,000
Income from operations		$ 187,000
Other income:		
Gain on sale of land	$ 12,000	
Other expense:		
Interest expense	8,000	4,000
Income before income tax		$ 191,000
Income tax expense		83,000
Net income		$ 108,000

The direct method reports cash flows from operating activities by major classes of operating cash receipts and operating cash payments. The difference between the major classes of total operating cash receipts and total operating cash payments is the net cash flow from operating activities.

Cash Received from Customers

The $1,180,000 of sales for Rundell Inc. is reported by using the accrual method. To determine the cash received from sales to customers, the $1,180,000 must be adjusted. The adjustment necessary to convert the sales reported on the income statement to the cash received from customers is summarized below.

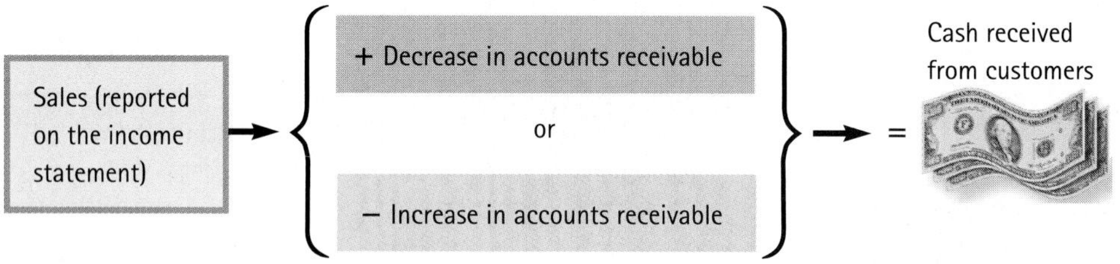

For Rundell Inc., the cash received from customers is $1,171,000, as shown below.

Sales	$1,180,000
Less increase in accounts receivable	9,000
Cash received from customers	$1,171,000

Sales reported on the income statement were $350,000. The accounts receivable balance declined $8,000 over the year. What was the amount of cash received from customers?

$358,000 ($350,000 + $8,000)

The additions to *accounts receivable* for sales on account during the year were $9,000 more than the amounts collected from customers on account. Sales reported on the income statement therefore included $9,000 that did not result in a cash inflow during the year. In other words, the increase of $9,000 in accounts receivable during 2005 indicates that sales on account exceeded cash received from customers by $9,000. Thus, $9,000 is deducted from sales to determine the cash received from customers. The $1,171,000 of cash received from customers is reported in the cash flows from operating activities section of the cash flow statement.

Cash Payments for Merchandise

The $790,000 of cost of merchandise sold is reported on the income statement for Rundell Inc., using the accrual method. The adjustments necessary to convert the cost of merchandise sold to cash payments for merchandise during 2005 are summarized on the following page.

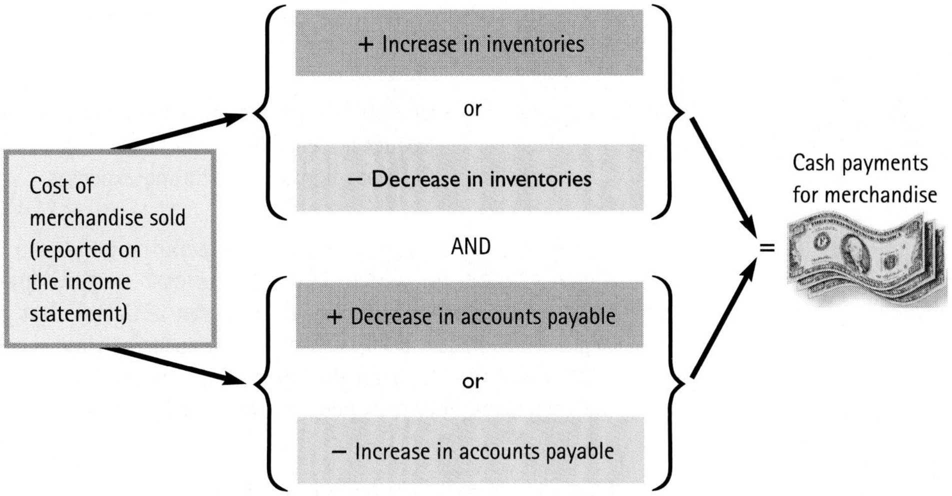

For Rundell Inc., the amount of cash payments for merchandise is $785,200, as determined below.

Cost of merchandise sold	$790,000
Deduct decrease in inventories	(8,000)
Add decrease in accounts payable	3,200
Cash payments for merchandise	$785,200

The $8,000 decrease in *inventories* indicates that the merchandise sold exceeded the cost of the merchandise purchased by $8,000. The amount reported on the income statement for cost of merchandise sold therefore includes $8,000 that did not require a cash outflow during the year. Thus, $8,000 is deducted from the cost of merchandise sold in determining the cash payments for merchandise.

The $3,200 decrease in *accounts payable* (merchandise creditors) indicates a cash outflow that is excluded from cost of merchandise sold. In other words, the decrease in accounts payable indicates that cash payments for merchandise were $3,200 more than the purchases on account during 2005. Thus, $3,200 is added to the cost of merchandise sold in determining the cash payments for merchandise.

Cash Payments for Operating Expenses

The $7,000 of depreciation expense reported on the income statement did not require a cash outflow. Thus, under the direct method, it is not reported on the statement of cash flows. The $196,000 reported for other operating expenses is adjusted to reflect the cash payments for operating expenses, as summarized below.

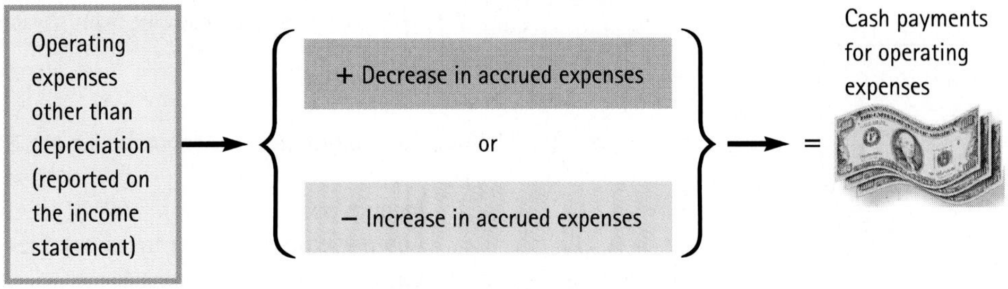

For Rundell Inc., the amount of cash payments for operating expenses is $193,800, determined as follows:

Operating expenses other than depreciation	$196,000
Deduct increase in accrued expenses	2,200
Cash payments for operating expenses	$193,800

The increase in *accrued expenses* (operating expenses) indicates that operating expenses include $2,200 for which there was no cash outflow (payment) during the year. In other words, the increase in accrued expenses indicates that the cash payments for operating expenses were $2,200 less than the amount reported as an expense during the year. Thus, $2,200 is deducted from the operating expenses on the income statement in determining the cash payments for operating expenses.

Gain on Sale of Land

The income statement for Rundell Inc. in Exhibit 7 reports a gain of $12,000 on the sale of land. As we discussed previously, the gain is included in the proceeds from the sale of land, which is reported as part of the cash flows from investing activities.

Interest Expense

The income statement for Rundell Inc. in Exhibit 7 reports interest expense of $8,000. The interest expense is related to the bonds payable that were outstanding during the year. We assume that interest on the bonds is paid on June 30 and December 31. Thus, $8,000 cash outflow for interest expense is reported on the statement of cash flows as an operating activity.

If interest payable had existed at the end of the year, the interest expense would be adjusted for any increase or decrease in interest payable from the beginning to the end of the year. That is, a decrease in interest payable would be added to interest expense and an increase in interest payable would be subtracted from interest expense. This is similar to the adjustment for changes in income taxes payable, which we will illustrate in the following paragraphs.

Cash Payments for Income Taxes

The adjustment to convert the income tax reported on the income statement to the cash basis is summarized below.

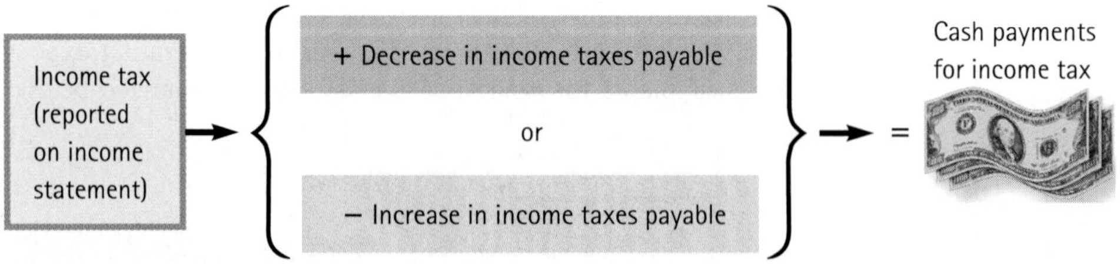

For Rundell Inc., cash payments for income tax are $83,500, determined as follows:

Income tax	$83,000
Add decrease in income taxes payable	500
Cash payments for income tax	$83,500

The cash outflow for income taxes exceeded the income tax deducted as an expense during the period by $500. Thus, $500 is added to the amount of income tax reported on the income statement in determining the cash payments for income tax.

Reporting Cash Flows from Operating Activities—Direct Method

Exhibit 8 is a complete statement of cash flows for Rundell Inc., using the direct method for reporting cash flows from operating activities. The portions of this statement that differ from the indirect method are highlighted in color. Exhibit 8 also includes the separate schedule reconciling net income and net cash flow from operating activities. This schedule must accompany the statement of cash flows when the direct method is used. This schedule is similar to the cash flows from operating activities section of the statement of cash flows prepared using the indirect method.

Exhibit 8

Statement of Cash Flows—Direct Method

Rundell Inc.
Statement of Cash Flows
For the Year Ended December 31, 2005

Cash flows from operating activities:			
Cash received from customers		$1,171,000	
Deduct: Cash payments for merchandise	$785,200		
Cash payments for operating expenses	193,800		
Cash payments for interest	8,000		
Cash payments for income taxes	83,500	1,070,500	
Net cash flow from operating activities			$100,500
Cash flows from investing activities:			
Cash from sale of land		$ 72,000	
Less: Cash paid to purchase land	$ 15,000		
Cash paid for purchase of building	60,000	75,000	
Net cash flow used for investing activities			(3,000)
Cash flows from financing activities:			
Cash received from sale of common stock		$ 48,000	
Less: Cash paid to retire bonds payable	$ 50,000		
Cash paid for dividends	24,000	74,000	
Net cash flow used for financing activities			(26,000)
Increase in cash			$ 71,500
Cash at the beginning of the year			26,000
Cash at the end of the year			$ 97,500

Schedule Reconciling Net Income with Cash Flows from Operating Activities:

Net income, per income statement		$108,000
Add: Depreciation	$ 7,000	
Decrease in inventories	8,000	
Increase in accrued expenses	2,200	17,200
		$125,200
Deduct: Increase in accounts receivable	$ 9,000	
Decrease in accounts payable	3,200	
Decrease in income taxes payable	500	
Gain on sale of land	12,000	24,700
Net cash flow from operating activities		$100,500

Analysis and Interpretation of Cash Flows

4 Calculate and interpret the cash conversion cycle, flow ratio, and free cash flow.

Managers want to generate cash from operations using a minimum of noncash working capital resources. The efficiency of a firm's noncash working capital policies can be measured using the cash conversion cycle and flow ratios. Cash-flow-generating ability can be measured by free cash flow.

Measuring Noncash Working Capital Efficiency

Noncash working capital consists of current assets and liabilities, other than cash. One way to view noncash working capital efficiency is to view operations as a cycle—from initial purchase of inventory to the final collection upon sale. The cycle begins with a purchase of inventory on account, after which the item is sold and the account collected. In each step, a current account is involved: accounts payable, inventory, and accounts receivable. These three balances can be translated into days of sales and used to measure how well a company efficiently manages noncash working capital. This measure is termed the **cash conversion cycle**, which is calculated as:

Cash conversion cycle (in days) = Number of Days' Sales in Receivables, Inventory, and Accounts Payable

Where,

Number of days' sales in accounts receivable = Accounts receivable, end of year/Average daily net sales
Number of days' sales in inventory = Inventory, end of year/Average daily cost of merchandise (goods) sold
Number of days' sales in accounts payable = Accounts payable, end of year/Average daily cost of merchandise (goods) sold

One way to generate cash from operations is to reduce the amount of noncash current assets and increase the level of current liabilities. Thus, the more positive the cash conversion cycle, the less efficient is the firm's operations from a cash flow perspective. The smaller the cash conversion cycle, the leaner are the working capital requirements for a given level of operations, thus releasing cash for other purposes. Negative cash conversion cycles indicate a highly efficient use of noncash working capital.

To illustrate the cash conversion cycle the following information was determined from the annual reports for selected companies in the computer industry:

	Dell Computer	Micron Technology	Hewlett-Packard	Gateway	Apple Computer	Compaq
Number of days' sales in:						
Receivables	33	72	47	20	32	71
Inventory	5	45	42	12	1	18
Accounts Payable	(61)	(49)	(53)	(38)	(71)	(48)
Cash conversion cycle	(23)	68	36	(6)	(38)	41

As can be seen from the table, Dell, Gateway, and Apple all have negative cash conversion cycles. For all three companies, their superior inventory management policies (low number of days' sales in inventory) explain this performance. Both Micron's and

Compaq's accounts receivable appear high for the industry, thus inefficiently committing cash to finance customers. Hewlett-Packard appears overinvested in inventory, compared to the industry, which contributes to its weaker cash conversion cycle.[5]

Another measure that is similar to the cash conversion cycle is the flow ratio. The **flow ratio** is calculated as:

$$\textit{Flow ratio} = \frac{\textit{Current assets} - (\textit{Cash} + \textit{Temporary investments})}{\textit{Current liabilities} - (\textit{Short-term debt or Current maturities})}$$

The flow ratio also measures the firm's noncash working capital efficiency. Again, efficient operations will use less noncash working capital, thus freeing up cash for other purposes. Thus, smaller values of the flow ratio are associated with more efficient use of noncash working capital.

The flow ratios for the selected companies in the computer industry for the latest available year are as follows:

	Dell Computer	Micron Technology	Hewlett-Packard	Gateway	Apple Computer	Compaq
Current assets	$ 9,491	$ 3,138	$23,244	$2,267	$ 5,143	$15,111
Cash	(4,910)	(469)	(3,415)	(484)	(2,310)	(2,569)
Marketable securities	(528)	(1,209)	(592)	(130)	(2,026)	
Numerator	$ 4,053	$ 1,460	$19,237	$1,653	$ 807	$12,542
Current liabilities	$ 6,543	$ 687	$15,197	$1,631	$ 1,518	$11,549
Short-term debt		(86)	(1,759)	(151)		(6,605)
Denominator	$ 6,543	$ 601	$13,438	$1,480	$ 1,518	$ 4,944
Flow ratio	0.62	2.43	1.43	1.12	0.53	2.54

As can be seen, the flow ratio is consistent with the cash conversion cycle. Micron, Hewlett-Packard, and Compaq all have the largest flow ratios, while Dell, Gateway, and Apple have the smallest ratios. Flow ratios near or less than 1.0 would indicate superior noncash working capital efficiency, while ratios greater than 2.0 would indicate less efficient use of noncash working capital.

In addition, the change in the flow ratio over time indicates the amount of cash generated from changes in noncash working capital. Thus, for example, as the flow ratio decreases, the cash flow from operating activities is enhanced from the more efficient use of working capital. As the flow ratio decreases, the numerator must increase, the denominator must decrease, or a combination of both. This analysis is consistent with our discussion for the indirect method of reporting cash flows from operating activities. That is, decreases in current assets and increases in current liabilities result in net cash inflows from operating activities, and *vice versa.* For example, the flow ratio for Apple Computer for the years 1998–2001 is shown graphically in Exhibit 9. As can be seen, Apple's flow ratio has improved from 0.92 in 1998 to 0.53 in 2001. Apple's improving flow ratio over this time period has provided operating cash flows from a more efficient use of working capital.

5 Hewlett-Packard and Compaq merged in 2002.

Exhibit 9

Flow Ratios for Apple Computer Company, 1998–2001

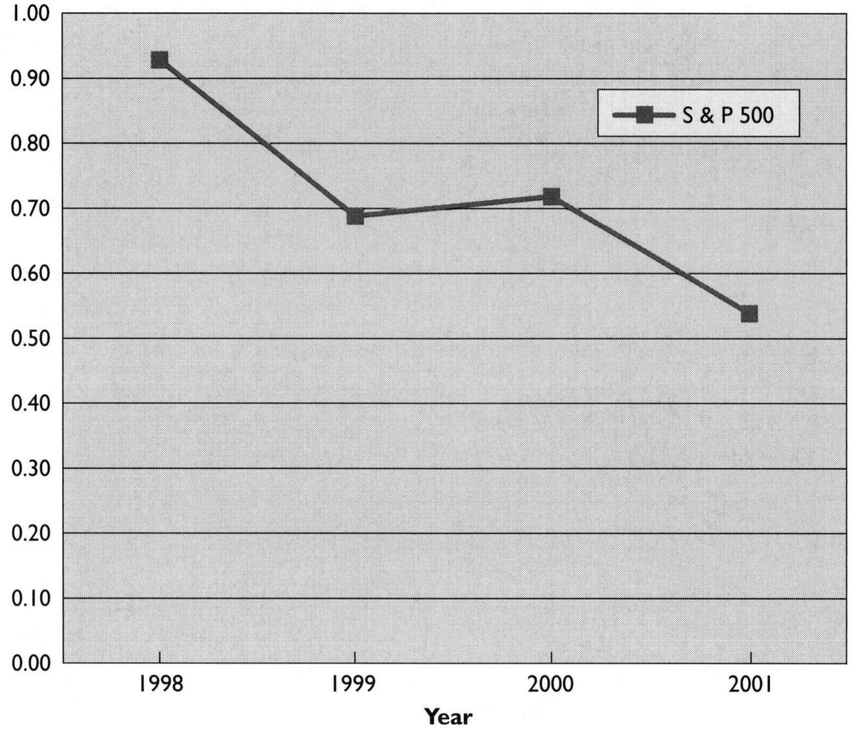

Free Cash Flow

Working capital efficiency explains how well a firm uses its working capital, but it does not indicate how much cash is actually being generated. A valuable tool for evaluating the cash flows of a business is free cash flow. **Free cash flow** is a measure of operating cash flow available for corporate purposes after providing sufficient fixed asset additions to maintain current productive capacity and dividends. Thus, free cash flow can be calculated as follows:

	Cash flow from operating activities
Less:	Cash used to purchase fixed assets to maintain productive capacity used up in producing income during the period
Less:	Cash used for dividends
	Free cash flow

Analysts often use free cash flow, rather than cash flows from operating activities, to measure the financial strength of a business. Many high-technology firms must aggressively reinvest in new technology to remain competitive. This can reduce free cash flow. For example, Motorola's free cash flow is less than 10% of its cash flow from operating activities. In contrast, Coca-Cola's free cash flow is approximately 75% of its cash flow from operating activities.

To illustrate, the cash flow from operating activities for Hewlett-Packard Co. was $3,460,000,000 in a recent fiscal year. The statement of cash flows indicated that the cash invested in property, plant, and equipment was $1,737,000,000, and $638,000,000 was paid for dividends. Assuming that the amount invested in property, plant, and equipment maintained existing operations, free cash flow would be calculated as follows:

Cash flow from operating activities		$3,460,000,000
Less: Cash invested in fixed assets to maintain productive capacity	$1,737,000,000	
Cash for dividends	638,000,000	2,375,000,000
Free cash flow		$1,085,000,000

During this period, Hewlett-Packard generated free cash flow in excess of $1 billion, which was 31% of cash flows from operations and over 2% of sales. The free cash flows for other companies in the computer industry are shown for comparison purposes below (in thousands).

	Dell Computer	Micron Technology	Gateway	Apple Computer	Compaq
Cash flow from operating activities	$4,195,000	$ 789,100	$ 288,772	$826,000	$ 565,000
Cash used to purchase property, plant, and equipment	(482,000)	(1,464,900)	(314,804)	(96,000)	(1,133,000)
Cash used to pay dividends	–	–	–	–	(170,000)
Free cash flow	$3,713,000	$ (675,800)	$ (26,032)	$730,000	$ (738,000)
Free cash flow as a percent of cash flow from operations	89%	−86%	−9%	88%	−131%
Free cash flow as a percent of sales	12%	−17%	0%	9%	−2%

Positive free cash flow is considered favorable. A company that has free cash flow is able to fund internal growth, retire debt, and enjoy financial flexibility. A company with no free cash flow is unable to maintain current productive capacity or dividend payouts to stockholders. Lack of free cash flow can be an early indicator of liquidity problems. Indeed, as stated by one analyst, "Free cash flow gives the company firepower to reduce debt and ultimately generate consistent, actual income."[6]

Appendix

Work Sheet for Statement of Cash Flows

A work sheet may be useful in assembling data for the statement of cash flows. Whether or not a work sheet is used, the concepts of cash flow and the statements of cash flows presented in this chapter are not affected. In this appendix, we will describe and illustrate the use of work sheets for the indirect method and the direct method.

Work Sheet—Indirect Method

We will use the data for Rundell Inc., presented in Exhibit 3, as a basis for illustrating the work sheet for the indirect method. The procedures used in preparing this work sheet, shown in Exhibit 10, are outlined below and on the next page.

1. List the title of each balance sheet account in the Accounts column. For each account, enter its balance as of December 31, 2004, in the first column and its balance as of December 31, 2005, in the last column. Place the credit balances in parentheses. The column totals should equal zero, since the total of the debits in a column should equal the total of the credits in a column.

6 Jill Krutick, *Fortune*, March 30, 1998, p. 106.

Exhibit 10

Work Sheet for Statement of Cash Flows–Indirect Method

Rundell Inc.
Work Sheet for Statement of Cash Flows
For the Year Ended December 31, 2005

	Accounts	Balance Dec. 31, 2004	Transactions Debit	Transactions Credit	Balance Dec. 31, 2005
1	Cash	26,000	(o) 71,500		97,500
2	Accounts receivable (net)	65,000	(n) 9,000		74,000
3	Inventories	180,000		(m) 8,000	172,000
4	Land	125,000	(k) 15,000	(l) 60,000	80,000
5	Building	200,000	(j) 60,000		260,000
6	Accumulated depreciation—building	(58,300)		(i) 7,000	(65,300)
7	Accounts payable (merchandise creditors)	(46,700)	(h) 3,200		(43,500)
8	Accrued expenses payable (operating expenses)	(24,300)		(g) 2,200	(26,500)
9	Income taxes payable	(8,400)	(f) 500		(7,900)
10	Dividends payable	(10,000)		(e) 4,000	(14,000)
11	Bonds payable	(150,000)	(d) 50,000		(100,000)
12	Common stock	(16,000)		(c) 8,000	(24,000)
13	Paid-in capital in excess of par	(80,000)		(c) 40,000	(120,000)
14	Retained earnings	(202,300)	(b) 28,000	(a) 108,000	(282,300)
15	Totals	0	237,200	237,200	0
16	Operating activities:				
17	Net income		(a) 108,000		
18	Depreciation of building		(i) 7,000		
19	Decrease in inventories		(m) 8,000		
20	Increase in accrued expenses		(g) 2,200		
21	Increase in accounts receivable			(n) 9,000	
22	Decrease in accounts payable			(h) 3,200	
23	Decrease in income taxes payable			(f) 500	
24	Gain on sale of land			(l) 12,000	
25	Investing activities:				
26	Sale of land		(l) 72,000		
27	Purchase of land			(k) 15,000	
28	Purchase of building			(j) 60,000	
29	Financing activities:				
30	Issued common stock		(c) 48,000		
31	Retired bonds payable			(d) 50,000	
32	Declared cash dividends			(b) 28,000	
33	Increase in dividends payable		(e) 4,000		
34	Net increase in cash			(o) 71,500	
35	Totals		249,200	249,200	

2. Analyze the change during the year in each account to determine the net increase (decrease) in cash and the cash flows from operating activities, investing activities, financing activities, and the noncash investing and financing activities. Show the effect of the change on cash flows by making entries in the Transactions columns.

Analyzing Accounts

An efficient method of analyzing cash flows is to determine the type of cash flow activity that led to changes in balance sheet accounts during the period. As we analyze each noncash account, we will make entries on the work sheet for specific types of cash flow activities related to the noncash accounts. After we have analyzed all the noncash accounts, we will make an entry for the increase (decrease) in cash during the period. These entries, however, are not posted to the ledger. They only aid in assembling the data on the work sheet.

The order in which the accounts are analyzed is unimportant. However, it is more efficient to begin with the retained earnings account and proceed upward in the account listing.

Retained Earnings The work sheet shows a Retained Earnings balance of $202,300 at December 31, 2004, and $282,300 at December 31, 2005. Thus, Retained Earnings increased $80,000 during the year. This increase resulted from two factors: (1) net income of $108,000 and (2) declaring cash dividends of $28,000. To identify the cash flows by activity, we will make two entries on the work sheet. These entries also serve to account for or explain, in terms of cash flows, the increase of $80,000.

In closing the accounts at the end of the year, the retained earnings account was credited for the net income of $108,000. The $108,000 is reported on the statement of cash flows as "cash flows from operating activities." The following entry is made in the Transactions columns on the work sheet. This entry (1) accounts for the credit portion of the closing entry (to Retained Earnings) and (2) identifies the cash flow in the bottom portion of the work sheet.

(a)	Operating Activities—Net Income	108,000	
	Retained Earnings		108,000

In closing the accounts at the end of the year, the retained earnings account was debited for dividends declared of $28,000. The $28,000 is reported as a financing activity on the statement of cash flows. The following entry on the work sheet (1) accounts for the debit portion of the closing entry (to Retained Earnings) and (2) identifies the cash flow in the bottom portion of the work sheet.

(b)	Retained Earnings	28,000	
	Financing Activities—Declared Cash Dividends		28,000

The $28,000 of declared dividends will be adjusted later for the actual amount of cash dividends paid during the year.

Other Accounts The entries for the other accounts are made in the work sheet in a manner similar to entries (a) and (b). A summary of these entries is as follows:

(c)	Financing Activities—Issued Common Stock	48,000	
	Common Stock		8,000
	Paid-In Capital in Excess of Par—Common Stock		40,000
(d)	Bonds Payable	50,000	
	Financing Activities—Retired Bonds Payable		50,000
(e)	Financing Activities—Increase in Dividends Payable	4,000	
	Dividends Payable		4,000

(continued)

(f)	Income Taxes Payable	500	
	Operating Activities—Decrease in Income Taxes Payable		500
(g)	Operating Activities—Increase in Accrued Expenses	2,200	
	Accrued Expenses Payable		2,200
(h)	Accounts Payable	3,200	
	Operating Activities—Decrease in Accounts Payable		3,200
(i)	Operating Activities—Depreciation of Building	7,000	
	Accumulated Depreciation—Building		7,000
(j)	Building	60,000	
	Investing Activities—Purchase of Building		60,000
(k)	Land	15,000	
	Investing Activities—Purchase of Land		15,000
(l)	Investing Activities—Sale of Land	72,000	
	Operating Activities—Gain on Sale of Land		12,000
	Land		60,000
(m)	Operating Activities—Decrease in Inventories	8,000	
	Inventories		8,000
(n)	Accounts Receivable	9,000	
	Operating Activities—Increase in Accounts Receivable		9,000
(o)	Cash	71,500	
	Net Increase in Cash		71,500

Completing the Work Sheet

After we have analyzed all the balance sheet accounts and made the entries on the work sheet, all the operating, investing, and financing activities are identified in the bottom portion of the work sheet. The accuracy of the work sheet entries is verified by the equality of each pair of the totals of the debit and credit Transactions columns.

Preparing the Statement of Cash Flows

The statement of cash flows prepared from the work sheet is identical to the statement in Exhibit 6. The data for the three sections of the statement are obtained from the bottom portion of the work sheet.

In the cash flows from operating activities section, the effect of depreciation is normally presented first. The effects of increases and decreases in current assets and current liabilities are then presented. The effects of any gains and losses on operating activities are normally reported last. The cash paid for dividends is reported as $24,000 instead of the amount of dividends declared ($28,000) less the increase in dividends payable ($4,000). Any noncash investing and financing activities are usually reported in a separate schedule at the bottom of the statement.

Work Sheet—Direct Method

As a basis for illustrating the direct method work sheet, we will use the balance sheet data for Rundell Inc. in Exhibit 3 and the income statement data in Exhibit 7. The procedures used in preparing the work sheet are outlined following Exhibit 11.

Exhibit 11

Work Sheet for Statement of Cash Flows–Direct Method

Rundell Inc.
Work Sheet for Statement of Cash Flows
For the Year Ended December 31, 2005

Accounts	Balance Dec. 31, 2004	Transactions Debit	Transactions Credit	Balance Dec. 31, 2005
Balance Sheet				
Cash	26,000	(t) 71,500		97,500
Accounts receivable (net)	65,000	(s) 9,000		74,000
Inventories	180,000		(r) 8,000	172,000
Land	125,000	(q) 15,000	(e) 60,000	80,000
Building	200,000	(p) 60,000		260,000
Accumulated depreciation—building	(58,300)		(c) 7,000	(65,300)
Accounts payable (merchandise creditors)	(46,700)	(o) 3,200		(43,500)
Accrued expenses payable (operating expenses)	(24,300)		(n) 2,200	(26,500)
Income taxes payable	(8,400)	(m) 500		(7,900)
Dividends payable	(10,000)		(l) 4,000	(14,000)
Bonds payable	(150,000)	(k) 50,000		(100,000)
Common stock	(16,000)		(j) 8,000	(24,000)
Paid-in capital in excess of par	(80,000)		(j) 40,000	(120,000)
Retained earnings	(202,300)	(i) 28,000	(h) 108,000	(282,300)
Totals	0	237,200	237,200	0
Income Statement				
Sales			(a)1,180,000	
Cost of merchandise sold		(b) 790,000		
Depreciation expense		(c) 7,000		
Other operating expenses		(d) 196,000		
Gain on sale of land			(e) 12,000	
Interest expense		(f) 8,000		
Income taxes		(g) 83,000		
Net income		(h) 108,000		
Cash Flows				
Operating activities:				
Cash received from customers		(a)1,180,000	(s) 9,000	
Cash payments:				
Merchandise		(r) 8,000	(b) 790,000	
			(o) 3,200	
Operating expenses		(n) 2,200	(d) 196,000	
Interest			(f) 8,000	
Income taxes			(g) 83,000	
			(m) 500	
Investing activities:				
Sale of land		(e) 72,000		
Purchase of land			(q) 15,000	
Purchase of building			(p) 60,000	
Financing activities:				
Issued common stock		(j) 48,000		
Retired bonds payable			(k) 50,000	
Declared cash dividends			(i) 28,000	
Increase in dividends payable		(l) 4,000		
Net increase in cash			(t) 71,500	
Totals		2,506,200	2,506,200	

1. List the title of each balance sheet account in the Accounts column. For each account, enter its balance as of December 31, 2004, in the first column and its balance as of December 31, 2005, in the last column. Place the credit balances in parentheses. The column totals should equal zero, since the total of the debits in a column should equal the total of the credits in a column.
2. List the title of each income statement account and "Net income" on the work sheet.
3. Analyze the effect of each income statement item on cash flows from operating activities. Beginning with sales, enter the balance of each item in the proper Transactions column. Complete the entry in the Transactions columns to show the effect on cash flows.
4. Analyze the change during the year in each balance sheet account to determine the net increase (decrease) in cash and the cash flows from operating activities, investing activities, financing activities, and the noncash investing and financing activities. Show the effect of the change on cash flows by making entries in the Transactions columns.

Analyzing Accounts

Under the direct method of reporting cash flows from operating activities, analyzing accounts begins with the income statement. As we analyze each income statement account, we will make entries on the work sheet that show the effect on cash flows from operating activities. After we have analyzed the income statement accounts, we will analyze changes in the balance sheet accounts.

The order in which the balance sheet accounts are analyzed is unimportant. However, it is more efficient to begin with the retained earnings account and proceed upward in the account listing. As each noncash balance sheet account is analyzed, we will make entries on the work sheet for the related cash flow activities. After we have analyzed all the noncash accounts, we will make an entry for the increase (decrease) in cash during the period.

Sales The income statement for Rundell Inc. shows sales of $1,180,000 for the year. Sales for cash provide cash when the sale is made. Sales on account provide cash when customers pay their bills. The entry on the work sheet is as follows:

(a)	Operating Activities—Receipts from Customers	1,180,000	
	Sales		1,180,000

Cost of Merchandise Sold The income statement for Rundell Inc. shows cost of merchandise sold of $790,000 for the year. The cost of merchandise sold requires cash payments for cash purchases of merchandise. For purchases on account, cash payments are made when the invoices are due. The entry on the work sheet is as follows:

(b)	Cost of Merchandise Sold	790,000	
	Operating Activities—Payments for Merchandise		790,000

Depreciation Expense The income statement for Rundell Inc. shows depreciation expense of $7,000. Depreciation expense does not require a cash outflow and thus is not reported on the statement of cash flows. The entry on the work sheet to fully account for the depreciation expense is as follows:

(c)	Depreciation Expense	7,000	
	Accumulated Depreciation—Building		7,000

Other Accounts The entries for the other accounts are made on the work sheet in a manner similar to entries (a), (b), and (c). A summary of these entries is as follows:

(d)	Other Operating Expenses	196,000	
	Operating Activities—Paid Operating Expenses		196,000
(e)	Investing Activities—Sale of Land	72,000	
	Land		60,000
	Gain on Sale of Land		12,000
(f)	Interest Expense	8,000	
	Operating Activities—Paid Interest		8,000
(g)	Income Taxes	83,000	
	Operating Activities—Paid Income Taxes		83,000
(h)	Net Income	108,000	
	Retained Earnings		108,000
(i)	Retained Earnings	28,000	
	Financing Activities—Declared Cash Dividends		28,000
(j)	Financing Activities—Issued Common Stock	48,000	
	Common Stock		8,000
	Paid-In Capital in Excess of Par—Common Stock		40,000
(k)	Bonds Payable	50,000	
	Financing Activities—Retired Bonds Payable		50,000
(l)	Financing Activities—Increase in Dividends Payable	4,000	
	Dividends Payable		4,000
(m)	Income Taxes Payable	500	
	Operating Activities—Cash Paid for Income Taxes		500
(n)	Operating Activities—Cash Paid for Operating Expenses	2,200	
	Accrued Expenses Payable		2,200
(o)	Accounts Payable	3,200	
	Operating Activities—Cash Paid for Merchandise		3,200
(p)	Building	60,000	
	Investing Activities—Purchase of Building		60,000
(q)	Land	15,000	
	Investing Activities—Purchase of Land		15,000
(r)	Operating Activities—Cash Paid for Merchandise	8,000	
	Inventories		8,000
(s)	Accounts Receivable	9,000	
	Operating Activities—Cash Received from Customers		9,000
(t)	Cash	71,500	
	Net Increase in Cash		71,500

Completing the Work Sheet

After we have analyzed all the income statement and balance sheet accounts and have made the entries on the work sheet, all the operating, investing, and financing activities are identified in the bottom portion of the work sheet. The mathematical accuracy of the work sheet entries is verified by the equality of each pair of the totals of the debit and credit Transactions columns.

Preparing the Statement of Cash Flows

The statement of cash flows prepared from the work sheet is identical to the statement in Exhibit 8. The data for the three sections of the statement are obtained from the bottom portion of the work sheet. Some of these data may not be reported exactly as they appear on the work sheet. The cash paid for dividends is reported as $24,000 instead of the amount of dividends declared ($28,000) less the increase in the dividends payable ($4,000).

Summary of Learning Goals

1 Summarize the types of cash flow activities reported in the statement of cash flows.

The statement of cash flows reports cash receipts and cash payments by three types of activities: operating activities, investing activities, and financing activities.

Cash flows from operating activities are cash flows from transactions that affect net income. There are two methods of reporting cash flows from operating activities: (1) the direct method and (2) the indirect method.

Cash inflows from investing activities are cash flows from the sale of investments, fixed assets, and intangible assets. Cash outflows generally include payments to acquire investments, fixed assets, and intangible assets.

Cash inflows from financing activities include proceeds from issuing equity securities, such as preferred and common stock. Cash inflows also arise from issuing bonds, mortgage notes payable, and other long-term debt. Cash outflows from financing activities arise from paying cash dividends, purchasing treasury stock, and repaying amounts borrowed.

Investing and financing for a business may be affected by transactions that do not involve cash. The effect of such transactions should be reported in a separate schedule accompanying the statement of cash flows.

Because it may be misleading, cash flow per share is not reported in the statement of cash flows.

2 Prepare a statement of cash flows, using the indirect method.

To prepare the statement of cash flows, changes in the noncash balance sheet accounts are analyzed. This logic relies on the fact that a change in any balance sheet account can be analyzed in terms of changes in the other balance sheet accounts. Thus, by analyzing the noncash balance sheet accounts, those activities that resulted in cash flows can be identified. Although the noncash balance sheet accounts may be analyzed in any order, it is usually more efficient to begin with retained earnings. Additional data are obtained by analyzing the income statement accounts and supporting records.

3 Prepare a statement of cash flows, using the direct method.

The direct method and the indirect method will report the same amount of cash flows from operating activities. Also, the manner of reporting cash flows from investing and financing activities is the same under both methods. The methods differ in how the cash flows from operating activities data are obtained, analyzed, and reported. The direct method reports cash flows from operating activities by major classes of operating cash receipts and cash payments. The difference between the major classes of total operating cash receipts and total operating cash payments is the net cash flow from operating activities.

The data for reporting cash flows from operating activities by the direct method can be obtained by analyzing the cash flows related to the revenues and expenses reported on the income statement. The revenues and expenses are adjusted from the accrual basis of accounting to the cash basis for purposes of preparing the statement of cash flows.

When the direct method is used, a reconciliation of net income and net cash flow from operating activities is reported in a separate schedule. This schedule is similar to the cash flows from operating activities section of the statement of cash flows prepared using the indirect method.

4 Calculate and interpret the cash conversion cycle, flow ratio, and free cash flow. The cash conversion cycle and flow ratio measure the efficiency of using noncash working capital for operations. The cash conversion cycle is calculated as the number of days' sales in accounts receivable, plus the number of days' sales in inventory, less the number of days' sales in accounts payable. Low or negative values for the cash conversion cycle are considered very efficient. The flow ratio is calculated as current assets less cash and temporary investments divided by current liabilities less short-term debt or current maturities. Flow ratios near or less than 1.0 would generally indicate superior noncash working capital efficiency, while ratios greater than 2.0 would generally indicate less efficient use of noncash working capital. Free cash flow is the amount of operating cash flow remaining after replacing current productive capacity and maintaining current dividends. Free cash flow is the amount of cash available to reduce debt, expand the business, or return to shareholders through increased dividends or treasury stock purchases.

Glossary

Cash conversion cycle The number of days' sales in accounts receivable, plus the number of days' sales in inventory, less the number of days' sales in accounts payable.

Cash flows from financing activities The section of the statement of cash flows that reports cash flows from transactions affecting the equity and debt of the business.

Cash flows from investing activities The section of the statement of cash flows that reports cash flows from transactions affecting investments in noncurrent assets.

Cash flows from operating activities The section of the statement of cash flows that reports the cash transactions affecting the determination of net income.

Direct method A method of reporting the cash flows from operating activities as the difference between the operating cash receipts and the operating cash payments.

Flow ratio Current assets less cash and temporary investments divided by current liabilities less short-term debt or current maturities.

Free cash flow The amount of operating cash flow remaining after replacing current productive capacity and maintaining current dividends.

Indirect method A method of reporting the cash flows from operating activities as the net income from operations adjusted for all deferrals of past cash receipts and payments and all accruals of expected future cash receipts and payments.

Statement of cash flows A summary of the major cash receipts and cash payments for a period.

Illustrative Accounting Application Problem

The comparative balance sheet of Dowling Company for December 31, 2004 and 2003, is shown on the next page.

Dowling Company
Comparative Balance Sheet
December 31, 2004 and 2003

	2004	2003
Assets		
Cash	$ 140,350	$ 95,900
Accounts receivable (net)	95,300	102,300
Inventories	165,200	157,900
Prepaid expenses	6,240	5,860
Investments (long-term)	35,700	84,700
Land	75,000	90,000
Buildings	375,000	260,000
Accumulated depreciation—buildings	(71,300)	(58,300)
Machinery and equipment	428,300	428,300
Accumulated depreciation—machinery and equipment	(148,500)	(138,000)
Patents	58,000	65,000
Total assets	$1,159,290	$1,093,660
Liabilities and Stockholders' Equity		
Accounts payable (merchandise creditors)	$ 43,500	$ 46,700
Accrued expenses (operating expenses)	14,000	12,500
Income taxes payable	7,900	8,400
Dividends payable	14,000	10,000
Mortgage note payable, due 2004	40,000	0
Bonds payable	150,000	250,000
Common stock, $30 par	450,000	375,000
Excess of issue price over par—common stock	66,250	41,250
Retained earnings	373,640	349,810
Total liabilities and stockholders' equity	$1,159,290	$1,093,660

The income statement for Dowling Company is shown below.

Dowling Company
Income Statement
For the Year Ended December 31, 2004

Sales		$1,100,000
Cost of merchandise sold		710,000
Gross profit		$ 390,000
Operating expenses:		
Depreciation expense	$ 23,500	
Patent amortization	7,000	
Other operating expenses	196,000	
Total operating expenses		226,500
Income from operations		$ 163,500
Other income:		
Gain on sale of investments	$ 11,000	
Other expense:		
Interest expense	26,000	(15,000)
Income before income tax		$ 148,500
Income tax expense		50,000
Net income		$ 98,500

An examination of the accounting records revealed the following additional information applicable to 2004:

a. Land costing $15,000 was sold for $15,000.
b. A mortgage note was issued for $40,000.
c. A building costing $115,000 was constructed.
d. 2,500 shares of common stock were issued at 40 in exchange for the bonds payable.
e. Cash dividends declared were $74,670.

Instructions

1. Prepare a statement of cash flows, using the indirect method of reporting cash flows from operating activities.
2. Prepare a statement of cash flows, using the direct method of reporting cash flows from operating activities.

Solution

1.

Dowling Company
Statement of Cash Flows—Indirect Method
For the Year Ended December 31, 2004

Cash flows from operating activities:			
Net income, per income statement		$ 98,500	
Add: Depreciation	$23,500		
Amortization of patents	7,000		
Decrease in accounts receivable	7,000		
Increase in accrued expenses	1,500	39,000	
		$137,500	
Deduct: Increase in inventories	$ 7,300		
Increase in prepaid expenses	380		
Decrease in accounts payable	3,200		
Decrease in income taxes payable	500		
Gain on sale of investments	11,000	22,380	
Net cash flow from operating activities			$115,120
Cash flows from investing activities:			
Cash received from sale of:			
Investments	$60,000		
Land	15,000	$ 75,000	
Less: Cash paid for construction of building		115,000	
Net cash flow used for investing activities			(40,000)
Cash flows from financing activities:			
Cash received from issuing mortgage note payable		$ 40,000	
Less: Cash paid for dividends		70,670	
Net cash flow used for financing activities			(30,670)
Increase in cash			$ 44,450
Cash at the beginning of the year			95,900
Cash at the end of the year			$140,350
Schedule of Noncash Investing and Financing Activities:			
Issued common stock to retire bonds payable			$100,000

2.

Dowling Company
Statement of Cash Flows—Direct Method
For the Year Ended December 31, 2004

Cash flows from operating activities:			
Cash received from customers[1]		$1,107,000	
Deduct: Cash paid for merchandise[2]	$720,500		
Cash paid for operating expenses[3]	194,880		
Cash paid for interest expense	26,000		
Cash paid for income tax[4]	50,500	991,880	
Net cash flow from operating activities			$115,120
Cash flows from investing activities:			
Cash received from sale of:			
Investments	$ 60,000		
Land	15,000	$ 75,000	
Less: Cash paid for construction of building		115,000	
Net cash flow used for investing activities			(40,000)
Cash flows from financing activities:			
Cash received from issuing mortgage note payable		$ 40,000	
Less: Cash paid for dividends[5]		70,670	
Net cash flow used for financing activities			(30,670)
Increase in cash			$ 44,450
Cash at the beginning of the year			95,900
Cash at the end of the year			$140,350
Schedule of Noncash Investing and Financing Activities:			
Issued common stock to retire bonds payable			$100,000

Computations:
[1]$1,100,000 + $7,000 = $1,107,000
[2]$710,000 + $3,200 + $7,300 = $720,500
[3]$196,000 + $380 − $1,500 = $194,880
[4]$50,000 + $500 = $50,500
[5]$74,670 + $10,000 − $14,000 = $70,670

Self-Study Questions

Answers at end of chapter

1. An example of a cash flow from an investing activity is:
   A. receipt of cash from the sale of equipment.
   B. receipt of cash from the sale of stock.
   C. payment of cash for dividends.
   D. payment of cash to acquire treasury stock.

2. An example of a cash flow from a financing activity is:
   A. receipt of cash from customers on account.
   B. receipt of cash from the sale of equipment.
   C. payment of cash for dividends.
   D. payment of cash to acquire land.

3. Which of the following methods of reporting cash flows from operating activities adjusts net income for revenues and expenses not involving the receipt or payment of cash?
   A. Direct method
   B. Purchase method
   C. Reciprocal method
   D. Indirect method

4. The net income reported on the income statement for the year was $55,000, and depreciation of fixed assets for the year was $22,000. The balances of the current asset and current liability accounts at the beginning and end of the year are as follows:

	End	Beginning
Cash	$ 65,000	$ 70,000
Accounts receivable	100,000	90,000
Inventories	145,000	150,000
Prepaid expenses	7,500	8,000
Accounts payable (merchandise creditors)	51,000	58,000

The total amount reported for cash flows from operating activities in the statement of cash flows, using the indirect method, is:
A. $33,000 C. $65,500
B. $55,000 D. $77,000

5. An analysis of the balance sheet of Getty Company revealed the number of days' sales in accounts receivable and inventory of 30 and 45 days, respectively. The number of days' sales in accounts payable was 25 days. What is Getty's cash conversion cycle?
A. 100 days C. 50 days
B. −40 days D. 75 days

Discussion Questions

1. What is the principal disadvantage of the direct method of reporting cash flows from operating activities?
2. What are the major advantages of the indirect method of reporting cash flows from operating activities?
3. A corporation issued $200,000 of common stock in exchange for $200,000 of fixed assets. Where would this transaction be reported on the statement of cash flows?
4. a. What is the effect on cash flows of declaring and issuing a stock dividend?
   b. Is the stock dividend reported on the statement of cash flows?
5. A retail business, using the accrual method of accounting, owed merchandise creditors (accounts payable) $290,000 at the beginning of the year and $315,000 at the end of the year. How would the $25,000 increase be used to adjust net income in determining the amount of cash flows from operating activities by the indirect method? Explain.
6. If salaries payable was $75,000 at the beginning of the year and $65,000 at the end of the year, should $10,000 be added to or deducted from income to determine the amount of cash flows from operating activities by the indirect method? Explain.
7. A long-term investment in bonds with a cost of $75,000 was sold for $80,000 cash. (a) What was the gain or loss on the sale? (b) What was the effect of the transaction on cash flows? (c) How should the transaction be reported in the statement of cash flows if cash flows from operating activities are reported by the indirect method?
8. A corporation issued $5,000,000 of 20-year bonds for cash at 105. How would the transaction be reported on the statement of cash flows?
9. Fully depreciated equipment costing $55,000 was discarded. What was the effect of the transaction on cash flows if (a) $5,000 cash is received, (b) no cash is received?
10. For the current year, Accord Company decided to switch from the indirect method to the direct method for reporting cash flows from operating activities on the statement of cash flows. Will the change cause the amount of net cash flow from operating activities to be (a) larger, (b) smaller, or (c) the same as if the indirect method had been used? Explain.
11. Name five common major classes of operating cash receipts or operating cash payments presented on the statement of cash flows when the cash flows from operating activities are reported by the direct method.

12. In a recent annual report, PepsiCo, Inc., reported that during the year it issued stock of $438 million for acquisitions. How would this be reported on the statement of cash flows?

Exercises

Exercise 13-1

Cash flows from operating activities—net loss

Goal 1

On its income statement for a recent year, Nortel Networks, Corp., a telecommunications equipment company, reported a net loss of $26.7 billion. A restructuring charge of $15.7 billion caused a significant portion of this loss. On its statement of cash flows, it reported $425 million of cash flows from operating activities.

Explain this apparent contradiction between the loss and the positive cash flows.

Exercise 13-2

Effect of transactions on cash flows

Goal 1

b. Cash payment, $501,000

STUDENT SOLUTIONS MANUAL

State the effect (cash receipt or payment and amount) of each of the following transactions, considered individually, on cash flows:

a. Purchased a building by paying $30,000 cash and issuing a $90,000 mortgage note payable.
b. Retired $500,000 of bonds, on which there was $2,500 of unamortized discount, for $501,000.
c. Paid dividends of $1.50 per share. There were 30,000 shares issued and 5,000 shares of treasury stock.
d. Sold a new issue of $100,000 of bonds at 101.
e. Purchased 5,000 shares of $30 par common stock as treasury stock at $50 per share.
f. Purchased land for $120,000 cash.
g. Sold equipment with a book value of $42,500 for $41,000.
h. Sold 5,000 shares of $30 par common stock for $45 per share.

Exercise 13-3

Classifying cash flows

Goal 1

Identify the type of cash flow activity for each of the following events (operating, investing, or financing):

a. Issued bonds.
b. Issued common stock.
c. Sold long-term investments.
d. Paid cash dividends.
e. Redeemed bonds.
f. Issued preferred stock.
g. Net income.
h. Sold equipment.
i. Purchased treasury stock.
j. Purchased buildings.
k. Purchased patents.

Exercise 13-4

Cash flows from operating activities—indirect method

Goal 2

STUDENT SOLUTIONS MANUAL

The following quote was from the footnotes of Hershey Foods Corporation's annual report:

> *Net write-downs of property, plant and equipment of $45.3 million were recorded to accumulated depreciation as a result of asset impairments associated with the Corporation's business realignment initiatives recorded in the fourth quarter of 2001. These initiatives included plans to close several manufacturing facilities and to sell certain businesses as part of product line rationalization programs.*

What impact would this write-down have on Hershey's statement of cash flows under the indirect method?

Exercise 13-5

Cash flows from operating activities—indirect method

Goal 2

Indicate whether each of the following would be added to or deducted from net income in determining net cash flow from operating activities by the indirect method:

a. Loss on disposal of fixed assets
b. Decrease in accounts payable
c. Decrease in salaries payable
d. Depreciation of fixed assets
e. Amortization of patent
f. Decrease in accounts receivable
g. Gain on retirement of long-term debt
h. Increase in merchandise inventory
i. Decrease in prepaid expenses
j. Increase in notes receivable due in 90 days from customers
k. Increase in notes payable due in 90 days to vendors

Exercise 13-6

Cash flows from operating activities—indirect method

Goals 2, 3

a. Cash flows from operating activities, $196,150

STUDENT SOLUTIONS MANUAL

SPREADSHEET

The net income reported on the income statement for the current year was $167,900. Depreciation recorded on equipment and a building amounted to $41,300 for the year. Balances of the current asset and current liability accounts at the beginning and end of the year are as follows:

	End of Year	Beginning of Year
Cash	$ 27,900	$ 30,900
Accounts receivable (net)	75,100	70,250
Inventories	120,400	110,900
Prepaid expenses	5,800	6,000
Accounts payable (merchandise creditors)	67,200	65,300
Salaries payable	7,150	7,950

a. Prepare the cash flows from operating activities section of the statement of cash flows, using the indirect method.
b. If the direct method had been used, would the net cash flow from operating activities have been the same? Explain.

Exercise 13-7

Cash flows from operating activities—indirect method

Goal 2

The net income reported on the income statement for the current year was $489,000. Depreciation recorded on store equipment for the year amounted to $135,700. Balances of the current asset and current liability accounts at the beginning and end of the year are shown on the next page.

Cash flows from operating activities, $657,200

SPREADSHEET

	End of Year	Beginning of Year
Cash	$420,400	$509,000
Accounts receivable (net)	625,100	693,200
Merchandise inventory	724,600	704,700
Prepaid expenses	32,000	30,500
Accounts payable (merchandise creditors)	432,700	452,500
Wages payable	40,600	35,000

Prepare the cash flows from operating activities section of the statement of cash flows, using the indirect method.

Exercise 13–8

Cash flows from operating activities—indirect method

Goal 2

STUDENT SOLUTIONS MANUAL

SPREADSHEET

Colgate Palmolive Company is a major consumer health care products company. The current assets and current liabilities from two recent balance sheet dates are reproduced below.

Colgate Palmolive Company
Current Assets and Current Liabilities
December 31, 2001 and 2000

	Dec. 31, 2001	Dec. 31, 2000
Current Assets		
Cash and cash equivalents	$ 172,700,000	$ 206,600,000
Receivables (less allowances of $45.6 and $39.8, respectively)	1,124,900,000	1,195,400,000
Inventories	677,000,000	686,600,000
Other current assets	228,800,000	258,600,000
Total current assets	$2,203,400,000	$2,347,200,000
Current Liabilities		
Notes and loans payable	$ 101,600,000	$ 121,100,000
Current portion of long-term debt	325,500,000	320,200,000
Accounts payable	678,100,000	738,900,000
Accrued income taxes	195,000,000	163,700,000
Other accruals	823,300,000	900,200,000
Total current liabilities	$2,123,500,000	$2,244,100,000

If we assume that there were no mergers, acquisitions, or divestitures that would impact consolidated current accounts during the year, determine the impact of changes in current accounts in reconciling net income to cash flows from operations.

Exercise 13–9

Determining cash payments to stockholders

Goal 2

The board of directors declared cash dividends totaling $280,000 during the current year. The comparative balance sheet indicates dividends payable of $60,000 at the beginning of the year and $70,000 at the end of the year. What was the amount of cash payments to stockholders during the year?

Exercise 13-10

Reporting changes in equipment on statement of cash flows

Goal 2

STUDENT SOLUTIONS MANUAL

An analysis of the general ledger accounts indicates that office equipment, which had cost $200,000 and on which accumulated depreciation totaled $95,000 on the date of sale, was sold for $125,000 during the year. Using this information, indicate the items to be reported on the statement of cash flows.

Exercise 13-11

Reporting changes in equipment on statement of cash flows

Goal 2

An analysis of the general ledger accounts indicates that delivery equipment, which had cost $50,000 and on which accumulated depreciation totaled $23,000 on the date of sale, was sold for $24,000 during the year. Using this information, indicate the items to be reported on the statement of cash flows.

Exercise 13-12

Reporting land transactions on statement of cash flows

Goal 2

STUDENT SOLUTIONS MANUAL

On the basis of the details of the following fixed asset account, indicate the items to be reported on the statement of cash flows:

LAND

Jan. 1	Balance	400,000	June 8	Sold for $105,000	80,000
Oct. 12	Purchased for cash	200,000			
		600,000			
Dec. 31	Balance	520,000			

Exercise 13-13

Reporting stockholders' equity items on statement of cash flows

Goal 2

On the basis of the following stockholders' equity accounts, indicate the items, exclusive of net income, to be reported on the statement of cash flows. There were no unpaid dividends at either the beginning or the end of the year.

COMMON STOCK

			Jan. 1	Balance	500,000
			Feb. 11	6,000 shares issued for cash	60,000
			June 30	2,750-share stock dividend	27,500
			Dec. 31	Balance	*587,500*

PAID-IN CAPITAL IN EXCESS OF PAR

			Jan. 1	Balance	90,000
			Feb. 11	6,000 shares issued for cash	240,000
			June 30	Stock dividend	137,500
			Dec. 31	Balance	*467,500*

RETAINED EARNINGS

June 30	Stock dividend	165,000	Jan. 1	Balance	475,000
Dec. 30	Cash dividend	180,000	Dec. 31	Net income	450,000
		345,000			925,000
			Dec. 31	Balance	580,000

Exercise 13–14

Reporting land acquisition for cash and mortgage note on statement of cash flows

Goal 2

STUDENT SOLUTIONS MANUAL

On the basis of the details of the following fixed asset account, indicate the items to be reported on the statement of cash flows:

LAND

Jan. 1	Balance	450,000	
Feb. 10	Purchased for cash	210,000	
Nov. 20	Purchased with long-term mortgage note	250,000	
Dec. 31	Balance	*910,000*	

Exercise 13–15

Determining net income from net cash flow from operating activities

Goal 2

SPREADSHEET

Tiger Golf Inc. reported a net cash flow from operating activities of $93,200 on its statement of cash flows for the year ended December 31, 2003. The following information was reported in the cash flows from operating activities section of the statement of cash flows, using the indirect method:

Decrease in income taxes payable	$ 1,600
Decrease in inventories	7,400
Depreciation	12,500
Gain on sale of investments	2,350
Increase in accounts payable	3,200
Increase in prepaid expenses	1,500
Increase in accounts receivable	4,850

Determine the net income reported by Tiger Golf Inc. for the year ended December 31, 2003.

Exercise 13–16

Cash flows from operating activities

Goal 2

Cash flows from operating activities, $9,191

STUDENT SOLUTIONS MANUAL

SPREADSHEET

Selected data derived from the income statement and balance sheet of Intel Corp. for a recent year are as follows:

Income Statement Data (dollars in millions)	
Net earnings	$6,068
Depreciation	2,807
Loss on sale of property, plant, and equipment	282
Other noncash expenses	242
Balance Sheet Data (dollars in millions)	
Increase in accounts receivable	$ 38
Decrease in inventories	167
Decrease in other operating assets	37
Decrease in accounts payable and accrued expenses	163
Decrease in income tax payable	211

Prepare the cash flows from operating activities section of the statement of cash flows (using the indirect method) for Intel Corp. for the year.

Exercise 13–17

Statement of cash flows

Goal 2

List the errors you find in the following statement of cash flows. The cash balance at the beginning of the year was $70,700. All other figures are correct, except the cash balance at the end of the year.

Cyber-Master Games Inc. Statement of Cash Flows For the Year Ended December 31, 2004			
Cash flows from operating activities:			
Net income, per income statement		$100,500	
Add: Depreciation	$ 49,000		
Increase in accounts receivable	11,500		
Gain on sale of investments	7,000	67,500	
		$168,000	
Deduct: Increase in accounts payable	$ 4,400		
Increase in inventories	18,300		
Decrease in accrued expenses	1,600	24,300	
Net cash flow from operating activities			$143,700
Cash flows from investing activities:			
Cash received from sale of investments		$ 85,000	
Less: Cash paid for purchase of land	$ 90,000		
Cash paid for purchase of equipment	150,100	240,100	
Net cash flow used for investing activities			(155,100)
Cash flows from financing activities:			
Cash received from sale of common stock		$107,000	
Cash paid for dividends		36,800	
Net cash flow provided by financing activities			143,800
Increase in cash			$132,400
Cash at the end of the year			105,300
Cash at the beginning of the year			$237,700

Exercise 13-18

Statement of cash flows

Goal 2

Net cash flow from operating activities, $22

STUDENT SOLUTIONS MANUAL

SPREADSHEET

The comparative balance sheet of Maria's Memories Inc. for December 31, 2004 and 2003, is as follows:

Maria's Memories Inc. Comparative Balance Sheet December 31, 2004 and 2003	Dec. 31, 2004	Dec. 31, 2003
Assets		
Cash	$ 54	$ 34
Accounts receivable (net)	23	27
Inventories	16	14
Land	20	30
Equipment	26	12
Accumulated depreciation—equipment	(8)	(5)
Total	$131	$112
Liabilities and Stockholders' Equity		
Accounts payable (merchandise creditors)	$ 17	$ 18
Dividends payable	8	6
Common stock, $1 par	3	2
Paid-in capital in excess of par—common stock	15	10
Retained earnings	88	76
Total	$131	$112

The following additional information is taken from the records:

a. Land was sold for $17.
b. Equipment was acquired for cash.
c. There were no disposals of equipment during the year.
d. The common stock was issued for cash.
e. There was a $25 credit to Retained Earnings for net income.
f. There was a $13 debit to Retained Earnings for cash dividends declared.

Prepare a statement of cash flows, using the indirect method of presenting cash flows from operating activities.

Exercise 13–19

Cash paid for merchandise purchases

Goal 3

The cost of merchandise sold for Toys"R"Us, Inc., for a recent year was $7,604 million. The balance sheet showed the following current account balances (in millions):

	Balance, End of Year	Balance, Beginning of Year
Merchandise inventories	$2,041	$2,307
Accounts payable	878	1,152

Determine the amount of cash payments for merchandise.

Exercise 13–20

Determining selected amounts for cash flows from operating activities–direct method

Goal 3

b. $87,500

STUDENT SOLUTIONS MANUAL

Selected data taken from the accounting records of Zippy Electronics Company for the current year ended December 31 are as follows:

	Balance, December 31	Balance, January 1
Accrued expenses (operating expenses)	$ 5,800	$ 6,200
Accounts payable (merchandise creditors)	35,700	39,100
Inventories	25,000	27,400
Prepaid expenses	3,000	3,500

During the current year, the cost of merchandise sold was $315,000 and the operating expenses other than depreciation were $87,600. The direct method is used for presenting the cash flows from operating activities on the statement of cash flows.

Determine the amount reported on the statement of cash flows for (a) cash payments for merchandise and (b) cash payments for operating expenses.

Exercise 13–21

Cash flows from operating activities–direct method

Goal 3

a. $723,000

The cash flows from operating activities are reported by the direct method on the statement of cash flows. Determine the following:

a. If sales for the current year were $685,000 and accounts receivable decreased by $38,000 during the year, what was the amount of cash received from customers?
b. If income tax expense for the current year was $72,000 and income tax payable decreased by $4,500 during the year, what was the amount of cash payments for income tax?

Exercise 13–22

Cash flows from operating activities–direct method

Goal 3

The income statement of Tender Memories Greeting Card Company for the current year ended June 30 is as follows:

Cash flows from operating activities, $51,800

STUDENT SOLUTIONS MANUAL

SPREADSHEET

Sales		$358,000
Cost of merchandise sold		163,400
Gross profit		$194,600
Operating expenses:		
Depreciation expense	$ 32,500	
Other operating expenses	142,600	
Total operating expenses		175,100
Income before income tax		$ 19,500
Income tax expense		7,300
Net income		$ 12,200

Changes in the balances of selected accounts from the beginning to the end of the current year are as follows:

	Increase Decrease*
Accounts receivable (net)	17,000*
Inventories	5,300
Prepaid expenses	3,100*
Accounts payable (merchandise creditors)	13,600*
Accrued expenses (operating expenses)	8,300
Income tax payable	2,400*

Prepare the cash flows from operating activities section of the statement of cash flows, using the direct method.

Exercise 13-23

Cash flows from operating activities—direct method

Goal 3

Cash flows from operating activities, $130,100

SPREADSHEET

The income statement for Wholly Donut Company for the current year ended June 30 and balances of selected accounts at the beginning and the end of the year are as follows:

Sales		$935,600
Cost of merchandise sold		534,200
Gross profit		$401,400
Operating expenses:		
Depreciation expense	$ 54,200	
Other operating expenses	195,700	
Total operating expenses		249,900
Income before income tax		$151,500
Income tax expense		65,300
Net income		$ 86,200

	End of Year	Beginning of Year
Accounts receivable (net)	$ 96,500	$ 93,000
Inventories	143,200	132,700
Prepaid expenses	7,500	8,900
Accounts payable (merchandise creditors)	102,300	98,400
Accrued expenses (operating expenses)	12,400	14,000
Income tax payable	2,000	2,000

Prepare the cash flows from operating activities section of the statement of cash flows, using the direct method.

Exercise 13-24

Calculate the cash conversion cycle

Goal 4

a. Wrigley: 105 days

STUDENT SOLUTIONS MANUAL

The December 31, 2001 end-of-year accounts receivable, inventory, and accounts payable information from a recent balance sheet for Wm. Wrigley Jr. Co. and Hershey Foods Corporation is provided below.

	Wm. Wrigley Jr. Dec. 31, 2001	Hershey Foods Dec. 31, 2001
Accounts receivable	$239,885,000	$361,726,000
Inventory	278,981,000	512,134,000
Accounts payable	91,225,000	133,049,000

In addition, the sales and cost of goods sold for the year ending December 31, 2001, for each company were reported as follows:

	Wm. Wrigley Jr. For the Year 2001	Hershey Foods For the Year 2001
Sales	$2,429,646,000	$4,557,241,000
Cost of goods sold	997,054,000	2,665,566,000

a. Calculate the cash conversion cycle for Wm. Wrigley and Hershey Foods. Round your calculations to the nearest whole day.

b. Interpret your results.

Exercise 13-25

Calculating the flow ratio

Goal 4

Saks, Inc., a major department store retailer, reported the following current asset and current liability information for two recent comparative year-ends:

a. 2002: 2.14

Saks, Inc.
Current Assets and Current Liabilities
February 2, 2002 and February 3, 2001

	Feb. 2, 2002 (in thousands)	Feb. 3, 2001 (in thousands)
Assets		
Current assets:		
Cash and cash equivalents	$ 99,102	$ 64,660
Receivables (net of allowances)	239,420	220,809
Inventories	1,295,878	1,522,203
Other current assets	135,529	108,566
Total current assets	$1,769,929	$1,916,238
Current liabilities:		
Current portion of long-term debt	$ 5,061	$ 5,650
Accounts payable	282,750	319,537
Accrued expenses	386,600	400,235
Other accruals	112,367	104,860
Total current liabilities	$ 786,778	$ 830,282

a. Determine the flow ratio for February 2, 2002, and February 3, 2001, using the information above. (Note: Exclude the current portion of long-term debt from the current liabilities.)
b. Given the change in the flow ratio between the two years, what general impact would this have on cash flow from operating activities as shown on the year ended February 2, 2002, statement of cash flows?

Exercise 13–26

Calculate free cash flow

Goal 4

STUDENT SOLUTIONS MANUAL

SPREADSHEET

The following information was available from selected financial statements of Island Retreat Hotels for a recent year.

Net income	$1,200,000
Depreciation expense	250,000
Cash flows provided from operating activities	1,500,000
Dividends paid	140,000
Cash used to purchase and improve fixed assets	900,000
Interest expense	35,000
Cash used to repay bank loans	400,000

Assume that the present capacity of the hotel chain can be maintained by investing an amount equal to 200% of the depreciation expense. Determine Island Retreat's free cash flow.

Exercise 13–27

Calculating the cash conversion cycle and flow ratio

Goal 4

The comparative current assets and current liabilities for Sun Microsystems, Inc., are shown on the next page.

a. Cash conversion cycle, 2001: 59 days

Sun Microsystems, Inc.
Consolidated Balance Sheet
June 30, 2001

	For Periods Ended	
	06/30/01	**06/30/00**
	(in millions)	
Current assets:		
Cash and cash equivalents	$1,472	$1,849
Short-term investments	387	626
Accounts receivable, net of allowances	2,955	2,690
Inventories	1,049	557
Other current assets	2,071	1,155
Total current assets	$7,934	$6,877
Current liabilities:		
Short-term borrowings	$ 3	$ 7
Accounts payable	1,050	924
Accrued payroll-related liabilities	488	751
Accrued liabilities and other	1,374	1,155
Deferred revenues and customer deposits	1,827	1,289
Estimated warranty reserve	314	211
Income taxes payable	90	209
Total current liabilities	$5,146	$4,546

The income statements indicated that the sales were $18,250 million and $15,721 million and the cost of goods sold were $10,041 million and $7,549 million for fiscal years 2001 and 2000, respectively.

a. Determine the cash conversion cycle and flow ratio for fiscal years ending 2001 and 2000.
b. Interpret the year-to-year change in your calculations.

Exercise 13-28

Calculate free cash flow

Goal 4

a. 2001: $690,800,000

STUDENT SOLUTIONS MANUAL

SPREADSHEET

An annotated statement of cash flows for Sara Lee Corporation is shown on the next page.

a. From Sara Lee's statement of cash flows, determine the free cash flow for the years ended June 30, 2001 and 2000. Assume that 60% of the acquisition of property and equipment is used to maintain productive capacity. The remaining 40% adds to productive capacity.
b. Determine the free cash flow as a percentage of sales. The sales were $17,747,000,000 and $17,511,000,000 for fiscal years ending 2001 and 2000, respectively.
c. Interpret your results.

Sara Lee Corporation
Statement of Cash Flows (Annotated)
For the Years Ended June 30, 2001 and 2000

	For the year ended, June 30, 2001	For the year ended, June 30, 2000
Operating Activities		
Net cash from operating activities	$ 1,496,000,000	$ 1,540,000,000
Investment Activities		
Purchases of property and equipment	$ (532,000,000)	$ (647,000,000)
Acquisitions of businesses and investments	(300,000,000)	(743,000,000)
Dispositions of businesses and investments	1,819,000,000	21,000,000
Sales of assets	65,000,000	64,000,000
Other	13,000,000	9,000,000
Net cash from (used in) investment activities	$ 1,065,000,000	$(1,296,000,000)
Financing Activities		
Issuances of common stock	$ 104,000,000	$ 84,000,000
Purchases of common stock	(643,000,000)	(1,032,000,000)
Issuance of equity securities by subsidiary	0	0
Borrowings of long-term debt	1,023,000,000	725,000,000
Repayments of long-term debt	(390,000,000)	(502,000,000)
Short-term (repayments) borrowings, net	(1,914,000,000)	1,022,000,000
Payments of dividends	(486,000,000)	(485,000,000)
Net cash used in financing activities	$(2,306,000,000)	$ (188,000,000)
Effect of changes in foreign exchange rates on cash	$(21,000,000)	$ (21,000,000)
Increase in cash and equivalents	$ 234,000,000	$ 35,000,000
Cash and equivalents at beginning of year	314,000,000	279,000,000
Cash and equivalents at end of year	$ 548,000,000	$ 314,000,000

Accounting Application Problems

Problem 13-1A

Statement of cash flows—indirect method

Goal 2

Net cash flow from operating activities, $139,800

SPREADSHEET

The comparative balance sheet of Everlast Flooring Co. for June 30, 2004 and 2003, is shown on the next page.

The following additional information was taken from the records of Everlast Flooring Co.:

a. Equipment and land were acquired for cash.
b. There were no disposals of equipment during the year.
c. The investments were sold for $50,000 cash.
d. The common stock was issued for cash.
e. There was a $126,000 credit to Retained Earnings for net income.
f. There was a $60,000 debit to Retained Earnings for cash dividends declared.

Instructions

Prepare a statement of cash flows, using the indirect method of presenting cash flows from operating activities.

	June 30, 2004	June 30, 2003
Assets		
Cash	$124,200	$ 67,900
Accounts receivable (net)	102,400	97,600
Inventories	142,700	123,500
Investments	0	58,000
Land	124,000	0
Equipment	373,400	201,400
Accumulated depreciation	(79,400)	(58,900)
	$787,300	$489,500
Liabilities and Stockholders' Equity		
Accounts payable (merchandise creditors)	$ 93,200	$ 84,600
Accrued expenses (operating expenses)	13,000	12,300
Dividends payable	15,000	12,500
Common stock, $10 par	120,000	80,000
Paid-in capital in excess of par–common stock	310,000	130,000
Retained earnings	236,100	170,100
	$787,300	$489,500

Problem 13-2A

Statement of cash flows–indirect method

Goal 2

Net cash flow from operating activities, $151,800

SPREADSHEET

The comparative balance sheet of Bon Voyage Luggage Company at December 31, 2004 and 2003, is as follows:

	Dec. 31, 2004	Dec. 31, 2003
Assets		
Cash	$ 155,400	$ 134,600
Accounts receivable (net)	192,400	176,400
Inventories	287,500	312,300
Prepaid expenses	8,500	6,000
Land	100,000	100,000
Buildings	550,000	415,000
Accumulated depreciation—buildings	(201,500)	(176,000)
Machinery and equipment	295,700	295,700
Accumulated depreciation—machinery & equipment	(119,800)	(84,600)
Patents	37,400	40,000
	$1,305,600	$1,219,400
Liabilities and Stockholders' Equity		
Accounts payable (merchandise creditors)	$ 131,400	$ 146,700
Dividends payable	12,000	10,000
Salaries payable	10,500	12,800
Mortgage note payable, due 2015	50,000	—
Bonds payable	—	164,000
Common stock, $1 par	19,000	15,000
Paid-in capital in excess of par—common stock	210,000	50,000
Retained earnings	872,700	820,900
	$1,305,600	$1,219,400

An examination of the income statement and the accounting records revealed the following additional information applicable to 2004:

a. Net income, $99,800.
b. Depreciation expense reported on the income statement: buildings, $25,500; machinery and equipment, $35,200.
c. Patent amortization reported on the income statement, $2,600.
d. A building was constructed for $135,000.
e. A mortgage note for $50,000 was issued for cash.
f. 4,000 shares of common stock were issued at $41 in exchange for the bonds payable.
g. Cash dividends declared, $48,000.

Instructions

Prepare a statement of cash flows, using the indirect method of presenting cash flows from operating activities.

Problem 13–3A

Statement of cash flows—indirect method

Goal 2

Net cash flow from operating activities, ($1,500)

SPREADSHEET

The comparative balance sheet of Union Wholesale Supply Co. at December 31, 2004 and 2003, is as follows:

	Dec. 31, 2004	Dec. 31, 2003
Assets		
Cash	$ 24,900	$ 27,400
Accounts receivable (net)	113,100	94,600
Inventories	194,000	176,500
Prepaid expenses	3,400	4,000
Land	60,000	80,000
Buildings	265,000	155,000
Accumulated depreciation—buildings	(55,800)	(43,500)
Equipment	195,600	185,600
Accumulated depreciation—equipment	(71,500)	(74,500)
	$728,700	$605,100
Liabilities and Stockholders' Equity		
Accounts payable (merchandise creditors)	$140,000	$143,700
Income tax payable	4,000	3,800
Bonds payable	50,000	—
Common stock, $1 par	26,000	25,000
Paid-in capital in excess of par—common stock	350,000	280,000
Retained earnings	158,700	152,600
	$728,700	$605,100

The noncurrent asset, the noncurrent liability, and the stockholders' equity accounts for 2004 are as follows:

LAND

Jan. 1	Balance	80,000	Apr. 20	Realized $34,000 cash from sale	20,000
Dec. 31	Balance	*60,000*			

BUILDINGS

Jan. 1	Balance	155,000			
Apr. 20	Acquired for cash	110,000			
Dec. 31	Balance	*265,000*			

ACCUMULATED DEPRECIATION—BUILDINGS

			Jan. 1	Balance	43,500
			Dec. 31	Depreciation for year	12,300
			Dec. 31	Balance	*55,800*

EQUIPMENT

Jan. 1	Balance	185,600	Jan. 26	Discarded, no salvage	30,000
Aug. 11	Purchased for cash	40,000			
		225,600			
Dec. 31	Balance	195,600			

ACCUMULATED DEPRECIATION—EQUIPMENT

Jan. 26	Equipment discarded	30,000	Jan. 1	Balance	74,500
			Dec. 31	Depreciation for year	27,000
					27,000
			Dec. 31	Balance	71,500

BONDS PAYABLE

			May 1	Issued 20-year bonds	50,000

COMMON STOCK, $1 PAR

			Jan. 1	Balance	25,000
			Dec. 7	1,000 shares issued for $71 per share	1,000
			Dec. 31	Balance	*26,000*

PAID-IN CAPITAL IN EXCESS OF PAR

			Jan. 1	Balance	280,000
			Dec. 7	1,000 shares issued for $71 per share	70,000
			Dec. 31	Balance	*350,000*

RETAINED EARNINGS

Dec. 31	Cash dividends	6,000	Jan. 1	Balance	152,600
			Dec. 31	Net income	12,100
					164,700
			Dec. 31	Balance	158,700

Instructions

Prepare a statement of cash flows, using the indirect method of presenting cash flows from operating activities.

Problem 13-4A

Statement of cash flows–direct method

Goal 3

Net cash flow from operating activities, $99,900

SPREADSHEET

The comparative balance sheet of Green Thumb Nursery Inc. for December 31, 2004 and 2003, is as follows:

	Dec. 31, 2004	Dec. 31, 2003
Assets		
Cash	$ 154,700	$ 176,500
Accounts receivable (net)	261,300	243,200
Inventories	317,800	303,300
Investments	—	65,000
Land	95,000	—
Equipment	365,000	275,000
Accumulated depreciation	(123,700)	(103,200)
	$1,070,100	$ 959,800
Liabilities and Stockholders' Equity		
Accounts payable (merchandise creditors)	$ 248,300	$ 235,700
Accrued expenses (operating expenses)	10,900	12,500
Dividends payable	24,000	20,000
Common stock, $1 par	15,000	12,000
Paid-in capital in excess of par—common stock	185,000	110,000
Retained earnings	586,900	569,600
	$1,070,100	$ 959,800

The income statement for the year ended December 31, 2004, is as follows:

Sales		$1,250,000
Cost of merchandise sold		759,000
Gross profit		$ 491,000
Operating expenses:		
Depreciation expense	$ 20,500	
Other operating expenses	284,500	
Total operating expenses		305,000
Operating income		$ 186,000
Other income:		
Gain on sale of investments		14,000
Income before income tax		$ 200,000
Income tax expense		85,000
Net income		$ 115,000

The following additional information was taken from the records:

a. Equipment and land were acquired for cash.
b. There were no disposals of equipment during the year.
c. The investments were sold for $79,000 cash.

(continued)

d. The common stock was issued for cash.
e. There was a $97,700 debit to Retained Earnings for cash dividends declared.

Instructions

Prepare a statement of cash flows, using the direct method of presenting cash flows from operating activities.

Problem 13-5A

Statement of cash flows—direct method applied to Problem 13-1A

Goal 3

Net cash flow from operating activities, $139,800

SPREADSHEET

The comparative balance sheet of Everlast Flooring Co. for June 30, 2004 and 2003, is as follows:

	June 30, 2004	June 30, 2003
Assets		
Cash	$124,200	$ 67,900
Accounts receivable (net)	102,400	97,600
Inventories	142,700	123,500
Investments	0	58,000
Land	124,000	0
Equipment	373,400	201,400
Accumulated depreciation	(79,400)	(58,900)
	$787,300	$489,500
Liabilities and Stockholders' Equity		
Accounts payable (merchandise creditors)	$ 93,200	$ 84,600
Accrued expenses (operating expenses)	13,000	12,300
Dividends payable	15,000	12,500
Common stock, $10 par	120,000	80,000
Paid-in capital in excess of par—common stock	310,000	130,000
Retained earnings	236,100	170,100
	$787,300	$489,500

The income statement for the year ended June 30, 2004, is as follows:

Sales		$543,800
Cost of merchandise sold		198,200
Gross profit		$345,600
Operating expenses:		
Depreciation expense	$ 20,500	
Other operating expenses	110,300	
Total operating expenses		130,800
Operating income		$214,800
Other expenses:		
Loss on sale of investments		8,000
Income before income tax		$206,800
Income tax expense		80,800
Net income		$126,000

The following additional information was taken from the records:

a. Equipment and land were acquired for cash.
b. There were no disposals of equipment during the year.
c. The investments were sold for $50,000 cash.
d. The common stock was issued for cash.
e. There was a $60,000 debit to Retained Earnings for cash dividends declared.

Instructions

Prepare a statement of cash flows, using the direct method of presenting cash flows from operating activities.

Alternate Accounting Application Problems

Alternate Problem 13–1B

Statement of cash flows—indirect method

Goal 2

Net cash flow from operating activities, $368,900

STUDENT SOLUTIONS MANUAL

SPREADSHEET

The comparative balance sheet of Idaho Al's Golf Shops Co. for December 31, 2004 and 2003, is as follows:

	Dec. 31, 2004	Dec. 31, 2003
Assets		
Cash	$ 524,300	$ 313,400
Accounts receivable (net)	132,500	126,700
Inventories	342,600	332,100
Investments	0	90,000
Land	125,000	0
Equipment	755,000	535,000
Accumulated depreciation—equipment	(189,000)	(158,000)
	$1,690,400	$1,239,200
Liabilities and Stockholders' Equity		
Accounts payable (merchandise creditors)	$ 85,200	$ 80,300
Accrued expenses (operating expenses)	4,300	7,400
Dividends payable	24,000	20,000
Common stock, $10 par	80,000	50,000
Paid-in capital in excess of par—common stock	335,000	200,000
Retained earnings	1,161,900	881,500
	$1,690,400	$1,239,200

The following additional information was taken from the records:

a. The investments were sold for $114,000 cash.
b. Equipment and land were acquired for cash.
c. There were no disposals of equipment during the year.
d. The common stock was issued for cash.
e. There was a $376,400 credit to Retained Earnings for net income.
f. There was a $96,000 debit to Retained Earnings for cash dividends declared.

Instructions

Prepare a statement of cash flows, using the indirect method of presenting cash flows from operating activities.

Alternate Problem 13–2B

Statement of cash flows—indirect method

Goal 2

Net cash flow from operating activities, $262,100

STUDENT SOLUTIONS MANUAL

SPREADSHEET

The comparative balance sheet of Gold Medal Athletic Apparel Co. at December 31, 2004 and 2003, is as follows:

	Dec. 31, 2004	Dec. 31, 2003
Assets		
Cash	$ 232,500	$ 257,900
Accounts receivable (net)	497,800	532,500
Merchandise inventory	635,200	621,300
Prepaid expenses	17,000	15,000
Equipment	720,000	600,000
Accumulated depreciation—equipment	(265,000)	(297,500)
	$1,837,500	$1,729,200
Liabilities and Stockholders' Equity		
Accounts payable (merchandise creditors)	$ 423,100	$ 397,600
Mortgage note payable	0	205,000
Common stock, $10 par	120,000	70,000
Paid-in capital in excess of par—common stock	820,000	620,000
Retained earnings	474,400	436,600
	$1,837,500	$1,729,200

Additional data obtained from the income statement and from an examination of the accounts in the ledger for 2004 are as follows:

a. Net income, $125,800.
b. Depreciation reported on the income statement, $92,000.
c. Equipment was purchased at a cost of $244,500, and fully depreciated equipment costing $124,500 was discarded, with no salvage realized.
d. The mortgage note payable was not due until 2006, but the terms permitted earlier payment without penalty.
e. 5,000 shares of common stock were issued at $50 for cash.
f. Cash dividends declared and paid, $88,000.

Instructions

Prepare a statement of cash flows, using the indirect method of presenting cash flows from operating activities.

Alternate Problem 13–3B

Statement of cash flows—indirect method

Goal 2

Net cash flow from operating activities, ($131,800)

The comparative balance sheet of Handyman's Helper Hardware Company at December 31, 2004 and 2003, is as follows:

STUDENT SOLUTIONS MANUAL

SPREADSHEET

	Dec. 31, 2004	Dec. 31, 2003
Assets		
Cash	$ 263,400	$ 275,400
Accounts receivable (net)	375,200	356,800
Inventories	543,200	512,400
Prepaid expenses	8,500	9,000
Land	95,000	120,000
Buildings	470,000	350,000
Accumulated depreciation—buildings	(182,300)	(170,000)
Equipment	198,700	185,500
Accumulated depreciation—equipment	(44,000)	(48,000)
	$1,727,700	$1,591,100
Liabilities and Stockholders' Equity		
Accounts payable (merchandise creditors)	$ 367,900	$ 377,100
Bonds payable	60,000	0
Common stock, $1 par	90,000	70,000
Paid-in capital in excess of par—common stock	450,000	250,000
Retained earnings	759,800	894,000
	$1,727,700	$1,591,100

The noncurrent asset, the noncurrent liability, and the stockholders' equity accounts for 2004 are as follows:

LAND

Jan. 1	Balance	120,000	Apr. 20	Realized $38,000 cash from sale	25,000
Dec. 31	Balance	*95,000*			

BUILDINGS

Jan. 1	Balance	350,000			
Apr. 20	Acquired for cash	120,000			
Dec. 31	Balance	*470,000*			

ACCUMULATED DEPRECIATION—BUILDINGS

			Jan. 1	Balance	170,000
			Dec. 31	Depreciation for year	12,300
			Dec. 31	Balance	*182,300*

EQUIPMENT

Jan. 1	Balance	185,500	Jan. 26	Discarded, no salvage	45,000
Aug. 11	Purchased for cash	58,200			
		243,700			
Dec. 31	Balance	198,700			

ACCUMULATED DEPRECIATION—EQUIPMENT

Jan. 26	Equipment discarded	45,000	Jan. 1	Balance	48,000
			Dec. 31	Depreciation for year	41,000
					89,000
			Dec. 31	Balance	44,000

BONDS PAYABLE

			May 1	Issued 20-year bonds	60,000

COMMON STOCK, $1 PAR

			Jan. 1	Balance	70,000
			Dec. 7	20,000 shares issued for $11 per share	20,000
			Dec. 31	Balance	*90,000*

PAID-IN CAPITAL IN EXCESS OF PAR

			Jan. 1	Balance	250,000
			Dec. 7	20,000 shares issued for $11 per share	200,000
			Dec. 31	Balance	*450,000*

RETAINED EARNINGS

Dec. 31	Cash dividends	20,000	Jan. 1	Balance	894,000
31	Net loss	114,200			
		134,200			
			Dec. 31	Balance	*759,800*

Instructions

Prepare a statement of cash flows, using the indirect method of presenting cash flows from operating activities.

Alternate Problem 13–4B

Statement of cash flows—direct method

Goal 3

Net cash flow from operating activities, $70,900

STUDENT SOLUTIONS MANUAL

SPREADSHEET

The comparative balance sheet of Nature's Bounty Markets, Inc., for December 31, 2004 and 2003, is as follows:

	Dec. 31, 2004	Dec. 31, 2003
Assets		
Cash	$ 65,800	$ 83,500
Accounts receivable (net)	101,200	95,800
Inventories	132,400	125,700
Investments	–	45,000
Land	70,500	–
Equipment	300,500	210,500
Accumulated depreciation	(65,900)	(45,600)
	$604,500	$514,900

(continued)

	Dec. 31, 2004	Dec. 31, 2003
Liabilities and Stockholders' Equity		
Accounts payable (merchandise creditors)	$ 93,500	$ 86,700
Accrued expenses (operating expenses)	10,200	12,000
Dividends payable	6,000	4,000
Common stock, $1 par	17,000	15,000
Paid-in capital in excess of par—common stock	200,000	150,000
Retained earnings	277,800	247,200
	$604,500	$514,900

The income statement for the year ended December 31, 2004, is as follows:

Sales		$545,000
Cost of merchandise sold		294,000
Gross profit		$251,000
Operating expenses:		
Depreciation expense	$ 20,300	
Other operating expenses	152,500	
Total operating expenses		172,800
Operating income		$ 78,200
Other expenses:		
Loss on sale of investments		4,000
Income before income tax		$ 74,200
Income tax expense		20,500
Net income		$ 53,700

The following additional information was taken from the records:

a. Equipment and land were acquired for cash.
b. There were no disposals of equipment during the year.
c. The investments were sold for $41,000 cash.
d. The common stock was issued for cash.
e. There was a $23,100 debit to Retained Earnings for cash dividends declared.

Instructions

Prepare a statement of cash flows, using the direct method of presenting cash flows from operating activities.

Alternate Problem 13-5B

Statement of cash flows—direct method applied to Alternate Problem 13-1B

Goal 3

The comparative balance sheet of Idaho Al's Golf Shops Co. for December 31, 2004 and 2003, is shown on the next page.

Net cash flow from operating activities, $368,900

STUDENT SOLUTIONS MANUAL

SPREADSHEET

	Dec. 31, 2004	Dec. 31, 2003
Assets		
Cash	$ 524,300	$ 313,400
Accounts receivable (net)	132,500	126,700
Inventories	342,600	332,100
Investments	0	90,000
Land	125,000	0
Equipment	755,000	535,000
Accumulated depreciation—equipment	(189,000)	(158,000)
	$1,690,400	$1,239,200
Liabilities and Stockholders' Equity		
Accounts payable (merchandise creditors)	$ 85,200	$ 80,300
Accrued expenses (operating expenses)	4,300	7,400
Dividends payable	24,000	20,000
Common stock, $10 par	80,000	50,000
Paid-in capital in excess of par—common stock	335,000	200,000
Retained earnings	1,161,900	881,500
	$1,690,400	$1,239,200

The income statement for the year ended December 31, 2004, is as follows:

Sales		$1,096,500
Cost of merchandise sold		401,200
Gross profit		$ 695,300
Operating expenses:		
Depreciation expense	$ 31,000	
Other operating expenses	163,400	
Total operating expenses		194,400
Operating income		$ 500,900
Other income:		
Gain on sale of investments		24,000
Income before income tax		$ 524,900
Income tax expense		148,500
Net income		$ 376,400

The following additional information was taken from the records:

a. The investments were sold for $114,000 cash.
b. Equipment and land were acquired for cash.
c. There were no disposals of equipment during the year.
d. The common stock was issued for cash.
e. There was a $96,000 debit to Retained Earnings for cash dividends declared.

Instructions

Prepare a statement of cash flows, using the direct method of presenting cash flows from operating activities.

Building Leadership Skills— Financial Analysis and Reporting

Case 13–1

Interpreting cash flows from operations

The operating activities section of the Statement of Cash Flows for Viacom, Inc., an entertainment company that owns CBS broadcasting, is shown as follows:

Viacom, Inc.
Statement of Cash Flows—Operating Activities
For the Year Ended Dec. 31, 2001

Operating Activities:	
Net earnings (loss)	$ (223,500,000)
Adjustments to reconcile net earnings (loss) to net cash flow from operating activities:	
Depreciation and amortization	3,087,000,000
Restructuring and merger-related charges	119,400,000
Inventory charges (write-downs)	392,100,000
(Gain) loss on transactions and other items, net	(284,600,000)
Equity in loss of affiliated companies, net of tax	127,000,000
Other adjustments	21,200,000
Change in operating assets and liabilities:	
Decrease (increase) in receivables	391,300,000
Decrease (increase) in inventory and related program liabilities	63,700,000
Decrease (increase) in other current assets	65,900,000
Increase in unbilled receivables	(107,500,000)
Decrease in accounts payable and accrued expenses	(519,200,000)
Increase (decrease) in income taxes payable and net deferred taxes	442,000,000
(Decrease) increase in deferred income	(67,200,000)
Other, net	1,500,000
Net cash flow provided by operating activities	$3,509,100,000

a. Why are restructuring and inventory charges added to the net loss in determining net cash flows provided by operating activities?
b. Why is the equity loss of affiliated companies added to the net loss in determining net cash flows provided by operating activities?
c. Viacom reported a gain on transactions of $284.6 million. Why is this amount subtracted from the net loss in determining net cash flows provided by operating activities?

Case 13–2

Interpreting the statement of cash flows

The statement of cash flows for Priceline.com, Inc., is shown on the next page.

Priceline.com, Inc.
Statement of Cash Flows
For the year ended December 31, 2001

OPERATING ACTIVITIES:	
Net loss	$ (7,303,000)
Adjustments to reconcile net loss to net cash (used in) provided by operating activities:	
Depreciation and amortization	16,578,000
Provision for uncollectible accounts	18,548,000
Net loss on disposal of fixed assets	17,000
Net loss on sale of equity investments	946,000
Equity in net income of pricelinemortgage	(551,000)
Noncash severance	3,076,000
Enhanced withholding on restricted shares	3,136,000
Compensation expense arising from deferred stock awards	13,395,000
Changes in assets and liabilities:	
Accounts receivable	(19,768,000)
Prepaid expenses and other current assets	699,000
Accounts payable and accrued expenses	(1,501,000)
Other	824,000
Net cash (used in) provided by operating activities	$ 28,096,000
INVESTING ACTIVITIES:	
Additions to property and equipment	$ (9,415,000)
Proceeds from sales of fixed assets	170,000
Proceeds from sales/maturities of investments	770,000
Funding of restricted cash and bank certificate of deposit	2,646,000
Investment in priceline.com europe Ltd.	(14,248,000)
Cash acquired from acquisition of priceline.com europe Ltd.	2,779,000
Investment in short-term investments/marketable securities	(38,878,000)
Net cash used in investing activities	$(56,176,000)
FINANCING ACTIVITIES:	
Shares reacquired for withholding taxes	$ (8,716,000)
Proceeds from sale of common stock, net	49,459,000
Proceeds from exercise of stock options and warrants	10,256,000
Net cash provided by financing activities	$ 50,999,000
Net increase (decrease) in cash and cash equivalents	$ 22,919,000
Cash and cash equivalents, beginning of period	77,024,000
Cash and cash equivalents, end of period	$ 99,943,000
Supplemental cash flow information:	
Acquisition of priceline.com europe Ltd.—net liabilities assumed	$ 7,896,000

a. What is the purpose of the supplemental schedule at the bottom of the statement of cash flows?

b. Interpret the provision for uncollectible accounts adjustment in the operating section of the statement of cash flows.

c. How does Priceline.com show a net loss of $7 million on the income statement, yet show positive cash flow from operating activities of over $28 million, a swing of $35 million dollars?

d. Evaluate Priceline's cash position. Specifically, do you believe it has sufficient cash to operate and grow the business?

Case 13-3

Analysis of statement of cash flows

Alan Hart is the president and majority shareholder of Elite Cabinets, Inc., a small retail store chain. Recently, Hart submitted a loan application for Elite Cabinets, Inc., to Montvale National Bank. It called for a $200,000, 11%, ten-year loan to help finance the construction of a building and the purchase of store equipment, costing a total of $250,000, to enable Elite Cabinets, Inc., to open a store in Montvale. Land for this purpose was acquired last year. The bank's loan officer requested a statement of cash flows in addition to the most recent income statement, balance sheet, and retained earnings statement that Hart had submitted with the loan application.

As a close family friend, Hart asked you to prepare a statement of cash flows. From the records provided, you prepared the following statement.

Elite Cabinets, Inc.
Statement of Cash Flows
For the Year Ended December 31, 2003

Cash flows from operating activities:			
Net income, per income statement		$ 86,400	
Add: Depreciation	$31,000		
Decrease in accounts receivable	11,500	42,500	
		$128,900	
Deduct: Increase in inventory	$12,000		
Increase in prepaid expenses	1,500		
Decrease in accounts payable	3,000		
Gain on sale of investments	7,500	24,000	
Net cash flow from operating activities			$104,900
Cash flows from investing activities:			
Cash received from investments sold		$ 42,500	
Less: Cash paid for purchase of store equipment		31,000	
Net cash flow from investing activities			11,500
Cash flows from financing activities:			
Cash paid for dividends		$ 40,000	
Net cash flow used for financing activities			(40,000)
Increase in cash			$ 76,400
Cash at the beginning of the year			27,500
Cash at the end of the year			$103,900
Schedule of Noncash Financing and Investing Activities:			
Issued common stock at par for land			$ 40,000

After reviewing the statement, Hart telephoned you and commented, "Are you sure this statement is right?" Hart then raised the following questions:

1. "How can depreciation be a cash flow?"
2. "Issuing common stock for the land is listed in a separate schedule. This transaction has nothing to do with cash! Shouldn't this transaction be eliminated from the statement?"
3. "How can the gain on sale of investments be a deduction from net income in determining the cash flow from operating activities?"
4. "Why does the bank need this statement anyway? They can compute the increase in cash from the balance sheets for the last two years."

After jotting down Hart's questions, you assured him that this statement was "right." However, to alleviate Hart's concern, you arranged a meeting for the following day.

a. How would you respond to each of Hart's questions?
b. Do you think that the statement of cash flows enhances the chances of Elite Cabinets, Inc., receiving the loan? Discuss.

Case 13–4

Analyzing noncash working capital efficiency

A schedule of current assets and current liabilities for Lexmark International Inc., a leading manufacturer of laser and ink-jet printers, for three comparative recent years is as follows:

Lexmark International Inc.
Schedule of Current Assets and Current Liabilities
December 31, 2001, 2000, and 1999 (in thousands)

	12/31/2001	13/31/2000	12/31/1999
Current assets:			
Cash and cash equivalents	$ 90,700	$ 68,500	$ 93,900
Accounts receivable	702,800	594,000	507,300
Inventories	455,100	412,300	387,700
Prepaid expenses and other current assets	244,500	168,900	99,800
Total current assets	$1,493,100	$1,243,700	$1,088,700
Current liabilities:			
Short-term debt	$ 11,000	—	$16,200
Accounts payable	384,700	$426,100	$300,900
Accrued liabilities	535,400	552,900	418,400
Total current liabilities	$ 931,800	$979,000	$735,500

In addition, sales and cost of goods sold information for the three fiscal years are as follows:

	For fiscal years ended		
	12/31/2001	12/31/00	12/31/99
Net sales	$4,142,800	$3,807,000	$3,452,300
Cost of goods sold	2,865,300	2,550,900	2,222,800

a. Determine the cash conversion cycles for the three balance sheet dates.
b. Determine the flow ratio for the three balance sheet dates.
c. Interpret your findings.

Case 13–5

Analyzing noncash working capital efficiency–Beer Industry

The current assets and current liabilities for Adolph Coors Co., Anheuser-Busch Co., and Boston Beer Company are shown below for a recent fiscal year-end.

	Adolph Coors Co.	Anheuser-Busch Co.	Boston Beer
Current Assets:			
Cash and short-term investments	$ 77,133,000	$ 162,600,000	$47,869,000
Temporary investments	232,572,000		
Accounts receivable (net)	108,732,000	620,900,000	19,219,000
Inventories	115,123,000	591,800,000	9,323,000
Other current assets	72,969,000	175,100,000	4,060,000
Total current assets	$606,529,000	$1,550,400,000	$80,471,000
Current Liabilities:			
Accounts payable	$222,493,000	$ 945,000,000	$11,201,000
Accrued expenses	210,052,000	787,300,000	13,196,000
Current portion of long-term debt	85,000,000		
Total current liabilities	$517,545,000	$1,732,300,000	$24,397,000

Sales and cost of goods sold information for the three companies are as follows:

	Adolph Coors Co.	Anheuser-Busch Co.	Boston Beer
Sales	$2,249,462,000	$12,911,500,000	$186,783,000
Cost of goods sold	1,537,623,000	7,950,400,000	81,693,000

a. Determine the cash conversion cycles for the three companies.
b. Determine the flow ratio for the three companies.
c. Interpret your findings.

Case 13–6

Free cash flow–general retail industry

The annotated statement of cash flows for Wal-Mart, Target, and Kmart for a recent fiscal year is shown on the next page (in millions). Assume that investments must be made in property, plant, and equipment equal to 150% of depreciation expense in order to maintain productive capacity.

a. Determine free cash flow for each company.
b. Determine the free cash flow as a percent of cash provided from operating activities.
c. Interpret your results.

	Wal-Mart	Target	Kmart
Cash flows from operating activities:			
Net income	$ 6,671	$ 1,374	$(2,587)
Adjustments to reconcile net income to net cash provided by operating activities:			
Depreciation and amortization	3,290	1,079	824
Restructuring, impairment, and other charges			1,078
Other noncash items affecting earnings		211	51
Increase in accounts receivable	(210)	(963)	
Increase in inventories	(1,235)	(201)	596
Other assets		(298)	222
Increase in accounts payable	368	584	996
Increase in accrued liabilities	1,125	29	
Deferred taxes	185	49	(55)
Other	66	128	(134)
Net cash provided by operating activities	$10,260	$ 1,992	$ 991
Cash flows from investing activities:			
Payments for property, plant, and equipment	$ (8,383)	$(3,163)	$(1,456)
Proceeds from sale of investments and fixed assets	1,134	32	
Other investing activities	103	(179)	(45)
Net cash used in investing activities	$ (7,146)	$(3,310)	$(1,501)
Cash flows from financing activities:			
Increase/(decrease) in notes and commercial paper	$ (1,533)	$ (808)	
Proceeds from issuance of long-term debt	4,591	3,250	$ 1,775
Purchase of Company stock	(1,214)	(20)	
Issue common stock			56
Dividends paid	(1,249)	(203)	(72)
Payment of long-term debt and other financing activities	(3,573)	(802)	(405)
Other		44	
Net cash provided by (used in) financing activities	$ (2,978)	$ 1,461	$ 1,354
Effect of exchange rate changes on cash	$ (29)		
Net increase/(decrease) in cash and cash equivalents	$ 107	$ 143	$ 844
Cash and cash equivalents at beginning of year	2,054	356	401
Cash and cash equivalents at end of year	$ 2,161	$ 499	$ 1,245

Building Leadership Skills—Responsible Leadership

Activity 13–1

Ethics and professional conduct in business

ETHICS

Toni Lance, president of Fine Fashions Inc., believes that reporting operating cash flow per share on the income statement would be a useful addition to the company's just completed financial statements. The following discussion took place between Toni Lance and Fine Fashions' controller, Tom Kee, in January, after the close of the fiscal year.

Toni: I have been reviewing our financial statements for the last year. I am disappointed that our net income per share has dropped by 10% from last year. This is not going to look good to our shareholders. Isn't there anything we can do about this?

Tom: What do you mean? The past is the past, and the numbers are in. There isn't much that can be done about it. Our financial statements were prepared according to generally accepted accounting principles, and I don't see much leeway for significant change at this point.

Toni: No, no. I'm not suggesting that we "cook the books." But look at the cash flow from operating activities on the statement of cash flows. The cash flow from operating activities has increased by 20%. This is very good news—and, I might add, useful information. The higher cash flow from operating activities will give our creditors comfort.

Tom: Well, the cash flow from operating activities is on the statement of cash flows, so I guess users will be able to see the improved cash flow figures there.

Toni: This is true, but somehow I feel that this information should be given a much higher profile. I don't like this information being "buried" in the statement of cash flows. You know as well as I do that many users will focus on the income statement. Therefore, I think we ought to include an operating cash flow per share number on the face of the income statement—someplace under the earnings per share number. In this way users will get the complete picture of our operating performance. Yes, our earnings per share dropped this year, but our cash flow from operating activities improved! And all the information is in one place where users can see and compare the figures. What do you think?

Tom: I've never really thought about it like that before. I guess we could put the operating cash flow per share on the income statement, under the earnings per share. Users would really benefit from this disclosure. Thanks for the idea—I'll start working on it.

Toni: Glad to be of service.

How would you interpret this situation? Is Tom behaving in an ethical and professional manner?

Activity 13–2

Using the statement of cash flows

You are considering an investment in a new start-up Internet company, VideoToGo.com Inc. A review of the company's financial statements reveals a negative retained earnings. In addition, it appears as though the company has been running a negative cash flow from operating activities since the company's inception.

How is the company staying in business under these circumstances? Could this be a good investment?

Activity 13–3

Profit vs. cash flows and management decision making

The Retailing Division of Biltmore Company provided information on its cash flow from operations as shown on the next page.

Net income	$ 450,000
Increase in accounts receivable	(340,000)
Increase in inventory	(300,000)
Decrease in accounts payable	(90,000)
Depreciation	100,000
Cash flow from operating activities	$(180,000)

The manager of the Retailing Division provided the accompanying memo with this report:

From: Senior Vice President, Retailing Division

I am pleased to report that we had earnings of $450,000 over the last period. This resulted in a return on invested capital of 10%, which is near our target for this division. I have been aggressive in building the revenue volume in the division. As a result, I am happy to report that we have increased the number of new credit card customers as a result of an aggressive marketing campaign. In addition, we have found some excellent merchandise opportunities. Some of our suppliers have made some of their apparel merchandise available at a deep discount. We have purchased as much of these goods as possible in order to improve profitability. I'm also happy to report that our vendor payment problems have improved. We are nearly caught up on our overdue payables balances.

Comment on the senior vice president's memo in light of the cash flow information.

Activity 13-4

Operating cash flow dialogue

Todd Manning is the president of Under Wraps, Inc., a chain of sandwich shops. Manning was meeting with his bank loan officer, Kim Wells. The following conversation took place:

Kim: Todd, I was looking at your income statement and you generated a loss during the last year. I'm really concerned about this.

Todd: I know, but you also need to look at the statement of cash flows. Our cash flow from operating activities was positive. Net income is just an accounting number. It's cash that's important. Wouldn't you agree?

Kim: Well, yes . . . cash is important. We want you to generate cash so you can pay back our loan. But your cash from operations, while positive, is not the end of the story.

Todd: What do you mean?

Kim: Well, don't you need cash for updating and replacing equipment in your shops? I don't think that's part of cash provided from operations.

Todd: I think that's why the accountant added back the depreciation. With the depreciation added back, we must be accounting for replacement of productive capacity somehow.

Is Kim's concern valid? Comment on Todd's analysis of Kim's concern.

Activity 13-5

Statement of cash flows

GROUP ACTIVITY

This activity will require two teams to retrieve cash flow statement information from the Internet. One team is to obtain the most recent year's statement of cash flows for Philip Morris Companies, and the other team the most recent year's statement of cash flows for Loral Space & Communications, LTD., a satellite-based mobile phone company.

The statement of cash flows is included as part of the annual report information that is a required disclosure to the Securities and Exchange Commission (SEC). The SEC, in turn, provides this information online through its EDGAR service. EDGAR (Electronic Data Gathering, Analysis, and Retrieval) is the electronic archive of financial statements filed with the Securities and Exchange Commission (SEC). SEC documents can be retrieved using the EdgarScan service from PricewaterhouseCoopers at edgarscan.pwcglobal.com.

To obtain annual report information, type in a company name in the appropriate space. EdgarScan will list the reports available to you for the company you've selected. Select the most recent annual report filing, identified as a 10-K or 10-K405. EdgarScan provides an outline of the report, including the separate financial statements. You can double-click the income statement and balance sheet for the selected company into an Excel™ spreadsheet for further analysis.

As a group, compare the two statements of cash flows. How are Philip Morris and Loral Space & Communications similar or different regarding cash flows?

Answers to Self-Study Questions

1. **A** Cash flows from investing activities include receipts from the sale of noncurrent assets, such as equipment (answer A), and payments to acquire noncurrent assets. Receipts of cash from the sale of stock (answer B) and payments of cash for dividends (answer C) and to acquire treasury stock (answer D) are cash flows from financing activities.
2. **C** Payment of cash dividends (answer C) is an example of a financing activity. The receipt of cash from customers on account (answer A) is an operating activity. The receipt of cash from the sale of equipment (answer B) is an investing activity. The payment of cash to acquire land (answer D) is an example of an investing activity.
3. **D** The indirect method (answer D) reports cash flows from operating activities by beginning with net income and adjusting it for revenues and expenses not involving the receipt or payment of cash.
4. **C** The cash flows from operating activities section of the statement of cash flows would report net cash flow from operating activities of $65,500, determined as follows:

Net income		$55,000
Add: Depreciation	$22,000	
Decrease in inventories	5,000	
Decrease in prepaid exp.	500	27,500
		$82,500
Deduct: Increase in accounts rec.	$10,000	
Decrease in accounts pay.	7,000	17,000
Net cash flow from oper. activities		$65,500

5. **C** The cash conversion cycle is calculated as the number of days' sales in accounts receivable, plus the number of days' sales in inventory, less the number of days' sales in accounts payable. Or, 30 days + 45 days − 25 days = 50 days (answer C).

Chapter 14
Financial Statement Analysis

THE LAW OF EXPLOSIVE GROWTH

"To add growth, lead followers–
To multiply, lead leaders."

–The 21 Irrefutable Laws of Leadership

Dr. John C. Maxwell

Learning Goals

1. Construct and interpret horizontal and vertical analyses.
2. Calculate and interpret the rate earned on stockholders' equity and the rate earned on total assets.
3. Analyze the rate earned on total assets by evaluating the profit margin and the asset efficiency of a business.
4. Determine and interpret leverage.
5. Calculate and interpret shareholder ratios: earnings per share, price-earnings ratio, and dividend yield.
6. Summarize the uses and limitations of analytical measures.
7. Describe the contents of corporate annual reports.

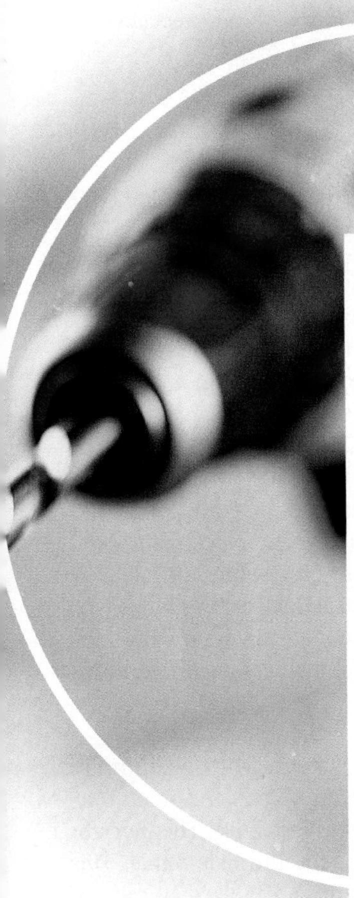

Home Depot

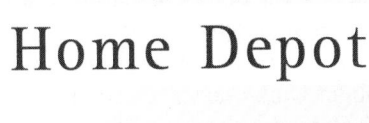

"You're fired!!" are the two words that marked the beginning of Home Depot in the spring of 1978. Bernie Marcus and Arthur Blank were fired from Handy Dan Stores. At the time, Bernie was the chief executive officer (CEO) and Arthur was the chief financial officer (CFO). Under their leadership, Handy Dan had grown to 66 stores with over $150 million in sales and had won the Home Center Retailer-of-the-Year award. Success, however, could not shield Bernie and Arthur from corporate politics.

Instead of feeling sorry for themselves, Bernie and Arthur viewed their firings as an opportunity to develop their own vision for a chain of home improvement stores. Their vision would challenge conventional wisdom and start a revolution in the home improvement industry.

Unfortunately, Bernie and Arthur had very little capital to start a new company. To raise financing, they courted potential investors, including H. Ross Perot, who at that time was relatively unknown. Bernie and Arthur agreed to give Perot 70 percent of the then unnamed company if he would invest $2 million in their vision. The negotiations broke down, however, when Perot would not let Bernie keep his four-year old Cadillac as a company car. Instead, Perot insisted that Bernie purchase a new, more expensive Chevrolet. Perot insisted that "My people don't drive Cadillacs."

By pleading with vendors, banks, and investors, Bernie and Arthur were able to scrape together enough money to open three stores in Atlanta. Preparing for the grand opening of their first store on Friday, June 22, 1979, Bernie placed an ad to be run on Thursday in the Atlanta Journal-Constitution. Unfortunately, the paper made a mistake and didn't run the ad. Thus, no customers showed up for the "grand" opening. To make up for the mistake, the newspaper gave Home Depot prime advertising for the next several weeks—advertising that otherwise it wouldn't have been able to afford.

Once in operation, Home Depot was slow to take off, but sales gradually increased in the early 1980s. Home Depot was continually short of cash and had to bargain with suppliers for increased credit limits. When a supplier asked for Home Depot's financial statements, Bernie and Arthur refused to disclose them, using the excuse that Home Depot was a private company. In truth, Bernie and Arthur were concerned that if suppliers examined their financial statements, they probably wouldn't extend credit to Home Depot.

Today, sales of Home Depot exceed $45 billion, and Bernie and Arthur are billionaires. Many of Home Depot's employees and managers have also become millionaires by participating in the company's stock ownership plan.

In this chapter, we focus on the important role that financial statements play in the analysis of a business's operations as well as how those operations are financed. The basic financial statements provide much of the information users need to make economic decisions about businesses.

Source: Bernie Marcus and Arthur Blank with Bob Andelman, "Built from Scratch," Times Business-Random House (New York: 1999).

Your Need to Know

Microsoft is a well-known, international company. However, U.S. Airways, Kmart, Worldcom, Polaroid, and Planet Hollywood were also well-known companies. These latter companies share the common characteristic of having declared bankruptcy!

Obviously, being well-known is not necessarily a good basis for investing. For example, Planet Hollywood sought bankruptcy protection, even though it was owned and promoted by such prominent Hollywood stars as Bruce Willis, Whoopi Goldberg, and Arnold Schwarzenegger. Knowledge that a company has a good product, by itself, may also be an inadequate basis for investing in the company. Even with a good product, a company may go bankrupt for a variety of reasons, such as inadequate financing.

How, then, does one decide on the companies in which to invest? Like any other significant purchase, you would need to do some research to guide your investment decision. Your research should be guided by your overall investment philosophy. If you were buying a car for performance, you would research performance characteristics; but if you were purchasing for economy, than you would research economy characteristics. You would research investment alternatives in the same way. The following four different investment philosophies match different investment preferences:

1. **Value Investing.** The value investor attempts to discover stocks with an intrinsic value that is greater than the stock price. Value investors often look for quiet, out-of-favor, "boring" companies that have excellent financial performance. The investor assumes that the stock price will eventually rise to match the intrinsic value. This method of investing was popularized by Benjamin Graham and is used by one of the most successful investors in the world, Warren Buffet. Naturally, the key to successful value investing is to accurately determine a stock's intrinsic value. This will often include analyzing company financial ratios, as discussed in this chapter, relative to target ratios and industry norms.
2. **Growth Investing.** The growth investor tries to identify companies that are growing sales and earnings through new products, markets, or opportunities. Growth companies are often young companies that are still unproven, but possess unique technologies or capabilities. Investors hope to "ride the wave" of growth by purchasing these companies before their potential becomes obvious. Growth investing carries the risk that the growth may not occur. When this happens, there is often severe price declines. Growth investors use many of the ratios discussed in this chapter to identify high-potential growth companies.
3. **Income Investing.** Income investors purchase common stocks for their dividend stream. High dividend paying companies are often in low growth and stable industries. The stock price of such companies is usually not very volatile. Thus, the majority of the investment return comes from dividends. Many of the ratios discussed in this chapter can help identify companies with financial strength and high dividends.
4. **Technical Investing.** Investors that use technical analysis do not concern themselves with the fundamental financial strength and performance of the business, but, instead, attempt to find clues of future performance from the past performance. Technical investors often use charts of the historical prices in order to discover recurring price patterns that will help them determine if the stock price is near a top (signal to sell) or near a bottom (signal to buy).

This chapter describes and illustrates common financial analyses used by managers, employees, customers, suppliers, and investors in decision making. We illustrate how to perform a complete analysis of these statements by integrating individual analytical measures. In addition, we discuss the contents of corporate annual reports.

Horizontal and Vertical Analysis

1 **Construct and interpret horizontal and vertical analyses.**

Basic financial statement analysis begins with evaluating the relative size of changes in account balances across time and the relative size of account balances within a statement. These are termed horizontal and vertical analyses.

Horizontal Analysis

The percentage analysis of increases and decreases in related items in comparative financial statements is called **horizontal analysis**. The amount of each item on the most recent statement is compared with the related item on one or more earlier statements. The amount of increase or decrease in the item is listed, along with the percent of increase or decrease. For example, cash of $150,000 on the current balance sheet may be compared with cash of $100,000 on the balance sheet of a year earlier. The current year's cash may be expressed as 1.5 or 150% of the earlier amount, or as an increase of 50% or $50,000.

When horizontal analysis compares two statements, the earlier statement is used as the base. Horizontal analysis may also compare three or more statements. In this case, the earliest date or period may be used as the base for comparing all later dates or periods. Alternatively, each statement may be compared to the immediately preceding statement. Exhibit 1 is a comparative balance sheet with horizontal analysis for two years for Home Depot Inc.

We cannot fully evaluate the significance of the various increases and decreases in the items shown in Exhibit 1 without additional information. Total assets on February 3, 2002, were $5.009 billion (23.4%) greater than at the beginning of the year. This increase is largely the result of an increase in cash of $2.31 billion (1,383%) and property, plant, and equipment of $2.307 billion (17.7%). In addition, liabilities increased significantly ($1.931 billion, or 30.3%), and stockholders' equity increased $3.078 billion (20.5%).

The changes in the current accounts in Exhibit 1 appear favorable. The increase in cash is explained on the statement of cash flows. Specifically, Home Depot more than doubled its cash flow from operations from the previous year to $5,963, explained largely by the increase in current liabilities. The accounts receivable grew 10.2%, while inventories grew only 2.6%. Given that sales increased 17.1% (from Exhibit 2), these lower percentage increases indicate favorable current asset management. The large increase in accounts payable of $1.46 billion (73.9%) may be due to delayed payment to suppliers.

Accounts Payable was $600,000 in the current year and $500,000 in the preceding year. What is the amount and the percentage of increase or decrease that would be shown in a balance sheet with horizontal analysis?

$100,000 or 20% ($100,000/$500,000) increase

Exhibit 2 (on page 669) shows the horizontal analysis for the income statement of Home Depot. The last line of the statement indicates that Home Depot has had a $463 million (17.9%) increase in net income. This is a strong improvement. The rest of the income statement indicates how Home Depot accomplished this. The net sales and cost of merchandise sold increased at nearly the same rate of approximately 17%. The selling and store operating costs increased slightly more than the sales growth rate (18.8%), while the general and administrative expenses grew less than the sales growth rate (12%). Thus, Home Depot's earnings improvement came from growing revenues while keeping costs near or below the sales growth rate.

Exhibit 3 (on page 669) illustrates the comparative retained earnings statement for Home Depot with horizontal analysis. It reveals that retained earnings increased 26.1% for the year (see also Exhibit 1). The increase is due to net income of $3,044 for the year, less dividends of $396.

Exhibit 1

Comparative Balance Sheet—Horizontal Analysis

HOME DEPOT INC.
Comparative Balance Sheets (In Millions)
February 3, 2002 and January 28, 2001

	Feb. 3, 2002	Jan. 28, 2001	Increase (Decrease) Amount	Increase (Decrease) Percent
Assets				
Current assets:				
Cash and cash equivalents	$ 2,477	$ 167	$2,310	1,383.2%
Temporary investments	69	10	59	590.0
Accounts receivable, net	920	835	85	10.2
Merchandise inventories	6,725	6,556	169	2.6
Other current assets	170	209	(39)	−18.7
Total current assets	$10,361	$ 7,777	$2,584	33.2
Property and equipment, net	15,375	13,068	2,307	17.7
Other assets	658	540	118	21.9
Total assets	$26,394	$21,385	$5,009	23.4
Liabilities				
Current liabilities:				
Accounts payable	$ 3,436	$ 1,976	$1,460	73.9%
Accrued salaries and related expenses	717	627	90	14.4
Sales taxes payable	348	298	50	16.8
Other accrued expenses	1,149	834	315	37.8
Unearned revenue	851	650	201	30.9
Total current liabilities	$ 6,501	$ 4,385	$2,116	48.3
Long-term debt, excluding current installments	$ 1,250	$ 1,545	$ (295)	−19.1
Other long-term liabilities	372	256	116	45.3
Deferred income taxes	189	195	(6)	−3.1
Total long-term liabilities	$ 1,811	$ 1,996	$ (185)	−9.3
Total liabilities	$ 8,312	$ 6,381	$1,931	30.3
Stockholders' Equity				
Common stock, par value $0.05	$ 117	$ 116	$ 1	0.9%
Paid-in capital	5,412	4,810	602	12.5
Retained earnings	12,799	10,151	2,648	26.1
Accumulated other comprehensive loss	(246)	(73)	(173)	237.0
Total stockholders' equity	$18,082	$15,004	$3,078	20.5
Total liabilities and stockholders' equity	$26,394	$21,385	$5,009	23.4

Exhibit 2

Comparative Income Statement–Horizontal Analysis

HOME DEPOT INC.
Income Statement (In Millions)
For Periods Ended February 3, 2002 and January 28, 2001

			Increase (Decrease)	
	2002	**2001**	**Amount**	**Percent**
Sales (net)	$53,553	$45,738	$7,815	17.1%
Cost of merchandise sold	37,406	32,057	5,349	16.7
Gross profit	$16,147	$13,681	$2,466	18.0
Selling and store operating expenses	10,280	8,655	1,625	18.8
General and administrative expenses	935	835	100	12.0
Total operating expenses	$11,215	$ 9,490	$1,725	18.2
Income from operations	$ 4,932	$ 4,191	$ 741	17.7
Other income and expenses:				
Interest and investment income	53	47	6	12.8
Interest expense	(28)	(21)	(7)	33.3
Income before income tax	$ 4,957	$ 4,217	$ 740	17.5
Income taxes	1,913	1,636	277	16.9
Net income	$ 3,044	$ 2,581	$ 463	17.9

Exhibit 3

Comparative Retained Earnings Statement–Horizontal Analysis

Home Depot Inc.
Comparative Retained Earnings Statement (In Millions)
For Periods Ended February 3, 2002 and January 28, 2001

			Increase (Decrease)	
	2002	**2001**	**Amount**	**Percent**
Retained earnings, beginning balance	$10,151	$ 7,941	$2,210	27.8%
Net income for the year	3,044	2,581	463	17.9
Total	$13,195	$10,522	$2,673	25.4
Dividends:				
On common stock	396	371	25	6.7
Retained earnings, ending balance	$12,799	$10,151	$2,648	26.1

Vertical Analysis

A percentage analysis may also be used to show the relationship of each component to the total within a single statement. This type of analysis is called **vertical analysis**. To illustrate, assume that cash of $50,000 and inventories of $250,000 are included in the total assets of $1,000,000 on a balance sheet. In relative terms, the cash balance is 5% of the total assets, and the inventories are 25% of the total assets.

Like horizontal analysis, the statements may be prepared in either detailed or condensed form. In the latter case, additional details of the changes in individual items may be presented in supporting schedules. In such schedules, the percentage analysis may be based on either the total of the schedule or the statement total. Although vertical analysis is limited to an individual statement, its significance may be improved by preparing comparative statements.

In vertical analysis of the balance sheet, each asset item is stated as a percent of the total assets. Each liability and stockholders' equity item is stated as a percent of the total liabilities and stockholders' equity. Exhibit 4 is a condensed comparative balance sheet with vertical analysis for Home Depot Inc. On January 28, 2001, current assets were 36.4% of total assets, and property, plant, and equipment was 61.1% of total assets. On February 3, 2002, the current assets increased to 39.3% of total assets, while property, plant, and equipment declined to 58.2% of total assets. The total liabilities as a percent of the total increased by 1.6 percentage points, while stockholders' equity as a percent of the total declined by the same amount over the two years.

At the end of the current year, Accounts Payable was $600,000 and total liabilities and stockholders' equity was $1,200,000. What percent would be shown for Accounts Payable in a balance sheet with vertical analysis?

50% ($600,000/$1,200,000)

Exhibit 4

Comparative Balance Sheet—Vertical Analysis

Home Depot Inc.
Comparative Balance Sheets (In Millions)
February 3, 2002 and January 28, 2001

	Feb. 3, 2002		Jan. 28, 2001	
	Amount	**Percent**	**Amount**	**Percent**
Assets				
Current assets	$10,361	39.3%	$ 7,777	36.4%
Property and equipment (net)	15,375	58.2	13,068	61.1
Other assets	658	2.5	540	2.5
Total assets	$26,394	100.0%	$21,385	100.0%
Liabilities				
Current liabilities	$ 6,501	24.6%	$ 4,385	20.5%
Long-term liabilities	1,811	6.9	1,996	9.3
Total liabilities	$ 8,312	31.5%	$ 6,381	29.8%
Stockholders' Equity				
Common stock and paid-in capital	$ 5,529	20.9%	$ 4,926	23.0%
Retained earnings & accum. comp. loss	12,553	47.6	10,078	47.1
Total stockholders' equity	$18,082	68.5%	$15,004	70.2%
Total liabilities and stockholders' equity	$26,394	100.0%	$21,385	100.0%

In a vertical analysis of the income statement, each item is stated as a percent of net sales. Exhibit 5 is a condensed comparative income statement with vertical analysis for Home Depot Inc. The vertical analysis indicates that the percentages of sales of each of the income statement items were very similar between the two years.

Exhibit 5

Comparative Income Statement—Vertical Analysis

Home Depot Inc.
Comparative Income Statements (In Millions)
For the Years Ended February 3, 2002 and January 28, 2001

	2002		2001	
	Amount	**Percent**	**Amount**	**Percent**
Sales (net)	$53,553	100.0%	$45,738	100.0%
Cost of merchandise sold	37,406	69.9	32,057	70.1
Gross profit	$16,147	30.1%	$13,681	29.9%
Selling expenses	$10,280	19.2%	$ 8,655	18.9%
Administrative expenses	935	1.7	835	1.8
Total operating expenses	$11,215	20.9%	$ 9,490	20.7%
Income from operations	$ 4,932	9.2%	$ 4,191	9.2%
Other income	53	0.1	47	0.1
Interest expense	(28)	(0.0)	(21)	(0.1)
Income before income tax	$ 4,957	9.3%	$ 4,217	9.2%
Income taxes	1,913	3.6	1,636	3.6
Net income	$ 3,044	5.7%	$ 2,581	5.6%

Strategy in Business

Cannibalization: Is It Desirable?

Since its beginning in the late 1970s, Home Depot has grown rapidly from one store to over 1,000 stores throughout the United States and Canada. But where should Home Depot build its stores? Does it make sense to build a new store near an existing store? Home Depot thinks so. This strategy of building a new store on the edge of the market area of an existing store may result in a negative impact on sales of the existing store. In other words, the new store "cannibalizes" the sales of the existing store. While Home Depot concedes that opening the new store may initially cannibalize sales of the existing store, management believes that such a strategy ultimately increases customer service levels and, in the long term, will increase overall sales and enhance market penetration. During a recent year, approximately 30 percent of Home Depot's existing stores were submitting to cannibalization by new store openings.

Source: Home Depot, Inc., Securities and Exchange Commission 10-K filing for the fiscal year ended January 28, 2001.

Common-Size Statements

Horizontal and vertical analyses with both dollar and percentage amounts are useful in assessing relationships and trends in financial conditions and operations of a business. Vertical analysis with both dollar and percentage amounts is also useful in comparing one company with another or with industry averages. Such comparisons are easier to make with the use of common-size statements. In a **common-size statement**, all items are expressed in percentages. An example of common-size income statements for Home Depot and Lowe's are shown later in this chapter.

Common-size statements are useful in comparing the current period with prior periods, individual businesses, or one business with industry percentages. Industry data are often available from trade associations and financial information services.

Other Analytical Measures

In addition to the preceding analyses, other relationships may be expressed in ratios and percentages. These relationships are described and illustrated in the following sections. Often, the items analyzed are taken from the financial statements, and thus the analysis is a type of vertical analysis. Comparing these items with items from earlier periods is a type of horizontal analysis.

Profitability Analysis

2 Calculate and interpret the rate earned on stockholders' equity and the rate earned on total assets.

The relative profitability of a firm can be analyzed by combining both profitability and balance sheet information into a single ratio. Two relative profitability ratios constructed in this way are the rate earned on stockholders' equity and the rate earned on total assets.

Rate Earned on Stockholders' Equity

The stockholder desires a return on his or her investment. One measure of this return is the rate earned on stockholders' equity. The **rate earned on stockholders' equity** is calculated as the net income divided by the average stockholders' equity. The average stockholders' equity is often calculated as the sum of the beginning and ending balance of the stockholders' equity, divided by two. Note that the average stockholders' equity is determined from the balance sheet and not by the market value of the common stock. To illustrate, the following information was provided in recent financial statements of Home

Ethics in Action

What Does It Take to Succeed in Life?

The answer to this question, according to Warren Buffett, the noted investment authority, is three magic ingredients: intelligence, energy, and integrity. According to Buffett, "If you lack the third ingredient, the other two will kill you." In other words, without integrity, your intelligence and energy may very well misguide you.

Source: Clifford, Eric, *University of Tennessee Torchbearer*, Summer 2002.

Depot and Lowe's Companies, Inc., a major competitor to Home Depot in the home improvement retail market:

	Home Depot (in millions) Year Ended Feb. 3, 2002	Lowe's (in millions) Year Ended Feb. 1, 2002
a. Net income	$ 3,044	$ 1,023
Stockholders' equity:		
Beginning of year	$15,004	$ 5,494
End of year	18,082	6,674
Total	$33,086	$12,168
b. Average (Total ÷ 2)	$16,543	$ 6,084
Rate earned on stockholders' equity (a. ÷ b.)	18.4%	16.8%

Home Depot earned an 18.4% return on stockholders' equity, while Lowe's is 1.6 percentage points less at 16.8%. Both companies are earning good returns for their shareholders.

Rate Earned on Total Assets

The **rate earned on total assets** is computed by dividing net income by the average total assets.[1] The rate earned on total assets measures the profitability of total assets, without considering how the assets are financed. That is, the rate is not affected by whether assets are financed primarily by creditors or stockholders.

The rate earned on total assets by Home Depot and Lowe's for a recent year is computed as follows:

	Home Depot (in millions) Year Ended Feb. 3, 2002	Lowe's (in millions) Year Ended Feb. 1, 2002
a. Net income	$ 3,044	$ 1,023
Total assets:		
Beginning of year	$21,385	$11,358
End of year	26,394	13,736
Total	$47,779	$25,094
b. Average (Total ÷ 2)	$23,890	$12,547
Rate earned on total assets (a. ÷ b.)	12.8%	8.1%

1 Alternatively, the numerator could be net income plus interest expense in order to remove the impact of the financing decision from the numerator. We select a simpler approach here to ease interpretation of the comprehensive analysis.

The rate earned on total assets of Home Depot was 12.8%, while Lowe's was 4.7 percentage points lower at 8.1%. Home Depot is performing better than Lowe's. A company's objective is to generate a return on total assets that exceeds the cost of capital. The **cost of capital** is the cost of financing its operations from both debt and common stock, expressed in percentage terms. For example, if a company borrows money at an 8% interest rate, the invested funds must generate a rate of return in excess of 8% to be successful.[2] However, a company will generally need to generate a rate earned on total assets in excess of 8–10% to exceed its cost of capital. The rate earned on total assets is widely acknowledged as a good summary measure of managerial performance, since it measures the return on total assets under management care and control, regardless of the method of financing those assets.

Sometimes it may be desirable to compute the *rate of income from operations to total assets.* This is especially true if significant amounts of nonoperating income and expense, such as interest income and expense, are reported on the income statement. In this case, any assets related to the nonoperating income and expense items should be excluded from total assets in computing the rate. In addition, using income from operations (which is before tax) has the advantage of eliminating the effects of any changes in the tax structure on the rate of earnings. When evaluating published data on rates earned on assets, you should be careful to determine the exact nature of the measure that is reported.

Comprehensive Profitability Analysis

Exhibit 6 diagrams the comprehensive ratio relationships that can be used to analyze the rate earned on stockholders' equity. The rate earned on stockholders' equity is the product of the rate earned on total assets and the amount of debt, or leverage, held by the firm. The rate earned on stockholders' equity is normally higher than the rate earned on total assets when a company uses debt, or **leverage**, in its capital structure.

The relationship between the rate earned on stockholders' equity and the rate earned on total assets can be computed using the following **leverage formula**:

$$\text{Rate earned on stockholders' equity} = \text{Rate earned on total assets} \times \text{Leverage}$$

$$\frac{\text{Net Income}}{\text{Average Stockholders' Equity}} = \frac{\text{Net Income}}{\text{Average Total Assets}} \times \frac{\text{Average Total Assets}}{\text{Average Stockholders' Equity}}$$

Home Depot's leverage is 1.44 ($23,890 ÷ $16,543). Thus, the rate earned on stockholders' equity for Home Depot is 18.4% (12.8% × 1.44). The leverage term (average assets divided by average stockholders' equity) measures the number of asset dollars supported by each dollar of stockholders' equity. The larger the value of this measure, the greater the leverage. For example, if a firm had no debt, than this ratio would be 1.0, thus causing the rate earned on stockholders' equity to equal the rate earned on total assets. If the firm had average debt equal to 50% of average total assets, then this leverage ratio would be 2.0. We will discuss leverage in greater detail in a later section of this chapter.

2 The cost of capital calculation is illustrated in finance textbooks.

Exhibit 6

Comprehensive Ratio Analysis

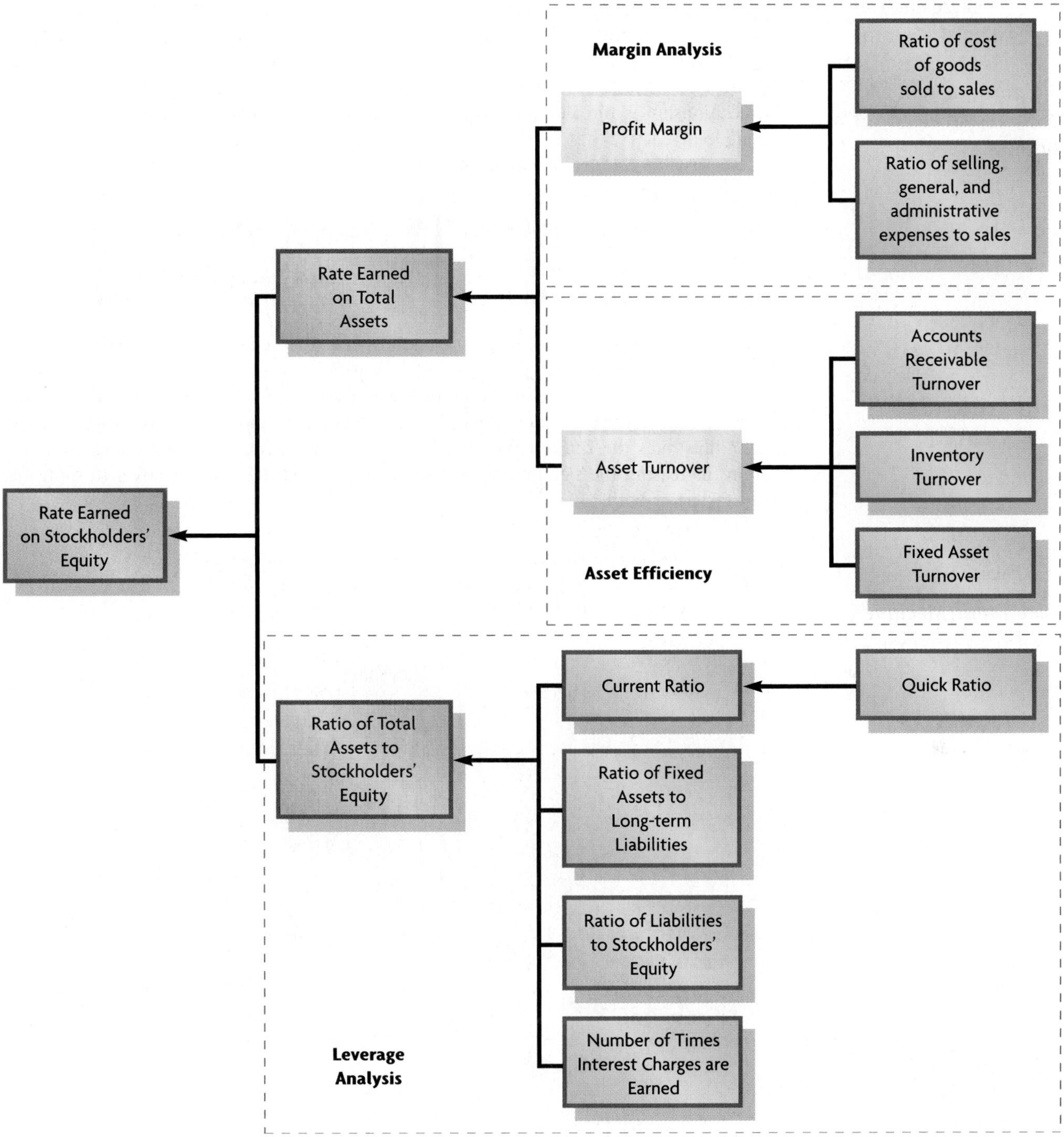

Margin Analysis and Asset Efficiency Analysis

3 Analyze the rate earned on total assets by evaluating the profit margin and the asset efficiency of a business.

In the previous section, we noted that Home Depot is earning 12.8% on its assets, while Lowe's is only earning 8.1% on its assets. In this section, we will more precisely explain this difference. The rate earned on total assets is the product of a firm's profit margin and the efficiency by which it uses its assets, as shown in Exhibit 6. One way to summarize this relationship is the DuPont formula. The **DuPont formula**, created by a financial executive of E.I. DuPont De Nemours & Co. in 1919, states that the rate earned on total assets is the product of two factors, the profit margin and the total asset turnover, shown as follows:

$$\text{Rate earned on total assets} = \text{Profit Margin} \times \text{Asset Turnover}$$

$$\frac{\text{Net Income}}{\text{Average Total Assets}} = \frac{\text{Net Income}}{\text{Net Sales}} \times \frac{\text{Net Sales}}{\text{Average Total Assets}}$$

The first factor is the ratio of net income to sales, often called the net **profit margin**. The profit margin shows the profit earned as a percent of sales. The second factor is the ratio of sales to total assets, or the **asset turnover**. The asset turnover is the number of sales dollars earned for each dollar of total assets. The "profit machine" shown in Exhibit 7 illustrates the DuPont formula. Profits are earned by either increasing the profit margin (increasing the size of the opening) or increasing the asset turnover (turning the crank faster) or both.

Exhibit 7

The "Profit Machine"

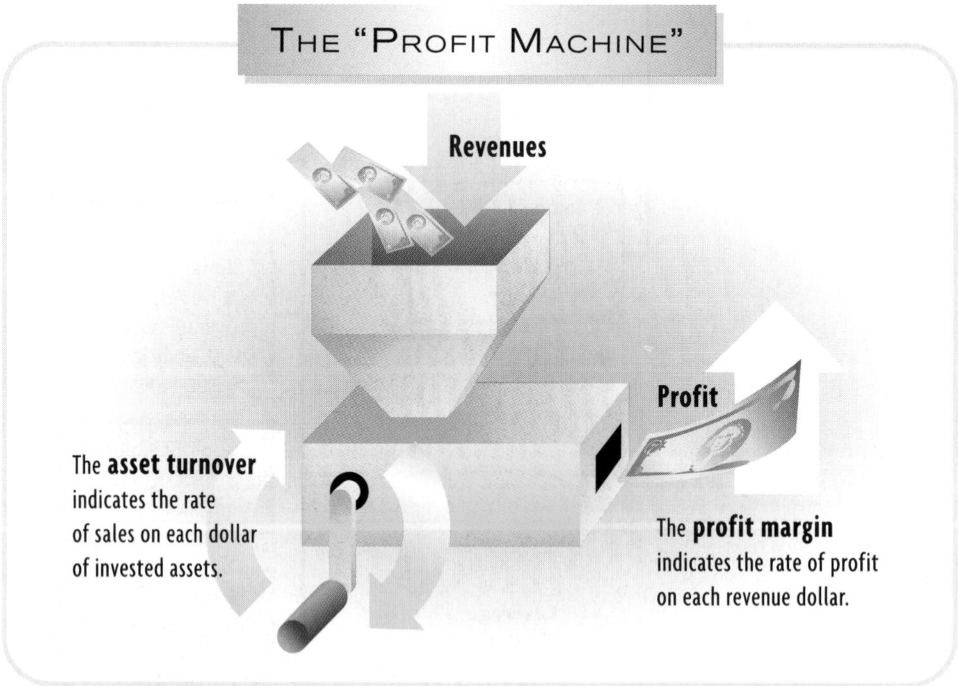
THE "PROFIT MACHINE"
Revenues
Profit
The asset turnover indicates the rate of sales on each dollar of invested assets.
The profit margin indicates the rate of profit on each revenue dollar.

The DuPont formula for Home Depot and Lowe's is as follows:

	Rate Earned on Total Assets	=	Profit Margin	×	Asset Turnover
Home Depot	12.8%	=	5.7%[1]	×	2.24[2]
Lowe's	8.1%	=	4.6%[3]	×	1.76[4]

[1]$3,044/$53,553 [2]$53,553/$23,890

[3]$1,023/$22,111 [4]$22,111/$12,547

We now have more insight into the difference between Home Depot and Lowe's. Home Depot's profit margin is over one percentage point better than Lowe's. While one percentage point may seem small, it can be significant in terms of dollars of potential profit. For example, if Lowe's could match Home Depot's rate of net income to sales, it would represent over \$220 million (\$22,111 million × 1%) of potential profit to Lowe's. In addition, Home Depot is more efficient in using its assets. Home Depot earns \$2.24 in net sales for each dollar of total assets, while Lowe's earns \$1.76 in net sales for each dollar of total assets. Again, this is a significant difference in asset efficiency. If Lowe's could match Home Depot's asset efficiency, it would be able to increase its rate earned on total assets to 10.3% (4.6% × 2.24), or recapture nearly half the difference. Thus, Home Depot is stronger than Lowe's on both dimensions.

Each of the two factors that determine the rate earned on total assets can be subjected to a more detailed analysis. The profit margin can be analyzed in more detail, using common-size information, while the total asset turnover can be segmented into a more detailed asset efficiency analysis.

Margin Analysis

Why is the profit margin of Home Depot over one percentage point stronger than Lowe's? This question can be addressed by analyzing the percentage of major expenses to net sales and comparing the percentages for the two companies.

Exhibit 8 is a comparative common-size income statement for Home Depot and Lowe's, wherein the major income statement items are translated into a percent of net sales. Exhibit 8 indicates that Home Depot has a higher rate of gross profit (or lower cost of merchandise sold) than Lowe's. The difference is more than one percentage point in favor of Home Depot. Home Depot's selling expenses are nearly a point higher than Lowe's, but its administrative expenses are lower, thus nearly equaling when summed. Lowe's has more interest expense as a percent of sales than does Home Depot, but its taxes are less as a percent of sales by nearly the same amount. Lowe's should focus on its cost of goods sold and its administrative expenses. That is, Lowe's management should review purchasing policies and attempt to get better pricing on merchandise, and it should review the efficiency of the administrative operations. Matching Home Depot in these two areas could improve Lowe's total profit margin relative to Home Depot's.

Exhibit 8

Common-Size Income Statement

Home Depot and Lowe's
Condensed Common-Size Income Statements
For the Year Ended February 3 and February 1, 2002

	Home Depot	Lowe's
Sales (net)	100.0%	100.0%
Cost of merchandise sold	69.9	71.2
Gross profit	30.1%	28.8%
Selling expenses	19.2%	18.3%
Administrative expenses	1.7	2.4
Total operating expenses	20.9%	20.7%
Income from operations	9.2%	8.1%
Other income	0.1	0.0
Interest expense	(0.0)	(0.8)
Income before income tax	9.3%	7.3%
Income tax expense	3.6	2.7
Net income	5.7%	4.6%

Asset Efficiency

We determined from the DuPont analysis that Home Depot's total asset turnover was 2.24, while Lowe's was only 1.76. What causes this difference? We can segment the total asset turnover into its component parts to address this question. The major components of total assets for a retailer are accounts receivable, inventory, and fixed assets (property and equipment). Thus, the total asset turnover can be evaluated in terms of these three subcategories of assets.

Accounts Receivable Analysis

The size and makeup of accounts receivable change constantly during business operations. Sales on account increase accounts receivable, whereas collections from customers decrease accounts receivable. Firms that grant long credit terms usually have larger accounts receivable balances than those granting short credit terms. Increases or decreases in the volume of sales also affect the balance of accounts receivable.

Collecting receivables as promptly as possible is desirable. The cash collected from receivables improves liquidity. In addition, the cash generated by prompt collections from customers may be used in operations for such purposes as purchasing merchandise in large quantities at lower prices. The cash may also be used for payment of dividends to stockholders or for other investing or financing purposes. Prompt collection also lessens the risk of loss from uncollectible accounts.

Accounts Receivable Turnover The relationship between credit sales and accounts receivable may be stated as the **accounts receivable turnover**. This ratio is computed by dividing net sales by the average net accounts receivable.[3] Basing the average on monthly balances, which allows for seasonal changes in sales, is desirable. When such data are not available, it may be necessary to use the average of the accounts receivable balance at the beginning and the end of the year. If there are trade notes receivable as well as accounts, the two may be combined. The accounts receivable turnover data for Home Depot and Lowe's are as follows:

	Home Depot (in millions)	Lowe's (in millions)
a. Net sales	$53,553	$22,111
Accounts receivable (net):		
Beginning of year	$ 835	$ 161
End of year	920	166
Total	$ 1,755	$ 327
b. Average (Total ÷ 2)	$ 878	$ 164
Accounts receivable turnover (a. ÷ b.)	61.0	134.8

Lowe's accounts receivable turnover is nearly twice that of Home Depot's. Thus, Lowe's appears to be more efficient than Home Depot in managing its accounts receivable.

3 Alternatively, the net sales *on account* can be used for the calculation. However, this number may not be publicly available; thus, net sales must be used. When so doing, the analyst must be aware that cash sales could impact the interpretation of the analysis.

Number of Days' Sales in Receivables Another measure of the relationship between net sales and accounts receivable is the **number of days' sales in receivables.** This ratio is computed by dividing the net accounts receivable at the end of the year by the average daily sales. Average daily sales is determined by dividing net sales by 365 days. The number of days' sales in receivables is computed for Home Depot and Lowe's as follows:

	Home Depot (in millions)	Lowe's (in millions)
a. Accounts receivable (net), end of year	$920	$166
Net sales	$53,553	$22,111
b. Average daily sales on account (net sales ÷ 365)	$147	$61
Number of days' sales in receivables (a. ÷ b.)	6.3	2.7

The number of days' sales in receivables is an estimate of the length of time (in days) the accounts receivable have been outstanding. As can be seen, the number of days' sales outstanding in accounts receivable is very low for both companies. Why is this? Undoubtedly, both Home Depot and Lowe's have significant "cash and carry" sales paid by credit cards (MasterCard and Visa) and checks. Thus, these sales would have no days outstanding in accounts receivable. The remaining sales would represent sales to contractors on account. These sales are apparently a small portion of either company's sales, thus creating very little accounts receivable as a percent of sales. Home Depot's slower turnover (or longer days' sales in accounts receivable) can be best interpreted as Home Depot having a larger percent of sales to contractors on account.

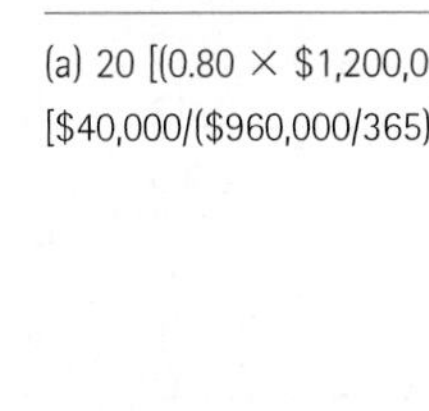

Sales are $960,000. The accounts receivable balance at the beginning of the year was $56,000, and at the end of the year it was $40,000. What are (a) the accounts receivable turnover and (b) the number of days' sales in receivables? [Hint: Use sales on account.]

(a) 20 [(0.80 × $1,200,000)/($56,000 + $40,000)/2]; (b) 15.2 days [$40,000/($960,000/365)]

Inventory Analysis

A business should keep enough inventory on hand to meet the needs of its customers and its operations. At the same time, however, an excessive amount of inventory reduces liquidity by tying up funds. Excess inventories also increase insurance expense, property taxes, storage costs, and other related expenses. These expenses further reduce funds that could be used elsewhere to improve operations. Finally, excess inventory also increases the risk of losses because of price declines or obsolescence of the inventory. Two measures that are useful for evaluating inventory efficiency are the inventory turnover and the number of days' sales in inventory.

Inventory Turnover The relationship between the volume of goods (merchandise) sold and inventory may be stated as the **inventory turnover**. It is computed by dividing the cost of goods sold by the average inventory. If monthly data are not available, the average of the inventory at the beginning and the end of the year may be used. The inventory turnover for Home Depot and Lowe's is computed as follows:

	Home Depot (in millions)	Lowe's (in millions)
a. Cost of merchandise sold	$37,406	$15,743
Inventories:		
Beginning of year	$ 6,556	$ 3,285
End of year	6,725	3,611
Total	$13,281	$ 6,896
b. Average (Total ÷ 2)	$ 6,641	$ 3,448
Inventory turnover (a. ÷ b.)	5.6	4.6

The inventory is the second largest asset category for each company, representing approximately 25% of total assets. Thus, inventory efficiency will be an important component of total asset efficiency. Home Depot's inventory turnover is one full turn faster than Lowe's. That is, Home Depot is over 20% [(5.6 − 4.6)/4.6] more efficient in moving inventory than is Lowe's. This is a significant difference.

Differences across inventories, companies, and industries are too great to allow a general statement on what is a good inventory turnover. For example, a firm selling food should have a higher turnover than a firm selling furniture or jewelry. Likewise, the perishable foods department of a supermarket should have a higher turnover than the soaps and cleansers department. However, for each business or each department within a business, there is a reasonable turnover rate. A turnover lower than this rate could mean that inventory is not being managed properly.

Number of Days' Sales in Inventory Another measure of the relationship between the cost of goods sold and inventory is the **number of days' sales in inventory**. This measure is computed by dividing the inventory at the end of the year by the average daily cost of goods sold (cost of goods sold divided by 365). The number of days' sales in inventory for Home Depot and Lowe's is computed as follows:

	Home Depot (in millions)	Lowe's (in millions)
a. Inventories, end of year	$6,725	$3,611
Cost of merchandise sold	$37,406	$15,743
b. Average daily cost of goods sold (COGS ÷ 365 days)	$102	$43
Number of days' sales in inventory (a. ÷ b.)	65.9	84.0

The number of days' sales in inventory is a rough measure of the length of time it takes to acquire, sell, and replace the inventory. This cycle is approximately 66 days for Home

Depot, while Lowe's is somewhat longer at 84 days. While there are a number of possible explanations for this difference, it does suggest that Lowe's has more "slower moving" merchandise items than does Home Depot. Thus, Lowe's management may wish to analyze the inventory turnover by each product class and replace the slower moving products with more popular items.

Fixed Asset Analysis

The fixed assets consist mostly of the property, plant, and equipment of a firm. These are usually the largest asset classification for most firms, especially manufacturing firms. Thus, the efficient deployment of fixed assets will significantly impact the overall asset efficiency of most firms. Businesses invest in fixed assets in order to create capacity to meet demand. If the capacity is not well-matched to the demand, either in terms of product volume or mix, then the fixed asset turnover can suffer adversely.

Fixed Asset Turnover A common financial measure of fixed asset efficiency is the fixed asset turnover. As in the other turnover measures, the **fixed asset turnover** measures the number of dollars of sales that are generated from each dollar of average fixed assets during the year. It is computed by dividing the net sales by the average fixed assets. If monthly data are not available, the average of the net fixed assets at the beginning and the end of the year may be used. The fixed asset turnover for Home Depot and Lowe's is computed as follows:

	Home Depot (in millions)	Lowe's (in millions)
a. Net sales	$53,553	$22,111
Fixed assets (net):		
Beginning of year	$13,068	$ 7,035
End of year	15,375	8,653
Total	$28,443	$15,688
b. Average (Total ÷ 2)	$14,222	$ 7,844
Fixed asset turnover (a. ÷ b.)	3.77	2.82

For Home Depot and Lowe's, the fixed asset turnover measures how many dollars of sales are being made from investments in stores and fixtures. Home Depot is able to generate $3.77 of revenue for each dollar invested in stores and fixtures, while Lowe's is only able to generate $2.82 per dollar invested in its stores. Again, this suggests that Lowe's merchandise may need to be re-evaluated in order to match Home Depot's sales rates.

Asset Efficiency Summary

The asset efficiency of the three major asset categories can now be compared for the two companies, as follows:

	Home Depot	Lowe's
Total asset turnover	2.24	1.76
Accounts receivable turnover	61.00	134.80
Inventory turnover	5.60	4.60
Fixed asset turnover	3.77	2.82

Lowe's total asset turnover is weaker than Home Depot's because both its inventory and fixed asset turnover are weaker. Lowe's stronger accounts receivable turnover is not sufficient to overcome these other two asset categories. That is, accounts receivable is a small asset category compared to inventory and fixed assets. As stated, Lowe's should work toward increasing sales. This can be done through a number of short- and long-term strategies, including adding advertising, changing product mix, or changing store locations.

Leverage Analysis

4 Determine and interpret leverage.

As we explained in a previous section, the excess of the rate earned by stockholders' equity over the rate earned on total assets is caused by leverage. Leverage measures the amount of debt used by a firm to finance its assets. Home Depot's rate earned on stockholders' equity of 18.4% is 5.6 percentage points greater than its rate of 12.8% earned on total assets, while Lowe's 16.8% rate earned on stockholders' equity is 8.7 percentage points higher than its rate of 8.1% earned on total assets.

Positive leverage will normally cause the rate earned on stockholders' equity to exceed the rate earned on total assets. It occurs when the rate earned on total assets is positive. *Negative* leverage will normally cause the rate earned on stockholders' equity to be less than the rate earned on total assets. It occurs when the rate earned on total assets is negative. Firms that have significant debt and have negative leverage are candidates for bankruptcy. Highly leveraged telecommunications companies, such as XO Communications and Global Crossing, faced this problem in the early 2000s.

The rate earned on stockholders' equity can be compared to the rate earned on total assets by using the leverage formula, shown previously, where leverage is measured as the average total assets divided by the average stockholders' equity:

Rate earned on stockholders' equity = Rate earned on total assets × Leverage

Both Home Depot and Lowe's have debt, but both have positive leverage. The impact of leverage for these two companies can be shown at the top of the following page. Lowe's rate earned on total assets was 4.7 percentage points (12.8 − 8.1) less than Home Depot's, indicating significantly weaker performance in margin and asset efficiency (as discussed in the previous section). However, Lowe's rate earned on stockholders' equity, which is the ultimate concern of stockholders, is only 1.6 percentage points less than Home Depot's. Lowe's supports more assets by each dollar of stockholders' equity than does Home Depot. As such, Lowe's generates more leverage and thus is able to turn a much weaker

	Rate Earned on Stockholders' Equity	=	Rate Earned on Total Assets	×	Leverage (Average Total Assets/Average Stockholders' Equity)
Home Depot	18.4%	=	12.8%	×	1.44*
Lowe's	16.7%	=	8.1%	×	2.06**

*$23,890/$16,543
**$12,547/$6,084

rate of return on asset performance into nearly the same rate of return on stockholders' equity as Home Depot's.

While positive leverage can improve a firm's financial performance for its stockholders, leverage also carries risk. A business that cannot pay its interest expense or debts on a timely basis may experience difficulty in obtaining further credit, and, thus, may be forced into liquidating assets, curtailing operations, or even filing for bankruptcy.

Leverage analysis focuses on the ability of a business to pay or otherwise satisfy its current and noncurrent liabilities. Thus, we can use leverage analysis to assess whether Lowe's use of leverage is too aggressive relative to its financial condition.[4] Leverage is normally assessed by examining current and long-term balance sheet relationships, using the following major ratios:

<u>Current Balance Sheet Relationships</u>
Current ratio
Quick ratio

<u>Long-Term Balance Sheet Relationships</u>
The ratio of fixed assets to long-term liabilities
The ratio of liabilities to stockholders' equity
The number of times interest charges are earned

Current Ratio

To be useful in assessing solvency, a ratio or other financial measure must relate to a business's ability to pay or otherwise satisfy its liabilities. Using measures to assess a business's ability to pay its current liabilities is called *current position analysis.* Such analysis is of special interest to short-term creditors.

An analysis of a firm's current position normally includes determining the current ratio and the quick ratio. The current and quick ratios are most useful when analyzed together and compared to previous periods and other firms in the industry.

The **current ratio** is computed by dividing the total current assets by the total current liabilities. For Home Depot and Lowe's, the current ratios on February 2, 2002, are at the top of the following page.

While Home Depot has nearly twice the working capital of Lowe's, working capital is not a relative measure of current position when making comparisons between firms or across time. Rather, the current ratio is a relative measure of current position. This ratio

4 Recall Lowe's high interest expense in the margin analysis on page 678.

	Home Depot (in millions)	Lowe's (in millions)
a. Current assets	$10,361	$4,920
b. Current liabilities	6,501	3,017
Working capital	$ 3,860	$1,903
Current ratio (a. ÷ b.)	1.59	1.63

is nearly equal for both firms, at approximately 1.60. A current ratio greater than 1.0 would indicate that a firm has more than enough current assets to meet short-term claims. Thus, most analysts would expect a current ratio greater than 1.0. Current ratios that exceed 1.5 are often considered acceptable for most industries, while a current ratio in excess of 2.0 is excellent and would indicate capacity for short-term borrowing.

Quick Ratio

The current ratio does not consider the makeup of the current assets. To illustrate the importance of this consideration, the current position data for Lincoln Company and Jefferson Corporation as of December 31, 2003, are as follows:

	Lincoln Company	Jefferson Corporation
Current assets:		
Cash	$ 90,500	$ 45,500
Marketable securities	75,000	25,000
Accounts receivable (net)	115,000	90,000
Inventories	264,000	380,000
Prepaid expenses	5,500	9,500
Total current assets	$550,000	$550,000
Current liabilities	210,000	210,000
Working capital	$340,000	$340,000
Current ratio	2.6	2.6

Both companies have a working capital of $340,000 and a current ratio of 2.6. But the ability of each company to pay its current debts is significantly different. Jefferson Corporation has more of its current assets in inventories. Some of these inventories must be sold and the receivables collected before the current liabilities can be paid in full. Thus, a large amount of time may be necessary to convert these inventories into cash. Declines in market prices and a reduction in demand could also impair Jefferson's ability to pay current liabilities. In contrast, Lincoln Company has cash and current assets (marketable securities and accounts receivable) that can generally be converted to cash rather quickly to meet its current liabilities.

A ratio that measures the "instant" debt-paying ability of a company is called the **quick ratio** or *acid-test ratio*. It is the ratio of the total quick assets to the total current liabilities. **Quick assets** are cash and other current assets that can be quickly converted to cash. Quick assets normally include cash, marketable securities, and receivables. The quick ratios for Lincoln Company and Jefferson Corporation are 1.3 ($280,500 ÷ $210,000) and 0.76 ($160,500 ÷ $210,000), respectively.

The quick ratios for Home Depot and Lowe's are as follows:

	Home Depot (in millions)	Lowe's (in millions)
Quick assets:		
Cash	$ 2,477	$ 799
Temporary investments	69	54
Accounts receivable (net)	920	166
a. Total quick assets	$ 3,466	$ 1,019
b. Current liabilities	÷6,501	÷3,017
Quick ratio	0.53	0.34

A balance sheet shows $300,000 of cash, marketable securities, and receivables, and $250,000 of inventories. Current liabilities are $200,000. What are (a) the current ratio and (b) the quick ratio?

(a) 2.75 ($550,000/$200,000); (b) 1.5 ($300,000/$200,000)

Home Depot's quick ratio (0.53) is stronger than Lowe's (0.34). The difference between the two quick ratios is caused by Home Depot's strong cash balance at 9.4% ($2,477 ÷ $26,394) of total assets, while Lowe's has a cash balance of only 5.8% ($799 ÷ $13,736) of total assets. Lowe's also has much less accounts receivable than does Home Depot, as we saw from the accounts receivable turnover ratio in the previous section. Lowe's quick ratio is still not so small as to be a concern. Lowe's is a strong company and would be able to obtain cash easily through short-term borrowing if necessary.

Ratio of Fixed Assets to Long-Term Liabilities

Long-term notes and bonds are often secured by mortgages on fixed assets. The **ratio of fixed assets to long-term liabilities** is a leverage measure that indicates the margin of safety of the noteholders or bondholders. It also indicates the ability of the business to borrow additional funds on a long-term basis. The ratio of fixed assets to long-term liabilities for Home Depot and Lowe's is as follows:

	Home Depot (in millions)	Lowe's (in millions)
Fixed assets (net)	$15,375	$ 8,653
Long-term liabilities	÷ 1,811	÷3,734
Ratio of fixed assets to long-term liabilities	8.5	2.3

Home Depot provides significant safety for its long-term creditors. The book value of the fixed assets exceeds the debt by 9.5 times. This is a very high ratio, indicating low use of leverage and extensive borrowing capacity. Lowe's also has good safety for its long-term creditors, with a ratio of 2.3, or a book value of net assets over twice the book value of long-term debt. This ratio shows the difference in leverage between the two companies. Home Depot is using long-term debt sparingly, while Lowe's is using long-term debt more aggressively, but not recklessly.[5] Lowe's use of debt is actually an advantage, due to positive leverage.

Ratio of Liabilities to Stockholders' Equity

Claims against the total assets of a business are divided into two groups: (1) claims of creditors and (2) claims of owners. The relationship between the total claims of the creditors and owners—the **ratio of liabilities to stockholders' equity**—is a leverage measure that indicates the margin of safety for creditors. This ratio is used widely to summarize a business's aggregate leverage. The ratio also indicates the ability of the business to withstand adverse business conditions. When the claims of creditors are large in relation to the equity of the stockholders, there are usually significant interest payments. If earnings decline to the point where the company is unable to meet its interest payments, the business may be taken over by the creditors.

The relationship between creditor and stockholder equity is shown in the vertical analysis of the balance sheet. For example, the balance sheet of Home Depot in Exhibit 4 indicates that on February 3, 2002, total liabilities represented 31.5% and stockholders' equity represented 68.5% of the total liabilities and stockholders' equity (100.0%). Instead of expressing each item as a percent of the total, this relationship may be expressed as a ratio of one to the other, as follows for both Home Depot and Lowe's:

	Home Depot (in millions)	Lowe's (in millions)
Total liabilities	$ 8,312	$ 7,062
Total stockholders' equity	÷18,082	÷6,674
Ratio of liabilities to stockholders' equity	0.46	1.06

The liability to stockholders' equity ratio of 1.0 occurs when half of the total assets are funded by debt and half are funded by stockholders' equity (that is, they are equal). This is an average ratio. Thus, Home Depot's ratio would be interpreted as very conservative, while Lowe's ratio is near average.

Number of Times Interest Charges Earned

Corporations in some industries, such as airlines, normally have high ratios of debt to stockholders' equity. For such corporations, the relative risk of the debtholders is normally measured as the **number of times interest charges are earned** during the year.

5 Home Depot is also using off-balance-sheet financing, which is described and explained in advanced accounting textbooks. Financial analysis may be distorted by off-balance-sheet financing.

The higher the ratio, the lower the risk that interest payments will not be made if earnings decrease. In other words, the higher the ratio, the greater the assurance that interest payments will be made on a continuing basis. This measure also indicates the general financial strength of the business, which is of interest to stockholders and employees as well as creditors.

The amount available to meet interest charges is not affected by taxes on income. This is because interest is deductible in determining taxable income. Thus, the number of times interest charges are earned for Home Depot and Lowe's is computed as shown below.

	Home Depot (in millions)	Lowe's (in millions)
Net income	$3,044	$1,023
Add income tax	1,913	601
a. Add interest expense	28	174
b. Amount available to meet interest charges	$4,985	$1,798
Number of times interest charges earned (b. ÷ a.)	178	10.3

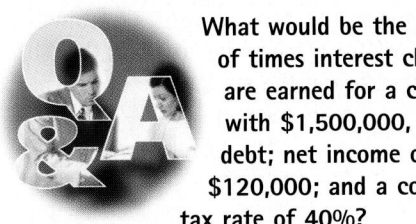

What would be the number of times interest charges are earned for a company with $1,500,000, 10% debt; net income of $120,000; and a corporate tax rate of 40%?

$$\frac{[\$120{,}000/(1.0 - 0.4)] + \$150{,}000}{\$150{,}000} = 2.33$$

Again, we see that Home Depot uses very little debt and thus has small interest payments. Its number of times interest charges are earned ratio is very high. Lowe's ratio is 10.3, which would be considered more than adequate.

Leverage Summary

We began this section by noting Lowe's advantageous use of positive leverage. However, since there are limits to the use of leverage, we next asked if Lowe's used too much leverage. After reviewing the additional leverage ratios in this section, Lowe's use of leverage is clearly not too aggressive. Home Depot, on the other hand, is not using leverage as aggressively as it might. By avoiding debt, Home Depot is forgoing the advantages to the stockholders in using leverage.

Stockholder Ratios

5 Calculate and interpret shareholder ratios: earnings per share, price-earnings ratio, and dividend yield.

The analytical approaches in the previous sections help shareholders and managers analyze the financial statements of companies. In this section, we will describe and illustrate analytical approaches used by shareholders to evaluate the stock price and/or dividend performance of their equity investments. The stock price and dividends on the common stock are the primary means by which an investor earns a return. Thus, additional ratios that relate to stock price and dividend information are of interest to shareholders. Three common shareholder ratios are earnings per share, the price-earnings ratio, and dividend yield.

Earnings per Share

One of the profitability measures often quoted by the financial press is **earnings per share (EPS)**. It is also normally reported in the income statement in corporate annual reports. If a company has issued only one class of stock, the earnings per share is computed by dividing net income by the number of shares of stock outstanding. If preferred and common stock are outstanding, the net income is first reduced by the amount of preferred dividend requirements.[6]

The data on the earnings per share of common stock for Home Depot and Lowe's are as follows:

	Home Depot (in millions)	Lowe's (in millions)
Net income	$ 3,044	$1,023
Shares of common stock outstanding	÷2,335	÷ 769
Earnings per share on common stock	$1.30	$1.33

INTERNATIONAL PERSPECTIVE

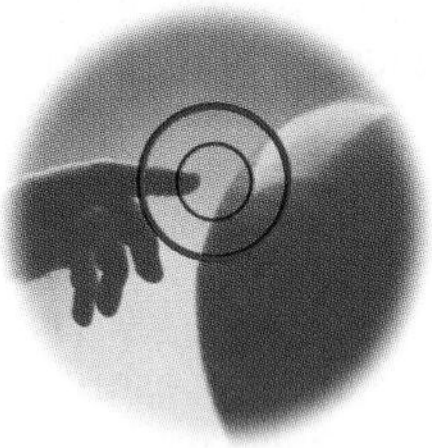

Germany's accounting standards and requirements do not require the disclosure of earnings per share.

The similarity in earnings per share between the two companies is coincidental. The earnings per share is difficult to interpret by itself. Rather, it should be compared to historical EPS trends and the stock price of a firm, as shown with the price-earnings ratio in the next section.

Price-Earnings Ratio

Another profitability measure quoted by the financial press is the **price-earnings (P/E) ratio** on common stock. The price-earnings ratio indicates a firm's future earnings prospects. It is computed by dividing the market price per share of common stock at a specific date by the annual earnings per share. To illustrate, the market prices per common share on February 2, 2002, for Home Depot and Lowe's were $50.00 and $46.15, respectively. Thus, the price-earnings ratio on common stock is computed as follows:

	Home Depot	Lowe's
Market price per share of common stock	$50.00	$46.15
Earnings per share on common stock	÷ 1.30	÷ 1.33
Price-earnings ratio on common stock	38	35

6 Additional details related to earnings per share were discussed in Chapter 12.

The price-earnings ratio indicates that a share of common stock of Home Depot sold for 38 times earnings, while for Lowe's it was 35 times earnings. At this time, both these amounts were above the market average of 24 times earnings. This means that market participants were optimistic about the future performance of both companies and were willing to price the common stock at a premium on the underlying earnings per share.

Dividend Yield

Since the primary basis for dividends is earnings, *dividends per share* and earnings per share on common stock are commonly used by investors in assessing alternative stock investments. The dividends per share for Home Depot and Lowe's were $0.20 and $0.08 per share, respectively, on February 2, 2002.

Dividends per share can be reported with earnings per share to indicate the relationship between dividends and earnings. The ratio of these two per share amounts, called the *dividend payout ratio*, indicates the extent to which the corporation is paying dividends to stockholders, versus retaining earnings for future growth. The dividend payout ratio for Home Depot is 15.4% ($0.20/$1.30), and for Lowe's it is 6% ($0.08/$1.33). These are modest payout ratios.

The **dividend yield** on common stock shows the rate of return to common stockholders in terms of cash dividends. It is of special interest to investors whose main investment objective is to receive current returns (dividends) on an investment, rather than an increase in the market price of the investment. The dividend yield is computed by dividing the annual dividends paid per share of common stock by the market price per share on a specific date. To illustrate, the dividend yield for Home Depot and Lowe's on February 2, 2002, is shown as follows:

	Home Depot	Lowe's
Dividends per share of common stock	$ 0.20	$ 0.08
Market price per share of common stock	÷50.00	÷46.15
Dividend yield on common stock	0.4%	0.2%

The dividend yields for both companies are small, indicating that stockholders expect to earn returns in appreciating share prices.

Summary of Analytical Measures

6 **Summarize the uses and limitations of analytical measures.**

Exhibit 9 presents a summary of the financial ratios that we have discussed for Home Depot, Lowe's, and the retail industry as a whole. Depending on the specific business being analyzed, some measures might be omitted or additional measures could be developed. The type of industry, the capital structure, and the diversity of the business's operations usually affect the measures used. For example, analysis for an airline might include revenue per passenger mile and cost per available seat as measures. Likewise, analysis for a hotel might focus on occupancy rates.

Exhibit 9

Summary of Analytical Measures

	Equation	Home Depot	Lowe's	Retail Industry
Profitability Analysis:				
Rate earned on stockholders' equity	$\frac{\text{Net income}}{\text{Average total stockholders' equity}}$	18.4%	16.8%	−3.1%
Rate earned on total assets	$\frac{\text{Net income}}{\text{Average total assets}}$	12.8%	8.1%	−0.2%
Margin Analysis:				
Ratio of net income to net sales	$\frac{\text{Net income}}{\text{Net sales}}$	5.7%	4.6%	0.5%
Ratio of cost of merchandise sold to net sales	$\frac{\text{Cost of merchandise sold}}{\text{Net sales}}$	69.9%	71.2%	67.7%
Ratio of selling, general, and administrative expenses to net sales	$\frac{\text{Selling, general and admin. expenses}}{\text{Net sales}}$	20.9%	20.7%	27.0%
Asset Efficiency Analysis:				
Asset turnover	$\frac{\text{Net sales}}{\text{Average total assets}}$	2.24	1.76	2.27
Accounts receivable turnover	$\frac{\text{Net sales}}{\text{Average accounts receivable}}$	61.0	134.8	117.4
Numbers of days' sales in receivables	$\frac{\text{Accounts receivable, end of year}}{\text{Average daily net sales}}$	6.3 days	2.7 days	3.1 days
Inventory turnover	$\frac{\text{Cost of goods sold}}{\text{Average inventory}}$	5.6	4.6	11.6
Number of days' sales in inventory	$\frac{\text{Inventory, end of year}}{\text{Average daily cost of goods sold}}$	65.9 days	84.0 days	31 days
Fixed asset turnover	$\frac{\text{Net sales}}{\text{Average fixed assets, net}}$	3.8	2.8	3.2
Leverage Analysis:				
Leverage ratio	$\frac{\text{Average total assets}}{\text{Average stockholders' equity}}$	1.44	2.06	2.15
Current ratio	$\frac{\text{Current assets}}{\text{Current liabilities}}$	1.59	1.63	2.29
Quick ratio	$\frac{\text{Quick assets}}{\text{Current liabilities}}$	0.53	0.33	1.02
Ratio of fixed assets to long-term liabilities	$\frac{\text{Fixed assets (net)}}{\text{Long-term liabilities}}$	9.5	2.3	2.1
Ratio of liabilities to stockholders' equity	$\frac{\text{Total liabilities}}{\text{Total stockholders' equity}}$	0.46	1.06	1.15
Number of times interest charges earned	$\frac{\text{Income before income tax + Interest expense}}{\text{Interest expense}}$	178	10.3	7.5
Stockholder ratios:				
Earnings per share	$\frac{\text{Net income − Preferred dividends}}{\text{Shares of common stock outstanding}}$	$1.30	$1.33	$1.08
Price-earnings ratio	$\frac{\text{Market price per share of common stock}}{\text{Earnings per share of common stock}}$	38	35	36.6
Dividend yield	$\frac{\text{Dividends per share of common stock}}{\text{Market price per share of common stock}}$	0.4%	0.2%	0.42%

Ethics in Action
Analyst Independence

Major investment banks, such as Salomon Smith Barney, underwrite new common stock offerings. They also provide investors with analyses of public companies. These two roles should be independent. Recently, however, research analysts have been accused of compromising independence by acting as cheerleaders for recent issues underwritten by their firm. Criticism has been leveled that such research may be misleading. Analysts behaving in this way have been partly blamed for the Internet and telecom bubble of the early 2000s.

Percentage analyses, ratios, turnovers, and other measures of financial position and operating results are useful analytical measures. They are helpful in assessing a business's past performance and predicting its future. They are not, however, a substitute for sound judgment. In selecting and interpreting analytical measures, conditions peculiar to a business or its industry should be considered. In addition, the analytical measures are not ends in themselves. They are only guides in evaluating financial and operating data. Many other factors, such as trends in the industry and general economic conditions, should also be considered.

In determining trends, the interrelationship of the measures used in assessing a business should be carefully studied. Comparable indexes of earlier periods should also be studied. Data from competing businesses or the industry may be useful in assessing the efficiency of operations for the firm under analysis. In making such comparisons, however, the effects of differences in the accounting methods used by the businesses should be considered.

Corporate Annual Reports

7 Describe the contents of corporate annual reports.

Corporations normally issue annual reports to their stockholders and other interested parties. Such reports summarize the corporation's operating activities for the past year and plans for the future. There are many variations in the order and form for presenting the major sections of annual reports. However, one section of the annual report is devoted to the financial statements, including the accompanying notes. In addition, annual reports usually include the following sections:

1. Financial Highlights
2. President's Letter to the Stockholders
3. Management Discussion and Analysis
4. Independent Auditors' Report
5. Historical Summary

In the following paragraphs, we describe these sections. Each section, as well as the financial statements, is illustrated in the annual report for Home Depot Inc. in Appendix D.

Financial Highlights

The Financial Highlights section summarizes the operating results for the last year or two. It is sometimes called *Results in Brief.* It is usually presented on the first one or two pages of the annual report.

There are many variations in the format and content of the Financial Highlights section. Such items as sales, net income, net income per common share, cash dividends paid, cash dividends per common share, and the amount of capital expenditures are typically presented. In addition to these data, information about the financial position at the end of the year may be presented. The Financial Highlights section for Home Depot includes the year-end amounts of net sales, net earnings, diluted earnings per share, assets, cash, and store count.

President's Letter to the Stockholders

A letter from the company president to the stockholders is also presented in most annual reports. These letters usually discuss such items as reasons for an increase or decrease in net income, changes in existing plants, purchase or construction of new plants, significant new financing commitments, social responsibility issues, and future plans. The President's Letter for Home Depot mentions the company's efforts to create a culture that would benefit employees, customers, vendors, and shareholders.

Management Discussion and Analysis

A required disclosure in the annual report filed with the Securities and Exchange Commission is the **Management Discussion and Analysis (MDA)**. The MDA provides critical information in interpreting the financial statements and assessing the future of the company.

The MDA includes an analysis of the results of operations and discusses management's opinion about future performance. It compares the prior year's income statement with the current year's to explain changes in sales, significant expenses, gross profit, and income from operations. For example, an increase in sales may be explained by referring to higher shipment volume or stronger prices.

The MDA also includes an analysis of the company's financial condition. It compares significant balance sheet items between successive years to explain changes in liquidity and capital resources. In addition, the MDA discusses significant risk exposure. For example, Home Depot has identified fluctuations in interest rates as its primary risk factor, since home building and improvement activities are sensitive to interest rates.

Ethics in Action

Do You Swear. . .

The Sarbanes-Oxley Act of 2002 was enacted in response to the perceived abuses in accounting, corporate responsibility, and public disclosure in the early part of this decade. One of the provisions of this act is to require the principal executive and financial officers to certify under oath and penalty of law that the financial statements have been personally reviewed, contain no material omissions, and present fairly the financial condition and results of operations.

Ethics in Action

One Bad Apple

A recent survey by *CFO* magazine reported that 17% of the chief financial officers were pressured by their chief executive officer to misrepresent financial results, while only 5% admitted to knowingly violating generally accepted accounting principles.

Independent Auditors' Report

Before issuing annual statements, all publicly held corporations are required to have an independent audit (examination) of their financial statements. For the financial statements of most companies, the CPAs who conduct the audit render an opinion on the fairness of the statements. The Independent Auditors' Report for Home Depot is included in the annual report in Appendix D.

The independence and objectivity of the independent auditor is critical to the integrity of the auditors' report. Recently, the independence of auditors has come into question due to the accounting scandals of the early 2000s. Auditors have been criticized for maintaining lucrative consulting relationships with their audit clients. These relationships were alleged to create conflicts of interest in order to avoid jeopardizing nonaudit fee business. This issue, among others, was believed to have led to the eventual demise of Arthur Andersen and the sale of consulting operations of the remaining large public accounting firms. In addition, legislation introduced by the Sarbanes-Oxley Act of 2002 created a Public Company Accounting Oversight Board, whose function is to provide regulatory guidance to audit practice.

Historical Summary

The Historical Summary section reports selected financial and operating data of past periods, usually for five or ten years. It is usually presented near the financial statements for the current year. There are wide variations in the types of data reported and the title of this section. In the annual report for Home Depot, this section is called "10-Year Summary."

Summary of Learning Goals

1 Construct and interpret horizontal and vertical analyses.

The analysis of percentage increases and decreases in related items in comparative financial statements is called horizontal analysis. The analysis of percentages of component parts to the total in a single statement is called vertical analysis. Financial statements in which all amounts are expressed in percentages for purposes of analysis are called common-size statements.

2 Calculate and interpret the rate earned on stockholders' equity and the rate earned on total assets.

The rate earned on stockholders' equity, which is net income divided by average stockholders' equity, is a widely acknowledged summary measure of financial performance from the stockholders' perspective. The rate earned on total assets, which is net income divided by average total assets, is an acknowledged summary measure of management performance.

3 Analyze the rate earned on total assets by evaluating the profit margin and the asset efficiency of a business.

The rate earned on total assets is the product of the profit margin and the total asset turnover, as shown below.

Rate earned on total assets = Profit Margin × Asset Turnover

$$\frac{\textit{Net Income}}{\textit{Average Total Assets}} = \frac{\textit{Net Income}}{\textit{Net Sales}} \times \frac{\textit{Net Sales}}{\textit{Average Total Assets}}$$

Management can evaluate the rate earned on total assets by conducting a margin analysis, which segments the profit margin into a vertical analysis of the income statement. Alternatively, management may evaluate the rate earned on total assets by conducting an asset efficiency analysis, which segments the total asset turnover into sub-asset categories.

4 Determine and interpret leverage.

Leverage measures the amount of debt used by the firm to finance its assets. The proper use of leverage can cause the rate earned on stockholders' equity to exceed the rate earned on total assets. This will occur when the return on borrowed funds exceeds the interest cost of those funds. A firm must be careful to avoid excess leverage, since debt requires fixed periodic interest payments, and the debt must eventually be repaid. The rate earned on stockholders' equity can be compared to the rate earned on total assets by using the leverage formula, as follows:

Rate earned on stockholders' equity = Rate earned on total assets × Leverage

Leverage analysis can be used to examine additional measures of current and long-term relationships, using the current ratio, the quick ratio, the ratio of fixed assets to long-term liabilities, the ratio of liabilities to stockholders' equity, and the number of times interest charges are earned.

5 Calculate and interpret shareholder ratios: earnings per share, price-earnings ratio, and dividend yield.

Shareholders are interested in making money on their stock investment. This return can come from stock appreciation or from dividends. Thus, earnings per share, the price-earnings ratio, and dividend yield, which relate to stock price and dividend information, are of interest to shareholders.

6 Summarize the uses and limitations of analytical measures.

In selecting and interpreting analytical measures, conditions peculiar to a business or its industry should be considered. For example, the type of industry, capital structure, and diversity of the business's operations affect the measures used. Thus, most analysts will compare a firm's ratios with competitors and averages for an industry. In addition, the influence of the general economic and business environment should be considered.

7 Describe the contents of corporate annual reports.

Corporate annual reports normally include financial statements and the following sections: Financial Highlights, President's Letter to the Stockholders, Management Discussion and Analysis, Independent Auditors' Report, and Historical Summary.

Glossary

Accounts receivable turnover The relationship between net sales and accounts receivable, computed by dividing net sales by the average net accounts receivable.

Asset turnover The number of sales dollars earned for each dollar of total assets, calculated as the ratio of net sales to total assets.

Common-size statement A financial statement in which all items are expressed only in percentages.

Cost of capital The cost of financing operations from both debt and common stock, expressed as a percentage rate.

Current ratio The ratio of current assets to current liabilities.

Dividend yield The rate of return to common stockholders in terms of cash dividends.

DuPont formula A formula that states that the rate earned on total assets is the product of two factors, the profit margin and the total asset turnover.

Earnings per share (EPS) The profitability ratio of net income available to common shareholders to the number of common shares outstanding.

Fixed asset turnover The number of dollars of sales that are generated from each dollar of average fixed assets during the year, computed by dividing the net sales by the average net fixed assets.

Horizontal analysis The percentage of increases and decreases in corresponding items in comparative financial statements.

Inventory turnover The relationship between the volume of goods sold and inventory, computed by dividing the cost of goods sold by the average inventory.

Leverage The amount of debt used by the firm to finance its assets; causes the rate earned on stockholders' equity to vary from the rate earned on total assets because the amount earned on assets acquired through the use of funds provided by creditors varies from the interest paid to these creditors.

Leverage formula A formula that states the rate earned on stockholders' equity as the product of the rate earned on total assets and the ratio of the average total assets divided by average stockholders' equity, or leverage.

Management Discussion and Analysis (MDA) An annual report disclosure that provides an analysis of the results of operations and financial condition.

Number of days' sales in inventory The relationship between the volume of sales and inventory, computed by dividing the inventory at the end of the year by the average daily cost of goods sold.

Number of days' sales in receivables The relationship between sales and accounts receivable, computed by dividing the net accounts receivable at the end of the year by the average daily sales.

Number of times interest charges are earned A ratio that measures creditor margin of safety for interest payments, calculated as income before interest and taxes divided by interest expense.

Price-earnings (P/E) ratio The ratio of the market price per share of common stock, at a specific date, to the annual earnings per share.

Profit margin A measure of the amount earned on each dollar of sales, calculated as the ratio of net income to net sales.

Quick assets Cash and other current assets that can be quickly converted to cash, such as cash, marketable securities, and receivables.

Quick ratio The ratio of the sum of cash, receivables, and marketable securities to current liabilities.

Rate earned on stockholders' equity A measure of profitability computed by dividing net income by total stockholders' equity.

Rate earned on total assets A measure of the profitability of assets, without regard to the equity of creditors and stockholders in the assets, calculated as the net income divided by average total assets.

Ratio of fixed assets to long-term liabilities A leverage ratio that measures the margin of safety of long-term creditors, calculated as the net fixed assets divided by the long-term liabilities.

Ratio of liabilities to stockholders' equity A comprehensive leverage ratio that measures the relationship of the claims of creditors to that of owners, calculated as total liabilities divided by total stockholders' equity.

Vertical analysis The percentage analysis of component parts in relation to the total of the parts in a single financial statement.

Illustrative Accounting Application Problem

Rainbow Paint Co.'s comparative financial statements for the years ending December 31, 2004 and 2003, are as follows. The market price of Rainbow Paint Co.'s common stock was $30 on December 31, 2003, and $25 on December 31, 2004.

Rainbow Paint Co.
Comparative Retained Earnings Statement
For the Years Ended December 31, 2004 and 2003

	2004	2003
Retained earnings, January 1	$723,000	$581,800
Add net income for year	245,000	211,200
Total	$968,000	$793,000
Deduct dividends:		
On preferred stock	$ 40,000	$ 40,000
On common stock	45,000	30,000
Total	$ 85,000	$ 70,000
Retained earnings, December 31	$883,000	$723,000

Rainbow Paint Co.
Comparative Income Statement
For the Years Ended December 31, 2004 and 2003

	2004	2003
Net sales	$5,000,000	$3,200,000
Cost of goods sold	3,400,000	2,080,000
Gross profit	$1,600,000	$1,120,000
Selling expenses	$ 650,000	$ 464,000
Administrative expenses	325,000	224,000
Total operating expenses	$ 975,000	$ 688,000
Income from operations	$ 625,000	$ 432,000
Other income	25,000	19,200
	$ 650,000	$ 451,200
Other expense (interest)	105,000	64,000
Income before income tax	$ 545,000	$ 387,200
Income tax expense	300,000	176,000
Net income	$ 245,000	$ 211,200

Rainbow Paint Co.
Comparative Balance Sheet
December 31, 2004 and 2003

	2004	2003
Assets		
Current assets:		
Cash	$ 175,000	$ 125,000
Marketable securities	150,000	50,000
Accounts receivable (net)	425,000	325,000
Inventories	720,000	480,000
Prepaid expenses	30,000	20,000
Total current assets	$1,500,000	$1,000,000
Long-term investments	250,000	225,000
Property, plant, and equipment (net)	2,093,000	1,948,000
Total assets	$3,843,000	$3,173,000
Liabilities		
Current liabilities	$ 750,000	$ 650,000
Long-term liabilities:		
Mortgage note payable, 10%, due 2008	$ 410,000	–
Bonds payable, 8%, due 2011	800,000	800,000
Total long-term liabilities	$1,210,000	$ 800,000
Total liabilities	$1,960,000	$1,450,000
Stockholders' Equity		
Preferred 8% stock, $100 par	$ 500,000	$ 500,000
Common stock, $10 par	500,000	500,000
Retained earnings	883,000	723,000
Total stockholders' equity	$1,883,000	$1,723,000
Total liabilities and stockholders' equity	$3,843,000	$3,173,000

Instructions

a. Determine the following measures for 2004:
   1. Working capital
   2. Current ratio
   3. Quick ratio
   4. Accounts receivable turnover
   5. Number of days' sales in receivables
   6. Inventory turnover
   7. Number of days' sales in inventory
   8. Ratio of fixed assets to long-term liabilities
   9. Ratio of liabilities to stockholders' equity
   10. Number of times interest charges earned
   11. Profit margin
   12. Asset turnover
   13. Rate earned on total assets
   14. Rate earned on stockholders' equity
   15. Earnings per share on common stock
   16. Price-earnings ratio
   17. Dividends per share of common stock
   18. Dividend yield

b. Compute the DuPont formula for 2004.

Solution

(Ratios are rounded to the nearest single digit after the decimal point.)

a. 1. Working capital: $750,000
   $1,500,000 − $750,000
   2. Current ratio: 2.0
   $1,500,000 ÷ $750,000
   3. Quick ratio: 1.0
   $750,000 ÷ $750,000
   4. Accounts receivable turnover: 13.3
   $5,000,000 ÷ [($425,000 + $325,000) ÷ 2]
   5. Number of days' sales in receivables: 31 days
   $5,000,000 ÷ 365 = $13,699
   $425,000 ÷ $13,699
   6. Inventory turnover: 5.7
   $3,400,000 ÷ [($720,000 + $480,000) ÷ 2]
   7. Number of days' sales in inventory: 77.3 days
   3,400,000 ÷ 365 = $9,315
   $720,000 ÷ $9,315
   8. Ratio of fixed assets to long-term liabilities: 1.7
   $2,093,000 ÷ $1,210,000
   9. Ratio of liabilities to stockholders' equity: 1.0
   $1,960,000 ÷ $1,883,000
   10. Number of times interest charges earned: 6.2
   ($545,000 + $105,000) ÷ $105,000
   11. Profit margin: 4.9%
   $245,000 ÷ $5,000,000
   12. Asset turnover: 1.4
   $5,000,000 ÷ [($3,843,000 + $3,173,000) ÷ 2]
   13. Rate earned on total assets: 7.0%
   $245,000 ÷ [($3,843,000 + $3,173,000) ÷ 2]
   14. Rate earned on stockholders' equity: 13.6%
   $245,000 ÷ [($1,883,000 + $1,723,000) ÷ 2]

(continued)

15. Earnings per share on common stock: $4.10
    ($245,000 − $40,000) ÷ 50,000
16. Price-earnings ratio: 6.1
    $25 ÷ $4.10
17. Dividends per share of common stock: $0.90
    $45,000 ÷ 50,000 shares
18. Dividend yield: 3.6%
    $0.90 ÷ $25

b. DuPont formula:

Rate earned on total assets = Profit Margin × Asset Turnover

$$\frac{\textit{Net Income}}{\textit{Average Total Assets}} = \frac{\textit{Net Income}}{\textit{Net Sales}} \times \frac{\textit{Net Sales}}{\textit{Average Total Assets}}$$

6.9% = 4.9% × 1.4

Self-Study Questions

Answers at end of chapter

1. What type of analysis is indicated by the following?

Amount		Percent
Current assets	$100,000	20%
Property, plant, and equipment	400,000	80
Total assets	$500,000	100%

A. Vertical analysis
B. Horizontal analysis
C. Profitability analysis
D. Asset efficiency analysis

2. Horizon Company has the following current account information for a recent balance sheet:

Cash	$ 25,000
Temporary investments	25,000
Accounts receivable	125,000
Merchandise inventory	100,000
Accounts payable	$ 75,000
Accrued expenses	25,000

What are the current and quick ratios?

A. 1.75, 2.50
B. 2.50, 1.50
C. 2.75, 0.50
D. 2.75, 1.75

3. Tiger Equipment Sales Co. had accounts receivable at the beginning and end of the year of $200,000 and $300,000, respectively. The net sales were $1,000,000. Determine the accounts receivable turnover and number of days' sales in accounts receivable.

A. 3.3, 109
B. 3.3, 91
C. 4.0, 91
D. 4.0, 109

4. The DuPont formula is:

A. Rate earned on total assets = Profit margin × Asset turnover.
B. Rate earned on total stockholders' equity = Rate earned on total assets × Leverage.
C. Rate earned on total assets = Rate earned on total stockholders' equity ÷ Leverage.
D. Rate earned on total assets = Profit margin × Leverage

5. A measure useful in evaluating the efficiency in the management of inventories is:

A. working capital ratio.
B. quick ratio.
C. number of days' sales in inventory.
D. ratio of fixed assets to long-term liabilities.

Discussion Questions

1. The current year's amount of net income (after income tax) is 15% larger than that of the preceding year. Does this indicate an improved operating performance? Discuss.
2. How would you respond to a horizontal analysis that showed an expense increasing by over 100%?
3. a. What measure is used by stockholders to assess the profitability of the firm?
   b. How is the ratio in (a) calculated?
4. a. What measure is used by managers in assessing the profitability of the firm?
   b. How is the ratio in (a) calculated?
5. What is the DuPont formula?
6. A company that grants terms of n/30 on all sales has a yearly accounts receivable turnover, based on monthly averages, of 6. Is this a satisfactory turnover? Discuss.
7. What does an increase in the number of days' sales in receivables ordinarily indicate about the credit and collection policy of the firm?
8. a. Why is it advantageous to have a high inventory turnover?
   b. Is it possible for the inventory turnover to be too high? Discuss.
   c. Is it possible to have a high inventory turnover and a high number of days' sales in inventory? Discuss.
9. Would a railroad be expected to have a high fixed asset turnover?
10. a. What is financial leverage?
    b. What impact does positive leverage have on the rate earned on stockholders' equity compared to the rate earned on total assets?
11. How would the current and quick ratios of a service business compare?
12. For Lindsay Corporation, the working capital at the end of the current year is $5,000 greater than the working capital at the end of the preceding year, reported as follows:

	Current Year	Preceding Year
Current assets:		
Cash, marketable securities, and receivables	$34,000	$30,000
Inventories	51,000	32,500
Total current assets	$85,000	$62,500
Current liabilities	42,500	25,000
Working capital	$42,500	$37,500

    Has the current position improved? Explain.
13. What do the following data taken from a comparative balance sheet indicate about the company's ability to borrow additional funds on a long-term basis in the current year as compared to the preceding year?

	Current Year	Preceding Year
Fixed assets (net)	$175,000	$170,000
Total long-term liabilities	70,000	85,000

14. What does a decrease in the ratio of liabilities to stockholders' equity indicate about the margin of safety for a firm's creditors and the ability of the firm to withstand adverse business conditions?
15. The price-earnings ratio for the common stock of Essian Company was 10 at December 31, the end of the current fiscal year. What does the ratio indicate about the selling price of the common stock in relation to current earnings?

16. Why would the dividend yield differ significantly from the rate earned on common stockholders' equity?
17. Favorable business conditions may bring about certain seemingly unfavorable ratios, and unfavorable business operations may result in apparently favorable ratios. For example, Sanchez Company increased its sales and net income substantially for the current year; yet the current ratio at the end of the year is lower than at the beginning of the year. Discuss some possible causes of the apparent weakening of the current position, while sales and net income have increased substantially.
18. Indicate the purpose of the Financial Highlights section and the Management Discussion and Analysis in a corporation's annual report.

Resources for your success online @ http://warren.swlearning.com

Remember! If you need additional help, visit South-Western's Web site. See page 30 for a description of the online and printed materials that are available.

Exercises

Exercise 14–1

Vertical analysis of income statement

Goal 1

2004 net income: $77,000; 10% of sales

SPREADSHEET

Revenue and expense data for Murry Cabinet Co. are as follows:

	2004	2003
Sales	$770,000	$700,000
Cost of goods sold	415,800	350,000
Selling expenses	138,600	140,000
Administrative expenses	84,700	105,000
Income tax expense	53,900	49,000

a. Prepare an income statement in comparative form, stating each item for both 2004 and 2003 as a percent of sales.
b. Comment on the significant changes disclosed by the comparative income statement.

Exercise 14–2

Vertical analysis of income statement

Goal 1

The following comparative income statement (in millions of dollars) for the fiscal years 2001 and 2000 was adapted from the annual report of Dell Computer Corporation:

a. Fiscal year 2000 income from operations, 8.3% of revenues

STUDENT SOLUTIONS MANUAL

SPREADSHEET

	Fiscal Year 2001	Fiscal Year 2000
Revenues	$31,168	$31,888
Costs and expenses:		
Cost of sales	25,661	25,445
Gross profit	$ 5,507	$ 6,443
Operating expenses	3,718	3,780
Income from operations	$ 1,789	$ 2,663

a. Prepare a comparative income statement for fiscal years 2001 (ended February 1, 2002) and 2000 (ended February 2, 2001) in vertical form, stating each item as a percent of revenues. Round to one digit after the decimal place.
b. Comment on the significant changes.

Exercise 14–3

Common-size income statement

Goal 1

a. Keystone net income: $218,500; 9.1% of sales

SPREADSHEET

Revenue and expense data for calendar year 2004 for Keystone Publishing Company and for the publishing industry are as follows. The Keystone Publishing Company data are expressed in dollars. The publishing industry averages are expressed in percentages.

	Keystone Publishing Company	Publishing Industry Average
Sales	$2,425,500	100.0%
Cost of goods sold	850,000	40.0
Selling expenses	970,000	39.0
Administrative expenses	280,000	10.5
Other income	30,000	1.2
Other expense	40,000	1.7
Income tax expense	97,000	4.0

a. Prepare a common-size income statement comparing the results of operations for Keystone Publishing Company with the industry average. Round to one digit after the decimal place.
b. As far as the data permit, comment on significant relationships revealed by the comparisons.

Exercise 14–4

Vertical analysis of balance sheet

Goal 1

Retained earnings, Dec. 31, 2004, 37.27%

STUDENT SOLUTIONS MANUAL

SPREADSHEET

Balance sheet data for Atlas Fitness Equipment Company on December 31, the end of the fiscal year, are as follows:

	2004	2003
Current assets	$180,000	$150,000
Property, plant, and equipment	340,000	330,000
Intangible assets	30,000	35,000
Current liabilities	120,000	125,000
Long-term liabilities	175,000	150,000
Common stock	50,000	40,000
Retained earnings	205,000	200,000

Prepare a comparative balance sheet for 2004 and 2003, stating each asset as a percent of total assets and each liability and stockholders' equity item as a percent of the total liabilities and stockholders' equity. Round to two digits after the decimal place.

Exercise 14–5

Horizontal analysis of the income statement

Goal 1

a. Net income decrease, 31.67%

SPREADSHEET

Income statement data for Neon Flashlight Company for the years ended December 31, 2004 and 2003, are as follows:

	2004	2003
Sales	$400,000	$460,000
Cost of goods sold	170,000	200,000
Gross profit	$230,000	$260,000
Selling expenses	$ 70,000	$ 60,000
Administrative expenses	50,000	40,000
Total operating expenses	$120,000	$100,000
Income before income tax	$110,000	$160,000
Income tax expense	28,000	40,000
Net income	$ 82,000	$120,000

a. Prepare a comparative income statement with horizontal analysis, indicating the increase (decrease) for 2004 when compared with 2003. Round to two digits after the decimal place.

b. What conclusions can be drawn from the horizontal analysis?

Exercise 14–6

Profitability ratios

Goal 2

a. Rate earned on total assets, 2004, 15.3%

STUDENT SOLUTIONS MANUAL

The following selected data were taken from the financial statements of Central States Transportation Co. for December 31, 2004, 2003, and 2002:

	December 31, 2004	December 31, 2003	December 31, 2002
Total assets	$3,200,000	$2,800,000	$2,200,000
Common stock	900,000	900,000	900,000
Preferred $12 stock, $100 par, cumulative, nonparticipating (no change during year)	500,000	500,000	500,000
Retained earnings	1,330,000	870,000	330,000

The 2004 net income was $460,000, and the 2003 net income was $540,000. No dividends on common stock were declared between 2002 and 2004.

a. Determine the rate earned on total assets and the rate earned on stockholders' equity for the years 2003 and 2004. Round to one digit after the decimal place.

b. Relate the rate earned on stockholders' equity to the rate earned on total assets using the leverage ratio for fiscal year 2004.

c. What conclusions can be drawn from these data as to the company's profitability?

Exercise 14–7

Profitability ratios

Goal 2

a. 2001 rate earned on total assets, 3.36%

Ann Taylor Inc. sells professional women's apparel through company-owned retail stores. Recent financial information for Ann Taylor is provided below (all numbers in thousands).

		Fiscal Year Ended	
		Feb. 2, 2002	Feb. 3, 2001
Net income		$29,105	$52,363
	Feb. 2, 2002	Feb. 3, 2001	Jan. 29, 2000
Total assets	$882,986	$848,115	$765,117
Total stockholders' equity	612,129	574,029	515,622

An analysis of 63 apparel retail companies indicates an industry average rate earned on total assets of 3.2% and an average rate earned on stockholders' equity of 7.6% for fiscal year 2001 (mostly February 2, 2002-dated statements).

a. Determine the rate earned on total assets for Ann Taylor for the fiscal years ended February 2, 2002, and February 3, 2001. Round to two digits after the decimal place.
b. Determine the rate earned on stockholders' equity for Ann Taylor for the fiscal years ended February 2, 2002, and February 3, 2001. Round to two digits after the decimal place.
c. Evaluate the two-year trend for the profitability ratios determined in (a) and (b).
d. Evaluate Ann Taylor's profit performance relative to the industry.

Exercise 14–8

Profitability ratios

Goal 2

a. 2003 rate earned on total assets, 8.61%

STUDENT SOLUTIONS MANUAL

The Starlight Production Company produces television shows. The company earned $450,000 and $500,000 in 2003 and 2004, respectively. The company had total assets of $5,000,000 and total liabilities of $1,000,000 on January 1, 2003. The company had no investing or financing transactions during 2003. On July 1, 2004, the company purchased studio property for $4,000,000 by issuing debt for the same amount.

a. Determine the average total assets and average stockholders' equity for 2003 and 2004.
b. Calculate the rate earned on total assets and rate earned on stockholders' equity for 2003 and 2004. Round to the nearest two decimal places.
c. Why did the profits increase from 2003 to 2004, but the rate earned on total assets decrease?
d. Why did the difference between the rate earned on stockholders' equity and rate earned on total assets increase from 2003 to 2004?

Exercise 14–9

DuPont formula

Goal 3

a. 2003 rate earned on total assets, 7.14%

The Chief Financial Officer (CFO) of Hopkins Flour Company has asked for a DuPont analysis of the company over the last two years. The CFO has requested that the rate earned on total assets be broken into its profit margin and asset turnover components. The following information is available, from the financial statements:

	2003	2004
Net income	$1,500,000	$1,200,000
Sales	25,000,000	20,000,000

	December 31, 2002	December 31, 2003	December 31, 2004
Total assets	$20,000,000	$22,000,000	$25,000,000

a. Perform a DuPont analysis for 2003 and 2004.
b. Analyze the change in the rate earned on total assets for the two years.

Exercise 14-10

DuPont formula

Goal 3

a. Profit margin, fiscal 2002, 7.50%

STUDENT SOLUTIONS MANUAL

Bed Bath and Beyond, Inc., is a major retailer of bed and bath products. During two recent fiscal years, the company reported the following information from the income statement:

	For the Year Ended	
	March 2, 2002	March 3, 2001
Sales	$2,927,962,000	$2,396,655,000
Net income	219,599,000	171,922,000

In addition, the balance sheet revealed the following information:

	March 2, 2002	March 3, 2001	March 3, 2000
Total assets	$1,647,517,000	$1,195,725,000	$865,800,000
Total liabilities	553,167,000	378,707,000	306,755,000
Total stockholders' equity	1,094,350,000	817,018,000	559,045,000

a. Determine the profit margin for fiscal years ending March 2, 2002, and March 3, 2001. Round to two decimal places.
b. Determine the asset turnover for fiscal years ending March 2, 2002, and March 3, 2001. Round to two decimal places.
c. Use the DuPont formula to determine the rate earned on total assets from (a) and (b).
d. Interpret the change in the rate earned on total assets between the two fiscal periods.

Exercise 14-11

DuPont formula and margin analysis

Goal 3

Taylor Foods Company disclosed the following comparative income statement information:

a. Rate earned on total assets, 2003: 15.5%

	For the Year Ended	
	Dec. 31, 2004	Dec. 31, 2003
Sales	$1,600,000	$1,400,000
Cost of goods sold	900,000	700,000
Gross profit	$ 700,000	$ 700,000
Operating expenses	450,000	390,000
Income from operations	$ 250,000	$ 310,000

The asset turnover for both 2003 and 2004 was 0.70.

a. Determine the rate earned on total assets for 2003 and 2004, using the DuPont formula. Round to one digit after the decimal place.
b. Prepare common-size income statements for 2003 and 2004.
c. Analyze the change in the rate earned on total assets between 2003 and 2004 by conducting a margin analysis on common-size statements.

Exercise 14–12

Accounts receivable analysis

Goal 3

a. Accounts receivable turnover, current year, 7.0

STUDENT SOLUTIONS MANUAL

The following data are taken from the financial statements of Northern Expressions Company. Terms of all sales are 1/10, n/60.

	Current Year	Preceding Year
Accounts receivable, end of year	$ 222,466	$ 235,068
Monthly average accounts receivable (net)	207,143	216,667
Net sales on account	1,450,000	1,300,000

a. Determine for each year (1) the accounts receivable turnover and (2) the number of days' sales in receivables. Round to one digit after the decimal place.
b. What conclusions can be drawn from these data concerning accounts receivable and credit policies?

Exercise 14–13

Accounts receivable analysis

Goal 3

a. (1) Coca-Cola's accounts receivable turnover, 11.04

Coca-Cola Company and PepsiCo Inc. are the two largest beverage companies in the United States. Both companies offer credit to their customers. Information from the financial statements for both companies for a recent year is as follows (all numbers are in millions):

	Coca-Cola	PepsiCo
Sales—fiscal 2001	$20,092	$26,935
Accounts receivable (net)—Dec. 31, 2001	1,882	2,142
Accounts receivable (net)—Dec. 31, 2000	1,757	2,129

a. Determine (1) the accounts receivable turnover and (2) the number of days' sales in receivables for both companies. Round to two digits after the decimal place.
b. Compare the two companies with regard to their credit policies.

Exercise 14–14

Inventory analysis

Goal 3

a. Inventory turnover, 2004, 6.0

STUDENT SOLUTIONS MANUAL

The following data were extracted from the income statement of Sierra Instruments Inc.:

	2004	2003
Sales	$3,600,000	$3,900,000
Beginning inventories	310,000	290,000
Cost of goods sold	2,010,000	2,400,000
Ending inventories	360,000	310,000

a. Determine for each year (1) the inventory turnover and (2) the number of days' sales in inventory. Round to two digits after the decimal place.

b. What conclusions can be drawn from these data concerning the inventories?

Exercise 14–15

Inventory analysis

Goal 3

a. (1) Dell inventory turnover, 75.7

Dell Computer Corporation and Gateway Inc. compete with each other in the personal computer market. Dell's strategy is to assemble computers from customer phone and Internet orders, rather than for inventory. Thus, for example, Dell will build and deliver a computer within four days of a customer entering an order on a Web page. Gateway, on the other hand, builds some computers prior to receiving an order, then sells from this inventory once an order is received. In addition, Gateway uses its own retail outlets to sell its computers. Below is selected financial information for both companies from a recent year's financial statements (in millions).

	Dell Computer Corporation	Gateway Inc.
Sales—fiscal 2001	$31,161	$6,080
Cost of goods sold	25,661	5,241
Inventory, beginning of fiscal 2001	400	315
Inventory, end of fiscal 2001	278	120

a. Determine for both companies (1) the inventory turnover and (2) the number of days' sales in inventory. Round to one digit after the decimal place.

b. Interpret the inventory ratios by considering Dell's and Gateway's operating strategies.

Exercise 14–16

Fixed asset analysis

Goal 3

a. Media Networks, 0.45

STUDENT SOLUTIONS MANUAL

The Walt Disney Co. reported segment information is as shown at the top of the following page.

A brief description of each segment is as follows:

Media Networks: The ABC television and radio network, Disney channel, ESPN, A&E, E!, and Disney.com.

Parks and Resorts: Disney World, Disneyland, Disney Cruise Line, and other resort properties.

Studio Entertainment: Walt Disney Pictures, Touchstone Pictures, Hollywood Pictures, Miramax, and Disney theatrical productions.

Consumer Products: Character merchandising and licensing, Disney stores, books, and magazines.

	Media Networks	Parks and Resorts	Studio Entertainment	Consumer Products
Sales—year ended Sept. 30, 2001	$ 9,596	$ 7,004	$6,106	$2,590
Identifiable fixed assets, Sept. 30, 2001	20,357	11,369	6,614	1,041
Identifiable fixed assets, Sept. 30, 2000	21,932	10,884	7,298	1,173

a. Determine for each business segment the fixed asset turnover for the year ended September 30, 2001. Round to the nearest two places after the decimal point.
b. Analyze your results.

Exercise 14–17

Leverage formula

Goal 4

a. 2000, 1.02%

International Paper Company is one of the world's largest manufacturers of paper and wood products. The following information (in millions) was disclosed on recent two-year comparative income statements:

	2001	2000
Net income (loss)*	$(1,142)	$368

*Before discontinued operations, extraordinary items, and cumulative effect from change in accounting principle.

Information (in millions) from three-year comparative balance sheets is as follows:

	Dec. 31, 2001	Dec. 31, 2000	Dec. 31, 1999
Total assets	$37,158	$42,109	$30,268
Total liabilities	26,867	30,075	19,964
Total stockholders' equity	10,291	12,034	10,304

a. Determine the rate earned on total assets for 2000 and 2001. Round to two decimal places.
b. Determine the rate earned on stockholders' equity, using the leverage formula, for 2000 and 2001. Round to two decimal places.
c. Analyze comparative ratios in (a) and (b) for the two years.

Exercise 14–18

Leverage formula

Goal 4

a. 16.51%

STUDENT SOLUTIONS MANUAL

Sigmund Psychiatric Hospitals, Inc., earned $180,000 in 2003 and $300,000 in 2004. The company began operations on January 1, 2003, with a $1,000,000 investment by stockholders and no debt. On January 1, 2004, the company borrowed $1,500,000 from a bank, payable in ten years.

a. Determine the rate earned on total assets and the rate earned on total stockholders' equity for 2003. Round to the nearest two decimal places.
b. Determine the rate earned on total assets for 2004. Round to the nearest two decimal places.
c. Use the leverage formula to determine the rate earned on stockholders' equity for 2004.

Exercise 14–19

Leverage analysis: current position

Goal 4

Current-year working capital, $1,085,000

The following data were taken from the balance sheet of Precision Gears Company:

	Current Year	Preceding Year
Cash	$280,000	$265,000
Marketable securities	131,000	121,000
Accounts and notes receivable (net)	395,000	384,000
Inventories	570,000	555,000
Prepaid expenses	19,000	40,000
Accounts and notes payable (short-term)	250,000	285,700
Accrued liabilities	60,000	64,300

a. Determine for each year (1) the working capital, (2) the current ratio, and (3) the quick ratio.
b. What conclusions can be drawn from these data as to the company's ability to meet its currently maturing debts?

Exercise 14–20

Leverage analysis: current position

Goal 4

a. (1) March 31, 2002 current ratio, 2.95

STUDENT SOLUTIONS MANUAL

Tommy Hilfiger Corp., the fashion apparel company, had the following current assets and current liabilities at the end of two recent years:

	March 31, 2002 (in thousands)	March 31, 2001 (in thousands)
Cash and cash equivalents	$387,247	$318,431
Accounts receivable	224,395	237,414
Inventories	184,972	205,446
Deferred tax and other current assets	97,274	90,353
Short-term borrowings	62,749	
Current portion of long-term debt	698	50,000
Accounts payable	28,980	38,628
Accrued expenses and other current liabilities	210,270	171,640

a. Determine the (1) current ratio and (2) quick ratio for both years. Round to two digits after the decimal place. Treat the deferred tax and other current assets as nonquick assets.
b. What conclusions can you draw from these data?

Exercise 14–21

Leverage analysis: current position

Goal 4

The bond indenture for the 10-year, $9\frac{1}{2}$% debenture bonds dated January 2, 2003, required working capital of $350,000, a current ratio of 1.5, and a quick ratio of 1 at the end of each calendar year until the bonds mature. At December 31, 2004, the three measures were computed as follows:

1. Current assets:

Cash	$245,000	
Marketable securities	123,000	
Accounts and notes receivable (net)	172,000	
Inventories	295,000	
Prepaid expenses	35,000	
Goodwill	150,000	
Total current assets		$1,020,000
Current liabilities:		
Accounts and short-term notes payable	$350,000	
Accrued liabilities	250,000	
Total current liabilities		600,000
Working capital		$ 420,000

2. Current ratio = 1.7 ($1,020,000 ÷ $600,000)
3. Quick ratio = 1.54 ($540,000 ÷ $350,000), rounded

a. Can you find any errors in the determination of the three measures of current position analysis?
b. Is the company satisfying the terms of the bond indenture?

Exercise 14–22

Leverage analysis: long-term debt position

Goal 4

a. Ratio of liabilities to stockholders' equity, Dec. 31, 2004, 0.63

STUDENT SOLUTIONS MANUAL

The following data were taken from the financial statements of Clear Spring Water Co. for December 31, 2004 and 2003:

	December 31, 2004	December 31, 2003
Accounts payable	$ 150,000	$ 204,000
Current maturities of serial bonds payable	300,000	300,000
Serial bonds payable, 8%, issued 1998, due 2008	1,800,000	2,100,000
Common stock, $1 par value	100,000	100,000
Paid-in capital in excess of par	800,000	800,000
Retained earnings	2,700,000	2,200,000

The income before income tax was $252,000 and $216,000 for the years 2004 and 2003, respectively.

a. Determine the ratio of liabilities to stockholders' equity at the end of each year. Round to two digits after the decimal place.
b. Determine the number of times the bond interest charges are earned during the year for both years.
c. What conclusions can be drawn from these data as to the company's ability to meet its currently maturing debts?

Exercise 14–23

Leverage analysis: Long-term debt position

Goal 4

Dow Jones & Co, Inc., and New York Times Co. are major publishers of financial and general news and information. Condensed financial statements for both companies for a recent year are as follows:

a. Ratio of fixed assets to long-term liabilities, Dow Jones, 1.16

Income Statements
For Year Ended December 31, 2001 (in thousands)

	Dow Jones	New York Times
Total revenues	$1,773,083	$3,015,958
Operating expenses	1,662,884	2,641,555
Income from operations	$ 110,199	$ 374,403
Other net gains or (losses)	(10,011)	12,650
Interest expense	500	47,199
Income before taxes	$ 99,688	$ 339,854
Income tax expense	10,794	137,632
Net income*	$ 88,894	$ 202,222

*From continuing operations before minority interest.

Balance Sheets
December 31, 2001 (in thousands)

	Dow Jones	New York Times
Current assets	$ 245,959	$ 559,890
Long-term investments	85,685	86,811
Property and equipment (net)	761,349	1,166,863
Intangible assets	205,347	1,625,120
Total assets	$1,298,340	$3,438,684
Current liabilities	$ 601,893	$ 860,876
Long-term debt	173,958	598,703
Other noncurrent liabilities	480,712	829,452
Total liabilities	$1,256,563	$2,289,031
Total stockholders' equity	41,777*	1,149,653
Total liabilities and stockholders' equity	$1,298,340	$3,438,684

*Includes treasury stock of $801,814.

a. Determine the following ratios for each company (round to nearest two digits):
   1. Ratio of fixed assets to long-term liabilities. Treat other noncurrent liabilities as long-term.
   2. Ratio of liabilities to stockholders' equity.
   3. Number of times interest charges earned.

b. Compare the debt position of the two companies from the ratios in (a).

Exercise 14–24

Stockholder ratios

Goal 5

b. Price-earnings ratio, 30

STUDENT SOLUTIONS MANUAL

The following information was taken from the financial statements of Arctic Air Conditioners Inc. for December 31 of the current fiscal year:

Common stock, $12 par value (no change during the year)	$4,800,000
Preferred $9 stock, $100 par, cumulative, nonparticipating (no change during the year)	1,200,000

The net income was $588,000, and the declared dividends on the common stock were $500,000 for the current year. The market price of the common stock is $36 per share.

For the common stock, determine the (a) earnings per share, (b) price-earnings ratio, (c) dividends per share, and (d) dividend yield. Round to two digits after the decimal place.

Exercise 14–25

Stockholder ratios

Goal 5

b. Dividends per share, $0.192

AFLAC, Inc., is the largest accident and health insurer in the United States. The stockholders' equity section of the balance sheet disclosed the following for December 31, 2001:

Shareholders' equity (in millions):	
Common stock	$ 403
Retained earnings	4,542
Accumulated other comprehensive income, net of taxes	2,091
Less: Treasury stock	1,611
Total shareholders' equity	$5,425

The Statement of Stockholders' Equity showed the following changes in the retained earnings balance for the year:

Retained earnings (in millions):	
Beginning of year (January 1, 2001)	$3,956
Net income	687
Dividends declared on common stock	(101)
End of year (December 31, 2001)	$4,542

During 2001, there were 525,098,000 shares outstanding for computing earnings per share. The market price of the common stock averaged $25 per share during January 2002.

Determine for the common stock (rounding to two decimal places):

a. Earnings per share.
b. Dividends per share.
c. Price-earnings ratio.
d. Dividend yield.

Exercise 14-26

Earnings per share

Goal 5

b. Earnings per share on common stock, $8.64

STUDENT SOLUTIONS MANUAL

The net income reported on the income statement of Southern Pulp and Paper Co. was $2,800,000. There were 250,000 shares of $20 par common stock and 80,000 shares of $8 cumulative preferred stock outstanding throughout the current year. The income statement included two extraordinary items: a $400,000 gain from condemnation of land and a $600,000 loss arising from flood damage, both after applicable income tax. Determine the per share figures for common stock for (a) income before extraordinary items and (b) net income.

Exercise 14-27

Leverage and stockholder ratios

Goals 4, 5

d. Price-earnings ratio, 20

The balance sheet for Aspen Properties Inc. at the end of the current fiscal year indicated the following:

Bonds payable, 12% (issued in 1993, due in 2013)	$3,000,000
Preferred $10 stock, $100 par	500,000
Common stock, $20 par	5,000,000

Income before income tax was $800,000, and income taxes were $200,000 for the current year. Cash dividends paid on common stock during the current year totaled $220,000. The common stock was selling for $44 per share at the end of the year. Determine each of the following: (a) number of times bond interest charges were earned, (b) earnings per share on common stock, (c) price-earnings ratio, (d) dividends per share of common stock, and (e) dividend yield. Round to two digits after the decimal place.

Exercise 14-28

Profitability and leverage ratios

Goals 2, 4

c. Ratio of net sales to assets, 1.09

STUDENT SOLUTIONS MANUAL

The following data were taken from the financial statements of Austin Labs Inc. for the current fiscal year:

Property, plant, and equipment (net)			$2,500,000
Liabilities:			
Current liabilities		$ 100,000	
Mortgage note payable, 7.5%, issued 1995, due 2010		1,200,000	
Total liabilities			$1,300,000
Stockholders' equity:			
Preferred $8 stock, $100 par, cumulative, nonparticipating (no change during year)			$ 600,000
Common stock, $10 par (no change during year)			1,600,000
Retained earnings:			
Balance, beginning of year	$900,000		
Net income	500,000	$1,400,000	
Preferred dividends	$ 48,000		
Common dividends	52,000	100,000	
Balance, end of year			1,300,000
Total stockholders' equity			$3,500,000
Net sales			$5,000,000
Interest expense			$ 90,000

Assuming that total assets were $4,400,000 at the beginning of the year, determine the following: (a) ratio of fixed assets to long-term liabilities, (b) ratio of liabilities to stockholders' equity, (c) asset turnover, (d) rate earned on total assets, and (e) rate earned on stockholders' equity. Round to two digits after the decimal place.

Accounting Application Problems

Problem 14–1A

Horizontal analysis for income statement

Goal 1

1. Sales, 30% increase

SPREADSHEET

For 2004, Better Biscuit Company reported its most significant increase in net income in years. At the end of the year, John Newton, the president, is presented with the following condensed comparative income statement:

Better Biscuit Company
Comparative Income Statement
For the Years Ended December 31, 2004 and 2003

	2004	2003
Sales	$715,000	$550,000
Sales returns and allowances	5,000	5,000
Net sales	$710,000	$545,000
Cost of goods sold	281,250	225,000
Gross profit	$428,750	$320,000
Selling expenses	$136,400	$110,000
Administrative expenses	42,350	35,000
Total operating expenses	$178,750	$145,000
Income from operations	$250,000	$175,000
Other income	3,500	3,000
Income before income tax	$253,500	$178,000
Income tax expense	85,000	60,000
Net income	$168,500	$118,000

Instructions

1. Prepare a comparative income statement with horizontal analysis for the two-year period, using 2003 as the base year. Round to two digits after the decimal place.
2. To the extent the data permit, comment on the significant relationships revealed by the horizontal analysis prepared in (1).

Problem 14–2A

Vertical analysis for income statement

Goal 1

1. Net income, 2004, 8.55%

SPREADSHEET

For 2004, Stainless Flow Systems Inc. initiated a sales promotion campaign that included the expenditure of an additional $50,000 for advertising. At the end of the year, Edwardo Gonzalez, the president, is presented with the following condensed comparative income statement shown at the top of the following page.

Instructions

1. Prepare a comparative income statement for the two-year period, presenting an analysis of each item in relationship to net sales for each of the years. Round to two digits after the decimal place.
2. To the extent the data permit, comment on the significant relationships revealed by the vertical analysis prepared in (1).

Stainless Flow Systems Inc.
Comparative Income Statement
For the Years Ended December 31, 2004 and 2003

	2004	2003
Net sales	$805,000	$770,000
Cost of goods sold	438,700	416,000
Gross profit	$366,300	$354,000
Selling expenses	$165,800	$115,800
Administrative expenses	96,600	93,400
Total operating expenses	$262,400	$209,200
Income from operations	$103,900	$144,800
Other income	2,000	1,800
Income before income tax	$105,900	$146,600
Income tax expense	37,000	51,000
Net income	$ 68,900	$ 95,600

Problem 14–3A

Effect of transactions on current position analysis

Goal 4

1. Quick ratio, 1.45

Data pertaining to the current position of Flintstone Aggregates Inc. are as follows:

Cash	$150,000
Marketable securities	64,000
Accounts and notes receivable (net)	221,000
Inventories	294,000
Prepaid expenses	11,000
Accounts payable	204,000
Notes payable (short-term)	66,000
Accrued expenses	30,000

Instructions

1. Compute (a) the working capital, (b) the current ratio, and (c) the quick ratio. Round to two digits after the decimal place.
2. List the following captions on a sheet of paper:

Transaction	Working Capital	Current Ratio	Quick Ratio

Compute the working capital, the current ratio, and the quick ratio after each of the following transactions, and record the results in the appropriate columns. Consider each transaction separately and assume that only that transaction affects the data given above. Round to two digits after the decimal point.

a. Sold marketable securities at no gain or loss, $34,000.
b. Paid accounts payable, $60,000.
c. Purchased goods on account, $40,000.
d. Paid notes payable, $20,000.
e. Declared a cash dividend, $25,000.
f. Declared a common stock dividend on common stock, $16,500.
g. Borrowed cash from bank on a long-term note, $120,000.
h. Received cash on account, $86,000.
i. Issued additional shares of stock for cash, $100,000.
j. Paid cash for prepaid expenses, $9,000.

Problem 14–4A

Profitability, asset efficiency, leverage, and stockholder ratios

Goals 2, 3, 4, 5

9. Ratio of liabilities to stockholders' equity, 0.7

The comparative financial statements of Integrity Technologies Inc. are shown on the next page. The market price of Integrity Technologies Inc. common stock was $80 on December 31, 2004.

Integrity Technologies Inc.
Comparative Retained Earnings Statement
For the Years Ended December 31, 2004 and 2003

	Dec. 31, 2004	Dec. 31, 2003
Retained earnings, January 1	$ 964,000	$ 689,000
Add net income for year	503,000	435,000
Total	$1,467,000	$1,124,000
Deduct dividends:		
On preferred stock	$ 48,000	$ 40,000
On common stock	120,000	120,000
Total	$ 168,000	$ 160,000
Retained earnings, December 31	$1,299,000	$ 964,000

Integrity Technologies Inc.
Comparative Balance Sheet
December 31, 2004 and 2003

	Dec. 31, 2004	Dec. 31, 2003
Assets		
Current assets:		
Cash	$ 200,000	$ 180,000
Marketable securities	923,000	215,000
Accounts receivable (net)	350,000	365,000
Inventories	500,000	480,000
Prepaid expenses	26,000	24,000
Total current assets	$1,999,000	$1,264,000
Property, plant, and equipment (net)	3,800,000	3,100,000
Total assets	$5,799,000	$4,364,000
Liabilities		
Current liabilities	$ 600,000	$ 400,000
Long-term liabilities:		
Mortgage note payable, 9%, due 2010	$ 800,000	—
Bonds payable, 8.5%, due 2014	1,000,000	$1,000,000
Total long-term liabilities	$1,800,000	$1,000,000
Total liabilities	$2,400,000	$1,400,000
Stockholders' Equity		
Preferred $8 stock, $100 par	$ 600,000	$ 500,000
Common stock, $10 par	1,500,000	1,500,000
Retained earnings	1,299,000	964,000
Total stockholders' equity	$3,399,000	$2,964,000
Total liabilities and stockholders' equity	$5,799,000	$4,364,000

Integrity Technologies Inc.
Comparative Income Statement
For the Years Ended December 31, 2004 and 2003

	2004	2003
Net sales	$6,100,000	$5,600,000
Cost of goods sold	2,800,000	2,550,000
Gross profit	$3,300,000	$3,050,000
Selling expenses	$1,450,000	$1,440,000
Administrative expenses	1,000,000	910,000
Total operating expenses	$2,450,000	$2,350,000
Income from operations	$ 850,000	$ 700,000
Other income	40,000	30,000
	$ 890,000	$ 730,000
Other expense (interest)	157,000	85,000
Income before income tax	$ 733,000	$ 645,000
Income tax expense	230,000	210,000
Net income	$ 503,000	$ 435,000

Instructions

Determine the following analyses for 2004, rounding to the nearest single digit after the decimal point:

1. Working capital
2. Current ratio
3. Quick ratio
4. Accounts receivable turnover
5. Number of days' sales in receivables
6. Inventory turnover
7. Number of days' sales in inventory
8. Ratio of fixed assets to long-term liabilities
9. Ratio of liabilities to stockholders' equity
10. Number of times interest charges earned
11. Asset turnover
12. Rate earned on total assets
13. Rate earned on stockholders' equity
14. Earnings per share on common stock
15. Price-earnings ratio
16. Dividends per share of common stock
17. Dividend yield
18. DuPont formula
19. Leverage formula

Problem 14–5A

Profitability and leverage trend analysis

Goals 2, 4

Jupiter Company has provided the following comparative information:

	2004	2003	2002	2001	2000
Net income	$ 100,000	$ 150,000	$ 150,000	$ 200,000	$ 250,000
Income tax expense	30,000	45,000	45,000	60,000	75,000
Interest	144,000	138,000	138,000	126,000	120,000
Average total assets	2,300,000	2,150,000	2,000,000	1,750,000	1,500,000
Average total stockholders' equity	1,100,000	1,000,000	850,000	700,000	500,000

You have been asked to evaluate the historical performance of the company over the last five years. Selected industry ratios have remained relatively steady for the last five years at the following levels:

	2000–2004
Rate earned on total assets	6%
Rate earned on stockholders' equity	15%
Number of times interest charges earned	3.0
Ratio of liabilities to stockholders' equity	1.5

Instructions

1. Prepare four line graphs, with the ratio on the vertical axis and the years on the horizontal axis for the following four ratios (round to two digits after the decimal place):
   a. Rate earned on total assets
   b. Rate earned on stockholders' equity
   c. Number of times interest charges earned
   d. Ratio of liabilities to stockholders' equity (using average balances)

   Display both the company ratio and the industry benchmark on each graph (each graph should have two lines).
2. Prepare an analysis of the graphs in (1).

Alternative Accounting Application Problems

Alternate Problem 14–1B

Horizontal analysis for income statement

Goal 1

1. Sales, 15% increase

STUDENT SOLUTIONS MANUAL

SPREADSHEET

For 2004, Chow Company reported its most significant decline in net income in years. At the end of the year, Hai Chow, the president, is presented with the following condensed comparative income statement:

Chow Company
Comparative Income Statement
For the Years Ended December 31, 2004 and 2003

	2004	2003
Sales	$690,000	$600,000
Sales returns and allowances	5,000	2,000
Net sales	$685,000	$598,000
Cost of goods sold	341,600	280,000
Gross profit	$343,400	$318,000
Selling expenses	$147,000	$105,000
Administrative expenses	81,250	65,000
Total operating expenses	$228,250	$170,000
Income from operations	$115,150	$148,000
Other income	2,500	2,000
Income before income tax	$117,650	$150,000
Income tax expense	32,000	40,000
Net income	$ 85,650	$110,000

Instructions

1. Prepare a comparative income statement with horizontal analysis for the two-year period, using 2003 as the base year. Round to two digits after the decimal place.
2. To the extent the data permit, comment on the significant relationships revealed by the horizontal analysis prepared in (1).

Alternate Problem 14–2B

Vertical analysis for income statement

Goal 1

1. Net income, 2004, 13.58%

STUDENT SOLUTIONS MANUAL

SPREADSHEET

For 2004, Guardian Home Security Company initiated a sales promotion campaign that included the expenditure of an additional $10,000 for advertising. At the end of the year, Gordon Kincaid, the president, is presented with the following condensed comparative income statement:

Guardian Home Security Company
Comparative Income Statement
For the Years Ended December 31, 2004 and 2003

	2004	2003
Net sales	$589,000	$480,000
Cost of goods sold	253,000	216,000
Gross profit	$336,000	$264,000
Selling expenses	$153,000	$136,500
Administrative expenses	71,000	64,500
Total operating expenses	$224,000	$201,000
Income from operations	$112,000	$ 63,000
Other income	2,500	2,000
Income before income tax	$114,500	$ 65,000
Income tax expense	34,500	20,000
Net income	$ 80,000	$ 45,000

Instructions

1. Prepare a comparative income statement for the two-year period, presenting an analysis of each item in relationship to net sales for each of the years. Round to two digits after the decimal place.
2. To the extent the data permit, comment on the significant relationships revealed by the vertical analysis prepared in (1).

Alternate Problem 14–3B

Effect of transactions on current position analysis

Goal 4

1. Current ratio, 1.96

STUDENT SOLUTIONS MANUAL

Data pertaining to the current position of Porter Glass Company are as follows:

Cash	$221,000
Marketable securities	95,000
Accounts and notes receivable (net)	345,000
Inventories	410,000
Prepaid expenses	22,000
Accounts payable	412,000
Notes payable (short-term)	100,000
Accrued expenses	45,000

Instructions

1. Compute (a) the working capital, (b) the current ratio, and (c) the quick ratio. Round to two digits after the decimal place.

2. List the following captions on a sheet of paper:

Transaction	Working Capital	Current Ratio	Quick Ratio

Compute the working capital, the current ratio, and the quick ratio after each of the following transactions, and record the results in the appropriate columns. Consider each transaction separately and assume that only that transaction affects the data given above. Round to two digits after the decimal point.

a. Sold marketable securities at no gain or loss, $56,000.
b. Paid accounts payable, $60,000.
c. Purchased goods on account, $80,000.
d. Paid notes payable, $40,000.
e. Declared a cash dividend, $25,000.
f. Declared a common stock dividend on common stock, $28,500.
g. Borrowed cash from bank on a long-term note, $120,000.
h. Received cash on account, $164,000.
i. Issued additional shares of stock for cash, $250,000.
j. Paid cash for prepaid expenses, $10,000.

Alternate Problem 14–4B

Profitability, asset efficiency, leverage, and stockholder ratios

Goals 2, 3, 4, 5

5. Number of days' sales in receivables, 45.4

STUDENT SOLUTIONS MANUAL

The comparative financial statements of Victor Audio Company are as follows. The market price of Victor Audio Company common stock was $105 on December 31, 2004.

Victor Audio Company
Comparative Balance Sheet
December 31, 2004 and 2003

	Dec. 31, 2004	Dec. 31, 2003
Assets		
Current assets:		
Cash	$ 87,000	$ 176,000
Marketable securities	258,000	335,000
Accounts receivable (net)	261,000	235,000
Inventories	212,000	190,000
Prepaid expenses	25,000	18,000
Total current assets	$ 843,000	$ 954,000
Property, plant, and equipment (net)	2,675,000	1,450,000
Total assets	$3,518,000	$2,404,000
Liabilities		
Current liabilities	$ 450,000	$ 310,000
Long-term liabilities:		
Mortgage note payable, 8%, due 2009	$ 400,000	—
Bonds payable, 12%, due 2013	600,000	$ 600,000
Total long-term liabilities	$1,000,000	$ 600,000
Total liabilities	$1,450,000	$ 910,000
Stockholders' Equity		
Preferred $6 stock, $100 par	$ 500,000	$ 300,000
Common stock, $10 par	800,000	800,000
Retained earnings	768,000	394,000
Total stockholders' equity	$2,068,000	$1,494,000
Total liabilities and stockholders' equity	$3,518,000	$2,404,000

Victor Audio Company
Comparative Retained Earnings Statement
For the Years Ended December 31, 2004 and 2003

	Dec. 31, 2004	Dec. 31, 2003
Retained earnings, January 1	$394,000	$ 50,000
Add net income for year	420,000	378,000
Total	$814,000	$428,000
Deduct dividends:		
On preferred stock	$ 30,000	$ 18,000
On common stock	16,000	16,000
Total	$ 46,000	$ 34,000
Retained earnings, December 31	$768,000	$394,000

Victor Audio Company
Comparative Income Statement
For the Years Ended December 31, 2004 and 2003

	2004	2003
Net sales	$2,100,000	$1,900,000
Cost of goods sold	840,000	770,000
Gross profit	$1,260,000	$1,130,000
Selling expenses	$ 410,000	$ 370,000
Administrative expenses	305,000	290,000
Total operating expenses	$ 715,000	$ 660,000
Income from operations	$ 545,000	$ 470,000
Other income	20,000	15,000
	$ 565,000	$ 485,000
Other expense (interest)	104,000	72,000
Income before income tax	$ 461,000	$ 413,000
Income tax expense	41,000	35,000
Net income	$ 420,000	$ 378,000

Instructions

Determine the following analyses for 2004, rounding to the nearest single digit after the decimal point:

1. Working capital
2. Current ratio
3. Quick ratio
4. Accounts receivable turnover
5. Number of days' sales in receivables
6. Inventory turnover
7. Number of days' sales in inventory
8. Ratio of fixed assets to long-term liabilities
9. Ratio of liabilities to stockholders' equity
10. Number of times interest charges earned

11. Asset turnover
12. Rate earned on total assets
13. Rate earned on stockholders' equity
14. Earnings per share on common stock
15. Price-earnings ratio
16. Dividends per share of common stock
17. Dividend yield
18. DuPont formula
19. Leverage formula

Alternate Problem 14–5B

Profitability and leverage and trend analysis

Goals 2, 4

STUDENT SOLUTIONS MANUAL

Nova Company has provided the following comparative information:

	2004	2003	2002	2001	2000
Net income	$ 400,000	$ 300,000	$ 200,000	$ 100,000	$ 50,000
Income tax expense	100,000	75,000	50,000	25,000	12,500
Interest	88,000	72,000	56,000	48,000	40,000
Average total assets	2,600,000	2,000,000	1,500,000	1,200,000	1,000,000
Average total stockholders' equity	1,500,000	1,100,000	800,000	600,000	500,000

You have been asked to evaluate the historical performance of the company over the last five years. Selected industry ratios have remained relatively steady for the last five years at the following levels:

	2000–2004
Rate earned on total assets	12%
Rate earned on stockholders' equity	18%
Number of times interest charges earned	5.0
Ratio of liabilities to stockholders' equity	0.9

Instructions

1. Prepare four line graphs, with the ratio on the vertical axis and the years on the horizontal axis for the following four ratios (rounded to two digits after the decimal place):
   a. Rate earned on total assets
   b. Rate earned on stockholders' equity
   c. Number of times interest charges earned
   d. Ratio of liabilities to stockholders' equity (using average balances)

   Display both the company ratio and the industry benchmark on each graph (each graph should have two lines).
2. Prepare an analysis of the graphs in (1).

Building Leadership Skills—Financial Analysis and Reporting

Case 14–1

Vertical analysis

The condensed income statements through income from operations for Dell Computer Corporation and Apple Computer Co. are reproduced below for recent fiscal years (numbers in millions):

	Dell Computer Corporation For the Year Ended February 1, 2002	Apple Computer Co. For the Year Ended September 29, 2001
Sales (net)	$31,168	$5,363
Cost of sales	25,661	4,128
Gross profit	$ 5,507	$1,235
Selling, general, and administrative expense	$ 2,784	$1,138
Research and development	452	430
Special charges	482	11
Operating expenses	$ 3,718	$1,579
Income from operations	$ 1,789	$ (344)

Prepare comparative common-size statements, rounding to two digits after the whole percent. Interpret the analyses.

Case 14–2

Comprehensive leverage analysis

Marriott International Inc. and Hilton Hotels Corp. are two major owners and managers of lodging and resort properties in the United States. Abstracted income statement information for the two companies is as follows for the year ended December 31, 2001:

	Marriott (in millions)	Hilton (in millions)
Operating profit before other expenses and interest	$ 590	$ 495
Other income (expenses)	(111)	48
Interest expense	(109)	(237)
Income before income taxes	$ 370	$ 306
Income tax expense	134	130
Net income	$ 236	$ 176

Balance sheet information is as follows:

	Marriott Dec. 31, 2001 (in millions)	Hilton Dec. 31, 2001 (in millions)
Total liabilities	$5,629	$7,498
Total stockholders' equity	3,478	1,642
Total liabilities and stockholders' equity	$9,107	$9,140

The average liabilities, stockholders' equity, and total assets for 2001 were as follows:

	Marriott (in millions)	Hilton (in millions)
Average total liabilities	$5,300	$7,250
Average total stockholders' equity	3,373	1,713
Average total assets	8,673	8,963

1. Determine the following ratios for both companies. (Round to the nearest two digits after the whole percent.)
   a. Rate earned on total assets
   b. Rate earned on total stockholders' equity
   c. Number of times interest charges are earned
   d. Ratio of liabilities to stockholders' equity
2. Determine the leverage formula for both companies
3. Analyze and compare the two companies, using the information in (1) and (2).

Case 14–3

Profitability and stockholder ratios

Ford Motor Company is the second largest automobile and truck manufacturer in the United States. In addition to manufacturing motor vehicles, Ford also provides vehicle-related financing, insurance, and leasing services. Historically, people purchase automobiles when the economy is strong and delay automobile purchases when the economy is faltering. For this reason, Ford is considered a cyclical company. This means that when the economy does well, Ford usually prospers, while when the economy is down, Ford usually suffers.

The following information is available for three recent years (in millions except per share amounts):

	2001	2000	1999
Net income (loss)	$(5,453)	$3,467	$7,237
Preferred dividends	$15	$15	$15
Shares outstanding for computing earnings per share	1,820	1,483	1,210
Cash dividend per share	$1.05	$1.80	$1.88
Average total assets	$279,967	$277,305	$256,887
Average stockholders' equity	$13,198	$23,107	$25,473
Average stock price	$21.32	$24.10	$29.55

1. Calculate the following ratios for each year:
   a. Rate earned on total assets
   b. Rate earned on stockholders' equity
   c. Earnings per share
   d. Dividend yield
   e. Price-earnings ratio
2. What is the leverage formula for 2001?
3. Why does Ford have so much leverage?
4. Explain the direction of the dividend yield and price-earnings ratio in light of Ford's profitability trend.

Case 14–4

Profitability and leverage analysis

AMC Entertainment Inc. is one of the largest exhibitors of motion pictures in the United States.

The condensed liabilities and stockholders' equity portion of AMC's balance sheet for March 28, 2002, is as follows:

Total current liabilities	$ 249,816,000
Long-term debt	650,969,000
Other long-term liabilities	120,029,000
Total liabilities	$1,020,814,000
Stockholders' equity (deficit):	
Series A Convertible Preferred	$ 175,000
Common Stock	20,025,000
Convertible Class B Stock	2,535,000
Additional paid-in capital	430,902,000
Accumulated other comprehensive loss	(16,967,000)
Accumulated deficit	(167,515,000)
	$ 269,155,000
Less:	
Common Stock in treasury, at cost, and other deductions	(10,799,000)
Total stockholders' equity	$ 258,356,000
Total liabilities and stockholders' equity	$1,279,170,000

Additional information:

Preferred dividends: $29,421,000
Common shares outstanding for computing earnings per share: 23,692,000
Total assets, March 29, 2001: $1,047,264,000
Total stockholders' equity, March 29, 2001: $(59,045,000)

AMC's income statement for a recent year-end was as follows:

AMC Entertainment Inc.
Income Statement
For the Year Ended March 28, 2002

	2002/03/28
Revenues	
Admissions	$ 901,566,000
Concessions	359,042,000
Other	80,898,000
Total revenues	$1,341,506,000
Expenses	
Film exhibition costs	$ 487,577,000
Concession costs	45,756,000
Theatre operating expense	327,665,000
Rent	236,829,000
Depreciation and amortization	99,742,000
Other	92,378,000
Total costs and expenses	$1,289,947,000
Operating income (loss)	$ 51,559,000
Other expense (income)	
Other expense (income)	$ 1,667,000
Interest expense	60,760,000
Loss before income taxes	$ (10,868,000)
Income tax provision	600,000
Net loss	$ (11,468,000)

1. Determine the following:
   a. DuPont formula
   b. Leverage formula
   c. Total operating profit as a percent of sales
   d. Concession operating profit as a percent of concession sales
   e. Number of times interest charges are earned
   f. Earnings per share
2. Evaluate AMC's financial performance, using the calculations in (1).
3. How do you believe AMC's stockholders' equity moved from a deficit of $59,045,000 on March 29, 2001, to $258,356,000 on March 28, 2002?

Case 14–5

Comprehensive DuPont analysis, company comparative

Merck & Co. is one of the largest global pharmaceutical companies in the world, and Amgen, Inc., is one of the largest biotechnology companies in the world. Both companies provide human health products. Merck develops new products principally by discovering new chemical combinations, while Amgen relies on using advanced cellular and molecular biology (gene therapies) to discover new products. Comparative condensed income statements for both companies are as follows:

Merck & Co. and Amgen, Inc.
Comparative Income Statements
For the Year Ended Dec. 31, 2001
(in thousands)

	Merck	Amgen
Sales	$47,715,700	$4,015,700
Costs, expenses, and other		
Cost of sales	28,976,500	443,000
Marketing and administrative	6,224,400	970,700
Research and development	2,456,400	865,000
Equity income from affiliates	(685,900)	2,700
Other (income) expense, net	367,100	203,100
Total expenses	$37,338,500	$2,484,500
Other income (expense):		
Interest and other income, net	490,100	168,700
Interest expense, net	(464,700)	(13,600)
Total other income	$ 25,400	$ 155,100
Income before taxes	$10,402,600	$1,686,300
Taxes on income	3,120,800	566,600
Net income	$ 7,281,800	$1,119,700

Average 2001 balances from the comparative balance sheets for both companies were as follows:

(in thousands)	Merck	Amgen
Average total assets	$42,080,800	$5,921,350
Average accounts receivable	5,238,900	443,200
Average inventory	3,300,400	330,400
Average fixed assets	12,292,750	1,863,800

1. Prepare a common-size income statement for both companies. (Round to the nearest single decimal place after the whole percent.)
2. Determine the DuPont formula for each company
3. Calculate the accounts receivable, inventory, and fixed asset turnovers for each company.
4. Analyze and compare the two companies, based on the analyses in (1)–(3).

Case 14–6

Comprehensive DuPont analysis, trend analysis

American Airlines Inc. is the largest passenger airline in the world. Condensed income statement information for American is as follows:

American Airlines Inc.
Comparative Income Statements
For the Years Ended December 31, 2001, 2000, 1999
(in millions)

	2001	2000	1999
REVENUES	$17,484	$18,117	$16,338
EXPENSES			
Wages, salaries, and benefits	$ 7,566	$ 6,354	$ 5,747
Aircraft fuel	2,744	2,372	1,622
Depreciation and amortization	1,257	1,068	977
Other rentals and landing fees	1,113	919	867
Maintenance, materials, and repairs	979	899	833
Aircraft rentals	799	561	582
Commissions to agents	786	973	1,090
Food service	771	769	734
Other operating expenses	3,322	2,958	2,866
Special charges, net of U.S. Government grant	421	0	0
Total operating expenses	$19,758	$16,873	$15,318
OPERATING INCOME (LOSS)	$ (2,274)	$ 1,244	$ 1,020
OTHER INCOME (EXPENSE)	(175)	38	34
EARNINGS (LOSS) BEFORE INCOME TAXES	$ (2,449)	$ 1,282	$ 1,054
Income tax provision (benefit)	(887)	504	427
NET EARNINGS (LOSS)	$ (1,562)	$ 778	$ 627

The average total assets for American Airlines for the comparative years were as follows:

	2001	2000	1999
Average total assets	$26,819	$22,440	$20,471

1. Prepare common-size statements for the three comparative years.
2. Calculate the DuPont formula for the three comparative years.
3. Analyze the company's performance trend for the three comparative years, using the information in (1) and (2).

Building Leadership Skills—Responsible Leadership

Activity 14–1

Ethics and professional conduct in business

ETHICS

Lee Camden, president of Camden Equipment Co., prepared a draft of the President's Letter to be included with Camden Equipment Co.'s 2004 annual report. The letter mentions a 10% increase in sales and a recent expansion of plant facilities, but fails to mention the net loss of $180,000 for the year. You have been asked to review the letter for the annual report.

How would you respond to the omission of the net loss of $180,000? Specifically, is such an action ethical?

Activity 14–2

Analysis of financing corporate growth

Assume that the president of Crest Brewery made the following statement in the President's Letter to Shareholders:

"The founding family and majority shareholders of the company do not believe in using debt to finance future growth. The founding family learned from hard experience during Prohibition and the Great Depression that debt can cause loss of flexibility and eventual loss of corporate control. The company will not place itself at such risk. As such, all future growth will be financed either by stock sales to the public or by internally generated resources."

As a public shareholder of this company, how would you respond to this policy?

Activity 14–3

Receivables and inventory turnover

Imex Computer Company has completed its fiscal year on December 31, 2004. The auditor, Sandra Blake, has approached the CFO, Travis Williams, regarding the year-end receivables and inventory levels of Imex. The following conversation takes place:

Sandra: We are beginning our audit of Imex and have prepared ratio analyses to determine if there have been significant changes in operations or financial position. This helps us guide the audit process. This analysis indicates that the inventory turnover has decreased from 5 to 2.8, while the accounts receivable turnover has decreased from 12 to 8. I was wondering if you could explain this change in operations.

Travis: There is little need for concern. The inventory represents computers that we were unable to sell during the holiday buying season. We are confident, however, that we will be able to sell these computers as we move into the next fiscal year.

Sandra: What gives you this confidence?

Travis: We will increase our advertising and provide some very attractive price concessions to move these machines. We have no choice. Newer technology is already out there, and we have to unload this inventory.

Sandra: . . . and the receivables?

Travis: As you may be aware, the company is under tremendous pressure to expand sales and profits. As a result, we lowered our credit standards to our commercial customers so that we would be able to sell products to a broader customer base. As a result of this policy change, we have been able to expand sales by 35 percent.

Sandra: Your responses have not been reassuring to me.

Travis: I'm a little confused. Assets are good, right? Why don't you look at our current ratio? It has improved, hasn't it? I would think that you would view that very favorably.

Why is Sandra concerned about the inventory and accounts receivable turnover ratios and Travis's responses to them? What action may Sandra need to take? How would you respond to Travis's last comment?

Activity 14–4

Projecting Microsoft financial statements

Go to the Microsoft Web site at www.microsoft.com and click on the "Investor Relations" area of Microsoft's Web environment. Select the menu item "analysis tools." Select the "what if" tool. With this tool, use horizontal and vertical information to create a full year's projection of the Microsoft income statement. Make the following assumptions:

Revenue growth	16%
Cost of goods sold as a percent of revenue:	18%
Research and development growth	12%
Sales and marketing as a percent of sales	20%
General and administrative as a percent of sales	4%
Tax rate	35%
Diluted shares outstanding	5,500

Activity 14–5

The role of the professional analyst

Henry Blodget was the famed Internet analyst for Merrill Lynch. The Attorney General of the State of New York released internal Merrill Lynch e-mails that gave a picture of the inside of the research arm of a major investment bank. The following article summarizes some of the insights:

> InfoSpace, *an investment banking client from August 2000 to December 2000, was featured as a "Favored 15" Merrill Lynch stock. During that time Blodget wrote* (internally) *that he had "enormous skepticism" about the stock and called it a "piece of junk," about which large investors had made "bad smell comments."*
>
> *However, InfoSpace wasn't downgraded until December 11, 2000, when it had fallen more than 90 percent from its high. And even then, it was only downgraded to "accumulate" for investors looking for gains within 12 months and "buy" for those with a longer-term horizon.*
>
> *Then there's* GoTo.com, *now known as* Overture Service. *Blodget got an inquiry from an institutional investor asking "what's so interesting about GoTo except banking fees?" Blodget replied "nothin." But that didn't stop his team from rating GoTo as a long-term "buy."*
>
> *In addition, in a move fraught with conflicts of interest, a junior analyst solicited input from GoTo management, which sometimes typed recommended changes right onto a draft report.*
>
> *Frustrated with pressures to inflate the rating, the junior analyst wrote to Blodget in an expletive-filled e-mail. The rating, she said, would mean "John and Mary Smith are losing their retirement because we don't want (GoTo's CFO) to be mad at us."*
>
> *She went on to say that "the whole idea that we are independent from banking is a big lie." Without the investment banking pressures, she said, she'd rate the stock "neutral" in the short term and "accumulate" in the longer term.*
>
> *Yet another case involved* Internet Capital Group, *an investment banking client that Merrill rated starting in August 1999 at "accumulate" for the next 12 months and "buy" in the longer term. After reaching a high of $212 in late 1999, the stock was trading at $12.38 in October 2000.*
>
> *Blodget confided in an e-mail to another analyst that he thought the stock was "going to 5," adding the next day that Internet Capital "has been a disaster . . . there really is no floor to the stock."*
>
> *However, it wasn't until a month later that Merrill downgraded the stock, and then only to "accumulate" for both the short and long term.*

Source: Deborah Lohse, "Probe Finds Analysts Recommending Stocks They Privately Bad-Mouthed," *San Jose Mercury News, Calif.*, 04/12/2002, KRTBN Knight-Ridder Tribune Business News: San Jose Mercury News

1. What is the nature of the problem identified in the article above?
2. How could it be solved?

Answers to Self-Study Questions

1. **A** Percentage analysis indicating the relationship of the component parts to the total in a financial statement, such as the relationship of current assets to total assets (20% to 100%) in the question, is called vertical analysis (answer A). Percentage analysis of increases and decreases in corresponding items in comparative financial statements is called horizontal analysis (answer B). An example of horizontal analysis would be the presentation of the amount of current assets in the preceding balance sheet, along with the amount of current assets at the end of the current year, with the increase or decrease in current assets between the periods expressed as a percentage. Profitability analysis (answer C) is the analysis of a firm's ability to earn income. Asset efficiency analysis (answer D) segments the asset turnover ratio into subcategories of assets.

2. **D** Current ratio: $\frac{\text{Current assets}}{\text{Current liabilities}} =$

$$\frac{\$275{,}000}{\$100{,}000} = 2.75$$

Quick ratio: $\frac{\text{Quick assets}}{\text{Current liabilities}} =$

$$\frac{\$175{,}000}{\$100{,}000} = 1.75$$

3. **D** Accounts receivable turnover:

$$\frac{\text{Sales (net)}}{\text{Average Accounts Receivable (net)}} =$$

$$\frac{\$1{,}000{,}000}{(\$200{,}000 + \$300{,}000)/2} = 4.0$$

Number of days' sales in accounts receivable:

$$\frac{\text{Accounts Receivable, ending bal. (net)}}{\text{Average daily sales}} =$$

$$\frac{\$300{,}000}{\$1{,}000{,}000 \div 365} = 109$$

4. **A** The DuPont ratio segments the rate earned on total assets into the product of the profit margin and the asset turnover (answer A). The rate earned on stockholders' equity is not explained by the DuPont ratio, but is explained by leverage. (Answers B and C are true statements, but they are not the Dupont formula.) Answer D is meaningless.

5. **C** The number of days' sales in inventory (answer C), which is determined by dividing the inventories at the end of the year by the average daily cost of goods sold, expresses the relationship between the cost of goods sold and inventory. It indicates the efficiency in the management of inventory. The working capital ratio (answer A) indicates the ability of the business to meet currently maturing obligations (debt). The quick ratio (answer B) indicates the "instant" debt-paying ability of the business. The ratio of fixed assets to long-term liabilities (answer D) indicates the margin of safety for long-term creditors.

Appendices

A Interest Tables

B Codes of Professional Ethics for Accountants

C Using the Internet for Fiancial Research

D The Home Depot Annual Report

Appendix A: Interest Tables

Present Value of $1 at Compound Interest Due in *n* Periods: $p_{\overline{n}\backslash i} = \frac{1}{(1+i)^n}$

n \ i	5%	5.5%	6%	6.5%	7%	8%
1	0.95238	0.94787	0.94334	0.93897	0.93458	0.92593
2	0.90703	0.89845	0.89000	0.88166	0.87344	0.85734
3	0.86384	0.85161	0.83962	0.82785	0.81630	0.79383
4	0.82270	0.80722	0.79209	0.77732	0.76290	0.73503
5	0.78353	0.76513	0.74726	0.72988	0.71290	0.68058
6	0.74622	0.72525	0.70496	0.68533	0.66634	0.63017
7	0.71068	0.68744	0.66506	0.64351	0.62275	0.58349
8	0.67684	0.65160	0.62741	0.60423	0.58201	0.54027
9	0.64461	0.61763	0.59190	0.56735	0.54393	0.50025
10	0.61391	0.58543	0.55840	0.53273	0.50835	0.46319
11	0.58468	0.55491	0.52679	0.50021	0.47509	0.42888
12	0.55684	0.52598	0.49697	0.46968	0.44401	0.39711
13	0.53032	0.49856	0.46884	0.44102	0.41496	0.36770
14	0.50507	0.47257	0.44230	0.41410	0.38782	0.34046
15	0.48102	0.44793	0.41726	0.38883	0.36245	0.31524
16	0.45811	0.42458	0.39365	0.36510	0.33874	0.29189
17	0.43630	0.40245	0.37136	0.34281	0.31657	0.27027
18	0.41552	0.38147	0.35034	0.32189	0.29586	0.25025
19	0.39573	0.36158	0.33051	0.30224	0.27651	0.23171
20	0.37689	0.34273	0.31180	0.28380	0.25842	0.21455
21	0.35894	0.32486	0.29416	0.26648	0.24151	0.19866
22	0.34185	0.30793	0.27750	0.25021	0.22571	0.18394
23	0.32557	0.29187	0.26180	0.23494	0.21095	0.17032
24	0.31007	0.27666	0.24698	0.22060	0.19715	0.15770
25	0.29530	0.26223	0.23300	0.20714	0.18425	0.14602
26	0.28124	0.24856	0.21981	0.19450	0.17211	0.13520
27	0.26785	0.23560	0.20737	0.18263	0.16093	0.12519
28	0.25509	0.22332	0.19563	0.17148	0.15040	0.11591
29	0.24295	0.21168	0.18456	0.16101	0.14056	0.10733
30	0.23138	0.20064	0.17411	0.15119	0.13137	0.09938
31	0.22036	0.19018	0.16426	0.14196	0.12277	0.09202
32	0.20987	0.18027	0.15496	0.13329	0.11474	0.08520
33	0.19987	0.17087	0.14619	0.12516	0.10724	0.07889
34	0.19036	0.16196	0.13791	0.11752	0.10022	0.07304
35	0.18129	0.15352	0.13010	0.11035	0.09366	0.06764
40	0.14205	0.11746	0.09722	0.08054	0.06678	0.04603
45	0.11130	0.08988	0.07265	0.05879	0.04761	0.03133
50	0.08720	0.06877	0.05429	0.04291	0.03395	0.02132

Present Value of $1 at Compound Interest Due in *n* Periods: $p_{\overline{n}\backslash i} = \dfrac{1}{(1+i)^n}$

n \ i	9%	10%	11%	12%	13%	14%
1	0.91743	0.90909	0.90090	0.89286	0.88496	0.87719
2	0.84168	0.82645	0.81162	0.79719	0.78315	0.76947
3	0.77218	0.75132	0.73119	0.71178	0.69305	0.67497
4	0.70842	0.68301	0.65873	0.63552	0.61332	0.59208
5	0.64993	0.62092	0.59345	0.56743	0.54276	0.51937
6	0.59627	0.56447	0.53464	0.50663	0.48032	0.45559
7	0.54703	0.51316	0.48166	0.45235	0.42506	0.39964
8	0.50187	0.46651	0.43393	0.40388	0.37616	0.35056
9	0.46043	0.42410	0.39092	0.36061	0.33288	0.30751
10	0.42241	0.38554	0.35218	0.32197	0.29459	0.26974
11	0.38753	0.35049	0.31728	0.28748	0.26070	0.23662
12	0.35554	0.31863	0.28584	0.25668	0.23071	0.20756
13	0.32618	0.28966	0.25751	0.22917	0.20416	0.18207
14	0.29925	0.26333	0.23199	0.20462	0.18068	0.15971
15	0.27454	0.23939	0.20900	0.18270	0.15989	0.14010
16	0.25187	0.21763	0.18829	0.16312	0.14150	0.12289
17	0.23107	0.19784	0.16963	0.14564	0.12522	0.10780
18	0.21199	0.17986	0.15282	0.13004	0.11081	0.09456
19	0.19449	0.16351	0.13768	0.11611	0.09806	0.08295
20	0.17843	0.14864	0.12403	0.10367	0.08678	0.07276
21	0.16370	0.13513	0.11174	0.09256	0.07680	0.06383
22	0.15018	0.12285	0.10067	0.08264	0.06796	0.05599
23	0.13778	0.11168	0.09069	0.07379	0.06014	0.04911
24	0.12640	0.10153	0.08170	0.06588	0.05323	0.04308
25	0.11597	0.09230	0.07361	0.05882	0.04710	0.03779
26	0.10639	0.08390	0.06631	0.05252	0.04168	0.03315
27	0.09761	0.07628	0.05974	0.04689	0.03689	0.02908
28	0.08955	0.06934	0.05382	0.04187	0.03264	0.02551
29	0.08216	0.06304	0.04849	0.03738	0.02889	0.02237
30	0.07537	0.05731	0.04368	0.03338	0.02557	0.01963
31	0.06915	0.05210	0.03935	0.02980	0.02262	0.01722
32	0.06344	0.04736	0.03545	0.02661	0.02002	0.01510
33	0.05820	0.04306	0.03194	0.02376	0.01772	0.01325
34	0.05331	0.03914	0.02878	0.02121	0.01568	0.01162
35	0.04899	0.03558	0.02592	0.01894	0.01388	0.01019
40	0.03184	0.02210	0.01538	0.01075	0.00753	0.00529
45	0.02069	0.01372	0.00913	0.00610	0.00409	0.00275
50	0.01345	0.00852	0.00542	0.00346	0.00222	0.00143

Present Value of Ordinary Annuity of $1 per Period: $p_{\overline{n}\backslash i} = \dfrac{1 - \dfrac{1}{(1+i)^n}}{i}$

$n \backslash i$	5%	5.5%	6%	6.5%	7%	8%
1	0.95238	0.94787	0.94340	0.93897	0.93458	0.92593
2	1.85941	1.84632	1.83339	1.82063	1.80802	1.78326
3	2.72325	2.69793	2.67301	2.64848	2.62432	2.57710
4	3.54595	3.50515	3.46511	3.42580	3.38721	3.31213
5	4.32948	4.27028	4.21236	4.15568	4.10020	3.99271
6	5.07569	4.99553	4.91732	4.84101	4.76654	4.62288
7	5.78637	5.68297	5.58238	5.48452	5.38923	5.20637
8	6.46321	6.33457	6.20979	6.08875	5.97130	5.74664
9	7.10782	6.95220	6.80169	6.65610	6.51523	6.24689
10	7.72174	7.53763	7.36009	7.18883	7.02358	6.71008
11	8.30641	8.09254	7.88688	7.68904	7.49867	7.13896
12	8.86325	8.61852	8.38384	8.15873	7.94269	7.53608
13	9.39357	9.11708	8.85268	8.59974	8.35765	7.90378
14	9.89864	9.58965	9.29498	9.01384	8.74547	8.22424
15	10.37966	10.03758	9.71225	9.40267	9.10791	8.55948
16	10.83777	10.46216	10.10590	9.76776	9.44665	8.85137
17	11.27407	10.86461	10.47726	10.11058	9.76322	9.12164
18	11.68959	11.24607	10.82760	10.43247	10.05909	9.37189
19	12.08532	11.60765	11.15812	10.73471	10.33560	9.60360
20	12.46221	11.95038	11.46992	11.01851	10.59401	9.81815
21	12.82115	12.27524	11.76408	11.28498	10.83553	10.01680
22	13.16300	12.58317	12.04158	11.53520	11.06124	10.20074
23	13.48857	12.87504	12.30338	11.77014	11.27219	10.37106
24	13.79864	13.15170	12.55036	11.99074	11.46933	10.52876
25	14.09394	13.41393	12.78336	12.19788	11.65358	10.67478
26	14.37518	13.66250	13.00317	12.39237	11.82578	10.80998
27	14.64303	13.89810	13.21053	12.57500	11.98671	10.93516
28	14.89813	14.12142	13.40616	12.74648	12.13711	11.05108
29	15.14107	14.33310	13.59072	12.90749	12.27767	11.15841
30	15.37245	14.53375	13.76483	13.05868	12.40904	11.25778
31	15.59281	14.72393	13.92909	13.20063	12.53181	11.34980
32	15.80268	14.90420	14.08404	13.33393	12.64656	11.43500
33	16.00255	15.07507	14.23023	13.45909	12.75379	11.51389
34	16.19290	15.23703	14.36814	13.57661	12.85401	11.58693
35	16.37420	15.39055	14.49825	13.68696	12.94767	11.65457
40	17.15909	16.04612	15.04630	14.14553	13.33171	11.92461
45	17.77407	16.54773	15.45583	14.48023	13.60552	12.10840
50	18.25592	16.93152	15.76186	14.72452	13.80075	12.23348

$$\text{Present Value of Ordinary Annuity of \$1 per Period: } p_{\overline{n}\backslash i} = \frac{1 - \frac{1}{(1+i)^n}}{i}$$

n \ i	9%	10%	11%	12%	13%	14%
1	0.91743	0.90909	0.90090	0.89286	0.88496	0.87719
2	1.75911	1.73554	1.71252	1.69005	1.66810	1.64666
3	2.53130	2.48685	2.44371	2.40183	2.36115	2.32163
4	3.23972	3.16986	3.10245	3.03735	2.97447	2.91371
5	3.88965	3.79079	3.69590	3.60478	3.51723	3.43308
6	4.48592	4.35526	4.23054	4.11141	3.99755	3.88867
7	5.03295	4.86842	4.71220	4.56376	4.42261	4.28830
8	5.53482	5.33493	5.14612	4.96764	4.79677	4.63886
9	5.99525	5.75902	5.53705	5.32825	5.13166	4.94637
10	6.41766	6.14457	5.88923	5.65022	5.42624	5.21612
11	6.80519	6.49506	6.20652	5.93770	5.68694	5.45273
12	7.16072	6.81369	6.49236	6.19437	5.91765	5.66029
13	7.48690	7.10336	6.74987	6.42355	6.12181	5.84236
14	7.78615	7.36669	6.96187	6.62817	6.30249	6.00207
15	8.06069	7.60608	7.19087	6.81086	6.46238	6.14217
16	8.31256	7.82371	7.37916	6.97399	6.60388	6.26506
17	8.54363	8.02155	7.54879	7.11963	6.72909	6.37286
18	8.75562	8.20141	7.70162	7.24967	6.83991	6.46742
19	8.95012	8.36492	7.83929	7.36578	6.93797	6.55037
20	9.12855	8.51356	7.96333	7.46944	7.02475	6.62313
21	9.29224	8.64869	8.07507	7.56200	7.10155	6.68696
22	9.44242	8.77154	8.17574	7.64465	7.16951	6.74294
23	9.58021	8.88322	8.26643	7.71843	7.22966	6.79206
24	9.70661	8.98474	8.34814	7.78432	7.28288	6.83514
25	9.82258	9.07704	8.42174	7.84314	7.32998	6.87293
26	9.92897	9.16094	8.48806	7.89566	7.37167	6.90608
27	10.02658	9.23722	8.54780	7.94255	7.40856	6.93515
28	10.11613	9.30657	8.60162	7.98442	7.44120	6.96066
29	10.19828	9.36961	8.65011	8.02181	7.47009	6.98304
30	10.27365	9.42691	8.69379	8.05518	7.49565	7.00266
31	10.34280	9.47901	8.73315	8.08499	7.51828	7.01988
32	10.40624	9.52638	8.76860	8.11159	7.53830	7.03498
33	10.46444	9.56943	8.80054	8.13535	7.55602	7.04823
34	10.51784	9.60858	8.82932	8.15656	7.57170	7.05985
35	10.56682	9.64416	8.85524	8.17550	7.58557	7.07005
40	10.75736	9.77905	8.95105	8.24378	7.63438	7.10504
45	10.88118	9.86281	9.00791	8.28252	7.66086	7.12322
50	10.96168	9.91481	9.04165	8.30450	7.67524	7.13266

Future Amount of $1 at Compound Interest Due in n Periods: $A_{\overline{n}\backslash i} = (1 + i)^n$

n \ i	5%	5.5%	6%	6.5%	7%	8%
1	1.05000	1.05500	1.06000	1.06500	1.07000	1.08000
2	1.10250	1.11303	1.12360	1.13423	1.14490	1.16640
3	1.15762	1.17424	1.19102	1.20795	1.22504	1.25971
4	1.21551	1.23882	1.26248	1.28647	1.31080	1.36049
5	1.27628	1.30696	1.33823	1.37009	1.40255	1.46933
6	1.34100	1.37884	1.41852	1.45914	1.50073	1.58687
7	1.40710	1.45468	1.50363	1.55399	1.60578	1.71382
8	1.54347	1.53469	1.59385	1.65500	1.71819	1.85093
9	1.55133	1.61909	1.68948	1.76257	1.83846	1.99900
10	1.62890	1.70814	1.79085	1.87714	1.96715	2.15892
11	1.71034	1.80209	1.89830	1.99915	2.10485	2.33164
12	1.79586	1.90121	2.01220	2.12910	2.25219	2.51817
13	1.88565	2.00577	2.13293	2.26749	2.40984	2.71962
14	1.97993	2.11609	2.26091	2.41487	2.57853	2.93719
15	2.07893	2.23248	2.39656	2.57184	2.75903	3.17217
16	2.18288	2.35526	2.54035	2.73901	2.95216	3.42594
17	2.29202	2.48480	2.69277	2.91705	3.15882	3.70002
18	2.40662	2.62147	2.85434	3.10665	3.37993	3.99602
19	2.52695	2.76565	3.02560	3.30859	3.61653	4.31570
20	2.65330	2.91776	3.20714	3.52365	3.86968	4.66096
21	2.78596	3.07823	3.39956	3.75268	4.14056	5.03383
22	2.92526	3.24754	3.60354	3.99661	4.43040	5.43654
23	3.07152	3.42615	3.81975	4.25639	4.74053	5.87146
24	3.22510	3.61459	4.04894	4.53305	5.07237	6.34118
25	3.38636	3.81339	4.29187	4.82770	5.42743	6.84848
26	3.55567	4.02313	4.54938	5.14150	5.80735	7.39635
27	3.73346	4.24440	4.82235	5.47570	6.21387	7.98806
28	3.92013	4.47784	5.11169	5.83162	6.64884	8.62711
29	4.11614	4.72412	5.41839	6.21067	7.11426	9.31728
30	4.32194	4.98395	5.74349	6.61437	7.61226	10.06266
31	4.53804	5.25807	6.08810	7.04430	8.14511	10.86767
32	4.76494	5.54726	6.45339	7.50218	8.71527	11.73708
33	5.00319	5.85236	6.84059	7.98982	9.32534	12.67605
34	5.25335	6.17424	7.25102	8.50916	9.97811	13.69013
35	5.51602	6.51383	7.68609	9.06225	10.67658	14.78534
40	7.03999	8.51331	10.28572	12.41607	14.97446	21.72452
45	8.98501	11.12655	13.76461	17.01110	21.00245	31.92045
50	11.46740	14.54196	18.42015	23.30668	29.45702	46.90161

Future Amount of \$1 at Compound Interest Due in *n* Periods: $A_{\overline{n}\backslash i} = (1 + i)^n$

$n \backslash i$	9%	10%	11%	12%	13%	14%
1	1.09000	1.10000	1.11000	1.12000	1.13000	1.14000
2	1.18810	1.21000	1.23210	1.25440	1.27690	1.29960
3	1.29503	1.33100	1.36763	1.40493	1.44290	1.48154
4	1.41158	1.46410	1.51807	1.57352	1.63047	1.68896
5	1.53862	1.61051	1.68506	1.76234	1.84244	1.92541
6	1.67710	1.77156	1.87041	1.97382	2.08195	2.19497
7	1.82804	1.94872	2.07616	2.21068	2.35261	2.50227
8	1.99256	2.14359	2.30454	2.47596	2.65844	2.85259
9	2.17189	2.35795	2.55804	2.77308	3.00404	3.25195
10	2.36736	2.59374	2.83942	3.10585	3.39457	3.70722
11	2.58043	2.85312	3.15176	3.47855	3.83586	4.22623
12	2.81266	3.13843	3.49845	3.89598	4.33452	4.81790
13	3.06580	3.45227	3.88328	4.36349	4.89801	5.49241
14	3.34173	3.79750	4.31044	4.88711	5.53475	6.26135
15	3.64248	4.17725	4.78459	5.47357	6.25427	7.13794
16	3.97031	4.59497	5.31089	6.13039	7.06733	8.13725
17	4.32763	5.05447	5.89509	6.86604	7.98608	9.27646
18	4.71712	5.55992	6.54355	7.68997	9.02427	10.57517
19	5.14166	6.11591	7.26334	8.61276	10.19742	12.05569
20	5.60441	6.72750	8.06231	9.64629	11.52309	13.74349
21	6.10881	7.40025	8.94917	10.80385	13.02109	15.66758
22	6.65860	8.14028	9.93357	12.10031	14.71383	17.86104
23	7.25787	8.95430	11.02627	13.55235	16.62663	20.36158
24	7.91108	9.84973	12.23916	15.17863	18.78809	23.21221
25	8.62308	10.83471	13.58546	17.00006	21.23054	26.46192
26	9.39916	11.91818	15.07986	19.04007	23.99051	30.16658
27	10.24508	13.10999	16.73865	21.32488	27.10928	34.38991
28	11.16714	14.42099	18.57990	23.88387	30.63349	39.20449
29	12.17218	15.86309	20.62369	26.74993	34.61584	44.69312
30	13.26768	17.44940	22.89230	29.95992	39.11590	50.95016
31	14.46177	19.19434	25.41045	33.55511	44.20096	58.08318
32	15.76333	21.11378	28.20560	37.58173	49.94709	66.21483
33	17.18203	23.22515	31.30821	42.09153	56.44021	75.48490
34	18.72841	25.54767	34.75212	47.14252	63.77744	86.05279
35	20.41397	28.10244	38.57485	52.79962	72.06851	98.10018
40	31.40942	45.25926	65.00087	93.05097	132.78155	188.88351
45	48.32729	72.89048	109.53024	163.98760	244.64140	363.67907
50	74.35752	117.39085	184.56483	289.00219	450.73593	700.23299

Future Amount of Ordinary Annuity of $1 per Period: $A_{\overline{n}\backslash i} = (1 + i)^n - 1/i$

n \ i	5%	5.5%	6%	6.5%	7%	8%
1	1.00000	1.00000	1.00000	1.00000	1.00000	1.00000
2	2.05000	2.05500	2.06000	2.06500	2.07000	2.08000
3	3.15250	3.16802	3.18360	3.19922	3.21490	3.24640
4	4.31012	4.34227	4.37462	4.40717	4.43994	4.50611
5	5.52563	5.58109	5.63709	5.69364	5.75074	5.86660
6	6.80191	6.88805	6.97532	7.06373	7.15329	7.33593
7	8.14201	8.26689	8.39384	8.52287	8.65402	8.92280
8	9.54911	9.72157	9.89747	10.07688	10.25980	10.63663
9	11.02656	11.25626	11.49132	11.73185	11.97799	12.48756
10	12.57789	12.87535	13.18080	13.49442	13.81645	14.48656
11	14.20679	14.58350	14.97184	15.37156	15.78360	16.64549
12	15.91713	16.38559	16.86994	17.37071	17.88845	18.97713
13	17.71298	18.28680	18.88214	19.49981	20.14064	21.49530
14	19.59863	20.29257	21.01505	21.76730	22.55049	24.21492
15	21.57856	22.40866	23.27597	24.18217	25.12902	27.15211
16	23.65749	24.64114	25.67253	26.75401	27.88805	30.32428
17	25.84037	28.99640	28.21288	29.49302	30.84022	33.75023
18	28.13238	29.48120	30.90565	32.41007	33.99903	37.45024
19	30.53900	32.10267	33.75999	35.51672	37.37896	41.44626
20	33.06595	34.86832	36.78559	38.82531	40.99549	45.76196
21	35.71925	37.78608	39.99273	42.34895	44.86518	50.42292
22	38.50521	40.86431	43.39229	46.10164	49.00574	55.45676
23	41.43048	44.11185	46.99583	50.09824	53.43614	60.89330
24	44.50200	47.53800	50.81558	54.35463	58.17667	66.76476
25	47.72710	51.15259	54.86451	58.88768	63.24904	73.10594
26	51.11345	54.96598	59.15638	63.71538	68.67647	79.95442
27	54.66913	58.98911	63.70577	68.85688	74.48382	87.35077
28	58.40258	63.23351	68.52811	74.33257	80.69769	95.33883
29	62.32271	67.71135	73.62980	80.16419	87.34653	103.96594
30	66.43885	72.43548	79.05819	86.37486	94.46079	113.28321
31	70.76079	77.41943	84.80168	92.98923	102.07304	123.34587
32	75.29883	82.67750	90.88978	100.03353	110.21815	134.21354
33	80.06377	88.22476	97.34316	107.53571	118.93342	145.95062
34	85.06696	94.07712	104.18376	115.52553	128.25876	158.62667
35	90.32031	100.25136	111.43478	124.03469	138.23688	172.31680
40	120.79977	136.60561	154.76197	175.63192	199.63511	259.05652
45	159.70016	184.11917	212.74351	246.32459	285.74931	386.50562
50	209.34800	246.21748	290.33591	343.17967	406.52893	573.77016

Future Amount of Ordinary Annuity of $1 per Period: $A_{\overline{n}\backslash i} = (1 + i)^n - 1/i$

n \ i	9%	10%	11%	12%	13%	14%
1	1.00000	1.00000	1.00000	1.00000	1.00000	1.00000
2	2.09000	2.10000	2.11000	2.12000	2.13000	2.14000
3	3.27810	3.31000	3.34210	3.37440	3.40690	3.43960
4	4.57313	4.64100	4.70973	4.77933	4.84980	4.92114
5	5.98471	6.10510	6.22780	6.35285	6.48027	6.61010
6	7.52334	7.71561	7.91286	8.11519	8.32271	8.53552
7	9.20044	9.48717	9.78327	10.08901	10.40466	10.73049
8	11.02847	11.43589	11.85943	12.29969	12.75726	13.23276
9	13.02104	13.57948	14.16397	14.77566	15.41571	16.08535
10	15.19293	15.93742	16.72201	17.54874	18.41975	19.33730
11	17.56029	18.53117	19.56143	20.65458	21.81432	23.04452
12	20.14072	21.38428	22.71319	24.13313	25.65018	27.27075
13	22.95338	24.52271	26.21164	28.02911	29.98470	32.08865
14	26.01919	27.97498	30.09492	32.39260	34.88271	37.58107
15	29.36092	31.77248	34.40536	37.27972	40.41746	43.84241
16	33.00340	35.94973	39.18995	42.75328	46.67173	50.98035
17	36.97370	40.54470	44.50084	48.88367	53.73906	59.11760
18	41.30134	45.59917	50.39594	55.74972	61.72514	68.39407
19	46.01846	51.15909	56.93949	63.43968	70.74941	78.96923
20	51.16012	57.27500	64.20283	72.05244	80.94683	91.02493
21	56.76453	64.00250	72.26514	81.69874	92.46992	104.76842
22	62.87334	71.40275	81.21431	92.50258	105.49101	120.43600
23	69.53194	79.54302	91.14788	104.60289	120.20484	138.29704
24	76.78981	88.49733	102.17415	118.15524	136.83147	158.65862
25	84.70090	98.34706	114.41331	133.33387	155.61956	181.87083
26	93.32398	109.18176	127.99877	150.33393	176.85010	208.33274
27	102.72314	121.09994	143.07864	169.37401	200.84061	238.49933
28	112.96822	134.20994	159.81729	190.69889	227.94989	272.88923
29	124.13536	148.63093	178.39719	214.58275	258.58338	312.09373
30	136.30754	164.49402	199.02088	241.33268	293.19922	356.78685
31	149.57522	181.94342	221.91317	271.29261	332.31511	407.73701
32	164.03699	201.13777	247.32362	304.84772	376.51608	465.82019
33	179.80032	222.25154	275.52922	342.42945	426.46317	532.03501
34	196.98234	245.47670	306.83744	384.52098	482.90338	607.51991
35	215.71076	271.02437	341.58955	431.66350	546.68082	693.57270
40	337.88244	442.59256	581.82607	767.09142	1013.70424	1342.02510
45	525.85873	718.90484	986.63856	1358.23003	1874.16463	2590.56480
50	815.08356	1163.90853	1668.77115	2400.01825	3459.50712	4994.52135

Appendix B: Codes of Professional Ethics for Accountants

In recent years, governments, businesses, and the public have given increased attention to ethical conduct. They have insisted upon a level of human behavior that goes beyond that required by laws and regulations. Thus many businesses, as well as professional groups (such as accountants) and governmental organizations, have established standards of ethical conduct. This appendix sets forth the standards expected of accountants in public accounting, the American Institute of Certified Public Accountants' *Code of Professional Conduct.*[1]

This text emphasizes the ethical conduct of accountants, who serve various business interests as well as the public. Supplementing the codes of professional ethics are ethics discussion cases that appear at the end of each chapter. These cases represent "real world" examples of ethical issues facing accountants. It should be noted that codes of professional ethics are general guides to good behavior and their application to specific situations often requires the exercise of professional judgment. In some cases, the line between right and wrong may be quite fine, and reasonable people may disagree. In addition, business is dynamic and everchanging, and what society considers to be acceptable behavior changes from time to time.

Code of Professional Conduct

Composition, Applicability, and Compliance

The Code of Professional Conduct of the American Institute of Certified Public Accountants consists of two sections—(1) the Principles and (2) the Rules. The Principles provide the framework for the Rules, which govern the performance of professional services by members. The Council of the American Institute of Certified Public Accountants is authorized to designate bodies to promulgate technical standards under the Rules, and the bylaws require adherence to those Rules and standards.

The Code of Professional Conduct was adopted by the membership to provide guidance and rules to all members—those in public practice, in industry, in government, and in education—in the performance of their professional responsibilities.

Compliance with the Code of Professional Conduct, as with all standards in an open society, depends primarily on members' understanding and voluntary actions, secondarily on reinforcement by peers and public opinion, and ultimately on disciplinary proceedings, when necessary, against members who fail to comply with the Rules.

Other Guidance

The Principles and Rules as set forth herein are further amplified by interpretations and rulings contained in *AICPA Professional Standards* (Volume 2).

1 *Code of Professional Conduct* (New York: American Institute of Certified Public Accountants, 2000), pp. 3–8. This Code may also be found at the AICPA's Web site, http://www.aicpa.org.

Interpretations of Rules of Conduct consists of interpretations which have been adopted, after exposure to state societies, state boards, practice units, and other interested parties, by the professional ethics division's executive committee to provide guidelines as to the scope and application of the Rules but are not intended to limit such scope or application. A member who departs from such guidelines shall have the burden of justifying such departure in any disciplinary hearing.

Ethics Rulings consist of formal rulings made by the professional ethics division's executive committee after exposure to state societies, state boards, practice units, and other interested parties. These rulings summarize the application of Rules of Conduct and interpretations to a particular set of factual circumstances. Members who depart from such rulings in similar circumstances will be requested to justify such departures.

Publication of an interpretation or ethics ruling in the *Journal of Accountancy* constitutes notice to members. Hence, the effective date of the pronouncement is the last day of the month in which the pronouncement is published in the *Journal of Accountancy.* The professional ethics division will take into consideration the time that would have been reasonable for the member to comply with the pronouncement.

Members should also consult, if applicable, the ethical standards of their state CPA society, state board of accountancy, the Securities and Exchange Commission, and any other governmental agency which may regulate their client's business or use their reports to evaluate the client's compliance with applicable laws and related regulations.

Section I—Principles

Preamble

Membership in the American Institute of Certified Public Accountants is voluntary. By accepting membership, a certified public accountant assumes an obligation of self-discipline above and beyond the requirements of laws and regulations.

These Principles of the Code of Professional Conduct of the American Institute of Certified Public Accountants express the profession's recognition of its responsibilities to the public, to clients, and to colleagues. They guide members in the performance of their professional responsibilities and express the basic tenets of ethical and professional conduct. The Principles call for an unswerving commitment to honorable behavior, even at the sacrifice of personal advantage.

Article I—Responsibilities

In carrying out their responsibilities as professionals, members should exercise sensitive professional and moral judgments in all their activities.

As professionals, certified public accountants perform an essential role in society. Consistent with that role, members of the American Institute of Certified Public Accountants have responsibilities to all those who use their professional services. Members also have a continuing responsibility to cooperate with each other to improve the art of accounting, maintain the public's confidence, and carry out the profession's special responsibilities for self-governance. The collective efforts of all members are required to maintain and enhance the traditions of the profession.

Article II—The Public Interest

Members should accept the obligation to act in a way that will serve the public interest, honor the public trust, and demonstrate commitment to professionalism.

A distinguishing mark of a profession is acceptance of its responsibility to the public. The accounting profession's public consists of clients, credit grantors, governments, employers, investors, the business and financial community, and others who rely on the objectivity and integrity of certified public accountants to maintain the orderly functioning of commerce. This reliance imposes a public interest responsibility on certified public accountants. The public interest is defined as the collective well-being of the community of people and institutions the profession serves.

In discharging their professional responsibilities, members may encounter conflicting pressures from among each of those groups. In resolving those conflicts, members should act with integrity, guided by the precept that when members fulfill their responsibility to the public, clients' and employers' interests are best served.

Those who rely on certified public accountants expect them to discharge their responsibilities with integrity, objectivity, due professional care, and a genuine interest in serving the public. They are expected to provide quality services, enter into fee arrangements, and offer a range of services—all in a manner that demonstrates a level of professionalism consistent with these Principles of the Code of Professional Conduct.

All who accept membership in the American Institute of Certified Public Accountants commit themselves to honor the public trust. In return for the faith that the public reposes in them, members should seek continually to demonstrate their dedication to professional excellence.

Article III—Integrity

To maintain and broaden public confidence, members should perform all professional responsibilities with the highest sense of integrity.

Integrity is an element of character fundamental to professional recognition. It is the quality from which the public trust derives and the benchmark against which a member must ultimately test all decisions.

Integrity requires a member to be, among other things, honest and candid within the constraints of client confidentiality. Service and the public trust should not be subordinated to personal gain and advantage. Integrity can accommodate the inadvertent error and the honest difference of opinion; it cannot accommodate deceit or subordination of principle.

Integrity is measured in terms of what is right and just. In the absence of specific rules, standards, or guidance, or in the face of conflicting opinions, a member should test decisions and deeds by asking: "Am I doing what a person of integrity would do? Have I retained my integrity?" Integrity requires a member to observe both the form and the spirit of technical and ethical standards; circumvention of those standards constitutes subordination of judgment.

Integrity also requires a member to observe the principles of objectivity and independence and of due care.

Article IV—Objectivity and Independence

A member should maintain objectivity and be free of conflicts of interest in discharging professional responsibilities. A member in public practice should be independent in fact and appearance when providing auditing and other attestation services.

Objectivity is a state of mind, a quality that lends value to a member's services. It is a distinguishing feature of the profession. The principle of objectivity imposes the obligation to be impartial, intellectually honest, and free of conflicts of interest. Independence precludes relationships that may appear to impair a member's objectivity in rendering attestation services.

Members often serve multiple interests in many different capacities and must demonstrate their objectivity in varying circumstances. Members in public practice render attest, tax, and management advisory services. Other members prepare financial statements in the employment of others, perform internal auditing services, and serve in financial and management capacities in industry, education, and government. They also educate and train those who aspire to admission into the profession. Regardless of service or capacity, members should protect the integrity of their work, maintain objectivity, and avoid any subordination of their judgment.

For a member in public practice, the maintenance of objectivity and independence requires a continuing assessment of client relationships and public responsibility. Such a member who provides auditing and other attestation services should be independent in fact and appearance. In providing all other services, a member should maintain objectivity and avoid conflicts of interest.

Although members not in public practice cannot maintain the appearance of independence, they nevertheless have the responsibility to maintain objectivity in rendering professional services. Members employed by others to prepare financial statements or to perform auditing, tax, or consulting services are charged with the same responsibility for objectivity as members in public practice and must be scrupulous in their application of generally accepted accounting principles and candid in all their dealings with members in public practice.

Activity V—Due Care

A member should observe the profession's technical and ethical standards, strive continually to improve competence and the quality of services, and discharge professional responsibility to the best of the member's ability.

The quest for excellence is the essence of due care. Due care requires a member to discharge professional responsibilities with competence and diligence. It imposes the obligation to perform professional services to the best of a member's ability with concern for the best interest of those for whom the services are performed and consistent with the profession's responsibility to the public.

Competence is derived from a synthesis of education and experience. It begins with a mastery of the common body of knowledge required for designation as a certified public accountant. The maintenance of competence requires a commitment to learning and professional improvement that must continue throughout a member's professional life. It is a member's individual responsibility. In all engagements and in all responsibilities, each member should undertake to achieve a level of competence that will assure that the quality of the member's services meets the high level of professionalism required by these Principles.

Competence represents the attainment and maintenance of a level of understanding and knowledge that enables a member to render services with facility and acumen. It also establishes the limitations of a member's capabilities by dictating that consultation or referral may be required when a professional engagement exceeds the personal competence of a member or a member's firm. Each member is responsible for assessing his or her own competence—of evaluating whether education, experience, and judgment are adequate for the responsibility to be assumed.

Members should be diligent in discharging responsibilities to clients, employers, and the public. Diligence imposes the responsibility to render services promptly and carefully, to be thorough, and to observe applicable technical and ethical standards.

Due care requires a member to plan and supervise adequately any professional activity for which he or she is responsible.

Article VI—Scope and Nature of Services

A member in public practice should observe the Principles of the Code of Professional Conduct in determining the scope and nature of services to be provided.

The public interest aspect of certified public accountants' services requires that such services be consistent with acceptable professional behavior for certified public accountants. Integrity requires that service and the public trust not be subordinated to personal gain and advantage. Objectivity and independence require that members be free from conflicts of interest in discharging professional responsibilities. Due care requires that services be provided with competence and diligence.

Each of these Principles should be considered by members in determining whether or not to provide specific services in individual circumstances. In some instances, they may represent an overall constraint on the nonaudit services that might be offered to a specific client. No hard-and-fast rules can be developed to help members reach these judgments, but they must be satisfied that they are meeting the spirit of the Principles in this regard.

In order to accomplish this, members should:

- Practice in firms that have in place internal quality-control procedures to ensure that services are competently delivered and adequately supervised.
- Determine, in their individual judgments, whether the scope and nature of other services provided to an audit client would create a conflict of interest in the performance of the audit function for that client.
- Assess, in their individual judgments, whether an activity is consistent with their role as professionals (for example, Is such activity a reasonable extension or variation of existing services offered by the member or others in the profession?).

Appendix C: Using the Internet for Financial Research

Investors, customers, suppliers, employees, and others have an interest in the financial prospects of a company. For analyzing these prospects, sophisticated analysis tools are available on private Internet sites through subscriptions or from online stockbrokers. Over the past five years, however, significant amounts of information have been made available on free Internet sites. Such readily available information simplifies company evaluations and analysis. In this appendix, we will review three public sites that you might find useful for analysis.

Thomson Analytics–*Business School Edition*

Thomson Analytics is a Web-based portal product that provides integrated access to Thomson Financial content for the purpose of financial analysis. An access card to the educational version of this rich resource is included with each new textbook. A view of a partial page from Thomson Analytics is shown in Exhibit 1.

Exhibit 1

Thomson Analytics Partial Page from Company Overview of Starbucks Corp.

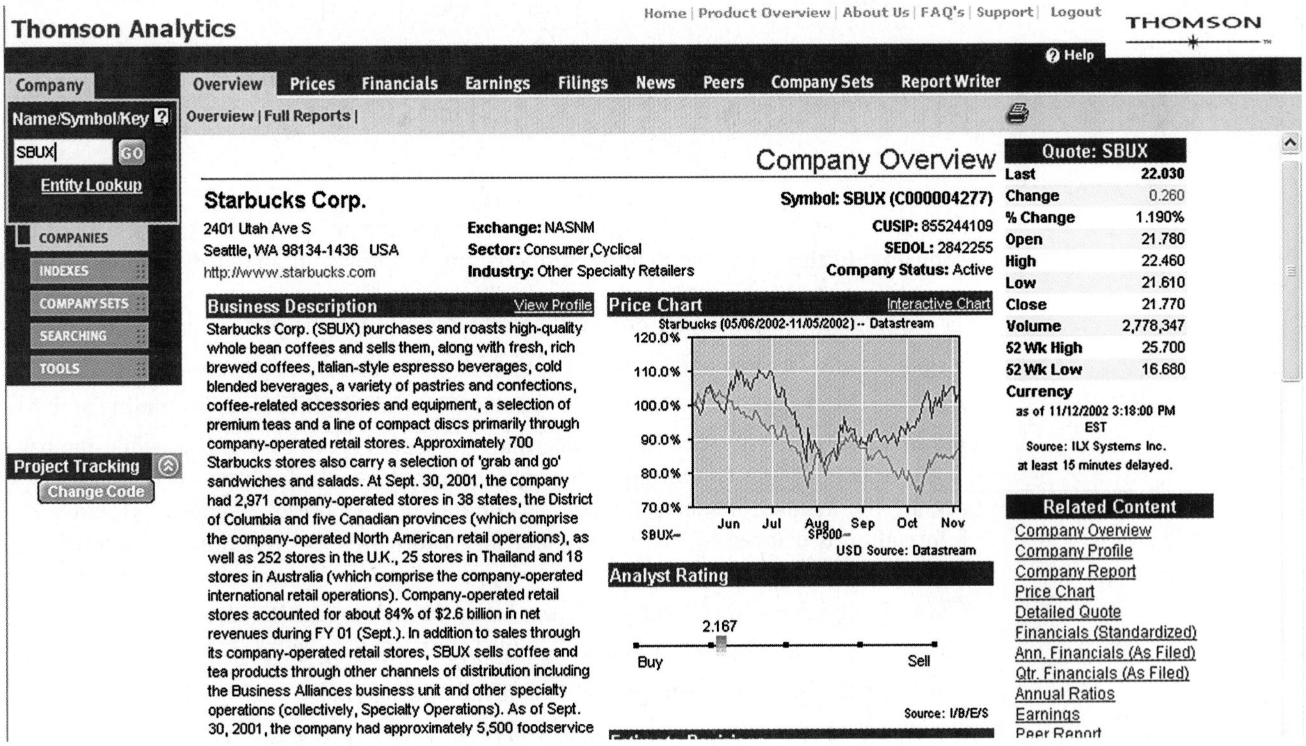

For 500 companies, the Thomson Analytics online resource provides seamless access to:

- **Current and Past Company Data:** Worldscope®, which includes company profiles, financials and accounting results, market per-share data, annual information, and monthly prices going back to 1980.
- **Financial Analyst Data and Forecasts:** I/B/E/S Consensus Estimates, which provides consensus estimates, analyst-by-analyst earnings coverage, and analysts' forecasts.
- **SEC Disclosure Statements:** Disclosure SEC Database, which includes company profiles, annual and quarterly company financials, pricing information, and earnings.

Yahoo! Finance

Yahoo! provides a free Internet research site for publicly listed companies in its finance Web environment, found at *http://finance.yahoo.com.* The finance home page provides real-time market statistics and business news. Entering a stock exchange symbol for a particular company at the top of the page will return individual company information. The symbol lookup feature is helpful when you are not sure of the company's symbol. For example, the symbol KO is used to designate the Coca-Cola Company. The detailed Yahoo! information about Coca-Cola (KO) for October 15, 2002, is illustrated in Exhibit 2.

Exhibit 2

Yahoo! Detailed Page View of the Coca-Cola Company

COCA COLA CO (NYSE:KO) - Trade: Choose Brokerage

Last Trade 11:10am · **47.73**	Change -4.75 (-9.05%)		Prev Cls 52.48	Open 50.00	Volume 8,846,700
Day's Range 47.26 - 50.00	Bid N/A	Ask N/A	P/E 32.00	Mkt Cap 118.5B	Avg Vol 5,523,409
52-wk Range 43.50 - 57.91	Bid Size N/A	Ask Size N/A	P/S 6.23	Div/Shr 0.80	Div Date Oct 1
1y Target Est 59.82	EPS (ttm) 1.64	EPS Est 1.78	PEG 2.46	Yield 1.52	Ex-Div Sep 11

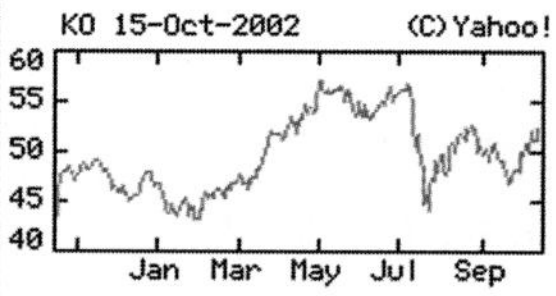

Small: 1d 5d **1y** none
Big: 1d 5d 3m 6m 1y 2y 5y max

Chart, Financials, Historical Prices, Insider, Messages, News, Options
Profile, Reports, Research, SEC Filings, Upgrades, **more...**

As can be seen, the Coca-Cola page view provides a number of market statistics about the company. In this view, the field descriptions are as follows, in alphabetical order:

1y Target Est: Median target price estimate as forecast by analysts covering the stock.

52-wk Range: The low and high range of prices over the last 52 weeks.

Avg Vol: The average daily volume determined from the last three-months' trading activity.

Bid and Ask (size): The bid is the price that you would receive on a sale, while the ask is the price that you would pay if you purchased the stock. The size of the bid and ask are the number of shares available at the bid and ask prices. Yahoo!'s bid and ask information is delayed by 20 minutes and not reported (N/A). Real-time bid and asks are available from online stock brokers.

Change: The price and percentage change from the previous day's close.

Day's Range: The range of trading prices during the trading day.

Div Date: The date on which the next dividend will be paid.

Div/Shr: Annual dividend per share of common stock.

EPS (ttm): Trailing twelve-month basic earnings per share.

EPS Est: Current-year analyst consensus earnings per share estimate.

Ex-Div: The last date for purchasing the stock to receive the dividend; the dividend record date.

Last Trade: The price of the last trade of the trading day (October 15, 2002).

Mkt Cap: The market value of the company determined by multiplying the closing market price by the number of common shares issued and outstanding.

Open: The opening price of the trading day.

P/E: The price-earnings ratio, defined as the closing market price divided by the trailing twelve months' earnings per share.

P/S: The price-to-sales ratio, calculated as the closing price divided by the revenue per share.

PEG: A ratio relating price to earnings growth, calculated by dividing the EPS (ttm) by the five-year annualized earnings growth rate.

Prev Cls: The closing price of the previous trading day.

Volume: The trading volume of common shares on the trading day.

Yield: The dividend per share divided by the closing market price.

As can be seen, this simple page view provides extensive market and financial information about The Coca-Cola Company. In addition, the Yahoo! detailed page view of Coca-Cola also allows an individual to retrieve quarterly financial statement information (financials), business news about the company (news), a profile of the company (profile), access to fee-based research reports (reports), and analyst forecasts (research). For example, a partial research page view for Coca-Cola is shown in Exhibit 3. In this exhibit, Coca-Cola has a buy rating of 2.3 on a five-point scale, with 3 out of 14 analysts recommending a strong buy.

Exhibit 3

Coca-Cola Research Page View (partial)

Current Broker Recommendations		Average Recommendation	
		(Buy) 1.00 - 5.00 (Sell)	
Strong Buy	3	This Week	**2.3**
Buy	4	Last Week	2.3
Hold	7	Change	0.0
Sell	0		
Strong Sell	0	Industry Mean	2.46
Covering Brokers	14	Sector Mean	2.34
		WSJ/Dow Jones Mean	2.33
Upgrades & Downgrades		S&P 500 Mean	N/A
		Industry: Beverage	

Overall, Yahoo Finance provides good but basic information about a company.

EDGAR

As stated by the Securities Exchange Commission,

> *EDGAR, the Electronic Data Gathering, Analysis, and Retrieval system, performs automated collection, validation, indexing, acceptance, and forwarding of submissions by companies and others who are required by law to file forms with the U.S.*

Securities and Exchange Commission (SEC). Its primary purpose is to increase the efficiency and fairness of the securities market for the benefit of investors, corporations, and the economy by accelerating the receipt, acceptance, dissemination, and analysis of time-sensitive corporate information filed with the agency.[1]

EDGAR provides free access to SEC submissions by public companies. The annual 10-K report is one of these submissions. The 10-K includes the complete audited financial statements of public companies, combined with the management discussion and analysis of the financial condition and results of operations. In addition, the 10-K report will often contain additional detailed financial information not formally disclosed in the annual report, which can be used by analysts in evaluating the financial prospects of a business. Thus, most professional researchers access and read 10-K reports.

The SEC provides many access points to the EDGAR system. For example, EDGAR can be accessed from Yahoo Finance and many other stock market sites. The SEC's EDGAR site can be accessed through links from the SEC home page: *http://www.sec.gov/*.

Alternatively, PricewaterhouseCoopers has developed a proprietary EDGAR interface that we recommend, called EDGARSCAN, at *http://edgarscan.pwcglobal.com/servlets/edgarscan*. As of this writing, EDGARSCAN is a free service. The initial EDGARSCAN page view asks for a company name. For example, assuming that we want to retrieve SEC information about The Coca-Cola Company, we would enter "KO" or the company name, as shown in Exhibit 4.

Exhibit 4

EDGARSCAN Initial Page View

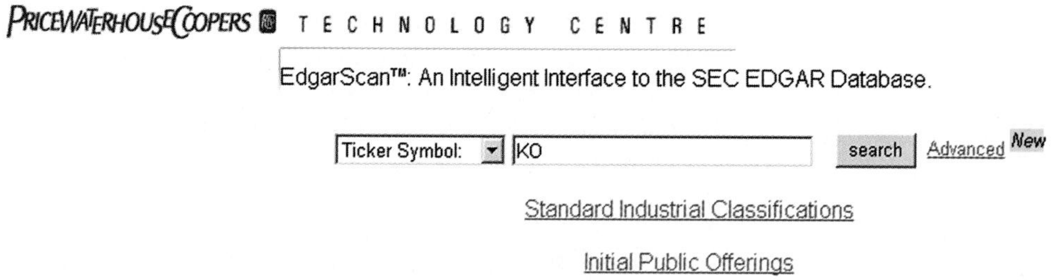

EDGARSCAN would then retrieve and list Coca-Cola filings as shown in Exhibit 5. The listings are separated into quarterly filings (10-Q), annual filings (10-K or 10-K405), and other types of filings, such as significant event filings (8-K). Notice, too, that EDGARSCAN also provides a tool, called Benchmarking Assistant, that graphs financial statement items.

If we select the 10-K 2001-12-31 filing for Coca-Cola, EDGARSCAN will return a table of contents of the filing as shown in Exhibit 6.

The financial statements can be retrieved by selecting from the income statement, balance sheet, or statement of cash flow titles under Item 14. The financial statement information can also be downloaded as a spreadsheet to conduct further vertical, horizontal, or ratio analyses.

Market Guide

The Market Guide site at *http://www.marketguide.com* is an excellent source for more advanced analysis tools. This site requires that you register as a member, but membership is free (as of this writing). The site provides individual company information, similar to

1 From *http://www.sec.gov/edgar/aboutedgar.htm* May 30, 2002.

Exhibit 5

SEC Filing Listing for Coca-Cola Company

Extracted Financial Data:

- hypertextual table
- slightly less hypertextual table -- recommended for slower connections
- Benchmarking Assistant
- Excel Spreadsheet

Recent Filings (by Filing Date):

4 2002-10-03 4 2002-10-03 4 2002-10-03 4 2002-10-03 8-K 2002-08-14

Quarterly Filings (10-Q's by Filing Period):

Q2 2002-06-30 Q1 2002-03-31 Q3 2001-09-30 Q2 2001-06-30 Q1 2001-03-31 Q3 2000-09-30 Q2 2000-06-30 Q1 2000-03-31
Q3 1999-09-30 Q2 1999-06-30 Q1 1999-03-31 Q3 1998-09-30 Q2 1998-06-30 Q1 1998-03-31 Q3 1997-09-30 Q2 1997-06-30
Q1 1997-03-31 Q3 1996-09-30 Q2 1996-06-30 Q1 1996-03-31 Q3 1995-09-30 Q2 1995-06-30 Q1 1995-03-31 Q3 1994-09-30
Q2 1994-06-30 Q1 1994-03-31

Annual Filings (10-K's by Filing Period):

10-K/A 2001-12-31 10-K 2001-12-31 10-K 2000-12-31 10-K 1999-12-31 10-K 1998-12-31 10-K 1997-12-31
10-K405 1996-12-31 10-K405 1995-12-31 10-K405 1994-12-31 10-K 1993-12-31

Exhibit 6

EDGARSCAN 10-K Table of Contents for Coca-Cola

COCA COLA CO 10-K for period ending 2000-12-31

Extracted Financial Data

Table of Contents

Yahoo Finance, but adds some additional analysis tools. For example, one tool is the ratio comparison. Market Guide can compare common financial ratios of your selected company with the industry, sector, and the Standard & Poor's 500 averages. This is one of the few online sites that provides ratio comparisons without a fee. For example, the financial strength of Coca-Cola, as measured by five leverage ratios, can be compared to the benchmarks, as shown in Exhibit 7.

Most of the ratios discussed in this text are provided by Market Guide's ratio comparison tool.

A second powerful tool provided by Market Guide is a stock-screening tool. This tool allows you to specify industry, geographic location, financial performance and valuation ratios, dividend information, and earnings estimates to screen a universe of over 9,000

Exhibit 7

Market Guide Benchmarks for Coca-Cola

Financial Strength	Company	Industry	Sector	S&P 500
Quick Ratio (MRQ)	0.58	0.70	0.63	1.11
Current Ratio (MRQ)	0.97	1.07	1.17	1.62
LT Debt to Equity (MRQ)	0.24	0.43	1.05	0.76
Total Debt to Equity (MRQ)	0.52	0.65	1.35	1.06
Interest Coverage (TTM)	24.28	23.24	13.60	9.60

companies into a specified list of companies that meet your criteria. Investors use screening tools to identify investment targets that meet a specified set of criteria. For example, an investor may be interested only in companies that have a dividend yield that exceeds 4% and a P/E ratio less than 12. The screening tool could be used to identify the list of companies that meet these two criteria.

Other Internet Sites

There are many other Internet sites that are helpful for analyzing and researching companies. The three provided in this appendix are a good start to successful company and investment research.

Appendix D: The Home Depot Annual Report

2001 Annual Report

FINANCIAL SUMMARY

amounts in millions, except per share and store data	2001	increase	2000	increase	1999	increase
Net sales	$53,553	17%	$45,738	19%	$38,434	27%
Net earnings	$ 3,044	18%	$ 2,581	11%	$ 2,320	44%
Diluted earnings per share	$ 1.29	17%	$ 1.10	10%	$ 1.00	41%
Assets	$26,394	23%	$21,385	25%	$17,081	27%
Cash	$ 2,477	1383%	$ 167	–	$ 168	171%
Store count	1,333	18%	1,134	22%	930	22%

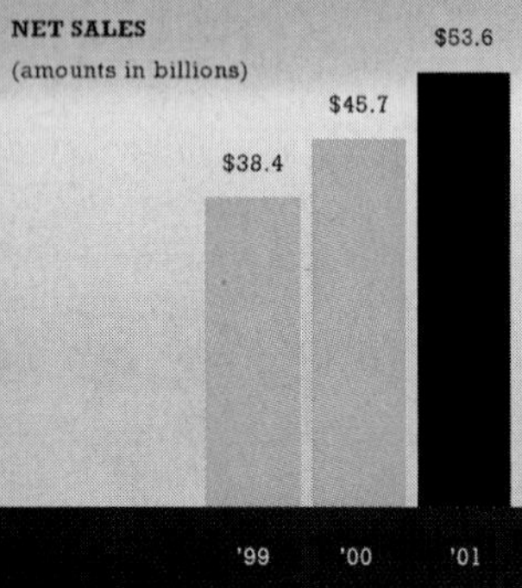

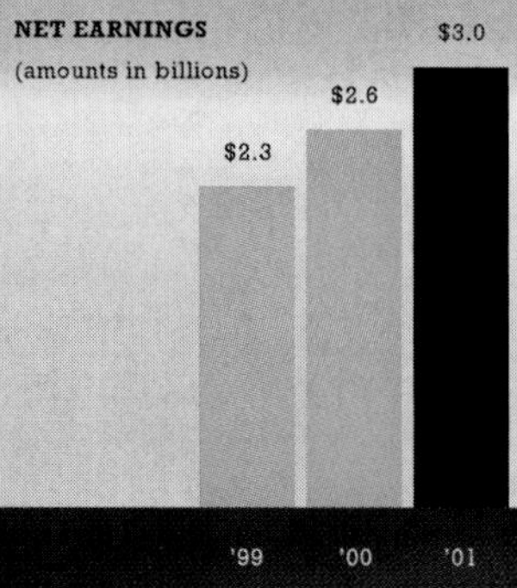

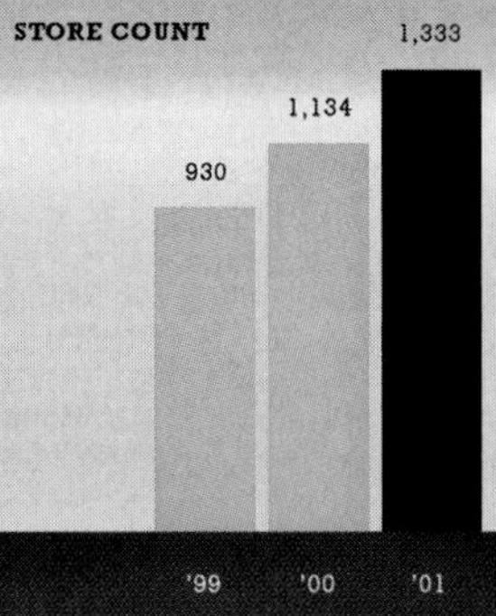

CORPORATE PROFILE FOUNDED IN 1978, THE HOME DEPOT® IS THE WORLD'S LARGEST HOME IMPROVEMENT RETAILER AND THE SECOND LARGEST RETAILER IN THE UNITED STATES, WITH FISCAL 2001 SALES OF $53.6 BILLION. AT THE CLOSE OF FISCAL 2001, THE HOME DEPOT OPERATED 1,333 RETAIL LOCATIONS, INCLUDING 1,201 HOME DEPOT STORES IN THE UNITED STATES, 78 HOME DEPOT STORES IN CANADA, AND EIGHT HOME DEPOT STORES IN MEXICO AND ARGENTINA. THE COMPANY ALSO OPERATED 41 EXPO DESIGN CENTERS®, FOUR VILLAGER'S® HARDWARE STORES, AND ONE HOME DEPOT FLOOR STORE℠. IN ADDITION, THE COMPANY OPERATED WHOLLY-OWNED SUBSIDIARIES APEX SUPPLY COMPANY, GEORGIA LIGHTING®, MAINTENANCE WAREHOUSE®, YOUR "OTHER" WAREHOUSE®, AND NATIONAL BLINDS AND WALLPAPER®. THE COMPANY EMPLOYED APPROXIMATELY 250,000 ASSOCIATES AT THE END OF FISCAL 2001. THE HOME DEPOT HAS BEEN PUBLICLY TRADED SINCE 1981. THE HOME DEPOT TRADES ON THE NEW YORK STOCK EXCHANGE UNDER THE TICKER SYMBOL "HD" AND IS INCLUDED IN THE DOW JONES INDUSTRIAL AVERAGE AND THE STANDARD AND POOR'S 500 INDEX.

BERNIE MARCUS, CO-FOUNDER

My mother taught me that every challenge brings an opportunity. Twenty-four years ago, I received a golden opportunity by being fired as president of what was then the nation's largest home improvement company. A door opened to a new vision of retailing, in which warehouse merchandising, contractor pricing and knowledgeable service would enable customers to take control of their home improvement needs. With the support of Ken Langone, our initial investors, and with the partnership of Arthur Blank, Pat Farrah, Ron Brill and countless others, this dream took shape as The Home Depot.

From the beginning, The Home Depot has marched under two standards. First, we set out to build a sound business, one that would create value for our customers, employees and shareholders while transforming the industry. I believe in the free enterprise system and am grateful that my parents settled in a country that makes it possible. The extent to which the company has achieved the first goal is a matter of financial record.

The second goal involves a different kind of value. One cannot see all that a company is by examining the bottom line. When we drew up our initial business plan, we talked about culture. Having seen a culture destroyed, we were determined to build our principles into the company's foundation and undergird it every step of the way.

Something special emerged, a culture in which employees were given the freedom, training and motivation to act as entrepreneurs, in which listening to customers improved us, in which vendors became partners in growth, and in which shareholders gained wealth by trusting in our abilities.

Behind these accomplishments, something more important has taken shape. The Home Depot gives back to the communities that support it. Most of this giving has been quiet, from employees building a wheelchair ramp for a disabled customer to clearing a park for inner city children. Some giving has involved corporate decisions, from refusing to raise prices in areas hit by natural disasters to sponsoring individual athletes in our Olympics program.

But the accomplishments of which we are most proud have come from spontaneous action in moments of need. When terrorists destroyed the World Trade Center, the only non-emergency vehicles permitted to enter the island of Manhattan were a stream of Home Depot trucks donating supplies and equipment to the rescue effort. Just as they did during the Oklahoma City tragedy several years earlier, our employees acted without seeking corporate approval. In them stands proof of the company's soul.

On January 1, 2002, I stepped down as company chairman, and in May of this year I will retire from the board to devote myself to philanthropic projects. The company finds itself in the excellent hands of Bob Nardelli, with whom I will continue a close relationship as mentor and friend. Bob and his staff have demonstrated during this past year that our culture is alive and well and that our business is running better than ever. I wish Bob and everyone involved with The Home Depot the best, and I have complete confidence in the company's future. Most importantly, I would like to thank all those who have helped make the Home Depot vision a reality. We could only have done it together.

TO OUR SHAREHOLDERS:

Having completed my first full year with this wonderful organization, I am more excited about this business and the opportunities for growth than ever before. In fact, I believe we have an infinite capacity for growth and value creation. My goal, when I arrived a year ago, was to build on this company's established tradition of growth, customer trust, corporate values, and brand recognition as the leader in home improvement retailing.

Since then, my confidence in the strength of The Home Depot has been confirmed and reconfirmed. Despite a turbulent economy that included massive corporate downsizings, consumer confidence hitting an eight-year low and the unthinkable disaster of September 11th, the 250,000 associates of The Home Depot delivered on our promise of improved performance in fiscal 2001. Not only did we stay on strategy, we embraced many new initiatives, accelerated existing programs, and delivered record results ... all while implementing a seamless transition in executive leadership.

2001 IN REVIEW

In many ways, this year's performance speaks for itself:

- Sales reached record levels, growing 17% to $53.6 billion. In fiscal 2001, The Home Depot became the second-largest retailer in the U.S.
- Net earnings grew 18% to exceed $3 billion for the first time, reaching $1.29 per share. Fiscal 2001 results included the second highest return on sales in company history.
- Cash reached a record $2.5 billion at year-end. Taken together with a debt-to-equity ratio of 6.9%, The Home Depot has one of the strongest balance sheets in retail, funding our ability to reinvest and generate additional growth.
- The Home Depot share price increased by 12.4%, outperforming both the S&P 500 and the Dow Jones Industrial Average, and ranking sixth among the Dow 30.
- In the fourth quarter, we increased the annual dividend 25%, allowing stockholders to benefit from the strong cash flows we produce.
- We reinvested more than $3.3 billion into our business through new stores, systems enhancements, and other initiatives.
- The Home Depot opened 204 new stores and added 40,000 incremental associates to staff them at a time when many corporations were downsizing.

In addition, we achieved several new milestones:

- Our loyal customers came to us for more than 1 billion transactions in a year for the first time ever.
- The Home Depot became the youngest retailer ever to reach $50 billion in revenue.
- We were named "#1 Specialty Retailer" by *Fortune Magazine* for the ninth consecutive year and "#6 Most Admired" company in America for the second consecutive year. Among the Top Ten Most Admired, The Home Depot was ranked fourth in return to stockholders.

I am immensely proud of these achievements. They're evidence of the pride, competitive enthusiasm, and drive of our "orange-blooded" associates. Our corporate values have also placed the highest emphasis on "giving back" to the communities in which we live and work. In fiscal 2001, that included:

- Six million volunteer hours including:
  - 16 KaBoom playgrounds built and 18 playgrounds refurbished
  - 17 Habitat For Humanity® homes built
  - 2,000 home repair projects completed in cooperation with Rebuilding Together™
- $20 million in grants to more than 7,500 organizations

Building value ... and values with Habitat for Humanity.

Our response to September 11th was proof positive of how thoroughly our values are engrained in every associate so that we "shine brightest during the darkest hours." Immediately following the attacks, our associates staffed our command center to coordinate delivering materials to the New York and Washington sites. Within hours, Home Depot trucks were on the road with supplies necessary for the rescue and recovery efforts. All told, as a company and as individuals, we contributed thousands of volunteer hours and more than $3 million in products, supplies and financial support.

In addition to driving record financial performance, 2001 was a year of driving change within the organization as we prepare to grow toward $100 billion in revenues. By introducing and implementing a Strategic Operating and Resource planning process or "SOAR", we focused the company on expanding our growth horizons. SOAR is a multi-step process focused on industry and economic data. SOAR allows us to see opportunities that otherwise might not have appeared, and in 2001 it validated our key initiatives, including:

Service Performance Improvement (SPI) – We implemented SPI across every division between June and October, the largest single shift in operating practice in Home Depot history. By receiving and processing inventory at night, SPI makes more hours available for associates to spend with customers during peak selling periods. SPI also provides us with a platform to improve store appearance, in-stock position, and operating efficiency. Perhaps the best part of SPI is that our associates can continue to improve their product knowledge and develop better customer service skills as SPI moves from an initiative to an everyday best practice ... SPI is the way we do business.

Merchandising Reorganization – In September, we centralized our buying function, allowing us to drive purchasing efficiencies while stores increased their focus on sales and service. We saw immediate improvement in merchandise assortment, the launch of new promotional activities, and the ability to deliver great values that our customers love. At the same time, we sustained the strongest field merchandising force in retail, ensuring that our stores maintain their neighborhood-specific, family-friendly emphasis.

We believe our greatest competitive advantage is our people.

The Pro Initiative – We grew this initiative, which provides specialized products and services to smaller professional customers, to 535 stores during 2001 and will maintain that momentum in 2002 by expanding to more than 950 stores. By dedicating trained staff to better service professional customers, we are attracting a greater percentage of the professional business, which typically spends $3 for every $1 spent by our traditional do-it-yourself (DIY) customer.

At-Home Services – We invested in our installation and service businesses to capture the market opportunity presented by a maturing population that is increasingly seeking a do-it-for-me (DIFM) solution to home projects. By building on years of experience in the installation business, The Home Depot is leveraging its brand to capture a greater share in a fragmented $180 billion marketplace.

In short, 2001 was a year of tremendous change and achievement, which demonstrated the resilience and capacity of our associates to deliver value to our stockholders, protect our values as a company, and absorb a host of transformational changes. It was also a year of building for our exciting future.

OPPORTUNITIES FOR FUTURE GROWTH

While The Home Depot's roots have been and will continue to be in the DIY market, we see vast new opportunities to increase our business and become the "home aggregator" of the home improvement business. To do that, our strategy is focused on generating growth in three ways.

Enhancing the core business – By focusing on improving store productivity, we can grow comparable sales and leverage operating efficiencies. We are investing in "game-changing" opportunities, for example, by tripling our investment in new systems initiatives, by applying Six Sigma business process improvement practices across the enterprise, and by rolling out efficient crossdock transit facilities. We will also build on our merchandising success by enriching the vitality and velocity of our inventory through programs that identify opportunities like energy conservation, environmentally-friendly products, and home security.

Extending the business – In 2002, The Home Depot will add 200 new stores in a variety of formats and sizes, reflecting customer demographics, buying preferences, and geography. We will also reach for new relationships with homebuilders and commercial and industrial customers through initiatives like Home Depot Supply and its "pro" stores. Home Depot Supply is our first step in realizing the business-to-business selling opportunity available to The Home Depot.

Expanding the business – In 2001, The Home Depot expanded its business with the acquisition of Your "other" Warehouse, a Louisiana-based specialty plumbing fixtures company that supports our stores in the special order plumbing and accessory areas. Customer response to these enhanced assortments and delivery has been very strong and we continue to be excited about potential expansion across other product lines.

We also entered Mexico through the acquisition of TotalHOME, the second largest home improvement retailer in that country. In March 2002, we announced plans to acquire the four-store Del Norte home improvement chain and build two additional Home Depot stores, which further consolidates our position in the $12.5 billion home improvement market in Mexico.

By analyzing and identifying ever-increasing concentric rings of market opportunity, we can continue to develop new products, services, and markets, both in this country and globally.

With thousands of volunteer hours and millions of donations, we showed our heart in the wake of September 11th.

SETTING THE HIGHEST STANDARDS

Leadership means holding ourselves to the highest business standards. During 2001, we completed a comprehensive review of our business to ensure that across every operation and in every functional area, The Home Depot is complying with not only the letter, but the spirit of the law.

INVESTING IN OUR PEOPLE

We believe our greatest competitive advantage is our people. That's why in 2001, we launched human resources initiatives designed to attract, motivate, and retain the best employees in the industry. Through new learning programs for associates and leadership development of district and store managers, we will increasingly shift our store management focus from "operating a box" to "managing a business."

Every Home Depot associate received a special lesson in leadership this year from our Olympic Job Opportunity Program (OJOP) athletes who competed in the 2002 Olympic and Paralympic Winter Games. I'm sure you share our pride in our orange-blooded athletes, who brought home eight medals, and agree that expanding our unique commitment to this program from 140 to 204 OJOP associates for the 2004 games is a great way to sustain and develop leadership in our stores.

LEADERSHIP TRANSITION

I can't thank Bernie Marcus enough for his support and guidance during this management transition. Without question, it has been extraordinarily smooth. Bernie has been both constructive and instructive, and I am grateful for his enormous support, his coaching, and his confidence in our management team to lead this great organization.

In closing, let me reiterate how excited I am about the future of The Home Depot. We have arguably the healthiest balance sheet in retailing and an enviable brand that offers tremendous opportunity for future growth. Our commitment to you, and to ourselves, is always to be the best, and improve what we do every day.

Sincerely,

Bob

Bob Nardelli
Chairman, President & Chief Executive Officer

MANAGEMENT'S DISCUSSION AND ANALYSIS OF RESULTS OF OPERATIONS AND FINANCIAL CONDITION

SELECTED CONSOLIDATED STATEMENTS OF EARNINGS DATA

The data below reflect selected sales data, the percentage relationship between sales and major categories in the Consolidated Statements of Earnings and the percentage change in the dollar amounts of each of the items.

	Fiscal Year[1]			Percentage Increase (Decrease) In Dollar Amounts	
	2001	2000	1999	**2001 vs. 2000**	2000 vs. 1999
NET SALES	**100.0%**	100.0%	100.0%	**17.1%**	19.0%
Gross Profit	**30.2**	29.9	29.7	**18.0**	19.9
Operating Expenses:					
Selling and Store Operating	**19.0**	18.6	17.8	**19.4**	24.8
Pre-Opening	**0.2**	0.3	0.3	**(17.6)**	25.7
General and Administrative	**1.7**	1.8	1.7	**12.0**	24.4
Total Operating Expenses	**20.9**	20.7	19.8	**18.2**	24.8
OPERATING INCOME	**9.3**	9.2	9.9	**17.7**	10.1
Interest Income (Expense):					
Interest and Investment Income	**0.1**	0.1	0.1	**12.8**	27.0
Interest Expense	**(0.1)**	(0.1)	(0.1)	**33.3**	(48.8)
Interest, net	**–**	–	–	**(3.8)**	750.0
EARNINGS BEFORE INCOME TAXES	**9.3**	9.2	9.9	**17.5**	10.9
Income Taxes	**3.6**	3.6	3.9	**16.9**	10.2
NET EARNINGS	**5.7%**	5.6%	6.0%	**17.9%**	11.3%
SELECTED SALES DATA[2]					
Number of Transactions (000s)	**1,090,975**	936,519	797,229	**16.5%**	17.5%
Average Sale per Transaction	**$ 48.64**	$ 48.65	$ 47.87	**–**	1.6
Weighted Average Weekly Sales per Operating Store	**$ 812,000**	$ 864,000	$ 876,000	**(6.0)**	(1.4)
Weighted Average Sales per Square Foot[3]	**$ 387.93**	$ 414.68	$ 422.53	**(6.5)**	(1.9)

(1) Fiscal years 2001, 2000 and 1999 refer to the fiscal years ended February 3, 2002; January 28, 2001; and January 30, 2000, respectively.
(2) Excludes Apex Supply Company, Georgia Lighting, Maintenance Warehouse, Your "other" Warehouse and National Blinds and Wallpaper.
(3) Adjusted to reflect the first 52 weeks of the 53-week fiscal year in 2001.

MANAGEMENT'S DISCUSSION AND ANALYSIS OF RESULTS OF OPERATIONS AND FINANCIAL CONDITION (CONTINUED)

FORWARD-LOOKING STATEMENTS Certain written and oral statements made by us or our authorized executive officers on our behalf constitute "forward-looking statements" as defined under the Private Securities Litigation Reform Act of 1995. Words or phrases such as "should result," "are expected to," "we anticipate," "we estimate," "we project" or similar expressions are intended to identify forward-looking statements. These statements are subject to certain risks and uncertainties that could cause actual results to differ materially from our historical experience and our present expectations or projections. These risks and uncertainties include, but are not limited to, unanticipated weather conditions; stability of costs and availability of sourcing channels; the ability to attract, train and retain highly-qualified associates; conditions affecting the availability, acquisition, development and ownership of real estate; general economic conditions; the impact of competition; and regulatory and litigation matters. You should not place undue reliance on forward-looking statements, since such statements speak only as of the date of the making of such statements. Additional information concerning these risks and uncertainties is contained in our filings with the Securities and Exchange Commission, including our Annual Report on Form 10-K.

RESULTS OF OPERATIONS For an understanding of the significant factors that influenced our performance during the past three fiscal years, the following discussion should be read in conjunction with the consolidated financial statements and the notes to consolidated financial statements presented in this annual report.

Fiscal year ended February 3, 2002 compared to January 28, 2001
Fiscal year 2001 consisted of 53 weeks compared to 52 weeks in fiscal 2000. Net sales for fiscal 2001 increased 17.1% to $53.6 billion from $45.7 billion in fiscal 2000. This increase was attributable to, among other things, the 204 new stores opened during fiscal 2001 and full year sales from the 204 new stores opened during fiscal 2000. Approximately $880 million of the increase in sales was attributable to the additional week in fiscal 2001. Comparable store-for-store sales were flat in fiscal 2001 due to the weak economic environment resulting from certain factors including, but not limited to, low consumer confidence and high unemployment.

Gross profit as a percent of sales was 30.2% for fiscal 2001 compared to 29.9% for fiscal 2000. The rate increase was primarily attributable to a lower cost of merchandise resulting from product line reviews, purchasing synergies created by our newly centralized merchandising structure and an increase in the number of tool rental centers from 342 at the end of fiscal 2000 to 466 at the end of fiscal 2001. We expect to have tool rental centers in approximately 600 stores by the end of fiscal 2002.

Operating expenses as a percent of sales were 20.9% for fiscal 2001 compared to 20.7% for fiscal 2000. Selling and store operating expenses as a percent of sales increased to 19.0% in fiscal 2001 from 18.6% in fiscal 2000. The increase was primarily attributable to growth in store occupancy costs resulting from higher depreciation and property taxes due to our investment in new stores, combined with increased energy costs. Also, credit card transaction fees were higher than the prior year due to increased penetration of total credit sales. These increases were partially offset by a decrease in store payroll expense caused by an improvement in labor productivity resulting from initiatives inside the store and new systems enhancements.

Store initiatives include our Service Performance Improvement ("SPI") initiative which was implemented in every Home Depot store in fiscal 2001. Under SPI our stores receive and handle inventory at night, allowing our associates to spend more time with customers during peak selling hours. In addition, our Pro program was in 535 of our Home Depot stores at the end of fiscal 2001, providing dedicated store resources to serve the specific needs of professional customers. We expect to have our Pro initiative in more than 950 stores at the end of fiscal 2002. SPI and Pro have resulted in improved operational efficiency, safety and customer service.

Pre-opening expenses as a percent of sales were 0.2% for fiscal 2001 and 0.3% for fiscal 2000. We opened 204 new stores in both fiscal 2001 and 2000. Pre-opening expenses averaged $569,000 per store in fiscal 2001 compared to $671,000 per store in fiscal 2000. The decrease in the average expense per store was primarily due to shorter pre-opening periods as we reengineered our store opening process.

MANAGEMENT'S DISCUSSION AND ANALYSIS OF RESULTS OF OPERATIONS AND FINANCIAL CONDITION (CONTINUED)

General and administrative expenses as a percent of sales were 1.7% for fiscal 2001 compared to 1.8% in fiscal 2000. This decrease was primarily due to cost savings associated with the reorganization of certain components of our general and administrative structure, such as the centralization of our merchandising organization, and our focus on expense control in areas such as travel.

Interest and investment income as a percent of sales was 0.1% for both fiscal 2001 and 2000. Interest expense as a percent of sales was 0.1% for both fiscal 2001 and 2000.

Our combined federal and state effective income tax rate decreased to 38.6% for fiscal 2001 from 38.8% for fiscal 2000. The decrease in fiscal 2001 was attributable to higher tax credits and a lower effective state income tax rate compared to fiscal 2000.

Net earnings as a percent of sales were 5.7% for fiscal 2001 compared to 5.6% for fiscal 2000, reflecting the increased gross profit rate, which was partially offset by higher store operating expenses, as described above. Diluted earnings per share were $1.29 for fiscal 2001 compared to $1.10 for fiscal 2000.

Fiscal year ended January 28, 2001 compared to January 30, 2000 Net sales for fiscal 2000 increased 19.0% to $45.7 billion from $38.4 billion in fiscal 1999. This increase was attributable to, among other things, full year sales from the 169 new stores opened during fiscal 1999, a 4% comparable store-for-store sales increase and 204 new store openings.

Gross profit as a percent of sales was 29.9% for fiscal 2000 compared to 29.7% for fiscal 1999. The rate increase was primarily attributable to a lower cost of merchandise resulting from product line reviews, benefits from global sourcing programs and an increase in the number of tool rental centers from 150 at the end of fiscal 1999 to 342 at the end of fiscal 2000.

Operating expenses as a percent of sales were 20.7% for fiscal 2000 compared to 19.8% for fiscal 1999. Selling and store operating expenses as a percent of sales increased to 18.6% in fiscal 2000 from 17.8% in fiscal 1999. The increase was primarily attributable to higher store selling payroll expenses resulting from market wage pressures and an increase in employee longevity. In addition, medical costs increased due to higher family enrollment in our medical plans, rising health care costs and higher prescription drug costs. Finally, store occupancy costs, including property taxes, property rent, depreciation and utilities, increased due to new store growth and energy rate increases.

Pre-opening expenses as a percent of sales were 0.3% for both fiscal 2000 and 1999. We opened 204 new stores in fiscal 2000, compared to opening 169 new stores in fiscal 1999. Pre-opening expenses averaged $671,000 per store in fiscal 2000 compared to $643,000 per store in fiscal 1999. The higher average expense was primarily due to the opening of more EXPO Design Center stores and expansion of Home Depot stores into certain new markets including international locations, which involved longer pre-opening periods and higher training, travel and relocation costs.

General and administrative expenses as a percent of sales were 1.8% for fiscal 2000 compared to 1.7% for fiscal 1999. The increase was primarily due to investments in Internet development and international operations, as well as a full year of payroll and other costs associated with operating four new divisional offices, which opened during the fourth quarter of fiscal 1999.

Interest and investment income as a percent of sales was 0.1% for both fiscal 2000 and 1999. Interest expense as a percent of sales was 0.1% for both comparable periods.

Our combined federal and state effective income tax rate decreased to 38.8% for fiscal 2000 from 39.0% for fiscal 1999. The decrease was attributable to higher tax credits in fiscal 2000 compared to fiscal 1999.

Net earnings as a percent of sales were 5.6% for fiscal 2000 compared to 6.0% for fiscal 1999, reflecting higher selling and store operating expenses as a percent of sales partially offset by a higher gross profit rate as described above. Diluted earnings per share were $1.10 for fiscal 2000 compared to $1.00 for fiscal 1999.

LIQUIDITY AND CAPITAL RESOURCES Cash flow generated from operations provides us with a significant source of liquidity. For fiscal 2001, cash provided by operations increased to $6.0 billion from $2.8 billion in fiscal 2000. The increase was primarily due to significant growth in days payable outstanding from 23 days at the end of fiscal 2000 to 34 days at the end of fiscal 2001, a 12.7% decrease in average inventory per store as of the end of fiscal 2001 and increased operating income. The growth in days payable and decrease in average inventory per store are the result of our efforts to improve our working capital position by extending our payment terms to industry standards and enhancing inventory assortments.

Cash used in investing activities, primarily comprised of capital expenditures, was $3.5 billion in both fiscal 2001 and 2000. We opened 204 new stores in both fiscal 2001 and 2000. We own 188 of the stores opened in 2001 and lease the remainder.

We plan to open 200 stores in fiscal 2002 and expect total capital expenditures to be approximately $3.6 billion.

MANAGEMENT'S DISCUSSION AND ANALYSIS OF RESULTS OF OPERATIONS AND FINANCIAL CONDITION (CONTINUED)

Cash used in financing activities in fiscal 2001 was $173 million compared with cash provided by financing activities of $737 million in fiscal 2000. The increase in cash used was primarily due to the net effect of repaying $754 million of commercial paper and issuing $500 million of $5^{3}/_{8}$% Senior Notes during fiscal 2001.

We have a commercial paper program that allows borrowings up to a maximum of $1 billion. As of February 3, 2002, there were no borrowings outstanding under the program. In connection with the program, we have a back-up credit facility with a consortium of banks for up to $800 million. The credit facility, which expires in September 2004, contains various restrictive covenants, none of which are expected to impact our liquidity or capital resources.

We use capital, operating and other off-balance sheet leases to finance about 20% of our real estate. Off-balance sheet leases include three leases created under structured financing arrangements to fund the construction of certain stores, office buildings and distribution centers. Two of these lease agreements involve a special purpose entity which meets the criteria established by generally accepted accounting principles and is not owned by or affiliated with the Company, its management or officers. Operating and off-balance sheet leases are not reflected in our balance sheet in accordance with generally accepted accounting principles. The net present value of capital lease obligations is reflected in our balance sheet in long-term debt. As of the end of fiscal 2001, our debt to equity ratio was 6.9%. If the estimated present value of future payments under the operating and other off-balance sheet leases were capitalized, our debt to equity ratio would increase to approximately 30%.

The following table summarizes our significant contractual obligations and commercial commitments as of February 3, 2002 (amounts in millions):

	Payments Due By Period				
Contractual Obligations(1)	Total	2002	2003-2004	2005-2006	Thereafter
Long-Term Debt	$1,023	$ 1	$ 502	$ 502	$ 18
Capital Leases	$ 791	$ 41	$ 85	$ 88	$ 577
Operating Leases	$7,407	$ 517	$ 942	$ 809	$ 5,139

	Amount of Commitment Expiration Per Period				
Commercial Commitments(2)	Total	2002	2003-2004	2005-2006	Thereafter
Letters of Credit	$ 557	$ 551	$ 6	–	–
Guarantees	$ 799	–	$ 504	$ 72	$ 223

(1) Contractual obligations consist of long-term debt comprised primarily of $1 billion of Senior Notes further discussed in "Quantitative and Qualitative Disclosures about Market Risk" and future minimum lease payments under capital and operating leases, including off-balance sheet leases, used in the normal course of business.

(2) Commercial commitments include letters of credit for certain business transactions and guarantees provided under certain off-balance sheet leases. We issue letters of credit for insurance programs, import purchases and construction contracts. Under certain off-balance sheet leases for retail locations, office buildings and distribution centers, we have provided residual value guarantees. The estimated maximum amount of the residual value guarantees at the end of the lease terms is $799 million. The leases expire at various terms from 2004 through 2008 with some carrying renewal options through 2025. The expiration date of the residual value guarantees in the table above is based on the original lease terms; however, the expiration period will change if the leases are renewed.

As of February 3, 2002, we had $2.5 billion in cash and cash equivalents. We believe that our current cash position, internally generated funds, funds available from the $1 billion commercial paper program and the ability to obtain alternate sources of financing should be sufficient to enable us to complete our capital expenditure programs through the next several fiscal years.

QUANTITATIVE AND QUALITATIVE DISCLOSURES ABOUT MARKET RISK Our exposure to market risks results primarily from fluctuations in interest rates. Although we have international operating entities, our exposure to foreign currency rate fluctuations is not significant to our financial condition and results. Our objective for holding derivative instruments is to decrease the volatility of earnings and cash flow associated with fluctuations in these rates.

We have financial instruments that are sensitive to changes in interest rates. These instruments include fixed rate debt and other contractual arrangements. We issued $500 million of $5^{3}/_{8}$% Senior Notes in fiscal 2001 maturing on April 1, 2006 and $500 million of $6^{1}/_{2}$% Senior Notes in fiscal 1999 maturing on September 15, 2004. As of February 3, 2002, the market values of the publicly traded $5^{3}/_{8}$% and $6^{1}/_{2}$% Senior Notes were approximately $511 million and $531 million, respectively. We have two interest rate swap agreements, both designed to hedge the market risk associated with interest rate volatility. We have one agreement in the notional amount of $300 million that swaps fixed rate interest on $300 million of our $500 million $5^{3}/_{8}$% Senior Notes for a variable interest rate equal to LIBOR plus 30 basis points and expires on April 1, 2006. We have another agreement expiring January 31, 2003 in the notional amount of $690 million that swaps a variable interest rate for a fixed rate of $6^{3}/_{4}$%, designed to mitigate the interest rate risk related to the portfolio of our proprietary credit card, which is serviced by a third party.

IMPACT OF INFLATION AND CHANGING PRICES Although we cannot accurately determine the precise effect of inflation on operations, we do not believe inflation has had a material effect on sales or results of operations.

MANAGEMENT'S DISCUSSION AND ANALYSIS OF RESULTS OF OPERATIONS AND FINANCIAL CONDITION (CONTINUED)

CRITICAL ACCOUNTING POLICIES Our significant accounting policies are disclosed in Note 1 to our consolidated financial statements. The following discussion addresses our most critical accounting policies, which are those that are most important to the portrayal of our financial condition and results, and that require judgment.

REVENUE RECOGNITION We recognize revenue, net of estimated returns, at the time the customer takes possession of the merchandise or receives services. We estimate the liability for sales returns based on the historical return levels. The methodology used is consistent with other retailers. We believe that our estimate for sales returns is an accurate reflection of future returns. When we collect payment from customers before ownership of the merchandise has passed or the service has been performed, the amount received is recorded as a deferred revenue liability.

INVENTORY Our inventory is stated at the lower of cost (first-in, first-out) or market, with approximately 94% valued under the retail method and the remainder under the cost method. Under the retail method, inventory is stated at cost which is determined by applying a cost-to-retail ratio to the ending retail value of inventory. As our inventory retail value is adjusted regularly to reflect market conditions, our inventory methodology approximates the lower of cost or market. Retailers with many different types of merchandise at low unit cost with a large number of transactions frequently use this method. In addition, we reduce our ending inventory value for estimated losses related to shrink. This estimate is determined based upon analysis of historical shrink losses and recent shrink trends.

SELF INSURANCE We are self-insured for certain losses related to general liability, product liability and workers' compensation. We maintain stop loss coverage with third party insurers to limit our total exposure. Our liability represents an estimate of the ultimate cost of claims incurred as of the balance sheet date. The estimated liability is not discounted and is established based upon analysis of historical data and actuarial estimates, and is reviewed by management and third party actuaries on a quarterly basis to ensure that the liability is appropriate. While we believe these estimates are reasonable based on the information currently available, if actual trends, including the severity or frequency of claims or fluctuations in premiums, differ from our estimates, our financial results could be impacted. In an attempt to mitigate our risks of workers' compensation and general liability claims, we have significantly enhanced our store safety procedures with SPI and other safety awareness programs.

USE OF ESTIMATES We have made a number of estimates and assumptions relating to the reporting of assets and liabilities, the disclosure of contingent assets and liabilities, and reported amounts of revenue and expenses in preparing our financial statements in conformity with generally accepted accounting principles. Actual results could differ from these estimates.

RECENT ACCOUNTING PRONOUNCEMENTS In July 2001, the Financial Accounting Standards Board ("FASB") issued Statement of Financial Accounting Standards ("SFAS") 142, "Goodwill and Other Intangible Assets." Under SFAS 142, which we will adopt on February 4, 2002, goodwill will no longer be amortized and will instead be evaluated for impairment at least annually. Without this change, amortization expense for goodwill in fiscal 2002 would have been approximately $11 million. We have reviewed our goodwill and completed our impairment analysis and, accordingly, have determined that the adoption of SFAS 142 will not have a material impact on our consolidated financial statements.

In October 2001, the FASB issued SFAS 144, "Accounting for the Impairment or Disposal of Long-Lived Assets," which amends Accounting Principles Board Opinion No. 30 ("APB 30"), "Reporting the Results of Operations - Reporting the Effects of Disposal of a Segment of a Business, and Extraordinary, Unusual and Infrequently Occurring Events and Transactions." SFAS 144 retains the fundamental provisions of SFAS 121, "Accounting for the Impairment of Long-Lived Assets and for Long-Lived Assets to be Disposed Of," for recognizing and measuring impairment losses on long-lived assets held for use and long-lived assets to be disposed of by sale, while resolving significant implementation issues. SFAS 144 retains the basic provisions of APB 30 on the presentation of discontinued operations in the income statement, but expands the scope to include all distinguishable components of an entity that will be eliminated from ongoing operations in a disposal transaction. We plan to adopt SFAS 144 on February 4, 2002 and do not expect the adoption to have a material impact on our consolidated financial statements.

CONSOLIDATED STATEMENTS OF EARNINGS

amounts in millions, except per share data	Fiscal Year Ended **February 3, 2002**	January 28, 2001	January 30, 2000
NET SALES	**$ 53,553**	$ 45,738	$ 38,434
Cost of Merchandise Sold	**37,406**	32,057	27,023
Gross Profit	**16,147**	13,681	11,411
Operating Expenses:			
Selling and Store Operating	**10,163**	8,513	6,819
Pre-Opening	**117**	142	113
General and Administrative	**935**	835	671
Total Operating Expenses	**11,215**	9,490	7,603
OPERATING INCOME	**4,932**	4,191	3,808
Interest Income (Expense):			
Interest and Investment Income	**53**	47	37
Interest Expense	**(28)**	(21)	(41)
Interest, net	**25**	26	(4)
EARNINGS BEFORE INCOME TAXES	**4,957**	4,217	3,804
Income Taxes	**1,913**	1,636	1,484
NET EARNINGS	**$ 3,044**	$ 2,581	$ 2,320
BASIC EARNINGS PER SHARE	**$ 1.30**	$ 1.11	$ 1.03
Weighted Average Number of Common Shares Outstanding	**2,335**	2,315	2,244
DILUTED EARNINGS PER SHARE	**$ 1.29**	$ 1.10	$ 1.00
Weighted Average Number of Common Shares Outstanding Assuming Dilution	**2,353**	2,352	2,342

See accompanying notes to consolidated financial statements.

CONSOLIDATED BALANCE SHEETS

amounts in millions, except share data	**February 3, 2002**	January 28, 2001
ASSETS		
Current Assets:		
Cash and Cash Equivalents	**$ 2,477**	$ 167
Short-Term Investments, including current maturities of long-term investments	**69**	10
Receivables, net	**920**	835
Merchandise Inventories	**6,725**	6,556
Other Current Assets	**170**	209
Total Current Assets	**10,361**	7,777
Property and Equipment, at cost:		
Land	**4,972**	4,230
Buildings	**7,698**	6,167
Furniture, Fixtures and Equipment	**3,403**	2,877
Leasehold Improvements	**750**	665
Construction in Progress	**1,049**	1,032
Capital Leases	**257**	261
	18,129	15,232
Less Accumulated Depreciation and Amortization	**2,754**	2,164
Net Property and Equipment	**15,375**	13,068
Notes Receivable	**83**	77
Cost in Excess of the Fair Value of Net Assets Acquired, net of accumulated amortization of $49 at February 3, 2002 and $41 at January 28, 2001	**419**	314
Other	**156**	149
	$26,394	$21,385
LIABILITIES AND STOCKHOLDERS' EQUITY		
Current Liabilities:		
Accounts Payable	**$ 3,436**	$ 1,976
Accrued Salaries and Related Expenses	**717**	627
Sales Taxes Payable	**348**	298
Other Accrued Expenses	**933**	752
Deferred Revenue	**851**	650
Income Taxes Payable	**211**	78
Current Installments of Long-Term Debt	**5**	4
Total Current Liabilities	**6,501**	4,385
Long-Term Debt, excluding current installments	**1,250**	1,545
Other Long-Term Liabilities	**372**	249
Deferred Income Taxes	**189**	195
Minority Interest	**–**	7
STOCKHOLDERS' EQUITY		
Common Stock, par value $0.05. Authorized: 10,000,000,000 shares; issued and outstanding – 2,345,888,000 shares at February 3, 2002 and 2,323,747,000 shares at January 28, 2001	**117**	116
Paid-In Capital	**5,412**	4,810
Retained Earnings	**12,799**	10,151
Accumulated Other Comprehensive Loss	**(220)**	(67)
	18,108	15,010
Less Unearned Compensation	**26**	6
Total Stockholders' Equity	**18,082**	15,004
	$26,394	$21,385

See accompanying notes to consolidated financial statements.

CONSOLIDATED STATEMENTS OF STOCKHOLDERS' EQUITY AND COMPREHENSIVE INCOME

amounts in millions, except per share data	Common Stock Shares	Common Stock Amount	Paid-In Capital	Retained Earnings	Accumulated Other Comprehensive Income (Loss)	Other	Total Stockholders' Equity	Comprehensive Income[1]
BALANCE, JANUARY 31, 1999	2,213	$111	$2,817	$ 5,876	$ (61)	$ (3)	$ 8,740	
Shares Issued Under Employee Stock Purchase and Option Plans	19	1	273	–	–	–	274	
Tax Effect of Sale of Option Shares by Employees	–	–	132	–	–	–	132	
Conversion of $3^{1/4}$% Convertible Subordinated Notes, net	72	3	1,097	–	–	–	1,100	
Net Earnings	–	–	–	2,320	–	–	2,320	$ 2,320
Translation Adjustments	–	–	–	–	34	–	34	34
Unearned Compensation	–	–	–	–	–	(4)	(4)	
Cash Dividends ($0.11 per share)	–	–	–	(255)	–	–	(255)	
Comprehensive Income for Fiscal 1999								$ 2,354
BALANCE, JANUARY 30, 2000	2,304	$115	$4,319	$ 7,941	$ (27)	$ (7)	$12,341	
Shares Issued Under Employee Stock Purchase and Option Plans	20	1	348	–	–	–	349	
Tax Effect of Sale of Option Shares by Employees	–	–	137	–	–	–	137	
Net Earnings	–	–	–	2,581	–	–	2,581	$ 2,581
Translation Adjustments	–	–	–	–	(40)	–	(40)	(40)
Stock Compensation Expense	–	–	6	–	–	–	6	
Unearned Compensation	–	–	–	–	–	1	1	
Cash Dividends ($0.16 per share)	–	–	–	(371)	–	–	(371)	
Comprehensive Income for Fiscal 2000								$ 2,541
BALANCE, JANUARY 28, 2001	2,324	$116	$4,810	$10,151	$ (67)	$(6)	$15,004	
Shares Issued Under Employee Stock Purchase and Option Plans	**22**	**1**	**448**	**–**	**–**	**–**	**449**	
Tax Effect of Sale of Option Shares by Employees	**–**	**–**	**138**	**–**	**–**	**–**	**138**	
Net Earnings	**–**	**–**	**–**	**3,044**	**–**	**–**	**3,044**	**$ 3,044**
Translation Adjustments	**–**	**–**	**–**	**–**	**(124)**	**–**	**(124)**	**(124)**
Unrealized Loss on Derivatives	**–**	**–**	**–**	**–**	**(29)**	**–**	**(29)**	**(18)**
Stock Compensation Expense	**–**	**–**	**16**	**–**	**–**	**–**	**16**	
Unearned Compensation	**–**	**–**	**–**	**–**	**–**	**(20)**	**(20)**	
Cash Dividends ($0.17 per share)	**–**	**–**	**–**	**(396)**	**–**	**–**	**(396)**	
Comprehensive Income for Fiscal 2001								**$ 2,902**
BALANCE, FEBRUARY 3, 2002	**2,346**	**$117**	**$5,412**	**$12,799**	**$(220)**	**$(26)**	**$18,082**	

(1) Components of comprehensive income are reported net of related taxes.

See accompanying notes to consolidated financial statements.

CONSOLIDATED STATEMENTS OF CASH FLOWS

		Fiscal Year Ended	
amounts in millions	**February 3, 2002**	January 28, 2001	January 30, 2000
CASH FLOWS FROM OPERATIONS:			
Net Earnings	**$ 3,044**	$ 2,581	$ 2,320
Reconciliation of Net Earnings to Net Cash Provided by Operations:			
Depreciation and Amortization	**764**	601	463
Increase in Receivables, net	**(119)**	(246)	(85)
Increase in Merchandise Inventories	**(166)**	(1,075)	(1,142)
Increase in Accounts Payable and Accrued Liabilities	**2,078**	754	820
Increase in Income Taxes Payable	**272**	151	93
Other	**90**	30	(23)
Net Cash Provided by Operations	**5,963**	2,796	2,446
CASH FLOWS FROM INVESTING ACTIVITIES:			
Capital Expenditures, net of $5, $16 and $37 of non-cash capital expenditures in fiscal 2001, 2000 and 1999, respectively	**(3,393)**	(3,558)	(2,581)
Payments for Businesses Acquired, net	**(190)**	(26)	(101)
Proceeds from Sale of Business, net	**64**	–	–
Proceeds from Sales of Property and Equipment	**126**	95	87
Purchases of Investments	**(85)**	(39)	(32)
Proceeds from Maturities of Investments	**25**	30	30
Other	**(13)**	(32)	(25)
Net Cash Used in Investing Activities	**(3,466)**	(3,530)	(2,622)
CASH FLOWS FROM FINANCING ACTIVITIES:			
(Repayments) Issuance of Commercial Paper Obligations, net	**(754)**	754	(246)
Proceeds from Long-Term Debt	**532**	32	522
Repayments of Long-Term Debt	**–**	(29)	(14)
Proceeds from Sale of Common Stock, net	**445**	351	267
Cash Dividends Paid to Stockholders	**(396)**	(371)	(255)
Minority Interest Contributions to Partnership	**–**	–	7
Net Cash (Used In) Provided by Financing Activities	**(173)**	737	281
Effect of Exchange Rate Changes on Cash and Cash Equivalents	**(14)**	(4)	1
Increase (Decrease) in Cash and Cash Equivalents	**2,310**	(1)	106
Cash and Cash Equivalents at Beginning of Year	**167**	168	62
Cash and Cash Equivalents at End of Year	**$ 2,477**	$ 167	$ 168
SUPPLEMENTAL DISCLOSURE OF CASH PAYMENTS MADE FOR:			
Interest, net of interest capitalized	**$ 18**	$ 16	$ 26
Income Taxes	**$ 1,685**	$ 1,386	$ 1,396

See accompanying notes to consolidated financial statements.

NOTES TO CONSOLIDATED FINANCIAL STATEMENTS

NOTE 1. **SUMMARY OF SIGNIFICANT ACCOUNTING POLICIES**

The Home Depot, Inc. and subsidiaries (the "Company") operates Home Depot stores, which are full-service, warehouse-style stores averaging approximately 109,000 square feet in size. The stores stock approximately 40,000 to 50,000 different kinds of building materials, home improvement supplies and lawn and garden products that are sold primarily to do-it-yourselfers, but also to home improvement contractors, tradespeople, and building maintenance professionals. In addition, the Company operates EXPO Design Center stores, which offer products and services primarily related to design and renovation projects, and Villager's Hardware stores, which offer products and services for home enhancement and smaller project needs in a convenience hardware store format. Additionally, the Company operates one Home Depot Floor Store, a test store that offers only flooring products and installation services. At the end of fiscal 2001, the Company was operating 1,333 stores, including 1,201 Home Depot stores, 41 EXPO Design Center stores, 4 Villager's Hardware stores and 1 Home Depot Floor Store in the United States; 78 Home Depot stores in Canada; 4 Home Depot stores in Argentina, which were sold on February 18, 2002; and 4 Home Depot stores in Mexico. Included in the Company's Consolidated Balance Sheet at February 3, 2002, were $946 million of net assets of the Canada, Argentina and Mexico operations. Also included in consolidated results are several wholly-owned subsidiaries. The Company offers facilities maintenance and repair products, as well as wallpaper and custom window treatments via direct shipment through subsidiaries Maintenance Warehouse and National Blinds and Wallpaper, Inc. Georgia Lighting is a specialty lighting designer, distributor and retailer to both commercial and retail customers. The Company offers plumbing, HVAC and other professional plumbing products through wholesale plumbing distributors Apex Supply Company and Your "other" Warehouse.

FISCAL YEAR The Company's fiscal year is a 52- or 53-week period ending on the Sunday nearest to January 31. Fiscal year 2001, which ended February 3, 2002, consisted of 53 weeks. Fiscal years 2000 and 1999, which ended January 28, 2001 and January 30, 2000, respectively, consisted of 52 weeks.

BASIS OF PRESENTATION The consolidated financial statements include the accounts of the Company, its wholly-owned subsidiaries, and its majority-owned partnership, The Home Depot Chile S.A. In October 2001, the Company sold its interest in The Home Depot Chile S.A. All significant intercompany transactions have been eliminated in consolidation.

Stockholders' equity, share and per share amounts for all periods presented have been adjusted for a three-for-two stock split effected in the form of a stock dividend on December 30, 1999.

CASH EQUIVALENTS The Company considers all highly liquid investments purchased with a maturity of three months or less to be cash equivalents. The Company's cash and cash equivalents are carried at fair market value and consist primarily of commercial paper, money market funds, U.S. government agency securities and tax-exempt notes and bonds.

MERCHANDISE INVENTORIES The majority of the Company's inventory is stated at the lower of cost (first-in, first-out) or market, as determined by the retail inventory method.

Certain subsidiaries and distribution centers value inventories at the lower of cost (first-in, first-out) or market, as determined by the cost method. These inventories represent approximately 6% of total inventory.

INVESTMENTS The Company's investments, consisting primarily of high-grade debt securities, are recorded at fair value and are classified as available-for-sale.

INCOME TAXES The Company provides for federal, state and foreign income taxes currently payable, as well as for those deferred because of timing differences between reporting income and expenses for financial statement purposes versus tax purposes. Federal, state and foreign incentive tax credits are recorded as a reduction of income taxes. Deferred tax assets and liabilities are recognized for the future tax consequences attributable to differences between the financial statement carrying amounts of existing assets and liabilities and their respective tax bases. Deferred tax assets and liabilities are measured using enacted tax rates expected to apply to taxable income in the years in which those temporary differences are expected to be recovered or settled. The effect of a change in tax rates is recognized as income or expense in the period that includes the enactment date.

The Company and its eligible subsidiaries file a consolidated U.S. federal income tax return. Non-U.S. subsidiaries, which are consolidated for financial reporting, are not eligible to be included in consolidated U.S. federal income tax returns. Separate provisions for income taxes have been determined for these entities. The Company intends to reinvest the unremitted earnings of its non-U.S. subsidiaries and postpone their remittance indefinitely. Accordingly, no provision for U.S. income taxes for non-U.S. subsidiaries was required for any year presented.

NOTES TO CONSOLIDATED FINANCIAL STATEMENTS (CONTINUED)

DEPRECIATION AND AMORTIZATION The Company's buildings, furniture, fixtures and equipment are depreciated using the straight-line method over the estimated useful lives of the assets. Improvements to leased premises are amortized using the straight-line method over the life of the lease or the useful life of the improvement, whichever is shorter. The Company's property and equipment is depreciated using the following estimated useful lives:

	Life
Buildings	10-45 years
Furniture, fixtures and equipment	5-20 years
Leasehold improvements	5-30 years
Computer software	3-5 years

REVENUES The Company recognizes revenue, net of estimated returns, at the time the customer takes possession of merchandise or receives services. When the Company collects payment from customers before ownership of the merchandise has passed or the service has been performed, the amount received is recorded as a deferred revenue liability.

SELF INSURANCE The Company is self-insured for certain losses related to general liability, product liability and workers' compensation. The Company has stop loss coverage to limit the exposure arising from these claims. The expected ultimate cost for claims incurred as of the balance sheet date is not discounted and is recognized as a liability. The expected ultimate cost of claims is estimated based upon analysis of historical data and actuarial estimates.

ADVERTISING Television and radio advertising production costs along with media placement costs are expensed when the advertisement appears. Included in current assets are $15 million and $20 million at the end of fiscal years 2001 and 2000, respectively, relating to prepayments of production costs for print and broadcast advertising.

SHIPPING AND HANDLING COSTS The Company accounts for certain shipping and handling costs related to the shipment of product to customers from vendors as cost of goods sold. However, costs of shipments to customers by the Company are classified as selling and store operating expenses. The costs of shipments included in selling and store operating expenses amounted to $122 million, $73 million and $40 million in fiscal years 2001, 2000 and 1999, respectively.

COST IN EXCESS OF THE FAIR VALUE OF NET ASSETS ACQUIRED Goodwill, which represents the excess of purchase price over fair value of net assets acquired, is amortized on a straight-line basis over 40 years. The Company assesses the recoverability of this intangible asset by determining whether the amortization of the goodwill balance over its remaining useful life can be recovered through undiscounted future operating cash flows of the acquired operation. The amount of goodwill impairment, if any, is measured based on projected discounted cash flows using a discount rate reflecting the Company's average cost of funds.

IMPAIRMENT OF LONG-LIVED ASSETS The Company reviews long-lived assets for impairment when circumstances indicate the carrying amount of an asset may not be recoverable. Impairment is recognized to the extent the sum of undiscounted estimated future cash flows expected to result from the use of the asset is less than the carrying value. Accordingly, when the Company commits to relocate or close a store, the estimated unrecoverable costs are charged to selling and store operating expense. Such costs include the estimated loss on the sale of land and buildings, the book value of abandoned fixtures, equipment and leasehold improvements, and a provision for the present value of future lease obligations, less estimated sublease income.

STOCK COMPENSATION Statement of Financial Accounting Standards No. 123 ("SFAS 123"), "Accounting for Stock-Based Compensation" encourages the use of a fair-value-based method of accounting. As allowed by SFAS 123, the Company has elected to account for its stock-based compensation plans under the intrinsic value-based method of accounting prescribed by Accounting Principles Board Opinion No. 25 ("APB 25"), "Accounting for Stock Issued to Employees." Under APB 25, compensation expense is recorded on the date of grant if the current market price of the underlying stock exceeds the exercise price. The Company complies with the disclosure requirements of SFAS 123.

DERIVATIVES On January 29, 2001, the Company adopted Statement of Financial Accounting Standards Nos. 133, 137, and 138 (collectively "SFAS 133"), "Accounting for Derivative Instruments and Hedging Activities." SFAS 133 requires an entity to measure derivatives at fair value and recognize these assets or liabilities on the balance sheet. Recognition of changes in the fair value of a derivative in the income statement or other accumulated comprehensive income (loss) depends on the intended use of the derivative and its designation. The Company designates its derivatives based upon criteria established by SFAS 133. The Company's objective for holding derivative instruments is to decrease the volatility of earnings and cash flow associated with fluctuations in interest rates and foreign currencies.

NOTES TO CONSOLIDATED FINANCIAL STATEMENTS (CONTINUED)

COMPREHENSIVE INCOME Comprehensive income includes net earnings adjusted for certain revenues, expenses, gains and losses that are excluded from net earnings under generally accepted accounting principles. Examples include foreign currency translation adjustments and unrealized gains and losses on certain hedge transactions.

FOREIGN CURRENCY TRANSLATION The assets and liabilities denominated in a foreign currency are translated into U.S. dollars at the current rate of exchange on the last day of the reporting period, revenues and expenses are translated at the average monthly exchange rates, and equity transactions are translated using the actual rate on the day of the transaction.

USE OF ESTIMATES Management of the Company has made a number of estimates and assumptions relating to the reporting of assets and liabilities, the disclosure of contingent assets and liabilities, and reported amounts of revenues and expenses in preparing these financial statements in conformity with generally accepted accounting principles. Actual results could differ from these estimates.

RECLASSIFICATIONS Certain amounts in prior fiscal years have been reclassified to conform with the presentation adopted in the current fiscal year.

NOTE 2. LONG-TERM DEBT

The Company's long-term debt at the end of fiscal 2001 and fiscal 2000 consisted of the following (amounts in millions):

	February 3, 2002	January 28, 2001
Commercial Paper; weighted average interest rate of 6.1% at January 28, 2001	**$ –**	$ 754
6 1/2% Senior Notes; due September 15, 2004; interest payable semi-annually on March 15 and September 15	**500**	500
5 3/8% Senior Notes; due April 1, 2006; interest payable semi-annually on April 1 and October 1	**500**	–
Capital Lease Obligations; payable in varying installments through January 31, 2027	**232**	230
Other	**23**	65
Total long-term debt	**1,255**	1,549
Less current installments	**5**	4
Long-term debt, excluding current installments	**$1,250**	$1,545

The Company has a commercial paper program with maximum available borrowings up to $1 billion. In connection with the program, the Company has a back-up credit facility with a consortium of banks for up to $800 million. The credit facility, which expires in September 2004, contains various restrictive covenants, none of which are expected to materially impact the Company's liquidity or capital resources. Commercial paper borrowings of $754 million outstanding at January 28, 2001, were classified as non-current pursuant to the Company's intent and ability to finance this obligation on a long-term basis.

The Company issued $500 million of 5 3/8% Senior Notes in fiscal 2001 and $500 million of 6 1/2% Senior Notes in fiscal 1999, collectively referred to as "Senior Notes." The Senior Notes may be redeemed by the Company at any time, in whole or in part, at a redemption price plus accrued interest up to the redemption date. The redemption price is equal to the greater of (1) 100% of the principal amount of the Senior Notes to be redeemed or (2) the sum of the present values of the remaining scheduled payments of principal and interest to maturity. The Senior Notes are not subject to sinking fund requirements.

Interest expense in the accompanying Consolidated Statements of Earnings is net of interest capitalized of $84 million, $73 million and $45 million in fiscal 2001, 2000 and 1999, respectively.

Maturities of long-term debt are $5 million for fiscal 2002, $6 million for fiscal 2003, $507 million for fiscal 2004, $8 million for fiscal 2005 and $509 million for fiscal 2006.

As of February 3, 2002, the market values of the publicly traded 5 3/8% and 6 1/2% Senior Notes were approximately $511 million and $531 million, respectively. The estimated fair value of all other long-term borrowings, excluding capital lease obligations, approximated the carrying value of $23 million. These fair values were estimated using a discounted cash flow analysis based on the Company's incremental borrowing rate for similar liabilities.

NOTE 3. INCOME TAXES

The provision for income taxes consisted of the following (in millions):

	Fiscal Year Ended		
	February 3, 2002	January 28, 2001	January 30, 2000
Current:			
U.S.	**$1,594**	$1,267	$ 1,209
State	**265**	216	228
Foreign	**60**	45	45
	1,919	1,528	1,482
Deferred:			
U.S.	**(12)**	98	9
State	**(1)**	9	(4)
Foreign	**7**	1	(3)
	(6)	108	2
Total	**$1,913**	$1,636	$ 1,484

NOTES TO CONSOLIDATED FINANCIAL STATEMENTS (CONTINUED)

The Company's combined federal, state and foreign effective tax rates for fiscal years 2001, 2000 and 1999, net of offsets generated by federal, state and foreign tax incentive credits, were approximately 38.6%, 38.8%, and 39.0%, respectively. A reconciliation of income tax expense at the federal statutory rate of 35% to actual tax expense for the applicable fiscal years is as follows (in millions):

	Fiscal Year Ended		
	February 3, 2002	January 28, 2001	January 30, 2000
Income taxes at U.S. statutory rate	**$1,735**	$ 1,476	$ 1,331
State income taxes, net of federal income tax benefit	**172**	146	145
Foreign rate differences	**4**	5	2
Other, net	**2**	9	6
Total	**$1,913**	$ 1,636	$ 1,484

The tax effects of temporary differences that give rise to significant portions of the deferred tax assets and deferred tax liabilities as of February 3, 2002 and January 28, 2001 were as follows (in millions):

	February 3, 2002	January 28, 2001
Deferred Tax Assets:		
Accrued self-insurance liabilities	**$ 220**	$ 151
Other accrued liabilities	**138**	118
Net loss on disposition	**31**	–
Total gross deferred tax assets	**389**	269
Valuation allowance	**(31)**	–
Deferred tax assets, net of valuation allowance	**358**	269
Deferred Tax Liabilities:		
Accelerated depreciation	**(492)**	(389)
Other	**(55)**	(75)
Total gross deferred tax liabilities	**(547)**	(464)
Net deferred tax liability	**$ (189)**	$ (195)

A valuation allowance was established in fiscal 2001 for a deferred tax asset generated from the net loss on disposition of a business. Company management believes the existing net deductible temporary differences comprising the deferred tax assets, net of the valuation allowance, will reverse during periods in which the Company generates net taxable income.

NOTE 4. **EMPLOYEE STOCK PLANS**

The 1997 Omnibus Stock Incentive Plan ("1997 Plan") provides that incentive stock options, non-qualified stock options, stock appreciation rights, restricted stock and deferred shares may be issued to selected associates, officers and directors of the Company. The maximum number of shares of the Company's common stock available for issuance under the 1997 Plan is the lesser of 225 million shares or the number of shares carried over from prior plans plus one-half percent of the total number of outstanding shares as of the first day of each fiscal year. In addition, restricted shares issued under the 1997 Plan may not exceed 22.5 million shares. As of February 3, 2002, there were 121 million shares available for future grants under the 1997 Plan.

Under the 1997 Plan, the Company has granted incentive and non-qualified options for 143 million shares, net of cancellations (of which 76 million had been exercised). Incentive stock options typically vest at the rate of 25% per year commencing on the first anniversary date of the grant and expire on the tenth anniversary date of the grant. The non-qualified options have similar terms but typically commence vesting on the second anniversary of the date of grant.

Under the 1997 Plan, 712,000 shares of restricted stock have been issued, net of cancellations (the restrictions on 4,600 shares have lapsed). Generally, the restrictions on 25% of the restricted shares lapse upon the third and sixth year anniversaries of the date of issuance with the restrictions on the remaining 50% of the restricted shares lapsing upon attainment of age 62. The fair value of the restricted shares is expensed over the period during which the restrictions lapse. The Company recorded compensation expense related to restricted stock in the amount of $3 million and $455,000 in fiscal 2001 and 2000, respectively.

Under the Non-Qualified Stock Option and Deferred Stock Unit Plans and Agreements, the Company issued 2.5 million non-qualified stock options with an exercise price of $40.75 per share in fiscal 2000. In addition, the Company granted 629,000 deferred stock units and 750,000 deferred stock units in fiscal years 2001 and 2000, respectively, to several key officers vesting at various dates. Each deferred stock unit entitles the officer to one share of common stock to be received up to five years after the vesting date of the deferred stock unit, subject to certain deferral rights of the officer. The fair value of the deferred stock units on the grant dates was $27 million and $31 million for deferred units granted in fiscal 2001 and 2000, respectively. These amounts are being amortized based upon the vesting dates. The Company recorded stock compensation expense related to deferred stock units in the amount of $16 million and $6 million in fiscal 2001 and 2000, respectively.

The per share weighted average fair value of stock options granted during fiscal years 2001, 2000 and 1999 was $20.51,

NOTES TO CONSOLIDATED FINANCIAL STATEMENTS (CONTINUED)

$31.96 and $18.86, respectively. The fair value of these options was determined at the date of grant using the Black-Scholes option-pricing model with the following assumptions:

	Fiscal Year Ended February 3, 2002	January 28, 2001	January 30, 2000
Risk-free interest rate	**5.1%**	6.4%	5.1%
Expected volatility of common stock	**48.1%**	54.6%	51.6%
Dividend yield	**0.4%**	0.3%	0.3%
Expected option term	**6 years**	7 years	5 years

The Company applies APB 25 in accounting for its stock plans and, accordingly, no compensation costs have been recognized in the Company's financial statements for incentive or non-qualified stock options granted. If, under SFAS 123, the Company determined compensation costs based on the fair value at the grant date for its stock options, net earnings and earnings per share would have been reduced to the pro forma amounts below (in millions, except per share data):

	Fiscal Year Ended February 3, 2002	January 28, 2001	January 30, 2000
Net Earnings			
As reported	**$3,044**	$2,581	$2,320
Pro forma	**$2,800**	$2,364	$2,186
Basic Earnings per Share			
As reported	**$ 1.30**	$ 1.11	$ 1.03
Pro forma	**$ 1.20**	$ 1.02	$ 0.97
Diluted Earnings per Share			
As reported	**$ 1.29**	$ 1.10	$ 1.00
Pro forma	**$ 1.19**	$ 1.01	$ 0.94

The following table summarizes options outstanding at February 3, 2002, January 28, 2001 and January 30, 2000 and changes during the fiscal years ended on these dates (shares in thousands):

	Number of Shares	Weighted Average Option Price
Outstanding at January 31, 1999	71,592	$ 13.45
Granted	14,006	37.81
Exercised	(13,884)	10.88
Cancelled	(3,295)	18.88
Outstanding at January 30, 2000	68,419	$ 18.79
Granted	14,869	49.78
Exercised	(14,689)	13.15
Cancelled	(2,798)	30.51
Outstanding at January 28, 2001	65,801	$ 26.46
Granted	25,330	40.33
Exercised	(16,614)	15.03
Cancelled	(5,069)	39.20
Outstanding at February 3, 2002	**69,448**	**$33.33**
Exercisable	26,777	$ 22.68

The following table summarizes information regarding stock options outstanding as of February 3, 2002 (shares in thousands):

Range of Exercise Prices	Options Outstanding	Weighted Average Remaining Life (Yrs)	Weighted Average Outstanding Option Price	Options Exercisable	Weighted Average Exercisable Option Price
$ 6.00 to 12.00	11,999	4.1	$ 10.10	11,631	$ 10.00
12.00 to 20.00	1,732	5.6	17.10	1,560	17.30
20.00 to 30.00	9,714	6.1	21.80	5,456	21.70
30.00 to 42.00	34,271	8.8	39.30	6,037	38.90
42.00 to 54.00	11,732	8.3	51.70	2,093	52.80
	69,448	7.0	$ 33.33	26,777	$22.68

In addition, the Company had 48 million shares available for future grants under the Employee Stock Purchase Plan ("ESPP") at February 3, 2002. The ESPP enables the Company to grant substantially all full-time associates options to purchase up to 152 million shares of common stock, of which 104 million shares have been exercised from inception of the plan, at a price equal to the lower of 85% of the stock's fair market value on the first day or the last day of the purchase period.

During fiscal 2001, 5.5 million shares were purchased under the ESPP at an average price of $35.87 per share. At February 3, 2002, there were 2.8 million options outstanding, net of cancellations, at an average price of $37.26 per share.

NOTE 5. LEASES

The Company leases certain retail locations, office space, warehouse and distribution space, equipment and vehicles. While the majority of the leases are operating leases, certain retail locations are leased under capital leases. As leases expire, it can be expected that in the normal course of business, leases will be renewed or replaced.

The Company has two off-balance sheet lease agreements totaling $882 million comprised of an initial lease agreement of $600 million and a subsequent agreement of $282 million. Off-balance sheet leases include leases created under structured financing arrangements. These lease agreements totaling $882 million involve a special purpose entity which meets the criteria established by generally accepted accounting principles and is not owned by or affiliated with the Company, its management or officers. The Company financed a portion of its new stores opened in fiscal 1997 through 2001, as well as a distribution center and office buildings, under these lease agreements. Under both agreements, the lessor purchases the properties, pays for the construction costs and subsequently leases the facilities to the Company. The lease term for the $600 million agreement expires in 2004 and includes four 2-year renewal options. The lease term for the $282 million agreement expires in 2008 with no renewal options. Both lease agreements provide for substantial residual value guarantees and include purchase options at original cost on each property.

NOTES TO CONSOLIDATED FINANCIAL STATEMENTS (CONTINUED)

The Company also leases an import distribution facility, including its related equipment, under an off-balance sheet lease arrangement totaling $85 million. The lease for the import distribution facility expires in 2005 and has four 5-year renewal options. The lease agreement provides for substantial residual value guarantees and includes purchase options at the higher of the cost or fair market value of the assets.

The maximum amount of the residual value guarantees relative to the assets under the off-balance sheet lease agreements described above is projected to be $799 million. As the leased assets are placed into service, the Company estimates its liability under the residual value guarantees and records additional rent expense on a straight-line basis over the remaining lease terms.

Total rent expense, net of minor sublease income, for the fiscal years ended February 3, 2002, January 28, 2001 and January 30, 2000, was $522 million, $479 million and $389 million, respectively. Real estate taxes, insurance, maintenance and operating expenses applicable to the leased property are obligations of the Company under the lease agreements. Certain store leases provide for contingent rent payments based on percentages of sales in excess of specified minimums. Contingent rent expense for the fiscal years ended February 3, 2002, January 28, 2001, and January 30, 2000 was approximately $10 million, $9 million and $11 million, respectively.

The approximate future minimum lease payments under capital and operating leases, including off-balance sheet leases, at February 3, 2002 were as follows (in millions):

Fiscal Year	Capital Leases	Operating Leases
2002	$ 41	$ 517
2003	42	495
2004	43	447
2005	44	415
2006	44	394
Thereafter	577	5,139
	791	$7,407
Less imputed interest	559	
Net present value of capital lease obligations	232	
Less current installments	4	
Long-term capital lease obligations, excluding current installments	$ 228	

Short-term and long-term obligations for capital leases are included in the Company's Consolidated Balance Sheets in Current Installments of Long-Term Debt and Long-Term Debt, respectively. The assets under capital leases recorded in Net Property and Equipment, net of amortization, totaled $199 million and $213 million at February 3, 2002 and January 28, 2001, respectively.

NOTE 6. EMPLOYEE BENEFIT PLANS

The Company maintains a defined contribution plan ("401(k)") that covers substantially all associates meeting certain service requirements. The Company makes weekly matching cash contributions to purchase shares of the Company's common stock, up to specified percentages of associates' contributions as approved by the Board of Directors.

The Company also maintains a 401(k) Restoration Plan to provide certain associates deferred compensation that they would have received under the 401(k) matching contribution if not for the maximum compensation limits under the Internal Revenue Code. The Company funds the 401(k) Restoration Plan through contributions made to a "rabbi trust," which are then used to purchase shares of the Company's common stock in the open market. Compensation expense related to this plan for fiscal years 2001, 2000 and 1999 was not material.

During February 1999, the Company made its final contribution to the Employee Stock Ownership Plan and Trust ("ESOP"), which was originally established during fiscal 1988.

The Company's combined contributions to the 401(k) and ESOP were $97 million, $84 million and $57 million for fiscal years 2001, 2000 and 1999, respectively. At February 3, 2002, the 401(k) and the ESOP held a total of 33 million shares of the Company's common stock in trust for plan participants.

NOTE 7. BASIC AND DILUTED EARNINGS PER SHARE

The calculations of basic and diluted earnings per share for fiscal years 2001, 2000 and 1999 were as follows (amounts in millions, except per share data):

	Fiscal Year Ended		
	February 3, 2002	January 28, 2001	January 30, 2000
Calculation of Basic Earnings Per Share:			
Net earnings	**$3,044**	$2,581	$ 2,320
Weighted average number of common shares outstanding	**2,335**	2,315	2,244
Basic Earnings Per Share	**$ 1.30**	$ 1.11	$ 1.03
Calculation of Diluted Earnings Per Share:			
Net earnings	**$3,044**	$2,581	$ 2,320
Tax-effected interest expense attributable to 3¼% Notes	**–**	–	17
Net earnings assuming dilution	**$3,044**	$2,581	$ 2,337
Weighted average number of common shares outstanding	**2,335**	2,315	2,244
Effect of potentially dilutive securities:			
3¼% Notes	**–**	–	51
Employee Stock Plans	**18**	37	47
Weighted average number of common shares outstanding assuming dilution	**2,353**	2,352	2,342
Diluted Earnings Per Share	**$ 1.29**	$ 1.10	$ 1.00

NOTES TO CONSOLIDATED FINANCIAL STATEMENTS (CONTINUED)

Employee stock plans represent shares granted under the Company's employee stock purchase plan and stock option plans, as well as shares issued for deferred compensation stock plans. For fiscal year 1999, shares issuable upon conversion of the Company's 3¼% Notes, issued in October 1996 and converted in 1999, were included in weighted average shares outstanding assuming dilution for purposes of calculating diluted earnings per share. To calculate diluted earnings per share, net earnings are adjusted for tax-effected net interest and issue costs on the 3¼% Notes (prior to conversion to equity in October 1999) and divided by weighted average shares outstanding assuming dilution.

NOTE 8. COMMITMENTS AND CONTINGENCIES

At February 3, 2002, the Company was contingently liable for approximately $557 million under outstanding letters of credit issued for certain business transactions, including insurance programs, import inventory purchases and construction contracts.

In addition, the Company has certain off-balance sheet leases that include residual value guarantees contingent on the value of underlying assets at the end of the lease term. The estimated maximum amount of the residual value guarantees at the end of the lease terms is $799 million. These leases expire at various terms from 2004 through 2008 with some containing renewal options through 2025.

The Company is involved in litigation arising from the normal course of business. In management's opinion, this litigation is not expected to materially impact the Company's consolidated results of operations or financial condition.

NOTE 9. ACQUISITIONS AND DISPOSITIONS

In 2001, the Company acquired Your "other" Warehouse and TotalHOME de Mexico, S.A. de C.V. These acquisitions were accounted for under the purchase method of accounting.

In October 2001, the Company sold all of the assets of The Home Depot Chile S.A., resulting in a gain of $31 million included in selling and store operating expenses.

On February 18, 2002, the Company sold all of the assets of The Home Depot Argentina S.R.L. In connection with the sale, the Company received proceeds comprised of cash and secured notes. An impairment charge of $45 million was recorded in selling and store operating expenses in fiscal 2001 to write down the net assets of The Home Depot Argentina S.R.L. to fair value.

During fiscal 2000, Maintenance Warehouse, a wholly-owned subsidiary of the Company, acquired N-E Thing Supply Company, Inc. The Company acquired Apex Supply Company, Inc. and Georgia Lighting, Inc. in fiscal 1999. These acquisitions were recorded under the purchase method of accounting.

Pro forma results of operations for fiscal years 2001, 2000 and 1999 would not be materially different as a result of the acquisitions discussed above and therefore are not presented.

NOTE 10. QUARTERLY FINANCIAL DATA (UNAUDITED)

The following is a summary of the quarterly results of operations for the fiscal years ended February 3, 2002 and January 28, 2001 (dollars in millions, except per share data):

	Net Sales	Increase (Decrease) In Comparable Store Sales	Gross Profit	Net Earnings	Basic Earnings Per Share	Diluted Earnings Per Share
Fiscal year ended February 3, 2002:						
First quarter	**$12,200**	**(3)%**	**$ 3,655**	**$ 632**	**$0.27**	**$0.27**
Second quarter	**14,576**	**1%**	**4,326**	**924**	**0.40**	**0.39**
Third quarter	**13,289**	**0%**	**4,010**	**778**	**0.33**	**0.33**
Fourth quarter	**13,488**	**5%**	**4,156**	**710**	**0.30**	**0.30**
Fiscal year	**$53,553**	**0%**	**$16,147**	**$3,044**	**$1.30**	**$1.29**
Fiscal year ended January 28, 2001:						
First quarter	$ 11,112	7%	$ 3,274	$ 629	$0.27	$ 0.27
Second quarter	12,618	6%	3,739	838	0.36	0.36
Third quarter	11,545	4%	3,450	650	0.28	0.28
Fourth quarter	10,463	0%	3,217	465	0.20	0.20
Fiscal year	$ 45,738	4%	$13,681	$ 2,581	$ 1.11	$ 1.10

Note: The quarterly data may not sum to fiscal year totals due to rounding.

MANAGEMENT'S RESPONSIBILITY FOR FINANCIAL STATEMENTS

The financial statements presented in this Annual Report have been prepared with integrity and objectivity and are the responsibility of the management of The Home Depot, Inc. These financial statements have been prepared in conformity with accounting principles generally accepted in the United States of America and properly reflect certain estimates and judgments based upon the best available information.

The Company maintains a system of internal accounting controls, which is supported by an internal audit program and is designed to provide reasonable assurance, at an appropriate cost, that the Company's assets are safeguarded and transactions are properly recorded. This system is continually reviewed and modified in response to changing business conditions and operations and as a result of recommendations by the external and internal auditors. In addition, the Company has distributed to associates its policies for conducting business affairs in a lawful and ethical manner.

The financial statements of the Company have been audited by KPMG LLP, independent auditors. Their accompanying report is based upon an audit conducted in accordance with auditing standards generally accepted in the United States of America, including the related review of internal accounting controls and financial reporting matters.

The Audit Committee of the Board of Directors, consisting solely of outside directors, meets five times a year with the independent auditors, the internal auditors and representatives of management to discuss auditing and financial reporting matters. The Audit Committee, acting on behalf of the stockholders, maintains an ongoing appraisal of the internal accounting controls, the activities of the outside auditors and internal auditors and the financial condition of the Company. Both the Company's independent auditors and the internal auditors have free access to the Audit Committee.

Carol B. Tomé
Executive Vice President and
Chief Financial Officer

INDEPENDENT AUDITORS' REPORT

The Board of Directors and Stockholders
The Home Depot, Inc.:

We have audited the accompanying consolidated balance sheets of The Home Depot, Inc. and subsidiaries as of February 3, 2002 and January 28, 2001 and the related consolidated statements of earnings, stockholders' equity and comprehensive income, and cash flows for each of the years in the three-year period ended February 3, 2002. These consolidated financial statements are the responsibility of the Company's management. Our responsibility is to express an opinion on these consolidated financial statements based on our audits.

We conducted our audits in accordance with auditing standards generally accepted in the United States of America. Those standards require that we plan and perform the audit to obtain reasonable assurance about whether the financial statements are free of material misstatement. An audit includes examining, on a test basis, evidence supporting the amounts and disclosures in the financial statements. An audit also includes assessing the accounting principles used and significant estimates made by management, as well as evaluating the overall financial statement presentation. We believe that our audits provide a reasonable basis for our opinion.

In our opinion, the consolidated financial statements referred to above present fairly, in all material respects, the financial position of The Home Depot, Inc. and subsidiaries as of February 3, 2002 and January 28, 2001, and the results of their operations and their cash flows for each of the years in the three-year period ended February 3, 2002 in conformity with accounting principles generally accepted in the United States of America.

KPMG LLP

Atlanta, Georgia
February 26, 2002

10-YEAR SUMMARY OF FINANCIAL AND OPERATING RESULTS

amounts in millions, except where noted	5-Year Compound Annual Growth Rate	10-Year Compound Annual Growth Rate	2001[1]
STATEMENT OF EARNINGS DATA			
Net sales	22.3%	26.4%	**$ 53,553**
Net sales increase (%)	–	–	**17.1**
Earnings before income taxes[2]	26.4	28.8	**4,957**
Net earnings[2]	26.5	28.4	**3,044**
Net earnings increase (%)[2]	–	–	**17.9**
Diluted earnings per share ($)[2,3]	24.6	25.8	**1.29**
Diluted earnings per share increase (%)[2]	–	–	**17.3**
Weighted average number of common shares outstanding assuming dilution	1.4	1.7	**2,353**
Gross margin – % of sales	–	–	**30.2**
Store selling and operating expense – % of sales	–	–	**19.0**
Pre-opening expense – % of sales	–	–	**0.2**
General and administrative expense – % of sales	–	–	**1.7**
Net interest income (expense) – % of sales	–	–	**–**
Earnings before income taxes – % of sales[2]	–	–	**9.3**
Net earnings – % of sales[2]	–	–	**5.7**
BALANCE SHEET DATA AND FINANCIAL RATIOS			
Total assets	23.1%	26.5%	**$ 26,394**
Working capital	15.6	20.0	**3,860**
Merchandise inventories	20.0	26.1	**6,725**
Net property and equipment	23.1	28.5	**15,375**
Long-term debt	0.1	16.5	**1,250**
Stockholders' equity	24.9	26.7	**18,082**
Book value per share ($)	22.9	24.1	**7.71**
Long-term debt to equity (%)	–	–	**6.9**
Current ratio	–	–	**1.59:1**
Inventory turnover	–	–	**5.4x**
Return on invested capital (%)[2]	–	–	**18.3**
STATEMENT OF CASH FLOWS DATA			
Depreciation and amortization	26.9%	30.8%	**$ 764**
Capital expenditures[5]	22.2	22.9	**3,398**
Cash dividends per share ($)	27.7	32.8	**0.17**
STORE DATA[4]			
Number of stores	21.1%	22.6%	**1,333**
Square footage at year-end	22.0	24.7	**146**
Increase in square footage (%)	–	–	**18.5**
Average square footage per store (in thousands)	0.8	1.4	**109**
STORE SALES AND OTHER DATA			
Comparable store sales increase (%)[6]	–	–	**–**
Weighted average weekly sales per operating store (in thousands)[4]	0.2%	2.5%	**$ 812**
Weighted average sales per square foot ($)[4,6]	(0.5)	1.1	**388**
Number of customer transactions[4]	18.6	22.3	**1,091**
Average sale per transaction ($)[4]	2.9	3.3	**48.64**
Number of associates at year-end (actual)	21.2	24.8	**256,300**

(1) Fiscal years 2001 and 1996 consisted of 53 weeks; all other fiscal years reported consisted of 52 weeks.
(2) Excludes the effect of a $104 million non-recurring charge in fiscal 1997.
(3) Diluted earnings per share for fiscal 1997, including a $104 million non-recurring charge, were $0.52.

2000	1999	1998	1997	1996[1]	1995	1994	1993	1992
$ 45,738	$ 38,434	$ 30,219	$ 24,156	$ 19,535	$ 15,470	$ 12,477	$ 9,239	$ 7,148
19.0	27.2	25.1	23.7	26.3	24.0	35.0	29.2	39.2
4,217	3,804	2,654	2,002	1,535	1,195	980	737	576
2,581	2,320	1,614	1,224	938	732	605	457	363
11.3	43.7	31.9	30.5	28.2	21.0	32.2	26.1	45.6
1.10	1.00	0.71	0.55	0.43	0.34	0.29	0.22	0.18
10.0	40.8	29.1	27.9	26.5	17.2	31.8	22.2	38.5
2,352	2,342	2,320	2,287	2,195	2,151	2,142	2,132	2,096
29.9	29.7	28.5	28.1	27.8	27.7	27.9	27.7	27.6
18.6	17.8	17.7	17.8	18.0	18.0	17.8	17.6	17.4
0.3	0.3	0.3	0.3	0.3	0.4	0.4	0.4	0.4
1.8	1.7	1.7	1.7	1.7	1.7	1.8	2.0	2.1
–	–	–	–	0.1	0.1	(0.1)	0.3	0.4
9.2	9.9	8.8	8.3	7.9	7.7	7.8	8.0	8.1
5.6	6.0	5.3	5.1	4.8	4.7	4.8	5.0	5.1
$ 21,385	$ 17,081	$ 13,465	$ 11,229	$ 9,342	$ 7,354	$ 5,778	$ 4,701	$ 3,932
3,392	2,734	2,076	2,004	1,867	1,255	919	994	807
6,556	5,489	4,293	3,602	2,708	2,180	1,749	1,293	940
13,068	10,227	8,160	6,509	5,437	4,461	3,397	2,371	1,608
1,545	750	1,566	1,303	1,247	720	983	874	844
15,004	12,341	8,740	7,098	5,955	4,988	3,442	2,814	2,304
6.46	5.36	3.95	3.23	2.75	2.32	1.69	1.39	1.15
10.3	6.1	17.9	18.4	20.9	14.4	28.6	31.1	36.6
1.77:1	1.75:1	1.73:1	1.82:1	2.01:1	1.89:1	1.76:1	2.02:1	2.07:1
5.1x	5.4x	5.4x	5.4x	5.6x	5.5x	5.7x	5.9x	6.3x
19.6	22.5	19.3	17.0	16.3	16.3	16.5	13.9	17.6
$ 601	$ 463	$ 373	$ 283	$ 232	$ 181	$ 130	$ 90	$ 70
3,574	2,618	2,094	1,464	1,248	1,308	1,220	900	437
0.16	0.11	0.08	0.06	0.05	0.04	0.03	0.02	0.02
1,134	930	761	624	512	423	340	264	214
123	100	81	66	54	44	35	26	21
22.6	23.5	22.8	23.1	21.6	26.3	33.2	26.3	26.8
108	108	107	106	105	105	103	100	98
4	10	7	7	7	3	8	7	15
$ 864	$ 876	$ 844	$ 829	$ 803	$ 787	$ 802	$ 764	$ 724
415	423	410	406	398	390	404	398	387
937	797	665	550	464	370	302	236	189
48.65	47.87	45.05	43.63	42.09	41.78	41.29	39.13	37.72
227,300	201,400	156,700	124,400	98,100	80,800	67,300	50,600	38,900

(4) Excludes Apex Supply Company, Georgia Lighting, Maintenance Warehouse, Your "other" Warehouse and National Blinds and Wallpaper.
(5) Excludes payments for businesses acquired (net, in millions) for fiscal 2001 ($190), fiscal 2000 ($26), fiscal 1999 ($101), fiscal 1998 ($6) and fiscal 1997 ($61).
(6) Adjusted to reflect the first 52 weeks of the 53-week fiscal years in 2001 and 1996.

CORPORATE AND STOCKHOLDER INFORMATION

STORE SUPPORT CENTER

The Home Depot, Inc.
2455 Paces Ferry Road, NW
Atlanta, GA 30339-4024
Telephone: 770-433-8211

THE HOME DEPOT WEB SITE

www.homedepot.com

TRANSFER AGENT AND REGISTRAR

EquiServe Trust Company, N.A.
P.O. Box 43010
Providence, RI 02940-3010
Telephone:
1-800-577-0177 (Voice)
1-800-952-9245
Internet address: www.equiserve.com

INDEPENDENT AUDITORS

KPMG LLP
Suite 2000
303 Peachtree Street, NE
Atlanta, GA 30308

STOCK EXCHANGE LISTING

New York Stock Exchange
Trading symbol - HD

ANNUAL MEETING

The Annual Meeting of Stockholders will be held at 10:00 a.m., May 29, 2002, at Cobb Galleria Centre, 2 Galleria Parkway, Atlanta, GA 30339.

NUMBER OF STOCKHOLDERS

As of April 1, 2002, there were approximately 206,988 stockholders of record. This number excludes individual stockholders holding stock under nominee security position listings.

DIVIDENDS PER COMMON SHARE

	First Quarter	Second Quarter	Third Quarter	Fourth Quarter
Fiscal 2001	**$0.040**	**$0.040**	**$0.050**	**$0.050**
Fiscal 2000	$0.040	$0.040	$0.040	$0.040

DIRECT STOCK PURCHASE/DIVIDEND REINVESTMENT PLAN

New investors may make an initial investment and stockholders of record may acquire additional shares of The Home Depot common stock through the Company's direct stock purchase and dividend reinvestment plan. Subject to certain requirements, initial cash investments, cash dividends and/or additional optional cash purchases may be invested through this plan.

To obtain enrollment materials, including the prospectus, access the Company's web site, or call 1-877-HD-SHARE. For all other communications regarding these services, contact the Transfer Agent and Registrar.

FINANCIAL AND OTHER COMPANY INFORMATION

To request a copy of the Company's Annual Report on Form 10-K for the fiscal year ended February 3, 2002, as filed with the Securities and Exchange Commission, to be mailed to you at no cost, please contact:

The Home Depot, Inc.
Investor Relations
2455 Paces Ferry Road, NW
Atlanta, GA 30339-4024
Telephone: 770-384-4388

In addition, financial reports, recent filings with the Securities and Exchange Commission (including Form 10-K), store locations, news releases and other Company information are available on The Home Depot web site.

For a copy of the 2001 Home Depot Corporate Social Responsibility Report, which also includes guidelines for applying for philanthropic grants, contact the Community Affairs Department at the Store Support Center, or access the Company's web site.

QUARTERLY STOCK PRICE RANGE

	First Quarter	Second Quarter	Third Quarter	Fourth Quarter
Fiscal 2001				
High	**$49.00**	**$53.73**	**$50.90**	**$52.04**
Low	**$38.11**	**$44.60**	**$30.30**	**$37.15**
Fiscal 2000				
High	$70.00	$58.75	$60.00	$52.50
Low	$51.00	$44.13	$34.69	$35.44

About this report:
Consistent with The Home Depot's commitment to the environment, this report is printed on paper that is certified in accordance with the Principles and Criteria of the Forest Stewardship Council (FSC). This certification ensures that the fiber from which the paper is manufactured comes partially from certified forests that are managed in a way that is socially beneficial, environmentally responsible and economically viable. The paper used in this report consists of at least 28% FSC fiber and at least 11% post consumer fiber.

Design: **Lucid Partners / Atlanta, GA**
Photography: **Scott Lowden Photography / Atlanta, GA**
Printing: **ACME Printing Company**

Glossary

A

Accelerated depreciation method A depreciation method that provides for a higher depreciation amount in the first year of the asset's use, followed by a gradual declining amount of depreciation. (p. 412)

Account The element of an accounting system that summarizes the increases and decreases in each financial statement item. (pp. 98, 153)

Accounting An information system that provides reports to stakeholders about the economic activities and condition of a business. (p. 13)

Accounting cycle The process that begins with the analysis of transactions and ends with preparing the accounting records for the next accounting period. (p. 114)

Accounting equation Assets = Liabilities + Stockholders' Equity. (p. 17)

Accounting information system An information system that consists of management reporting, transaction processing, and financial reporting subsystems that processes financial and operational data into reports useful to internal and external stakeholders. (p. 151)

Accounting period concept A concept of accounting in which accounting data are recorded and summarized in a period process. (p. 22)

Accounts payable A liability for an amount incurred from purchases of products or services in the normal operations of a business. (pp. 11, 101)

Accounts receivable A receivable created by selling merchandise or services on credit. (pp. 12, 101, 314)

Accounts receivable turnover The relationship between net sales and accounts receivable, computed by dividing net sales by the average net accounts receivable. (pp. 328, 678)

Accrual basis of accounting A system of accounting in which revenue is recorded as it is earned and expenses are recorded when they generate revenue. (p. 55)

Accruals A revenue or expense that has not been recorded. (p. 103)

Accrued expense An expense that has been incurred at the end of an accounting period but has not been recorded in the accounts; sometimes called an accrued liability. (p. 104)

Accrued revenue A revenue that has been earned at the end of an accounting period but has not been recorded in the accounts; sometimes called an accrued asset. (p. 104)

Accumulated depreciation An offsetting or contra asset account used to record depreciation on a fixed asset. (p. 106)

Adequate disclosure concept A concept of accounting that requires that the financial statements include all relevant data a reader needs to understand the financial condition and performance of a business. (p. 22)

Adjusted trial balance The trial balance prepared after the adjusting entries have been posted to the ledger. (p. 162)

Adjusting entries The entries necessary to bring the accounts up to date before preparing financial statements. (p. 161)

Adjustment process A process required by the accrual basis of accounting in which the accounts are updated prior to preparing financial statements. (p. 102)

Administrative expenses Expenses incurred in the administration or general operations of the business. (p. 213)

Aging the receivables The process of analyzing the accounts receivable and classifying them according to various age groupings, with the due date being the base point for determining age. (p. 320)

Allowance for doubtful accounts The contra asset account for accounts receivable. (p. 318)

Allowance method The method of accounting for uncollectible accounts that provides an expense for uncollectible receivables in advance of their write-off. (p. 317)

Amortization The periodic transfer of the cost of an intangible asset to expense. (p. 422)

Appropriation An act by the board of directors to restrict the amount of retained earnings available for use as dividends. (p. 520)

Asset turnover The number of sales dollars earned for each dollar of total assets, calculated as the ratio of net sales to total assets. (p. 676)

Assets The resources owned by a business. (p. 12)

Available-for-sale securities Securities that management expects to sell in the future but which are not actively traded for profit. (p. 561)

Average cost method The method of inventory costing that is based upon the assumption that costs should be charged against revenue by using the weighted average unit cost of the items sold. (p. 364)

B

Balance of an account The amount of the difference between the debits and the credits that have been entered into an account. (p. 154)

Balance sheet A list of the assets, liabilities, and stockholders' equity *as of a specific date*, usually at the close of the last day of a month or a year. (p. 14)

Bank reconciliation The analysis that details the items responsible for the difference between the cash balance reported in the bank statement and the balance of the cash account in the ledger. (p. 281)

Bank statement A summary of all transactions is mailed to the depositor by the bank each month. (p. 279)

Bond A form of interest-bearing note used by corporations to borrow on a long-term basis. (p. 462)

Bond indenture The contract between a corporation issuing bonds and the bondholders. (p. 462)

Bonds payable A type of long-term debt financing with a face amount that is due in the future with interest that is normally paid semiannually. (p. 11)

Book inventory The amount of inventory recorded in the accounting records. (p. 226)

Book value The cost of a fixed asset minus accumulated depreciation on the asset. (p. 411)

Business An organization in which basic resources (inputs), such as materials and labor, are assembled and processed to provide goods or services (outputs) to customers. (p. 4)

Business entity concept A concept of accounting that limits the economic data in the accounting system to data related directly to the activities of a specific business or entity. (p. 21)

Business information system A system that collects and processes company data into information that is distributed to users. (p. 150)

Business stakeholder A person or entity who has an interest in the economic performance of a business. (p. 9)

Business strategy An integrated set of plans and actions designed to enable the business to gain an advantage over its competitors and, in doing so, maximize its profits. (p. 6)

C

Capital expenditures The cost of acquiring fixed assets, adding a component, or replacing a component of fixed assets. (p. 418)

Capital stock Types of stock a corporation may issue. (p. 11)

Carrying amount The balance of the bonds payable account (face amount of the bonds) less any unamortized discount or plus any unamortized premium. (p. 466)

Cash Coins, currency (paper money), checks, money orders, and money on deposit that is available for unrestricted withdrawal from banks and other financial institutions. (p. 275)

Cash basis of accounting A system of accounting in which only transactions involving increases or decreases of the entity's cash are recorded. (p. 54)

Cash conversion cycle The number of days' sales in accounts receivable, plus the number of days' sales in inventory, less the number of days' sales in accounts payable. (p. 616)

Cash dividend A cash distribution of earnings by a corporation to its shareholders. (p. 515)

Cash equivalents Highly liquid investments that are usually reported with cash on the balance sheet. (p. 285)

Cash flows from financing activities The section of the statement of cash flows that reports cash flows from transactions affecting the equity and debt of the business. (p. 598)

Cash flows from investing activities The section of the statement of cash flows that reports cash flows from transactions affecting investments in noncurrent assets. (p. 598)

Cash flows from operating activities The section of the statement of cash flows that reports the cash transactions affecting the determination of net income. (p. 598)

Cash short and over account An account used to record the difference between the amount of cash in a cash register and the amount of cash that should be on hand according to the records. (p. 276)

Chart of accounts The list of accounts in the general ledger. (p. 157)

Classified balance sheet A balance sheet prepared with various sections, subsections, and captions that aid in its interpretation and analysis. (p. 111)

Closing entries The entries necessary at the end of an accounting period to transfer the balances of revenue, expense, and dividend accounts to retained earnings. (p. 165)

Closing process The process of transferring the balances of the revenue, expense, and dividends accounts to retained earnings in preparation for the next accounting period. (p. 115)

Combination strategy A business strategy that includes elements of both the low-cost and differentiation strategies. (p. 8)

Common stock The stock outstanding when a corporation has issued only one class of stock. (pp. 11, 505)

Common-sized financial statement A financial statement in which all items are expressed only in percentages. (pp. 115, 672)

Comprehensive income All changes in stockholders' equity during a period except those resulting from dividends and stockholders' investments. (p. 559)

Consignee The retailer carrying an item for sale (consignment) that is owned by another retailer (consignor). (p. 229)

Consignment Merchandise that is owned by a retailer (consignor) that is being carried for sale by another retailer (consignee). (p. 229)

Consignor A retailer who allows another retailer (consignee) to carry and sale its merchandise (consignment). (p. 229)

Consolidated financial statements Financial statements resulting from combining parent and subsidiary statements. (p. 567)

Consolidation The creation of a new corporation by the transfer of assets and liabilities of two or more existing corporations, which are then dissolved. (p. 567)

Contingent liability An obligation from a past transaction that is contingent upon a future event. An example would be product warranty payable. (p. 454)

Contract rate The periodic interest to be paid on the bonds that is identified in the bond indenture; expressed as a percentage of the face amount of the bond. (p. 463)

Controlling account The account in the general ledger that summarizes the balances of the accounts in a subsidiary ledger. (p. 217)

Copyright An exclusive right to publish and sell a literary, artistic, or musical composition. (p. 423)

Corporation A business organized under state or federal statutes as a separate legal entity. (p. 5)

Cost concept A concept of accounting that determines the amount initially entered into the accounting records for purchases. (p. 21)

Cost of capital The cost of financing operations from both debt and common stock, expressed as a percentage rate. (p. 674)

Cost of goods sold The cost of product sold. (p. 361)

Cost of merchandise sold The cost that is reported as an expense when merchandise is sold. (p. 209)

Credit memorandum A form used by a seller to inform the buyer of the amount the seller proposes to credit to the account receivable due from the buyer. (p. 219)

Credit period The amount of time the buyer is allowed in which to pay the seller. (p. 218)

Credit terms Terms for payment on account by the buyer to the seller. (p. 218))

Creditor A lender of money, such as a bank or bondholder. (p. 450)

Credits Amounts entered on the right side of an account. (p. 154)

Cumulative preferred stock A class of preferred stock that has a right to receive regular dividends that have been passed (not declared) before any common stock dividends are paid. (p. 507)

Current assets Cash and other assets that are expected to be converted to cash or sold or used up within one year or less, through the normal operations of the business. (p. 112)

Current liabilities Liabilities that will be due within a short time (usually one year or less) and that are to be paid out of current assets. (p. 113)

Current ratio A financial ratio that is computed by dividing current assets by current liabilities. (pp. 461, 683)

D

Days' purchases in accounts payable ratio A measure of the vendor payment velocity (measured in days of accounts payable to gross purchases). (p. 451)

Debit memorandum A form used by a buyer to inform the seller of the amount the buyer proposes to debit to the account payable due the seller. (p. 221)

Debits Amounts entered on the left side of an account. (p. 154)

Debtor A borrower of money. (p. 450)

Declining-balance method A method of depreciation that provides periodic depreciation expense based on the declining book value of a fixed asset over its estimated life. (p. 411)

Deferrals The delayed recording of an expense or revenue. (p. 103)

Deferred expense Items that are initially recorded as assets but are expected to become expenses over time or through the normal operations of the business; sometimes called prepaid expenses. (p. 103)

Deferred revenues Items that are initially recorded as liabilities but are expected to become revenues over time or through the normal operations of the business; sometimes called unearned revenues. (p. 103)

Depletion The process of transferring the cost of natural resources to an expense account. (p. 415)

Depreciation The systematic periodic transfer of the cost of a fixed asset to an expense account during its expected useful life. (pp. 106, 408)

Differentiation strategy A business strategy in which a business designs and produces products or services that possess unique attributes or characteristics for which customers are willing to pay a premium price. (p. 7)

Direct method A method of reporting the cash flows from operating activities as the difference between the operating cash receipts and the operating cash payments. (p. 599)

Direct write-off method The method of accounting for uncollectible accounts that recognizes the expense only when accounts are judged to be worthless. (p. 317)

Discontinued operations Operations of a major line of business or component for a company, such as a division, a department, or a certain class of customer, that have been disposed of. (p. 553)

Discount The interest deducted from the maturity value of a note or the excess of the face amount of bonds over their issue price. (pp. 453, 463)

Discount rate The rate used in computing the interest to be deducted from the maturity value of a note. (p. 453)

Dishonored note receivable A note that the maker fails to pay on the due date. (p. 324)

Dividend payout ratio A ratio computed by dividing the annual cash dividends (per share) by the annual net income (per share); indicates dividend safety. (p. 518)

Dividend yield A ratio computed by dividing the annual dividends paid per share of common stock by the market price per share at a specific date; indicates the rate of return to stockholders in terms of cash dividend distributions. (pp. 517, 689)

Dividends Distributions of earnings of a corporation to stockholders. (p. 12)

DuPont formula A formula that states that the rate earned on total assets is the product of two factors, the profit margin and the total asset turnover. (p. 676)

E

Earnings before interest, taxes, depreciation, and amortization (EBITDA) A type of pro forma computation used by financial analysts as a rough estimate of operating cash flows that are available to pay interest and other fixed charges. (p. 168)

Earnings per [common] share (EPS) The profitability ratio of net income available to common shareholders to the number of common shares outstanding. (pp. 558, 688)

Effective interest rate method A method of amortizing a bond discount or premium using present value techniques. (p. 464)

Effective rate of interest The market rate of interest at the time bonds are issued. (p. 463)

Electronic funds transfer (EFT) A system in which computers rather than paper (money, checks, etc.) are used to effect cash transactions. (p. 278)

Elements of internal control The control environment, risk assessment, control activities, information and communication, and monitoring. (p. 265)

Employee fraud The intentional act of deceiving an employer for personal gain. (p. 265)

Equity method A method of accounting for an investment in common stock by which the investment account is adjusted for the investor's share of periodic net income and cash dividends of the investee. (p. 563)

Equity securities The common and preferred stock of a firm. (p. 561)

Expenses Costs used to earn revenues. (p. 12)

Extraordinary items Events and transactions that (1) are significantly different (unusual) from the typical or the normal operating activities of a business and (2) occur infrequently. (p. 554)

F

FICA tax Federal Insurance Contributions Act tax used to finance federal programs for old-age and disability benefits (social security) and health insurance for the aged (Medicare). (p. 456)

Financial Accounting Standards Board (FASB) The authoritative body that has the primary responsibility for developing accounting principles. (p. 21)

Financial accounting system A system that includes (1) a set of rules for determining what, when, and the amount that should be recorded for economic events, (2) a framework for facilitating preparation of financial statements, and (3) one or more controls to determine whether errors may have arisen in the recording process. (p. 52)

Financial reporting system A subsystem of accounting that produces financial statements and other reports for external stakeholders. (p. 152)

Financial statements Financial reports that summarize the effects of events on a business. (p. 14)

Financing activities Business activities that involve obtaining funds to begin and operate a business. (p. 11)

Finished goods inventory The cost of finished products on hand that have not been sold. (p. 361)

First-in, first-out (fifo) method A method of inventory costing based on the assumption that the costs of merchandise sold should be charged against revenue in the order in which the costs were incurred. (p. 364)

Fiscal year The annual accounting period adopted by a business. (p. 164)

Fixed asset impairments A condition when the fair value of a fixed asset falls below its book value and is not expected to recover. (p. 555)

Fixed asset turnover The number of dollars of sales that are generated from each dollar of average fixed assets during the year, computed by dividing the net sales by the average net fixed assets. (pp. 421, 681)

Fixed assets Long-lived or relatively permanent tangible assets that are used in the normal business operations; sometimes called plant assets. (pp. 112, 404)

Flow ratio Current assets less cash and temporary investments divided by current liabilities less short-term debt or current maturities. (p. 617)

FOB (free on board) destination Freight terms in which the seller pays the transportation costs from the shipping point to the final destination. (p. 222)

FOB (free on board) shipping point Freight terms in which the buyer pays the transportation costs from the shipping point to the final destination. (p. 222)

Free cash flow The amount of operating cash flow remaining after replacing current productive capacity and maintaining current dividends. (p. 618)

Fringe benefits Benefits provided to employees in addition to wages and salaries. (p. 459)

G

General ledger The group of accounts of a business. (p. 157)

Generally accepted accounting principles (GAAP) Rules for how financial statements should be prepared. (p. 20)

Going concern concept A concept of accounting that assumes a business will continue operating for an indefinite period of time. (p. 21)

Goodwill An intangible asset of a business that is created from such favorable factors as location, product quality, reputation, and managerial skill, as verified from a merger transaction. (p. 424)

Gross pay The total earnings of an employee for a payroll period. (p. 456)

Gross profit Sales minus the cost of merchandise sold. (pp. 23, 209)

H

Held-to-maturity securities Investments in bonds or other debt securities that management intends to hold to their maturity. (p. 470)

Horizontal analysis A method of analyzing financial performance that computes percentage increases and decreases in related items in comparative financial statements. (pp. 23, 667)

I

Income from operations (operating income) The excess of gross profit over total operating expenses. (p. 213)

Income statement A summary of the revenue and expenses *for a specific period of time*, such as a month or a year. (p. 14)

Indirect method A method of reporting the cash flows from operating activities as the net income from operations adjusted for all deferrals of past cash receipts and payments and all accruals of expected future cash receipts and payments. (pp. 215, 599)

Intangible assets Long-lived assets that are useful in the operations of a business, are not held for sale, and are without physical qualities; examples are patent or copyright rights. (pp. 12, 112, 422)

Interest payable A liability to pay interest on a due date. (p. 11)

Internal controls The policies and procedures used to safeguard assets, ensure accurate business information, and ensure compliance with laws and regulations. (p. 264)

Inventory ledger The subsidiary ledger that shows the amount of each type of inventory. (p. 363)

Inventory shrinkage The amount by which the merchandise for sale, as indicated by the balance of the merchandise inventory account, is larger than the total amount of merchandise counted during the physical inventory. (p. 226)

Inventory turnover The relationship between the volume of goods sold and inventory, computed by dividing the cost of goods sold by the average inventory. (pp. 375, 679)

Investing activities Business activities that involve obtaining the necessary resources to start and operate the business. (p. 12)

Investments The balance sheet caption used to report long-term investments in stocks not intended as a source of cash in the normal operations of the business. (p. 563)

Invoice The bill that the seller sends to the buyer. (p. 218)

J

Journal The record in which the effects of transactions are recorded in chronological order. (p. 156)

Journal entry The transaction record entered in the journal. (p. 156)

Journalizing The process of recording transactions in the journal. (p. 156)

L

Last-in, first-out (lifo) method A method of inventory costing based on the assumption that the most recent merchandise inventory costs should be charged against revenue. (p. 364)

Leverage The amount of debt used by the firm to finance its assets; causes the rate earned on stockholders' equity to vary from the rate earned on total assets because the amount earned on assets acquired through the use of funds provided by creditors varies from the interest paid to these creditors. (pp. 471, 674)

Leverage formula A formula that states the rate earned on stockholders' equity as the product of the rate earned on total assets and the ratio of the average total assets divided by average stockholders' equity, or leverage. (p. 674)

Liabilities The rights of creditors that represent a legal obligation to repay an amount borrowed according to terms of the borrowing agreement. (pp. 11, 113)

Lifo conformity rule A financial reporting rule requiring a firm that elects to use lifo inventory valuation for tax purposes to also use lifo for external financial reporting. (p. 372)

Lifo reserve A required disclosure for lifo firms, showing the difference between inventory valued under fifo and inventory valued under lifo. (p. 377)

Liquidity Measures the ability of a business to pay or otherwise satisfy its current liabilities. (p. 461)

Long-term liabilities Liabilities that will not be due for a long time (usually more than one year). (p. 113)

Low-cost strategy A business strategy in which a business designs and produces products of acceptable quality at a cost lower than competitors. (p. 6)

Lower-of-cost-or-market (LCM) method A method of valuing inventory that reports the inventory at the lower of its cost or current market value (replacement cost). (p. 373)

M

Management Discussion and Analysis (MDA) An annual report disclosure that provides an analysis of the results of operations and financial condition. (p. 692)

Management reporting system A subsystem of accounting that provides internal information to assist managers in making decisions. (p. 152)

Manufacturing A type of business that changes basic inputs into products that are sold to individual customers. (p. 4)

Matching concept A concept of accounting in which expenses are matched with the revenue generated during a period by those expenses. (p. 22)

Materials inventory The cost of materials that have not yet entered into the manufacturing process. (p. 361)

Maturity value The amount that is due at the maturity or due date of a note. (p. 324)

Merchandise available for sale The cost of merchandise available for sale to customers. (p. 212)

Merchandise inventory Merchandise on hand and available for sale to customers. (pp. 210, 360)

Merchandising A type of business that purchases products from other businesses and sells them to customers. (p. 8)

Merger The joining of two corporations in which one company acquires all the assets and liabilities of another corporation, which is then dissolved. (p. 566)

Minority interest The portion of a subsidiary corporation's stock owned by outsiders. (p. 568)

Multiple-step income statement A form of income statement that contains several sections, subsections, and subtotals. (p. 211)

N

Natural business year The fiscal year that ends when a business's activities reach their lowest point in the operating cycle. (p. 165)

Net income The excess of revenues over expenses. (p. 13)

Net loss The excess of expenses over revenues. (p. 13)

Net pay Gross pay less payroll deductions; the amount the employer is obligated to pay the employee. (p. 456)

Net realizable value The amount of cash expected to be realized in the future from a receivable; the estimated selling price of an item of inventory less any direct costs of disposal, such as sales commissions. (pp. 318, 374)

Net sales Revenue received for merchandise sold to customers less any sales returns and allowances and sales discounts. (p. 209)

Note payable A type of short or long-term financing that requires payment of the amount borrowed plus interest. (p. 11)

Notes receivable Written claims against debtors who promise to pay the amount of the note plus interest at an agreed-upon rate. (pp. 112, 315)

Number of days' sales in inventory The relationship between the volume of sales and inventory, computed by dividing the inventory at the end of the year by the average daily cost of goods sold. (pp. 376, 680)

Number of days' sales in receivables The relationship between sales and accounts receivable, computed by dividing the net accounts receivable at the end of the year by the average daily sales. (pp. 329, 679)

Number of times interest charges are earned A ratio that measures creditor margin of safety for interest payments, calculated as income before interest and taxes divided by interest expense. (pp. 471, 686)

O

Objectivity concept A concept of accounting that requires accounting records and the data reported in financial statements be based on objective evidence. (p. 22)

Operating activities Business activities that involve using the business's resources to implement its business strategy. (p. 12)

Other expense Expenses that cannot be traced directly to operations. (p. 213)

Other income Revenue from sources other than the primary operating activity of a business. (p. 213)

Outstanding stock The stock in the hands of stockholders. (p. 505)

Owners' equity The rights of the owners of a company. (p. 17)

P

Par The monetary amount printed on a stock certificate. (p. 505)

Parent company The corporation owning all or a majority of the voting stock of the other corporation. (p. 567)

Partnership A business owned by two or more individuals. (p. 5)

Patents Exclusive rights to produce and sell goods with one or more unique features. (p. 423)

Payroll The total amount paid to employees for a certain period. (p. 456)

Periodic inventory method The inventory method in which the inventory records do not show the amount available for sale or sold during the period. (p. 213)

Perpetual inventory system The inventory system in which each purchase and sale of merchandise is recorded in an inventory account. (p. 213)

Petty cash fund A special-purpose cash fund to pay relatively small amounts. (p. 284)

Physical inventory The detailed listing of merchandise on hand. (pp. 226, 363)

Post-closing trial balance The trial balance prepared after the closing entries have been posted to the ledger. (p. 165)

Posting The process of transferring the debits and credits from the journal entries to the accounts in the ledger. (p. 157)

Preferred stock A class of stock with preferential rights over common stock. (p. 506)

Premium The excess of the issue price of a stock over its par value. (pp. 463, 508)

Prepaid expenses Items that are initially recorded as assets but are expected to become expenses over time or through the normal operations of the business; often called deferred expenses. (pp. 12, 103)

Price-book ratio The ratio of the market value of a share of common stock to the book value of a share of common stock. (p. 569)

Price-earnings (P/E) ratio The ratio computed by dividing a corporation's stock market price per share at a specific date by the company's annual earnings per share. (pp. 568, 688)

Prior period adjustment An adjustment to retained earnings arising from material errors in a prior period's net income as a result of mathematical mistakes or mistakes in applying accounting principles. (p. 519)

Proceeds The net amount available from discounting a note payable. (p. 453)

Profit margin A measure of the amount earned on each dollar of sales, calculated as the ratio of net income to net sales. (p. 676)

Proprietorship A business owned by one individual. (p. 5)

Purchase method The accounting method used when a corporation acquires the controlling share of the voting common stock of another corporation by paying cash, exchanging other assets, issuing debt, or some combination of these methods. (p. 567)

Purchase return or allowance From the buyer's perspective, returned merchandise or an adjustment for defective merchandise. (p. 212)

Purchases discounts Discounts taken by the buyer for early payment of an invoice. (p. 212)

Q

Quick assets Cash and other current assets that can be quickly converted to cash, such as cash, marketable securities, and receivables. (pp. 461, 685)

Quick ratio A financial ratio that measures the ability to pay current liabilities with quick assets (cash, marketable securities, accounts receivable). (pp. 461, 685)

Quick response A method for optimizing inventory levels in the value chain by electronically sharing common forecast, inventory, sales, and payment information between manufacturers and merchandisers, using the Internet or other electronic means. (p. 375)

R

Rate earned on stockholders' equity A measure of profitability computed by dividing net income by total stockholders' equity. (p. 672)

Rate earned on total assets A measure of the profitability of assets, without regard to the equity of creditors and stockholders in the assets, calculated as the net income divided by average total assets. (p. 673)

Ratio of fixed assets to long-term liabilities A leverage ratio that measures the margin of safety of long-term creditors, calculated as the net fixed assets divided by the long-term liabilities. (p. 685)

Ratio of liabilities to stockholders' equity A comprehensive leverage ratio that measures the relationship of the claims of creditors to that of owners, calculated as total liabilities divided by total stockholders' equity. (p. 686)

Ratio of total liabilities to total assets The percent of total assets that are funded by total liabilities; a measure of solvency. (p. 472)

Receivables All money claims against other entities, including people, business firms, and other organizations. (p. 314)

Report form The form of balance sheet in which assets, liabilities, and stockholders' equity are reported in a downward sequence. (p. 214)

Residual value The estimated value of a fixed asset at the end of its useful life. (p. 408)

Restructuring charge The cost of accrued employee termination benefits associated with a management-approved employee termination plan. (p. 556)

Retained earnings Net income retained in a corporation. (p. 16)

Retained earnings statement A summary of the changes in the retained earnings in a corporation for *a specific period of time*, such as a month or a year. (p. 14)

Revenue The increase in assets from selling products or services to customers. (p. 12)

Revenue expenditures Costs that benefit only the current period or costs incurred for normal maintenance and repairs of fixed assets. (p. 418)

Rules of debit and credit Standardized rules for recording increases and decreases in accounts. (p. 154)

S

Sales The total amount charged to customers for merchandise sold, including cash sales and sales on account. (p. 211)

Sales discounts From the seller's perspective, discounts that a seller may offer the buyer for early payment. (p. 211)

Sales return or allowance From the seller's perspective, returned merchandise or an adjustment for defective merchandise. (p. 211)

Selling expenses Expenses that are incurred directly in the selling of merchandise. (p. 213)

Service A type of business that provides services rather than products to customers. (p. 5)

Single-step income statement A form of income statement in which the total of all expenses is deducted from the total of all revenues. (p. 213)

Special-purpose fund A cash fund used for a special business need. (p. 284)

Stated value A value, similar to par value, approved by the board of directors of a corporation for no-par stock. (p. 505)

Statement of cash flows A summary of the cash receipts and cash payments *for a specific period of time*, such as a month or a year. (pp. 15, 598)

Statement of stockholders' equity This statement is often prepared in a columnar format, where each column shows the change in each major stockholders' equity classification. (p. 519)

Stock Shares of ownership of a corporation. (p. 503)

Stock dividend A distribution of shares of stock to stockholders. (p. 516)

Stock option The right to purchase common stock at a fixed price over a limited period of time, often used to provide employee incentives to enhance stock price. (p. 510)

Stock split A reduction in the par or stated value of a common stock and the issuance of a proportionate number of additional shares. (p. 512)

Stockholders Investors who purchase stock in a corporation. (pp. 12, 503)

Stockholders' equity The stockholders' rights to the assets of a business. (pp. 17, 113)

Straight-line method A method of depreciation that provides for equal periodic depreciation expense over the estimated life of a fixed asset. (pp. 410, 464)

Subsidiary company The corporation that is controlled by a parent company. (p. 567)

Subsidiary ledger A ledger containing individual accounts with a common characteristic. (p. 217)

T

Taxable income The income according to the tax laws that is used as a base for determining the amount of taxes owed. (p. 549)

Temporary differences Differences between taxable income and income before income taxes, created because items are recognized in one period for tax purposes and in another period for income statement purposes. Such differences reverse or turn around in later years. (p. 550)

Temporary investments The balance sheet caption used to report investments in income-yielding securities that can be quickly sold and converted to cash as needed. (p. 562)

Trademark A name, term, or symbol used to identify a business and its products. (p. 423)

Trading securities Securities that management intends to actively trade for profit. (p. 561)

Transaction An economic event that under generally accepted accounting principles affects an element of the accounting equation and, therefore, must be recorded. (p. 53)

Transaction processing system A subsystem of accounting that records and summarizes the effects of financial transactions on the business. (p. 152)

Treasury stock Stock that a corporation has once issued and then reacquires. (p. 510)

Trial balance A summary listing of the accounts and their balances in the ledger. (p. 158)

U

Uncollectible accounts expense The operating expense incurred because of the failure to collect receivables. (p. 317)

Unearned revenues Items that are initially recorded as liabilities but are expected to become revenues over time or through the normal operation of the business; often called deferred revenues. (p. 99)

Unit of measure concept A concept of accounting requiring that economic data be recorded in dollars. (p. 22)

Units-of-production method A method of depreciation that provides for depreciation expense based on the expected productive capacity of a fixed asset. (p. 411)

Unrealized holding gain or loss The difference between the fair market values of the securities and their cost. (p. 562)

V

Value chain The way a business adds value for its customers by processing inputs into a product or service. (p. 8)

Vertical analysis A method of analyzing comparative financial statements in which percentages are computed for each item within a statement to a total within the statement. (pp. 66, 670)

Voucher Any document that serves as proof of authority to pay cash. (p. 277)

Voucher system A set of procedures for authorizing and recording liabilities and cash payments. (p. 277)

W

Work in process inventory The direct materials costs, the direct labor costs, and the factory overhead costs that have entered into the manufacturing process, but are associated with a product that has not been finished. (p. 361)

Company Index

T

U

V

W

X

Y

Z

Subject Index

C

D

E

F

T

U

V

W

Y

Z